权威·前沿·原创

皮书系列为
“十二五”“十三五”国家重点图书出版规划项目

BLUE BOOK OF
NATIONAL CENTRAL CITY

Consultants: Qiu Baoxing Zhang Dawei

ANNUAL REPORT OF THE CONSTRUCTION OF NATIONAL CENTRAL CITIES (2019)

National Central City Construction and Coordinated Regional Development

Editors-in-Chief: Zhao Jian Sun Xianke
Executive Editors: Chen Yao Yu Xin'an
Associate Editors: Jiang Lizhu Zhao Hong
Yang Dongfang Shi Yu

社会科学文献出版社
SOCIAL SCIENCES ACADEMIC PRESS (CHINA)

Editorial Commission for Report of National Central City Construction (2019)

Introduction of Major Editors

Zhao Jian Doctor of management, Party Secretary of Zhengzhou Normal University, Professor and research fellow, Former Director of Zhengzhou Finance Bureau, Deputy to the 11th, 12th and 13th National People's Congress of Zhengzhou municipality, and Deputy to the 12th National People's Congress of Henan Province. He had been awarded with the titles of Outstanding Worker of the National Financial System, Excellent Party Worker of Henan Province, and Excellent Educational Manager of the Education Department of Henan Province.

Research fields: regional economy and lean management. He had published 6 academic monographs, with the representative being *On Development of Local Finance*, presided over the provincial-level key research programs including *Urban Agricultural Development Model Innovation—Case Study of Zhengzhou*, and *Study on the Opportunities Brought by the National Policy of Expanding Domestic Demand to Zhengzhou's Economy and Its Responses*, published more than 70 papers, including 20 plus papers on national core journals, and won the provincial and ministerial level science and technology achievement award as well as 5 provincial and ministerial level excellent achievement awards.

Sun Xianke Doctor of literature, Current President of Zhengzhou Normal University, Professor, PhD Supervisor for the Modern and Contemporary Literature major of Henan University, Expert enjoying the special allowance of State Council, and former Vice-president of Henan Normal University.

Research fields: China's contemporary literary trends and contemporary novel studies. He has published academic works including *Prayer and Soliloquy: Narrative Features and Cultural Consciousness of Novels in the New Stage, Meaning of Narration*, and *Speakers and Their Words*, published a wordage exceeding 600,000 characters in authoritative academic periodicals such as *Literary Review* and *Theoretical Studies in Literature and Art.* He has presided over 3 projects under the National Social Science Fund, 3 Henan's provincial philosophy and social science planning projects, winning 2 Frist Prizes and 1 Second Prize for "Henan Provincial Social Science Outstanding Achievement Award".

Chen Yao PhD of economics, Dean of the National Central City Research Institute of Zhengzhou Normal University, Research Fellow, Professor and PhD supervisor for the Institute of Industrial Economics of CASS, Vice President and Secretary General of China Association of Regional Economy, Deputy Director of Western Development Research Center of CASS, Editor-in-chief of Regional Economic Reivew, and Chief expert for major programs under the National Social Science Fund enjoying the special allowance of the State Council. He had been one of the invited experts for the academicians' trip to western regions organized by the Organization Department of the CPC Central Committee, the inspection delegation of Standing Committee of CPPCC and the activitites organized by National Development and Reform Commission, and member of Chinese Regional Economists 50 Forum.
Research fields: regional economy, industrial space organization and government policy. Representative monographs include *Study on the National Policies on the Central-and-Western Regions' Development, Frontierof Regional Economics in China, Regional Economics, Regional Economics Dictionary*, etc. He had published nearly 100 papers and special research reports on the periodicals such as *Economic Research Journal, China Industrail Economics, Business Management Journal* and *Regional Economic Review.* He has won 10 plus awards including the National Science and Technology Progress Award, China Development Research Award, China Academy of Social Sciences Outstanding Achievements Award.

Yu Xin'an Doctor of economics, Honorary Dean of National Central City Research Institute of Zhengzhou Normal University, Chief Expert, Former President of Henan Academy of Social Sciences, Second-level Research Fellow, expert enjoying the special allowance from the State Council, Excellent Expert of Henan Province, one of the first Outstanding Professional Technicians of Henan Province, Henan Economic Figure for the second year, Vice President of China Regional Economic Society, Vice President of Henan Social Sciences Association, specially invited economist for the "Confidence Survey of China's Hundred

Economists" conducted by the National Bureau of Statistics, and Member of the Expert Team for the 10th and 13th Five-year Plans of Henan province.
Research Fields: regional economy, industrial economy and economic system reform. Representative works include *The Rising of Great Province, Research on the Construction of the New Urban Area in China, Study on the Central Economic Region, On the New Leading Urbanization, Toward the Rise of the Central Region, the Henan Model of Coordinated Industrial and Agricultural Development*, etc. He has presided over more than 30 national, provincial and ministerial projects. He has published more than 400 papers in newspapers and magazines such as *Qiushi, China Industrial Economics, China Reform, Reform, People's Daily, Guangming Daily and Economic Daily.*

Jiang Lizhu PhD of education, Professor, Vice President of Zhengzhou Normal University, Visiting Scholar to Birmingham City University in the U.K., and postgraduate supervisor. She is the member of the Second National Expert Committee on Teachers' Education Curriculum Resources under the Ministry of Education, an expert for the "National Teachers Training Program" under the Ministry of Educationin on both theory and practice, Theoretical Talent of Henan province, one of the first batch of teachers and educational experts of Henan, one of the tenth batch of professional top talent of Zhengzhou, and Excellent Manager of Education in Education Department of Henan Province.
Research fields: education economy and management. She proposed the study model of CEA Hybrid Learning (C-class learning, E-e-learning, A-action learing) and the venue learning model, which have been presented in the book *Classic Cases for National Teachers Training Program* compiled by the Ministry of Education. She has presided over six provincial and ministerial research projects, received 2 provincial and ministerial awards, a number of local and municipal level awards, published a monograph, chaired the editing of 5 books, edited 3 books and published nearly 20 papers.

Zhao Hong PhD, postdoctoral supervisor, Member of the Party Group and Deputy President of Beijing Academy of Social Sciences, Research Fellow, Consultant in the Expert Board for Beijing Municipality, expert with special allowances of the State Council, Vice-President of China Regional Economic Society, Vice-President of Beijing Industrial Economy Research Society and other academic positions.

Research fields: regional economy, industrial economy, science and technology innovation, industrial park development, urban governance, etc. He initiated the "Headquarter Economy" theory, published the first relevant monograph in China—*Headquarter Economy*, which has aroused strong responses in academia and the real economy sector. He has published more than 100 academic papers, over 10 monographs, won 6 provincial and ministerial level outstanding scientific and technological achievements awards, presided over the major project under the National Social Science Fund "Study on the Major Issues for Beijing-Tianjin-Hebei Synergetic Development" and nearly 100 other national, municipal and various horizontal projects, providing reference to the government with many of his research results.

Yang Dongfang Party secretary and director of Zhengzhou development and reform commission, national registered cost engineer, registered supervision engineer, registered consulting engineer (investment), registered first-class construction engineer.Edited or organized the compilation and compilation of books or periodicals such as *Zhengzhou national central city planning and construction outline*, *Zhengzhou index study of Zhengzhou central city*, *Zhengzhou bridge, Planning innovation and practice of national aviation economic zone*, *New York street design manual* and *Zhengzhou planning*; Pushed to carried out the "zhengzhou airport economic comprehensive experimental area planning in low carbon ecological wisdom key technology research and application" project which was awarded in henan province and zhengzhou city science and technology achievement prizes of science and technology progress second prize, "zhengzhou city planning 'picture' system project" won the award for the best engineering survey and design industry in henan province of urban planning and design of the second prize and excellent in Zhengzhou city won the first prize in the urban and rural planning and design.

Shi Yu PhD, Zhengzhou normal university institute of national central city, associate professor, master tutor, the executive vice President of China's regional economic association professional committee of the national center city secretary general, outstanding young and middle-aged backbone teachers, Zhengzhou city, Henan province education department technical academic leader, the backbone of middle-aged and young teachers in Henan province department of education funding.The main research areas are application of statistics and government evaluation.In recent years, Presided over and participated in 13 scientific research projects at all levels, including 4 national natural science foundation projects, 1 achievement appraisal of Henan provincial science and technology department, 1 project of Henan provincial social science federation, 1 key scientific and technological project of Henan provincial education department, 1 project of Zhengzhou municipal science and technology bureau, 5 teaching and research projects of Zhengzhou normal university.Published 17 papers, 7 of which were indexed by SCI and EI, 1 by CSSCI and 7 by Chinese core, and won 2 provincial excellent papers.Participated in compiling one textbook for the 12th five-year plan;Won 11 teaching and scientific research awards.

Abstract

This book is the second blue book of the national central city organized by the National Central City Research Institute of Zhengzhou Normal University, with nearly 30 scientific research institutions and more than 50 experts and scholars at home and abroad participating in the research. Based on the latest requirements of the coordinated development of national regions, this book takes "the construction of national central cities and the coordinated development of regions" as the theme, objectively evaluates the current level and developing trend of China's national central cities in 2018, and comprehensively reflects the exploration and practice of Beijing, Shanghai, Tianjin, Chongqing, Guangzhou, Chengdu, Wuhan, Zhengzhou and Xi'an in undertaking the mission of the construction of national central cities and the coordinated development of regions. This paper discusses the current hot issues in the construction of national central city and its radiation-driven role in regional coordinated development, which has important guiding significance theoretically in high-quality construction of a national central city and the effective promotion of regional coordinated development.

The book is divided into six parts, its structure and contents are as follows.

The first part is the General Report. The general report points out that the implementation of the strategy of coordinated regional development and the establishment of a more effective new mechanism for coordinated regional development are important strategies to solve the unbalanced and insufficient development in the new era. Since 2018, the construction of nine national central cities have shown a lot of outstanding results, and remarkable achievements have been made in comprehensive services, scientific and technological innovation, and opening-up exchanges and cooperation with the outside world. At the same time, measures such as speeding up planning and guidance, promoting the interconnection of transportation infrastructure, promoting the co-construction and sharing of factor resource platforms, and promoting the effective convergence of rules and systems have effectively driven the development of surrounding regions and promoted the implementation of the national regional coordinated development strategy. In the new era and new development stage, the implementation of the national central city construction and regional coordinated development strategy not only faces rare development opportunities, but also needs to actively and steadily face various unfavorable factors and challenges. In order to promote the optimization of land and space development pattern and balanced regional development, the national central city will continue to expand, at the same time, it is necessary to continue to improve the thinking of promoting coordinated regional development and enrich the path of promoting coordinated regional development.

The second part is Evaluation Report. In order to accurately grasp the construction level and development of China's national central cities in 2018 in six aspects: comprehensive services, network hubs, scientific and technological innovation, open communication, cultural cohesion and ecological livability, growth indexes are added to the national central city construction index and measured separately. In terms of construction index, compared with 2016, 9 national central cities still have obvious stratification phenomenon, among which Chongqing, Chengdu and Tianjin have undergone great changes in the ranking of construction indexes. In the growth index, Zhengzhou, Xi'an, Chengdu, Wuhan and other cities ranked lower in the construction index among the nine national central cities, and the growth index ranked in the top four, indicating that they are all in rapid development, while the growth index of the other five cities is relatively low, indicating that the urban development tends to be stable. Based on the measurement results, the report puts forward that the national central city construction should pay attention to the coordinated development of various functional layers, the coordinated relationship between economic development and ecological livability, promote the construction of an open city, gradually establish a brand image of city culture, and effectively solve urban diseases, so as to better play the leading, demonstrating, radiating and driving role of the national central city in metropolitan areas and urban agglomerations, and further promote regional coordinated development.

The third part is Cities' Reports. It is composed of nine reports reflecting the construction achievements and development trends of the national central cities since 2018. They were written by relevant experts from nine key research institutions of the national central cities, including Beijing, Shanghai, Tianjin, Guangzhou, Chongqing, Chengdu, Wuhan, Zhengzhou and Xi 'an. The reports comprehensively show the unique strategic measures of the national central cities since 2018 under the requirements of thoroughly implementing the relevant national policies. They reflect the process, characteristics and effects of the high-quality development and construction of each city, as well as its radiation and driving role in regional coordinated development. At the same time, they analyze the shortcomings and challenges in the high-quality development and construction of the national central cities, and put forward targeted countermeasures and suggestions.

The fourth part is Case Studies. This part of the content fully combines the development characteristics of each national central city at the present stage, and in view of the hot issues in promoting the high-quality development of national central cities and the coordinated development of regions, it selects topics such as cultural and tourism integration, public services, e-commerce, and the radiation belt power of national central cities in metropolitan areas to carry out special studies, thus effectively enriching and supplementing the content of the urban chapter.

The fifth part is Exploration Reports. This part mainly includes forward-looking articles aiming at the hot and difficult issues in the construction of national central cities and the coordinated development of regions, and exploring the high-quality development of China's national central cities on the basis of drawing lessons from the experiences and laws of the construction of international metropolises and modern metropolitan areas. The exploration article is very problem-oriented and stands in the perspective of international development. Its purpose is to enhance the forward-looking of the construction of national central cities and to promote the solution of the most urgent and critical problems encountered by the construction of national central cities and the coordinated development of regions.

Part VI is Appendix. It is composed of three types of important data, namely, the main data on the construction of nine national central cities in 2018, excerpts from the main documents on regional coordinated development at the national level, and memorabilia on the construction of national central cities since 2018. These data truly present the objective process of the construction of the national central city since 2018, and at the same time provide basic data for the vast number of scientific researchers to track and deepen the research on major issues in the construction of the national central city.

Key words: National Central City; Coordinated Regional Development; High Quality Development

Preface

In celebrating the 70th anniversary of the founding of the People's Republic of China, led by The National Central City Research Institute(NCCRI) of Zhengzhou Normal University, the second "national center city blue book" the national center for urban development report (2019) is published, I expressed warm congratulations and express my sincere admiration and gratitude to the leaders of Zhengzhou Normal University who strongly supported the establishment of the think tank.

National central city, known as the "spire" of China's urban system, is the core city of urban agglomeration and occupies the highest position in the central city. Building national central cities is a major strategic plan made by the central government to improve the national urban system, promote coordinated development among regions, boost the power of megacities , and win the global competition. There are three main missions of national central cities: national strategic importance, participating in global competition on behalf of the country, and promoting regional development.

In recent years, the central government attaches great importance to the construction and development of central cities and has taken a series of major measures. First, November 18, 2018, the central committee of the communist party of China and the state council promulgated a official document on establishing a more effective regional coordination development mechanism of opinions , explicitly proposed to "establish a central city leading the development of urban agglomeration and urban agglomeration drive the new pattern of regional development, promoting the development of regional plate interaction between", and focus on planning for seven large urban agglomeration and its corresponding led 12 central cities, including nine national center city: Beijing, Tianjin, Shanghai, Guangzhou, Chongqing, Chengdu, Wuhan, Zhengzhou, Xi'an. Second, in

February 2019, the National Development and Reform Commission issued the guiding opinions on cultivating and developing a modern metropolitan area, which proposed that the metropolitan area is an urbanization spatial form within the urban agglomeration centering on megacities or large cities with strong driving functions and taking the 1-hour commuting circle as the basic range. And to promote the central city and surrounding cities (towns) urban development as the direction, cultivate and develop a number of modern urban circle. Third, on August 26, 2019, President Xi Jinping hosted the fifth meeting of the central finance and economics committee, pointed out the current economy development of spatial structure of our country is undergoing profound changes, the central city and urban agglomeration is becoming a main space form of bearing development elements. To promote coordinated development among regions under the new situation, we need to adjust and improve the regional policy system in accordance with objective economic laws, give full play to the strengths of various regions, and enhance the economic and population carrying capacity of central cities and city clusters.

These important central documents and meetings show that, in order to promote the high-quality development of China's economy and the coordinated development of regional economies, as well as to cope with the complicated international environment, we must attach great importance to the leading and leading role of central cities and optimize the strategic layout of regional economy. These basic principles have pointed out the direction and provided us with strong impetus and confidence to build a national central city in the future.

At present, in order to implement the requirements of the central government and relevant arrangements, all regions are actively studying and planning the development of central cities, metropolitan areas and city clusters. For example, how to improve the primacy of the central city of the provincial capital, how to promote the integration of the central city and neighboring cities, and how to realize the integration within the large urban agglomeration; The national central city is thinking about how to build a city with higher quality. The cities with certain strength are actively creating conditions and striving to be approved to build a national central city. I have noticed that after the National Development and Reform Commission officially issued the guidance on supporting Zhengzhou's construction of a national central city in January 2017, Henan province soon formulated and issued the program of action for Zhengzhou's construction of a national central city (2017-2035).In June 2019, the Henan provincial government issued "several opinions on supporting the construction of Zhengzhou national center city", required to accelerate construction of Zhengzhou "three center a hub a portal", further expand the opening to the outside world, stimulate endogenous impetus, construction has the creativity and cultural charm, and the ecological wisdom and open inclusive national center city, led driving the development of Zhongyuan urban agglomeration and central parts of high quality. In 2018, Zhengzhou's economic aggregate exceeded one trillion yuan, its permanent resident population exceeded 10 million, and significant progress was made in scientific and technological innovation, ecological environment, and development of an open highland. These practices show that national central cities are becoming an important force and starting point for China to push forward the construction of new urbanization and promote the coordinated development of regions.

Of course, the better construction and better layout of the national central city, still need in-depth study and discussion. Happily, the Blue Book of National Central City combines the latest requirements of national regional coordinated development and establishes a new research theme, namely "National Central City Construction and Coordinated Regional Development", on the basis of the first blue book "the Mission and Commitment of National Central City". The book comprehensively evaluated the current level and development trend of China's national central city construction in the past year, especially reflected the exploration and practice of 9 cities in undertaking the mission of national central city construction and regional coordinated development, and discussed the hot and difficult issues in the current development in depth. I have noticed that this blue book not only has a new theme, comprehensive content and professional rigor, but also has a lot of innovations in research methods. It is truly comprehensive, objective, authentic and professional.

I'm looking forward to NCCRI continue to adhere to the theory with practice, adhere to the theory and method innovation, to build the national central city blue book into a well-known academic brand for urban development research in China, build the NCCRI into a national first-class research base for central cities, so that the results of think tanks can be better translated into government decisions, guide urban practice, and serve urban development.

Vice-president and Secretary General of China Center for International Economic Exchanges
Chief Consultant for National Central City Research Institute of Zhengzhou Normal University
Zhang Dawei
September, 2019

CONTENTS

I General Report

II Evaluation Report

III Cities' Reports

Ⅳ Exploration Reports

General Report

B.1

China's National Central City Construction and Coordinated Regional Development: New Development Momentum and New Measures

Research Team of National Central City Research Institute of Zhengzhou Normal University[*]

Abstract: Implementing a coordinated regional development strategy and establishing a more effective mechanism in this regard is an important measure to resolve the problem of imbalanced and inadequate development in the new era. Since 2018, numerous highlights have emerged from the construction of nine national central cities and remarkable achievements have been made in comprehensive services, technological innovation, and open exchanges and cooperation. At the same time, a series of measures have been taken, including accelerating the formation of the guiding

* Directors of Research Team: Chen Yao, Yu Xin'an; Deputy-directors: Wang Jianguo, Shi Yu; Writers: Wang Xintao, Zuo Wen, Li Jianhua, Yi Xueqin and Guo Zhiyuan.

role of planning, promoting the connectivity of transportation infrastructure, facilitating the joint construction and sharing of factor resources platforms, and boosting the effective connection of rules and systems. They have effectively propelled the development of surrounding areas and the implementation of national coordinated regional development strategies. In the new era and new development stage, the implementation of the national central city construction and coordinated regional development strategies not only coincides with valuable development opportunities, but also has to be confronted with various unfavorable factors and challenges actively and steadily. In order to promote the optimization of national land space development pattern and balanced regional development, on the one hand, the national central cities will continue to expand; on the other hand, they will continue to perfect the concept of driving coordinated regional development and design more paths leading to this end.

Keywords: national central cities; coordinated regional development; new development momentum

The coordinated regional development strategy is a major national strategy in the new era and is an important part of the new development concept and the modern economic system. In 2018, the State Council of the CPC Central Committee issued the *Opinions on Establishing a More Effective New Coordinated Regional Development Mechanism* which drew a road map for coordinated regional development in the coming period. National central cities assume national missions, lead regional development, participate in international competition, and represent the national image. They are the "spire" cities of China's urban system that play a vital role in promoting coordinated regional development. At present, there are nine national central cities in China, i.e. Beijing, Tianjin, Shanghai, Guangzhou, Chongqing, Chengdu, Wuhan, Zhengzhou and Xi'an. Since 2018, the construction of the nine national central cities has been accelerated, and many of them have developed clearly defined timetables and roadmaps, with clearer development goals, priorities and tasks. These cities develop with distinctive initiatives, and remarkable achievements have been made in comprehensive services, technological innovation, and open exchanges and cooperation. They have become "leaders" of high-quality development in China.

I The Latest Developments and Characteristics of National Central City Construction Since 2018

(I) Overview of the Construction of Nine National Central Cities

Since the concept of national central city construction was first proposed by the Ministry of Housing and Urban-Rural Development of the People's Republic of China in the *National Urban System Plan* in 2005, nine cities, i.e. Beijing, Tianjin, Shanghai, Guangzhou, Chongqing, Chengdu, Wuhan, Zhengzhou and Xi'an, have been designated as national central cities under national support. As important platforms and strategic fulcrums of national development strategies, these cities assume national political goals and strategic tasks, and enjoy concentrated advantages in economy, population, resources and policies among Chinese cities. At the same time, with a focus on their respective functional positioning, their construction has been promoted by improving infrastructure, upgrading industrial structure, and expanding opening-up. By the end of 2018, according to relevant public data of the country as well as its provinces and cities, the total population of the nine national central cities was 154.8488 million, accounting for 11% of the national total population of 1.39538 billion; their total GDP was RMB 17.371527 trillion, accounting for 19.3% of the national GDP of RMB 90.0309 trillion; their per capita GDP was RMB 112,200, 1.7 times of the national per capita GDP (RMB 64,600); Wuhan, Chengdu, Zhengzhou and Xi'an reported a GDP growth rate higher than the national rate of 6.6%; their general public budget income was RMB 2.368775 trillion, accounting for 13% of the national level of RMB 18.3352 trillion; their urbanization rate was 78.9%, 1.32 times of the national average level (about 59.58%) (see Table 1).

Table 1 Main Economic and Social Development Indicators of Nine Cities in 2018

	Resident Population (10,000)	Regional GDP (RMB 100 Million)	Regional GDP Per Capita (RMB 10,000)	GDP Growth Rate (%)	General Public Budget Income (RMB 100 Million)	Resident Urbanization Rate (%)
Beijing	2154.2	30320	14.08	6.6	5785.9	86.5
Tianjin	1559.6	18809.64	12.06	3.6	2106.19	83.15
Shanghai	2423.78	32679.87	13.48	6.6	7108.15	88.1
Chongqing	3101.79	20363.19	6.59	6.0	2265.5	65.5
Guangzhou	1490.44	22859.35	15.55	6.2	1632.3	86.38
Wuhan	1108.1	14847.29	13.51	8	1528.7	80.29
Chengdu	1633	15342.77	9.48	8	1424.2	73.12
Zhengzhou	1013.6	10143.3	10.14	8.1	1152.1	73.4
Xi'an	1000.37	8349.86	8.51	8.2	684.71	74.01
Nine Cities	15484.88	173715.27	11.22	—	23687.75	78.9
Nationwide	139538	900309	6.46	6.6	183352	59.58

Source: Statistical Communiqué of the People's Republic of China on 2018 National Economic and Social Development for the nine national central cities

(II) Characteristics of National Central City Construction

1 Clearer Construction Progress Roadmap

As urban competition becomes increasingly fierce, many regional central cities dream of being promoted to the national rank. Many cities are actively applying for a position in the national rank. For those cities that have been designated as national central cities, especially Wuhan, Zhengzhou and Xi'an, which were latecomers, planning a strategic blueprint for national central city construction has become the most urgent task. The *Plan on Implementation of National Central City Construction of Wuhan* introduced in April 2018 by Wuhan proposes a three-stage strategy for the national central city construction of Wuhan: By 2021, the GDP of Wuhan should reach RMB 2 trillion or so; by 2035, Wuhan should be basically built into a national central city with certain competitiveness and influence on a global scale; by the middle of this century, Wuhan should be at the forefront of the country in the process of building China a prosperous, democratic, civilized, harmonious and beautiful modern socialist country and become a world prominent city with international influence, global competitiveness and sustainable development capabilities. In the *Plan on Implementation of National Central City Construction of Xi'an*, Xi'an develops a "three-step" strategy: the first step is to build Xi'an into a well-off society whose economic aggregate will hit the trillion level and shape the Xi'an Metropolitan Area by 2020; the second step is to basically realize modernization, to fully build Xi'an into a national central city that represents the national image, takes the lead in implementing the Belt and Road Initiative and has important international influence, and to make significant progress in the international metropolis construction by 2035; the third step is to basically achieve common prosperity, to further increase international characteristics, to fully improve its modernization, ecologicalization and internationalization levels, to fully build Xi'an into an international metropolis that takes the lead in implementing the Belt and Road Initiative and Asia-Europe cooperation and exchanges, and to be listed as a world city, and an international culturally prominent city by 2050. Moreover, the *Action Plan for National Central City Construction of Zhengzhou (2017-2035)* issued in February 2018 by Zhengzhou defines its goal of national central city construction: In the short term (2017-2020), a new process of national central city construction should be started to fully build Zhengzhou into a high-quality and high-level well-off society that is recognized by the people and that can withstand the tests of history; in the medium term (2021-2035), Zhengzhou should grow into a leading innovative city in China and become an international comprehensive hub, an international logistics center, and an important national economic growth center; in the long term (2036-2050), Zhengzhou should be built into a prosperous, democratic, civilized, harmonious and beautiful modern socialist city with global influence. It can be found that these "design sketches", "construction drawings" and "assignment books" for national central city construction have become clearer, more well-defined and more specific. As concentrated efforts and continuous progress are made under the guidance of the existing blueprints, the national central city construction enjoys a bright prospect.

2 Further Highlighting Theme of New Era

A new era for the socialism with Chinese characteristics and the economic development of China has approached. The basic feature in the new era is that

China's economy has moved from a high-speed growth stage to a high-quality development stage. Promoting high-quality development is the fundamental requirement for framing development ideas, formulating economic policies, and implementing macro-control in the current and future periods. High-quality development has become the theme of the new era. The nine national central cities regard high-quality development as the fundamental requirement and goal of development, carrying out urban planning and policy design under the principle. For example, Xi'an issued the *Decision of CPC Xi'an Municipal Committee on Accelerating National Center City Construction and Promoting High-Quality Development*, in which clear requirements for the key points and objectives of high-quality development of Xi'an as a national center city are put forward. In the process of moving from a regional center city to a national center city and an international metropolis, Xi'an focuses on building six major functions: an important economic center in West China, a foreign exchange center, a Silk Road technological innovation center, a Silk Road cultural base, an inland opening-up base, and a national comprehensive transportation hub. Xi'an exerts itself to set a high-quality development model while seeking breakthroughs in key areas and links. It promotes high-quality development with "three focuses": focusing on high-end and high-tech industries, especially industrial transformation and upgrading; focusing on high-speed growth, especially optimization of investment structure; focusing on innovation as a driving force, especially the replacement of old growth drivers with new ones. The "three focuses" have become important forces driving Xi'an towards high-quality development. The other national central cities also work closely under the requirements of the new era, new missions, and new tasks. In line with the new situation of urban work, new requirements for reform and development, and new expectations of the people, they make practical exploration and innovation on the path of high-quality development and inject important impetus to high-quality development.

3 Attaching More Importance to Strengthening Areas of Weakness for People's Well-being

Since the 18th National Congress of the Communist Party of China, the new central leadership with Comrade Xi Jinping at the core has treated people's well-being as the starting point and the foothold of governing the country and people's yearning for a better life as the objective of their endeavor. To this end, by national strategic needs, new research and development institutions such as Beijing Academy of Quantum Information Sciences, Chinese Institute for Brain Research, and Beijing Academy of Artificial Intelligence were founded; the construction of a comprehensive national science center was launched in full swing; a dazzling array of landmark original achievements such as Majorana anyon and new ultra-low-power transistors were made. In Shanghai, big scientific facilities such as soft X-ray free electron laser facility and ultra-intense and ultra-short lasers basically took shape; a number of scientific research institutions such as the National Innovation Center of Integrated Circuit Manufacturing and the Shanghai Institute for Brain Research were founded; a series of sci-tech achievements such as new drugs targeting at Alzheimer's disease and hyperspectral comprehensive observation satellites were successively introduced to the market. Guangzhou strongly pushed the construction of the Guangzhou Regenerative Medicine and Health Laboratory and the Provincial Laboratory of Southern Marine Science and Engineering; Guangzhou High-tech Zone was selected as one of the top ten world-class high-tech parks in the country. Tianjin attracted 10 national scientific research institutions to settle, including the China Institute of Atomic Energy, the CAS Institute of UAV Application, and the Tianjin Artificial Intelligence Innovation Center, as well as a number of national innovation platforms such as large-scale earthquake engineering simulation research facility and the China University of Nuclear Industry. By the end of 2018, there had been 672 national key laboratories, national engineering technology research centers, and national key laboratories run by enterprises, as well as 535,134 patent grants in the nine national central cities. The in-depth implementation of the innovation-driven development strategy of these cities has promoted the deep integration of innovation elements and further enhanced the independent innovation vitality of the country.

3 Increased Open Exchange and Cooperation Level

National central cities are important carriers for opening up to the outside world. They represent the country to participate in international competition and make extensive exchanges and cooperation with foreign countries in political, economic, cultural and social fields. Since 2018, highlights have been found in the foreign exchanges and cooperation of the nine national central cities. More and more enterprises gain access to the international economic arena, speaking with the strongest voice of China's full open development, by making use of the open platforms and service channels of national central cities. In November 2018, the people of Shanghai made concerted efforts to successfully host the first Import Expo supported by first-class urban environment and services. It attracted a total of 172 countries, regions and international organizations and 3,617 overseas enterprises. More than 800,000 visitors negotiated, placed orders and experienced the expo. The transaction volume reached USD 57.8 billion, and a number of international expo records were set. As one of the top ten commercial expos in the world at its first try, the Import Expo marked a major pioneering attempt in the history of international expo industry. Tianjin successfully hosted a series of major international conferences such as the Summer Davos, the Second World Intelligence Congress, and the China Mining. Its exchanges and cooperation with international sister cities were further consolidated and expanded. Guangzhou held 61 international conferences including the World Route Development Conference, the Imperial Springs International Forum and the Global Mayors' Forum. Beijing successfully hosted the 3rd World Winter Sports Expo. Tianjin successfully hosted the China-Russia Youth Ice Hockey Friendly Match and other major events. Chengdu successfully hosted international exchange activities such as the 2nd China-CEE Art Cooperation Forum, the 4th Arabic Arts Festival, the 2018 European Culture Season, and the International Sister Cities Youth Music Festival. Xi'an successfully held major international events such as the Silk Road International Film Festival, and the Global Programmers' Festival. By the end of 2018, the nine national central cities reported actual used foreign investment of USD 117.649 billion, accounting for 13.3% of the national total amount. There had been 16 comprehensive bonded zones and 333 international sister cities. By organizing these large-scale events, exhibitions and important international conferences, they gather high-end resources from the whole country and even the whole world, strengthen the ties with the world, and deepen China's integration into the global urban network system to comprehensively enhance the convenience and closeness of international contacts and exchanges and boost the international image and influence of Chinese cities.

4 Enhanced Network Hub Function

National central cities are information, logistics and e-commerce centers that serve important transportation network hub function in the country.

Since 2018, the nine national central cities have made major breakthroughs in hub construction. Guangzhou strengthened its function as an international comprehensive transportation hub by pushing forward the construction of 18 international shipping hub projects, 11 international aviation hub projects, 5 national railway projects, 6 intercity railway projects, 9 metro projects and 10 expressway projects. So far, metros have run through all its administrative districts. In Beijing, Daxing International Airport was officially named, with the main works of its terminal building basically completed. In Shanghai, the reconstruction of Terminal 1 of Hongqiao International Airport was completed. This airport has the third largest cargo and mail handling capacity and the fourth largest passenger volume in the world. The Port of Shanghai has maintained the largest container handling capacity for 9 consecutive years and the fourth largest passenger volume from cruise home port in the world. The Jinxiong Intercity Railway was included in the national plan; the 100,000t waterway in the Dagang District of Tianjin Port was completed and put into used; the shipping service center was officially put into operation. In Chengdu, the "Rongou+" ASEAN Rail-Ocean Intermodal Train and Railway Train are able to reach 24 overseas cities, and 1,591 "Rongou+" trips are operated in the whole year, remaining the No. 1 in the country. In Wuhan, the 1,000-container demonstration vessel designed for river-to-sea transportation successfully set off on its maiden voyage. Xi'an was recognized as a national-level airport economic demonstration zone and cross-border e-commerce comprehensive test zone. In Zhengzhou, the construction of Zhengji, Zhengwan and Zhengfu High-speed Railway, Zhengzhou South Railway Station, and Airport-to-South Station Intercity Railway was quickened, and a Union Jack-shaped high-speed rail network took shape. By the end of 2018, the nine national central cities reported RMB 220.732 billion of postal services, which accounted for 17.9% of the national service volume; 8,679.32 telecommunications services, which accounted for 13.2% of the national service volume; 1.108691 trillion passenger kilometers of passenger volume, which accounted for 32.4% of the national passenger volume; 5.832362 trillion tons of freight transport rotation volume, which accounted for 28.4% of the national volume; 476 international airport routes; and 4,183 trip/day of high-speed trains. China's Internet + Index is an important indicator to measure the construction of information hub. In the 2018 China's Internet + Index ranking, seven national central cities made into the top ten except Zhengzhou and Xi'an. The construction and improvement of airports, railways, ports, highways, information and other facilities in the nine national central cities facilitates the formation of an international trade and business circulation network in China and lends solid support to accelerate the construction of a modern three-dimensional integrated network hub connecting the East and the West, the North and the South, and radiating to all directions, and to promote regional economic cooperation and coordinated development.

5 Increased Ecological Livability Level

Ecological livability is the pursuit of a beautiful urban environment that is vibrant, ecologically sound and livable. Ecological livability is also an important goal of national central city construction. The nine national central cities thoroughly implement the development concept that "Clear waters and green mountains are as good as mountains of gold and silver" and continuously promote ecological environment management and the construction of ecologically livable green cities. Many ecological and environmental indicators continue to be positive; remarkable achievements have been made in the green development process; the people's sense of gains is significantly enhanced. Xi'an took active measures to turn the "two mountains" concept into reality, green both sides of "five roads", and carry out the campaign of "Beautiful Xi'an · Green Home". Wuhan launched greening and quality upgrading campaign that expanded green land by 7.58 million square meters. Guangzhou polished its reputation as a flower city and a green city by holding the China Forest Tourism Festival, planting 100,000 themed flowers and trees, and adding 100,000 square meters of vertical planting and 80km of ecological landscape forest belts. Shanghai vigorously promoted whole-process classification of household garbage, built 3,374 resources recycling points, and commenced the construction of 15 garbage resource disposal facilities. Beijing launched a "River Cleaning" campaign and a special operation of water source environmental protection and completed the task of treating 84 sections of black and odorous water body in non-built up areas. Zhengzhou vigorously propelled a land greening speed-up action that added urban green space of 13.56 million square meters and completed 411 parks, gardens and micro-parks such as the High-speed Rail Park. By the end of 2018, the urban green coverage rate of the nine national central cities had reached 41.3%, 3.4

percentage points higher than the national average; the per capita park green area of Beijing, Chongqing and Guangzhou had exceeded the national average; the annual average concentration of PM2.5 and the daily Traffic Performance Index of the nine national central cities had declined to varying degrees compared to the previous year. This data shows that the ecological livability of the national central cities has been further increased and that people and nature are more harmonious.

II New Phenomena, Measures and Experiences in National Central City Construction Since 2018

(I) New Development Concepts Guide the Comprehensive Development of National Central Cities

As important carriers that assume national missions, reflect the national will, represent the national image, and lead regional development, the national central cities unswervingly implement the concept of "innovative, coordinated, green, open, and sharing" development and fully follow the guidance of the new development concept. In February 2018, when General Secretary Xi Jinping visited Sichuan, he put forward a series of major requirements for the construction of Chengdu. He clearly stated that Chengdu would receive support in its attempt to fully follow the guidance of the new development concept. His instructions indicated the political direction and provided a basis for the construction of Chengdu as a national central city. At the third plenary meeting of the 13th Committee of Chengdu held on July 6-7, 2018, the *Decision of CPC Chengdu Municipal Committee on Comprehensively Implement the New Development Concept and Accelerating the Promotion of High-quality Development* and the *Decision of CPC Chengdu Municipal Committee on In-depth Implementation of the Important Instructions Given by General Secretary Xi Jinping on Accelerating the Construction of Chengdu as a Beautiful Livable Park City during His Inspection in Sichuan* were adopted. Chengdu aims to realize "five city" goals in its pursuit of becoming a national central city fully guided by the new development concept: Firstly, it will implement the innovative development concept and become an innovation-driven pilot city; secondly, it will implement the coordinated development concept and become an urban-rural coordinated development demonstration city; thirdly, it will implement the green development concept and become a beautiful Chinese model city; fourthly, it will implement the open development concept and become a modern international city; fifthly, it will implement the sharing development concept and become a harmonious and livable city. The other eight national central cities also take responsibility and work hard to become national central cities that fully follow the guidance of the new development concept, reflect the level and quality of national urban development, display the national image to the outside world, and play a leading, exemplary and radiating role in the country.

(II) "Hard Technology" Boosts High-Quality Economic Development

"Hard technology" is a general term for high-tech original technologies in terms of artificial intelligence, aerospace, biotechnology, photoelectric chip, information technology, new material, new energy, and intelligent manufacturing. Technological innovation provides strategic support for promoting high-quality development and building a modern and powerful country, and it is also one of the core functions of national central cities. Relying on their rich technological innovation elements, the nine national central cities keep quickening the pace of technological innovation, and the role of technological innovation in guiding the city's high-quality development is further strengthened. In November 2018, the Institute of International Technology and Economy of the Development Research Center of the State Council published the *2018 Hard Technology Innovation Index of Global Major Cities*, in which Beijing and Shanghai were ranked 2nd and 3rd, and Guangzhou and Xi'an 9th and 12th, respectively. This result demonstrated the strong innovation capabilities of national central cities. For example, Xi'an vigorously implemented the "hard technology +" strategy, clearly proposing to build itself into a city of hard technology. To this end, it compiled and introduced nine hard technology industry plans and held "The Global Hard & Core Technology Innovation and The Belt and Road Innovative Cooperation Conference 2018". Xixian New District took the lead in building the first hard technology town in the country. "Hard technology" is included in the national discourse system as an original concept from Xi'an. Beijing set up an RMB 30 billion technology innovation fund of funds focused on the layout of hard technology and early innovation attempts. The Zhongguancun Management Committee designated the first batch of 27 hard technology incubation platforms, each of which can receive a support fund up to RMB 10 million per year. Guangzhou also set up a RMB 5 billion industrialization guidance fund for technological achievements. The technology credit risk fund pool fueled bank loans by more than RMB 10 billion, and the number of equity investment institutions increased to 6,192. The city successfully held the "Convention on Exchange of Overseas Talents" and Canton Tower Science & Technology Conference. Wuhan had two new Nobel Prize workstations, 28 academician expert workstations, 47 well-known enterprise R&D institutions, 41 innovation platforms above the provincial level, and 51 provincial-level crowd innovation incubators; 1,237 new technology "little giants" and 500 gazelle enterprises were founded; the five unicorn enterprises put Wuhan in the 5th position among Chinese cities. Strengthening "hard technology" to lead the high-quality economic development of national central cities has become the biggest highlight in the national central city construction.

(III) "Coordination in Four Directions" to Build Inland Opening-up Bases

Participating in international competition is the responsibility and mission for every national central city. In 2018, the nine national central cities made full use of their own advantages and foundations in location, transportation and industry to respond actively to the Belt and Road Initiative and increase their level of opening up. In particular, the inland cities of Zhengzhou, Xi'an, Chengdu and Wuhan exerted forces "air", "onshore", "online" and "maritime", and made abundant achievements in the construction of inland opening-up bases. The "Air Silk Road" is getting wider and wider. Zhengzhou Airport obtained the Fifth Freedom and accommodates flights along 236 routes. An international hub route network spanning the three major economic zones of Europe, America and Asia has taken shape, making the airport the second transfer airport to integrate aviation, railway, rail transit and expressway in the country. Xi'an added seven international passenger routes to make the total number reach 64. Its air passenger volume jumped to the seventh in the country, and its cargo and mail handling capacity exceeded 310,000t, equivalent to the largest growth rate among the top ten airports in China. Xi'an Xianyang International Airport obtained the Fifth Freedom. Chengdu opened 12 new international regular direct passenger and cargo routes and had a total of 11 international (regional) routes. Shuangliu International Airport was the 26th busiest airport in the world. The "Onshore Silk Road" is running faster and faster. The China-Europe train (Zhengzhou) runs under a high frequency of "nine departure and eight return trips" every week. The new Central Asia and ASEAN routes are travelled in 752 trips throughout the year, keeping the main indicators at the national leading levels. The Railway Port Supervision Zone at Xi'an Port was officially put into use, and the China-Europe train "Chang'an" sets off on 1,235 trips. The train boasts the most actual total trips, the largest heavy load rate and the highest freight volume in the country. The new "Rongou+" ASEAN Rail-Ocean Intermodal Train and Railway Train drives to 24 overseas cities from Chengdu, and 1,591 "Rongou+" trips are operated in the whole year, still the No. 1 in the country. The "Online Silk Road" is getting more and more convenient. The construction of EWTO core function cluster was commenced in Zhengzhou, and 45 new contracted projects were signed. The 2nd Global Cross-Border E-Commerce Conference was successfully held, and the cross-border e-commerce transaction volume increased by 25.1%. Xi'an Branch of the People's Bank of China and Xi'an Municipal Government joined hands to actively build the "RMB Silk Road" cross-border e-commerce RMB settlement platform that provides ten "one-stop services" including RMB cross-border settlement, customs declaration and inspection, credit guarantee and trade financing. The platform builds an "Online RMB Silk Road" toward the global market. The "Maritime Silk Road" is becoming smoother. A total of 206 rail-ocean intermodal trips are provided from Zhengzhou to Lianyungang, Qingdao, Tianjin and other domestic ports. Wuhan now is connected to Ningbo via rail-ocean intermodal train.

(IV) "Talent Competition" Injects Forces to National Central City Construction

Talent is the first driving force for economic and social development and the most important resource for national central city construction. Both traditional first-tier cities like Beijing, Shanghai and Guangzhou and newcomers like by Wuhan, Chengdu and Zhengzhou quicken the pace of "talent competition" with intensified effort. In 2018, Wuhan continued to optimize its settlement policy by building "Yangtze Science City" and "Yangtze Youth City" and financing university rental houses to attract talents vigorously. In 2018 alone, Wuhan introduced 45 academicians and 281 high-level talents from foreign countries and other cities; 406,000 college graduates chose to stay in Wuhan and start their business, which set a record high. Wuhan had one of the largest net inflow of population among Chinese cities, reporting 300,800 new registered households and a total of 8.8373 million registered population. Xi'an actively implemented the recruitment policy of "retaining local talents and introducing foreign ones" and made great efforts to attract and train high-end scientific research talents, scarce management talents, and skilled and practical talents that are urgently needed for city development. In 2018, a total of 386,000 talents engaged in various specialties were introduced and trained, and 800,000 residents settled down. Chengdu issued "12 New Talents Polices" and introduced 34 experts under the national "Thousand Talents Program". More than 250,000 graduates holding bachelor degree or above chose to settle down in the city. Shanghai promulgated the *Action Plan for Shanghai to Accelerate the Implementation of Talent Peak Project* focused on 13 key fields that gather top talents such as cosmogony and celestial observation, photonic science and technology, and life sciences and biomedicine. The city also quickened the establishment of an internationally accepted selection mechanism, built internationally competitive career development platforms, and implemented an internationally accepted work system. A "talent peak" is looming on the basis of a "talent base" to gather and draw on talents from the world. Guangzhou has held the "Guangzhou Convention of Overseas Chinese Scholars in Science and Technology" (later renamed the "Convention on Exchange of Overseas Talents") for 20 consecutive years, which has become the "No. 1 brand of exchange of overseas Chinese scholars". In June 2019, Guangzhou issued the *Opinions on Implementing the Talent Attraction Plan*, which included 19 innovative initiatives designed to gather "highly educated, top, advanced and scarce" talents at home and abroad. Gathering and drawing on talents from the world and building talent bases to inject a steady stream of forces to the sustainable development of cities has become a consensus among the nine national central cities.

(V) Business Environment Is Optimized to Enhance the Competitiveness of Cities

Business environment is an important part of the comprehensive competitiveness of a country or region. The national central cities use the business environment assessment standards of the World Bank as a benchmark and have made remarkable results in the process of optimizing their business environment. They have become the epitome in this regard in the country. Beijing implemented in all round manners General Secretary Xi Jinping's request that Beijing should take the lead in reinforcing the business environment reform. It successively introduced the "9+N" policy measures and the three-year action plan for further optimizing the business environment. The city was the champion in a business environment trial evaluation of 22 Chinese cities and made contributions to the great progress of China in the ranking of the World Bank's Doing Business list. Shanghai established a big data center and put online a general portal of "one network processing" to integrate examination and approval into one process, one network and one government department. 1,274 formalities are now connected to the whole-process integrated online service platform. 90% of transactions require "only one errand" and can be "done with one try"; 99% of people's livelihood services can be processed in any competent department throughout the city. Tianjin accelerated the examination and approval system reform of "commitment system, and standardization, smartness and facilitation", the "Five Reductions" reform, the "Multi-certificate Integration" reform, managing to integrate 24 certificates; it has built "Tianjin Online Service Hall" and 50 "unmanned supermarkets" of government services. Over 90% of approval applications can be handled in "one network" with "one errand at most". Business registration can be done "without leaving home". "Eight Regulations of Tianjin" have become the highlight of its efforts in business environment optimization. Guangzhou has begun to implement the "20 Measures for Promoting the Development of Private Economy". The "one-day acceptance of business starting application" implemented in its Yuexiu District was commended by the State Council in the great inspection. Xi'an continued to deepen "Three Major Revolutions" and upgrade "Three Major New Policies". Xi'an government service network was put into use. 90% of transactions require "one errand at most" and 96% can be "done online". With this progress, Xi'an rose to the list of top ten cities with the best business environment in the country.

III Status Quo and Characteristics of Coordinated Regional Development Driven by National Central Cities

(I) Trends of Regional Interactive Development Are Looming after Persistence in Following the Guidance of Planning and Making Overall Progress

In recent years, the national central cities have followed the guidance of planning and coordinated the functional, spatial, transportation, facility and environmental connection with surrounding areas in fully implementing the national regional development strategy. For example, Beijing formulated and implemented the *New Three-year Action Plan for Beijing-Tianjin-Hebei Coordinated Development (2018-2020)*, which is closely linked with the *Planning Outline of Xiong'an New Area in Hebei*, the *Master Plan of Xiong'an New Area in Hebei (2018-2035)* and the Controlled *Detailed Planning of Deputy Urban Center in Beijing (Block Level) (2016-2035)*. The city also introduced a series of special plans and policies concerning industry, transportation, science and technology, ecology, facility and institutional mechanism to support the construction of areas assuming non-capital functions and the commencement of deputy urban center and Xiong'an New Area construction in all round manners. Shanghai worked actively with Jiangsu, Zhejiang and Anhui in facilitating the implementation of the first regional integrated development planning outline, the *Planning Outline of Regional Integrated Development in the Yangtze River Delta*, and signed special action plans including the *Framework Agreement on Cooperation in Connecting Inter-Provincial Dead End Highways in the Yangtze River Delta Region*, the *Cooperation Agreement on Jointly Promoting the Coordinated Development of Civil Aviation and Building a World-Level Airport Group in the Yangtze River Delta* and the *Six Action Plans for Jointly Promoting the Integrated Development of Port and Shipping in the Yangtze River Delta*, in order to deeply promote the integrated development of the Yangtze River Delta. While thoroughly implementing the plans of Guangzhou-Foshan integration, Guangzhou-Qingyuan integration and Guangzhou-Dongguan strategic cooperation, Guangzhou started with the approval of the *Development Plan Outline of Guangdong-Hong Kong-Macao Greater Bay Area* and actively participated in the design of the "1+N" planning system for the Greater Bay Area. Multiple plans and action plans for coordinated regional development in terms of industry, innovation and ecology were formulated. Chongqing and Sichuan signed the *Action Plan for Deepening Cooperation between Sichuan and Yunnan to Promote the Development of the Yangtze River Economic Belt (2018-2022)*, and initially established a joint meeting system that requires joint convening and rotary presiding by main leaders, driving the Chengdu-Chongqing city cluster to transform from concept to reality under the radiating effects of Chongqing and Chengdu. On the basis of the *Regional Development Plan for Wuhan Metropolitan Area (2013-2020)*, Wuhan further accelerated the preparation and implementation of special plans and action plans, and signed with three provincial capital cities (Changsha, Nanchang and Hefei) the *Action Plan for the Cooperation of Capital Cities in the City Cluster along the Middle Reaches of the Yangtze River (2017-2020), the Recent Key Cooperation Projects in the Construction of City Clusters along the Middle Reaches of the Yangtze River, the Framework Agreement on the Development of New Areas in Capital Cities in the City Cluster along the Middle Reaches of the Yangtze River*, and *the Cooperation Agreement on Joint Construction of Science and Technology Service Resources Sharing Platform in Capital Cities in the City Cluster along the Middle Reaches of the Yangtze River*, in order to deepen and refine exchange and cooperation. With an aim to accelerate the building of the core area in the Central Plains city cluster, Zhengzhou compiled the *Spatial Planning of Zhengzhou Metropolitan Area (2018-2035)* to accelerate the deep integration of Zhengzhou with Kaifeng, Xuchang, Xinxiang and Jiaozuo, and at the same time quickened the submission of six special plans on Zhengkai Innovative and Entrepreneurial Corridor, Kaigang Industrial Belt and Xugang Industrial Belt for approval. Xi'an issued the *2019 Action Plan for Promoting the Construction of the Guanzhong Plain Urban Cluster in Shaanxi Province* at the provincial level, which provides support for the construction of national central city later radiating to the development of the urban cluster. Generally speaking, these cities pay attention to the pioneering role of planning in guiding and driving regional development. By giving full play to the role of national central cities and implementing the national regional development strategy, they join hands with surrounding cities to accelerate concrete or new top-level design targeting at promoting regional cooperation and integrated development. Through the top-level design, they define the phased goals, strategic paths and main tasks for the national central cities to drive regional development. Some national central cities have basically erected "multiple pillars" in their attempt to drive coordinated regional development. The surrounding cities also respond to and integrate with the process actively, participating in the preparation and implementation of the overall planning and special action plans. They cooperate with the national central cities in terms of space, industry, infrastructure, public services, sharing of factors, ecological governance, and institutional mechanism. The breadth and depth of regional cooperation are constantly expanding, and trends of interactive regional development are looming.

(II) The Basic Support for Regional Coordination Is Constantly Strengthened after Persistence in Connectivity of Transportation Infrastructure

The connectivity of infrastructure is essential to the process of exploiting the radiating effect of the central cities, and it also lends a basic support for promoting coordinated regional development. Under the guidance of various regional development plans, the national central cities accelerate inter-regional connectivity of infrastructure. For example, Beijing and Tianjin accelerated the construction of rail transit projects such as Shijiazhuang-Jinan High-speed Railway, Tianjin-Baoding Railway, Beijing-Tangshan Railway, Beijing-Binhai Railway, Beijing-Xiongan Railway and Tianjin-Xiongan Intercity Railway, as well as the construction of expressways around the capital region. Active efforts were made to linking a number of "dead end highways" and "bottleneck roads". The preliminary work of the new Tianjin-Beijing airport connecting line progressed at faster speed, and a traffic pattern with four high-speed railways connecting Beijing with Tianjin is taking shape. At the same time, Tianjin also manages traffic control over visiting small-sized and mini buses carrying Beijing license. China T-union for Beijing-Tianjin-Hebei Region covers all bus and metro lines in the region. Shanghai worked with Jiangsu, Zhejiang and Anhui to jointly promote the work for road connection at provincial level. By the end of 2018, 19 provincial-level "dead end highways" spanning all of the four regions were constructed and 2 of them had been put into use. At the same time, 37 inter-provincial and intercity bus routes were opened to neighboring regions in the Yangtze River Delta, and zero bus transfer is about to become reality. On the basis of connectivity with Foshan,

Zhongshan and Zhuhai, Guangzhou promoted the opening the Guangzhou-Shenzhen-Hong Kong High-speed Railway and accelerated the construction of the Guangzhou-Hong Kong-Macao exit and entry building to efficiently connect the water routes to Hong Kong Airport and Macau Airport. As the Hong Kong-Zhuhai-Macao Bridge was put into operation, a one-hour convenient living circle and a 1.5h economic circle in the Guangdong-Hong Kong-Macau Greater Bay Area are able to take shape. As two of the first pilot cities to break the existing regional expressway network in the country, Chengdu and Chongqing had completed the transformation of a networked toll collection system by the end of 2018 on the basis of connectivity between high-speed rail and expressway. They technically implemented "separate billing and unified toll collection" for expressway traffic. The two cities also put into operation nearly 80 trips of bullet train and "midnight bullet train" per day. The bus-like operation of bullet train deepens the economic ties between small and medium-sized cities in the two places. Wuhan led the city cluster along the middle reaches of the Yangtze River to successively link more than 10 "dead end highways", and successively built special intercity railways to connect with Huangshi, Ezhou, Xishui, Xianning, Xiaogan, Xiantao, Qianjiang and Tianmen. It also gradually promoted "bus-like" operation of intercity railways and established a rail transit network in the city circle. While accelerating the construction of an international airport logistics hub and a Union Jack-shaped high-speed rail network, Zhengzhou quickened the pace of realizing connectivity with neighboring cities. At present, three intercity railways from Zhengzhou to the airport, Kaifeng and Jiaozuo have been put into operation. Within the metropolitan area of Zhengzhou, the expressway networks of all counties have been initially connected. In addition, partial integration of pipe corridors has been realized between Zhengzhou and Xinxiang. Zhengzhou also joined hands with Xuchang to construct and operate the Remote Terminal at Zhengzhou Airport. Xi'an formulated a subway construction plan for the Greater Xi'an Area (including Xixian New Area and Xianyang City) and quickened the implementation of the Union Jack-shaped high-speed rail network plan and the Guanzhong intercity railway network plan featuring "one core, double rings and six radiations". It also actively promoted the construction of intercity railways to the Famen Temple and Hancheng and from the airport to the Famen Temple and Yanliang, as well as the construction of high-speed railways to Yinchuan, Yan'an, Shiyan and Ankang. The main skeleton of the Guanzhong intercity railway network has basically taken shape. Connectivity of transportation infrastructure enables the national central cities and surrounding areas to gradually establish an efficient, convenient and integrated transportation network system, effectively breaks their physical space constraints, and continuously strengthens the basic support for coordinated regional development. Regional contacts of the central cities are thus continuously intensified, and personnel, logistics, information, capital and innovation flows between regions become frequent and efficient, which generates new factor flow modes such as "rail talent" ① and facilitates efficient flow and optimal allocation of production factors.

(III) Coordinated Development of Regional Industries Gains Momentum after Persistence in Joint Construction and Sharing of Element Resources Platforms

Shanghai actively promotes the coordinated innovation of 11 industrial parks in the Yangtze River Delta and plans to build the G60 S&T Innovation Valley② with other three provinces. It implements the *Action Outline for High-Quality Integrated Development of Industry Clusters in the G60 S&T Innovation Valley of Yangtze River Delta*, trying to drive high-quality integrated development of industries based on seven strategic emerging industries: artificial intelligence, integrated circuit, biomedicine, high-end equipment, new energy, new material and new energy vehicle. At the same time, a series of institutional mechanisms such as joint construction and sharing of scientific instrument and facility zone, universal acceptance and circulation of innovation vouchers, regional coordination along innovation chain, and investment data sharing will be built in the S&T Innovation Valley. Joint investment alliance, joint procurement alliance and industrial park alliance will be established to facilitate free flow of sci-tech innovation resources in the Yangtze River Delta and effectively push sci-tech innovation projects and new achievements. Shanghai also joined hands with the three other provinces to

① Rail talent mainly refers to the effective flow of talents due to connection between the central city and the surrounding areas that are connected by convenient rail transit, which allows high-end talents in the central city to commute between the central city and the surrounding areas at weekends or other non-working hours and thereby exploits talent efficiency.

② Songjiang District in Shanghai is the birth place of the S&T Innovation Valley, which was jointly established by Songjiang (Shanghai), Jiaxing, Huzhou, Hangzhou and Jinhua (Zhejiang), Suzhou (Jiangsu), Xuancheng, Wuhu and Hefei (Anhui). It is positioned as "a pioneering pilot valley driven by scientific and technological and institutional innovation and aimed to realize integrated development of industries and cities" in the regional planning of the Yangtze River Delta.

set up an RMB 100 billion Collaborative Advantage Industry Fund of the Yangtze River Delta which aims to accelerate the deep integration of the industrial chain in the Yangtze River Delta by investing in "hard technology" and other key fields. At the same time, in order to accurately connect the sci-tech innovation board, Pudong New Area and Shanghai Stock Exchange jointly planned and constructed a Capital Market Service Base of the Yangtze River Delta in Zhangjiang Science City to provide one-stop services for enterprises in the region to dock the capital market, strengthen collaborative innovation in the region, enhance the economic capabilities of financial service entities, and boost the integration and development of financial centers and S&T innovation centers. Following the regional innovation system that defines "original innovation in Beijing, research and development and transformation in Tianjin, application and promotion in Hebei", Beijing and Tianjin improved the results transformation mechanism and support policies and built a high-level national major sci-tech infrastructure and innovation platform and a display and trading platform of scientific research achievements to encourage the transfer and transformation of scientific and technological achievements in Tianjin, which would complement the advantages and maintain rational division of labor and orderly collaboration with Beijing and Hebei. Tianjin actively assumed the non-capital functions from Beijing and built a "1+16" pattern with Binhai New Area as the comprehensive platform and the other districts as specialized platforms. It also actively reinforced the effective cooperation with national ministries, central enterprises and large institutions. By the end of 2018, Binhai-Zhongguancun Science and Technology Park had added another 941 registered enterprises to its resident base, which had already occupied by a number of excellent projects including Baidu Innovation Center, JD Cloud Innovation Space, Tianjin Deepinfar Ocean Technology Co., Ltd., and China Intellectual Property Rights Protection Center. From 2014 to 2018, Beijing enterprises invested over RMB 640 billion in Tianjin, accounting for more than 40% of the total attracted domestic investment. Guangzhou lent active support to the construction the headquarters of Sinovation Ventures in the Guangdong-Hong Kong-Macao Greater Bay Area, and a local investment and AI R&D and service team consisting of dozens of members was established. A fund of RMB 2.5 billion was raised to invest in such fields as artificial intelligence and big data. Great efforts into extensive research, teaching and talent cultivation were made at well-known universities including The Hong Kong University of

Science and Technology, Nanjing University, Chinese Academy of Sciences, Peking University, Tsinghua University, and Shanghai Jiaotong University, for the purpose of training scientific and technological talents that are able to solve real-world problems with AI in the Greater Bay Area and contributing to technology progress and talents take-off. At the same time, relying on the advantages in smart manufacturing, Guangzhou seized the opportunity of re-industrialization in Hong Kong and commenced the construction of Guangzhou-Hong Kong Special Cooperation Zone for Smart Manufacturing, striving to establish cooperation in such fields as great biomedical health, artificial intelligence, electronic information, financial service, new energy and new material. Concerted efforts were made to build an innovation chain of "basic research + technology development + achievements transformation" in the Greater Bay Area and the Guangzhou-Shenzhen-Hong Kong Science and Technology Innovation Corridor. Taking advantage of scientific research resources and the high-tech industry foundation, Chengdu and Chongqing fully utilized the high-end factor gathering platforms of Tianfu New Area and Liangjiang New Area to jointly build a number of innovation parks and strategic emerging industrial bases that accommodate industry clusters of electronic core components, new materials, the Internet of Things and smart equipment, high-end transportation equipment and biomedicine. Wuhan and the other three provincial capital cities in Central China jointly set up the Union for Transfer of Scientific and Technological Achievements in the city cluster along the middle reaches of the Yangtze River to accelerate the transfer of scientific and technological achievements through the intercity sci-tech interoperability platform. More than 3,300 enterprises from Changsha, Nanchang and Hefei invested and registered in Wuhan, and more than 4,500 enterprises from Wuhan invested and registered in these three capital cities. Together with the other three capital cities in the city cluster along the middle reaches of the Yangtze River, Wuhan also promoted the establishment of a government-led "scientific and technological service resources sharing platform in the city cluster along the middle reaches of the Yangtze River" that operates both online and offline. The scientific and technological service industries of the four capital cities along the middle reaches of the Yangtze River form cooperation ecology, regular working platform and market-oriented cooperation mechanism to serve superior industry chains in the city cluster along the middle reaches of the Yangtze River. Relying on the Zhengzhou Airport Economy Zone as a platform that is involved in multiple national strategies, Zhengzhou built with surrounding cities an expansion area and a supporting area on the basis of the economy zone and promoted the transfer of a number of industries to Xinxiang, Xuchang and Jiaozuo, seeking complementary advantages, tax sharing and coordinated development between places through the "enclave economy" mode. In short, the national central cities are accelerating the coordinated development of regional industries through joint construction and sharing of element resources platforms, and a regional industrial ecosystem characterized by industry complementarity, chain extension and structural optimization is generated at a faster pace.

(IV) Regional Market Integration Is Accelerated after Persistence in Effective Connection of Rules and Systems

The decisive role of market in resources allocation is the fundamental driving force of regional economic cooperation. Observing market laws means breaking rules and institutional barriers between regions and establishing a unified and standardized rule and institutional system. In recent years, the national central cities have accelerated the integration of regional markets according to the requirement of building a unified, open, competitive and orderly market system. For example, the nine cities (districts) resident in the G60 S&T Innovation Valley of Yangtze River Delta initiated by Shanghai pioneered the operation of "one network processing" that allows 30 kinds of licenses across different provinces to "be certified in one place and processed on one network" online. Such "one network processing" model has now been extended to 14 cities in the Yangtze River Delta and applies to 51 transactions, including 30 business service transactions and 21 personal service transactions. At the same time, business license, resident ID card, driver's license, marriage certificate, residence permit and birth certificate, can be electronically certified in the government service APPs of the three provinces and Shanghai. A regional credit cooperation mechanism was built in the Yangtze River Delta and introduced an exploratory cross-regional credit joint reward and punishment model in the country. The first identification criteria for regional serious moral crisis in the field of environmental protection were issued, and 40 joint disciplinary measures classified into eight categories that cover administrative, social, market and industrial fields were introduced. The Beijing-Tianjin-Hebei region took the lead in implementing the integration of customs clearance that shortens the customs clearance time by an average of 41 days. At the same time, under the leadership of the Ministry of Public Security, Beijing introduced and implemented 20 innovative entry and exit policies. Positive progress has also been made in mechanism integration reforms such as risk sharing, payment and settlement, and reciprocal and interoperable deposits in different places in the banking industry in Beijing-Tianjin-Hebei region. Relying on the construction of the Greater Bay Area, Guangzhou promoted the interconnection with financial markets in Hong Kong and Macao in an orderly manner and advanced institutional, market and product synergies; it also promoted the implementation of the "exit and entry inspections in one place" policy applicable to Guangdong, Hong Kong and Macao; Guangzhou also joined hands with Hong Kong and Macao to strengthen safety cooperation in markets of edible agricultural products through active explorations and trials by creating a "vegetable basket" information-based product circulation platform in the Guangdong-Hong Kong-Macao Greater Bay Area and by adopting the operation mode of "one market standard, one circulation platform, and one quality safety supervision system" to build a strict quality safety supervision network system of agricultural products in Guangdong-Hong Kong-Macao Greater Bay Area; Guangzhou High-tech Zone took the lead in setting up the Entry and Exit Public Service Platform for Biomaterials from South China in Guangzhou International Bio Island. An innovative supervision model featuring "release from port, inspection by platform and follow-up supervision" was adopted to greatly reduce the time for customs clearance of biological reagents; policies and measures that offer convenience to Hong Kong and Macao residents who wish to develop in the Mainland are implemented under the support of institutional innovation, and breakthroughs have been made in cross-border use of research funds, cancellation of employment permit, and residence permit policy for Hong Kong and Macao residents. Together with Changsha, Nanchang and Hefei, Wuhan called for 26 cities in the city cluster along the middle reaches of the Yangtze River signed the *Memorandum of Cooperation between Non-governmental Chambers of Commerce in the Four Cities of the City Cluster (Nanchang) and Associated City Circles along the Middle Reaches of the Yangtze River*. The purpose of cooperation is to fully integrate various resources from the city circles associated with the four cities, chambers of commerce in cities (prefecture-level cities) involved in the "integration" strategy and their non-governmental peers based in different regions, industries and other cities. A "great chamber of commerce" cooperation mechanism in the middle reaches of the Yangtze River is built to promote a new model for regional integration, coordinated development and win-win among non-governmental chambers of commerce. The 4 cities also promoted the integration and sharing of business and government information, established an integrated mechanism of quality and technology supervision and a coordination mechanism of food and drug inspection, and initially realized the integration of customs clearance. At the same time, they quickened the pace of breaking regional administrative barriers to boost market integration and built the first cross-regional, inter-provincial government cloud project in the country-the business and government cloud platform of provincial capital cities (regions) in the city cluster along the middle reaches of the Yangtze River. They canceled the verification of qualification certificates, personal practice certificates and related credit status required for enterprises that seek access from other cities in the city cluster. Instead, corporate information is collected directly, and newcomers are treated in the same way as local enterprises. Direct competent departments from different provinces agreed to cancel the registration of construction enterprises coming from anywhere within the scope of the four provincial capital cities; Wuhan and Changsha also jointly built the first cross-provincial cooperation platform for public resources transactions in the middle reaches of the Yangtze River, which makes remote bid evaluation spanning two cities possible. Chengdu and Chongqing, Zhengzhou and Xi'an are also exploring the establishment of a cost and benefit sharing mechanism for coordinated development. Thcy promoted capital, technology and other market integration mechanisms, established and improved the horizontal coordination mechanism of the hinterland economic zone around Chongqing, and set up a rotating joint conference system joined by counties, cities and districts concerned to negotiate and resolve issues related to regional cooperation. In short, these national central cities make active explorations based on the integration of regional markets, accelerate pioneering attempts, and focus on removing institutional mechanism obstacles. They also press for the unification of inter-regional market rules and systems and encourage the formation of a unified open market supporting free flow of elements. With a series of institutional mechanism barriers broken, they also actively explore a new mechanism for integrated development of regional markets, one that features unified rules and systems, joint development models, consistent governance approaches, and interactive regional markets to inject more endogenous dynamics to regional integrated development.

(V) The Social Environment for Regional Integration Is Continuously Improved after Persistence in Mutual Recognition and Sharing of Public Service Systems

A regional integrated public service system can enhance social adhesion and recognition between regions. The national central cities put effort in promoting mutual recognition and sharing of public service systems within regions and effectively enhanced the mobilization of regional factors and the social recognition of residents. For example, Shanghai and 17 cities including Nanjing, Taizhou, Lianyungang, Hangzhou and Wenzhou jointly established a cross-provincial pilot coordinated zone for remote settlement of clinical services in the Yangtze River Delta, which has realized direct settlement of clinical service expenses incurred in other places. At the same time, the medical insurance departments of Jiangsu, Zhejiang, Anhui and Shanghai included four prioritized insured groups, i.e. relocated retirees, permanent residents in other places, resident workers in other places, and referrals from other places, into the pilot scope, optimize the services, streamline the procedures, and expand the channels of registration and referral. Beijing, together with Tianjin and Hebei, ran schools on the basis of cross-regional cooperation, and such schooling projects allowed primary and secondary schools in Tianjin and Hebei to share high-quality digital resources in Beijing. Nine innovative development alliances, including Beijing-Tianjin-Hebei Alliances of Industrial and Normal Colleges, were founded. At the same time, the new rural cooperative information platforms from the three places were connected. Beijing and Hebei continued to promote two-way referral and mutual recognition of examination and inspection results. A pilot project of direct settlement of clinical service expenses and joint procurement of medical consumables in public hospitals were carried out in Beijing, Tianjin and Hebei. Tianjin and Xiong'an New Area strengthened cooperation in vocational education and social insurance system construction in all aspects.

Tianjin Vocational Institute, Tianjin the First Business School and Tianjin Garden School all set up their branch in Xiong'an New Area. In addition, the coordinated development of "Small Beijing-Tianjin-Hebei" in Tongwulang was accelerated. The mutual recognition of clinical examination results, sharing of medical imaging examination data, and mutual recognition and approval of professional qualifications among medical institutions in the three places were realized. During the process of integrating with neighboring cities, Guangzhou effectively allocated public resources in education, medical care, social security and culture. Unemployment insurance of mobile workers can be transferred barrier-free between different regions. Mutual recognition of medical insurance designated hospitals between any two cities has become a reality. The mutual recognition of medical examinations and imaging examination results and the direct settlement of medical expenses of insured patients were advanced. At the same time, faster progress was made for connectivity of education metropolitan areas network. Secondary vocational school enrollment is no longer subject to geographic restrictions, and integration of mobile communication rates has been realized in some cities. Wuhan accelerated the connectivity and mutual recognition of medical expenses, social security and education with the city cluster along middle reaches of the Yangtze River represented by Changsha and Nanchang. On-spot settlement of remote medical expenses covered by medical insurance for workers is realized among Wuhan, Changsha and Nanchang. They also explored mutual recognition and mutual mortgage of inter-provincial housing provident funds and issued unified policy and procedures for applying for long-distance housing provident fund loans. These four central capital cities also founded the "Public Health Collaboration Center in the city cluster along the middle reaches of the Yangtze River" and a first-aid alliance, which has been developed from the four cities to 20 cities along the middle reaches of the Yangtze River. Integration of telecommunications services has been realized among Zhengzhou, Kaifeng and Xinxiang, and they are speeding up the study on sharing of transportation services, financial services and public resources. By constructing mutually recognized and shared regional public service systems, the barriers to public service mechanisms among the national central cities and surrounding areas are gradually eliminated, and the social environment for regional integration is continuously optimized. Regional frictions are effectively reduced by improved social welfare.

(VI) A Regional Ecological Security Pattern Is Being Shaped At Faster Speed after Persistence in Coordinated Governance of Regional Ecological Environment

Ecological environmental protection is a hard task and a major premise in regional governance. The national central cities adhere to the concept of "ecological priority, green development", focus on improving the regional environmental governance capacity, strengthen ecological protection and restoration, promote prevention and control of air, water and soil pollution, carry out join treatment of regional pollution and joint ecological construction, and inject green power to coordinated regional development. For example, Shanghai led the establishment of the Regional Pollution Prevention Collaboration and Water Pollution Prevention Collaboration Group in the Yangtze River Delta, held a meeting on the regional pollution prevention coordination mechanism in the Yangtze River Delta in conjunction with other provinces and municipalities, and established a regional meteorological integration business platform in the Yangtze River Delta to "trace the source" of regional air pollution and control pollution from the source. At the regional level, synchronous observation with big data radar and information sharing between meteorological and environmental protection departments of different cities have become practice, which effectively improves the observation ability in pollution transmission and practically addresses the previous time lag of weather forecast. At the same time, a pollution transmission evaluation system was established to conduct quantitative assessment of key meteorological conditions and contributions to transmission in the Yangtze River Delta and the three provinces and Shanghai, which further provides good information and data support for environmental protection departments in different regions to prevent and control pollution sources; credit offices and ecological environment departments in the three provinces and Shanghai also signed the *Memorandum of Understanding on Implementing Joint Credit Reward and Punishment in the Field of Environmental Protection in the Yangtze River Delta*, and strengthened cooperation in mutually recognizing the evaluation criteria of moral crisis, establishing a data collection and sharing mechanism, promoting joint disciplinary measures, and creating a good environmental credit environment. Enterprises committing serious environmental discredit from different regions are exposed in the joint credit platform and subject to restrictions in market access and financial credit as joint disciplinary measures taken by the coordinated regions. Beijing, in conjunction with Tianjin and Hebei, accelerated the coordinated regional management of air, water and soil, strengthened joint prevention and control, and unified their efforts in planning, standardizing, monitoring and emergency response to heavy air pollution. At the same time, the construction of major ecological projects such as the Beijing-Tianjin-Baoding plain ecotone and the comprehensive treatment and ecological restoration project of Yongding River were accelerated; the ecological compensation mechanism for water source protection in the upper reaches of Miyun Reservoir and the horizontal ecological compensation mechanism for upstream and downstream of Luanhe River diverted to Tianjin were constructed and improved. The competent department of the state also worked with Beijing, Tianjin, Hebei, Shanxi and Henan governments to distribute a work plan on air pollution prevention and control in the Beijing-Tianjin-Hebei region and surrounding areas; Beijing, Tianjin and Hebei jointly formulated the "2+26" work plan on urban air pollution prevention and control, in which "2+26" means Beijing and Tianjin Municipalities, as well as eight cities in Hebei Province including Shijiazhuang, Tangshan and Langfang, four cities in Shanxi Province including Taiyuan, Yangquan and Changzhi, seven cities in Shandong Province including Jinan, Zibo, Jining and Dezhou, and seven cities in Henan Province including Zhengzhou, Kaifeng, Anyang and Hebi, all of which together form an air pollution control channel in the Beijing-Tianjin-Hebei region. Within the framework of advancing integrated development with neighboring cities, Guangzhou coordinated regional environmental protection work such as cross-basin management of the Pearl River, cross-regional control of atmospheric environment and treatment of automobile exhaust, helping make the Pearl River Delta the first demonstration zone of national-level forest city cluster. Wuhan took the lead in formulating and implementing an overall plan on ecological protection and green development of the Yangtze River Economic Belt at the provincial level, setting up the rule of prioritizing ecological protection from the source. At the same time, the first pilot ecological civilization demonstration zone along the Yangtze River Economic Belt was built in Qingshan District of Wuhan to promote the planning, construction of ecological reserve forests, ecological restoration, water environment management, land consolidation, three old transformations, infrastructure upgrading, construction of characteristic town, and city-industry integrated development within the ecological civilization pilot scope (Beihu Lvcheng) in Beihu, Qingshan District. These are all exploratory attempts in the whole province. Other cities are also accelerating the establishment of institutional mechanisms for regional joint ecological prevention and control. In short, these cities have always regarded ecological civilization construction and ecological environmental protection as matters essential to the overall picture. They emphasize and strengthen the top-level design of ecological civilization construction, and establish and perfect a working mechanism featuring national guidance, local responsibility, regional cooperation, and ministerial and provincial collaboration. They also gain momentum in advancing sharing of ecological environment data and information, carry out joint ecological construction and governance at multiple levels and in multiple forms, and practically manage pollution control and ecological restoration. Thanks to these efforts, a regional ecological security pattern is being shaped at faster speed.

IV Environmental Analysis of the Coordinated Regional Development Driven by National Central Cities

(I) Opportunities

1 China has entered a stage of high-level and high-quality coordinated regional development

Since the reform and opening up, China has implemented a regional development strategy which schedules coastal areas to develop earlier and get richer first, followed by strategies such as the Western Development Strategy, the Revitalization of the Northeast Strategy, and the Rise of Central China Strategy. All regions actively foster regional economic growth poles, allowing resources to pool in developed areas and spread to economic hinterlands. New regional development patterns of "east-middle-west cascade" and "south-south differentiation" have taken shape. Imbalanced regional development remains a conspicuous issue. Therefore, the coordinated regional development strategy was put forward at the 19th National Congress of CPC and was incorporated as one of the seven national major strategies, which marked the new stage of coordinated regional development strategy in China. On November 18, 2018, the CPC Central Committee and the State Council issued the *Opinions of the CPC Central Committee and the State Council on Establishing a More Effective Coordinated Regional Development Mechanism*, proposing to establish a more effective coordinated regional development mechanism, fully implement the tasks set out in the coordinated regional development strategy, and move toward a higher-level and high-quality stage. It was clearly stated at the Central Economic Working Conference held at the end of 2018 that coordinated regional development should be promoted by coordinating the development of the Western Region, the comprehensive revitalization of the Northeast, the rise of Central China, and the forerunner development of the Eastern Region. This also provides a new historical opportunity for the construction of national central cities, which requires adaptation to local conditions, coordinated development of the Eastern, Central and Western regions in spite of their differences, and rational layout of national central cities. Each region has its own national central cities to support and lead the regional development. As for the selection and layout of national central cities, five out of nine are located in the Central and Western regions. They are expected to seize opportunities and drive the development of surrounding small and medium-sized cities to seek coordinated development. They should also actively foster regional economic growth poles, lead regional economy, optimize regional development patterns, and become important driving forces to narrow the gap in regional development.

2 Five Regional Development Strategies Contribute to the Formation of New Regional Development Patterns

On November 5, 2018, President Xi Jinping stated in his keynote speech at the opening ceremony of the First China International Import Expo held in Shanghai that "We will support integrated development of the Yangtze River Delta. We will make it a national strategy and implement our new development concept in real earnest. We will build a modern economic system, adopt higher standards for reform and opening-up and achieve a higher level of opening to the outside world. The region will develop in tandem with the Belt and Road Initiative, the Beijing-Tianjin-Hebei coordinated development area, the Yangtze River Economic Belt and the Guangdong-Hong Kong-Macao Greater Bay Area, and will help improve the overall layout of China's reform and opening-up." This declaration marked that advancing the integrated development of the Yangtze River Delta officially becomes a national strategy and a network of five major regional development strategies is shaped to break the constraints of administrative division, allocate and optimize resource elements on a larger scale, and focus more on coordinated development across administrative regions. Not only is the radiating effect of developed coastal cities is exploited, but also more efforts and more support are involved for the economic development of the whole country and to foster multiple economic centers nationwide. Of the five national-level regional development strategies, the regional integration of the Yangtze River Delta, the construction of the Guangdong-Hong Kong-Macao Greater Bay Area, and the coordinated development of the Beijing-Tianjin-Hebei region are concerned about the Yangtze River Delta, the Pearl River Delta, and the Beijing-Tianjin-Hebei region, respectively, all of which have already been highly integrated. The national central cities of Shanghai, Guangzhou, Beijing and Tianjin are located in the "spire" and central positions of regional development in these regions. They have become engines that fuel regional development and are on their way to the status of world-class cities. Chongqing, Chengdu, Wuhan, Zhengzhou and Xi'an, on the other hand, are involved in the Yangtze River Economic Belt and the Belt and Road Innovative. They should seize opportunities brought about by the Yangtze River Economic Belt and the Belt and Road Innovative, speed up the opening up as inland areas, and enhance their radiating effect as central cities to drive regional development and become important driving forces for high-quality development.

3 Metropolitan Areas and City Clusters Will Become the Main Patterns of City Development in China

China's city development will follow the trajectory of "central cities-metropolitan areas-city clusters-regional economic integration", which means a process of expanding from central cities, to metropolitan areas, to city clusters and to a regional economic integration development pattern with city clusters as the main body while large, medium-sized and small cities as well as small towns develop in an coordinated manner. Regional integration with metropolitan areas and city clusters as the main carriers will become the core driving force for future regional development. In 2018, 34 metropolitan areas led by the central cities accounted for 24% of the country's total area, 59% of the national total population, and 77.8% of the national total GDP. China's new urbanization development officially ushered in the era of metropolitan areas. The development of metropolitan areas is a general law and a common phenomenon in the urbanization process in the world. Powerful metropolitan areas can help magnify the radiating capacity of the central cities in city clusters and strengthen the ties between the central cities and the surrounding small and medium-sized cities. On September 28, 2018, while presiding over a symposium on promoting the revitalization of the Northeast China in Shenyang, General Secretary Xi Jinping put forward for the first time the requirement for "developing modern metropolitan areas." In February 2019, the National Development and Reform Commission issued the *Guiding Opinions on Developing Modern Metropolitan Areas*, requiring all localities and departments to unify their thinking, strengthen organizational leadership, sharpen their sense of responsibility, and actively develop modern metropolitan areas with methods of reform and innovative spirits. City cluster represents the very top spatial organization form in the mature stage of urban development. It is the main form of new-type urbanization in China. However, most of the city clusters in China now are in their infancy, and metropolitan areas have not yet entered a mature stage. Development of central cities should be prioritized in more city clusters and metropolitan areas, and core growth poles of regional development should be fostered and radiate to the surrounding areas. The nine national central cities are all strategically located in regional centers or hubs. They are positioned in the centers of their respective city clusters and metropolitan areas, shouldering the important task of and driving regional development. These national central cities should be upgraded by gathering high-end elements, optimizing transportation networks and accelerating industrial upgrading to truly become "strong cores" of their own metropolitan areas and city clusters.

(II) Challenges

1 The Challenge of Improving International Competitiveness under the Context of World Economic Pattern Being Adjusted and Reformed

The world economic pattern has come to the critical turning point of major reforms. In 2018, the world economy grew moderately, and the growth rate slowed down. Although peace and development were still the theme of the times, the trend of "reverse globalization" emerged; trade protectionism and unilateralism gained ground; global economic and trade rules undergone profound adjustment. The United States not only imposed tariffs on Chinese exports through a series of policies such as "normalization of monetary policy", "protectionism" and "high standardization of trade agreements", but also took a lot of restrictive measures in the fields of high-tech transfer, investment, research and development, and personnel exchanges. It also tried to conspire with other developed countries to establish new trade rules that exclude China. This will have different impacts on China's exports, investment and even consumption. For some time to come, China will have to rebuild its relations with the world. It will be faced with a more complicated external environment where unfavorable factors will increment. This will introduce more challenges to China, which is making great efforts to transform its economic development mode and growth momentum and to promote high-quality development. Trade protectionism will hinder the national central cities from using and allocating resources on a global scale, from participating in international division of labor and cooperation, and from advancing their internationalization process. The supreme goal of national central city construction is to become world cities with international influence and competitiveness. Some of the central cities are not strong enough and have to further improve their ability to participate in international competition.

2 The Challenge of Coordinating Agglomeration Development and Driving Regional Development

The national central cities are the "spire" of the new pyramid spatial pattern of city development, shouldering the dual tasks of seeking development on their own and driving regional development. On the one hand, national central city construction needs to gather various element resources, accelerate their own development, and become bases and growth poles for regional development. In this process, a siphon effect or a polarization effect will result as funds, talents and quality industries can be attracted easily to big cities from the surrounding small cities, posing challenges on the development of small cities. On the other hand, the agglomeration of the national central cities themselves can powerfully pool high-quality resource elements, transfer element resources and some industries to surrounding areas, and generate radiating effects to drive the development of surrounding areas and narrow the gap between the central cities and the surrounding small and medium-sized cities. Thus, how to balance the siphon effect and the radiating effect is a major challenge for national central city construction. Due to the different locations of the national central cities, they stay in different development stages and assume different functions. For example, Shanghai and Guangzhou are more capable of pooling elements and have better economic strength, so they are better at driving the development of the surroundings and have been part of an integrated development pattern with the surrounding areas. In spite of their great comprehensive strength, Beijing and Tianjin play a weaker role in driving the development of the surroundings. How to drive the development of the surrounding areas and allow the radiating effect to outweigh the siphon effect is a tough issue for them. Other national central cities, i.e. Chongqing, Chengdu, Wuhan, Zhengzhou and Xi'an, are tempering their ability to pool population and production factors in an attempt to develop and empower themselves. They are not strong enough to drive the surroundings. For them, how to drive the weaker surrounding small and medium-sized cities is a huge challenge, and how to balance the siphon effect and the radiating effect is another problem.

3 The Challenge of Maintaining Sustainable Competitiveness

National central cities should own sustainable competitiveness. In other words, while making full use of the existing factors to gain development advantages and seek economic growth, they can shape their future development advantages and accumulate the factors that can contribute to long-term growth. To maintain sustainable competitiveness, they have to be able to keep long-term economic growth. During the construction process, some of the national central cities are undergoing industrial restructuring and are still in transition from old growth drivers to new ones before their industrial upgrading is completed. They have not fostered new impetus to fuel long-term economic development. Sustainable competitiveness requires a balance between multiple goals, such as economic development, ecological environment, social welfare, and scientific and technological innovation, and further improvement in economic efficiency on this basis. As large populations move to the national central cities, some of them have found their resources and environment tightening and approaching the upper limit of carrying capacity. Environmental pollution such as haze and water pollution can hardly be addressed in the short term. There is still a huge gap between improvement in environmental quality and the expectations of the people, which restricts the development of cities. In addition, improving sustainable competitiveness requires the national central cities to increase urban residents' access to more welfare while improving their quality of life and social welfare. Some of the central cities are now stuck in growing pains manifested in traffic congestion, shortage of public resources and management malfunctions. There is a long way to go before people's longing for a better life is turned into reality. To improve the environment, increase the living standards and welfare level of the people, and enhance the ability and competitiveness of sustainable development while achieving economic growth is another challenge facing the national central cities in the future.

V Prospects and Suggestions for Coordinated Regional Development Driven by National Central Cities

(I) Prerequisites for Inclusion of New National Central Cities

From the perspectives of basic connotation, strategic positioning, and functions, two basic conditions have to be met in order to be qualified as national central cities:

The first condition is to meet the functional requirements for national central cities. Such functional requirements mainly include driving capacity and market recognition. In terms of the capacity to drive regional development, candidates for national central cities must have a high functional level, one that is higher than other cities in the same region or city cluster, and must be able to play a central role in the economic, social, cultural, and innovative development processes in a larger scale in the country. They are also supposed to be economic centers, cultural centers, management centers, innovation centers, financial centers, logistics centers, foreign exchange centers, and probably, the political centers of the local administrative region. The strong pooling and driving capacity of national central cities should enable them to effectively transfer their production capacity, innovation capacity and service capacity to other node towns in the national or regional urban system, thus driving the efficient development of the entire region. In terms of gaining wide market recognition, the qualification to be a national central city is ultimately determined by market, rather than by government planning or arbitrary will. The key is whether the candidate has the basic functions expected in a national central city. Although national planning defines the goal of national central city construction, the final historical status has yet to be established by market recognition. New national central cities must be screened by market recognition in terms of historical status, comprehensive strength, education and research, health care, and transportation location.

The second condition is to fit with the overall layout of coordinated regional development in the country. Judging from the existing nine national central cities, a basic requirement for becoming a national central city is strong centrality: First of all, the candidates should be central cities in the national urban system. The concept of "national central city" was first proposed by the former Ministry of Housing and Urban-Rural Development in an official document titled the *National Urban System Plan (2006-2020)*, which clearly positioned Beijing, Tianjin, Shanghai, Guangzhou, and Chongqing as five national central cities. In the national urban system plan, the national central cities are selected from central cities in the national urban system. In the short term, other cities are unlikely to be included in the central city rank under the national urban system and least likely to be further included in the national central city rank. Secondly, the candidates should be core cities in state-level city clusters. Their predecessors are Chengdu, Zhengzhou, Wuhan and Xi'an. For example, the *Development Plan of City Clusters along the Middle Reaches of the Yangtze River* issued in 2015 clearly indicated that Wuhan is the central city in the city cluster along the middle reaches of the Yangtze River. In 2016, the National Development and Reform Commission issued the *Development Plan of Chengdu-Chongqing City Cluster*, which clearly stated that Chengdu should pursue the goal of becoming a national central city to strengthen its functions as an important economic center, science and technology center, cultural and creative center, foreign exchange center and integrated transportation hub in the Western Region. In December 2016, with the official approval of the State Council, the National Development and Reform Commission issued the *13th Five-Year Plan for Promoting the Rise of the Central Region*, which explicitly supported Wuhan and Zhengzhou to obtain the qualification for being national central cities. The status of Zhengzhou as a national central city was later identified in the development plan for the urban cluster in the Central Plains. On February 2, 2018, the *Notice on Distributing Plan on the Development of*

Guanzhong Plain City Cluster issued by the National Development and Reform Commission and the Ministry of Housing and Urban-Rural Development clearly stated that Xi'an would be built into a national central city to strengthen its functions as comprehensive service and foreign exchange portal in the Northwest Region. From this perspective, another significant channel leading to the rank of national central cities is to become a core city in a state-level city cluster. Fourthly, the candidates should be central cities in regional development. As the national central city rank is expanding, Chongqing, Wuhan and Xi'an are highly recognized as national central cities as they are the primate cities in Southwest China, Central China, and Northwest China, respectively. New national central cities must also be central cities in large regions of China and are able to effectively drive the development of a particular region.

New national central cities should not only perform the core functions granted by the title, but also put in place the strategic layout for coordinated regional development. Some cities have been put in the waiting list to be national central cities, such as Shenzhen, Nanjing, Shenyang and Xiamen given the current national macro-strategic layout, land development pattern and opening-up layout of China, in response to the comprehensive strength and dynamic development evolution of major mega-cities and large cities, and according to the adjustment and changes in the current coordinated regional development policies of China.

(II) Thinking and Tasks in Coordinated Regional Development Driven by National Central Cities

1 General Thinking in Coordinated Regional Development Driven by National Central Cities

The general thinking in coordinated regional development driven national central cities is as follows: to optimize the spatial combination and factor flow channels constituted by central cities-metropolitan areas-city clusters-regions, build new models of city cluster development led by central cities and regional development driven by city clusters, and exploit the strength of Beijing and Tianjin to lead the development of Beijing-Tianjin-Hebei city cluster and drive the coordinated development of the Bohai Sea rim area; to lead the development of city clusters in the Yangtze River Delta with Shanghai as the center to drive the development of the Yangtze River Economic Belt; to lead the construction of Guangdong-Hong Kong-Macao Greater Bay Area with Guangdong, Hong Kong, Macao and Shenzhen as the centers to drive the innovative and green development of the Pearl River-Xijiang Economic Belt; to lead the development of city clusters in such areas as Chengdu-Chongqing, the middle reaches of the Yangtze River, the Central Plains, the Guanzhong Plain, Harbin-Changchun, and the Western Taiwan Strait with Chongqing, Chengdu, Wuhan, Zhengzhou, Xi'an, Changchun and Xiamen as the centers, and finally to further promote inter-regional and inter-sectoral integrated and interactive development, at a faster speed and under the guidance of major strategies like the Belt and Road Initiative, the coordinated development of Beijing-Tianjin-Hebei, the development of the Yangtze River Economic Belt, the construction of Guangdong-Hong Kong-Macao Greater Bay Area, and the integration of the Yangtze River Delta in the four major sectors of the Eastern Region, the Central Region, the Western Region, and the Northeast Region.

2 Key Tasks of Coordinated Regional Development Driven by National Central Cities

Plan a functional system for coordinated regional development driven by national central cities. China has a total land area of about 9.6 million square kilometers. By the end of 2018, its total population had been nearly 1.4 billion. Considering that regional development remains unbalanced, a number of strategic fulcrums to support the entire country and a "network system of national central cities" with reasonable layout are needed. Within such a network system, Beijing, Shanghai and Guangzhou should aim at becoming global cities that also serve as the hubs for allocation of global resources and that occupy global competitive advantages; Chongqing, Chengdu, Wuhan, Zhengzhou and Xi'an should try to develop outstanding specialized advantages in such fields as technological innovation, cultural exchanges, commercial trade, transportation hub and advanced manufacturing throughout the country so as to occupy a niche in the global division of labor network. At the same time, they should be positioned as central cities in sub-regions of the country to support national land development and drive coordinated regional development.

Construct a carrier platform for coordinated regional development driven by national central cities. As a geographical form on a large spatial scale, the development of regions driven by the national central cities as single "energy sources" is limited on a large scale, coupled with the attenuation of interaction between cities with spatial distance. It is necessary to establish sound and complete central city-level energy transmission mechanism and channel to facilitate coordinated development of regions. Thus, a strategic pattern of "urban system-characteristic towns-rural revitalization for coordinated development of national central cities-metropolitan areas-large, medium and small cities" along the full spatial combination chain should be established more quickly to drive free flow and efficient configuration of factors between regions and between urban and rural areas. Now a more important development carrier is metropolitan areas. Currently, different regions have come to different development stages, and intra-regional development is imbalanced as well. Therefore, some part of the full spatial combination chain should be highlighted, especially the national central cities, in the active building of metropolitan areas, which should be advanced according to local conditions. Successful experience should be summed up in a timely manner. Metropolitan areas should be treated as an important foundation for the construction of city clusters to promote their integrated development.

Strengthen the strategic coordination of national central cities to drive coordinated regional development. This is carried out at mainly two levels: First, the national central cities must strengthen coordination of their strategic planning platforms. Take Zhengzhou as an example. When a number of national strategic planning platforms are deployed in Henan, Zhengzhou is positioned as an important component of those national strategic planning platforms. In particular, the implementation of leading strategies such as Zhengzhou Airport Economy Zone, the China (Henan) Pilot Free Trade Zone, and the Zheng-Luo-Xin National Innovation Demonstration Area has made Zhengzhou an important gateway to the outside world, an experimental field for comprehensively deepening reform, and a core carrier for seeking innovation-driven development. Since the provincial capital of Henan Province was relocated from Kaifeng to Zhengzhou in 1954, Zhengzhou had faced with historical opportunities brought by many national strategies by early 2017. Becoming a national central city under state support not only means to Zhengzhou a new national strategy, but also is an inevitable result of the integration of many national strategic plans and strategic platforms and an intensive representation of its function and role in the regional structure of the country. In other words, the central government supports

Zhengzhou as a national central city not only because its development potential and strategic status are highly recognized, but also because its comparative advantages and shortcomings in development are well understood. In order to maximize the superposition effect of the national strategic planning platforms and accelerate the pace of building Zhengzhou into a national central city, a systemic thinking should be established and the coordinated and interactive development of the strategic planning platforms should be pursued. Secondly, strategic coordination between the national central cities and their city clusters and others of their countries should be strengthened. The strategic coordination between city clusters such as Beijing-Tianjin-Hebei City Region, Guangdong-Hong Kong-Macau Greater Bay Area, the Yangtze River Delta, the middle reaches of the Yangtze River, Chengdu-Chongqing City Cluster, the Central Plains City Cluster, and Harbin-Changchun City Cluster with strategies like the Belt and Road Initiative and the Yangtze River Economic Belt to drive coordinated development the Eastern Region, the Northeast Region, the Central Region and the Western Region.

Strengthen the cooperation and mutual assistance between the national central cities in driving coordinated regional development. Deepen cooperation and mutual assistance between city clusters, metropolitan areas and the national central cities, and increase the quality and level of cooperation. Develop various social intermediary organizations vigorously and regional industry associations and chambers of commerce in an orderly manner, and encourage enterprises to set up cross-regional and cross-sectoral cooperation platforms in industry, technology, innovation and talents. Actively explore the city cluster coordinated governance model and encourage the establishment of various forms of city alliances. At present, a transition is gradually made from hardware connectivity to software linkup between and within regions. The connection in terms of medical care, education and social security between regions and especially neighboring areas should be strengthened in order to realize optimal allocation of social resources and equalization of public services.

(III) Measures and Suggestions for Strengthening Regional Coordinated Development Driven by the National Central Cities

Build a fast transit network system. A fast transit system is the basic support for the flow of various production factors between the natural central cities and hinterlands and other national central cities and regions. The expansion of city clusters undermines the closeness of ties between cities in China. To drive coordinated regional development, the national central cities have, first of all, to speed up factor flows on a large spatial scale. The construction of high-speed railways should be advanced on a large scale to form an integrated rail transit system that integrates intercity high-speed railways, regional express trains, metro system with light rail system, so as to extend urban public transportation to urban-regional systems and boost rapid flows of factors like population, goods, services, funds and information. For example, as the Nanning-Guangzhou High-Speed Railway and Guiyang-Guangzhou High-Speed Railway were put into operation, the channel connecting the Pearl River Delta with the Southwest Region has been opened. Guangdong, Guangxi and Guizhou jointly built a high-speed railway economic belt on the basis of high-speed railways. The provinces and cities along those railways cooperate and share resources, forming an economic integration zone.

Optimize the spatial layout of industries. The important role of the national central cities in regional development is leading regional industries to medium- and high-end development until they finally form industrial clusters that are competitive in the country and even in the world. To this end, the national central cities have to, on the basis of a rational division of labor within their own system, guide the regions they are located in to cultivate and develop leading industries with their innovative development capabilities and driving capacity. By taking advantage of the forward and backward linkage and spillover effects of leading industries, industrial parks and industrial bases occupied by enterprises of similar natures or associated in the upstream and downstream chains should be built. The connection between leading enterprises and small and medium-sized enterprises should be deepened. The leading, radiating and demonstration roles of leading industries should be strengthened. A number of characteristic industrial clusters that have outstanding strengths and clear advantages and that are intensive and efficient should be developed to continuously increase the level of regional industrial clusters and promote optimal layout in the entire industrial chain and coordinated regional development.

Promote two-way flow of production factors. The construction of national central cities contributes to the establishment of a unified market and differentiated but orderly competition within regions, thus promoting regional growth. While further opening themselves to the market, they will also serve as benchmarks in forming a unified market with the surrounding areas. At the same time, their construction will break and reshape the existing inter-regional competition pattern, and facilitate the building of a more open, unified, differentiated but orderly regional market environment. Specifically, the national central cities will play a leading role in the following aspects: First, they can speed up the integration of human resources markets. They will take the lead in accepting and mutually recognizing accumulated years of residence required for household registration access, to speed up the elimination of household registration barriers between urban and rural areas, to coordinate the citizenization of local and migrant populations, to promote the sharing of human resources information, and to jointly build public employment service platforms. Second, they can promote the integration of technology market. They will accelerate the joint construction of science and technology resources sharing service platform, encourage concerted efforts in building science and technology, research and development, and transformation bases, explore the establishment of a joint release mechanism for corporate needs and a mechanism on financial support for sharing of scientific and technological achievements, remove barriers posed by inconsistent technical standards between cities, establish a technology trading market alliance, and build a multi-level trading market system of intellectual property rights. Third, they can promote the integration of financial services. They will strengthen the construction of integrated financial infrastructure, information network and service platforms, and encourage a coordinated layout of financial institutions. Fourth, they can eliminate the invisible obstacles to the registration of change in domicile of commercial subjects relocated to a different place, explore the business operation model of "one license and one certificate indicating multiple business addresses", quicken the cancellation of registration requirements for design and construction enterprises with required qualifications in other places, and promote the standardization of various approval processes and the connectivity and sharing of approval information. Fifth, they can improve the credit system with a quicker pace and implement joint trustworthiness incentives and joint dishonesty punishments. They will jointly crack down on infringements and counterfeiting, explore the establishment of a real-time linkage monitoring platform for food and drugs, and promote mutual recognition of food safety inspection and test results.

Innovate institutional mechanisms for coordinated development. Accelerate the creation of mechanisms for consultation and cooperation, planning and coordination, policy coordination, and social participation. Create a multi-level cooperation and negotiation mechanism between cities. Where conditions permit, explore coordination and promotion mechanisms focused on development and key areas, and promote the implementation of major issues concerning integrated development. Strengthen the organic connection between city cluster planning and urban planning to ensure coordination and synthetic forces. Strengthen the policy coordination mechanism. Actively build a mutually beneficial and win-win tax sharing mechanism and a collection and management coordinated mechanism to strengthen coordination in preferential tax policies between cities. Encourage social capital to participate in project construction and operations. Allow cross-regional adjustments in surplus from increase or decrease in urban and rural construction land. Perfect the supply system of commodity housing and strengthen the policy coordination in regulation and control of urban and rural real estate markets. Strengthen public opinion guidance, innovate propaganda methods, enhance the sense of identity and mobilize the enthusiasm of all sectors of society, and pool strong joint forces for joint participation and support for coordinated development of urban regions.

Give play to the roles of market and government according to local conditions. The construction of national central cities is part of the construction of the national urban system, a process in which market and the government play dominant roles. Respect and adapt to the natural laws of economic development, and give full play to the decisive role of market in allocating resources in the process of national central city construction and coordinated regional growth. At the same time, give full play to and enhance the leading role of government agencies at all levels in this process. On the one hand, different plans for the construction of national urban system should be advanced actively in the correct direction and to the appropriate extent of the construction process; on the other hand, the regional development and governance concepts of local governments should be changed positively to weaken "administrative district economy" and shortsighted local protectionism, break regional homogeneous competition, and achieve regional diversified development for mutual prosperity.

References

[1] Sun Jiuwen. Study on the Development and Innovation of Coordinated Regional Development Strategy in the New Era [J]. Journal of Chinese Academy of Governance, 2018 (8).

[2] Jin Bei, Chen Yao, Zhang Keyun, and Yu Xin'an. Establishing More Effective Coordinated Regional Development Mechanisms [J]. Regional Economic Review, 2019 (1).

[3] Yang Xiaolan, and Ni Pengfei. Review on the Origin and Development of Urban Sustainable Competitiveness [J]. Economics Perspectives, 2017 (9).

[4] Yang Guoliang, Cheng Hao, and Ouyang Hui. Can National Central City Construction Promote Regional Coordinated Growth? [J]. Finance & Economics, 2018 (5).

[5] Liu Zhiyan. How Do National Central Cities Lead Regional Development? [J]. People's Tribune, 2017 (20).

[6] Bai Hua, and Tan Deqing. Research on the Economic Development Path of National Inland Central Cities-Taking Inland Free Trade Areas as an Example [J]. Inquiry into Economic Issues, 2018 (10).

[7] Tu Yong. Strategic Thinking on the Coordinated Regional Development with Central Cities Playing a Leading Role [J]. Theory Front, 2003 (12).

[8] Wang Wei, Luo Xinyue, and Feng Yu. Advancement and Coordination Assessment of Regional Development in Four National Central Cities [J]. Beijing Planning Review, 2017 (1).

[9] Chen Jiewen. Strengthening the Construction of Chengdu-Chongqing Central Cities and Promoting the Coordinated Development of Regional Economy [J]. Fortune Today, 2017 (10).

[10] Wang Yuhu. Thoughts on the Planning from Provincial "Edges" to Regional "Centers" [C]. Annual National Planning Conference. 2014.

[11] Sun Bindong, Jin Xiaoxi and Lin Jie. China's New Pattern of Urbanization toward Coordinated Development of Large, Medium and Small Cities: Evolution and Determinants of City Size Distribution Since 1949 [J]. Geographical Research, 2019 (1).

Evaluation Report

B.2

Analysis of China's National Central City Construction Indexes and Growth Indexes in 2018

*Research Team of National Central City Research Institute of Zhengzhou Normal University**

Abstract: In order to accurately understand the construction levels and development of China's national central cities in terms of integrated services, network hubs, science and technology innovation, open exchanges, humanistic cohesion and ecological livability in 2018, this study adds new growth indexes to the original construction indexes and measure these two kinds of indexes for the nine national central cities. As a whole, the measurement of construction indexes shows that the nine cities are clearly stratified, with Shanghai, Beijing and Guangzhou still in the first echelon that boasts of strong growth momentum as a whole; with Chongqing, Chengdu, Tianjin and Wuhan in the second echelon that shows relatively good

* Directors of Research Team: Chen Yao, Yu Xin'an; Deputy-directors: Wang Jianguo, Shi Yu; Writers: Chen Yao, Shi Yu, and Xu Yanhong.

development trends; with Xi'an and Zhengzhou in the third echelon that still has much room for improvement in all indexes. The results of six functions measured as construction indexes for the cities are analyzed and suggest that attention should be paid to ensuring the coordinated development of various functions and the coordination between economic development and ecological livability during national central city construction. The construction of open cities should be promoted, a cultural brand image should be built, and urban diseases should be effectively cured. Only in this way will the national central cities play a better role in leading, demonstrating, radiating and driving the development of metropolitan areas and city clusters and thereby promote coordinated regional development.

Keywords: national central cities; construction indexes; growth indexes; coordinated regional development

National central city construction is a major strategic measure taken by the Party Central Committee and the State Council to improve the national urban system, promote coordinated regional development, enhance the radiating and driving capacity of mega-central cities, and win the global city competition. The coordinated regional development strategy is one of the seven major strategies to be implemented in the decisive period of building a well-off society in an all-round way that was adopted at the 19th National Congress of the Communist Party of China. On November 18, 2018, the *Opinions of the Central Committee of the Communist Party of China and the State Council on Establishing More Effective Coordinated Regional Development Mechanisms* was issued and it included a proposal to "promote strategic and integrated development of major regions in China". It also pressed for the development of city clusters centering round and led by the nine national central cities, which should drive the integration of relevant sectors and promote coordinated regional development. In 2018, in order to promote the national central city construction, Beijing, Shanghai, Guangzhou, Tianjin, Chongqing, Chengdu, Wuhan, Zhengzhou and Xi'an formulated a series of relevant policies and measures to continuously promote the construction in integrated services, network hubs, science and technology innovation, open exchanges, humanistic cohesion and ecological livability. And these efforts have been exchanged for varying degrees of progress.

I Comparison of Basic Economic Development Indicators among China's National Central Cities

Considering their key positions in the global urban network and core functions in the national urban system, the national central cities are required to strictly observe the concept of "innovative, coordinated, green, open and sharing" development to move from high-speed development to high-quality development in urban construction and to drive regional coordination and sustainable development. In order to fully understand and analyze the economic development status and index progress of the nine cities in 2018, they are compared from ten basic indicators of resident population, GDP, per capita GDP, general public budget income, social fixed assets investment, total value of import and export, the number of patents granted, the balance of domestic and foreign currency deposits in financial institutions, the balance of foreign currency loans of financial institutions, and disposable income per capita.

The comparison of the absolute values and growth of 10 basic indicators associated with economic development among the nine national central cities shows that both measures varied greatly (see Figure 1 to Figure 10).

In 2018, Chongqing had the largest resident population, followed by Shanghai and Beijing. Zhengzhou and Xi'an, whose resident populations exceeded 10 million for the first time, ranked eighth and ninth, respectively; in terms of annual growth rate, however, Xi'an had the highest annual growth rate of resident population, followed by Guangzhou and Zhengzhou, while Beijing experienced a negative trend in resident population growth.

In 2018, Shanghai had the largest GDP, followed by Beijing. Zhengzhou ranked eighth with its GDP topped trillion for the first time, followed by Xi'an; in terms of annual GDP growth rate, Xi'an was champion, followed by Zhengzhou, Chengdu and Wuhan.

In 2018, the top three cities in terms of per capita GDP were Guangzhou,

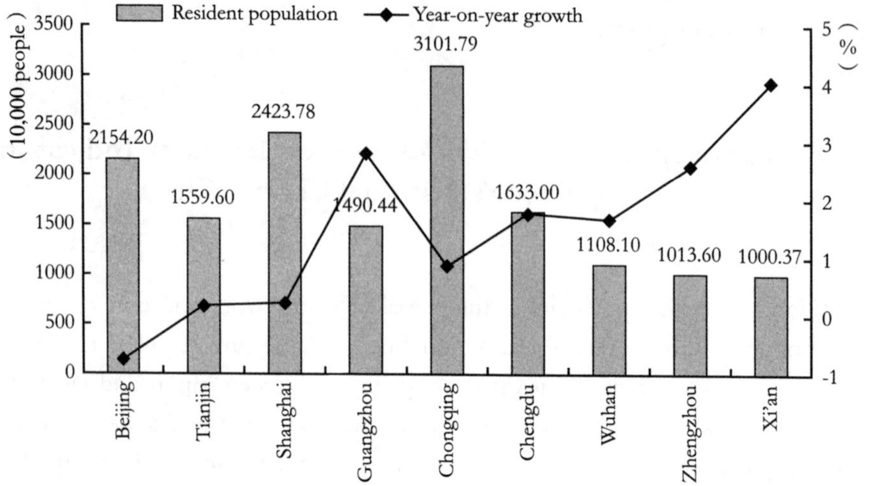

Figure 1 Comparison of the Number and Growth of Resident Population among the National Central Cities in 2018

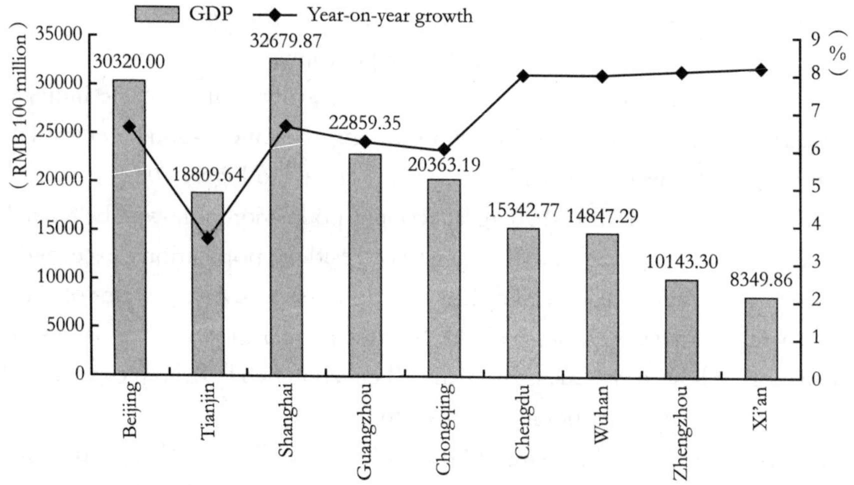

Figure 2 Comparison of the GDP and GDP Growth among the National Central Cities in 2018

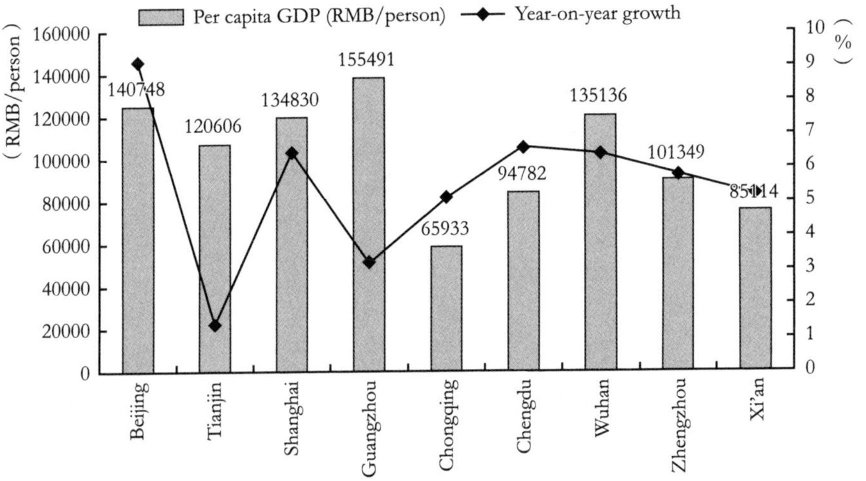

Figure 3 Comparison of the GDP and GDP Per Capita among the National Central Cities in 2018

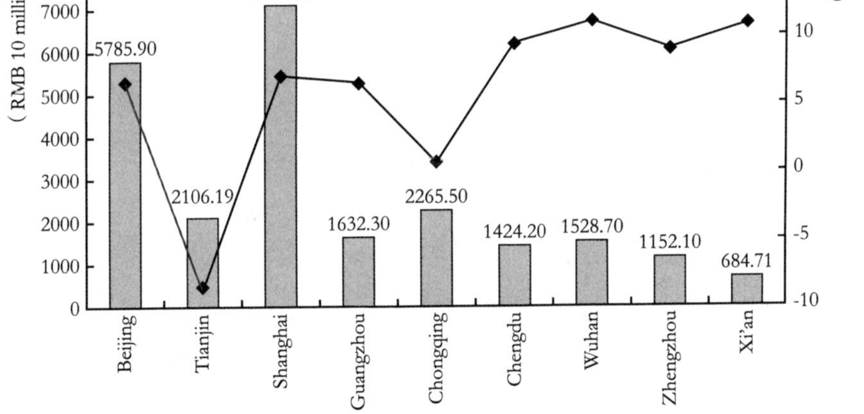

Figure 4 Comparison of the General Public Budget Income and Its Growth among the National Central Cities in 2018

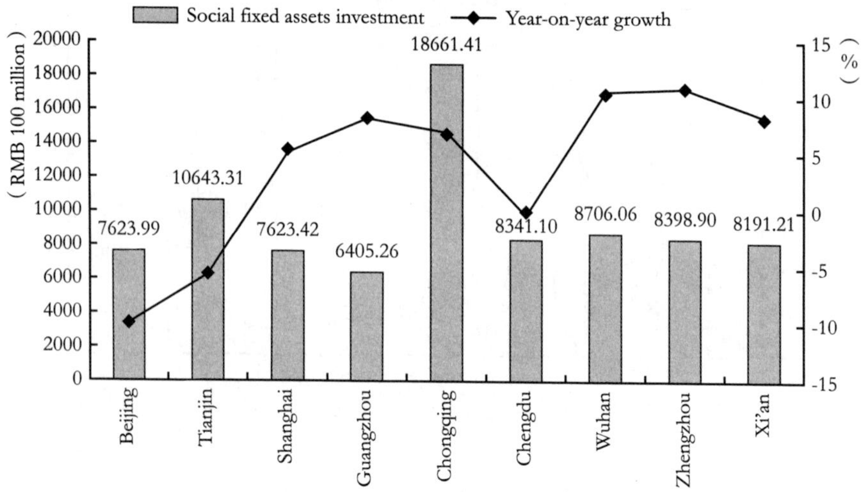

Figure 5 Comparison of the Social Fixed Assets Investment and Its Growth among the National Central Cities in 2018

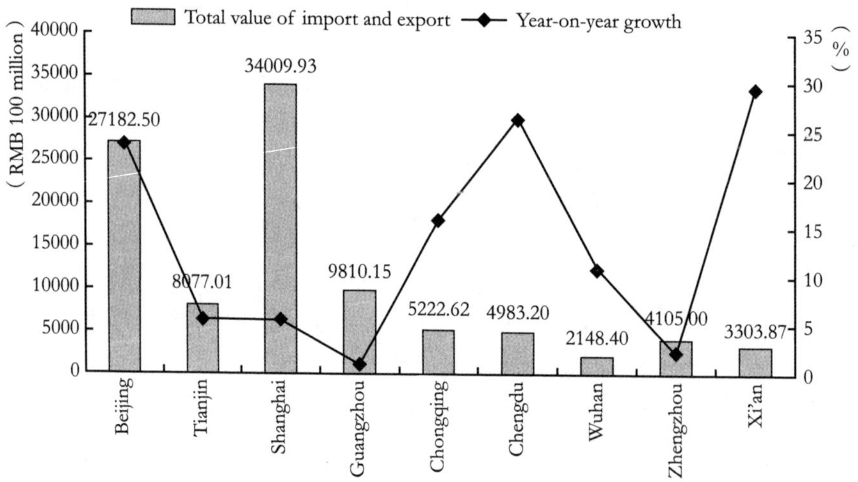

Figure 6 Comparison of the Total Value of Import and Export and Its Growth among the National Central Cities in 2018

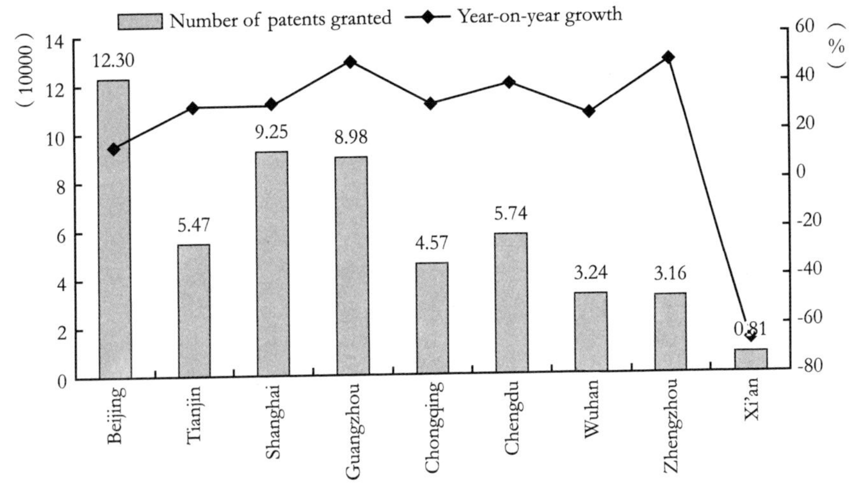

Figure 7 Comparison of the Number of Patents Granted and Its Growth among the National Central Cities in 2018

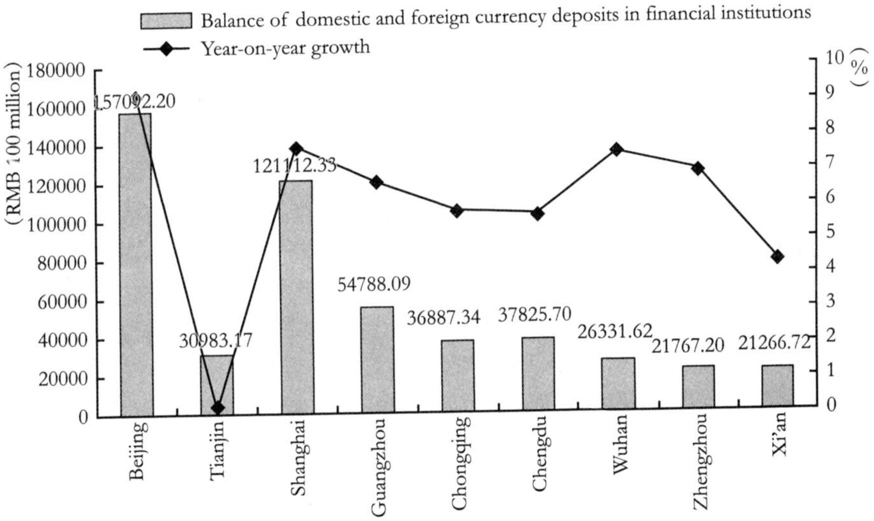

Figure 8 Comparison of the Balance of Domestic and Foreign Currency Deposits in Financial Institutions and Its Growth among the National Central Cities in 2018

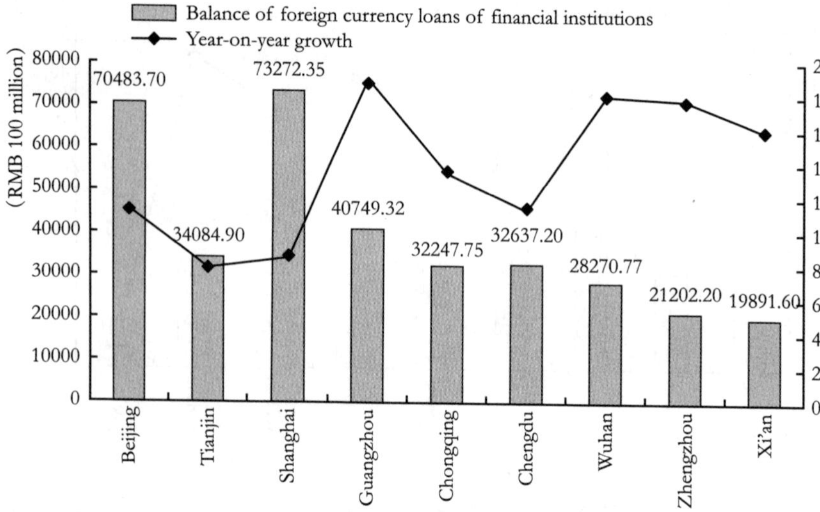

Figure 9 Comparison of the Balance of Foreign Currency Loans of Financial Institutions and Its Growth among the National Central Cities in 2018

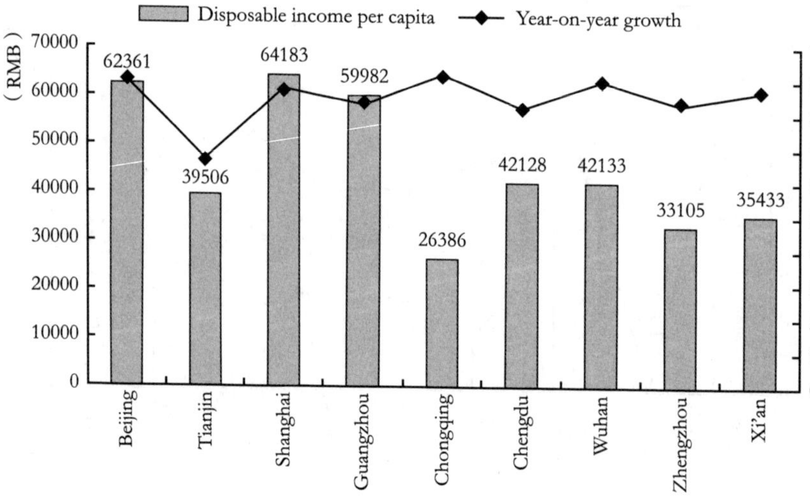

Figure 10 Comparison of the Disposable Income Per Capita and Its Growth among the National Central Cities in 2018

Beijing and Shanghai, while Xi'an and Chongqing ranked eighth and ninth, respectively. Zhengzhou's per capita GDP exceeded RMB 100,000 for the first time, which secured it in the sixth position; in terms of annual growth rate of per capita GDP, Beijing was the champion while on the other side of the spectrum was Tianjin.

In 2018, Shanghai led the national central cities in the general public budget income, followed by Beijing, while Xi'an was at the bottom; in terms of its annual growth rate, Wuhan was the very top one, while Tianjin suffered a certain drop.

In 2018, Chongqing had the highest social fixed assets investment, followed by Tianjin, while Guangzhou had the lowest; in terms of annual growth rate, Zhengzhou's social fixed assets investment grew most, followed by Wuhan's. In contrast, the social fixed assets investments in Chengdu, Tianjin and Beijing all declined to varying degrees.

In 2018, Shanghai and Beijing ranked first and second in terms of the total value of import and export, while Xi'an and Wuhan ranked eighth and ninth, respectively. In terms of its annual growth rate, Xi'an ranked first, Chengdu second, Beijing third, and Guangzhou ninth.

In 2018, Beijing had the most patent grants, followed by Shanghai and Guangzhou, while Xi'an had the least; in terms of its annual growth rate, the top three cities were Guangzhou, Zhengzhou and Chengdu, while Xi'an was at the bottom.

In 2018, the top three cities having most balance of domestic and foreign currency deposits in financial institutions were Beijing, Shanghai and Guangzhou, while Xi'an ranked ninth; in terms of its annual growth rate, the top three cities were Beijing, Shanghai and Wuhan, while Tianjin ranked ninth.

In 2018, the top three positions in the ranking of the balance of foreign currency loans of financial institutions were occupied by Shanghai, Beijing and Guangzhou, while Xi'an placed last; in terms of its annual growth rate, the top three positions were occupied by Guangzhou, Wuhan and Zhengzhou.

In 2018, Shanghai, Beijing and Guangzhou had the highest disposable income per capita in order, while on the other side of the spectrum were Zhengzhou and Chongqing; in terms of its annual growth rate, Chongqing ranked first, followed by Beijing and Wuhan.

The preliminary analysis shows that Shanghai, Beijing and Guangzhou are apparently the best economic performers among the nine national central cities, with rapid growth trends observed in many indicators such as GDP, per capita GDP, general public budget income, the balance of domestic and foreign currency deposits in financial institutions, and disposable income per capita; in spite of their relatively weak overall economic strength, Zhengzhou and Xi'an show rapid growth trends in various basic indicators, especially population concentration and social fixed assets investment. Therefore, in order to promote the construction of modern metropolises and to better play their leading role in city clusters and regional development, the national central cities still need to further accelerate their economic development and increase the scope of their radiating effect.

II Ranking of China's National Central City Construction Indexes

(I) Determination of the Weights of China's National Center City Construction Indexes

This evaluation adopts the comprehensive index evaluation system of national central cities cited in the *Report on National Center City Construction (2018)*.

1 Date Sources

The research data comes from the *Statistical Bulletin of National Economic and Social Development in 2018* from the nine cities, the official websites of the People's Government Offices of these cities and Gaotie.cn, the 2018 statistical yearbooks from the cities, *Blue Book on Innovation and Entrepreneurship: Annual Report on the Development of China's Innovation and Entrepreneurship (2017-2018)* published by the Research Center of China's Special Economic Zones of Shenzhen University, *Top 100 Chinese Cities in Sports Vitality in 2017* jointly issued by the sport.people.com and the Public Opinion Data Center of people.com.cn, *Digital China Index Report (2019)* issued by Tencent Research Institute, *China E-Commerce Development Index Report (2018)* issued jointly by the National Engineering Laboratory for E-Commerce Technologies of Tsinghua University and other institutions, *Report on Traffic Analysis of Major Chinese Cities in 2018* issued by Amap, and *Annual Report on China's Exhibition Industry (2018)* issued by the Department of Trade and Investment Promotion of China Council for the Promotion of International Trade.

2 Quantitative Method

This evaluation adopts the quantitative method used in the *Report on National Center City Construction (2018)*. Considering that direct comparison and calculation is unfeasible due to the inconsistent characterization data units in the national central city construction indexes, all data should be standardized with TOPSIS; then, the weights of the indexes are determined using the variation coefficient method; finally, the construction indexes of the nine national central cities are determined by weighting each index.

3 Weight Distribution

The weight distribution of the evaluation indexes determined using the method above and in combination with the relevant data analysis is as follows:

Table 1 Weights of China's National Center City Construction Indexes

Functions	Weights	Dimensions	Weights	Indexes	Weights
Comprehensive services	0.2694	Economic vitality	0.0347	X1	0.0086
				X2	0.0073
				X3	0.0050
				X4	0.0138
		Production services	0.1788	X5	0.0312
				X6	0.0288
				X7	0.0084
				X8	0.0752
				X9	0.0145
				X10	0.0207
		Public services	0.0559	X11	0.0130
				X12	0.0191
				X13	0.0033
				X14	0.0205

Continued

Functions	Weights	Dimensions	Weights	Indexes	Weights
Network hubs	0.2323	Information hubs	0.0676	X15	0.0187
				X16	0.0206
				X17	0.0283
		Transportation hubs	0.1647	X18	0.0209
				X19	0.0495
				X20	0.0181
				X21	0.0415
				X22	0.0213
				X23	0.0134
Scientific and technological innovation	0.1855	Innovative resources	0.0426	X24	0.0349
				X25	0.0077
		Scientific research platforms	0.0440	X26	0.0391
				X27	0.0049
		Factor input	0.0523	X28	0.0209
				X29	0.0314
		Innovative achievements	0.0466	X30	0.0202
				X31	0.0264
Open exchanges	0.1968	International trade	0.0725	X32	0.0204
				X33	0.0339
				X34	0.0182
		Foreign exchanges	0.1243	X35	0.0155
				X36	0.0353
				X37	0.0498
				X38	0.0237
Humanistic cohesion	0.0955	City brands	0.0479	X39	0.0469
				X40	0.0010
		Cultural atmosphere	0.0476	X41	0.0134
				X42	0.0198
				X43	0.0144

Continued

Functions	Weights	Dimensions	Weights	Indexes	Weights
Ecological livability	0.0205	Beautiful environment	0.0107	X44	0.0080
				X45	0.0027
		Harmony and livability	0.0098	X46	0.0074
				X47	0.0024

According to the variation coefficient method and the weight distribution of indexes, from the perspective of functions, the weight of comprehensive services is 0.2693, which is the largest; the weight of network hubs is 0.2323, ranking the second; the weights of scientific and technological innovation and open exchanges are relatively close; humanistic cohesion and ecological livability have the smallest weights. These results show that the construction levels of the nine national central cities mainly differed in comprehensive services and network hubs. From the perspective of dimensions, the weights of production services, transportation hubs and foreign exchanges are 0.1787, 0.1647 and 0.1244, respectively, accounting for 46.78% of the total weight of 15 dimensions. This fully indicates that the nine national central cities differed greatly in these three dimensions.

Compared with the weights of national central city indexes in 2016, the order of index weights in 2018 does not change much, although the weights of factor input, international trade and foreign exchanges increase greatly while the weights of beautiful environment and harmony and livability decrease greatly, which suggests that the nine national central cities differed more in open exchanges while got close in ecological livability (see Figure 11).

(II) Ranking and Analysis of China's National Central City Construction Indexes

1 Analysis of the Ranking of Comprehensive Scores of Construction Indexes

In general, except for some cities, the ranking of construction indexes did not change a lot from the result in 2016. Shanghai, Beijing and Guangzhou still maintained strong development momentum, while Xi'an and Zhengzhou lagged behind as shown in Table 2. However, the comparison of the basic indicators

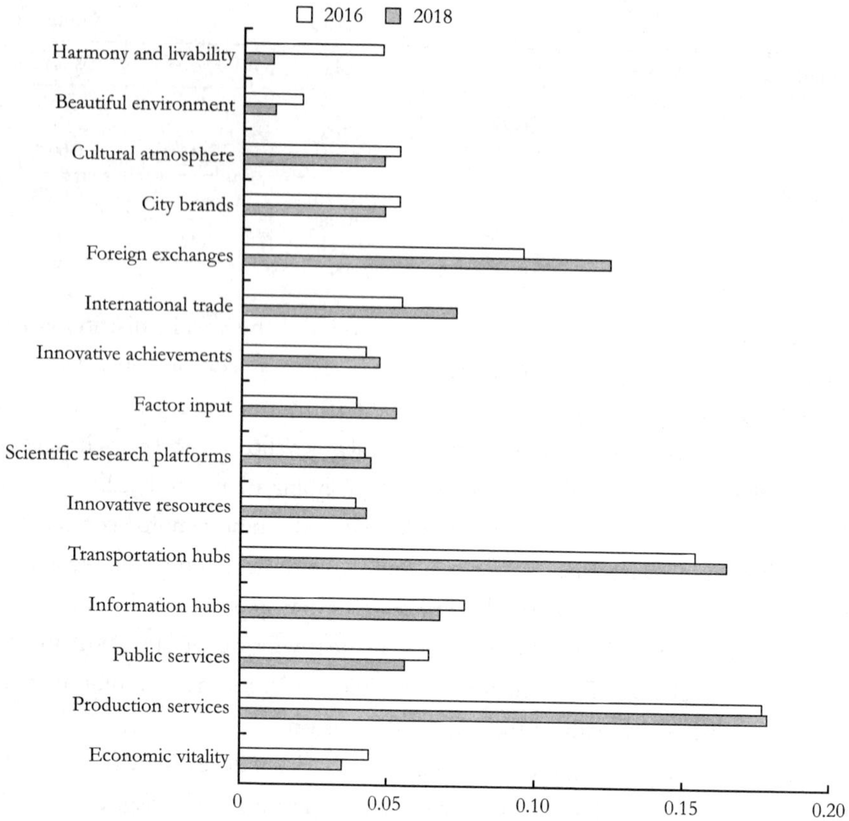

Figure 11 Comparison of the Weights of Dimensions in Construction Indexes between 2018 and 2016

of economic development between the nine national central cities shows that all of them were under constant optimization and development with good momentum.

From a hierarchical perspective, the nine national central cities were quite different in their development level, and three echelons can be observed clearly. Shanghai, Beijing and Guangzhou were still in the first echelon of national central city construction with strong overall development momentum; Chongqing, Chengdu, Tianjin and Wuhan were members of the second echelon, with sound development trends; Xi'an and Zhengzhou were in the third echelon with much to improve in all indicators. Compared with their rankings in 2016, Chongqing moved forward from the fifth place to the fourth and Chengdu from the sixth place to the fifth, both of which made progress of one place; Tianjin dropped from the fourth place to the sixth, a two-place decline; the rankings of the other cities remained basically unchanged.

Table 2 Scores and Rankings of National Central City Construction Index in 2018

Cities	Scores	Rankings
Shanghai	0.5284	1
Beijing	0.4991	2
Guangzhou	0.2770	3
Chongqing	0.1863	4
Chengdu	0.1816	5
Tianjin	0.1671	6
Wuhan	0.1643	7
Xi'an	0.1505	8
Zhengzhou	0.1204	9

2 Analysis of the Construction Indexes of Six Functions

In line with overall analysis, the nine cities differed greatly in the indexes of all the functions, except ecological livability (see Figure 12). However, the transition from high-speed growth to high-quality development for the national central cities requires coordination and coordinated development of all the six functions. They have to start from making quality changes and improving efficiency and reform the growth engines to effectively promote coordinated regional development (Yu Xin'an, 2019).

Through the comparison of functional indexes inherent to the nine cities, Shanghai maintained its advantages in comprehensive services, network hubs and open exchanges as it ranked first in all of them. Beijing ranked first in scientific and technological innovation and humanistic cohesion and the second in comprehensive services and open exchanges; the relatively large weights of these functions had great influences on the overall construction indexes

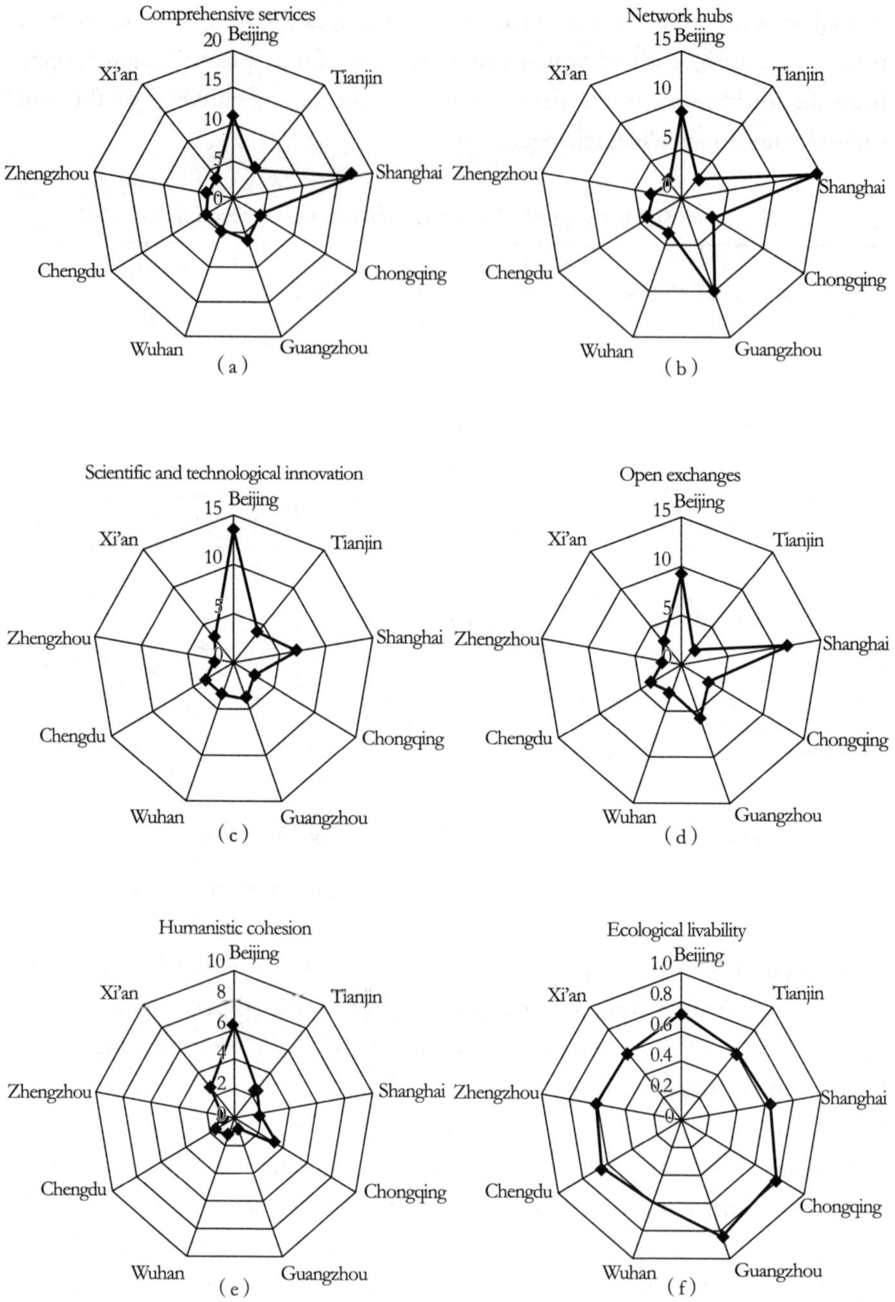

Figure 12 Comparison of Functional Indexes among the National Central Cities in 2018

of Shanghai and Beijing, making them the best and the runner-up in the construction indexes ranking, respectively. Guangzhou ranked first in ecological livability, second in network hubs, and third in comprehensive services as well as open exchanges, but there are still big gaps between it and the top performer Shanghai in all of the three functions, and it also needed to further improve its humanistic cohesion. Chongqing ranked second in both humanistic cohesion and ecological livability, but more improvements were needed in comprehensive services and in scientific and technological innovation. Chengdu made a 2-place progress from 2016 in scientific and technological innovation to rank fifth, and enjoyed certain advantages in network hubs and open exchanges, but it needed to improve its comprehensive services. Tianjin showed obvious advantages in comprehensive services and in scientific and technological innovation but not in network hubs and open exchanges. Wuhan had good comprehensive services, but there were gaps to fill in humanistic cohesion and ecological livability. Xi'an had an advantage in humanistic cohesion, but comprehensive services and network hubs were the directions for future progress. Zhengzhou lagged behind the other cities in all functional indexes and needed urgently to accelerate development, particularly comprehensive services and scientific and technological innovation.

The coordinated regional development strategy in the new era is an important measure to effectively resolve imbalanced regional development (Chen Yao, 2019). As the core cities in the national urban system, the nine national central cities are key contributors that lead the development of their respective city cluster and promote the strategic integrated development of major regions in the country. Therefore, their healthy and orderly development is vital to coordinated regional development. To solve the problem of imbalanced and inadequate development among them, the focus should be placed on relatively backward cities like Xi'an and Zhengzhou. Their development shortcomings should be addressed and targeted measures should be taken to increase their development levels and gradually narrow their gap with the other national central cities.

III Ranking of China's National Central City Construction Growth Indexes

(I) Growth Evaluation Method of National Central City Construction

1 Evaluation Indicators

The concept of "growth" is derived from biology. The word itself means change, which represents a trend and process of change in research objectives and reflects the comprehensive change characteristics of research objectives in manifold indicators (Wu Shinong, 1999).

Judging from the ranking of national central city construction indexes in 2018, except for certain changes in the rankings of a few cities, the nine cities remained relatively stable in their respective tier: Shanghai and Beijing were still far ahead the others, while Xi'an and Zhengzhou did not break from the bottom. The gap was attributed to the different positioning and basic development levels of the nine cities. In spite of varying degrees of development, no visible differences could be found in the evaluation results of these cities for different years, given the influence of various indicator bases in 2018.

Therefore, in order to more effectively characterize their development speed of the national central cities, this study further analyzes their growth since the "13th Five-Year Plan" was started on the basis of the original evaluation indicators of national central city construction indexes. This study focuses on six functional layers of national central city construction, namely comprehensive services, network hubs, scientific and technological innovation, open exchanges, cultural cohesion and ecological livability, They are refined into 15 dimensional layers, namely economic vitality, production services, public services, information hubs, transportation hubs, innovative resources, scientific research platforms, factor input, innovative achievements, international trade, foreign exchanges, city brands, cultural atmosphere, beautiful environment, harmony and livability. Under these layers, 33 indicators are selected for growth evaluation. The purpose is to explore and evaluate the growth of the nine cities by analyzing the growth of national central city construction indicators since the "13th Five-Year Plan" was started (2016-2018). The specific evaluation indicators are shown in Table 3.

Table 3 Growth Evaluation Indicators of National Central City Construction in China

Functions	Dimensions	Indicators
Comprehensive services	Economic vitality	GDP growth rate
		Growth rate of the proportion of added value of the tertiary industry
		Growth rate of resident population
	Production services	Growth rate of the number of listed companies
		Growth rate of the balance of domestic and foreign currency deposits in financial institutions
		Growth rate of insurance penetration
		Growth rate of e-commerce development index
	Public services	Growth rate of residents' basic medical insurance coverage
		Growth rate of the local general public budget income as a percentage of GDP
		Growth rate of urban rail transit operation mileage
Network hubs	Information hubs	Growth rate of business volume of telecommunications
		Growth rate of China's Internet Plus index
		Growth rate of business volume of express delivery
	Transportation hubs	Growth rate of passenger volume
		Growth rate of freight volume
Scientific and technological innovation	Innovative resources	Growth rate of the number of undergraduates enrolled in junior college and above
	Scientific research platforms	Growth rate of the number of national key laboratories, national engineering technological research centers and national key laboratories affiliated to enterprises
	Factor input	Growth rate of R&D input
		Growth rate of R&D personnel
	Innovative achievements	Growth rate of the number of authorized patents
		Growth rate of the number of national awards won for scientific achievements
Open exchanges	International trade	Growth rate of economic extroversion
		Growth rate of actually used foreign investment
	Foreign exchanges	Growth rate of the number of exhibitions
		Growth rate of inbound international tourists

Continued

Functions	Dimensions	Indicators
Humanistic cohesion	City brands	Growth rate of AAAA tourist destinations and above
	Cultural atmosphere	Growth rate of the number of public libraries
		Growth rate of the number of museums
		Growth rate of the number of cultural centers
Ecological livability	Beautiful environment	Growth rate of the per capita park greenery area
		Growth rate of the urban green coverage
	Harmony and livability	Scale of decrease in PM 2.5 annual average density
		Scale of decrease in all-day traffic congestion index

2 Data Sources

Apart from the data used for the construction index evaluation, the other data used for growth evaluation of national central city construction in the calculation of different indicators comes from the 2015-2017 National Economic and Social Development Statistics Reports and the 2016-2018 Statistical Yearbooks of the nine national central cities, the 2016-2018 Statistical Yearbooks of Guangzhou, Sichuan, Hubei, Shaanxi and Henan Provinces, government websites of the nine national central cities, *China E-Commerce Development Index Reports (2017), (2016) & (2014-2015)* issued jointly by the National Engineering Laboratory for E-Commerce Technologies of Tsinghua University and other institutions, *Reports on Traffic Analysis of Major Chinese Cities in 2017, 2016 and 2015* issued by Amap, *Annual Report on China's Exhibition Industry (2017), (2016) & (2015)* issued by the Department of Trade and Investment Promotion of China Council for the Promotion of International Trade, and *China "Internet Plus" Index Report (2018), (2017) & (2016)* issued by Tencent Research Institute.

(II) Analysis of the Ranking of Growth Indexes

1 Ranking of Comprehensive Scores of Growth Indexes

According to the statistics and data analysis, the growth index ranking of the nine national central city construction is shown in Table 4.

Table 4 Scores and Ranking of Growth Indexes of China's National Central City Construction in 2018

Cities	Scores	Rankings
Zhengzhou	0.3439	1
Xi'an	0.2353	2
Chengdu	0.2069	3
Wuhan	0.1579	4
Guangzhou	0.1253	5
Chongqing	0.1176	6
Shanghai	0.1132	7
Beijing	0.0362	8
Tianjin	0.0261	9

Judging from the comprehensive scores, all of the nine national central cities showed positive growth indexes, indicating that they were under different levels of continuous optimization and development. Among them, Zhengzhou, Xi'an, Chengdu and Wuhan led the list as the top four, and their scores were all above 0.15. In contrast, Guangzhou, Chongqing, Shanghai, Beijing and Tianjin had relatively low growth indexes. It can be seen that Zhengzhou, Xi'an and Wuhan, in spite of their relatively low construction indexes among the nine national central cities, were under rapid development due to their great development potential; Chengdu moved slightly upward in the ranking of construction indexes and was also a relatively fast grower. Beijing, Shanghai and Guangzhou, which had relatively high construction indexes, tended to remain stable; when its growth indexes were combined with its construction indexes, Tianjin still needed to further accelerate its development speed in line with its current status.

Based on the analysis of the growth index weight of the national central city construction (see Table 5), the weights of comprehensive services and scientific and technological innovation still accounted for more than 50%, which was 5 percentage points higher than their weights in the national central city construction indexes. Among the weights of growth indexes, those of production services, public services, factor input and cultural atmosphere were higher than those of the other 11 dimensional layers, accounting for 43.84% of the total weights, which marked a huge difference from the weights of the same dimensional layers in the construction index evaluation. This indicated that there was a huge gap among the nine national central cities in the growth rate of these four dimensions.

Table 5 Weights of Growth Evaluation Indexes of Chinese National Central Cities

Functions	Weights	Dimensions	Weights	Indexes		Weights
Comprehensive services	0.2815	Economic vitality	0.0687	GDP growth rate	Y1	0.0063
				Growth rate of the proportion of added value of the tertiary industry	Y2	0.0268
				Growth rate of resident population	Y3	0.0356
		Production services	0.1007	Growth rate of the number of listed companies	Y4	0.0218
				Growth rate of the balance of domestic and foreign currency deposits in financial institutions	Y5	0.0143
				Growth rate of insurance penetration	Y6	0.0301
				Growth rate of e-commerce development index	Y7	0.0345
		Public services	0.1121	Growth rate of residents' basic medical insurance coverage	Y8	0.0574
				Growth rate of the local general public budget income as a percentage of GDP	Y9	0.0260
				Growth rate of urban rail transit operation mileage	Y10	0.0287
Network hubs	0.0957	Information hubs	0.0486	Growth rate of business volume of telecommunications	Y11	0.0285
				Growth rate of China's Internet Plus index	Y12	0.0093
				Growth rate of business volume of express delivery	Y13	0.0108
		Transportation hubs	0.0471	Growth rate of passenger volume	Y14	0.0169
				Growth rate of freight volume	Y15	0.0302

Continued

Functions	Weights	Dimensions	Weights	Indexes		Weights
Scientific and technological innovation	0.2262	Innovative resources	0.0426	Growth rate of the number of undergraduates enrolled in junior colleges and above	Y16	0.0426
		Scientific research platforms	0.0186	Growth rate of the number of national key laboratories, national engineering technological research centers and national key laboratories affiliated to enterprises	Y17	0.0186
		Factor input	0.1060	Growth rate of R&D input	Y18	0.0418
				Growth rate of R&D personnel	Y19	0.0642
		Innovative achievements	0.0591	Growth rate of the number of authorized patents	Y20	0.0192
				Growth rate of the number of national awards won for scientific achievements	Y21	0.0399
Open exchanges	0.1044	International trade	0.0531	Growth rate of economic extroversion	Y22	0.0330
				Growth rate of actually used foreign investment	Y23	0.0201
		Foreign exchanges	0.0513	Growth rate of the number of exhibitions	Y24	0.0298
				Growth rate of inbound international tourists	Y25	0.0214
Humanistic cohesion	0.1456	City brands	0.0260	Growth rate of AAAA tourist destinations and above	Y26	0.0260
		Cultural atmosphere	0.1196	Growth rate of the number of public libraries	Y27	0.0430
				Growth rate of the number of museums	Y28	0.0463
				Growth rate of the number of cultural centers	Y29	0.0303
Ecological livability	0.1465	Beautiful environment	0.0838	Growth rate of the per capita park greenery area	Y30	0.0473
				Growth rate of the urban green coverage	Y31	0.0365
		Harmony and livability	0.0627	Scale of decrease in PM 2.5 annual average density	Y32	0.0229
				Scale of decrease in all-day traffic congestion index	Y33	0.0398

Compared with their weights in the construction indexes (see Table 1), the weights of network hubs and open exchanges declined, by more than 50% and nearly 47%, respectively. This indicated that these two functions of the nine national central cities grew slightly from what they were in the construction indexes. The weights of four functions, namely comprehensive services, scientific and research innovation, humanistic cohesion and ecological livability, increased to varying degrees: the weight of humanistic cohesion increased by more than 50%, and the weight of ecological livability increased by about 6 times. The reason was that some of the national central cities have increased their investment in environmental construction and thus widened the gap with the other cities (see Figure 13).

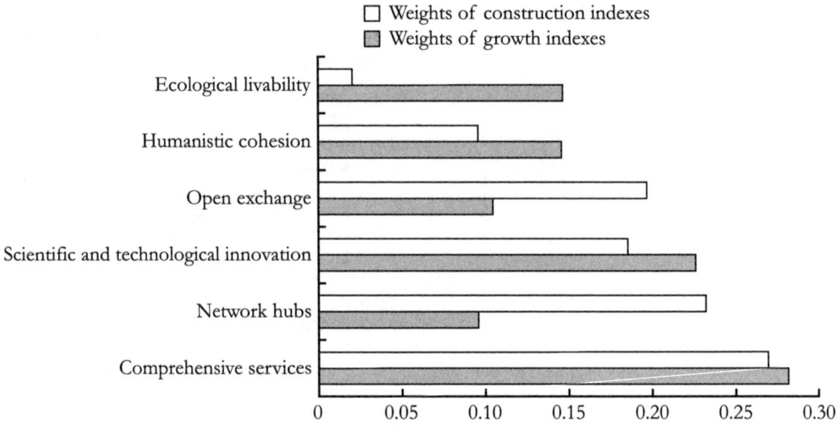

Figure 13 Comparison of Dimensional Weights between Construction Index Evaluation and Growth Index Evaluation in 2018

Comparison analysis shows that the dimensional weights of the construction indexes and the growth indexes of national central city construction were significantly different. In the growth index evaluation, the weights of the eight dimensional layers, namely economic vitality, public services, innovative resources, factor input, innovative achievements, cultural atmosphere, beautiful environment, and harmony and livability, increased to varying degrees. The weight of beautiful environment increased by nearly 7 times; the weight of harmony and livability increased by 5.4 times; the weight of cultural atmosphere increased by 1.5 times;

the weights of economic vitality, public services and factor input were nearly doubled. However, the weights of other seven dimensions, namely production services, information hubs, transportation hubs, scientific research platforms, international trade, foreign exchanges, and city brands, declined to varying degrees. The weights of transportation hubs, foreign exchanges and scientific research platforms were only 29%, 41%, and 42% of those in the construction index evaluation, hence a great gap (see Figure 14).

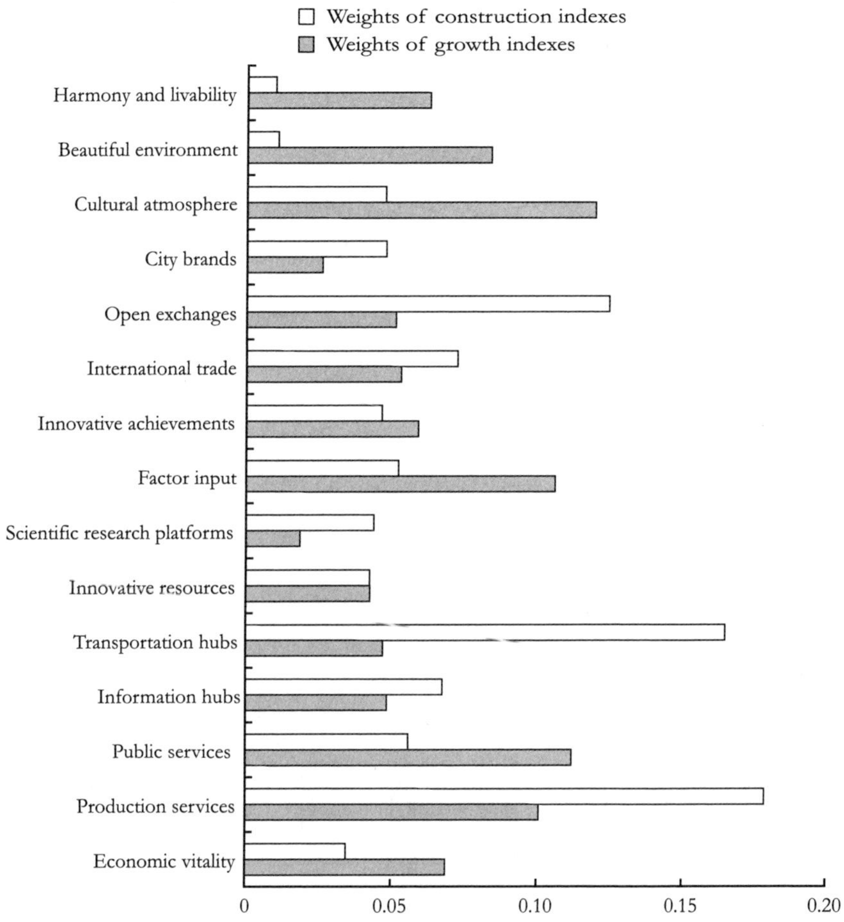

Figure 14 Comparison of Dimensional Weights between Construction Index Evaluation and Growth Index Evaluation in 2018

2 Analysis of Growth Indexes of Six Functions

Generally, all of the nine national central cities showed positive growth of varying degrees in such indexes as comprehensive services and network hubs, in spite of several exceptions. This indicated that the nine national central cities were under stable development in terms of these two functions; however, some of cities showed a downward trend in the growth indexes of four functions: scientific research innovation, open exchanges, humanistic cohesion and ecological livability (see Figure 15-20). The comparative analysis of the growth indexes of the cities' functions is indicated below:

Zhengzhou was among the best performers in the growth indexes of many functions, and it was the leader that grew fast in comprehensive services, network hubs, humanistic cohesion and ecological livability; however, its growth was relatively slow in scientific and technological innovation and open exchanges due to poor scientific research platform construction, inadequate scientific research input, and slow international trade development in import and export trade and the use of foreign investment. Given its construction indexes in 2018, Zhengzhou was an underachiever among the nine national central cities when evaluated from the comprehensive construction indexes, and still needed to focus on improving its comprehensive services, scientific and technological innovation

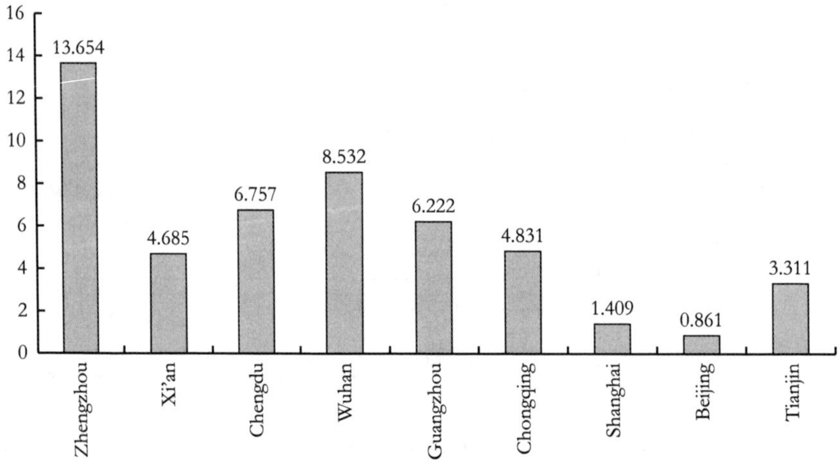

Figure15 Comparison of Growth Indexes of Comprehensive Services among Chinese National Central Cities

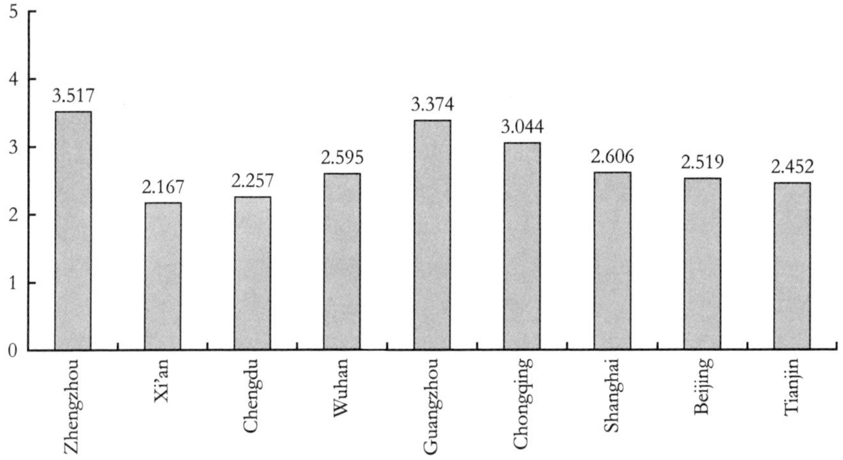

Figure 16　Comparison of Growth Indexes of Network Hubs among Chinese National Central Cities

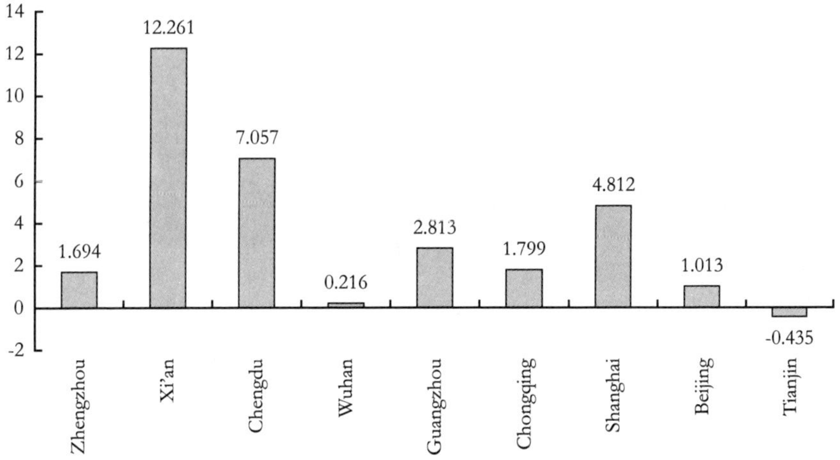

Figure 17　Comparison of Growth Indexes of Scientific and Technological Innovation among Chinese National Central Cities

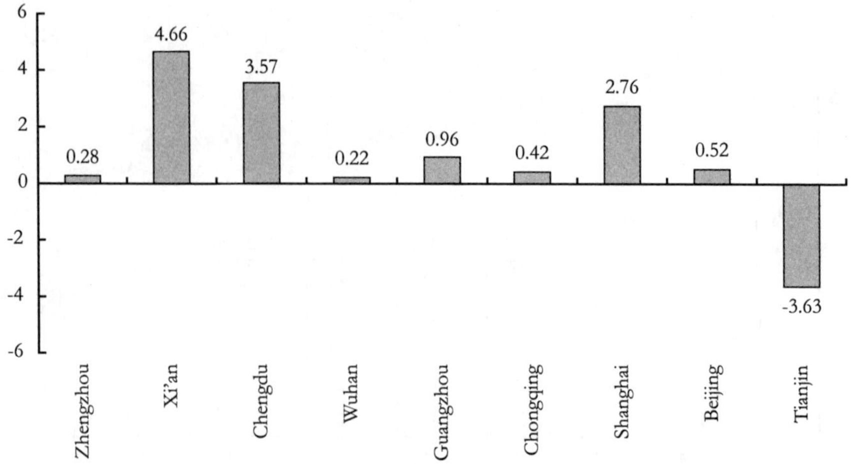

Figure 18 Comparison of Growth Indexes of Open Exchanges among Chinese National Central Cities

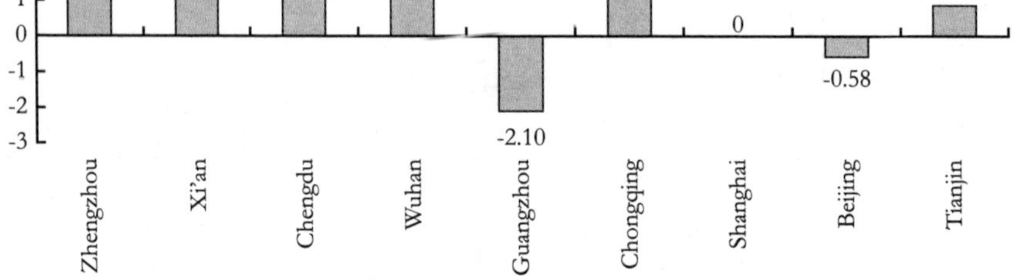

Figure 19 Comparison of Growth Indexes of Humanistic Cohesion among Chinese National Central Cities

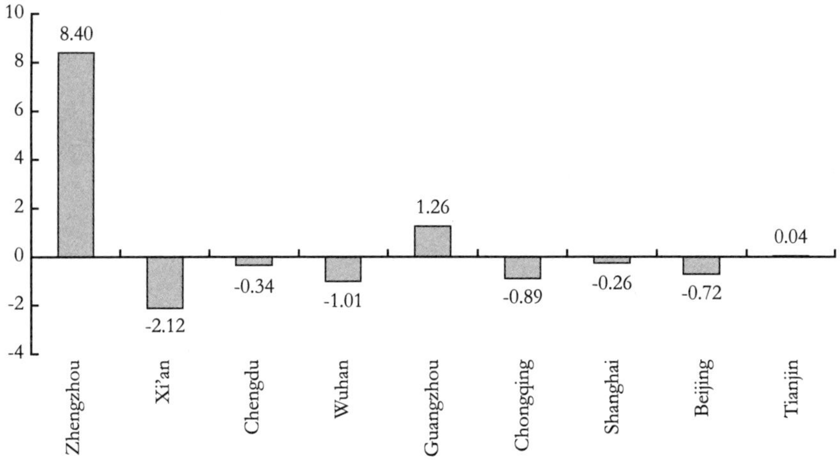

Figure 20 Comparison of Growth Indexes of Ecological Livability among Chinese National Central Cities

and open exchanges while maintaining rapid development in all functional aspects. Although its ecological livability grew fast, the overall development speed should be further increased as it lagged behind the other cities in the other urban environment related indicators.

Xi'an had the fastest growing scientific and technological innovation and open exchanges and the fourth fastest growing humanistic cohesion, but its growth indexes of the other functions remained relatively low. In particular, it had the lowest growth indexes and construction indexes of network hubs and ecological livability. These results could be explained by the low and slowly growing business volume of express delivery on the one hand, and by the all-time high PM 2.5 density and the continued urban traffic congestion as indicators of ecological livability. Therefore, in addition to comprehensive services, network hubs and ecological livability should also be the focus of future upgrades.

Chengdu was ranked second in the growth rate of scientific and technological innovation and fifth in the construction index of the same function, having moved up from the seventh place in 2016; it was ranked second in the growth rate of open exchanges and third in the growth rate of comprehensive services, but its ranking was low in the construction index of comprehensive services among all the nine national central cities, thus calling for improvement; its ecological habitability showed negative growth, mainly because of the declining per capita park greenery area and the increasing traffic congestion index since the "13th Five-Year Plan" was started. The results of comprehensive construction index evaluation and growth index evaluation suggested that comprehensive services and ecological livability should be the focus of future upgrades for Chengdu.

In recent years, Wuhan has maintained relatively rapid economic development. At the same time, having invested in humanity and tourism facilities, it was ranked second in the fasting growing comprehensive service and humanistic cohesion; however, it did not enjoy advantage in the growth indexes or construction indexes of open exchanges and ecological livability among the nine national central cities. For ecological livability in particular, its growth indexes was negative due to decreases in per capita park greenery area and urban green coverage and increase in all-day traffic congestion index. Therefore, it should strengthen the construction of ecological livability. At the same time, Wuhan also needed to increase investments in the construction of humanistic cohesion, considering its low performance in the indicators in this regard.

Guangzhou was ranked second in both network hubs and ecological livability. When combined with its construction indexes, the growth index analysis shows that it had made great achievements in information hubs, transportation hubs, environmental construction and urban construction; however, it was the poorest performer in humanistic cohesion, both for the growth index and the construction index, mainly because it had fewer public libraries, museums and cultural centers than the other national central cities and even showed a downward trend in recent years. In addition, the number of AAAA tourist destinations in its land grew more slowly than those in the other cities. Thus, the construction of humanistic cohesion should be the focus of future upgrades.

Chongqing was ranked third in network hubs and humanistic cohesion, functions that it performed better in than the others, but more efforts were required; in spite of the leading construction index of ecological livability owned by Chongqing among the nine national central cities, its growth index was negative, mainly because of its high all-day traffic congestion index, second only to Beijing's. What's more, it had the highest average growth rate of traffic congestion index among the nine national central cities. The worsening traffic congestion had affected the livability of the city and became an issue to be addressed in the future. When these results are combined with the construction index analysis, Chongqing still needed to pay attention to the construction of comprehensive services and scientific and technological innovation.

Shanghai has entered a relatively stable period of urban development in all aspects, but its scientific and technological innovation and open exchanges have maintained relatively rapid development, whose growth indexes were ranked third. The growth index of network hubs was ranked fourth. Comprehensive analysis of the six functions of national central city construction suggests that Shanghai should strengthen its humanistic cohesion and ecological livability. The latter was particularly urgent as it showed a negative index. It had the same problems as Chongqing, a city that it was ranked only second to in terms of all-day traffic congestion index and its average growth rate, which should be the focus of future upgrades.

According to the results of growth evaluation of Beijing in all the defined functions, all showed positive development to varying degrees, except humanistic cohesion and ecological livability. The main reasons for the negative growth included decreases in the number of public libraries and the urban green coverage and the ever increasing all-day traffic congestion index. Thus, Beijing should continue to develop all the functions, especially those associated with urban environment and city livability.

Benefiting from the increased per capita park greenery area and the decreased PM 2.5 annual average density, Tianjin significantly outgrew the other cities and the adverse effects of decreased urban green coverage and the clear increase in all-day traffic congestion index were offset to some extent. As a result, it was ranked third in the growth indexes of functions. However, when the construction index analysis was involved, Tianjin did not grow adequately in the other functions. In particular, its scientific and technological innovation and open exchanges showed negative growth as a consequence of the rapid declines in the numbers of national key laboratories, national engineering technological research centers and national key laboratories affiliated to enterprises and the reduction in the number of national awards won for scientific achievements in 2017. When these results were combined with the construction indexes, Tianjin should pay particular attention to the development of open exchanges and ecological livability and should strengthen the development of network hubs while maintaining balanced development of different functions.

Based on the analysis above, serious imbalances can be detected in the urban development of the nine national central cities. Among them, ecological livability is a common obstacle to their healthy and orderly development. The analysis of the growth characterization index of this function suggests that the main reasons for the negative growth of ecological livability plaguing most of the cities include: (1) Most of them have suffered somehow worse traffic congestion index all the year round since the "13th Five-Year Plan" was started; (2) In some of the cities, the construction of park green space and urban green space is outpaced by the increase in urban resident population and the expansion of urban area, resulting in varying decreases in per capita park green area and urban green coverage. As leaders in regional development, the uncoordinated development within the national central cities severely restricts their role in driving the transition to high-quality development of their respective region (Liu Guobin and Song Jinze, 2019).

IV Matters to Attend to in National Central City Construction

National central cities occupy a key position in the global urban network and play leading, demonstrating, radiating and driving roles in the national urban system. Therefore, national central city construction must be guided by the new concept of "innovative, coordinated, green, open and sharing" development, must move from high-speed development to high-quality development, and must drive coordinated regional development and sustainable development. Based on the construction indexes of the nine national central cities in 2018 and their growth indexes since the "13th Five-Year Plan" was started, the following matters should be attended to during the national central city construction process:

1 Pay Attention to the Coordination of Economy and Ecological Environment and Pursue Green Development of the National Central Cities

The national central city construction should focus closely on the six functions of comprehensive services, network hubs, technological innovation, open exchanges, humanistic cohesion and ecological livability. Ecological livability is an indispensable and important function that is as essential as the other five ones. Nevertheless, according to the construction indexes and growth indexes of ecological livability for the nine national central cities in 2018, this function has not received equal attention as the others. The national central cities should build a consensus of green development, integrate green development into coordinated regional development, bear in mind the constrained carrying capacity of ecological environment, enhance the awareness of ecological environmental protection, correctly deal with the balance between urban and regional economic development and the development of ecological environment, improve the social environment conducive to optimal allocation of resources and structural optimization and upgrading, pursue low-carbon urban development, build a beautiful, harmonious and livable urban environment, and maintain the overall ecological environment of the region. This is not only a practical prerequisite for pursuing high-quality urban development, but also an important means of implementing the coordinated regional development strategy.

2 Pay Attention to the Construction of Open Cities and Improve the Quality and Benefits of National Central City Construction

Currently, most of the national central cities do not perform well in open exchanges. However, with the ongoing economic globalization and regional economic integration processes, to be an open city and developing an open economy are important focuses and paths leading to the goals of comprehensively deepening the reform and opening up, promoting the replacement of old driving forces, and achieving high-quality development. According to the results of construction index evaluation and growth index evaluation of the national central cities in 2018, the open exchanges indexes of Shanghai and Beijing were 2 to 6 times of those of the other cities. The development of open economy is spatially uneven. Thus, cities in the Central and Western Regions, such as Zhengzhou, Wuhan, Xi'an, Chengdu and Chongqing, as well as Tianjin in the Eastern Region should promote development on the basis of deepening the reform and opening up, and build mechanisms encouraging mutual opening between metropolitan districts (areas) and city clusters centering round national central cities and opening up of the regions to the outside world. They should also shape a pattern of all-round opening up and make full use of regional, domestic and international markets and resources to enhance their open economy development level and effectively improve the quality and benefits of urban economic growth.

3 Pay Attention to City Culture Construction and Enhance the Unique Soft Power of the National Central Cities

At present, the cultural construction of the national central cities needs to be strengthened, and some of the cities have not established a unique city brand image. Specific city cultural labels and good cultural forms represented by city symbols, city slogans, historical cultures and architectural styles are important means to highlight a city's quality and charm and enhance a city's connotation. They are not only important elements of a city's core competitiveness, but also important means to make a city's international competitiveness prominent. Thus, the national central city construction needs to be deeper rooted in the profound history and culture and combined with modern life. An urban culture with distinctive characteristics and profound foundation should be shaped. Cultural construction should be combined with urban spatial layout, technological innovation and development, regional open exchanges and ecological environment upgrade. A concise and unique urban brand image should be established. The goal is to promote the coordinated development of urban culture and economy and to transform intangible soft power of culture into realistic hard power of competitiveness.

4 Avoid or Eliminate Urban Diseases and Effectively Exploit the Leading and Driving Role of the National Central Cities

National central cities are the spire and core cities in the national urban system that play leading, demonstrating, radiating and driving roles in metropolitan areas, city clusters and coordinated regional development. However, in order to effectively act as models for surrounding cities and lead surrounding areas and the city clusters where they are located, they should fully understand, respect and conform to the laws of urban development, uncover the constraints of sustainable urban development, identify the root causes of urban diseases, and explore ways and methods that can improve their carrying capacity and operational efficiency. Emphasis should be placed on the integrated development of metropolitan areas and city clusters centering round the national central cities in industrial collaboration, infrastructure, ecological environment and public services to achieve high-quality development of the cities, effectively resolve urban diseases, and then exploit the role of the national central cities in driving the development of urbanization and coordinated regional development.

References:

[1] Chen Yao. Institutional Advantages Should Be Fully Reflected in the Construction of New Regional Coordination Mechanisms [J]. Regional Economic Review, 2019, 37 (01): 8-11.

[2] Liu Guobin and Song Jinze. Research on High-quality Development of China's Regional Economy [J]. Regional Economic Review, 2019, (2): 55-60.

[3] Wang Lin. Cultural Soft Power of National Central Cities: A Case Study of Top Five National Central Cities in China [J]. Urban Insight, 2009, 3 (3): 71-78.

[4] Wu Shinong, Li Changqing and Yu Wei. Decision Analysis and Empirical Research on the Growth of Chinese Listed Companies [J]. Nankai Business Review, 1999, (4): 49-57.

[5] Yu Xin'an. Realizing Coordinated Regional Development Under the Continuous Promotion of Driving Force Transformation [J]. Regional Economic Review, 2019, 37 (01): 15-18.

[6] Zhong Maochu. The Countermeasure Thinking of Green Development Concept into Regional Coordinated Development Strategy [J]. Regional Economic Review, 2018, (05): 84-88.

Cities' Reports

B.3

National Central City Construction of Beijing: Effectiveness and Outlook

*Li Ruipeng and An Shuwei**

Abstract: Beijing assumes different functions when it is measured on three different spatial scales: municipal, the Beijing-Tianjin-Hebei Region, and the country. As a national central city, Beijing experienced stable economic and social development in all areas at the municipal level in 2018; it effectively promoted the Beijing-Tianjin-Hebei collaboration at the Beijing-Tianjin-Hebei level; the status of Beijing as the "four centers" has been constantly increased at the national

* This study is part of the research project "New Urbanization and Industrial Agglomeration: Pattern, Process and Mechanism" (Approval No.: CIT&TCD20180336) funded by the "Training Program of the Great Wall Scholars", a program supporting the construction of high-level faculty in universities affiliated to Beijing Municipality.

Li Ruipeng, a Ph.D. student majored in Regional Economics at School of Urban Economics and Public Administration, Capital University of Economics and Business; An Shuwei, Ph.D. Economics, Professor and Doctoral Supervisor at School of Urban Economics and Public Administration, Capital University of Economics and Business.

level. However, the capital is still stuck in the "dilemmas" such as lack of core supporting force in high-grade, precision and advanced industries, failure to properly respond to the impact of the special relief of non-capital functions actions, poor attractiveness of deputy urban center, and imperfect Beijing-Tianjin-Hebei coordinated development mechanism. High-quality development is the choice and inevitable requirement for the national central city construction of Beijing. To become a high-quality national central city in the future, Beijing should change the means of urban governance, promote the relief of non-capital functions in a people-oriented manner, enhance its radiating and driving capacity, and build innovative coordinated regional development mechanism until it gradually becomes a world-class harmonious and livable capital.

Keywords: national central cities; relief of non-capital functions; coordinated development of Beijing-Tianjin-Hebei Region

As a national central city, Beijing is at the top of the national urban system and acts as a leader in the new urbanization construction of China. China has moved from a stage of high-speed economic growth to a stage of high-quality economic development. At present, high-quality development is an objective requirement for Beijing, which is required to focus on reduced quantity development, that is, to move from the mere pursuit of speed and aggregate to the pursuit of high efficiency and high quality (An Shuwei & Sun Wenqian, 2019). How effective was the national central city construction of Beijing in 2018? What problems were there? What is the focus of the future? The following is an analysis that starts from the functions of Beijing as a city.

I Changing Functional Positioning of Beijing as a City

The functions of Beijing as a city has been redefined several times (Table 1).

Beijing is the capital of China and a city in the country. It assumes different functions when it is measured on three different spatial scales: municipal, the Beijing-Tianjin-Hebei Region, and the country (see Figure 1).

Table 1 Changing Urban Positioning of Beijing Municipality

Year	Plan	Urban Positioning of Beijing
1953	*Key Points for Rebuilding and Expanding the Draft Plan for Beijing Municipality*	Political, economic, and cultural centers, industrial base, and scientific and technological center of the country
1958	*Tentative Program for the General Construction Planning of Beijing Municipality*	Political center, cultural and educational center, modern industrial base, and center of science and technology
1973	*Program for the General Construction Planning of Beijing Municipality*	Basically consistent with urban planning in the 1950s
1982	*Program for the General Construction Planning of Beijing Municipality*	Political center and cultural center of the country, and international exchange center
1993	*General Plan of Beijing Municipality (1991-2010)*	The capital, political center and cultural center of the country, a world famous ancient capital and modern international city.
2005	*General Plan of Beijing Municipality (2004-2020)*	The capital, political center and cultural center of the country, a world famous ancient capital and modern international city.
2017	*General Plan of Beijing Municipality (2016-2035)*	Political center, cultural Center, international exchange center, and scientific and technological innovation center of the country

Sources: Liu Xinkui: *Urban Planning and Management of Beijing for 60 Years*, Guangming Daily Press, 2010; Zou Biying: *A Study on the Evolution of Functional Division among Beijing-Tianjin-Hebei Region As Cities*, Capital University of Economics and Business, 2019, complied from pp. 26-27.

At the municipal level, as a mega-city, Beijing has to meet the needs of 21.542 million urban residents for a better life, providing them with quality, convenient and efficient services for life and a livable environment. At the same time, Beijing must guarantee economic growth at a certain speed and continuous growth of government fiscal revenue in order to provide material security for improving the quality of urban development, the quality of living environment, and the quality of people's life.

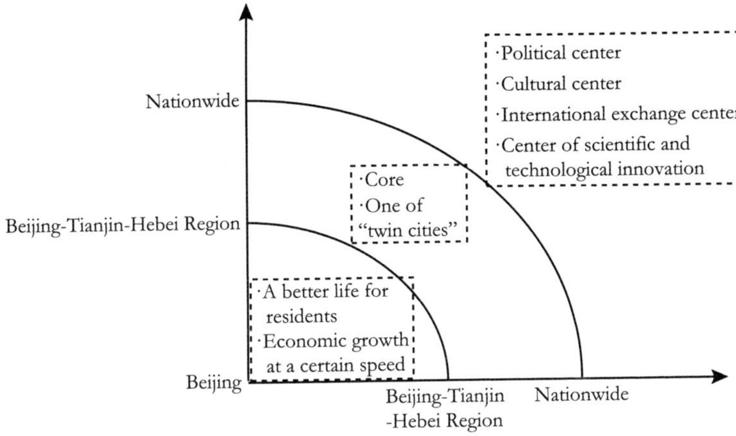

Figure 1 Functions of Beijing Measured on Different Spatial Scales

Source: *Industry Collaboration among Three Major Coastal City Clusters* by An Shuwei and Yu Peng et al., Economy & Management Publishing House, 2019, pp. 238-240; *A Study on Optimizing the Radiating and Driving Function of Beijing* by Wu Xiaoxia, Shi Chen and Gao Jian, *City*, 2019 (2), pp.28-36.

At the Beijing-Tianjin-Hebei level, Beijing is the core and one of the "dual engines" of the Beijing-Tianjin-Hebei coordinated development. As a "core", it should focus on adjusting and relieving its non-capital functions, optimizing and upgrading its core functions as the capital, and solving the "urban diseases". The optimization and upgrading of its core functions as the capital is required by its position as the center of scientific and technological innovation and the cultural center. As one of the "dual engines", Beijing should further strengthen the linkage with Tianjin as twin cities, and the two cities should follow their functional division, expand the breadth and depth of mutual cooperation, accelerate integrated development, and jointly play leading, radiating and driving roles as top cities.

At the national level, Beijing is the symbol of the great motherland as the capital. Beijing should fully perform its functions as the political center, cultural center, international exchange center, and center of scientific and technological innovation in the country, and should also strengthen its uniting, demonstrating, leading, radiating and driving roles as the cultural center, international exchange center, and center of scientific and technological innovation in the country

II Characteristics of Current Social and Economic Development of Beijing

In 2018, Beijing maintained stable economic and social development, with GDP increasing by 6.6%. The high-grade, precision and advanced industries developed rapidly, and the industrial structure was continuously optimized; the total resident population continued to decline, and its growth rate also continued to decline at a negative level, and the number of migrants dropped significantly; the ecological and environmental quality was improved; and Beijing was ranked second among the nine national central cities in many economic and social indicators.

(I) Economic Aggregate Grew Steadily, But Growth Rate Shown a Downward Trend

In 2018, Beijing adhered to the general direction of seeking improvement in stability and maintained rapid economic development. From 2010 to 2018, Beijing's GDP increased from RMB 1.44416 trillion to RMB 3.032 trillion; its per capita GDP increased from RMB 73,610.3 to RMB 140,748.3; nevertheless, its regional GRP growth rate decreased from 10.4% to 6.6% (see Figure 2). As

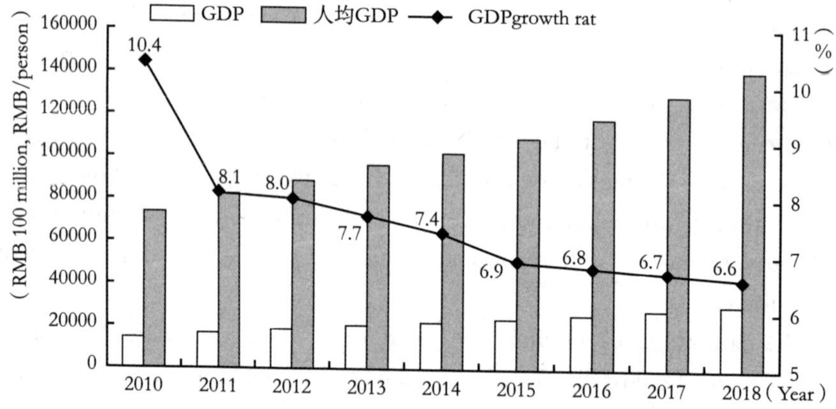

Figure 2 Beijing's GDP, Per Capita GDP and GDP Growth Rates for 2010-2018 (with 1978 as the Base Year)

Source: *Beijing Statistical Yearbook (2018), Statistical Communiqué of Beijing Municipality on the 2018 National Economic and Social Development.*

a whole, its economic aggregate continued to grow, but its economic growth rate showed a downward trend, which has remained at around 6.6% in recent years.

(II) Industry Structure Was Continuously Optimized, and Each District Had A Differentiated Industrial Structure

From 2010 to 2018, Beijing's industry structure changed from 0.8:23.5:75.7 to 0.4:18.6:81.0. The proportions of the primary industry and the secondary industry continued to decline, while the proportion of the tertiary industry continued to increase (see Figure 3). The added value of the primary industry decreased from RMB 12.28 billion to RMB 11.87 billion; the added value of the secondary industry increased from RMB 338.79 billion to RMB 564.77 billion; the added value of the tertiary industry increased from RMB 1.09309 trillion to RMB 2.45536 trillion.

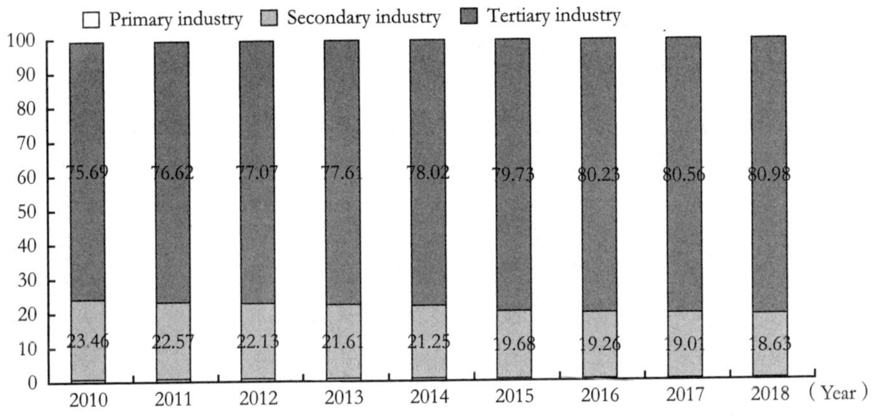

Figure 3 Beijing's Industry Structure for 2010-2018

Source: *Beijing Statistical Yearbook (2018), Statistical Communiqué of Beijing Municipality on the 2018 National Economic and Social Development.*

Further breakdown analysis suggests that the added value of agriculture, forestry, animal husbandry, fishery and real estate industries of Beijing decreased in 2018, and the added value of other industries increased. The top five growing industries were information transmission, software and information technology services, scientific research and technological services, health and social work, finance, transportation, warehousing and postal services. The proportions of information transmission, software and information technology services, and scientific research and technological services in GDP also significantly increased (see Figure 4).

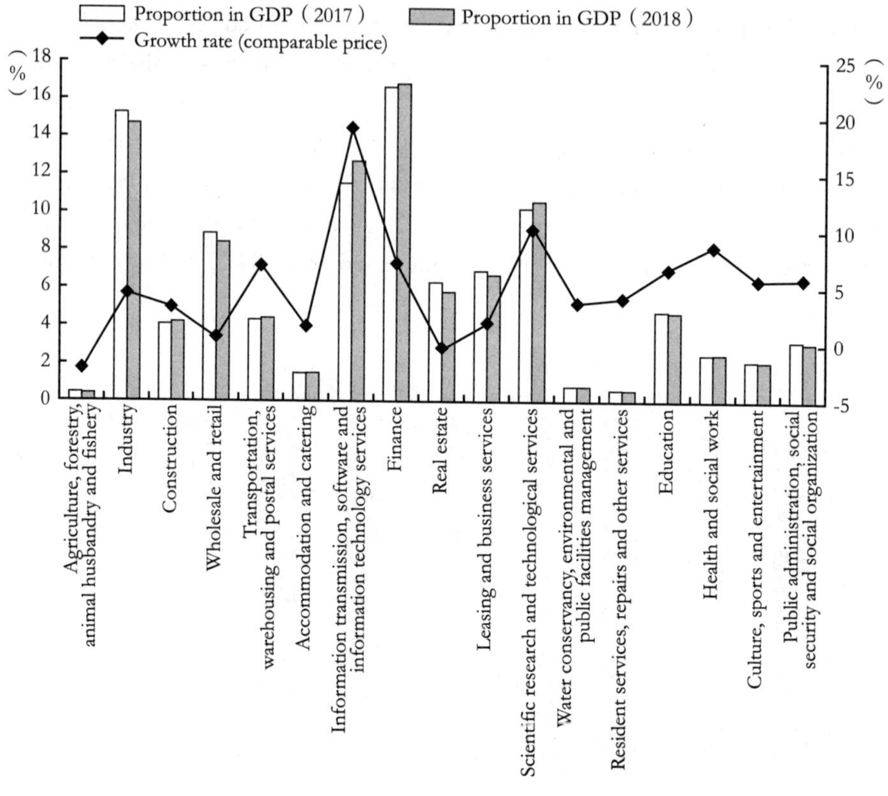

Figure 4 Proportions in GDP and Growth Rates of the Added Value of Breakdown Industries of Beijing in 2018

Source: *Beijing Statistical Yearbook (2018), Statistical Communiqué of Beijing Municipality on the 2018 National Economic and Social Development.*

The changed industry structure of Beijing was attributed to the development of "high-grade, precision and advanced" industries in recent years. The top ten "high-grade, precision and advanced" industries in 2018, i.e. the new generation of information technology, integrated circuits, medical health, intelligent equipment, energy conservation and environmental protection, new energy smart cars, new materials, artificial intelligence, software and information services, and technological service industry, reported a total operating income of RMB 3.2548 trillion.① New driving forces grew rapidly, and the industry structure was continuously optimized. The added value of the high-tech industry, strategic emerging industries and the information industry of Beijing in 2018 ② were RMB 697.68 billion, RMB 489.34 billion and RMB 494.07 billion, accounting for 23.0%, 16.1% and 16.3% of GDP and up 9.4%, 9.2% and 14.3%, respectively, from 2017 (measured at current prices). ③

(III) Total Resident Population Had Declined for Two Consecutive Years

According to the *General Plan for Beijing (2016-2035)*, Beijing is required to constrain its city scale based on the carrying capacity of resources and environment and strictly control its population size within 23 million. To this end, Beijing took special actions for the relief of non-capital functions and the enhancement of capital functions. In 2016, the resident population of Beijing reached a peak of 21.729 million. After that, the total resident population showed a downward trend. In 2018, it was 21.542 million, a decrease of 187,000 from 2016. From 2010 to 2018, the growth rate of Beijing's resident population continued to decline and turned from positive to negative, down from 5.5% to-0.8%. In 2015, the resident population without Beijing household registration reached a peak and then began to decrease. From 2010 to 2018, the number and growth rate of resident population without Beijing household registration showed basically the same trend as those of the total resident population, but it changed more than greatly than the resident population (see Figure 5).

① *Beijing Reported Results from High-quality Development: Top Ten High-grade, Precision and Advanced Industries Earned RMB 3,2548 trillion in 2018*, chinadaily.com, March 25, 2019

② The high-tech industry, strategic emerging industries and the information industry overlap.

③ *Statistical Communiqué of Beijing Municipality on the 2018 National Economic and Social Development.*

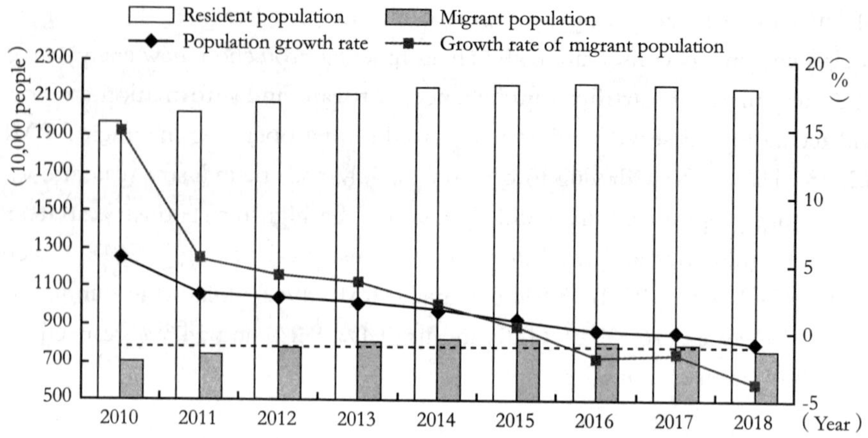

Figure 5 Numbers and Growth Rates of Residents and Migrants in Beijing for 2010-2018

Source: *Beijing Statistical Yearbook (2018)*, *Statistical Communiqué of Beijing Municipality on the 2018 National Economic and Social Development.*.

(IV) Significant Achievements Were Made from Ecological and Environmental Governance

Beijing is a world-class harmonious and livable capital to which ecological environment protection and governance matters. In 2018, Beijing, on the one hand, took a special relief and remediation action by "opening up empty spaces and adding green areas" to enhance the sense of gain among the people. It opened up a total land area of 6,828ha and added a total green area of 1,683ha by demolishing illegal structures; it built 28 new leisure parks and 121 small and micro green spaces and increased the coverage of the 500m service radius of park green spaces to 80%; on the other hand, it strengthened the pollution management of diesel trucks, dust and volatile organic compounds, eliminated 47,000 trucks fueled by the National III standard diesel, increased the new process rate of road cleaning by 89%, reduced the emissions of volatile organic compounds from key industrial sectors by 2,000t, promoted "the replacement of coal with clean energy", and increased the proportion of clean and high-quality energy in the plain areas of the city to more than 96%. [1] Remarkable achievements were made in ecological environment construction. Since 2013, the

① Chen Jining: *Report on the Work of Beijing Municipal Government*, January 23, 2019.

annual average concentrations of PM2.5, SO_2 and NO_2 in Beijing had continued to decline and were measured at 51μg/m³, 6μg/m³ and 42μg/m³, respectively, in 2018; from 2010 to 2018, the urban forest greening rate, forest coverage rate and green coverage rate continued to increase, reaching 61.5%, 43.5% and 48.4%, respectively, in 2018. The number of days with good air increased significantly and air quality continued to improve when compared with the levels in 2013 (Table 2).

Table 2 Main Ecological and Environmental Indicators of Beijing for 2010-2018

Year	PM2.5 (μg/m³)	SO_2 (μg/m³)	NO_2 (μg/m³)	Urban forest greening rate (%)	Forest coverage rate (%)	Woody plant coverage rate (%)	Number of days with good air (days)
2010	—	32	57	45.0	37.0	53.0	286
2011	—	28	55	45.6	37.6	54.0	286
2012	—	28	52	46.2	38.6	55.5	281
2013	90	27	56	46.8	40.1	57.4	167
2014	86	22	57	47.4	41.0	58.4	168
2015	81	14	50	48.4	41.6	59.0	186
2016	73	10	48	48.4	42.3	59.3	198
2017	58	8	46	48.4	43.0	61.0	226
2018	51	6	42	48.4	43.5	61.5	227

Source: *Beijing Statistical Yearbook (2018)*, *Statistical Communiqué of Beijing Municipality on the 2018 National Economic and Social Development*..

(V) Beijing Was Ranked Second in Major Economic and Social Indicators among the Nine National Central Cities

Large population, large scale, and concentrated functions are prominent features of national central cities (Wu Aizhi and Li Guoping, 2017). National central city construction is based on strong economic strength. This paper measures the comprehensive economic strength of the national central cities by economic scale, financial strength, consumer market, people's living standards, industry structure, and urbanization rate. Compared with the other eight national central cities, Beijing had the second highest GDP, general public budget income, total retail volume of social consumer goods, per capita disposable income, and urbanization rate in 2018, second only to Shanghai; its per capita GDP was RMB 141,000, second only to that of Guangzhou; it had the highest proportion of the tertiary industry in the industry structure (see Table 3).

Table 3 Major Economic and Social Indicators of the Nine National Central Cities in 2018

City	GDP (RMB 100 million)	Per capita GDP (RMB 10,000)	General public budget income (RMB 100 million)	Per capita disposable income (RMB)	Total retail volume of social consumer goods (RMB 100 million)	Industry structure	Urbanization rate (%)
Shanghai	32679.9	13.5	7108.2	64183.0	12668.7	0.3:29.8:69.9	88.1
Beijing	30320.0	14.1	5785.9	62361.0	11747.7	0.4:18.6:81.0	86.5
Guangzhou	22859.4	15.5	1632.3	59982.1	9256.2	1.0:27.2:71.8	86.4
Chongqing	20363.2	6.6	2265.5	26386.0	8769.6	6.8:40.9:52.3	65.5
Tianjin	18809.6	12.1	2106.2	39506.0	5533.0	0.9:40.5:58.6	83.2
Chengdu	15342.8	9.5	1424.2	36753.9	6801.8	3.4:42.5:54.1	73.1
Wuhan	14847.3	13.5	2900.2	42133.0	6843.9	2.4:43.0:54.6	80.3
Zhengzhou	10143.3	10.1	1152.1	33105.0	4268.1	1.5:43.9:54.7	73.4
Xi'an	8349.9	8.5	684.7	35432.9	4658.7	3.1:35.0:61.9	74.0

Source: Statistical Communiqués of the Cities on the 2018 National Economic and Social Development

III Beijing's Achievements in Driving Beijing-Tianjin-Hebei Coordinated Development

At the Beijing-Tianjin-Hebei regional level, Beijing has made some achievements in promoting the Beijing-Tianjin-Hebei coordinated development strategy by relieving non-capital functions. On the one hand, it optimized its radiating and driving role under the new urban pattern featuring "one core and two wings". On the other hand, it promoted the development of Beijing, Tianjin and Hebei in such fields as industrial cooperation, transportation integration, and ecological joint prevention and control.

(I) Resident Population of Beijing Decreased and the Construction of "Two Wings" Continued to Advance

Beijing has alleviated the "urban diseases" to a certain extent by relieving non-capital functions. Firstly, its population decreased. In 2017, the resident population of Beijing dropped by 22,000 from the previous year, and in 2018 it further dropped by 165,000 from the previous year. Secondly, Beijing's urban environment was further improved. Its air quality was constantly improved due to a series of measures such as relieving and shutting down energy-intensive or highly polluting industries and regulating "scattering, disorderly and polluting" enterprises.

At the same time, Beijing promoted the construction of the "two wings" in the Beijing-Tianjin-Hebei coordinated development. The first batch of municipal-level agencies has moved into the administrative office in the deputy urban center of Beijing, and the Tongzhou Campus of Beijing No. 5 High School and the Tongzhou Branch of Beijing Friendship Hospital have been put into operation. In Xiong'an New Area, paired assistance to four schools continued to progress, and 12 enterprises from Zhongguancun have settled down: Beijing Origin Water Technology Co., Ltd., Beijing Orient Landscape Investment Holdings Co, Ltd., Beijing Oriental Yuhong Technology Co., Ltd., Glodon Technology Holdings Co., Ltd., Beijing SDL Technology Co., Ltd., Beijing SPC Environment Protection Tech Co., Ltd., Beijing Shenwu Technology Group Co., Ltd., Beijing Creative Distribution Automation Co., Ltd., Beijing Xiaoju Technology Co., Ltd., Kingsoft Holding Co., Ltd., Beijing Shouhang IHW Resources Saving Technology Company Co., Ltd., and Beijing Eyecool Science and Technology Co., Ltd.

(II) Industrial Transfer and Undertaking Proceeded in an Orderly Manner

In 2018, Beijing signed a new round of strategic cooperation agreements with Tianjin and Hebei, and implemented a new three-year action plan for coordinated development to strengthen the construction of industrial undertaking platforms. Tianjin basically formed a "1+16" undertaking pattern: the Binhai New Area plus 16 key undertaking platforms. From 2015 to the first quarter of 2019, Tianjin had introduced a total of 72,300 enterprises and 7,879 investment projects from

Beijing and Hebei, whose total investment was maintained at more than 40% of the domestic investment actually used by Tianjin and mostly came from Beijing.① Hebei promoted the construction of key undertaking platforms such as Xiong'an New Area, Caofeidian Coordinated Development Demonstration Zone, Zhangjiakou-Chengde Ecological Function Zone, Bohai New Area, and Zhangbei Economic Development Zone. It focused on the construction of incubation bases and absorbed the transformed achievements of scientific and technological innovation from Beijing and Tianjin, such as the Beijing-Tianjin-Hebei (Langfang) Collaborative Innovation and Entrepreneurship Base, the Pilot Scale Test and Incubation Base of Tsinghua University (Gu'an), and the Beijing-Hebei New Airport Economic Zone. The Beijing-Tianjin-Hebei "4+N" industrial cooperation pattern was getting more stable.

From the perspective of capital flows in Beijing, Tianjin and Hebei, Beijing's capital had prominent radiating effects on Tianjin and Hebei. From 2014 to 2018, Beijing's investments in Tianjin and Hebei increased from RMB 105.88 billion to RMB 362.86 billion, equivalent to an increase in the proportion of Beijing's total investment in the country from 4.7% to 8.1%. The investments from Beijing were far higher than the investments from Tianjin and Hebei to the other two places (see Table 4). From the perspective of technology spillovers in the Beijing-Tianjin-Hebei Region, Beijing's technology had still minor radiating effects on Tianjin and Hebei, although they were getting stronger. From 2014 to 2017, the number of technological contracts and business volume from Beijing to the other two places increased significantly, and Hebei benefited more than Tianjin in both. In 2018, the total value of technological contracts flowing from Beijing to Tianjin and Hebei was RMB 22.74 billion, an increase of 11.7% from the previous year. The proportions of technological contracts and business volume benefiting Tianjin and Hebei were increasing in the total number benefiting the other provinces (municipalities and autonomous regions), but they were still at small levels, measured at 10.5% and 8.7% in 2017 (see Table 5).

---

① *Tianjin Gains Momentum to Introduce Projects from Beijing and Hebei*, Beijing Municipal People's Government, June 14, 2019, http://www.beijing.gov.cn/ywdt/zwzt/sjfsdgn/zxjz/ybxzzy/t1590856.htm.

Table 4 Capital Flows in Beijing, Tianjin and Hebei for 2014-2018

Year	Beijing's investments in Tianjin and Hebei (RMB 100 million)		Tianjin's investments in Beijing and Hebei (RMB 100 million)		Hebei's investments in Beijing and Tianjin (RMB 100 million)		Beijing's investments across the country (RMB 100 million)	Beijing's investments in Tianjin and Hebei/ Beijing's investments across the country (%)
	Tianjin	Hebei	Beijing	Hebei	Beijing	Tianjin		
2014	783.8	275.0	169.4	42.4	264.8	57.1	22553.0	4.7
2015	1138.9	923.4	337.1	48.2	101.1	55.0	33160.1	6.2
2016	1927.1	997.0	605.7	47.2	231.0	107.2	67939.2	4.3
2017	1520.3	1484.6	266.0	141.3	264.5	189.9	57140.4	5.3
2018	1327.4	2301.2	289.9	120.0	207.6	85.1	44540.2	8.1

Source: Beijing-Tianjin-Hebei Big Data Research Center.

Table 5 Number of Technological Contracts and Business Volume from Beijing to Tianjin and Hebei for 2014-2018

Year	Number of technological contracts				Business volume of technological contracts (RMB 100 million)			
	To Tianjin	To Hebei	To Tianjin and Hebei	To other provinces	To Tianjin	To Hebei	To Tianjin and Hebei	To other provinces
2014	1376	2099	3475	37212	20.4	62.7	83.1	1722
2015	1407	2291	3698	37447	57.6	53.9	111.5	1878.7
2016	1486	2362	3848	38928	56.0	98.7	154.7	1997.2
2017	1766	2880	4646	44287	49.3	154.2	203.5	2327.3
2018	—	—	—	—	—	—	227.4	—

Source: *Statistical Communiqué of Technical Market of Beijing* over the years and the *2019 Report on the Work of Beijing Municipal Government.*

(III) Regional Integrated Transportation Network Was Increasingly Improved

Since 2014, "Beijing-Tianjin-Hebei on track" has been under construction, and the construction of transportation infrastructure such as roads, railways, airports and public transportation in the region has been advanced (An Shuwei, 2017). At present, all the national "dead end highways" within Beijing have been connected, and the Beijing sections of the 7 capital lines radiating from the national expressway network have been completed. The construction of Beijing-Xiongan Expressway is about to commence; the construction of Beijing-Zhangjiakou, Beijing-Tangshan, Beijing-Binhai New Area, Beijing-Caofeidian and Beijing-Xiong'an Railways proceeds; Beijing Daxing International Airport is about to be put into operation, and the construction of airport lines connecting the new airport to Tianjin and Hebei is also about to commence; there are 41 bus routes departing from Beijing, and they basically cover 17 adjacent areas including Langfang, Laishui and Chicheng in Hebei Province. Now, the Beijing-Tianjin-Hebei T-Union has been more and more functional, and more than 1.8 million cards have been distributed. A "one-hour" traffic circle is just around the corner to promote the rapid flow of resources among Beijing, Tianjin and Hebei.

(IV) Remarkable Results Have Been Made in Joint Ecological and Environmental Protection

In 2018, the "2+26" cities in the Beijing-Tianjin-Hebei and surrounding areas① reported a PM2.5 annual average density as 60μg/m^3, down 11.8% from the previous year; Beijing, Tianjin and Hebei jointly revised a new emergency plan against heavy air pollution.② They also worked together to promote the comprehensive management and ecological restoration of the Yongding River,

---

① In order to ensure the completion of the 2017 target tasks as defined in the *Action Plan of Air Pollution Prevention and Control*, the Ministry of Environmental Protection formulated the *Work Plan for Air Pollution Prevention and Control in Beijing-Tianjin-Hebei and Surrounding Areas in 2017*, which covers the air pollution transmission channels in the Beijing-Tianjin-Hebei Region, including Beijing; Tianjin; Shijiazhuang, Tangshan, Langfang, Baoding, Cangzhou, Hengshui, Xingtai and Handan in Hebei Province; Taiyuan, Yangquan, Changzhi and Jincheng in Shanxi Province; Jinan, Zibo, Jining, Dezhou, Liaocheng, Binzhou and Heze in Shandong Province; Zhengzhou, Kaifeng, Anyang, Hebi, Xinxiang, Jiaozuo and Puyang in Henan Province, namely "2+26" cities.

② "Five-year collaborative efforts into ecological environment coordinated governance bear fruits in Beijing-Tianjin-Hebei and upstream water channel of Yongding River is refilled in 2019", Beijing Municipal People's Government, February 25, 2019, http://www.beijing.gov.cn/ywdt/zwzt/jjjyth/hbgj/t1578413.htm。

the North Canal and the Chaobai River. Beijing and Tianjin signed the *Agreement on Compensation for Horizontal Ecological Protection of the Water Conservation Area in the Chaobai River Basin Upstream of Miyun Reservoir*; the Beijing-Tianjin-Hebei collaborative efforts have produced afforestation of 114,700 ha to control windblown sand and protect water sources over the past five years.

IV Results from the Construction of Beijing as "Four Centers"

As the capital of China, Beijing represents the image of the country. Its urban functions not only meet its own needs as a city, but also serve the whole country. As the "four centers" of China, Beijing's ability to support national government activities continues to improve, and its advantages in gathering cultural, scientific and technological resources are constantly exploited. Beijing's role as the national scientific and technological innovation center makes it more influential throughout the country, and it continues to provide a good environment for international exchanges of China.

(I) Continuous Improvement in the Ability to Support Government Activities

Beijing is the political center of the country, which is also its primary function. It is intended to providc top quality services and support for the central leading party, government and military agencies. Firstly, it must adhere to the party's leadership, safeguard the authority of the party and the central government, and build a good political ecological environment. It continues to spread the core values of socialism and builds a spiritual civilization base through theme education, series exhibitions and cultural activities in parks and museums. Secondly, it actively implements the special relief and remediation plan designed to provide conditions for optimal layout of the central Party and state organs. This special plan focuses on the six districts of the city and puts the core areas as top priorities. In 2018, the comprehensive remediation of 29 old districts in the central city moved on smoothly. The 80km road electric overhead wire was grounded along the core areas. Thirdly, Beijing must ensure that the national government activities carried out within its scope are safe, efficient, and orderly. In 2018, Beijing well served and supported the hosting of government activities like the NPC and the CPPCC, the celebration of the 200th anniversary of Marx's birth, the celebration of the 40th anniversary of reform and opening up, and diplomatic activities of the country.

(II) Constantly Enhanced Cultural Center

Beijing has a profound cultural background and a gathering of cultural resources. In recent years, it has reinforced its cultural protection efforts. In 2018, Beijing continued to enhance its status as the national cultural center around "One Core, One City, Three Belts and Two Zones".① Beijing published and implemented the new version of the *Protection and Development Plan for the Historical and Cultural City*, completed the protection and construction planning for the northern Great Wall, the eastern canal and the western Xishan cultural belts, and moved forward the application of the Central Axis into the world heritage list. The Tiananmen Gate Tower and its tower platform were rehabilitated, and the renovation of the East Square of the Great Hall of the People and the landscape upgrading project were completed.

The cultural and creative industry developed rapidly. From 2010 to 2017, the added value of Beijing's cultural and creative industry increased from RMB 169.77 billion to RMB 390.88 billion, with an average annual growth rate of 14.9% and accounting for 11.4% of the city's GDP, second only to the finance industry.② By 2018, there had been 34 cultural and creative Industrial Parks in Beijing, including 4 in Dongcheng District, 8 in Xicheng District, 11 in Chaoyang District, 5 in Haidian District, 3 in Daxing District, 1 in Tongzhou District, 1 in Changping District, and 1 in the Beijing Economic-Technological Development Area. Among them, Chaoyang District had the best developed cultural and

① "One Core" represents the socialist core values; "One City" represents its status as a historical and cultural city; "Three Belts" represent the Grand Canal Cultural Belt, the Great Wall Cultural Belt, and the Xishan Yongding River Cultural Belt; "Two Zones" represents the demonstration zone for the public cultural service system and the leading zone for development of cultural and creative industries.

② In 2017, the finance industry of Beijing contributed 16.6% of the total municipal GDP.

creative industry: there were nearly 81,000 registered cultural enterprises; its inhabitants include 798 Art District, the 751D·park, Laijin Cultural and Creative Industrial Park, Langyuan Vintage Park, Maolong Cultural and Creative Industrial Park, Universal Creative Park and many other distinctive cultural Industrial Parks. In 2018, there were more than 4,000 legal entities in the cultural industry above designated size whose income reached RMB 1.0173 trillion, an increase of 11.9% over the previous year, in Beijing. At the same time, more favorable policies were introduced for the cultural and creative industry. The Beijing Municipal Committee of the Communist Party of China and the Beijing Municipal People's Government issued the *Opinions on Promoting the Innovation and Development of the Cultural and Creative Industry*. The Beijing Municipal People's Government issued the *Guiding Opinions on Protection and Utilization of Old Factory Buildings to Expand Cultural Space*.

The quality of cultural services was constantly improved. In 2018, the amount of books in libraries, the number of collected files in archives, the total number of newspapers and the number of publication distributors in Beijing registered year-on-year increase by 1.732 million, 410,000, 116, and 324 to 67.012 million, 8.687 million, 3,491, and 7,922, respectively. A low fare subsidy policy for commercial performances and a rent subsidy policy for 151 physical bookstores were promulgated.

(III) The Construction of National Scientific and Technological Center Gained Momentum

Beijing's innovation vitality was constantly enhanced due to the gathering of high-end talents and the strong technology foundation. In 2018, Beijing was home to 25,000 national high-tech enterprises, which marked an increase of 25% from the previous year. On average, 199 new innovative enterprises were established every day. The Zhongguancun Demonstration Zone registered a total revenue of more than RMN 5.8 trillion. Beijing was the champion city in the country for having more than 80 unicorn companies.① The list of scientific and technological innovation achievements was still extending in Beijing. From 2010 to 2018,

---

① Unicorn company generally refers to an unlisted startup that has a history of not more than 10 years and is valued more than USD 1 billion.

the numbers of patent applications, patent grants, technological contracts and business volume of technological contracts all showed increasing trends. In 2018, these numbers increased by 13.6%, 15.5%, 1.5% and 10.5%, respectively, over the previous year (see Figure 6). In the same year, Beijing contributed 55.7% of the world-leading technology achievements,[①] such as breakthroughs in a number of key core technologies including the Chinese laser phototypesetting system and the 5G mobile communication, the discovery of threefold degeneracy fermion and Majorana anyon, and the successful development of carbon-based optoelectronic integrated circuits, Beidou series satellites, and "Insight" satellites.

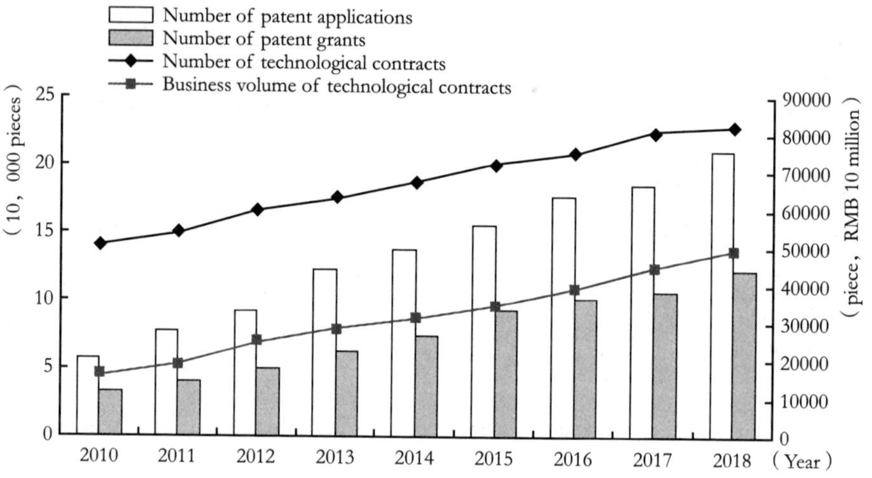

Figure 6 Patents and Technological Contracts in Beijing for 2010-2018

Source: *Beijing Statistical Yearbook (2018), Statistical Communiqué of Beijing Municipalty on the 2018 National Economic and Social Development.*

Beijing has basically formed a technological innovation pattern of "three science parks plus one area". Among them, Zhongguancun Science Park upgraded its innovation capability and strengthened its top-level design by compiling the *Zhongguancun Science Park Planning*; the Co-construction Joint Conference of Zhongguancun Science Park was set up to approach various

① "Contributing 55.7% of the world-leading technology achievements, Beijing becomes a high-speed growth technology center", China Finance, December 7, 2018.

"innovation partners"; it served as a "cornerstone" in basic research and original innovation and bred major landmark original achievements such as the Majorana anyon and the new ultra-low power consumption transistor. Huairou Science Park completed the *Huairou Science Park Planning*; five cross-research platforms for integrated extreme condition experiments, scientific equipment and material genomes and so on were completed; a number of innovative entities including the National Laboratory of Space Science, the Nano Energy Institute, China Automatic Battery Research Institute, and Haichuang Industry Research Institute, were born. The Future Science Park completed the *Future Science Park Planning*, focusing on revitalizing a complex of 60,000m^2 idle buildings by introducing open platforms for scientific research and mass entrepreneurship and innovation. Beijing Economic-Technological Development Area has fostered two hundred billion-level industrial clusters of high-end automobile and industrial Internet which have contributed 35 new products and 31 new technologies, as well as 350 practical invention patents owned by per 10,000 people; it was also the only national-level green industrial park in the city.[①]

Beijing has a strong radiating and driving effect on the innovation and development of the whole country, and such effect is increasingly strengthened. From 2010 to 2017, the number and business volume of technological contracts from Beijing to the other provinces (municipalities and autonomous regions) as percentages in the total number and business of technological contracts signed by Beijing tended to increase slowly, and both have exceeded 50% in recent years. In 2017, 44,287 technological contracts flowed from Beijing to the other provinces (municipalities and autonomous regions), accounting for 54.5% of the total technological contracts signed by the city and marking an increase of 2.6 percentage points over the previous year; the business volume from Beijing to the other provinces (municipalities and autonomous regions) was RMB 232.73 billion, accounting for 51.9% of the total business volume happening in the city and marking an increase of 1.2 percentage points over the previous year (see Figure 7).

---

① "The construction of 'three science parks plus one area' is in full swing", Xinhuanet, January 14, 2019.

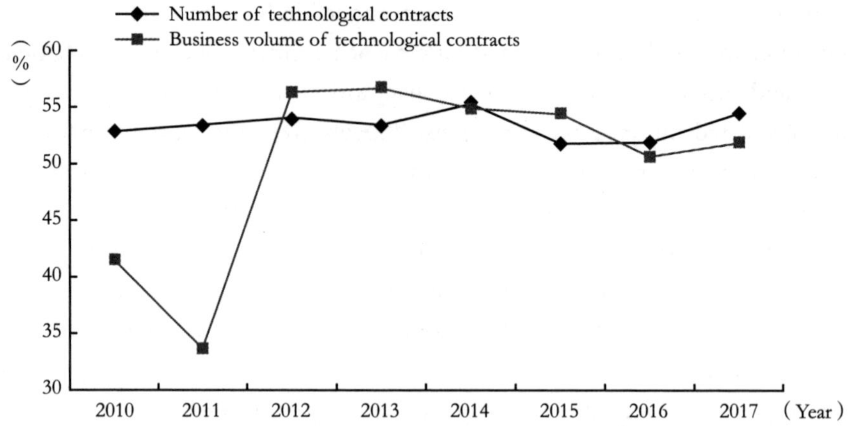

Figure 7 Number and Business Volume of Technological Contracts from Beijing to the Other Provinces (Municipalities and Autonomous Regions) for 2010-2017 as Percentages of the Total in Beijing

Source: *Statistical Communiqué of Technical Market of Beijing* over the years.

(IV) Continuously Optimized Environment for International Exchanges

"Going out" is an important way to increase international influence. As the capital, Beijing is an important window for China to go to the outside world. The achievements of Beijing as the international exchange center were made in four aspects. Firstly, it actively hosted various international conferences, events and activities. In terms of international conferences, Beijing hosted the Forum on China-Africa Cooperation, Beijing International Horticultural Exhibition, World Winter Sports Expo, China Cultural Finance Summit, etc. in 2018. In terms of international events, Beijing participated in the closing ceremonies of the Pyeongchang Winter Olympics and Winter Paralympics and actively organized the 2022 Beijing Winter Olympics; in terms of international activities, Beijing hosted the Beijing International Film Festival, the Beijing Music Festival, the Beijing Design Week and the Beijing International Cultural & Creative Industry Expo. Secondly, it vigorously promoted exchanges with other international sister cities. By December 1, 2018, Beijing had been a sister city to 56 cities in the world and was the champion in the country for that matter (Wang Yiwei and Liu Xuejun,

2019). At the same time, it actively implemented the Belt and Road Initiative and introduced a three-year action plan for this initiative. Thirdly, the scale of international exchanges made by Beijing has gradually picked up in recent years. From 2010 to 2018, the total export-import volume and the number of inbound tourists in Beijing declined, but both figures have increased in recent years (see Figure 8). In 2018, the total export-import volume and the number of inbound tourists in Beijing were RMB 2.71825 trillion and 4.004 million, respectively, up 23.9% and 2.0% from the previous year. Beijing took positive actions to build a "quasi-overseas" environment that is favorable to both living and entrepreneurship for international talents. Seven hospitals became international hospital pilots, and 618 foreign high-level talents chose to settle down in Beijing. Fourthly, the international communication hardware continued to improve. The main works of the terminal building of Beijing Daxing International Airport were basically completed and would be put into operation soon; the main venue of the Jinhai Lake International Convention and Exhibition Center was basically completed and would host the Pinggu 2020 World Leisure Congress Beijing China; the Yanqi Lake International Convention Center was expanded to provide venue support for more high-end conferences.

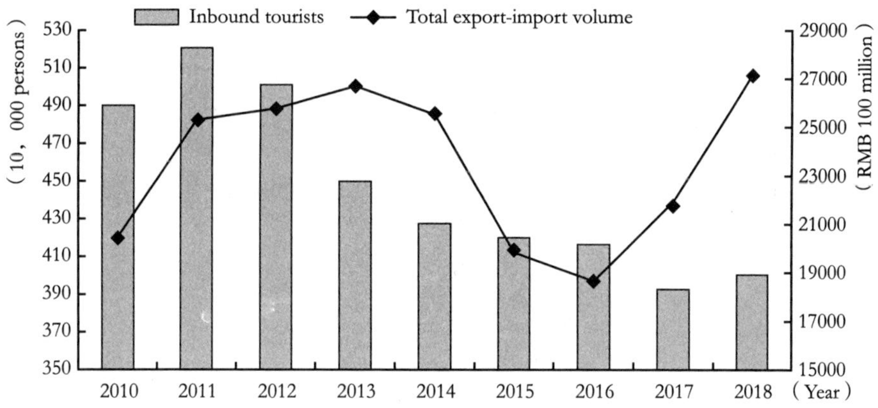

Figure 8 Total Export-Import Volume and Number of Inbound Tourists in Beijing for 2010-2018

Source: The same as Figure 2.

References

[1] Wu Aizhi and Li Guoping. Beijing: Building Multi-center, Networked Spatial Structure of National Central City. Beijing Planning Review, 2017 (1): 11-15.

[2] An Shuwei and Sun Wenqian. Reduced Quantity Development of Beijing. Qian Xian, 2019 (1): 68-70.

[3] Liu Xinkui. Urban Planning and Management of Beijing for 60 Years. Guangming Daily Press, 2010.

[4] Zou Biying. A Study on the Evolution of Functional Division among Beijing-Tianjin-Hebei Region As Cities, Capital University of Economics and Business, 2019, pp. 26-27.

[5] An Shuwei and Yu Peng et al. Industry Collaboration among Three Major Coastal City Clusters, Economy & Management Publishing House, 2019, pp. 238-240.

[6] Wu Xiaoxia, Shi Chen and Gao Jian. A Study on Optimizing the Radiating and Driving Function of Beijing, City, 2019 (2): 28-36.

[7] Wang Yiwei and Liu Xuejun. The Belt and Road Initiative and the Construction of Beijing as the International Exchange Center. Qian Xian, 2019 (2): 39-42.

[8] Wu Aizhi. Double-Chain Integration Strengthens the "High-grade, Precision and Advanced Industries. Beijing Daily, June 10, 2019.

[9] Li Yao and An Shuwei. Formation Mechanism, Path and Countermeasures of Beijing's Deputy Urban Center. City, 2018 (8): 24-32.

[10] Gao Yue, He Dishen and Li Siying et al. Research on the Contribution of Beijing's Deputy Urban Center to the Relief of Non-Capital Functions. The World of Survey and Research, 2019 (2): 55-59.

[11] An Shuwei and Xiao Jincheng. Beijing-Tianjin-Hebei Coordinated Development: Beijing's "Dilemma" and Hebei's "Role". Social Sciences in Guangdong, 2015 (4): 5-11.

[12] An Shuwei, Yan Chengli and Wang Yuguang. Following the Law of Urban Development and Promoting the Coordinated Development of Beijing-Tianjin-Hebei Region. Financial Minds, 2017 (3): 37-47, 139-140.

[13] An Shuwei, Li Ruipeng and Li Yao. The Influence of Relocating Non-core Functions in Beijing on Residents' Lives-An Analysis Based on Questionnaires. Journal of Hebei University of Economics and Trade, 2018 (6): 70-78, 101.

B.4

National Central City Construction of Shanghai and Coordinated Development of the Yangtze River Delta: Retrospect and Prospect

Zhen Jie[*]

Abstract: Shanghai has made many achievements as a national central city in economic development, innovation development and urban renewal since 2018. Owing to its construction achievements, it plays an important role in driving the coordinated development of the Yangtze River Delta. At the same time, Shanghai is still confronted with important challenges in innovation-driven capability, business environment, ecological resources and environment, city cluster competitiveness, regional coordination efficiency and joint construction of industrial parks. Based on the national strategic requirement for regional integration of the Yangtze River Delta, Shanghai should improve the level of regional integration development in all round manners, accelerate industrial transformation and structural upgrading based on high standards, promote regional interaction and coordinated governance at multiple levels, advance cooperated and joint construction of industrial parks, and take on the responsibility of urban construction in the new era.

Keywords: Shanghai; national central city; coordinated development of the Yangtze River Delta

* Zhen Jie, Ph.D., Associate Professor of Business School of East China University of Political Science and Law, Secretary General of the Development Research Institute of Tongji University, and Executive Director of China Industrial Park Development Research Center, majors in strategic management and industrial park management.

By the end of 2018, among the nine national central cities, Shanghai had the highest total GDP. However, from the perspective of global city construction, Shanghai still needs to review and evaluate its performance in economy, innovation, ecology and regional coordination. While summing up the development experience, it should pay attention to the gap with the benchmark, further improve the construction results from top-level design and key tasks, and enhance its ability to drive the coordinated development of the Yangtze River Delta.

I Analysis of Progress and Trend of the National Central City Construction of Shanghai

(I) Analysis of the Overall Economic Development

In 2018, Shanghai's GDP increased by 6.6% over the previous year, and the growth rate was equal to the national average (see Figure 1). In the first quarter of 2019, its GDP increased by 5.7% on a year-on-year basis, but the growth rate dropped. From the perspective of three industrial structures, the industrial structures of Shanghai in 2018 were 0.3:29.8:69.9. The added value of the primary industry decreased significantly on a year-on-year basis and was measured at-6.9%; the added value of the secondary industry increased slightly by 1.8%; the added value of the tertiary industry registered a great year-on-year increase by 8.7%. In the first quarter of 2019, the value added of the primary industry decreased by 3.4% on a year-on-year basis; the added value of the secondary industry decreased by 1.7%; the added value of the tertiary industry increased by 8.8%. The total output of industrial enterprises above designated size had registered a sharp decline for five quarters. In the first quarter of 2019, the year-on-year growth rate declined to-4.8%. Clearly, although the economic growth of Shanghai remained generally stable, its industrial structure was undergoing rapid adjustments. Among them, the tertiary industry developed rapidly with a high growth rate and prominent characteristics of industrial transformation.

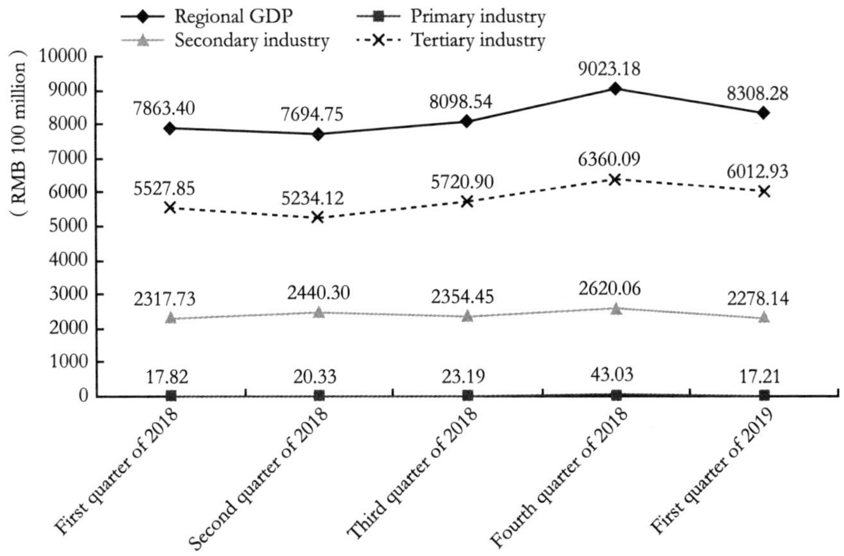

Figure 1 GDP and Growth Rates of Three Industries Structures in Shanghai over Five Quarters during 2018-2019

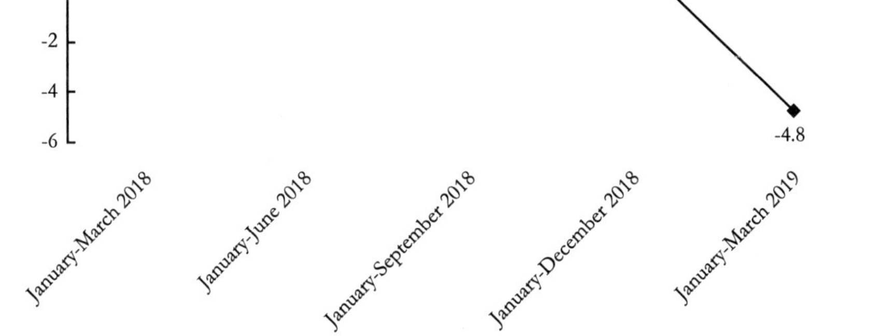

Figure 2 Quarterly Accumulated Growth Rates of the Total Output of Industrial Enterprises Above Designated Size in Shanghai for 2018-2019 (%)

Source: Adapted from the statistics of Shanghai, tjj.sh.gov.cn

1 Performance of Main Industries

In 2018, the transportation, warehousing and postal services industries in Shanghai grew significantly on a year-on-year basis, with an average growth rate of 10.4%. The finance, real estate, wholesale and retail industries maintained steady growth. In the first quarter of 2019, the finance industry reported a high year-on-year increase of 13.3%, and the real estate and construction industries also showed relatively high year-on-year growth (see Table 1). The year-on-year growth rate of the industry was relatively low, even falling to-2.8% in the first quarter of 2019, and the industrial product price index has been falling since the second half of 2018 (see Figure 3). However, Shanghai maintained growing total fixed assets investment (see Figure 4). Generally speaking, Shanghai developed rapidly in finance and trade, which was in line with its urban positioning.

Table 1 Total Outputs and Year-on-Year Growth Rates of Main Industries in Shanghai Since 2018

Indicators	2018		In the First Quarter of 2019	
	Total output (RMB 100 million)	Year-on-Year growth rate (%)	Total output (RMB 100 million)	Year-on-Year growth rate (%)
Agriculture, forestry, animal husbandry and fishery	111.98	-3.6	18.18	-1.4
Industry	8694.95	1.9	2015.29	-2.8
Construction	1071.75	1.1	270.76	7.3
Wholesale and retail	4581.49	3.3	1075.87	2.0
Transportation, warehousing and postal services	1533.36	10.4	378.26	4.3
Accommodation and catering	421.46	-2.8	98.05	0.3
Finance	5781.63	5.7	1709.59	13.3
Real estate	1992.52	4.8	509.34	8.3

Source: Shanghai Municipal Statistics Bureau, tjj.sh.gov.cn

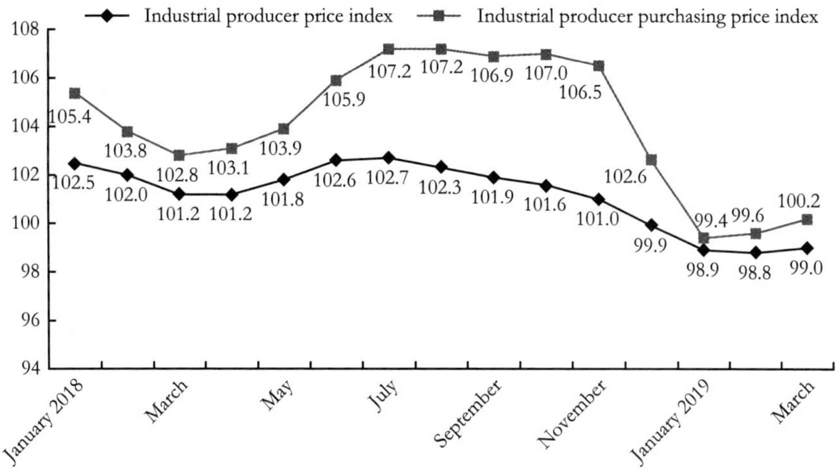

Figure 3 Growth Rate of Industrial Product Price Index on Monthly Basis in Shanghai during 2018-2019

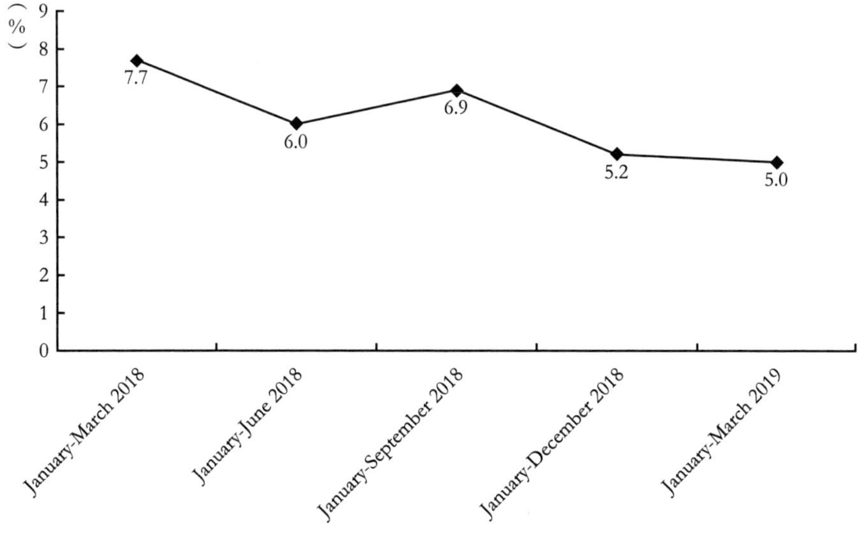

Figure 4 Growth Rate of Total Fixed Assets Investment on Quarterly Basis in Shanghai during 2018-2019 (%)

Source: Adapted from statistics of Shanghai, tjj.sh.gov.cn

2 Development of Strategic Emerging Industries

In 2018, the added value of strategic emerging industries in Shanghai increased by 8.2% over the same period, accounting for 16.7% of its GDP. Of the added value, the industry contributed 43.5%, up 4.2% over the previous year; the tertiary industry contributed 56.5%, up 11.3% over the previous year (see Table 2). The proportion of the tertiary industry in strategic emerging industries in Shanghai was 13 percent points higher than that of the industry, and so was its growth rate. This performance has further enhanced the modern service function of Shanghai.

Table 2 Added Value and Growth Rate of Strategic Emerging Industries in Shanghai in 2018

Indicators	Absolute value (RMB 100 million)	YoY Growth (%)
Added value of strategic emerging industries	5461.91	8.2
Industry	2377.60	4.2
Service industry	3084.31	11.3

Source: *Statistical Communiqué of Shanghai Municipality on the 2018 National Economic and Social Development*

3 Total Output of Six Key Industries

As a whole, the key industries in Shanghai continued to grow in 2018, but their total year-on-year growth rate was as low as only 1.4%; in the first quarter of 2019, this year-on-year growth rate even fell to a negative value. Automobile manufacturing and electronic information product manufacturing were two industries reporting low growth rates in 2018, and both of them showed sharp declines in the first quarter of 2019. In contrast, biomedicine and complete equipment manufacturing grew rapidly (see Table 3). It can be seen that Shanghai showed clear advantages in advanced manufacturing typified by biomedicine, but its total output value only accounted for 4.9% of the total output of the six key industries. In the future, the overall development level of the key industries should be further increased.

Table 3 Total Output and YoY Growth Rates of Key Industries in Shanghai for 2018-2019

Indicators	2018		In the First Quarter of 2019	
	Total output (RMB 100 million)	YoY growth rate (%)	Total output (RMB 100 million)	YoY growth rate (%)
Total output of six key industries	23870.78	1.4	5176.89	-5.7
Electronic information product manufacturing	6450.23	1.9	1292.28	-7.0
Automotive manufacturing	6832.07	0.8	1471.54	-17.2
Petrochemical and fine chemical manufacturing	4006.76	-1.5	938.80	5.2
High-end steel manufacturing	1233.42	-6.5	276.38	-4.4
Complete equipment manufacturing	4171.70	4.8	898.68	2.3
Biomedicine manufacturing	1176.60	9.8	299.21	10.2

Source: Shanghai Municipal Statistics Bureau, tjj.sh.gov.cn

4 Development Level of Service Enterprises Above Designated Size

Judging from the operating income of service enterprises above designated size (see Table 4), high growth rates were reported from high-end production service industries in Shanghai. As a national central city, Shanghai's rapid development in scientific research and technological service industries has effectively contributed to the process of building itself into a high-tech industrial production and R&D base and has facilitated the continuous upgrading and optimization of its industrial structure. It seems that the continued concentration of high-end R&D, information technology services and other productive service industries in Shanghai also drives its innovation capability to grow rapidly.

Table 4 Operating Incomes and YoY Growth Rates of Service Industries Above Designated Size in Shanghai for 2018-2019

Indicators	2018		In the First Quarter of 2019	
	Operating Income (RMB 100 million)	YoY Growth Rate (%)	Operating Income (RMB 100 million)	YoY Growth Rate (%)
Transportation, warehousing and postal services	9298.13	13	2363.15	11.7
Information transmission, software and information technology services	5094.3	12.7	1083.90	14.1
Leasing and business services	8673.26	9.8	2144.10	6.1
Scientific research and technological services	2330.18	16	531.58	17
Water conservancy, environmental and public facilities management	402.81	4	91.99	-2.7
Resident services, repairs and other services	298.63	9.7	98.05	8.7
Education	129.02	6.5	75.13	10.6
Health and social work	154.93	13.1	39.06	12.3
Culture, sports and entertainment	419.6	1.8	85.48	1.5

Source: Shanghai Municipal Statistics Bureau, tjj.sh.gov.cn

(II) Analysis of Overall Innovation Development

1 R&D Funding and High-tech Enterprises

In 2018, Shanghai spent 4.00% of its GDP on R&D undertakings (see Figure 5). The growth rate of projects for transformation of high-tech achievements was 33.1% over the same period of the previous year, and the number of identified achievements created a new record for the past five years. Moreover, these projects were mainly concentrated in key areas such as electronic information, biomedicine and new materials, which accounted for 86.3% of the total.

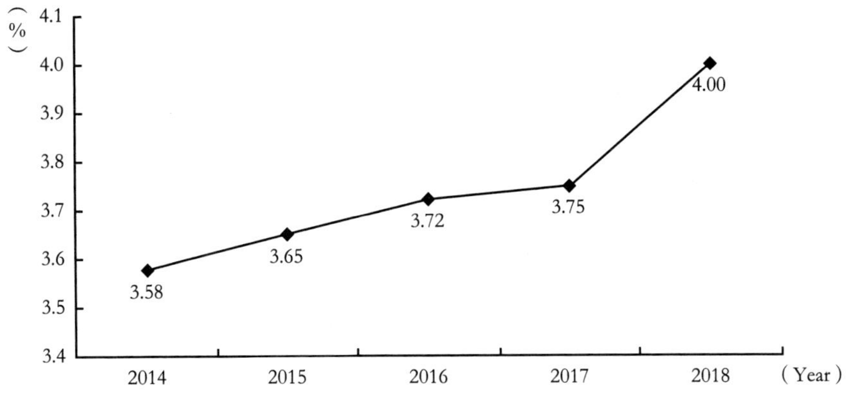

Figure 5 R&D Expenditure as Percentage of GDP in Shanghai for 2014-2018

Source: *Statistical Communiqué of Shanghai Municipality on the 2018 National Economic and Social Development*

2 Patents

In 2018, Shanghai reported rapid growth in key patent-related indicators such as the number of patent applications on a year-on-year basis (see Table 5). Moreover, despite the low growth rate of the number of various technology transaction contracts that were registered, their total value reached RMB 130.32 billion, up 50.2% over the previous year.

Table 5 Patent Development of Shanghai in 2018

Indicators	Number (Piece)	YoY Growth (%)
Number of patent applications	150233	14.0
Patent for invention	62755	14.9
Patent for utility models	69564	14.2
Design patent	17914	10.7
Number of patents granted	92460	27.0
Patent for invention	15548	3.1
Patent for utility models	55581	39.2
Design patent	15548	27.6
Number of PCT international patents	2500	19.1
Valid patent for invention	114966	14.5
Invention patents owned by per 10,000 people	47.5	14.5
Number of various technology transaction contracts registered	21630	0.3

3 Innovation of Industrial Parks

The agglomeration effect of industrial parks makes them important media for regional development. The sustained competitiveness of industrial parks in innovation development, reflected in the richness of innovation resources, construction of innovation platforms and the number and level of innovation achievements, can speak well for the innovation level and capability of the region where the industrial parks are located. In 2018, in the ranking of sustained competitiveness of national industrial parks in innovation development, Zhangjiang National Innovation Demonstration Zone in Shanghai occupied the second place, and Caohejing High-tech Park occupied the ninth place. The ranking included one industrial park from Jiangsu and another one from Zhejiang: Suzhou Industrial Park was ranked fourth and Hangzhou High-Tech Development Zone was ranked sixth (see Table 6). Zhangjiang National Innovation Demonstration Zone in Shanghai demonstrated obvious advantages in the numbers of high-tech enterprises, national engineering technology centers, and patents granted.

Table 6 Top 10 National Industrial Parks in Sustained Competitiveness of Innovation Development in 2018 ①

Ranking	Name of Development Zone	Ranking	Name of Development Zone
1	Zhongguancun Science Park	6	Hangzhou High-Tech Development Zone
2	Zhangjiang National Innovation Demonstration Zone in Shanghai	7	Nanchang Economic and Technological Development Zone
3	Wuhan East Lake Hi-tech Development Zone	8	Nanjing High-tech Development Zone
4	Suzhou Industrial Park	9	Caohejing High-tech Park
5	Guangzhou Economic & Technological Development District	10	HZZK High-tech Industrial Development Zone

① Ren Hao and Zhen Jie, et al. *Blue Book on Sustainable Development of Industrial Parks in China in 2018*, Tongji University Press, November 2018.

(III) Analysis of General Urban Renewal

Structural adjustment, industrial transformation and urban renewal are systematic projects. Shanghai, as a mega national central city, is also a pioneer in urban renewal in the important form of cultural and creative industrial park (hereinafter referred to as CCIP) when it encounters bottlenecks in land, environment, ecology and public resources.

1 Methods for Re-utilizing CCIPs

The rich industrial heritage provides the main venue for urban renewal in Shanghai. Under the industrial restructuring context of "exiting from the secondary industry and entering into the tertiary industry", a large number of industrial enterprises have moved out of the city territory, and cultural and creative bases become the mainstream form of re-utilizing stock industry in Shanghai. By June 2018, there had been more than 170 CCIPs in Shanghai. In February 2019, Shanghai identified 137 municipal-level CCIPs, as well as 10 demonstration buildings and 20 demonstration spaces. ① At present, Shanghai re-utilizes the CCIPs in the city in four ways (see Table 7).

Table 7 Main Methods for CCIP Re-Utilization in Shanghai

No.	Re-Utilization Method	Percentage (%)	Example
1	Protective development of excellent historical buildings	8.57	1933 Shanghai, Husizhan, Mengqing Garden, 800 Show
2	Renovation and transformation of old industrial heritages	76.43	Option 1: renovation of a single original factory: Westbank Talent Valley, Creater Space Yuan, Shanghai Fashion Center Option 2: Renovation by combining multiple factories: Huxi Yuefang, Tianzifang, Bridge 8
3	New buildings on the original industrial sites through conversion of land nature	7.14	Haishanghai, KIC
4	New buildings in the location of the original industrial agglomeration	7.86	Shanghai Zhengda Himalayas Center, Songjiang Fashion Valley Creative Park

Source: Cai Qing, "Research on Data Analysis and Development of Shanghai Industrial Heritage Transformation into Creative Industrial Park", *Research on Heritages and Preservation*, July 2018.

① Notice put up by the Shanghai Municipal Leading Group Office of Cultural and Creative Industry Promotion about city-level CCIPs for 2019-2020.

2 Development Law of CCIPs

The development content of CCIPs in Shanghai is divided into business type, development mode, development organizer and capital participation mode. It is undergoing corresponding changes, and showing corresponding development characteristics (see Table 8). The government has pressed for the unified planning of CCIPs and improved the scientific re-utilization of old industrial areas and the concentration of projects. The construction and development of CCIPs has become more flexible.

Table 8 Development Content and Characteristics of Cultural and Creative Industrial Parks in Shanghai

No.	Development Content	Characteristics
1	Business type	From a single office to a mix of multiple business types, including co-working space, cloud space, creative market and other new formats
2	Development mode	From bottom-up spontaneous behavior to top-down government-advocated behavior
3	Development organizer	From the earliest separation of property rights and investment as a result of industrial leasing development, to the intermediary development mode of companies founded by property rights owners, and to the present combination of various development forms.
4	Capital participation mode	From private investments to corporate investment and to the present combination of government, business and individual investments

Source: Cai Qing, "Research on Data Analysis and Development of Shanghai Industrial Heritage Transformation into Creative Industrial Park", *Research on Heritages and Preservation*, July 2018

3 Industrial Forms of CCIPs

CCIPs in urban renewal are operated in such industrial forms as design, fashion consumption, entertainment and leisure, and business office (see Table 9), and transform from the traditional single production to modern composite urban public services by embracing multiple and innovative urban public services.

Table 9　Industries Before and After Transformation in Typical Urban Renewal Projects in Shanghai

No.	Project name	Predecessor	Transformed Industry							
			Status quo	Commercial recreation			Creative office		Other supporting facilities	
				Retail	Catering	Culture and entertainment	Office	Art studio	Hotel	Exhibition space
1	Bridge 8	SABS	Architectural design, design consulting, film production		●		●	●		●
2	Hongfang	The 10th Steel Factory of Shanghai	Culture, design, media, sculpture		●		●	●		●
3	Park Space (Phase I)	Shanghai Purlux	Creative design, business office				●	●		●
4	Tianzifang	Shangshi Machinery Factory etc.	Interior design, visual arts, arts and crafts	●	●		●	●		●
5	Tonglefang	Sentai Milling Machinery Factory etc.	Entertainment and recreation, fashion and creativity	●	●	●		●		
6	The Cool Docks	Shanghai Oil and Grease Plant	Commercial recreation, fashion consumption	●	●	●	●	●	●	
7	1933 Shanghai	Slaughter House of Shanghai Municipal Council	Fashion experience, film and television creativity, exhibition and trade	●	●	●	●	●		●

Source: Zeng Rui and Li Zao. "Research on Mechanism of Transformation and Regeneration in Urban Industrial Heritage: Taking Shanghai as an Example." *Urban Development Studies*, May 2019

II Analysis of the Driving Effect of Shanghai on the Coordinated Development of the Yangtze River Delta

(I) Radiating Effect of A World Class City

1 City Ranking by GaWC

GaWC (Globalization and World Cities) offers an authoritative ranking of world cities by mainly evaluating their finance, accounting, advertising, law, and management consulting sectors. The evaluated cities are classified by their ranking.① This ranking emphasizes the "high-level producer service organizations" and pays attention to the leading role and driving capacity of a city in activities around the world. It serves as an important reference for the national central city construction of Shanghai and its role in coordinated regional development.

Table 10 Top 100 Chinese Cities and Their Rankings by GaWC for 2010-2018

	Ranking in 2010	Ranking in 2013	Ranking in 2016	Ranking in 2018
Hong Kong	3	3	4	3 (Alpha+, first-tier)
Shanghai	7	7	9	6 (Alpha+, first-tier)
Beijing	12	10	6	4 (Alpha+, first-tier)
Taipei	43	42	36	26 (Alpha, first-tier)
Guangzhou	67	53	40	27 (Alpha, first-tier)
Shenzhen	—	—	85	55 (Alpha-, first-tier)
Chengdu	—	—	100	71 (Beta+, second-tier)
Hangzhou	—	—	—	75 (Beta+, second-tier)
Tianjin	—	—	—	86 (Beta, second-tier)
Nanjing	—	—	—	94 (Beta, second-tier)
Wuhan	—	—	—	95 (Beta, second-tier)

Source: Adapted by the author

① GaWC divides the world cities into four major levels: Alpha (first-tier cities), Beta (second-tier cities), Gamma (third-tier cities), and Sufficiency (self-sufficient cities, also known as fourth-tier cities). Cities in each level are subdivided by adding a plus or minus sign.

In the 2000 GaWC ranking, Shanghai was the only city from the Chinese mainland that was listed in the first-tier rank, and it was put in the 31st place. In recent years, Chinese cities have shown increasing strength and climbed up the ladder of the ranking with strong momentum. In 2018, 10 cities from the Chinese mainland made into the top 100 list (see Table 10). Among them, Shanghai has been ranked among the top 10 since 2010, which represent the "first-tier" cities in the world. Meanwhile, Hangzhou of Zhejiang Province and Nanjing of Jiangsu Province entered the top 100 list for the first time in 2018. This progress epitomized the leading role of Shanghai in the coordinated development of the Yangtze River Delta.

2 UNESCO's "Design City"

At present, three cities in the Yangtze River Delta, namely Shanghai, Hangzhou and Suzhou, are included in the UNESCO's "Creative Cities Network", accounting for one-third of the nine nominated Chinese cities. Among them, Shanghai is awarded the title of "Design City". Since 2013, Shanghai has formulated two three-year action plans for the construction of design city, sending a clear message about boosting the driving effect of the cultural and creative industries, serving the Yangtze River Delta as a whole, and driving the development of other parts of the country. By the end of 2018, the output of cultural and creative industries accounted for 12.6% of the city's GDP. ① In July 2018, Shanghai defined the development goal of the creative and design industries: the growth rate of the added value of these industries should be 2 to 3 percentage points faster than the growth rate of the city's GDP.② In terms of industrial layout, Shanghai attaches importance to the driving force of design, catches up closely with cutting-edge technologies, and makes great efforts to build itself into an international design city, fashion city, brand city, and exhibition city.

To develop creative and design industries, Shanghai strives to promote multi-party cooperation in the Yangtze River Delta and has established different special features to strengthen regional coordination and interaction. The thread of

① *Three-Year Action Plan for the Development of Cultural and Creative Industries in Shanghai (2016-2018)*, Shanghai Creative Industry Association, 2016

② Notice of the Shanghai Municipal Economic and Information Technology Commission and other departments on printing and distributing the *Implementation Measures for Promoting the Development of Creative and Design Industries in Shanghai*, Hu Jing Xin Du [2018] No. 339, June 19, 2018.

design runs through industry, exhibition and other specific fields to promote the overall development level of manufacturing in the Yangtze River Delta. High-quality supporting services are provided to facilitate industrial transformation and upgrading. At the same time, brand building at all levels receives due attention so as to foster quality and strong brands that promote regional development. E-commerce platforms are encouraged to provide special services to facilitate the important role of "Shanghai Design" in regional coordination.

In April 2018, the *Report on the Brand Development of City Clusters in the Yangtze River Delta* released in the first Yangtze River Delta (Shanghai) Brand Expo,[①] showing that more than one-third of the China time-honored brands are born in the Yangtze River Delta, with Shanghai as the biggest contributor. In addition, organizations like the Brand Building Alliance in the Yangtze River Delta are committed to integrating brands, talents, finance and other resources to build a "brand building ecosystem" in the region; the formation of international strong brand clusters contributes to the formation of an ecological chain of professional services dedicated to brand building.

(II) Intensive Development and Joint Construction of Industrial Parks

As the main form of enterprise agglomerations and industry clusters, industrial parks are important platforms and main fronts to implement the national strategy of regional integration of the Yangtze River Delta.

1 Intensive Use of Land in Industrial Parks in the Yangtze River Delta

With rapid economic and social development, Shanghai is under more pressure posed by limited land resources, and industrial parks provide important opportunities for intensive land use, which is an important part of regional integration in the Yangtze River Delta. In national development zones, those located in the Yangtze River Delta centering round Shanghai perform well in

① Yangtze River Delta (Shanghai) Brand Expo was an event stipulated in the *Agreement on Jointly Promoting Platform Construction and Organizing Social Forces and Main Market Players for Urban Cooperation in the Yangtze River Delta* signed by the main leaders of Shanghai, Jiangsu, Zhejiang and Anhui at a seminar of main leadership in the Yangtze River Delta held in Suzhou on January 12, 2018.

intensive land use (see Table 11). A total of 13 industrial parks from the Yangtze River Delta were among the top 30 list in this regard, accounting for 43%. They showed a high level of intensive land use as a whole.① In terms of land nature, the proportion of industrial land dropped slightly, while the proportions of supporting land for residential, commercial and transportation purposes increased. On the basis of clear leading industries, the industrial structure demonstrated transformation and upgrading characteristics.

Table 11 Comprehensive Ranking of Intensive Land Use Evaluation of Industrial-Oriented Development Zones in 2018

Ranking	Name of Development Zone	Ranking	Name of Development Zone
1	Futian Bonded Area in Guangdong	16	SND Integrated Free Trade Zone
2	Comprehensive Bonded Area of Wuxi High-tech District	17	Pingdingshan National Hi Tech Industrial Development Zone
3	Guangzhou Economic and Technological Development Zone	18	Guangzhou Bonded Area
4	Wuhan Economic and Technological Development Zone	19	Xishan Economic and Technological Development Zone
5	Kunshan Integrated Free Trade Zone	20	Xi'an Hi-tech Industries Development Zone
6	Caohejing Export Processing Zone in Shanghai	21	Waigaoqiao Free Trade Zone in Shanghai
7	Dalian Free Trade Zone	22	Shantou High-tech Industrial Development Zone
8	Songshan Lake National Hi-tech Industrial Development Zone in Dongguan	23	Kunshan Economic and Technological Development Zone
9	Foshan High-tech Industrial Development Zone	24	Tianjin Economic-Technological Development Area
10	Logistics Park of Guangzhou Free Trade Zone	25	Xi'an Export Processing Zone in Shaanxi

① Indicators considered in the evaluation of intensive land use in development zones include land supply rate, land completion rate, land development rate, proportion of industrial land, comprehensive plot ratio, building density, plot ratio of industrial land, building coefficient of industrial land, input intensity of fixed assets in industrial land, average tax revenue from industrial land, and comprehensive average land tax, etc.

Continued

Ranking	Name of Development Zone	Ranking	Name of Development Zone
11	Changshu Economic & Technological Development Zone	26	Wuxi High-tech Industrial Development Zone
12	Hefei Export Processing Zone in Anhui	27	Langfang Comprehensive Bonded Zone
13	Shenzhen High-tech Industrial Park	28	Taicang Port Comprehensive Bonded Zone
14	Nanjing Economic and Technological Development Zone	29	Beichen Economic and Technological Development Area
15	Kunshan Hi-tech Industrial Development Zone	30	Xiyong Comprehensive Bonded Zone in Chongqing

Source: Circular on the Evaluation of Intensive Land Use in National Development Zones in 2018 by the State Council ①

2 Sustained Competitiveness of Industrial Parks in Industrial Cooperation in the Yangtze River Delta

As venues to accommodate agglomeration of enterprises and various types of institutions, industrial parks have created a new model of resource linkage and a new way of market competition that enhance the comprehensive competitiveness of the local region. At the same time, the cooperation is not limited to the parks, but organically involving external partners. Effective external collaborative research helps the parks to obtain diversified resources for sustainable development and is conducive to reallocation and integration of resources in the parks and the local regions. Therefore, cooperation of industrial parks can further reflect the coordinated development of the local region. As shown in Table 12, two parks from Shanghai were ranked among the top 5 industrial parks in terms of sustainable competitiveness in industrial cooperation, and Zhangjiang National Innovation Demonstration Zone was the champion. In addition, among

① In order to thoroughly implement the message of the 19th National Congress of the Communist Party of China and the *13th Five-Year Plan for National Economic and Social Development* and to improve the land supply quality in development zones, the Ministry of Natural Resources organized the evaluation of intensive land use in development zones across the country in 2018. A total of 520 national development zones were subject to a comprehensive evaluation of intensive land use based on relevant technical standards.

the top 10 parks in the country, 4 were from the Yangtze River Delta. In addition to Shanghai, the other two parks were from Jiangsu Province and Zhejiang Province. Obviously, with industrial parks as important carriers and by seizing these opportunities, Shanghai plays an important role in promoting the regional cooperation and development of the Yangtze River Delta.

Table 12 Top 10 National Industrial Parks with Best Sustained Competitiveness of Industrial Cooperation in 2018

Ranking	Name of Development Zone	Ranking	Name of Development Zone
1	Zhangjiang National Innovation Demonstration Zone in Shanghai	6	Shenzhen High-tech Industrial Development Zone
2	Zhongguancun Demonstration Zone	7	Xiamen Torch Development Zone for High Technology Industries
3	Guangzhou Economic and Technological Development Zone	8	Suzhou Industrial Park
4	Chengdu Hi-Tech Industrial Development Zone	9	Wuhan East Lake National Innovation Demonstration Zone
5	Caohejing Hi-Tech Park	10	Ningbo Hi-Tech Industrial Development Zone

Source: Ren Hao and Zhen Jie, et al. *Blue Book on Sustainable Development of Industrial Parks in China in 2018*, Tongji University Press, November 2018.

3 Joint Construction of Industrial Parks in the Yangtze River Delta

In order to solve the problem of land constraints, joint construction of industrial parks within or across provinces was carried out in various forms such as enclave economy and land functional replacement in the Yangtze River Delta to improve the efficiency of land output in 2018. Currently, special industrial park coordinated development organizations have been set up in the Yangtze River Delta, such as the Coordinated Development Alliance for Development Zones; G60 S&T Innovation Valley promoted cooperation among industrial parks in nine cities in the Yangtze River Delta by establishing a joint office mechanism and implementing specific reform measures; Songjiang District in Shanghai and Xuancheng City in Anhui Province jointly established the "Xuanzhou-Songjiang Industrial Park"; Jinshan District in Shanghai and Pinghu City in Zhejiang jointly

Table 13 Some of the Industrial Park Joint Construction Examples in the Yangtze River Delta in 2018

No.	Park/Joint Construction Activity	Location	Nature	Specific Activity/Effect	Date
1	Binhai Port Industrial Park	Shanghai	Inter-provincial	Yancheng (Shanghai) Industrial Park Cooperation Investment Promotion Conference	June 5, 2019
2	South-North Joint Park in Jiangsu (43 residents)	/	Intra-provincial	Assessment of South-North Joint Park	April 2019
3	South-North Joint Park in Anhui (3+7)	/	Intra-provincial	Assessment of South-North Joint Park	April 2019
4	Suzhou Yancheng Coastal Cooperation Development Park	Yancheng	Intra-provincial	Confirmed settlement of intelligent park of low-carbon metal materials project	February 2019
5	Wuxi-Xuzhou Joint Park (7 residents)	/	Intra-provincial	Significant achievements from the development of Wuxi-Xuzhou Joint Park in 2018	February 2019
6	Anqing (Shanghai) Park Cooperation	Shanghai	Inter-provincial	Anqing (Shanghai) Industrial Park cooperation meeting and signing ceremony as part of a series of activities	December 18, 2018
7	Suzhou-Yinchuan Industrial Park	Yinchuan	Inter-provincial	Suzhou Industrial Park and Binhe New Area will form partnership	August 20, 2018
8	Haining Branch of Caohejing Development Zone, and other seven residents	Haining, etc.	Inter-provincial	One of the first demonstration parks in joint construction of the Yangtze River Delta	July 10, 2018
9	Chengtou (Qidong) Jianghai Industrial Park in Shanghai and other 3 residents	Qidong etc.	Inter-provincial	One of the first demonstration parks in joint construction of the Yangtze River Delta	July 10, 2018

Continued

No.	Park/Joint Construction Activity	Location	Nature	Specific Activity/Effect	Date
10	Langxi Industrial Park in Qingpu	Langxi	Inter-provincial	Precision investment attraction in Langxi Economic Development Zone and undertake industrial transfer in clusters	June 2018
11	Mountain-Sea Cooperation Industrial Park in Zhejiang Province (9 residents)	/	Intra-provincial	Several Opinions of the CPC Zhejiang Provincial Committee and the People's Government of Zhejiang Province on Deeply Implementing the Mountain-Sea Cooperation Project to Promote Coordinated Regional Development	May 31, 2018
12	Jingjiang Branch of Jiangyin Economic and Development Zone	Jingjiang	Intra-provincial	Integrated development meeting and seminar on experiment for Jiangyin-Jingjiang high-quality cross-river integrated development	August 29, 2018
13	Shanghai-Jiangsu Dafeng Industry Linkage Cluster	Shanghai	Inter-provincial	The second joint session of the leading group on promoting coordination in Shanghai-Jiangsu Dafeng industry linkage development and construction	May 8, 2018

Source: Adapted by the author.

built the Zhangjiang Yangtze River Delta Sci-Tech City; Qingpu (Shanghai), Kunshan (Jiangsu) and Jiashan (Zhejiang) around the Dianshan Lake region jointly signed a memorandum of cooperation on the coordinated development of strategic collaborative areas; Jiading in Shanghai joined hands with Kunshan and Taicang in Jiangsu to found the Jiading-Kunshan-Taicang Industrial Chain Innovation Alliance and Jiading-Kunshan-Taicang Scientific Innovation Industrial Park. At the same time, Jiading District in Shanghai and Wenzhou City jointly built the "Technological Innovation (R&D) Park" in Jiading and the "Wenzhou Park of Jiading Industrial Zone" in Wenzhou, which is also a demonstration zone for deep integration of advanced manufacturing.

(III) Performance and Potential of Regional Innovation

1 Enhanced Innovation Capabilities of Cities

According to the *Top 30 Most Innovative Chinese Cities 2018* by Forbes (see Table 14), 18 cities in the Yangtze River Delta were shortlisted, accounting for 60%, and 4 of them were new on the list. In contrast, only 6 cities from the Pearl River Delta and one city from the Beijing-Tianjin-Hebei Region were included, and both of the regions lost one city from the list when compared with their respective results in the previous year. The city clusters in the Yangtze River Delta showed strong overall innovation advantages. Suzhou had already climbed to the third place as a result of benefiting from coordinated regional development.

2 Strong Momentum for Institutional Innovation

On June 25, 2019, Shanghai issued the *Several Opinions on Supporting the New Round of Reform and Opening up of Pudong New Area to Achieve High-Quality Development in the New Era* and put forward 20 important measures. These measures were intended for "decentralization" to improve the institutional supply capacity, systematically support the reform and pioneering exploration of Pudong New Area, and achieve high-quality development. The specific measures are as follows: ①

①

Table 14 Top 30 Most Innovative Chinese Cities

Ranking	City	Province / Municipality / Autonomous Region	City Cluster	Ranking	City	Province / Municipality / Autonomous Region	City Cluster
1	Shenzhen	Guangdong	Pearl River Delta	16	Xi'an	Shaanxi	Guanzhong Plain City Cluster
2	Beijing	Beijing	Beijing-Tianjin-Hebei	17	Shaoxing	Zhejiang	Yangtze River Delta
3	Suzhou	Jiangsu	Yangtze River Delta	18	Zhenjiang	Jiangsu	Yangtze River Delta
4	Shanghai	Shanghai	Yangtze River Delta	19	Taicang	Jiangsu	Yangtze River Delta
5	Guangzhou	Guangdong	Pearl River Delta	20	Hefei	Anhui	Yangtze River Delta
6	Zhuhai	Guangdong	Pearl River Delta	21	Qingdao	Shandong	Shandong Peninsula
7	Dongguan	Guangdong	Pearl River Delta	22	Huzhou	Zhejiang	Yangtze River Delta
8	Zhongshan	Guangdong	Pearl River Delta	23	Wuhan	Hubei	City clusters along the middle reaches of the Yangtze River
9	Hangzhou	Zhejiang	Yangtze River Delta	24	Zhengzhou	Henan	Central Plains City Cluster
10	Nanjing	Jiangsu	Yangtze River Delta	25	Changzhou	Jiangsu	Yangtze River Delta
11	Kunshan	Jiangsu	Yangtze River Delta	26	Wuhu	Anhui	Yangtze River Delta
12	Foshan	Guangdong	Pearl River Delta	27	Cixi	Zhejiang	Yangtze River Delta
13	Chengdu	Sichuan	Chengdu-Chongqing City Cluster	28	Yixing	Jiangsu	Yangtze River Delta
14	Ningbo	Zhejiang	Yangtze River Delta	29	Nantong	Jiangsu	Yangtze River Delta
15	Wuxi	Jiangsu	Yangtze River Delta	30	Jiaxing	Zhejiang	Yangtze River Delta

Source: *Top 30 Most Innovative Chinese Cities in 2018*

Table 15 20 Measures for the New Round of Reform and Opening Up of Pudong New Area

No.	Positioning	Thoughts	Measures
1	Be a good explorer in deepening the reform	Support Pudong New Area to build a world-class business environment by working around institutional innovation and drawing on the highest standards and best reference with boldness, exploratory spirit and independence.	Grant city-level economic management authority to the Pudong New Area according to law; deepen the reform of market access management system; deepen the reform of "Internet + government service"; deepen the innovation of comprehensive government supervision; deepen the reform of industrial land use system.
2	Create an all-round window at the forefront of opening to the world	Actively explore the expansion from the opening of commodity and factor flows to the opening of rules and institutions, increase the risk and pressure tests entailed by open economy, and promote all-round, high-level opening at a deeper level, in wider fields, and with greater efforts.	Deepen the opening of key pilot areas; enhance the liberalization and facilitation level of investment and trade; build a globally connected platform; better serve the national construction of the Belt and Road Initiative and the integrated development strategy of the Yangtze River Delta.
3	Build a core bearing science and technology center with global influence	Strengthen the forward-looking layout and integrated development of scientific and technological innovation, improve the technology innovation system and the technology service system, participate in global collaborative innovation, create a "strong magnetic field" that pools global innovation resources, keep introducing "places of origin" of innovation achievements, and promote "preferred areas" where scientific results are transformed efficiently.	Improve the ability to develop the origins of scientific and technological innovation; build a more attractive innovation ecosystem; create a more competitive integrated service environment for talents. Support the Pudong New Area to explore a population management mechanism focused on optimizing population structure and talent services. Authorize the Pudong New Area to approve the direct household registration of introduced domestic talents and overseas returnees.
4	Building a new industrial base with global competitiveness	Concentrate efforts to pursue high-quality development of the real economy, focus on improving economic density, foster a group of strategically advanced modern industrial clusters and vital innovative enterprise clusters, and develop new advantages in international competition.	Build a world-class advanced manufacturing cluster; enhance the global competitiveness of the merchant service industry.
5	Building a high-quality modern urban area	Pursue eco-priority and green development, strive to improve the refined management level of the city, and enhance the city's attractiveness	Build a world-class hub-like and networked integrated transportation system; accelerate urban-rural development integration at a higher level; build a complete "urban brain" system.

Source: www.gov.cn

It can be concluded that Pudong will have a huge and far-reaching impact on the high-level reform and opening up, high-quality development and better living standards of the Yangtze River Delta as a whole during the institutional innovation process.

III Suggestions on the National Central City Construction of Shanghai and Coordinated Development of the Yangtze River Delta

1 Improve the Level of Regional Integration Development in an All-Round Manner

The integrated development of the Yangtze River Delta is a systematic project. On the one hand, the connectivity of infrastructures in such fields as transportation, logistics, environmental protection, new energy and big data should be realized to substantially enhance the new location advantages and economic development potential of the cities in the region; on the one hand, obstacles imposed by administrative boundaries should be broken in order to increase the efficiency of resource allocation for the purpose of science and technology innovation, and the relevant systems that promote regional integration development should be improved to give full play to the decisive role of the market. Care should be taken to draw on the environmental and resource carrying capacities of different places to form a clear hierarchical spatial structure of "central city-metropolitan area-city cluster-small and medium-sized towns" and the industrial structure of "production + life" and "leading industries + supporting industries".

2 Accelerate Industrial Transformation and Structural Upgrading Based on High Standards

Continue to optimize the talent structure, stimulate the vitality of innovation subjects, explore regional integrated innovation models, accelerate the transformation of innovation results, and improve the mechanism of joint intra-regional construction and benefit sharing around the core task of enhancing innovation capability; accelerate industrial linkage, promote the transformation and upgrading of traditional industries, and increase the development level of advanced manufacturing based on the penetration and interaction of new-generation information technology; promote urban renewal, increase land use efficiency and benefits from both stock and increment, develop deep-rooted urban cultural connotation, and boost the modern service industry; improve the business environment in Shanghai and even the Yangtze River Delta to meet the highest standards and hit the best level at a faster speed, and enhance the soft power of urban construction.

3 Advance Regional Interaction and Coordinated Governance at Multiple Levels

A cooperative network formed by the main participants of "government, industrial parks, enterprises", supplemented by other organizations should be established in the Yangtze River Delta led by Shanghai; an institutional system that integrates "law, system and mechanism" should be established at the content level; a balanced management pattern that combines "hard foundation" with "soft environment" should be formed; an ecosystem in which "industrial forms, spatial forms, and relational forms" evolve to higher orders should be shaped; a governance structure that includes "reform and innovation at multiple points, coordination among multiple parties, and evaluation in multiple dimensions" should be built. The ultimate goal is to achieve coordination and joint governance of the Yangtze River Delta.

4 Promote Joint Construction of Industrial Parks by Category

The joint construction of industrial parks should be strongly promoted in the coordinated regional development of the Yangtze River Delta, and especially key tasks should be advanced by category. For example, paired cooperation between economic development zones, high-tech zones and bonded zones should be encouraged in view of zone functions. Favorable policies should be offered to support industrial parks, agricultural parks, tourist complexes and business parks in view of business activities. Innovation support should be lent to science and technology parks, headquarters, and cultural and creative parks in view of park residents. Overall planning and management supplemented by optimized management systems and prioritized strategic positioning should be guaranteed. Operational work should be refined; international rules should be observed; efforts in investment attraction should be optimized systematically. The innovation and entrepreneurship ecosystems should be improved to support sustainability. Various platforms should be perfected, and quality supporting public services should be strengthened.

References

[1] Statistical Communiqué of Shanghai Municipality on the 2018 National Economic and Social Development.

[2] Ren Hao and Zhen Jie, et al. Blue Book on Sustainable Development of Industrial Parks in China in 2018. Tongji University Press, November 2018.

[3] Cai Qing, Research on Data Analysis and Development of Shanghai Industrial Heritage Transformation into Creative Industrial Park. Research on Heritages and Preservation, July 2018.

[4] Zeng Rui and Li Zao. Research on Mechanism of Transformation and Regeneration in Urban Industrial Heritage: Taking Shanghai as an Example. Urban Development Studies, May 2019

[5] Circular on the Evaluation of Intensive Land Use in National Development Zones in 2018 by the State Council.

B.5 National Central City Construction of Tianjin: Progress, Feature and Trend

*Li Hui and Zhou Liqun**

Abstract: Some changes have occurred during the urban development of Tianjin since 2018, such as the decline of economic growth rate, the continuous upgrading of the three-industry structure, the further deepening of the supply-side structural reform, and the steady advancement of eco-city construction. In order to achieve the basic positioning in national central city construction, Tianjin promoted the Beijing-Tianjin-Hebei coordinated development strategy, the construction of "one base and three zones", and the strategy driven by openness and innovation, which have produced some results. However, Tianjin is still confronted with three major problems during the process of national central city construction. First, its economic growth is declining, and it is under a great pressure for transformation and upgrading. Secondly, further improvement is required in the platform construction intended to undertake non-capital functions from Beijing. Thirdly, the development of intelligent technology industry is still hindered by shortcomings of core technologies and relatively weak basic industries. Only by focusing on solving these problems, promoting the development of

* Li Hui, Doctor of School of Economics, Nankai University; Zhou Liqun, Professor of Binhai Development Institute, Nankai University, President of Tianjin Think-tank Alliance

intelligent technology industry, improving the platform construction to undertake non-capital functions, and sharing accurate innovative resources with Zhongguancun, can Tianjin be truly built into a national central city with guiding, driving and distributing functions.

Keywords: high-quality development; intelligent technology industry; Beijing-Tianjin-Hebei coordination; sharing of resources

I Basic Progress in the Central City Construction of Tianjin

Tianjin has fully implemented the message of the 19th National Congress of the Communist Party of China since 2018. In June 2013, when General Secretary Xi Jinping inspected Tianjin, he indicated three priorities to work for: "to improve the quality and benefits of development, to safeguard and improve people's livelihood, and to strengthen and improve party leadership." Following his instructions, Tianjin has worked to promote high-quality economic development in an all-round way by taking the intelligent technology industry as an important starting point. As a result, important progress has been made in different aspects of urban construction, such as economic growth, industrial development, structural adjustment, population change, ecology and environment.

(I) Economic Growth

1 The Economic Aggregate Slipped in the Ranking, with Widening Gap to Close

In 2018, Tianjin delivered the worst GDP of RMB 188 million among all of the municipalities directly under the central government and became the only municipality that did not enter the "2 trillion club". From 2011 to 2016, Tianjin had maintained a GDP higher than that of Chongqing and secured the third place among the four municipalities; however, Chongqing surpassed Tianjin in 2017 by nearly RMB 100 billion, dragging Tianjin down the economic aggregate ladder. At the same time, among the four municipalities, Tianjin suffered the biggest declining growth rate of GDP, with an economic growth rate significantly lower than those of the other three cities. A conclusion could be drawn that Tianjin has got huge gaps in both economic aggregate and economic growth rate to close with Beijing, Shanghai and Chongqing since 2018 and that it has been under a great downward pressure on economic growth.

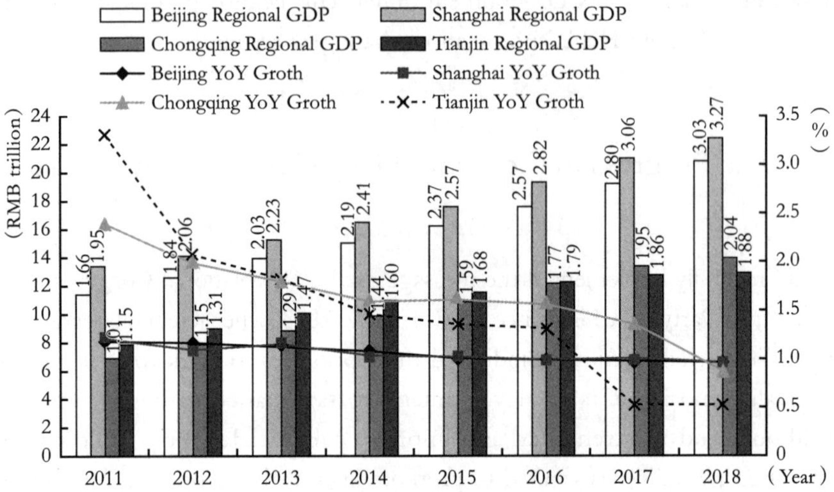

Figure 1 GDP and Growth Rates of Four Municipalities for 2011-2018

2 The Economic Growth Was Still Stalling, but Better Signs Have Appeared Quarter by Quarter

In 2018, Tianjin's GDP was RMB 1.880964 trillion, a growth rate of 3.6% over 2017 (measured at comparable price). The data showed that Tianjin had the lowest economic growth rate among the 31 provinces, autonomous regions and municipalities in the country in 2018. Its economic growth was still stalling.

2018 presented a good historical opportunity for Tianjin and marked a critical transition from high-speed growth to high-quality development. In order to accelerate the transition to high-quality economic development, Tianjin abandoned the scale-and speed-oriented growth mode and closely followed the "three priorities" instructed by General Secretary Xi Jinping. Centering round the general tasks of deepening reform and seeking innovation driven development, it mapped the general layout of the intelligent technology industry, actively cultivated new economic growth points, and vigorously promoted quality, efficiency and power reforms. As a result, the economic growth has been improved quarter by quarter, and a high-quality development trend is looming. By the first quarter of 2019, the growth rate of Tianjin's GDP had risen to 4.5%, which was 2.6, 1.1 and 0.9 percentage points higher than the levels in the first quarter of 2018, the first half of 2018 and the previous whole year, respectively.

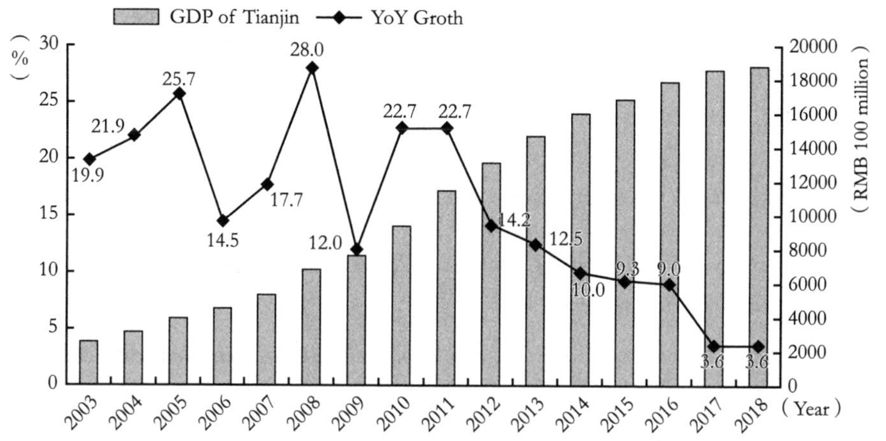

Figure 2 GDP and Growth Rates of Tianjin for 2003-2018

(II) Industrial Development

1 Modern Urban Agriculture Continued to Upgrade

In 2018, modern urban agriculture in Tianjin developed rapidly and was upgraded continuously. The progress was mainly reflected in six aspects. First, the grain production remained stable. Second, the agricultural industry became further information-based, brand-oriented and functional, with 800 demonstration bases of the Internet of Things application in farming and breeding and an agricultural big data application platform basically built. Third, the mayor accountability system was put into operation for the "vegetable basket" project, and the construction of "a city with agricultural quality and safety" was advanced in an orderly manner. Basically over 98% of local agricultural products passed random tests, one of the highest pass rates in the country. Fourth, remarkable results were made in agricultural green development. Ten Sino-Israel agricultural and scientific cooperation demonstration parks were completed, and the construction of 10 green recycling animal by-product bases and 100 demonstration parks with large-scale standardized facilities was commenced. Fifth, the pilot project of rural "five initiatives" proceeded step by step, and new types of business such as rural complex, modern agricultural industrial parks, and shared farms developed at quicker pace. Sixth, the pilot work of national rural reform experiment zones was carried out steadily; the reform of rural collective property rights system was fully unfolded; the confirmation, registration and certification of rural land contractual management right was basically completed; the pilot project of mortgage on rural property rights made solid progress; the perfection of agricultural insurance system was quickened; a rural property rights trading market that covered cities, districts and towns/streets that served as a pioneer in the country was established.

2 Quality and Benefits of Advanced Manufacturing Industry Were Significantly Improved

In 2018, the added value of high-tech industry (advanced manufacturing industry) in Tianjin increased by 4.4%, 2.0 percentage points higher than the added value of industrial enterprises above designated size in the city and accounting for its 13.3%; the added value of strategic emerging industries increased by 3.1%, accounting for 21.8% of the added value of industrial enterprises above designated size in the city and 1.0 percentage point higher than the added value in 2017; the advanced manufacturing industry contributed 61.8% of the total industrial output, and the profits of industrial enterprises increased by 17.6% from 2017. This clearly showed that the industrial development of Tianjin progressed steadily and the quality and benefits of advanced manufacturing industry were improved significantly. In order to comprehensively promote the construction of national advanced manufacturing R&D base, foster and expand emerging industries, and accelerate the replacement of old driving forces with new ones, Tianjin promulgated a three-year (2018-2020) action plan for four industries: new-generation artificial intelligence, biomedicine, new energy and new materials. It also implemented another three-year action plan for 13 key industries including aerospace, intelligent terminals and robots. The output of key products such as integrated circuit wafers, service robots and wind turbine generator sets doubled. All of these achievements fueled the rapid development of the advanced manufacturing industry. At the same time, the Internet and the real economy were further integrated. A number of cloud platforms such as Binhai Industrial Cloud and Troila Technology Cloud added wings to the upgrading of the manufacturing industry. Furthermore, in order to explore the important developments of big data industry in commercial, civil and political applications, the *Regulations of Tianjin on Promoting the Applications of Big Data Developments* was issued to actively cultivate and empower strategic emerging industries and intelligent economy forms and to accelerate the construction of digital economy and smart city construction.

3 The Modern Service Industry Played A Stronger Supporting Role

The proportion of service industry in Tianjin was continuously improved, and the modern service industry played a stronger role. In 2018, the added value of the service industry in Tianjin reached RMB 1.102712 trillion, a year-on-year increase of 5.9%, which was 2.3 percentage points higher than the growth rate of the city's GDP. It accounted for 58.6% of the city's GDP, 0.4 percentage points higher than its proportion in 2017. The service industry took up a larger share in the city's economy. Specifically, the added value of the finance sector was 196.689 billion, a year-on-year increase of 7.2%; capital-and technology-intensive sectors such as finance, technology services, information services, and business leasing accounted for 42.1% of the service industry, up 1.4 percentage points from 2017; of service enterprises above designated size, the operating incomes of technology service, high-tech service and strategic emerging service sectors increased by 12.2%, 11.9% and 9.2% respectively, and their profit margins amounted to 7.5%, 7.3% and 8.5% respectively; the internal structure of the service industry continued to be optimized. At the same time, 183,000 market entities were added to the service industry in the city in 2018, accounting for 90.6% of all the new market entities. A number of emerging service companies like Heer Technology, Yiyun Sharing, and Toutiao grew rapidly. New driving forces for the development of the service industry were cultivated at quicker pace.

(III) Population Changes

In terms of population, the resident population of Tianjin increased slightly in 2018 (see Table 1). In terms of population growth rate, statistics showed that the birth rate of resident population in Tianjin was 6.67‰, the death rate was 5.42‰, and the natural growth rate was 1.25‰ in 2018.

Table 1 Resident Population of Tianjin by the End of 2018

	By the End 2018	Increase (10,000 persons)	Percentage as Total Resident Population (%)
Resident population (10,000 persons)	1559.60	2.73	100.0
Migrant population (10,000 persons)	499.01	0.78	32.0
Urban population (10,000 persons)	1296.81	5.70	83.15
Registered population (10,000 persons)	1081.63	31.64	—

Tianjin introduced 22 policies that favored entrepreneurship and employment of college students, made proper arrangements for enterprise workers rendered unemployed due to excess capacity, and ensured that at least one person from a zero-employment family or a low-income family was employed. With these efforts, both the number and quality of employment continued to increase. In 2018, the total employment population of Tianjin was 8.9656 million, including 3.5978 million migrant workers, which marked a year-on-year increase of 16,000; the urban employment population was 7.1421 million, which marked a year-on-year increase of 41,000. The year-end registered unemployment rate was 3.5%; the all-year new employment population was 490,000.

In 2018, Tianjin took 17 measures to increase income, and the incomes and expenditures of residents increased steadily. As shown in Table 2, the per capita disposable income and the per capita consumption expenditure of residents in Tianjin showed steady growth in 2018; among the per capita consumption expenditure, those spent on education, culture, entertainment, transportation, communication and health care rose rapidly and were 9.0, 5.9, and 4.6 percentage points higher the per capita consumption expenditure, respectively.

Table 2 Incomes and Expenditures of Tianjin Residents in 2018

	Income and Expenditure (RMB)	Growth Rate (%)
Per capita disposable income of total residents (RMB)	39506	6.7
Per capita disposable income of urban residents (RMB)	42976	6.7
Per capita disposable income of rural residents (RMB)	23065	6.0
Per capita consumption expenditure of total residents (RMB)	29903	7.4
Including: education, culture and entertainment	—	18.4
Transportation and communication	—	14.3
Health care	—	12.0

(V) Ecology and Environment

In order to fight the battle against pollution, Tianjin organized thorough study and comprehensive implementation of the new concept of innovative, coordinated, green, open and sharing development. The construction of ecological city was promoted steadily. Significant results have been made in pollution prevention and control.

First of all, Tianjin continuously strengthened ecological environment protection mainly in four aspects. First, sea and land areas totaling 1,393.79 square kilometers were put under red line ecological protection, and they accounted for 9.91% of the total sea and land area of Tianjin. Second, the *Wetland Nature Reserve Planning of Tianjin Municipality* was implemented, and the protection of important ecological wetlands such as Qilihai and Beidagang was comprehensively upgraded. The area of land conversion to ecological wetland core areas totaled 98.1 square kilometers. Third, the *Detailed Rules on Strengthening the Planning and Management of Central Zones in Binhai New Area and Central Urban Area to Construct Green Ecological Barriers in Tianjin Municipality* was formulated according to high standards, aiming to strengthen the management and construction of "green ecological barriers in twin cities" and complete the greening of the starting area of 7,400 mu faster. Fourth, measures were taken to protect the migration channel of migratory birds, and special actions were taken to crack down crimes such as destructing migratory birds and other wild animal resources.

Next, the prevention and control of air, water, soil and solid waste pollution was deepened. To start with, Tianjin deepened the prevention and control of air pollution by implementing the *Three-Year Plan for the Blue Sky Protection Campaign of Tianjin Municipality (2018-2020)*. As a result, 25 key industries controlled their emissions within the special limits of atmospheric pollutants, and the annual average PM2.5 concentration was reduced by 16.1% from the level in 2017. Secondly, Tianjin also deepened the prevention and control of water pollution by implementing the *Special Action Plan on Environmental Protection of the Sources of Centralized Drinking Water in Tianjin Municipality*. All of the sources of centralized drinking water were delineated as protected areas, and 258 enterprises that discharged waste water directly were upgraded and renovated. More than 40% of the surface water reached or exceeded the Grade-III sediment water quality level in national assessment, which was 5 percentage points higher than that in

2017, and 25% was found to have the Grade-V sediment water quality, which was 15 percentage points lower than that in 2017. Thirdly, a detailed investigation of soil pollution was conducted, including the test of 4,725 soil samples and data reporting. Finally, Tianjin also strengthened the prevention and control of solid waste pollution by taking special actions to curb illegal dumping of solid waste and regulate the disposal of waste acid and by reducing the volume of licensed solid waste import.

II Main Results from the Central City Construction of Tianjin

As a national central city, Tianjin is always the economic center of the Bohai Sea rim area. Under the great context of Beijing-Tianjin-Hebei coordinated development, Tianjin established the positioning as "one base and three zones": the national R&D base of advanced manufacturing, the northern core zone of international shipping, the demonstration zone of financial innovation operation, and the pilot zone of reform and opening-up. In moving towards the high-quality development stage, Tianjin established a new position as a pioneer of artificial intelligence. In order to achieve the basic positioning in national central city construction, Tianjin promoted the Beijing-Tianjin-Hebei coordinated development strategy, the construction of "one base and three zones", and the strategy driven by openness and innovation, which have produced remarkable results.

(I) Significant Results Have Been Made in Regional Integration from Advancing the Beijing-Tianjin-Hebei Coordinated Development Strategy

On the one hand, Tianjin has made a number of achievements in its efforts to further promote the major national strategy of Beijing-Tianjin-Hebei coordinated development, seize the critical opportunity of relieving non-capital functions from Beijing, and deepen the functional exchanges and cooperation in related fields. First, in order to accurately undertake the non-capital functions relieved, Tianjin continued to build a "1+16" pattern framed by several professional platforms such as the comprehensive undertaking platform of Binhai New Area as the strategic cooperation zone and the Zhongguancun Scientific and Technology Park in Baodi. Second, a number of projects were started or contracted. For example, the construction of the National Convention and Exhibition Center was commenced, and the contract on the building of China University of Nuclear Industry was signed. Third, the construction of key carriers such as the Binhai Zhongguancun Science and Technology Park and the Beijing-Tianjin Zhongguancun Scientific Park in Baodi, as coordinated development centers, was accelerated. The Binhai Zhongguancun Science and Technology Park has attracted 941 enterprises to register and high-quality projects such as China (Binhai New Area) Intellectual Property Rights Protection Center to settle down.

On the other hand, Tianjin took the initiative to participate in the critical arrangements for the construction of Xiong'an New Area and served for it. First, according to the *Strategy Cooperation Agreement between the People's Government of Hebei Province and Tianjin Municipal People's Government on Actively Promoting the Construction and Development of Xiong'an New Area*, Tianjin accelerated the implementation of eight cooperation matters identified in the agreement, and planned and perfected the transportation network connecting it to the Xiong'an New Area. It also formulated the *Implementation Plan for Building Tianjin Port into a World-Class Port (2019-2023)*, which defined the goal to build Tianjin Port and Huanghua Port in Hebei Province into two estuaries for Xiong'an New Area. Second, Tianjin maintained in-depth cooperation with Xiong'an New Area in the fields of vocational education and social insurance system building. The two places established cooperation in school running, which led to the founding of the Xiong'an Branch of Tianjin the First Commercial School and the Xiong'an Branch of Tianjin Landscape Architecture School, as well as the commencement of the training base of Tianjin Vocational Institute in Xiong'an New Area.

(II) A Project-based Support List System Was Created and Practical Results Were Harvested in the Positioning as "One Base and Three Zones"

In order to implement the major national strategy of Beijing-Tianjin-Hebei coordinated development and comprehensively promote the construction of "one base and three zones", Tianjin formulated a plan of project-based support list system to accelerate the realization of functional positioning. By the end of 2018, 45 of the first 126 major projects and matters had been completed, signifying substantial results in living up to the positioning as "one base and three zones".

Firstly, the construction of a national advanced manufacturing R&D base was fully launched. Fueled by the engine of innovation driven strategy, guided by manufacturing power strategy, and focused on intelligent manufacturing, Tianjin promoted stock upgrading and incremental transformation of the manufacturing industry toward the goal of building a national advanced manufacturing R&D base. It proposed to build "Tianjin Smart Port" and become a pioneer of artificial intelligence. To this end, it introduced more than 300 intelligent technology projects including Unicloud, JD Cloud, Toutiao, Yonyou Software and CASICloud. These projects have initially formed industry clusters in such fields as autonomous and controllable cloud, intelligent equipment and intelligent networked vehicles.

Next, its function as the northern core area of international shipping was significantly improved. Tianjin launched a special campaign to improve the environment of Tianjin Port by reducing charges, increasing efficiency and rectifying chaos. In 2018, 1.38 million TEUs benefited from the "one-stop transparent price list", and port charges were reduced by more than RMB 290 million. At the same time, the "one-stop transparent price list" adopted by Tianjin Port was copied nationwide as a model of business environment optimizing recognized by the General Office of the State Council.

Thirdly, good progress was made in the construction of demonstration zone of financial innovation operation. Tianjin continued to intensify its financial innovation endeavors which produced over 200 innovative financial products; 11 measures such as paying finance lease in foreign currency were copied nationwide; the pilot policy favoring leasing enterprises' external debt facilitation was implemented; cross-border aircraft, ship and offshore platform leasing business created leading models in the country, accounting for more than 80% of the national total business volume.

Finally, important results were achieved in the construction of the pilot zone of reform and opening-up. Tianjin accelerated the building of an experiment and demonstration zone for Tongzhou-Wuqing-Langfang coordinated development, implemented 60 cooperation agreements at quicker pace, and pushed forward mutual recognition and approval of talents among the three places in an orderly manner. It also opened up a two-way green channel for the registration of relocated enterprises in Beijing, Tianjin and Hebei and facilitated "six unifications" (name, basis, licensed content, application conditions, application materials, and form of licensed result) in administrative approval among the three places. It explored the creation of innovation vouchers and their cross-regional mutual recognition mechanism, and signed cooperation agreements on the creation of innovation voucher cooperation mechanism in the Beijing-Tianjin-Hebei Region with the other two places. The Beijing-Tianjin-Hebei (Tianjin) experiment zone for comprehensive reform of inspection and quarantine was officially launched.

(III) The General Layout of the Intelligent Technology Industry Was Mapped and Prominent Achievements Were Made in the Construction of Pioneering Artificial Intelligence City

In order to go with the new tide of scientific revolution and industrial transformation in the world, the Municipal Party Committee and the Municipal Government of Tianjin attached great importance to the development of the intelligent technology industry and mapped a general layout in which it was treated as a major means and key breakthrough to promote industrial restructuring, accelerate industrial transformation and upgrade, and foster new driving forces. To this end, Tianjin was the first city to propose the building of "Tianjin Smart Port" and to hold the World Intelligence Congress. It also issued a series of favourable policies, carried out a number of pilot and demonstration projects, and took the lead in raising the banner of intelligent development in the country.

At present, Tianjin has issued a series of policy measures, created a sound policy support system, gathered a number of platforms and carriers that support industrial development, introduced and cultivated a lot of backbone enterprises engaged in intelligent technologies. The Research Institute of the New Generation of Artificial Intelligence Development Strategies in China released the *Development of Intelligent Industry Driven by a New Generation of Artificial Intelligence Technology* in 2018. The report showed that the regional competitiveness index of AI industry in Tianjin was 5.9, which was ranked 9th in the country. This result put it in the second-tier rank with Shandong, Anhui and Hubei. The overall development level of its AI industry was in the middle upper level of the country. The intelligent technology industry is becoming an important driving force for the industrial transformation and upgrading of Tianjin, which is moving towards a pioneer of artificial intelligence steadily.

Ⅲ Suggestions on the Central City Construction of Tianjin

Based on the basic positioning as a national central city, the further positioning as "one base and three zones" in the Beijing-Tianjin-Hebei coordinated development strategy, and the goal to become a pioneer of artificial intelligence, Tianjin will continue to implement the major national strategy of Beijing-Tianjin-Hebei coordinated development and the strategy driven by openness and innovation, and build "Tianjin Smart Port" during the national central city construction process. It should also focus on addressing the problems arising from this process and build itself into a leading innovative city and intelligent technology innovation center in the country at a faster speed.

1 Promote the Development of Intelligent Technology Industry and Inject New Driving Forces into Industrial Transformation and Upgrading

To build "Tianjin Smart Port", Tianjin should actively promote the deep integration of intelligent technology and the real economy, strive to create a new system of intelligent technology industry that is driven by innovation, guided by applications, upheld by industrial collaboration, supported by carriers, and assisted by cross-border integration. It should seek new driving forces for the construction of a pioneer of artificial intelligence and an intelligent technology innovation center with international influence. It should also add new engines to realize the "five modernizations of Tianjin" and promote Beijing-Tianjin-Hebei coordinated development.

First, pay attention to the construction of open innovation platforms. On the one hand, build a platform for sharing resources in the intelligent technology industry, and provide cooperation channels for intelligent technology enterprises, universities and scientific research institutions on a global scale by building innovation exchange platforms for intelligent technology enterprise, founding intelligent technology innovation alliances, and holding global high-end intelligent technology conferences. On the other hand, seek partners to jointly build empowering platforms in the intelligent technology industry. Cooperate with leading companies in the field of intelligent technologies, such as iFLYTEK, Alibaba and Tencent, and leverage the technological advantages and industry resources of such enterprises to facilitate effective connection of upstream and downstream industry chains. At the same time, build an intelligent technology incubator base and a "mass entrepreneurship and innovation" platform to reduce the costs of innovation and entrepreneurship that intelligent technology enterprises have to bear, increase public supplies such as supercomputing and intelligent cloud services, and enhance professional public service level for innovation and entrepreneurship.

Second, strengthen the training and introduction of talents. On the one hand, strengthen the introduction of high-end talents. Introduce a number of talents specialized in strategic technologies, industry leaders, academic leaders and outstanding young technology talents who master international level skills in the field of intelligent technology through the Haihe Talent Program and the Thousand Talents Program, etc. On the other hand, accelerate the training of intelligent technology professionals. Rely on the Institute of Artificial Intelligence of Nankai University, the Institute of Artificial Intelligence of Tianjin University and related institutes of other universities to step up the training of professionals in intelligent technology; promote the interdisciplinary integration and specialty adjustment and reform of universities to meet industrial needs, with the focus on cultivating a team of scientific and technological entrepreneurs with good technical skills, global strategic vision, management and innovation capabilities.

Third, build a national high-end intelligent manufacturing industry cluster. On the one hand, encourage advanced and advantageous manufacturing industries such as electronic information, biomedicine and equipment manufacturing to focus on the R&D and innovation of advanced manufacturing technologies and systems; promote the development of R&D-focused manufacturing and service-oriented manufacturing industries, expand and extend the high-end manufacturing industry chain to complement Beijing as a global R&D center and form distributed collaboration with the manufacturing base in Hebei. On the other hand, improve the industrial technology collaboration chain, actively explore cooperation mechanisms used in scientific and technological systems, industrial environment, collaborative complex, and technological services, and gather technology resources with market power. In addition, strengthen technological exchanges and cooperation with the Bohai Sea rim area, open up markets with product demand, increase the transformation level of innovation achievements, and actively build a national high-end intelligent manufacturing industry cluster.

2 Improve the Construction of Undertaking Platforms to Actively Undertake Non-capital Functions Relieved from Beijing

As the Beijing-Tianjin-Hebei coordinated development strategy is further advanced, Tianjin should optimize the overall undertaking pattern to address the problems arising from the construction of undertaking platforms, explore a more effective mechanism for coordinated regional development, actively undertake the non-capital functions relieved from Beijing, and take over the industrial transfer and technological innovation resources from Beijing in an orderly manner.

To begin with, Tianjin should put the "1+16" platforms to undertake industrial transfer in the greater "2+4+46" pattern of industrial transfer in the Beijing-Tianjin-Hebei Region and redefine the functions and industries of each undertaking platform to highlight their respective advantages in attracting investments and industrial characteristics. Complementary layouts of undertaking platforms should be formed to promote effective connection of industrial transfer.

Next, improve the working mechanism featuring up and down linkage and internal and external combination. Strengthen the horizontal communication and interests coordination between the undertaking platforms, and enable them to complement each other in undertaking industrial transfer based on their own functional positioning and leading industries and pool upstream and downstream related industries together. Make sure that there are smooth channels to connect the releasing site and the undertaking site. Promote centralized and group undertaking. Improve mutual restraint and homogeneous competition among undertaking platforms in different places.

Finally, the "1+16" undertaking platforms in Tianjin should be integrated organically. Those stuck in slow construction progress, backward supporting facilities, poor undertaking capacity and bad undertaking effect should be subject to timely adjustments. Focus on building an "East-South-West-

North" undertaking pattern composed of the Binhai Zhongguancun Science and Technology Park, the South Station Technological Business District in Tianjin, the Jinbin Industrial Park in Wuqing, and the Zhongguancun Scientific and Technology Park in Baodi. Form a cluster to undertake the non-capital functions relieved from Beijing and a base to take over the industrial transfer and technological innovation resources from Beijing.

Share Accurate Innovative Resources with Zhongguancun and Accelerate the Concentration of Intelligent Technology Elements

With the further relief of non-capital functions, innovative resources and high-tech enterprises will be diffused and transferred from Zhongguancun faster. As the intelligent technology industry is under a critical development stage, the integration of artificial intelligence and innovative resources from Zhongguancun is particularly important to the rapid concentration of intelligent technology elements in the manufacturing industry of Tianjin. Therefore, it should share accurate innovative resources with Zhongguancun.

On the one hand, Tianjin must share innovative resources in intelligent technology with Zhongguancun, keep a close eye on the project sources to be released and key technology partners, and build a Beijing-Tianjin intelligent industry chain and innovation chain composed of "original innovation-hardware manufacturing-R&D of software technology-general platform support-terminal industry applications". First, focus on introducing integrators and key industry solution providers along the intelligent manufacturing industry chain; increase the connection of local big data, computing power and service platforms with intelligent technologies, algorithms and solutions; integrate upstream and downstream intelligent enterprises and resources; upgrade Tianjin's ability in intelligent solutions. Second, attract and support the deep application of key intelligent technologies from Zhongguancun in R&D and design, production, logistics and warehousing, and after-sales services of the manufacturing industry in Tianjin through visits to investors, professional investment attraction, and investment attraction along industrial chain in combination with the precision innovation action plan for "seven chains" associated with AI in Tianjin. The ultimate purpose is to form an "organic chain" of application scenarios and system applications.

On the other hand, seize the opportunity presented by the opening of service industries from Beijing, explore new ways to attract modern service industries from Zhongguancun to settle down in Tianjin, and increase the scale and level of productive service industries. In the new round of Beijing-Tianjin-Hebei coordinated development, productive service industries are the key targets to be attracted from Zhongguancun to settle down in Tianjin. Tianjin needs to rectify the shortcomings and increase the strength of its productive service industries. First of all, accelerate the construction of productive service industry systems in terms of science and technology services, intermediary services and transformation support in the building of undertaking platforms such as the Binhai Zhongguancun Science and Technology Park, the Beijing-Tianjin Zhongguancun Science and Technology Park in Baodi, and the Beijing and Tianjin Scientific Town in Wuqing, as well as in the construction of demonstration zone of financial innovation operation and national demonstration zone of leasing innovation. Second, strive to introduce upstream and downstream associated industries and extension service agencies to closely meet the needs of industrial transfer undertaking projects and intelligent technology industry projects; foster and attract follow-up sci-tech finance, sci-tech intermediary, commercial logistics and legal services to form a comprehensive service pattern in which the real economy and productive services support and promote each other, assemble to exert supporting force, and develop in cluster.

References

[1] Zhou Liqun et al. "The Rise of the Beijing-Tianjin-Hebei Metropolitan Circle and China's Economic Development" [M]. Beijing, Economic Science Press, 2012.

[2] Zhou Liqun, Li Jiaxiang, et al. "The Annual Development Report of Binhai New Area (2014)" [M]. Tianjin, Tianjin People's Publishing House, 2014.

[3] Zhou Liqun et al. "Regional Economy: A New Map of China" [M]. Nanjing, Jiangsu People's Publishing Ltd., 2017.

[4] Zhou Caiyun and Zhou Liqun. "Status Quo and Measures to Attract High-tech Resources from Beijing into Tianjin" [J]. Tianjin Government Affairs Reference, 2018 (11).

[5] Zhou Caiyun and Zhou Liqun. "Suggestions on Attracting and Undertaking High-tech Innovation Resources from Beijing to Hebei" [J]. Special Information Report (Office of the CPC Hebei Provincial Committee), 2018 (09).

[6] Wang Jinjie and Zhou Liqun. "Complete Thoughts on the Relief of Non-Capital Functions and Undertaking Platforms in Tianjin and Hebei-A Series Research on the

Beijing-Tianjin-Hebei Coordinated Development Strategy for Five Years" [J]. Tianjin Social Sciences, 2019 (01).

[7] Wang Jinjie and Zhou Liqun. "The Orientation and Path of Coordinated Regional Development under the New Normal-A Case Study of the Exploration and Practice of Beijing-Tianjin-Hebei Region" [J]. Jianghai Academic Journal, 2015 (04).

[8] Bo Wenguang and Chen Fei. "Beijing-Tianjin-Hebei Coordinated Development: Challenges and Dilemmas" [J]. Nankai Journal (Philosophy, Literature and Social Science Edition), 2015 (01).

[9] Zhang Jie and Zheng Ruoyu. "Multiple Predicament and Reform Orientation in the Industrial Coordinated Development of Beijing-Tianjin-Hebei Region" [J]. *Journal of the Party School of the Central Committee of the C.P.C.*, 2017 (04).

[10] Expert Advisory Committee of the Intelligent Technology Industry in Tianjin. "Annual Report on the Development of Intelligent Technology Industry in Tianjin (2019)" [R]. Tianjin, 2019.

[11] Tianjin Municipal People's Government. "Report on the Implementation of the 2018 National Economic and Social Development Plan and the Draft of 2019 National Economic and Social Development Plan of Tianjin Municipality" [EB/OL].(2019-02-15) [2019-06-26].http://www.tj.gov.cn/zw/zfgb/rdhwj/201903/t20190304_3650546.html。

[12] ChinaTimes. "With GDP growth rate hitting the bottom, Tianjin is deeply mired in stalling economic growth" [EB/OL]. (2019-02-15) [2019-06-26]. http://new211.com/cjfg/43429.html.

[13] The Paper. "Tianjin's economic growth rate drops to multi-year low, and the People's Daily has three questions about how it could get through" [EB/OL].(2018-01-20)[2019-06-26]. http://news.163.com/18/0120/07/D8IVDVM0000187VE.html.

B.6
The Construction of Guangzhou as a Technological, Educational and Cultural Center: Goal, Connotation, Path and Strategy

Qin Jian and Yin Tao[*]

Abstract: Developing and upgrading the functions as a technological, educational and cultural center lends an important support for Guangzhou to serve as the core engine for the development of the Guangdong-Hong Kong-Macau Greater Bay Area. It is also an important step for Guangzhou to rejuvenate as an old city. As a national central city, Guangzhou owns strong and relatively balanced comprehensive strength in technology, education and culture. Looking into the future, Guangzhou will develop and upgrade the functions as a technological, educational and cultural center with modern education as the foundation, technological innovation as the focus, urban culture as the soul, and integration as the key. Its goal is to become a model city that develops socialist science, technology, education and culture with Chinese characteristics together. To achieve this goal, Guangzhou should start with building an ideal city for world scientists, a world-class university sci-tech park, the Chinese "Silicon Alley", and innovative neighborhoods.

Keywords: technological, educational and cultural center; urban function; Silicon Alley model; Guangzhou

* Qin Jian, Deputy Head and Associate Research Fellow of Regional Economy Research Institute of Guangzhou Academy of Social Sciences; Yin Tao, Vice President and Research Fellow of Guangzhou Academy of Social Sciences.

On February 18, 2019, the *Development Plan for Guangdong-Hong Kong-Macau Greater Bay Area* was officially released, which put forward the new requirement that Guangzhou further develop and upgrade the functions as a technological, educational and cultural center. Among the major cities in the Guangdong-Hong Kong-Macau Greater Bay Area, Guangzhou has laid a good foundation in technological innovation, education, scientific research and cultural undertakings, and it has maintained relatively balanced development, which gives it the first-mover advantage in building a technological, educational and cultural center that integrates "technology + education + culture". Therefore, it is important for Guangzhou to seize the great development opportunity presented by the Guangdong-Hong Kong-Macau Greater Bay Area and play the radiating and driving role as a national central city to further pool high-quality technological, educational and cultural resources, create and develop new driving forces, stimulate new possibilities and brilliance in comprehensive urban functions, and enable rejuvenation of old city.

I Basic Conditions for Building Guangzhou into a Technological, Educational and Cultural Center

(I) Continuously Enhanced Comprehensive Economic Strength

Since the reform and opening up, Guangzhou has generally embarked on a steady and rapid growth trajectory. In 2018, Guangzhou's GDP grew by 6.2%, and its total GDP increased from RMB 4.309 billion in 1978 to RMB 2.285935 trillion; the three-industry structure evolved from 11.67:58.59:29.74 in 1978 to 0.98:27.27:71.75. The urbanization rate of resident population reached 86.4%; the per capita GDP amounted to RMB 155,491; the per capita consumption expenditure of urban permanent household was RMB 42,180.96, 13.4% of which was spent on education, culture and entertainment. From the perspective of economic development level and current development stage, Guangzhou takes on a new development trend driven by the two wheels of "innovation + culture", which lays a solid foundation for the construction of a technological, educational and cultural center.

Table 1 Main Economic Indicators of Some Chinese Cities in 2018

City	Total resident population (10,000 persons)	Regional GDP (RMB 100 million)	Regional per capita GDP (RMB 10,000)	GDP growth rate (%)	General public budget income (RMB 100 million)	Urbanization rate of resident population (%)
Beijing	2154.20	30320.00	14.00	6.6	5785.90	86.5
Shanghai	2423.78	32679.87	13.50	6.6	7108.15	88.1
Tianjin	1559.60	18809.64	12.10	3.6	2106.19	83.2
Chongqing	3101.79	20363.19	6.59	6.0	2265.50	65.5
Guangzhou	1490.44	22859.35	15.55	6.2	1632.30	86.4
Wuhan	1108.10	14847.29	13.51	8.0	1528.70	80.3
Chengdu	1633.00	15342.77	9.50	8.0	1424.20	73.1
Zhengzhou	1013.60	10143.30	10.13	8.1	1152.10	73.4
Xi'an	1000.37	8349.86	8.51	8.2	684.71	74.0

Source: Statistical communiqué of each city on the 2018 national economic and social development

(II) Continuously Enhanced Scientific and Technological Innovation Strength

According to the deployment requirements of national and provincial innovation-driven development strategies and in view of the goal to build a national innovation central city, Guangzhou has accelerated the construction of Guangzhou Science City, Nansha Science City, Sino-Singapore Knowledge City, Small Science and Technology Innovation Town, value innovation parks and other innovation functional zones and innovation carriers. It also actively participates in the construction of the new comprehensive national science center in the Guangdong-Hong Kong-Macau Greater Bay Area. Its comprehensive innovation strength has been substantially enhanced due to its continued investment in innovation, enhanced basic innovation capability, improved international innovation cooperation network, and preemptive actions to occupy the frontier of innovation industry development. According to the *2017 Evaluation Report on Global Scientific and Technological Innovation Centers* released by Shanghai Information Center in December 2017, Guangzhou was ranked 41st among all nominated global cities. According to the *2018 Hard Technology Innovation Indexes of Global*

Table 2 Rankings of Guangzhou in Some Innovation City Lists

Time	Publisher	Index Report	Evaluate System	Ranking of Guangzhou
2018	Supplement to *Nature*, a British journal	*Nature Index 2018 Science Cities*	A ranking of scientific research strength from analysis of the number of scientific research papers published in international high-quality natural science journals and the output performance of high-quality scientific researchers from research institutions and enterprises in major cities.	25
2018	Development Research Center of the State Council	*2018 Hard Technology Innovation Indexes of Global Major Cities*]	"Hard technology" refers to any high-grade, precision and advanced technology in such fields as information technology, artificial intelligence, biotechnology, new materials, aerospace, smart manufacturing, new energy, and chips. The hard technology innovation indexes are analysis and evaluation results from two aspects: innovation input and innovation output. Innovation input indicators include organizational input, talent input and capital investment, and innovation output indicators include knowledge output and business transformation.	9
2017	Shanghai Information Center	*2017 Evaluation Report on Global Scientific and Technological Innovation Centers*	This reports includes four firs-level indicators of basic research, innovation environment, innovation economy and industrial technology, and 25 second-level indicators, and it assesses 165 cities and metropolitan areas with high global visibility, developed economy and strong innovation capability.	41
2018	Capital Institute of Science and Technology Development Strategy	*Building a City of Innovation: Insight from TOP10 Chinese Innovation Cities*	This report builds an "indicator system of scientific and technological development of Chinese cities" by selecting 26 specific indicators in four dimensions of innovation resources, innovation environment, innovation service and innovation performance.	4
2018	Fujian Normal University, etc.	*Report on the Innovation Competitiveness Development of Chinese Cities (2018)*	This reports establishes an indicator system in the five dimensions of basic innovation competitiveness, innovation environmental competitiveness, innovation input competitiveness, innovation output competitiveness and innovation sustainable development competitiveness to comprehensively evaluate the innovation competitiveness of 274 cities in China.	5

Major Cities released by CASSTAR in November 2018, Guangzhou was ranked 9th in the world. According to the *Nature Index 2018 Science Cities*, a supplement to *Nature*, a British journal, issued in November 2018, Guangzhou was ranked 25th among global cities.

The status of innovation enterprises as hubs has basically taken root. Enterprises are the mainstay of market innovation. Recent years have witnessed comprehensive innovation capability of enterprises in Guangzhou continuously improve and the number of R&D-focused enterprises increase. The number of various R&D platforms created within enterprises has risen rapidly, and innovative enterprises have grown at faster speed. In 2018, 3,104 new high-tech enterprises were founded in Guangzhou, adding its total number of high-tech enterprises to 11,794. A number of high-growth and dynamic innovative enterprises with great development potential, such as EHang, Pony.ai, Xpeng Motors, Cloudwalk, Chengxing Zhidong Automobile Technology, XAG, and Burning Rock Dx, have emerged in strategic emerging industries such as biomedicine, artificial intelligence, information technology, cloud computing, new materials, new energy and big data. According to the *2018 Technology Fast 50* released by Deloitte on November 20, 2018, Guangzhou had 8 companies included in the list, second only to Beijing (12 companies). Huizheng Zhilian Technology Co., Ltd., a Guangzhou-based company, was ranked second in the list.

Guangzhou has initially secured the status as an innovative activity hub. In 2018, 173,124 patent applications and 50,169 invention patent applications were filed in Guangzhou, an increase of 46.3% and 35.8%, respectively. Guangzhou reported the highest growth rate among 19 cities at sub-provincial level and above nationwide. It was only next to Beijing and Shenzhen and occupied the third place among major domestic cities in terms of the number of PCT international patent applications. The proportion of corporate invention patent applications hit a new high at 63.4%. In addition, Guangzhou had the vast majority of institutions of higher learning and scientific research institutions in Guangdong Province. In 2018, it had 20 national key laboratories, 18 national engineering technological research centers, 27 state-level enterprise technological centers, and 8 national and provincial university science and technology parks. This endowed the city with profound knowledge reserve and foundation in scientific and technological innovation. Various types of technology incubation platforms and crowd innovation spaces in the city developed rapidly, with a total of 196 crowd innovation spaces, including 53 at the national level. There were 26 state-level incubators covering an incubation area of 10.5 million square meters. A group of high-level innovative talents gathered in the city as well, including 98 academicians of the Chinese Academy of Sciences and the Chinese Academy of Engineering, as well as 490 national high-level talents.

Table 3 Invention of Patents in Guangzhou

Indicator (Piece)	2017	2018	YoY Growth (%)
Number of patent applications	118332	173124	46.30
Number of invention patent applications	36941	50169	35.80
Number of patent grants	60201	89826	49.20
Number of invention patent grants	9345	10797	15.50
Invention patent applications by enterprises as a percentage of the total applications (%)	56.30	63.40	7.10

Sources: *Statistical Communiqué of Guangzhou Municipality on the 2017 National Economic and Social Development; Statistical Communiqué of Guangzhou Municipality on the 2018 National Economic and Social Development*

The international innovation network is continuously improved. In recent years, Guangzhou's network for open international innovation cooperation has been continuously improved, and its ability to attract international high-end innovative resources has been continuously enhanced. It has attracted SRI International, the Cold Spring Harbor Laboratory, the Wanda Pittsburgh University International Hospital in Guangzhou, and the Barcelona International Hospital in Guangzhou to settle down from European countries and the United States. It established intergovernmental framework partnership and cooperation with the University of Birmingham and signed an agreement with Heidelberg, Germany, on building Sino-Germany Science and Education Park. It founded offices in the Silicon Valley, Boston, and Tel Aviv, Israel, to actively promote project cooperation and talent introduction. Enterprises and institutions in Guangzhou established more than 150 bilateral research projects with partners and scientific research institutions in countries involved in the Belt and Road Initiative. China Innovation Conference, Fortune International Brainstorming Conference on Technology,

China Innovation and Entrepreneurship Fair, Guangzhou Convention of Overseas Chinese Scholars in Science and Technology, Canton Tower Science & Technology Conference, China Venture Capital & Private Equity Forum and other international innovation events successfully promoted the sharing of innovation resources in the world and contributed to Guangzhou's integration into the global innovation network.

(II) Intensive and Rich Resources of Higher Education

As one of the Chinese cities that enjoy best higher education, Guangzhou had more than 80 institutions of higher education above junior college in 2018. Sun Yat-sen University and South China University of Technology are included in the world-class university construction program, while Jinan University and South China Normal University are included in the world-class discipline construction program in China. There are 1.0864 million college and university students in the city, which is the largest number in the country. In January 2003, the construction of Guangzhou Higher Education Mega Center with a total area of 34.4 square kilometers was officially launched. After years of development and construction, this constantly improved environment has gathered more than ten universities famous at home and abroad, including Sun Yat-sen University, South China University of Technology, Jinan University and South China Normal University. Its residents also include a number of national key laboratories, engineering laboratories and other R&D innovation platforms which boast of some international and domestic leading R&D technologies. More than 200,000 innovative talents at high end level, in middle and young age groups and in collective teams, as well as university teachers and students gather here to form talent, technological and platform advantages that all fuel technological innovation. Relying on the scientific research advantages of Sun Yat-Sen University and its surrounding areas, Guangzhou is planning to build the Zhongda International Innovation Valley, a high-level headquarters based on first-class world standards to focus on key industries such as smart manufacturing, information technology, new energy, biomedicine, and creative design. The new sci-tech innovation park that integrates innovation, technology transfer, result incubation, entrepreneurship centers and talent innovation bases is expected to become sources of new paths and new models for the exploration of new industry-university-research integration modes in Guangzhou.

(III) Profound Historic and Cultural Backgrounds

Guangzhou is one of the first 24 famous historic and cultural cities announced in China. It has built a complete public cultural facilities system and owns the most distinctive and competitive resource advantages such as the Lingnan cultural center, the birthplace of ancient Maritime Silk Road, the source of modern democratic revolution, and the frontier of the reform and opening up. Relying on the rich cultural resources and profound historical background of Lingnan, Guangzhou is also active in promoting the integration of culture, business and tourism. The Beijing Road Cultural Tourism Zone is rated as a national 4A-level tourist attraction and has been recognized as a national-level cultural industry demonstration park that carries the mission of exploring ten new models for "revitalization" of inherited historical and cultural resources, for strategic cooperation in branded cultural activities, and for new types of business under "culture +" cross-sector integration and development of new formats, to name just a few. It is a pioneer to explore experiences and provide demonstrations for the whole country. Guangzhou Cultural and Financial Service Center Co., Ltd. was founded and initiated the establishment of the National Alliance of Cultural and Financial Center with about 20 cultural and financial centers, as well as cultural investment institutions across the country. In doing so, Guangzhou tried to establish an investment and financing system in the cultural industry with other parts of the country. The ultimate goal was to promote cross-sector innovation, finance and culture integration and the prosperity of the cultural market.

In recent years, the cultural industry in Guangzhou has developed rapidly, further enhancing its cultural influence. Companies or brands that are prestigious in the world have emerged, such as Netease, WeChat, Kugou, UC, YY, Alpha Animation, Comic Fans, and Leafun. Pleasant Goat and Big Big Wolf, Happy Q-Bot, GG Bond, and Balala the Fairies were rated among the top ten brands of Chinese animation. *Nanfang Daily* had the best brand value among all the provincial party newspapers in China, and *Guangzhou Daily* was also the champion among city newspapers. According to the 2018 "China Top 500 Most Valuable Brands" released by the World Brand Lab on June 20, 2018, the total value of

Nanfang Daily, *Nanfang Metropolis Daily* and *Southern Weekly* reached RMB 93.371 billion. Nanfang Media Group was the third largest media organizations in the country, second only to China Media Group and People's Daily. *Nanfang Daily, People's Daily and Reference News* were the top valuable print media brands in China. Branded events such as the Guangzhou International Documentary Film Festival, China, the China International Children's Film Festival, the Chinese Golden Bell Award for Music, the China International Performing Arts Fair, the Guangzhou Cultural Industry Fair and the Guangzhou International Art Fair has growing international influence. In order to further enhance the development level of the cultural industry and enhance the soft power of city culture, the *Opinions of Guangzhou City on Accelerating the Innovation and Development of the Cultural Industry* was formulated in 2018, in which a proposal was made to build the cultural industry into an important strategic pillar industry in the city, to steadily increase the proportion of the added value of the cultural industry in GDP and to basically make Guangzhou a hub for international cultural industries by 2035. To this end, Guangzhou will foster 20 digital content leaders, build 10 digital content industrial parks at city level and above that will have great influence at home and abroad, and strive to win the titles of the city of cartoon game industry, the national art industry center, the global cultural and creative design city, the global cultural equipment manufacturing center, the global cultural exhibition center, and the national venture capital and startup capital center of the cultural industry.

II Connotation in the Goal of Constructing Guangzhou as a Technological, Educational and Cultural Center

Based on its basic advantages and drawing on the development experience of international advanced cities, the goal of Guangzhou as a technological, educational and cultural center is to train high-end talents who can adapt to the needs of scientific and technological innovation through modern innovation education and consolidate the basic capability in technological innovation; to drive the development of new technologies and new industries through technological innovation and accelerate the transition from old to new industries and from old to new driving forces; to enhance the city's appeal, creativity, influence and recognition through cultural means, accelerate the formation of a technology, education and culture ecosystem that maintains virtuous circle, promote the integration and holistic effect of technology, education and culture, and take the lead in exploring the construction of a model city in the integrated development of technology, education and culture in China. Specifically, such goal has the following four aspects of connotation:

(I) Modern Education is the Foundation for the Construction of Guangzhou as a Technological, Educational and Cultural Center

Education determines what humans are and will be. It is an important symbol of the development level and potential of a city. Relying on first-class universities and first-class disciplines, building major infrastructures and large-scale instruments used for scientific research, carrying out national major science and technology projects and even participating in global scientific research projects can effectively enhance the basic innovation capability of a city. Developed vocational education can feed a variety of application-oriented talents and human resources to enterprises, thereby driving the development of industries. It is the developed vocational education that provides a number of excellent industrial workers and technical talents for "Made in Germany" and "German quality" [1]. In fact, internationalized and quality basic education is not only a means to enhance the cultural quality and sustained competitiveness of urban citizens, but also a magic formula for a city to attract international talents to settle down.

(II) Technological Innovation is the Priority in the Construction of Guangzhou as a Technological, Educational and Cultural Center

In April 2019, General Secretary Xi Jinping attended the opening ceremony of the Second Belt and Road Forum for International Cooperation and delivered a keynote speech stating that "Innovation produces productivity, helping make companies competitive and countries prosperous." For cities, the combination of technological innovation with institutional innovation, management innovation, business type innovation, cultural innovation and business model innovation can move a city from a labor and capital intensive stage to a knowledge and technological progress intensive stage and lead its economy toward a more advanced, high-end, and high-quality level. Looking into the future when digitalization, networking and intelligence trends take hold, mass technological revolution characterized by intelligence, greenness and ubiquity will trigger major adjustments in division of labor in international industries. Emerging cutting-edge and disruptive technologies will accelerate the restructuring of global innovation landscape. Under this context, the ability to grasp the development trends presented in the new round of scientific and technological revolution and strengthen the driving forces of technological innovation will directly determine the competitiveness of a city and its position in the global urban network system. Therefore, the top priority in developing and upgrading the functions as a technological, educational and cultural center is to strengthen the technological innovation function and enhance the driving forces behind it.

(III) City Culture is Fundamental to the Construction of Guangzhou as a Technological, Educational and Cultural Center

City culture is a unique spiritual character of a city. It tells the whole story of a city about its historical tradition, cultural heritage, contemporary spirit and values over years of development [2]. The cultural soft power bred from city culture is an important driving force for a city to move towards a high-level development stage and will ultimately determine how it will be written in history. According to the "Evaluation Report of International Cultural Metropolises" jointly released by Shanghai Jiaotong University and the University of Southern California on March 11, 2019, the top ten cities were New York, London, Paris, Tokyo, San Francisco, Berlin, Beijing, Los Angeles, Shanghai and Rome. However, the top ten cities in the "Global City Rankings" published by GaWC in November 2018 were London, New York, Hong Kong, Beijing, Singapore, Shanghai, Sydney, Paris, Dubai, and Tokyo. Overlaps in these two lists are obvious, which testifies that the culture of a city is closely related to its comprehensive competitiveness. In fact, all the world-famous cities are often imbued with certain spiritual disposition. Obviously, to develop and upgrade the functions as a technological, educational and cultural center that demonstrates visible and distinctive disposition,

Guangzhou must resort to its rich historical and cultural resources to improve the spiritual and cultural quality of citizens, cultivate the humanistic spirit as a modern city, and seek support and driving force for its technological innovation, economic development and social progress from increasingly enhanced cultural soft power.

(IV) Integration is the Key to the Construction of Guangzhou as a Technological, Educational and Cultural Center

Technology, education and culture are inextricable. Education is not only the basis for the transformation of science and technology into productivity, but also a cultural form per se. Education development can boost technological innovation capability and the inheritance, preservation, exchange and innovation of social cultures. Technological progress can aid the modernization of education, cultural renewal and the development of new cultural forms, and substantially boost the influence and communication of education and culture. Profound historical and cultural backgrounds and advanced cultural concepts are the sources of technological innovation and the development of modernized and international education. Thus, developing and upgrading technological, educational and cultural functions is by no means a simple combination and assembly of the three; instead, it is all about their deep integration and the resulting comprehensive competitiveness. This requires both profound historical background and a dynamic modern innovation culture and innovative spirit in the city. Technological innovation and cultural soft power are two driving forces to fuel city development.

III The Path for the Construction of Guangzhou as a Technological, Educational and Cultural Center

(I) Positioned as an Ideal City for Scientists and Aimed to be a Technological, Educational and Cultural Center in the Guangdong-Hong Kong-Macau Greater Bay Area

A group of outstanding scientists are required to support the building of

Guangdong-Hong Kong-Macau Greater Bay Area into an international technological innovation center. In October 2018, the Shanghai Institute for Science of Science and Springer Nature jointly released the *2018 Survey Report on the "Ideal Cities" for Global Scientists.* According to this questionnaire survey that engaged in 654 front-line scientists in major countries and regions around the world, when choosing a city to work in, scientists mainly consider whether there are world leading scientific research institutions, leading research infrastructures, generous research fund support, extensive global technological innovation exchange and cooperation opportunities, status as a global technology center, and adequate research work opportunities and income, etc.

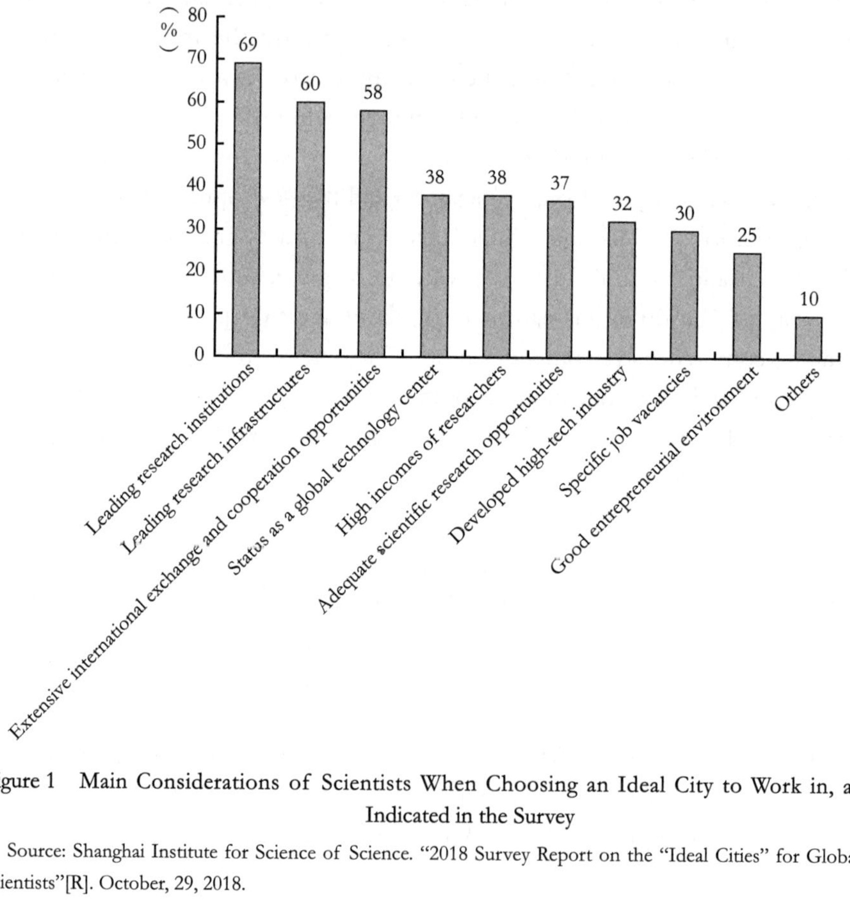

Figure 1 Main Considerations of Scientists When Choosing an Ideal City to Work in, as Indicated in the Survey

Source: Shanghai Institute for Science of Science. "2018 Survey Report on the "Ideal Cities" for Global Scientists"[R]. October, 29, 2018.

When choosing a city to live in, scientists mainly consider whether the city has an open and inclusive innovation culture, convenient living conditions, a modern, beautiful and fashionable lifestyle, clean air and environment, convenient transportation, a good education environment for children, and a comfortable climate, etc.

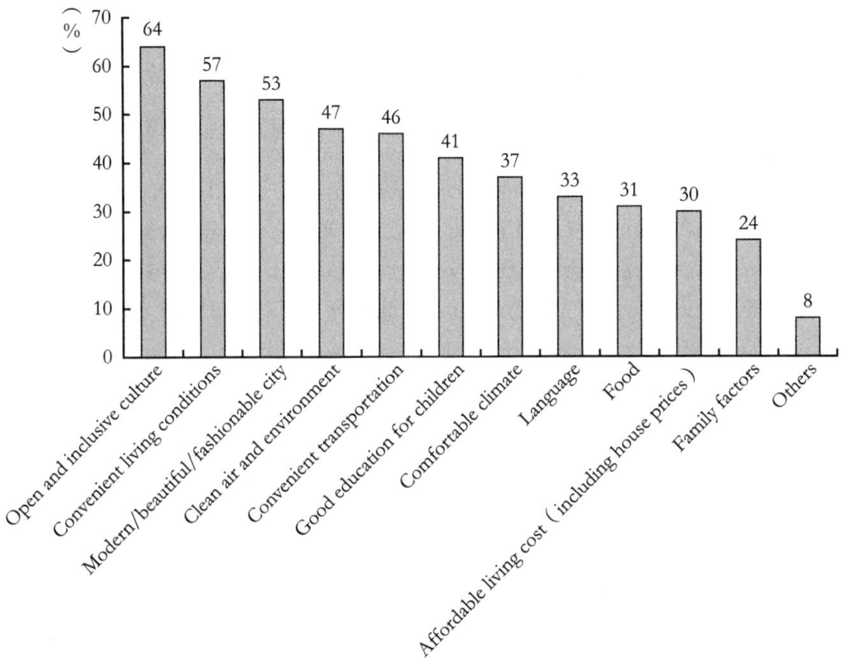

Figure 2 Main Considerations of Scientists When Choosing an Ideal City to Live in, as Indicated in the Survey

Source: Shanghai Institute for Science of Science. "2018 Survey Report on the "Ideal Cities" for Global Scientists" [R]. October, 29, 2018.

On the whole, Guangzhou gathers about 70% of the universities, research institutes and key laboratories at national, provincial and departmental levels in Guangdong Province. It has one of the most developed higher education systems in China, plus an open and inclusive culture and convenient living conditions, which makes it the most likely ideal city for scientists in the Guangdong-Hong Kong-Macau Greater Bay Area. Therefore, to be an ideal city for scientists in the

Guangdong-Hong Kong-Macau Greater Bay Area should be an important goal in the construction of Guangzhou as a technological, educational and cultural center. With the main considerations of global scientists when choosing the cities to work and live in as benchmark, Guangzhou should define priorities, improve weak links, and make up for deficiencies. First, it should continue to boost its comprehensive competitiveness in higher education. Taking advantage of the status as the provincial capital and educational resources, it should launch the "Four Batches" project that is intended to promote a batch of high-quality secondary specialized schools to junior colleges, a batch of high-quality junior colleges to undergraduate colleges, a batch of high-quality undergraduate colleges to be universities, and a batch of high-quality universities and disciplines to be first-class universities and first-class disciplines in the world. Second, Guangzhou should strive to build a world-class scientific research platform and to create superior scientific research infrastructure conditions, an inclusive innovation system environment and an open and inclusive urban cultural environment. It should also continue to maintain a relatively reasonable housing price level and establish a sound service system that offers convenience to the work and life of talents. It should try to attract innovative and creative scientists from all over the world and become a base that pools international talents and innovation. Third, the Canton Tower Science & Technology Conference should be made into an annual event for the global scientific and technological community, a high-level dialogue platform around global technology, industry and capital, and a press conference of global new sciences, new technologies, new products and various innovation indexes, innovation standards and innovation reports that will enhance Guangzhou's reputation and visibility in the global urban system of technological innovation centers. Fourth, Sino-Singapore Guangzhou Knowledge City and Guangzhou Science City should serve as models in comprehensive innovation reform and intellectual property rights protection. Guangzhou should take the lead in exploring the institutional environment, policy environment and business environment favourable to technological innovation, fostering professional, internationalized and branded science and technology service agencies and organizations, and establishing an influential market for transformation of technological innovation and scientific research knowledge that turns innovation into real value. Fifth, Guangzhou should strengthen international cooperation in technological innovation with a global vision and build a sound national technological innovation cooperation network. By "going out" and "bringing in", it should seek to build new scientific research institutions, carry out scientific and technological projects, and organize technological innovation activities with international partners to attract more attention and time of world-class brains and high-level experts.

(II) Explore the Integration of Technological Innovation and Business Culture by Referring to the Development Model of the Silicon Alley in New York

Guangzhou has a profound historical and cultural background, but its cultural industry and especially the cultural and creative industries are relatively backward. The prevalence of business culture does not well activate the innovation culture and innovative genes in the entire city. However, as the new round of scientific and technological revolution boosts the development of new technologies, new industries, new business types and new models in the future, they will provide new opportunities of exploring innovative development modes, promoting the integration of technological innovation and business culture, and activating the development of business culture in Guangzhou. In fact, in the list of unicorn companies that have been born in China in recent years, most of those from Guangzhou are specialized in e-commerce, software applications, culture and entertainment, and epitomize the unique development model of "technology + business + culture". The listed unicorn companies from Shenzhen, which is also located in the Guangdong-Hong Kong-Macau Greater Bay Area, are mostly specialized in hardware and finance, and epitomize another new development model of "technology + hardware + finance". In fact, the two development models adopted by Guangzhou and Shenzhen respectively share many similarities with the "East Coast Model" represented by the Silicon Alley and the "West Coast Model" represented by the Silicon Valley.

In the future, based on their respective strengths, Shenzhen will refer to the development model of the Silicon Valley while Guangzhou is likely to refer to that of the Silicon Alley from the Guangdong-Hong Kong-Macau Greater Bay Area. Guangzhou will pay more attention to the application of new technologies and focus on the combination of new Internet technologies with fashion, media, commerce, culture and service industries. It will vigorously develop Internet

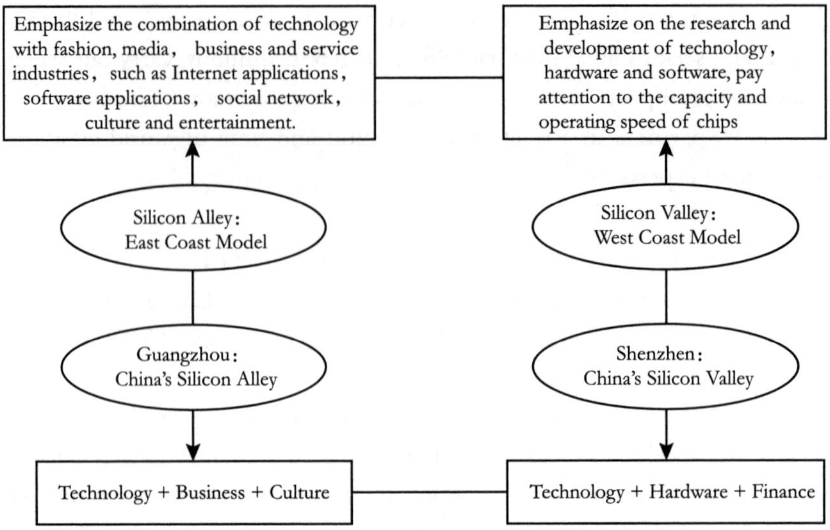

Figure 3 Integration of Technological Innovation and Business Culture by Referring to the Development Model of the Silicon Alley

applications, software applications, social network, culture, entertainment and e-commerce, promote deep integration of technological innovation and business culture, and create new economic development models with Guangzhou characteristics. In order to better tap this new development model, it is essential to seize the opportunity of the construction of Guangdong-Hong Kong-Macau Greater Bay Area to cooperate with Hong Kong and Shenzhen. Guangzhou is deeply penetrated by a business culture, Hong Kong has a unique fashion and creative culture, while Shenzhen boasts of a dynamic and innovative culture. Thus, Guangzhou may attract giants from the cultural industries in Hong Kong and Shenzhen to build a number of high-level demonstration parks in deep integration of culture and technology, facilitate the superposition of different types of cultures from the three places, and inject innovative factors into its business culture.

Guangzhou should ride the wave of the "Internet +" and explore the founding of "Internet Technology University of China". It should focus on the development and application of the Internet technology to support the deep integration of the Internet, big data, artificial intelligence and the real economy and the creation of "China's Silicon Alley" by training talents, nurturing industries and promoting transformation of scientific results. To form scale advantages through accumulation, it should carefully tap and foster a number of leading enterprises and unicorn companies in the fields of Internet applications, software applications, social network, culture and entertainment, and e-commerce. It should also draw on international advanced experience, actively explore the "sandbox" supervision model, create a more tolerant and liberal environment for the new economy, new business types and new models emerging from the integration of technological innovation and business culture, and build a testing ground and demonstration zone for the integration of technology, business and culture in the Guangdong-Hong Kong-Macau Greater Bay Area.

(IV) Learn from the Famous Innovation Districts in the World and Incorporate Technology, Education and Culture into the Development of the Central Urban Area Again

In 2014, the Brookings Institution of the United States released a research report titled *The Rise of Innovation Districts*, in which the concept of "Innovation District" was first introduced. According to the report, innovation districts built by integrating elements of economic activities in innovative enterprises, educational institutions, financial institutions, multiculturalism, and consumer services via convenient transportation and the Internet environment in the high-density central urban area can be an important feasible solution for the revitalization of the central urban area. The concept of innovation district, following its birth, has been put into practice in many foreign cities. The Silicon Roundabout in London, the Kendall Square in Cambridge, the Harbour Plaza in Boston, and the South Lake in the Seattle were all examples of successful innovation districts. [3]

To promote the rejuvenation of old city, a key task is to accelerate the renovation of the old urban quarter and inject new vitality. By drawing on international advanced experience, combining this task with the goal of building an ideal city for scientists in the Guangdong-Hong Kong-Macau Greater Bay Area, and making use of the convenient conditions for work and living in the downtown area, Guangzhou may build a number of high-level innovation districts, creative districts, entrepreneurial districts, cultural districts, and historical districts with distinctive features and meeting high standards. It may also plan to build distinctive laboratories, SME incubators, research facilities, design offices and studios. The purpose is to integrate technological innovation with history and culture, promote spatial renewal and transformation and the expansion of new economic spaces, incorporate innovation to the central urban area again, and support the spatial transformation and functional improvement of the old urban quarter.

By drawing on the experience of the international innovation districts, Guangzhou may start from details in exploring the construction of innovation districts. Firstly, it should promote the renovation of infrastructures, such as roads, pipelines and parks, in the central urban area, especially in the old urban quarter, cover all the public spaces with 5G signals, and provide high-speed free Wi-Fi. Secondly, it should design and construct a number of open and open-air offices and venues for innovative activities, projecting technological innovation conceptualized indoors onto public spaces in the city, and introduce distinctive technological interfaces that make technology visible to all and create an innovative atmosphere. Thirdly, it should explore and transform inefficient or deteriorating urban spaces, retain and inject fashionable breath to historical customs and cultural heritage, and build some design offices, creative bookstores, cafes and mini-bars where creative workers communicate with each other and get inspired. Fourthly, given the large number of flyovers in the city, Guangzhou should learn from the Down Under the Manhattan-Brooklyn Bridge Overpass and make use of spaces under bridges in the central urban area through micro-renovation and functional development so that they will be windows and pools of city culture and technology trends [4].

References:

[1] Yuan Bo and He Xianyun. "Research and Reference of German Dual-System Vocational Education" *Education and Teaching Forum*, 2009 (1).

[2] Fan Ruiping. "Accelerate the Construction of a Famous Cultural City with Unique Humanistic Charm in the World" *Guangming Daily*, January 14, 2019.

[3] Deng Zhituan. "On Innovation Square: Concept, Motive Force and Development Path" *Urban Studies*, 2017 (8).

[4] Qin Jian. "Research on the Function Development and Governance of Space under Bridge in City" *Construction Economy*, 2019 (5).

B.7

National Central City Construction of Chongqing: New Progress, Main Features and Development Trend

*Peng Jinsong, Zhu Xusen and Lu Fei**

Abstract: In 2018, Chongqing's GDP topped RMB 2 trillion, entering a new stage of development. However, due to the intertwining effects of internal factors and the external environment, it ushered in a critical period that witnessed the falling of growth rate to bottom, transformation of development mode and deep structural adjustment. Bearing important missions and responsibilities in national strategies deployed by the Central Government, Chongqing should give full play to its comprehensive integration advantages and continuously promote high-quality development.

Keywords: development status; four cycles; four advantages

In the central and western regions, Chongqing is the only municipality directly under the Central Government and a national central city. In 2018, in spite of the complicated international situation, Chongqing clung to the overall direction of seeking improvement in stability, continuing to promote the supply-side structural

* Peng Jinsong: Deputy Director of Urban Development Institute, Chongqing Academy of Social Sciences, Director and Research Fellow of Chongqing Research Center of Urban Promotion Strategy; Zhu Xusen, Associate Researcher of Chongqing Academy of Social Sciences; Lu Fei, Associate Researcher of Chongqing Academy of Social Sciences.

reform and concentrating efforts on the "Eight Action Plans". Approaching from rural revitalization and urban upgrading, its efforts to actively advance high-quality construction of national central city paid off with new results.

I Development Status and Foundation

(I) Economic Development

In 2018, Chongqing's GDP topped RMB 2 trillion and was measured at RMB 2.036319 trillion, an increase of 6.0%. The double-digit high-speed growth rate that had sustained for many years was replaced by a single-digit growth rate, which was lower than the national average for the first time. A critical period that witnessed the falling of growth rate to bottom, transformation of development mode and deep structural adjustment has arrived. By industry, the tertiary industry registered the fastest growth rate at 9.1%, while the secondary industry had a growth rate of 4.4% and the figure for the primary industry was 3.0%. The three-industry structural ratio was 6.8:40.9:52.3.

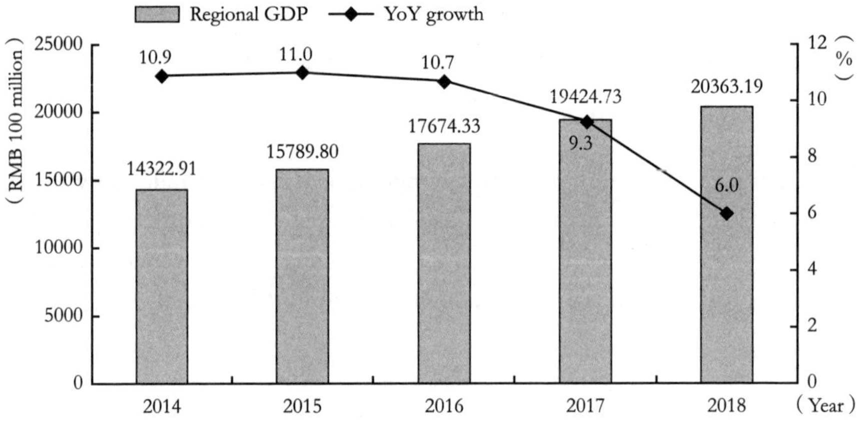

Figure 1 Chongqing's GDP and Growth Rate for 2014-2018

In 2018, Chongqing's fixed asset investment increased by 7.0% on a year-on-year basis. The investments in the secondary and tertiary industries maintained stability and steady progress and increased by 7.3% and 7.4%, respectively. In contrast, the investment in the primary industry experienced a negative growth. By field, industry and infrastructure remained important forces supporting the city's fixed asset investment. As its investment and business service environment continued to improve, Chongqing showed good private investment performance, of which the annual growth rate reached 12.8%, 5.8 percentage points higher than the total investment growth rate of the city and accounting for more than half of the total investment.

In 2018, the foreign trade of Chongqing rose against the deteriorating external trade environment. Its imports and exports amounted to RMB 522.262 billion, equal to a year-on-year increase of 15.9% and marking a good growth level in recent years. Owing to its active measures to attract foreign investors, its annual foreign direct investment (FDI) was USD 3.25 billion, an increase of 43.8%, which was the largest growth rate in the central and western regions and the ninth largest in the country.

In 2018, the consumer market in Chongqing maintained moderate and stable. The total retail volume of social consumer goods increased by 8.7% compared with the last year. As Internet infrastructures and service platforms were built and improved, the online retail industry developed rapidly and grew more than three times faster than the traditional retail industry. The e-commerce transaction volume exceeded RMB 1.1 trillion, and the cross-border e-commerce imports, exports and settlements exceeded RMB 20 billion.

(II) Industrial Construction

In 2018, the industrial added value of Chongqing reached RMB 599.77 billion, a year-on-year increase of 1.1%. There was a sharp contrast between two groups of key pillar industries in the city as "seven of them grew and two declined". The seven growing industries were electronics, equipment, chemical, pharmaceutical, materials, consumer goods and energy, which increased by 13.6%, 4.8%, 1.5%, 9.3%, 11.0%, 1.9%, and 1.7%, respectively. As the first pillar industries contributing to industrial development, the automobile and motorcycle industries showed a downward trend. The added value of the automobile industry decreased by 17.3%, and that of the motorcycle industry decreased by 0.3%. New driving forces of industrial development developed with good momentum. Both high-tech industries and strategic emerging industries grew faster than traditional industries. Industrial enterprises above designated size became the main sources of R&D investments, which approximated RMB 32 billion, up 13.9%.

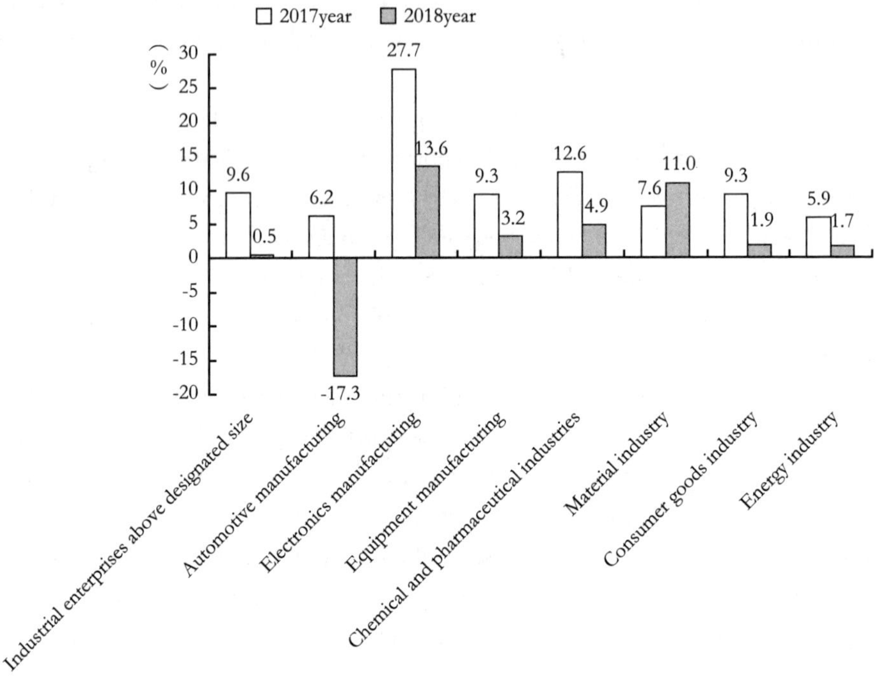

Figure 2 Comparison of Growth Rates among Pillar Industries in Chongqing for 2017-2018

In order to maintain the stability and continuity of industrial development, Chongqing intensified the structural adjustment and optimization of the automobile industry, gathered strength to quicken its transformation and upgrading, and introduced the "1+2" policy system that cast the initial shape of a new energy automobile industry system with relatively reasonable product structure. It was composed of 9 passenger car enterprises including Changan Automobile, 3 coach enterprises including Hengtong, and 5 special-purpose car enterprises including Isuzu. With a view to the development of complete vehicle industry, Chongqing also lent strong support to more than 30 producers of core components that had strong market competitiveness.

Chongqing actively extended towards the two ends of R&D and market application in the manufacturing industry and built a value chain ecosystem that ran through the entire industry. For R&D purposes, a number of new energy vehicle testing and inspection agencies with strong innovation capabilities were founded, such as China Automotive Research Institute and Chongqing Vehicle Test Institute. Concerning commercial applications, online ride hailing and time-sharing car lease brands such as Changan Travel and Pand-auto were developed from the existing complete vehicle manufacturing advantages of Changan Automobile and Lifan Motors. Statistics showed that a total of 15,146 new energy vehicles were produced in Chongqing from January to April, 2019, which marked an increase of 32.6% over the same period of previous year; the production of intelligent networked vehicles was 50,600, which marked an increase of 10%.

The intelligent manufacturing industry was also an emerging growth point in the development of manufacturing industry in Chongqing. In 2018, the sales revenue of this industry amounted to RMB 464 billion, a year-on-year increase of 19.2%. The most fast growing products were robots and smart phones.

(III) Opening to the Outside World

Chongqing has continuously improved its infrastructure to serve for its opening up to the outside world, upgraded the major channel used for outbound logistics, and pushed the construction of inland open base to a new level.

Firstly, an open platform system was formed. Jiangjin Comprehensive Bonded Zone and Guoyuangang Bonded Logistics Center (Type B) were approved. Yongchuan and Rongchang in the western part of Chongqing were elevated to national high-tech industry development zones. There were 18 platform systems of various types mainly in the Liangjiang New Area and 4 state-level open ports that were designated ports for 9 types of special imported goods. The total import and export volume of these major open platforms accounted for more than 80% of the total volume in the city, and their FDI accounted for more than 70% of the total. They have become the main forces in the open development of the city.

Secondly, an overall open channel was further expanded. Based on the unique advantage of being located in the junction of the "Belt and Road" and the Yangtze River Economic Belt, Chongqing coordinated a variety of transportation modes such as railway, highway, air and waterway to vigorously develop multi-modal transport and built an overall all-directional, three-dimensional open channel. The southward channel is supported by the "New International Land-Sea Trade Corridor" for Sino-Singapore interconnection, and multi-modal trains like railway, sea and highway have been put into operation. The westward channel is supported by the China-Europe train and the construction of network system, with more than 3,000 trains put into operation on an accumulated basis and more than 40 foreign distribution points built in countries like Germany and Russia. The eastward channel mainly relies on the golden waterway of the Yangtze River, and the northward channel has the China-Mongolia-Russia economic corridor under construction. The air corridor is backed by the construction of international aviation hub.

Thirdly, new progress was made in the construction of an international business environment. Chongqing deepened the construction of "a single window" that serves international trade, and the benefits cover 100% of customs inspection and clearance zones. It also deepened 7×24 customs clearance services, accelerated the construction of smart ports, shortened the overall customs import and export clearance time by half, and was the first city to perform nine innovative functions like online international settlement and whole-process traceability of imported medical equipment. It accelerated the construction of pilot free trade zone and explored a series of institutional innovations in investment, trade, finance, interim-and post-supervision and land borne trade rules. The projects of pilot automobile parallel importing and of deepening innovative development of service trade were approved. The commercial system reform resulted in "31-certificates-in-one" and shorted the approval time for business startup within 5 working days. New progress was made in the construction of the pilot free trade zone, which has attracted well-known domestic Internet companies like Baidu, Alibaba and Tencent to set up their regional headquarters. There were 287 Fortune Global 500 companies in Chongqing, 8 of which were newcomers compared with 2017.

II Development Environment

(I) Superposition of Four Cycles Led to Declining Growth Rates

In 2018, the growth rates of major economic indicators such as industry, investment, consumption and output in Chongqing were lower than expected. Subjectively, delay and failure in the adjustment of industrial technology structure were to blame. Objectively, the complicated international and domestic macroeconomic changes were culprits. It was, in a nutshell, the result of industry, technology, finance and population cycles intertwined in time and space and the combination of effects from the external great environment and the local microclimate.

1. Pillar industries had come to the "end point" of the shrinking stage in the global industrial development cycle. Automobile manufacturing and electronics manufacturing took up half of the industry and were the two driving wheels of industrial development in Chongqing. The automobile industry, in particular, had a long industrial chain and a lasting history. It has been the traditional advantageous industry in Chongqing for a long time. In 2018, the growth rate of the automobile industry was-17.3%, and that of the electronic information industry fell back to 13.6%, putting an end to the several fold growth rates that had sustained over the past few years. The falling growth rates of these two pillar industries seriously dragged down the already slow growth of industries.

According to statistics, the automobile sales in China totaled 28.08 million in 2018, down 2.8% from the previous year. This was the first decline suffered by the automobile sales market of China. The production and sales volume of passenger cars, which accounted for 85% of those in the automobile industry, also fell by 5.2% and 4.1%, respectively. In fact, as more and more Chinese families afforded to own a car, the recession of the traditional automobile industry worldwide has been doomed since 2016. The automobile industry of Chongqing simply enjoys quantity and scale advantages in the national market competition. Statistics showed that the single vehicle value in the Chongqing market was about RMB 80,000, converted to tax revenue of about RMB 6,000. It was far lower than the national averages of RMB 140,000 and RMB 18,000, respectively. The output of new energy vehicles accounted for 1.9%, which was lower than the national average (2.7%). Changan Ford and CCAG, two major automobile producers in Chongqing, suffered declining production and sales in 2018, which pulled down the industrial output of the city by at least 3 percentage points. Suzuki, BAIC Yinxiang and Lifan were under the stage of deep adjustment, while commercial vehicle companies like Isuzu and SAIC Hongyan grew slowly and played weaker supporting role. The automobile industry, as a pillar industry in Chongqing, was indeed trapped in a hard time.

2. The global technological development cycle stalled at "breakpoint" during the increasing marginal process. With the advent of the fourth industrial science and technology revolution, a large number of new technologies, new business types, new industries, and new models have been widely applied in the economic world. It has also promoted industries to become high-end, intelligent, intensive, service-oriented and globalized. To promote the development of new driving forces for industries, Chongqing, first of all, must focus on the development of "hard technology" industries that master core technologies in China instead of merely "soft technology" industries such as business model innovation.

With R&D as an indicator of innovation input, R&D investment accounted for 1.95% of Chongqing's GDP in 2018, which was far lower than the percentages in first-tier cities such as Beijing, Shanghai and Shenzhen, as well as in provincial capitals such as Wuhan, Xi'an, Nanjing and Hangzhou. Chongqing had only one unicorn company listed among the national ranking, a type of business that represents a city's innovative vitality, lagging seriously behind some cities in developed city clusters along the Pearl River Delta and the Yangtze River Delta. The technology development structure of Chongqing has come to a "break point". Large traditional industrial technologies grow very slowly as a variable. New strategic technologies nurtured in the new technological revolution are still in infancy and have not formed a scale advantage as a cluster. This new technological revolution of Industry 4.0 completely subverts the development path dependent on traditional technologies. As the new technological revolution paradigm prevails, both the weak and the strong will find their fate change. The conversion between advantages and disadvantages is not completely based on the original economic and technological structure. Even some disadvantages may be converted to advantages, while traditional advantages turn out to be obstacles in the new technology era. Chongqing has not been well integrated into this technological revolution that is under the increasing marginal process.

3. The corporate thirty for capital coincided with the "game point" of structural de-leverage in the financial development cycle in China. Over the past two years, steady progress has been made in the prevention and mitigation of financial risks intended to promote structural de-leverage and ensure financial stability, and substantial results have been achieved. Data showed that the broad money supply M2 fell from a multi-year double-digit high growth rate to 8% in 2017 and 2018, approaching the GDP growth rate. The "gap" between the two rates was greatly reduced; at the same time, the YoY growth rate of social financing scale inventory came to a level around 10%, which was 4.6 percentage points lower than the high level in early 2017.

All the signs showed that the battle to fight against financial systemic risks and curb expanding financial bubble in the real economy of China has come to the critical "game point", and phased substantial achievements have been made in the de-leveraging of financial structure. During this period, banks tightened their on-balance sheet credits and strengthened risk prevention and control. However, some enterprises in Chongqing tasted the "bitterness" of inadequate liquidity backup because they did not have sufficient mortgage ability and credit level, although they had a desperate "thirsty" for capital in the current transformation and takeoff period. Research found that private enterprises in Chongqing generally find that formal financing channels can hardly satisfy their great production needs for short-term liquid funds. Difficulty and high cost entailed by financing endeavors affect the production and operation of enterprises.

(II) Four Major Advantages Consolidated the Foundation for Sustainable Development

In the new era, Chongqing is faced with the transformation and development challenge, but it also receives a new round of strong support at the state level. It should systematically integrate the four unique advantages in location, ecology, industry and system with system thinking and innovative thinking to fully promote the high-quality development as a national central city.

1. Chongqing has an irreplaceable location advantage. The Belt and Road Initiative involves 71 countries, whose combined economic output accounts for about 18% of the world's total GDP. Promoting joint efforts in the construction of "Belt and Road" and establishing a new cooperation mechanism for achieving

shared benefits through extensive consultation and joint contribution are not only a basic policy supporting China's opening up to the outside world, but also an important part of the continuous advancement and deepening of the reform. Chongqing is at a strategic link between the "Belt and Road" and the Y-shaped layout of the Yangtze River Economic Belt. It plays a unique and important role in advancing the Western Development Strategy and building a balanced inland and coastal development pattern. Especially as the New International Land-Sea Trade Corridor is constructed and rises to be a national strategy, Chongqing's location advantage will be even more prominent. Chongqing should make full use of its unique and irreplaceable location advantage to strengthen the construction of major channels, ports and platforms. Standing as an international logistics hub, it should strive to build a major channel extending to all directions towards Europe, Southeast Asia, the Indo-China Peninsula, the Russian Far East, and Mongolia. It should create an open major port where personnel flow, logistics, business flow, capital flow and information flow gather and distribute. This is what it can do to lead, drive and make new contributions to the development and opening up of the western inland areas.

2. Chongqing has a distinct and unique ecological advantage. Chongqing is located in the upper reaches of the Yangtze River, where a strip-shaped reservoir with a length of more than 600km, as part of the Three Gorges Dam Project, is situated in Chongqing. To protect the Mother River, Chongqing is responsible for the upstream ecological environmental protection, which is related to the overall picture of national ecological security development. In the national central city construction, Chongqing can make full use of the unique natural resources to enhance the city's quality and urban environment and create a beautiful view of the city surrounded by mountains and rivers. It should try to make mountains clearer, waters greener, the sky bluer, and the air fresher. It should fully highlight ecological livability, greenness and low carbon, and sustainable development in the construction of national central city. While building an important ecological barrier in the upper reaches of the Yangtze River, Chongqing should continue to integrate ecological resources in ecological economy and strive to develop ecological products incorporated in sustainable recycling, which can greatly facilitate the optimization of development environment and enhance the city's competitiveness in sustainable development.

3. Chongqing has a strong industrial advantage. Chongqing has developed

into an important industrial city in the upper reaches of the Yangtze River over a history of nearly one hundred years. It is now moving towards an important modern manufacturing base in the country. Chongqing boasts of complete industries, relatively sound industrial infrastructures, and a solid manufacturing foundation. Of the 41 industrial categories available in the country, 39 complete ones are developed in Chongqing. In particular, the electronic information industry and the automobile manufacturing industry have formed two major manufacturing clusters as a result of long-term industrial changes and adjustments. In spite of the recent declining growth rate, the outputs of these two industries still secure relatively important positions both nationally and internationally. In addition, located near mountains and reservoirs, Chongqing also has abundant agricultural resources. The modern high-efficiency agriculture specific to mountainous areas and eco-tourism in Chongqing will benefit from important growth potential under the context of rural revitalization.

III Countermeasures and Suggestions

(I) Further Optimize the Regional Spatial Layout

Chongqing should further optimize the spatial layout of its urban area in combination with the ongoing construction of the metropolitan area in the main urban district. The plan is to erect a framework of the metropolitan area consisting of "one core, two deputy centers and multiple centers" in the main urban district. Firstly, increase and strengthen the scale and volume of the core of the metropolitan area in the main urban district by incorporating the whole Bishan district in the west and Shuangfu New Area in Jiangjin into the main urban district and extending the main urban district westward until it crosses Zhongliang Mountain and further Jinyun Mountain. This will further upgrade the spatial framework of Chongqing for the national central city construction. Meanwhile, the traditional spatial pattern of "four mountains surrounding three valleys" in the main urban district will be changed into "five mountains surrounding four valleys". That means five south-north roughly parallel urban mountains, i.e. Mingyue Mountain, Tongluo Mountain, Zhongliang Mountain,

Jinyun Mountain and Yunwu Mountain, will surround four urban valleys from east to west. The geological eastern, central and western parts of the metropolitan area in the main urban district will be redefined conceptually. The eastern, central and western parts of the new main urban district should be geologically divided into: Longxing-Yufu-Chayuan-Lujiao Valley in the east; Xiyong-University Town-Jinfeng-Baishiyi Valley and the traditional Central Valley in the center; Bishan Valley in the west. Secondly, build two deputy urban centers in the eastern and western wings of the metropolitan area of the main urban district. The eastern deputy urban center is Yongchuan, which will be the "bridgehead" for the cooperation of the Chengdu-Chongqing city cluster, while the western deputy urban center is Fuling, which will be the "relay station" to radiate the effects of the core area to southeastern and northeastern Chongqing. Thirdly, encourage small and medium-sized cities in other non-core areas to pursue collaborative and integrated development in line with their own characteristics. Fourthly, accelerate the collaboration between Sichuan and Guizhou Provinces at city, district, county and township levels and encourage active integration into the metropolitan areas around the main urban districts so as to promote the high-quality integration process of Chengdu-Chongqing city cluster. Fifthly, speed up the construction of infrastructures to improve the operational efficiency of the metropolitan area. Accelerate the planning and construction of subways, intercity rail services and suburban trains, build a network-like rail transit system in the metropolitan area as soon as possible, speed up the construction and deployment of urban smart facilities, and promote the application of public services such as smart transportation, smart education and smart communities.

(II) Build a Complete Modern Industry System

Intensify the transformation and upgrading of advantageous industries such as the automobile industry, increase the R&D investments in intelligent manufacturing and Internet technology as two starters, improve the product quality and brand connotation of the automobile industry, strengthen the quality and level of vehicle manufacturing, and accelerate R&D and market launch of mid-and high-end automobile products. Continue to enhance the technical content of traditional motorcycles, constantly improve their quality while reducing the production, focus on making breakthroughs in sport and recreational motorcycle products, and increase their share in the high-end market. Improve the independent manufacturing capacity of key automobile assemblies such as parts, engine systems and transmission systems in Chongqing. Increase the concentration of the automobile industry in the whole city through mergers and acquisitions, and shape an industrial layout led by 2 to 3 large-scale automobile producers. Strongly develop the basic equipment manufacturing industry to fit the key areas and key needs of national economic construction. As for traditional equipment, focus on the rail transit equipment industry in view of the ongoing development of rail transit. Given the promotion and application of new energies and the increasingly important ecological environmental protection, actively develop energy-saving, environmental protection and new energy equipment industries with leading technological advantages. Try to introduce and cultivate an aerospace equipment industry to catch up with the development of the aerospace industry. Vigorously develop intelligent manufacturing equipment and strive to improve the development capability and level of key basic parts under the context of the digitalization and intelligent transformation of traditional industries. Hold on to new strategic opportunities from a new round of scientific and technological revolution and industrial transformation in the world. On the basis of a large-scale electronic information industry that has taken shape in the early stage, actively extend it further towards integrated circuits, new displays, intelligent terminals, smart sensors and instrumentation, and build an intelligent industry cluster that embraces "chips, LCD panels, smart terminals, core components, and Internet of Things". Actively develop new industries such as new energy vehicles, biomedicine, new materials, and energy-saving and environmental protection. Promote aerospace, communication manufacturing, digital mapping and geographic information industries under the guidance of the *Action Plan for the Military-Civilian Integration Development Strategy*, and build a national-level demonstration base for transformation of military-civilian integration industrial technologies. Expand the digital economy and the digital industry, build a research institute of digital economy, and strengthen the utilization of digital resources.

(III) Quicken the Development and Opening up Attempts

Accelerate the construction of international channels in "water, land, air, and information highway", encrypt the route network, upgrade channel level, build a fully open transportation system that connects South Asia, Central Asia and Europe, and form a pattern in which the "Belt and Road", the New International Land-Sea Trade Corridor and the Yangtze River Economic Belt integrate in Chongqing. Construct an international information portal hub, set up an international offshore data center and an onshore data center, and develop an international data reserve, distribution and application system. Accelerate the construction of internal and external opening platforms, and explore and strengthen cooperation with countries involved in the Belt and Road Initiative and the New International Land-Sea Trade Corridor based on the construction of platforms like industrial parks, enclaves, development zones and free trade ports. Enhance the convenience of opening up, promote the connectivity between the electronic port in Chongqing with the "Belt and Road" and the New International Land-Sea Trade Corridor, maintain information exchange and business coordination in logistics, customs clearance and inspection, and improve the integration, traceability and timeliness of "a single customs window". Deeply integrate into the construction of global industrial chain, and develop an economy that is driven by both domestic demand and export. On the one hand, accelerate the development of modern service industries and strategic emerging industries towards the high ends of industrial chain and value chain, and build an inland service trade center and an advanced manufacturing base. On the other hand, vigorously promote the upgrading of traditional manufacturing industries and develop an export-oriented economy targeted at markets such as ASEAN and Central Asia by making use of geographical and transportation advantages and relying on the technology accumulation, manufacturing capabilities and supporting systems of traditional industries. Introduce international trade as soon as possible, optimize and develop the processing trade and general trade, apply innovation to the development of service trade, and cultivate an inland industrial cluster of international trade. Strengthen international cultural exchanges and cooperation, and take the initiative to undertake major influential international exchange activities in the fields of culture, tourism, exhibition, science and technology, and transportation.

(IV) Strive to Improve the Ecological Quality

Keep improving the ecological, production and living spaces of the city under the new regional development pattern of "one metropolitan area and two city clusters", and promote rational allocation of regional ecological resources and production factors. Solidly propel the governance of "two rivers and four banks" in the main urban district and the protection of the "four mountains", concentrate efforts to build an ecological network system that highlights the characteristics of Chongqing as a city situated amid mountains and rivers, organically combine the beautiful scenery of the city with its culture and livability. Provide urban ecological quality and living quality comparable to international levels. Build urban walkways that reflect the cultural characteristics of a mountainous city, and build community-based sports and cultural parks in different marginal land parcels and idle places in the city to beautify the urban environment. Facilitate the construction of urban public transportation, increase the coverage of urban rail to new towns and new districts, advocate the use of public transportation, and reduce urban carbon emissions and traffic congestion. Propel the construction of demonstration sponge city, promote green and energy-saving building technologies and materials, reduce urban consumption, and promote the disposal of municipal waste by classification. Accelerate the construction of green ecological corridor along the Yangtze River, and build a series of visible ecological landmarks such as Guangyang Island and other urban ecological islands, as well as the scenery zone along the Yangtze River. Strive to increase forest coverage and urban green coverage, build more intensive, human-oriented and dynamic new blocks that manifest the unique charm of Chongqing as a beautiful city amid mountains and waters, and finally build it into an international city that satisfy both local and migrant people with its cultural temperament and special landscape.

(V) Establish an Internationalized Cultural Image

Chongqing should improve its inner quality and spirit, deeply explore and inherit its historical heritage, continuously improve its spiritual temperament, and consolidate a cultural foundation with international quality. It should strongly support influential cultural construction projects with local characteristics, such as the Bayu culture, the anti-Japanese war culture and the Three Gorges immigrant culture on the way to becoming a lively, vigorous, positive, elegant, civilized and attractive city. It should intensify the collation and research of city culture, protect and make good use of outstanding historical buildings within its scope, inherit and enrich the historical and cultural heritages. Chongqing should also protect its unique natural conditions and special buildings, create an undulating, smooth, multi-level and three-dimensional city landscape in which natural environment is perfectly combined with buildings, and exert fine urban management to make the city more graceful and stylish. It should improve the city image, regulate the city appearance, improve the quality of citizens, staff and services, and enhance the quality, responsibility and impartiality of law enforcement and administrative personnel. By taking the opportunities of national civilized city and hygienic city construction, it should continuously increase the humanistic quality and knowledge of citizens and become a learning city and a learning society.

B.8

National Central City Construction of Chengdu: Progress, Achievements and Outlook

Luo Ruoyu and Yang Jing

Abstract: 2018 witnessed the full implementation of various actions for economic and social development in Chengdu. Positioned as "five centers and one hub" in central city construction, Chengdu steadily promoted the national central city construction and made new breakthroughs in enhancing urban vitality, promoting the development of new economy, and improving the business environment and the ecological environment, which were all highlighted characteristics of Chengdu over the development process. However, Chengdu is still hindered by weak economic strength, poor radiating role as a "main trunk" city, insufficient supply factors for innovation, huge traffic congestion pressure, and unbalanced sharing of development benefits in its national central city construction. In the future, Chengdu should focus on improving its economic strength, promoting regional integration development, increasing investments in innovation factors, rationally planning the urban transportation system, and enhancing people's sense of well-being.

Keywords: Chengdu; central city construction; high-quality development; regional coordination

I Progress in the National Central City Construction of Chengdu

National central cities are the "spire cities" in regional development that bear the mission and function of national development. In 2018, Chengdu was still positioned as "an important center of economy, science and technology, finance, culture and creativity, and foreign relations, and as an integrated transportation hub" in the national central city construction. In this process, it made sound development achievements in the development of new economy, nurturing of new technologies, growth of "Jiaozi Finance", advancement of "Six Famous Cities", an increase of opening up.

(I) Results from the Construction of Chengdu as an Economic Center in 2018

In 2018, guided by the new development concept, Chengdu made steady progress in economic development. All the economic indicators met or exceeded the targets set at the beginning of the year. The regional GDP exceeded RMB 1.5 trillion and was measured at RMB 1.534277 trillion, up 8% over the previous year and 1.4 percentage points higher than the national GDP. The total fixed assets investment amounted to RMB 834.11 billion, equal to a year-on-year increase of 10%. The public budget income was RMB 142.42 billion, equal to a year-on-year increase of 9.4%. The total retail volume of social consumer goods reached RMB 680.18 billion, equal to a year-on-year increase of 10%. The price rise remained stable at the basic level.

At present, Chengdu exerts great efforts to develop economy and has established a "5+5+1" ① modern industry system. The added value of the five major advanced manufacturing industries increased by 10.8%, while that of the five new service industries increased by 9%. Meanwhile, new economy became a new growth point for the economic development of Chengdu. For

① 5+5+1: the first "5" refers to five advanced manufacturing industries: electronic information, equipment manufacturing, medical health, new materials, and green food; the second "5" refers to five emerging service industries: financial services, modern logistics, exhibition economy, cultural tourism, and life services; "1" refers to new economic industries represented by "artificial intelligence+, big data+, 5G+ clean energy+, and supply chain+".

the whole year, 41,000 new economic enterprises were registered and made outstanding contributions to economic development. In order to promote economic development, 66 industrial functional zones were established, operated as industrial clusters classified by division of labor in the five districts. The newly established "headquarters economy" model guided the layout of "R&D in Chengdu and manufacturing in Deyang and Mianyang" and accelerated the division of labor and cooperation between regions. The healthy development of the private economy was supported and yielded added value of RMB 746.479 billion, up 8.1% from the previous year and accounting for 48.7% of Chengdu's GDP. The private economy has become an important part of the city's economic development. (See Figure 1)

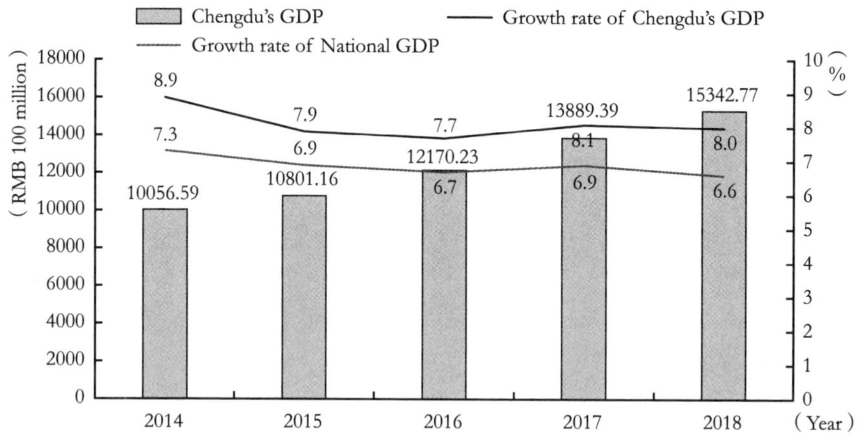

Figure 1 Chengdu's GDP and Its Growth Rate and Growth rate of National GDP for 2014-2018

(II) Results from the Construction of Chengdu as a Technological Center in 2018

In 2018, Chengdu remained committed to the goal of building itself into "the technological center" in the Western Region and followed closely the "industry-university-research" cooperation development direction. It increased the investment of scientific and technological innovation resources, built the foundation for innovative development, fostered new driving forces of innovation, and protected intellectual property rights for technological innovation and development. As a result, new results were produced in the city's technological innovation and development. Chengdu increased investments in technological innovation. The annual R&D investment increased by 12%. The number of invention patents owned by per 10,000 people increased by 15.8% to 22. There were 7 new national enterprise technology centers and 8 new industrial technology institutes. Chengdu provided 9 innovation reform experiences that could be copied nationwide. Its new achievement lists also included 1,200 industry, university and research platforms of various types, 491 completed Torch Programs, 935 technical breakthroughs, and 29 national technology awards. As a technological center, the numbers of patent applications and patent grants in Chengdu have increased year by year. In 2018, a total of 107,801 applications were accepted and 57,730 patents were granted. The total number of applications declined slightly, but the number of patent grants increased dramatically by 39.62% from the previous year. At the same time, Chengdu also established an intellectual property right trading center to protect achievements of scientific and technological innovations. Enterprises engaged in technological innovation developed rapidly. By the end of May 2019, there had been 2,703 small and medium-sized sci-tech enterprises, 3,112 high-tech enterprises and 53 technologically advanced service enterprises registered in Chengdu. For the whole year, 1,980 products of mass entrepreneurship and innovation, 2,234 scientific and technological achievements, and a cumulative technical transaction volume of RMB 397.8 billion were reported. In order to support the development of innovation and entrepreneurship, 691 service organizations, 289 carriers of various types, and 200 carriers of technological entrepreneurship and innovation were created; 28,645 entrepreneurial and innovation teams in enterprises were set up, which gathered 897 instructors. At the same time, Chengdu kept facilitating the development of university-enterprise alliances to realize joint innovation and development on a large scale. In order to encourage innovation and entrepreneurship, the government facilitated corporate financing by offering "technological innovation loans", "technological innovation investments", and "technological innovation vouchers". The accumulated credit loan distributed amounted to RMB 4.309 billion; the total investment reached RMB 644 million; the technological innovation vouchers offered offset RMB 5.2729 million of corporate financing. (See Figure 2)

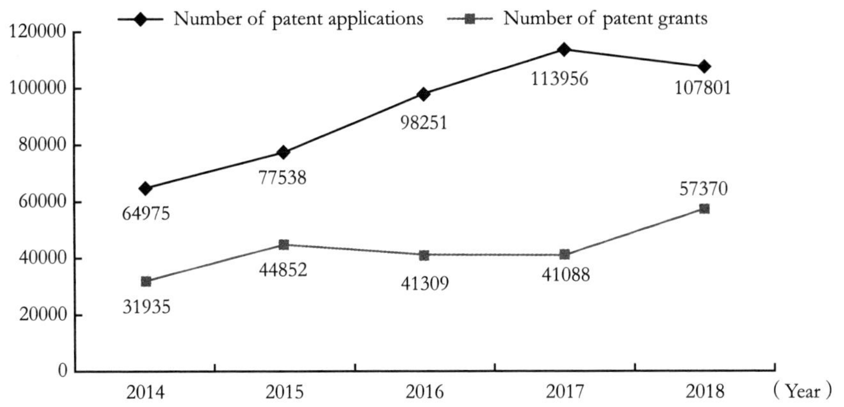

Figure 2 Numbers of Patent Applications and Patent Grants in Chengdu for 2014-2018

(III) Results from the Construction of Chengdu as a Financial Center in 2018

According to the "10th China Financial Center Index in 2018", the "2018 Tianfu Financial Index" and the "Global Financial Center Index", Chengdu's financial industry was ranked 6th in the country and 79th in the world. These rankings testified its remarkable development results. Meanwhile, new development trends could be observed in the construction of Chengdu as a financial center. Three major changes, from volume and scale to core functions, from traditional finance to new financial business types, and from self-adsorption to opening up and radiation, have occurred. Chengdu strengthened the five core functions of the financial industry in "capital market, wealth management, innovation investment and financing, financial settlement and new finance". The added value of its financial industry reached RMB 175.002 billion; the balance of local and foreign currency deposits was RMB 3.78257 trillion; the loan balance was RMB 3.26372 trillion. There were 11 new listed companies in the capital market, and the distributed bail-out funds totaled RMB 7.6 billion. The innovation investment and financing remained active, and the direct financing amount of the whole city reached RMB 360.92 billion and the cross-border settlement amount in RMB was 81.1 billion. More financial service institutions were put into service. By the end of 2018, there had been more than 2,500 financial institutions and service organizations of various types, 94 insurance institutions, 84 banking and financial institutions, 334 securities institutions, and more than 900 local financial institutions in Chengdu. At the same time, Chengdu concentrated on building six new financial industry ecosystems of "technology finance, consumer finance, rural finance, supply chain finance, green finance, and cultural finance" in a transition from traditional finance to new financial business types so as to better serve the new economy, the rural economy, and the cultural and creative industries. To further opening up and tap radiating effects, it became the first Chinese city to host the annual meeting of the board of governors of Inter-American Development Bank, signed cooperation agreements with Ziyang and Meishan, established an integrated financial service market, and strengthened international financial cooperation.

(IV) Results from the Construction of Chengdu as a Cultural and Creative Center in 2018

Culture is a unique mark of a city that carries its history and civilization. Culture and economy can complement each other, and intensive cultural innovation can add new vitality to economic development. In 2018, Chengdu took the crown in the *China's New Cultural and Creative Vitality List* due to its unique advantages in cultural policy, talents, communication and industries. In 2018, the city's cultural and creative industries created some new records. The annual added value of the industries totaled RMB 112.9 billion, up 43.79% from the previous year and accounting for 7.4% of the total GDP. A cultural and creative investment fund of RMB 10 billion and 31 cultural and entrepreneurial parks were established, which introduced 5 leading enterprises engaged in cultural and creative industries and 142 well-known music enterprises and key projects. More than 800 cultural and creative districts, towns and spaces were created. New progress was made in the construction of "Six Famous Cities". ① Chengdu received tourist income of RMB 371.26 billion, of which the total inbound tourist income reached USD 1.45 billion. Chengdu is committed to becoming a city famous for world events that shares the sports economy pie and aims to build a sports economy consumer industry. It was the host city of 21 successful international sports events

① Six Famous Cities: To be a city famous for culture, tourism, events, food, music and exhibition in the world.

throughout the year, and it also won the bid for the 31st Universiade Chengdu 2021 and the 12th World Games. To be a world-renowned music city, it held more than 1,640 music performances, introduced 103 music companies including Migu Music and Chengdu Performance & Arts Group Co. LTD, and reported a total revenue of RMB 39.786 billion from the music industry. To be an international consumption city, Chengdu introduced more than 300 international premium brands and attracted 200 brands to open their first store in the city. The inclusion of these brands drove innovation in consumption modes and models. To be a world famous exhibition city, Chengdu held 689 major events which brought a total revenue exceeding RMB 100 billion, and the exhibition industry became an independent industry for the first time. Culture and creativity have increasingly important influence on Chengdu.

(V) Results from the Construction of Chengdu as an Opening Center in 2018

In 2018, Chengdu made remarkable results in the construction of central opening city. According to the *Vitality Index of Chinese Cities in International Communication*, Chengdu was ranked 5th in the comprehensive vitality indexes of international communication and was ranked 4th in international communication in social and political fields. The city's influence from opening to the outside world was growing. Chengdu pursued an export-oriented economy. Its total volume of imports and exports has risen year by year. In 2018, its total import and export volume almost topped RMB 500 billion, accounting for 83.87% of the total foreign trade volume of the province. The growth rate of total import and export volume was as high as 26.40%, the second highest rate among the nine central cities. Chengdu promoted the development of the pilot free trade zone by improving its business environment and implementing tax reduction and exemption policies. For the whole year, 27,000 new enterprises registered, including 359 foreign-funded enterprises. The new registered capital totaled RMB 700.85 billion. Chengdu also attracted 285 Fortune Global 500 companies to settle down. It strengthened the cooperation with partners from France, Italy and South Korea in building industrial parks which introduced a total of 124 projects. Twenty "Chengdu Overseas" workstations were set up. In terms of foreign affairs, the Consulate General of Austria in Chengdu was founded in 2018, making the total number of consulate generals reach 17, and Chengdu then had the third most consulate generals in China. With the advancement of the Belt and Road Initiative, Chengdu expanded its international friend circle by strengthening exchanges with coastal and border cities. By the end of 2018, it had established friendly relations with 93 international cities. Its foreign exchanges were constantly deepened, and the 144-hour transit visa-free policy for visitors from some countries has been approved. Chengdu also successfully held a series of international events such as the 2nd China-CEEC Art Cooperation Forum, the 4th Arabic Arts Festival, the 2018 Europe Culture Season, and the International Sister Cities Youth Music Week. With growing international influence, Chengdu has become a central city of international communication in the Western Region. (See Figure 3 and Figure 4)

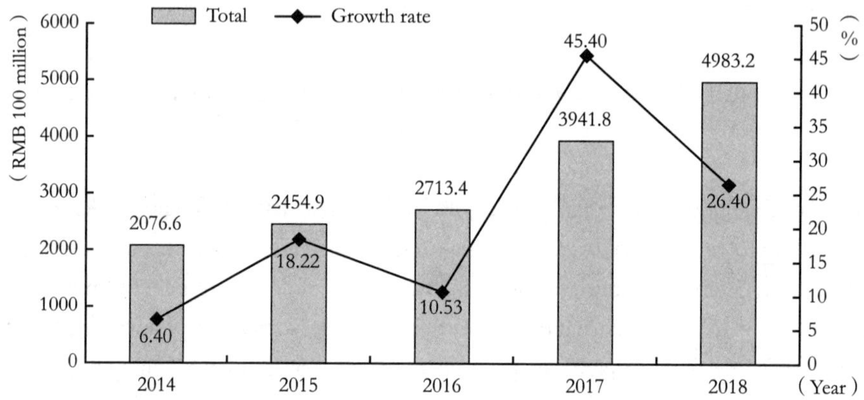

Figure 3 Total Import and Export Volume of Chengdu and Its Growth Rate for 2014-2018

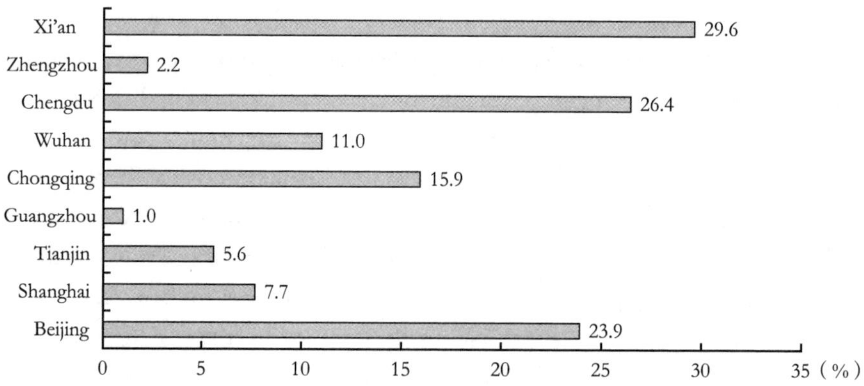

Figure 4 Growth Rates of Total Import and Export Volumes of Nine Central Cities in 2018

(VI) Results from the Construction of Chengdu as an Integrated Transportation and Communication Hub in 2018

Chengdu is an open gateway in the Western Region and an important hub connecting the border cities involved in the Belt and Road Initiative. To be an integrated transportation and communication hub meets the need of the national development strategy and helps stimulate the economic development of the mainland. It mainly means to enhance the position of Chengdu as an international integrated hub by improving its international air transportation and railway transportation and creating a three-dimensional transportation and communication network. In terms of air transportation, 12 new routes to 12 cities including St. Petersburg, Bangkok and Phuket were opened in 2018, adding the total number of international routes to 114. The international flight network was further improved. In terms of airport throughput, Shuangliu International Airport had a total passenger volume of 52.95 million in 2018, which meant it was the 26th busiest airport in the world. In terms of railway transportation, Chengdu built the "7+5" ① international railway channels in 2018 as part of the "international land and sea combined transportation" corridor. For the whole year, 2,619 international trains, an increase of 159% from the previous year, were operated to connect 38 domestic and foreign cities. Among them, the China-Europe freight train continued to extend in all directions and a total of 1,591 trips were recorded in 2018, an increase of 85%. In order to promote regional coordination, the newly operated "Rongou+" train covered 14 coastal and border cities including Neijiang, Zigong, Luzhou and Deyang, which shaped an international logistics network to achieve coordinated development among cities. To list some development results, the annual social passenger person-kilometers reached 38.18 billion tons passenger-kilometers and the annual rotation volume of freight transport reached 111.53 billion tons passenger-kilometers, increasing by 7.3% and 12.3% from the previous year, respectively. The status of Chengdu as an integrated transportation and communication hub was enhanced.

① "7+5" means 7 international railway channels and 5 international rail and sea transport channels

II Main Achievements in the National Central City Construction of Chengdu in 2018

(I) Chengdu Developed with Great Dynamics and Optimized Industrial Structure

Since the Western Development Strategy was implemented, Chengdu has maintained development at a relatively fast pace. The economic growth rate has remained above 8% for many years. Investment and consumption make increasingly important contributions to economic growth. The fiscal revenue has increased year by year, and the income level of the people has improved significantly. All the economic indicators grew rapidly, demonstrating the development vitality of the city. In terms of industrial structure, the annual added value of the three industries accounted for 3.4%, 42.5% and 54.1 of the GDP, and the tertiary industry was making more and more contribution to the economy, with a growth rate of 9%, which was 1 percentage point higher than the growth rate of GDP. The three-industry structure was adjusted and optimized, and the proportion of the tertiary industry increased by 0.9 percentage point. At the same time, the industrial structure was also internally optimized. Advanced manufacturing and service industries developed faster and made more contributions to economic development. The added value of the automobile industry, the petrochemical industry and the building material industry from the eight special industries and the added value of some traditional low-level manufacturing and raw material extraction industries took up lower proportions in the added value of enterprises above designated size. The total revenue of the five advanced manufacturing industries, namely "electronic information, equipment manufacturing, medical health, new materials, and green food", was RMB 970.54 billion, up 10.9% from the previous year. It took up 82% of the total industrial added value in the city, which was 2.4 percentage points higher than the growth rate of the total added value. The value-added of high-tech industries grew by 15.3%, which was 6.8 percentage points higher than the growth rate of the added value of industries above designated size. Among the service industries, finance, tourism, and post and telecommunications all grew rapidly. (See Table 1 and Figure 5)

Table 1 Economic Indicators of Chengdu for 2014-2018

Year	GDP growth rate	Growth rate of fixed asset investment	Growth rate of total consumption	Growth rate of fiscal revenue
2018	8.00%	9.40%	10.00%	10.00%
2017	8.10%	11.30%	11.50%	12.30%
2016	7.70%	7.00%	10.40%	14.30%
2015	7.90%	11.90%	10.90%	5.80%
2014	8.90%	14.10%	12.10%	1.80%

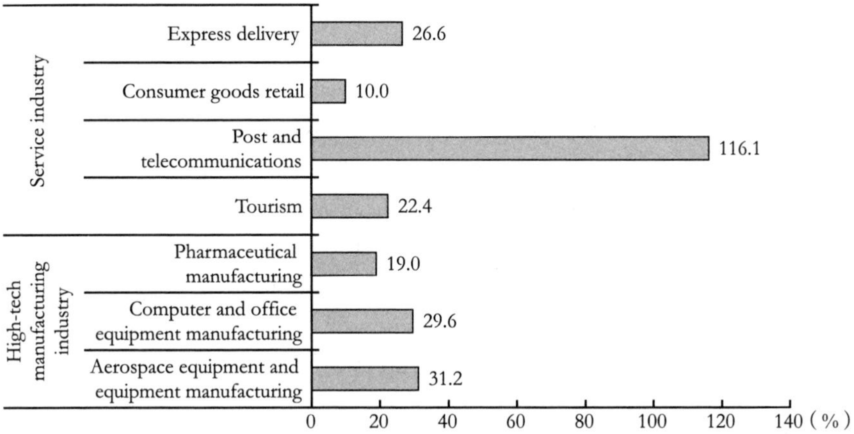

Figure 5 Growth Rates of High-tech Manufacturing Industry and Service Industry in Chengdu in 2018

(II) Establish a New Economy Policy System and Promote the Development of New Economy

In 2018, Chengdu made remarkable achievements in the development of the new economy, which developed vigorously. According to the *2018 China Vitality Index Ranking of New Economy*, Chengdu was ranked third in the vitality of new economy in the country. In order to better guide the development of new economy, Chengdu was the first city that proposed to build a new economic city systematically. It founded the Chengdu New Economic Development Committee. It also established a new economy policy system that consisted of "six economic forms" and "seven application scenarios"① to guide the development of new economy. In 2018, Chengdu launched the "Double Hundred Program" among new economy enterprises that was intended to train key enterprises and outstanding talents by providing targeted services and development platforms for new economy enterprises and by founding an angel fund to support the development of new economy. For the whole year, 41,000 new economy enterprises were fostered, 245 of which received a total investment of RMB 17.021 billion, and 100 enterprises above designated size reported a total income of RMB 25.147 billion, up 40.24% from the previous year. The government made active preparations for the building of a "Unicorn Island" in Tianfu New Area of Chengdu, where 4 new unicorn companies were fostered. Concerning new products, the output of urban rail transit vehicles, industrial robots and solar cells increased by 31.6%, 12.6%, and 110.1%, respectively. In terms of new business types, the online retail business increased by 29.4%, and the online retail sales reached RMB 66.95 billion. At the same time, the government promoted "three changes"② in its service function in order to create a good business environment for the development of the new economy. Policies about "capital, technology, talent and data" were promulgated to support the development of new economy and the conception for the new economy 2.0 in Chengdu.

(III) Government Reinforced Regulation and the Business Environment Was Substantially Improved.

In 2018, Chengdu was committed to improving the business environment.

① The "six economic forms" refer to digital economy, smart economy, green economy, creative economy, flow economy and sharing economy. The "seven application scenarios" refer to innovation applications in improving the ability to service the real economy, promoting the construction of smart city, technological innovation and entrepreneurship, human capital synergy, consumption upgrading, green and low-carbon development, and modern supply chain.

② Three changes: from "prescription" to "customization" in policy formulation; from "offering preferential treatment" to "providing opportunities", and from "individual service" to "ecosystem creation".

According to the *2019 Evaluation Report on the Business Environment Index of Chinese Cities*, Chengdu was ranked 6th among major cities in the country, 7 places higher than where it was in the previous year. Among the nine central cities, it rose from the last but one in 2017 to the 5th, showing a positive trend in business environment development. In terms of government services, the government continued to promote the reform of "streamlining administration, delegating power, strengthening regulation and improving services". Business formalities were streamlined by "separating certificate from license", "integrating forty-three-in-one" and "requiring only one seal in approval application". More efforts were made to push the reform of going through formalities with "one errand" and through "one window". As a result, 85% of approval applications could be processed with "one errand", and 95% of public services could be processed online. In order to enhance market vitality, a market access negative list was adopted, and controls on enterprises were relaxed. Enterprises were encouraged to maintain various forms of cooperation and exchanges with partners along the "Belt and Road". In 2018, due to the improved investment environment in Chengdu, investments of about USD 10 billion were made to support 150 projects in countries along the "Belt and Road". In terms of scientific research and innovation, Chengdu encouraged universities and enterprises to be committed to innovation and creation, made active investments to build key laboratories and purchase large-scale instruments and equipment to facilitate scientific research, encouraged enterprises to be committed to independent innovation and independent R&D, provided policy incentives and fiscal and tax subsidies for innovative enterprises, and nurtured leading and benchmark technology-oriented enterprises. Chengdu also attracted talents by implementing "12 New Measure" for Talents and establishing the service system of "Green Cards for Talents to Chengdu". Now 659 experts and 64 teams are supported by the independently selected "Rongpiao Plan". The total number of talents specialized in various trades was about 5 million, which formed an excellent talent base for enterprise development. In terms of the legal environment, the People's Court and Arbitration Center of the Sichuan Pilot Free Trade Zone was founded, and the Chengdu Intellectual Property Rights Tribunal was established to guarantee the normal business environment. (See Table 3)

Table 2 Business Environment Index of Chinese Cities and Their Rankings

City	Rankings in 2017	Rankings in 2018	Business Environment Index
Shenzhen	3	1	0.611
Shanghai	4	2	0.524
Guangzhou	1	3	0.512
Beijing	2	4	0.510
Chongqing	5	5	0.478
Chengdu	13	6	0.405
Nanjing	6	7	0.398
Hangzhou	7	8	0.397
Changsha	20	9	0.391
Wuhan	10	10	0.388
Xi'an	12	11	0.377
Qingdao	9	12	0.375
Kunming	22	13	0.359
Guiyang	30	14	0.350
Ningbo	8	15	0.331
Xiamen	28	16	0.330
Zhengzhou	23	17	0.324
Tianjin	11	18	0.322
Dalian	19	19	0.318
Nanchang	17	20	0.313

Source: *The 2019 Evaluation Report on the Business Environment Index of Chinese Cities*

(IV) The "Blue Sky Protection Campaign" Paid Off and the Ecological Environment Was Substantially Improved

In 2018, Chengdu was determined to improve its ecological environment by adhering to the new development concept, building itself into a park city at a quicker pace, resolutely following the green development concept and promoting "three control initiatives and one greening measure". It has explored a new path to realize "value conversion" between environmental protection and development during the central city construction process. In the field of pollution control, the three control initiatives to tackle "air, water pollution and traffic congestion" paid off. After the "Blue Sky Protection Campaign" was launched, Chengdu had 16 more days with air quality up to the standard and 251 days with good air quality. The average concentrations of PM10 and PM2.5 as two harmful substances decreased by 8.0% and 8.9%, and those of SO_2, NO_2 and CO decreased by 12.8%, 9.4%, and 17.6%, respectively. Chengdu was among the first winner of "Blue Sky Award for Global Green and Low-carbon Pioneer Cities". In the field of water pollution control, the focus was on treating black and odorous waters. 7.2% of the surface water was found to have the Grade-1 to Grade-111 sediment water quality. The ecological environments in Jinjiang River, Tuojiang River and Jinma River basins were improved. 45 solid waste pollution control projects were launched. To tackle traffic congestion, the *2018 Plan for Scientific Control of Traffic Congestion in Chengdu* was issued to scientifically control traffic congestion. In terms of ecological environment, Chengdu was committed to becoming a park city and implemented "Ten Regulations on the Greening of Chengdu". Last year witnessed a series of remarkable achievements: 6 new parks with a total area of 20,000 square meters, 839 greening projects under planning, Tianfu Green Road with a length of 2,607km, and a new greening area of nearly 65,000 mu in Longquan Forest Park; the forest coverage rate increased to 39.5%, the green area coverage increased to 41.7% in the built-up area, and the per capita park area increased to 12.7 square meters.

III Challenges in the National Central City Construction of Chengdu

(I) Economic Factors Are not Strong Enough to Lend Comprehensive Support

Regional GDP, fixed asset investment, public budget income, total retail volume of social consumer goods, and per capita GDP income are economic indicators that reflect the comprehensive economic strength of a region. In 2018, Chengdu's GDP totaled RMB 1.534277 trillion, and its annual income was slightly over RMB 1.5 trillion, compared to more than 2 trillion long reported by Beijing, Shanghai, Guangzhou and Chongqing. From the perspective of fixed investment, Chengdu's fixed investments in 2020 totaled RMB 834.11 billion, which was equal to only 78.37% of Tianjin's fixed investments and 44.7% of Chongqing's. From the perspective of public budget income for the whole year, the public budget income of Chengdu in 2018 was RMB 142.42 billion, which was the third lowest and made it only superior to Zhengzhou and Xi'an among the nine central cities. Its total income took up only about 25% of Beijing's total income, 20% of Shanghai's, and 63% of Chongqing's. From the perspective of per capita GDP, Chengdu performed better than Chongqing and Xi'an only. Economic factors lend important support to the construction of central cities. The comprehensive economic indicators are not strong enough to support the construction of Chengdu as an important national central city. (See Table 3)

Table 3 Economic Indicators of the Nine Central Cities in 2018

City	GDP (RMB 100 million)	Fixed asset investment (RMB 100 million)	Total retail volume of social consumer goods (RMB 100 million)	General public budget income (RMB 100 million)	Regional GDP per capita (RMB 10,000)
Beijing	30320.0	8062.1	11747.7	5785.9	13.5
Shanghai	32679.9	7622.8	12668.7	7108.2	2.1
Tianjin	18809.6	10642.7	5533.1	2106.2	5.5
Guangzhou	22859.4	6404.4	9256.2	1632.3	6.6
Chongqing	20363.2	18660.1	6960.1	2265.5	13.5
Wuhan	14847.3	8705.3	6843.9	1528.7	9.5
Chengdu	15342.8	8341.1	6801.8	1424.2	10.1
Zhengzhou	10143.3	8398.5	4268.1	1152.1	8.7
Xi'an	8349.9	8190.7	4658.7	684.7	14.0
Ranking of Chengdu	6	3	5	7	7

(II) Chengdu Needs to Improve Its Capacity as a "Trunk" to Drive Regional Coordination

In 2018, Chengdu attached importance to coordinated regional development and followed the regional development concept of "one trunk and multiple branches" and "concerted development of five districts" to seek common development among the regions. It solidly advanced the "Ten Key Projects" of rural revitalization. It also deeply promoted the integration of Chengdu, Deyang, Meishan and Ziyang to develop deputy central cities in different regions. It propelled other cities (prefectures) to sign comprehensive cooperation agreements for the purpose of common development. However, generally speaking, Chengdu failed to significantly drive coordinated regional development. The economic gap between different regions in the province remained huge. Chengdu, as the provincial capital, was the pillar of economic development in Sichuan Province. Its annual GDP was RMB 1.524277 trillion, accounting for roughly 37.72% of the provincial GDP, but the GDP of secondary cities Mianyang, Deyang, Yibin and Nanchong accounted for only 5.66%, 5.44%, 4.89% and 4.83%, respectively. The GDP of Chengdu was about 6 to 7 times that of these places. From the perspective of per capita GDP, an indicator that reflected people's living standards, all the other cities fell far behind Chengdu, except Panzhihua, whose per capita GDP was just slightly lower than that of the provincial city due to its abundant mineral resources such as titanium, vanadium and graphite. From the perspective of regional synergy, the annual GDP of "Chengdu Plain, South Sichuan, Northeast Sichuan, Panxi, and Northwest Sichuan" was RMB 2.566554 trillion, RMB 653.98 billion, RMB 639.417 billion, 270.671 billion, and RMB 59.787 billion, respectively. The GDP of Chengdu Plain alone accounted for 61% of the total GDP of Sichuan Province, which was 22 percentage points higher than the sum of the other four regions. The GDP of Northeast Sichuan and Northwest Sichuan accounted for only 25.48% and 2.33% of the GDP of Chengdu Plain, although they were the second and the fifth largest contributors, respectively. Such economic performance suggested that Chengdu played a weak role in driving regional development and failed to fully tap its radiating advantages as a central city. At the same time, the regional coordination mechanism was not perfect, and industrial isomorphism and disorderly competition became problems. Transportation facilities, joint environmental governance, equalization of public services and free movement of market factors were not satisfactory. The development levels of different regions varied greatly due to poor overall coordination. (See Figure 6 and Figure 7)

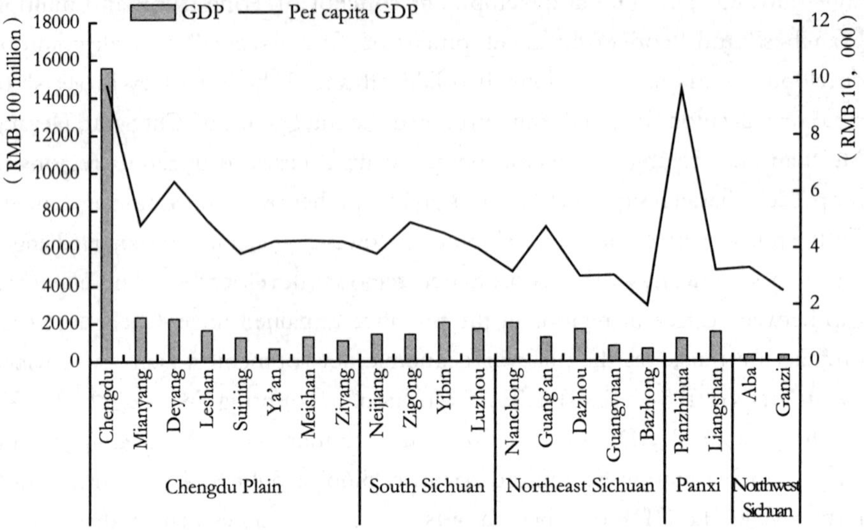

Figure 6 GDP and Per Capita Incomes of Cities in Sichuan Province in 2018

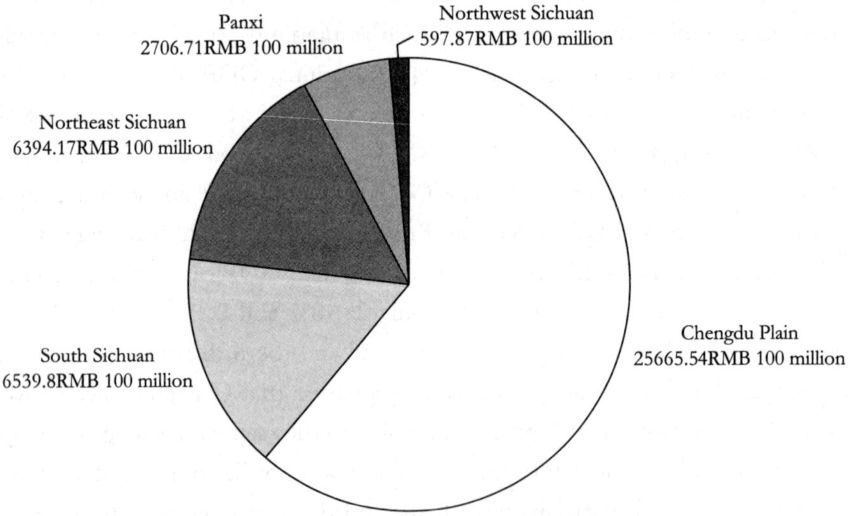

Figure 7 GDP of Five Regions in Sichuan Province in 2018

(III) The Supply Factors Supporting Innovation Development Were Inadequate

Innovation is the first driving force for the future development of a city, and all the central cities are trying to inject momentum into their development by increasing investments in innovation. Chengdu was ranked 16th in the *2018 Innovation Capability Ranking of Cities*, superior to Zhengzhou only among the nine central cities. Total R&D investment and the number of postgraduates devoted to R&D reflect how technological innovation is valued and how much room for innovation to progress in a city. In 2017, Beijing and Shanghai were rated as the biggest investors, both reporting R&D investments of more than RMB 100 billion. Chengdu was only about 20% and 27% of them in this regard. Chengdu also had to catch up with Wuhan, Chongqing and Xi'an, which were actually in the similar rank with it. Chengdu was last but one in terms of both total R&D investment and input intensity among the nine central cities, and these rankings were not in the interest of its positioning as a new science and technology city. Chengdu was striving to build new economy and high-tech industries. The amount of research funding determines the vitality and dynamics of emerging industries. In addition, Chengdu lacked a good research and innovation environment, adequate supplies for innovation, and sufficient resources such as national key sci-tech infrastructures and innovation bases. This, combined with the weak ability to gather talents and the shortage of leading talents, limited improvement in innovative and creative capabilities of the city. (See Figure 8)

(IV) The Health Level of Urban Traffic Remains to be Improved

In recent years, Chengdu's economy has developed rapidly, which is an increasingly strong magnet to population. At present, the city actually holds a population of over 2 million, and more is to be added. As the economy and population grow, traffic congestion is inevitable. Traffic congestion not only brings about inconvenience in people's lives, but also affects the economic development of a region. According to the *Analysis Report on Traffic in Chinese Major Cities in 2018* issued by Amap, Chengdu was ranked 9th among major cities in the country when measured for the mileage of traffic congestion during rush hours and 42th in terms of traffic health index, which was 64.33%. Its high

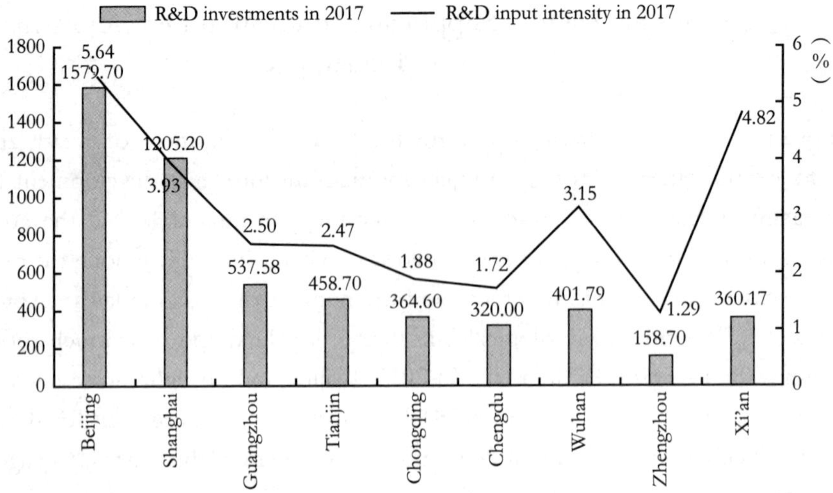

Figure 8　Total R&D Investments and Input Intensity of the Nine Central Cities in 2017

delay time ratio in the time-road network took up 41.8%, and its space-constant congestion distance ratio was 0.176%. Chengdu residents spent 72.60 minutes on commuting on average, and the average congestion duration during working days was 32.78 minutes, which caused an economic loss of RMB 15 per day. According to the ranking of traffic health estimate, Chengdu was still in a sub-health state in the traffic field. (See Figure 9)

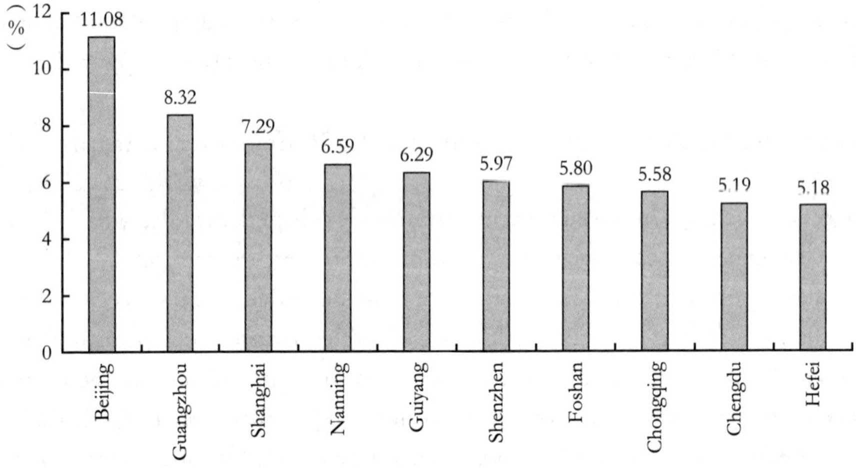

Figure 9　Top 10 Chinese Cities in Ratio of Congestion Mileage during Rush Hours in 2018

Source: *Analysis Report on Traffic in Chinese Major Cities in 2018* by Amap

(V) Development Benefits Should Be Shared by More

The economic development of Chengdu grew well, but the development benefits have not been shared by the people equally. Chengdu was still hindered by generally low urban and rural incomes, insufficient resources for primary and secondary education, uneven distribution of medical resources, and inadequate pension infrastructures. Although the income and consumption levels of Chengdu residents grew rapidly in 2018, they were seriously behind the levels of first-tier cities due to the original small bases. Kindergartens and primary and middle schools were faced with a shortage of teaching resources. 87.3% of the kindergartens in the city were public and non-profit, but difficulty in admission and high cost remained unsolved for many kids. The limited number of secondary and primary schools led to perennial "oversized classes". In terms of medical health, there were 10,755 medical health institutions in Chengdu, providing 8.38 beds per 1,000 people. However, because Chengdu received a large number of patients from other places, medical resources were still urgently needed. From the perspective of regional distribution, Grade-3 hospitals at ministerial, provincial and municipal levels were mainly distributed within the Second Ring Road. As a result, hospitals in the central urban area were heavily loaded, and well-known medical experts were hardly accessible. In terms of pension for the aged, 2,089 pension facilities and 30,000 beds were available in the communities in Chengdu. The supply of these pension infrastructures could hardly meet the needs of the aging population.

V Countermeasures and Suggestions on the National Central City Construction of Chengdu in the Future

1 Pursue High-quality Economic Development and Boost Comprehensive strength

Economic strength is an important basic indicator about the development and construction of a region. Chengdu is the most developed city in the central and western regions. However, comparison from various economic indicators shows that it still has to catch up with the other central cities. This is the main challenge for Chengdu for a future period of time. Going forward, Chengdu should continue to transform the economic development mode under the guidance of the new concept, and guide the three industries to the path of high-quality development. First, it should establish a modern economic system and build a sound industrial chain around the "5+5+1" key industries to strengthen the industrial strength. It should improve the 66 key industrial parks with strong carrying capacity, optimize the layout of industrial functional zones, attract leading enterprises, strengthen the strength of industrial parks, and try to build four new industrial towns with strong comprehensive strength. Second, it should quicken industrial transformation and upgrading, upgrade the manufacturing industry, promote the five major industries to form clusters, expand the industrial scale, increase the added value of industries, increase the R&D and manufacturing capabilities of high-tech industries, and embark on the path of high-end industrial development. At the same time, it should pay attention to the high-end and digital transformation of key industries to enhance the technological content of products. Third, it should focus on supporting new economies such as "artificial intelligence +, big data +, 5G+, clean energies + and supply chain +" that are highly technological and competitive and allow them to play an important role in the future economic development. Fourth, it should value the role of investment and consumption in boosting economic development, make investments in project construction, and exploit the role of investment in macroeconomic development. It should expand the consumer market, support internationalized Chengdu brand, aid the construction of "world consumption city", and increase its overall economic strength.

2 To Be a Strong "Trunk" that Leads Regional Integration Construction

Chengdu is the "trunk" of Sichuan Province and the "core" of the Chengdu-Chongqing city cluster. It is also an important central city and an open base of international exchanges in the Western Region. The construction of Chengdu bears many historical and realistic missions. One of the most important missions is to drive development of the regions to achieve coordinated regional development. In the future, Chengdu should pay attention to regional coordination and strive to achieve regional integration. Firstly, it should try to be a strong "trunk" that leads balanced development of the regions by sticking to multi-point and multi-polar strategies. It should pay attention to the top-level design of coordinated regional development, make rational industrial planning, adopt the strategy of complementary development, uphold rational division of labor and industrial collaboration among the regions, and form a complete industrial ecological chain. Secondly, it should foster secondary central cities and satellite cities, make concerted efforts to promote deep integration of designated cities, and upgrade the regional development level. Thirdly, it should change the way of government governance, optimize the business environment in the regions, and facilitate free flow of factors in the market to inject vitality to the economic development of regional markets. Fourthly, it should intensify the planning and construction of transportation infrastructures that are put into service all over the regions, combine urban railways with expressways, vigorously develop intercity public transportation, and provide integrated services. Fifthly, it should work with the other cities in regional coordination planning to ensure orderly advancement of coordinated regional development. Chengdu should put in place a sound coordination mechanism between local governments at all levels, form regional cooperation alliances, deepen regional cooperation in division of labor along the industrial chain, technological innovation, infrastructure co-construction, and joint environmental governance, and build a regional development community.

3 Increase the Factor Inputs in Innovation and Enhance Innovation Capability

Science and technology constitute the primary productive force, and innovation is the only driver. The development of high-tech industries and new economies in Chengdu requires intensive input of innovation resources. Given its current development status, Chengdu, on the one hand, should increase investments in scientific research to lend strong support to research and innovation activities. On the other hand, it should encourage enterprises to carry out independent R&D activities and innovation, add investments to develop scientific and technological products, and offer tax incentives or subsidies to technological and innovative enterprises to stimulate their innovative and creative vitality. It should also intensify the input of educational resources, purchase major experimental instruments for colleges and universities, build key laboratories, and fund research activities. It should increase the enrollment of graduate students, integrate educational resources, and cultivate first-class universities and first-class disciplines to lay the foundation for innovation. It should actively recruit high-end innovative talents and perfect the existing talent recruitment programs.

4 Make Rational Urban Planning and Increase the Carrying Capacity

Chengdu should rationally plan its spatial structure, scientifically optimize the urban transportation system, and learn from strategies of urban traffic congestion mitigation that are applied in other cities. To solve urban traffic congestion, Chengdu needs rational planning and construction of urban spatial structure that divides different industrial areas reasonably and diverts people to different workplaces. On the other hand, it needs to optimize the comprehensive urban traffic construction, promote the formation of a dense urban traffic network, and build half-hour commuter circles by rail transit. It should increase investments in the construction of buses, subways and trams, increase their operational coverage, and develop a convenient transportation network system. It should promote smart buses, connect them with subways and trams, optimize bus scheduling to reduce congestion during rush hours, and shorten commuting time. It should also control congestion scientifically by referring to congestion control strategies of other cities, such as "improved intersection channelization", "optimized signal timing during morning/evening peaks", and "signal linkage control and shunt at regional junctions".

5 Enhance People's Sense of Happiness and Allow Development Benefits to Be Shared by All

The uneven development of districts within Chengdu results in huge income differences among urban and rural residents. The uneven distribution of educational, medical care and infrastructure resources affects the improvement of living standards for urban and rural residents. In order to achieve "perceivable development", Chengdu must first steadily push forward the rural revitalization project and explore the potential of rural development. It should support some enterprises to build production and processing bases in rural areas, which can contribute to rural industrialization and increase farmers' production and income. Next, it must develop high-quality education, build and expand kindergartens and primary and secondary schools, and introduce excellent teachers to support education development and improve people's literacy. At the same time, it should also expand key hospitals, allocate high-quality medical resources in different regions rationally, and create a "15-minute medical health circle" to meet people's needs. Last but not least, it must provide active social security for the aged and increase fiscal investments to the construction of infrastructures to safeguard the life of this population group.

References

[1] Chengdu Municipal People's Government: "The Government Work Report of Chengdu City in 2019", https://www.is97.com/doc-173925-1.html

[2] The People's Government of Sichuan Province: "Chengdu's GDP exceeds RMB 1.5 trillion in 2018, a YoY growth rate of 8.0%", http://www.sc.gov.cn/10462/10464/10465/10595/2019/1/29/3b3fb4caca5b462fb292833ff6195d00.shtml

[3] Hou Chuchu: "Keep in mind the commitment and seize the opportunity: Chengdu makes positive progress in high-quality development", http://sc.cri.cn/20190123/389e5237-7107-ef37-998d-9cb2cf81165c.html

[4] "As new economy enterprises continue to emerge, the 'city opportunity list' of Chengdu is extended", http://www.p5w.net/news/gncj/201906/t20190613_2303777.htm

[5] "The construction of 'Six Famous Cities' is pushed forward", http://sc.people.com.cn/n2/2019/0603/c379471-33003170.html

[6] Wen Gongzhu. "Treating the creation of first-class business environment as the top priority, Chengdu is committed to building an international business environment in 2019", http://www.sohu.com/a/294098142_120066169

[7] "Chengdu delivers good performance in fully opening up to the outside world in 2018", http://www.yybnet.net/news/china/201903/8818265.html

[8] "Chengdu: to play a "trunk" role in pooling strength to empower the development of the province", http://sc.people.com.cn/n2/2018/1203/c379471-32357801.html

[9] "Threc 'changes' have occurred to the construction of Chengdu as the financial center in the Western Region", http://scnews.newssc.org/system/20190222/000945142.html

[10] "Chengdu has formulated a medical and health layout plan and will launch a number of general hospital projects", http://sc.sina.com.cn/news/b/2018-05-01/detail-ifzvpatr7223565-p2.shtml

B.9
National Central City Construction of Wuhan: Progress and Prospects

*Deng Hongbing and Li Shiran**

Abstract: Judging from the overall situation of the Central Region and the geographical location, Wuhan is located strategically as a hub. It is the core to the Yangtze River Economic Belt, the city cluster along the middle reaches of the Yangtze River and the Wuhan metropolitan area. Having been an important growth pole in the national spatial development strategy, Wuhan serves as an important portal that drives the rise of the Central Region and leads the development of city clusters along the middle reaches of the Yangtze River and the Yangtze River Economic Belt, as the national urban spatial system is improved. With a clear understanding of its own advantages and disadvantages, Wuhan should make breakthroughs and achieve transformation and upgrading by superimposing and maximizing the effects of development strategies. The next step is to assume the major responsibility as the national spatial fulcrum and complete the great mission of building itself into a national central city.

Keywords: national central city; Wuhan metropolitan area; city clusters along the middle reaches of the Yangtze River

---

* Deng Hongbing, Professor and Ph.D. Supervisor, Director of Regional Economy and Investment Environment Research Center of China University of Geosciences (Wuhan), whose research orientation is regional economy and regional innovation. Li Shiran, doctoral student of Regional Economy and Investment Environment Research Center of China University of Geosciences, whose research orientation is regional economy.

I Progress and Achievements in the National Central City Construction of Wuhan in 2018

In 2018, the total output of intelligent manufacturing and service industries above designated size in Wuhan was 18.8% and 23.6%, respectively, and the investments in strategic emerging industries increased by 24.3% from the previous year. As the modern industrial system pooled advanced manufacturing, new economy and modern service industries, the industrial structure was further optimized; more investments were attracted, and the actually used foreign investments reached USD 10.927 billion, converted to a year-on-year increase of 13.3%; another 10 Fortune Global 500 companies settled down in the city. As poverty alleviation actions were taken, 87 poverty-stricken villages and 21,600 people got rid of poverty. The economic and social reforms were pushed forward steadily. The incomes of urban and rural residents maintained steady growth, and the modern, international and ecological construction of the city was accelerated. The national central city construction was advanced with high quality.

In 2018, Wuhan's GDP was RMB 1.484729 trillion, with a growth rate of 8.0%, and its per capita GDP was RMB 123,900. The annual per capita disposable income of residents was RMB 42,133, an increase of 9.0% from the previous year. The income and the economy generally grew stably. Over the past five years, Wuhan's GDP has kept climbing up the trillion ladder, maintaining a growth rate of 8.0% or so. The steady economic development has laid a solid foundation for the central city construction of Wuhan (Figure 1).

In 2018, the total retail volume of social consumer goods in Wuhan was RMB 684.390 billion, and the growth rate of consumption was 10.5% on a year-on-year basis, which was slightly higher than the growth rate of income. From 2014 to 2018, the total retail volume of social consumer goods rose fast, and its growth rate began to stabilize at about 10% in 2016 (Figure 2). According to statistics, the retail business area per capita in Wuhan was more than two square meters, and there were 369,000 commercial outlets throughout the city. The annual growth rates of per capita consumption expenditure of urban and rural residents in Wuhan were 0.3% and 1.8% higher than the growth rates of income, respectively, which pointed to strong consumer demand and the effectiveness of policy measures that were intended to stimulate domestic demand.

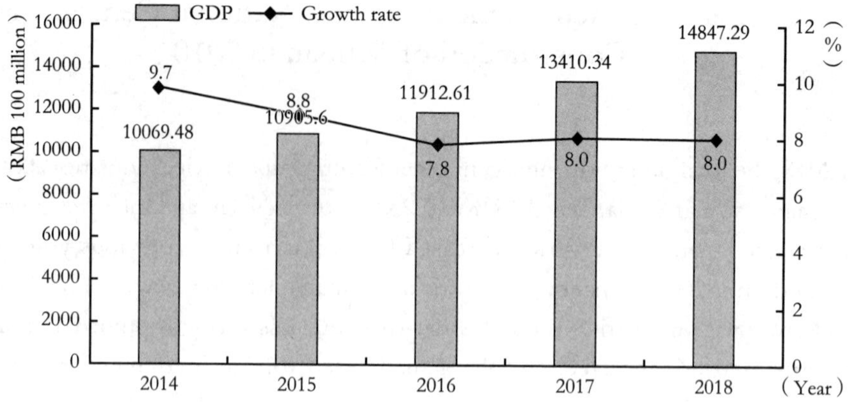

Figure 1 Wuhan's GDP and Its Growth Rate for 2014-2018

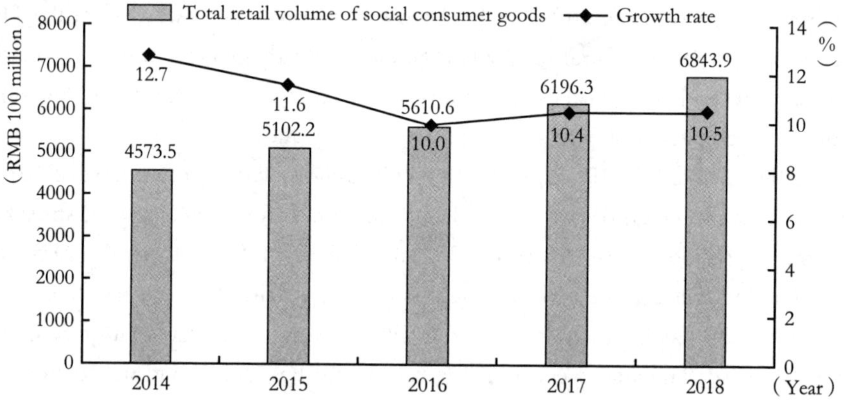

Figure 2 Wuhan's Total Retail Volume of Social Consumer Goods and Its Growth Rate for 2014-2018

Improvement-oriented consumption led the consumption expenditure of residents in Wuhan. In 2018, the residents in Wuhan spent 27.4% of their consumption on living expenses, and the expenditure on education, culture and entertainment kept growing rapidly, accounting for 10.5%. The expenditure on health care grew rapidly, accounting for 7.6%. According to the resident consumption data in 2018, the growth rate in December showed an upward trend amid fluctuations compared to the last December, with the peak of 2.6% appearing in September (Figure 3). The data showed that both the consumption and its level moved towards a new height after the urban and rural residents of Wuhan met their basic needs.

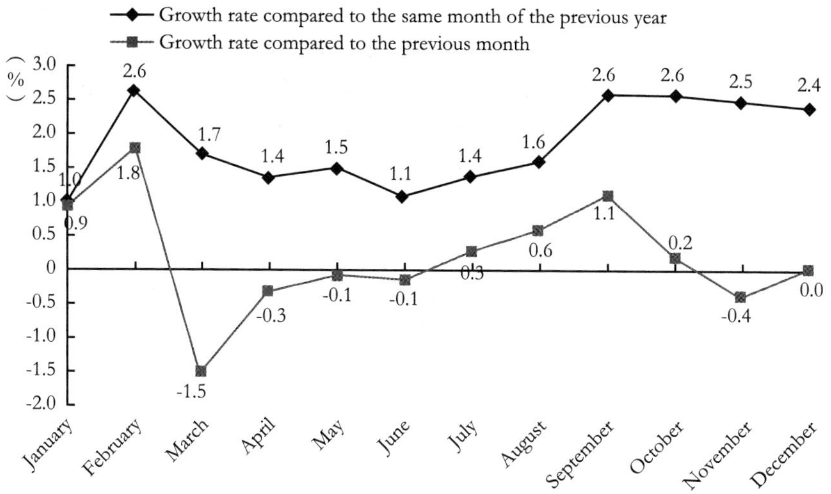

Figure 3 Monthly Data of Consumer Prices of Wuhan in 2018

According to statistical results, the employment, entrepreneurship and incomes of urban and rural residents in Wuhan all maintained steady growth, showing good fundamentals in 2018. For the whole year, 191,200 jobs were created, and the registered urban unemployment rate was 2.14%, which was controlled within the target range; market vitality was continuously stimulated, attracting 191,200 new market participants, which marked an increase of 5.2% from the previous year, including 94,600 new registered enterprises. The annual income and expenditure of residents also manifested Wuhan's transformation and upgrading to innovative development and high-quality development.

The industrial layout was optimized and the industrial structure was subject to constant adjustments and upgrading. More high-paying jobs were created. In the composition of total output value, the proportion of the tertiary industry kept increasing from 2014 to 2018 to finally reach 54.6% (Figure 4). For the whole year, the total output value of three strategic emerging industries grew substantially. Among them, intelligent manufacturing delivered the most growing business revenue at a rate of 21.5%. Among the service industries above designated size, the tourism industry reported the most growing business revenue at a rate of 23.6%, followed by the productive service industry and the technological service industry, at 21.2% and 20.1%, respectively, on a year-on-year basis. At the same time, the investments in strategic emerging industries grew at a faster rate of 24.3%. As Wuhan accelerated the construction of a modern industry system supported by advanced manufacturing and emerging service industries, residents were provided with excellent job opportunities, and the proportion of those engaged in information transmission, software and information technology services, and finance was substantially increased from the previous year.

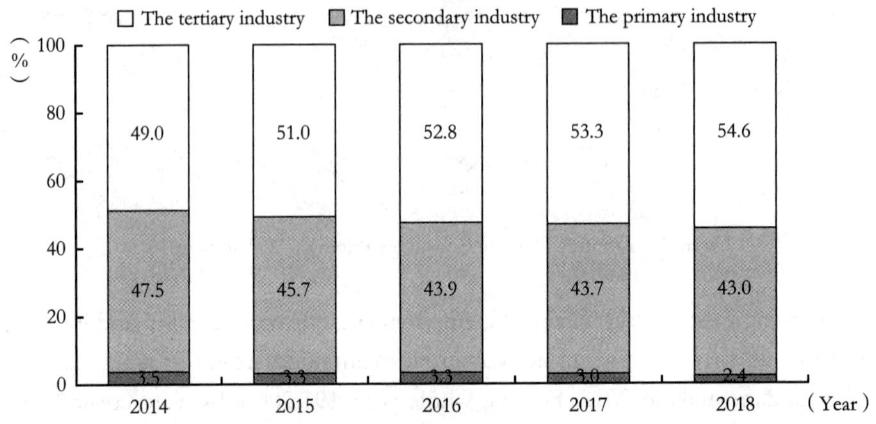

Figure 4 Composition of the Total Output Value of Wuhan for 2014-2018

In terms of ecological environment, the ambient air quality of the city remained relatively stable in 2018 compared with the previous year. Wuhan had 249 days with good air quality and two days less than the number of days with severe pollution in 2017. The annual concentrations of sulfur dioxide, nitrogen dioxide, and particulate matters dropped from the levels in the previous year. The water quality of rivers and lakes continued to be positive while maintaining stability.

In terms of technological innovation, Wuhan strictly followed the strategy of rejuvenating the nation through science and education and the innovation driven strategy, a focus on "five major projects and two major reforms". It was committed to being a national city of intellectual property rights protection. In 2018, the output value of high-tech industries in the city grew by 13.5%. The numbers of patent applications and grants grew significantly, keeping a relatively obvious upward trend over the past five years (Figure 5). Wuhan also supported scientific research and development of key universities and institutions in the city and devoted energy to the transformation of their scientific and technological achievements via special pairing activities. It promoted the construction of innovative industrial parks, and 25 new mass innovation incubators at provincial level and above were built; it gathered concerted efforts to build a modern industrial system and optimize the future industrial layout around three key industries: information technology, life health and intelligent manufacturing. By accelerating the cultivation of new economic growth points, it propelled the sustained and rapid development of high-tech industries.

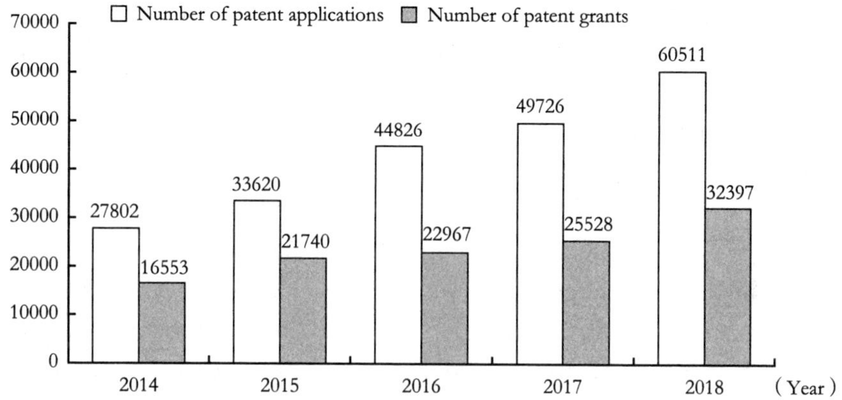

Figure 5 Numbers of Patent Applications and Grants in Wuhan for 2014-2018

II Characteristics, Potential and Main Problems of the National Central City Construction of Wuhan

The characteristics and potential of national central city construction of Wuhan are analyzed on the basis of quantitative comparison through an evaluation index system. The analysis results are then used to identify existing problems.

(I) Analysis of the Characteristics and Potential of the National Central City Construction of Wuhan

The connotation and functions of national central cities are reflected in the development foundations stage, including economic development level, agglomeration level, radiation level and communication level; the potential and competitiveness of national central cities are fully demonstrated in the rapid growth stage, mainly including innovation capability and information sharing ability; the future development directions of national central cities are indicated in the construction goal, including humanistic communication, ecological livability and green development. Based on this, a comprehensive evaluation index system for the national central cities is built according to the scientific and systematic principles (Table 1). It reflects the status quo, construction process and final state of the national central cities during the foundation, growth and goal realization stages. With Wuhan as the benchmark, the 9 national central cities (Beijing, Shanghai, Tianjin, Guangzhou, Chongqing, Chengdu, Wuhan, Zhengzhou and Xi'an) are compared through an analytic hierarchy process by assigning weight to each factor in the comprehensive system. The decision-making layer is about a city's comprehensive strength; the target layer is divided into basic function, growth function, and target function; the intermediate layer is divided into economic development center, open and agglomeration center, radiating and driving center, interactive and communication center, technological innovation center, information sharing center, livable and entrepreneurial center, humanistic and social center, and green development center. The characteristics, potential and existing problems of the national central city construction of Wuhan are evaluated in a systematic, quantitative manner.

First, contrary indicators are processed reversely, including unemployment rate, per capita water consumption, per capita electricity consumption, per capita urban built-up area, industrial wastewater discharge, industrial fume emissions, and industrial waste emissions. Because of the different natures and units of the indicators, the raw data of the indicators are made dimensionless with the extremum method to eliminate the error caused by dimensional differences. Positive indicators are processed based on Equation (1), and negative indicators are processed based on Equation (2). $\max_{xij}$ and $\min x_{ij}$ represent the maximum and minimum values, and X_{ij} represents the processed standard value. The value of the processed data is [0.1]. In order to ensure that the values of the variables are greater than zero, 0.00001, instead of zero, is taken for zero values.

Table 1 Comprehensive Evaluation Index System for National Central Cities

Decision-making Layer	Target Layer	Intermediate Layer	Indicator Layer	Unit
Comprehensive strength	Basic function	Economic development center	GDP	RMB 100 million
			Per capita GDP	RMB 10,000
			Proportion of tertiary industry output	%
			Local fiscal revenue	RMB 100 million
			GDP growth rate	%
		Open and agglomeration center	Registered population	10,000 persons
			Employment population	10,000 persons
			Permanent migrants	10,000 persons
			Number of foreign enterprises	
			Number of state-owned enterprises	
			Actually used foreign investments	USD 100 million
		Radiating and driving center	Total retail volume of social consumer goods	RMB 100 million
			Opening function	10, 000 persons
			Total exports	USD 100 million
		Interactive and communication center	Freight volume	10,000 tons
			Passenger volume	10,000 tons

Continued

Decision-making Layer	Target Layer	Intermediate Layer	Indicator Layer	Unit
Comprehensive strength	Growth function	Technological innovation center	Number of graduate students	10, 000 persons
			Number of scientific research institutions	
			Research expenditure	RMB 100 million
			Number of invention patent grants	
			Number of scientific papers	
		Information sharing center	Number of broadband users	10,000 households
			Per capita mobile phone ownership	set/person
	Target function	Livable and entrepreneurial center	Average life expectancy of residents	
			Per capita housing area	square meters
			Unemployment rate	%
			Per capita disposable income	RMB
			Public transportation mileage	km
		Humanistic and social center	Number of higher education beneficiaries	10,000 persons
			GDP of cultural industries	RMB 100 million
			Number of medical beds	
			Number of books in public libraries	10,000 volumes
			Volume of periodical publishing	100 million volumes
		Green development center	Per capita water consumption	cubic meters
			Per capita electricity consumption	Kilowatt hours
			Green coverage rate in built-up areas	square meters
			Per capita park green area	square meters
			Industrial wastewater discharge	100 million tons
			Industrial fume emissions	100 million tons
			Industrial waste emissions	100 million tons

Note: From the statistical communiqué of Wuhan in 2018

$$X_{ij}=\frac{x_{ij}\text{-}\min_{xij}}{\max_{xij}\text{-}\min_{xij}} \tag{1}$$

$$X_{ij}=\frac{\max_{xij}\text{-}x_{ij}}{\max_{xij}\text{-}\min_{xij}} \tag{2}$$

In order to overcome subjectivity, the indicator weights are determined with the entropy method. Firstly, an evaluation matrix is established, which is an m×n raw data matrix $X=(xij)_{m\times n}$, in which m is the number of the studied administrative districts and n is the number of indicators; then, information entropy is calculated with the standard value based on Equation (3) where $k=(\ln m)^{-1}$ and $0 \leqslant H_j \leqslant 1$. Finally, the indicator weights are calculated according to Equation (4).

$$\mathrm{Hj}=-k\sum_{i=1}^{m}\frac{Xij}{\sum_{i=1}^{m}Xij}\ln\frac{Xij}{\sum_{i=1}^{m}Xij} \tag{3}$$

$$\mathrm{Wj}=\frac{1-Hj}{\sum_{i=1}^{m}(1-Hj)} \tag{4}$$

The comprehensive evaluation indexes of the nine national central cities are calculated from the weights of indicators and the total scores (Table 2).

Table 2 List of Comprehensive Evaluation Indexes for National Central Cities in 2018

Functional Layer	Beijing	Shanghai	Guang zhou	Chengdu	Wuhan	Zheng zhou	Chong qing	Tianjin	Xi'an
Economic development center	0.8	0.8	0.7	0.5	0.5	0.6	0.4	0.2	0.4
Open and agglomeration center	0.55	0.65	0.38	0.45	0.09	0.25	0.45	0.33	0.12
Radiating and driving center	0.55	1.00	0.45	0.18	0.01	0.13	0.29	0.15	0.05
Interactive and communication center	0.15	0.52	0.71	0.59	0.18	0.26	0.76	0.55	0.04
Technological innovation center	0.39	0.21	0.24	0.24	0.23	0.15	0.18	0.04	0.12

Continued

Functional Layer	Beijing	Shanghai	Guang zhou	Chengdu	Wuhan	Zheng zhou	Chong qing	Tianjin	Xi'an
Information sharing center	0.46	0.32	0.26	0.26	0.04	0.03	0.89	0.03	0.03
Livable and entrepreneurial center	0.63	0.71	0.73	-0.09	0.33	0.49	0.13	0.37	-0.09
Humanistic and social center	0.19	0.49	0.48	0.48	0.40	0.38	0.59	0.19	0.47
Green development center	0.50	0.63	0.68	0.09	-0.24	0.12	0.67	-0.16	-0.41
Total score	0.77	0.76	0.71	0.47	0.42	0.33	0. 31	0.28	0.13
Ranking	1	2	3	4	5	6	7	8	9

The comparative analysis of the comprehensive evaluation of the 9 national central cities (see Figure 6) shows that Beijing had the best comprehensive strength, followed by Shanghai, Guangzhou, Chengdu, Wuhan and Zhengzhou, and the last three cities were Chongqing, Tianjin and Xi'an. The average comprehensive index of the national central cities was 0.53, and Beijing, Shanghai and Tianjin were all above this average. The comprehensive development levels of the other six national central cities were lower than the national average. The three leaders also showed faster development speeds, while the results show that the six laggards were still confronted with unbalanced comprehensive development. From the functional perspective, the nine cities all paid more attention to the basic function while devoting insufficient input to the growth function. According to the comprehensive evaluation results of the 9 national central cities in 2018, most of them still prioritized economic expansion over innovation factor inputs and green development. More attention is needed on innovation, humanistic and green development.

From a comprehensive perspective, there were huge gaps between Wuhan and the other national central cities on average. Wuhan was ranked 5th among the 9 national central cities; among the second batch of the 4 national central cities, Wuhan was ranked 2nd (after Chengdu, which was slightly better than Wuhan) as a regional central city, while far ahead of Zhengzhou and Xi'an. From an average functional perspective, Wuhan had huge gaps to fill with the averages

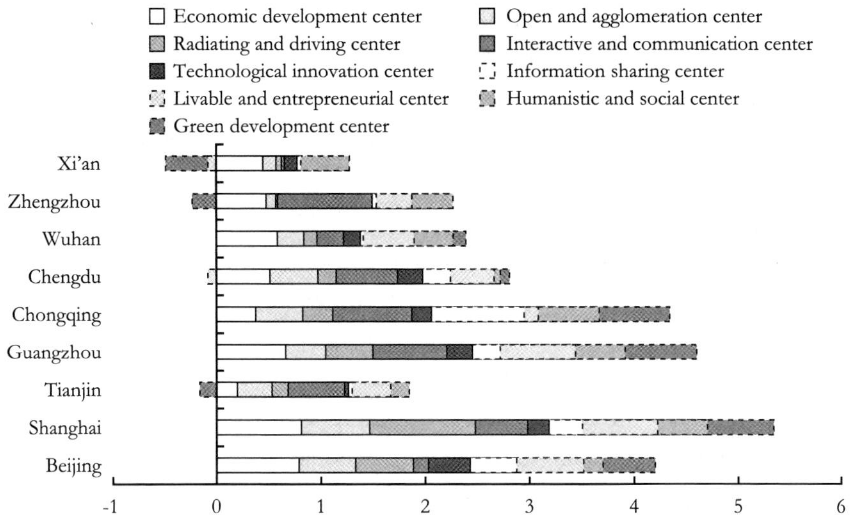

Figure 6 Comparison of Comprehensive Results among the National Central Cities in 2018

of the national central cities in 9 indicators. At the same time, Wuhan went beyond the national averages in 7 indicators, which indicated that Wuhan had its advantages and disadvantages at play in the national central city construction. It should give full play to its own advantages, recognize its shortcomings, and identify its core functions in the development path. From the perspective of sub-functions, Wuhan demonstrated strong radiating and driving ability and technological innovation capability, but its radiating and driving ability was still not comparable to the national average level. It did not perform well in the open and agglomeration function and the interactive and communication function, and its ability to absorb and circulate passengers and freight still needed to be improved. Nevertheless, Wuhan enjoys a good location advantage and will be a national transportation hub in the future. At the target function level, Wuhan fell behind the other national central cities in terms of the livable and entrepreneurial level. At the green development level, although Wuhan had high scores, it still needed to catch up with the national comprehensive average; its humanistic and social development was above the national comprehensive average. To sum up, in the process of building itself into a national central city in 2018, Wuhan got two messages based on indicator breakdown at two levels: the first message was about the functions to be improved, including open and agglomeration center, interactive and communication center, livable and entrepreneurial center, information sharing center and green development center; the second message was about the functions to be strengthened, including economic development center, radiating and driving center, technological innovation center, and humanistic and social center.

(II) Existing Problems in the National Central City Construction of Wuhan

Judging from the objective evaluation result of the comprehensive strength of the nine national central cities and the comprehensive comparative analysis on Wuhan, it shows outstanding advantages in national central city construction, but its shortcomings remain noticeable. The main problems are as follows:

Firstly, advantageous scientific and educational resources are not well integrated, and the transformation of results should be more efficient. Wuhan owns a wealth of scientific and educational as well as think tank resources, but they have not been integrated into a systematic system. As one of the central cities in the Central Region and a megacity in the middle reaches of the Yangtze River, Wuhan is supposed to play a radiating and driving role and become a complete and strategic place that has comparative advantage in decision-making research. It should make full use of its scientific and educational resources to gather high-quality think tanks. According to the research results mentioned above, Wuhan fails to enhance its overall competitiveness by tapping its abundant scientific and educational resources. At the same time, the quality and efficiency of the transformation of scientific and technological achievements are not satisfactory, which undermines the integration of scientific and educational resources and the advancement of think tank construction.

Secondly, Wuhan needs to further open up to the outside world. Although Wuhan is located strategically in the city cluster along the middle reaches of the Yangtze River, it is an inland city that has little access to communication with surrounding areas and foreign countries. It is relatively closed. Among all the national central cities, Wuhan falls far behind in comprehensive evaluation from the perspectives of opening and interaction. The evaluation results show that Wuhan does not regard openness and communication as priorities and has inadequate regional and international exchanges and cooperation.

Thirdly, the ecological, productive and living environments need to be improved. Although Wuhan has vigorously developed its infrastructures, subways and convenient transportation to support its rapid development, the comprehensive evaluation results show that Wuhan is not comparable to Beijing, Shanghai, Guangzhou, Tianjin and Zhengzhou in terms of livable and entrepreneurial environment. It has less foreign exchanges and cooperation, and provides only a moderate living and employment environment. It is expected to attract foreign investments or establish foreign cooperation and improve its living and employment environment in order to enhance its influence.

III Analysis and Evaluation of the Radiating and Driving Role of the National Central City Construction of Wuhan

The focus of this section is the radiating and driving role of Wuhan in the Wuhan metropolitan area and the Yangtze River Economic Belt.

In 2016, the *Outline of Development Plan for the Yangtze River Economic Belt* was issued by the Central Government, which indicated the leading role of Wuhan in the Yangtze River Economic Belt. In 2018, the Central Government decided the coordinated regional development strategy as one of the major strategies in the new era, which once again highlighted the role of the Wuhan in leading the development of the city cluster along the middle reaches of the Yangtze River. Based on the scientific, systematic and comparable research principles, 17 indicators in the dimensions of economic development, city scale, scientific and technological capability, opening up, information sharing and traffic accessibility are selected to reveal the comprehensive strength of Wuhan. The role of Wuhan in driving coordinated regional development is objectively analyzed with the principal component analysis method. The research objects are 11 provincial capitals (Changsha, Guiyang, Chengdu, Hangzhou, Chongqing, Kunming, Hefei, Nanchang, Wuhan, Shanghai and Nanjing) in the Yangtze River Economic Belt. The raw data first goes through standardized processing, and then the comprehensive radiating roles of the nine cities are objectively analyzed with the principal component analysis method.

Table 3 Evaluation Index System of the Radiating Role of Wuhan

Target Layer	Criterion Layer	Field Layer	Indicator Layer	Unit
Radiating role	Internal economic strength (radiating source)	Economic development	Per capita GDP	RMB 10,000
			The tertiary industry as a percentage of GDP	%
			Per capita fixed assets investment	RMB/person
			total retail volume of social consumer goods	RMB 100 million
		City scale	Built-up area	Square kilometer
			Total permanent population	10,000 persons
		Scientific and technological capability	Number of higher education institutions	
			Number of college and university students	Person
			Number of patent grants	
			Transaction volumes at technological markets	RMB 100 million
	External contacts (radiating flow)	Opening up	Total imports and exports	USD 100 million
			Actually used foreign investments	USD 100 million
			International tourism income	USD 100 million
		Information sharing	Number of broadband users	10,000 households
			Total post and telecommunications business volume	RMB 100 million
		Traffic accessibility	Total regional passenger volume	10,000 persons
			Total regional freight volume	10,000 tons

Note: From the statistical communiqué of Wuhan in 2018.

According to the calculation, the cumulative contribution rate of the first four principal components is 97.07%, so they can well explain all the selected indicators (not listed for limited length). All the indicators contribute to these four components. Based on the contributions to the extraction of principal components, the variables that contribute most are summarized as: F1 for economic development level, F2 for city development scale, F3 for capital investment scale, and F4 for technological innovation level (see Table 4).

Table 4 Rankings of Four Components in Radiating Role of Wuhan in 2018

	F1	Ranking	F2	Ranking	F3	Ranking	F4	Ranking	E	Ranking
Shanghai	6.876	1	-0.927	10	-0.501	10	-0.226	11	0.786	1
Nanjing	2.470	6	-0.199	8	0.879	4	0.309	5	0.577	4
Hangzhou	3.478	4	-1.339	11	1.097	3	1.663	1	0.663	2
Hefei	1.447	8	-0.040	7	0.750	5	0.349	4	0.353	8
Nanchang	0.935	9	0.111	5	0.734	6	-0.218	10	0.141	11
Wuhan	3.095	5	0.595	2	1.584	1	-0.075	9	0.378	6
Changsha	1.959	7	-0.274	9	0.536	7	0.187	7	0.640	3
Chongqing	4.819	2	2.489	1	0.298	8	0.968	2	0.377	7
Chengdu	3.543	3	0.580	3	1.191	2	0.195	6	0.478	5
Guiyang	0.407	11	0.486	4	-1.004	11	0.852	3	0.169	10
Kunming	0.869	10	0.066	6	0.058	9	0.107	8	0.211	9

F1 comprehensively reflects the economic development level of a city. The main contributing variables are per capita GDP, total retail volume of social consumer goods, proportion of the added value of the tertiary industry, and total postal and telecommunications business volume. It can be shown from Table 5 that the economic development levels of Shanghai, Chongqing, Chengdu, Hangzhou, Wuhan, Nanjing, Changsha and Hefei were greater than 1, indicating that their economic development levels were higher than the overall average. Wuhan was ranked 5th, with a comprehensive evaluation index of 3.095, which put it in the second-tier rank. The results show that Wuhan developed stably and positively in the process of national central city construction.

F2 comprehensively reflects the urban development scale. The main contributing indicators are built-up area, number of college and university students, and total permanent population. Among the comprehensive rankings, Wuhan was placed the second. Wuhan is strong in education and owns abundant scientific and educational resources. In 2018, its total permanent population was 11.081 million. With its continuous expansion, Wuhan placed equal emphasis on quantity and quality, which made great contributions to the improvement in its overall competitiveness.

The main contributing indicators of F3 are per capita fixed capital investments, passenger volume and freight volume, which comprehensively reflect the scale of capital investment. Negative values make Shanghai and Guiyang the only two provincial capitals among 11 in the Yangtze River Economic Belt that have capital investment scales smaller than the overall average. Wuhan is ranked first. The results show that Wuhan boasts of a large scale of capital investments due to its pivotal role in the rise of the Central Region, the development of Yangtze River Economic Belt, and the "Belt and Road" construction. Chengdu and Hangzhou are ranked 3rd and 4th, respectively.

The main contributing variables of F4 are the number of patent grants, transaction volumes at various technological markets, and the number of higher education institutions, which mainly reflect the technological innovation capability of Wuhan. Shanghai, Nanchang and Wuhan are put on the negative list, which means that their technological innovation capabilities are lower than the overall level. Among the cities with positive technological innovation capability, only Hangzhou has a value greater than 1. As a city with abundant scientific and educational resources in China, Wuhan has 88 colleges and universities, but its scientific and educational innovation capability is poor. This fully exposes the dispersal of scientific and educational and think tank resources and the room for improvement in the efficiency of transforming scientific and technological achievements in Wuhan.

A city's comprehensive radiating role, E, depends on the weights of the four principal components, and it comprehensively reflects the economic development, city size, capital investment, and technological innovation of the 11 provincial capitals in the Yangtze River Economic Belt. As shown in Table 5, Shanghai leads the ranking of the 11 provincial capitals in the Yangtze River Economic Belt due to its strong comprehensive capability in politics, economy, culture, science and technology. Wuhan is placed the 6th that belongs to the second-tier rank and has considerable gaps to fill with Shanghai, Hangzhou and Changsha in the first-tier rank. However, Wuhan has a moderate to high radiating capacity in the Yangtze River Economic Belt as a whole. Therefore, as an important central city in the Central Region and a national transportation hub, Wuhan should accurately identify its shortcomings, take full advantage of its human resources, scientific and educational resources, and think tank resources, enhance the radiating role, and play its due role in promoting the development of the Yangtze River Economic Belt.

IV Countermeasures and Suggestions on the National Central City Construction of Wuhan

1 Leverage the Superposition of National Strategies and Absorb Strategic Dividends

Wuhan has obvious advantages in transportation, affluent human capital, abundant historical and cultural resources, a vast radiating area, and an economic aggregate steadily climbing up the trillion rank. It has outstanding comparative advantages in the process of national central city construction, but it is also hindered by shortcomings such as relatively backward urban construction management, poor innovation output, and low public service supply capacity. In fact, Wuhan is facing a major opportunity from the superposition of many national strategies. Therefore, Wuhan needs to be highly fit with the national strategies and build platforms from major national strategic planning such as the rise of the Central Region, the development of the Yangtze River Economic Belt, and the "Belt and Road" construction. Relying on its own advantages and following systemic thinking with a global picture in mind, it should accurately identify its shortcomings, strengthen interactions among strategic platforms, and strive to exploit potential in various aspects such as technological innovation and information hub. The purpose is to play a core role in promoting the Yangtze River Economic Belt and in radiating to the Wuhan metropolitan area and the city cluster along the middle reaches of the Yangtze River, and to maximize the superimposed effect of national strategic plans.

2 Strengthen Connectivity with Neighboring cities and Integrated Development of Cities within the Wuhan Metropolitan Area

From the perspective of the functional positioning in the national central city construction, Wuhan is one of the core cities that drive the rise of the Central Region, and has much to catch up with the already recognized national central cities. Therefore, Wuhan needs to strengthen linkage development with neighboring cities, such as Zhengzhou, which is also a national central city. From the perspective of national central city construction, Zhengzhou and Wuhan are both strategically located in the coordinated regional development pattern and important core cities that drive the rise of the Central Region. From the perspective of urban space development, the two cities should establish a close coordination and communication mechanism, fully tap their own advantages to achieve south-north complementarity in the Central Region, and become integrated transportation hubs that provide traffic support. From the perspective of coordinated regional development, the cooperation between the cities as important nodes in the Yangtze River Economic Belt and the Lanzhou-Lianyungang Economic Belt is conducive to the cultivation of new growth poles in the region and the acceleration of regional connectivity and development. At the same time, as a key element support, Wuhan should follow the development plan of urban agglomeration to promote the optimization and upgrading of the spatial structure of Wuhan metropolitan area and drive it towards rapid and positive development through breakthroughs in key elements. At present, Wuhan has played a significant siphon effect and far outperforms the other cities in the metropolitan area, which is not favourable to the coordinated regional development within the Wuhan metropolitan area. Thus, with well-defined functions and directions of future urban development, Wuhan should strengthen basic infrastructure and the effective connection with cities within the metropolitan area. In line with the overall interests and general picture of the integrated development of Wuhan metropolitan area, Wuhan should play a core role in building a community of shared interests within the metropolitan area and put forward an innovative model of sustainable development.

3 Make Use of Scientific and Educational Advantages and Seek Support from High-quality Think Tanks

To be a national central city is not only an important mission posed by history, but also a strategic task assigned by the country in the new era. Given the urgent need for the national central city construction, Wuhan needs high-quality think tanks to provide decision-making support as the core city in the Yangtze River Economic Belt. Given the current development status of think tanks in Wuhan, persistent, focused and comprehensive high-quality research think tanks are needed. As a city with a strong education base, Wuhan owns abundant resources and outstanding innovation capability in scientific and educational fields. Its comprehensive strength in science and education still occupies the leading position in the country. To meet the huge social needs from the national central city construction, Wuhan should concentrate more efforts to the construction of high-quality think tanks. To begin with, with profound understanding of the message about the construction of a new type of think tanks with Chinese characteristics delivered at the 19th National Congress of the Communist Party of China, Wuhan should formulate a systematic development plan for high-quality think tanks in the city. Secondly, considering the scattering and inefficiency of the existing think tank resources in Wuhan, plus the main shortcomings in the development of existing think tank resources, the key is to integrate the think tank resources in Hubei Province with those in universities in Wuhan. Market mechanism should play a decisive role in the full allocation of think tank resources, and equal emphasis should be placed on the efficiency and quality of think tank resources in Wuhan. Finally, Wuhan should actively build and continuously improve think tank resources that offer core support, vigorously promote the construction of high-quality institutional information platforms, and encourage applications of achievements from high-quality think tanks.

4 Innovate Green Development and Improve "Productive, Living and Ecological" Environments in Wuhan

Judging from the objective indicators selected to evaluate the national central cities, they have larger populations, more complex population structures, and people there have higher demand for better livable and entrepreneurial environments. However, with the continuous expansion of the city size, Wuhan finds its original city scale continuously broken while enjoying the demographic dividend, resulting in the short supply of urban public goods. Moreover, because the urban management departments fail to have a clear idea about city scale expansion, the transformation of management model has lagged behind and the urban environment has not been improved accordingly. From the perspective of economic development, the human capital engaged in the productive service sector of Wuhan has higher requirements for the "productive, living and ecological" environments. Thus, Wuhan should not only meet the demand of innovative and green industries for a better city environment, but also strive to improve the "productive, living and ecological" environments for the people. Whiling enhancing the competitiveness in economy, innovation and openness, Wuhan should also make improvement in the ecological and livable environment, so as to attract more excellent human capital and develop towards a more civilized, more comfortable and safer path.

References

[1] Li Xia and Dai Shengli. Research on Development Evaluation and Mode Optimization of Smart Wuhan Oriented to National Central City: Theory and Empirical Analysis. [J]. *China Soft Science*, 2018 (01): 77-89.

[2] Tian Meiling and Fang Shiming. Study on the Strategy of Constructing Wuhan into a National Central City [J]. *Beijing Planning Review*, 2017 (01): 16-20.

[3] Peng Limin. Thoughts on National Central City Construction of Wuhan: Taking Dynamic Coupling of Urban Functions and National Strategy as a Clue [J].*Urban Studies*, 2013, 20 (01): 14-22.

[4] Liu Lan and Luo Fan. Study on Enhancing the Radiating Role of Wuhan as a National Central City [J]. *Journal of Jianghan University: Social Science*, 2015, 32 (01): 44-50+124.

[5] Li Xia and Dai Shengli. Research on Development Evaluation and Mode Optimization of Smart Wuhan Oriented to National Central City: Theory and Empirical Analysis. [J].*China Soft Science*, 2018 (01): 77-89.

[6] Afzalan, N., Sanchez, T. W., & Evans-Cowley. Creating smarter cities: Considerations for selecting online participatory tools [J].Cities, 2017, (67): 21–30.

[7] Aina, Y. A. Achieving smart sustainable cities with GeoICT support: The Saudi evolving smart cities [J].Cities, 2017, (71): 49–58.

[8] Ben Sta, H. Quality and the efficiency of data in "smart-cities" [J]Future Generation Computer Systems, 2017, (74): 409–416.

[9] Cicirelli, F., Guerrieri, A., Spezzano, G., & Vinci, A. An edge-based platform for dynamic smart city applications[J].Future Generation Computer Systems, 2017, (76): 106–118.

[10] Deloitte LLP. Assessing the value of TfL's open data and digital partnerships[R]. July 2017.

B.10

National Central City Construction of Zhengzhou: New Achievement, Problems and Suggestions

*Chen Xichuan**

Abstract: With the steady advancement of the national central city construction of Zhengzhou, a number of national strategies that support the development of this city have begun to show superimposed effects, including the established Central Plains city cluster, the Zhengzhou Airport Economy Zone, the Zheng-Luo-Xin National Innovation Demonstration Area, and the Zhengzhou Free Trade Zone. Zhengzhou plays an increasingly important role in the overall development of the country. This paper analyzes the history, advantages and foundation, problems and challenges of the national central city construction of Zhengzhou. Suggestions and future priorities are put forward based on the positioning of Zhengzhou in the national central city construction.

Keywords: Zhengzhou; national central city; construction process

* Chen Xichuan, Doctor of Management, Professor and Dean of School of Economics and Management, Zhengzhou Normal University, whose research orientation is science and technology policy and management, as well as lean management.

I History of the National City Construction of Zhengzhou

(I) Proposal and Social Influence of National Central City Construction

Central cities are spatial representations of functional division of city clusters and production layouts of economic zones. They are regional economic centers with strong innovation, service, gathering and diffusion functions. Both regional central cities and national central cities carry the essential characteristics of central cities. National central cities are best representatives of a country's internationalization and modernization levels. They are not confined to the domestic market, but participate in global economic competition. That's why they have functions and attributes different from those of regional central cities. National central cities are central centers that perform national-level strategic functions. They are social and economic centers in certain regions that combine administrative, social and economic organizations as a whole to radiate to the economic development of surroundings.

In 2005, when the Ministry of Housing and Urban-Rural Development compiled the *National Urban System Plan*, national central city construction was first introduced as a concept. In December 2008, "national central cities" officially appeared in the *Outline of the Plan for the Reform and Development of the Pearl River Delta*, which clarified that "Guangzhou should strengthen its status as a national central city, a comprehensive gateway city and a regional cultural education center." In 2010, the Ministry of Housing and Urban-Rural Development compiled the *National Urban System Plan (Draft)*, clarifying Beijing, Tianjin, Shanghai, Guangzhou and Chongqing as five national central cities.

On February 5, 2016, the State Council approved the *Urban Master Plan of Guangzhou (2011-2020)*, positioning Guangzhou as a national famous historical and cultural city, an important national central city, an international business center and an integrated transportation hub.

On April 27, 2016, with the approval of the State Council, the National Development and Reform Commission and the Ministry of Housing and Urban-Rural Development jointly issued the *Plan on Development of Chengdu and Chongqing*

City Clusters, positioning Chengdu as a national central city and requiring it to "realize the goal of becoming a national central city and enhance its functions as an important economic center, scientific and technological center, cultural and creative center, foreign exchange center and integrated transportation hub in the Western Region."

On December 14, 2016, the National Development and Reform Commission issued the *Guide to Supporting Wuhan as a National Central City*, clearly putting forward the requirement of "accelerating the construction of national central cities that serve as national economic centers, high-level technological innovation centers, trade and logistics centers, and international exchange centers".

On December 20, 2016, the National Development and Reform Commission officially printed and distributed the *"Thirteenth Five-year" Plan to Promote the Rise of Central China*, clearly proposing to "support the construction of Wuhan and Zhengzhou as national central cities."

On January 22, 2017, the National Development and Reform Commission officially issued the *Guide to Supporting Zhengzhou as a National Central City*, clearly stating that "Zhengzhou, as the core city of the Central Plains city cluster, has clear location advantages, a vast hinterland market, abundant human resources, and profound cultural heritage."

On February 2, 2018, with the approval of the State Council, the National Development and Reform Commission and the Ministry of Housing and Urban-Rural Development printed and distributed the *Development Plan of Guanzhong Plain City Cluster*, clearly stating "Xi'an should be built into a national central city." "It should quicken the pace of central city construction." "It is positioned as an important economic center, a foreign exchange center, a Silk Road scientific innovation center, a Silk Road cultural base, an inland open base, and a national integrated transportation hub in the Western Region."

(II) Strategic Vision for Zhengzhou

1 Short Term (Starting Stage: 2017-2020)

This stage witnesses the start of a new journey for the national central city construction of Zhengzhou, which is aimed to be a high-quality and high-level well-off society that is recognized by the people and that can withstand historical tests. During this stage, Zhengzhou will continue to improve its comprehensive competitiveness and make into the rank of cities with a total economic output at trillion level while improving the balance, inclusiveness and sustainability of development. In this short term, Zhengzhou will significantly improve the development quality and efficiency, accelerate the establishment of a modern economic system, make great progress in the high-end, clustering, intelligent, integrated, and green development, basically establish itself as an international hub, and greatly enhance its opening up level and technological innovation capability. At the same time, it will also effectively improve its ecological environment, fully hit various obligatory targets of ecological construction, make remarkable achievements in the construction of a resource-saving and environment-friendly society, and substantially improve the quality of the ecological environment. The people's living standards will be significantly improved, and Zhengzhou will be one of the earliest cities to fully complete the task of poverty alleviation. It will find its urban and rural infrastructure carrying capacity and public service security level greatly boosted. The income level of residents will grow simultaneously with economic development. A higher employment rate will be measured and the social security system will be further improved. All undertakings will develop in full swing; cultural characteristics will be more prominent; democracy and the rule of law will be better upheld; the governance system will be sounder; the civilization level will be clearly increased; the society will be more stable, united, civilized and harmonious.

2 Mid-term (Accelerating and Advancing Stage: 2021-2035)

The status of Zhengzhou as a national central city will be more prominent, and Zhengzhou will be a top national innovative city. It will be built into an international integrated hub, an international logistics center, an important national economic growth center, a national dynamic innovation and entrepreneurship center, a national inland gateway to the outside world, and an inheritance and innovation center of Chinese history and civilization. Its outstanding role in driving the Central Plain and in supporting the overall picture of the country will be fully highlighted. Its governance system and capacity will be basically modernized; the ecological environment will be fundamentally improved; people's living standards will be enhanced. Hopefully it will accomplish socialist modernization five years in advance by 2030.

3 Long Term (Full Completion Stage: 2036-2050)

By the middle of this century, Zhengzhou will have comprehensively upgraded its material civilization, political civilization, spiritual civilization, social civilization, and ecological civilization levels. Its governance system and capacity will have been modernized, and common prosperity will have been universally true. People will enjoy a happier and healthier life. Zhengzhou will become a powerful socialist modern city and a world city with global influence.

II Positioning, Foundation and Advantages of Zhengzhou in National Center Construction

(I) Positioning of Zhengzhou in National Central City Construction Defined by the Central Government

In the *Guide to Supporting Zhengzhou as a National Central City*, the National Development and Reform Commission made specific arrangements for the national central city construction of Zhengzhou, requiring Zhengzhou to build itself into an internationalized modern city, to upgrade its comprehensive economic strength in all round manners, to foster new driving forces for economic development quickly, to become a logistics and transportation hub, to be an open economic base in the inland, and to make greater contributions in leading the integrated development of the Central Plains city cluster, supporting the rise of the Central Region and serving the overall development of the country. Zhengzhou will receive, according to this document, support in its endeavor to "develop the hub economy, improve the technological innovation capability, strengthen the comprehensive economic strength, and become a national central city that crystallizes in itself innovative vitality, humanistic charm, ecological wisdom, openness and inclusiveness."

(II) Foundation and Advantages of Zhengzhou in National Central City Construction

1 Significant Advantages in Location and as a Transportation Hub

From the perspective of regional distribution in the country, Zhengzhou is part of the Central Region located between the southeast coast and the Western Region. From the perspective of economic belt, belonging to both the Lanzhou-Lianyungang Economic Belt and the Beijing-Guangdong Economic Belt, Zhengzhou acts as a bridge that ties the east with the west and the south with the north and plays a core role in the rise of the Central Region. In view of the Central Region, Zhengzhou is located at the intersection of the Zhengzhou-Kaifeng-Luoyang Industrial Corridor and the Xinzheng-Zhengzhou-Luohe Industrial Development Belt. It is an important railway, aviation, highway, electric power, postal and telecommunication hub in the country. It is also one of the first national pilot cities in cross-border e-commerce trade and a direct link on the state-level connectivity backbone network. Zhengzhou North Railway Station is the largest railway marshaling station in Asia. Zhengzhou Xinzheng International Airport is one of the eight regional hub airports in China that have passed the Fifth Freedom approval. The airport now operates 236 routes and becomes the second airport that supports integrated transfer among aviation, railway rail transit and expressway in China. Zhengzhou owns one railway port and one air port at the first class, as well as one railway port and one highway port at the second class. It has a good foundation for port economy development, with "four-road coordination"[①], domestic and overseas double hubs, and multi-point gathering and distribution pattern all initially in place. The rapid road network system consisting of "two horizontal and two vertical routes + loops" has basically taken shape. Intercity bus lines to Kaifeng, Jiaozuo, Xuchang, Xinxiang and other cities have been put into operation. The total length of urban bus lines exceeds 5,000km, transporting a total of 1 billion passengers annually, which made Zhengzhou the "National Bus Construction Demonstration City". *The Strategic Plan of Zhengzhou International Air Cargo Hub (2018-2035)* and the *Master Plan of Zhengzhou Railway*

① "Four-road coordination" refers to "the Air Silk Road (Aviation)", "the Silk Road (the China-Europe Train)", "the Online Silk Road" and "the Maritime Silk Road (ocean-rail combined transport trains have travelled 206 trips from Zhengzhou to Lianyungang, Qingdao and Tianjin Ports).

Hub (2016-2030) were successfully approved, and the *White Paper of Smooth Transportation in Zhengzhou (2019-2021)* was compiled. A Jack Union-shaped high-speed rail network is under progress quickly, and Zhengzhou shows an increasing advantage as a transportation hub.

2 The Modern Industrial System Develops Rapidly

By the end of 2018, there had been two industrial clusters, namely electronic information plus automobile and equipment manufacturing, in Zhengzhou, and both of them were valued over RMB 500 billion. Zhongmu Automobile Industry Cluster has become a new national industrialized demonstration base. The added value of seven leading industries grew by 7.6%, which contributed 93.9% of the growth of total industries in the city. Zhengzhou Airport Economy Zone was commended by the State Council as a national demonstration base of mass entrepreneurship and innovation. The Central Business District of Zhengdong New Area is one of the "most dynamic central business districts" in China. The International Logistics Park was promoted to a national-level demonstration logistics park, and Zhengzhou was simultaneously recognized as national logistics hub based on land port and used for production services and business services. Zhengzhou was also recognized as a national service-oriented manufacturing demonstration city and a strategic demonstration city of "variety, quality and brand" in the consumer goods industry of China. The investments in industrial technology reform increased by 35.4%; manufacturing investments accounted for 79.5% of the total industrial investment; the investments in strategic emerging industries increased by 26.4%, and those in high-end equipment manufacturing and new-generation information technology industries grew by 380.5% and 734.7%, respectively. The production and sales volume of new energy passenger cars exceeded 25,000, accounting for 27% of the total in the country. The ratio of three industries in the city was adjusted from 2.1:49.5:48.4 to 1.81:42.43:55.76 in late 2015.

(III) Progress in the National Central City Construction of Zhengzhou

1 Major Economic and Social Development Indicators Hit Historic Records

By the end of 2018, with the solid advancement of the national central city construction, Zhengzhou had stood at a new starting point that led to high-quality development. The city's regional GDP totaled RMB 1.01433 trillion, with a growth rate of 8.1%, which moved it one place forward to be the 16th among 298 cities above prefecture level in the country. The added value of industrial enterprises above designated size increased by 6.8%. The proportion of high energy consumption industries fell below 40% for the first time. The fixed asset investments increased by 10.9%; the industrial investments increased by 11.8%; the total retail volume of social consumer goods increased by 9.7%; the local fiscal general public budget income increased by 9% to RMB 115.21 billion, and the proportion of taxes reached 74.6%, 4 percentage points higher than the provincial level. The total number of market entities was 1.075 million, added by 252,000 new comers, which made Zhengzhou the eighth provincial capital with over one million market entities. The private economy accounted for 58.9% of GDP, and the proportion of employees engaged in private economy accounted for 87.3% of the urban employment population. The energy consumption per unit of production decreased to 7%, and the energy consumption per RMB 10,000 of industrial added value decreased by 14.8%. The consumer price index increased by 2.4%, and the prices of eight categories of commodities covering "clothing, food, housing and transportation" all maintained moderate increases. The per capita disposable income of residents was RMB 33,105, with a growth rate of 8.3%, and the urban-rural resident income ratio was narrowed to 1.8.

2 The City's Carrying Capacity and Service Functions are Increasingly Improved

By the end of 2018, the built-up area of the urban area in Zhengzhou was 1,055.27 square kilometers, with 224.3 square kilometers added on the basis of the existing area in the previous year. The urbanization rate of the city was 73.4%. Public service facilities for education, health, medical care, and pension purposes were provided at faster pace. The "four centers"① in the Central

① "Four centers" cover an area of about 1.53 square kilometers that extends to the south of the main canal of the South-to-North Water Diversion Project, the west of Kaixuan Road, and the north of Bohai Road. There were 16 single projects planned from west to east: the Olympic Sports Center (stadium, gymnasium, natatorium), the Cultural, Museum and Art Center (art museum, archive and annals museum, museum, grand theatre), the Citizen Activity Center (science museum, mass art center, acrobatic center, youth activity center, women and children activity center, health center), and the Modern Media Center (newspaper building, radio station, television station).

Cultural Districts" (CCD) were basically completed. Comprehensive pilot projects such as integrated pipe gallery and clean heating were advanced in an orderly manner, adding a new heating area of 16 million square meters and a new daily domestic sewage treatment capacity of 200,000 tons. A garbage power plant with a daily processing capacity of 4,000 tons and a kitchen waste treatment plant with a capacity of 600 tons were soon put into operation. A three-year action plan for refined urban management was fully launched, whose coverage scope was expanded from the Third Ring Road to 48 townships in the suburbs, with an area of 1,440 square kilometers. A three-level "road accountability system" was fully implemented within the Fourth Ring Road. Zhengzhou was selected as one of the 35 pilot cities for nationwide construction waste control, and was ranked among the top ten of the 46 pilot cities in urban household waste classification. The national land greening speed-up action was vigorously promoted, and all illegal constructions by railways, trunk roads, highway overpasses and at entrances and exits of the city were all demolished. Ecological corridors with a total length of 528 kilometers were improved and connected; an afforestation area of 115,000 mu and a forest tending area of 78,000 mu were added. In the urban area, new green spaces covering a total area of 13.56 million square meters were built, and 411 parks, gardens and micro-parks, including the High-speed Rail Park, were put into service, adding up to a total area of 2,431 hectares. There were 966 public toilets available in the city. The Zhengzhou Green Expo Garden and Zhengzhou Garden Expo Park were regularly open. The centralized domestic sewage treatment facilities were provided at a faster pace in 27 beautiful villages and 364 planned reserve villages, and 1,037 grassroots comprehensive cultural service centers were completed and put into use. The green coverage rate of the built-up area reached 40.3%. All public resource transactions were under online supervision. Zhengzhou won the national "Award for Innovating Incentives for Integrity" for its social credit system.

3 The City's Spatial Layout and Functional Positioning Are Constantly Optimized

The Action Plan for the National Central City Construction of Zhengzhou (2017-2035) issued in February 2018 put forward the development concept of "eastward expansion, westward reclamation, southward extension, northward linkage and central optimization" to constantly optimize the spatial layout of the city and form a spatial pattern dominated by two cities①, integrating three green belts②, interconnected by three-axis railways③, and linking multipoles,④ as well as an urban system of "main urban area, aviation city, multi-groups, multi-nodes"; the plan also required efforts to pursue group-based development, highlight industrial differentiation, identify development orientation, give prominence to comparative advantages, demonstrate city characteristics, promote integrated development of new city groups and the central urban area bounded by fast and convenient three-dimensional transportation, with large-scale green spaces and ecological communities as barriers; the plan made the transformation of Zhongmu, Xingyang and Xinzheng Counties (Cities) into counties a priority and pressed for faster construction of Xinmi Group, Dengfeng Group and Gongyi Group to include them into the urban area as soon as possible; the plan urged faster functional dispersal of the central urban area, which would be taken as a pioneering breakthrough to guide orderly industrial transfer, drive population transfer, support optimization of urban layout, and help get rid of "big urban diseases"; the plan finally prescribed that Zhengzhou should optimize the layout of public service organizations at provincial and municipal levels, facilitate the migration of general wholesale markets and manufacturing industries, speed up the relocation of long-distance bus stations such as the central bus station near the railway station, and encourage the transfer of high-quality educational and medical resources to new city groups. It is estimated that by 2035 the total GDP of Zhengzhou will reach RMB 3 trillion, the per capita GDP RMB 220,000, the population 13.5 million, the proportion of urban population 90%; and an urban population increase by about 5.5 million from 2016.

---

① A spatial pattern dominated by two cities: refers to the linkage of the optimized central urban area and the accelerated construction of aviation city (the Zhengzhou Airport Economy Zone with an area of 415 square kilometers) to lead the development of the city and the greater region.

② Three green belts: the Yellow River, the mountain areas and the rural ecological and cultural belts).

③ Three-axis railways: Beijing-Guangzhou Railway, Lanzhou-Lianyungang Railway, and Zhengzhou-Dengfeng-Luoyang Intercity Railway.

④ Multipoles: regional function centers, new functional groups, and peripheral small characteristic towns.

III Goals for the National Central City Construction of Zhengzhou

(I) To Actively Promote Construction of Innovation and Entrepreneurship Centers and Gradually Enhance Innovation Leading Function

In recent years, Zhengzhou has taken active measures to guide the innovation factors such as talents, technology and capital to flow towards enterprises and has tried to make enterprises the mainstay that meets technological innovation demand, makes R&D investments, and applies technological innovation results; in addition, it has further promoted the joint construction of independent technological innovation service platforms by universities, research institutes and enterprises leading different industries; it has also made active commitment to government policy inputs in various aspects such as taxation and finance and has established a diversified, multi-level and multi-channel technology investment system contributed by social capital; it has implemented the strategy of reinvigorating the city through human resource development and a series programs such as "Zhengzhou Brains • 1125 Talent Recruitment Program" and "Zhengzhou Brains • 1+7 Talent Introduction Program" and has quickened the pace of introducing and cultivating talents and teams for innovation and entrepreneurship. As a result, its ability to lead innovation and entrepreneurship has been gradually enhanced. By the end of 2018, the number of scientific and technological projects organized in the city grew by 8.8% over the previous year to reach 1,336, which included 436 projects at the provincial level and above, equal to an increase by 43.9%. There were 6 national engineering research centers and 19 national enterprise technology centers, 355 provincial engineering technology research centers and 280 provincial enterprise technology centers, and 117 provincial key laboratories. The city won 9 prizes for progress in science and technology at national level and 38 at provincial level. The number of patent applications in 2018 increased by 38.8% to 70,128; the number of patent grants increased by 48.6% to 31,585; the number of technological contracts signed increased by 15.1% to 4,349, and the turnover of technology contracts increased by 136.8% to RMB 8.24 billion. In 2018, the added value of high-tech industries amounted to RMB 45.76 billion, 10.4 times that of 2010, which lent strong support to the improved entrepreneurial and innovative capabilities of Zhengzhou (see Figure 1).

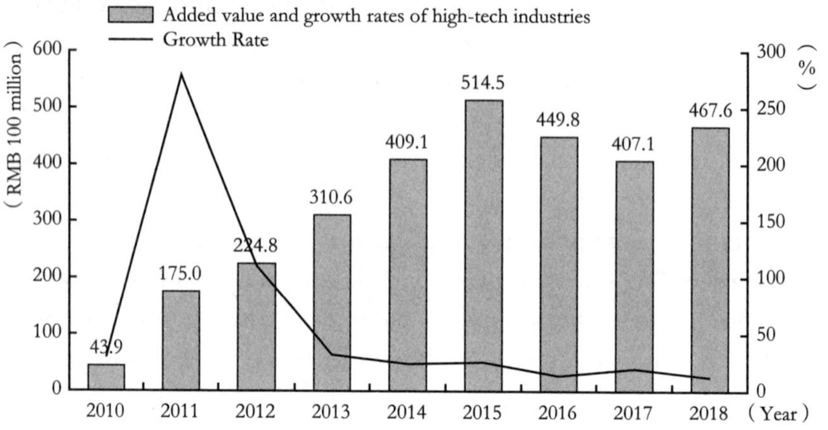

Figure 1 Added Value and Growth Rates of High-tech Industries in Zhengzhou for 2010-2018.

Sources: Adapted from the *Economic Operation of Zhengzhou* and the *Statistical Communiqué of Zhengzhou Municipality on the 2017 National Economic and Social Development.*

(II) To Actively Promote Construction of Economic Growth Center and Gradually Improve Industrial Driving Capacity

Zhengzhou accelerated the construction of advanced manufacturing industries which were the pillar of the economy, modern service industries which played a dominant role in economic development, and urban ecological agriculture which served as the economic foundation. At the same time, it promoted coordinated development of the real economy, technological innovation, modern finance and human resources. In order to stabilize growth, adjust the industrial structure and promote transformation, the industrial and information sector of the city took the following measures to promote industrial agglomeration, upgrading and transformation: strengthening industrial operation monitoring, promoting investment attraction and project construction, accelerating industrial transformation and upgrading, quickening the innovation and development of manufacturing industries, and reinforcing policy support and other initiatives.

These measures have enhanced the factor agglomeration and driving capacity of industries in Zhengzhou and pushed the industries to develop towards the mid and high ends of the industry chain. By enhancing the vitality of micro market entities and cultivating a more efficient market system, Zhengzhou is positioned as the economic growth pole of the Central Plains Economic Zone to drive the rise of the Central Region. By the end of 2018, the year-end total population of the city increased by 2.6% to 10.136 million; its GDP increased by 8.1% to RMB 1.01433 trillion; its per capita GDP increased by 5.8% to RMB 101,349; its urbanization rate increased by 1.2 from the previous year to 73.4%. In 2018, the industrial driving capacity of Zhengzhou was gradually enhanced (see Figure 2).

(III) To Actively Promote Construction of Historical and Cultural Inheritance Center and Gradually Improve Living Quality of Urban and Rural Residents

In recent years, seizing the opportunity of building itself into the innovation and inheritance center of Chinese historical civilization, Zhengzhou has combined protection with utilization and inheritance with innovation, and continuously improved the civilization quality of citizens and urban civilization.

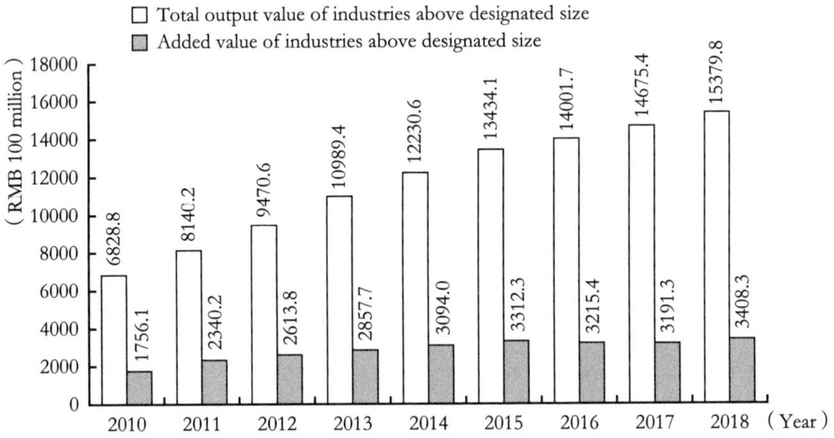

Figure 2 Total Output Value and Added Value of Industrial Enterprises above Designated Size in Zhengzhou for 2010-2018.

Sources: Adapted from the *Zhengzhou Statistical Yearbook* and the *Statistical Communiqué of Zhengzhou Municipality on the National Economic and Social Development.*

It has created an open and inclusive culture that is in line with the status of national central city and that reflects the socialist core values. It is committed to shaping the humanistic spirit of a modern metropolis and becoming an international cultural metropolis where traditional cultures and modern civilization complement each other. It strengthened the exploration, protection and inheritance of historical and cultural heritages by building characteristic cultural districts, promoting cultural quality projects, constructing and improving the quality of museums, and actively applying for inclusion in the list of world cultural heritage. Making use of the cultural resources of Songshan Mountain, Zhengzhou increased publicity, actively participated in various major international events, and carried out a number of city image promotion activities to further enhance the international influence of the Central Plain culture. Solid steps have been taken to strengthen the integration of Central Plain culture with world cultures. By the end of 2018, there had been 15 art performance groups, 17 public libraries, 14 cultural centers, 38 museums, 13 general archives, 1.578 million volumes (pieces) of various files open to the public, 74 national key cultural relic protection units, and 6 items included in the national intangible cultural heritage list in the city. All the city population was covered by radio and television, and the number of cable TV users was 1.558 million. The living quality of residents was gradually improved.

(IV) To Actively Promote Construction of International Integrated Transportation and Logistics Hub and Gradually Enhance Radiating and Agglomerating Functions

The transportation in Zhengzhou was led by the aviation network, framed by the railway network as the backbone and supported by the high-grade road network. Its plan was to build a spoke-structured aviation network that reaches the world and radiates to the whole country, to accelerate the construction of a Jack Union-shaped railway network and a intercity railway network, to continuously improve the expressway network pattern, the national highway network pattern and the provincial road network pattern within the city, and to establish a modern integrated transportation system mainly composed of international aviation, high-speed railway and expressway; it optimized the comprehensive layout of freight hub formed by "four ports and multiple stations", improved the functions of airport, railway port, highway port and seaport, and enhanced service capabilities; it promoted the construction of "four hubs and multiple stations" with an aim to shape an integrated hub system in which the four ports are linked and connected seamlessly; it strengthened the overall layout of international, domestic and urban transportation corridors, expanded international routes, improved domestic corridors, and built city corridors with reasonable structure, clear hierarchy, complete functions, high coverage rate and deep accessibility; it made concerted effort to put into place a transportation hub characterized by "integration of three networks, linkage of four ports, and multimodal transportation"; it constantly strengthened the construction of national main power, information and pipeline hubs, tried to upgrade its status as a global node city, and was committed to being an international integrated hub city. The transportation status of Zhengzhou over the past 5 years was shown in Table 1.

Table 1 Transportation Status of Zhengzhou over the Past 5 Years

Year	Rotation Volume of Freight Transport			Passenger Volume		
	Railway (100 million ton-km)	Air (100 million ton-km)	Highway (100 million ton-km)	Railway (100 million passenger-km)	Air (100 million passenger-km)	Highway (100 million passenger-km)
2013	217.2	0.5849	467.5	128	26.6	188
2014	199.9	4.7139	332.4	130.2	61.2	83.6
2015	172.7	5.4276	370	134.5	65.4	79.7
2016	176.8	14.7	494.8	138.2	65.9	107.7
2017	202.5	18.6	558.2	152.4	72.4	104.4
2018	213.8	29.1	621.4	157.1	87.3	97.1

Sources: Adapted from the *Zhengzhou Statistical Yearbook* and the *Statistical Communiqué of Zhengzhou Municipality on the National Economic and Social Development.*

(V) To Actively Promote Construction of Opening-up Gateway in Inland Area and Gradually Improve Trade Logistics Center

Zhengzhou coordinated the construction of important open platforms such as Zhengzhou Airport Economy Zone, Zhengzhou Economic Development Zone and Zhengdong New Area. It erected a supporting system of opening platforms, further improved the gateway role of international ports, built and improved the customs clearance and logistics mechanisms adopted by international air and railway hub ports and the innovation port in Zhengzhou, enhanced the cross-border customs clearance and logistics functions of these ports, strengthened their freight transportation function, improved their passenger transportation function, and developed an international mail transshipment function. It also strengthened cross-regional cooperation with cities along the Silk Road Economic Belt, the Yangtze River Economic Belt, the Beijing-Tianjin-Hebei Region, the Pan-Pearl River Delta Region and Northeast China.

Table 2 Trade Logistics Developments of Zhengzhou over the Past Three Years

Year	Freight Volume			Passenger Volume		
	Railway (10,000 tons)	Air (10,000 tons)	Highway (10,000 tons)	Railway (10,000 persons)	Air (10,000 persons)	Highway (10,000 persons)
2016	2750	19	19269	4875	479	11007
2017	3034.2	22.9	22073.2	5418.2	518.7	8815.4
2018	1920.3	31.5	25679	5780.5	813.1	8236

Source: Adapted from the *Zhengzhou Statistical Yearbook and the Statistical Communiqué of Zhengzhou Municipality on the National Economic and Social Development.*

It promoted the interconnection of transportation infrastructures, information and communication infrastructures, and port opening platforms, strengthened interoperability in key areas, and explored the possibilities of global port alliance. To deeply integrate into the "Belt and Road" strategy, Zhengzhou relied on its advantageous tourism resources to build an important platform for dialogues between world civilizations and cultural exchanges, maintained close humanistic exchanges, and introduced high-quality education resources from foreign countries. It created a favorable international business environment, innovated and developed cross-border E-trade industries, carried out high-level international economic exchanges and cooperation, enhanced its international level, and built itself into an opening gateway in the inland area of China. The freight transportation developments in Zhengzhou over the past three years are shown in Table 2.

IV National Central City Construction of Zhengzhou: Problems and Thoughts

(I) Limited Economic Output and Inadequate Comprehensive Carrying Capacity

Zhengzhou's GDP, though exceeding RMB 1 trillion, was less than 50% of Tianjin's and Chongqing's, and only 70% of Wuhan's and Chengdu's. Zhengzhou was not comparable to Wuhan, Guangzhou, Chengdu and Xi'an in terms of the proportion of their respective GDP to the provincial total. Among all the national central cities, Zhengzhou has a small area, about just half of Chengdu's (14,312 square kilometers). Its ecological construction relatively lags behind; its environmental capacity tends to be saturated; its ecological environment has a low carrying capacity. The per capita water resources of Zhengzhou are less than one-tenth of the national average, and it has bad air quality among 74 cities in the country. Zhengzhou does not stand at the forefront of either population or economic rankings in the province and the Central Plains city cluster. Modern service industries in the city, such as finance, information services, and scientific research and development, have limited coverage, and the comprehensive service function is not strong enough to support the capacity of the city to radiate to the surroundings. The economic indicators of Zhengzhou and the other national central cities are compared in Table 3.

Table 3 Comparison of Economic Indicators between Zhengzhou and the Other Eight National Central Cities in 2018

City	GDP (RMB 100 Million)	Total Industrial Added Value (RMB 100 Million)	Fixed Asset Investment (RMB 100 Million)
Beijing	30320	4464.6	8062.2
Shanghai	32679.87	8694.95	7623.4
Tianjin	18809.64	6962.71	10643.3
Guangzhou	22859.35	5621.73	5938.4
Chongqing	20363.19	5997.7	18661.4
Chengdu	15342.77	5663.75	8341.1

Continued

City	GDP (RMB 100 Million)	Total Industrial Added Value (RMB 100 Million)	Fixed Asset Investment (RMB 100 Million)
Wuhan	14847.29	5076.21	8706
Zhengzhou	10143.3	3746.2	8398.9
Xi'an	8349.86	1874.36	8090.2

Source: Adapted from the statistical communiqué of each city on the 2018 national economic and social development.

(II) Obvious Shortcomings in Industrial Development and Development Potential to be Further Exploited

Zhengzhou's industries excel in size but not in strength, and traditional resource-intensive industries still account for about 40% of the industries. There are few large-scale leading enterprises, and advanced manufacturing and modern service industries need to play a more leading role. The tertiary industry accounted for 50.7% of GDP, which put Zhengzhou in the 22nd place among 35 large and medium-sized cities nationwide and the 17th place among provincial capital cities.

1 Industrial Structural Problems Still Exist

The city's industries are concentrated in the front end of the industrial chain and the mid-and low-end of the value chain. The products do not provide high added value, and high energy consumption industries still account for nearly 40% of the total industries; strategic emerging industries do not play a prominent driving role; traditional trade and real estate in the service industry account for more than 30%, while emerging services such as technological services, R&D and design take up low proportions.

2 Poor Core Competitiveness of Modern Service Industries

The total economic output of the service industry remains relatively small. Of the fixed assets investments in the service industry, only a few go to finance, cultural and creative tourism, logistics, and technological services, which result in weak momentum for industrial development. In terms of the added value of the cultural industry as a percentage in the city's GDP, Zhengzhou lags behind the other national central cities. It has such problems as small-scale cultural management enterprises, which have weak competitiveness and influence, scattered industrial operations, small industrial scale and low intensive degree, few large-scale key enterprise groups and cultural brands that are famous at home and abroad, and incapacity to "go out". In addition, the contradiction between the development of the cultural industry and the total number of competent talents is conspicuous, which greatly restricts the improvement of the overall cultural industry. The per capita disposable incomes of urban and rural residents in Zhengzhou in recent years are shown in Figure 3.

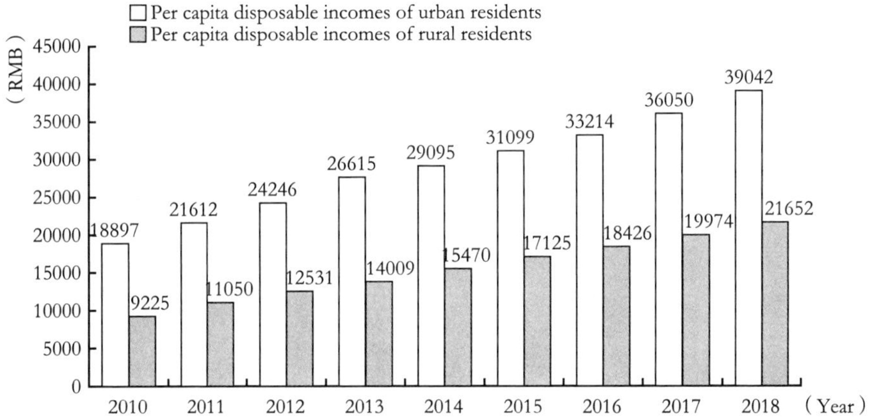

Figure 3 Per Capita Disposable Incomes of Urban and Rural Residents in Zhengzhou for 2010-2018

Sources: Adapted from the statistical communiqué of Zhengzhou Municipality on the national economic and social development over the years.

3 The Quality of Agricultural Development Needs to be Improved

The intensive degree and scale of agriculture needs to be improved. The rural land transfer rate in Zhengzhou was lower than 25%, far lower than the average levels of the province (38%) and the whole country (35%). The output rate of agricultural land per mu remains low (RMB 3,760 per mu), less than one-third of the level in Wuhan (RMB 12,980 per mu). Thus, its agricultural labor productivity needs to be improved. The number of employees in the primary industry of Zhengzhou (917,000) was twice that of Wuhan (456,000), but its added value of the industry was less than 1/2 of that of Wuhan. According to the data of 35 large and medium-sized cities in China published by the Ministry of Agricultural and Rural Affairs, the added value of agriculture, forestry, animal husbandry and fishery in Zhengzhou had the highest energy consumption per unit production and the lowest output. Its energy consumption per unit production was about 4 times that of Wuhan and 3 times that of Chengdu.

(III) The City Has a Weak Technological Innovation Foundation and Needs to Improve Its Comprehensive Competitiveness

1 Insufficient Social Inputs of Innovation Resources and Weak Innovative Capability

The R&D activities of Zhengzhou are mainly concentrated in advantageous industries and large-scale enterprises. SMEs generally do not pay due attention to R&D and need to enhance their awareness of independent innovation. The overall ability of innovation subjects needs to be improved. High-tech enterprises are too few, small, and impotent to play a radiating role. Leading innovation-based enterprises and technology-based enterprises develop at a slow speed and with low quality. Zhengzhou is hindered by a shortage of high-end innovation resources. There are only 12 national-level research institutes, only one research institute affiliated to the Chinese Academy of Sciences, and only four national key laboratories. In terms of innovation mechanism, Zhengzhou needs to improve the environment that encourages innovation and entrepreneurship. The system and mechanism for strengthening domestic and foreign communication and cooperation still need to be improved. The public service system for innovation and entrepreneurship is not complete; the universities and research institutes are not closely combined with industry development in Zhengzhou and the transformation rate of scientific and technological achievements is too low to serve and support economic and social development. The R&D expenditures of Zhengzhou and the other national central cities are compared in Table 4.

Table 4 Comparison of Industrial Structures (in 2018) and R&D Expenditure (in 2017) between Zhengzhou and the Other National Central Cities

City	Added Value of the Tertiary Industry as Percentage of GDP (2018)	R&D Expenditure (RMB 100 Million) (in 2017)	R&D Expenditure as Percentage of GDP (%) (in 2017)	Number of Patent Grants (in 2018)
Beijing	80.98%	1579.7	5.64%	123000
Shanghai	69.9%	1205.2	3.93%	92460
Tianjin	58.6%	458.7	2.47%	54700
Guangzhou	71.75%	537.58	2.5%	89826
Chongqing	52.3%	364.6	1.88%	45688
Chengdu	61.3%	331.3	2.39%	57370
Wuhan	54.6%	429.13	3.2%	32397
Zhengzhou	54.7%	158.7	1.29% (for the whole province)	31583
Xi'an	61.9%	360.17	4.82%	71250 (Number of applications)

Source: Adapted from the statistical communiqué of each city on the national economic and social development from 2016 to 2018.

2 The Construction of the Core Area of Zheng-Luo-Xin National Innovation Demonstration Zone Should be Promoted to a New Level

At present, the core area of Zheng-Luo-Xin National Innovation Demonstration Zone has not built an institutional mechanism that fully adapts to its own development needs, stimulates vitality and motivation, and mobilizes enthusiasm and creativity, and the lack of such mechanism to some extent restricts its development; in terms of the spatial layout of the core area, the development hinterland of 99 square kilometers (including construction land of 77 square kilometers, basic farmland of 4.67 square kilometers, and other conditional and limited land of about 17 square kilometers outside planning) cannot satisfy the actual construction and development needs of the core area; in respect of various innovative resources, there is a shortage of human resources in high-tech industries, and there are huge gaps between Zhengzhou and other national central cities in terms of the number of colleges and universities, the number of college students, the number of academicians of the two academies, the number of experts included in the "Thousand Talents Program", the number of high-tech enterprises, and the number of national technology business incubators. Such shortages fail to meet the needs of technological innovation and the district development of Zhengzhou; as for the overall scale of emerging industries, the strategic emerging industries in the core area are generally small and few. No large-scale leading enterprises with strong driving capacity have emerged. No strong industry-driven effect has been formed, and the industrial system needs to be improved.

(IV) The Construction of Modern International Logistics Center Is Relatively Backward and the Construction of Logistics Center with Great International Influence Should be Accelerated

1 The International Logistics Park in Zhengzhou Still Has Shortcomings and Deficiencies

The International Logistics Park in Zhengzhou has a short industry chain and a low input-output ratio. The main business scope of the park is traditional warehousing and transportation. The logistics projects are generally small and scattered, with few headquarters, platform and supply chain projects. Dominant projects fail to exert a driving force, and most of the projects are small and medium-sized ones that do not generate productivity and contribute little to operating income and taxation. They need to be integrated and upgraded. The park is not intelligent enough. Key logistics enterprises are highly information-based, but small and medium-sized ones are not. Various information systems are widely applied in logistics enterprises, but the construction of public information service platform for government logistics lags behind. There is a shortage of comprehensive logistics information service providers in the park, and in-the-majority small and medium-sized logistics enterprises are engaged in the low end of the industrial chain, with a low logistics informationization degree and poor information integration capability. There is an urgent need for resource integration and information transformation. The logistics infrastructures are not complete, and the information integration is unsatisfactory in the park. The park has not been fully connected with the main urban area, the airport, Zhengdong New Area or trunk highways such as the Zhengmin Expressway, and the new National Highway 107. Special facilities used for logistics purposes, such as public parking lots, public goods yards, and public information platforms, are not fully in place. With bad weather such as rain, snow and fog, or during rush hours, disorderly parking and traffic jams become serious problems. The overall supporting capacity of the park needs to be further improved.

2 The Construction of Modern Logistics Infrastructures Is Relatively Backward

As the status of Zhengzhou as a transportation hub is enhanced, general small scale, unreasonable structure, incomplete supporting facilities and low carrying capacity of logistics infrastructures have become bottlenecks that restrict the development of the modern logistics industry and the construction of modern international logistics center in Zhengzhou. For example, at present there are only two loading and unloading lines operating at the Railway Container Central Station of Zhengzhou. With more intensive operation of the China-Europe train (Zhongzhou), the loading and unloading capacity of the railway port cannot meet the actual needs. Currently, the logistics industry of Zhengzhou is at preliminary transportation and storage stage. There is a big gap between Zhengzhou and other similar cities in the country in terms of logistics infrastructures. Many less-than-carload logistics enterprises do not have stable business premises, and their development is seriously restricted.

3 The Financial Support Systems and the Connection between Multimodal Transportation Means Need to be Improved

At present, the financial support and policy support systems for aviation, Zhengzhou-European Train, port construction, and cross-border e-commerce services are relatively scattered. No unified logistics policy support system is available for smooth international logistics channels, strengthening the functional level of the international hub, upgrading port clearance services, increasing the modernization level of logistics, and introducing innovative logistics organization models. Inconsistent standards, uncoordinated connection, inefficient transfer, and inconvenient customs clearance are serious problems that hinder connection between different modes of transportation such as aviation, railway and highway. In particular, railway manifests and other modes of transportation are not mutually recognized and effectively docked, which has become a major obstacle to the development of international logistics in Zhengzhou. The airports, railways and postal ports are not closely connected and effectively interacted. According to the Zhengzhou Customs, there is a conflict between the customs supervision and the safety inspection of the railway department. In order to ensure effective supervision of goods, the customs will affix a seal or lock on the inspected containers, while the railway department has to unpack the containers to check their loading status in order to prevent lateral weight. Containers that are transferred from other modes of transportation such as road transport are sealed, and the railway department is not able to unpack the goods for their name and add reinforcement to the loading. This is a conflict between customs supervision and transportation safety.

(V) The Investment Environment and "Internet + Government Services" Should be Improved

1 Government Services Should be More Efficient

In recent years, Zhengzhou has started to develop the top-level design and standards of e-government, and a number of policy documents in the field of e-government have been issued. The lack of a unified standard system between departments and inconsistency between systems and data standards have seriously affected the development and advancement of data sharing and business collaboration, resulting in delays and deviations in data navigation, data acquisition and exchange and further inefficiency of government affairs.

There Is a Shortage of Professionals Working by Government Service Windows

E-government construction is a systematic project. Basic cloud platform erection, data sharing and top-level planning and design all require a large number of professional and technical personnel armed with advanced e-government concepts. Due to the low informationization degree in the early stage, there is a serious shortage of window clerks and professionals, which has dragged Zhengzhou seriously behind other advanced cities in terms of government administration. There is still a big gap to fill in order to meet the national requirement for "Internet + government services" and adapt to the reform of "streamlining of administration, delegation of power to lower level, governance and service reform". More support in aspects such as funds and talents should be increased to improve the government service environment and the investment environment.

(VI) The Open Economy Develops Slowly and Further Opening Up Is Urgently Needed

In recent years, Zhengzhou has shown a good development trend in opening up to the outside world, but it still needs to fill the gap and overcome its shortcomings when compared with the other national central cities.

1 The Function of Zhengzhou in the China (Henan) Pilot Free Trade Zone Should be Improved

Zhengzhou has a low opening level as a whole and is not attractive enough to international innovation resources. It is also a weak magnet for innovative resources or entities such as foreign capital, foreign companies and international high-end talents. The inter-departmental communication and coordination mechanism needs to be further improved. The coordination and promotion mechanism for the departments that lead and assist in reforms and pilot innovation tasks needs to be improved; the mechanism for communication and coordination between the management committee of Zhengzhou and other government departments needs to be strengthened; more improvements should be made in inter-departmental work coordination and information sharing in order to form synergy with Kaifeng and Luoyang; cooperation with other free trade pilot zones at home and abroad should be continuously strengthened; the coordinated development with the Central Plains Economy Region should be strengthened.

2 Zhengzhou Needs to be More International

Zhengzhou is not a coastal city and has no sea port, which is why its marine economy and port industry development is limited. Although the Zhengzhou-European Train and cross-border E-trade have performed well and the Zhengzhou Airport Economy Zone gets increasingly functional, Zhengzhou apparently has much less international exchange channels than Beijing, Shanghai and Guangzhou, where the airports are more international. This restricts the internationalization, the development of tourism and exhibition and other relevant industries in Zhengzhou. At present, real estate and related industries take up a lion's share in the service industry of Zhengzhou. The low levels, low proportions, obscure characteristics, and generally small scale of enterprises in the service economy and the creative economy can be directly explained by the internationalization degree of Zhengzhou.

3 The Foreign Trade Structure Should be Optimized

Although the total import and export volume of Zhengzhou is higher than those of the surrounding cities, the problem of excessive dependence on the trade of single enterprises still exists. The import and export of Foxconn alone accounted for 80% of the total import and export volume of the city. This fact seriously affects the stable development of import and export of Zhengzhou. Major projects that attract foreign investments in high-end manufacturing and modern service industries are few and far between. Industrial transformation and upgrading is backed up by weak momentum. Few large-scale central enterprises and industry leading enterprises are introduced to drive related industries strongly. Thus, the adjustments in the economic structure and foreign trade structure are limited and the breadth and depth of economic opening up of Zhengzhou are affected.

(VII) The Airport Economy Zone Plays A Limited Leading Role and Has Much Room for Improvement

1 The Aviation Hub Construction and the Industrial Development Need to be Strengthened

At present, the Zhengzhou Airport Economy Zone has only one base company which is a joint venture base airline of China Southern Airlines (Henan). It has much to catch up with the target of supporting the construction of an international air passenger and freight hub. There is an urgent need to increase the number and scale of passenger and freight base companies. The industries in the Airport Economy Zone are generally positioned at the lowest end of the industrial chain. There are few major innovative, leading and radiating projects, and the industries do not master strong core competitiveness.

2 Innovative Mechanisms for Domestic and International Economic Cooperation Should be Established

The status of aviation hub can, to some extent, be translated to the expansion of business scopes, including aviation logistics, equipment manufacturing, freight forwarder, high-end technical maintenance, investment and financing. On the one hand, it relies on professionals. On the other hand, it requires connection between various systems and regulations and innovation in this regard. Without complete institutional mechanisms as guarantee, the depth, breadth and intensity of economic cooperation would be restricted and affected, so will be the functions of the hub.

3 The Gathering Capability of the International Aviation Logistics Center in the Airport Economy Zone Should be Improved

The market entities are small, scattered and weak, and there is a shortage of large-scale and networked air transport groups and big air logistics integrated service providers; effective connection is not accomplished in port infrastructure construction, and multimodal transportation development is slower and not smooth; the center is not international enough and the clustering effect of the aviation transportation industry is not obvious; the docking efficiency between information platforms of ports, enterprises and industries should be improved. These problems affect the customs clearance efficiency and the transit efficiency. The international aviation logistics centre needs to further clarify its capabilities.

V Suggestions on the National Central City Construction of Zhengzhou

(I) Build An Innovative and Entrepreneurial Center with Vitality and Regional Competitiveness and Create a New Engine for Innovation and Entrepreneurship in Zhengzhou

1 Support the Expansion of Zheng-Luo-Xin National Innovation Demonstration Zone

Zhengzhou National High & New Technology Industries Development Zone (Zhengzhou Development Zone for short) is the core area of Zheng-Luo-Xin National Innovation Demonstration Zone. With a total planned area of 99 square kilometers, it is far smaller than the Wuhan East Lake National Innovation Demonstration Zone (518 square kilometers), and Xi'an High-Tech Industries Development Zone (307 square kilometers), Jinan Innovation Zone (191 square kilometers) and Changsha High-tech Industries Development Zone (140 square kilometers), which have similar rankings in the statistics of the Torch Program. Because delineated permanent basic farmlands are prevalent in the spaces available for development around the Zhengzhou Development Zone, the provincial and municipal self-coordination capabilities are limited and the implementation of the national independent innovation demonstration strategy will be seriously affected. It is recommended that the relevant state departments be involved to coordinate the land used for the demonstration zone at the national level.

2 Build a National Key Innovative and Entrepreneurial Center

Build an open innovation base; fully integrate into the global innovation system; build a high-standard Science and Innovation Valley in the Central Plain; introduce, cultivate and attract world-class research institutes, support industrial backbone enterprises to carry out product R&D and provide innovative designs by making use of global innovation resources; enhance the core competitiveness of enterprises. Strengthen collaborative innovation; facilitate and encourage enterprises, universities and research institutes to build strategic alliances for industrial technology innovation; intensify the radiating effects of the National Technology Transfer Center in Zhengzhou and the Patent Examination Collaboration (Henan) Center; build Zhengzhou into a key national trading center and transformation base of scientific and technological achievements. Deploy the innovation chain based on the industrial chain; continue to strengthen progressive innovation; keep abreast of disruptive innovations that lead industrial transformation; enhance the status of industries and enterprises in the global value chain. Encourage enterprises to integrate into the global division of labor and cooperation in industries; enhance the ability to integrate domestic and foreign markets, as well as upstream and downstream industries.

3 Actively Promote the Combination of Technology and Finance

Promote the deep integration of industries, universities, research and finance;

strengthen the integration of the industrial chain, the innovation chain and the capital chain; support the national initiative of constructing a pilot city that integrates technology with finance and accumulates experience that can be replicated. Establish a guidance fund for the transformation of scientific and technological achievements in the Zheng-Luo-Xin National Innovation Demonstration Zone to guide social capital to scientific and technological innovation and develop technological industries through provincial and municipal linkages. Make use of the provincial special fund for science and technology to provide "technological guarantee" and "technological loans" on both provincial and municipal scales, establish a technological loan risk compensation mechanism, guide banks to increase credit support for technological enterprises, and resolve the difficulty in access to loans by small and medium-sized technological enterprises. Encourage innovation of products and services provided by banking and financial institutions, and provide loans such as those accepting intellectual property rights and equity as pledges to financially support the transformation of scientific and technological achievements. Cultivate and support qualified technological enterprises to go listed and raise capital in domestic and overseas capital markets. Allow the Henan Technology Stock Exchange to serve the financing of technological SMEs. Support qualified technological SMEs to expand financing channels by issuing bonds and through asset securitization. Encourage the development of equity investment funds and venture capital funds, standardize the development of equity-based crowdfunding, improve the investment and financing mechanisms of technological enterprises, and further improve innovative development policies and measures such as technology credit and technology insurance. Actively try a pilot project of investment and credit linkage in the Zheng-Luo-Xin National Innovation Demonstration Zone.

(II) Build a Key National Economic Growth Center and Provide New Support for the Industrial Transformation and Upgrading in Zhengzhou

1 Develop Advanced Manufacturing Industries

Fully integrate with the national strategy and development plan of "Made in China 2025", strengthen planning, and make top-level design. With consideration to the new urban master plan of Zhengzhou, make full use of high-quality development factors such as new technologies, new industries, new business types and new models, identify the prioritized leading industries and emerging industries to be developed in the next step, determine the industrial spatial layout, and boost the radiating and driving role of the national central cities; take the opportunities of key projects and other important matters to form national and world-class industrial clusters, accelerate industrial optimization and upgrading, and speed up high-quality development. Put quality in the first place, give priority to benefits, accelerate the intelligent, green and technological transformation of traditional industries through supply-side structural reform, and promote the intelligent upgrading of traditional industries; introduce special policies supporting the building of carrier platforms for high-quality development of industries, integrate resource elements such as talents, capital, land and energy, form ecosystems of key industries, and shape the overall sustainable and healthy development pattern of industries.

2 Vigorously Develop Modern Service Industries

Build a financial service system that "adopts multiple financing methods, provides efficient services, and applies integrated control" in the international hub logistics center and the national modern financial center in the region; manage the construction of a pilot city in the innovation and the development of modern logistics in the country, strengthen the logistics industry, and lay a solid foundation for the international logistics center; continue to advance the online publicity of resettlement housing agreements, and promote the stable and healthy development of the real estate market; cultivate cultural and creative tourism with local characteristics, promote the development of elderly care industry by allowing for the actual condition of Henan, and increase the development level of modern trade and exhibition industries.

3 Make up for the Shortcomings in Modern Agricultural Development

Provide accurate support and benefits for the agricultural industry, use the fiscal fund for agricultural purposes for good reasons; develop efficient farming such as vegetables, flowers, fruits and edible fungi, as well as animal husbandry; learn from experiences of other regions, substituting subsidies with rewards to effectively promote the construction of agricultural projects while ensuring that the financial fund for agricultural purposes are fully used; formulate a negative list of agricultural construction projects in line with the actual development of Zhengzhou, stimulate social forces to enliven urban ecological agriculture, foster new growth points of the agricultural industry, promote the rural development and help farmers get rich in Zhengzhou.

(Ⅲ) Building an Innovation and Inheritance Center of Chinese Historical Civilization and a Livable International Metropolis Favorable to Business and Tourism

1 Inherit, Protect and Innovate the Ancient Capital Culture, the Kung Fu Culture, the Root Culture, and the Confucianism, Buddhism and Taoism Cultures, and Enhance the Gathering, Radiating and Communicating Functions of the City

Zhengzhou is a significant birthplace of Chinese civilization, a national famous historical and cultural city, one of the eight major ancient capitals in China, and one of the six major historic sites supported by the state, and a member of the League of Historical Cities. According to the traditional world view of the Chinese nation, Zhengzhou stands in the "center of the heavens and the earth". It has been the critical crossroad of civilization exchanges since ancient times and preserves rich cultural heritages. By taking advantage of these resources, Zhengzhou should try to enhance the influence of the Songshan Forum as an important platform for dialogue and exchange between Chinese and world civilizations. It should strengthen urban cultural design and shape a city image carrying the cultural characteristics of the Central Plain and combining tradition with modernity. It should deepen exchanges with foreign culture and create a number of well-known cultural brands. It should cultivate high-end cultural talents and a group of cultural masters, art masters and cultural ambassadors who enjoy fame at home and abroad.

2 Vigorously Develop Cultural and Creative Industries Such As Digital Media, Creative Design, and Cartoon Game

In the maker era marked by technological innovation, the costs of established "hi-tech" technologies such as "smart technology", "Internet technology" and "image processing technology" have been greatly reduced. These relatively readily available technologies are always applicable to solve problems in practical scenarios or used as a certain technical link in artistic expression, no matter in what way. Zhengzhou should apply modern information and image processing technologies to promote integrated development of culture and tourism, build a national tourism demonstration zone, and become a global key city that is livable and favorable to cultural tourism.

(IV) Build An International Integrated Transportation and Logistics Hub and An Upgraded Version of Integrated Transportation Hub

1 Introduce the "Integrated Hub" Strategy to Base Cargo Airlines and Build A Global Air Cargo Channel

With the deepening of the "Belt and Road" construction, Zhengzhou will speed up the implementation of the international and domestic "integrated hub" strategy that covers air, railway and highway. It will enhance its radiating function as a main node city and promote joint construction and efficient connection of inter-regional infrastructures. It will build the Silk Road in the air, on land and online. It will build efficient and convenient railway, air and highway networks and become a fully functional integrated transportation hub. It will build a multimodal transportation system and an all-round logistics assembling and distributing network.

2 Strengthen Cooperation with International Logistics Integrators and Other Freight Service Enterprises and Improve the Air Freight Assembling and Distributing System

Based on the principle of appropriate advancement, Zhengzhou should push forward the construction of large-scale aviation hub, strengthen the connection of land and air transportation, and build an air freight assembling and distributing system characterized by advanced facilities, complete network, strong support, and efficient operation. It should accelerate the construction of cold chain logistics system, extend the industry chain and improve the development level of cold chain logistics; it should create a characteristic logistics center and strive to be an international trading center of bulk commodities, a global online commodity distribution center, and a national express and logistics center. It should increase the intelligent level of transportation and logistics, build transportation and logistics information platforms and a multimodal national information center, open up the logistics information chain, and promote the deep integration of cutting-edge technologies, such as big data, the Internet of Things and next-generation information technology, with transportation and logistics.

(V) Build an Opening-up Gateway in the Inland Area and a National Trade Logistics Center with Better Exchange Function

1 Build An All-round Opening-up Gateway in the Inland Area That Serves National Strategies

Vigorously develop the port economy and build an all-round opening up gateway in the inland area that serves national strategies. Port is a symbol and gateway to the economic development and opening up of a region. Taking the opportunity of constructing an international logistics corridor in the air and an international logistics hub on the railway, Zhengzhou should vigorously develop the port economy and accelerate the integration into the great development pattern of the Belt and Road Initiative. Zhengzhou Airport provides 7×24 customs clearance services and examines documents quickly. The transfer of Grade-I railway port has been completed and accepted. The customs supervision center for multimodal transportation, which was the third of its kind in China and the first of its kind in the Central Region, was put into operation, and the "four-port-in-one" multimodal transportation function covering air, railway, highway and shipping is getting mature. A port customs clearance system is gradually established. Zhengzhou has become an "international logistics channel hub", a global online commodity distribution center supporting deals at every corner of the world, and the most active logistics channel hub along the Silk Road Economic Belt.

2 Improve the Construction of Compound Port Platform

Advance the construction of a modern international logistics information platform, and build a public logistics information platform consisting of three levels: logistics public management information, logistics business information exchange, and industry/enterprise logistics information processing; explore and support new establishments jointly founded by Henan Province Airport Group, Zhengzhou International Hub Development and Construction Co., Ltd. and Henan Bonded Logistics Center with large-scale leading logistics enterprises inside and outside the province and international strategic investors to manage the data exchange service platform for multi-modal transportation of logistics enterprises; upgrade the functions of modern integrated transportation hub and modern logistics center.

3 Build a National Trade Logistics Center with Better Exchange Function

Promote the integration of aviation hub, railway hub and highway hub; coordinate the construction of assembling and distributing network; tap the advantage of integrated hub that is dominated by air transport and supports land-air connection, assembling and distributing on highways and railways, internal rapidness and external smoothness; build an international multimodal combined transport logistics center with accessible network, efficient connection, low costs, and multiple transportation means; encourage logistics enterprises to invest in M&As, assets restructuring, alliances between giants and strategic cooperation, and increase the scale and intensive level of logistics enterprises; consolidate the status of Zhengzhou as a global intelligent terminal production base and an international aviation logistics center through the airport project (Phase II), Foxconn's "Five Hundred Billion in Five Years Program", the development of three districts, the commencement of major contracted projects, the introduction of major investment projects, and the construction of major factor platforms; provide all-round support from the aspects of talent, land and fund for the construction of trade logistics center through the talent program of "Zhengzhou Brains" and the "1+N" policy system.

References

[1] Statistical Bureau of Zhengzhou Municipality. "Economic Operations of Zhengzhou Municipality (2010-2018)" http://tjj.zhengzhou.gov.cn/fxtj/1579608.jhtml.

[2] Statistical Bureau of Zhengzhou Municipality. "Statistical Communiqué of Zhengzhou Municipality on the National Economic and Social Development (2010-2018)" http://

www.zhengzhou.gov.cn/tjgb/715921.jhtml.

[3] National Development and Reform Commission. "Guide of the National Development and Reform Commission to Supporting Zhengzhou as a National Central City (Fa Gai Gui Hua [2017] No. 154)"

[4] Zhengzhou Municipal People's Government. "*The Circular on the Action Plan for the National Central City Construction of Zhengzhou (2017-2035)*"

B.11

National Central City Construction of Xi'an: Main Measures, Opportunities and Challenges, and Suggestions

Wang Xiaojuan *

Abstract: In 2018, Xi'an officially launched the national central city construction and accomplished initial results in the first year. New progress has been made in economic indicators, and economic restructuring was accelerated. Factors for the development of Greater Xi'an were gathered at faster speed, and Xi'an significantly increased its openness level and strongly advanced its ecological civilization construction. At the same time, due to the late start of the national central city construction, Xi'an is stilled confronted with problems such as weak economic foundation, low industrialization degree of scientific and technological achievements, and inactivation of the private economy. This paper proposes targeted countermeasures and suggestions on the major issues to be solved urgently in the current national central city construction of Xi'an.

Keywords: Xi'an; national central city; Belt and Road Initiative; internationalization

---

* Wang Xiaojuan, Assistant Researcher at Shaanxi Academy of Social Sciences, research direction: regional economy, financial investment.

I A Good Start in the National Central City Construction of Xi'an

(I) Main Economic Indicators Moved to New Heights

Xi'an launched the national central city construction in 2018, from which it began to develop more quickly. Its GDP reached a new height with a growth rate of 8.2% from the previous year, which was equal to an increase of 0.5 percentage point and 1.6 percentage points higher than the national average. It had the highest growth rate among all the sub-provincial cities in the country. Its GDP reached RMB 834.986 billion, which made itself among the top 20 cities in the country. Xi'an found its comprehensive economic strength further conspicuous in the Guanzhong city cluster and Shaanxi. In 2018, its GDP accounted for 34.2% of the provincial GDP, a record high. Thanks to the International freight train "Chang'an", the foreign trade of the city registered a super-high growth rate of 29.6%, putting Xi'an in the first place among all the sub-provincial cities. The total volume of imports and exports exceeded RMB 300 billion for the first time. The social fixed assets, total retail volume of social consumer goods and local fiscal revenue also grew significantly, with growth rates of 8.4%, 9.6% and 10.8%, respectively. In 2018, the cultural tourism of Xi'an experienced explosive growth. Benefiting from the influence of Xi'an as a popular city online and the publicity and influence of tourism planning projects such as "The Most Characteristic Chinese Spring Festival in Xi'an", "Immersed in China's Spring in Xi'an", and "Chang'an as the Capital of Tang Dynasty in 1400", Xi'an quickly became one of the most popular tourist cities of the year and was rated by *China National Travel* as the "Best Cultural Tourism Destination" in 2018. In 2018, the number of tourists and tourism revenue of Xi'an grew rapidly. The number of tourists exceeded 247 million, with a growth rate of 36.7%; the total tourism revenue amounted to RMB 255.481 billion, with a growth rate of 56.4%. The status of Xi'an as an international city brand and its influence were further enhanced.

Table 1 Main Economic Indicators of Xi'an in 2018

Main Indicator	Total	Growth Rate (%)
GDP (RMB 100 million)	8349.86	8.2
Social fixed asset investment (RMB 100 million)	8191.21	8.4
Total retail volume of social consumer goods (RMB 100 million)	4658.72	9.6
Total import and export volume (RMB 100 million)	3303.87	29.6
FDI actually used (USD 100 million)	63.54	14.9
Total tourism revenue (RMB 100 million)	2554.81	56.4
General public budget income of local finance (RMB 100 million)	684.71	10.8

Data source: Website of the Statistical Bureau of Xi'an

(II) The Economic Structure Continued to be Optimized

In 2018, strongly driven by the accelerated transformation of investment structure, the economic structure of Xi'an was continuously optimized. Xi'an began to feel spurring economic forces, with investment momentum quickly transformed, industries moving towards the high-end direction, and surging technological innovation. The main changes could be observed in the industrial investment growth rate that was turned from negative to positive more quickly and the added value of industrial growth that was steadily rising to become the economic mainstay of the city. In 2018, the added value of the primary industry was RMB 25.882 billion; the added value of the secondary industry was RMB 292.561 billion, an increase of 8.5%; the added value of the tertiary industry was RMB 516.543 billion. The three-industry ratio was 3.1:35.0:61.9. The three-industry structure was continuously optimized. The secondary industry resumed strong growth, receiving industrial investments more quickly. The tertiary industry developed rapidly, and its proportion increased by 0.4 percentage point from the previous year to contribute more to GDP. In particular, strategic emerging industries grew rapidly with strong momentum, injecting a powerful endogenous force into the economic development of Xi'an. The industries developed towards the mid-to-high ends at a faster pace. In 2018, the total output value of strategic emerging industries above designated size amounted to RMB 233.416 billion, accounting for 40.7% of the total industries, which made them an important force supporting the economic development of the city. Among the seven strategic new industries, the new-generation information technology industry and the new energy industry took up the highest shares of 28.6% and 22.8%, respectively, and they together accounted for half of the total scale. From the perspective of industrial growth rate, high-end equipment manufacturing, new materials industry, new energy vehicle industry and new energy industry all registered rapid growth rates of 14.5%, 15.1%, 34.3% and 14.1%, respectively, showing great development potential.

Table 2 Statistics of Indicators for Strategic Emerging Industries above Designated Size in Xi'an in 2018

	Total Industrial Output (RMB 100 Million)	Growth Rate (%)	Percentage (%)	Contribution Rate (%)	Increase (%)
Industries above designated size	5734.50	12.2	—	—	—
#Strategic emerging industries above designated size	2334.16	11.1	40.7	37.3	4.5
New-generation information technology	668.22	1.0	28.6	2.8	0.3
High-end equipment manufacturing	222.37	14.5	9.5	12.1	1.3
New material industry	237.27	15.1	10.2	13.4	1.5
Bio-industry	274.73	10.1	11.8	10.9	1.2
New energy vehicle industry	247.67	34.3	10.6	27.2	3.0
New energy industry	531.23	14.1	22.8	28.3	3.1
Energy-saving and environmental protection industry	152.67	8.7	6.5	5.2	0.6

Data source: Website of the Statistical Bureau of Xi'an

(III) Factors Gathering for the Development of Greater Xi'an

The household registration policy of Xi'an has proven more effective since 2018, and Xi'an has been more attractive to talents. In 2018, nearly 800,000 people moved to Xi'an, and more than 60% of them, as settled population or recruited talents, held Bachelor degree or above. The settlement of high-quality talents would undoubtedly contribute more to the construction and development of

Xi'an as a national central city. As the business environment of Xi'an has been constantly improved in recent years, various types of entrepreneurial talents have emerged. In 2018, the number of new market players in the city grew rapidly. There were 543,000 newly registered market players, a year-on-year increase of 91.7%. Achievements of technological innovations were made in an endless stream, supporting the construction of Xi'an as a new scientific research base, and also boosting and inspiring the vigorous development of "mass entrepreneurship and innovation". More and more subjects of scientific research and innovation emerged. According to the data of the science and technology department, 1,156 platforms and carriers for mass entrepreneurship and innovation had been built by the end of 2018, with a total area of 32.81 million square meters. They attracted 41,000 enterprises and created more than 400,000 jobs. In 2018, there were 26,675 invention patents and 8,096 patent grants, and the turnover of technological contract was RMB 103 billion, equal to a year-on-year increase of 21%.

(IV) The Openness Level Was Significantly Increased

In 2018, the construction of Xi'an as a new base for the reform and opening up in inland was further advanced. Riding the waves of developing "the hub economy, the gateway economy and the mobility economy", Xi'an continued to expand opening up, increased its international level, and quickened the opening pace as a national central city. It strengthened the construction of an opening platform in the Free Trade Zone, continuously promoted investment convenience, and successfully introduced a number of major projects such as Samsung Phase II, Huawei Global Technology Center, and Alibaba's headquarters in the Western Region to settle down. At the same time, the Free Trade Zone continued to attract more market players. In 2018, it received more than 15,000 new enterprises, which brought total registered capital of more than RMB 250 billion. They included more than 200 new foreign enterprises and 347 enterprises each with registered capital of more than RMB 100 million. The vitality of market entities was further highlighted. At the same time, as efforts to support the "Belt and Road" and the national central city construction, Xi'an got approval to build a provincial comprehensive reform and opening pilot zone under the Belt and Road Initiative, an airport economic demonstration zone, the "Silk Road" cross-border e-commerce RMB settlement platform in the cross-border e-commerce comprehensive pilot zone, and a great science and technology market, all of which would further promote the opening of Xi'an. The China-Europe train "Chang'an" further developed as an important means to support the foreign trade of Xi'an. For the whole year, 1,235 trips were scheduled, and the train boasted the most actual total trips, the highest freight volume and the largest heavy load rate in the country. Xi'an Xianyang International Airport obtained the "Fifth Freedom", which greatly enhanced the aviation operation capacity of the city. In 2018, 7 new international passenger routes were opened, adding up to a total of 64. The passenger volume of the airport rose to the 7th in the country, and the cargo and mail handling capacity exceeded 310,000 tons, with the biggest growth rate among the top ten airports in the country. With the establishment of the Second International Commercial Court, Xi'an further increased its international level. It added another 8 international sister cities and friendly exchange cities, attracted 215 Fortune Global 500 companies, and actually used foreign capital of USD 6.354 billion. Xi'an earned a good reputation for its efforts in the opening up and gathered powerful momentum to accelerate catch-up actions.

(V) Ecological Civilization Construction Was Strongly Propelled

In 2018, the construction of national ecological civilization demonstration zone was begun in Xi'an. Guided by the concept of "two mountains" put forward by the state, Xi'an deeply promoted the "five actions" of ecological civilization construction and accelerated the pace of construction that was intended to make Xi'an an ecologically livable city. It was awarded as the "2018 Green Development Model City" and was included in the first batch of the "2018 Eco-Cities". Over the past year, the city appearance and refined management level of Xi'an was substantially improved. By strengthening the gardening construction to "add greening, flowers and colors to the city", Xi'an built 62 green squares, put into service 15 free green parks, and successfully passed the review of national garden city. Further advancement of the "cigarette butt revolution", urban and rural household waste management, and the "greening, cleaning and beautification campaign" for both sides of roads and railways enhanced the internal quality of Xi'an as a national central city. The "Blue Sky Protection Campaign" proved effective. Following the working idea of haze control with an iron hand, Xi'an exerted powerful air pollution control and outperformed the governance targets in 2018. According to the air quality monitoring data in 2018, Xi'an had 188 days with good air quality, 8 days more than the same period of the previous year, and 21 days with excellent air quality. Water environment governance was progressed steadily. Xi'an resorted to the "five strategies to control water pollution" and actively promoted the ecological restoration project of "eight rivers running across Chang'an", the "top ten projects" to tackle polluted water, and the sponge city construction. In 2018, ecological water surface covering an area of 2,590 mu was built, and the rainwater system construction mode was promoted and applied throughout the city. As a development zone named after ecology, Chanba adhered to the development idea of "driving regional development with river management and supporting ecological construction with new district development". As a result, it gradually established a development mode that combines "urban development with green development" and that is eco-friendly and favourable to entrepreneurship. With these accomplishments, Chanba Development Zone was rated as "2018 Model Development Zone of Ecological Civilization Construction".

II Restraints on the Further National Central City Construction of Xi'an

(I) Weak Foundation of Comprehensive Economic Strength and Limited Radiating and Driving Capacity

Historically, there is a big gap between Xi'an and the eastern coastal areas. Influenced by the market economy, the imbalanced and inadequate development remains a lasting problem. The proposal to build Xi'an into a national central city is intended to promote coordination and balance between the Western Region and the eastern coast, thereby driving balanced regional development in the entire country. Located in the northwest and the Silk Road Economic Belt, Xi'an possesses an important location and economic development advantage. It is expected to drive the development of the entire northwest and the Silk Road

Economic Belt. Xi'an started the national central city construction in 2018. In spite of a good start and observed economic acceleration, the national central city construction and radiating role of Xi'an seems fragile on a weak foundation and the city has to bear more daunting tasks than the other national central cities due to its inland location. Judging from the basic elements of economic development, Xi'an cannot rival the other national central cities in terms of economic aggregate, population size and regional area. It is still at a stage of self-growth and Greater Xi'an development for the purpose of national central city construction. What it does now is to absorb resources, spaces and population from the surrounding Guanzhong Plain city cluster. It has only a limited radiation effect as the central city of the city cluster. The entire Guanzhong Plain city cluster and the wider Northwestern Region have large land areas and low economic densities. Therefore, Xi'an now is struggling to drive the development of Guanzhong Plain city cluster for some time to come.

(II) The Scientific and Technological Strength Does not Match the Economy, and Scientific and Technological Achievements Are Not Well Transformed

Xi'an has many universities and research institutes that harbor strong scientific and technological strength, which lays a good foundation for economic development. In particular, there is still ample room for military-civilian integration. However, the superior resources in the fields of science and education and military in Xi'an have not been fully mobilized and utilized. This is manifested in the imbalance between technological innovation capability and economic strength. Xi'an is still stuck in low creation and manufacturing levels. At present, Xi'an has plenty of researchers, and many large companies operate their R&D department in this city. However, many research achievements are separated from the economic market, without being transformed into effective productivity, and even more weirdly the transformation happens in other places. From the perspective of enterprise innovation, large and technological innovation enterprises in Xi'an are not ideal in quantity and quality. Due to the deficient systems and mechanisms in the field of science and technology, some enterprises in Xi'an are not capable enough to carry out technological innovation and transform resulting achievements. It is necessary to provide scientific and technological resources and transformation channels for enterprises by formulating appropriate policies, systems and mechanisms which open up communication and connection between scientific research institutions and enterprises and combine research achievements with productivity. At the same time, enterprises should make consistent efforts in facilitating innovation by industries, academia and research institutes and in transformation of research achievements as preparations for going listed.

(III) The Development of Private Economy Is Relatively Backward and Enterprises Need to Enhance Their Strength and Vitality

The private economy of Xi'an has many problems to be solved in expanding opening up, intensifying technological innovation, optimizing resources allocation, and promoting transformation and upgrading. Currently, the private non-public economy is still dominated by traditional industries, mainly concentrated in manufacturing, retail and catering industries. There are still horizontal and vertical gaps between the private economies of Xi'an and the other central cities such as Chengdu, Wuhan and Zhengzhou. The private enterprises in Xi'an need to improve their vitality. Most of the enterprises are small or micro. Private enterprises are mostly small and micro, while large and medium-sized enterprises take up only about 20%. The total assets and operating income show a clearer picture. Private enterprises are hindered by many obstacles and constraints to technological innovation capability and technical talents. Financing is particularly difficult and costly for them. At present, many preferential policies related to the private economy have not been put in place, which restricts the development and growth of the private economy. In addition, it involves few emerging industries and has a low-level industrial structure. The private investments are relatively concentrated. They mainly target at real estate, with few going to strategic emerging industries with high technological and financial requirements, such as information transmission, software and information services. The investments are excessively concentrated and vulnerable to macro policies. As more and more regulation and control policies are promulgated, the real estate investment growth slows down and private investments will surely be under great impact.

(IV) Countermeasures and Suggestions on the National Central City Construction of Xi'an

(I) Build Greater Xi'an Metropolitan Area and Drive the Rapid Rise of the Guanzhong City Cluster

1 Promoted the Xi'an-Xianyang Administrative Integration at a Faster Speed

Xi'an Municipal Party Committee and Municipal Government pledged to build a Greater Xi'an metropolitan area by 2020 in the *Implementation Plan for the National Central City Construction of Xi'an*. This goal is, first of all, based on the construction of Greater Xi'an. Only the Greater Xi'an metropolitan area centering round Greater Xi'an could support and assume the mission of national central city construction and make Xi'an a true core of the "Belt and Road" and an international metropolis for exchanges and cooperation between Europe and Asia. Therefore, the construction of central Greater Xi'an is the priority, and the Xi'an-Xianyang integration should be further promoted on the premise that Xi'an is now governing the Xixian New Area. Reasonable adjustments of administrative divisions should be made step by step to achieve the goal of building Greater Xi'an and support the quickening formation of Greater Xi'an metropolitan area, which is expected to further drive and radiate to the development and growth of surrounding city clusters.

2 Promote Connectivity of Facilities and Transportation

Starting with a high-standard plan with global vision, Xi'an should continue to promote the construction of infrastructure and transportation logistics hub leading to the goal of building Greater Xi'an and becoming an international city. It should establish a comprehensive public service facility system with excellent quality, complete composition, clear hierarchy and balanced radiation. It should increase the international livable environment standard and strengthen the two-way flow of various resource factors between cities in the Greater Xi'an metropolitan area. It should speed up the construction of the Jack Union-shaped high-speed rail network, the Guanzhong intercity railway network and the expressway network to further improve the rapid accessibility to cities in the Guanzhong Plain city cluster and realize regional transportation integration. On the basis of the transportation connectivity in the Guanzhong Plain city cluster, the connectivity of the multimodal transportation information platform should be further promoted to facilitate the effective matching of freight supplies with transportation resources such as "highways", "railways", "airlines", and "sea transportation". It should create a "highway-flight combined transportation" demonstration route to promote the "multimodal highway-flight" service model.

3 Accelerate the Coordinated Regional Development

As the core city in the Guanzhong city cluster, Xi'an must start with developing industrial clusters and concentrate advantageous resources to push industries towards high ends and develop high-end manufacturing and modern service industries in order to fulfill the mission as a national central city. It may plan to move some resource-intensive or labor-intensive industries to the surrounding Guanzhong city cluster and thus drive the supporting service capability of the entire industrial chain there. In terms of policy and system, a regional social and economic alliance initiated by Xi'an and participated by cities and counties in the Guanzhong city cluster should be built to strengthen communication and transportation, and a regular cooperation and communication mechanism should also be established to forge joint forces in connectivity of facilities, industrial division of labor, scientific and technological exchange, public services, and environmental protection. The alliance may promote the implementation of large projects and shape a long-term mechanism for the coordinated development of the Guanzhong city cluster. In terms of spatial construction, Xi'an should promote regional connection and integrated development and accelerate the Xi'an-Xiangyang and Xi'an-Tongchuan integration and the formation of a regional development community to drive and radiate to the interactive and integrated development of the entire Guanzhong region and even the Northwestern Region.

(II) Take the Opportunity of Industrial Transformation and Upgrading to Establish a Modern Characteristic Industrial System in Xi'an

1 Establish a Modern Characteristic Industrial System

The high-quality development of Xi'an as a national central city requires strong support from a characteristic modern industrial system. According to the requirement for an industrial system in which "four elements develop in coordination" proposed at the 19th National Congress of the Communist Party of China, Xi'an should speed up the establishment of a modern industrial system driven by innovation to better promote the growth of the real economy. Following the development trends in scientific and technological resources, industrial base and future industrial revolution, Xi'an should focus on developing four trillion-level big industries, promote the growth of high-tech industries, advanced manufacturing industries, modern service industries and cultural tourism, and form a competitive modern industrial system with its own characteristics. The development of high-tech industries should stick to the core of new-generation information technology industry, mobilize the technological innovation resources in the city, and concentrate on the high-end information technology industry. Breakthroughs should be made in drones, new materials, integrated circuits and robots. New driving forces for high-tech industry development should be fostered. The development of advanced manufacturing industries should focus on new energy vehicles, artificial intelligence, and aerospace and let them drive upstream and downstream industries to gradually form an advanced manufacturing industry cluster. The high-quality development of the modern service industries should be promoted, with the focus on the trade logistics industry, scientific and technological information service, financial services and other productive service industries which are closely related to the real economy, in order to contribute to the real economy of Xi'an. Cultural tourism is a big industry that enjoys unique advantages in Xi'an. Xi'an should continue to make innovation and make use of its historical and cultural resources to become a tourist and fashionable city with world influence and let tourism drive the development of related industries.

2 Create a Good Industrial Development Environment

A good industrial development environment expects guidance and support from the government. In terms of industrial policy, the local government of Xi'an should formulate a reasonable industrial policy system, establish a dynamic management system of market access and withdrawal, and provide policy support for industry cultivation and development in all aspects including taxation, finance, talents, and science and technology. They should establish a leadership accountability system for industrial projects, strengthen project performance evaluation, handle special cases with special methods, mobilize various resources, apply for green channels for land, capital and management related projects, increase the operating rate and completion rate of projects, and quicken the implementation of major industrial projects. Xi'an should persist in overcoming and solving chronic institutional obstacles, gradually improve information consultation, guarantee and financing service systems, strengthen the existing intellectual property rights protection, and effectively protect the legitimate rights and interests of property rights owners. It should particularly lend support to the prioritized industrialization of scientific and technological achievements in strategic emerging industries. The city should also further strengthen the intensity of foreign investment attraction and ensure high-quality investment during the process by taking precise and professional investment attraction actions and focusing on industries and enterprises that can promote effective extension of the industrial chain. New breakthroughs should be made to make the industrial chain and industrial clusters in Xi'an stronger.

(III) Rely on the Construction of a Comprehensive Innovation and Reform Pilot Zone to Promote the Industrialization of Scientific and Technological Achievements

1 Accelerate Technological Innovation Reform

Fully utilize and give full play to the abundant scientific and educational resources, great innovative strength, and complete science and technology platforms mastered by Xi'an. Make breakthroughs in the efforts to invigorate institutional mechanisms, create a supportive environment, formulate accurate policies, and exploit the role of leading subjects. Carry out scientific and technological research based on the actual needs of economic development, promote the constant transformation of old driving forces to new ones, and encourage the transformation and upgrading of enterprises. Keep abreast of cutting-edge technologies, conduct forward-looking theoretical innovation research, attract national key laboratories, more large scientific installations, major technological infrastructures, cutting-edge technology innovation platforms and industrial innovation platforms to settle down, and attract top scientists at home and abroad and innovation teams to carry out scientific research in

Xi'an. This can grab the commanding height of innovation and development, fully unleash the city's scientific and technological advantages, lead coordinated regional innovation and development, and make innovation a source of high-quality development. Accelerate the ongoing construction of research centers and academies; pay attention to the building of the Xi'an Science Park of the Chinese Academy of Sciences, the Science and Technology Innovation Harbor in Western China, and the Soar Town of Northwestern Polytechnical University; create important science and technology platforms and carriers, such as the Silk Road Science and Technology Innovation Center and the National Innovation Hub.

2 Promote Military-Civilian Integration and Innovation

Xi'an should continue to utilize its own advantages to solve system and mechanism problems, speed up the deployment of strategies and emerging industries about military-civilian integration, and let military-civilian integration become "a new engine" for it to catch up with those forerunners. It may take the opportunity of military-civilian integration to encourage and guide non-public enterprises into the military industry, open up channels for civilian applications of military technologies, and strengthen the two-way flow of knowledge and technology. It should transform the strong scientific and technological resources into great productivity to push economic development to a new level. It is advised to make full use of the existing technologies and platform resources associated with military-civilian integration, serve the "civilian enterprises that venture into the military industry", and issue relevant policies to encourage basic and qualified private enterprises to enter military-civilian integration related industries. It should boost a mixed ownership reform among military enterprises and exercise the government's fiscal leverage to guide social capital to military enterprises and promote the military-civilian integration. It should focus on driving the formation of military-civilian integration industry clusters through pilot programs and projects and maximize the military-civilian integration through "base + center + market + platform" model. It should strengthen the recruitment and cultivation of talents, attract and retain more excellent management and technical talents, and gradually establish a talent database and a talent system that serves military-civilian integration and innovation.

(IV) Optimize the Private Investment Environment and Develop the Private Economy in Xi'an

1 Continue to Optimize the Business Environment

Seriously study and comprehend the message from the speech of General Secretary Xi at the Central Symposium on Private Enterprises, try to improve the administrative efficiency, and conscientiously study the ideological concepts, institutional mechanisms, and business environment that currently restrict the development of Xi'an's private economy. Then, develop a targeted policy system that is in line with the actual situation of Xi'an and support the private economy to blaze a new path in the national central city construction. Deeply promote the reform of "streamlining of administration, delegation of power to lower level, governance and service reform", make continuous innovations in service methods, make use of the Internet, establish a service system operated online and offline, improve law enforcement methods in aspects of supervision, taxation and environmental protection to private enterprises, and reduce unnecessary transaction costs, and strive to provide "golden services" for them. Incorporate the development of the private economy into the regular assessment of the Xi'an Municipal Party Committee and Municipal Government and as an important indicator for assessing cadres; stimulate the vitality of market players in the private economy; conduct regular investigations on the implementation of policies and systems for the private economy and the business environment satisfaction survey. Strengthen the mechanisms for government-enterprise interaction, supervision and assessment; implement a strict accountability system; steer a clear direction and create a first-class environment for the development of the private economy; truly solve the last mile problems in the implementation of central, provincial and municipal policies favorable to enterprises.

2 Guide the Healthy Development of the Private Economy

Deeply explore and mobilize the potential of social private capital, guide private capital to make effective investments, regularly compile an investment catalogue of major projects for the national central city construction of Xi'an, indicate the key directions for investments to expand, reduce investment risks, reduce investment restrictions, and enhance the investment willingness, intensity and enthusiasm of private enterprises. Explore and develop economic forms of mixed ownership, provide channels for private capital and private enterprises to participate in the state-owned enterprise reform of Xi'an, allow private capital to enter competitive industries in various ways, such as capital contribution and subscription of convertible bonds, encourage different types of capital to complement and integrate with each other. Strengthen the supporting role of scientific and technological resources in the private economy, encourage and support scientific and technological talents from universities and research institutes to engage in the private economy and contribute to the development of private enterprises in the city. Scientific and technological talents who serve the private economy may be given more autonomy to break through the institutional constraints of scientific research units. Explore feasible paths for the decentralization of results and income ownership division to scientific and technological talents, further revitalize scientific and technological resources, and unleash innovation vitality. Gradually establish a market withdrawal mechanism for private enterprises and resolve overcapacity in some industries. Guide and encourage qualified private enterprises or private capital to expand the industrial development space and to invest in emerging industries such as elderly care, the Internet of Things, and electronic information, and accelerate the transformation and upgrading of the private economy.

References

[1] Zhang Ni. "A New National Central City: Missions and Challenges of Xi'an" [J] *China Development Observations*, 2018.

[2] Kang Qiaona. "Contribute the "Xi'an Solution" to the Construction of Pilot Free Trade Zone" [J] *New Silk Road Horizon*, 2018

Exploration Reports

B.12

Guangzhou: Renewal and Revival of A National Central City

*Zhang Dawei**

Abstract: The *Development Plan for Guangdong-Hong Kong-Macau Greater Bay Area* redefines the positioning of Guangzhou. According to this development plan, there will be four central cities, namely Guangzhou, Shenzhen, Hong Kong and Macao in South China. The "one country, two systems" policy and the "three customs areas" are unique in the world city clusters. As a national central city, Guangzhou has a solid foundation and enjoys advantages that are incomparable within a certain period of time. Of the four central cities listed above, Guangzhou is the only one that possesses

* Zhang Dawei, male, Doctor of Economics, PhD Supervisor, Vice-president and Secretary General of China Center for International Economic Exchanges, former Deputy Governor of Henan Provincial People's Government. This paper is a speech given by the author at the 2019 Guangzhou Forum on Global Cities Research" on June 21, 2019.

a broad economic hinterland and a multi-level urban system. Its economic space can even be constantly expanded amid competition and cooperation through planning of metropolitan areas. To this end, the following suggestions arc provided: It should accelerate institutional innovation, technological innovation and industrial innovation; it should quicken the pace of urban renewal and further revitalize the "old Guangzhou"; it should maintain the youthfulness of the city; it should be built into a fashion and consumption center with international influence.

Keywords: Guangzhou; new positioning; Guangdong-Hong Kong-Macau Greater Bay

I New Positioning of Guangzhou in the Guangdong-Hong Kong-Macau Greater Bay Area

In this February, the Central Government officially released the *Development Plan for Guangdong-Hong Kong-Macau Greater Bay Area* (hereinafter referred to as "Plan"), which positioned the construction of the Greater Bay Area as a major regional development strategy of the country, which is joined by the development of the "Belt and Road", the Beijing-Tianjin-Hebei coordinated development, and the development of the Yangtze River Economic Belt.

The Plan defines the strategic positioning of the Guangdong-Hong Kong-Macau Greater Bay Area as: 1. a dynamic world city cluster; 2. an international technological innovation center with global influence; 3. an important support for the construction of the "Belt and Road"; 4. a demonstration zone for deep cooperation between the Mainland and Hong Kong and Macao; 5. a high-quality living circle that is livable and favorable to entrepreneurship.

This positioning clearly reflects the state's vision for the Greater Bay Area. However, the significance of its construction goes beyond that. Both the *Plan* and some relevant documents issued by the Central Government clearly indicated the national will embodied in this regional strategy: to enrich the implication of "one country, two systems" and maintain long-term stability in Hong Kong and

Macao; to implement new development concepts, develop new driving forces, and achieve innovation-driven development; to deepen reform, expand opening up, and participate in international economic cooperation; to boost the "Belt and Road" construction and build a converging and supporting zone in the Maritime Silk Road; to drive the green and innovative development of the Pearl River-Xijiang Economic Belt.

Whether out of the strategic meaning or the national will, we, indeed, should truly comprehend the profound implication of this regional strategy from its contributions to the deepening of reform, the furthering of opening up, the sustainable and healthy development of economy, the implementation of "one country, two systems" policy, and the peaceful reunification of the motherland. My understanding of this regional strategy can be elaborated below:

1. It can promote the integration of regional advantageous resources such as innovation, advanced manufacturing, and modern service industries, stimulate market vitality, build a pioneering modern economic system, and produce engines that drive the sustained growth of the national economy.

2. It complies with changes in economic globalization and the international trade pattern, helps comprehensively construct a new open economic system and a new international opening base, and participates in the competition among world city clusters on behalf of China.

3. It can accelerate the institutional compatibility and integration between regions under the framework of "one country, two systems", provide opportunities for exchange and mutual learning of civilizations, and offer a regional model for the great rejuvenation of the Chinese nation and the building of a community with a shared future for mankind.

4. It can promote coordinated economic and social development and meet the needs of people for consumer welfare, talents, environment, ecology, and other public goods and public services as they live a better and better life by transforming development methods and through industrial changes.

While defining the overall positioning of the Guangdong-Hong Kong-Macau Greater Bay Area, *the Plan* also clarifies the strategic positioning of Guangzhou, Shenzhen, Hong Kong and Macao in order to uphold advantages, rational division of labor, complementary functions and staggered development. Guangzhou is one of the four central cities in the Greater Bay Area. As defined

Table 1 Comparison of Competitiveness between Guangdong-Hong Kong-Macau Greater Bay Area and Other World City Clusters

Indicator (2017)	Tokyo Bay Area	San Francisco Bay Area	New York	Guangdong-Hong Kong-Macau Greater Bay Area			
			Bay Area	Grand Port District	Nine cities in Chinese Mainland	Hong Kong	Macau
Population (10,00 persons)	4347	473	2032	6951	6150	739	62
GDP (USD trillion)	1.82	0.48	1.74	1.51	1.12	0.34	0.05
Per capita GDP (USD 10,000)	4.19	10.15	8.56	2.17	1.82	4.6	8.06
Economic growth rate	2.30%	2.30%	4.70%	7.00%	7.90%	3.70%	9.10%
Area (10,000/km^2)	3.68	1.79	2.15	5.6	5.47	0.11	0.003
Container throughout at the port (10,000/TPU)	798	242	671	7809	5719	2076	13
Passenger volume at airport (100 million person-time)	1.24	0.79	1.32	2.02	1.22	0.73	0.07
Ranking among global financial centers	5	8	2	—	18 (Shenzhen) 28 (Guangzhou)	3	—
Ranking in global innovation index	13	6	6	17 (China)	—	14	—
Number of top 100 universities in the world	2	2	3	4	0	4	0
Number of Fortune Global 500 headquarters	39	28	26	19	11	8	0

in *the Plan*, it is positioned as:

1.To be a national central city and a comprehensive gateway city;

2. To be an international business center and an integrated transportation hub;

3. To be a scientific and technological, cultural and educational center;

4. To be an international metropolis.

The positioning of Guangzhou has been "elevated" in the plans after revisions approved by the State Council since the 21st century.

Table 2 Planning Outline

The Plan for 2001-2011 (2005)	The Plan for 2011-2020 (2016)	The Plan for 2017-2035 (2018)
The provincial capital of Guangdong Province; One of the central cities in South China; A national famous historical and cultural city.	The provincial capital of Guangdong Province; A national famous historical and cultural city; An important central city in China; An international trade center and an integrated transportation hub.	The provincial capital of Guangdong Province; A national key central city; A famous historical and cultural city; An international integrated transportation hub; A business, communication and technological innovation center and a leading global city.

Compared with other central cities positioned in *the Plan*, Guangzhou has the unique advantage of being recognized as "a national central city"; Hong Kong as "an international metropolis" and an international financial center (offshore business hub, fund management and risk management center), an international legal and dispute resolution service center, a shipping center, and an aviation hub; Shenzhen as "a national innovation city", "a modern international city" and "an innovative and creative city with world influence".

Table 3 Plan for the Greater Bay Area and Strategic Positioning of the Four Central Cities

Guangdong-Hong Kong-Macau Greater Bay Area	Guangzhou	Shenzhen	Hong Kong	Macao
1. A dynamic world city cluster; 2. An international technological innovation center with global influence; 3. An important support for the construction of the "Belt and Road"; 4. A demonstration zone for deep cooperation between the Mainland and Hong Kong and Macao; 5. A high-quality living circle that is livable and favourable to business and tourism.	1. To be a national central city and a comprehensive gateway city; 2. To be an international business center and an integrated transportation hub; 3. To be a scientific and technological, cultural and educational center; 4. To be an international metropolis.	1. A national economic central city; 2. An international innovation city; 3. A modern international city; 4. An innovative and creative city with world influence.	1. An international finance, shipping and trade center and an international aviation hub; 2. A global offshore RMB business hub, an international asset management and risk management center; 3. An international legal dispute resolution center in the Asia-Pacific region; 4. An international metropolis	1. A world tourism and leisure center; 2. A cooperation service platform between China and Portuguese-speaking countries; 3. A communication and cooperation base with the Chinese culture as the mainstream and coexistence of different cultures.

The comparison above shows that any of the four cities alone cannot assume the historical mission of realizing the strategic goals of the Greater Bay Area. To accomplish this mission requires synergy and joint forces of the four cities.

International experience shows that excessive customs zones and special zones can result in isolation between cities and isolated development of central cities. Thus, the four cities should both compete and cooperate with each other, but make competition a driving force for cooperation. They should resolve structural contradictions in the region through cooperation among governments, enterprises and the public. Based on the positioning as a "national central city", Guangzhou, in particular, should seize strategic opportunities, make up for its shortcomings, and embark on a right development path in the new era.

II Historical Thoughts on the Positioning of Guangzhou as a National Central City

Cities are not isolated. The so-called central city earns its name from its position in an urban system. The urban system in China has gone through a historical development process:

1. Xia, Shang and Zhou Dynasties witnessed the beginning of Chinese cities. Due to the political "enfeoffment system", cities were generally separated and closed in space. They were often political centers at different levels, without any vertical connection from the bottom up or horizontal connection between one and the other.

2. From the prefecture and county system in the Qin Dynasty to the Ming Dynasty, although the enfeoffment system was abandoned, cities in a greater administrative region were politically governed by a dominant city due to the social limitations of the small-scale peasant economy. There was still a lack of spontaneous and equal economic ties between cities.

3. During the Ming Dynasty, as commercial activities became thriving and the commercial economy got a higher status in China, industrial and commercial towns emerged in large numbers. Influenced by political and economic forces, the urban spatial system began to get complicated, with administrative subordination and economic connection emerging as two systems, as an American scholar put it. Generally speaking, the city where bureaucrats were located and the cities under its jurisdiction were both administratively and economically connected. The city where government offices with a larger jurisdiction were located was often both an administrative and economic "center".

4. With the development of modern economy and especially under the context of economic globalization, resources are allocated in a larger geographical space, and the urban system in which economic activities were governed by the administrative center has changed. For a city, the unique functions, the connection with the hinterland, the economic strength, the convenience of transportation, and the position in the global supply chain all become important factors. The concept of administrative subordination is gradually undermined, while economic connection formed by the market division of labor matters. Some cities that become economic centers may become more essential than administrative centers.

New York v.s. Washington in the United States and Qingdao v.s. Jinan, Dalian v.s. Shenyang, and Xiamen v.s. Fuzhou in China are paired examples.

Guangzhou was established as the central city of South China after General Ren Xiao pacified Lingnan in the 33rd year of the rule of the First Emperor of Qin (214 BC). Guangzhou "is located between Guangdong and Guangxi, adjacent to Nanxiong and Zhaozhou in the north and near Jiangxi and Hubei and Hunan; it borders Chaozhou and Huizhou in the east and can deter Zhejiang and Fujian; it can defend Gao and Lian in the west and guards against Jiao and Yong; it surrounds the Hainan Island in the south, controlling the portal of the Li nationality." This ancient passage described the location advantage and the military control ability of Guangzhou.

It "leads to sea in all directions and is divided in half by a mountain." "The seas, the fields, the rivers, and the city lie progressively in a profound landscape; towers, buildings, pavilions, and terraces echo each other with distinctive meanings and symbolize cities in Lingnan." This passage described the profound cultural heritage, distinctive urban characteristics and traditional settlement wisdom reflected in the urban construction of Guangzhou.

In the modern society, the implementing the open door policy made Guangzhou the first Chinese city that was open to the outside world, that was exposed to modern civilization and international trade, and that led China into the era of democratic revolution. Since the late 1970s, Guangzhou has led the reform and opening up, prosperity and development of the country because of its proximity to Hong Kong and Macao and its cultural diversity. Its status as the central city in South China is nonparallel and unquestionable.

Nowadays, the plan for the Greater Bay Area designates four central cities in South China, namely Guangzhou, Shenzhen, Hong Kong and Macao. The "one country, two systems" policy and the "three customs areas" are unique in the world city clusters. For Guangzhou, it is particularly meaningful to find itself compete with Shenzhen, a peer central city that developed quickly from a small fishing village after decades. Guangzhou should objectively analyze and hold a correct attitude towards the changes that are taking place.

III Reflections on the Growth and Development of Guangzhou and Shenzhen

Radical changes have occurred to Shenzhen over the past four decades of reform and opening up. In recent years, it has firmly seized the great opportunity of new technological revolution and industrial transformation to push the replacement of old driving forces with new ones during economic structure adjustments. It is under this context that Shenzhen once again quickens the pace of economic development. In 2017, Guangzhou's GDP was surpassed by Shenzhen's; in 2018, the gap between the two cities in GDP and per capita GDP was further widened.

Table 4 Economic Structures of Guangdong and Shenzhen in 2017

2017	GDP (RMB 100 million)	Per capita GDP (RMB)	Three-industry ratio	Resident population (10,000 persons)	Urbanization rate of resident population	Registered population (person)	Urbanization rate of registered population	Municipal district area (square kilometers)
Guang zhou	22859.35	155491	0.98: 27.27: 71.75	1490.44	86.38%	927.69	79.78%	7434.4
Shen zhen	24221.98	189568	0.4: 41.1: 58.8	1302.66	100%	454.7	34.90%	1997.47

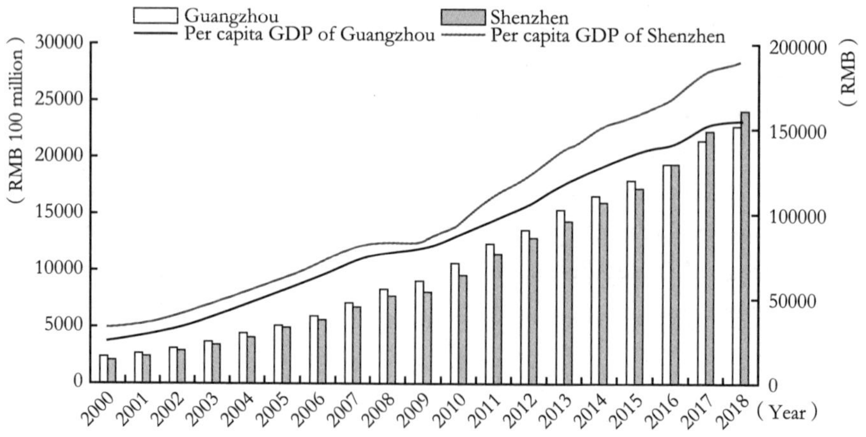

Figure 1 GDP and Per Capita GDP of Guangzhou and Shenzhen for 2000-2018

The miracle of Shenzhen is not reproducible. There are profound reasons and inherent laws behind the fact that the GDP of Guangzhou was surpassed by that of Shenzhen. Careful analysis shows that the key lies in the different economic structures and factor endowments of the two cities.

(1) Guangzhou is under industrial structure adjustments. As an old industrial base, traditional manufacturing takes up a large share in the industrial economy of Guangzhou. In recent years, Guangzhou has quickened the replacement of old driving forces with new ones and has shown good performance in such indicators as speed, efficiency and quality investment. However, 12 of 35 industrial sectors showed negative growth in 2018. The annual industrial added value of Guangzhou increased by 5.5%, 4 percentage points lower than the 9.5% of Shenzhen.

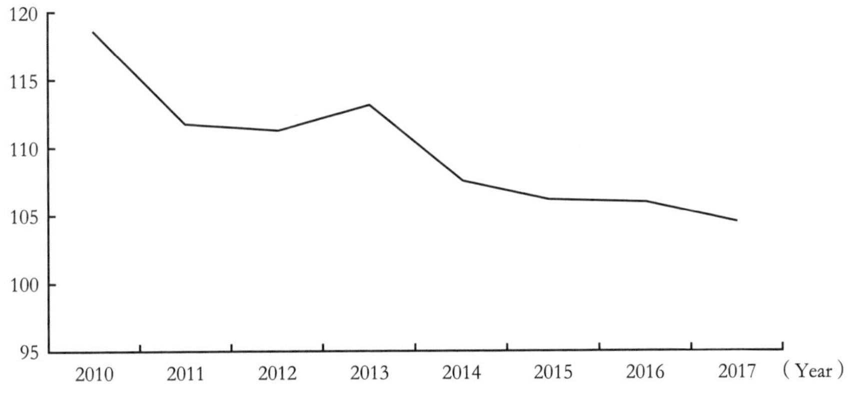

Figure 2 Total Industrial Output Index of Guangzhou (2010-2017)

Source: Derived from the Guangzhou Statistical Yearbook (2018)

(2) As a provincial capital, Guangzhou has a good foundation and a large base for the development of the service industry. In 2018, the tertiary industry of the city grew by 6.6%, accounting for 71.75%, up 0.73 percentage point from 2017; the growth rate of the tertiary industry in Shenzhen was 6.4%, accounting for 58.8%.

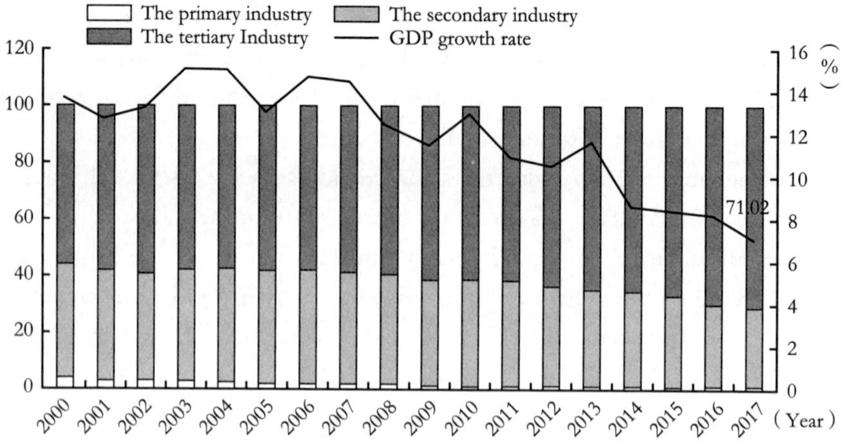

Figure 3 Three-industry Structure and GDP Growth Rate of Guangzhou

Source: Derived from the Guangzhou Statistical Yearbook (2018)

The increases in the growth rate and proportion of the service industry were attributed to the optimized economic structure. However, the service industry was often not as efficient as the industrial sector, which could affect the growth rate of GDP as well.

By comparison from the perspectives of innovation power and enterprise vitality, Shenzhen had stronger industrial development momentum:

(1) It had a huge high-end manufacturing industry cluster. Its top ten industries above designated size rated by industrial added value were: computer, communication and other electronic equipment manufacturing; electrical machinery and equipment manufacturing; special equipment manufacturing; electric power, heat production and supply; oil and gas extraction; rubber and plastic products industry; general equipment manufacturing; metal products industry; automobile manufacturing; pharmaceutical manufacturing.

Table 5 Production of Main Industrial Products in Shenzhen in 2018

Name	Unit	Production	YoY Growth Rate (%)
Mobile communication base station	10,000 channels	42427.60	63.5
New energy vehicle	10,000 sets	9.99	191.1
Satellite navigation positioning receiver	10,000 sets	541.85	33.2

Continued

Name	Unit	Production	YoY Growth Rate (%)
Mobile communication handset (mobile phone)	10,000 sets	30870.73	-15,3
Civilian drone	10,000 sets	294.50	4.4
Industrial robot	Set	21283.00	34.0
STB	10,000 sets	9861.67	-0.9
Discrete semiconductor devices	100 million piece	98.88	-30.9
Integrated circuit	100 million pieces	255.11	8.0
LCD	100 million pieces	11.08	-11.6
Electronic component	100 million pieces	1591.17	7.7
Optical fiber	10,000 km	1240.71	12.8
Server	10,000 sets	89.19	35.5
Solar battery (photovoltaic battery)	Kw	239361.49	33.6
Graphite and carbon product	Ton	12095.63	-31.4

The production of mobile communication base station equipment from Shenzhen accounted for 98.15% of the national total production; the production of mobile communication handset (mobile phone) accounted for 17.16%; the production of industrial robot accounted for 14.41%.

(2) There were large numbers of listed companies with high market value.

Table 6 Statistics of Listed Companies in Major Cities by December 31, 2018

(RMB 100 Million)

	Beijing	Shanghai	Guangzhou	Shenzhen	Tianjin	Chongqing
Number	319	319	101	303	53	52
Market value (RMB 100 Million)	145807.7	44366.91	12284.24	54458.31	4511.002	5031.504

Shenzhen showed encouraging development trends. However, the advantages and development momentum of Guangzhou as a historical central city cannot be underestimated. Analysis shows that:

1 Guangzhou Has Great Development Space.

Guangzhou has a total area of 7,434.4 square kilometers, 3.72 times an area of 1,997.47 square kilometers covered by Shenzhen. Guangzhou has a built-up area of 1,294 square kilometers, compared to 973 square kilometers built by Shenzhen. The undeveloped area (i.e., potential development space) of Guangzhou is 5.9 times that of Shenzhen.

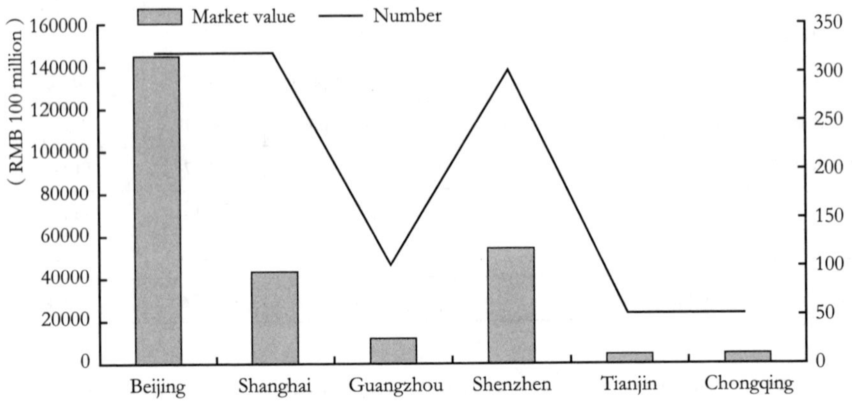

Figure 4 Total Output Value and Number of Listed Companies in Major Cities by the end of 2018

Source: Statistical Yearbook of City Construction in China

2 Guangzhou Has a Relatively Balanced Economic Structure.

Guangzhou has a complete industrial system and the basic characteristics of a modern economic system. Strategic emerging industries such as automobile manufacturing and electronic product manufacturing in the industrial sector develop with good momentum. Traditional industries are upgraded at quicker pace, and basic industries grow with strong dynamics. Guangzhou is a millennium business capital with a developed business culture and numerous commercial scenarios. A closer connection between commercial capital and industries can be found here. In 2018, the total merchandise wholesale and retail volume of Guangzhou was 2.36 times that of Shenzhen; its express business volume increased by 28.8% to exceed 5 billion parcels, maintaining the top one position in the country. The service industry of Guangzhou took up a large share and possessed strong growth momentum. The foreign trade dependence of the industrial system in Shenzhen was as high as 123.79%. In order to reduce the excessive dependence on foreign markets and meet the needs of domestic consumption and industrial upgrading, the next step for Shenzhen should be adapting industrial institutions to the domestic demand market.

Table 7 Foreign Trade Dependence of Guangzhou and Shenzhen in 2018

	GDP (RMB 100 Million)	Import (RMB 100 Million)	Export (RMB 100 Million)	Balance of Import and Export (RMB 100 Million)	Total Import and Export (RMB 100 Million)	Export to the US (RMB 100 Million)	Export to Hong Kong (RMB 100 Million)	Foreign Trade Dependence (%)
Guangzhou	22859.35	4202.57	5607.58	1405.01	9810.15	821.49	808.72	42.92
Shenzhen	24221.98	13709.05	16274.69	2565.64	29983.94	2383.94	6758.33	123.79

Source: Statistical Communiqués of Guangzhou and Shenzhen on the 2018 National Economic and Social Development

3 Guangzhou Has Strong Public Service Capacities

Guangzhou gathers high-quality medical, educational, sci-tech and cultural resources that can serve the South China and even the whole country. These public service capacities that other cities cannot rival are the most commendable soft power owned by Guangzhou.

(1) Health care

Table 8 Comparison of Health Care Institutions between Guangzhou and Shenzhen in 2018

	Hospital	Grade-3 hospitals	Number of total beds (10,000)	Number of beds in hospitals (10,000)	Number of beds per 1,000 people	Number of health workers (10,000 people)	Number of health workers per 1,000 people
Guangzhou	255	57	9.51	8.6	5.77	15.65	10.5
Shenzhen	139	18	4.76	4.36	3.35	9.37	7.19

Source: Statistical Communiqués of Guangzhou and Shenzhen

In the *Top 100 Hospitals of 2018* in the Chinese mainland, 11 come from Guangzhou, ranking third after 16 from Beijing and 13 from Shanghai. Shenzhen has only one hospital in this list.

(2) Education

Guangzhou has the strongest capability of high-quality talent training in South China. In 2018, the numbers of admissions, students and graduates in universities and junior colleges in Guangzhou were more than 10 times those in Shenzhen. The numbers of admissions, students and graduates in postgraduate schools in Guangzhou were also more than five times those in Shenzhen.

Table 9 Comparison of Education between Guangzhou and Shenzhen in 2018

(Unit: 10,000 People)

	Admissions in universities and junior colleges	Number of students	Number of graduates	Admissions in postgraduate schools	Number of graduate students	Number of postgraduates graduated
Guangzhou	32.36	108.64	29.04	3.74	10.11	2.54
Shenzhen	2.71	8.82	2.31	0.65	1.76	0.49

Source: Statistical Communiqués of Guangzhou and Shenzhen in 2018

(3) Culture

Guangzhou has a history of 2,233 years since it was built as Panyu City during the reign of the First Emperor of Qin. The Central Plain culture and the ethnic cultures in Nanyue were blended to form a unique Lingnan-Guangfu culture. Facing the sea and leaning against the hinterland of China, Guangzhou not only passes down and spreads the Chinese cultures and civilization, but also serves as a window to accept and assimilate foreign cultures and civilizations.

Guangzhou is an important starting point of the Maritime Silk Road. Arabic traders came here to do business during the Tang and Song Dynasties. While recommending the Chinese civilization to Europe, they also introduced religions and cultures from India, Central Asia and Europe. In the modern society, Guangzhou was the first place to experience the clash between the Chinese traditional culture and the Western industrial civilization. While accepting western advanced thoughts and science and technology, numerous Chinese pioneers left for Southeast Asia, Europe and the United States from Guangzhou.

The exchanges and mutual understanding of different civilizations temper the characteristics and heritage of regional culture in Guangzhou, making it highly inclusive and globally influential. Guangzhou has become a model in successful blending of Eastern and Western civilizations and cultures.

3 Science and Technology

Many renowned universities such as Sun Yat-Sen University, South China University of Technology, and Jinan University, as well as many national first-class research institutions such as the Guangzhou Branch of the Chinese Academy of Sciences are situated in Guangzhou. This is a city which gathers scientific and technological talents, owns complete scientific research facilities, and has strong advantages in basic scientific research that make it a potential source of scientific thinking and inventions. Shenzhen is the "Silicon Valley in the East". Its advantage comes from the innovation activities carried out by enterprises, so it is more favorable to market-oriented technological innovation and industrialization. The two cities are mutually complementary.

(1) Patents

Although Guangzhou cannot compete with Shenzhen in terms of the numbers of patent applications, invention patents, patent grants, and invention patent grants, it grew faster than Shenzhen in all of these numbers in 2018.

Table 10 Comparison of Patent Applications between Guangzhou and Shenzhen

	Number of patent applications (10,000)	Growth rate (%)	Number of patent grants (10,000)	Growth rate (%)	Number of invention patents (10,000)	Growth rate (%)	Number of invention patent grants (10,000)	Growth rate (%)
Guangzhou	17.31	46.3	8.98	49.2	5.02	35.08	1.08	15.5
Shenzhen	22.86	29.1	14.02	48.8	7	16.1	2.13	12.6

Source: Statistical Communiqués of Guangzhou and Shenzhen in 2018

(2) Scientific Research Institutions

Guangzhou has much more national and provincial high-end scientific research platforms than Shenzhen.

Table 11 Number of Scientific Research Institutions

City	National Engineering Technology Center	National Enterprise Technology Center	National Key Laboratory	Provincial Engineering Technology Center	Provincial Key Laboratory	Municipal Key Laboratory
Guangzhou	18	27	20	956	233	165
Shenzhen	7	26	14	218	24	238

Note: The data of Guangzhou came from 2018, while the data of Shenzhen came from 2017.

Sources: Statistical Communiqués of Guangzhou and Shenzhen in 2018 and the Shenzhen Statistical Yearbook in 2018.

5 Guangzhou Has a More Balanced Population Structure

In 2018, Guangzhou had a resident population of 14.9044 million, 62.2% of which, or 9.2769 million, was registered residents; Shenzhen had a resident population of 13.0266 million, only 34.9% of which, or 4.547 million, was registered residents. A relatively stable population is attributed to good public policies and lays the foundation for further improvement. Most importantly, it is conducive to sustainable economic development and social stability and harmony.

In addition, judging from the composition of resident population (refer to Figure)

Table 12 Age Compositions of Resident Population in National Central Cities and Shenzhen, Hong Kong, Macao and Hangzhou (By the End of 2017)

Region	Resident Population (10,000 persons)	Age Composition			Percentage (%)		
		Age 0-14	Age 15-64	Age 65+	Age 0-14	Age 15-64	Age 65+
Beijing	2170.7	225.8	1706.2	238.8	10.4	78.6	11.0
Shanghai	2418	240.5	1832.7	344.8	9.9	75.8	14.3
Tianjin	1557	175.8	1205.5	175.7	11.3	77.4	11.3
Chongqing	3075	504.1	2131.8	439.1	16.4	69.3	14.3
Zhengzhou	988	190.7	694.6	102.7	19.3	70.3	10.4
Wuhan	854	116.0	621.1	116.8	13.6	72.7	13.7
Xi'an	883	120.4	664.0	98.6	13.6	75.2	11.2
Chengdu	1604	253.9	1126.7	223.4	15.8	70.2	13.9
Guangzhou	1450	249.5	1075.5	125.0	17.2	74.2	8.6

Note: The data was calculated from the summary of sample survey of population in 2017.

Among the 9 national central cities, the population aged 0-14 accounted for 17.2% of the total population, which was only next to 19.3% in Zhengzhou and was even higher than the percentage in Shenzhen; the population aged over 65 accounted for 8.6%, the lowest percentage among all the compared cities. This pointed to a moderate aging population in Guangzhou, which is still considered a "young" city. It also registers a high percentage of settled migrants who constitute ample reserves of labor resources. The data about "demographic dividends" indicate that Guangzhou is a city with great growth and innovation potential.

The analysis above showed that Guangzhou has a strong foundation as a national central city and that its advantages are irreplaceable within a certain period of time. It has strong public service capacities in the fields of integrated transportation, culture, education, medical care, science and technology that are incomparable to other cities in South China.

In particular, different from the other central cities, namely Shenzhen, Hong Kong and Macao, Guangzhou possesses a broad economic hinterland and a multi-level urban system. Its economic space can even be constantly expanded amid competition and cooperation through planning of metropolitan areas. Economic and social development is an ever-changing process. Being surpassed by another city in individual GDP indicators is nothing to worry about.

IV Several Suggestions for Guangzhou

Guangdong-Hong Kong-Macau Greater Bay Area can be understood both from physical geography and from economic geography, cultural geography and political geography.

From the perspective of natural geography, it enjoys a good location backed by the hinterland of the mainland and facing the western Pacific. It has blessed natural endowments for building a world-class bay region and a world-class city cluster in the Blue Harbor and the Pearl River Delta.

From the perspective of economic geography, it is located at the intersection of the forefront of opening up in China and the "Belt and Road" as a strategic hub for opening up, exchanges and cooperation by China. After 40 years of reform and opening up, it has developed a unique advantage from the integration of systems, institutions, mechanisms and markets and has become an engine that drives national innovation and development and an economic support belt that radiates to East Asia, South Asia and Southeast Asia.

From the perspective of cultural geography, Guangzhou has formed a special cultural ecosystem with deep roots, long-lasting charm, inclusive property, and unfading quality due to the long-term blending and collision of traditional culture and industrial civilization, Eastern culture and Western civilization. Its development, integration and dissemination carry the national cultural ideals, and it has a strong potential to expand spatially.

From the perspective of political geography, it bears the national vision and historical mission of governing the South China Sea, maintaining friendly relations with the neighboring Southeast Asia, resolving geopolitical conflicts, keeping long-term prosperity and stability, and facilitating peaceful reunification of the country with the "one country, two systems" policy. It is a leading platform for China to enable its national strategies to interact with global governance under the conditions of globalization.

The new mission of the Greater Bay Area is to promote institutional innovation, deeply connect with world rules and standards, forge regional breakthrough capabilities, and lead China's towards modernization and great rejuvenation through competition and cooperation and by making full use of factor advantages.

Guangzhou is a national central city. National central cities are assigned with three main tasks: (1) To be national strategic posts; (2) To participate in global competition on behalf of the country; and (3) To drive the development of a greater region. In order to better assume the mission and responsibility as a national central city in the construction of the Guangdong-Hong Kong-Macau Greater Bay Area, Guangzhou is advised to:

1 Accelerate Institutional Innovation, Technological Innovation and Industrial Innovation

Firstly, strengthen economic and cultural ties with Hong Kong and Macao, seize opportunities to cooperate with them at system level, and make full use of the advantages of Hong Kong and Macao in system, mechanism and business environment; actively refer to international rules and standards, promote reform and institutional innovation with a broad vision, create an innovative and upgraded export-oriented economic system and a new socialist market economy system, and to be a forerunner in the country in deepening reform and expanding opening up by making prior attempts.

Secondly, seize the historical opportunities presented by the new technological revolution and industrial transformation in reshaping the global innovation landscape, the global economic structure and the global supply chain, enhance the ability to manage innovative resources, promote the development of new driving forces and the transformation and upgrading of traditional industries, and replace old driving forces with new ones; join hands with Hong Kong and Macao to integrate elements and industrial advantages in innovation, finance, commerce intermediary, free trade, and integrated transportation in the region, foster world-class advanced manufacturing clusters, and temper the ability to lead global industries and manage value chain.

Thirdly, create an innovation platform that is led by enterprises as main subjects, pay attention to model innovation, develop a platform economy mainly characterized by the digital economy, and promote a transition from linear structure and mesh structure to matrix structure in economic organizations and industrial ecology; transform production, transaction and consumption processes into value creation, cultural identity, resources sharing, and market interaction processes across regions and communities, and make these highly informative and intelligent platforms into unique nodes and central hubs in the new production relationship network in Guangzhou.

Fourthly, effectively combine the national innovation system, the industrial innovation system and the social innovation system, build a platform for connecting and converting these systems, reduce frictions among national innovation strategies, industrial innovation willingness and innovation energies from society and market, enhance innovation efficiency, and reduce innovation costs.

2 Accelerate the Pace of City Renewal to Further Revitalize the "Old Guangzhou"

Firstly, make the city more intelligent, low-carbon and livable, strengthen the overall design and coordination for the construction of smart city, smart transportation, smart municipalities and smart management, avoid fragmented and conceptualized intelligent renewal of the city, create a more convenient, comfortable and livable environment for citizens at all ages.

Secondly, strengthen the construction of an international integrated transportation hub and a modern logistics system, perform powerful allocation, assembling and distributing, and transshipment functions, and develop the hub economy.

Thirdly, boost urban industrial upgrading, and position advanced manufacturing and modern service industries as the main business types in the city. Highlight the industrialization of industrial Internet, life science, artificial intelligence, new energies, space and marine technologies, and new energy technologies based on the advantages and characteristics of Guangzhou. Transfer traditional manufacturing industries to the surroundings, and lay out a scientific industrial chain and supply chain within a reasonable space. At the same time, pay attention to the needs of the city and its industries for the ecosystem in the service industry and frame a reasonable employment structure.

Finally, adapt to the replacement of manual labor with technological advances and the trend that more employment opportunities will come from the service industry than from the manufacturing industry, and promote changes in the nature of work. Increase government and social investments in human capital and human resources, help urban employees improve their skills and professional quality, and provide more employment choices for residents. Guide enterprises to strengthen on-the-job training for employees so that they can adapt to new skill requirements put forward by technological progress and business type changes, and support enterprises to maintain sustainable innovation capability.

3 Keep the City Young

Firstly, vigorously develop new technologies and new industries, especially new business types and models that can attract more young people to work, and provide more innovation, entrepreneurship and creation spaces and employment opportunities for young people.

Secondly, continue to increase the proportion of registered population to the resident population, and reduce the scissors difference between resident population and total population. Turn more mobile employed population to new citizens and make their children, the "second and third generations of Guangzhou natives" who integrate into the local culture and living environment, have access to local education and enjoy urban public services equally. Explore the potential of human resources and maintain sufficient and dynamic backup human resources.

Thirdly, break the institutional barriers that restrict talent inflows and population mobilization, implement tolerate, open and loose policies on employment, housing, home purchase, car purchase and migration to city, exert inclusive and prudent management, attract more domestic and international talents and ordinary residents to start a business, seek employment, settle down, and consume in Guangzhou.

4 Build Guangzhou into a Fashion Center and Consumer Center with International Influence

Firstly, continually refine the traditional "Lingnan culture" and "Guangfu culture" native to Guangzhou, and pay due attention to their inheritance, spreading, innovation and enrichment. Maintain cultural diversity, deepen the integration and interaction with Hong Kong, Macao and Taiwan cultures and Nanyang culture, strengthen exchanges and mutual understanding with foreign cultures and civilizations, and try to be a model city that upholds multiculturalism and coexistence of different civilizations. Use the weapon of inclusiveness and vitality rooted in Guangzhou's cultural environment to break the curse of "clash of civilizations", and advocate the consensus that exchanges and mutual understanding are the mainstream in the development of human civilization and cultural progress.

Secondly, further enhance the status of Guangzhou as a consumer center, promote cooperation with the free trade port in Hong Kong, strengthen the concept of free trade development, introduce Hong Kong's trade and tariff systems when appropriate, encourage innovations in government regulatory systems and mechanisms, and develop new trade methods and new trade forms. Enhance the supply capacity of public goods and public services to provide high-quality and readily accessible medical, educational, elderly, child care, technological, cultural, tourist and other consumer services for the Greater Bay Area and the vast South China, and boost the soft power and influence of Guangzhou as a national central city.

Thirdly, tap the profound business culture and consumer culture of Guangzhou; pay attention to changes in consumer sentiment and consumer psychology triggered by consumption upgrades; support the development of personalized design, customization, consumer experience, cultural spaces and consumer communities; promote the prosperity of creativity, fashion, apparel, beauty, food, drama, classical and pop music, tea house culture, bar culture, health and wellness, recreational travel, social salons, and popular digital products to provide residents with more creation and consumption choices and scenario; make Guangzhou a truly fashionable and charming city that leads new consumption trends with "low business costs and high-quality life".

B.13

Reflections on Several Issues about Integration of Greater Metropolitan Areas

*Chen Yao**

Abstract: At present, generally three issues need to be solved or eliminated in promoting the integration of metropolitan areas in China: excessive concentration of core cities; ambiguous functions and serious homogenization of cities in an area; weak comprehensive strength and low primacy ratio of central cities that limit their radiating effects on the surrounding areas. The fundamental difficulty and key lie in systems and mechanisms, including the existing fiscal and taxation systems and the administrative division. The measures to promote integration include: plan the development of greater metropolitan areas, attach importance to the generation of peripheral sub-growth poles, strengthen the linked division of labor between central cities and surrounding cities as well as sub-centers, and form complementarity between functional industries; reduce administrative intervention and encourage free and orderly flow of elements; establish benefit-sharing mechanisms, including the tax sharing mechanism for industrial transfer and undertaking, and the ecological compensation mechanism between the ecological beneficial zone and the damaged zone; convene city head or departmental joint meetings and allow social institutions

* Chen Yao, PhD of Economics, Dean of the National Central City Research Institute of Zhengzhou Normal University, Research Fellow, Professor and PhD Supervisor for the Institute of Industrial Economics of CASS, Vice President and Secretary General of China Association of Regional Economy, Deputy Director of the Western Development Research Center of CASS.

to be organizers and coordinators. The integration of greater metropolitan areas in Zhengzhou should serve the mission of national central city construction. Its purpose is to strengthen the leading, gathering and radiating functions of the central city, accelerate the expansion of supporting space in the surrounding cities, and form an influential modern metropolitan circle.

Keywords: greater metropolitan areas (metropolitan circles); integration; national central city

Greater metropolitan areas, or greater metropolitan circles, are products of industrialization or urbanization that has developed to a certain degree. The new-type urbanization in China should mainly take on the form of greater metropolitan area and city cluster and should focus on promoting the integration of metropolitan areas and city clusters. This paper discusses the concept, theory and significance of greater metropolitan areas integration, challenges and solutions to this process, and the ideas and suggestions on the integration of greater metropolitan areas in Zhengzhou.

I Concept, Theory and Significance of Greater Metropolitan Area Integration

How do the public or people understand the differences between city cluster, greater metropolitan area, and national central city? How are they defined? The academic circle has been trying to answer these questions, but no consensus has been reached. As far as the author is concerned, "metropolitan circle" has the same meaning as "metropolitan area", in spite of different wording. In the past, metropolitan circle was taken in a larger sense, because it was mistaken as "city cluster". According to the definition given by the National Development and Reform Commission, metropolitan area, as we put it, is equal to metropolitan circle, which was a concept originated from Japan. Japan had a very detailed definition of the earliest planning of metropolitan circle, including the population size of the central city, the ratios of commuting population and cargo flows between surrounding areas and the central city, etc.

The author believes that a greater metropolitan area is an intermediate layer in the urban spatial structure and is an integral part of the spatial pattern under the new-type urbanization. What we are discussing is the integration of greater metropolitan areas, while in the past we talked about integration inside a city cluster. In fact, the sequence that started with the integration of city cluster has been mistaken both by the competent department and at the local operational level in the first place. Now according to the national plan, there are 19 city clusters of different sizes all over the country. For example, Chengdu-Chongqing city cluster and Central Plains city cluster include more than 30 cities, and the city cluster along the Yangtze River Delta includes 26 ones. These city clusters are vast and internally varied. Although the integration of city clusters is proposed, it is like a castle in the air in practice and closely connected urbanized areas are rare to see.

Based on international and domestic experience, especially the international one, the integration of metropolitan areas should precede the integration of city clusters. A city cluster is larger than a metropolitan area. In other words, the integration of metropolitan areas is an important step and prerequisite for the integration of city cluster. For example, the East Coast city cluster in the United States incorporated Boston in the northeast, New York, Philadelphia and Baltimore in the southwest, and Washington. It was formed on the basis of the Greater New York metropolitan area, the Washington metropolitan area, and the Boston metropolitan area, which were gradually integrated with their own characteristics preserved and functions complemented.

The integration of greater metropolitan areas can contribute to the construction of central cities. It plays a significant role in upgrading the functions and development levels of central cities and driving the development of surrounding areas. In the future, it will become a focus in the process of new-type urbanization in the country. Although 19 city clusters have been defined, more progress is hardly made at the local level. On the one hand, as work has to be done on a large spatial scale and across provincial administrative divisions, metropolitan areas and integration of cities should be the starting points. In other words, the integration of metropolitan areas in existing city clusters should be the first step to take in the future urbanization process.

The guidance given by the National Development and Reform Commission

("NDRC") clearly states the necessity of building metropolitan circles. However, the metropolitan circles here come with an attribute: modern metropolitan circles, which mean they are different from the past or foreign concept of the term. The guidance clearly defines a city cluster as one that has a central city of a super or mega size or with strong radiating and driving capacity. This is a requirement on the volume of the central city. The population thresholds are over 10 million for a super city, over 5 million for a mega city, and over 1 to 5 million for a large city, which is further divided into two levels of 1 to 3 million and 3 to 5 million. Cities with a population of over 3 million are arguably central cities with strong radiating and driving capacity. A metropolitan area, as we put it, should meet the basic standard of being at least as big as a one-hour commuting circle. The "one hour" was measured as a driving duration, but now it is associated with "commuting", which means a metropolitan area refers to the urban spatial pattern within the scope of one-hour commuting.

The NDRC's guidance actually takes the construction of modern metropolitan circles as a starting point to push forward the new-type urbanization in the new era. This initiative can not only optimize the urban spatial structure, but also deliver great economic benefits by activating effective investments and potential consumer demand and enhancing endogenous power. The basic idea behind the development of metropolitan circles is promoting the integration of central cities with surrounding towns through innovative systems and mechanisms and ultimately propelling the development of modern metropolitan circles. This development goal can be achieved through two stages. By 2022, the prospected modern metropolitan circle should have a clear spatial structure, complementary urban functions, coordinated industrial division of labor, unimpeded traffic, balanced public services, and a harmonious and livable environment. By 2035, several modern metropolitan circles with global influence will have basically taken shape.

The construction of modern metropolitan circles involves seven major tasks: infrastructure integration, industrial division of labor, construction of a unified open market, joint construction and sharing of public services, joint protection and control of ecological environment protection, urban and rural integration development, and integrated institutional mechanisms. A national guide has been provided for cultivating modern metropolitan circles and for different regions and provinces to follow in the future. At present, apart from the Shanghai metropolitan circle in the city cluster along the Yangtze River Delta, Nanjing metropolitan circle, Hangzhou metropolitan circle and Hefei metropolitan circle are also under planning. The so-called integration of metropolitan circles is actually about breaking barriers between central cities and surrounding cities as soon as possible, in order to promote coordinated and linkage development.

Why is the concept of greater metropolitan circle put forward? In fact, it is closely related to the rapid development of urbanization in the country. The emergence of greater metropolitan circles and metropolitan areas is actually the product of urbanization and industrialization that has developed to a certain degree. In the early days of reform and opening up, China had an urbanization rate of only 17%, which increased to 29% in 2000, 58.52% in 2017, and about 60% in 2018. In other words, 60% of the population in China now lives in cities. Traffic congestion in cities is a perceived problem during the rapid development of urbanization when we drive and commute. This process is also accompanied by problems like environmental pollution and haze, high housing prices, heavy pressure on public facilities and services, and social governance. As a result, the spatial form is also changing in the urbanization process. In the past, the single center of a city kept expanding and spreading to the surrounding areas. Now a single center is replaced by multiple ones in order to relieve the functions and the excessive concentration of population and industries in the central city, or to integrate the central city with surrounding towns and form metropolitan circles of different scales and levels.

China is a big country with a population of nearly 1.4 billion. The division of cities here is obviously different from that in foreign countries. For example, a foreign city with a population of 50,000 is a big city indeed, while it is commensurate with a town in China. Humen, the largest town in China, has a resident population of 600,000. Now, super and mega cities are born on the basis of the original large, medium and small cities. The traditional threshold for a small city was a population of 100,000, but now the population thresholds are a population of 500,000 for small cities, 5 to 10 million for mega cities, and over 10 million for super cities. The resident population of Zhengzhou has exceeded 10 million, which makes it a mega city by population size of the urban central area. At present, there are 19 city clusters in the national plan, 7 of which are most important, namely the Beijing-Tianjin-Hebei city cluster, the city cluster along the Yangtze River Delta, the city cluster along the Pearl River Delta (now known as the Guangdong-Hong Kong-Macau Greater Bay Area), the city cluster along the middle reaches of the Yangtze River, the Central Plains city cluster, the Guanzhong Plain city cluster, and the Chengdu-Chongqing city cluster. All of these 7 city clusters have clearly defined central cities which total 12 (the Beijing-Tianjin-Hebei city cluster and the Chengdu-Chongqing city cluster both have two central cities, and the Greater Bay Area has 4 central cities). Except Hong Kong, Macau and Shenzhen, the remaining 9 central cities are also designated as national central cities. Zhengzhou, for example, is clearly identified as the national central city that leads the development of the Central Plains city cluster. Generally speaking, the 7 city clusters are evenly distributed: 3 in the eastern coastal area and 2 in the Central and Western Regions, respectively. This layout is conducive to the coordinated development of various regions in the country (the Beijing-Tianjin-Hebei city cluster is supposed to drive the entire Bohai Sea rim area and hopefully the Northeast).

The concept of greater metropolitan circles has long been introduced. In 1957, Gottman, a French geographer, first proposed the concept of megalopolis (greater metropolitan circle). In his view, megalopolis refers to "a giant centering around one or more super cities with a total population of more than 10 million and significant political and economic influence." His definition is still accepted in researches nowadays. There are many theories about metropolitan areas. For example, John Friedmann, an American economist, applied Schumpeter's innovation theory to formulate a spatial polarization theory named the Core and Periphery Theory. The "growth pole" theory proposed by the French economist Perroux, the "cumulative causation" proposed by Myrdal, a Nobel Prize winner in economics, and the new economic geography proposed by Krugman are also examples. The metropolitan circle theory is based on the urban spatial form of metropolis. This theory originated from the location theory by the German economist von Thünen, emphasizing that the metropolitan circle is a circular structure composed of urban systems at different levels, on different scales, with different functions and spatial structures within the area. There are one or two central big cities or mega cities within a certain geographical or administrative region that radiate to and drive a number of smaller and medium-sized cities within a certain range, in which way the metropolitan circle grows to be a city cluster or city belt that is influential and competitive.

What is the integration of metropolitan areas (metropolitan circles)? The so-called integration mainly refers to coordination and cooperation between different entities (including governments, enterprises, residents and associations) in a metropolitan area for the purpose of optimizing resource allocation and improving the overall competitiveness of the metropolitan area. For example, in the Greater London, Greater New York, and Greater Tokyo metropolitan areas, the central cities and surrounding small and medium-sized cities are actually different administrative areas, which bring about a coordination problem. International cooperation is mainly established by creating alliances or other cooperation mechanisms. The requirements and tasks in the integration of metropolitan areas mainly include infrastructure connectivity, industrial division of labor and cooperation, market integration, joint prevention and control of ecological environment, joint protection and governance, and mutual recognition of social security policies, etc. In China, the integration of metropolitan circles is actively explored and advanced in many places. I participated in several investigations last year, one of which was about the Chengdu-Chongqing metropolitan circle, which is now under strong and relatively solid progress. As a central city, Chengdu is integrated with its neighbors, namely Meishan, Ziyang and Deyang, in prioritized fields such as transportation, industry, ecology, social security, household registration, education and medical care. Solid progress is made in each field. The integration can constantly increase the development quality and primacy ratio of central cities and also substantially radiate to the development of surrounding cities. Then, what is the goal of city integration? In a nutshell, it is intended to narrow the gap between central cities and peripheral areas (also between urban and rural areas) in per capita income level and GDP. Different places fully exert their comparative advantages, while the leading and radiating functions of central cities are enhanced. That will help eliminate both big city diseases and "rural diseases" (poverty, infertility and hollowing out).

II Difficulties in Promoting the Integration of Metropolitan Areas and Solutions

At present, many difficulties get in the way of the integration of metropolitan areas in China. In general, there are three major difficulties to be solved. The first one is excessive functions of core cities. Beijing is the most typical example, and Shanghai is joining as well. High concentrations of urban population, industries and high-quality resources and indiscriminate assembling of core and non-core functions have resulted in great gaps within metropolitan areas. Central cities have a huge "siphon effect" on surrounding and peripheral areas. For example, there is a poverty zone around Beijing and Tianjin, which is quite an obstacle in the integration process.

The second difficulty is ambiguous functions and serious homogenization of cities in metropolitan areas. This is typical of metropolitan circles without prominent central cities. For example, in the "Chuannan metropolitan circle" (including Yibin, Zigong, Neijiang and Luzhou) of the Chengdu-Chongqing city cluster, cities are very homogeneous due to similarities in scale, function and industry. For them, competition outweighs cooperation. Not only does vicious competition occur in industrial development and investment attraction, but also consensus can hardly be reached on infrastructure planning and policy interaction. Thus, it is necessary to work out solutions to the integration of such metropolitan circles.

The third difficulty is universal among metropolitan areas. Central cities have weak comprehensive strength and low primacy ratio. They function like small horses trying to pull big wagons and has limited radiating effects on surrounding urban areas. Jinan, Nanjing and Shijiazhuang in the Eastern Region, Zhengzhou in the Central Region, and Nanning and Hohhot in the Western Region are typical provincial capitals with low primacy ratio. In recent years, capital cities have been trying to increase their primacy ratio. Some attempts have been successful, while others remain to pay off. It is worth mentioning that the intention has to be accomplished in a proper way. Many cities hope to grow quickly by transforming counties into districts and by merging other cities. Some approaches are praiseworthy. For example, the merger of Chaohu into Hefei not only streamlined government agencies, but also facilitated the ecological protection of Chaohu Lake and opened up a new space for the development of the provincial capital. Nevertheless, to expand city scale by transforming counties or merging other cities is generally not an admirable antidote; instead, adjustment of administrative division should be strictly controlled. Fundamentally, to increase primacy ratio requires endogenous growth and innovation driven forces. In this regard, Zhengzhou pool resources to invest in innovative development during the process of national central city construction. Its primacy ratio is continuously improved to have now exceeded 20%, registering delightfully three percentage points higher from 2010 to 2017. Only when central cities increase their primacy ratio, will they be able to drive the development of surrounding areas and promote the integration process.

Fundamentally, the difficulty and key lie in systems and mechanisms. Since the reform and opening up in the early 1980s, the fiscal system of "dividing revenue and expenditure between the central and local governments" has been implemented. Under this fiscal system, all regions have to seek financial resources by themselves. Only those enterprises that pay taxes in dependent territories and create more local jobs are supported by local governments. Otherwise, they would be restricted. Under this system, redundant construction, mismatched resources and inefficient investment began to take hold. Another problem is inconsistent administrative levels, which makes connection between cities difficult. Many surrounding areas find it hard to approach the central city within the same region. An effective mechanism for interaction and cooperation is absent. All of these are problems to be solved during the integration process.

So, how to promote the integration of metropolitan areas under the current system? Here are some solutions. The first one is to further refine the existing city cluster plans by giving priority to the integration of metropolitan circles. By comparing several city cluster plans that have been announced so far, I found that the plan for the Central Plains city cluster is relatively rough as it involves a large scope and a number of cities, and low operability. If it could be further refined to focus on the integration of Zhengzhou metropolitan area and be specific to urban districts and counties, the construction of the Central Plains city cluster would no doubt be easier. Thus, a good plan for metropolitan areas is the first step to promote the integration of city clusters. Secondly, attention should be paid to the development of peripheral growth poles. Henan is now working on it, and the development of Luoyang as a sub-center is evidence. Meanwhile, the division of labor between the central city and surrounding cities and sub-centers should be strengthened to make differentiated functional industries complement each other. Next, reducing administrative intervention and encouraging free and orderly flow of elements are important. Benefit-sharing mechanisms should also be established. Last year, the Central Committee of the Communist Party of China and the State Council introduced a new mechanism for more effective regional coordination. The most important part of the mechanism is about strengthening the coordination of inter-regional interest relations, because it is the key to the promotion of integration. Indeed, more exploration is needed, including the tax sharing mechanism for industrial transfer and undertaking, and the ecological compensation mechanism between the ecological beneficial zone and the damaged zone. In addition, city head or departmental joint meetings should be convened in metropolitan circles, and social institutions should be encouraged to serve as organizers and coordinators.

Here are some domestic and foreign examples. The Shandong Peninsula city cluster is a domestic example. Although it is a city cluster within a province, it has a wide coverage. The provincial capital, Jinan, and sub-provincial cities Qingdao and Yantai are central cities in this city cluster. The integration of metropolitan circles centering round these cities must be well planned in order to achieve the integration of the entire city cluster. The plan clearly defines the Jinan metropolitan circle, the Qingdao metropolitan circle and the Yantai metropolitan area, and the integration of the three metropolitan circles is the basis and premise for the integration of Shandong Peninsula city cluster. There is also a foreign example. There are five internationally influential city clusters, and their huge expanse is constituted by numerous metropolitan circles. There are 11 city clusters in the United States, the most important of which is the northeastern city cluster centering round New York in the East Coast, plus the central Great Lakes Megalopolis centering round Chicago and the West Coast city cluster centering round Los Angeles in California. However, the city clusters in the United States are conceptually megalopolises rather than metropolitan areas. A metropolitan area is similar to the Greater New York Area, an area where New York, as the core, is closely connected with its neighbors. Having developed for a period of time, the East Coast city cluster has shown distinct functional division, with New York as an international financial center, Boston as a scientific and educational center, Philadelphia and Baltimore as manufacturing and trade centers, and Washington as the political center of the country. The large cities are functionally complementary and clearly divided in labor. They provide a good reference.

III Thoughts and Suggestions for the Integration of Zhengzhou Metropolitan Area

Concerning the integration of Zhengzhou metropolitan area, the author contends that national central city construction provides a good opportunity to strengthen the leading and radiating capacity of the central city, to accelerate the expansion of supporting space for surrounding cities, and to form an influential modern metropolitan circle. At present, the Central Government has clearly defined seven major city clusters to be developed in the future as well as the leading and driving central cities inside them. For example, Zhengzhou is the central city that leads the development of the Central Plains city cluster. Thus, to promote the construction of Zhengzhou metropolitan area and the Central Plains city cluster, Zhengzhou, as the central city, should be the top priority. The national central city construction of Zhengzhou should be the first step to promote the integration of Zhengzhou metropolitan area and even the integration of the Central Plains city cluster.

National central cities bear national missions, and they also assume some functions that serve the whole country. Their functions are classified into several specific categories: comprehensive services, technological innovation, network hubs, opening and exchanges, humanistic cohesion, and ecological livability. All of the six functions carry profound connotations, based on which a complete indicator system has been built to evaluate the nine national central cities. The evaluation results showed that Zhengzhou cannot rival the other cities in many aspects, but it has certain strengths. For example, it has better GDP, larger resident population, and greater foreign trade growth rate than Xi'an. It is also a stronger network hub. Nevertheless, Zhengzhou is generally in a take-off stage. For example, Zhengzhou, as an inland city, has many internationalization related indicators that underperform, although it is aimed to become an open base. Its internationalization has many indicators that are significantly lower. It has the least foreign investments actually used and fewer international sister cities. I attended a city forum the other day and found that a county in the Central Region has six international sister cities; now no foreign consulates have stepped in Zhengzhou yet, and the record will probably be broken soon. Compared with other central cities in China, Zhengzhou still has obvious shortcomings, but it has entered the fast track of growth. In the future, comprehensive services, technological innovation, opening and exchanges should be the focus of development.

Based on the national deployment of metropolitan circle development, Zhengzhou should seize the opportunity of national central city construction to develop a modern metropolitan circle. It should bear the national missions assigned to the national central cities and enhance its ability to serve the whole country. This is an important perspective of consideration. We need to identify the fields where Zhengzhou has the potential to serve the whole country. For example, is it possible for it to become a medical health center that serves the country? Now, Beijing definitely offers the best medical services and receives tremendous patients. Statistics show that Beijing receives 720,000 patients across the country every day, which partly accounts for the traffic congestion in the capital. So we need to relieve this medical service function from the capital. Zhengzhou, located in the Central Plains, is an important integrated transportation hub in the country that connects the east with the west, and the south with the north conveniently. The transportation is convenient there as well. There are hence many possibilities for Zhengzhou to serve the country. I recently heard that the National Health Commission has approved of building a children's medical service center in Zhengzhou.

In order to improve the leading and radiating function and the primacy ratio as a central city, Zhengzhou may continue to increase its population and economic concentrations. Currently, Zhengzhou covers 1/20 of the province, holds one-tenth of the total population in the province, and accounts for one-fifth of the provincial GDP. However, compared with other provincial capitals in the country, Zhengzhou has a low degree of concentration. Population concentration represents one direction of improvement. Taking up only 1/10 of the provincial population of 100 million, the population in the provincial capital is no doubt not concentrated enough. I think that the proportion could be increased to 20% or so, and its primacy ratio could be raised from 20% to 30%. Indeed, the primacy ratio of a central city should be reasonably high. Excessive primacy ratio will result in imbalanced development. Over-concentration is also a source of problems like "urban diseases". From a comprehensive perspective, an economic primacy ratio of 30% would be appropriate. At the same time, the urban built-up area needs to be further expanded. Now, Zhengzhou has a built-up area of only a few hundred square kilometers. The development space cannot meet the needs for national central city construction and is much smaller than those in many provincial capitals. This area should at least be expanded to somewhere between 1,500 and 2,000 square kilometers in the future.

We also need to study the core functions of Zhengzhou as a central city, considering gradually transferring some non-core functions to neighboring cities to avoid "urban diseases" that may appear during the rapid advance of urbanization, which is also an inherent implication in the integration of Zhengzhou metropolitan area. The construction of metropolitan areas should not only allow for concentrations in the central city, but also drive the development of neighboring cities such as Kaifeng, Xuchang, Jiaozuo and Xinxiang. Thus, some functions should be planned to shift to the surrounding areas, such as manufacturing of primary products, large road logistics and warehousing, and urban agriculture. We need to carefully study the national plan of metropolitan circle and try to build the Zhengzhou metropolitan area into a model of metropolitan circle construction in the country.

Other suggestions include to put the innovation-driven force in the first place and to improve hard and soft connectivity continuously. Now, the Jack Union-shaped high-speed railway in Zhengzhou is considered a feat. In fact, there are still more improvements to be made, including air-rail, ocean-rail and other multi-modal combined transportation. Soft connections via the Internet, the Internet of Things and information can also be improved to strengthen the pivotal position of Zhengzhou. Attention should also be paid to the urban cultural characteristics of Zhengzhou and enhancing the brand influence of the city. Zhengzhou not only is a millennium commercial city, but also has a profound cultural background. More of its cultural characteristics need to be excavated.

References:

[1] Chen Yao and Wang Bin. "Research on the Collaborative Development Obstacle and Implementation Mechanism of Large Urban Agglomerations" [J] *Regional Economic Review*, 2016 (2).

[2] Lu Daodao. "The Development and Planning of Metropolitan Areas" [J] *Economic Geography*, 2009 (10).

[3] Qin Chenglin. "Research on the Economic Marketization and Integration of the Central Plains City Cluster" [J] *Jiangxi Social Sciences*, 2005 (12).

[4] Miao Jianjun. "Theoretical and Empirical Research on the Conflict of Interest in City Clusters" [N] Beijing: Economy & Management Publishing House, 2014.

B.14
Pay Due Attention to the Construction of Modern Metropolitan Circles in Promoting the High-quality Development of National Central Cities

Zhao Hong[*]

Abstract: Fully understanding, respecting and conforming to laws of urban development is essential in constructing and developing national central cities. National central cities are different from small and medium-sized cities in many ways, especially in spatial and traffic structures, and they have their own inherent development requirements. To promote the high-quality development of national central cities, efforts are required to deeply study and explore the inherent development laws of mega cities. Continued actions should be taken to optimize spatial and traffic structures as they are key issues that have fundamental and lasting impact on urban development. Another suggestion is establishing sound systems and mechanisms suitable for the implementation of spatial strategies for metropolitan circles, thereby contributing to the formation of a development pattern of metropolitan circles and promoting the high quality and sustainable development of cities.

Keywords: national central cities; spatial structure of metropolitan circle; suburban railway construction

---

* Zhao Hong, male, Deputy Dean and Research Fellow of Beijing Academy of Social Sciences, whose main research fields include regional economy, industrial economy, headquarters economy, and urban governance.

I The Spatial Structure of A Metropolitan Circle Is an Important Space Strategy to Improve the Carrying Capacity and Operational Efficiency of Cities

Judging from the development laws of mega cities, many international metropolises experienced the spatial evolution process of "single core city-multi-core metropolitan circle-city cluster". In the early development stage, cities often expanded outward from the single core of a central city. With the expansion of city scale, some cities find themselves trapped in a conflict between functional clustering and operational efficiency, and "urban diseases" appear. In order to address "urban diseases", new cities and satellite cities are built outside the central city to share its functions, and administrative boundaries are even broken to optimize the allocation of resources in a larger spatial scope and coordinate the relationship of population, resources and the environment. As the regional spatial organization converts from quantitative to qualitative changes, an inter-regional spatial organization called "metropolitan circle" emerges. Through fast transportation, a metropolitan circle can have a radius of 100 kilometers. Several developed central cities form metropolitan circles with overlapping radiation ranges, which further constitutes a city cluster with wider geographical coverage and stronger carrying capacity (see Table 1). For example, Tokyo, Osaka and Nagoya formed different metropolitan circles where the central cities are connected with surrounding satellite cities and new cities through fast transportation. These three metropolitan circles jointly support the "Pacific Coast city cluster in Japan".

Table 1 Evolution of Spatial Pattern in International Metropolises in Different Development Stages

Development Stage	Single-core City	Multi-core Metropolitan Circle	City Cluster
Dynamic mechanism	· Clustering economy and scale effect give rise to cities which expand around the central city · A conflict between clustering and efficiency and urban diseases may appear when the cities have developed to a certain degree	· From "single-core" to "multi-core", administrative boundaries are broken to deploy resources within 100 kilometers with modern transportation technology	· Many central cities form metropolitan circles whose radiation ranges overlap, giving birth to larger clusters.
Spatial pattern			

Drawing on the development histories and practice in addressing urban disease of foreign mega cities such as New York, London and Tokyo, mega cities are fundamentally different from small and medium-sized cities in spatial and traffic structures. Compared with small and medium-sized cities, mega cities are special at least in two ways. Firstly, they are particularly strong magnet to population and resources. Mega cities have unique brand value and charm that form a strong "magnetic field" to attract and gather resource elements. Secondly, they perform diverse and complex functions. The diverse functions in education, medical care, culture, science and technology, industry and residence make a huge population base in such cities. Therefore, mega cities must "combat" "diseconomies of scale" brought by large-scale population aggregation within a single specific space through urban planning. Decentralized urban functions and a traffic supply structure in line with the traffic needs of mega cities are two key factors to avoid and address urban diseases.

International metropolises like London and New York went through urban development processes in which they were plagued by urban diseases triggered by unreasonable spatial and traffic structures. In exploring the practice of urban disease control, urban planning experts and urban economic experts proposed different urban development theories and formed into different schools. For example, "urban decentralism" rejects spontaneous expansion of cities. When a certain city scale is reached, new expansion should only occur to surrounding new towns. "Urban centralism" advocates creating a modern living environment by increasing the plot ratio, constructing a modern transportation network, and opening up a large area of green space. The confrontation and integration of these two different development concepts led to the "scattered concentration" theory, which emphasizes the isolation of dense urban core areas from other central functional areas by ecological space and connection of urban core areas with surrounding functional areas through a public transportation system between cities, especially a rail transit system, until a multi-center, networked urban spatial structure is formed.

Combining the theoretical research results and the practical research on foreign mega cities, we believe that mega cities have to take the following two actions in order to achieve efficient and sustainable development:

Firstly, decentralize the diversified, complex and extremely rich urban functions. Adopt a scattered group layout, build "new towns", "satellite cities" and "business nuclear cities" to guide the scattered distribution of urban functions and population. This is an important means for many cities in the world to solve urban diseases such as overpopulation and traffic congestion brought by "single core concentration". For example, London issued the *New Town Act* in 1946, raising a "New Town Movement" and a hard journey of satellite city exploration that spanned four generations.

(1) In the 1940s, London planned to build the first-generation satellite cities. The satellite cities were close to the mother city and mainly undertook the single residential function. They depended heavily on the mother city and were functionally incomplete. As a result, these first-generation satellite cities developed slowly.

(2) In the 1950s and 1960s, London planned to build the second-generation satellite cities. On the basis of the single residential function of the first generation, the second-generation satellite cities were equipped with considerable industries and service facilities and became more independent. However, due to the proximity to the mother city, they were expanded with limitations and did not develop smoothly.

(3) In the 1960s and 1970s, London planned to build new towns, which could be regarded as third-generation satellite cities. These new towns and satellite cities were distant from the mother city. In addition to the residential function, they also performed certain industrial functions and allowed residents to work nearby. In fact, it was believed at that time that such satellite cities should not be too large and were expected to accommodate a population between 30,000 and 50,000. Due to small sizes, incomplete services and weak attraction, the third-generation satellite cities failed to develop satisfactorily.

(4) After the 1980s, London began to build the fourth-generation satellite cities. This generation was characterized by greater distances from the mother city, expanding city scales, and an average population of 200,000 people; they had more functions and were able to replace some functions of the mother city. They became important nodes in the multi-center regional network of the Greater London metropolitan circle. The fourth-generation satellite cities turned out to be a success.

After decades of practice and exploration, London has built 33 new towns and satellite cities which hold nearly one-quarter of urban residents from London, reducing the pressure on the central city, completing the spatial structure of the

London metropolitan circle, and effectively alleviating urban diseases in London.

Secondly, establish a public transportation system dominated by rail transit that is compatible with the spatial structure and traffic volume of metropolis. The transportation supply structure of a city is determined by its spatial structure and urban transportation demand. According to the data provided by the Transportation Research Institute of Tsinghua University, with equal space resources, the hourly passenger capacity is 3,000 for cars, 3,000 to 6000 for buses, 10,000 to 30,000 for rapid rail on the ground, and 30,000 to 70,000 for subways (networked).

Judging from the histories of urban disease governance in international metropolises like London, New York and Tokyo, setting up a public transportation system dominated by rail transit is the fundamental and only solution to the traffic congestion so prevailing in mega cities. We summarize it as "two dominances". First, public transportation (70%-80%) should be dominant in the urban transportation system; second, all kinds of rail transit means (70%-80%) should be dominant in the public transportation structure. For example, public transportation accounts for about 90% of the urban transportation in Tokyo, and rail transit accounts for 90% of the public transportation. Thus, the latter dominance is key and fundamental. It must be planned with a strategic forward-looking vision and constructed preemptively to safeguard efficient and sustainable development of a city.

Over the years, the mega cities in China simply emphasize the importance of ground buses while neglecting the construction of rail transit in the urban transportation supply structure. As a consequence, their urban rail transit construction is backward and their urban transportation structures are fundamentally defective. Take Beijing as an example. Now Beijing has to resolve two shortcomings in its rail transit system: First, the urban rail transit has low density, big capacity and short supply. The carrying capacity of urban transportation remains impotent. Currently, the operating mileage of urban rail transit in Beijing is only 1/4 of that in Tokyo. Second, the suburban railway construction is backward. International metropolises like London, New York, Tokyo have large-scale and well-developed suburban railway systems. However, Beijing's suburban railway construction lags behind and is now in its infancy. Its suburban railway system operates few lines and short mileage, not able to divert population and guide the urban functional layout.

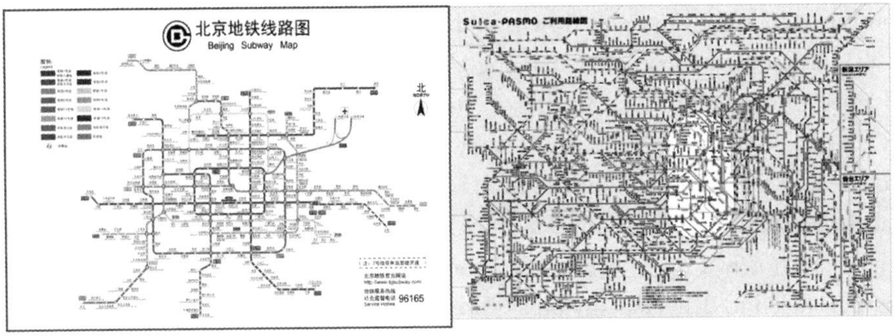

Figure 1 Subway Maps of Beijing (Left) and Tokyo Bay (Right)

Table 2 Suburban Railway and Subway Mileages of Some International Metropolises

City	Suburban Railway (km)	Subway (km)
London	3650	402
New York	3000	368
Tokyo	2031	291
Paris	1867	214
Beijing	238	609

From the perspective of the operation scopes of metropolitan rail transit abroad, different rail transit modes have different optimal traffic intervals due to different service functions. Subway is the most important mode in dense urban areas. It is characterized by short station distance, high frequency of departure, relatively slow running speed, and an average operating radius of less than 15km. Express railway mainly meets the transportation demand in the central urban area and suburbs. It has such characteristics as long station distance, fast speed and an average operating radius of generally around 15-30km. Suburban railway can operate within a range of 30-70km and usually provides large capacity, high speed and low fare. It mainly meets the commuting needs between the central urban area and satellite cities as well as new towns.

The decentralized layout of urban functions and the rail transit system mentioned above are two aspects of a problem that affect each other.

A study on the development history of mega cities in China revealed that the idea of decentralized layout has long been proposed. For example, Beijing proposed to build 13 satellite towns in the suburbs in the 1983 master plan. In the 1993 master plan, the goal of building 14 satellite towns and 10 fringe groups was defined. A general spatial pattern of "two axes, two belts and multiple centers" was proposed in the 2004 master plan, which also included a plan to build 11 new towns and 8 functional zones. However, in practice, the idea of decentralized layout adopted by Chinese mega cities was not well implemented. The satellite cities did not live up to the expectations, and the "single-center" development pattern failed to delivered any breakthrough.

After studying and analyzing the experience in foreign satellite city construction, we believe that the following five elements are the key to the success of satellite cities.

The first one is urban functions and industries. Satellite cities should not be built for the residential purpose only; instead, they should allow some inhabitants to live and work in them. For example, the new town of Milton Keynes in England, often known as a third-generation satellite city in London, is 80km from London downtown and stands between University of Cambridge and University of Oxford, two top universities in the world. Relying on superior location conditions and advanced modern infrastructures, Keynes focuses on developing modern service industries such as information technology, business consulting, finance and insurance, technological research and development, education and training, and has attracted hundreds of famous companies to build their headquarters there, including Mercedes-Benz, Volkswagen, Mobil, Nissan, Yamaha, Domino, and BP, as well as more than 5,000 resident companies. With a population of 260,000, the town has become a well-known economic center in the London metropolitan circle and even the UK. Two-thirds of its residents are locally employed, but the remaining population has to work in London; two-thirds of the employed population in Keynes is local residents, and the remaining employees come from London and surrounding areas. Satellite cities should also have a good public service base to narrow the gap with the mother city and enhance the attractiveness to the population from there.

The second element is distance. Satellite cities should be reasonably distant from the mother city to ensure that sufficient development space is left in the mother city. At the same time, the development boundary of the mother city should be well defined. The mother city and satellite cities should be "separated" by strictly delineating ecological red lines and building large green ecological spaces around the mother city to prevent it from sprawling irrationally. The distances between satellite cities and the mother city should be moderate. A shorter distance may stick a satellite city to the mother city, while a longer distance can make it hard to be driven by the mother city. International experience suggests that a suitable distance is generally around 30-70km.

The third element is passage. The attractiveness of a satellite city depends on its close contact with the mother city. Satellite cities and new towns must be linked to the central city to be attractive, and thus passages are needed. Many central urban areas in foreign metropolises are connected to surrounding new towns and satellite cities by suburban railways with large capacity, high speed, one-stop services and low fares. Highways are only optional, because they have limited traffic capacity during rush hours and are prone to congestion.

The fourth element is scale. To follow the development concepts of mother city-satellite cities and mother city-new towns, the central city must be well controlled rather than sprawling irrationally. Satellite cities are generally positioned as small and medium-sized cities that perform certain urban functions or foster certain industries. Therefore, they should not be too small. Otherwise, they would not be able to effectively relieve the population and functions of the mother city. Generally, satellite cities should not be built for the residential purpose only. Otherwise, the transportation demand would be huge. In addition, the overall size of a satellite city should also be controlled. An excessive size will pose layout problems. If residents have to spend too much time on commuting between the residential area and the station and the work site in the mother city, satellite cities would not be efficient or attractive at all.

The fifth element is the construction sequence. The construction sequence in a satellite city significantly influences its ability to guide the optimization of the spatial structure of a metropolitan city. Based on international experience, rail transit, stations and other infrastructures are generally put on the top of the construction list of foreign satellite cities; they are followed by public service facilities, such as hospitals and schools, and the final projects are residential buildings. This sequence will allow the satellite city to prepare good traffic conditions and public service supply capacity before the completion of residential construction. It is helpful for rail transit and public services to guide the decentralized layout of cities so that the satellite city is a more attractive living and working place to population from the mother city and the goal of absorbing population and decentralize resources can be finally achieved. On the contrary, if the construction sequence is reversed, with houses built before public service and transportation facilities, the residents of the satellite city would have to go to work in the mother city by car. Chances are that tidal traffic congestion is caused by excessive use of cars, which in turn weakens the appeal of the satellite city. Take Malmo, the third largest city in Sweden, as an example. The plan of its satellite city was to build a suburban railway station first, followed by public service facilities and residential buildings.

II Promote High-quality Development of National Central Cities and Work on Four Key Elements to Create Modern Metropolitan Circles

First, innovate urban development concepts and follow the common development laws of mega cities. Cities have strong assembling capacity. The assemblage of various functions and elements can generate economies of scale and increase the efficiency of urban operation; however, if a city is so large that it holds more functions and elements than it could carry, declining operational efficiency, increasing operating costs, and eventually "urban diseases" would result.

Therefore, when a city has assembled functions and elements to a certain scale, a decentralized layout should be put on the agenda. According to the law of differential rent, some non-cost-oriented city functions or strongly profitable functions are often deployed in the downtown of a city. These functions are mostly indispensable to a city, such as administrative office and financial business; other city functions, such as those in the fields of housing, education, medical care, science and technology, and economy, may be deployed by building new science and education, medical health and industry towns in the form of satellite city in the surrounding areas to decentralize the functions of the city. Through reasonable urban spatial layout, various functions and elements in a city can be "largely dispersed and narrowly concentrated" to avoid diseconomies of scale and ensure effective improvement in operational efficiency and carrying capacity of cities.

Second, build a decentralized, group-like and multi-center metropolitan circle structure to enhance the overall carrying capacity of a region. A metropolitan circle has a strongly radiating central city that cooperates with neighboring cities (like new towns and satellite cities) on the basis of complementary functions and interdependence to form an integrated region. The formation and development of metropolitan circles can greatly optimize the functional layout of the central city. The decentralization of functions, on the one hand, can effectively avoid "urban diseases", and, on the other hand, effectively radiate to and drive the integrated development of surrounding areas, thereby enhancing the comprehensive strength of metropolitan circles. Metropolitan circle and city cluster are two concepts that are both interrelated and different. The former is the basis for the development of the latter. Only those city clusters built on metropolitan circles are more efficient and vibrant.

Table 3 Metropolitan Circle V.S. City Cluster

	Metropolitan Circle	City Cluster
Function	Increase the carrying capacity and operational efficiency of large cities through functional decentralization and reasonable layout	Strengthen economic and social ties between different big cities to enhance regional competitiveness
Scope	Usually with a radius of 70km	With an area of 50,000-150,000 square kilometers
Scale	For big cities with a population of more than 1 million, a multi-center model is more efficient than a single-center model and metropolitan circle is the development direction	A city cluster based on several metropolitan circles
Core supporting condition	"One-hour commuting circle" formed by subway, suburban railway, and light rail	Integration of intercity railway, trunk railway and expressway, without requirement for "one-hour commuting circle"
Realistic value	It is a direct, critical and decisive means to address urban diseases. This is an indispensable and insurmountable stage.	Connecting big cities for linkage development, while allowing small and medium-sized cities to participate directly in the division of labor in metropolitan circles

In recent years, while more studies have focused on city clusters, metropolitan circles are not adequately studied and noticed. This cognitive "gap" is not good for the treatment of urban diseases. The 19th National Congress of the Communist Party of China put forward the proposal for high-quality development. Our offspring should not be rendered into the irreversible predicament of urban diseases. Currently, to address urban diseases and especially to avoid them in the future (especially in the second-tier, third-tier and fourth-tier cities), metropolitan circle construction must be elevated to a strategic height.

Thus, to promote high-quality development of national central cities, we should conscientiously summarize the experiences and lessons we learn in the urban development process in China, revisit the strategic value of metropolitan circle construction, and reexamine the relationship between metropolitan circle and city cluster. We should also learn from the experience of international metropolises in city evolution and expansion. It is urgent to put metropolitan circle construction at top priority. Based on the "distributed compactness" theory and the "largely dispersed and narrowly concentrated" principle, new towns, satellite cities and micro-centers should be planned and constructed, and spatial patterns like "mother city-new towns", "mother city-satellite cities" and "mother city-micro-centers" should be built in multi-center, decentralized and networked metropolitan circles to enhances the overall carrying capacity of the region.

Third, highlight suburban railway construction and make a forward-looking plan for suburban railway construction. Within a metropolitan circle, an efficient and close relationship should be maintained between the mother city and various functional groups to attract city functions and population, and only in this way will a decentralized and networked urban spatial pattern be a reality. Highways have limited capacity and are very vulnerable to weather and other factors. Using highway as the main transportation means to connect the center city and new towns and satellite cities may trigger tidal congestion. In contrast, rail transit and especially suburban railway can provide important transportation guarantee to efficient connection between the mother city and functional groups in a metropolitan circle due to their large capacity, fast speed and resistance to weather factors. Thus, the main transportation means to connect the mother city and satellite cities and new towns in a metropolitan circle should be rail transport, complemented by road transport.

For the sake of national central city construction, we may draw inspiration from the development of international metropolises such as the Tokyo metropolitan circle and the Paris metropolitan circle, which put suburban railway construction on the top of the agenda and promoted it proactively. We should accelerate the construction of a transportation structure that adapts to the traffic volumes of mega cities and the spatial layout of metropolitan circles, so as to provide strong support for the construction of modern metropolitan circles. Suburban railways should be planned in a systematic way that ensures independent construction, operation and management. Routes should be reserved in cities that are temporarily not able to build suburban railway. That will help avoid finding routes "passively" or "with hindsight" after congestion becomes a headache. Suburban railway construction is a huge project with tremendous capital needs. The construction and operation needs of suburban railway can hardly be met by the single investments from the government. The comprehensive development model of "rail transportation + land" can be explored, and the proceeds from land resources development can be used to meet the huge capital needs of suburban railway construction.

Fourth, establish systems and mechanisms for the implementation of metropolitan circle strategy. The formation and evolution of metropolitan circle is a long process that usually takes decades or even hundreds of years. To promote the high-quality development of national central cities, sufficient patience and strategic willpower are required. Upholding the spirit of "I sow the seeds, but I don't have to be the reaper", government officials involved should stick to the blueprint, and ensure that the metropolitan circle plan centering round national central cities is implemented smoothly.

At the same time, metropolitan circle construction is also a complex system project that requires not only forward-looking urban spatial and rail transit planning, but also innovative and planned mechanism guarantee, including planning examination, city examination, supervision mechanism and accountability mechanism. Avoid short-term and short-sighted behavior accompanied by the tenure system; otherwise, the result would be a "pie" rather than a "circle". An important reason why Washington DC is immune from urban diseases is that the urban planning is strictly implemented. Generally speaking, over the 200 years of urban development in Washington, the framework and spatial pattern of the city have always been observed as they were in the original plan. Although some adjustments and improvements were made at different stages of historical development, the overall pattern remained intact. Scientific planning and good execution repressed the impulse of reckless sprawl in downtown Washington.

At the same time, residential, commercial and other urban functions are decentralized in the surrounding areas, and a number of satellite cities developed along six radiation axes and finally formed the Washington metropolitan circle.

Learning from international experience, we should establish a regular planning examination and evaluation mechanism to examine and comprehensively evaluate the implementation of the master plan and regulatory detailed planning for national central cities with the approach of "one examination every year and one evaluation every five years". The examination and evaluation reports should be submitted to relevant departments for approval. We should also establish a monitoring mechanism and an accountability mechanism for planning implementation, and extensively solicit opinions from people's congresses, governments, and the public at all levels through demonstration meetings, hearings or other means. Failure to observe the plan or poor performance must be resolutely held accountable and corrections should be made in a timely manner to maintain the rigidity and authority of urban planning and ensure that the relevant planning and the metropolitan circle strategy are truly implemented.

References

[1] Zhao Hong. "Promote the Coordinated Development of Beijing-Tianjin-Hebei Region through Modern Metropolitan Circle Construction" [J]. *Economic Forum*, 2018 (07).

[2] Zhao Hong. "Address Beijing's 'Urban Diseases' with the Concept of Sustainable City" [M]. Annual Report on *Economic Development of Beijing (2015-2016)*. Beijing: Social Sciences Academic Press, 2016.

[3] Li Guoping. "Spatial Structure Serves as an Important Factor Affecting Urban Development" [N]. *Beijing Daily*, 14th edition, August 28, 2017.

[4] Wu Jianhong and Shen Lizi. "The Characteristics of Suburban Railway in the Tokyo Metropolitan Circle and the Reference for China" [J]. *China Railway*, 2019 (09).

B.15

Promote the High-quality Development of Zhengzhou through Deep Culture-Tourism Integration

Sun Xianke and Du Xuexia[*]

Abstract: Deep culture-tourism integration is the future development direction of the tourism industry and an important driving force for the high-quality development of Zhengzhou. To achieve deep culture-tourism integration, Zhengzhou should value cultural resources and advantages, focus on the inheritance and innovation of Chinese historical civilization, and utilize representative cultural items; it should also combine various business types and embark on the path of "cultural tourism +"; it should promote "great integration", plan "great projects", develop "great products", and improve the "great environment"; it should frame high-quality design, supply high-quality products, achieve high-quality integration of industries, and shape high-quality brand; it should uphold the principle of sustainable development of economy and culture. Deep culture-tourism integration can promote the high-quality development of Zhengzhou and carry on the Chinese culture.

Keywords: culture-tourism integration; high quality; cultural tourism+; Chinese culture

---

* Sun Xianke, male, born in 1964, Ph.D. in Literature, President, Professor and Doctoral Supervisor of Zhengzhou Normal University.; Du Xuexia, female, born in 1965, Ph.D. in Literature, Professor of the National Central City Research Institute of Zhengzhou Normal University.

With the advent of mass tourism and all-for-one tourism, tourism has become a pillar industry in China's economy. Under the new normal, deep culture-tourism integration becomes an important driving force for tourism development. For the development of tourism, Zhengzhou enjoys obvious advantages in population, location and cultural resources. The tourism industry in Zhengzhou has such problems as poor culture-tourism integration, lack of the all-for-one tourism awareness, and absence of prominent tourism brands. How to make full use of the cultural resources and advantages to solve the existing problems in the tourism industry and how to promote high-quality development and national central city construction through deep culture-tourism integration in Zhengzhou are questions worthy of in-depth discussion.

I Overview of Tourism Development in China

1 The Era of Mass Tourism Has Arrived

Mass tourism usually refers to a form of tourism with a high participation rate in the tourism industry, and it is attributed to reduced travel costs, better living standards and progress in transportation technology. In recent years, with the rapid growth of the national economy, the living standards of Chinese residents have been considerably improved. With great progress in aviation and high-speed rail, the tourism industry in China has been developing rapidly. Various data sources indicate that an era of mass tourism has arrived and the tourism industry is becoming an important industry in the national economy.

2 All-for-One Tourism Has Become an Important Strategy for the Tourism Development in China

In order to support tourism development, all-for-one tourism is strongly promoted at the national level. In March 2018, the General Office of the State Council issued the *Guiding Opinions on Promoting the Development of All-for-One Tourism* to accelerate the transformation and upgrading of the tourism industry, improve efficiency and quality in this regard, comprehensively optimize the environment for tourism development, and embark on the new path of all-for-one tourism development. All-for-one tourism is the product of tourism development strategy redesign in the new era and marks a far-reaching change in the tourism industry.

3 Tourism Is an Important Growth Pole of the National Economy

In 2014, President Xi Jinping indicated that the national economy entered a new normal, which meant that it has shifted from high-speed growth to medium-to-high-speed growth. Under this stage, the economic structure is continuously optimized; the consumption demand in the tertiary industry has gradually become dominant; transition is made from factor-driven and investment-driven to innovation-driven growth. Under the new normal, the tourism industry in China still maintains good performance, with a growth rate far outpacing the growth rate of GDP. This good performance is shown in the following data:

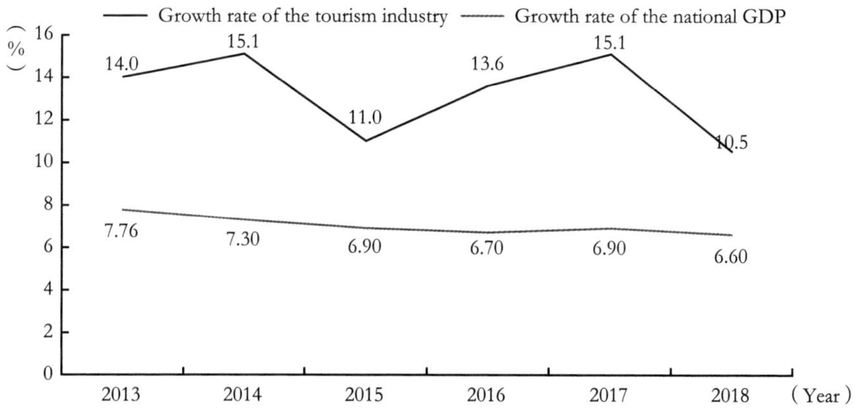

Figure 1 Growth Rate of Tourism Industry V.S. Growth Rate of the National GDP over the Past Six Years

Source: This figure is plotted by the authors based on the data estimate concerned.

The data above shows that while the GDP growth took on an L-shaped development trend, the tourism industry grew significantly faster than GDP, showing a general trend of rapid growth. Capital is always profit-driven. All kinds of capital flow into the tourism industry, substantially driving up tourism investments. This shows that tourism is regarded as a promising industry at the capital market. The investment scales of tourism industry in China over the past few years are shown as follows:

In 2014, the total investment actually completed in the tourism industry was RMB 705.3 billion, up 32% from the previous year.

In 2015, the total investment actually completed in the tourism industry was RMB 1.0072 trillion, up 43% from the previous year.

In 2016, the total investment actually completed in the tourism industry was RMB 1.2997 trillion, up 29% from the previous year.

In 2017, the total investment actually completed in the tourism industry was over RMB 1.5 trillion, up 15% from the previous year.

From January to July 2018, the total investment reached RMB 580 billion (incomplete data).

The total investment is expected to reach RMB 2 trillion by 2020.

Domestic tourism, inbound tourism and outbound tourism has kept growing since 2014, and so has been the proportion of tourism in GDP. This indicates that tourism has become an important growth pole in the economic development of China given its increasing proportion in GDP under the new normal:

Table 1 Income of the Tourism Industry as Percentage of GDP Since 2014

Year	Total Annual Tourism Income (RMB Trillion)	YoY Growth Rate (%)	Total Annual GDP (RMB Trillion)	Total Annual Contribution of National Tourism to GDP (RMB Trillion)	Percentage in GDP (%)
2014	3.73	11%	63.64	6.61	10.39
2015	4.13	11%	67.67	7.34	10.8
2016	4.69	13.6%	74.41	8.19	11.01
2017	5.4	15.1%	82.71	9.13	11.04
2018	5.97	10.5%	90.03	9.94	11.04

Source: This table is plotted by the authors based on the data estimate concerned.

4 Mission of Culture-Tourism Integration under the New Normal

In March 2018, the Ministry of Culture and the National Tourism Administration were formally combined as the Ministry of Culture and Tourism. In April, the new Ministry of Culture and Tourism was officially founded. The merger of these departments was a big event in China, which marked the institutional integration of culture and tourism in China.

The merger of the Ministry of Culture and the National Tourism

Administration was in line with the great context and the great trend of the increasing association between culture and tourism. The merger was significant in the following ways. Firstly, it met the actual needs of both the culture industry and the tourism industry as they have been increasingly correlated and overlapping. Cultural tourism will assume the mission of national economic transformation and play an important role in promoting the high quality economic development of China. Secondly, it met the urgent needs of tourism development in China. In spite of the recent excellent performance of the tourism industry in China, low product quality and poor brand benefits remain salient problems. The most intensive and serious problem is the low integration of culture and tourism in the tourism industry. Pure natural sightseeing can no long meet the tourism needs of ordinary people. There is an urgent need to enrich tourism by adding cultural colors. With culture-tourism integration, the cultural and economic benefits of tourism on the basis of "culture+" and "tourism+" are the future development direction and path of tourism. Thirdly, the merger also manifested the cultural strategic thinking of the nation. Cultural tourism is not only a cultural economy, but also an important mission of inheriting, innovating and carrying on the excellent Chinese culture and enhancing the country's cultural soft power. Since the 18th National Congress, the Party Central Committee and the State Council have vigorously advocated the inheritance and promotion of excellent traditional Chinese culture. Cultural tourism is an important means to inherit, innovate and promote the excellent traditional Chinese culture. As far as domestic tourism is concerned, the tourism industry should be endowed with more cultural connotations in order to spread and popularize the excellent Chinese culture to the public. At the same time, as China becomes more and more international, the numbers of outbound and inbound tourists have increased dramatically. Outbound and inbound travel has also become important ways to spread and promote excellent Chinese culture. Thus, the merger of the Ministry of Culture and the National Tourism Administration marked the first step in culture-tourism integration, and more steps will have to be taken to deepen the integration. Culture-tourism integration not only adapts to the needs of national strategic development under the new normal, but also helps to increase the quality of economic development. It meets the needs of economic transformation under the new normal, while enhancing cultural consciousness, demonstrating cultural self-confidence, and propelling the internationalization of excellent Chinese culture.

II Status Quo and Existing Problems of the Tourism Development in Zhengzhou

In combination with the development of the tourism industry in China, the tourism development in Zhengzhou over the past five years is shown below:

Table 2 Growth Rate of Tourism in Zhengzhou for the Past 5 Years

Year	Annual Tourism Income (RMB 100 Million)	YoY Growth Rate (%)	Tourism		International Tourism		Domestic Tourism	
			Number of Tourists (10,000 Persons)	YoY Growth Rate (%)	Number of Tourists (10,000 Persons)	YoY Growth Rate (%)	Number of Tourists (10,000 Persons)	YoY Growth Rate (%)
2014	892.6	11.4	7766	10.6	45.1	2.7	7720.9	10.7
2015	1004.2	12.5	8674.4	11.7	47.3	4.9	8627.1	11.7
2016	1053.9	4.9	8933.6	3.0	48.1	1.7	8885.5	3.0
2017	1195	13.4	10092	13.0	50.3	4.6	10042	13.0
2018	1387.4	16.1	11410	13.1	52.7	4.8	11357.3	13.1

Source: This table is based on the data provided by the Culture, Broadcasting and Tourism Bureau of Zhengzhou.

As shown in Table 2, the growth rate of tourism in Zhengzhou has outpaced the growth rate of the national tourism industry over the past five years. The data above also showed that the tourism development in Zhengzhou has a good foundation.

Under the new normal, although the annual GDP of Zhengzhou outgrew the national GDP, the GDP growth in the earliest days of new normal remained lower than the growth of tourism in Zhengzhou, as shown in the table below:

Table 3 Growth Rate of Zhengzhou under the "New Normal"

Year	GDP of Zhengzhou (RMB 100 Million)	YoY Growth Rate	Growth Rate of National GDP
2014	6800	9.3%	67.3%
2015	7315.2	10.1%	6.9%
2016	7994.2	8.4%	6.7%
2017	9130.2	8.2%	6.9%
2018	10143.3	8.1%	6.6%

Source: This table is based on the data published by relevant departments in Zhengzhou.

Although the tourism industry of Zhengzhou outgrew its GDP, it has to overcome many difficulties and problems, which are partly consistent with those bothering the development of national tourism. These difficulties and problems mainly include:

First, culture and tourism are not well integrated, and the cultural resources and advantages of Zhengzhou are not fully utilized. As a national famous historical and cultural city, Zhengzhou undoubtedly owns rich cultural resources. However, such cultural resources and advantages are not fully utilized in the actual development of the tourism industry. In particular, Zhengzhou's core position in the Central Plain culture and in the historical civilization of Chinese nation is not reflected. This is an important reason why culture and tourism is not well integrated or even separated in the tourism development of Zhengzhou. As a result, Zhengzhou natives are not well aware of their cultural identity. They mention only the specific locations and landscapes of Songshan Mountain, Shaolin Temple and Yellow River when asked about Zhengzhou, without realizing the core position of the city in the Chinese historical civilization, its status as one of the eight ancient capitals, or the Yellow Emperor culture as the origin of the Chinese history of five thousand years. Besides, many visitors to the city not only know little about its rich history and culture, but also assume that this is a cultural desert. Tourists are interested in natural landscapes like Songshan Mountain, Shaolin Temple and Yellow River instead of the culture of the city.

Second, the tourism industry of Zhengzhou fails to grasp and adapt to the current trend of tourism stratification. With the advent of mass tourism, tourists develop stratified demand, just as tourists with different levels of cultural literacy travel for different purposes and with different requirements. However, now Zhengzhou simply provide "one-size-fits-all" and "undifferentiated" tourist products, without paying due attention to tourism stratification or fully studying and actively responding to the new needs. This has, to some extent, affected and restricted the development of cultural tourism in Zhengzhou.

Third, the tourism industry is not well prepared for the advent of all-for-one tourism. "All-for-one tourism" is a proposal based on the status quo and future demand of tourism development in China, and it is intended to increase the tourism development level in China. However, the all-for-one tourism in Zhengzhou has not proved effective. This can be explained by the fact that some tourism companies and groups do not well understand all-for-one tourism and have weak awareness of tourism services. Not well prepared for the advent of all-for-one tourism, the tourism industry in Zhengzhou still relies heavily on ticket proceeds, without improving the overall tourist environment and services accordingly.

Fourth, there are few well-known brands, and the established brands are not able to play a leading role. Tourists are often interested in Songshan Mountain, Shaolin Temple and the hometown of the Yellow Emperor when they visit Zhengzhou. Indeed, they are well-known tourist brands in the country and even the world. However, there are few well-known tourist brands as a whole in Zhengzhou. As a result, the existing tourist brands do not match the cultural resources owned by Zhengzhou. Some nationally influential cultural issues from Zhengzhou have not been taken seriously, let alone deeply explored. Well-known brands are able to drive certain associated cultural products. However, the driving force of well-known cultural brands in Zhengzhou has not been fully developed, and the driving force remains weak. The lack of well-known brands is also an important factor that restricts the tourism development in Zhengzhou.

The most fundamental cause for the problems in the tourism development of Zhengzhou mentioned above is the low integration of culture and tourism, which hinders the full utilization of its rich historical and cultural resources and advantages.

III The Role of Deep Culture-Tourism Integration in Driving the National Central City Construction of Zhengzhou

Under the new normal, the mission of national central city construction is to deeply integrate culture with tourism, to make full use of the population, location and especially cultural resource advantages of Zhengzhou, to develop its tourism, and to promote the Central Plain culture and the excellent Chinese culture. This is also required in the Zhengzhou metropolitan area construction, the rise of Central China and the active integration into the national Belt and Road Initiative.

Zhengzhou's demographic and location advantages and its importance in national strategies can be testified in the following figures:

In late 2017, Zhengzhou was approved to build national central city and became one of the nine national central cities in China. In 2018, its total population reached 10 million, and GDP reached RMB 1 trillion. This showed that the city construction and development of Zhengzhou had ushered in a new stage. At the end of 2018, the provincial government passed the *Spatial Planning of Zhengzhou Metropolitan Area (2018-2035)*, supporting the building of the Zhengzhou metropolitan area on the basis of the national central city construction (Zhengzhou metropolitan area, which is centered on Zhengzhou, includes the central cities of Zhengzhou, Kaifeng, Xinxiang, Jiaozuo and Xuchang, and Gongyi City, Wuzhi County, Yuanyang County, Xinxiang County, Weishi County, Changge City, and Pingyuan Urban-Rural Integration Demonstration Zone). Zhengzhou metropolitan area covers a total area of about 15,900 square kilometers, accounting for 9.6% of the province's land area. It gathers nearly 20% of the population and more than 30% of the total economic output in the province. It is the most economically developed and fastest growing region in the Central Plains city cluster. It is also the most economically dynamic region in the economic corridor in the Eurasian Continental Bridge.

Zhengzhou has the following location advantages:

The table above shows that Zhengzhou has remarkable population and location advantages. Zhengzhou has a strong foundation and unique advantages in developing tourism.

The cultural advantage of Zhengzhou is even more remarkable. Zhengzhou is the core area of Chinese historical civilization. It was built as a capital for five times and prefecture for eight times. It is the birthplace and capital of the Yellow Emperor, the first ancestor of the Chinese people. It used to be the capital of the King Yu of Xia Dynasty (Gaocheng Town in Dengfeng City was the historical site of Yangcheng, the capital of the King Yu), the early Shang Dynasty (when it was known as Bodu), the Kingdom of Zheng in the Zhou Dynasty, and the Kingdom of Han during the Warring States Period... Zhengzhou left a clear mark in every stage of the Chinese civilization, so to speak. A large number of tangible and intangible cultural heritages have been preserved during the long-term historical development. The most famous ones here include the hometown of the Yellow Emperor, the Dahe Village ruins where large ancient settlements containing four archaeological cultures of Yangshao, Longshan Xia and Shang, the historical site of the King Yu of Xia Dynasty, the early historical site of the Shang Dynasty, the Zhengzhou section of Tongji Canal in the Grand Canal, and the Historical Building Complex between the Heaven and the Earth... There are also national intangible cultural heritages: the ritual in memory of the birthday of the Yellow Emperor, Chaohua blowing song, Chang-style boxing, Shaolin Kungfu, and Xiaoxiang lion dance...

Under the new normal, to improve its urban development quality and cultural taste, Zhengzhou should make full use of its cultural advantages. In particular, it should place cultural tourism as a priority, trying to carry on cultural heritage with the assistance of the tourism industry, promote transformation and upgrading of the tourism industry by exploiting and utilizing cultural resources, and truly realize the integrated development of cultural tourism. While promoting the economic development, deep culture-tourism integration can also contribute to the creative transformation and innovative development of the excellent Chinese traditional culture and the promotion of the historical and contemporary humanistic spirit of the Central Plains; since Zhengzhou is an important node in the Belt and Road, deep culture-tourism integration can also facilitate Zhengzhou to become an international famous cultural tourism destination and promote the internationalization of excellent Chinese culture.

IV Create High-quality Development Model Based on Zhengzhou through Deep Culture-Tourism Integration

Zhengzhou has a solid foundation for deep culture-tourism integration. As mentioned above, Zhengzhou is the core area of Chinese historical civilization and has abundant historical and cultural resources. At the same time, located in the middle reaches of the Yellow River, it also owns important and abundant natural landscape tourism resources from the Yellow River beach and Songshan Mountain. Deep culture-tourism integration can combine the rich historical culture with natural resources, making nature and culture as a whole in which nature brings enjoyment while culture refines the mind.

So, how to create a high-quality development model based on the case of Zhengzhou through deep culture-tourism integration? The following are specific suggestions:

1. The inheritance and innovation of Chinese historical civilization is the soul. In culture-tourism integration, culture is the soul and tourism the medium. In the past, cultural tourism was nothing but to develop tourism in the name of

culture. Now it is about cultural revival via tourism. As the core area of Chinese historical civilization, Zhengzhou should pay attention to the following aspects in pursuing deep culture-tourism integration: cultural creativity should be guided by the inheritance and innovation of Chinese historical civilization and consciously highlight the status of Zhengzhou as the core area of Chinese historical civilization; quality tourist routes should be designed with the focus on showing and experiencing main cultural events in the Chinese historical civilization; cultural concepts should be established to achieve the important goal of carrying forward Chinese historical civilization, the humanistic spirit of the Central Plain, and the spirit of Chinese civilization; inbound tourism must cooperate with the Belt and Road Initiative by valuing and seizing tourism and cultural shares of involved countries, strengthening cultural interaction with them, and encouraging exchanges and mutual understanding between Chinese culture and diverse cultures in the world.

2. The deep culture-tourism integration in Zhengzhou should cling to representative cultural events. Zhengzhou should make full use of its own cultural resources and publicize well-known domestic and international tourism brands and cultural tourism events that are closely related to the Chinese historical civilization in order to realize deep culture-tourism integration. The Yellow Emperor Culture, the Ancient Capital Culture and the Shaolin Culture are all exemplary tourism brands and events famous at home and abroad that can be used to promote cultural tourism around the themes of ancestor tracing, ancient capital revival, Shaolin Kung Fu, and Yellow River. At the same time, it is also necessary to analyze the needs of different tourists through big data, and then design layered cultural tourism routes in Zhengzhou to meet the interest of different tourists.

3. Deep culture-tourism integration should always be guided by the combination of "culture +" and "tourism +" to promote the integration of culture and tourism with multiple business types. To integrate culture into tourism and to integrate tourism with other business types can produce a nuclear fission effect on cultural tourism. For example, Zhengzhou should adhere to the strategy of "culture +" and "tourism +" combination or the "culture + tourism +" strategy and promote deep integration of culture and tourism with agriculture, industry, service industry, sports and fitness; as for investors, state-owned, collective, individual, and foreign investors should all be encouraged to participate in all-for-one tourism development; from the perspective of the entire

industry, it is necessary to extend the industrial chain, upgrade the value chain, and foster new business types in emerging industries to support the high-quality development of Zhengzhou.

4. The deep culture-tourism integration in Zhengzhou should serve the important goal of building it into an international cultural metropolis. Currently, the city is not international enough, and it receives only a small number of inbound tourists. However, with the construction of Zhengzhou Airport and the operation of China-Europe train (Zhengzhou), which makes eight round trips every week, along with the establishment of the global e-commerce platform and the status of Zhengzhou as an important node city along the Belt and Road and thus an inland open base, Zhengzhou will be more and more recognized and understood by people around the world. The Belt and Road Initiative involves 65 countries and regions, covering a population of 4.4 billion (about 63% of the world population). It forms a huge tourist market that presents huge opportunities in cultural tourism. As the core area of Chinese historical civilization, Zhengzhou should embrace a forward-looking vision, seize the great opportunities in history, grab an international share in the field of cultural tourism, and promote the construction of Zhengzhou as an international cultural metropolis. This is not only an important way to realize deep culture-tourism integration, but also a critical means to promote the high-quality development of Zhengzhou accordingly.

5. The deep culture-tourism integration in Zhengzhou should be steered to the following breakthroughs:

- Focus on "great integration". Promote culture-tourism integration, industry-city integration and industrial integration; follow the development trend of multi-field, multi-industry and multi-regional integration, and make integration an important fulcrum to fuel economic growth.
- Plan "great projects": Let project construction be a powerful engine to drive structural optimization; promote the clustering development of cultural tourism; push the cultural tourism industry on broader time and space scales and towards broader fields.
- Develop "great products": Optimize product structure; build high-quality products to meet the high-end needs of consumers;
- Optimize the "great environment": Improve service quality and supporting

facilities to create a high-quality development environment.

Paths for deep culture-tourism integration of Zhengzhou:

- To frame a high-quality design: formulate a planning system for the high-quality development of the tourism industry, integrate regional tourism resources, promote institutional mechanism reforms, establish high-quality development demonstration zones, and build an overall framework to support high quality economic development.
- To supply high-quality products: implement differentiated development strategies, promote quality improvement in tourism products and services, cultivate high-quality tourist attractions, improve the quality of tourism products, advance the construction of key tourism projects, and let high quality economic development play a leading role.
- High-quality integration of industries: starting from all-for-one tourism, continuously promote the organic integration of cultural tourism with other industries, propose innovative integration methods, facilitate multi-factor agglomeration and multi-industry superposition, foster new business types, and breed new driving forces to support high-quality economic development.
- To shape high-quality brands: create an overall tourism brand, establish a tourism brand system with multiple levels and covering the entire industry chain, adopt innovative marketing methods for cultural tourism, strengthen publicity and guidance, tell a good "Zhengzhou story", and breed new highlights in the high-quality development process.
- To construct a high-quality public service system: provide "comprehensive and convenient" tourism distribution and consulting services, "fast-moving and slow-traveling" tourism transportation systems, "smart and intelligent" tourism management services, and a new model of high-quality development.
- High-quality development of rural tourism: promote tourism-based comprehensive revitalization of rural areas and incorporate it into the course of high-quality development by building rural tourist destinations, famous villages and towns, and tourism-oriented poverty alleviation.
- High-quality guarantees: continuously improve the quality of cultural tourism industry and create a new high-quality development environment through policy support, talent recruitment, assessment and supervision.

References:

[1] Hu Xiaofen and Li Xinjian. "Urban Development and Culture-Tourism Integration from Eight Perspectives" [N]. *Chinese Culture Daily*, 2019-4-13 (007).

[2] Zhong Sheng. "Promote Culture-Tourism Integration and Build a Spiritual Homeland for the Chinese" [N]. *Chinese Culture Daily*, 2019-7-26 (003).

[3] Qian Chunxian. "Deepening Culture-Tourism Integration Can Pass on Excellent Traditional Cultures" [N]. *China Tourism News*, 2019-6-12 (003).

[4] Xinhuanet. "Conference on Dialogue of Asian Civilizations: Beijing Consensus in 2019" [EB/OL]. http://www.xinhuanet.com/world/2019-05/24/c_1124539189.htm, 2019-5-24.

[5] Luo Shugang. "Promote Quality Tourism with Culture-Tourism Integration" [J]. *China Real Estate*, 2019, (14): 13.

[6] Wu Xue'an. Culture-Tourism Integration: Combination of Poetry and Travels" [N]. *China Reading Weekly*, 2019-7-3 (008).

B.16

Study on the Integrated Development of Chongqing Metropolitan Area

*Tu Jianjun, Chu Jie, Mao Kai, Huang Yan and Ding Weizhen**

Abstract: This study adopts the urban centrality, field strength and economic relation force model and Wilson Index to explore the spatial structure and integrated development level of the Chongqing metropolitan area and put forward the paths of integrated development for metropolitan areas. The results show that: (1) The Chongqing metropolitan area has an urban spatial structure of "the central city + peripheral affected zones"; (2) The spatial pattern of "the central city" (the built-up area in the main city) is extended mainly westward and northward along the focused paths of "Yubei District, Shapingba District, Nan'an District → Jiangbei District, Shapingba District → Jiangbei District, Yubei District and Beibei District"; the spatial economic relations in the peripheral affected areas of the metropolitan area is continuously strengthened; (3) The comprehensive integration level of the Chongqing metropolitan

* Tu Jianjun (1973-), Ph.D., Professor and Doctoral Supervisor of College of Economics and Management of Southwest University; Chu Jie (1996-), a postgraduate of Geographical Science in School of Geographical Sciences of Southwest University; Mao Kai, a postgraduate of Geographical Science in School of Geographical Sciences of Southwest University; Huang Yan, a postgraduate of Geographical Science in School of Geographical Sciences of Southwest University; Ding Weizhen, a postgraduate of Geographical Science in School of Geographical Sciences of Southwest University.

area has been significantly improved since Chongqing became a municipality, which is closely related to the spatial expansion of the built-up area, the varying economic development levels, national strategies and government policies; (4) The key path for the integrated development of the Chongqing metropolitan area is to construct a spatial pattern of "one city-five districts-multi-center groups".

Keywords: metropolitan areas; integrated development; spatial structure; Chongqing

I Introduction

Metropolitan area is a special form of spatial organization in a region that is formed in the process of urban evolution. It is an inevitable product of economic and social development of a city reaching to a certain degree. Over the years, experts, scholars, as well as urban management and construction departments around the world have explored the overall trends and salient characteristics of urban development under new historical development stages from theoretical and practical perspectives and have studied the regional evolution and organizational laws of different spatial organization forms such as metropolitan area, metropolitan circle, city cluster, and metropolitan interlocking region.

Chongqing is both a mega city and a province with moderate scale. It is the only municipality and national central city in the Western Region. However, the main urban area of Chongqing has a small population and limited economic and land use scales, which, to some extent, weakens the size effect of economic and social development in the city. Therefore, to promote integrated development, Chongqing should boost a rational layout of population, land, industry and transportation based on the metropolitan area and enhance its comprehensive strength. This is the only way to promote coordinated development of various regions in the city and realize comprehensive, coordinated and sustainable development. This study explores the spatial characteristics, current status, development trajectory and driving mechanism of the Chongqing metropolitan area from the perspectives of spatial structure, integrated development evaluation, influencing factors and development path. It is expected to provide empirical basis for the future development strategy making of Chongqing.

II Research Methods and Data

2.1 Research Methods

2.1.1 Urban Centrality

Centrality is an indicator of central level of a place, reflecting the relative importance of the central place in serving other areas.

$$U=\sum_{i=1}^{m} x_{ij}w_j \tag{1}$$

In Equation (1), U is the central value of the city, m is the year, X_{ij} is the normalized value of the indicator j in the year i, and W_j is the weight of the indicator j (this study adopts the entropy method for weight calculation).

2.1.2 Economic Relation Force and Economic Subordination Models

In this study, an economic relation force model formula and an economic subordination formula consisting of urban population size, administrative area and GDP as three parameters are used, and the weights are corrected.

Economic distance refers to the intensity of communication between the central city and other core towns. The greater the distance is, the smaller the intensity of communication is. This parameter mainly requires the correction of commuting time. This study is based on spatial distance, and the economic distance obtained after two weight corrections is:

$$E=a\times\beta\times D \tag{2}$$

In Equation (2), E is the economic distance, D is the spatial distance from the central city to other towns, and a and β are correction weights.

The economic relation force model characterizes the absolute economic relation between the central city and the surrounding core towns, reflecting the external economic relation of the central city based on the following formula:

$$T_{ij}=\frac{\sqrt[3]{P_i\times G_i\times R_i}\times\sqrt[3]{P_i\times G_i\times R_i}}{D_{ij}^2} \tag{3}$$

Economic subordination model is used to measure the economic radiation intensity of surrounding core areas by the central city based on the following formula:

$$L_{ij}=\frac{T_{ij}}{\sum_{i=1}^{n}T_{ij}} \tag{4}$$

In which, T is the economic relation force, i is the core towns around the metropolitan area, j is the central city, P is the total population of the city, G is the GDP of the city, R is the administrative area, D is the economic distance, and L_{ij} is the economic subordination degree.

2.1.3 Urban economic field strength model

Urban economic field strength is used to identify the location in the "force field" where the economic force applied by the central city is rapidly decreased on the surrounding core towns. It is used to measure the "force field diagram" of the economic force applied by the central city to surrounding core towns in a metropolitan area and reflects the spatial structure of economic interaction between cities and towns in the metropolitan area based on the following formula:

$$S_j=\frac{\sqrt[3]{P_i\times G_i\times R_i}}{D_{ij}^2} \tag{5}$$

In which, S is the urban field strength, i is the surrounding core towns in a metropolitan area, j is the central city, P is the total population of the city, G is the GDP of the city, R is the administrative area, and D is the economic distance.

2.1.4 Wilson Index

The Wilson Index is extended from the coefficient of variation and is a weighted coefficient of variation. It describes the degree of dispersion of flag values with the same properties. [8]

$$V_u=\frac{1}{x'}\times\sqrt{\sum_{i=1}^{n}\frac{(x_i-\bar{x})^2 p_i}{p}} \tag{6}$$

In which, x' is per capita GDP of the background region, x is per capita GDP of the region i, p is the total population of the background region, and p_i it the population of the region i. Other economic indicators can certainly also be included. For example, this study uses GDP and per capita GDP to fully measure the different development levels within a metropolitan area.

2.1.5 Theil Index

Proposed by Thail and using the concept of entropy in the information theory in 1967, Theil Index is an inequality coefficient that can be decomposed according to the addition rule. This index has been gradually applied to the empirical analysis of regional difference measurement for being able to decompose general regional differences into differences between and within groups based on the following formula: [9]

$$T=\frac{1}{N}\sum_{i\in N}\frac{y_i}{\mu}\ln\frac{y_i}{\mu} \tag{7}$$

In Equation (7), N is the number of regions studied, y is the integration level of the region i, and μ is the integration level of all the four regions in the Chongqing metropolitan area. The logarithmic differential value is the Theil Index T. Smaller T suggests smaller regional differences and higher integration level, and vice versa. This study measures the Theil Indexes of economy, infrastructure and public services to generate the total integrate index that reflects the integration level of the Chongqing metropolitan area.

2.2 Data Sources and Processing

The research data in this paper mainly comes from the *1997-2017 China City Statistical Yearbook* and the *Statistical Chongqing Yearbook*. Some of the data comes from the website of the National Bureau of Statistics (http://data.stats.gov.cn/). The traffic data of the city come from http://tools.2345.com/jiaotong/lc.htm and https://www.qichezhan.cn/, and the spatial data come from the National Geomatics Center of China (http://www.ngcc.cn/).

This study uses the geospatial remote sensing (RS) technology to process the remote sensing data of the main districts of Chongqing on the ENVI software. Remote sensing data samples collected since Chongqing became a municipality were selected and processed by radiation correction, geometric correction, mosaic cutting and image enhancement. NDBI (Normalized Difference Build-up Index) and NDVI (Normalized Difference Vegetation Index) models were built and the urban area and spatial distribution data were extracted from the processed satellite remote sensing data to yield the spatial structure evolution of the urban built-up area of Chongqing's main districts.

III Spatial Structure of Chongqing Metropolitan Area

Metropolitan area is not only a term of regional concept, but also a mature urbanization form of a region and one of the main forms of progressed urban agglomerations. Metropolitan area is a complex system centering round a central city with strong urban functions and consisting of neighboring towns it is closely related to. Therefore, a metropolitan area is often formed by one or more "central cities" with strong economic strength to play an important role in the formation and development of the metropolitan area. The Chongqing metropolitan area is formed by "a central city" with 9 districts together with 12 influenced peripheral districts (Fuling District, Jiangjin District, Yongchuan District, Hechuan District, Bishan District, Qijiang District, Changshou District, Dazu District, Tongnan District, Rongchang District, Tongliang District, and Nanchuan District). It covers a total area of 28,700km^2.

3.1 Spatial Structure Evolution of the "Central City" in the Chongqing Metropolitan Area

The formation and development of a metropolitan area is a dynamic evolution process, and any metropolitan area will evolve from formation to maturity. As the "central city" of the Chongqing metropolitan area, the main urban built-up area in Chongqing has become the fastest growing, most urbanized and strongest expanded area since the reform and opening up, and especially since Chongqing became a municipality. It is now a strong cornerstone that radiates to and drives the coordinated development of the metropolitan area.

The spatial expansion of the main urban built-up area in Chongqing mainly went through the following three stages:

Stage I (1997-2005): The main urban area was expanded mainly northward and westward. By 2005, the core part of the main urban area had extended to somewhere between Jinyun Mountain and Mingyue Mountain, and the peripheral areas developed rapidly in a dot-like pattern. The urban built-up area was mainly expanded in Yubei District, Shapingba District and Nan'an District, significantly extending along the traffic arteries. Compared with 1997, 2005 saw no change in Yuzhong District, although the compactness indexes increased for Dadukou District and Yubei District and decreased for all the other districts. This suggested that Dadukou District and Yubei District were expanded mainly by internal filling, while the other districts by external sprawling to form multi-center groups. The city developed outward rapidly (see Figure 1).

Stage II (2006-2010): The main urban area began to develop westward and northward. As urban development was affected by transportation, the urban built-up area obviously extended along highways, and the direct result was that Shapingba District and Jiangbei District situated in these two directions expanded fastest. Jiangbei District, in particular, developed most rapidly and expanded most intensively. Except for slight declines in Dadukou District and Nan'an District, the compactness indexes of all the other districts increased. This indicated that the districts moved from outward sprawl to internal filling after the period of rapid development during 1997-2005 (see Figure 2).

Stage III (2011-2015): After the internal absorption of built-up area during 2006-2010, the urban construction once again expanded outwards, mainly in two directions. First, the city continued to develop westward. With the opening of several tunnels in Zhongliang Mountain, the urban construction was able to cross the geographical restrictions brought by Zhongliang Mountain and reach Jinyun Mountain, turning the linkage development between valleys

Figure 1 Built-up Area of Chongqing's Main Districts (1997-2005)

Figure 2 Built-up Area of Chongqing's Main Districts (2006-2010)

Figure 3 Built-up Area of Chongqing's Main Districts (2011-2015)

in Zhongliang Mountain and Jinyun Mountain into a reality. Second, with the establishment and development of Liangjiang New Area (including the original Northern New Ara) in 2010, the construction of the main urban area gradually expanded northwestward to cover Jiangbei District, Yubei District and Beibei District. Jiangbei Financial Town, Yuelai International Convention and Exhibition City and the Guoyuan Port have been developing rapidly ever since (see Figure 3).

3.2 Economic Relation Characteristics of Peripheral Affected Areas in the Chongqing Metropolitan Area

The integrated development of the Chongqing metropolitan area is not only reflected in the further expansion of "the central city" (the main urban built-up area), but also in the strengthened economic relation of its peripheral affected areas. By the end of 2016, the "the central city" of "Chongqing metropolitan area" had a population of 8.518 million, and the urbanization level reached 89.03%. In addition, its urban centrality level reached 69.21 (see Table 1 for the structure and weights of the urban centrality level indicator system).

Table 1 Weight of Each Index of Urban Centrality Level

Target Layer	Criteria Layer	Index Layer	Weight
Urban centrality level	Urban economic development level	GDP (RMB 10,000)	0.1355
		Per captain GDP (RMB)	0.0958
		Percentage of non-agricultural output value (%)	0.0935
		Total retail volume of social consumer goods (RMB 10,000)	0.1105
	Urban material factor construction level	Urbanization rate of resident population (%)	0.1002
		Total social fixed asset investment (RMB 10,000)	0.0836
		Total output value of construction industry (RMB 10,000)	0.0522
		Traffic convenience index	0.0673
	Level of urban public services and residents' living standard	Public budget expenditure of Z District/County (RMB 10,000)	0.0629
		Number of primary and secondary school students (person)	0.0455
		Average wage of urban employees (RMB)	0.0793
		Per capita deposit in financial institutions (RMB)	0.0737

Note: The traffic convenience index was the weighted sum of five indexes that were normalized: expressway mileage, classified highway mileage, high-speed rail mileage, railway mileage, and total number of traffic exits (including highway exits, high-speed rail station exits, and railway station exits). According to the *Technical Standards for Highway Engineering* (JTG B01-2014) and national railway regulations, as well as the road conditions in Chongqing, the weights of the five indexes based on highway (60km/h), railway (100km/h), expressway (120km/h) and high-speed railway (200km/h) were 0.19, 0.13, 0.32, 0.16, and 0.2, respectively.

Table 2 Characteristics of Spatial Economic Relations between "Central City" in Chongqing Metropolitan Area and Districts and Counties in Peripheral Affected Areas

District/ County	Economic Distance	Field Strength	Relation Force	Subordination Degree (%)
Bishan District	12.15	21.67	66.28	3.02
Jiangjin District	23.7	5.70	37.87	1.73
Qijiang District	47.7	1.51	7.04	0.32
Hechuan District	22.4	6.38	35.44	1.61
Yongchuan District	29.4	3.70	17.81	0.81
Tongliang District	46.68	1.57	5.71	0.31
Changshou District	39.55	2.05	7.70	0.35
Dazu District	38.52	2.16	7.57	0.34

Continued

District/ County	Economic Distance	Field Strength	Relation Force	Subordination Degree (%)
Rongchang District	45.18	1.57	5.76	0.32
Tongnan District	41.7	1.84	5.94	0.37
Nanchuan District	131.4	1.90	5.80	0.33
Fuling District	32.36	3.06	20.52	0.93

Comparing the economic distance, economic relation force and economic subordination between the "central city" and the surrounding core districts and counties in the Chongqing metropolitan area and the "central city's field strength on the 12 surrounding core districts and counties showed the following characteristics values: field strength >1.50, economic relation force > 5.0, economic subordination > 0.3 (see Table 2). The combination of the population size, urbanization level and centrality of the "central city" in the Chongqing metropolitan area with the spatial economic relation characteristics of the peripheral affected areas further rationalized the urban spatial structure of the "central city + peripheral affected areas" in the metropolitan area.

IV Integration Level Evaluation of the Chongqing Metropolitan Area

The integration of the Chongqing metropolitan area is not only reflected in the spatial structure expansion of the "central city" (the main urban built-up area) in the metropolitan area, but also in the strengthened economic relation between the "central city" and peripheral affected areas and the higher integration level of the metropolitan area. The strong economic foundation of Chongqing is the basic condition to promote the integrated development of the Chongqing metropolitan area. The steady advancement of new-type urbanization and the evolution of regional development strategy also lend strong support. The economic development of Chongqing has made a qualitative leap since 2000. The per capita GDP of the city increased from RMB 5,616 in 2000 to RMB 52,549.71 in 2015, an increase of nearly 9 times. In addition, the social fixed assets investment of Chongqing reached RMB 1.548033 trillion, 22 times the RMB 65.581 billion in 2000. Given the increasing economic development level of Chongqing, this study evaluates the integration level of the Chongqing metropolitan area from the single perspective of varying economic development levels and the multiple perspectives of economic, infrastructure and public service integration level.

4.1 Measurement of Varying Economic Development Levels

The economic development level of a region is a key factor to determine the coordinated comprehensive development within the region. Regional economic disparities should include regional variations in total economic growth, growth rate, economic structure, and even economic development conditions. The economic development variations (the Wilson Index) in 21 districts within the Chongqing metropolitan area since Chongqing became a municipality were calculated using the GDP and per capita GDP of each district, as shown in Figure 4:

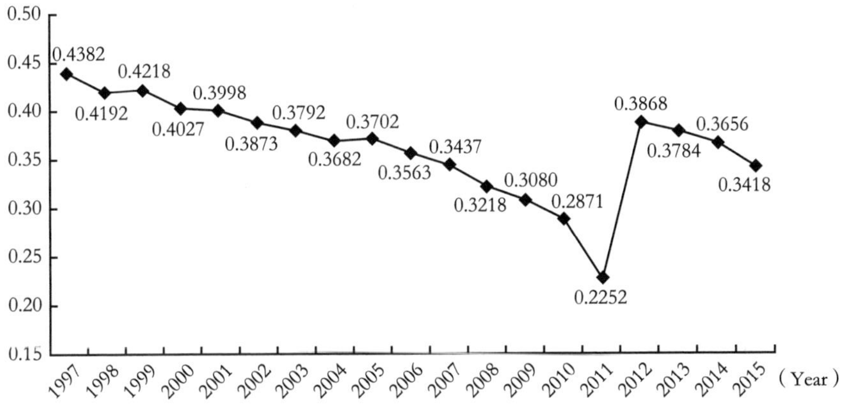

Figure 4 Wilson Index of the Chongqing Metropolitan Area (1997-2015)

The figure showed that the economic development variations in 21 districts within the Chongqing metropolitan area since Chongqing became a municipality have been generally declining over the past 20 years, from 0.4382 in 1997 to 0.3418 in 2015. This result indicated that these variations kept shrinking. It should be noted that the Wilson Index of the metropolitan area showed a significant rebound during 2011-2012 after 2011, from the historic low record of 0.2252 in 2011 to 0.3868 in 2012, due to the impact of the global financial crisis and the strategy of "Five Functional Zones in Chongqing". However, it resumed decline during 2012-2015. It showed that the international environmental and regional development strategies and policies can greatly influence regional integrated development.

4.2 Evaluation of Integrated Development Level

Based on the evolution of economic development variations (the Wilson Index) in 21 districts within the Chongqing metropolitan area since Chongqing became a municipality, this study adopts the coordinated regional development index (the Theil Index) to calculate changes in economic, infrastructure and public service integration during 2000-2015 (see Table 3 for the construction and weights of the index system). The Theil index about integration level is shown in Figure 5:

Table 3 Evaluation Index System and Weight of Chongqing Metropolitan Area Integrated Development Level

Target Layer	Criteria Layer	Index Layer	Weight
Regional integrated development level	Economic development integration	Non-agricultural output value (RMB 10,000)	0.1282
		Per capita GDP (RMB)	0.0392
		Average wages of employees (RMB)	0.0131
		Total retail volume of social consumer goods (RMB 10,000)	0.1571
	Infrastructure integration	Urbanization rate (%)	0.0250
		Total social fixed assets investment (RMB 10,000)	0.1591
		Classified highway mileage (km)	0.0365
		Total output value of construction industry (RMB 10,000)	0.1793
	Public service integration	Public budget expenditure (RMB 10,000)	0.0662
		Number of students in secondary schools and above (person)	0.0914
		Number of health institutions	0.0544
		Number of books in public libraries (10,000 volumes)	0.0504

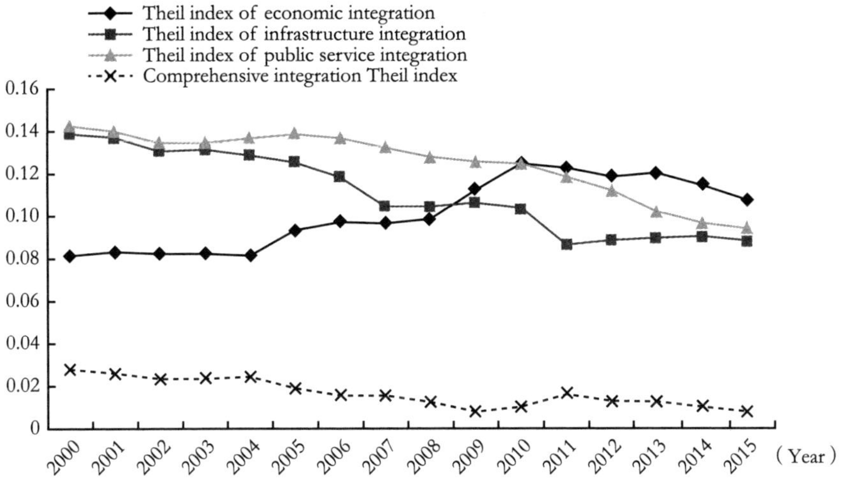

Figure 5 Theil Index of Chongqing Metropolitan Area Integration Development Level (2000-2015)

As shown in the figure, the comprehensive integration Theil index of the Chongqing metropolitan area dropped from 0.028 in 2000 to 0.008 in 2015, but the regional integrated development level increased greatly. Concerning the economic development of the metropolitan area, the Theil index of regional economic integration rose, stabilized and then gradually dropped after 2004. It can be found that the economic development differences in the metropolitan area have begun to shrink and the economic integration process has accelerated since 2010. The infrastructure and public service integration went through similar development processes. In spite of occasional fluctuations during 2007-2011, the integrated development levels were greatly increased from 2000 as a whole.

V Analysis of the Integrated Development Paths of the Chongqing Metropolitan Area

5.1 Build a Metropolitan Area of "One City-Five Districts-Multi-center Groups"

First, build "one city" as the core, which means building a "central city" in the core area of the metropolitan area that bear the functions of national central city.

Second, provide strategic support from "five districts". That is, build a "1+4" urban spatial pattern within the entire metropolitan area. "1" refers to the combination of 21 towns and streets in the peripheral areas on the basis of the spatial scope of the main urban area for the purpose of integrated development of the main urban area. "4" refers to the four major urban groups within the metropolitan area: Tongliang-Tong'an Group in the north, Yongchuan-Rongchang-Dazu Group in the west, Qijiang-Nanchuan Group in the south, and Changshou-Fuling Group in the east.

Third, build a "multi-center group" network structure. On the basis of the "1+4" overall spatial pattern of the metropolitan area, the spatial structure within each group should be deepened. Within the main urban area group ("1"), a multi-level central system around business districts, residential areas (large settlements) and industrial parks should be created. A multi-level central system centering round Tongliang and Tongnan should be created along the G93 line in the Tongliang-Tongnan Group. A multi-level central system centering round Yongchuan, Rongchang and Dazu should be created along the G85 line in the Yongchuan-Rongchang-Dazu Group. A multi-level central system centering round Qijiang, Nanchuan and Wansheng should be created along the G210 and G65 lines in the Qijiang-Nanchuan Group. A multi-level central system centering round Changtao and Fuling should be created along the G69 and G50 lines in the Changshou-Fuling Group. (A multi-level central system includes regional center-counties-key towns-key villages). The "4" groups are connected by expressways in three rings to form another ring within the metropolitan area after the internal and external ones, thereby greatly enhancing the interconnection and communication between the groups.

5.2 Building an Efficient and Convenient Modern Integrated Transportation System

First, improve the rail transit network system in the metropolitan area and increase the rail travel ratio among citizens. Advocate the prevailing travel modes of rail + walk and rail + bus in the "central city" in the metropolitan area.

Second, accelerate the construction of transfer stations and hubs to achieve zero transfer in the metropolitan area. Construct a public travel information service system, a vehicle operation dispatch management system, a safety monitoring system and an emergency response system. Speed up the construction of bus transfer stations, focusing on transfer nodes at Chongqing Railway Station, Chongqing North Railway Station, Longtou Temple and Jiangbei Airport and transfer solutions with bus, rail transit, taxis and suburban railway.

Third, connect suburban railway with urban rail and promote interconnection within the metropolitan area. Operate suburban trains by utilizing the surplus capacity of national railway trunk lines, add suburban railway lines in areas not covered by the trunk railway lines and connect them with the trunk railway lines, and ensure convenient transfer with the urban rail. Complete and put into operation the Bishan-Tongliang and Jiangjin-Jiulongpo section of suburban railway by 2020 to achieve transportation connectivity in the metropolitan area.

5.3 Optimize the Industrial Division of Labor and Promote Industrial Clusters and Networked Linkage in the Metropolitan Area

First, highlight the high-end service functions of the "central city" in the metropolitan area, with the focus on modern service industries such as financial services, international commerce, high-end commerce, culture and creativity, and urban tourism, and build a central business district and several clusters of emerging modern service industry.

Second, highlight the advanced manufacturing and regional comprehensive service functions of peripheral affected areas in the metropolitan area, with the focus on "national strategic" manufacturing industries such as electronics, automobile and motorcycle, materials, aviation equipment, and rail transit equipment, and develop regional integrated service industries such as logistics exhibitions, warehousing and distribution, software R&D, service outsourcing and service trade.

Third, highlight the modern manufacturing and local service functions in the potential expansion area of the metropolitan area integration, with the focus on large-scale manufacturing industries such as chemicals, steel, equipment, consumer goods, electronic equipment, and automobile and motorcycle parts, and develop supporting industries such as comprehensive logistics, leisure tourism, commerce and trade, and modern agriculture to make the area a predominant place with industrial economy.

VI Conclusion and Discussion

6.1 Conclusion

The Chongqing metropolitan area has an urban spatial structure of "central city + peripheral affected areas". The main urban built-up area is the "central city" whose spatial structure evolution lays the foundation for the formation and integrated development of the Chongqing metropolitan area. The spatial economic relation with the peripheral affected areas in the metropolitan area further strengthens the integrated development of the Chongqing metropolitan area.

The spatial expansion of the main urban built-up area in Chongqing happens in three main stage: the first stage, from 1997 to 2005, recorded the expansion to Yubei District, Shapingba District and Nan'an District, significantly extending along the traffic arteries and dominated by outward sprawl; the second stage, from 2006 to 2010, recorded the westward and northward construction and development of the main urban area, and the direct result was that Shapingba District and Jiangbei District expanded fastest, while Jiangbei District, in particular, developed most rapidly, with a transition from outward sprawl to internal filling; the third stage, from 2011 to 2015, recorded the further westward development of the city, with the main urban area gradually extending northwestward to cover Jiangbei District, Yubei District and Beibei District after 2010.

The economic development variations in the 21 districts of the Chongqing metropolitan area kept declining as a whole, and there was a brief period of expansion between 2011 and 2012. The gap continued to narrow after 2012. Since 2000, the economic integration level of the Chongqing metropolitan area has been fluctuating, while the infrastructure and public service integration levels increased simultaneously. The integration level of the Chongqing metropolitan area was generally improved. The main factors affecting the integration level of the Chongqing metropolitan area include spatial expansion of built-up areas, social and economic development variations, government policies and development strategies.

The most important path for the integrated development of the Chongqing metropolitan area is to form a spatial pattern of "onc city-five districts-multi-center groups", or a "1+4" urban spatial pattern within the entire metropolitan area. "1" refers to the combination of 21 towns and streets in the peripheral areas on the basis of the spatial scope of the main urban area for the purpose of integrated development of the main urban area. "4" refers to the four major urban groups within the metropolitan area: Tongliang-Tongnan Group in the north, Yongchuan-Rongchang-Dazu Group in the west, Qijiang-Nanchuan Group in the south, and Changshou-Fuling Group in the east. The "4" groups are connected by expressways in three rings to form another ring within the metropolitan area after the internal and external ones, thereby greatly enhancing the connectivity and communication between the groups.

6.2 Discussion

Due to the availability of data and the dynamic characteristics of regional integration, there is still room for improvement and refinement in this study: (1) There is a need to further explore the new pattern of metropolitan area integrated development under the new situation. Inter-regional economic relations have been continuously strengthened since Chongqing became a municipality directly under the Central Government, and more and more elements are assembled in the "central city". The traditional integration of metropolitan area divided by administrative boundaries is constantly changing, requiring academic attention to the new integration pattern of the metropolitan area. (2) Dynamic evaluation of regional integration level is needed. This study adopts the Wilson Index and the Theil index to evaluate the integration level of the Chongqing metropolitan area. The data used is only the cross-section data in 2016, but the spatial scope of the Chongqing metropolitan area integration is constantly changing. The next step is to evaluate the integration level of the metropolitan area in different time periods. (3) Future research may rely on big data and artificial intelligence platforms. This study adopts remote sensing image to analyze the spatial structure evolution of the "central city" in the Chongqing metropolitan area and applies road mileage data and economic data in quantitative analysis of urban spatial economic relation. However, inter-regional element "flows" happen all the time. Future research may use real-time big data to detect the dynamic characteristics of inter-regional population, economy and transportation and analyze the spatial dynamic evolution of metropolitan area integration.

References

[1] Liang Shuangbo, Cao Youhui, and Wu Wei. "Spatial Pattern Evolution of Port Logistics Enterprises in Shanghai Metropolitan Area" [J]. *Geographical Research*, 2013, 32 (08): 1448-1456.

[2] Ning Yuemin. "Definition of Chinese Metropolitan Areas and Large Urban Agglomerations: Role of Large Urban Agglomerations in Regional Development" [J]. *Scientia Geographica Sinica*, 2011,31 (03): 257-263.

[3] Fang Chuanglin and Yehua Dennis Wei. "Evaluation on the Sustainable Development Capacity and Regularity of its Regional Differentiation in Hexi Region" [J]. *Acta Geographica Sinica*, 2001 (05): 560-568.

[4] Chen Xiaofei, Zhang Luocheng, and Yao Shimou. "Spatial Pattern of the Yangtze River Delta Urban Agglomeration: from the New Economic Geography Perspective" [J]. *Progress in Geography*, 2015, 34 (02): 229-236

[5] Ou Xiangjun, Xue Liping, and Gu Wenjuan. "Space Characteristics of Economic Contacts between Cities and Counties in Jiangsu Province" [J]. *Economic Geography*, 2015, 35 (08): 24-31.

[6] Yan Guanghua. "Geographic Area and Fractal Study of Towns Spatial Distribution of Shenyang Metropolitan Area" [J]. *Scientia Geographica Sinica*, 2016, 36 (11): 1736-1742.

[7] Wang Bin and Chen Yao. "Measurement of the Development Gap of Beijing-Tianjin-Hebei city cluster and Study on Their Coordination Development" [J]. *Shanghai Economic Review*, 2015 (08): 109-116.

[8] Hu Zhiyuan and Ou Xiangjun. "Analysis of Regional Inequality in Jiangsu Province by Multi-target Measure Based on Theil Index" [J]. *Economic Geography*, 2007 (05): 719-724.

B.17
Study on the Effects of Administrative Division Adjustment on Public Service Supply in Chengdu*

*Luo Ruoyu and Liu Junjie***

Abstract: Administrative division adjustment is a policy arrangement by the government to change the trajectory of urban development and reshape the urban development dynamics and regional development pattern. Currently, promoting urban-rural coordination and accelerating urban-rural integration are main objectives of administrative division adjustment. Administrative division adjustment can reduce administrative costs, optimize resource allocation, and improve the conflict between supply and demand of public services. Meanwhile, it also affects the supply-demand structure of public resources and the spatial layout of public service facilities. This paper is a case study of Chengdu that discusses the relationship between administrative division adjustment and changes in public service supply system in Chengdu from the longitudinal historical trajectory. It also explores the specific mechanism of public services and explains the dual effects of administrative division adjustment on public service supply.

* This paper is a phased outcome of a general research project in humanities and social sciences (19YJA630051) funded by the Ministry of Education.

** Luo Ruoyu, Professor of School of Public Affairs and Administration, University of Electronic Science and Technology of China, whose research orientation is urban and regional governance; Liu Junjie, a postgraduate of School of Public Affairs and Administration, University of Electronic Science and Technology of China, whose research orientation is urban and regional governance.

Keywords: Chengdu; administrative division adjustment; urban spatial structure; public service supply

As a public management measure that the government applies in social governance, administrative division adjustment drives optimization and upgrading of urban spatial structure by systematically changing the administrative structure within a region. When urbanization development has come to a certain stage, expanding urban space and increased urban population will inevitably have a significant impact on public services in a city. The development and improvement of public services can affect the satisfaction and happiness of urban residents and thus is an important indicator to measure the healthy development of modern society and the construction of service-oriented government. Thus, in order to meet the needs of urban development, attention should be paid to public service supply and alleviation of its unbalanced spatial structure in the process of administrative regional adjustment.

I Process and Characteristics of Administrative Division Adjustment in Chengdu

(I) Historical Development of Administrative Division Adjustment in Chengdu

1. First adjustment of administrative division. Relevant information revealed that the first adjustment of administrative division in Chengdu happened from the early days of the New China to the 1960s, when the adjustment focused on the municipal district. In the early days of the New China, there were eight municipal districts in Chengdu. From 1950 to 1960, the administrative division was under frequent adjustments. In 1960, Chengdu was administratively divided into five districts: Dongcheng District, Xicheng District, Suburb, Qingbaijiang District and Longquanyi District. In the urban spatial structure, Chengdu adopted the Soviet model, emphasizing a basic development pattern with core radiation. At the same time, in line with the national five-year plan, Chengdu focused on the industrial layout, dividing the industrial area in the west and the residential area in the east to separate them more clearly.

Table 1 Changes in Administrative Division Adjustment in Chengdu (from Early Days of the New China to the 1960s)

Year	Changes in post-administrative division adjustment
1950	Incorporated the section of Desheng Township to Huayang County and Yongfeng Township into No. 5 and 6 Districts, and incorporated No. 7 and 8 Districts
1952	Canceled Chengdu County, incorporated Tianhui Taihua, Jinma, Taiping and Hongxing Townships that originally belonged to Chengdu County into No.3 District, incorporated Baohe, Desheng and Xinglong Townships (Longtan Temple) from Huayang County No.4 District.
1953	The number of municipal districts was adjusted from eight districts to five: Dongcheng, Xicheng, Wangjiang, Wannian and Longtan.
1960	Incorporated Cuqiao Commune from Wenjiang County to Suburb. In July, Suburb was renamed as Jinniu District in Chengdu. It developed from three districts in 1957 to five districts: Dongcheng District, Xicheng District, Suburb, Qingbaijiang District and Longquanyi District.

2. The second adjustment of administrative division. The second adjustment of administrative division in Chengdu occurred roughly from the 1970s to the early 1990s. The main representation of administrative division adjustment during this period was "incorporating counties into the city". From 1976 to 1983, Jintang and Shuangliu Counties, as well as some sections of Jianyang and Wenjiang were put under the jurisdiction of Chengdu, and a system of city leading counties was implemented. This administrative division adjustment not only expanded the municipal scope of Chengdu, but also improved its service functions.

Table 2 Changes in Administrative Division Adjustment in Chengdu (from the 1980s to the Early 1990s)

Year	Specific Administrative Division Adjustment
1976	Incorporated Jintang and Shuangliu Counties to Chengdu, Luodai District from Jianyang to Longquanyi District, and Jitian District from Renshou County to Shuangliu County.
1983	Incorporated Wenjiang area (except Guanghan and Shiyu Counties) to Chengdu, and implemented the system of city leading counties.

3. The third administrative division adjustment. The third administrative division adjustment in Chengdu happened from the 1990s to the early 21st century. During this period, the focus was placed on "adjustment in administrative boundaries" and "transforming counties to districts". From 1990 to 1994, the administrative boundary adjustment transformed Dongcheng, Xicheng and Jinniu Districts into Jinjiang, Qingyang, Jinniu, Wuhou and Chenghua Districts, and an urban-rural integration system and a management system of districts leading townships were adopted in administrative governance. In "transforming counties to cities", four counties including Guanxian were selected under the administrative division adjustment reform to expand the scope of administrative region. In general, Chengdu expanded the built-up area and pushed the patchy spatial structure towards an axial structure by expanding the administrative boundary and transforming counties into cities.

Table 3 Administrative Division Adjustment in Chengdu (from the 1990s to the Early 21st Century)

Year	Administrative Adjustment	Specific Program
1990	Administrative boundary adjustment	Transformed Dongcheng, Xicheng and Jinniu Districts into Jinjiang, Qingyang, Jinniu, Wuhou and Chenghua Districts, and adopted the urban-rural system and the system of districts leading townships.
1994	Transform counties into cities	Transformed Guan County (Dujiangyan City), Peng County, Dengxia County, and Chongqing County into cities.

4. The fourth administrative division adjustment. The fourth administrative division adjustment occurred roughly in the early 21st century. During this period, the administrative division adjustments were most frequent, involving the most changes. These mainly included the construction of new urban areas, township reform and reorganization of districts. The construction of new urban areas mainly included transforming counties into districts and setting up new national districts. In 2002, Xindu County and Wenjiang County were successively transformed into districts; in 2013, a national new district named "Tianfu New District" was founded; in 2015, Shuangliu County was transformed into Shuangliu District; in 2016, Pi County was adjusted to Pidu District. The township reform mainly included township system reform. In 2004, Chengdu reformed the administrative townships through cancellation and merger and replaced it with an administrative system based on sub-district office. The district reorganization began roughly in the early 21st century and mainly included adjustments in the areas of cities, townships and different districts. Due to the locality and flexibility of boundary adjustments, district reorganization will be continued to adapt to the continuous urbanization process.

(II) Characteristics of Administrative Division Adjustment in Chengdu

Historical development documents revealed that the adjustment of administrative division in Chengdu showed different characteristics in different stages. According to the timeline of administrative division adjustments in Figure 1, Chengdu first adjusted the administrative boundaries. This adjustment generally featured the gradual expansion of administrative scope to suburbs. In the early 1970s, with the development of urbanization, Chengdu began to build satellite cities on its original borders. In 1983, Chengdu carried out an administrative reform and a round of district reorganization, and implemented the management system of city leading counties. The administrative district reorganization not only affected administrative management and personnel arrangements, but also caused the residential relocation of administrative agencies. In the 21st century, there were two major administrative division adjustments in Chengdu: "transforming counties into districts" and "township institutional reform", both starting at almost the same time and showing synchronous characteristics in the general project construction process. The pr ojects were basically independent of each other during the implementation process, except some adjustments made to the direction of administrative division. The adjusted projects were coordinated, and there was no separate administrative reform project.

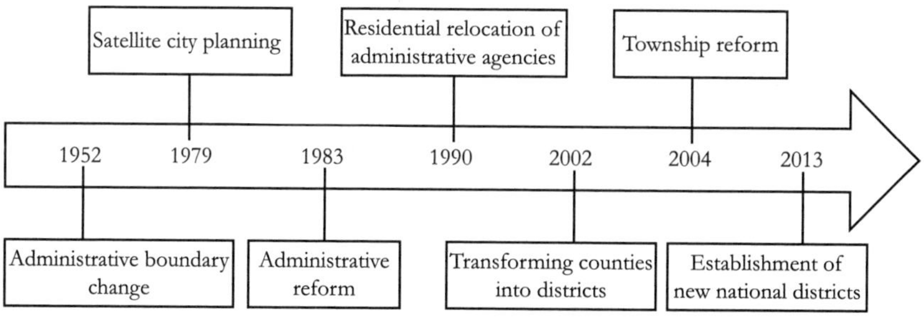

Figure 1 Timeline of Administrative Division Reform in Chengdu

In fact, the spatial and temporal distribution of administrative division adjustment in Chengdu is closely related to the evolution of urban development strategies and macroeconomic policies in China. Based on the characteristics of administrative division adjustments mentioned above in Chengdu, four periods can be roughly framed: the period of urban geospatial expansion, the period of administrative mechanism changes, the period of urban-rural coordination planning, and the period of urban regional transformation.

1 Period of Urban Geospatial Expansion

(1) Changes in administrative boundaries. Administrative boundary is the dividing line between districts. It can facilitate refined management of the city by dividing its jurisdictions. Administrative boundary changes in Chengdu began in 1952, when the transformation of counties into cities was started. As the administrative division was regulated by macroeconomic policies, administrative boundary changes have been particularly active since the early 21st century. These changes are mostly local changes caused by administrative cancellations and mergers, district reorganization, and new streets. Administrative cancellation and mergers mainly include cancellation and merger of streets into townships. District reorganization is mainly about formation of new streets and expansion of district and town jurisdiction through merger of streets. New streets mainly mean addition of new streets. All of these three forms have spurred administrative boundary changes and optimized the spatial structure of the city.

(2) Establishment of satellite cities. Satellite cities must perform the functions of the secondary industry: on the one hand, they relieve industries from the central city; on the other hand, they intercept large-scale foreign industries and population from the central city. The planning of satellite cities in Chengdu began around 1979. In 1996, the master plan of the city adjusted the setting and spatial layout of satellite cities. As a result, eight satellite towns were built: Huayang, Longquanyi, Xindu, Xinfan, Pi County, Wenjiang, Shuangliu and Qingbaijiang. The 2003 master plan of Chengdu clearly stated that six surrounding groups, including Xindu, Wenjiang and Pi County, would be planned and constructed in the southward, northward and eastward directions. Through the construction of satellite cities, Chengdu formed a multi-core urban spatial structure, which helps relieve the development pressure of the central city, further expands the urban development space, optimizes the industrial and population structures of the city, and promotes the economic development of the entire region.

2 Period of Administrative Mechanism Changes

(1) Administrative System Reform. Administrative system reform is an institutional reform, which means adjusting the original administrative system through top-level design and planning to increase the work efficiency and quality of administrative agencies. The administrative system reform of Chengdu began in 1952 and became active in the early 21st century. During this period, the administrative reforms at the municipal level mainly included "transforming counties into cities", "the system of cities leading counties", and "the system of county-level cities under custody of cities". For example, during the process of administrative division adjustment, Chengdu County was canceled and incorporated into Chengdu City in 1952, together with Wenjiang County, Xindu County, Pi County and Xinfan County, and some counties were incorporated into the suburbs of Chengdu City. In 1983, Wenjiang area was canceled, and all the 12 counties under its jurisdiction were incorporated into Chengdu City, and a system of cities leading counties was implemented. In 2015, the system of county-level cities under custody of cities was introduced. At present, five county-level cities are under the custody of Chegndu: Dujiangyan City, Chongzhou City, Pengzhou City, Qionglai City and Jianyang City. The administrative system reforms at district and county levels mainly included canceling the township system and replacing it with the sub-street office management system. According to the Chengdu Statistical Yearbook, 42 township governments and 4 sub-street offices were canceled from 2000 to 2010. After the administrative division adjustments in 2005, townships were almost completely canceled in Qingyang District, Jinjiang District, Wuhou District, Jinniu District and Chenghua District, and they were replaced by sub-street offices as administrative unit. Although more streets were added to Xindu District, Longquanyi District, Shuangliu District, Qingbaijiang District, Wenjiang District and Pidu District, the administrative system reforms mostly included township mergers, town mergers, and adoption of town as the main administrative unit. In 2014, Chengdu implemented five reforms that streamlined administration and instituted decentralization, and government services were comprehensively improved; the administrative examination and approval system was streamlined and optimized, and one-stop services were promoted to meet the needs of administrative division adjustment.

(2) The residential relocation of administrative agencies. The relocation of administrative agencies in Chengdu coincided with administrative division adjustments. With administrative division adjustments such as township reform, transformation of counties into districts, and street reorganization, the institutional setup and personnel composition of the original administrative unit had to be changed. At the same time, due to the expansion of jurisdictions, only by relocating administrative agencies would the whole administrative area be managed more conveniently. Chengdu has been relocating administrative agencies along with administrative division adjustments since 1990, and such relocation was most active in the early 21st century. At present, with the administrative boundary reform, the cancellation and merger of administrative agencies are still in progress, and administrative agencies will also change accordingly to adapt to changing jurisdictions.

3 Period of Urban-Rural Coordination Planning

(1) Cancellations and mergers of towns and townships, transformation of townships into towns and towns into streets. In 2004, Chengdu launched the township reform. In the same year, the most intensive administrative adjustments were made, including changes in the number, area and population of towns and townships. After the reform, the number of townships was reduced from 71 to 27; the number of towns was reduced from 247 to 200; the area of towns and townships was increased from 37.5 square kilometers to 49.7; the population was increased from 24,000 to 32,000. Along with the township reform, Chengdu also began to cancel the township system and replaced it with the sub-district office management system to meet the requirements of urban management. The number of streets began to increase, and in the same year, 13 new sub-district offices were added in Chengdu. These reforms played an important role in achieving fiscal centralization and improving government quality while at the same time promoting urban-rural integrated development.

Table 4 Before and After Township Reforms in Chengdu City

	Before Reforms	After Reforms
Number of townships	71	27
Number of towns	247	200
Area of towns and townships (square kilometres)	37.5	49.7
Population of towns and townships (10,000 persons)	2.4	3.2

(3) Transforming counties into districts. Transforming counties into districts means that municipal administrative units change their subordinate county-level administrative units into district-level ones. Such transformations in Chengdu were intensive in 2002, 2015 and 2016. Xindu County and Wenjiang County were transformed into districts in 2002, Shuangliu County in 2015, and Pidu County in 2016. Transforming counties into districts allowed surrounding counties to be deeply integrated into the central city. Traditional county-level public services would be replaced by powerful municipal ones, which would benefit residents more.

4 Period of Urban Regional Transformation

The administrative division adjustment during this period mainly included the establishment of new national districts, especially around 2013. For example, the national-level Tianfu New District was established in 2013 mainly due to the effects of economic and social development. The accelerating urbanization process has attracted a large number of migrants to the urban area, posing severe pressure on urban management and public service supply. The planning and construction of the new national districts in Chengdu can absorb some of the population from the central city while retaining some of the migrant population to reduce the burden on the central city. At the same time, the establishment of the new district assumes important national development and reform tasks and plays an important role in driving regional economic development, leading comprehensive reform and opening up, promoting institutional mechanism innovation, boosting industry-city integration and urban-rural integrated development.

II Changes in Public Service Supply after Administrative Division Adjustment in Chengdu

(I) Changes in Public Service Supply after Administrative Division Adjustment in Chengdu

As shown in Figure 2, the administrative division adjustment in Chengdu has short-term and long-term effects on public service supply. Short-term effects mainly include transformation of counties into districts and township reform. In the short term, "transformation of counties into districts" can have an impact on per capita economic growth in the post-reform administrative region and drive the inflow of social capital. Township reform can directly change the urban and rural public fiscal structures. In the long term, the spatial layout of public service facilities and the spending preferences of public finance can be affected by the expansion of administrative regions. However, public service facilities require long investment cycle and construction period, and the effect of administrative division adjustment may not be evident in them in the short term. Changes in administrative boundaries will lead to redefinition of the main public service supplier in a region. With some counties transformed into districts, some of the administrative authorities granted to counties were still retained, resulting in overlapping of responsibilities for providing public services at city and county levels, which in turn affected public service supply.

1 Increased Scale of Public Service Supply

Administrative division adjustment can stimulate the vitality of urban development and drive the economic and social development of a region. According to the relevant statistical yearbooks, the public service expenditure of Chengdu has been continuously increased after administrative division adjustments. The public service expenditures were mainly concentrated in education, medical care, transportation, and pension insurance. Chengdu tries to build a sound public service system and expand the coverage of public services (as shown in Table 5).

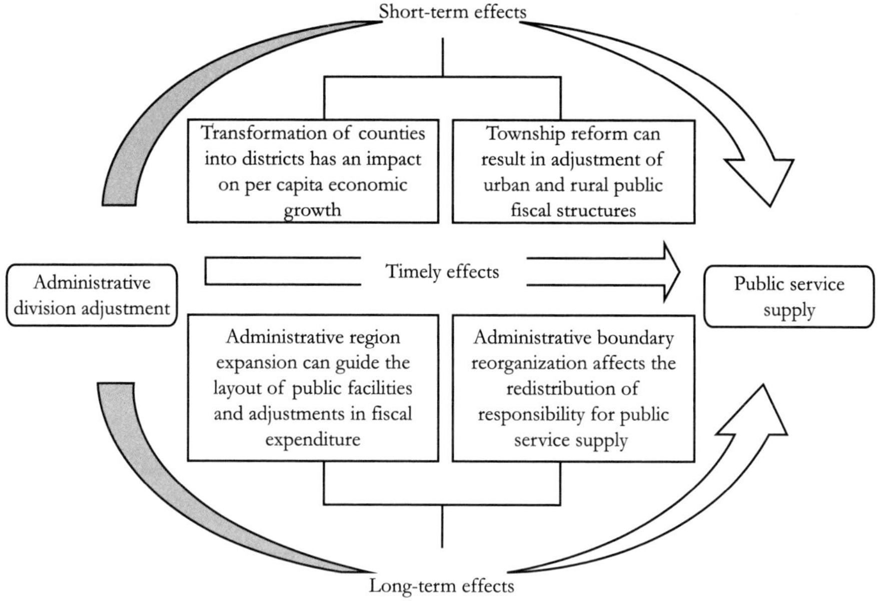

Figure 2 Short-term and Long-term Effects of Administration Division on Public Services

Table 5 Expenditures on General Public Services in Districts and Counties in Chengdu (2013-2017)

Unit: (RMB 10,000)

	2013	2014	2015	2016	2017
Chengdu	1309986	1311174	1533158	1577380	1806007
Jinjiang District	72683	70925	78118	73061	75409
Qingyang District	53233	54553	65651	68266	72293
Jinniu District	48426	53299	42861	45976	52883
Wuhou District	71676	71879	91841	112334	149060
Chenghua District	51985	57053	58498	65773	79235
Longquanyi District	73272	67404	82088	87882	102863
Qingbaijiang District	34226	34040	36423	39872	44384
Xindu District	59289	74804	64728	53759	74946
Wenjiang District	65486	58219	52890	57734	69222
Shuangliu District	96835	113709	179722	160054	213307
Pidu District	59034	68488	97297	89472	73446

2 Improved ability of medical health services.

This paper measures the medical health service ability of Chengdu from the indicators of the number of medical health institutions, the number of health technicians and the number of medical treatments in the whole year. As shown in Table 6, in terms of the scale and number of health facilities, the increases in the number of health institutions and the number of health technicians in Chengdu were 2,779 and 49,000, respectively, over the past 6 years. In terms of the number of people who receive medical services in Chengdu every year, the total number of medical treatments increased by 43.65 million during the same period, up 43%. This showed that Chengdu's medical service ability was greatly improved.

Table 6 Statistics of Medical Health Service Indicators in Chengdu (2013-2018)

	2013	2014	2015	2016	2017	2018
# Number of health institutions	7976	8190	8481	9853	10183	10755
# Number of hospitals and health centers	724	746	768	866	888	892
# Number of centers for disease control and prevention	22	22	22	23	23	23
# Number of maternal and child health care centers	21	21	21	22	22	21
# Number of beds in health institutions (10,000)	10. 1	10.8	11.5	12.8	13.5	14.3
# Number of health technicians (10,000 persons)	12	12.8	13.5	14.8	15.8	16.9
# Number of medical treatments on a yearly basis (10,000 person-times)	10148	10928	11344	12762	13575	14513

(1) Public transport services. The direct benefit for public transportation from the transformation of counties into districts is longer bus routes in the city center. As Xindu, Wenjiang, Shuangliu and Pi County were put under the jurisdiction of Chengdu, the overall area of the city has been expanded and makes increasing bus routes in the city center inevitable in order to improve public transportation infrastructure in all districts and counties. Chengdu basically built a transformation network of "Two Rings and Eight Main Roads" in the metropolitan area in 2003. Over the past five years, the number of bus routes in the city center has increased by 8,299km (see Table 7), and transportation networks in different cities and counties were integrated. The expressway network runs through all counties in Chengdu, and the urban and rural transportation construction has been constantly improved. At the same time, the government lent preferential financial support to rural transportation construction. New rural road networks were established, and 98% of the villages had access to passenger transport within the village. After the urban and rural passenger transportation network was improved, the efficiency and quality of public transportation services in urban and rural areas were increased, which made people's work and life more convenient.

Table 7 Statistics of Public Transportation Service Indicators in Chengdu (2013-2017)

	2013	2014	2015	2016	2017
# Built-up area in the municipal districts (square kilometer)	528.9	604.1	615.5	837.3	885.6
# Length of bus routes in the city center (km)	4019	6421	6785	6777	12318
Number of buses put into operation (unit)	10176	11447	11294	10781	14402
Length of paved roads (km)	2845	2633	2739	3700	4125

(2) Social security and employment services. Chengdu solidly promoted the efforts in employment and social security improvement. The number of insured employees and the amount of social security fund in the city were continuously increased. The numbers of people covered by urban basic pension and medical insurances have increased by 2.704 million and 2.624 million over the past five years, with growth rates of 49% and 45%, respectively. Judging from the number of residents covered by the government's subsistence allowances, the number of people enjoying subsistence allowances from governments in urban and rural areas has been decreasing year by year. This proved the remarkable results of poverty alleviation efforts in Chengdu. In addition, Chengdu paid attention to the employment and entrepreneurship of key population groups and dynamically eliminated "zero-employment" families. As a result, the number of new urban employees has increased year by year. Finally, Chengdu continued to improve the social security mechanism, established a sound employment injury insurance system, and applied supervision over the social security fund to promote "fine, standardized and specialized" social security management. (See Table 8)

Table 8 Statistics of Social Service Indicators in Chengdu (2013-2018)

	2013	2014	2015	2016	2017	2018
# Number of people covered by urban basic pension insurance (10,000 persons)	514.5	547.5	570.8	657.1	719.6	817.9
# Number of insured employees (10,000 persons)	377.6	401.7	417.7	474.9	529.1	614.9
# Number of people covered by urban basic medical insurance (10,000 persons)	555.2	588.4	620.8	675.3	743.9	850.8
# Number of insured employees (10,000 persons)	416.7	442.2	468.7	506.5	562.0	655
# Number of urban residents enjoying subsistence allowances from the government (10,000 persons)	4.1	3.6	3.4	3.4	2.8	2.5
# Number of rural residents enjoying subsistence allowances from the government (10,000 persons)	12.1	11.3	10.9	11.4	10.6	8.9

2 Unbalanced Public Service Supply Structure

(1) The spatial supply structure of public services was unbalanced. In the urban spatial pattern, inequality in public service supply is more obvious. The spatial imbalance of public service supply is mainly reflected in the uneven expenditures on specific public service indicators by district governments. (See Figure 3)

Public service expenditure, social security and employment, education, and government fund expenditure are four indicators to measure the public service supply level of a region. The financial expenditures on these four indicators in Chengdu in 2017 can roughly reflect the public service supply capacity of different districts.

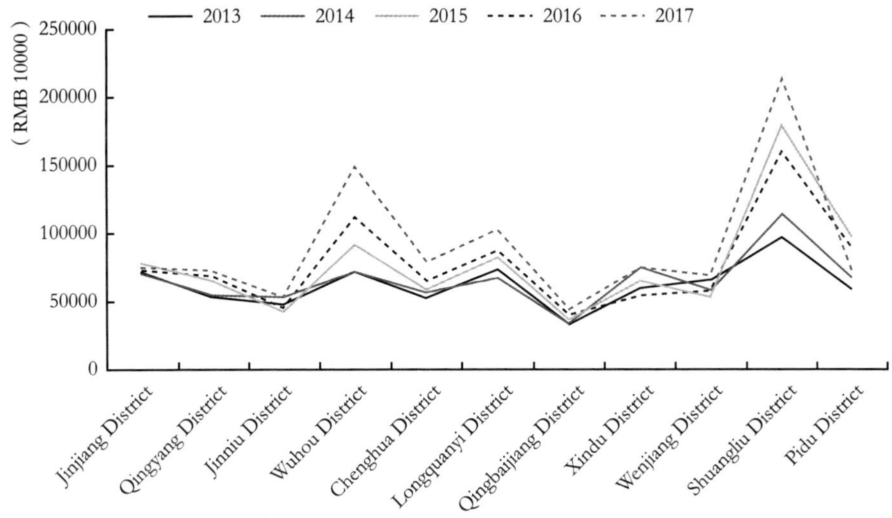

Figure 3 Financial Expenditures on Public Services in Different Districts in Chengdu (2013-2017)

Table 9 Comparison of Financial Expenditures on Public Services in Different Districts in Chengdu (2017)

Unit: RMB 10,000

	General Public Services	Educational Services	Social Security and Employment	Government Subsidy Expenditure
Jinjiang District	75409	75260	72232	3798
Qingyang District	72293	88548	71414	24574
Jinniu District	52883	115650	54926	24281
Wuhou District	149060	134404	97265	31886
Chenghua District	79235	102101	47236	254941
Longquanyi District	102863	178196	50568	759014
Qingbaijiang District	44384	60713	34306	451752
Xindu District	74946	144248	55846	440341
Wenjiang District	69222	87425	29133	374261
Shuangliu District	213307	240321	87165	2690234
Pidu District	73446	81372	54354	397226

The statistics in Table 9 reflects the different spatial structures of public services throughout the urban area. Longquanyi District and Shuangliu District had higher overall public service expenditures, while Jinjiang District and Jinniu District were on the other side of the spectrum. Public service projects consumed different proportions of investments in different districts. However, all districts generally attached importance to investments in public education services, although social security and employment received less attention. The unbalanced spatial structure of public services was attributed to both historical and realistic reasons. In practice, due to the differences in public finance system, the degree of financial preferences to public service expenditure also varied in different districts. It was the main reason for the unbalanced spatial structure of public services.

(2) The social supply structure of public services was unbalanced. Due to the urban-rural dual structure and the household registration system, Chengdu provided different public services for urban and rural residents, mobile population and registered population. This difference in supply was converted into unbalanced social supply structure of public services. During the process of administrative division adjustment in Chengdu, the supply difference caused by urban-rural variations and household registration system always remained.

Table 10 Changes in the Income and Expenditure Structure of Urban and Rural Residents after Administrative Division Adjustment in Chengdu

(Unit: RMB)

Year	2013	2014	2015	2016	2017	2018
Per capita disposable income of urban residents (RMB)	29968	32665	33476	35902	38918	42128
Per capita disposable income of rural residents (RMB)	12985	14478	17690	18605	20298	22135
Per capita consumption expenditure of urban residents (RMB)	20362	21711	21825	23514	25314	27312
Per capita consumption expenditure of rural residents (RMB)	8866	9697	12711	13428	14616	15977

Over the past five years, the per capita disposable incomes of urban and rural residents have increased by 29% and 53% respectively, and the per capita consumption expenditures of the two groups have increased by 26% and 25% respectively. However, due to the low bases of these two indicators among rural residents, the income gap between urban and rural residents remains huge. The gap between the income and expenditure of residents results in a gap in the payment level for public services and thus the gap in the level of public services in education for their children, employment and pension security.

(II) Changes in Public Service Supply after Administrative Division Adjustment

At present, "diverse" public service suppliers, "one-stop" supply management and "decentralized" supply method are the main changes following the administrative division adjustment in Chengdu.

1 Toward "Diverse" Public Service Suppliers

In the urbanization process, the government increases financial investments to support the construction of urban public service infrastructures and optimize the urban development environment. This can attract considerable population and capital inflows. However, the government, as the single provider of public services, is not able to meet residents' demand. Therefore, diverse suppliers must be sought to solve the problem and dilemma of public service supply and rectify the spatial imbalance of public service supply and demand structure. The municipal government of Chengdu should encourage market entities and non-government entities to participate in public service supply, and the costs of public services should be "shared" by the government and the community. In addition, by "transforming counties into districts" and establishing new districts, Chengdu absorbs not only high-quality talents but also huge social capital. The assemblage of these resources can promote the optimization and upgrading of industries and drive the regional economy. Tianfu New District has utilized its own policy advantages to attract and pool social capital and technologies. Thus, it not only promotes its economic transformation and upgrading, but also drives the "diversification" of public service suppliers.

2 Toward "One-Stop" Public Service Supply Management

In the process of administrative division adjustment, administrative agencies are streamlined and redundant functional departments are reduced through cancellations, adjustments and mergers. This is conducive to the refined and efficient management on government departments. By the end of 2018, the Chengdu Municipal Government was able to process 699 government affairs online and required "one errand at most" for 91% of approval services through construction of websites and municipal government cloud platform. These changes have improved the previously cumbersome government services and the efficiency of public services.

3 Toward "Decentralized" Public Service Supply

The acceleration of urbanization process has attracted a huge population to gather in Chengdu, imposing serious public service supply pressure on the central city. Therefore, Chengdu pays attention to the planning and construction of new districts in the process of administrative division adjustment and reasonably guides the layout and flow of element resources in the city. This has prompted the government to shift from "centralized" to "decentralized" public service investments. At the same time, in the urban planning and design, the government provides more policy support for the development of public services to adapt to changes in urban spatial structure. This not only eases the contradiction of urban public service supply, but also guides the city to the path of high-quality and sustainable development.

III Analysis of the Dual Effects of Administrative Division Adjustment on Public Service Supply in Chengdu

(I) Direct Effects of Administrative Division Adjustment on Public Service Supply in Chengdu

1 Administrative System Reform Helped to Save Public Service Costs

The administrative system reform that integrates the number of administrative agencies is significant mainly because it can improve the administrative efficiency of public services and establish a government that people are satisfied with. The system of "districts leading townships" and the sub-district office management system in Chengdu are intended to narrow the jurisdiction of administrative agencies and achieve the goal of "limited but effective government". The administrative reform system improves the efficiency of government to supply public services, promotes effective cooperation among multiple suppliers, and further reduces the administrative costs for public service supply.

Table 11 Changes in the Number of Administration Division Agencies in Chengdu (2000-2005)

Unit: piece

Studied Area	2000	2001	2002	2003	2004	2005
Township government	37	25	22	22	3	3
Town government	92	101	104	102	71	69
Sub-street office	96	88	88	83	85	90

According to the changes in the number of administrative agencies shown in Table 11, the number of administrative agencies in Chengdu was clearly decreasing between 2000 and 2005. The most obvious change occurred in 2004, when the number of township governments was 18 less than the number in the previous year; the number of town governments was 31 less in the same period. The reason was that Chengdu unfolded a township reform in its jurisdiction which incorporated 78 townships into towns and changed the township system into a sub-street office management system in that year.

2 The "Transformation of Counties into Districts" Increased the Investments in Public Service Supply

After the system of transforming counties into districts was implemented in Chengdu, the already existing public service infrastructures in counties were put under "coordination of the city" instead of "being managed by counties". At the same time, the jurisdictions that originally belonged to the transformed counties became part of the main urban area, with their infrastructure planning gradually synchronous with that of the main urban area. The main urban area could also drive the economic development of new districts. In addition, the transformation of counties into districts could actively guide the inflow of social capital. With the improvement of infrastructures, transformed counties would attract substantial inflows of population and social capital, thereby increasing the regional fiscal revenue and social investments in public services. For example, after Xindu County and Wenjiang County were transformed into districts in 2002, their fiscal revenue increased by 1.18% and 1.31%, respectively, over the previous year. In 2015, after being transformed into districts, Shuangliu County saw its fiscal revenue increase by 1.07% and its public financial investments increase by 0.9% to reach RMB 11.82 billion from the previous year. In 2016, Pi County was transformed into a district, and its fiscal revenue increased by 0.96% from the previous year, reaching RMB 3.97 billion. Its public financial expenditure increased as well by 1.057%, reaching RMB 600.6 million.

3 The Planning of New Cities and New Districts Helped to Alleviate the Supply-Demand Structure of Public Services

The planning and construction of new districts in Chengdu could alleviate the contradiction between supply and demand of urban public services. By building new districts and satellite cities to accommodate some of the population and industries, the central city could be relieved from the pressure on public service supply and the urban economic development space could be expanded. At the same time, the new urban areas could also become transitional zones for urban-rural coordinated development, help the government coordinate public services between urban and suburban areas, and optimize the spatial layout of public service facilities. In building new districts, the government increased financial support for areas where meager public service expenditures were made and built a public transportation network between old and new urban areas to facilitate free flow of factors in regional markets. In addition, the development of new districts inevitably radiated to the development of township and village industries around the suburbs in a way that "cities drove the development of townships" and "the integration of industries, cities and townships was realized". While new districts promoted the development of township industries, the income gap between urban and rural areas was naturally narrowed, and thus the "class" difference between urban and rural public service supplies shrank.

(II) Indirect Effects of Administrative Division Adjustment on Public Service Supply in Chengdu

1 Administrative Division Adjustment Affected the Optimization of Economic Structures Indirectly

The effect mechanism of administrative division adjustment on urban economic structure was mainly manifested in the change of administrative boundaries and the reform of administrative management system. The "transformation of counties into districts" and the establishment of new districts and satellite cities were two important measures to adjust administrative boundaries. They helped expand the space for urban economic development, and the economic radiation of the central urban area could drive the economic growth of new urban areas, which further improved the ability of local governments to supply public services. At the same time, the "cancellation and incorporation of townships" and "township custody" encouraged cooperative development of regional industries, optimized the industrial structure, and improved the regional economic structure, which in turn boosted improvement in regional economic strength. Thus, administrative division adjustment could facilitate public services indirectly.

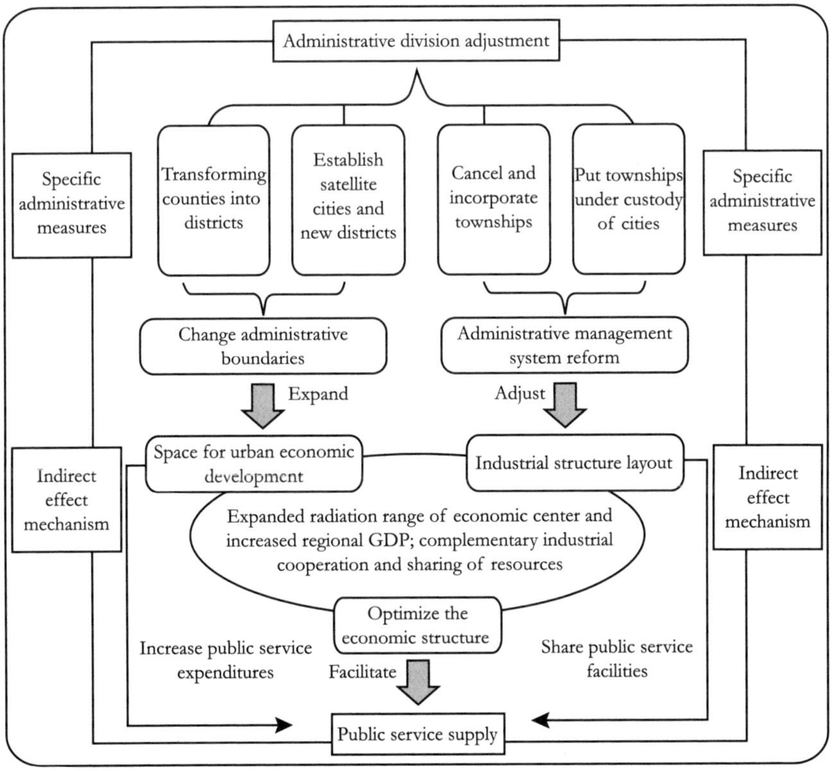

Figure 4 Effect Mechanism of Administrative Division Adjustment on the Urban Economic Structure in Chengdu

Fiscal revenue and regional GDP were main economic indicators that affected the public service supply capacity. As shown in Figure 5 and Figure 6 below, the GDP and general public budget revenues of Chengdu as well as districts and counties grew significantly from 2011. Research showed that the administrative division adjustment in Chengdu adapted to the requirements of economic development, played a positive role in the economic development within the administrative scope, and therefore improved the public service supply capacity.

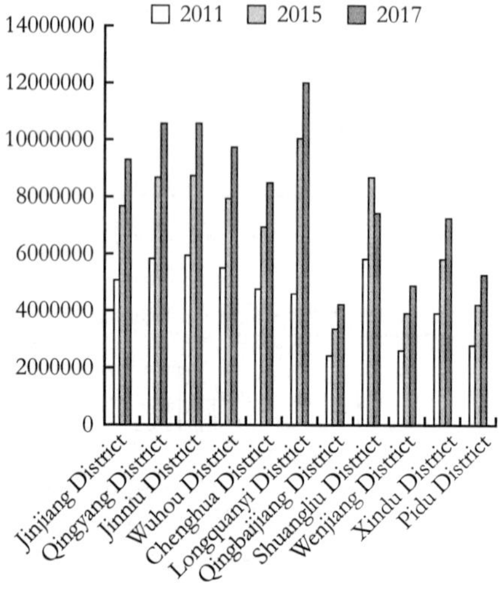

Figure 5 Recent GDP of Districts in Chengdu

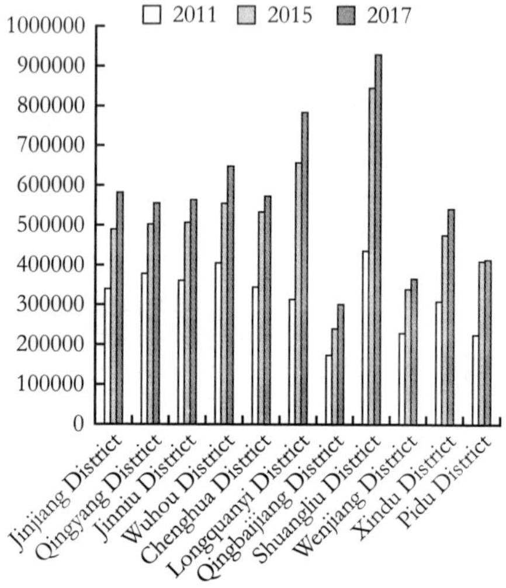

Figure 6 Recent Changes in General Public Budget Revenue of Chengdu

2 Administrative Division Adjustment Affected the Population Structure

Administrative division affected population mobility mainly via its public policy attributes. For example, establishment of new national districts and satellite cities might lead to large-scale population movements. However, the planning of public service system was not included in the policy planning of new districts. Some public service projects involved designated facilities that required long construction periods, such as schools, hospitals and welfare houses for the aged. Thus, short-term imbalance between public service supply and demand caused by lagging availability of public facilities might trigger new social conflicts. In addition, Chengdu also implemented the township system reform and the sub-district office management system reform. As a result, more extensive urban land was utilized and rural surplus labor migrated to cities. Administrative division adjustment promoted population concentration in cities, which brought about economic benefits. However, since entitlement to public services was associated with household registration, not only did the mobile population and rural population migrating to cities affect the process and effects of public service entitlement granted to urban residents, the household registration system also deprived them of equal access to public services like medical treatment and educational services. (See Figure 7)

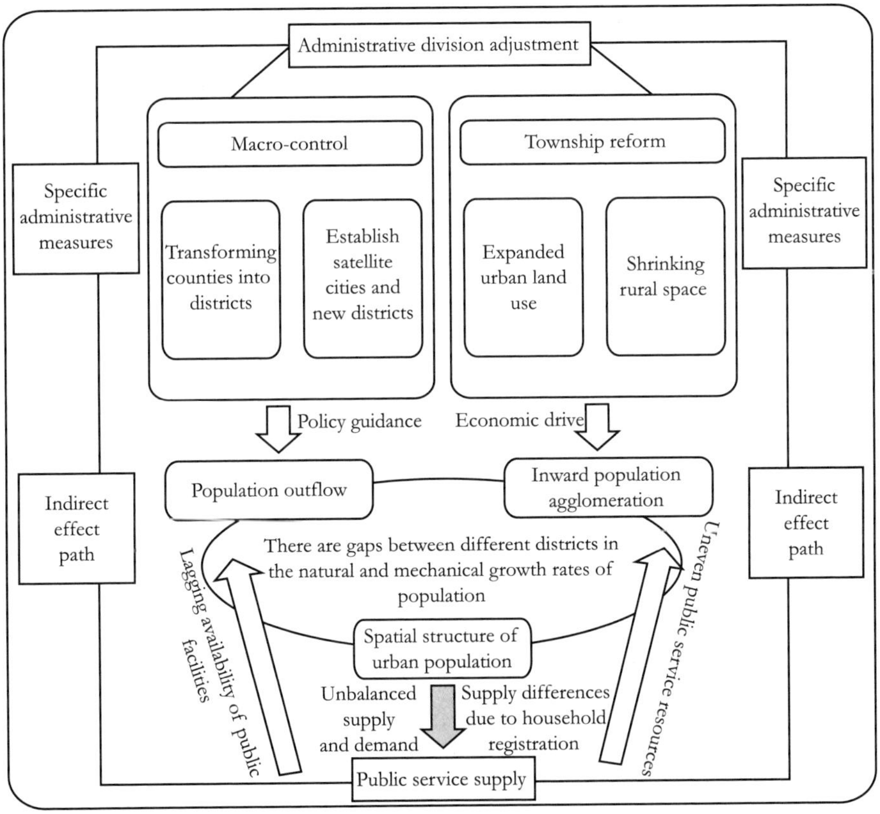

Figure 7 Effect Mechanism of Administrative Division Adjustment on Urban Population Structure in Chengdu

Table 12, on the one hand, showed that the administrative division adjustment in Chengdu boosted population increase in the city. On the other hand, it also revealed huge gaps in the mechanical population growth rates of different districts in Chengdu. In 2017, the growth rate of Shuangliu District was 90.12% higher than that of the Qingbaijiang District, which had the lowest growth rate. Faced with fast-growing migrants, some districts were certainly not able to provide public services that met public needs in the short term. Contrarily, other districts and counties found their public services apparently oversupplied due to sluggish population growth. This suggested that public resources allocation was not adjusted in time to adapt to changes in the spatial structure of population.

Table 12 Mechanical Growth Rates of Population in Different Districts in Chengdu (2013-2017)

Unit: %

	2013	2014	2015	2016	2017
Chengdu	9.69	14.3	8.77	11.01	25.02
Jinjiang District	24.47	31.22	19.57	25.16	40.86
Qingyang District	28.49	31.66	18.96	17.39	30.59
Jinniu District	14.56	18.82	8.51	11	22.55
Wuhou District	14.33	26.3	18.74	18.6	62.5
Chenghua District	17.14	25.09	17.92	19.69	35.76
Longquanyi District	13.43	20.3	10.34	17.02	29.86
Qingbaijiang District	2.63	2.5	0.03	2.33	2.01
Shuangliu District	15.97	25.02	19.48	25.93	92.13
Wenjiang District	14.82	27.67	20.15	26.76	49.92
Xindu District	9.87	18.43	15	15.71	26.28
Pidu District	10.38	24.54	20.98	19.7	37.41

IV Summary

By examining relationship between administrative division adjustment and public services, this paper concludes that administrative division adjustment affects public service supply mainly in five ways. Firstly, the administrative system reform can improve the efficiency of public services and reduce the administrative costs for the government to supply public services. Secondly, the reorganization of administrative boundaries can facilitate rational allocation of resources between urban and rural areas and accomplish the integration of public services. Thirdly, the transformation of counties into districts can guide the inflow of social capital and labor resources, thereby increasing social capital investments in public services. Fourthly, the establishment of satellite cities and new districts can guide the rational flow of population, relieve the public service pressures of the central city, and improve the supply-demand structure of public services. Fifthly, the mergers and reorganization of administrative agencies can increase the efficiency and quality of public services, which further enhance the overall supply level of public services in Chengdu.

The municipal administrative division has direct positive and indirect negative effects on the supply of public services in Chengdu. The administrative division adjustment results in cancellations or mergers of township and town administrative units, strengthens the flow of population between different regions, and integrates the existing public service supply institutions and facilities. All of this leads to unbalanced spatial and social structures of public service supply and thus has negative effects on public services.

References:

[1] Tong Yan and Xie Yufu. "A Quantitative Analysis of the City Administrative Division Adjustment to Space Layout Optimization: A Case Study of Shenyang" [J]. *Modern Urban Research*, 2013, 28 (07): 37-42.

[2] Gu Chaolin, Wang Ying, Shao Yuan and Gu Jiang. "Research on Administrative Divisions Based on Functional Areas Analysis: A Case Study of Shaoxing Metropolitan Area" [J]. *Acta Geographica Sinica*, 2015, 70 (08): 1187-1201.

[3] Hu De and Liu Junde. "The Relationship among the Administrative Regional Registration, Right and the Regional Economy—the Inter-Spaces Process and Its Influence of Governmental Power in China" [J]. *Chinese Public Administration*, 2007 (06): 11-13.

[4] Wei Heng, Wei Qingquan, Cao Tianyan, and Zhao Jing. "Types, Problems and Changes for Readjustment of Administrative Divisions in the Process of Urbanization" [J]. *Human Geography*, 2009, 24 (06): 55-58.

[5] Liu Zhihui. "Transforming Counties into Districts: Status Quo · Problems · Measures" [J]. *The Journal of Yunnan Provincial Committee School of CPC*, 2017, 18 (02): 164-168.4
[6] Yin Jie and Luo Xiaolong. "From Turning County into District to District Restructuring: A New Trend in County-level Administrative Division Adjustment in China" [J]. *City Planning Review*, 2013, 37 (06): 9-15.
[7] Zhao Peihong and Sun Jiuwen. "The Impact and Enlightenment of Beijing Administrative Division Adjustment on Urban Development" [J]. *Urban Insight*, 2011 (05): 107-117.
[8] Yan Yana. "Research on Financial Countermeasures for Equalization of Basic Public Services" [D]. Shanxi University of Finance and Economics, 2017.
[9] Jin Meijuan and Zhang Zhibin. "A Review on the Study of Urban Spatial Structure Home and Abroad" [J]. *Tropical Geography*, 2006 (02): 134-138+172.
[10] Geng Weijun. "'Transforming Counties into Districts': Transformation of Administrative Division System and Regional Economic Development" [D]. Zhejiang University of Finance & Economics, 2016.
[11] Shang Zhengyong, Lu Xiaoxu, Zhang Xiaolin, and Wu Qiyan. "The Impacts of Administrative District Adjustment on the Evolution of Urban Spatial Structure: A Case of Huai'an in Jiangsu Province" [J].*Economic Geography*, 2015, 35 (08): 61-67.
[12] Li Yixuan. "Analysis on the Impact of Urban Spatial Expansion on Economic Effects from a Macro Perspective" [J]. *New West (Theoretical Edition)*, 2016 (16): 61+50.

B.18
Study on the Green Development Evaluation Index System of National Central Cities

*Gao Xin**

Abstract: It is of great strategic significance to promote green development of national central cities. Focusing on the strategic positioning of national central cities, this paper draws on existing research results to construct a green development evaluation index system of national central cities that includes 32 specific evaluation indicators in green production, green life and green ecology. This study uses the synthetic index method to quantitatively measure the green development level of national central cities based on the available statistical yearbooks and statistical communiqué of the nine national central cities on national economic and social development. The results show that these cities vary greatly in the green development level due to the differences in green development concepts, policies and technological supply. To promote green development of national central cities, the focus should be placed on concept renewal, policy supply, and technological innovation.

Keywords: national central cities; green development; green production; green life

City is an important symbol of human civilization. The formation and development of a city is not only a process when human beings occupy and transform the natural environment, but also a process when they accept

---

* Gao Xin, female, Ph.D. in Economics, Associate Professor of the School of Business of Huanghe S&T University, whose research orientation is industrial economy as well as agricultural and rural development.

and adapt to it. As important platforms and strategic fulcrums of national development strategies, national central cities are pools of space, population, resource and factor advantages and perform the strategic functions of leading the implementation of new development concepts, leading coordinated regional development, participating in international competition and cooperation, and demonstrating the comprehensive strength of the country. By the end of 2017, the resident population of the existing nine national central cities had accounted for 11.01% of the total population in the country; in terms of economic scale, the total GDP of these cities had accounted for 19.4% of the national GDP; their per capita GDP was 1.76 times the national average level; most of them had outpaced the national average in GDP growth rate; in terms of fiscal revenue, the public budget revenue of these cities had accounted for 13.07% of the total in the country; their urbanization rate of resident population was 1.33 times the national average. Most of these cities took the lead in the country in terms of economic and social development indicators. Some of them have made into the rank of the most economically competitive cities in the country and even the world and have initially been secured as "central status" leading regional and urban development in China. They also show momentum of accelerating development and fully demonstrate, upgrade and play their roles in leading development, international competitiveness, and driving the growth of surrounding areas. With the acceleration of urbanization, quickening the green development pace of national central cities has become the theme of the times. This is not only an inherent requirement for national central cities, but also an important way for them to play a leading and demonstration role. Building an evaluation index system, measuring the quality, monitoring the process, guiding the direction, and identifying major problems in the green development of national central cities has both practical and theoretical value.

I Literature Review

In recent years, as the concept of green development is gradually prevailing, some institutions and scholars at home and abroad have begun to build an index system of urban green development. In 2004, the EU built a comprehensive evaluation index system of urban green space that included 64 specific indicators in terms of quantity, quality, use, and planning and development management (Chen Chundi et al., 2009). In 2009, the US Green Building Council built a green community certification system and divided communities into four levels based on evaluation scores: certified, silver, golden and platinum. In 2011, the Japanese Sustainable Building Federation proposed a comprehensive evaluation system for urban built-up environmental efficiency and evaluated the efficiency of urban built-up environment in a scale from 1 to 5 (Zhao Ge, 2017). In 2011, the Economist Intelligence Unit introduced the Green City Index that included 29 indicators in 8 categories. The evaluation index systems of green development for cities from foreign countries mentioned above provide useful references for the construction of one for Chinese cities. However, when constructing green development indicators of national central cities, we also need to allow for China's basic conditions and functional positioning of national central cities when we draw on references.

China's cities started late to pursue green development, and the evaluation index system in this regard is still in the exploration stage. In 2011, the Ministry of Housing and Urban-Rural Development, as well as other ministries and commissions, put forward the "Evaluation Index System for Construction of Green and Low-carbon Key Small Towns (Trial)", which included 62 specific indicators in 7 categories including economic and social development, utilization of land resources, and public service level. In 2012, Beijing Normal University worked with other relevant units to propose the concept of green development index for China and defined 43 indicators in greening degree of economic growth, resource and environmental carrying capacity, and government policy support at the city level. In 2016, the National Development and Reform Commission ("NDRC") and the Ministry of Environmental Protection built 56 green development indicators in seven dimensions: resource utilization, environmental governance, ecological protection, environmental quality, green life, growth quality, and public satisfaction. In the same year, a target system of ecological civilization construction assessment was also introduced. In 2017, the Standardization Administration of China ("SAC") selected 12 secondary indicators and 65 tertiary indicators in green production, green life and environmental quality to construct a green city evaluation index system. Among all of the urban green development index systems mentioned above, the "Evaluation Index System for Construction of Green and Low-carbon Key Small Towns (Trial)" issued by the Ministry of Housing and Urban-Rural

Development focuses on the green development evaluation of small towns with many qualitative indicators but few quantitative ones, and thus it is not operable enough. The China Green Development Index released by Beijing Normal University pays attention to urban industry development more than ecological environment, and it is not systematic enough. The green development index system and the assessment system of ecological civilization construction issued by the NDRC are an important basis for the evaluation and assessment of ecological civilization construction in China and can serve as an important reference for constructing a green city index system in China; the green city evaluation indicators proposed by the SAC are systematic and complete, but they don't allow for variations among cities of different types, in different regions and under different development stages. In addition, some local governments have proposed their own green development evaluation index systems in combination with regional characteristics in recent years, such as the green development index systems of Shanghai and Shandong, the urban green ecology index system of Shaanxi, the green and ecological city construction index system of Anhui Province, and the green development index system of Chengdu. Some scholars constructed urban green development index systems for specific regions or cities, such as the green index system of Beijing (Shao Quan et al., 2015), the evaluation index system of green city construction in Nanjing (Wang Wanjing et al., 2012), the green development evaluation indexes of four provinces and cities in the upper reaches of the Yangtze River (Geng Zhi, 2019), the urban green development evaluation index system of the Beijing-Tianjin-Hebei Region (Wang Guoli and Han Huihui, 2019), the evaluation index system of green economy development in Yunnan Province (Ma Xing, 2018), and the evaluation index systems of green development in Xinjiang (Xiao Chunmei and Zhu Pingping, 2018) and Sichuan (Li Xue, 2018). These evaluation index systems are mostly based on the actual situation of specific regions or cities and have certain practical value and regional characteristics. However, the statistical calibers and calculation methods vary greatly with different regions, and these systems are too locally limited to be helpful to the evaluation and comparison of all cities in China.

As "spire cities" in the urban system planning of China, national central cities play an extremely strategic role in leading green development. Currently, although the nine national central cities share similarities in the overall strategic positioning, they assume different tasks based on specific functional positioning and follow different tasks, directions and paths of green development due to their disparities in location, cultural background, resource factors, endowment conditions, and development level. Given this fact, this paper tries to construction a green development evaluation index system for the nine cities on the basis of analyzing their green development levels and constraints and took the pulse of their current green development status. This paper expects to provide a theoretical decision-making reference for designing the strategic layout to thoroughly implement the "Four-Pronged Comprehensive Strategy", turning the five development concepts into actions, and promoting the high-quality development of national central cities.

II Constructing the Green Development Evaluation Index System of National Central Cities

(I) Theoretical Connotation of the Green Development of National Central Cities

As core cities in the national urban system, national central cities are centers and hubs of science and technology, finance, industry, ecology, culture, transportation and information. They have centrality on the national scale and certain basic international characteristics at the regional level. They play guiding, radiating, assembling and distributing roles. Compared with ordinary cities, national central cities play stronger leading and demonstration roles in promoting urban-rural integration development, industrial transformation and upgrading, and harmonious coexistence between man and nature. Meanwhile, since they mostly have dense populations, abundant resources and huge traffic volumes, their ecological environments are highly sensitive issues and they stand at the very forefront of green development. Their green development not only affects their own sustainability, but also directly influences and guides the green development direction and trend throughout the country. As a developmental revolution, green development involves economic, social, ecological and other subsystems, each of which is both interconnected and independent. The economic system, social system and ecosystem are based on production, life and environment, respectively. Henceforth, the green development of a city is, in a sense, a collection of green production, green life and green ecology. The green production, life and ecology levels of a city, to some extent, indicate its green development performance.

Green production is the premise and foundation for green development of national central cities. Production is the premise and foundation for economic and social development. Without production, development would be impossible. Green production is characterized by green resources utilization, green development of driving forces, and green output. The green production level of a city should be measured by resource utilization efficiency, industrial structure, and green kinetic energy. Green life is an important symbol of green development of national central cities. Green urban life is a goal and an objective manifestation for the green development of a city. The income level, life expectancy, material supply, cultural products, service guarantee, and consumption concept of urban residents are, on the one hand, important goals of urban development, and on the other hand, they reflect the self-renewal and sustainable development abilities of a city. That's why they are important representation of urban green development. Green ecology is a requirement for green development of national central cities. Ecological resources are not only the basic conditions for human survival, but also important guarantee for better development quality. The history of human civilization is essentially a history of interactions between man and nature. Ecological protection and economic development complement each other and form a dialectical unity. The utilization and quality of natural resources such as air, soil and water profoundly reflects the scale and level of green development.

(II) Principles for Selection of Green Development Indicators for National Central Cities

The principle of index system construction can significantly influence the evaluation results (Chai Yanni et al., 2018; Gan Lin et al., 2018). Based on the connotation of urban green development and the functional positioning of national central cities, we draw on the results of green city evaluation researches by domestic and foreign scholars and follow the principles below to support indicators calculation, data collection, methodological comparison, and result interpretation.

The first principle is being both systemic and hierarchical. The green development of national central cities involves many fields, such as production, life and ecology. These fields restrict and influence each other. The indicators in each field are both independent and interrelated, together forming a unified holistic system. Therefore, the selection of evaluation indicators should take into account the independence of indicators and the integrity of evaluation system, so as to comprehensively reflect the green development level of national central cities.

The second principle is being both scientific and operable. The green development of national central cities is inherently regular. The selection of evaluation indicators should respect the internal rules of green development of national central cities, and the evaluation methods and indicators should be selected in scientific and normative manners. At the same time, the selection of indicators should fully consider the availability of data so as to be more operable in practical applications.

The third principle is being both comparable and forward-looking. Due to different statistical calibers, different cities and different indicators may yield different values. Thus, the selection of indicators should follow unified and comparable standards. In order to make the evaluation results usable for development, the index evaluation system should also be foresighted and forward-looking enough to guide future green development of national central cities.

(III) Construction of Green Development Index System for National Central Cities

Based on the green development connotation of national central cities and the principles for constructing an evaluation index system of urban green development, this paper approaches the topic from 15 dimensions in the City Competitiveness Index by the World Bank (2015), the Sustainable Cities Index by the Forum for the Future from the UK (2007), the green development index system and the target system for ecological civilization construction assessment by the National Development and Reform Commission of China (2016), the index system for construction of pilot demonstration cities in ecological civilization by the Ministry of Environmental Protection of China (Version 2013), and the green city evaluation indexes by the Standardization Administration of China (2017). With reference to existing research results, these studies select 32 indicators including per capita GDP, GDP growth rate, proportion of the tertiary industry and GDP energy consumption per unit in green production, green life and green ecology to construct a green development index system of national central cities, as shown in Table 1. The entropy method is adopted to determine the weight of each indicator.

Table 1 Evaluation Index System of Green Development of National Central Cities

	Secondary Indicators	Tertiary Indicators	Type	Weight
Green development indexes of national central cities	Green production index 0.4623	Per capita GDP (RMB 10,000/person)	+	0.0257
		GDP growth rate (%)	+	0.0158
		Proportion of the tertiary industry (%)	+	0.0670
		GDP energy consumption per unit (SCE/RMB 10,000)	–	0.0501
		Nitrogen oxide emissions per industry output of RMB 10,000 (kg)	–	0.0283
		Industrial fume (dust) emissions per industry output of RMB 10,000 (kg)	–	0.0281
		Industrial wastewater emissions per industry output of RMB 10,000 (ton)	+	0.0299
		Comprehensive utilization rate of general industrial solid waste (%)	+	0.0304
		R&D input intensity (%)	+	0.0556
		Number of invention patent ownership per 10,000 persons (piece)	+	0.0554
		Number of secondary school and college students per 10,000 persons (person)	+	0.0513
		Urban registered unemployment rate (%)	–	0.0248
	Green life index 0.2840	Per capita disposable income of urban residents (RMB)	+	0.0390
		Average life expectancy of residents (year)	+	0.0317
		Population density (persons per square kilometer)	–	0.0176
		Per capita daily living water consumption (L)	–	0.0276

Continued

	Secondary Indicators	Tertiary Indicators	Type	Weight
Green development indexes of national central cities	Green life index 0.2840	Water supply penetration rate (%)	+	0.0169
		Gas penetration rate (%)	+	0.0283
		Sewage treatment rate (%)	+	0.0284
		Harmless treatment rate of domestic garbage (%)	+	0.0172
		Urban natural gas utilization rate (%)	+	0.0159
		Per capita domestic sewage discharge (ton)	–	0.0203
		Per capita living nitrogen oxide emissions (kg)	–	0.0261
		Per capita living dust emissions (kg)	–	0.0149
	Green ecology index 0.2536	Per capita road area (square meter)	+	0.0258
		Per capita park green area (square meter)	+	0.0313
		Green coverage of built-up areas (%)	+	0.0295
		Greening rate of built-up areas (%)	+	0.0431
		Air quality comprehensive index	–	0.0236
		Excellent air quality as a percentage (%)	+	0.0280
		Mean urban noise (decibel)	–	0.0391
		Mean road traffic noise in daytime (Decibel)	–	0.0333

Based on available statistical yearbooks and statistical communiqué of the nine national central cities on national economic and social development in 2018, the raw data of 32 indicators for the national central cities in 2017 are processed with the extreme value method, combined with the weight of each indicator to calculate the overall green development score of each national central city, as shown in Table 2. The nine national central cities are ranked for green development performance according to the score of each indicator.

Table 2 Measurement Results of the Green Development of Nine National Central Cities in 2017

	Green Production Index	Ranking	Green Life Index	Ranking	Green Ecology Index	Ranking	Green Development Index	Ranking
Beijing	0.3748	1	0.2404	1	0.1710	2	0.7862	1
Guangzhou	0.2363	3	0.1617	5	0.1513	3	0.5493	2
Shanghai	0.2076	4	0.2291	2	0.0729	7	0.5096	3
Wuhan	0.1954	5	0.1799	3	0.0752	6	0.4506	4
Xi'an	0.2618	2	0.1068	9	0.0612	8	0.4298	5
Tianjin	0.1311	8	0.1749	4	0.1076	5	0.4135	6
Chengdu	0.1760	6	0.1171	8	0.1179	4	0.4109	7
Chongqing	0.0445	9	0.1517	6	0.1735	1	0.3698	8
Zhengzhou	0.1453	7	0.1327	7	0.0541	9	0.3321	9

III Multidimensional Analysis of the Green Development of National Central Cities

The green development levels of the nine national central cities vary due to the differences in geographical location, natural environment, population distribution, energy reserves, economic base, new technology development and application, and policy support.

In terms of the green production index (see Figure 1), Beijing was ranked first among the nine national central cities with 0.3748, while Chongqing was ranked last with 0.0445. The average green production index of the nine national central cities was 0.1970. Beijing, Xi'an, Guangzhou and Shanghai scored above the average, more than the average score, while Wuhan, Chengdu, Zhengzhou, Tianjin and Chongqing scored below it. The nine cities showed great differences in green production. Numerically, Beijing's green production level was almost twice the average level, while Chongqing's was only a little more than a quarter of the average. Further analysis showed that Chongqing, Tianjin and Zhengzhou, which had relatively low green production levels, were restricted by inadequate driving forces in the green industry. In 2017, the numbers of invention patents per 10,000 persons in Chongqing and Zhengzhou were 9.1 and 12.9, respectively, while the number in Beijing in the same year was 111.2. In terms of the R&D input intensity, Zhengzhou invested only RMB 15.87 billion in scientific research and experimental development, with an R&D input intensity rate of only 1.74%, compared to RMB 159.53 billion in Beijing, which was 10 times that in Zhengzhou, and 5.64% of an R&D input intensity rate in Beijing, which was more than three times that in Zhengzhou, respectively.

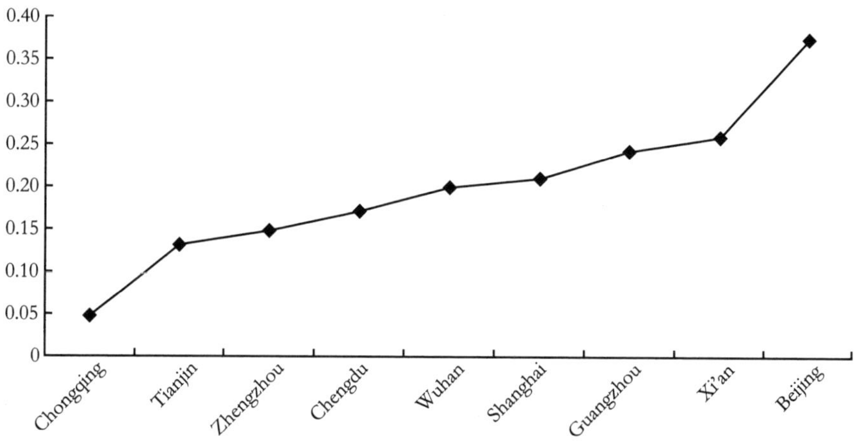

Figure 1 Green Production Indexes of National Central Cities in 2017

In terms of the green life index (see Figure 2), the ranking of the nine national central cities was Beijing, Shanghai, Wuhan, Guangzhou, Tianjin, Guangzhou, Chongqing, Zhengzhou, Chengdu and Xi'an, whose green production indexes were 0.2404, 0.2291, 0.1799, 0.1749, 0.1617, 0.1517, 0.1327, 0.1171 and 0.1068, respectively. Compared to the case of green production index, they were less different in the green life index. The main reasons for the differences in the green life level were resource utilization method and pollutant discharge. The per capita living nitrogen oxide emissions in Xi'an and Zhengzhou were 686 g and 640 g in 2017, respectively, which were almost twice those in Beijing.

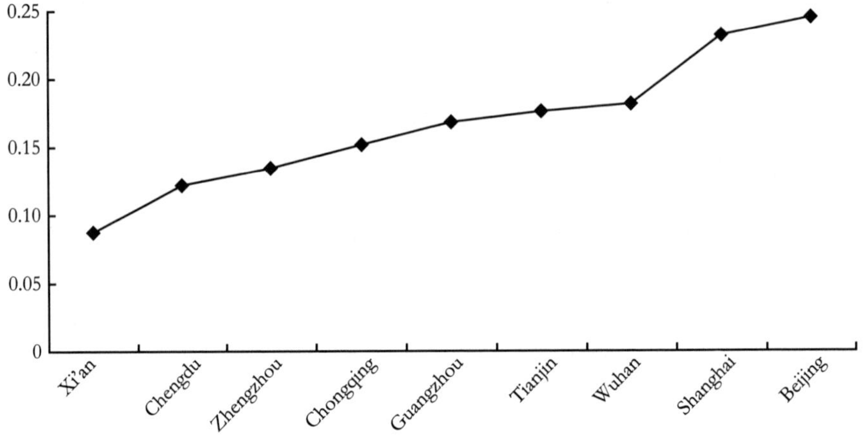

Figure 2 Green Life Indexes of National Central Cities in 2017

In terms of the green ecology index (see Figure 3), Chongqing was the champion among the nine national central cities with 0.1710, followed by Beijing with 0.1513, while on the other end of the spectrum were Zhengzhou and Xi'an, with 0.0541 and 0.0612 respectively. Generally speaking, the nine national central cities were most different in the green ecology index. Such regional differences were attributed to, on the one hand, geographical location and natural conditions, and on the one hand, the green production and living conditions. Chongqing, located in the southwest of China and the upper reaches of the Yangtze River, has a subtropical monsoon humid climate, abundant natural resources and a good ecological foundation. That's why it got a relatively high green ecology index, while Beijing credited its high score to a series of new green development policies that have been implemented in recent years.

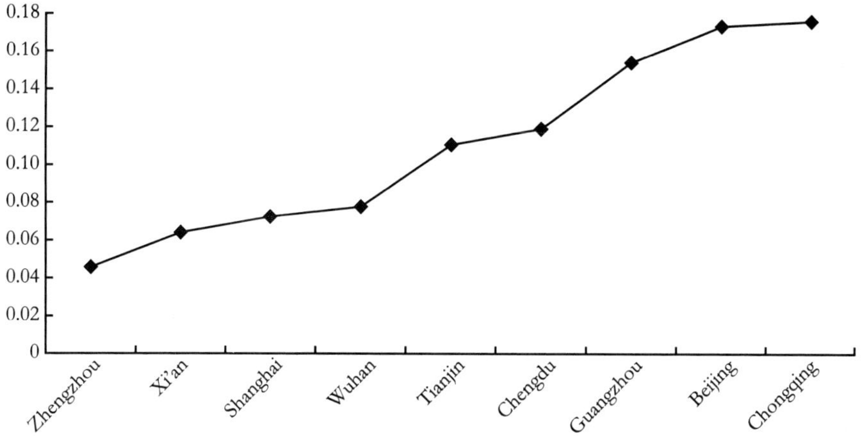

Figure 3　Green Ecology Indexes of National Central Cities in 2017

In terms the green development index (see Figure 4), Beijing occupied the first place among the nine national central cities with 0.7862, 0.2369 higher than the score of the runner-up, Guangzhou. They were followed by Shanghai, Wuhan, Xi'an, Tianjin, Chengdu, Chongqing and Zhengzhou from top to bottom. By comparing the green development levels of the nine national central cities, we found that Beijing, as the capital city, was ranked first in terms of the green production level and the green life level, although it came off second to Chongqing in the green ecology level. These results also suggested that introducing more green development policies is an important means to promote the green development of a city under the context of economic and social transformation. In fact, when it comes to green development, the "invisible hand" of the market is by no means "the hand of God". Confronted with the growth paradigm of materialism, the profit-oriented technical rationality, the environmental differentiation of regional development and the materialism steered consumption concept during the economic and social transformation and development stage, the market mechanism is not able to totally curb the scale of macro-economy and excessive consumption of natural resources although it can function naturally well on allocation of natural ecological resources. The intangible benefits of green waters and mountains, the intangible costs of environmental pollution, and the integrity, publicity and externalities of resources and environment secure the presence of the government in promoting green development.

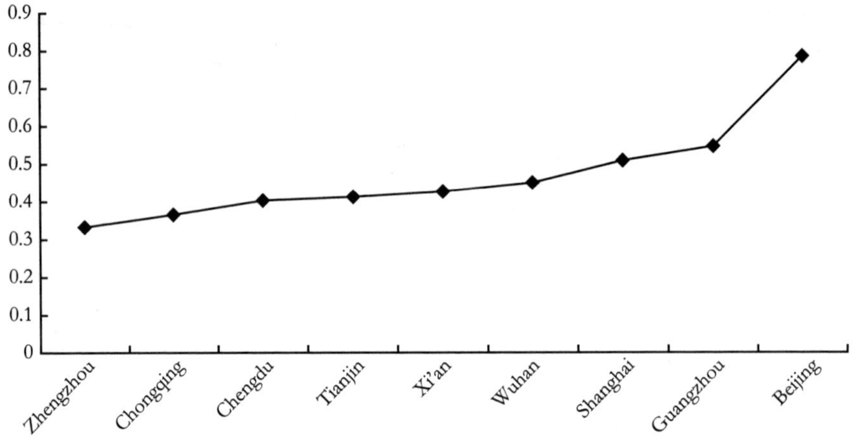

Figure 4 Green Development Indexes of National Central Cities in 2017

IV Paths for Green Development of National Central Cities

The multidimensional measurements of the green development of national central cities showed that they vary significantly for the time being. Such variations can be explained by the differences in renewal of green development concept, provision of green development policies, and cultivation of driving forces for green development. Therefore, the national central cities should promote green development by renewing their green development concept, optimizing the provision of green development policies, and cultivating new driving forces for green development.

First, remain conceptually steered. As General Secretary Xi Jinping put it, mankind has created unprecedented material wealth as well as irreparable ecological trauma since the industrial civilization era came. As the main contradiction in society is between people's growing needs for a better life and the inadequate and unbalanced development, people's cry for a beautiful ecological environment has become an important aspect of this contradiction. People are eager to see the quality of ecological environment improved more quickly, especially one with fresh air, clear water and clean environment. The ecological civilization construction in China has entered a critical, crucial and window period. Local governments of central cities around the world must firmly establish the green development concept that "protecting the ecological environment is equal to protecting productivity and improving the ecological environment to developing the productivity" as the rule. Firstly, deepen the reform of environmental protection management system and mechanism. Establish and improve a responsibility system that clearly defines powers and responsibilities and division of labor among different government departments, and an integrated ecological environmental governance and protection mechanism across sectors, industries and fields. Seize the opportunity of institutional reform launched by the Party and the state to accelerate the optimization of environmental protection organization systems in national central cities, and combine resource management, environmental governance and ecological protection as a whole under unified management and deployment. Secondly, reform the government performance evaluation mechanism. Make environmental governance and ecological protection important indicators for government performance assessment; coordinate departmental assessment, public evaluation, and social evaluation; adopt differentiated assessment mechanisms for different regions; highlight the dominant role of "green achievements" in selecting and employing talents, appointing cadres, and making promotion decisions. Thirdly, promote the construction of a green development responsibility supervision mechanism. Considering the backward, public and long-term nature of ecological environment construction, establish an off-office auditing and lifelong accountability system for cadres in terms of green development in order to ensure that they perform their duties under the accountability system. Supervise and restrict exercise of power, and further standardize and strengthen the environmental decision-making behavior of governments in national central cities. At the same time, broadly guide the public to establish a green life concept, advocate green consumption concepts in the whole community, and develop modest, scientific, low-carbon, environmentally friendly, and recyclable green consumption. Establish a sound eco-ethic education system; strengthen education on environmental science; further disseminate ecological science knowledge; help people develop conservation, low-carbon, environmental protection and ecological awareness; plant green life concept in people's minds; popularize green lifestyles. Incorporate environmental science education into the national education system; help individuals develop the concept that they are responsible for the environment; integrate the green and environmental protection concept with the construction of civic morality and spiritual civilization; enhance the public consciousness, enthusiasm, responsibility and sense of mission about maintaining the ecological environment; create a dynamic and positive cultural atmosphere in which citizens develop green lifestyles and behaviors.

Next, strictly follow policy guidance. To promote green development, national central cities should unswervingly carry out supply-side structural reforms and follow the guidance of fiscal and taxation, financial, monetary and industrial policies. Combine policy optimization with market guidance to promote overcapacity cut, cost reduction, and addressing of shortcomings. National central cities in different regions and under different stages should clearly define the focus and objectives of policy regulation and guide green economic and social development by addressing shortcomings and providing effective policies. Firstly, choose reasonable policy tools to support urban green development. Make full use of price, taxation and subsidy policy tools; guide and motivate enterprises to optimize their production methods and the public to improve their lifestyles; reduce energy consumption and pollution emissions; improve resources utilization efficiency. National central cities should explore the adoption of differentiated water, electricity, gas, and heat pricing policies, rationally share energy consumption costs, and convert energy conservation awareness into behaviors. They should also implement financial subsidy policies for enterprises engaged in energy conservation and emission reduction to encourage them to prioritise technological innovation, transformation and upgrading; they should significantly increase the percentages of renewable and clean energy as well as energy-saving and environmentally friendly products, reduce or limit the circulation and supply of polluting and unsafe products and non-clean energy in the market, encourage enterprises to embark on the green development path, accelerate green transformation, and develop green production. Secondly, continuously improve green procurement. National and local governments should erect and constantly improve laws and regulations, and encourage government agencies at all levels, enterprises, institutions and NGOs to purchase environmentally-certified products and services. Government finance may be leveraged to guide and support, in various forms and through different means, enterprises and residents to use energy-saving and environmentally-friendly products, and to reward enterprises that provide environmentally-certified products and services. Governments should actively guide and rationally use social capital in public environmental projects, while managing, using, and liquidating social capital well. Local governments may purchase environmental protection services and use the in-house facilities of large enterprises to treat urban wastewater and garbage. They should also encourage, with flexible management methods, private enterprises to feed green services to the community and increase the cash flow and competitiveness of green investment projects. They should use tax, interest, debt and fee oriented administrative means to increase enterprises' proceeds from green production or increase the costs of pollution. They should foster an open and transparent government procurement market supported by institutional system and create a fair and just business environment. Thirdly, formulate a green financial policy. Leverage financial support by providing loan interest subsidies or risk compensation; encourage social capital to flow spontaneously to environmental projects; introduce innovative green financial instruments; develop new financial instruments such as green bonds, green loans, green insurance, and green funds; shape a green financial system. Fourthly, strengthen the provision of basic systems. Improve the carbon emission trading market, and promote the construction of institutional system, regulatory system, reporting system, distribution system in this market phase by phase and step by step; enhance the basic capability of upholding the consistency of industry standards and trading mechanisms, the effectiveness of policies, regulations and system design, and the transparency of quota allocation and information disclosure; give full play to the role of the carbon market in reducing emissions of greenhouse gases; make concerted efforts to reduce the cost of emissions reduction in the community.

Third, rely on scientific and technological support. To promote green development, national central cities must firmly exploit technological innovation, establish and improve the technology support system for urban green development, push the transition to urban green development under the assistance of market-oriented technologies, use core technologies to promote urban green revolution, try to considerably improve the quality and efficiency of urban green development through information and intelligent technologies, and provide scientific basis and technical support for green development. Firstly, establish a market-oriented green technology innovation system. Take into account economic, social and ecological benefits, and use an effective market mechanism to guide the development of low-carbon and green technologies; continue to strengthen the R&D of industrial technologies that support energy-saving, environmentally-friendly, clean, low-carbon and efficient production. Combine economic benefits with ecological benefits; promote the application of efficient and energy-saving technologies in national central cities; apply green concept, green technologies and green processes to the production technology revolution and the industrial transformation and upgrading; connect traditional industries with green technologies; promote the development of green industries while improving the green development level of traditional industries. In particular, national central cities with relatively low green development levels should allow for regional development characteristics, focus on industrial structure transformation and upgrading, increase investments in scientific research, optimize scientific research input methods, promote the upgrading of traditional industries, develop new business types in modern emerging industries, and increase the green development quality of industries. Secondly, promote the systematic integration of the green technology support system. As a systematic project, the green development of national central cities requires not only changes in production methods, management methods and lifestyles, but also knowledge innovation, technological changes and product upgrades. To promote the R&D, application and promotion of green technologies, national central cities should build a systematic and integrated green technology support system. They must pay close attention to the basic and cutting-edge green technologies in the world, build a high-standard technological support system for green development from a high starting point, gather talents, resources, information, products and other factors, combine R&D subjects such as enterprises, universities and scientific research institutions, and connect the processes of R&D, production, sales, and service to form a systematic and integrated technology innovation support system for green development. Thirdly, create a green core technology system that leads industrial development based on local conditions. Different industrial development foundations exist in national central cities. They should learn from each other in promoting green technology revolution. At the same time, they should allow for local realities and characteristics of regional development, focus on the key constraints and critical conflicts that restrict local green development, and continue to build a green core technology system that is aimed to solve problems and is able to lead the transformation of industrial development. National central cities with relatively low green development levels should identify key technical breakthroughs to make in different phases, attach importance to the R&D and application of technologies in new energies, new materials and high-end equipment, and transform traditional industries with high energy consumption, high inputs and high pollution. At the same time, they should enrich talent and technology reserves to inject endless impetus and inspiration to technological innovation that fuels green development. National central cities with relatively high green development levels should focus on the development and application of cutting-edge, key and core technologies, try to occupy the science and technology frontier in the world, and serve national major strategies.

References:

[1] Chen Chundi, Rong Bingling, and Deng Hongbing. "Comprehensive Assessment System of Urban Green Spaces in the European Union" [J]. *Chinese Landscape Architecture*, 2009, 25 (03): 66-69.

[2] Shao Quan, Xiao Yang, and Liu Na. "Study on the Construction and Evaluation of Green Beijing Index System" [J]. *Ecological Economy*, 2015, 31 (06): 92-94+102.

[3] Wang Wanjing, Zhao Rongqin, Chuai Xiaowei, and Gao Shan. "Study on the Green City Construction Evaluation Index System for Nanjing" [J]. *Areal Research and Development*, 2012, 31 (02): 62-66.

[4] Geng Zhi. "Analysis on Green Development Level and Influencing Factors of Four Provinces in the Upper Reaches of the Yangtze River" [J]. *Journal of Wuhan Engineering Institute*, 2019, 31 (01): 17-20+32.

[5] Wang Guoli and Han Huihui. "Regional Difference Analysis of Urban Green Development Level in Beijing-Tianjin-Hebei Region" [J]. *Journal of Liaoning Normal University (Natural Science Edition)*, 2019, 42 (01): 106-111.

[6] Ma Xing. "Study on the Evaluation Index System of Green Economic Development in Yunnan Province" [J]. *Journal of Southwest University for Nationalities (Humanities and Social Sciences Edition)*, 2018, 39 (12): 128-136.

[7] Xiao Chunmei and Zhu Pingping. "Comprehensive Evaluation and Countermeasure Study of Green Development Level in Xinjiang" [J]. *Journal of Shihezi University (Philosophy and Social Science)*, 2018, 32 (03): 41-49.

[8] Li Xue. “Study on the Evaluation of Green Development Level and Its Spatial and Temporal Differentiation in Sichuan Province” [D]. *Sichuan Normal University*, 2018.

[9] Chai Yanni, Wei Guanjun, Hou Wei, Feng Zhixian, and Zhai Liang. “Multi-scale Eco-environmental Quality Evaluation Method from a Spatial Perspective” [J]. *Chinese Journal of Ecology*, 2018, 37 (02): 596-604.

B.19

Inspiration from International Data Strategies under the Context of National Central City Construction

Zhang Bing[*]

Abstract: In the information age, city data is an important resource, capital and asset of a city. Fully apply city data in policy decision-making, management and innovation can improve the competitiveness and achieve sustainable development of a city. This paper analyzes an international model of city data application, the City Data Strategy of London, and draws inspiration from it to put forward six suggestions for the data application of national central cities: giving full play to the leading role of government in the central cities, establishing a shared city data platform, developing a dynamic data market, building an effective data governance system, protecting citizens' data privacy, and promoting collaborative innovation based on city data.

Keywords: national central cities; city data of London; international inspiration

In February 2010, the former Ministry of Construction first proposed the construction of national central cities in the *National Urban System Plan (2010-2020)*. By 2019, nine national central cities have been designated: Beijing, Tianjin, Shanghai, Chongqing, Guangzhou, Chengdu, Wuhan, Zhengzhou and Xi'an. The national central cities represent the level and quality of urban development in

* [UK] Zhang Bing, female, Ph.D. from Heriot-Watt University, UK, Research Fellow of China (Henan) Innovation Development Institute of Huanghe S&T University, whose research orientation is finance and urban economy.

the country. They are and will be benchmarks in implementing new development concepts. The report of the 19th National Congress proposed the construction of a "smart society" and digital China. The Chinese government will continue to empower cities by taking advantage of the Internet, information technology, big data, and artificial intelligence. In the new era, city data is an important resource, capital and asset of a city. It can be fully used to make policy decisions, develop data management, carry out data-driven innovation, improve the quality of government management and public services, create new business opportunities, and improve the living quality of urban residents. Especially in the process of national central city construction, these central cities can lead, demonstrate and radiate to other cities in the country by embracing innovative development concepts, effectively using city data to lead data-driven innovation, realize the social, economic and environmental benefits of city data.

I Economic and Social Value of City Data

1 Definition and Classification of City Data

City data refers to a large amount of dynamic and static data generated by subjects and objects including various urban facilities, organizations and individuals using the new generation of information technology to be collected by city governments, institutions, enterprises and individuals (Pan et al., 2016). City data comes in many forms, including those from government public service departments and from private organizations, such as utilities, infrastructure providers, retailers, and land developers. Depending on source and purpose, city data can be classified as open data, private data, business data, sensor collected data and citizen sourced data. Open data is non-private and non-confidential data from both public and private sectors, and it can be provided without any restrictions, such as open map data. Private data is restricted and/or licensed data, as well as current privately held data. Business data is licensed data, including data license and charging data, such as consumer data about urban residents. Sensor collected data is the data collected by sensors, actuators and other devices owned by public and private sectors as well as citizens, such as urban noctilucent data. Citizen sourced data is the data generated by citizens using digital technology and social media data, such as cell phone data.

2 Mechanism for City Data to Deliver Economic and Social Value

City data can be fully used to improve urban governance, integrate urban resources, improve the efficiency of resource allocation, increase the science and technology of a city, promote urban industrial transformation and upgrading, and improve people's quality of life. The release of city data calls for an innovative ecosystem to create innovative products and services, one that include governments, companies and some non-profit organizations. Data-driven innovation is innovation based on published data, including innovative products and services. Such innovation creates social and economic value and has positive economic and social influences (Jetzek et al., 2014). Figure 1 presents the three stages of a data innovation ecosystem, from data collection to data processing, development of products and services, and the generation of economic and social value. The first stage focuses on data quality and availability. If the data is usable, the city data will be used to develop products and services in the second stage. The second stage focuses on how these data sources are converted to innovative services and generate products and services through data-driven innovation (Schaffers et al., 2011). The third stage promotes and commercializes the products and services generated during the second stage, and assesses their economic and social effects. In this data ecosystem, cities are the source of data while citizens are the end users of the ultimate innovative products and services (Alberto et al., 2017).

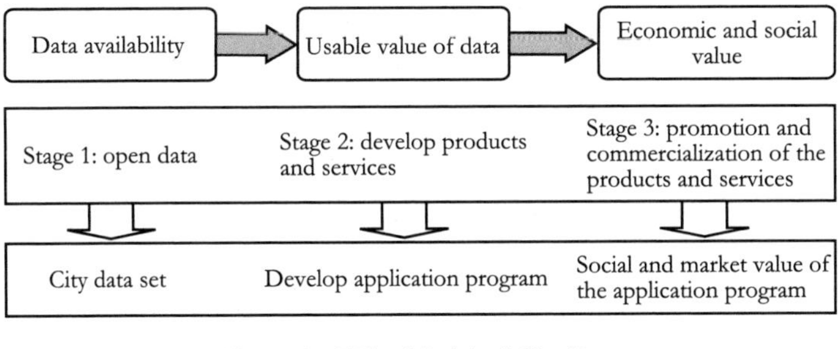

Figure 1 Value Model of City Data

Source: A Model of the Analysis of Data-Driven Innovation and Value Generation in Smart Cities' Ecosystems (Alberto et al., 2017) Updated by the Author Based on Translation.

3 Key Elements in the Application Process of City Data

The following six key elements should be noted in the application of city data. 1) Data quality management. The prerequisite for city data application is the availability of high-quality city data. Some city data comes from different data collection devices, and huge differences may result during the collection process. Another source is irregular database or inaccurate data (Ben Sta, 2017). Thus, to ensure the success of urban development projects, the quality of existing data should be taken into account and approaches to improve data quality should be identified. 2) Integration of data from different sources. Different types of city data may come from different city resources. What matters is to integrate them to provide high-level and high-quality information (Ruijer et al., 2017). Different organizations use different data structures, making data integration and standardization in different domains one of the most pressing issues when city data is used. 3) Knowledge about the needs of citizens, urban tourists and employees. Data used to upgrade public services should be citizen-driven rather than information-driven. Identifying the most important and valuable information for citizens, tourists and employees is critical in data-based urban development projects, and identifying the information transmitted by citizens is directly related to the value and attractiveness of public services (Afzalan et al., 2017). 4) Protection of data privacy. Survey showed that citizens were willing to accept new products and services generated on the basis of data analysis, but it also clearly indicated that the prerequisite for using their data should be privacy protection. Examining and addressing data privacy issues are critical to urban development projects based on city data. 5) Visualization of geographic information. Another key element in the use of city data is using geographic information systems (GIS) to achieve information visualization and effective transmission, such as visualized information about urban buildings and different bus lines. The visualized information should be clear and substantial (Aina, 2017). 6) Design of city data service projects. Make full use of city data to create value and provide it for citizens and tourists in the form of products and services, and increase the efficiency of city operations. This requires an effective mechanism for collaboration between governments, research institutions and citizens (Cicirelli et al., 2017). The six key elements mentioned above are closely related and complement each other.

II International Experience in City Data Strategy-A Case Study of London

London sets a model in city data application in the UK. It is committed to encouraging public participation to solve city problems by implementing strategies such as open data. The open data strategy is also conducive to the innovative applications of data and helps fully exploit the added economic value of city data. The *2013 Smart London Plan* focused on the openness of open data and the use of data to plan and operate the city. This document clearly noted that data is the backbone of urban planning and operations. Data dashboard and other digital tools are used in London to encourage the public and developers to participate in data development and applications. *Toward a Smarter London through Concerted Efforts*, a 2018 roadmap to build London into a smart city, illustrated London's plan on better digital services, open data, connectivity, digital inclusion, network security, and data-driven innovation. In order to maximize the potential of city data in different sectors and enhance its value, the government of London formulated the *City Data Strategy* in 2016, with the vision of building the most dynamic and productive city data market in the world. City data will be seen as part of infrastructure in London to save money, foster innovation and drive economic growth, so that London will be globally renowned for its data influence.

1 The *2016 City Data Strategy* for London

The government of London formulated the *2016 City Data Strategy* to support the initiatives and multifaceted urban policies of the City Hall. In the field of urban assets management, data is used to develop and manage infrastructures in the city more efficiently. In terms of energy, the *London Energy Plan* describes the modeling of complex data from a series of sources to better understand the energy needs and supply pattern of the city and achieve the goal of more efficient energy use. By placing city data and the London Datastore at the heart of smart city development, coordinated urban platform development methodology and city data architecture can be framed to integrate data streams and optimize urban services. For city-level collaborative strategic decision-making, data and computational science expertise across business and academia can be combined to better aid in urban policy formulation and strategic development, as well as solve problems in complex urban systems. To improve the quality of public services, the sharing and analysis of city data can be applied in different links from integrating health and social care services to optimizing routes in waste management to become a key element that can help effectively manage urban technology infrastructures, improve service efficiency and save costs. This strategic plan includes six priorities: developing a data market in London, organizing city data to expand its influence, fully understanding the value of city data, aiding public acceptance, establishing a positive and effective governance system, and mapping a technical route (Larissa, 2015). The specific messages are as follows.

(1) Develop A Data Market in London

Build and operate an efficient city data market and create support tools to fully tap the value of city data. This requires the city to provide data in order to deliver better urban services and better urban infrastructures and serve economic development. It is also about open innovation that can change organizational culture, improve analytical capability, and encourage participation and performance of different parties. Better city data can bring about better urban services and better urban policies, and can propel innovation. To this end, the government of London needs to consider building data-based business and financial models, formulating relevant policies and data licensing agreements, and deploying the most advanced data management strategy to lay the foundation for long-term, wide applications of data. The government of London will build a strong value-oriented partner network to reduce the complexity and costs associated with data-driven infrastructure development, ensure the quality of data in London, and create new data-driven services and smart infrastructures.

(2) Organize City Data to Expand Its Influence

To lend stronger support in public service decision-making, infrastructure investment decision-making, and broader innovation, city data should be better organized for more systematic and rigorous use in the management of urban services and assets. City data, when well organized, can also contribute more effectively to the building of a true "city as a platform" approach and new business models. The government of London has established the London Datastore based on the Internet of Things and cloud computing, making data a core to the infrastructures in the city. As shown in Figure 2, the London

Datastore, which was started in 2010, is one of the earliest platforms to provide open and accessible public data in the world. It now has 827 data sets that cover eight fields including economy, transportation, environment, security and medical care, helping to solve urban challenges and improve public services. The second-generation London Datastore was a partnered project with Barcelona and other cities that was commenced from 2013 as part of the iCity Program of the EU that cost EUR 5.2 million. The goal was to build "a city platform" to test public and private data acquired, captured and stored by millions of sensors from across the capital. London provides a city data roadmap that details the architectural features of existing city data, including its sources, quantity, types, time factor and sensitivity to determine the processes and resources needed for managing the city data supply chain. To secure the leading position of London in the data-driven world, more investments have been made in the data infrastructures operating in the city. During this process, data integration in the urban environment and consistency of standards for presenting city data are particularly important. Thus, London provides "core reference data" to support the integration of data from different sources. It also discloses methods for integrating design and service delivery in city data-driven infrastructures in order to ensure consistency of data standards.

Figure 2 A Screenshot of London Datastore

Source: the website of Greater London Authority, accessed on June 27, 2019

Website: https://data. london.*gov.uk*

(3)Fully recognize the value of city data

To measure the value of city data, one must take into account the social, environmental, economic, and financial sectors. The way is to build better value-based measurement method and pricing system to help all partners correctly recognize the value of data and trade in the city data market. So far little has been known about the uses of data, both in the private sector and in the public sector. The public sector fails to regard data as a value-added asset and has limited understanding of sharing data and open data and the ensuing value generation potential. There is hence a need for cultural and organizational changes. One of the reform proposals that have been put into actions is the London infrastructure map application, which is targeted to the Mayor's Infrastructure Delivery Committee, with data from a range of public utility companies and organizations outside the public sector. Actions to be taken include launching deep data mining to boost the public services and the construction of smart city in London, conducting academic researches and developing new products to improve the city, enterprises and living quality of residents in the city and realize the value of data. Necessary licensing agreements should be prepared for open and business data to ensure that London maximizes and recycles the potential of each city data set.

(4) Enhance trust in city data

Only by fully addressing the security, privacy and trust issues associated with personal data, will the next era of data use and the possibilities of resulting service creation become realities. Once the public fully understand how to use their personal data to create economic, social and personal value, data supply will increase and the public's acceptance of data services will be ultimately enhanced. The public is an important part of the city data market and the source of a large portion of city data in London. Basically, the data primarily come from their daily activities with services, social media, mobile devices, vehicles and smart cards. In the future, smart homes, other smart city services, new autonomous technologies, and artificial intelligence will increase the amount of personal data generated. Working with the personal data and trust network at Digital Catapult can promote responsible personal data innovation. A consumer data committee may be founded to enable Londoners to participate in discussions on how to publish and use their data in the city data market. Partnerships with a range of personal data protection and consumer groups can ensure that Londoners better understand laws about personal privacy. It is necessary to learn about the privacy needs concerning personal data, develop data management strategies for data infrastructures in the city, ensure data integrity and comply with national, European and international data protection regulations. A data ethics committee needs to be established to address legal and ethical challenges in order to balance privacy, data security, and public interest (Larissa, 2015).

(5) Establish an active and effective data governance system

Efforts should be made to actively govern the city data market in London so as to address the challenges imposed on the *City Data Strategy,* anticipate and leverage opportunities brought about by the strategy. Good governance will help the public better understand regulatory and legal issues, promote data sharing and maximize public interest, while limiting negative effects. Since the implementation of the open data strategy, the city data market in London has been increasingly complex. The governance system should not only attach importance to data quality and data release, but also pay attention to the interoperability and coordination of data operations. The establishment of a city data committee in London will significantly strengthen the governance of city data and set the strategic direction for the London Data Innovation Center. Set up a "city data exchange" department in the London Datastore to encourage all partners in the city data market to develop their data requirements, identify the expected data demand and data uses, and address outstanding issues concerning data sharing and coordination, data value measurement, and data monetization. The Data Committee of the City of London Corporation should be required to put forward a range of data supply requirements covering supply contracts in the public sector and business models in the private sector lest valuable data should be ignored. The City Data Committee should prompt various government departments in London (such as the Department of Taxation and the Department of Work and Pensions) to acquire data widely and overcome obstacles to further data sharing opportunities inside and outside departments and to the value creation of data. Convene a group within the City Data Committee to provide professional guidance for informed individual decisions concerning data publishing and data sharing.

(6) Data technical roadmap

Effectively coordinate the data infrastructures in the city based on the technical roadmap. This is a key strategy for London to integrate data, accomplish digital innovation, provide true public service opportunities in the 21st century, and increase its economic competitiveness. At the heart of this strategy are advanced methods for organizations and individuals to share and use data. London needs to improve its data infrastructures by taking a series of initiatives as follows. They include initiatives about sharing data: sharing information and functions with city data partners (citizens, city managers, and other third parties) through various tools; building the London Super Cloud (a city-wide cloud-based digital infrastructure) to lay the foundation for a range of digital innovation applications in public services and broader services. Here are the initiatives about understanding data: effectively improving processing and analysis capabilities and allowing cities or citizens to optimize and utilize data and information. There are also initiatives about storing data: the stored data should be clearly categorized to make searching and access from a single point easier. Finally, there are initiatives about advanced analysis: providing appropriate software, hardware, and storage capabilities to help data scientists process unstructured big data technologies (Larissa, 2015). In 2018, London set up the Data Analysis and Planning Office and introduced a new data sharing initiative to the City Hall and public service departments to facilitate data sharing and collaboration. This initiative emphasized partnerships with the public and technology sectors in creating a new city data innovation center to develop data application paradigms.

2 The Economic and Social Value of Data Policy in London

The data use practice by the Transport for London (TFL) is one successful example of the *City Data Strategy* in London. The TFL released open data and created a virtuous cycle to improve traffic quality by providing passengers with real-time information that can be embedded into applications. So far, the TFL has maintained more than 80 data sources covering operational and corporate information and all modes of transportation. Approximately 75% of the data is available through API; 42% of Londoners use the TFL data-driven applications; 83% of Londoners use their website. The TFL has established significant data partnerships with major application developers and digital partners and owns over 12,000 registered developers.

The economic benefits of the TFL data can be divided into direct economic benefits and broad economic benefits. The former include increased employment rates, more jobs and new business units. In 2016, the number of employees in the digital sector in London increased by 13%, and it was expected that the open data business of the TFL would directly create 500 new jobs or so. Moreover, 230 indirect job opportunities were created in the supply chain and broader economic fields. Many companies that use and reuse the TFL data have created some new businesses to introduce a range of new applications and services to market. Many of these companies are based in London, and conservative estimates showed that the total added value of broader supply chain and consumer spending by these companies amounted to £14 million per year. As for the broad economic benefits, London benefited from new development opportunities as well as innovation encouragement and facilitation stimulated by the open data of the TFL (Deloitte, 2017). The TFL open data saves times for passengers and allows passengers to better plan their trips through the applications. The applications also help them adjust routes based on new information, offer more certainty when they have to transfer to different vehicles, and help them avoid traffic congestion and save time. In all the public transport applications, the economic benefits created by saving time costs were measured between £70 million and £90 million. They also offer more certainty about transfer to different modes of transport, helping passengers avoid traffic congestion and save time (Deloitte, 2017).

The direct and indirect social and environmental benefits for passengers using the TFL open data include increased passenger satisfaction with trips and a healthier lifestyle. The open data helps to integrate the first mile with the last one, advocates the use of public transportation, and encourages healthier, greener ways of getting around. The number of travelers who choose walking as the main mode of transportation has increased by 13% since 2007.

III Thoughts and Suggestions on the Inspiration from Data Strategies of International Metropolises to National Central City Construction

In the process of urban construction, London is committed to promoting strategies like city data to boost innovative applications of data, solve urban development problems, fully exploit the economic and social values of government public data, and drive sustainable development of the city. The city data strategy promotes economic growth mainly by creating an ecosystem of open database applications to lay the foundation for the open data industry, promoting innovative applications of data, and fully exploiting the added economic value of city data. Enterprises can use open data resources associated with urban operations to provide open data services and products. The city data strategy facilitates urban governance by better sharing information across local authorities based on consistent data standards, providing greater transparency and better information sharing opportunities, providing analytical tools and utilizing urban networks to expand city data innovation, and improving services in key sectors such as transportation and public security to better meet the needs of citizens and businesses. The central city construction in China should be inspired by certain practices in London and make full use of city data to improve competitiveness and achieve sustainable development of central cities.

1 Insist on the Leading Role of Central City Governments

At the national level, the British government released *Digital Britain* in 2009 and officially published the *Digital Britain Strategy* in 2017. At the city level, the City Hall of London released the *Smart London Plan* in 2013, the *City Data Strategy of London* in 2016, and the *Toward a Smarter London through Concerted Efforts* in 2018. All of these initiatives are committed to urban infrastructure construction, universal digital applications, and sharing and innovative development and utilization of open data. They constitute a series of government-led city data policies that are designed to promote collection, integration, storage, sharing and development of city data. At the national level, China also attaches great importance to data development and utilization. The *Outline of the Thirteenth Five-Year Plan for National Economic and Social Development of the People's Republic of China*, which was formulated in 2016, states that big data is a basic strategic resource and that actions should be taken to fully promote big data development. In the process of national central city construction, governments should pay attention to the value of city data, formulate data policies suitable for the development of central cities, make city data an important resource, capital and asset for cities and an element of urban innovation and development, develop a city data strategy, and set up a data analysis department to fully dig the added value of city data.

2 Establish a Shared City Data Platform

The London Datastore offers 827 data sets covering eight economic and social sectors. The city data is updated in real time and effectively encourages research institutions, companies and citizens to participate in innovation and development of new applications. The London Datastore attracts developers in London, creates new markets by acquiring public data, develops a number of data-based applications, and drives efficient allocation and rational use of existing resources in the city to aid in city operations, improve the ecological environment, promote the digital economy, and facilitate energy conservation. It also treats London as a large data development base that sets an example of data development for other cities in Britain. National central cities should break data barriers between existing city departments and industries and enable authorized and orderly data sharing between departments. They should integrate data resources, standardize and normalize data from multiple channels, set up data management processes and standards, and ensure data quality. They should also actively release real-time data, develop versatile, interoperable and easy-to-use city data platforms, work with other cities and organizations to release more data to support the development of new business models by developers, and deliver better, more convenient and more cost-effective services to urban residents.

3 Develop a Dynamic Data Market

An efficient data market can drive governments, research institutions, companies and citizens to get involved and play their part in promoting open data innovation. According to an investigation report released by Intelligence Research Group (2018), the market scale of the big data industry in China is expected to reach RMB 1.0100 trillion, with a compound growth rate of 29.25% during 2015-2020. Shanghai has been actively developing a city data market. In 2016, the Shanghai Data Exchange Corporation (2016) was founded with the approval of the Shanghai Municipal People's Government. It adopts the mechanism of "trading organizations + innovation bases + industry funds + development alliances + research centers" to promote data circulation, inter-regional institutional cooperation, and interconnection and integrated applications of data. So far, no city data markets have been built in other central cities in China. National central cities should be innovators and models in utilizing city data as an important city asset and in developing a dynamic data market and a data valuation and pricing system. They should engage specialized agencies to conduct economic analysis and design a monetization framework for the prospective city data market. They should also frame value-based measurement method and pricing system for city data so that all partners can correctly understand the value of data and be able to trade openly and transparently in the data market.

4 Build an Effective Data Governance System

While building a city data market, national central cities should consider an effective data governance system to promote public understanding of data governance and related laws and to limit the negative effects of data sharing and data applications. They may establish regulatory agencies associated with city data to strengthen urban data governance and steer strategic directions for the city data innovation center. They may also establish a city data committee or a data exchange department to identify the expected data demand and data uses, and address outstanding issues concerning data sharing and coordination, data value measurement, and data monetization. The city data committee is supposed to unify the standards for multiple public agencies to publish data on different websites, publish city data regulations, formulate a standardized format of city data, overcome obstacles to data sharing among various departments, and develop a set of standards and principles for open data to improve data applicability. Finally, national central cities are advised to regulate necessary authorizations and license agreements for open city data so as to ensure maximum use and recycling of city data potential.

5 Protect Citizens' Data Privacy

Public social media, mobile devices and intelligent services are important sources of city data. That's why protecting the data security and privacy of citizens is an important premise for city data utilization. In city data-based construction projects, national central cities need to pay attention to city data security and privacy. They should develop a city-wide cyber security strategy to coordinate and respond to cyber threats confronting citizens. Data security defense should shift from the present ex post defense to active and efficient ex ante defense, and the security defense technology and management should be put under continuous supervision. National central cities should also strengthen citizens' trust in data rights, data accountability and data usage. For example, they may set up a consumer data committee to organize urban citizens to discuss about how to publish and use their data in the city data market. They may also work with personal data protection and consumer groups concerned to ensure public understanding of the laws regarding personal privacy. They should learn about the demand for personal data privacy to guide informed data management strategies for data infrastructures in the city.

6 Promote Collaborative Innovation Based on City Data

Build an ecological system for urban digital innovation, strengthen city data-based collaborative innovation and open innovation between governments, enterprises and academia, improve the quality of government management and public services, create new business opportunities for enterprises, and improve the living quality of urban residents. National central cities may adopt the open innovation model and establish a data collaborative innovation center. Government may utilize city data and the platform of collaborative innovation center to encourage the participation of scholars, enterprises, developers and the public to stimulate city data innovation and application. In particular, urban planners are unlikely to master and understand preference of local citizens and local knowledge in the urban design process. They are recommended to fully use the analysis results of open source city data, mobilize the wisdom of citizens, and transmit local information and needs to urban planners and decision makers to help them make the most informed urban planning decisions.

References

[1] Hong Xuehai, Fan Lingjun, Hong Xiaonan, and Li Guojie. "Government Big Data Opening and Market Utilization for Smart City Construction" [J]. *Big Data Research*, 2016, 2 (03): 17-26.

[2] Deloitte Research. "Super Smart City—A Higher Quality Happy Community" [R].2018.

[3] The Editorial Department. "The Sustainable Development of Big Data Served Cities" [J]. *Informatization of China Construction*, 2018 (19): 3.

[4] "Shanghai Data Exchange Corporation Is Founded" -Xinhuanet http://www.xinhuanet.com//politics/2016-04/01/c_128856527.htm

[5] A. Abella, M. Ortiz-de-Urbina-Criado, C. De-Pablos-Heredero. A model for the analysis of data-driven innovation and value generation in smart cities' ecosystems[J].Cities, 2017, (64) : 47-53.

[6] Afzalan, N., Sanchez, T. W., & Evans-Cowley. Creating smarter cities: Considerations for

selecting online participatory tools [J].Cities, 2017, (67): 21–30.

[7] Aina, Y. A. Achieving smart sustainable cities with GeoICT support: The Saudi evolving smart cities [J].Cities, 2017, (71): 49–58.

[8] Ben Sta, H. Quality and the efficiency of data in "smart-cities" [J]Future Generation Computer Systems, 2017, (74): 409–416.

[9] Cicirelli, F., Guerrieri, A., Spezzano, G., & Vinci, A. An edge-based platform for dynamic smart city applications[J].Future Generation Computer Systems, 2017, (76): 106–118.

[10] Deloitte LLP. Assessing the value of TfL's open data and digital partnerships[R]. July 2017.

S 基本子库
UB DATABASE

中国社会发展数据库（下设 12 个子库）

全面整合国内外中国社会发展研究成果，汇聚独家统计数据、深度分析报告，涉及社会、人口、政治、教育、法律等 12 个领域，为了解中国社会发展动态、跟踪社会核心热点、分析社会发展趋势提供一站式资源搜索和数据分析与挖掘服务。

中国经济发展数据库（下设 12 个子库）

基于"皮书系列"中涉及中国经济发展的研究资料构建，内容涵盖宏观经济、农业经济、工业经济、产业经济等 12 个重点经济领域，为实时掌控经济运行态势、把握经济发展规律、洞察经济形势、进行经济决策提供参考和依据。

中国行业发展数据库（下设 17 个子库）

以中国国民经济行业分类为依据，覆盖金融业、旅游、医疗卫生、交通运输、能源矿产等 100 多个行业，跟踪分析国民经济相关行业市场运行状况和政策导向，汇集行业发展前沿资讯，为投资、从业及各种经济决策提供理论基础和实践指导。

中国区域发展数据库（下设 6 个子库）

对中国特定区域内的经济、社会、文化等领域现状与发展情况进行深度分析和预测，研究层级至县及县以下行政区，涉及地区、区域经济体、城市、农村等不同维度。为地方经济社会宏观态势研究、发展经验研究、案例分析提供数据服务。

中国文化传媒数据库（下设 18 个子库）

汇聚文化传媒领域专家观点、热点资讯，梳理国内外中国文化发展相关学术研究成果、一手统计数据，涵盖文化产业、新闻传播、电影娱乐、文学艺术、群众文化等 18 个重点研究领域。为文化传媒研究提供相关数据、研究报告和综合分析服务。

世界经济与国际关系数据库（下设 6 个子库）

立足"皮书系列"世界经济、国际关系相关学术资源，整合世界经济、国际政治、世界文化与科技、全球性问题、国际组织与国际法、区域研究 6 大领域研究成果，为世界经济与国际关系研究提供全方位数据分析，为决策和形势研判提供参考。

法律声明

权威·前沿·原创

皮书系列为

“十二五”“十三五”国家重点图书出版规划项目

国家中心城市蓝皮书
BLUE BOOK OF NATIONAL CENTRAL CITY

顾　问／仇保兴　张大卫

国家中心城市建设报告（2019）

ANNUAL REPORT OF THE CONSTRUCTION OF NATIONAL CENTRAL CITIES (2019)

国家中心城市建设与区域协调发展

主　　编／赵　健　孙先科
执行主编／陈　耀　喻新安
副 主 编／蒋丽珠　赵　弘　杨东方　石　玉

社会科学文献出版社
SOCIAL SCIENCES ACADEMIC PRESS (CHINA)

图书在版编目(CIP)数据

国家中心城市建设报告. 2019：全两册：汉英对照/赵健，孙先科主编. -- 北京：社会科学文献出版社，2019.10

（国家中心城市蓝皮书）

ISBN 978 - 7 - 5201 - 5591 - 5

Ⅰ.①国… Ⅱ.①赵… ②孙… Ⅲ.①城市建设 - 研究报告 - 中国 - 2019 - 汉、英 Ⅳ.①F299.2

中国版本图书馆 CIP 数据核字（2019）第 210630 号

国家中心城市蓝皮书

国家中心城市建设报告（2019）

——国家中心城市建设与区域协调发展

主　　编 / 赵　健　孙先科

执行主编 / 陈　耀　喻新安

副 主 编 / 蒋丽珠　赵　弘　杨东方　石　玉

出 版 人 / 谢寿光

责任编辑 / 李　淼

文稿编辑 / 徐　宇

出　　版 / 社会科学文献出版社 · 城市和绿色发展分社（010）59367143

地址：北京市北三环中路甲 29 号院华龙大厦　邮编：100029

网址：www.ssap.com.cn

发　　行 / 市场营销中心（010）59367081　59367083

印　　装 / 三河市东方印刷有限公司

规　　格 / 开　本：787mm × 1092mm　1/16

印　张：62.5　字　数：1127 千字

版　　次 / 2019 年 10 月第 1 版　2019 年 10 月第 1 次印刷

书　　号 / ISBN 978 - 7 - 5201 - 5591 - 5

定　　价 / 288.00 元（全 2 册）

《国家中心城市建设报告（2019）》
编　委　会

主要编撰者简介

赵　健　天津大学管理学博士，郑州师范学院党委书记，教授、研究员，中国区域经济学会国家中心城市专业委员会主任委员，郑州市财政局原局长，郑州市第十一、十二、十三届人大代表，河南省第十二届人大代表。全国财政系统先进工作者，河南省优秀党务工作者，河南省教育厅优秀教育管理人才。主要研究领域为区域经济，精益管理。出版学术专著6部，代表性论著《地方财政发展论》，主持省级重点课题“都市农业发展模式创新研究——以郑州为例”“国家实施扩大内需政策给郑州市经济发展带来的机遇和对策问题研究”，发表论文70余篇，其中核心期刊20余篇，获得省部级科技成果奖、省部级优秀成果奖5项。

孙先科　文学博士，现任郑州师范学院校长、教授，河南大学现当代文学专业博士生导师，享受国务院特殊津贴专家，河南师范大学原副校长。主要研究领域为中国当代文学思潮和当代小说研究。出版学术著作《颂祷与自诉——新时期小说的叙述特征及其文化意识》《叙述的意味》《说话人及其话语》，在《文学评论》《文艺理论研究》等权威学术期刊发表论文60余万字。主持国家社科基金项目3项，主持完成河南省哲学社会科学规划项目3项，获“河南省社会科学优秀成果奖”一等奖2项、二等奖1项。

陈　耀　经济学博士，郑州师范学院国家中心城市研究院院长，中国社会科学院工业经济研究所研究员、教授、博士生导师，中国区域经济学会副会长兼秘书长，中国社会科学院西部发展研究中心副主任，《区域经济评论》主编，国家社会科学基金重大项目首席专家。享受国务院特殊津贴，中央组织部“院士专家西部行”、全国政协常委视察团和国家发展改革委等活动受邀专家，中国区域经济50人论坛成员。主要研究领域为区域经济、产业空间组织和政府政策。代表性论著有《国家中西部发展政策研究》《中国区域经济学前沿》《区域经济学》《区域经济辞典》等，在《经济研究》《中国工业经济》《经济管理》《区域经济评论》等刊物发表论文和各项研究报告数百篇，获得国家科技进步奖、中国发展研究奖、中国社会科学院优秀成果奖等十余项奖励。

喻新安　经济学博士，郑州师范学院国家中心城市研究院名誉院长，首席专家，河南省社会科学院原院长，二级研究员，享受国务院特殊津贴，河南省优秀专家，河南省首批杰出专业技术人才，第二届河南经济年度人物（2011），兼任中国区域经济学会副会长，河南省社科联副主席，国家统计局“中国百名经济学家信心调查”特邀经济学家。郑州大学、河南大学、河南工业大学等高校客座教授。主要研究领域为区域经济、产业经济、经济体制改革。代表作有《大省崛起》《中国新城区建设研究》《全面建设小康社会的目标体系》《中原经济区研究》《新型城镇化引领论》《中原崛起之路》《工农业协调发展的河南模式》等，主持完成国家级、省部级课题30余项；在《求是》《中国工业经济》《中国改革》《改革》《人民日报》《光明日报》《经济日报》等报刊发表论文400多篇，获省部级特等奖、一等奖12项。

蒋丽珠　北京师范大学教育学博士，现任郑州师范学院副校长、教授，中国区域经济学会国家中心城市专业委员会副主任委员，英国伯明翰城市大学访问学者，研究生导师。教育部第二届全国教师教育课程资源专家委员会委员，教育部“国培计划”教师培训理论与实践专家，河南省“四个一批”理论人才，河南省首批教师教育专家，郑州市第十批专业技术拔尖人才，河南省教育厅优秀教育管理人才。主要研究领域为教育经济与管理。提出CEA混成学习模式（C-class learning，E-e-learning，A-action learning）和场馆学习模式，被收入教育部编写的《国培计划经典案例》一书。主持省部级课题6项，获得省部级奖励2项、地厅级奖励多项，出版专著1部，主编5部、参编3部，发表论文20余篇。

赵　弘　博士，北京市社会科学院党组成员、副院长，研究员，博士后合作导师，北京市人民政府专家顾问团顾问，享受国务院特殊津贴专家，兼任中国区域经济学会副会长、北京产业经济研究会副会长等学术职务。主要研究领域为区域经济、产业经济、科技创新、园区发展、城市治理等。在国内首创"总部经济"理论，出版了我国第一部总部经济理论专著——《总部经济》，在学术界和实际经济部门引起强烈反响。发表学术论文100余篇，出版专著10余部，获省部级优秀科技成果奖6项，主持国家社科基金重大项目"京津冀协同发展重大问题研究"以及其他国家级、市级及各类横向课题100余项，多项研究成果为政府决策提供参考。

杨东方　郑州市发展和改革委员会党组书记、主任，国家注册造价工程师、注册监理工程师、注册咨询工程师（投资）、注册一级建造师。主编或组织编制、编译了《郑州国家中心城市规划建设纲要》《国家中心城市郑州指数研究》《郑州桥梁》《国家航空经济区规划创新与实践》《纽约街道设计手册》《郑州规划》等书籍或期刊；推动开展的"郑州航空港经济综合实验区规划中生态智慧低碳关键技术研究与应用"项目荣获河南省科学技术成果奖和郑州市科学技术进步奖二等奖，"郑州市规划'一张图'系统"项目荣获河南省优秀工程勘察设计行业奖（城市规划设计）二等奖和郑州市优秀城乡规划设计奖一等奖。

石　玉　博士，郑州师范学院国家中心城市研究院常务副院长、副教授、硕士生导师，中国区域经济学会国家中心城市专业委员会秘书长，郑州市优秀中青年骨干教师，河南省教育厅学术技术带头人，河南省教育厅中青年骨干教师资助对象。主要研究领域为统计学应用及政府评价等。近年来主持、参与各级各类科研项目13项，其中国家自然科学基金项目4项，河南省科技厅成果鉴定1项，河南省社科联课题1项，河南省教育厅科学技术重点项目1项，郑州市科技局项目1项，郑州师范学院教科研项目5项。发表论文17篇，其中SCI、EI检索7篇，CSSCI 1篇，中文核心7篇，获得省级优秀论文成果奖2项；参与编写十二五规划教材1部；获得各级各类教学科研奖励11项。

摘 要

本书是郑州师范学院国家中心城市研究院牵头组织，国内外近30个科研机构、50多位专家学者参与创研的第二本“国家中心城市蓝皮书”。本书结合国家区域协调发展的最新要求，以“国家中心城市建设与区域协调发展”为主题，客观地评估了2018年我国国家中心城市的现状水平和发展态势，全面地反映了北京、上海、天津、重庆、广州、成都、武汉、郑州、西安9个城市在承担国家中心城市建设使命和区域协调发展方面的探索与实践，探讨了当前国家中心城市建设的热点问题和在区域协调发展中的辐射带动作用，对于高质量建设国家中心城市、有效带动区域协调发展具有重要理论指导意义。

本书共分为6个部分，其结构和内容如下。

第一部分，总报告。总报告指出，实施区域协调发展战略，建立更加有效的区域协调发展新机制，是解决新时代发展不平衡、不充分矛盾的重要举措。2018年以来，9个国家中心城市建设亮点纷呈，在综合服务、科技创新、对外开放交流合作等方面取得了显著成效。同时，通过加快规划引领、推进交通基础设施互联互通、推动要素资源平台共建共享、促进规则和制度的有效衔接等举措，有力带动了周边区域发展，推动了国家区域协调发展战略的实施。在新时代和新的发展阶段，国家中心城市建设与区域协调发展战略的实施，既面临难得的发展机遇，也需要积极稳妥面对各种不利因素和挑战。为推动国土空间开发格局优化和区域均衡发展，国家中心城市将继续进行扩容，同时要继续完善带动区域协调发展的思路，丰富带动区域协调发展的路径。

第二部分，评价篇。为准确把握2018年中国国家中心城市在综合服务、网络枢纽、科技创新、开放交流、人文凝聚和生态宜居六个方面的建设水平和发展情况，在国家中心城市建设指数之外，新增成长性指数，分别进行测度。在建设指数上，与2016年相比，9个国家中心城市仍旧存在明显的分层现象，其中重庆、成都、天津的建设指数排名发生了较大变化。在成长性指数上，9个国家中心城市中建设指数排名靠后的郑州、西安、成都、武汉等城市，成长性指数位列前四位，表明其均处于快速发展中，其他五个城市成长性指数相对较低，表明城市发展趋于平稳。报告结合测度结果，提出国家中心城市建设中应注重各功能层的协调发展，要注重经济发展与生态宜居的协调关系，推进开放型城市建设，逐步树立城市文化品牌形象，有效解决城市病，才能更好地发挥国家中心城市在都市圈、城市群中的引领、示范、辐射、带动作用，进而促进区域协调发展。

第三部分，城市篇。由9篇反映国家中心城市2018年以来建设成效和发展趋势的报告组成，分别由北京、上海、天津、广州、重庆、成都、武汉、郑州、西安等9个国家中心城市重点研究机构的相关专家撰写。各报告全方位地展现了2018年以来国家中心城市在深入贯彻国家相关政策要求下，独具特色的战略措施，反映了各个城市高质量发展建设的进程、特点和成效，以及在区域协调发展中发挥的辐射和带动作用，同时剖析了国家中心城市高质量发展建设中存在的短板以及面临的挑战，并提出了针对性的对策建议。

第四部分，案例篇。该部分内容充分结合各国家中心城市现阶段发展特点，针对促进国家中心城市高质量发展和区域协调发展中的热点问题，选择文旅融合、公共服务、电子商务，以及国家中心城市在大都市区的辐射带动力等论题进行了专题研究，有效地丰富和补充了城市篇的内容。

第五部分，探索篇。该部分主要收录针对国家中心城市建设和区域协调发展中的热点和难点问题，在借鉴国际大都市、现代都市圈建设经验、规律的基础上，探索我国国家中心城市高质量发展的前瞻性文章。探索篇文章具有很强的问题导向性，并站在国际发展视角，目的是增强国家中心城市建设的前瞻性，推动解决国家中心城市建设、国家中心城市在带动区域协调发展中遇到的最迫切最关键的难题。

第六部分，附录。由3类重要资料组成，即9个国家中心城市2018年建设情况的主要数据、国家层面有关区域协调发展的主要文件内容摘编、2018年以来国家中心城市建设大事记。这几项资料真实呈现2018年以来国家中心城市建设的客观进程，同时为广大科研工作者跟踪和深化国家中心城市建设重大问题的研究提供了基础资料。

关键词： 国家中心城市　区域协调发展　高质量发展

序

在举国欢庆新中国成立70周年之际，由郑州师范学院国家中心城市研究院（简称“国中院”）牵头组织创研的第二本“国家中心城市蓝皮书”《国家中心城市建设报告（2019）》正式出版，我对此表示热烈的祝贺，向大力支持智库建设的郑州师范学院领导表示由衷的钦佩和感谢！

国家中心城市，被称为是我国城镇体系的“塔尖”，是城市群的核心城市，居于中心城市的最高位置。建设国家中心城市，是中央着眼完善全国城镇体系、促进区域协调发展、提升特大超大中心城市辐射力带动力、赢得全球城市竞争做出的重大战略部署。国家中心城市的使命任务主要有三：国家战略要津、代表国家参与全球竞争、辐射带动大区域发展。

近年来中央高度重视中心城市的建设和发展，采取了一系列重大举措，特别值得关注的有以下几个：一是，2018年11月18日，中共中央国务院发布《关于建立更加有效的区域协调发展新机制的意见》，明确提出要“建立以中心城市引领城市群发展、城市群带动区域发展新模式，推动区域板块之间融合互动发展”，并重点规划了七大城市群及其相应引领的12个中心城市，其中北京、天津、上海、广州、重庆、成都、武汉、郑州、西安等9个为获得批复支持建设的国家中心城市。二是，2019年2月，国家发展改革委发布《关于培育发展现代化都市圈的指导意见》，提出都市圈是城市群内部以超大特大城市或辐射带动功能强的大城市为中心、以1小时通勤圈为基本范围的城镇化空间形态；并且要以促进中心城市与周边城市（镇）同城化发展为方向，培育发展一批现代化都市圈。三是，2019年8月26日，习近平总书记主持召开中央财经委员会第五次会议，指出当前我国经济发展的空间结构正在发生深刻变化，中心城市和城市群正在成为承载发展要素的主要空间形式，新形势下促进区域协调发展，要按照客观经济规律调整完善区域政策体系，发挥各地区比较优势，增强中心城市和城市群等经济发展优势区域的经济和人口承载能力。

以上这些重要的中央文件和会议表明，为促进我国经济的高质量发展和区域经济协调发展以及应对纷繁复杂的国际环境，必须高度重视发挥中心城市的引领和辐射带动作用，优化区域经济战略布局。这些基本精神，为我们今后建设好国家中心城市进一步指明了方向，提供了强大的动力和信心。

目前，为贯彻落实中央要求和相关部署，各地区都在积极研究谋划中心城市、都市圈和城市群的发展，比如，如何提升省会中心城市的首位度，如何推动中心城市与周边相邻城市的同城化，如何实现大城市群内部的一体化；已获批的国家中心城市在研究思考如何更高质量的建设城市，已具备一定实力的城市在积极创造条件力争获批建设国家中心城市。我注意到，2017 年 1 月国家发改委正式发布《关于支持郑州建设国家中心城市的指导意见》后，河南省很快就编制出台了《郑州建设国家中心城市行动纲要（2017 ~ 2035 年）》，2019 年 6 月，河南省委省政府又专门出台了《关于支持郑州建设国家中心城市的若干意见》（豫发〔2019〕18 号），提出加快推进郑州“三中心一枢纽一门户”建设，进一步扩大对外开放，激发内生动力，建设具有创新活力、人文魅力、生态智慧、开放包容的国家中心城市，引领带动中原城市群乃至中部地区高质量发展。正是由于有了这种高度重视的使命感、责任感和科学规划，郑州在 9 个国家中心城市中的实力虽较弱，但近些年的上升势头却很强劲。2018 年郑州经济总量跨入“万亿元俱乐部”，常住人口突破一千万，科技创新、生态环境、开放高地建设都取得明显进步。这些实践说明，国家中心城市正在成为我国推进新型城镇化建设、促进区域协调发展的重要力量和抓手。

当然，如何更好地建设和更好地布局国家中心城市，目前仍然需要深入研究和探讨。令人欣喜的是，这本国家中心城市建设蓝皮书结合国家区域协调发展的最新要求，在首部蓝皮书“国家中心城市的使命与担当”主题的基础上，确立了新的研究主题，即“国家中心城市建设与区域协调发展”，该皮书全面评估了一年来我国国家中心城市建设的现状水平和发展态势，特别是反映了现有 9 个城市在承担国家中心城市建设使命与区域协调发展方面的探索与实践，深入探讨了当前发展中的热点和难点问题。我注意到，这本蓝皮书不仅主题新颖、内容全面、专业严谨，而且研究方法上也有不少创新，比如，采用 6 个功能指标、15 个维度指标和 47 个评价指标，编制国家中心城市建设指数，而以往的评价指数只是反映一个年度时点上的总体水平，很难揭示城市发展的变动状况，这次创研团队经过大量数据指标测试后新增了“成长性指数”，结果显示，有些中心城市尽管综合实力较弱，但近几年增速快，按成长性指数排序呈现“后来居上”态势。这样的研究报告可以说真正做到了“全面、客观、真实、专业”。

期待郑州师范学院国中院继续坚持理论联系实际，坚持理论方法创新，努力把“国家中心城市蓝皮书”打造成中国城市发展研究的学术品牌，把国中院建设成为全国一流的国家中心城市研究基地，让智库成果更好地转化为政府决策，指导城市实践，服务城市发展。

中国国际经济交流中心副理事长兼秘书长

郑州师范学院国家中心城市研究院首席顾问

张大卫

2019 年 9 月 15 日

目 录

Ⅰ 总报告

Ⅱ 评价篇

Ⅲ 城市篇

Ⅳ　案例篇

Ⅴ　探索篇

Ⅵ 附录

皮书数据库阅读**使用指南**

总 报 告

General Report

B.1

中国国家中心城市建设与区域协调发展报告（2019）

郑州师范学院国家中心城市研究院课题组*

摘 要： 实施区域协调发展战略，建立更加有效的区域协调发展新机制，是解决新时代发展不平衡、不充分矛盾的重要举措。2018年以来，9个国家中心城市建设亮点纷呈，在综合服务、科技创新、对外开放交流合作等方面取得了显著成效。同时，通过加快规划引领、推进交通基础设施互联互通、推动要素资源平台共建共享、促进规则和制度的有效衔接等举措，有

* 课题组长：陈耀、喻新安；副组长：王建国、石玉；执笔：王新涛，硕士，河南省社会科学院城市与环境研究所副所长、副研究员，研究方向为城市规划、经济学；左雯，硕士，河南省社会科学院城市与环境研究所副研究员，研究方向为宏观经济管理；李建华，硕士，河南省社会科学院城市与环境研究所助理研究员，研究方向为环境经济；易雪琴，硕士，河南省社会科学院城市与环境研究所助理研究员，研究方向为区域经济；彭俊杰，硕士，河南省社会科学院城市与环境研究所助理研究员，研究方向为生态经济；郭志远，博士，河南省社会科学院城市与环境研究所助理研究员，研究方向为城市经济。

力带动了周边区域发展，推动了国家区域协调发展战略的实施。在新时代和新的发展阶段，国家中心城市建设与区域协调发展战略的实施，既面临难得的发展机遇，也需要积极稳妥地面对各种不利因素和挑战。为推动国土空间开发格局优化和区域均衡发展，一方面，国家中心城市将继续进行扩容；另一方面，国家中心城市要继续拓展带动区域协调发展的思路，丰富带动区域协调发展的路径。

关键词： 国家中心城市　区域协调发展　新发展理念

实施区域协调发展战略是新时代国家重大战略之一，是贯彻新发展理念、建设现代化经济体系的重要组成部分。2018 年，中共中央、国务院发布了《关于建立更加有效的区域协调发展新机制的意见》，绘就了今后一段时期区域协调发展的路线图。国家中心城市肩负国家使命，引领区域发展，参与国际竞争，代表国家形象，处于全国城镇体系的“塔尖”，对于促进区域协调发展战略具有举足轻重的作用。目前，国家明确了北京、天津、上海、广州、重庆、成都、武汉、郑州、西安 9 个国家中心城市。2018 年以来，这 9 个国家中心城市建设加速推进，多个城市都明确了时间表和路线图，其发展目标更加清晰，发展重点和任务更加具体，9 个国家中心城市推进建设的举措各具特色，在综合服务、科技创新、对外开放交流合作等方面取得了显著成效，成为我国高质量发展的“领跑者”。

一　2018年以来国家中心城市建设最新进展及特点

（一）9个国家中心城市建设总体情况

自 2005 年住房和城乡建设部编制《全国城镇体系规划》首次提出建设国家中心城市这一概念起，国家目前已经明确支持北京、天津、上海、广州、重庆、成都、武汉、郑州、西安9座城市建设成为国家中心城市。作为国家发展战略的重要平台和战略支点，这些城市承载了国家的政治目标和战略任务，集中了中国城市在经济、人口、资源和政策上的主要优势。同时，紧紧围绕各自的功能定位，从完善基础设施、产业结构升级、扩大开放等多个方面推进国家中心城市建设。截止到2018年底，根据国家和各省市相关公开数据，在人口规模上，9个国家中心城市的常住人口总量为15484.88万，在全国139538.00万人口中占比为11%；在经济规模上，9个国家中心城市的GDP总量为173715.27亿元，在全国900309.00亿元GDP中占比为19.3%；在人均GDP上，9个国家中心城市的人均GDP为11.22万元人民币，是全国人均水平（6.46万元人民币）的1.7倍；在GDP增长速度上，9个国家中心城市中有武汉、成都、郑州、西安4个城市超过国家6.6%的增长速度；在一般公共预算收入上，9个国家中心城市的一般公共预算收入为23687.75亿元，占全国一般公共预算收入183352.00亿元的13%；在城镇化率上，9个国家中心城市的城镇化率为78.90%，是全国平均水平（约为59.58%）的1.32倍（见表1）。

表1　2018年9个国家中心城市主要经济社会发展指标

	常住人口总量（万人）	GDP（亿元）	人均GDP（万元）	GDP增速（%）	一般公共预算收入（亿元）	城镇化率（%）
北京	2154.20	30320.00	14.08	6.6	5785.90	86.50
天津	1559.60	18809.64	12.06	3.6	2106.19	83.15
上海	2423.78	32679.87	13.48	6.6	7108.15	88.10
重庆	3101.79	20363.19	6.59	6.0	2265.50	65.50
广州	1490.44	22859.35	15.55	6.2	1632.30	86.38
武汉	1108.10	14847.29	13.51	8.0	1528.70	80.29
成都	1633.00	15342.77	9.48	8.0	1424.20	73.12
郑州	1013.60	10143.30	10.14	8.1	1152.10	73.40
西安	1000.37	8349.86	8.51	8.2	684.71	74.01
9市	15484.88	173715.27	11.22	—	23687.75	78.90
全国	139538.00	900309.00	6.46	6.6	183352.00	59.58

资料来源：9个国家中心城市2018年国民经济和社会发展统计公报。

（二）国家中心城市建设特点

1. 建设推进路线图更加明确

在城市发展竞争日趋激烈的当下，成为国家中心城市是很多区域性中心城市的梦想，很多城市还在积极争取加入国家中心城市的行列。对于已经进入国家中心城市的这几个城市，尤其是武汉、郑州和西安这三个后进入的国家中心城市来说，如何谋划国家中心城市建设的战略蓝图就成为最迫切的工作。武汉于2018 年4 月出台了《武汉建设国家中心城市实施方案》，该方案提出：武汉国家中心城市分三个阶段建设，到 2021 年，武汉地区生产总值要达到 2 万亿元左右；到 2035 年，武汉初步建成在全球范围内具有一定竞争力和影响力的国家中心城市；到 21 世纪中叶，武汉在富强民主文明和谐美丽的社会主义现代化建设中走在全国前列，建成具有国际影响力、全球竞争力和可持续发展能力的世界亮点城市。西安制定了《西安国家中心城市建设实施方案》，该方案提出了“三步走”战略：第一步，到 2020 年全面建成小康社会，地区生产总值迈上万亿元台阶，大西安都市圈全面形成；第二步，到 2035 年基本实现现代化，全面建成代表国家形象、引领“一带一路”、具有重要国际影响力的国家中心城市，国际化大都市建设取得重大进展；第三步，到 2050 年基本实现共同富裕，城市国际性特征进一步完备，现代化、生态化、国际化水平全面提升，全面建成引领“一带一路”、亚欧合作交流的国际化大都市，努力跻身世界城市、国际文化名都行列。郑州市也在 2018 年 2 月出台了《郑州建设国家中心城市行动纲要（2017—2035 年）》，提出郑州国家中心城市建设的发展目标：近期（2017—2020 年），开启郑州全面建设国家中心城市新征程，全面建成人民群众认可、经得起历史检验的高质量、高水平小康社会；中期（2021—2035 年），跻身国家创新型城市前列，建成国际综合枢纽、国际物流中心、国家重要的经济增长中心等；远期（2036—2050 年），建成富强民主文明和谐美丽的社会主义现代化强市，成为具有全球影响力的城市。可以看出，这些国家中心城市建设的“效果图”、“施工图”和“任务书”已经变得愈加清晰、明确和具体，围绕既定蓝图聚焦聚力、持续推进，国家中心城市建设的未来可期。

2. 更加突出新时代主题

中国特色社会主义进入了新时代，我国经济发展也进入了新时代，新时代的基本特征就是我国经济已由高速增长阶段转向高质量发展阶段。推动高质量发展是当前和今后一个时期发展思路、制定经济政策、实施宏观调控的根本要求，高质量发展成为新时代的主题。9 个国家中心城市把高质量发展作为发展的根本要求和目标，在高质量发展的导向下进行城市各项规划和政策设计。比如西安，就高质量发展出台了《中共西安市委关于加快国家中心城市建设 推动高质量发展的决定》，对西安国家中心城市高质量发展的重点和目标提出明确要求。西安以建设西部重要的经济中心、对外交往中心、丝路科创中心、丝路文化高地、内陆开放高地、国家综合交通枢纽六大功能为重点，推动西安从区域中心城市向国家中心城市、国际化大都市跨越。西安提出要着力打造高质量发展样板，在打造高质量发展样板中寻求在重点领域关键环节求突破，以“三个聚焦”来推动高质量发展。一是聚焦高端高新，在产业转型升级上下功夫；二是聚焦高速增长，在投资结构优化上下功夫；三是聚焦创新驱动，在新旧动能转换上下功夫，这“三个聚焦”，成为西安推动高质量发展的重要发力点。其他几个国家中心城市也紧扣新时代、新使命、新任务要求，顺应城市工作新形势、改革发展新要求和人民群众新期待，在高质量发展路径方法上进行了实践探索和创新，成为高质量发展的重要推动力。

3. 更加注重补齐民生短板

党的十八大以来，以习近平同志为核心的新一代中央领导集体将民生问题作为治国理政的出发点和落脚点，把满足人民对美好生活的向往作为自己的奋斗目标，提出了一系列关于民生保障的新理念、新目标和新要求。十九大更是强调要坚持在发展中保障和改善民生，将增进民生福祉作为发展的根本目的。9 个国家中心城市在建设中致力于解决发展中的不平衡不充分问题，把补齐民生短板作为城市发展的重点任务来抓。其中，天津市财政支出 75% 以上用于民生，全面完成 20 项民心工程；成都全面完成十大民生实事，连续 10 年位居“中国最具幸福感城市”榜首；武汉持续加大民生投入，公共财政用于民生领域支出 1402. 7 亿元，增长 15%；西安全市财政用于民生支出达 921. 5 亿元，增长 9. 7%；郑州坚持在发展中补齐民生短板，全年财政民生支出 1402. 9 亿元，增长 17%，占全市财政一般公共预算支出的 79. 6%。这些城市通过不断加大财政投入用于民生领域，基础设施、住房、就业创业、医疗、教育、养老等民生短板正在加快补齐，群众共享改革发展成果的获得感、幸福感、安全感进一步增强。

4. 更加注重城市品质提升

城市品质是人民群众感受和评价城市工作的重要标准，是城市发展建设成果与水平的整体展现，也是衡量一个城市规划、建设、管理、服务质量和效果的重要尺度。9个国家中心城市在城市品质提升方面各有侧重，其中，广州开展广州大道、人民桥等路桥品质提升工程和桥下空间整治，优化调整部分街道行政区划，规范命名城乡道路3200条，加大违法建设治理力度，拆除违法建设7.3万宗、3600万平方米；成都通过建设美丽宜居公园城市、优化慢行交通体系、1918条背街小巷提升整治和109条特色街区打造来全面提升城市品质；重庆制定城市综合管理提升行动方案，推进大城细管、大城智管、大城众管，“马路办公”成为常态，城市面貌发生巨大变化；上海结合城市有机更新，较好地保护了历史建筑和风貌街区；郑州大幅提升环卫保洁标准，城市管理范围从三环内拓展至近郊48个乡镇，四环内全面推行三级“路长制”，管理责任落实到了最后一米、最后一人。9个国家中心城市都把城市品质提升工作作为规划建设的根本落脚点，从城市基础设施细节入手，在精细化管理上下功夫，使城市更有序、更安全、更干净、更有温度、更有品位。

5. 更加注重营商环境优化

营商环境是企业生存发展的土壤，体现着一个城市的经济竞争力。城市营商环境的优劣直接影响到企业的设立和经营状况，并对其经济发展、财税收入、就业状况等产生重要影响。国家中心城市要发展更高层次的开放型经济，就要在优化营商环境上下更大功夫。2018年，9个国家中心城市在优化营商环境方面出台了很多举措，如北京开办企业时间压缩至5天，成为全球开办企业完全免费的两个城市之一；上海深入实施以“一网通办”为重要标志的“放管服”改革，取消行政审批事项100项、评估评审40项，获得电力、开办企业、办理施工许可、跨境贸易、纳税、登记财产等领域的办事和审批环节减少30.5%、时间缩短52.8%；广州出台实施营商环境综合改革试点方案，企业开办时间压减至4个工作日以内，政府投资工程建设项目审批时间压减至90个工作日以内，社会投资项目压减至50个工作日以内；成都全面推开“证照分离”改革，实现涉企证照“四十三证合一”，推广全程电子化网上登记；武汉大幅压减行政审批时限，企业开办、工程建设项目审批时间实现“双减半”，商事制度改革、政务服务改革经验受到国务院通报表扬。9个国家中心城市持续简化各类行政审批，推进公平公正监管，提高政府服务效能，加强产权保护，废除妨碍统一市场和公平竞争的各种规定和做法，推动我国营商环境不断优化，助力我国在2018世界银行营商环境报告中的排名从78位提升到46位。

（三）国家中心城市建设成效

1. 城市综合服务功能进一步提高

国家中心城市是全国的经济中心、金融中心，第三产业发达，为周边地区乃至全国提供优质的生产服务和社会服务。9个国家中心城市依托全国性市场体系和科技教育人才等高端要素优势，通过产业互补协作，构建信息技术产业、现代服务业及其他战略性新兴产业体系，经济活力进一步增强，经济中心带动区域协调发展的作用进一步凸显。9个国家中心城市大力发展银行、保险、证券、广告、审计、电子商务等中介机构，为经济发展提供服务的能力进一步增强。其中，武汉推进中心城区现代服务业创新升级，涌现出50余栋纳税亿元以上商务楼宇；广州建设国家绿色金融改革创新试验区，获批国家服务型制造示范城市；天津推出金融服务实体经济创新产品138项，设立百亿元智能制造财政专项资金，依托海河产业基金打造千亿元级新一代人工智能科技产业基金和项目群、300亿元生物医药产业母基金群。9个国家中心城市不断加强医疗、教育、文化等公共服务设施建设，社会服务能力稳步提高。截止到2018年底，9个国家中心城市上市公司数量达1036家，金融机构本外币存款余额达508054.37亿元，占全国的27.8%。第三产业增加值比重均超过全国52.2%的平均水平；三甲医院数量达429个，包括博物馆、文化馆、公共图书馆在内的文化场馆共1077个。9个国家中心城市的服务能级显著提高，在世界城市体系、全球金融中心等排名中地位明显提升，在服务国家发展大局方面发挥出更加重要的战略支点作用，成为中国城市发展的“加速器”。

2. 科技创新能力进一步增强

当今世界，科技创新能力成为国家综合实力最集中的体现。在经济全球化时代，一个国家具有强大的科技创新能力，就能在世界产业分工链条中处于高端位置，就能创造激活国家经济的新产业，就能拥有重要的自主知识产权，从而推动社会发展。尤其是当前的中美经贸摩擦，让中国认识到自主创新和科技赶超的重要性和紧迫性。科技创新是国家中心城市应具有的一项核心功能，2018 年，9 个国家中心城市高度重视科技创新，围绕实施创新驱动发展战略、加快推进以科技创新为核心的全面创新，在全国科技中心、创新中心建设，高端人才集聚，发明专利，科技成果等方面取得丰硕成就。其中，北京以国家战略需求引导创新方向，组建北京量子信息科学研究院、脑科学与类脑研究中心、智源人工智能研究院等新型研发机构，综合性国家科学中心建设全面展开，涌现出马约拉纳任意子、新型超低功耗晶体管等重大标志性原创成果；上海基本建成软 X 射线自由电子激光装置、超强超短激光等大科学设施，成立国家集成电路制造业创新中心、脑与类脑研究中心等一批科研机构，阿尔茨海默病治疗新药、高光谱综合观测卫星等一批科创成果相继问世；广州高水平推进再生医学与健康、南方海洋科学与工程省实验室建设，广州高新区入选国家十大世界一流高科技园区；天津引进中国原子能科学研究院、中科无人机应用研究院、人工智能军民融合创新中心等 10 家国家级科研院所，大型地震工程模拟研究设施、中国核工业大学等一批国家级创新平台相继落户。截止到 2018 年底，9 个国家中心城市共有国家重点实验室、国家工程技术研究中心、企业国家重点实验室数量 672 个，专利授权数达 53.5134 万件。9 个国家中心城市创新驱动发展战略的深入实施，促进了中国创新要素的深度融合，进一步增强了国家自主创新活力。

3. 对外开放交流合作水平进一步提升

国家中心城市是对外开放的重要载体，能代表国家参与国际竞争，在政治、经济、文化、社会等领域与国外开展广泛交流合作。2018 年以来，9 个国家中心城市在对外交流合作方面亮点纷呈，越来越多的企业借助国家中心城市的开放平台和服务通道，登上国际经济大舞台，向世界发出中国全面开放发展的最强音。2018 年 11 月，上海全市人民齐心协力，以一流的城市环境、一流的服务保障成功举办了首届中国国际进口博览会，共有 172 个国家、地区和国际组织参会，3617 家境外企业参加首届中国国际进口博览会，80 多万人进馆洽谈采购、参观体验，成交额达 578 亿美元，创造了多项国际博览会纪录，首次举办就跻身全球十大商业展会，中国国际进口博览会成为国际博览业史的一大创举。天津成功举办了夏季达沃斯论坛、第二届世界智能大会、国际矿业大会等一系列重大国际会议，国际友城交流合作进一步巩固拓展。广州举办世界航线发展大会、从都国际论坛、全球市长论坛等国际性会议61次。北京成功举办第三届国际冬季运动博览会。天津成功承办中俄青少年冰球友谊赛等重大赛事活动。成都成功承办第二届中国—中东欧国家艺术合作论坛、第四届阿拉伯艺术节、2018欧洲文化季、国际友城青年音乐周等国际交流活动。西安成功举办丝路国际电影节、全球程序员节等重大国际活动。截止到2018年底，9个国家中心城市实际利用外资投资额达1176.49亿美元，占全国总额的13.3%，综合保税区个数达16个，国际友好城市个数达333个。国家中心城市通过举办这些大型的赛事、展会和重要国际会议，集聚全国甚至全球的高端资源，强化与世界的联系，促进中国深度融入全球城市网络体系中，进而全面提升国际交往便利度和交流合作紧密度，提升中国城市的国际形象和影响力。

4. 网络枢纽功能进一步增强

国家中心城市是全国的信息中心、物流中心、电子商务中心，承担着重要的交通网络枢纽功能。2018年以来，9个国家中心城市在枢纽建设方面取得了重大突破。广州强化国际综合交通枢纽功能，推进18项国际航运枢纽工程、11项国际航空枢纽工程建设，推进5个国铁、6个城际铁路、9个地铁和10个高速公路项目建设，实现所有行政区通地铁。北京大兴国际机场正式命名，航站楼主体工程基本完工。上海完成虹桥国际机场一号航站楼改造，上海机场航空货邮吞吐量、旅客吞吐量分别保持世界第三、世界第四，上海港集装箱吞吐量连续9年位居世界第一，邮轮母港旅客发送量保持世界第四。天津的津雄城际纳入国家规划，天津港大港港区10万吨级航道建成使用，航运服务中心正式运营。成都新开通“蓉欧+”东盟铁海联运班列和铁路班列，国际班列通达24个海外城市，蓉欧班列全年开行1591列，开行量继续保持全国第一；武汉的江海直达千箱级集装箱示范船成功首航，西安获批国家级临空经济示范区和跨境电商综合试验区，郑州的郑济、郑万、郑阜高铁及郑州南站、机场至南站城际铁路加快建设，“米”字形高铁网络正在形成。截止到2018年底，9个国家中心城市邮政业务量达2207.32亿元，占全国业务量的17.9%；电信业务总量达8679.32亿元，占全国业务量的13.2%；客运周转量达11086.91亿人公里，占全国客运周转量的32.4%，货运周转量达58323.62亿吨公里，占全国货运周转量的28.4%，机场国际航线数量达476个，高铁车次数量达4183次/天。“中国互联网+指数”是反映信息枢纽建设的重要指标，2018年中国互联网+指数排名中，除了郑州和西安，其他7个城市都位居全国前十。9个国家中心城市的机场、铁路、港口码头、公路、信息等设施的建设和完善，促进了中国国际商贸流通节点网络的形成，对于加快构建连接东西、贯通南北、辐射八方的现代化立体综合网络枢纽，促进区域经济合作和协调发展提供了坚实支撑。

5. 生态宜居水平进一步提升

生态宜居是人们对拥有充满活力、生态良好、适宜居住生活的城市环境的美好追求，生态宜居也是国家中心城市建设的一个重要目标。9个国家中心城市深入贯彻“绿水青山就是金山银山”的发展理念，持续推进生态环境治理，全力推动生态宜居的绿色城市建设，多项生态环境指标持续向好，绿色发展成效显著，人民群众获得感显著增强。西安积极践行“两山”理念，深入开展“五路”两侧增绿美化、“美丽西安·绿色家园”行动；武汉开展增绿提质行动，新增绿地758万平方米；广州擦亮花城绿城品牌，举办中国森林旅游节，种植主题花树10万株，新增立体绿化10万平方米、生态景观林带80公里；上海大力推进生活垃圾全程分类，建成再生资源回收点3374个，开工建设15个垃圾资源化利用设施；北京开展“清河行动”和水源地环境保护专项行动，完成非建成区84条段黑臭水体治理任务；郑州强力推进国土绿化提速行动，市区新增绿地1356万平方米，建成高铁公园等公园、游园、微公园411个。截止到2018年底，9个国家中心城市城市绿化覆盖率达41.3%，比全国平均水平高3.4个百分点；北京、重庆、广州的人均公园绿地面积超过全国平均水平；PM2.5年平均浓度值和全天交通拥堵指数都比上年有不同程度下降。这些数据表明，国家中心城市的生态宜居水平进一步提高，人与自然更加和谐发展。

二 2018年以来国家中心城市建设新现象、新举措、新经验

（一）新发展理念引领国家中心城市全面发展

国家中心城市作为肩负国家使命、体现国家意志、代表国家形象、引领区域发展的重要载体，坚定不移贯彻“创新、协调、绿色、开放、共享”的发

展理念，建设全面体现新发展理念引领的城市。2018 年 2 月，习近平总书记到四川视察时，对成都工作提出了一系列重大要求，明确表示支持成都建设全面体现新发展理念的城市，为成都国家中心城市建设指明了政治方向，提供了根本遵循。2018 年 7 月 6 日至 7 日召开的中共成都市第十三届委员会第三次全体会议上，审议通过了《中共成都市委关于全面贯彻新发展理念加快推动高质量发展的决定》《中共成都市委关于深入贯彻落实习近平总书记来川视察重要指示精神加快建设美丽宜居公园城市的决定》。成都建设全面体现新发展理念的国家中心城市，具体体现为建设“五个城市”：一是贯彻创新发展理念，建设创新驱动先导城市；二是贯彻协调发展理念，建设城乡统筹示范城市；三是贯彻绿色发展理念，建设美丽中国典范城市；四是贯彻开放发展理念，建设现代化国际城市；五是贯彻共享发展理念，建设和谐宜居生活城市。其他 8 个国家中心城市也担当尽责勇作为，努力建设全面体现新发展理念的国家中心城市，体现着全国城市发展的水平和品质，对外展示国家形象，对内发挥引领、示范和辐射带动效应。

（二）“硬科技”推动经济高质量发展

“硬科技”是对人工智能、航空航天、生物技术、光电芯片、信息技术、新材料、新能源、智能制造等领域中的高精尖原创技术的统称。科技创新是推动高质量发展、建设现代化强国的战略支撑，也是国家中心城市承担的核心职能之一。9 个国家中心城市依托自身丰富的科技创新要素，不断加快科技创新步伐，科技创新引领城市高质量发展能力进一步增强。2018 年 11 月国务院发展研究中心国际技术经济研究所发布的《2018 年度全球主要城市硬科技创新指数》中，北京、上海高居第二和第三位，广州和西安位居第九和第十二位，展示了国家中心城市强大的创新能力。比如，西安大力实施“硬科技 +”战略，明确提出要打造硬科技之都，编制出台 9 个硬科技产业规划，举办 2018 全球硬科技创新暨“一带一路”创新合作大会，西咸新区已率先在全国建成硬科技小镇，“硬科技”作为西安原创概念进入国家话语体系。北京设立 300 亿元规模的科技创新母基金，专注布局硬科技和创新早期，中关村管委会认定了首批 27 家硬科技孵化平台，每个平台年度支持可达 1000 万元。广州也设立了 50 亿元科技成果产业化引导基金，科技信贷风险资金池拉动银行贷款超过 100 亿元，股权投资机构达到6192家，成功举办了海交会、小蛮腰科技大会。武汉新增诺贝尔奖工作站2个、院士专家工作站28个、知名企业研发机构47个、省级以上创新平台41个、省级众创孵化机构51个；新增科技“小巨人”企业1237户、瞪羚企业500户；独角兽企业达到5户，居全国第五位。做强“硬科技”，引领国家中心城市经济高质量发展，成为国家中心城市建设的最大亮点。

（三）“四路协同”打造内陆开放高地

参与国际竞争是每一个国家中心城市都必须承担的责任和使命。2018年，9个国家中心城市都充分依托自身在区位、交通、产业等方面的优势和基础，积极响应国家“一带一路”建设号召，提升对外开放水平。尤其是郑州、西安、成都、武汉等几个内陆城市，“空中”“陆上”“网上”“海上”四路并进，内陆开放高地建设成果丰硕。“空中丝绸之路”越飞越广，郑州机场获批第五航权，已开通航线236条，横跨欧美亚三大经济区的国际枢纽航线网络初步形成，成为全国第二个实现航空、铁路、轨道交通、高速公路一体化换乘机场。西安新增7条国际客运航线，总数达64条，航空旅客吞吐量跃居全国第七，货邮吞吐量突破31万吨，增速位居全国十大机场第一，西安咸阳国际机场获批第五航权。成都新开通国际定期直飞客货运航线12条，国（地区）际航线达到11条，双流国际机场位居全球最繁忙机场第二十六位。“陆上丝绸之路”越跑越快，中欧班列（郑州）每周“去九回八”高频次运行，新开通中亚、东盟线路，全年开行752班，主要指标继续保持全国前列。西安港铁路口岸监管区正式投用，中欧班列“长安号”开行1235列，实际开行总量、重载率、货运量均位居全国第一。成都新开通“蓉欧+”东盟铁海联运班列和铁路班列，国际班列达24个海外城市，蓉欧班列全球开行1591列，开行量继续保持全国第一。“网上丝绸之路”越来越便捷，郑州EWTO核心功能集聚区启动建设，新签约项目45个，成功举办第二届全球跨境电子商务大会，跨境电商交易额增长25.1%。中国人民银行西安分行与西安市积极打造“通丝路”跨境电子商务人民币结算平台，在线提供人民币跨境结算、报关报检、信用担保、贸易融资等10项“一站式服务”，面向全球市场搭建“人民币网上丝绸之路”。“海上丝绸之路”越来越顺畅，郑州至连云港、青岛、天津等港口海铁联运班列累计开行206班，武汉也开通了至宁波的铁海联运班列。

（四）“抢人才”为国家中心城市建设添动力

人才是经济社会发展的第一动力，也是国家中心城市建设的第一资源。无论是北京、上海、广州等传统一线城市，还是以武汉、成都、郑州为代表的新一线城市，都在加快“抢人”步伐，加大“抢人”力度。2018 年武汉继续优化落户政策，新建“长江科学城”“长江青年城”，筹集大学租赁房，大力引进人才。仅 2018 年，武汉就新引进外籍外地院士 45 名、高层次人才 281 名；留汉创业就业大学毕业生 40.6 万名，创历史新高，人口净流入量居全国城市前列，新增户籍 30.08 万，户籍总人口达到 883.73 万人。西安积极实施“内留外引”招贤纳才工作，大力引进、培养大西安发展急需的高端科研人才、稀缺管理人才和技能型、实用型人才，2018 年共引进培养各类人才 38.6 万人，新落户人口 80 万人。成都出台了“人才新政 12 条”，新引进国家“千人计划”专家 34 人，累计吸引超过 25 万名本科及以上学历毕业生落户。上海出台了《上海加快实施人才高峰工程行动方案》，明确了要围绕宇宙起源与天体观测、光子科学与技术、生命科学与生物医药等 13 个集聚造就高峰人才的重点领域，加快建立国际通行的遴选机制，打造具有国际竞争力的事业发展平台，实施国际通行的工作体制，在“人才高地”基础上筑起“人才高峰”，聚天下英才而用之。广州连续 20 年举办中国留学人员广州科技交流会（后更名为“中国海外人才交流大会”），成为中国海外留学人员交流第一品牌。2019 年 6 月，广州市发布了《关于实施“广聚英才计划”的意见》，提出了 19 项创新举措，全力集聚国内外“高精尖缺”人才。聚天下英才而用之，打造人才高地，为城市可持续发展注入源源不断的动力，成为 9 个国家中心城市建设的共识。

（五）优化营商环境，增强城市竞争力

营商环境是一个国家或地区综合竞争力的重要内容，国家中心城市积极对标世界银行营商环境评估标准，优化营商环境工作亮点不断，成为全国优化营商环境的窗口和名片。北京市全面贯彻落实习近平总书记关于北京要率先加大营商环境改革力度的要求，先后出台“9 + N”系列政策措施和进一步优化营商环境三年行动计划，在国内 22 个城市营商环境试评价中综合排名第一，为

我国营商环境世行排名大幅提升做出贡献。上海市组建大数据中心，开通运行“一网通办”总门户，推进审批服务事项全程通办、全网通办、全市通办，1274个事项接入全流程一体化在线服务平台，90%的事项实现“只跑一次、一次办成”，99%的民生服务事项实现全市通办。天津市加快推进“一制三化”审批制度改革、“五减”改革、“多证合一”改革，实现“24证合一”，建成“天津网上办事大厅”和50个政务服务“无人超市”，90%以上审批事项实现“一网通办”“最多跑一次”，企业登记做到“一次都不用跑”，“天津八条”成为优化营商环境的亮丽名片。广州“民营经济20条”落地，越秀区“企业开办最快1天”受国务院大督查通报表扬。西安不断深化“三大革命”，持续升级“三大新政”，西安政务服务网建成投用，“最多跑一次”和“网上办”分别达90%和96%，营商环境综合排名跃进全国前十。

（六）实施乡村振兴战略，开创城乡融合新局面

实施乡村振兴战略，是党中央在中国特色社会主义新时代和奋力实现“两个一百年”目标的历史进程中，对我国城乡关系的准确研判和重大部署。国家中心城市的建设也离不开乡村的振兴，正是有了乡村的滋养，城市才能生生不息、持续发展。9个国家中心城市也积极实施乡村振兴战略，不断开创城乡融合发展新局面。比如，重庆立足大城市、大农村、大山区、大库区基本市情，统筹抓好乡村振兴和城市提升，加快城乡一体化建设，新发展农林特色产业166万亩，“巴味渝珍”品牌首批授权产品438个；农村“三变”改革、“三社”融合发展试点稳步推进，减少村级集体经济“空壳村”1224个；启动农村人居环境整治三年行动，行政村生活垃圾有效治理率超过90%、污水处理率达到63%。成都加快培育乡村产业新优势，加快建设“6+7”现代农业产业功能区，启动“农村集体经济+农商文旅体融合发展”试点项目30个，有力推动了乡村产业跨界融合；广泛开展文明村镇创建和乡村文脉保护传承行动，实施农村人居环境整治提升“百镇千村”攻坚行动，完成农村户厕改造提升24.8万户，培育“美丽四川·宜居乡村”达标村1500个。郑州市出台了《中共郑州市委郑州市人民政府关于推进乡村振兴战略的实施意见》和《郑州市人民政府关于加快推进乡村振兴战略2018年实施方案》，谋划540个项目，计划总投资超过3600亿元，27个美丽乡村建设正在加快推进。西安市紧紧围

绕“五个振兴”，加快推进“五个美丽”建设，不断加大农村人居环境整治力度，实施“百村示范、千村整治”工程，开展农村垃圾、污水、厕所“新三大革命”。推进行政村规划编制全覆盖，完成400个村庄基础设施和公共服务设施建设，创建50个“五个美丽”样板村，累计建成300个美丽宜居示范村。武汉市创新提升“三乡工程”，持续推动人才、资本、技术下乡，打造“一乡一村一品”。

三　国家中心城市带动区域协调发展的现状特点

（一）坚持规划引领和统筹推进，区域联动发展的态势初步显现

近年来，国家中心城市坚持规划引领，统筹推进中心城市与周边地区在功能、空间、交通、设施、环境等方面的衔接，全面落实国家区域发展战略。比如，北京制定并实施了京津冀协同发展新三年行动计划（2018—2020年），紧密对接《河北雄安新区规划纲要》、《河北雄安新区总体规划（2018—2035年）》和《北京城市副中心控制性详细规划（街区层面）（2016—2035年）》等规划，出台了产业、交通、科技、生态、设施、体制机制等一系列支持建设非首都功能集中承载地的专项规划和政策，全方位支持城市副中心建设和雄安新区开局起步。上海与江苏、浙江、安徽三省积极联动，推动了首个区域一体化发展规划纲要《长江三角洲区域一体化发展规划纲要》落地实施，签署了《长三角地区打通省际断头路合作框架协议》《关于共同推进长三角地区民航协同发展　努力打造长三角世界级机场群合作协议》《关于协同推进长三角港航一体化发展六大行动方案》等专项行动计划，深度推进长三角一体化发展。广州在深入落实广佛同城化、广清一体化、穗莞战略合作规划的同时，以《粤港澳大湾区发展规划纲要》获批实施为新起点，积极参与到大湾区“1 + N”规划体系编制中，制订了产业、创新、生态等多个区域协同发展的相关规划和行动计划。重庆与四川省签署了《深化川渝合作深入推动长江经济带发展行动计划（2018—2022年）》，初步建立了主要领导共同召集、轮流主持的联席会议制度，以重庆、成都引领带动成渝城市群发展从概念逐步走向现实。武汉在落实《武汉城市圈区域发展规划（2013—2020年）》基础上，进一步加

快专项规划和行动计划的编制和实施，同时与中部三个省会城市（长沙、南昌、合肥）共同签署了《长江中游城市群省会城市合作行动计划（2017—2020）》《长江中游城市群建设近期合作重点事项》《长江中游城市群省会城市新区发展合作框架协议》《长江中游城市群省会城市共建科技服务资源共享平台合作协议》等多个行动计划，进一步深化细化交流合作。郑州立足于加快打造中原城市群核心区，编制规划了《郑州大都市区空间规划（2018—2035年）》以加快推动郑州与开封、许昌、新乡、焦作的深度融合发展，同时加快推进郑开双创走廊、开港产业带、许港产业带等6个专项规划报审。西安从省级层面印发了《陕西省2019年推进关中平原城市群建设行动计划》，为支持先建设国家中心城市并以中心城市引领城市群发展提供了支撑。总体来看，这些城市都注重发挥规划在引领带动区域发展过程中的先行先导作用，站在发挥国家中心城市和落实国家区域发展战略的高度，联合周边城市加快推进区域合作和一体化发展的具体的或者新一轮的顶层设计，通过顶层设计明确国家中心城市带动区域发展的阶段性目标、战略路径和主要任务，部分国家中心城市带动区域协调发展的“四梁八柱”基本建立。这些国家中心城市周边的城市也积极响应，主动融入，共同参与总体规划和专项行动计划的编制和实施当中来，从空间、产业、基础设施、公共服务、要素共享、生态治理、体制机制等多个角度展开合作，区域合作的广度和深度不断拓展，区域联动发展的态势已初步显现。

（二）坚持交通基础设施互联互通，区域协同的基础支撑不断强化

基础设施的互联互通是发挥中心城市带动作用的重要方面，也是推动区域协同发展的基础支撑。国家中心城市在各类区域发展的规划指引下，加快推动区域之间的基础设施互联互通。比如，北京、天津加快推动石济客专，津保铁路，京唐铁路，京滨铁路，京雄、津雄城铁等轨道交通以及环首都地区高速公路建设，积极打通扩容一批“断头路”“瓶颈路”，天津至北京新机场联络线前期工作加速推进，4条高铁通道联通京津双城的交通格局正在形成，同时天津对来津北京牌照小型、微型客车限行，实行同城化管理，京津冀交通“一卡通”覆盖全部公交和地铁线路。上海与江苏、浙江、安徽三省共同推进省级对接道路各项工作，截至2018年底三省一市的省级“断头路”开工19条，

通车 2 条，同时，长三角各相邻地区开通了 37 条跨省市公交线路并逐步推动实现公交零换乘。广州在实现与佛山、中山、珠海等交通互联互通基础上，又推动了广深港高铁的开通运营，同时加快推进穗港澳出入境大楼建设以高效连接香港机场、澳门机场的水上航线，伴随着港珠澳大桥的通行，粤港澳大湾区 1 小时便捷生活圈、1.5 小时经济圈正在加快形成。成渝作为全国打破高速公路区域网络格局的首批试点，在实现高铁和高速公路互联互通的基础上，两市已于 2018 年底完成了联网收费系统改造，从技术上实现了高速公路通行费“分省计费、统一收费”，两市还推出了每天近 80 趟的动车和“深夜动车”，动车公交化的运行使两地之间的中小城市的经济联系更加密切。武汉牵头长江中游城市群相继打通了十余条高速公路“断头路”，先后建设了武汉至黄石、鄂州、浠水、咸宁、孝感、仙桃、潜江、天门等城市的城际铁路专用线，并逐步推进了城际铁路“公交化”运行，形成城市圈轨道交通网。郑州在加快航空港国际物流枢纽和“米”字形高铁网络建设的同时，加快与周边城市交通互联互通建设，目前已开通了郑州到机场、开封、焦作三条城际铁路，郑州大都市区范围内已初步实现了各县市区高速公路网相连，同时郑州与新乡实现了部分管廊的一体化，联合许昌建设运行了郑州航空港异地候机楼。西安编制了大西安地区（含西咸新区、咸阳市）地铁建设规划，加快实施“米”字形高速铁路网规划和“一核、双环、六辐射”的关中城际铁路网规划，同时积极推进西安至法门寺、韩城，机场至法门寺、阎良的城际铁路建设和西安至银川、延安、十堰、安康等地的高速铁路建设，基本形成了关中城际铁路网的主骨架。通过交通基础设施的互联互通，国家中心城市与周边地区逐步建立起高效、便捷、一体化的交通网络体系，有效打破了中心城市与周边地区的物理空间限制，不断强化区域协同发展的基础支撑，使得中心城市的区域联系强度不断提升，推动人流、物流、信息流、资金流、创新流在区域之间的高频高效流动，催生了如“轨道人才”① 之类的新的要素流动模式，推动生产要素实现高效流动和最佳配置。

① “轨道人才”主要是指中心城市与周边通过便捷的轨道交通连接的地区，实现人才的有效流动，中心城市的高端人才利用周末或其他非上班时间往返于中心城市与周边地区，发挥了人才效能。

（三）坚持要素资源平台共建共享，区域产业协同发展动力更加强劲

上海积极推动长三角区域的11家产业园协同创新，与其他三省共同规划建设G60科创走廊①，实施《长三角G60科创走廊产业集群高质量一体化发展行动纲要》，立足人工智能、集成电路、生物医药、高端装备、新能源、新材料、新能源汽车七大战略性新兴产业，推进产业高质量一体化发展，同时依托科创走廊构建科学仪器设施区域共建共享、创新券通用通兑、创新链区域协同、投资数据共享等体制机制，组建联合招商联盟、联合采购联盟，成立产业园区联盟，促进长三角科创资源自由流动，有效推动科创项目和新成果落地。上海还联动其他三省成立了总规模达到1000亿元的长三角协同优势产业基金，将通过对“硬科技”等方向的重点投资加速长三角产业链深度融合，同时，为了精准对接科创板，上海推动浦东新区和上海证券交易所在张江科学城共同规划建设了长三角资本市场服务基地，为长三角企业对接资本市场提供一站式服务，加强长三角区域的协同创新，增强金融服务实体经济能力，促进金融中心和科创中心融合发展。北京、天津按照“北京原始创新、天津研发转化、河北应用推广”区域创新体系，完善成果转化体制机制和支持政策，高水平打造国家级重大科技基础设施和创新平台、科研成果展示交易平台，鼓励科技成果在天津转移转化，实现与京冀优势互补、合理分工和有序协作。天津积极承接北京非首都功能，构建起以滨海新区为综合承载平台、各区专业承载平台为支撑的“1+16”承接格局，主动加强与国家部委、中央企业、大院大所的有效合作，截至2018年底，滨海—中关村科技园已新增注册企业941家，百度创新中心、京东云创空间、深之蓝、中国知识产权保护中心等一批优质项目在这里安家落户，扎根发展。2014～2018年，北京企业在津投资到位金额超过6400亿元，占引进内资的40%以上。广州积极建设创新工场粤港澳大湾区总部，搭建了一支数十人的本地化投资及AI研发团队、服务团队，募集25亿元投资在人工智能、大数据等领域，在香港科技大学、南京大学、北京大

① 科创走廊以上海松江区为牵头发起地，由上海松江、浙江嘉兴、浙江湖州、浙江杭州、浙江金华、江苏苏州、安徽宣城、安徽芜湖、安徽合肥共同组建，在长三角区域规划中被定位为“科技和制度创新双轮驱动、产业和城市一体化发展的先行先试走廊”。

学、清华大学、上海交通大学等知名高校开展了广泛的科研教学和人才培养工作，为大湾区培育用AI解决真实世界问题的科技人才，助力技术和人才腾飞。同时，广州依托智能制造优势，对接香港再工业化，启动建设了穗港智造特别合作区，力求在生物医药大健康、人工智能、电子信息、金融服务、新能源新材料等领域展开合作，着力打造湾区“基础研究+技术开发+成果转化”的创新链，合力建设广深港澳科技创新走廊。成渝两地依托科研资源优势、高新技术产业基础，充分发挥了天府新区、两江新区高端要素集聚平台作用，联合打造了一批创新型园区和战略性新兴产业基地，形成电子核心部件、新材料、物联网及智能装备、高端交通装备、生物医药等产业集群。武汉联合中部其他三个省会城市组建了长江中游城市群科技成果转化促进联盟，通过城市间科学技术互通平台，加快了科技成果转化。长沙、南昌、合肥三市在武汉投资注册企业超过3300家，武汉在三市投资注册企业超过4500家。武汉还和长江中游城市群其他三个省会城市着力推动共同搭建政府主导、线上线下“长江中游城市群科技服务资源共享平台”，形成长江中游城市群四省会城市科技服务业合作生态化、工作平台常态化、合作机制市场化，共同服务长江中游城市群优势产业链。郑州依托郑州航空港区承载多个国家战略的平台优势，与周边城市联合打造郑州航空港区的拓展区和配套区，推进一批产业向新乡、许昌、焦作等地转移，通过“飞地经济”等模式，实现了两地优势互补、税收共享、协调发展。总之，国家中心城市通过要素资源平台的共建共享，加快推动区域产业协同发展，产业互补、链条延伸、结构优化的区域产业生态正在加快形成。

（四）坚持规则和制度的有效衔接，区域市场一体化建设加速推进

市场在资源配置中的决定性作用是区域经济合作的根本动力，尊重市场规律，意味着打破地域之间的规则约束和制度壁垒，建立统一规范的规则和制度体系。近年来，国家中心城市按照建设统一、开放、竞争、有序的市场体系要求，加快推进区域市场一体化建设。比如，由上海牵头建设的长三角G60科创走廊的九城（区）率先探索跨省市“一网通办”，实现30种证照跨省异地线上“一地认证、全网通办”。这种“一网通办”模式目前已扩展到长三角地区14个城市和51种事项，包括30种企业服务事项和21种个人服务事项，同

时，企业营业执照、居民身份证、驾驶证、结婚证、居住证、行驶证、出生医学证明 7 种证照在三省一市的政务服务 App 上都实现了电子亮证。长三角地区还建立完善了区域信用合作机制，在国内率先探索形成跨区域的信用联合奖惩模式，针对环境保护领域发布了首个区域严重失信行为认定标准及覆盖行政、社会、市场、行业四个方面 8 大类 40 项联合惩戒措施。京津冀地区则率先实行通关一体化改革，通关时间平均缩短 41 天，同时，在公安部牵头下，北京出台实施创新发展 20 条出入境政策措施，京津冀区域银行业风险分担、支付清算和异地存储互惠互通等机制一体化改革也取得积极进展。广州依托大湾区建设，有序推进香港、澳门的金融市场互联互通，推动实现机构协同、市场协同和产品协同；推动广东、香港、澳门“一地两检”通过政策落地；广州还联合香港、澳门积极探索，先行先试，加强粤港澳地区食用农产品市场安全合作，建立了粤港澳大湾区“菜篮子”信息化产品流通平台，采取“一个标准供市场、一个平台流通、一个体系监管质量安全”的运行模式，构建大湾区严密的农产品质量安全监管网络体系；广州高新区牵头在广州国际生物岛设立了华南生物材料出入境公共服务平台，采取“口岸放行、平台查验、后续监管”的创新监管新模式，大幅压缩生物试剂通关时间；聚焦体制机制创新，落实便利港澳居民到内地发展的政策措施，在科研经费跨境使用、取消办理就业许可证、实施港澳居民居住证政策等方面取得突破。武汉联合长沙、南昌、合肥四市牵头发动长江中游城市群 26 个城市共同签署了《长江中游城市群（南昌）四市暨相关城市圈民间商会合作备忘录》，全面融合四市相关城市圈、“一体化”战略城市（地级市）商会和各区域、行业、外埠、异地民间商会各类资源，创建长江中游城市群“大商会”合作机制，推进民间商会区域一体化和协调合作共赢发展的新模式。四市推动了工商政务信息整合共享，建立了质量技术监督一体化机制、食品药品稽查协作机制，初步实现了通关一体化，同时加快打破区域行政壁垒促进市场融通，构建了全国第一个跨区域、跨省市的政务云项目——长江中游城市群省会城市（区域）工商政务云平台，取消了对进入本市的城市群企业的资质证书、个人执业证书及相关的信用状况核验，直接采集企业信息，与本地企业同等待遇，并协调各省直部门对于四省会范围内的建筑企业取消进入本省的外来备案注册。武汉还与长沙联手打造长江中游地区首个跨省级公共资源交易合作平台，实现了两市远程异地项目评标。

成渝两地、郑州、西安也正在探索建立成本共担利益共享协同发展机制，推动资本、技术等市场一体化的体制机制，建立健全环渝腹地经济区块横向协调机制，设立由有关县、市、区为成员单位的轮值联席会议制度，协商解决区域合作的有关问题。总之，这些国家中心城市立足于区域市场一体化进行积极探索，加快先行先试，着力解决和破除体制机制障碍，推动区域间市场规则和制度的统一，促进形成要素自由流动的统一开放市场，一系列体制机制障碍的破除，积极探索建立规则制度统一、发展模式共推、治理方式一致、区域市场联动的区域市场一体化发展新机制，为带动区域一体化发展带来更多的内生动力。

（五）坚持公共服务体系互认共享，区域融合的社会环境不断优化

构建区域一体化公共服务体系，能够增强区域之间的社会黏合度和认同度。国家中心城市着力推动区域内的公共服务体系互认共享，有效增进了区域要素流动的积极性和区域内居民的社会认同度。比如，上海与南京、台州、连云港、杭州、温州等17个城市联合建立了长三角地区跨省异地就医门诊结算试点统筹区，实现了异地就医门诊费用直接结算，同时，苏浙皖沪的医保部门将异地安置退休人员、异地长期居住人员、常驻异地工作人员、异地转诊人员四类人员优先纳入试点范围，优化备案及转诊服务，精简备案及转诊手续，扩充备案及转诊渠道。北京与天津、河北开展跨区域合作办学，实现津冀中小学北京优质数字资源共享，组建了京津冀工业院校、师范院校等9个创新发展联盟，同时三地的新农合信息平台完成了对接，京冀两地不断推进双向转诊和检查检验结果互认，开展了京津冀门诊异地直接结算试点和公立医院医用耗材联合采购。天津与雄安新区在职业教育、社会保险制度体系建设等方面全面加强合作，天津职业大学、天津市第一商业学校、天津市园林学校在雄安新区设立分校，同时加快推进通武廊“小京津冀”协调发展，实现了三地医疗机构临床检验结果互认、医疗影像检查资料共享、人才职称资格互认互准。广州与周边城市同城化过程中，推动了教育、医疗、社保、文化等公共资源的有效配置，在区域之间的流动就业人员实现失业保险关系无障碍转移，两市之间相互认定医保定点医疗机构，推进医学检验、影像检查结果互认和医院参保人员医疗费用直接结算，同时加快推进教育城域网实现互联互通，中等职业学校招生

不受地域限制，与部分城市实现了移动通信资费一体化。以武汉与长沙、南昌等为代表的长江中游城市群在医疗、社保、教育等方面加快互联互认，三地之间的职工医保异地就医实现了即时结算，探索了省际住房公积金异地互认互贷，并统一住房公积金异地贷款政策和操作流程。同时，4 个中部省会城市还建立了“长江中游城市群公共卫生协作中心”，成立了急救联盟，该联盟已由 4 市发展至长江中游城市群中的 20 个城市。郑州与开封、新乡逐步实现了电信同城，同时正在加快研究城市之间的交通服务、金融同城及公共资源的共享。通过构建互认共享的区域公共服务体系，国家中心城市与周边地区的公共服务机制壁垒逐渐消除，区域融合的社会环境不断优化，有效发挥出社会福利增进对区域摩擦的消减作用。

（六）坚持区域生态环境协同治理，区域生态安全格局加快形成

生态环境保护是区域治理的硬任务和大前提，国家中心城市坚持“生态优先，绿色发展”的发展理念，着眼于提升区域环境治理能力，强化生态保护与修复，推进气水土等污染防治，实现区域污染同治、生态同建，为区域协调发展增添绿色动力。比如，上海牵头成立了长三角区域污染防治协作和水污染防治协作小组，联合其他省市召开了长三角区域污染防治协作机制会议，建成了长三角区域环境气象一体化业务平台，区域大气污染实现“追本溯源”，进行源头治理。在区域层面实现了大数据雷达同步观测和气象和环保部门信息共享，有效提升了对污染输送的组网观测能力，切实改善了之前气象预报的时间滞后。同时，建立污染输送评估系统，实现对长三角区域及三省一市关键气象条件的定量评估和对输送贡献的定量评估，为各地区环保部门防控污染源排放提供了良好的信息和数据支撑；三省一市信用办及生态环境部门还共同签署了《长三角地区环境保护领域实施信用联合奖惩合作备忘录》，并在实施失信行为评价标准互认、建立数据归集共享机制、推动联合惩戒措施落地、营造良好环保信用环境等方面加强合作，将区域之间环保严重失信企业推送到联合信用平台上，实施区域联合惩治，在市场准入、金融信贷等方面对其加以限制。北京联合天津和河北加快推进区域大气、水、土壤协同治理，加强区域联防联控，实现了规划、标准、监测和重污染天气应急响应“四个统一”，同时加快推进北京、天津、保定平原生态过渡带等重大生态工程建设和永定河综合治理

与生态修复工程，构建和完善了密云水库上游地区的水源保护生态补偿机制和引滦入津上下游横向生态补偿机制。国家相关部门还连同北京、天津、河北、山西、河南等多省份印发了京津冀及周边地区大气污染防治工作方案，京津冀形成了“2＋26”城市大气污染防治工作方案，包括北京、天津，以及河北石家庄、唐山、廊坊等8个城市，山西太原、阳泉、长治等4个城市，山东济南、淄博、济宁、德州等7个城市，河南郑州、开封、安阳、鹤壁等7个城市，形成京津冀大气污染共治通道。广州在推进与周边城市同城化发展的框架内，协调推进珠江跨流域治理、大气环境跨区治理以及汽车尾气的治理等区域环保工作，推动珠三角成为首个国家级森林城市群建设示范区。武汉率先从省级层面编制实施长江经济带生态保护和绿色发展总体规划，从源头上立起生态优先的规矩，同时在武汉青山区试点打造湖北长江经济带首个生态文明示范区，推动青山区北湖生态文明试验区（北湖绿城）范围的规划编制、生态储备林建设、生态修复、水环境治理、土地整理、三旧改造、基础设施提升、特色小镇打造、产城融合发展等方面的合作，为全省探路。其他城市也正在加快构建区域生态联防联治的体制机制。总之，这些城市始终把生态文明建设和生态环境保护工作摆在事关全局的重要位置来抓，突出加强生态文明建设顶层设计，建立健全国家指导、地方担责、区域协作、部省协同的工作机制，加快推动生态环境数据信息共享，通过开展多层次、多形式的生态共建共治，扎实抓好污染治理与生态修复，区域生态安全格局正在加快形成。

四　国家中心城市带动区域协调发展面临的环境分析

（一）面临的机遇

1. 我国进入区域高水平和高质量协调发展阶段

改革开放以来，我国实施了沿海地区率先发展，让一部分地区先富起来的区域发展战略，之后实施了西部大开发、振兴东北老工业基地、中部崛起等战略，各地区积极打造区域经济增长极，形成了资源向发达地区集聚和向经济腹地扩散的态势，呈现“东中西阶梯化”和“南北分化”的区域发展新特征，区域发展不平衡的问题依旧突出。因此，党的十九大正式提出区域协调发展战略，并将其纳入国家七大战略之中，意味着我国进入了实施区域协调发展战略的新阶段。2018 年 11 月 18 日，党中央、国务院印发《中共中央、国务院关于建立更加有效的区域协调发展新机制的意见》，提出建立更加有效的区域协调发展新机制，全面落实区域协调发展战略各项任务，促进区域协调发展向更高水平和更高质量迈进。2018 年底召开的中央经济工作会议明确提出，要统筹推进西部大开发、东北全面振兴、中部地区崛起、东部率先发展，促进区域协调发展。这也为国家中心城市建设提供了新的历史机遇，建设国家中心城市要因地制宜，统筹东、中、西部区域发展的差异性，合理布局国家中心城市，各区域都有国家中心城市支撑和引领区域发展。在国家中心城市的选择和布局中，目前的 9 个国家中心城市中，中西部地区城市占了 5 个席位，中西部地区的国家中心城市要抢抓机遇，辐射带动周边中小城市协同发展，积极打造区域经济增长极，形成区域经济发展高地，优化区域发展格局，成为缩小区域发展差距的重要推动力量。

2. 五大区域发展战略推动形成区域发展新格局

2018 年 11 月 5 日，习近平主席在上海召开的首届中国国际进口博览会开幕式的主旨讲演中提出，“将支持长江三角洲区域一体化发展并上升为国家战略，着力落实新发展理念，构建现代化经济体系，推进更高起点的深化改革和更高层次的对外开放，同‘一带一路’建设、京津冀协同发展、长江经济带发展、粤港澳大湾区建设相互配合，完善中国改革开放空间布局”。标志着长江三角洲区域一体化发展正式上升为国家战略，形成了五大区域发展战略体系，打破了行政区划的制约，在更大范围内配置和优化资源要素，更加注重跨行政区域的协调发展，不能仅靠沿海发达城市带动，需要多点发力、多点支撑全国经济的发展，在全国范围内形成多个经济中心。在五大国家级区域发展战略中，长三角区域一体化、粤港澳大湾区建设、京津冀协同发展分别对应的是长三角、珠三角、京津冀地区，一体化程度已经处于较高水平，上海、广州、北京、天津 4 个国家中心城市在这一区域，处于区域发展的“塔尖”和中心，已经成为引领区域发展的引擎，正在向世界级城市的目标迈进。而重庆、成都、武汉、郑州、西安处于长江经济带、“一带一路”建设的区域，抢抓长江经济带、“一带一路”建设带来的机遇，加快内陆地区对外开放，增强中心城市辐射带动力，引领带动区域发展，形成高质量发展的重要推动力。

3. 城镇化由快速推进向高质量推进阶段转变

我国正处于由高速度发展向高质量转变的关键期，城镇化仍是我国经济增长的巨大引擎。2018 年我国城镇化率达到 59.6%，户籍人口城镇化率为 43.37%，与发达国家相比，无论是在绝对量还是相对量上都仍有较大的发展空间，发展潜力巨大。但是我国户籍人口城镇化率远远低于常住人口城镇化率，两者相差 16.23 个百分点，城市常住非户籍人口并没有享受到与城市居民平等的公共服务。此外，人们对城市生活的理解和需求也在发生代际转换，距离高质量的城镇化还有较长的路要走。与此同时，在城镇化快速推进过程中，少数大城市由于承担过多的功能，产业、人口等资源要素高度集聚，“职住分离”导致城市规模扩张过快，房价居高不下、交通拥堵、人居环境恶化等“城市病”凸显。为有效推进新型城镇化，提高城镇化质量，党中央、国务院先后出台一系列重大举措，2014 年中共中央、国务院印发《国家新型城镇化规划（2014—2020 年）》，随后国务院发布《关于进一步推进户籍制度改革的意见》《关于深入推进新型城镇化建设的若干意见》《关于实施支持农业转移人口市民化若干财政政策的通知》《2019 年新型城镇化建设重点任务》等文件。未来一段时间我国仍处于城镇化快速发展期，人口将不断向各类中心城市，特别是向国家中心城市集聚，人口持续地流入将为国家中心城市经济发展创造持久动力。国家中心城市一方面要推进农业转移人口市民化，使其享受到与户籍居民同等的公共服务；另一方面加快疏解城市功能，缓解大城市病，进一步发挥其辐射和带动作用，推动城乡、中心城市和周边中小城市协调发展。

4. 都市圈和城市群将成为我国城市发展的主体形态

我国的城市发展将沿着“中心城市—都市圈—城市群—区域经济一体化”的轨迹发展，即由中心城市向都市圈扩散，由都市圈向城市群蔓延，最终形成以城市群为主体、大中小城市和小城镇协调发展的区域经济一体化发展格局，以都市圈和城市群为主要载体的区域一体化将成为未来区域发展的核心动力。2018 年，34 个中心城市引领的都市圈占到全国总面积的 24%，总人口的 59%，GDP 的 77.8%，中国新型城镇化发展正式进入都市圈时代。都市圈发展是世界城市化进程中的一般性规律和普遍现象，通过强有力的都市圈，能够放大城市群中心城市的辐射能力、加深中心城市与周边中小城市的各方面联系。2018 年 9 月 28 日，习近平总书记在沈阳主持召开深入推进东北振兴座谈会，首次提出“要培育发展现代化都市圈”。2019 年 2 月，国家发展改革委出台了《关于培育发展现代化都市圈的指导意见》，要求各地区各部门要统一思想认识、加强组织领导、强化责任意识，用改革的办法和创新的精神，积极培育发展现代化都市圈。城市群是城市发展到成熟阶段的最高空间组织形式，城市群是我国新型城镇化的主体形态。但是，现阶段我国的城市群大多处于发展初级阶段，都市圈发展也未进入成熟阶段，更多的城市群和都市圈需要优先发展中心城市，打造区域发展的核心增长极，进而辐射带动周边区域发展。我国确认的 9 个国家中心城市，都处于国家区域中心或枢纽的关键位置，在各自的城市群和都市圈中处于核心位置，肩负辐射带动区域发展的重任，通过集聚高端要素、优化交通网络、加快产业升级等举措提升城市能级，使国家中心城市真正成为都市圈和城市群的“强核”。

（二）面临的挑战

1. 世界经济格局调整变革背景下提高国际竞争力的挑战

世界经济格局正处于大调整、大变革的关键转折期，2018 年世界经济温和增长，增速放缓。和平和发展仍是时代发展主题，但是“逆全球化”倾向出现，贸易保护主义和单边主义抬头，全球经贸规则正面临深刻调整。美国通过“货币政策正常化”“保护主义”“贸易协定高标准化”等一系列政策，不仅对中国的出口商品加征关税，还在高新技术转让、投资、研发、人员交流等领域，采取各种限制性举措，同时试图联合其他发达国家创建新的贸易规则，将中国排除在外，这些将会对我国的出口、投资甚至消费产生程度不同的冲击。未来一段时期，中国与世界的关系将处于一个重新调适和相互建构的过程之中，中国的外部环境发展将更加复杂，不利因素逐渐增多。这些将给正在大力转变经济发展方式、转换增长动力、推动高质量发展的中国增添更多挑战，贸易保护主义将不利于国家中心城市在全球范围内运用和配置各种资源，参与国际分工与协作，阻碍国家中心城市的国际化进程。国家中心城市建设的最高目标是打造世界城市，建设具有国际影响力和竞争力的城市，而部分中心城市自身实力还不强，参与国际竞争的能力需要进一步提升。

2. 统筹集聚发展和辐射带动区域发展的挑战

国家中心城市是城市发展新金字塔形空间格局的塔尖城市，肩负着自身发展壮大和辐射带动区域发展的双重使命。一方面，国家中心城市建设需要集聚各种要素资源，加快自身发展，使之成为一个区域发展的高地和增长极，在这个过程中会产生虹吸效应或极化效应，中心城市周边小城市的资金、人才、优质产业容易被吸引转移到大城市，进而使小城市发展面临挑战。另一方面，国家中心城市自身集聚吸引优质资源要素的能力较强，可以将要素资源和部分产业向周边地区转移，产生辐射效应，带动周边区域发展，缩小中心城市与周边中小城市发展的差距。因此，如何平衡虹吸效应和辐射效应，是国家中心城市建设面临的一大挑战。各国家中心城市区位不同，发展阶段不同，承担的职能也不同，如上海、广州集聚要素能力和经济实力较强，对周边辐射带动作用明显，已经形成与周边区域一体化发展格局；北京、天津整体实力较强，但是对周边辐射带动作用较弱，如何带动辐射周边区域发展，使辐射带动效应大于虹吸效应是其面临的难题。重庆、成都、武汉、郑州、西安等国家中心城市仍处于集聚人口和生产要素、努力发展壮大自身实力的阶段，其自身实力还不够强大，辐射带动能力不足，如何带动更加弱小的周边中小城市是巨大的挑战，平衡好虹吸效应和辐射效应也是一个难题。

3. 提升城市人口吸引力的挑战

人口吸引力是城市竞争力的重要体现，在全国人口总量增长趋缓、人口红利下降的背景下，区域间、城市间的人口竞争日益激烈。2017 年以来，强二线城市纷纷出台“人才政策”，如实行购房租房优惠、落户放宽、就业创业给予补贴等措施，以吸引更多的人口落户到该城市，“抢人大战”愈演愈烈。由于各国家中心城市对人才的需求不同，各城市出台政策的侧重点也不同，对于落户要求，大多城市本科学历即可落户，郑州、重庆两市专科学历即可落户；在出台了《西安市深化人才发展体制机制改革，打造“一带一路”人才高地若干政策措施》后，2018 年西安又出台了《西安市进一步加快人才汇聚若干措施》，首创 13 条措施以吸引更多的人才留在本地就业创业；2017 年 7 月，《成都实施人才优先发展战略行动计划》（简称“成都人才新政 12 条”）正式实施；2017 年 11 月，郑州市委市政府正式公布了《关于实施“智汇郑州”人才工程加快推进国家中心城市建设的意见》。各城市人才政策出台两年来，成效显著，除北京常住人口仍保持负增长外，各城市人口规模持续增长。上海、天津常住人口规模“止负回升”，在 2017 年人口负增长后 2018 年常住人口分别增长 5.5 万人和 2.7 万人；广州人口增长较快，2018 年常住人口新增 40.6 万人；西安、成都、重庆、郑州在“引才政策”带动下，常住人口均增长超过 20 万人，人口吸引力较强（见图 1）。但是，提高城市对人口的吸引力，不仅要靠出台的人才引进政策，还要依靠城市自身的产业发展、就业机会、人居环境等方面的提升，未来的人口竞争格局将更加激烈，如何吸引人口、留住人口对各国家中心城市将是一个挑战。

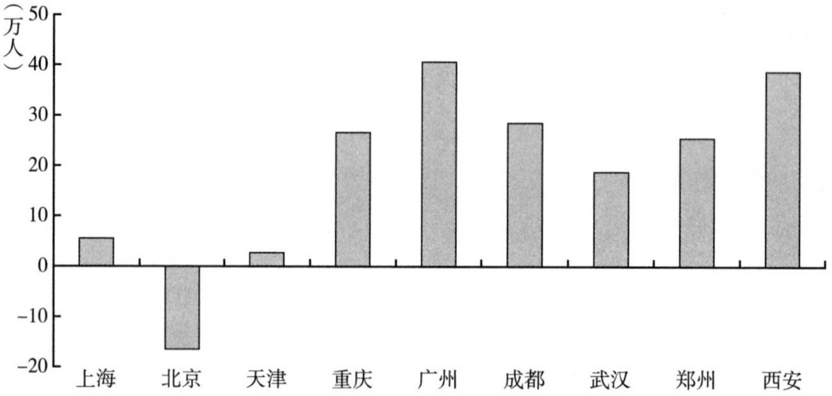

图 1　2018 年 9 个国家中心城市常住人口增加量

资料来源：9 个国家中心城市 2018 年国民经济和社会发展统计公报。

4. 城市之间竞争日益激烈的挑战

建设国家中心城市是适应中国经济新常态、促进区域协调发展、构建中国特色新型城镇体系的重大创新，国家中心城市将集聚国家战略性资源、享受更多的政策红利，一些城市认识到国家中心城市的重要地位，竞相提出要建设国家中心城市，未纳入的城市正在积极争取戴上“国家中心城市”的帽子。但是国家中心城市建设应该重质而不重量，控制中心城市的数量，不拔苗助长、不撒胡椒面、不搞平衡主义，避免将不够条件的城市纳入国家中心城市，保证国家中心城市的国家级地位。除了争取政策支持外，现有的国家中心城市间也面临着激烈的竞争，特别是在地缘相近、优势相近的城市间竞争更加激烈，如武汉、郑州的中部龙头之争，成都、重庆的西南地区龙头之争，各个城市都在争取国家政策支持，在产业、人才、资金、交通等方面争夺资源。从经济实力看，2018 年郑州迈入万亿元俱乐部后，9 个国家中心城市中只有西安的 GDP

还没有破万亿元；从人口规模看，2018 年 9 个国家中心城市常住人口均突破 1000 万人。除了硬指标，各城市在营商环境、文化等软实力上也存在激烈的竞争，各城市依托自身优势，推动城市特色发展和城市功能的提升。各中心城市如何在竞争中提升自身综合实力和竞争力，形成城市间良性竞争还是一个挑战。

5. 保持城市可持续竞争力的挑战

国家中心城市应是具有可持续竞争力的城市，即城市在充分利用现有要素获得发展优势和经济增长的同时，能够形成城市未来发展优势，并积累能够促进城市长期增长的要素。保持城市可持续竞争力，要求国家中心城市要具有长期经济增长的能力，在国家中心城市建设中，有些城市正在进行产业结构调整，产业升级尚未完成，仍处于新旧动能转化过程中，支撑经济长期发展的新动力尚未形成。城市可持续竞争力要求兼顾经济发展、生态良好、社会福利、科技创新等多方面的目标，在此基础上实现经济效率的提升。随着大量人口向中心城市集聚，部分国家中心城市资源环境约束趋紧，城市资源环境承载力达到上限，雾霾、水污染等环境污染短期内难以改善，环境质量改善的程度与人民群众的期盼还有较大的差距，制约了城市的发展。此外，提升城市可持续竞争力要求国家中心城市在确保当前城市居民生活质量提升和社会福利增加的同时，提升城市居民未来获得更多的福利，当前部分中心城市正处于交通拥堵、公共资源短缺、管理失效的发展阵痛期，距离人民群众对美好生活的向往还有一定的距离。如何实现经济增长的同时使环境改善、人民群众生活水平和福利水平提高，提升可持续发展能力和竞争力是国家中心城市未来一段时期面临的又一挑战。

五　国家中心城市带动区域协调发展的展望与建议

（一）新增国家中心城市的必备条件

从国家中心城市的基本内涵、战略定位、功能作用上看，进入国家中心城市行列，要满足两个基本条件。

第一个条件是要体现国家中心城市的职能要求。职能要求主要包括辐射带动能力和市场认可程度两个方面。从辐射带动区域发展的角度看，要成为国家中心城市，必须具备强大的城市能级，而且要展现出比所在区域或者城市群范围内的其他城市更强大的能级，在全国较大区域范围内的经济、社会、文化、创新发展过程中发挥核心作用，是区域的经济中心、文化中心、管理中心、创新中心、金融中心、物流中心、对外交往中心，还可能是所在行政区的政治中心。国家中心城市具有强大的集聚辐射带动能力，能够将自身的生产能力、创新能力、服务能力等内容高效地传递到全国城市体系或区域城镇体系中的其他节点城镇，从而带动整个区域的高效发展。从获得广泛市场认可的角度看，一个城市究竟能不能成为国家中心城市，最终并不由政府规划说了算，也不是主观上想成就成，从根本上讲是市场选择的结果，核心是看这个城市是否具备了国家中心城市的基本功能。尽管国家可以通过规划等方式确立建设国家中心城市的目标，但是国家中心城市最终历史地位的确立，还有待于市场的认可。新增国家中心城市，必须在历史地位、综合实力、教育科研、医疗卫生、交通区位等方面获得市场的认可。

第二个条件是要体现国家区域协调发展的总体布局。从我国目前已经明确的九大国家中心城市来看，成为国家中心城市的基本要求，是必须具有较强的中心性特征：一是全国城镇体系的中心城市。我国官方文件中第一次明确提出国家中心城市的概念，就是在原住房和城乡建设部发布的《全国城镇体系规划（2010—2020 年）》中，其中明确将北京、天津、上海、广州、重庆定位为五大国家中心城市。在全国城镇体系规划中，国家中心城市的定位非常明确，是全国城镇体系的中心城市，短期内其他城市进入全国城镇体系中心城市行列的概率相对较低，以全国城镇体系中心城市来入围国家中心城市行列的难度较大。二是国家级城市群的核心城市。成都、郑州、武汉、西安等城市进入国家中心城市行列，均是作为国家级城市群的核心城市。例如，2015 年在《长江中游城市群发展规划》中，明确武汉是长江中游城市群的中心城市。2016 年国家发改委发布的《成渝城市群发展规划》中明确提出，成都要以建设国家中心城市为目标，增强成都西部地区重要的经济中心、科技中心、文创中心、对外交往中心和综合交通枢纽功能。2016 年 12 月，经国务院正式批复，国家发改委发布《促进中部地区崛起“十三五”规划》，明确支持武汉、郑州建设国家中心城市，随后进一步在中原城市群发展规划中明确郑州的国家中心城市地位。2018 年 2 月 2 日，国家发展改革委、住房和城乡建设部《关于印发关中平原城市群发展规划的通知》明确提出，建设西安国家中心城市，强化面向西北地区的综合服务和对外交往门户功能。从这个角度来看，进入国家中心城市行列的另一条主要路径是成为国家级城市群的核心城市。三是区域发展的中心城市。在国家中心城市梯队扩容的背景下，重庆、武汉、西安分别作为我国西南、华中、西北地区的首位城市，作为国家中心城市的认可度也相对较高。新增国家中心城市，也必须是我国大区域的中心城市，能够有效辐射带动某一区域的发展。

新增国家中心城市，要具备国家中心城市的核心职能，更要具备贯彻落实国家区域协调发展的战略布局。根据当前我国的国家宏观战略布局、国土开发格局和对外开放布局，根据主要特大城市和大城市自身综合实力和所处发展阶段的动态演变，根据我国当前的区域协调发展政策的调整与变化，未来仍有一些城市有望进入国家中心城市行列，比如深圳、南京、沈阳、厦门等。

（二）国家中心城市带动区域协调发展的思路和任务

1. 国家中心城市带动区域协调发展的总体思路

国家中心城市带动区域协调发展的总体思路是：以“一带一路”建设、京津冀协同发展、长江经济带发展、粤港澳大湾区、长三角一体化等重大战略为引领，以东部、中部、西部、东北四大板块为基础，加快优化中心城市—都市圈—城市群—区域所组成的空间组合模式和要素流动通道，加快构建以中心城市引领城市群发展、城市群带动区域发展新模式，以北京、天津为中心引领京津冀城市群发展，带动环渤海地区协同发展；以上海为中心引领长三角城市群发展，带动长江经济带发展；以广州和香港、澳门、深圳为中心引领粤港澳大湾区建设，带动珠江—西江经济带创新绿色发展；以重庆、成都、武汉、郑州、西安、长春、厦门等为中心，引领成渝、长江中游、中原、关中平原、哈长、海峡西岸等城市群发展，进而推动区域板块之间融合互动发展。

2. 国家中心城市带动区域协调发展的重点任务

谋划国家中心城市带动区域协调发展的功能体系。我国陆地总面积约为 960 万平方公里，2018 年末总人口将近 14 亿，区域发展还不平衡，需要打造多个支撑整个国土的战略性支点，构建起布局合理的“国家中心城市网络体系”。在国家中心城市网络体系内部，北京、上海、广州等要瞄准全球城市的目标，努力成为全球资源的配置中枢，占据全球竞争优势；重庆、成都、武汉、郑州、西安等国家中心城市，要努力在全国范围内，在科技创新、文化交流、商业贸易、交通枢纽、先进制造等专项方面形成突出优势，在全球分工网络中占据一席之地；同时，成为国家各自区域板块的中心城市，支撑国土开发、辐射带动区域协同发展。

构建国家中心城市带动区域协调发展的载体平台。区域作为一个较大空间尺度的地域形式，单靠国家中心城市的单核能级，再加上城市之间作用强度存在的空间距离衰减规律，国家中心城市在较大范围内的带动能力有限，必须通过建立健全较为完善的中心城市量级传导机制和作用通道才能有利于实现区域的协调发展。因此，必须加快构建“国家中心城市—都市圈—大中小城市协调发展的城镇体系—特色小镇—乡村振兴”的全尺度空间组合链条和战略格局，从而带动要素在区域之间、城乡之间自由流动和高效配置。当前，较为重要的发展载体是都市圈的建设。当前我国区域发展存在一定的阶段差异，各个区域内部也存在发展不均衡的情况，因此，要在全尺度空间组合链条突出重点，特别是以国家中心城市为中心，积极打造都市圈，应当因地制宜推进都市圈建设，及时总结成功经验，把都市圈作为城市群建设的重要基础，推动城市群一体化发展。

增强国家中心城市带动区域协调发展的战略统筹。国家中心城市带动区域协调发展的战略统筹主要包括两个层面：第一，国家中心城市必须加强自身诸多战略规划平台的统筹。以郑州为例，国家在赋予河南诸多战略规划平台时，将郑州作为承载国家战略规划平台的重要组成区域，特别是郑州航空港经济综合实验区、中国（河南）自由贸易试验区、郑洛新国家自主创新示范区等引领性战略的实施，使郑州拥有了对外开放的重要门户、全面深化改革的试验田、实施创新驱动发展的核心载体。自 1954 年河南省会从开封西迁以来，到 2017 年初，郑州开始面临诸多国家战略叠加的历史机遇。对于郑州来讲，国家支持郑州建设国家中心城市，既是赋予郑州一个新的国家战略，也是诸多国家战略规划和战略平台融合叠加的必然结果，是郑州在全国区域格局功能与作用的集中体现。可以说，中央支持郑州建设国家中心城市，不仅是对郑州发展潜力和战略地位的高度认可，也是对郑州的比较优势和发展短板的精准把握。

为使国家战略规划平台的叠加效应最大化，加快郑州建设国家中心城市步伐，必须树立系统思想，加强战略规划平台的协同联动发展。第二，加强国家中心城市及其所在城市群与其他国家中心城市和城市群之间的战略统筹。推进京津冀、粤港澳大湾区、长三角、长江中游、成渝、中原、哈长等城市群与“一带一路”、长江经济带等战略统筹，带动东部、东北、中部和西部四大板块的协调发展。

强化国家中心城市带动区域协调发展的合作互助。深化城市群、都市圈、国家中心城市之间的合作互助，提升合作层次和水平。积极发展各类社会中介组织，有序发展区域性行业协会商会，鼓励企业组建跨地区跨行业产业、技术、创新、人才等合作平台。积极探索建立城市群协调治理模式，鼓励成立多种形式的城市联盟。当前，区域之间、区域内部开始逐渐从硬件相通阶段走向软件对接阶段，要加强区域之间，特别是区域相邻地区之间在医疗、教育和社保等方面的对接，以实现社会资源的优化配置和公共服务的均等化。

（三）国家中心城市增强带动区域协调发展的对策与建议

构建快速交通运输体系。快速交通运输体系是国家中心城市与腹地、国家中心城市与其他国家中心城市和区域之间进行各种生产要素流动的基础支撑。由于我国城市群的扩容，导致城市之间的联系紧密度下降。国家中心城市要带动区域协调发展，首先是要在较大空间尺度上实现各种要素流的快速交换。要大规模推进高速铁路建设，形成集城际高速铁路、区域快速火车、地铁系统及轻轨系统为一体的综合轨道交通系统，使城市公共交通扩展至城市—区域系统范围，促进人口、商品、服务、资金和信息等要素快速流动。如随着南广（南宁—广州）高铁、贵广（贵阳—广州）高铁的开通，珠三角面向大西南的通道随之打开。广东与广西、贵州联手打造高铁经济带，即以高铁线路为基础，沿线各省市互相合作、共享资源，形成一个经济一体化区域。

优化产业空间布局。国家中心城市在区域发展中的重要作用就是引领区域产业向中高端发展，形成在全国乃至全球具有竞争力的产业集群。为此，要在国家中心城市体系内部进行合理分工的基础上，通过国家中心城市的创新发展能力和辐射带动能力，引领各个区域培育发展主导产业，并利用主导产业的前、后向关联效应和外溢影响，建设同类企业或上下游关联企业集聚的产业园区、产业基地等，深化龙头企业与中小微企业之间的联系衔接，强化主导产业的引领辐射示范作用，努力打造一批实力突出、优势明显、集约高效的特色产业集群，不断提升区域的产业集群水平，推动全产业链布局优化和区域协调发展。

推动生产要素双向流动。国家中心城市建设有助于区域内部统一市场的构建和错位有序的竞争，从而促进区域增长。国家中心城市在自身市场开放程度提升的时候，也会在与周边区域形成统一市场上发挥标杆作用。同时，国家中心城市建设会打破现有的区域间竞争态势，重新塑造区域间的竞争格局，构建更为开放、统一、错位有序的区域市场环境。具体展开，国家中心城市将在以下几方面发挥引领作用：一是加快人力资源市场一体化。率先实现户籍准入年限同城化累积互认，加快消除城乡区域间户籍壁垒，统筹推进本地人口和外来人口市民化，推动人力资源信息共享、公共就业服务平台共建。二是推动技术市场一体化。加快联合建设科技资源共享服务平台，鼓励共建科技研发和转化基地。探索建立企业需求联合发布机制和财政支持科技成果共享机制。清理城市间因技术标准不统一形成的各种障碍。建立技术交易市场联盟，构建多层次知识产权交易市场体系。三是推动金融服务一体化。加强金融基础设施、信息网络、服务平台一体化建设，鼓励金融机构协同布局。四是消除商事主体异地迁址变更登记隐形阻碍，探索“一照多址、一证多址”企业开办经营模式，加快取消具有相应资质的设计、施工企业异地备案手续，推动各类审批流程标准化和审批信息互联共享。五是加快完善信用体系，实施守信联合激励和失信联合惩戒。联合打击侵权假冒行为，探索建立食品药品联动实时监控平台，推进食品安全检验检测结果互认。

创新协同发展的体制机制。加快构建协商合作、规划协调、政策协同、社会参与等机制。建立城市间多层次合作协商机制。有条件的地方可以探索设立发展及重点领域协调推进机制，负责推动落实一体化发展重大事项。强化城市群规划、城市规划的有机衔接，确保协调配合、同向发力。强化政策协同机制。积极构建互利共赢的税收分享机制和征管协调机制，加强城市间税收优惠政策协调。鼓励社会资本参与建设与运营。允许城乡建设用地增减挂钩节余指标跨地区调剂。健全商品房供应体系，强化城市间房地产市场调控政策协同。加强舆论引导，创新宣传方式，增强社会各方的认同感和积极性，汇聚形成共同参与和支持城市区域协同发展的强大合力。

因地制宜地发挥市场和政府作用。国家中心城市建设是全国城镇体系建设中的一部分，城镇体系的建设过程中两个主要的作用方面是市场和政府。尊重和适应经济发展的自然规律，积极发挥市场在国家中心城市建设和区域协同增长过程中资源配置的决定性作用。同时，应当充分发挥和完善各级政府机构在此过程中的统领作用，一方面，把握全国城镇体系建设的方向和程度，积极推动全国城镇体系建设的各项规划实施；另一方面，积极转变地方政府在区域发展和治理的观念，弱化“行政区经济”和狭隘的地方保护主义，打破区域同质化竞争，实现区域多元化互补共荣发展。

参考文献

[1] 孙久文：《论新时代区域协调发展战略的发展与创新》，《国家行政学院学报》2018 年第 8 期。

[2] 金碚、陈耀、张可云、喻新安：《建立更加有效的区域协调发展新机制》，《区域经济评论》2019 年第 1 期。

[3] 杨晓兰、倪鹏飞：《城市可持续竞争力的起源与发展评述》，《经济学动态》2017 年第 9 期。

[4] 阳国亮、程皓、欧阳慧：《国家中心城市建设能促进区域协同增长吗?》，《财经科学》2018 年第 5 期。

[5] 刘治彦：《国家中心城市怎样引领区域发展》，《人民论坛》2017 年第 20 期。

[6] 白桦、谭德庆：《内陆国家级中心城市经济发展路径研究——基于内陆自贸区视角》，《经济问题探索》2018 年第 10 期。

[7] 涂勇：《中心城市引领区域协调发展的战略思考》，《理论前沿》2003 年第 12 期。

[8] 王伟、罗鑫玥、冯羽：《四大国家中心城市区域发展进阶与协调性测评》，《北京规划建设》2017 年第 1 期。

[9] 陈杰文：《加强成渝中心城市建设促进区域经济协调发展》，《今日财富》2017 年第 10 期。

[10] 王玉虎：《从省际“边缘”到区域“中心”的规划思考》，中国城市规划年会，2014。

[11] 孙斌栋、金晓溪、林杰：《走向大中小城市协调发展的中国新型城镇化格局——建国以来中国城市规模分布演化与影响因素》，《地理研究》2019 年第 1 期。

评 价 篇

Evaluation Report

B.2
2018年中国国家中心城市建设指数及成长性指数评价分析

郑州师范学院国家中心城市研究院课题组*

摘 要： 为准确把握2018年中国国家中心城市在综合服务、网络枢纽、科技创新、开放交流、人文凝聚和生态宜居6个方面的建设水平和发展情况，本研究在国家中心城市建设指数之外，新增成长性指数，分别对9个城市的建设指数和成长性指数进行测度。总体来看，从建设指数上，9个国家中心城市仍旧存在明显的分层现象，上海、北京、广州依旧处于国家中心城市建设的第一梯队，总体发展强势；重庆、成都、天津、武汉处于第二梯队，发展态势相对较好；西安、郑州处于第

* 课题组组长：陈耀、喻新安；副组长：王建国、石玉；执笔：陈耀，经济学博士，郑州师范学院国家中心城市研究院院长，中国社会科学院工业经济研究所研究员、教授、博士生导师，研究方向为区域经济、产业空间组织和政府政策；石玉，博士，郑州师范学院国家中心城市研究院常务副院长，副教授，研究方向为统计学应用、政府评价；徐艳红，博士，郑州师范学院讲师，研究方向为城市发展、城市生态。

三梯队，各项指标均存在很大的提升空间。与2016年相比，9个国家中心城市中部分城市的建设指数排名发生了较大变化：重庆从第五位提升至第四位、成都从第六位提升至第五位，而天津从第四位下降为第六位。从成长性指数上，9个国家中心城市中建设指数排名靠后的城市，均处于快速发展中，其中排在前四位的分别为郑州、西安、成都、武汉，其成长性指数值均在0.15以上；广州、重庆、上海、北京、天津的成长性指数相对较低，城市发展趋于平稳。根据9个国家中心城市建设评价中六大功能层测度结果分析，国家中心城市建设中应注重各功能层的协调发展，要注重经济发展与生态宜居的协调关系，推进开放型城市建设，逐步树立城市文化品牌形象，有效解决城市病，才能更好地发挥国家中心城市在都市圈、城市群中的引领、示范、辐射、带动作用，进而促进区域协调发展。

关键词： 国家中心城市　建设指数　成长性指数　区域协调发展

建设国家中心城市，是党中央、国务院着眼完善全国城镇体系，促进区域协调发展，提升特大中心城市辐射力、带动力，赢得全球城市竞争的重大战略手段；实施区域协调发展战略，是党的十九大确定的我国全面建成小康社会决胜期的七大战略之一。2018年11月18日，《中共中央国务院关于建立更加有效的区域协调发展新机制的意见》中提出了“推动国家重大区域战略融合发展”的意见，并要求以9个国家中心城市为中心分别引领相应城市群发展，带动相关板块融合，促进区域协调发展。2018年，为促进国家中心城市建设，北京、上海、广州、天津、重庆、成都、武汉、郑州、西安等城市分别制定了一系列相关政策、措施，持续推进城市综合服务、网络枢纽、科技创新、开放交流、人文凝聚和生态宜居六大功能的建设，并取得了不同程度的发展。

一　中国国家中心城市经济发展基础指标对比

鉴于国家中心城市在全球城市网络中的关键地位和在国家城镇体系中的核心功能，要求国家中心城市发展中应严格遵循“创新、协调、绿色、开放、共享”的发展理念，实现城市建设从高速发展向高质量发展转变，带动区域协调、可持续发展。为充分了解并分析对比9个国家中心城市2018年的经济发展现状水平及相关指标增长情况，从常住人口、GDP、人均GDP、一般公共预算收入、全社会固定资产投资额、进出口总额、专利授权数量、金融机构本外币存款余额、金融机构本外币贷款余额、人均可支配收入10项基础指标出发，对9个国家中心城市的经济发展现状水平及指标增速进行初步比较。

通过对9个国家中心城市中选取的10项表征经济发展的基础指标绝对值及增长情况对比发现，各国家中心城市之间不仅基础指标绝对值差异比较大，同时其指标的增长情况也呈现较大差异（见图1～图10）。

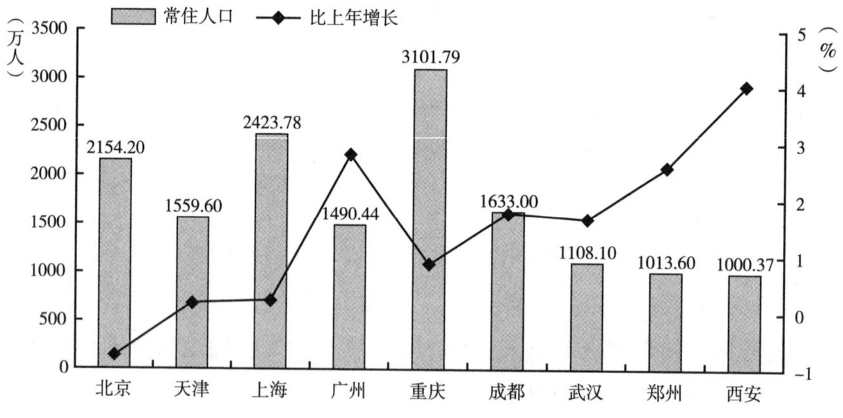

图1　2018年国家中心城市常住人口数及增长情况对比

资料来源：各城市2018年国民经济和社会发展统计公报。

2018年常住人口最多的城市是重庆，其次是上海和北京，而常住人口首次突破千万的郑州和西安分别排名第八和第九；但从年增长率来看，西安常住人口的年增长率最大，其次是广州和郑州，而北京的常住人口则呈负增长态势。

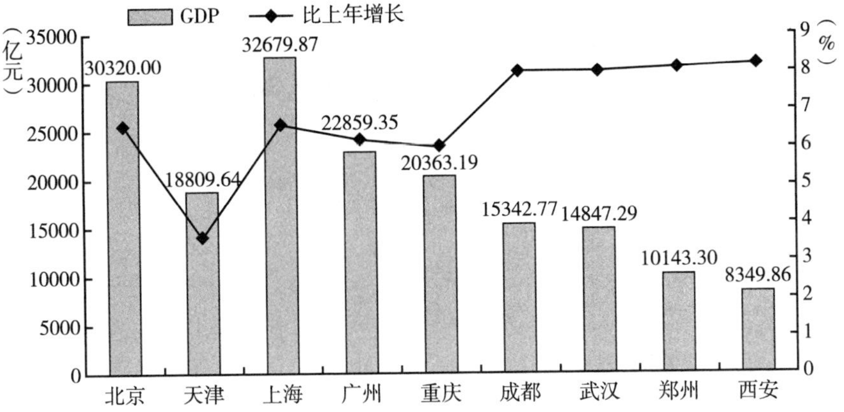

图2　2018 年国家中心城市 GDP 及增长情况对比

资料来源：各城市 2018 年国民经济和社会发展统计公报。

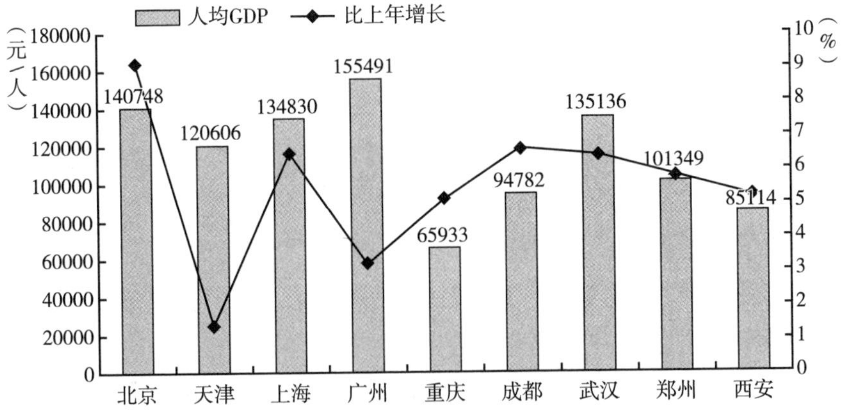

图3　2018 年国家中心城市人均 GDP 及增长情况对比

资料来源：各城市 2018 年国民经济和社会发展统计公报。

2018 年地区生产总值上海排名第一，北京排名第二，首次突破万亿元的郑州排名第八，西安排名第九；从年增长率来看，西安生产总值的年增长率最大，其次是郑州、成都和武汉。

2018 年人均 GDP 广州排名第一，北京排名第二，上海排名第三，西安和重庆分别排名第八、第九，郑州的人均 GDP 首次突破十万元，排名第六；从年增长率来看，北京人均 GDP 年增长率排名第一，天津排名第九。

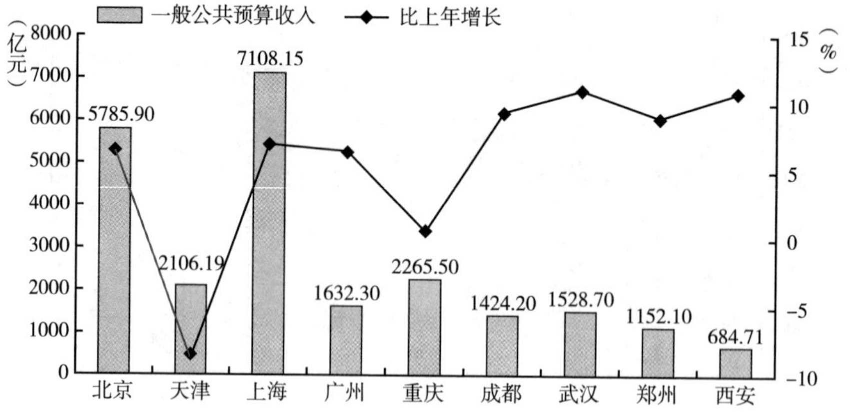

图 4　2018 年国家中心城市一般公共预算收入及增长情况对比

资料来源：各城市 2018 年国民经济和社会发展统计公报。

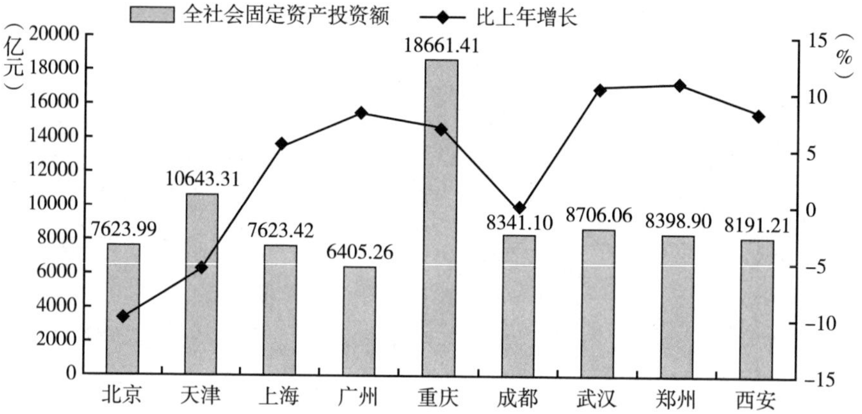

图 5　2018 年国家中心城市全社会固定资产投资额及增长情况对比

资料来源：各城市 2018 年国民经济和社会发展统计公报。

2018 年一般公共预算收入上海排名第一，北京排名第二，西安排名第九；从年增长率来看，武汉的一般公共预算增长率最大，而天津有一定幅度下降。

2018 年全社会固定资产投资额重庆排名第一，天津排名第二，广州排名第九；从年增长率来看，郑州全社会固定资产投资额增长率排名第一，武汉排名第二，而成都、天津、北京均有不同程度下降。

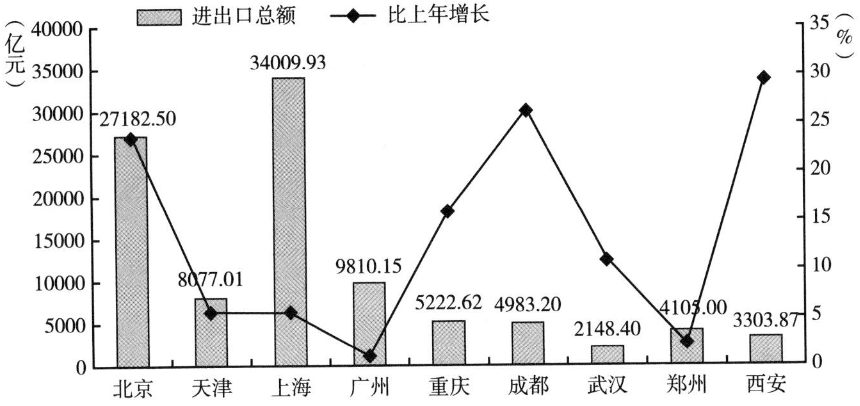

图6　2018年国家中心城市进出口总额及增长情况对比

资料来源：各城市2018年国民经济和社会发展统计公报。

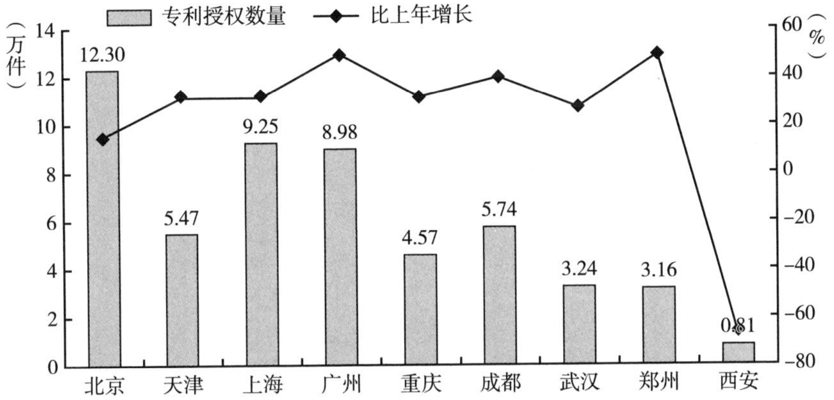

图7　2018年国家中心城市专利授权数量及增长情况对比

资料来源：各城市2018年国民经济和社会发展统计公报。

2018年进出口总额上海排名第一，北京排名第二，西安排名第八，武汉排名第九；从年增长率来看，西安排名第一，成都排名第二，北京排名第三，而广州排名第九。

2018年专利授权数量北京排名第一，上海排名第二，广州排名第三，西安排名第九；从增长率来看，广州排名第一，郑州排名第二，成都排名第三，西安排名第九。

2018年金融机构本外币存款余额北京排名第一，上海排名第二，广州排

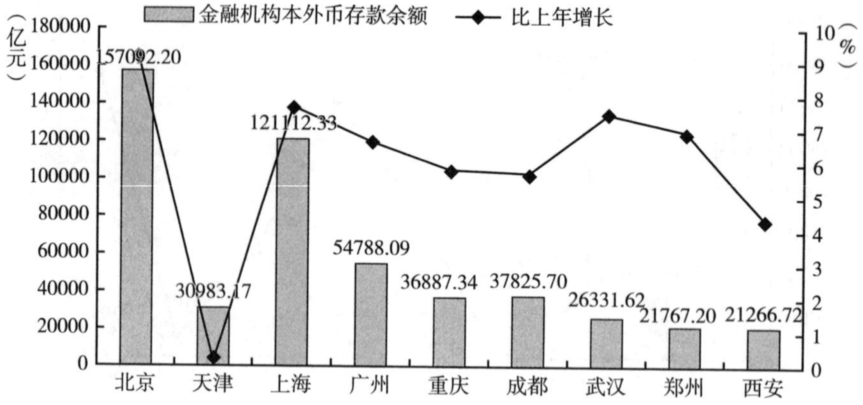

图8　2018年国家中心城市金融机构本外币存款余额及增长情况对比

资料来源：各城市2018年国民经济和社会发展统计公报。

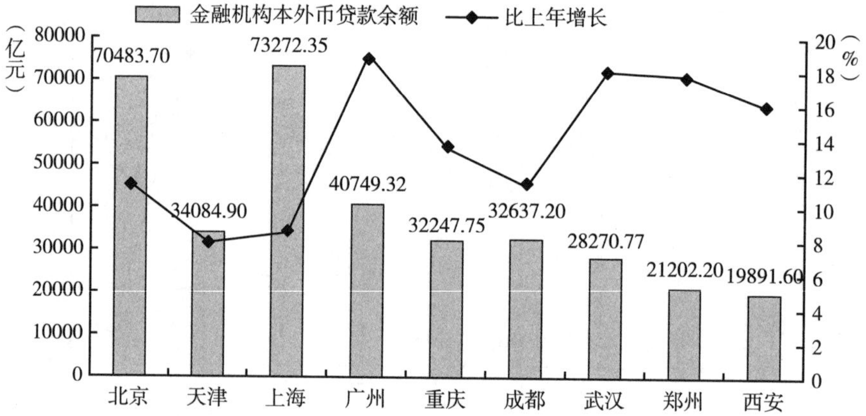

图9　2018年国家中心城市金融机构本外币贷款余额及增长情况对比

资料来源：各城市2018年国民经济和社会发展统计公报。

名第三，西安排名第九；从年增长率来看，北京排名第一，上海排名第二，武汉排名第三，天津排名第九。

2018年金融机构本外币贷款余额上海排名第一，北京排名第二，广州排名第三，西安排名第九；从年增长率来看，广州排名第一，武汉排名第二，郑州排名第三。

2018年人均可支配收入上海排名第一，北京排名第二，广州排名第三，郑州排名第八，重庆排名第九；从年增长率来看，重庆排名第一，北京和武汉

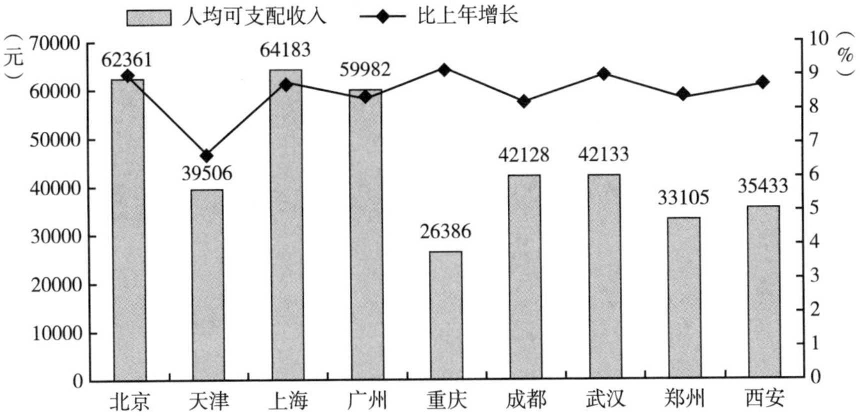

图10 2018年国家中心城市人均可支配收入及增长情况对比

资料来源：各城市2018年国民经济和社会发展统计公报。

排名第二、第三。

初步分析结果表明，目前9个国家中心城市中，上海、北京、广州的经济发展水平优势显著，同时GDP、人均GDP、一般公共预算收入、金融机构本外币存款余额、人均可支配收入等多项指标仍呈现高速增长的态势；而郑州、西安总体经济实力虽依旧相对较弱，但各项基础指标也多呈快速增长趋势，尤其在人口聚集力度、全社会固定资产投资方面增长较快，因此，为促进现代大都市建设，并能够更好地发挥其在城市群和区域发展中的引领作用，仍需进一步加快其经济发展，增大城市辐射范围。

二　中国国家中心城市建设指数排序

（一）中国国家中心城市建设指标权重确定

本次评价采用《国家中心城市建设报告（2018）》中所用的国家中心城市建设指数综合评价体系。

1. 数据来源

研究数据来源于各城市2018年国民经济和社会发展统计公报、各城市人民政府办公室官网、高铁网、各城市2018年统计年鉴、深圳大学中国经济特区研究中心发布的《双创蓝皮书：中国双创发展报告（2017～2018）》、人民体育和人民网舆情数据中心发布的《2017 中国最具体育活力城市排行榜TOP100》、腾讯研究院发布的《数字中国指数报告（2019）》、清华大学电子商务交易技术国家工程实验室等发布的《中国电子商务发展指数报告（2018）》、高德地图发布的《2018 年度中国主要城市交通分析报告》、中国贸促会贸易投资促进部发布的《中国展览经济发展报告（2018）》。

2. 定量方法

本次评价采用《国家中心城市建设报告（2018）》中所用定量方法，考虑到国家中心城市建设评价指标的表征数据单位不统一，无法进行直接比较计算，因此需对所有数据进行 TOPSIS 标准化处理；然后采用变异系数法确定各指标权重；最后通过各指标加权分别确定 9 个国家中心城市的建设指数。

3. 权重分布

根据以上方法，结合相关数据分析，得到各评价指标权重分布情况如表 1。

根据变异系数法以及指标的权重分配显示：从功能层角度分析，综合服务

表 1　2018 年中国国家中心城市建设评价指标权重

功能层	权重	维度层	权重	指标层	权重
综合服务	0. 2694	经济活力	0. 0347	X1	0. 0086
				X2	0. 0073
				X3	0. 0050
				X4	0. 0138
		生产服务	0. 1788	X5	0. 0312
				X6	0. 0288
				X7	0. 0084
				X8	0. 0752
				X9	0. 0145
				X10	0. 0207
		公共服务	0. 0559	X11	0. 0130
				X12	0. 0191
				X13	0. 0033
				X14	0. 0205

续表

功能层	权重	维度层	权重	指标层	权重
网络枢纽	0.2323	信息枢纽	0.0676	X15	0.0187
				X16	0.0206
				X17	0.0283
		交通枢纽	0.1647	X18	0.0209
				X19	0.0495
				X20	0.0181
				X21	0.0415
				X22	0.0213
				X23	0.0134
科研创新	0.1855	创新资源	0.0426	X24	0.0349
				X25	0.0077
		科研平台	0.0440	X26	0.0391
				X27	0.0049
		要素投入	0.0523	X28	0.0209
				X29	0.0314
		创新成果	0.0466	X30	0.0202
				X31	0.0264
开放交流	0.1968	国际商贸	0.0725	X32	0.0204
				X33	0.0339
				X34	0.0182
		对外交流	0.1243	X35	0.0155
				X36	0.0353
				X37	0.0498
				X38	0.0237
人文凝聚	0.0955	城市名片	0.0479	X39	0.0469
				X40	0.0010
		文化氛围	0.0476	X41	0.0134
				X42	0.0198
				X43	0.0144
生态宜居	0.0205	环境优美	0.0107	X44	0.0080
				X45	0.0027
		和谐宜居	0.0098	X46	0.0074
				X47	0.0024

功能权重为0.2694，所占比重最大；网络枢纽功能权重为0.2323，排名第二；科研创新功能、开放交流功能的权重较为接近，人文凝聚功能和生态宜居功能所占权重最小。这一结果表明9个国家中心城市建设水平的差异主要表现在综合服务和网络枢纽两方面。从维度层角度分析，9个国家中心城市在生产服务、交通枢纽、对外交流3个层面的权重分别为0.1788、0.1647、0.1243，占15个维度总权重的46.78%，充分说明9个中心城市在这三个方面的差异较大。

与2016年国家中心城市评价指标权重相比，指标所占权重排序差别不大，但要素投入、国际商贸、对外交流等维度层的权重增加较大，而环境优美、和谐宜居维度层权重降低较大，表明9个国家中心城市在开放交流功能上差异变大，而在生态宜居功能上的差距在逐步缩小（见图11）。

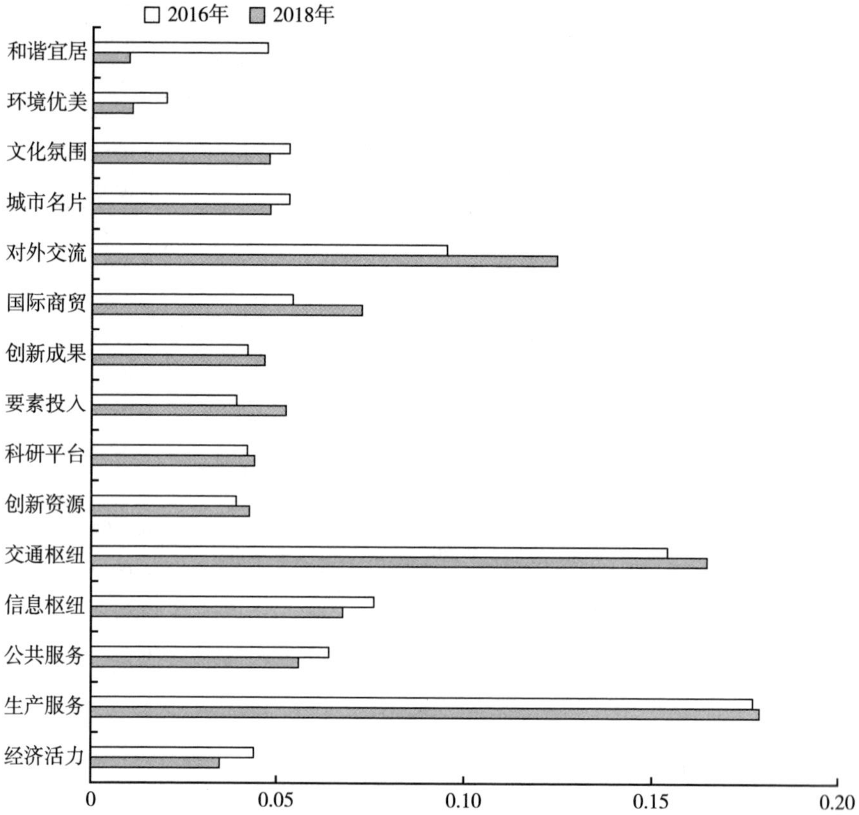

图11　2016年和2018年国家中心城市评价指标权重对比

资料来源：《国家中心城市建设报告（2018）》。

（二）中国国家中心城市建设指数排序及分析

1. 建设指数综合得分排序分析

从总体上看，除部分城市外，建设指数排名与2016年相比总体变化不大，上海、北京、广州总体发展仍旧强势，西安、郑州发展相对落后，见表2。但从9个国家中心城市的经济发展基础指标对比发现，各个城市的建设均处于不断优化发展中，具有良好的发展势头。

从层次上看，9个国家中心城市发展差异较大，明显分为三个梯队，其中上海、北京、广州依旧处于国家中心城市建设的第一梯队，总体发展势头强劲；重庆、成都、天津、武汉处于第二梯队，发展态势相对较好；西安、郑州处于第三梯队，各项指标均存在很大的提升空间。与2016年中国国家中心城市建设指数排名相比，重庆从原来的第五位上升至第四位，成都从原来的第六位上升至第五位，排名均提升1位；天津从原来的第四位下降至第六位，排名下降2位，其他城市排名基本不变。

表2　2018年中国国家中心城市建设指数评分及排名

城市	分值	排名
上海	0.5284	1
北京	0.4991	2
广州	0.2770	3
重庆	0.1863	4
成都	0.1816	5
天津	0.1671	6
武汉	0.1643	7
西安	0.1505	8
郑州	0.1204	9

2. 六大功能层建设指数分析

从总体分析，除生态宜居功能外，9个城市其他5项功能层指数的差距均较大（见图12）。但国家中心城市的经济从高速增长转向高质量发展，需要的是六大功能的协调、协同发展，需要从质量改变、效率提升着手，开展动力变革，才能有效促进区域协调发展。

通过对9个城市内部各功能指数对比，上海持续保持了其在综合服务功能、网络枢纽功能、开放交流功能的优势，均排名第一。北京的科研创新功能、人文凝聚功能排名第一，综合服务功能、开放交流功能排名第二。由于这几项功能的权重相对较大，对上海和北京的总体建设指数有较大影响，上海和北京的综合建设指数分别位列第一和第二位。广州的生态宜居功能排名第一，网络枢纽功能排名第二，综合服务功能和开放交流功能排名第三，但这三项功能与均排名第一的上海相比仍有较大差距，同时人文凝聚功能有待提升。重庆的人文凝聚功能和生态宜居功能均排名第二，综合服务功能和科研创新功能有待提升。成都的科研创新功能排名第五，排名与2016年相比提升了2位，网络枢纽功能和开放交流功能也有一定优势，但综合服务功能还需进一步提升。天津的综合服务功能、科研创新功能优势明显，网络枢纽功能、开放交流功能有待提升。武汉的综合服务功能具有一定优势，但人文凝聚功能、生态宜居功能有待加强。西安有一定人文凝聚功能优势，但综合服务功能和网络枢纽功能还需加强提升。郑州的各项功能发展与其他城市相比优势不明显，均亟须加速发展，综合服务功能和科研创新功能是今后提升的重点。

新时期的区域协调发展战略，是有效解决地区间发展不平衡矛盾的重要举措。9个国家中心城市，作为国家城镇体系的核心城市，是引领相应城市群发展，推动国家重大区域战略融合发展的关键城市。因此，国家中心城市的健康有序发展对区域协调发展起着重要作用。要解决国家中心城市发展不平衡不充分问题，应重点解决西安、郑州等发展相对落后城市，针对其发展短板，针对性提升发展水平，逐步缩小其与其他国家中心城市的差距。

三　中国国家中心城市建设成长性指数排序

（一）国家中心城市建设成长性评价方法

1. 评价指标

“成长性”的概念来源于生物学，该词本身意味着变化，代表了研究目标的一种变化趋势和过程，反映的是研究目标在多方面指标的综合变化特征（见图12）。

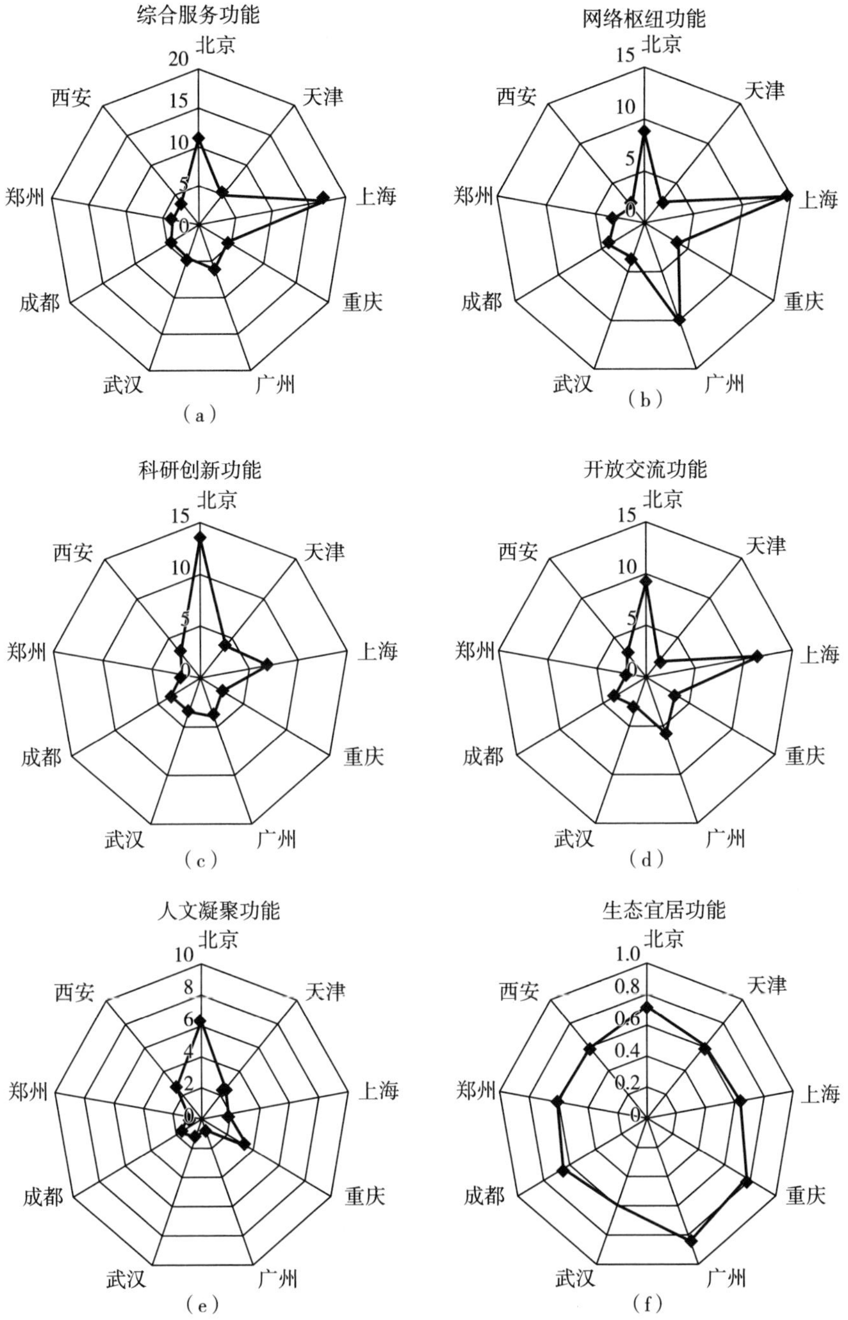

图 12　2018 年中国国家中心城市各功能指数对比

根据2018年国家中心城市建设指数排序结果，发现除少数城市的建设指数排序发生了变化外，9个国家中心所处梯度位次变化不大，上海、北京的建设指数仍远远高于其他国家中心城市，与此同时，西安、郑州的建设指数也依旧远低于其他国家中心城市。这主要是由于9个国家中心城市的城市定位不同，基础发展情况也有较大差异，因此导致2018年虽然9个国家中心城市发展程度有所差异，但在各指标基数的影响下，不同年度的评价结果差异不明显。

因此，为更有效地表征各个国家中心城市的发展速度情况，本研究在原国家中心城市建设指数评价指标基础上，进一步分析“十三五”以来9个国家中心城市成长性变化情况。本研究围绕国家中心城市建设的综合服务、网络枢纽、科研创新、开放交流、人文凝聚和生态宜居六大功能层，从经济活力、生产服务、公共服务、信息枢纽、交通枢纽、创新资源、科研平台、要素投入、创新成果、国际商贸、对外交流、城市名片、文化氛围、环境优美、和谐宜居15个维度层出发，选择了33个指标进行增长率评价，分析“十三五”以来（2016—2018年）国家中心城市建设指标的增长情况，探索评价9个国家中心城市建设的成长性。具体评价指标见表3。

表3　中国国家中心城市建设成长性评价指标

功能层	维度层	指标层
综合服务	经济活力	GDP增速
		第三产业增加值比重增速
		常住人口增速
	生产服务	上市公司数量增速
		金融机构本外币存款余额增速
		保险深度增速
		电商发展指数增速
	公共服务	居民基本医疗保险覆盖率增速
		地方一般公共预算收入占GDP比重增速
		城市轨道交通运营里程增速
网络枢纽	信息枢纽	电信业务总量增速
		中国互联网+指数增速
		邮政业务量增速
	交通枢纽	客运周转量增速
		货物周转量增速

续表

功能层	维度层	指标层
科研创新	创新资源	本专科以上在校生数量增速
	科研平台	国家重点实验室、国家工程技术研究中心、企业国家重点实验室数量增速
	要素投入	R&D 投入强度增速
		R&D 人员增速
	创新成果	专利授权数量增速
		国家级科技成果获奖数增速
开放交流	国际商贸	经济外向度增速
		实际利用外资投资额增速
	对外交流	展览数量增速
		入境国际旅游人数增速
人文凝聚	城市名片	4A 以上景区数量增速
	文化氛围	公共图书馆数量增速
		博物馆数量增速
		文化馆增速
生态宜居	环境优美	人均公园绿地面积增速
		城市绿化覆盖率增速
	和谐宜居	PM 2.5 年平均浓度值下降率
		全天交通拥堵指数下降速率

2. 数据来源

国家中心城市建设成长性评价研究数据来源除建设指数评价中所用数据外，为进行各指标增速统计，同时搜集统计了 9 个国家中心城市 2015～2017 年国民经济和社会发展统计公报；9 个国家中心城市 2016～2018 年统计年鉴，广州、四川、湖北、陕西、河南等省 2016～2018 年统计年鉴；9 个国家中心城市相关政府网站；清华大学电子商务交易技术国家工程实验室等发布的《中国电子商务发展指数报告（2017）》《中国电子商务发展指数报告（2016）》《中国电子商务发展指数报告（2014—2015）》；高德地图发布的《2017 年度中国主要城市交通分析报告》《2016 年度中国主要城市交通分析报告》《2015 年度中国主要城市交通分析报告》；中国贸促会贸易投资促进部发布的《中国展览经济发展报告（2017）》《中国展览经济发展报告（2016）》《中国展览经济发展报告（2015）》；腾讯研究院发布的《中国“互联网+”指数报告

(2018)》《中国“互联网+”指数报告(2017)》《中国“互联网+”指数报告(2016)》。

(二)成长性指数得分排序分析

1. 成长性指数综合得分排序

根据数据统计与分析,9 个国家中心城市建设成长性指数得分排序见表 4。

表 4　2018 年中国国家中心城市建设成长性指数评分及排名

城市	分值	排名
郑州	0.3439	1
西安	0.2353	2
成都	0.2069	3
武汉	0.1579	4
广州	0.1253	5
重庆	0.1176	6
上海	0.1132	7
北京	0.0362	8
天津	0.0261	9

从 9 个城市成长性指数的综合评分来看,成长性指数均为正,说明 9 个国家中心城市建设均处于不同程度的持续优化发展中。其中,郑州、西安、成都、武汉位列成长性指数排名的前四位,其分值均在 0.15 以上,广州、重庆、上海、北京、天津的成长性指数相对较低。由此可以看出,9 个国家中心城市中建设指数排名相对靠后的郑州、西安、武汉等城市由于发展潜力较大,均处于快速发展中;成都的建设指数排名提升,同时成长性也相对较快。而建设指数相对靠前的北京、上海、广州等城市发展趋于平稳;结合天津的建设指数评价结果,该城市仍需结合发展现状,进一步加快发展速度。

通过国家中心城市建设成长性指数权重分析(见表 5),综合服务、科研创新功能权重仍旧占据超过 50% 的比重,与国家中心城市建设指数权重相比增加 5 个百分点。在成长性评价指数各权重中,生产服务、公共服务、要素投入和文化氛围 4 个维度权重高于其他 11 个维度层的权重,占总权重的 43.84%,与建设指数评价中对应维度权重差距较大,说明 9 个国家中心城市在这 4 个维度的发展增速上有较大差距。

表 5　中国国家中心城市成长性评价指标权重

功能层	权重	维度层	权重	指标层		权重
综合服务	0.2815	经济活力	0.0687	GDP 增速	Y1	0.0063
				第三产业增加值比重增速	Y2	0.0268
				常住人口增速	Y3	0.0356
		生产服务	0.1007	上市公司数量增速	Y4	0.0218
				金融机构本外币存款余额增速	Y5	0.0143
				保险深度增速	Y6	0.0301
				电商发展指数增速	Y7	0.0345
		公共服务	0.1121	居民基本医疗保险覆盖率增速	Y8	0.0574
				地方一般公共预算收入占 GDP 比重增速	Y9	0.0260
				城市轨道交通运营里程增速	Y10	0.0287
网络枢纽	0.0957	信息枢纽	0.0486	电信业务总量增速	Y11	0.0285
				中国互联网+指数增速	Y12	0.0093
				邮政业务量增速	Y13	0.0108
		交通枢纽	0.0471	客运周转量增速	Y14	0.0169
				货物周转量增速	Y15	0.0302
科研创新	0.2263	创新资源	0.0426	本专科以上在校生数量增速	Y16	0.0426
		科研平台	0.0186	国家重点实验室、国家工程技术研究中心、企业国家重点实验室数量增速	Y17	0.0186
		要素投入	0.1060	R&D 投入强度增速	Y18	0.0418
				R&D 人员增速	Y19	0.0642
		创新成果	0.0591	专利授权数量增速	Y20	0.0192
				国家级科技成果获奖数增速	Y21	0.0399
开放交流	0.1043	国际商贸	0.0531	经济外向度增速	Y22	0.0330
				实际利用外资投资额增速	Y23	0.0201
		对外交流	0.0512	展览数量增速	Y24	0.0298
				入境国际旅游人数增速	Y25	0.0214

续表

功能层	权重	维度层	权重	指标层		权重
人文凝聚	0.1456	城市名片	0.0260	4A 以上景区数量增速	Y26	0.0260
		文化氛围	0.1196	公共图书馆数量增速	Y27	0.0430
				博物馆数量增速	Y28	0.0463
				文化馆增速	Y29	0.0303
生态宜居	0.1465	环境优美	0.0838	人均公园绿地面积增速	Y30	0.0473
				城市绿化覆盖率增速	Y31	0.0365
		和谐宜居	0.0627	PM 2.5 年平均浓度值下降率	Y32	0.0229
				全天交通拥堵指数下降速率	Y33	0.0398

与建设指数权重相比（见表 1），网络枢纽、开放交流功能权重下降，其中，网络枢纽功能权重下降超过 50%，开放交流功能权重下降 47%，这说明 9 个国家中心城市在以上两个功能层相关指标的成长性差别与建设现状值相比差距较小。综合服务、科研创新、人文凝聚、生态宜居 4 个功能层权重均有不同程度增加，其中人文凝聚功能权重增加超过 50%，生态宜居功能层权重增加约 6 倍，可见部分国家中心城市加强了环境建设方面的相关投入，并与其他城市拉开了差距（见图 13）。

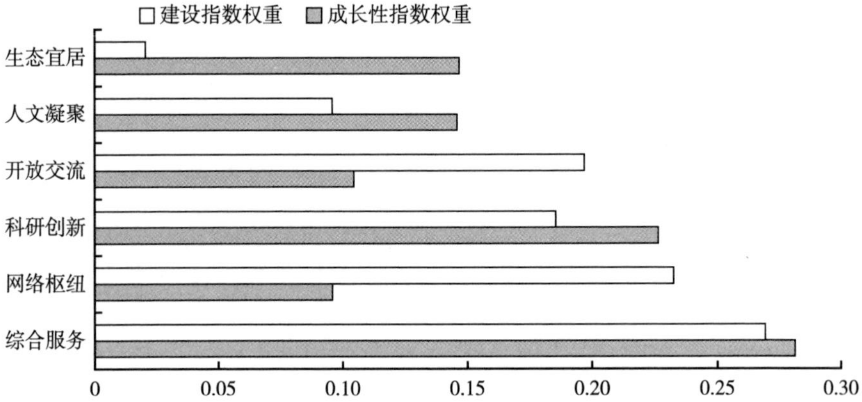

图 13　2018 年建设指数评价和成长性评价各功能层权重对比

在国家中心城市建设成长性指数评价和建设指数评价的维度层权重对比显示，两种评价方法中维度层权重变化相对较大。成长性指数评价中，经济活力、公共服务、创新资源、要素投入、创新成果、文化氛围、环境优美、和谐宜居 8 个维度层的权重均有不同程度增加，其中环境优美权重增加近 7 倍，和谐宜居权重增大 5.4 倍，文化氛围权重增大 1.5 倍，经济活力、公共服务、要素投入权重增加 1 倍左右。但其他 7 个维度，生产服务、信息枢纽、交通枢纽、科研平台、国际商贸、对外交流、城市名片等的权重呈不同程度下降，其中交通枢纽、对外交流、科研平台等维度的权重分别仅为建设指数评价权重的 29%、41%、42%，变化幅度较大（见图 14）。

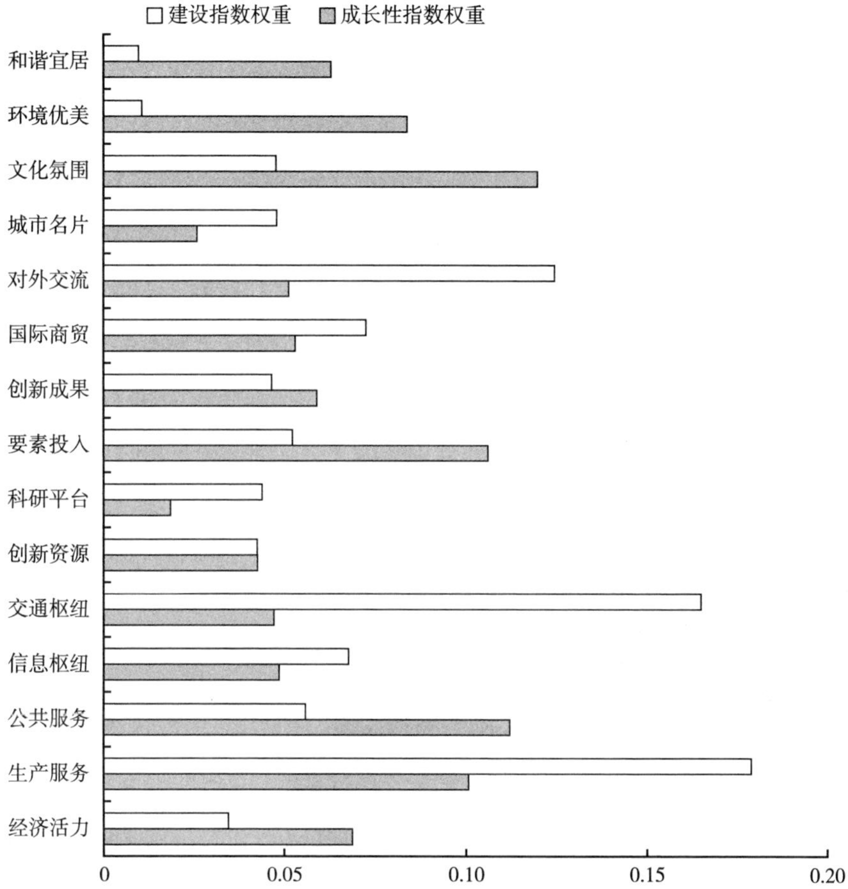

图 14　2018 年建设指数评价和成长性评价各维度层权重对比

2. 六大功能层成长性指数分析

从总体上看，除部分城市外，9 个国家中心城市的综合服务功能、网络枢纽功能的成长性指数均有不同程度的正向增长，说明这9个国家中心城市的这两项功能均处于稳定发展中；但科研创新、开放交流、人文凝聚、生态宜居4项功能成长性指数评价中，个别城市涉及这几项功能的表征指标值处于下降态势（见图15～图20所示）。各城市功能层成长性指数结果对比分析如下。

郑州多项功能的成长性指数均排在前列，其中综合服务、网络枢纽、人文凝聚、生态宜居等功能成长性排名第一，正处于快速发展中；但由于科研平台建设不足，科研投入较低，进出口贸易和利用外资等国际商贸发展缓慢等原因，郑州在科研创新功能、开放交流功能方面成长性相对较低。结合郑州2018年建设指数分析，其综合建设指数在9个国家中心城市中仍较为落后，亟须在继续保持各项功能快速发展的情况下，尤其注意综合服务功能、科研创新功能、开放交流功能的提升与发展。生态宜居功能虽成长性较快，但由于城市环境各项指标与其他城市相比基数较低，仍需加快发展。

西安的科研创新功能和开放交流功能的成长性指数排名第一，人文凝聚功能成长性指数排名第四，其他功能成长性指数排名相对较低，特别是网络枢纽和生态宜居功能，成长性指数和建设指数排名均为末位，一方面是由于邮电业务量低也增长缓慢，另一方面也有生态宜居指标中可吸入颗粒物PM 2.5浓度居高不下、城市交通拥堵持续加剧等原因。因此，除综合服务功能外，网络枢纽功能、生态宜居功能也是今后提升的重点。

成都科研创新功能成长性排名第二，该功能的建设指数排名第五，与2016年排名第七相比，该功能有了较大提升；开放交流功能成长性排名第二，综合服务功能的成长性排名第三，但综合服务功能的建设指数在9个国家中心城市中排名仍较靠后，需继续加强；生态宜居功能呈负增长，主要原因是“十三五”以来成都的人均公园绿地面积呈递减态势，且交通拥堵指数不断上升。综合建设指数和成长性指数评价结果，综合服务功能和生态宜居功能是今后提升的重点。

武汉近几年经济发展速度相对较快，同时注重了在人文、旅游等设施中的投入，其综合服务功能、人文凝聚功能成长性均排名第二，发展相对较快；但开放交流功能、生态宜居功能的成长性指数和建设指数在9个国家中心城市中还处于劣势，尤其是生态宜居功能，受人均公园绿地面积、城市绿化覆盖率降低及全天交通拥堵指数不断上升的影响，其成长性指数呈负数。因此，需要加强生态宜居功能的建设，同时由于武汉市人文凝聚相关表征指标基数不足，还需持续加大在人文凝聚功能建设上的投入。

广州的网络枢纽功能和生态宜居功能成长性均排名第二，综合其建设指数分析，近几年广州在信息枢纽、交通枢纽，以及环境建设和城市建设上均取得了较大成绩；但人文凝聚功能成长性和建设指数均在9个国家中心城市中排名第九，主要原因是广州的公共图书馆、博物馆和文化馆等的数量与其他国家中心城市相比较少，且近几年还呈下降趋势，同时4A以上景区数量增长也比其他城市低，因此，人文凝聚功能建设是今后提升的重点。

重庆网络枢纽功能、人文凝聚功能成长性排名第三，与其他功能相比具有一定优势，但仍需继续加强这两个功能的建设；生态宜居功能建设指数虽然在9个国家中心城市中排名靠前，但其成长性为负，主要原因是其全天交通拥堵指数仅次于北京排在第二位，同时交通拥堵指数平均增长率居9个国家中心城市之首，交通拥堵程度不断上升，城市宜居性受到影响，今后需加强该方面的提升。结合建设指数分析，重庆仍需重视综合服务功能、科研创新功能方面的建设。

上海各项城市发展均已进入相对稳定期，但其科研创新功能、开放交流功能仍保持较为快速的发展，其成长性均排名第三，网络枢纽功能成长性排名第四。综合国家中心城市建设六项功能分析，上海还需加强人文凝聚功能和生态宜居功能的建设，尤其是生态宜居功能，其成长性指数为负，主要原因与重庆相同，其全天交通拥堵指数与平均增长率均仅次于重庆，是今后提升的重点。

北京各项功能成长性评价中，除人文凝聚功能、生态宜居功能外，其他功能均有不同程度正向发展，造成这两项功能成长性为负的主要原因是，公共图书馆数量的降低、城市绿化覆盖率的降低，以及全天交通拥堵指数不断上升。因此，北京在今后的发展中需要持续各项功能的发展，尤其需要注重城市环境和城市宜居的建设。

天津生态宜居功能成长性因人均公园绿地面积增长率和PM 2.5年平均浓度下降速率明显高于其他城市，并在一定程度上平衡了城市绿化覆盖率降低和全天交通拥堵指数明显增加的不利影响，该功能成长性指数为正，排名第三；但结合城市建设指数分析，天津其他功能成长性均不足，尤其是科研创新功能和开放交流功能，受2017年国家重点实验室、国家工程技术研究中心、企业国家重点实验室数量快速缩水，以及国家级科技成果获奖数降低的影响，导致其成长性为负。结合建设指数分析，天津在重视各项功能均衡发展的同时，尤其需要重视开放交流、生态宜居功能的发展，同时还需加强网络枢纽功能的发展。

综合以上分析，9 个国家城市发展仍存在严重的不均衡性。其中生态宜居功能方面的问题是 9 个国家中心城市健康有序发展的共性问题，通过该功能成长性表征指标分析，造成多数城市该功能成长性指数为负的主要原因是：①“十三五”以来多数城市全年交通拥堵指数每年均有不同程度地增加；②部分城市的公园绿地和城市绿地的建设速度，赶不上城市常住人口的增加和城市区域面积的扩张速度，造成人均公园绿地面积、城市绿化覆盖率不同程度下降。作为区域发展的引领者，国家中心城市内部的不协调发展，严重制约着国家中心城市带动区域经济向高质量发展的转变。

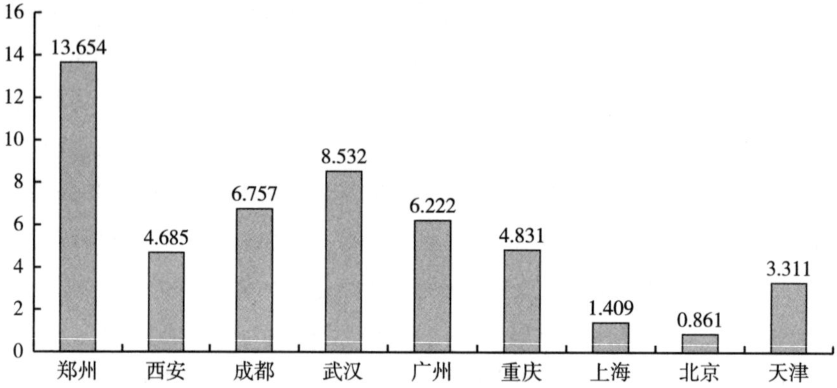

图 15　中国国家中心城市综合服务功能成长性指数对比

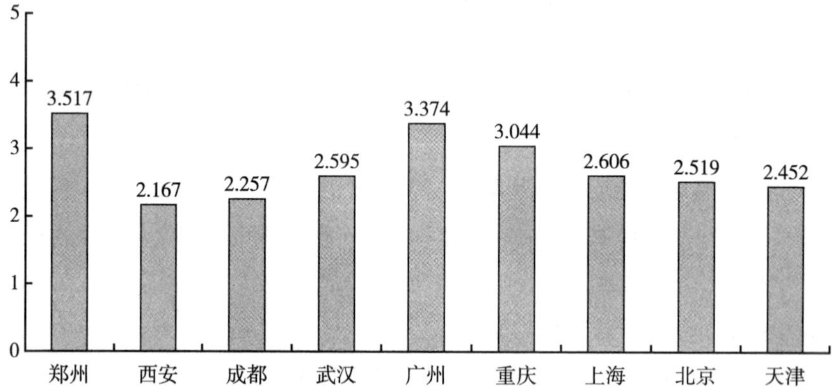

图 16　中国国家中心城市网络枢纽功能成长性指数对比

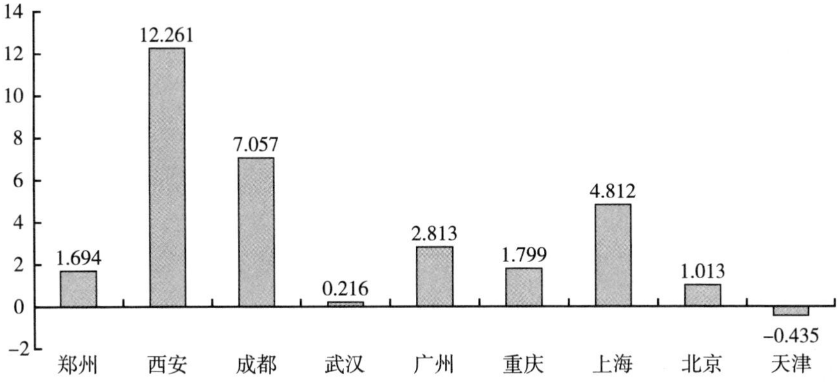

图 17　中国国家中心城市科研创新功能成长性指数对比

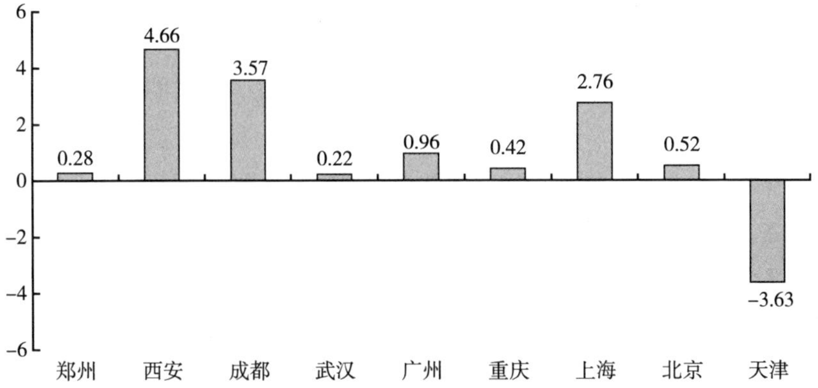

图 18　中国国家中心城市开放交流功能成长性指数对比

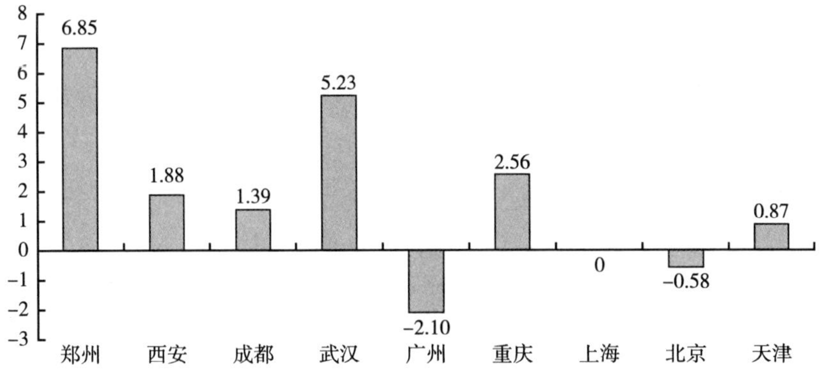

图 19　中国国家中心城市人文凝聚功能成长性指数对比

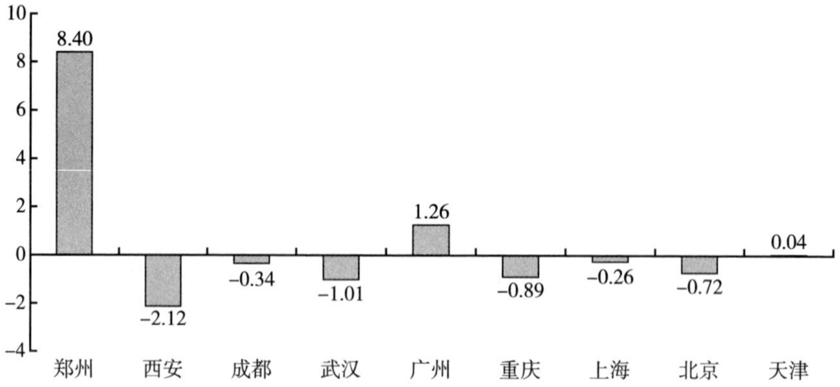

图 20　中国国家中心城市生态宜居功能成长性指数对比

四　国家中心城市建设要注意的问题

国家中心城市在全球城市网络中具有关键地位，在国家城镇体系中具有引领、示范、辐射带动等核心功能，因而，建设国家中心城市必须按照“创新、协调、绿色、开放、共享”的新发展理念，努力实现城市建设由追求高速度向追求高质量转变，并带动区域协调、可持续发展。基于 9 个国家中心城市 2018 年建设指数和“十三五”以来成长性指数评价结果，国家中心城市在建设中应着重注意以下几方面问题。

1. 注重经济与生态环境协调度，实现国家中心城市绿色发展

国家中心城市建设要紧密围绕综合服务、网络枢纽、科研创新、开放交流、人文凝聚和生态宜居六大功能，生态宜居功能是其不可或缺的重要组成部分，与其他五项功能具有同等重要的地位。但根据 2018 年 9 个国家中心城市建设指数和成长性指数评价结果，该功能尚未得到与其他功能同等的地位。在国家中心城市建设中构建绿色发展共识，将绿色发展融入区域协调发展中，树立生态环境承载力约束理念，增强生态环境保护意识，正确处理城市、区域经济发展与生态环境均衡发展的关系，完善有利于资源优化配置和结构优化升级的社会环境，实现城市低碳发展，构建环境优美、和谐宜居的城市环境，维护区域整体生态环境。这不仅是构建城市高质量发展的有效前提，同时也是落实

区域协调发展战略的重要手段。

2. 注重开放型城市建设，实现国家中心城市建设质效提升

现阶段多数国家中心城市开放交流功能还比较弱，但在经济全球化、区域经济一体化的今天，建设开放型城市、发展开放型经济是全面深化改革开放、推动动能转化、实现高质量发展的重要着力点和实施途径。根据2018年国家中心城市建设指数和成长性指数评价，与其他城市相比，上海、北京的开放交流功能建设指数是其他城市的2~6倍，开放型经济发展水平空间分布不均衡。因此，位于中西部的郑州、武汉、西安、成都、重庆等，以及东部天津等城市应在深化改革开放的基础上，以改革推动发展，以开放促进发展，构建以国家中心城市为中心的大都市区（圈）、城市群等区域内部互相开放，以及区域对外开放体制，建设全方位开放格局，充分利用区域内、国内、国际的市场和资源，提升城市开放型经济发展水平，有效提高城市经济增长的质量和效益。

3. 注重城市文化建设，增强国家中心城市独特软实力

目前国家中心城市的文化建设还需加强，部分城市还缺乏独特的城市品牌形象。城市符号、城市口号、历史文化、建筑风格等特定的城市文化标签和良好的文化形式，是彰显城市品质和魅力、提升城市内涵的重要途径。它不仅是城市核心竞争力的重要组成部分，同时也是凸显城市国际竞争力的重要手段。因此，在国家中心城市建设中，需要进一步扎根于深厚的历史文化中，并与现代生活相结合，注重塑造特色鲜明、底蕴深厚的城市文化，将文化建设与城市空间布局、科技创新发展、区域开放交流、生态环境提升等紧密结合，树立简明、独特的城市品牌形象，推动城市文化与经济协同发展，将无形的文化软实力转变为现实的城市竞争硬实力。

4. 避免或消除城市病，有效发挥国家中心城市的引领辐射作用

国家中心城市是全国城镇体系的塔尖城市、核心城市，在都市圈、城市群和区域协调发展中起着引领、示范、辐射、带动作用。但要切实发挥国家中心城市对周边城市的示范作用，实现国家中心城市对周边地区、城市群的引领功能，就要充分认识、尊重、顺应城市发展规律，探明城市可持续发展的制约因素，找到城市病的根源，探索能够提升城市承载能力和运行效率的方式方法，强调以国家中心城市为辐射中心的都市圈、城市群在产业协作、基础设施、生态环境、公共服务等领域的一体化发展，实现城市高质量发展，有效解决城市

病问题，进而实现国家中心城市在城镇化发展中的带动作用，促进区域协调发展。

参考文献

[1] 陈耀：《构建区域协调新机制应充分体现制度优势》，《区域经济评论》2019年第1期，第8～11页。

[2] 刘国斌、宋瑾泽：《中国区域经济高质量发展研究》，《区域经济评论》2019年第2期，第55～60页。

[3] 王琳：《国家中心城市文化软实力评价研究——以港京沪津穗城市为例》，《城市观察》2009年第3期，第71～78页。

[4] 吴世农、李常青、余玮：《我国上市公司成长性的判定分析和实证研究》，《南开管理评论》1999年第4期，第49～57页。

[5] 喻新安：《在动能转化的持续推动中实现区域协调发展》，《区域经济评论》2019年第1期，第15～18页。

[6] 钟茂初：《绿色发展理念融入区域协调发展战略的对策思考》，《区域经济评论》2018年第5期，第84～88页。

城 市 篇

Cities' Reports

B.3 北京建设国家中心城市的成效与展望*

李瑞鹏 安树伟**

摘 要： 在北京市域、京津冀、全国三个不同空间尺度下，北京承担的功能存在差异。作为国家中心城市，在市域层面，2018年北京经济社会各领域发展平稳；在京津冀层面推动京津冀协同成效明显；在全国层面“四个中心”地位不断提升。但是仍存在高精尖产业尚未形成核心支撑力，未能对“疏解整治促提升”行动的影响妥善应对，城市副中心吸引力不强，京津冀协同发展机制尚不健全等“困境”。高质量发展是北京建设国家中心城市的选择与必然要求，未来北京建设高质量的国家中心城市，应该着手于城市治理手段的转变、以人为

* 北京市属高校高水平教师队伍建设支持计划“长城学者培养计划”资助项目：“新型城镇化与产业集聚：格局、过程与机理”（批准号：CIT&TCD20180336）。

** 李瑞鹏，首都经济贸易大学城市经济与公共管理学院区域经济学专业博士生，研究方向为城市与区域发展；安树伟，经济学博士，首都经济贸易大学城市经济与公共管理学院教授、博士生导师，研究方向为城市与区域发展。

本推进非首都功能疏解、提高北京辐射带动作用、创新区域协同发展机制等方面，逐步建成国际一流的和谐宜居之都。

关键词： 国家中心城市　非首都功能疏解　京津冀协同发展

改革开放以来，北京出现了人口膨胀、交通拥挤、住房困难、环境恶化、资源紧张、物价过高等一系列“大城市病”现象，这主要与北京城市职能的过度集中有关。北京作为国家中心城市，处于国家城镇体系的顶层，是我国新型城镇化建设的引领者。我国经济已由高速增长阶段转向高质量发展阶段，目前，高质量发展是北京发展的客观要求，要注重减量发展，即从单一追求速度和总量转向追求高效率和高质量的发展。2018 年北京国家中心城市建设成效如何？遇到了什么问题？未来的着力点是什么？下文以北京城市功能分析为切入点对这些方面进行分析。

一　北京城市功能定位的演变

北京城市功能经历了多次演变（见表 1）。北京是我国的首都，同时也是我国的一个城市，在北京市域、京津冀、全国三个不同空间尺度下，其承担的功能存在差异（见图 1）。

表 1　北京市城市功能定位演变情况

年份	规　划	北京城市定位
1953	《改建与扩建北京市规划草案的要点》	全国的政治、经济、文化的中心，工业基地和科学技术中心
1958	《北京城市建设总体规划初步方案》	政治中心、文化教育中心，现代化的工业基地和科学技术的中心
1973	《北京城市建设总体规划》	与 20 世纪 50 年代城市规划基本一致
1982	《北京城市建设总体规划方案》	全国政治中心和文化中心，国际交往中心
1993	《北京城市总体规划(1991—2010 年)》	首都，全国的政治中心和文化中心，是世界著名的古都和现代国际城市

续表

年份	规　划	北京城市定位
2005	《北京城市总体规划(2004—2020 年)》	首都,全国的政治中心、文化中心,是世界著名的古都和现代国际城市
2017	《北京城市总体规划(2016—2035 年)》	全国政治中心、全国文化中心、国际交往中心、科技创新中心

资料来源：刘欣葵：《北京城市规划与管理 60 年》，光明日报出版社，2010；邹碧莹：《京津冀城市功能分工演化研究》，首都经济贸易大学，2019，第 26 ~ 27 页等。

在北京市域层面，作为超大城市，北京要满足 2154.2 万城市居民对美好生活的需求，为居民提供优质、便捷、高效的生活服务和宜居的生活环境。同时，北京要保证一定速度的经济增长，确保政府财政收入不断增长，为提高城市发展质量、人居环境质量和人民生活品质提供物质保障。

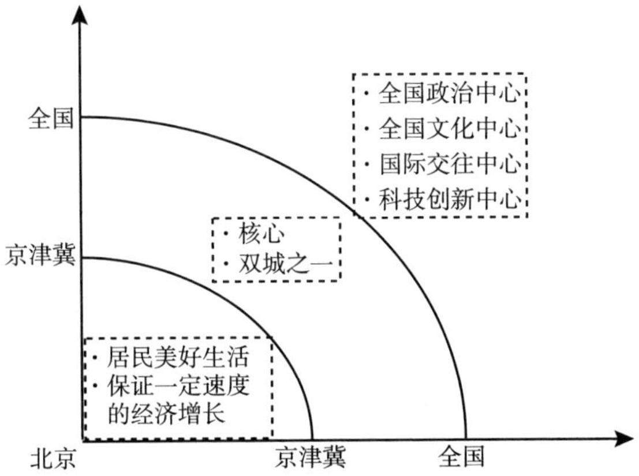

图 1　不同空间尺度下的北京功能

资料来源：安树伟、郁鹏等：《沿海三大城市群产业协作》，经济管理出版社，2019，第 238 ~ 240 页；邬晓霞、时晨、高见：《优化北京辐射带动功能研究》，《城市》2019 年第 2 期，第 28 ~ 36 页等。

在京津冀层面，北京是京津冀协同发展的核心，也是京津冀协同发展的“双引擎”之一。作为“一核”，要重点调整疏解北京非首都功能，优化提升首都核心功能，解决北京“大城市病”。其中，优化提升首都核心功能，需要在科技创新中心和文化中心两个领域进行。作为“双引擎”之一，要进一步强化京津双城联动，贯彻落实京津双城的职能分工，全方位拓展京津合作的广度和深度，加快实现同城化发展，共同发挥高端引领和辐射带动作用。

在全国层面，北京作为首都，是伟大祖国的象征。北京要充分发挥全国政治中心、文化中心、国际交往中心和科技创新中心功能，强化全国文化中心、国际交往中心、科技创新中心的凝聚示范引领和辐射带动作用。

二　北京市经济社会发展现状特征

2018 年北京经济社会发展平稳，地区生产总值增长 6.6%。“高精尖”产业快速发展，产业结构不断优化；常住人口总量持续下降，增速持续下降且为负，外来人口显著减少；生态与环境质量得到改善；北京经济和社会的多个指标位居 9 个国家中心城市第二位。

（一）地区生产总值平稳增长，增速呈现下降趋势

2018 年，北京坚持稳中求进的工作总基调，保持了经济平稳较快发展。2010～2018 年，北京地区生产总值由 14441.6 亿元增长为 30320.0 亿元；人均地区生产总值由 73610.3 元增加至 140748.3 元；但地区生产总值增速由 10.4% 下降至 6.6%（见图 2）。总体来看，地区生产总值在持续增长，但是增速呈现下降趋势，近年来增速维持在 6.6% 左右的水平。

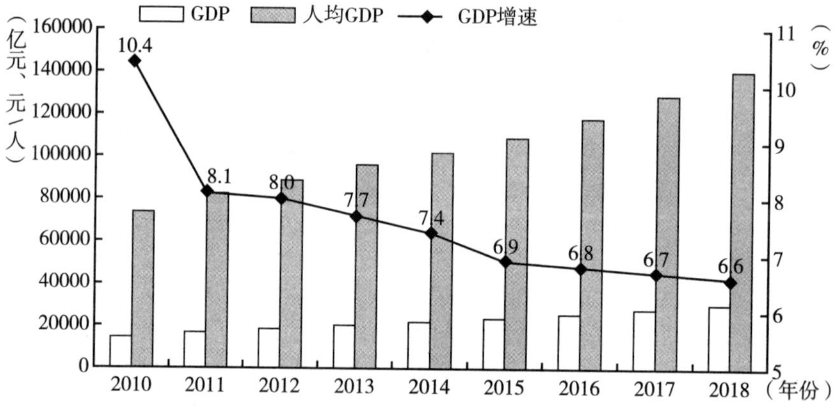

图 2　2010～2018 年北京市 GDP、人均 GDP 以及 GDP 增速（以 1978 年为基期）

资料来源：《北京统计年鉴（2018）》《北京市 2018 年国民经济和社会发展统计公报》。

（二）产业结构不断优化，各区产业结构差异明显

2010～2018 年，北京产业结构由 0.85∶23.46∶75.69 演变为 0.39∶18.63∶80.98，第一产业、第二产业比重不断下降，而第三产业比重不断增加（见图 3）。第一产业增加值由 122.8 亿元降低至 118.7 亿元，第二产业由 3387.9 亿元增加至 5647.7 亿元，第三产业由 10930.9 亿元增加至 24553.6 亿元。

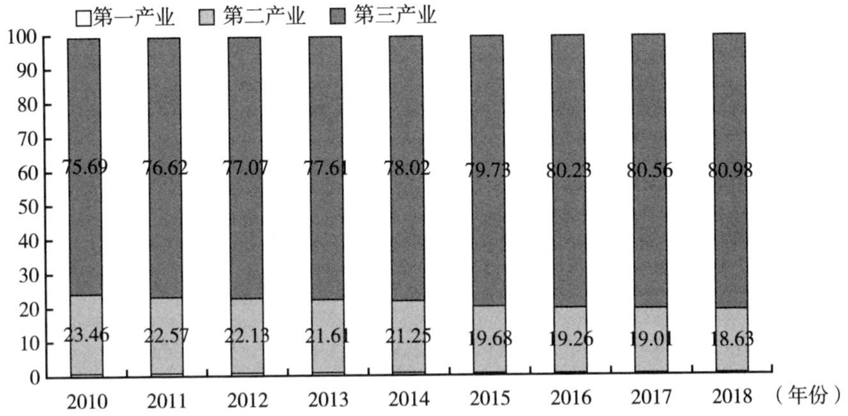

图 3　2010～2018 年北京市三次产业结构

资料来源：《北京统计年鉴（2018）》《北京市 2018 年国民经济和社会发展统计公报》。

进一步分析细分行业，2018 年北京农、林、牧、渔业和房地产业的增加值在减少，其余产业增加值在增加。增速居前五位的行业从高到低依次是信息传输、软件和信息技术服务业，科学研究和技术服务业，卫生和社会工作，金融业，交通运输、仓储和邮政业。信息传输、软件和信息技术服务业，科学研究和技术服务业占 GDP 的比重也显著增加（见图 4）。

北京产业结构的变化与近年来“高精尖”产业的发展有关。2018 年新一代信息技术、集成电路、医药健康、智能装备、节能环保、新能源智能汽车、新材料、人工智能、软件和信息服务、科技服务业十大“高精尖”产业，实现营业收入 32548 亿元①。新动能成长迅速，产业结构不断优化，2018 年北京

① 《北京发布高质量发展见成效：2018 年十大高精尖产业收入 32548 亿元》，中国日报网，2019 年 3 月 25 日。

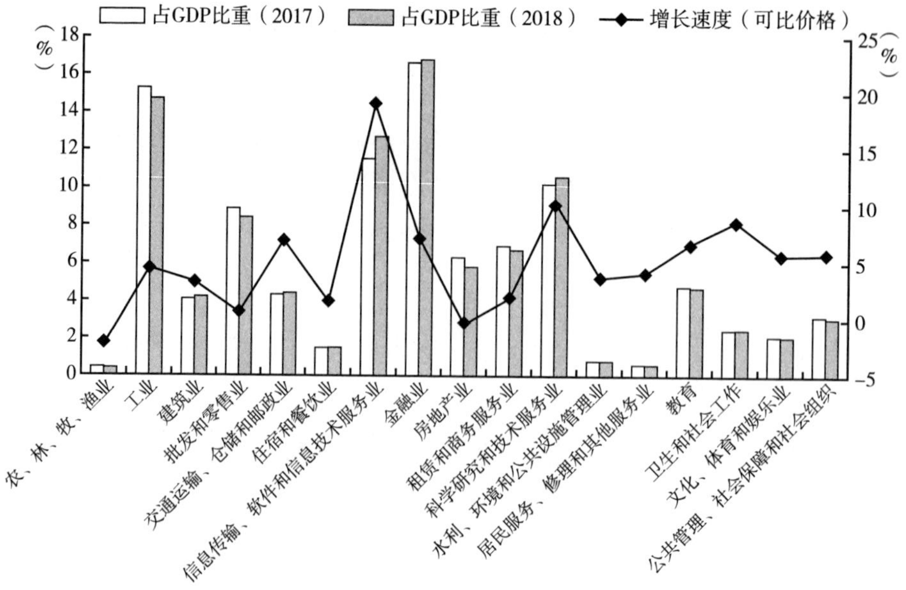

图4　2018年北京市细分行业的增加值占GDP的比重与增长速度

资料来源：《北京统计年鉴（2018）》《北京市2018年国民经济和社会发展统计公报》。

高技术产业增加值、战略性新兴产业增加值和信息产业增加值①分别为6976.8亿元、4893.4亿元和4940.7亿元，占GDP的比重分别为23.0%、16.1%和16.3%，与2017年相比分别增长9.4%、9.2%和14.3%（按现价计算）②。

对2018年北京各区产业结构进行分析可知，各区产业结构存在明显差异。房山区、怀柔区为“二三一”结构，其余各区为“三二一”结构，其中，东城区、西城区和石景山区已无第一产业。

（三）常住人口总量连续两年下降

根据《北京城市总体规划（2016—2035年）》，北京城市规模以资源环境承载能力尤其是水资源为硬性约束条件，严格控制人口规模，维持在

① 高技术产业、战略性新兴产业和信息产业三者存在交叉。

② 《北京市2018年国民经济和社会发展统计公报》。

2300 万人以内这一水平。为此，北京积极推进疏解整治促提升，大力疏解非首都功能，提升首都功能。2016 年北京常住人口达到峰值，为 2172.9 万人，之后常住人口总量呈现下降趋势，2018 年北京常住人口为 2154.2 万人，比 2016 年减少了 18.7 万人。2010～2018 年，北京常住人口增速持续下降且由正转负，由 5.5% 下降为 -0.8%。2015 年无北京户籍常住人口达到最大值，之后开始减少。2010～2018 年，无北京户籍常住人口数量、增速的变化趋势与总的常住人口基本一致，但是变动幅度大于常住人口（见图 5）。

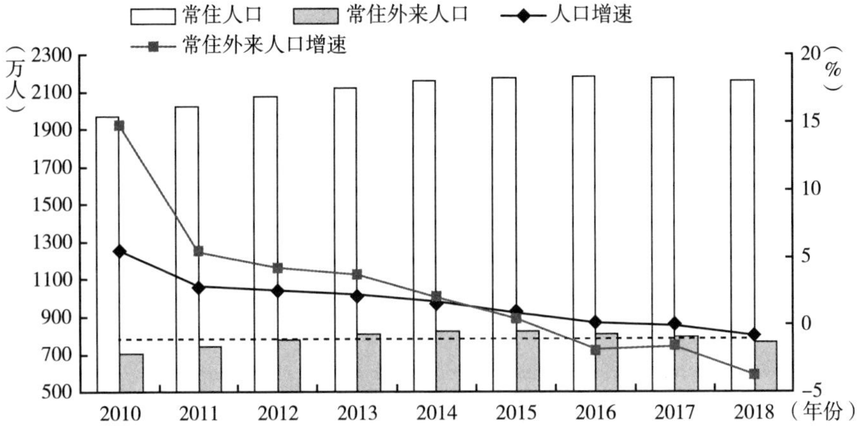

图 5　2010～2018 年北京常住人口、常住外来人口的总量与增速

资料来源：《北京统计年鉴（2018）》《北京市 2018 年国民经济和社会发展统计公报》。

（四）生态与环境治理成效显著

北京建设国际一流的和谐宜居之都，生态环境保护与治理是关键之一。2018 年，北京一方面实施疏解整治促提升专项计划，“留白增绿”，增强群众获得感。拆违腾退土地 6828 公顷、还绿 1683 公顷，建成城市休闲公园 28 处、小微绿地 121 处，全市公园绿地 500 米服务半径覆盖率提高到 80%。另一方面加强治理柴油货车、扬尘、挥发性有机物污染，淘汰国Ⅲ标准柴油货车 4.7 万辆，道路清扫保洁新工艺作业率达到 89%，重点工业行业减排挥发性有机物

2000 吨，实施“煤改清洁能源”，全市平原地区清洁优质能源所占比重超过 96%①。生态环境建设也取得显著成效，2013 年以来北京的 PM2.5、SO_2、NO_2 的年均浓度均持续下降，2018 年分别为 51μg/m³、6μg/m³、42μg/m³；2010～2018 年，全市林木绿化率、森林覆盖率、绿化覆盖率均持续增加，2018 年分别达到 61.5%、43.5%、48.4%。与 2013 年相比较，空气优良天数显著增加，空气质量持续改善（见表 2）。

表 2　2010～2018 年北京主要生态与环境指标

年份	PM 2.5（μg/m³）	SO_2（μg/m³）	NO_2（μg/m³）	绿化覆盖率(%)	森林覆盖率(%)	林木绿化率(%)	空气优良天数(天)
2010	—	32	57	45.0	37.0	53.0	286
2011	—	28	55	45.6	37.6	54.0	286
2012	—	28	52	46.2	38.6	55.5	281
2013	90	27	56	46.8	40.1	57.4	167
2014	86	22	57	47.4	41.0	58.4	168
2015	81	14	50	48.4	41.6	59.0	186
2016	73	10	48	48.4	42.3	59.3	198
2017	58	8	46	48.4	43.0	61.0	226
2018	51	6	42	48.4	43.5	61.5	227

资料来源：《北京统计年鉴（2018）》《北京市 2018 年国民经济和社会发展统计公报》。

（五）主要经济和社会指标位居9个国家中心城市第二位

人口多、规模大、功能集中是国家中心城市的显著特征。国家中心城市建设，是建立在较强的经济实力基础上的。本文选取经济规模、财政实力、消费市场、人民生活水平、产业结构、城镇化率反映城市综合经济实力。与其余 8 个国家中心城市相比较，2018 年北京的 GDP、一般公共预算收入、社会消费品零售总额、人均可支配收入、城镇化率均处于第二位，仅次于上海；人均 GDP 为 14.1 万元，仅次于广州，处于第二位；产业结构中第三产业所占比重最高（见表 3）。

① 陈吉宁：《北京市政府工作报告》，2019 年 1 月 23 日。

表 3　2018 年 9 个国家中心城市主要经济社会指标

城市	GDP（亿元）	人均 GDP（万元）	一般公共预算收入（亿元）	人均可支配收入（元）	社会消费品零售总额（亿元）	产业结构	城镇化率（%）
上海	32679.9	13.5	7108.2	64183.0	12668.7	0.3∶29.8∶69.9	88.1
北京	30320.0	14.1	5785.9	62361.0	11747.7	0.4∶18.6∶81.0	86.5
广州	22859.4	15.5	1632.3	59982.1	9256.2	1.0∶27.2∶71.8	86.4
重庆	20363.2	6.6	2265.5	26386.0	8769.6	6.8∶40.9∶52.3	65.5
天津	18809.6	12.1	2106.2	39506.0	5533.0	0.9∶40.5∶58.6	83.2
成都	15342.8	9.5	1424.2	36753.9	6801.8	3.4∶42.5∶54.1	73.1
武汉	14847.3	13.5	2900.2	42133.0	6843.9	2.4∶43.0∶54.6	80.3
郑州	10143.3	10.1	1152.1	33105.0	4268.1	1.5∶43.9∶54.7	73.4
西安	8349.9	8.5	684.7	35432.9	4658.7	3.1∶35.0∶61.9	74.0

资料来源：2018 年各市国民经济和社会发展统计公报。

三　北京促进京津冀协同发展的成效

在京津冀区域层面，北京通过疏解非首都功能，在促进京津冀协同发展战略的实施中取得了一些成效。一方面优化了“一核两翼”的辐射带动功能，另一方面也推动了京津冀三地在产业协作、交通一体化、生态联防联治等领域的发展。

（一）北京常住人口有所减少，“两翼”建设持续推进

北京通过非首都功能疏解，在一定程度上缓解了“大城市病”。一是北京人口有所减少，2017 年北京常住人口较上一年下降了 2.2 万人，而 2018 年较上一年下降了 16.5 万人。二是北京的城市环境进一步改善，通过疏解和关停高耗能高污染的产业、整治“散乱污”企业等一系列措施，空气质量不断提高。

同时，北京推动了京津冀协同发展中“两翼”的建设。对于北京城市副中心，第一批市级机关已搬至城市副中心行政办公区，北京五中通州校区、友谊医院通州院区已经投入使用。对雄安新区，4 所对口帮扶学校持续推进，北京碧水源科技股份有限公司、北京东方园林投资控股有限公司、北京东方雨虹

防水技术股份有限公司、广联达科技股份有限公司、北京雪迪龙科技股份有限公司、北京清新环境技术股份有限公司、神雾科技集团股份有限公司、北京科锐配电自动化股份有限公司、北京小桔科技有限公司、金山软件股份有限公司、北京首航艾启威节能技术股份有限公司、北京眼神科技有限公司 12 家中关村企业入驻。

（二）产业转移与承接有序进行

2018 年北京与天津、河北签订了新一轮的战略合作协议，并实施协同发展新三年行动计划，加强产业承接平台的建设。天津已基本形成“1 + 16”的承接格局，即滨海新区与 16 个重点承接平台，2015 年至 2019 年第一季度，天津累计引进京冀企业 7.23 万家，投资项目 7879 个，投资额占天津实际利用内资比重一直保持 40% 以上，且绝大部分来自北京①；河北推进雄安新区、曹妃甸协同发展示范区、张（家口）承（德）生态功能区、渤海新区、张北经济开发区等重点承接平台建设，注重孵化基地的建设，吸纳京津两地科技创新成果到河北转化，如京津冀（廊坊）协同创新创业基地、清华大学（固安）中试孵化基地等；京冀共建新机场临空经济区。京津冀“4 + N”的产业合作格局更加稳定。

从京津冀三地的资本流动情况看，北京的资本辐射作用凸显。2014 ~ 2018 年，北京对津冀两地的投资额由 1058.8 亿元增加至 3628.6 亿元，占同期北京对全国的投资额的比重由 4.7% 增加至 8.1%。北京对津冀两地的投资额明显高于天津与京冀、河北与京津之间的资本流动额（见表 4）。从京津冀三地科技溢出情况来看，北京向津冀两地的科技辐射作用在增强但是仍然较小。2014 ~ 2017 年，北京向津冀两地输出的技术合同数及成交额明显增加，且流向河北的合同数和成交额高于天津。2018 年，北京流向津冀的技术合同成交额为 227.4 亿元，与上一年相比增加了 11.7%。北京向津冀两地输出的技术合同数及成交额占流向外省（直辖市、自治区）的比重不断增加，但是仍然较小，2017 年分别为 10.5%、8.7%（见表 5）。

---

① 《天津引进京冀项目持续高涨》，北京市人民政府，2019 年 6 月 14 日，http://www.beijing.gov.cn/ywdt/zwzt/sjfsdgn/zxjz/ybxzzy/t1590856.htm。

表 4　2014～2018 年京津冀三地资本流动情况

年份	北京对津冀投资（亿元）		天津对京冀投资（亿元）		河北对京津投资（亿元）		北京对全国投资(亿元)	北京对津冀投资/北京对全国投资(%)
	天津	河北	北京	河北	北京	天津		
2014	783.8	275.0	169.4	42.4	264.8	57.1	22553.0	4.7
2015	1138.9	923.4	337.1	48.2	101.1	55.0	33160.1	6.2
2016	1927.1	997.0	605.7	47.2	231.0	107.2	67939.2	4.3
2017	1520.3	1484.6	266.0	141.3	264.5	189.9	57140.4	5.3
2018	1327.4	2301.2	289.9	120.0	207.6	85.1	44540.2	8.1

资料来源：京津冀大数据研究中心。

表 5　2014～2018 年北京向津冀两地输出的技术合同项数与成交额

年份	技术合同数(项)				技术合同成交额(亿元)			
	流向天津	流向河北	流向津冀	流向外省	流向天津	流向河北	流向津冀	流向外省
2014	1376	2099	3475	37212	20.4	62.7	83.1	1722
2015	1407	2291	3698	37447	57.6	53.9	111.5	1878.7
2016	1486	2362	3848	38928	56.0	98.7	154.7	1997.2
2017	1766	2880	4646	44287	49.3	154.2	203.5	2327.3
2018	—	—	—	—	—	—	227.4	—

资料来源：历年北京技术市场统计公报以及 2019 年《北京市政府工作报告》。

（三）区域综合交通网络日趋完善

2014 年以来，“轨道上的京津冀”正在形成中，区域内公路、铁路、机场、公交等交通基础设施建设不断推进。目前，北京市域内国家高速公路“断头路”全部贯通，国家高速公路网 7 条首都放射线北京段全部建成，（北）京雄（安）高速即将开工；（北）京张（家口）、（北）京唐（山）、（北）京滨（海新区）、（北）京曹（妃甸）、（北）京雄（安）铁路建设持续推进；北京大兴国际机场即将投入运营，新机场与津冀两地的机场线也即将开工；出京公交线路达到 41 条，公交已基本覆盖河北省廊坊、涞水、赤城等 17 个毗邻区。目前，京津冀一卡通功能不断拓展，发卡数量累计超过 180 万张，“一小时交通圈”的网络化格局正加速形成，将促进京津冀三地的资源要素快速流动。

（四）生态环境保护联防联治成效显著

2018年，京津冀及周边地区“2+26”城市① PM2.5年均浓度为60μg/m³，比上年下降11.8%；三地还修订了新一轮重污染天气应急预案②。京津冀三地联合推进永定河、北运河、潮白河综合治理与生态修复，京津两地签署了《密云水库上游潮白河流域水源涵养区横向生态保护补偿协议》；京津冀协同5年来，累计造林11.47万公顷治理风沙与保护水源。

四　北京“四个中心”建设成效

北京作为我国的首都，代表着国家的形象，北京的城市职能不仅仅是满足北京自身的需求，同时也为全国提供服务。作为我国的“四个中心”，北京对于国家政务活动的保障能力不断提升，文化资源和科技资源集聚的优势不断发挥，科技创新中心在全国更具影响力，并且持续为国家的国际交往提供良好的环境。

（一）政务保障能力不断提升

北京作为全国的政治中心，旨在为中央党政军领导机关提供最优质的服务和保障，这也是城市的第一功能。一是坚持党的领导，维护党中央的权威，建设良好的政治生态环境，不断通过在公园、博物馆等举办主题教育、系列展览和文化活动传播社会主义核心价值观，建设精神文明高地。二是积极实施“疏解整治促提升”专项计划，为中央和国家机关优化布局提供条件。主要体现在该专项计划以城六区为重点、以核心区为重中之重，2018年中心城区29

① 为确保完成《大气污染防治行动计划》所确定的2017年各项目标任务，环保部制定了《京津冀及周边地区2017年大气污染防治工作方案》，实施范围为京津冀大气污染传输通道，包括北京市，天津市，河北省石家庄、唐山、廊坊、保定、沧州、衡水、邢台、邯郸，山西省太原、阳泉、长治、晋城，山东省济南、淄博、济宁、德州、聊城、滨州、菏泽，河南省郑州、开封、安阳、鹤壁、新乡、焦作、濮阳，即“2+26”城市。

② 《京津冀生态环境协同治理5年结硕果永定河上游2019年实现通水》，北京市人民政府网，2019年2月25日，http：//www.beijing.gov.cn/ywdt/zwzt/jjjyth/hbgj/t1578413.htm。

个老旧小区综合整治试点进展顺利，核心区 80 千米道路电力架空线入地。三是保障国家政务活动安全、高效、有序运行。2018 年北京完成了全国“两会”、马克思 200 周年诞辰大会、改革开放 40 周年大会以及国家外交活动等政务活动的服务和保障任务。

（二）文化中心地位不断增强

北京文脉底蕴深厚和文化资源集聚，近年来持续加强文化保护。2018 年北京继续以“一核一城三带两区”① 为抓手，建设全国的文化中心，发布实施了新版《历史文化名城保护发展规划》，编制完成北部长城、东部运河和西部西山三条文化带保护建设规划，推进中轴线申遗保护。开展天安门城楼及城台修缮，完成人民大会堂东广场改造修复和环境景观提升工程。

文化创意产业快速发展。2010 ~ 2017 年，北京文化创意产业增加值由 1697.7 亿元增加至 3908.8 亿元，年均增速为 14.9%，占全市 GDP 的比重由 11.8% 增加至 14.0%，仅次于金融业②。截至 2018 年，北京文化创意产业园区共 34 个，东城区、西城区、朝阳区、海淀区、大兴区、通州区、昌平区、北京经济技术开发区分别为 4 个、8 个、11 个、5 个、3 个、1 个、1 个、1 个。其中，朝阳区文化创意产业发展较好，登记注册文化企业有近 8.1 万家，拥有 798 艺术区、751D · park 北京时尚设计广场、莱锦文化创意产业园、郎园文化创意园、懋隆文化产业创意园、恒通国际创新园等多家各具特色的文化产业园区。2018 年北京规模以上文化产业法人单位 4000 余家，收入达到 10173 亿元，比上年增长 11.9%。同时，文化创意产业的支持政策也在不断地完善，中共北京市委、北京市人民政府出台了《关于推进文化创意产业创新发展的意见》，北京市人民政府发布了《关于保护利用老旧厂房拓展文化空间的指导意见》等相关政策。

文化服务质量不断提升。2018 年北京图书馆的藏书量、档案馆的馆藏案卷数、报刊总量、出版物发行单位数等文化基础设施相比 2017 年在不断增加，

---

① “一核”为社会主义核心价值观，“一城”为历史文化名城，“三带”是大运河文化带、长城文化带、西山永定河文化带，“两区”为公共文化服务体系示范区和文化创意产业发展引领区。

② 2017 年北京金融业占全市 GDP 的比重为 16.6%。

分别达到6701.2万册、868.7万卷件、3491种、7922家，分别增加了173.2万册、41万卷件、116种、324家。对营业性演出实施低票价补贴政策，对151家实体书店实施房租补贴政策。

（三）全国科技创新中心建设提速

北京高端人才集聚，科技基础雄厚，创新活力不断增强。2018年全市国家高新技术企业达到2.5万家，与2017年相比增长25%，平均每天新设创新型企业199家。中关村示范区总收入超过5.8万亿元，独角兽企业①超过80家，居全国首位。北京科技创新成果不断增加，2010～2018年，全市专利申请数、专利授权数、技术合同数、技术合同成交额均呈现增长的态势，2018年全市专利申请数、专利授权数、技术合同数和技术合同成交额比2017年分别增长13.6%、15.5%、1.5%和10.5%（见图6）。2018年在全国领跑世界的技术成果中北京占55.7%②，如汉字激光照排系统、5G移动通信等一批关键核心技术的突破，三重简并费米子、马约拉纳任意子的发现，碳基光电集成电路、北斗系列卫星、“慧眼”等的研制成功。

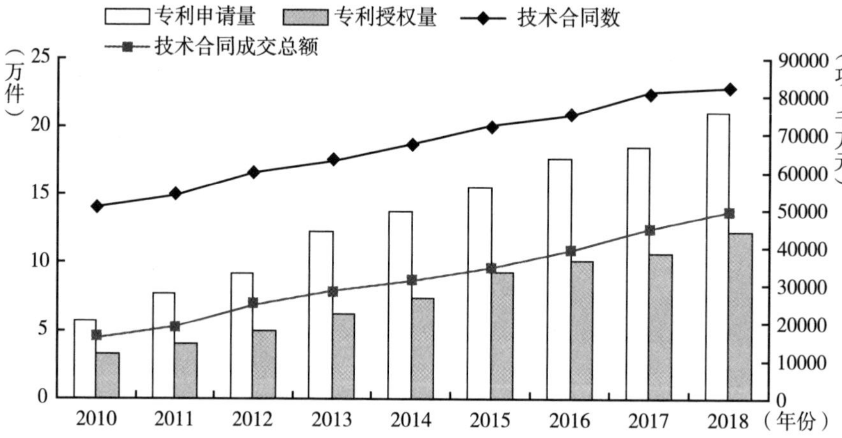

图6　2010～2018年北京专利与技术合同情况

资料来源：《北京统计年鉴（2018）》《北京市2018年国民经济和社会发展统计公报》。

---

① 一般指成立时间不超过10年、估值超过10亿美元的未上市创业公司。

② 《全国领跑世界技术成果中北京占55.7%成高速成长科技中心》，《中国财经》2018年12月7日。

北京基本形成了“三城一区”的科技创新格局。其中，中关村科学城创新提级，强化顶层设计，编制完成了《中关村科学城规划》；组建了中关村科学城共建联席会，联系各类“创新合伙人”；在基础研究、原始创新领域发挥着“基石”作用，出现了马约拉纳任意子、新型超低功耗晶体管等重大标志性原创成果。怀柔科学城完成了《怀柔科学城规划》，综合极端条件实验等科学装置和材料基因组等5个交叉研究平台完工，空间科学国家实验室、纳米能源所、国联动力电池、海创产业研究院等一批创新主体落地。未来科学城完成了《未来科学城规划》，着力盘活6万平方米闲置楼宇，引进开放性科研平台和双创平台。北京经济技术开发区形成了高端汽车和产业互联网两个千亿元级产业集群，新产品、新技术分别达到35项、31项，万人实用发明专利拥有量为350件；建成了全市唯一国家级绿色工业园区。①

北京对全国创新发展有较强的辐射带动作用，且呈现增强态势。2010～2017年，北京流向外省（直辖市、自治区）的技术合同数以及合同成交额占全市的比重呈现缓慢增加的趋势，近年来二者均高于50%。2017年北京流向外省（直辖市、自治区）技术合同数为44287项，占市内总技术合同数的54.5%，比2016年增加2.6个百分点；北京流向外省（直辖市、自治区）技术合同成交额为2327.3亿元，占市内总技术合同成交额的51.9%，比2016年增加1.2个百分点（见图7）。

（四）国际交往环境不断优化

“走出去”是国际影响力提升的重要途径。北京作为首都，是我国走向世界的重要窗口。北京的国际交往中心的建设成效主要体现在4个方面：一是积极承办各种国际会议、赛事与活动。国际会议方面，2018年北京承办了中非合作论坛峰会、中国北京世界园艺博览会、国际冬季运动博览会、中国文化金融峰会等多项会议；国际赛事方面，北京完成了平昌冬奥会、冬残奥会闭幕式主办城市交接仪式等，并积极筹办2022年北京冬奥会；国际活动方面，举办了北京国际电影节、国际音乐节、国际设计周和国际文化创意产业博览会等活动。二是大力推进与其他国际友好城市的交往。截至2018年12月1日，北京

① 《北京“三城一区”建设全面发力》，新华网，2019年1月14日。

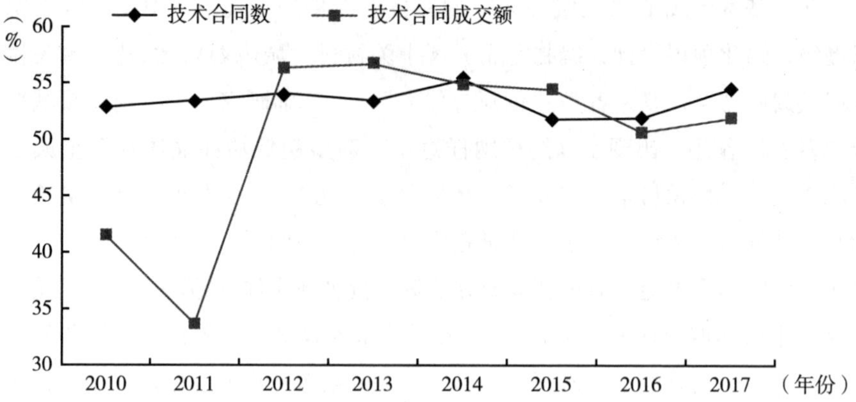

图 7　2010～2017 年北京流向外省（直辖市、自治区）技术合同数与成交额占全市的比重

资料来源：历年北京技术市场统计年报。

与 56 个城市建立了国际友好城市关系，居于全国首位。同时，积极落实“一带一路”倡议，出台共建“一带一路”三年行动计划。三是近年来国际交流规模逐渐回升。2010～2018 年，北京进出口总额、接待入境旅游者数量呈现下降的趋势，近年来开始增加（见图 8）。2018 年，北京进出口总额、接待入境旅游者分别为 27182.5 亿元、400.4 万人，比上一年分别增长 23.9%、2.0%。

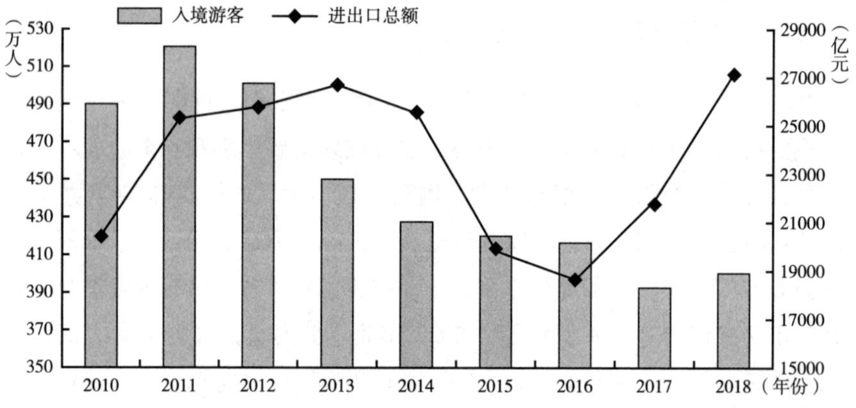

图 8　2010～2018 年北京进出口总额、接待入境旅游者

资料来源：《北京统计年鉴（2018）》《北京市 2018 年国民经济和社会发展统计公报》。

北京积极为国际人才打造宜居宜业的“类海外”环境，7 家医院成为国际医院试点，618 位外籍高层次人才永久居住。四是国际交流硬件持续完善。北京大兴国际机场航站楼主体工程基本完工，即将投入运营；金海湖国际会展中主场馆基本完成，助力 2020 年北京·平谷世界休闲大会顺利进行；雁栖湖国际会都扩容，为更多高端会议会展提供场地支持。

五　北京国家中心城市建设的“困境”

北京旨在疏解非首都功能，同时发展“高精尖”产业，做到经济有增有减，疏解与发展共存。而目前，北京非首都功能疏解逐渐对居民的生活以及北京的经济发展产生一些不利影响，而“高精尖”产业尚未形成首都经济的核心支撑力量。作为北京的“两翼”之一的城市副中心，公共服务仍然与城六区存在较大差距，吸引力不足。从京津冀区域层面来看，区域协调机制仍未建立。

（一）“高精尖”产业尚未形成首都经济的核心支撑力

产业是城市发展的根本。非首都功能被疏解之后，北京靠什么来实现经济高质量发展？“腾笼”之后要换什么“鸟”？2017 年，北京市人民政府发布了《加快科技创新发展新一代信息技术等十个高精尖产业的指导意见》给出了方向，即要构建高精尖的产业体系。通过“一减一增”实现首都的高质量发展。但是，目前高精尖产业的发展过程中存在如下问题：一是创新链与产业链的融合水平低。目前，北京不同程度面临着高技术不高、产业技术含量不足的问题，科技创新能力并没有真正转化为高新技术产业创新能力和国际竞争力。北京市的全球创新要素资源聚集能力、原始创新能力、创新成果转化能力正处于发展提高阶段，尚不具备有效的经济支撑作用，对新动能的支撑作用还有很大提升空间。二是随着非首都功能的疏解，高精尖产业很难在短时间内壮大成为支柱产业，这也使部分地区容易产生新旧动能衔接断崖，进而影响地区的经济发展。

（二）“疏整促”专项行动的实施对居民生活和经济发展的影响

“疏解整治促提升”专项行动，是对疏解非首都功能的进一步细化与完善。其中，多次提到“低端业态”，而实际上什么是“低端业态”，相关文件并没有明确的定义，对它的认识与理解也比较主观。同时，关于什么是“非首都功能”，学术界对其的看法并不一致，实际上这本身并不是一个科学的概念。非首都功能是指与北京城市定位不符合的功能，而在疏解非首都功能的时候，一定要注意该功能是属于城市的基础部门还是非基础部门。根据城市经济增长的基础模型理论，城市的经济增长取决于基础部门和非基础部门的比例，基础部门是城市增长与发展的动力，但是基础部门的增加会对非基础部门产生需求。同时，根据大城市劳动力结构变动的规律可知，随着劳动力收入水平的提高，每一个高收入的劳动者需要更多的普通服务人员为他们提供服务。而在政府的强力作用下，如果将城市非基础部门或普通服务人员疏解，必然会影响城市的经济增长与城市活力。近年来，北京经济增速持续下降与此有关。

目前，“疏解整治促提升”专项行动疏解“低端业态”，比如部分一般性制造业、街边小店、菜市场和批发市场被搬迁和拆除。实际上，把“大城市病”的产生归结于外来人口和低端产业并不合适，东京、纽约、洛杉矶等国际化大城市也并未采用清理低端产业的模式来优化城市管理。[①] 简单地疏解北京非首都功能，不仅会对居民的生活、工作造成影响，还会增加政府的城市管理成本。根据 2017 年一项关于非首都功能疏解对居民生活影响的问卷调查，年龄在 18～45 岁、没有北京户口、在京居住时间 15 年以内、月收入为 2000 元及以下、居住地离市中心较远的居民更认为疏解对其生活有影响。鉴于政策的滞后性以及随着北京非首都功能疏解的不断实施，疏解对于居民生活、工作的影响将会越来越明显。而且，随着非首都功能的推进以及“疏解整治促提升”专项计划的实施，北京产业投资动力将在一定程度上弱化，2018 年北京全社会固定资产投资与上年相比下降了 9.9%。因此，需要妥善应对北京非首都功能疏解对居民生活、工作的影响，以及对北京经济发展的影响，这是非首都功能疏解的关键，否则会事倍功半。

---

① 袁晓彬：《大城市离不开“低端产业”》，网易新闻，http：//view.163.com/special/reviews/low－endindustry1231.html。

（三）北京城市副中心吸引力不足

完善的配套基础设施和高水平的公共服务是北京城市副中心发展的重要保障，这为企业提供了好的生产环境，也为人类提供了好的生活环境。高越、何迪燊和李思莹等于2019年测度了北京城市副中心对于非首都功能疏解的贡献度，发现在北京产业转移方面，城市副中心在科技创新产业方面发挥了一定的作用，而就业和人口方面效果一般。根据托罗达的人口流动理论，人口流动与对一个地方的预期收入有关，预期收入与一个地方的实际收入和在这个地方找到工作的概率有关，即“预期收入 = 城市实际收入 × 在城市找到工作的概率”。实际中，城市副中心通州与北京中心城区在经济发展水平、公共服务等方面具有较大的差距。2018年城市副中心的GDP仅为海淀区的13.0%，人均GDP远低于城六区，经济发展水平会在经济收入上体现，2018年城市副中心的人均可支配收入是城六区平均水平的56.0%；通州区每千人拥有的医疗卫生机构床位数、卫生人员数以及每万人普通中学、小学、幼儿园班数，均远低于城六区平均水平（见表6）。客观而言，北京市优质的教育、医疗资源也集中在城六区，比如位于城六区的中国人民大学附属中学、北京市第四中学、北京师范大学附属实验中学、北京大学附属中学等学校，以及协和医院、同仁医院、北京医院、中国人民解放军总医院、北京大学第三医院等医院。需要说明的是，2018年北京五中通州校区、人大附中通州校区小学部相继建成招生，城市副中心的教育资源在不断壮大。

表6　2018年城市副中心与中心城区经济发展水平与公共服务

城区	GDP（亿元）	人均GDP（万元）	人均可支配收入（元）	每千人常住人口的医疗卫生机构床位数（个）	每千人常住人口卫生人员数（个）	每万人的普通中学班数（个）	每万人的小学班数（个）	每万人的幼儿园班数（个）
东城区	2425.7	29.5	75547	12.1	38.0	14.2	20.3	7.0
西城区	4243.9	36.0	81678	13.9	37.6	12.1	19.6	6.5
朝阳区	6093.5	16.9	70746	6.6	18.7	5.7	13.3	8.8
丰台区	1551.1	7.4	60144	5.9	13.4	3.9	9.4	7.3

续表

城区	GDP（亿元）	人均 GDP（万元）	人均可支配收入（元）	每千人常住人口的医疗卫生机构床位数（个）	每千人常住人口卫生人员数（个）	每万人的普通中学班数（个）	每万人的小学班数（个）	每万人的幼儿园班数（个）
石景山区	584.6	9.9	71244	8.1	17.0	6.8	12.5	9.2
海淀区	6400.0	19.1	78178	4.0	13.2	9.2	13.7	6.5
城六区平均水平	3549.8	18.3	72442	6.9	19.3	7.7	13.8	7.6
通州区	832.4	5.3	40553	2.4	8.0	5.0	11.4	6.2
通州区/城六区平均水平（%）	23.4	29.0	56.0	34.8	41.5	64.9	82.6	81.6

资料来源：经济发展水平相关指标来源于2018年各区的国民经济和社会发展统计公报，卫生数据来自北京市卫生健康委员会网站，教育数据来自北京市教育委员会网站。

（四）区域利益协调机制尚不完善

京津冀协同发展有利于实现北京的可持续发展。在区域协调发展问题上，参与方之间能否建立完善协调和合作制度是基础和关键。而目前，北京与天津、河北两地在产业协同、创新协同、财税制度协同、生态协同机制方面尚不完善。在产业协同方面，三地的产业发展仍然过度依赖于政府规划，未能在市场的作用下形成合理的产业链分工；在创新协同方面，创新成果利益分配方式与机制不明确；在财税制度协同方面，北京仍以“项目式”方式来给予天津、河北两地财政支持；在生态协同方面，现有的补偿机制尚未处理好政府补偿与市场补偿、直接成本与间接成本、“输血”与“造血”三个关系。在一定程度上，这与京津冀三地不同的政治地位和经济地位有关。在政治地位上，北京既是直辖市，又是中央政府所在地，天津是直辖市，河北仅仅是一个省。京津冀三地分属不同行政区域，基于中国特殊的行政发包和属地制及官员晋升机制，地方政府为追求各自的地方利益，打理各自的一亩三分地，整体的合作意识较弱。各地虽然从政策层面都制定了一系列政策，但较多考虑本地利益，忽视整体发展。在经济地位上，2018年北京的GDP是天津的1.6倍，是河北省的84.2%，与2017年[1]相比均有所增加。

北京与天津、河北三地的协同发展，要保障在执行层面上务实项目合作的跟进，否则实际效果会大打折扣，应警惕京津冀地区协同发展中出现“三个和尚没水吃”的“三地共输”局面。

六　北京高质量建设国家中心城市的建议

高质量的发展是北京建设国家中心城市的选择与必然要求。综合目前北京建设国家中心城市的成效以及遇到的“困境”，未来应该从城市治理手段的转变、以人为本推进非首都功能疏解、提高北京辐射带动作用、创新区域协调机制等方面着手，提高北京城市发展质量。

（一）促进城市治理手段的转变

区域政策手段主要有行政手段、经济手段和法律手段三种，行政手段短期效果显著，但是由于过多重视“领导”忽视“公众”，长期来看会出现许多负面影响。经济手段是一种长期才会见效且有效的手段，法律手段效果稳定、连续。目前，非首都功能疏解以及城市副中心、雄安新区的建设等过多地依赖于行政手段，如各地政府部门都出台了大量的规划、意见和建议，而经济手段和法律手段的应用很少，虽然在短期内非首都功能疏解有序推进，成效显著，但是从长期来看并非如此。北京向河北各地转移的产业由于人才流失、当地机制落后等原因出现了“水土不服”的现象，遭遇发展困境。未来，北京城市治理手段应由行政手段为主逐渐向法律手段和经济手段为主转变。

（二）以人为本推进非首都功能疏解

随着北京“低端产业”被疏解整治，会影响常住居民的生活与工作，尤其是北京的外来务工人员，这与他们从事的行业有关系，他们多数从事的是所谓“低端”的第二、第三产业。如何妥善处理非首都功能疏解对居民生活、工作的影响？一是要建立良好的协商机制，通过多主体参与协商和表达意见，

① 2017年北京的GDP是天津的1.5倍，是河北省的77.9%。

决定产业是否被疏解或整治；二是要及时完善便民服务基础设施，新建或改造社区便民服务中心，实现“一刻钟社区服务圈”，新建物美价廉的综合商业街或零售市场；三是要重视产业被疏解整治后所产生的失业问题，主要是北京外来务工人员，这与和谐宜居之都的建设目标息息相关。具体来说，需要各级政府做好转出产业失业人员的安置工作，加强对失业人员的教育培训，尽快实现再就业。

只有这样才能使北京非首都功能真正得到疏解，进而在解决北京“大城市病”，调整优化京津冀区域城市布局和空间结构的同时，实现京津冀协同发展的目标。

（三）提高北京的辐射带动作用

提高北京的带动作用，先要提高北京自身的带动作用。一方面要加速创新驱动，改变传统的生产方式。竞争优势经历从生产要素导向到投资导向，再到创新导向，最后到富裕导向四个发展阶段。对于现阶段的北京城市发展来讲，城市的竞争力提高要注重向创新阶段转变，即竞争优势产业是技术密集型企业，这主要来源于企业创新，依赖于城市和企业的技术创新愿望和技术创新能力。依据钻石理论，这就要求北京注重基础设施创新，重视培育高级要素（如人力资源）、最挑剔的消费者、具有竞争力的供应商和相关产业，保持企业之间的有序竞争状态。与此同时，要抓住机遇，处理好政府与市场的关系，最终实现创新链、产业链与价值链的融合。另一方面要完善城市副中心的基础设施和公共服务，加快与城市副中心职能相匹配的各种配套服务业的发展，实现中心城区与城市副中心以副辅主、主副共兴的目标。

除了北京自身的带动作用，北京的辐射带动作用也与周围城市的承接能力有关。这就要求注重在河北建设抗衡京津双城极化效应的反磁力中心城市。建设产业承接平台来积极承接北京和天津两地的制造业等产业转移，同时，不应该单纯地承接北京和天津的产业转移，而应抓住承接北京和天津转移产业的机会，以提高地区整体发展水平和竞争力为核心。通过对接北京相关产业，进一步推动本地的机制体制改革以及产业转型升级，推动反磁力中心城市的基础设施建设和公共服务水平提高，增强城市的综合实力。

（四）创新区域协调机制，推进京津冀协同发展

京津冀协同发展关系到北京未来的发展，京津冀协同成效如何取决于协调机制是否有效，即该机制能否处理好京津冀三地的利益关系。区域发展机制是为实现国家区域发展战略目标而形成的长期化、规范化甚至是法律化的办法或手段，包括区域规划与区域政策。创新京津冀协调发展机制，第一，要注重多主体参与顶层设计，主要有中央政府、地方政府、企业和个人 4 个主体，在保证中央政府在顶层设计的主导地位时，仍然要重视其余主体的创造力对于顶层设计的不断完善作用，最大限度满足各方主体的利益诉求且实现利益最大化。第二，对于北京来说，要处理好非首都功能疏解与京津冀协同发展的关系。而根据《北京城市总体规划（2020—2035 年）》，京津冀协同发展的首要任务却是优化提升首都功能，解决北京“大城市病”问题。实际上，北京非首都功能疏解只是北京的利益诉求，或者说这应该仅仅是京津冀协同发展的一个短期目标，长期来讲京津冀协同目标的实现应该是建立满足三地的利益诉求，建立利益共享机制和成本分摊机制，逐步建成世界级城市群。第三，要重视发挥市场的决定性作用。在京津两地与河北存在较大落差的情况下，依赖政府力量推动京津冀协同发展很容易演变成对政府干预发展模式的路径依赖，制约协同的长远发展。今后，要适度约束政府行为，充分发挥“有为政府”和“有效市场”相互结合的综合作用，要综合运用行政、法治、市场手段，分类施策、多措并举、标本兼治，引导企业转移、压减过剩产能、淘汰落后产能，倒逼经济发展方式转变。

参考文献

［1］吴爱芝、李国平：《北京：打造国家中心城市多中心、网络化空间结构》，《北京规划建设》2017 年第 1 期，第 11～15 页。

［2］安树伟、孙文迁：《北京的减量发展》，《前线》2019 年第 1 期，第 68～70 页。

［3］刘欣葵：《北京城市规划与管理 60 年》，光明日报出版社，2010。

［4］邹碧莹：《京津冀城市功能分工演化研究》，首都经济贸易大学硕士学位论文，2019，第 26～27 页。

[5] 安树伟、郁鹏等：《沿海三大城市群产业协作》，经济管理出版社，2019，第238～240页。
[6] 邬晓霞、时晨、高见：《优化北京辐射带动功能研究》，《城市》2019年第2期，第28～36页。
[7] 王义桅、刘雪君：《“一带一路”与北京国际交往中心建设》，《前线》2019年第2期，第39～42页。
[8] 吴爱芝：《双链融合做强“高精尖”产业》，《北京日报》2019年6月10日。
[9] 李瑶、安树伟：《北京城市副中心的形成机制、路径与对策》，《城市》2018年第8期，第24～32页。
[10] 高越、何迪燊、李思莹等：《北京城市副中心对疏解非首都功能贡献度研究》，《调研世界》2019年第2期，第55～59页。
[11] 安树伟、肖金成：《京津冀协同发展：北京的“困境”与河北的“角色”》，《广东社会科学》2015年第4期，第5～11页。
[12] 安树伟、闫程莉、王宇光：《遵循城市发展规律，促进京津冀协同发展》，《财经智库》2017年第3期，第37～47+139～140页。
[13] 安树伟、李瑞鹏、李瑶：《北京非首都功能疏解对居民生活的影响——基于问卷调查的分析》，《河北经贸大学学报》2018年第6期，第70～78+101页。

B.4 上海国家中心城市建设与长三角区域协调发展：回顾与展望

甄　杰*

摘　要： 2018年以来，上海作为国家中心城市在经济发展、创新发展、城市更新等方面取得了诸多成绩，并以其自身的建设成就在长三角区域协调发展中发挥着重要的核心带动作用。同时，上海在创新驱动能力、营商环境、生态资源环境、城市群竞争力、区域协调效率以及产业园区共建等方面仍面临着重要挑战。基于长三角区域一体化的国家战略要求，上海应全方位提升区域一体化发展水平、高标准加快产业转型和结构升级、多层次推进区域互动与协调共治、分类别推进产业园区合作共建，担当起新时代赋予的城市建设重任。

关键词： 上海　国家中心城市　“长三角”　区域协调发展

截至2018年底，在全国9个国家中心城市中，上海的GDP位居榜首。但从上海建设全球城市的角度看，还需要从经济、创新、生态、区域协调等诸多方面进行回顾与评价，在总结发展经验的同时，着重寻找对标差距，从顶层设计和重点任务等层面进一步提高城市建设成效，增强上海对长三角区域协调发展的辐射带动能力。

---

* 甄杰，博士，华东政法大学商学院副教授，同济大学发展研究院秘书长、中国产业园区发展研究中心执行主任，主要研究方向为战略管理、产业园区管理。

一 上海国家中心城市建设进展与态势分析

（一）经济发展总体情况分析

2018 年，上海市 GDP 比上年增长 6.6%，增速与全国平均水平持平（见图 1）。2019 年第一季度 GDP 同比增长 5.7%，增幅有所下降。从三次产业情况看，2018 年上海市三次产业结构为 0.3∶29.8∶69.9。其中，第一产业增加值同比降幅明显，为 -6.9%；第二产业增加值小幅增长，增幅为 1.8%；第三产业增加值同比增幅较大，达到 8.7%。2019 年第一季度，第一产业增加值同比下降 3.4%，第二产业增加值同比下降 1.7%，第三产业增加值同比增长 8.8%。其中，规模以上工业 5 个季度以来同比连续大幅下降，2019 年第一季度，同比增幅跌至 -4.8%（见图 2）。可见，上海市经济增长虽然总体平稳，但三次产业结构正经历快速调整，第三产业发展较快，增速较高，产业转型特征明显。

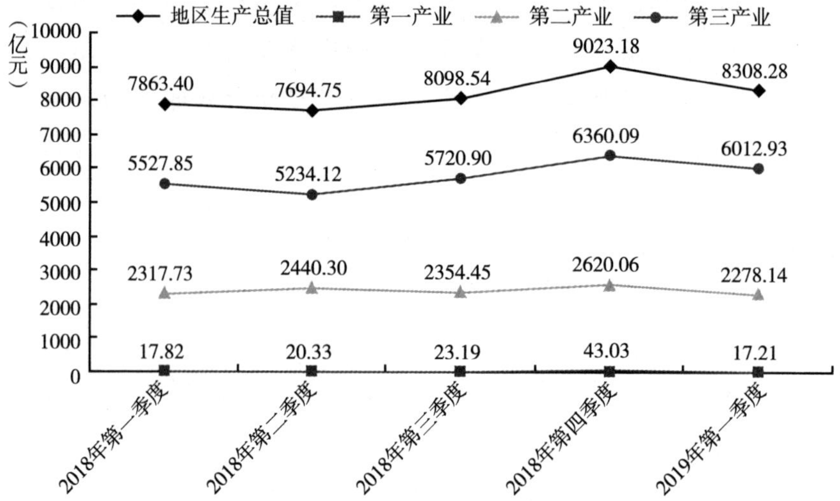

图 1 上海市 2018 ~ 2019 年五个季度 GDP 及三次产业的增长情况

资料来源：根据上海市相关统计数据整理。

1. 主要行业表现

2018 年，上海市的交通运输、仓储和邮政业同比增长明显，达到 10.4%，

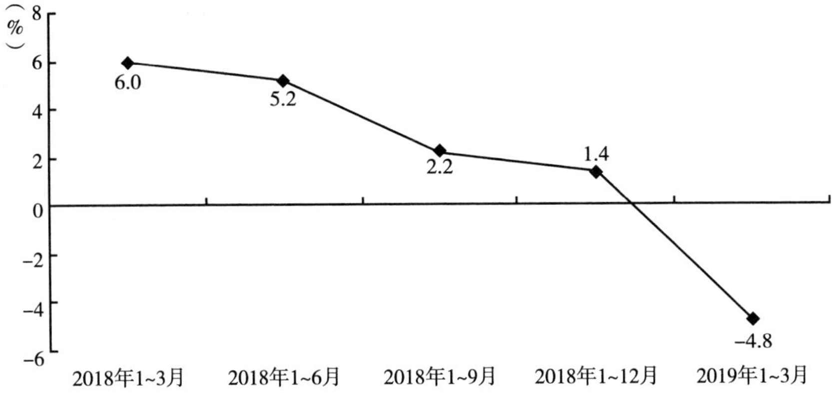

图2　上海市2018～2019年规模以上工业总产值季度累计同比增速

资料来源：根据上海市相关统计数据整理。

金融业、房地产业、批发和零售业保持稳定增长；2019年第一季度，金融业同比增幅显著提高，达到13.3%，房地产业和建筑业同比增长也呈现较高态势（见表1）。工业的同比增速较低，甚至在2019年第一季度降至－2.8%，工业品价格指数也从2018年下半年开始不断走低（见图3）。但从固定资产投资总额来看，上海一直保持增长态势（见图4）。总体上，上海市在金融、贸易方面发展较快，符合其城市定位要求。

表1　2018年以来上海市主要行业生产总值及其同比增长

指标	2018年		2019年第一季度	
	总产值(亿元)	同比增长(%)	总产值(亿元)	同比增长(%)
农林牧渔业	111.98	－3.6	18.18	－1.4
工业	8694.95	1.9	2015.29	－2.8
建筑业	1071.75	1.1	270.76	7.3
批发和零售业	4581.49	3.3	1075.87	2.0
交通运输、仓储和邮政业	1533.36	10.4	378.26	4.3
住宿和餐饮业	421.46	－2.8	98.05	0.3
金融业	5781.63	5.7	1709.59	13.3
房地产业	1992.52	4.8	509.34	8.3

资料来源：上海市统计局。

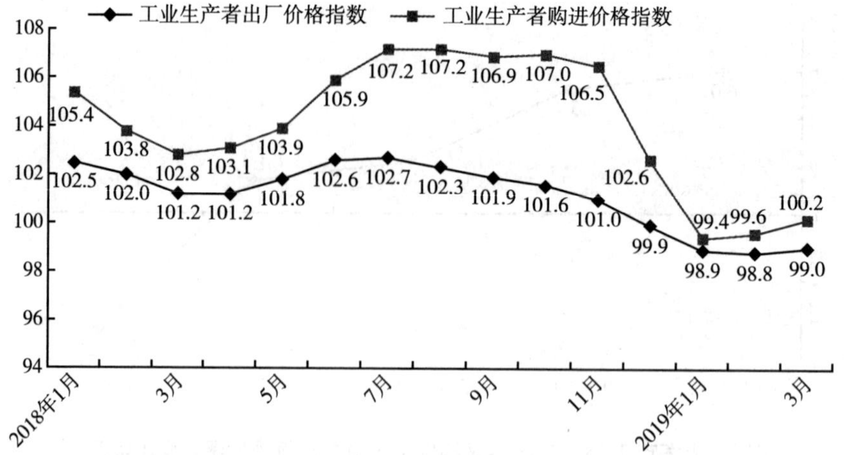

图3　上海市2018～2019年工业品价格指数（月度同比）

资料来源：根据上海市相关统计数据整理。

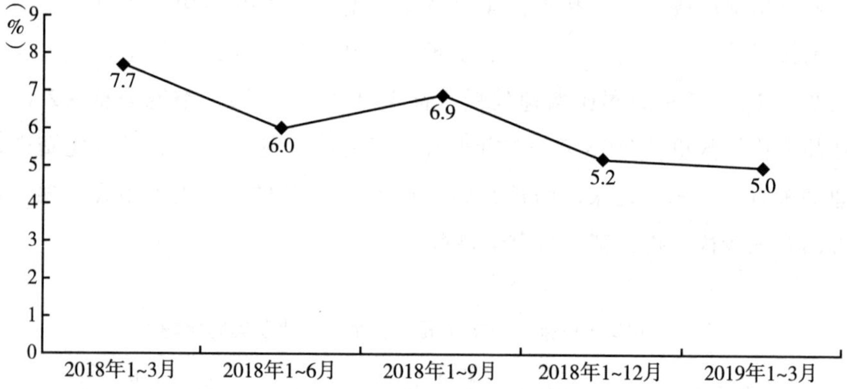

图4　上海市2018～2019年固定资产投资总额季度累计同比增速

资料来源：根据上海市相关统计数据整理。

2. 战略性新兴产业发展情况

2018年，上海市的战略性新兴产业增加值同比增长了8.2%，占上海市GDP的16.7%。其中，工业贡献了43.5%，比上年增长4.2%；服务业贡献了56.5%，比上年增长11.3%（见表2）。服务业在上海市战略性新兴产业中的比重已经高出工业13个百分点，在同比增幅方面也远高于工业，进一步提升了上海市的现代服务功能。

表 2　2018 年上海市战略性新兴产业增加值及其增长速度

指标	绝对值(亿元)	比上年增长(%)
战略性新兴产业增加值	5461.91	8.2
工业	2377.60	4.2
服务业	3084.31	11.3

资料来源：《2018 年上海市国民经济和社会发展统计公报》。

3. 六大重点行业工业总产值

总体来看，2018 年上海市的六大重点行业工业总产值保持增长，但同比增幅较低，仅为 1.4%；2019 年第一季度，同比增幅更是跌为负值。汽车制造业、电子信息产品制造业两个产业 2018 年的增幅较低，而在 2019 年第一季度均呈现较大跌幅。相比之下，生物医药制造业、成套设备制造业两个产业则增长较快（见表 3）。可见，上海凸显了以生物医药为主的先进制造业优势，但其总产值仅占六大重点行业工业总产值的 4.9%，未来应进一步提升重点行业的总体发展水平。

表 3　2018 ~ 2019 年上海市重点行业工业总产值及其同比增速

指标	2018 年全年		2019 年第一季度	
	总产值(亿元)	同比增长(%)	总产值(亿元)	同比增长(%)
六大重点行业工业总产值	23870.78	1.4	5176.89	-5.7
电子信息产品制造业	6450.23	1.9	1292.28	-7.0
汽车制造业	6832.07	0.8	1471.54	-17.2
石油化工及精细化工制造业	4006.76	-1.5	938.80	5.2
精品钢材制造业	1233.42	-6.5	276.38	-4.4
成套设备制造业	4171.70	4.8	898.68	2.3
生物医药制造业	1176.60	9.8	299.21	10.2

资料来源：上海市统计局。

4. 规模以上服务业企业发展水平

从规模以上服务业企业的营收来看（见表 4），上海市增长率较高的领域主要集中在高端生产性服务业。作为国家中心城市，上海在科学研究和技术服务业等方面的快速发展，有力地促进了自身建设成为高新技术产业生产和研发基地的过程，推动其产业结构不断升级优化。可以看到，高端研发、信息技术服务等生产性服务业在上海持续集聚，创新驱动能力也得到较快的提升。

表4 2018~2019年上海市规模以上服务业企业营业收入及其同比增长

指标	2018年		2019年第一季度	
	营业收入（亿元）	比上年同期增长(%)	营业收入（亿元）	比上年同期增长(%)
交通运输、仓储和邮政业	9298.13	13	2363.15	11.7
信息传输、软件和信息技术服务业	5094.3	12.7	1083.90	14.1
租赁和商务服务业	8673.26	9.8	2144.10	6.1
科学研究和技术服务业	2330.18	16	531.58	17
水利、环境和公共设施管理业	402.81	4	91.99	-2.7
居民服务、修理和其他服务业	298.63	9.7	98.05	8.7
教育	129.02	6.5	75.13	10.6
卫生和社会工作	154.93	13.1	39.06	12.3
文化、体育和娱乐业	419.6	1.8	85.48	1.5

资料来源：上海市统计局。

（二）创新发展总体情况分析

1. 研发经费及高新技术企业情况

2018年，上海市用于研究与试验发展（R&D）的经费支出相当于全市生产总值的4.00%（见图5）。当年认定的高新技术成果转化项目同比增长达到33.1%，认定数量为2014~2018年的最高水平。并且，这些项目主要集中在电子信息、生物医药、新材料等重点领域，占比达到86.3%。

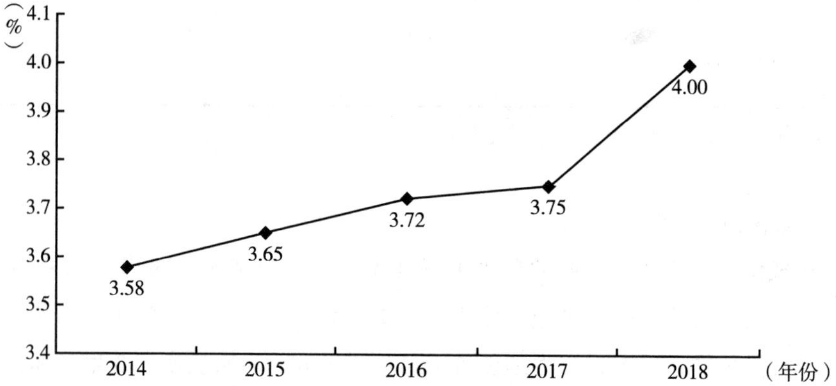

图5 2014~2018年R&D经费支出相当于上海市GDP的比例

资料来源：《2018年上海市国民经济和社会发展统计公报》。

2. 专利情况

2018 年，上海市在专利申请量等主要指标上与上年相比均有高速增长（见表 5）。并且，经认定登记的各类技术交易合同数量虽增幅较低，但其金额达到 1303.20 亿元，比上年增长了 50.2%。

表 5　上海市 2018 年专利发展情况

指标	数量(件)	比上年增长(%)
专利申请量	150233	14.0
发明专利	62755	14.9
实用新型专利	69564	14.2
外观设计专利	17914	10.7
专利授权量	92460	27.0
发明专利	21331	3.1
实用新型专利	55581	39.2
外观设计专利	15548	27.6
PCT 国际专利申请量	2500	19.1
有效发明专利	114966	14.5
每万人口发明专利拥有量	47.5	14.5
经认定登记的各类技术交易合同	21630	0.3

3. 产业园区创新情况

产业园区的集聚效应使其成为区域发展的重要载体，由园区拥有的创新资源丰富程度、创新平台建设情况、创新成果数量水平所反映的产业园区创新发展持续竞争力，可以较好地说明所在地区的创新水平与创新能力。2018 年，在国家级园区创新发展持续竞争力榜单中，上海张江国家自主创新示范区排名第二位，漕河泾经济技术开发区排名第九位。江苏和浙江分别有 1 家园区入榜，即苏州工业园区排名第四位，杭州高新技术产业开发区排名第六位（见表 6）。其中，上海张江国家自主创新示范区在高新技术企业、国家工程技术中心、获得专利授权数量方面都具有明显优势。

4. 产业创新资源分布情况

根据上海市产业地图，按照高等院校、科研院所、创新平台、协会联盟四类创新资源对行业进行梳理①，可以得到上海市融合性数字产业、战略性新兴产业的创新资源分布情况②，并基本是以中心城区为核心，结合各类产业布局特征进行集聚。

表6　2018年国家级产业园区创新发展持续竞争力10强

排名	开发区名称	排名	开发区名称
1	中关村国家自主创新示范区	6	杭州高新技术产业开发区
2	上海张江国家自主创新示范区	7	南昌经济技术开发区
3	武汉东湖国家自主创新示范区	8	南宁高新技术产业开发区
4	苏州工业园区	9	漕河泾经济技术开发区
5	广州经济技术开发区	10	惠州仲恺高新技术开发区

资料来源：任浩、甄杰等《2018中国产业园区持续发展蓝皮书》，同济大学出版社，2018。

（三）城市更新总体情况分析

结构调整、产业转型和城市更新是一项系统工程，上海作为特大型的国家中心城市，在土地、环境、生态、公共资源等方面遇到了瓶颈，也以文化创意产业园（以下简称文创园）等重要形式率先在城市更新方面做出了表率。

1. 文创园再利用方式

上海丰富的工业遗存为城市更新提供了主要空间。在“退二进三”产业结构调整的背景下，大量工业企业迁出市域范围，文化创意基地成为上海存量工业再利用的主流形式。截至2018年6月，上海共有170余个文创园。2019年2月，上海市共认定了137家市级园区，并同时认定了10家示范楼宇以及20家示范空间。③ 目前，上海市文创园区的再利用主要有4种方式（见表7）。

① 梳理内容包括行业所拥有的国家或本市高校、科研院所、工程研究中心、工程技术研究中心、重点实验室、制造业创新中心、研发与转化功能型平台、质量监督检验中心、计量测试中心、测试与评定中心、行业协会或联盟等。

② 根据2018年上海市经济和信息化委员会《上海市产业地图》整理。

③ 上海市文化创意产业推进领导小组办公室对2019～2020年度市级文创园的公示。

表7　上海市文创园再利用的主要方式

序号	再利用方式	占比(%)	示例
1	以优秀历史建筑保护性开发为主	8.57	1933老场坊，湖丝栈，梦清园，800秀
2	在旧工业遗存的基础上，以改造转化为主	76.43	形式1：基于原单个厂区建筑的改造：西岸才谷、创邑·源、国际时尚中心 形式2：对多个厂区进行整合性改造：沪西乐坊、田子坊、8号桥
3	依托旧工业原址，通过土地性质转化，在工业原址上以新建为主	7.14	海上海、创智天地
4	依托原产业集聚区位，完全采用新建的方式建设	7.86	上海证大喜玛拉雅艺术中心、松江时尚谷创意园

资料来源：蔡青：《上海工业遗产转型创意产业园区数据分析与发展研究》，《遗产与保护研究》2018年第7期。

2. 文创园发展规律

上海文创产业园的发展内容涉及业态类型、开发模式、开发组织者、资本参与方式4个方面，且正在经历相应的转变，表现出相应的发展特征（见表8）。政府推动了文创园的统一规划，提高了旧工业区再利用的科学性和项目的集聚程度，文创园的建设开发形式也更加灵活。

表8　上海市文化创意产业园的发展内容及其特征

序号	发展内容	特征
1	业态类型	从单一办公走向多种业态混合模式，包括联合办公、云space、创意集市等新业态
2	开发模式	由自下而上的自发性行为向自上而下的政府倡导行为转变
3	开发组织者	从最早的产业租赁式开发形成的产权、投资相分离的模式，到中期的产权方自主成立公司开发再到目前多种开发形式相结合
4	资本参与方式	由民间自发性投资到企业投资再到目前的政府、企业、个人多种投资相结合

资料来源：蔡青：《上海工业遗产转型创意产业园区数据分析与发展研究》，《遗产与保护研究》2018年第7期。

3. 文创园产业形态

城市更新中的文创园主要集聚了设计、时尚消费、娱乐休闲、商务办公等业态（见表9），并通过植入多元创新的城市公共服务功能，促进由传统单一的生产向现代复合的城市公共服务进行转变。

表9　上海市城市更新典型项目转型前后的产业变化

序号	项目名称	前身	转型后产业							
			现状	商业休闲			创意办公		其他配套	
				零售	餐饮	文娱	办公	艺术工作室	酒店	展示空间
1	8号桥	上汽制动器公司	建筑设计、设计咨询、影业制作		●		●	●		●
2	红坊	上钢十厂	文化、设计、传媒、雕塑		●		●	●		●
3	智造局（一期）	上海紫光机械厂	创意设计、商务办公				●	●		●
4	田子坊	上食机械厂等	室内设计、视觉艺术、工艺美术	●	●		●	●		●
5	同乐坊	森泰机器铣牙厂等	娱乐休闲、时尚创意	●	●	●		●		
6	老码头	上海油脂厂	商业休闲、时尚消费	●	●	●	●	●	●	
7	1933老场坊	上海工部局宰牲场	时尚体验、影视创意、展示交易	●	●	●	●	●		●

资料来源：曾锐、李早：《城市工业遗产转型再生机制探析——以上海市为例》，《城市发展研究》2019年第5期。

二　上海带动长三角区域协调发展成效分析

（一）世界城市能级的辐射影响

1. GaWC 城市排名

GaWC（Globalization and World Cities）对世界城市进行了权威的排名，主

要是对全球城市进行评测，内容涉及金融、会计、广告、法律、管理咨询5个行业，并在排名中对这些城市进行级别划分。① 这份排名重视“高级生产者服务业机构”，关注城市在世界各地活动中所表现出来的主导作用和带动能力，对上海国家中心城市建设和区域协调发展具有重要的借鉴意义。

表10 2010～2018年中国GaWC百强城市及其排名

	2010年排名	2013年排名	2016年排名	2018年排名
香港	3	3	4	3(Alpha＋,一线强)
上海	7	7	9	6(Alpha＋,一线强)
北京	12	10	6	4(Alpha＋,一线强)
台北	43	42	36	26(Alpha,一线中)
广州	67	53	40	27(Alpha,一线中)
深圳	—	—	85	55(Alpha－,一线弱)
成都	—	—	100	71(Beta＋,二线强)
杭州	—	—	—	75(Beta＋,二线强)
天津	—	—	—	86(Beta,二线中)
南京	—	—	—	94(Beta,二线中)
武汉	—	—	—	95(Beta,二线中)

资料来源：作者整理。

在2000年的GaWC排名中，中国大陆仅有上海入围全球一线城市，排在第三十一位。近年来，中国城市的实力不断提升且上升势头强劲，2018年已有10座大陆城市进入百强榜单（见表10）。其中，上海自2010年以来一直稳居前10名，为全球“一线强”城市。同时，浙江的杭州市、江苏的南京市也于2018年首次进入前100强名单，这也是上海在长三角区域协调发展中发挥“龙头”带动作用的成效表现。

2. 联合国“设计之都”

目前，长三角区域共有上海、杭州和苏州3座城市入选了联合国教科文组织的“创意城市网络”，在已入选的9个中国城市中占了1/3。其中，上海被

① GaWC将世界城市分为四个大的等级，即Alpha（一线城市）、Beta（二线城市）、Gamma（三线城市）、Sufficiency（自给自足城市，也可理解为四线城市），同时，每个大的等级中又区分出多个带加、减号的次等级。

授予“设计之都”称号。自2013年起，上海先后两次制订设计之都建设三年行动计划，明确提出要提高文化创意产业的带动效应，整体服务于长三角，并辐射带动全国其他地区发展。2018年末，上海文创产业产值占全市GDP的12.6%。① 2018年7月，上海市在创意与设计产业方面明确了发展目标，即其增加值增速要比全市GDP增速快2~3个百分点。② 在产业布局方面，重视设计驱动，紧密融合前沿科技，大力建设国际设计之都、时尚之都、品牌之都、会展之都。

在创意与设计产业发展方面，上海着力推进长三角区域的多方深入合作，形成了加强区域协调互动的各类专题，并以设计为主线，通过工业设计、会展设计等具体领域提升长三角制造业的整体发展水平，提供高质量的配套服务，并促进产业转型升级。同时，注重各层次的品牌建设，以优质强势品牌带动区域发展；并激励电子商务平台提供专项服务，以有利于“上海设计”在区域协调中发挥重要作用。

2018年4月，首届长三角（上海）品牌博览会③发布了《长三角城市群品牌发展报告》，显示长三角各地所拥有中华老字号超过了全国的1/3。其中，上海的数量最多。同时，长三角品牌建设联盟等机构将品牌、人才、金融等资源进行整合，在长三角区域构建了“品牌建设生态系统”；并通过培育国际强势品牌集群，在品牌建设方面推动形成了专业服务的生态链条。

（二）产业园区集约发展与合作共建

产业园区作为企业集聚、产业集群的主要载体，是实现长三角区域一体化这一国家战略的重要平台与主要阵地。

1. 长三角产业园区土地集约利用

在经济社会快速发展的背景下，上海的土地资源更加趋紧，产业园区成为

---

① 《上海文化创意产业发展三年行动计划（2016—2018年）》，上海市创意产业协会，2016。

② 《上海市经济和信息化委员会等关于印发〈促进上海创意与设计产业发展的实施办法〉的通知》，沪经信都〔2018〕339号，2018年6月19日。

③ 长三角（上海）品牌博览会是2018年1月12日在苏州召开的长三角地区主要领导座谈会上，由沪、苏、浙、皖四地主要领导签署的《长三角地区共同推进平台建设、组织社会力量和市场主体推进城市合作协议》中明确的一项活动。

土地集约利用的重要抓手。长三角区域一体化的重要内容之一即是土地集约利用，在国家级开发区中，以上海为核心的长三角区域在土地集约利用方面具有较好表现（见表11）。长三角区域共有13家园区进入前30强榜单，占比高达43%，整体上显示出在土地集约利用方面的较高水平。[①] 在用地性质方面，工业用地率略有下降，住宅、商服、交通运输等配套用地的比重则有所提升，在明确主导产业内容的基础上，产业结构呈现转型升级的特征。

表11　2018年工业主导型开发区土地集约利用评价结果综合排序

排序位次	开发区名称	排序位次	开发区名称
1	广东福田保税区	16	苏州高新技术产业开发区综合保税区
2	无锡高新区综合保税区	17	平顶山高新技术产业开发区
3	广州经济技术开发区	18	广州保税区
4	武汉经济技术开发区	19	锡山经济技术开发区
5	昆山综合保税区	20	西安高新技术产业开发区
6	上海漕河泾出口加工区	21	上海外高桥保税区
7	大连保税区	22	汕头高新技术产业开发区
8	东莞松山湖高新技术产业开发区	23	昆山经济技术开发区
9	佛山高新技术产业开发区	24	天津经济技术开发区
10	广州保税物流园区	25	陕西西安出口加工区
11	常熟经济技术开发区	26	无锡高新技术产业开发区
12	安徽合肥出口加工区	27	廊坊综合保税区
13	深圳市高新技术产业园区	28	太仓港综合保税区
14	南京经济技术开发区	29	北辰经济技术开发区
15	昆山高新技术产业开发区	30	重庆西永综合保税区

资料来源：国务院《关于2018年度国家级开发区土地集约利用评价情况的通报》②。

2. 长三角产业园区合作持续竞争力

产业园区作为企业及其他各类机构的空间聚集体，创造了资源联结的新模

① 开发区土地集约利用状况评价涉及的指标包括土地供应率、土地建成率、土地开发率、工业用地率、综合容积率、建筑密度、工业用地综合容积率、工业用地建筑系数、工业用地固定资产投入强度、工业用地地均税收、综合地均税收等。

② 为深入贯彻落实党的十九大精神和《国民经济和社会发展第十三个五年规划纲要》，促进开发区提升土地供给质量，自然资源部组织开展了2018年度全国开发区土地集约利用评价工作，共有520个国家级开发区依据相关技术标准，对土地集约利用状况进行了全面评价。

式以及市场竞争的新方式，从而提升了区域的综合竞争力。同时，合作行为并不仅限于园区内部，而且还与外部合作进行有机结合，有效的外部合作科研帮助园区获取持续发展的多样化资源，有利于园区以及所在区域的资源重新配置与整合。因此，产业园区合作进一步反映了其所在区域的协同发展情况。由表12可知，上海有2个园区进入产业合作持续竞争力全国5强，其中，上海张江国家自主创新示范区排在全国首位。同时，在全国前10名园区中，长三角区域共有4个园区入围，除上海市以外，另外两家分别来自江苏省和浙江省。可见，以产业园区为重要载体和抓手，上海在带动长三角区域合作发展方面发挥着重要的作用。

表12　2018年国家级产业园区产业合作持续竞争力10强

排序位次	开发区名称	排序位次	开发区名称
1	上海张江国家自主创新示范区	6	深圳高新技术产业开发区
2	中关村国家自主创新示范区	7	厦门火炬高技术产业开发区
3	广州经济技术开发区	8	苏州工业园区
4	成都高新技术产业开发区	9	武汉东湖国家自主创新示范区
5	漕河泾经济技术开发区	10	宁波高新技术产业开发区

资料来源：任浩、甄杰等：《2018中国产业园区持续发展蓝皮书》，同济大学出版社，2018。

3. 长三角产业园区合作共建

为了解决土地约束问题，2018年，长三角各地利用飞地经济、土地置换等多种形式，实现了省内或省际的园区合作共建，提高了土地产出效率（见表13）。目前，长三角区域成立了专门的产业园区协同发展组织，如开发区协同发展联盟等；G60科创走廊通过建立联席办公机制，施行具体的改革举措，在长三角区域9个城市的产业园区之间推进相关合作；上海松江区与安徽宣城市合作成立了“宣州松江产业园”；上海金山区与浙江平湖市共建了张江长三角科技城；环淀山湖区域的上海青浦、江苏昆山与吴江、浙江嘉善共同签署了战略协同区一体化发展合作备忘录；上海的嘉定、江苏的昆山与太仓共同打造了嘉昆太产业链创新联盟以及嘉昆太科创产业园。同时，上海嘉定区同温州市共同设立了位于嘉定的“科技创新（研发）园”和位于温州的“嘉定工业区温州园”，后者也是先进制造业深度融合发展示范区。

表 13　2018 年以来长三角园区共建部分活动情况

序号	园区/共建活动	地点	属性	具体活动/成效	时间
1	滨海港工业园区	上海	省际	盐城（上海）产业园区合作共建投资推介会	2019.6.5
2	江苏南北共建园区（43 家）	—	省内	南北共建园区考核	2019.4
3	安徽南北合作共建园区（3+7）	—	省内	南北共建园区考核	2019.4
4	苏州盐城沿海合作开发园区	盐城	省内	低碳金属材料智造产业园项目确定落户	2019.2
5	无锡与徐州共建园区（7 家）	—	省内	2018 年无锡与徐州共建园区发展成效明显	2019.2
6	安庆（上海）园区合作共建	上海	省际	安庆（上海）园区合作共建对接会暨项目签约仪式等系列活动	2018.12.18
7	苏银产业园区	银川	省际	苏州工业园区与滨河新区将合作共建	2018.8.20
8	漕河泾开发区海宁分区等 8 家	海宁等	省际	推进长三角园区合作共建首批示范园区	2018.7.10
9	上海城投（启东）江海产业园等 4 家	启东等	省际	推进长三角园区合作共建首批试点园区	2018.7.10
10	青浦郎溪工业园	郎溪	省际	在郎溪经济开发区实行精准招商，集群式承接产业转移	2018.6
11	浙江省山海协作产业园（9 家）	—	省内	中共浙江省委、浙江省人民政府关于深入实施山海协作工程促进区域协调发展的若干意见	2018.5.31
12	江阴经济开发区靖江园区	靖江	省内	融合发展协调会暨创建江阴—靖江高质量跨江融合发展实验区研讨会	2018.8.29
13	沪苏大丰产业联动集聚区	上海	省际	沪苏大丰产业联动开发建设推进协调领导小组第二次联席会议	2018.5.8

资料来源：作者整理。

（三）区域创新的表现与潜力

1. 城市创新力增强

根据《2018 福布斯创新力最强的 30 个城市》排名（见表 14），长三角共有 18 个城市入围，占比 60%，比 2017 年增加 4 个城市。相比之下，珠三角、京津冀入围城市分别只有6个、1个，均比上年减少1个。长三角城市群的整体创新优势非常明显，其中，在区域协同发展的作用下，苏州已经跃居全国第三位。

表14　中国大陆最具创新力的30个城市

排名	城市	省/直辖市/自治区	所属城市群	排名	城市	省/直辖市/自治区	所属城市群
1	深圳	广东	珠三角	16	西安	陕西	关中平原城市群
2	北京	北京	京津冀	17	绍兴	浙江	长三角
3	苏州	江苏	长三角	18	镇江	江苏	长三角
4	上海	上海	长三角	19	太仓	江苏	长三角
5	广州	广东	珠三角	20	合肥	安徽	长三角
6	珠海	广东	珠三角	21	青岛	山东	山东半岛
7	东莞	广东	珠三角	22	湖州	浙江	长三角
8	中山	广东	珠三角	23	武汉	湖北	长江中游城市群
9	杭州	浙江	长三角	24	郑州	河南	中原城市群
10	南京	江苏	长三角	25	常州	江苏	长三角
11	昆山	江苏	长三角	26	芜湖	安徽	长三角
12	佛山	广东	珠三角	27	慈溪	浙江	长三角
13	成都	四川	成渝城市群	28	宜兴	江苏	长三角
14	宁波	浙江	长三角	29	南通	江苏	长三角
15	无锡	江苏	长三角	30	嘉兴	浙江	长三角

资料来源：《2018福布斯创新力最强的30个城市》。

2. 制度创新强劲

2019年6月25日，上海出台《关于支持浦东新区改革开放再出发实现新时代高质量发展的若干意见》，明确了20条重要措施。这些措施重在“放权”，旨在提升制度供给能力，系统支持浦东新区锐意改革、先行先试，实现高质量发展。其主要内容包括见表15。

表15　浦东新区改革开放再出发措施内容

序号	定位	思路	内容举措
1	当好全面深化改革的探路尖兵	支持浦东新区以制度创新为核心，对标最高标准、最好水平，大胆试、大胆闯、自主改，打造国际一流营商环境	依法赋予浦东新区市级经济管理权限；深化市场准入管理制度改革；深化“互联网+政务服务”改革；深化政府综合监管创新；深化产业用地制度改革

续表

序号	定位	思路	内容举措
2	打造全方位开放的前沿窗口	积极探索从商品和要素流动型开放向规则等制度型开放拓展，加大开放型经济风险压力测试力度，在更深层次、更宽领域，以更大力度推进全方位高水平开放	深化重点领域开放先行先试；提升投资贸易自由化便利化水平；打造联通全球大平台；更好服务国家“一带一路”建设和长三角一体化发展战略
3	建设具有全球影响力的科创中心核心承载区	强化科技创新前瞻布局和融通发展，完善技术创新体系和科技服务体系，参与全球协同创新，打造集聚全球创新资源的“强磁场”，不断推出创新成果的“原产地”、促进成果高效转化的“首选区”	加快提升科技创新策源能力，构建更具吸引力的创新生态，打造更具竞争力的人才综合服务环境；支持浦东新区探索以优化人口结构和人才服务为重点的人口管理机制，赋予浦东新区国内人才引进直接落户审批权和留学人员落户审批权
4	建设具有国际竞争力的产业新高地	坚持把高质量发展着力点放在实体经济上，着力提高经济密度，打造一批战略领先的现代产业集群和充满生机的创新企业集群，增创国际竞争新优势	打造世界级先进制造业集群，提升高端服务业全球竞争力
5	建设高品质的现代化城区	生态优先，绿色发展，全力提升城市精细化管理水平，增强城市吸引力	构建国际一流的枢纽型、网络化综合交通体系，加快实现更高水平的城乡发展一体化，建设更加完善的“城市大脑”体系

资料来源：《关于支持浦东新区改革开放再出发实现新时代高质量发展的若干意见》。

可见，浦东在制度创新的过程中，将对长三角区域整体的高水平改革开放、高质量发展、高品质生活带来巨大和深远的影响。

三 上海国家中心城市建设与长三角区域协调发展的特征与挑战

（一）主要特征

1. 城市功能定位明确统一

上海无论是作为直辖市、国家中心城市，还是作为特大型城市、长三角一体化的龙头城市、全球城市，都具有明确且内涵统一的城市功能定位。在总体上，上海要建设成为国际经济、金融、贸易、航运、科技创新中心，[①] 成为国际性综合交通枢纽[②]以及全球高端要素网络的重要枢纽，加快发展先进制造业、强化现代服务功能，提升城市创新能力，持续优化服务为主的产业结构，提高辐射带动长三角、长江流域以至全国发展的能力。[③]

2. 产业结构优化转型明显

2018 年以来，上海市三次产业中第一、第二产业同比增幅持续走低，但第三产业同比增幅明显较大。2019 年第一季度，三次产业结构已经调整为 0.2∶27.4∶72.4，服务业产值占比已经超过了 70%。2018 年，上海市战略性新兴产业增长较快，其中，服务业增幅明显高于工业，增幅是工业的 2.7 倍。从具体行业看，高端服务业、生产性服务业表现尤为抢眼，而工业中的生物医药制造等先进制造业增长显著。

3. 创新发展重点持续突出

上海市用于研究与试验发展（R&D）的经费支出占全市生产总值的比重逐年提高。2018 年上海市认定的高新技术成果转化项目中，电子信息、生物医药、新材料等重点领域表现突出，占比达到 86.3%，专利发展的各项内容均有快速增长；产业园区的创新持续竞争力在全国具有优势；以中心城区为重点，在融合性数字产业、战略性新兴产业方面表现出鲜明的创新资源持续集聚的分布特征。

4. 城市更新示范效应显著

上海的城市更新已经形成了以改造转化旧工业遗存为主的 4 种再利用类型，在发展内容、产业转型等方面具有明显特征。通过实践探索与理论研究，上海将大数据分析等内容融入城市更新领域，关注城市的整体空间形态、局部设计内容、深层文化内涵，并注重高频客群的价值挖掘、目的客群的网红打卡效应，在长三角区域乃至全国具有积极的示范意义。

5. 区域协调发展提速换挡

2018 年以来，上海深入构建了长三角区域一体化发展的各项机制，设立

---

① 《国务院关于上海市城市总体规划的批复》，国函〔2017〕147 号。

② 《国务院关于印发"十三五"现代综合交通运输体系发展规划的通知》，国发〔2017〕11 号。

③ 《国务院关于印发全国主体功能区规划的通知》，国发〔2010〕46 号。

了区域合作专门机构；通过政策文件明确了区域一体化的战略方向与工作内容，施行《长三角地区一体化发展三年行动计划（2018—2020 年）》，制定了长三角一体化发展的时间表，描绘了路线图，并开展立法对接，在机制和法律层面上为区域协调发展提供保障。

（二）重要挑战

1. 创新驱动能力不足

上海虽然在以产业园区为载体的土地集约利用方面做出了成绩，但从整体来看，由于对土地资源高度依赖，其发展的内生动力逐渐表现出财富与投资“双轮驱动”的特征，使得经济难以保持稳定增长，产业转型升级遇到瓶颈，科技创新内生动力不足，发展质量和效益不能快速提升。从全球城市创新力排行中可以看出，2018 年上海在创新力方面已经被苏州超越，由 2017 年的全国第三位下降至第四位。同时，由于科创中心应具有全球影响力，上海的经济转型、产业结构升级带来了对技术型、研发型人才的大幅需求，引起了国际化人才、创新创业人才的紧缺，这也要求上海尽快解决高端人才的培育、吸引和留住问题。

2. 营商环境有待提高

《2019 全球营商环境报告》显示，我国营商环境整体向好，上海在办理施工许可等一些指标方面有显著改善，并且，与国内其他城市相比，上海的营商环境具有较大竞争力。然而，相较于建设卓越全球城市的要求，上海城市发展的软环境仍待改善，法治化、国际化、便利化水平尚显不足，市民素质和城市文明程度亟须提高。长三角区域营商环境的评估显示，① 该区域营商环境总体虽处于全国领先水平，但平均得分仍有很大成长空间。上海虽然在城市排名中位居榜首，然而在省级层面上浙江则领先于上海。长三角城市间注重自身发展、强调自身特色，但容易忽略区域协同发展和一体化机制的完善。

3. 生态资源环境约束

2018 年，上海市常住人口增长到 2423.78 万人，老龄化率达到 14% 左右，位居全国之首。与其他国际大都市相比，上海建设用地规模过高。“十三五”期

① 《首届（2019）长三角地区营商环境发展水平评估报告》。

间，上海建设用地增量有限，用地结构中生产用地占比较大，生活用地结构亟须优化，公共服务设施用地占比较低。同时，能源资源供给有限，水资源安全保障风险较高，资源环境紧约束的局面已经形成。地表水环境的氮磷污染问题在一定程度上得到改善，但仍然是主要的污染来源。环境空气质量虽有持续改善，但与美好生活的标准还相去甚远，臭氧污染问题仍比较严重。上海、江苏的森林覆盖率均只有16%左右，在全国内地31个省份中居第二十五、第二十六位，处于落后状态。此外，上海的浓雾、雷电、地质灾害等也给生产生活带来了诸多影响。

4. 城市群竞争力亟待提升

上海的中心城区人口密集，但国际大都市的功能表现不足。落户上海的世界500强企业总部仅为纽约的10%，外国人口占常住人口比重仅有0.9%。制造业和服务业的中低端内容较多，“大城市病”问题突出。与世界先进城市群相比，长三角城市群的发展处于滞后状态（见表16）。制造业附加值不高，创新性不足，城市间分工协作不够，人均GDP、地均GDP等指标差距巨大，甚至GDP也明显落后。城市建设中的空间利用效率不高，国土开发强度远高于法国大巴黎地区、英国大伦敦地区。此外，上海大都市圈生态安全屏障较为脆弱；缺乏统一的生态体系建设规划，难以统筹安排，生态协同效益不高。

表16　世界城市群对标分析

城市群	北美五大湖城市群	美国东北部大西洋沿岸城市群	英国中南部城市群	日本太平洋沿岸城市群	欧洲西北部城市群	中国长三角城市群
面积（万平方公里）	24.5	13.8	4.5	3.5	14.5	21.2
人口（万人）	5000	6500	3650	7000	4600	15033
GDP（亿美元）	33600	40320	20186	33820	21000	20652
人均GDP（美元/人）	67200	62030	55305	48315	45652	13737
地均GDP（万美元/平方公里）	1370	2920	4485	9662	1448	974

资料来源：作者整理。

5. 区域协调效率尚需提高

当前，上海及长三角其他地方在区域一体化发展中均出台了相关推进性政策，但总体上各地政策仍不完全一致，需要尽快完善推进和保障机制。在跨区域信息平台建设、资源整合与重新配置、工作推进与监管、利益协调共享、考核机制建设与完善等方面需要进行系统考虑，切实提高长三角区域协同治理的效率。要在打破行政壁垒的基础上，高效率多层次地推进市场、政策、公共服务、民生服务等方面的一体化工作，形成开发区、城市、区域等相互之间的独特竞争优势，避免同质化发展和过度竞争问题，构建长三角区域良好的经济与社会的生态系统空间。此外，目前上海大都市圈轨道交通满足高强度出行需求的能力还比较弱，地铁与轻轨兴建力度大，但尚未形成“地铁、市郊铁路、干线”的交通模式，不利于人口由中心城区向郊区疏散，也不利于产业的优化布局。

6. 产业园区共建难以深化

产业园区合作共建是快速高效推进区域协调发展的重要抓手，长三角区域内部的园区合作共建工作得到了不断推进，但在实践中遇到了不少瓶颈问题，难以持续深化。一是园区现有飞地合作模式急需优化，需重点考量自身发展的可持续性与飞地园区发展的自主性；二是在当前区域一体化与融合化发展的大背景下，园区需进一步推动各地区创新资源与要素的自由流动与集聚；三是在完成自身存量优化的基础上，仍要实现增量改革目标。因此，上海及其他长三角地方应考虑如何在园区共建合作中进行重要调整，包括战略定位要更加精准、政策激励要更加有效、利益分配要更加合理、管理权限要更加科学等。另外，长三角区域一体化发展示范区的建设已经成为各方共识，但该示范区跨越沪苏浙三地，要真正打破行政边界建设统一性园区，也将在诸多方面面临挑战。

四　上海国家中心城市建设与长三角区域协调发展展望与建议

（一）展望

1. 三重压力下城市建设进入深化制度改革关键时期。改革开放 40 周年之际，上海作为开放的前沿窗口和改革的探路尖兵，在中美经贸摩擦不断升级、供给侧结构性改革深入推进和体制机制改革持续深化的三重压力下，加快产业结构转型升级，并将会继续从供给侧探索解决土地利用、人才引进、资源优化配置、创新驱动等方面的问题。同时，浦东实现新时代高质量发展等重要举措是上海在制度改革进入攻坚阶段的进一步深化和推进，并将为上海后续的国家中心城市建设与推进长三角区域协调发展夯实基础并打开局面。

2. 营商环境优化将成为城市建设发展的重要手段。长期以来，上海同国内其他城市都比较重视基础设施等硬环境建设，而在营商环境所涉及的软环境方面，上海虽然在国内具有相应的竞争优势，但仍远落后于其他国际大都市。上海未来仍将结合国际通行评价指标和中国改革时代要求和地方特色，系统地营造亲商、安商、富商的良好环境，并从制度方面为法制化营商环境提供保障。未来将持续做好知识产权保护工作，深化“放管服”改革，完善科技金融服务体系，打造更加安全、高效、透明的便利化营商环境。

3. 以园区为载体构建区域创新生态系统是协调重点。长三角区域协调发展需要构建有效的创新生态系统，其重点在于通过创新引领产业发展，实现区域发展的高质量。不同于微观的企业创新生态系统和宏观的区域创新生态系统，园区创新生态系统的构建是以产业园区为重要平台的中观新型视角，这既是基于产业集聚层面寻找促进企业有效关联的重要抓手，也是推动长三角区域经济协调发展必须直面的重要问题。目前，区域创新效率较低，而基于园区从“制度—产业—网络”层面系统地构建区域新型创新生态系统则是破题的有效路径。

4. 飞地经济作为区域一体化的主要形式将不断深化。2017 年，国家发展改革委等联合印发了《关于支持“飞地经济”发展的指导意见》，提出应大力发展“飞地经济”，通过资金输出、技术输出、管理输出等举措，提升“飞入地”园区的建设与管理水平，实际上，这种形式近两年也在推进区域一体化方面扮演着重要角色。不过，由于飞地经济在战略定位、政策激励、利益分配、管理权限等方面都具有一些瓶颈性问题，长三角区域在协调发展过程中也要持续探索“飞地经济”的发展模式，通过不断创新“飞地经济”合作机制，进一步优化资源配置、提升区域整体发展水平。

5. 区域协调发展内生驱动机制将得到进一步强化。中共中央、国务院在《关于建立更加有效的区域协调发展新机制的意见》中指出，小尺度城市合作是区域发展的主要形式。从都市圈建设来看，长三角区域相关政府协调与沟通机制将进一步得到加强，在统一规划、区域共治、利益共享等方面要具体落实。同时，长三角区域应重点建立市场一体化发展机制，建设统一的要素和产品市场，加强市场监管合作，优化区域产业布局。2019 年 5 月 13 日，在中共中央政治局会议审议的《长江三角洲区域一体化发展规划纲要》中，“一体化”和“高质量”的重要性被特别强调，并成为进一步加强区域内生驱动机制建设的明确要求。

（二）建议

1. 全方位提升区域一体化发展水平

长三角区域一体化发展是一项系统工程，一方面要尽快完善交通、物流、环保、新能源、大数据等方面基础设施的互联互通，大幅提升各城市新的区位优势与经济发展潜力；另一方面要以提升科技创新资源配置效率为核心，消除行政边界带来的阻碍，完善促进区域一体化发展的相关制度，充分发挥市场的决定性作用。依托各地环境资源承载力条件，形成“中心城市—都市圈—城市群—中小城镇”梯次清晰的空间结构，以及“生产 + 生活”“主导产业 + 配套产业”的产业结构。

2. 高标准加快产业转型和结构升级

围绕提升创新能力的核心任务，持续优化人才结构，激发创新主体活力，探索形成区域集成创新模式，加快创新成果转化，完善区域内合作共建与利益共享机制；基于新一代信息技术的渗透与贯通作用，加速产业联动，推动传统产业转型升级，提高先进制造业的发展水平；推进城市更新，从存量与增量两个方面提高土地利用效率和效益，厚植城市文化内涵，提升现代服务业水平；以最高标准和水平加快改善上海乃至长三角区域的营商环境，提升城市建设的软实力。

3. 多层次推进区域互动与协调共治

在以上海为龙头的长三角区域，从主体上形成“政府、园区、企业”以及其他各类组织共同参与的合作网络，从内容上形成“法制、体制、机制”三位一体的制度体系，从方式上形成“硬基础”与“软环境”齐抓共管、融合发力的均衡格局，从形态上形成“产业形态、空间形态、关系形态”不断向高阶演进的生态系统，从结果上形成“多点改革创新、多方统筹协调、多元评估考核”的治理结构。最终，达成长三角区域协调共治的良好局面。

4. 分类别推进产业园区合作共建

在长三角区域协调发展中以产业园区为抓手，大力推进园区的合作共建工作，特别是应该分类别地对园区合作共建进行重点推进。例如，根据园区功能对经开区、高新区、保税区等进行对口合作，根据园区经营活动内容对工业园区、农业园区、旅游园区、商业园区等进行政策配套，根据园区依托对象对科技园、总部基地、文化创意园等进行创新支持。总体上做好规划管理工作，优化管理体制，重视战略定位；细化运营工作，对接国际规则，系统优化招商工作；持续创新创业，完善创新创业生态系统；完善各类平台建设，强化优质公共服务支撑。

参考文献

[1]《2018 年上海市国民经济和社会发展统计公报》。

[2] 任浩、甄杰等:《2018 中国产业园区持续发展蓝皮书》，同济大学出版社，2018。

[3] 蔡青:《上海工业遗产转型创意产业园区数据分析与发展研究》，《遗产与保护研究》2018 年第 7 期。

[4] 曾锐、李早:《城市工业遗产转型再生机制探析——以上海市为例》，《城市发展研究》2019 年第 5 期。

[5] 国务院:《关于 2018 年度国家级开发区土地集约利用评价情况的通报》。

B.5

天津国家中心城市建设的进展、特点及趋势

李 慧 周立群*

摘 要： 2018年以来，天津城市发展以“三个着力”为元为纲，以智能科技产业为重要抓手，全方位推进经济高质量发展，呈现经济增长速度下滑、三次产业结构持续升级、供给侧结构性改革进一步深化、生态城市建设稳步推进等变化特点。为实现国家中心城市建设的基本定位，天津从京津冀协同发展战略实施、“一基地三区”定位落实、开放创新“双驱动”战略实施等各方面深入推进，取得了显著成效。然而，天津国家中心城市建设仍面临着三大问题：一是经济增长下滑，转型升级压力较大；二是承接北京非首都功能疏解的平台建设仍需完善；三是智能科技产业发展仍存在核心技术有短板、基础产业相对薄弱等不足。只有着力解决这些问题，推动智能科技产业发展、完善非首都功能承接平台建设、精准对接中关村创新资源，才能真正将天津建设成为具备引领、辐射、集散功能的国家中心城市。

关键词： 高质量发展 智能科技产业 京津冀协同 资源对接

---

* 李慧，南开大学经济学院博士，研究方向为产业组织、企业创新；周立群，南开大学滨海开发研究院教授、天津市智库联盟理事长，研究方向为市场结构、企业组织、区域经济。

一　天津市中心城市建设的基本进展

2018年以来，天津市全面贯彻落实党的十九大精神，以2013年5月习近平总书记考察天津时提出的“着力提高发展质量和效益、着力保障和改善民生、着力加强和改善党的领导”“三个着力”为元为纲，以智能科技产业为重要抓手，全方位推进经济高质量发展，在经济增长、产业发展、结构调整、人口变化、生态与环境等城市建设方面取得了重要进展。

（一）经济增长

1. 地区生产总值排名下滑，且差距拉大

2018年，天津市地区生产总值为1.88万亿元，在直辖市中排在末位，且成为唯一一个未进入“2万亿元俱乐部”的直辖市。2011～2016年，在4个直辖市的地区生产总值中，天津市一直高于重庆市，处于第三位；然而，2017年，重庆市地区生产总值超过天津市，比天津市高出近1000亿元，天津市地区生产总值排名下滑。同时，在4个直辖市中，天津市地区生产总值增速下滑幅度最大，经济增速显著低于其他三市。可见，无论是地区生产总值还是经济增速，与北京市、上海市、重庆市相比，2018年以来，天津市的差距均较为明显，经济增长下行压力较大（见图1）。

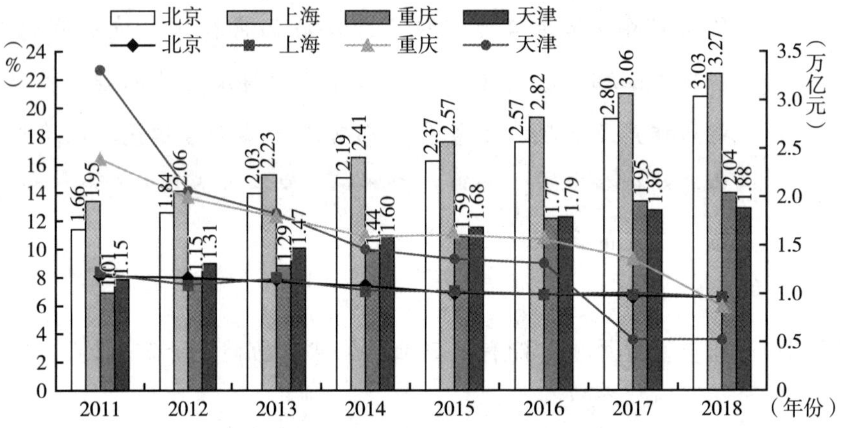

图1　2011～2018年4个直辖市地区生产总值及增长率

资料来源：2011～2018年北京、上海、重庆、天津各市国民经济和社会发展统计公报及统计年鉴。

2. 经济增长仍然失速，但逐季向好

2018 年，天津市实现生产总值 18809.64 亿元，比 2017 年增长 3.6%（按可比价格计算）（见图 2）。从数据上看，2018 年天津市经济增速在内地 31 个省份当中名列倒数第一，经济增长仍然失速。

对天津市而言，2018 年是抢抓历史性窗口期，实现由高速增长向高质量发展转变的生死攸关的一年。为加速经济向高质量发展迈进，天津市摒弃规模速度型增长方式，深入践行“三个着力”，以深化改革、创新驱动为统领，全方位布局智能科技产业，积极培育新的经济增长点，大力推动质量变革、效率变革、动力变革，经济增长逐季向好，高质量发展态势正在形成。到 2019 年一季度，天津市地区生产总值增速回升至4.5%，分别比2018 年一季度、上半年和全年加快 2.6 个、1.1 个和 0.9 个百分点。

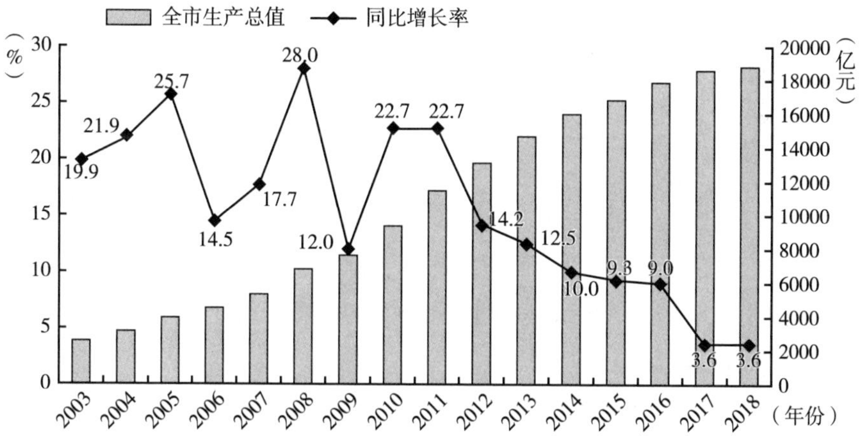

图 2　2003 ~ 2018 年天津市生产总值及增长率

资料来源：《2018 年天津统计年鉴》《2018 年天津市国民经济和社会发展统计公报》。

（二）产业发展

1. 现代都市型农业持续升级

2018 年，天津市现代都市型农业快速发展、持续升级，主要体现在 6 个方面：一是粮食生产保持稳定；二是农业信息化、品牌化、功能化不断延伸、拓展，建设物联网种植养殖应用示范基地达 800 个，基本建成农业大数据应用平台；三是“菜篮子”工程市长负责制得以落实，“农产品质量安全市”创建工作有序推进，地产农产品抽检合格率基本保持在98%以上，居全国前列；四是农业绿色发展成效显著，已建成农业科技合作示范园区10个，先后开展10个绿色循环畜产品生产基地、100个规模化规范化设施示范园区的建设工作；五是乡村“五创行动”试点工作逐步推进，田园综合体、现代农业产业园、共享农庄等新业态加快发展；六是国家农村改革试验区的改革试点工作稳步开展，农村集体产权制度改革全面推开、农村土地承包经营权确权登记颁证工作基本完成，农民住房财产权抵押贷款试点扎实推进、农业保险制度体系加速完善，在全国范围内率先建成了覆盖市、区、镇街三级的农村产权交易市场。

2. 先进制造业明显提质增效

2018年，天津市高技术产业（先进制造业）增加值增长4.4%，比全市规模以上工业增加值增速高2.0个百分点，占全市规模以上工业增加值的比重为13.3%；战略性新兴产业增加值增长3.1%，占全市规模以上工业增加值的比重为21.8%，比2017年提高1.0个百分点；先进制造业产业在工业总产值中的比重高达61.8%，工业企业利润比2017年增长17.6%。显见，天津市工业发展稳步向好，先进制造业质量效益提升明显。为全面推进全国先进制造研发基地建设，培育壮大新兴产业，加速新旧动能转换，天津市为挖掘大数据产业发展在商用、民用、政用方面的重要作用，制定出台《天津市促进大数据发展应用条例》，积极培育壮大战略性新兴产业和智能经济形态，加快构建数字经济和智慧城市建设。

3. 现代服务业支撑作用增强

天津市服务业比重不断提高，现代服务业支撑作用增强。2018年，天津市服务业增加值为11027.12亿元，同比增长5.9%，高于全市生产总值2.3个百分点，占全市生产总值的比重达58.6%，比2017年提高0.4个百分点，服务业在全市经济中的比重进一步提高。其中，金融业增加值为1966.89亿元，同比增长7.2%；金融业、科技服务业、信息服务业、商务租赁业等资本技术密集型行业占服务业比重达42.1%，比2017年提高1.4个百分点；在规模以上服务业中，科技服务业、高技术服务业、战略性新兴服务业的营业收入分别增长12.2%、11.9%、9.2%，利润率分别达7.5%、7.3%、8.5%；服务业内部结构持续优化。同时，2018年，全市新增服务业市场主体达18.3万户，占全部新增市场主体的比重达90.6%，合尔科技、忆云共享、今日头条等一批新兴服务业企业快速成长，服务业新动能培育不断加速。

（三）结构调整

1. 三次产业结构持续调整

为实现高质量发展这一根本要求，天津市坚持以创新驱动发展战略为引领，加速构建现代化经济体系，创新发展现代都市型农业、先进制造业、现代服务业，三次产业结构持续调整，产业内部结构不断优化。

一方面，三次产业结构持续调整。2018年，天津市三次产业结构由2017年的1.2∶40.8∶58.0调整为0.9∶40.5∶58.6，服务业对天津市产业发展的主导作用日益增强。

另一方面，产业内部结构不断优化。一是为扎实推进习近平总书记“三农”思想在天津落地生根，天津市以实施乡村振兴战略为抓手，大力发展科技农业、工程农业、都市农业，打造现代都市型农业升级版。自2017年以来，天津市先后出台《天津市乡村振兴战略规划（2018—2022年）》《关于推进现代都市型农业绿色发展的实施意见》等文件，有效引导天津市打造国家级现代都市型农业示范区、农业高新技术产业园区、农产品物流中心区、国家农业农村改革试验区和农业信息化平台、农业对外合作平台的“四区两平台”建设工作稳步推进，切实促进了天津市现代都市型农业持续向形态更高级、结构更合理、融合更深入迈进。二是为全面推进全国先进制造研发基地建设，天津市全面布局智能科技产业，自2017年以来，密集制订出台《天津市加快推进智能科技产业发展总体行动计划》和《天津市智能制造发展专项行动计划》等10项专项计划，以及生物医药、新能源、新材料等4个产业发展三年行动计划、“智造十条”等实施细则，助力天津市先进制造业、智能科技产业发展。其中，智能科技产业迅猛发展，自主可控、大数据和云计算、智能网联车、智能终端、先进通信、机器人、智能安防、智能制造及智慧医疗等领域的产业特色逐步形成，竞争优势快速显现。三是为切实推进经济由高速增长转向高质量发展，在《中共天津市委　天津市人民政府关于加快现代服务业发展的若干意见》的指导下，天津市不断加快现代服务业发展，服务业内部结构持续优化，新兴金融、电子商务、文化创意、旅游会展、科技服务等现代服务业快速发展。其中，融资租赁业务稳步发展，业务总量仍处于全国领先态势，截止到2018年底，天津市共有各类融资租赁公司总部（不包括单一项目租赁公司、分公司、SPV子公司、海外收购的公司、已注销的公司）2008家，比2017年底增加434家。

2. 供给侧结构性改革进一步深化

2018年，天津市全面落实深化供给侧结构性改革的年度任务，加快新旧动能转换，为经济战略性调整增添新动力。在“去产能”方面，天津市积极开展违法违规钢铁产能大排查大整治、落后产能淘汰工作，全年共处置“僵尸企业”365家；在“去库存”方面，天津市积极盘活空置楼宇和低效闲置土地资源，全年共盘活空置楼宇、示范工业园区低效闲置土地分别为238.5万平方米、2679亩；在“去杠杆”方面，天津市稳步推进规模以上工业企业去杠杆、国有企业混合所有制改革去杠杆等工作，促进了企业杠杆率持续降低，2018年末规模以上工业企业资产负债率降至60.3%，比2017年同期降低了0.2个百分点；在“降成本”方面，为持续降低实体经济企业成本，天津市陆续制定出台了《天津市进一步推进供给侧结构性改革降低实体经济企业成本政策措施》（2018年5月）等一系列降成本政策措施，2018年全年共计为企业减负600亿元左右，工业企业每100元主营业务收入的成本降低为83.90元，比全国平均水平低0.29元；在“补短板”方面，针对科技教育、基础设施等薄弱环节，天津市不断加大补短板工作力度，精准发力找差距、强弱项，在“美丽天津”城乡建设、地铁建设等方面取得了积极成效。

（四）人口变化

从人口数量看，2018年，天津市常住人口呈现小幅度增长（见表1）。从人口增长率看，统计数据显示，2018年，天津市常住人口出生率为6.67‰，死亡率为5.42‰，自然增长率为1.25‰。

天津市积极实施22项促进大学生创业就业政策，妥善安置化解过剩产能企业职工，保证零就业家庭、低保家庭至少有1人实现就业，就业数量持续增加，就业质量不断提升。2018年，天津市全社会就业人口达896.56万人；其中，外来就业人口为359.78万人，比2017年增加1.6万人；城镇就业人口为

714.21 万人，比 2017 年增加 4.1 万人，年末城镇登记失业率为 3.5%；全年新增就业人口为 49 万人。

表 1　2018 年末天津市常住人口情况

	人数	增加(万人)	占全市常住人口比重(%)
常住人口(万人)	1559.60	2.73	100.0
外来人口(万人)	499.01	0.78	32.0
城镇人口(万人)	1296.81	5.70	83.15
全市户籍人口(万人)	1081.63	31.64	—

资料来源：《2018 年天津市国民经济和社会发展统计公报》。

2018 年，天津市贯彻落实 17 项增收措施，居民收支稳定增长。由表 2 可见，2018 年天津市居民人均可支配收入、人均消费支出均呈现稳定增长；在人均消费支出中，教育文化娱乐、交通通信、医疗保健的支出增长较快，分别比人均消费支出的增长高出 11.0 个、6.9 个、4.6 个百分点。

表 2　2018 年天津市居民收支状况

	收入与支出(元)	增长(%)
全市居民人均可支配收入(元)	39506	6.7
城镇居民人均可支配收入(元)	42976	6.7
农村居民人均可支配收入(元)	23065	6.0
全市居民人均消费支出(元)	29903	7.4
其中:教育文化娱乐	—	18.4
交通通信	—	14.3
医疗保健	—	12.0

资料来源：《2018 年天津市国民经济和社会发展统计公报》。

（五）生态与环境

为打好污染防治攻坚战，天津市深入学习、全面贯彻创新、协调、绿色、开放、共享的新发展理念，稳步推进生态城市建设，污染防治工作取得显著成效。

首先，不断加强生态环境保护，主要开展四方面工作：一是划定面积为 1393.79 平方公里的海域、陆域生态保护红线，占天津市海陆总面积的比重达

9.91%；二是落实《天津市湿地自然保护区规划》，全面升级对七里海、北大港等重要生态湿地的保护力度，共计完成生态湿地核心区土地流转98.1平方公里；三是高标准制定《天津市加强滨海新区和中心城区中间地带规划管控建设绿色生态屏障实施细则》，加强“双城绿色生态屏障”的管控、建设，加速完成7400亩起步区的绿化任务；四是为保护候鸟迁徙通道，针对破坏候鸟等野生动物资源的违法犯罪行为，积极开展专项打击行动。

其次，深化大气、水、土壤、固体废物等污染防治。一是深化大气污染防治，二是深化水污染防治，三是开展土壤污染状况详细调查工作，四是强化固体废物污染防治，开展遏制固体废物非法转移倾倒、废酸整治等专项治理行动，降低进口固体废物许可量。

二 天津市中心城市建设的主要成效

作为国家中心城市，天津一直是环渤海地区的经济中心。在京津冀协同发展的大格局中，天津确立了“一基地三区”的定位，即全国先进制造研发基地、北方国际航运核心区、金融创新运营示范区、改革开放先行区。在推动经济迈向高质量发展阶段，天津确立了打造人工智能先锋城市的新定位。为实现中央关于天津市国家中心城市建设的基本定位，天津市从京津冀协同发展战略实施、“一基地三区”定位落实、开放创新“双驱动”战略实施等方面，联合推进中心城市建设，取得了显著成效。

（一）深入推进京津冀协同发展战略，区域一体化发展成效明显

一方面，深入推进京津冀协同发展重大国家战略，紧抓疏解北京非首都功能这个“牛鼻子”，深化相关领域的功能对接与合作，取得了一系列成效。一是为精准承接非首都功能疏解，天津市持续打造以滨海新区战略合作功能区为综合承载平台、宝坻中关村科技城等若干专业承载平台为框架的“1+16”承接平台。二是启动建设或签约一批项目，例如，启动建设国家会展中心项目，成功签约中国核工业大学等项目。三是滨海中关村科技园、宝坻京津中关村科技城协同发展中心等重点载体建设不断加快，其中，滨海中关村科技园累计注册941家企业，并吸引了中国（滨海新区）知识产权保

护中心等优质项目落户。

另一方面，主动对接雄安新区建设重大部署，为雄安新区建设发展提供服务。一是根据《河北省人民政府　天津市人民政府关于积极推进河北雄安新区建设发展战略合作协议》，加快落实协议所确定的 8 方面合作事项，规划完善天津市联通雄安新区的交通网络，制定实施《关于天津港建设世界一流港口的实施方案（2019—2023 年）》，天津港与河北省黄骅港共同打造雄安新区出海口。二是与雄安新区在职业教育、社会保险制度体系建设等领域开展深入合作，实施天津和雄安两地合作办学，设立天津市第一商业学校雄安分校、天津市园林学校雄安分校，启动天津职业大学雄安新区培训基地建设等。

（二）构建项目化清单化支撑体系，“一基地三区”定位取得实效

为落实京津冀协同发展重大国家战略，全面推进“一基地三区”建设，天津市制定出台了加快实现功能定位的项目化清单化支撑体系实施方案，截止到 2018 年底，首批 126 个重大项目和事项已完成 45 个，“一基地三区”定位取得实效。

一是全国先进制造研发基地建设全面展开。天津市以创新驱动战略为引擎，以制造强国战略为引领，以智能制造为主攻方向，促进制造业存量升级增量转型，打造全国先进制造研发基地。天津市提出打造“天津智港”、建设人工智能先锋城市，引进了紫光云、京东云、今日头条、用友软件、航天云网等 300 多个智能科技项目，初步形成了自主安全可控、智能装备、智能网联车等产业集群。

二是北方国际航运核心区功能显著提升。

三是金融创新运营示范区建设取得良好进展。

四是改革开放先行区建设取得重要成果。加速打造“通武廊”协同发展试验示范区，加快实施 60 项合作协议，三地人才互认互准得以有序推进；开辟京津冀三地迁移企业注册登记双向绿色通道，推动三地行政许可事项“六统一”（包括名称、设定依据、许可内容、申请条件、申请材料、许可结果形式）；探索建立创新券、创业券跨区域互通互认机制，三地签订创新券合作协议，建立京津冀科技创新券合作机制；京津冀（天津）检验检疫综合改革试验区挂牌运营。

（三）全面布局智能科技产业，人工智能先锋城市建设成效显著

为顺应全球新一轮科技革命和产业变革趋势，天津市委、市政府高度重视智能科技产业发展，全面布局智能科技产业，将其作为推进产业结构调整、加快产业转型升级、培育新动能的重大举措和重要突破口。为此，天津市第一个提出打造“天津智港”，第一个举办世界智能大会，出台了一系列支持政策，开展了一系列试点示范，在全国率先举起了智能发展的旗帜。

目前，天津市先后出台了一系列政策措施，形成了完善的政策支撑体系；聚集了一批支撑产业发展的平台和载体；引进和培育了一批智能科技骨干企业。智能科技产业正成为天津市产业转型升级、高质量发展的重要驱动力，人工智能先锋城市建设有序推进。

三　城市建设新突破：大力发展智能科技产业

天津市贯彻创新驱动发展等国家战略，立足发展实际，创造性地将“智能”与“科技”两个领域有机衔接，率先提出了“智能科技产业”的概念，在全国率先举起了智能发展的旗帜，把发展智能科技产业作为推动科技跨越发展、产业优化升级、生产力整体跃升的战略抓手。以此为突破口，天津市委市政府相继制定出台了一系列文件，通过完善顶层设计，整合优势资源，推动互联网、大数据、人工智能和实体经济深度融合，着力发展智能经济，加快打造人工智能先锋城市。

2018 年以来，为推动高质量发展、创新发展，天津市中心城市建设的推进工作主要围绕智能科技产业的布局展开，致力于加快建设全国领先的创新型城市和智能科技产业创新中心，以智能科技产业引领经济转型升级、实现中心城市建设定位。

（一）区域间错位发展布局

在智能科技产业顶层设计及相关规划指导下，天津市各区依托自身区域优势及产业基础，选择发展具有比较优势的产业及应用领域，逐步形成了以滨海新区为引领、各区协同发展的智能科技产业错位发展格局。

1. 滨海新区

滨海新区依托雄厚制造业为基础，以人工智能和智能制造为主攻方向，积极布局和发展智能科技产业，形成了自主可控、大数据 + 云计算、模式识别、机器人 + 无人装备、工业互联网 + 智能制造、智能网联车、智能终端 + 核心元器件、智能医疗等具有竞争力的产业链，成为天津市智能科技产业核心集聚区。

2. 中心城区

中心城区充分发挥现代服务业先发优势，以智能科技服务业为主导方向，布局智能科技产业发展。

其中，河东区作为天津市区连接滨海新区的前沿，依托天津音乐街、棉三创意街区、先之科技园等文化产业载体，大力发展智能文化创意产业；依托河东金贸产业园区，聚焦智能电气方向，打造特色产业科技创新示范区；依托天津站交通枢纽，深化智能交通场景应用。

河北区具有深厚的文化底蕴、良好的产业基础、深厚的产业潜能，在传统产业基础上加快智能文化创意产业发展，依托天津美术学院、天津工艺美术职业学院、通广智能科技产业园、1946 创意产业园、巷肆创意产业园等载体，打造智能文化创意产业集聚区。

红桥区是天津市的发祥地，占据三岔河口和“三河五岸”的独特区位优势，依托天津西站坐落区内及京沪、津秦、津保、京津城际四条高铁全线贯通的优越发展条件，以大数据、云计算等为主要方向，打造人工智能和研发服务的创新生态系统。

河西区是天津市委、市政府所在地，也是全市政治活动和国际交往的重要场所、对外开放交流的重要窗口，主要依托北方设计联盟、陈塘自主创新示范区等平台载体，以设计产业为主导，致力于智慧城市建设和人工智能产业发展。

和平区作为全市金融、商贸、教育和医疗卫生中心，围绕建设世界级智慧中央活力区的目标，实施金融、商贸、文化旅游等行业智能化升级，以智慧金融为主，推动智能医疗健康、智能政务、智能交通、智能社区等领域形成区域特色。

南开区以“一座古城、两位总理、三所名校”闻名遐迩，主要依托南开大学、天津大学等优质教育资源和以中汽工程为代表的创新联盟优势，打造高水平研发与成果转化平台，重点培育大数据、云计算、机器人等产业。

3. 其他城区

东丽区、西青区、津南区、北辰区和武清区以“提升研发创新能力、促进智能科技创新要素聚集”为主线，主要聚焦软件信息业、智能科技解决方案，重点引进云服务、大数据、电子商务、智能硬件、智能物流、智能家居等领域企业，重点发展智能网联车、智能机器人、智能制造、智慧城市等产业领域，大力建设智能制造小镇，快速打造工业互联网产业集聚区。

宁河区地处京津唐大城市群中间地带，聚焦于系统谋划智能科技产业战略布局，强化招商对接，高水平打造未来科技城人工智能产业基地，推动引导传统产业智能化改造。

宝坻区、静海区和蓟州区则充分发挥在农业、商贸物流和旅游等领域的资源禀赋优势，积极拓展智能农业、智能商贸物流和智慧旅游，形成优势特色领域。

（二）“智能＋”多领域深度融合

天津市以重点行业为突破口，推动传统产业智能化改造，打造“智能＋”应用新高地。围绕制造业、医疗与健康、交通运输、智慧城市建设等行业领域，布局行业特色智能化应用，打造一批典型行业应用场景，提升行业智能化解决方案能力。

1. 智能制造领域

为深入推进全国先进制造研发基地建设，天津市制定发布《天津市智能制造发展专项行动计划》，实施智能制造创新中心建设专项行动、智能制造装备与系统创新、智能制造系统解决方案供应商培育等专项行动。依托爱波瑞、天津智慧城市研究院等智能化转型升级咨询诊断服务机构，长荣科技、天汽模等垂直领域解决方案供应商，航天云网、阿里云计算、紫光云技术等国内知名的行业智能化解决方案服务商，开展智能解决方案和场景应用布局，分步推进智能技术在智能制造企业研发设计、生产制造、物流仓储、售后服务等环节的深度应用，加快工业互联网综合创新平台和关键技术试验平台建设。截至2018年底，累计获得国家智能制造项目19个，龙头示范带动产业转型效果显著，新技术、新模式快速涌现，智能制造发展迅速。

2. 智能医疗与健康领域

天津市先后印发《智能健康与医疗专项行动计划》《关于促进“互联网＋医疗健康”发展的实施意见》《关于印发“互联网＋医疗健康”便民惠民服务行动方案的通知》等文件，全面推进以“智能＋”为依托的智慧医院、远程医疗平台、智慧健康管理等应用场景的发展。依托零氪科技、天堰科技、GE医疗、国际生物医药联合研究院等代表性企业和科研院所，天津市基本形成了从智能医疗检测分析设备、新型医用诊断仪器、健康大数据、基因测序到可穿戴智能健康设备的智能医疗产业链。基于此，积极推动传统就医方式变革，全市43家三级医疗机构中39家完成智慧门诊建设并上线运行，移动终端预约率达到65%，自助缴费率达到30.6%；建成市级数据中心，实现了电子病历与健康档案核心数据关联，医疗数据与健康数据集成加速。

3. 智能交通领域

依据《天津市智能交通专项行动计划》，实施“智能交通335专项行动”，以完善智能交通制度建设，加强数据资源整合、数据协同应用，加快智慧港口建设等。一方面，加速建设智能交通数据资源交换共享与开放应用平台、天津市综合交通数据分析服务系统，通过整合分散在各部门的数据资源，形成可视、可测、可控的数据资源交换共享体系与应用整合平台和以路网、公共交通、综合运输和停车慢行四大交通指数为核心的大数据分析服务平台，实时综合分析各项综合交通数据，推动实现决策科学、管理智慧、生产智能、服务人文的智能交通运输系统。另一方面，完善天津港集团智能调度指挥系统，推动“一港多区”管理一体化，推进所属6家集装箱码头“操作系统一体化”切换，在全国沿海港口中率先实现集装箱码头生产作业全过程集成化运营管理。

4. 智慧城市领域

根据《天津市智慧城市专项行动计划》，推进基础设施智能化、基础信息安全化、民生服务均等化、城市治理精细化、数字经济高端化5项任务。实施专项行动计划以来，天津市围绕政务、社保、环保等领域实施11项重点工程，推动新型智慧城市建设。现已建成全市信息资源统一共享交换平台——智慧政务平台，涵盖42个市级政务部门、16个区以及能源集团等3家公共服务机构，上线数据总量超过35亿条；同时，建设智慧城市运行平台，例如，完成数字化城市管理平台视频监控系统提升改造，建立查缉布控体系“慧眼”系统助力交管工作；探索实践智慧城区建设，建成社区管理服务平台，覆盖全市每个区、街镇、社区。

（三）逐步强化政策环境支撑

自2017年起，天津市委、市政府陆续出台了多项促进智能科技产业发展的扶持政策，相关委办局出台各细分领域行动计划和配套支持政策，所辖16个区因地制宜量身打造区级政策，形成从点到面、上下联动的格局，政策环境支撑逐步强化，有力推动了天津市智能科技产业创新能力、综合实力和核心竞争力的提升。

1. 政策密度和力度空前

为促进智能科技产业发展，2017年至2018年底，天津市委、市政府、相关委办局、各区政府共出台了115项扶持政策。按时间划分，2017年出台32项，2018年出台83项；按级别划分，市级政策44项，区级政策71项；按发布单位划分，天津市委、市政府出台21项，相关委办局出台23项，各区政府出台71项；按类型划分，综合类政策36项，专项类政策79项。这些政策涵盖了人工智能、机器人、大数据、集成电路、智能制造以及“智能+”等多个领域，呈现“数量多、覆盖广、针对性强、力度大”等特点。

2. 市级政策体系较完善

天津市在市级层面搭建了智能科技产业政策体系的四梁八柱，打造最优政策组合，基本形成了“顶层设计引领—行动计划深化—实施细则支撑—人才资金保障”的政策框架体系。

一是顶层设计引领。2017年9月，天津市委、市政府印发了《关于大力发展智能科技产业推动智能经济发展建设智能社会的实施意见》（以下简称《实施意见》），明确了天津市智能科技产业发展目标、重点推进的五大工程和五大政策体系，是天津市加快推进智能科技产业发展的顶层设计，是智能科技产业发展的总纲，为行动计划、实施细则、金融人才政策和方案意见制定出台指明了方向。

二是行动计划深化。在《实施意见》的基础上，天津市陆续出台了《“1+10”行动计划》《天津市新一代人工智能产业发展三年行动计划（2018—2020

年)》《天津市人工智能“七链”精准创新行动计划》等行动计划和相关规划。其中,《“1+10”行动计划》提出了天津市智能科技产业发展的总体策略、路径和着力点,并根据各分领域特点和需求明确了相应的目标和任务。

三是实施细则支撑。2018年5月,天津市政府印发了《天津市关于加快推进智能科技产业发展的若干政策》(以下简称《若干政策》),明确设立智能制造财政专项资金、新一代人工智能科技产业基金等,并依照《若干政策》要求,天津市各委办局结合自身特点,因地制宜研究制订了相应的实施细则。

四是人才资金保障。为培育智能科技产业市场主体、加速企业和人才聚集、催生新经济新业态,天津市从人才引育、财政金融等方面,出台新一代人工智能科技产业基金、智能制造专项资金、“海河英才”行动计划等多个配套政策。这些政策对天津市招商引资、人才引入、智能制造发展起到了显著促进作用。

3. 搭建专家决策支撑体系

2018年10月19日,成立了天津市智能科技产业专家咨询委员会,由16名委员构成,涵盖人工智能、智能制造等智能科技产业重点领域,其中两院院士8名,占专家委员总数的一半。同时,遴选出186名来自高校、代表性企业、科研院所、行业协会等领域的专家,成立了智能制造、智能医疗与健康、智能农业、智能文化创意、智能交通等共10个分领域专家组,构建形成“1+10”专家决策支撑体系,为天津市委、市政府智能科技产业发展的重大决策提供智力支持。

4. 借力世界智能大会

截止到2019年7月,天津市已连续成功举办三届世界智能大会,产业合作平台影响力快速提升,向世界智能科技领域发出了“中国声音”,同时还签署落地了一批重大项目,有效促进了智能科技产业资源要素的加速聚集。

四 天津市中心城市建设面临的问题与挑战

随着天津市智能科技产业的全面布局与发展,天津市国家中心城市建设呈现智能天津、数字天津、新型智慧城市建设的特点,在打造人工智能先锋城市、建设全国领先的创新型城市和智能科技产业创新中心方面,取得了显著成效。然而，其建设中仍面临着一些问题。

1. 天津经济增长下滑，转型升级压力较大

多年以来，天津市以政府主导的投资拉动经济增长模式为主，随着供给侧结构性改革、污染防治攻坚战等的深入推进，压缩淘汰低效落后产能、环保限产风暴等持续进行，天津市传统工业对经济增长的拉动减弱，经济增长陷入下滑，转型升级压力加大。这使得天津市迫切需要以创新驱动代替投资驱动，加速新旧动能转换，培育新的经济增长点，从而推动经济发展方式转变、实现高质量发展。

2. 承接北京非首都功能疏解的平台建设仍需完善

一方面，承接平台较多，部分平台定位重叠，产业承接同质化竞争。为承接北京非首都功能疏解，促进三地产业有序转移、精准对接，京津冀联合发布《关于加强京津冀产业转移承接重点平台建设的意见》，初步明确“2 +4 +46”个平台，即北京城市副中心、河北雄安新区两个集中承载地，四大战略合作功能区，46 个专业化、特色化承接平台。天津市布局了“1 +16”承接平台格局。河北省确立了 11 个省级重大承接平台及一批县级承接平台。尽管各地承接载体较多，但载体布局较为分散，载体之间功能定位重叠、主导产业同质化，再加上承接平台管委会之间缺乏横向沟通和利益协同，导致各承接平台缺乏合作、各自为战，不利于产业转移和造成承接的错位，无法形成优势产业集聚和上下游产业间联动，难以实现产业精准转移。

另一方面，部分平台建设进展缓慢、配套能力欠佳、承接能力不强。在天津市分设在 16 个城区的承接平台中，一半以上处于开发水平较低区域或成立时间较短，甚至尚处于规划阶段或基础设施施工建设阶段，平台建设缓慢、配套设施不足，尚不具备产业承接能力；在已经建成的承接平台中，也存在承接项目偏少、配套建设放缓、招商引资吸引力不足的问题；同时，多数承接平台仅依靠政策红利招商引资、承接项目，在体制机制创新、产业生态环境营造方面较为滞后，也不利于其承接能力提高。

3. 智能科技产业发展仍存在一些不足

第一，核心技术存在短板。目前，天津市侧重于技术追踪和技术引进，核心技术掌控不足，例如，核心工业软件受制于人，南大通用数据库、麒麟操作系统等自主产品普及率较低。第二，基础产业相对薄弱。天津市出台的一系列

意见、政策契合时代潮流、符合天津实际，但总体来看，主要集中于自动驾驶、智能机器人等应用推广方面，在处理器、芯片等基础产业领域投入相对较少，产业竞争力较弱。第三，专业领域人才不足。从天津市人工智能人才数量看，高层次领军人才、高技能人才不足，基础理论、核心算法以及高端芯片等专业人才缺乏。第四，应用广度和深度不够。尽管天津市智能制造新模式推广取得初步成效，但目前还处于自动化向数字化过渡的低层次阶段，整体水平不高；且梯次培育机制不健全，财政专项资金支持的亮点项目、标志性项目数量不够多。

五　天津市中心城市建设的展望与对策

依据天津国家中心城市建设的基本定位、京津冀协同发展战略关于天津“一基地三区”的定位、天津市打造人工智能先锋城市的目标，天津国家中心城市建设将继续通过深入推进京津冀协同发展重大国家战略、实施开放创新“双驱动”战略、打造“天津智港”等，着力解决当前天津国家中心城市建设中面临的问题，加快建设全国领先的创新型城市和智能科技产业创新中心。

1. 推动智能科技产业发展，为转型升级发展注入新动能

围绕打造“天津智港”，天津市要积极推进智能科技与实体经济深度融合，着力构建创新驱动、应用牵引、产业协同、载体支撑、跨界融合的智能科技产业新体系，为建设人工智能先锋城市、创建具有国际影响力的智能科技产业创新中心注入新动能，为打造“五个现代化天津”、推动京津冀协同发展塑造新引擎。

一要重视开放创新平台的搭建。一方面，搭建智能科技产业资源对接平台，通过搭建智能科技企业创新交流平台、组建智能科技创新联盟、举办全球智能科技高端会议等方式，构建起全球范围内的智能科技企业、高校、科研机构等的合作渠道。另一方面，共建智能科技产业赋能平台，通过与科大讯飞、阿里巴巴和腾讯等智能科技领域领先企业合作，借助企业的技术优势和行业资源，推动上下游产业链的有效对接。同时，打造智能科技孵化基地和“双创”平台，降低智能科技企业创新创业成本，提高超级计算、智能云服务等公共供给以及专业化的创新创业公共服务水平。

二要加大人才培养和引进力度。一方面，要加大高端人才引进力度。借助海河英才计划、千人计划等，重点引进一批智能科技领域具有国际水平的战略科技人才、行业领军人才、学术带头人和优秀青年科技人才。另一方面，要加快智能科技人才培养步伐。依托南开大学人工智能研究院、天津大学人工智能研究院及其他高校的相关研究院所，加紧培养智能科技方面的专业人才；以产业需求为导向，推进天津市高校学科交叉融合和专业调整改革，重点培养造就一批具有较高技术水平、全球战略眼光、管理创新能力的科技型企业家队伍。

三要构筑全国高端智能制造产业集聚区。一方面，依托电子信息、生物医药、装备制造等先进制造优势产业，主攻先进制造技术和系统的研发创新，推动研发型制造业、服务型制造业的发展，拓展和延伸高端制造业产业链条，与北京全球研发中心形成错位，与河北的制造业基地形成异地协同化。另一方面，完善产业技术协同链条，在科技制度、产业环境、协同联合体、科技服务等方面积极探索协作机制，以市场力量汇聚科技资源。此外，加强与环渤海地区的技术交流与合作，开拓产品需求市场，提高创新成果转化水平，积极打造全国高端智能制造产业核心聚集区。

2. 完善承接平台建设，积极承接北京非首都功能疏解

在京津冀协同发展战略深入推进的背景下，天津市应针对承接平台建设中存在的问题，统筹优化承接格局，探索建立更为有效的区域协调发展新机制，积极承接北京非首都功能疏解，有序对接北京产业转移及科技创新资源。

首先，将天津市“1＋16”产业转移承接平台格局置于京津冀产业转移“2＋4＋46”大格局中，对各个承接平台的功能和产业进行重新定位，突出各自的引资优势、产业特色，形成承接平台的错位布局，促进产业转移有效对接。

其次，健全上下联动、内外结合的工作机制，强化承接平台之间的横向沟通和利益协同，依据各自功能定位和主导产业，开展错位承接、上下游关联产业聚集，畅通疏解地、承接地对接渠道，推进集中承接、团组承接，改善各地承接平台间的相互牵制、同质化竞争。

最后，对天津市“1＋16”承接平台进行有机整合，适时调整建设进度缓慢、配套设施滞后、承接能力较低、对接效果较差的承接平台，重点打造以滨海—中关村科技园、天津南站科技商务区、武清津滨工业园、宝坻中关村科技城为主的“东—南—西—北”承接格局，形成承接北京非首都功能疏解的聚

集地、对接北京产业转移和科技创新资源的高地。

3. 精准对接中关村创新资源，加速智能科技要素集聚

随着非首都功能的进一步疏解，中关村创新资源和高科技企业外扩和转移步伐在加快。在智能科技产业发展的关键时期，中关村人工智能创新资源融入天津制造对于快速集聚智能科技要素尤为重要。为此，应精准对接中关村创新资源。

一方面，要对接中关村智能科技创新源，盯准承接的项目源和关键技术合作方，构建由“原始创新—硬件制造—软件技术研发—通用平台支持—终端产业应用”构成的京津智能产业链和创新链。一是重点引进智能制造产业链集成商和重点行业解决方案商，加大本地大数据、算力、服务平台与智能技术、算法、解决方案的对接，整合上下游智能企业和智能资源，提升天津市智能化解决方案的能力。二是结合天津市人工智能“七链”精准创新行动计划，通过敲门招商、专业招商、产业链招商有针对性地吸引和扶持中关村关键智能技术在天津制造的研发设计、生产制造、物流仓储、售后服务环节深度应用，形成应用场景的“有机串链”和系统应用。

另一方面，要把握北京服务业开放的契机，探索吸引中关村现代服务业在津发展的新路径，提升生产性服务业的规模和层次。在新一轮的京津冀协同中，吸引中关村企业在天津发展的重点是生产性服务业，天津市需在生产性服务业领域补短板、增强项。首先，在滨海—中关村科技园、宝坻京津中关村科技城、武清京津产业新城等承接平台以及金融创新运营示范区、国家租赁创新示范区建设中，应加快构建科技服务、中介服务、转化支持等生产性服务业体系。其次，重点围绕产业转移承接项目、智能科技产业项目，着力引入上下游关联产业和延伸服务机构，培育吸引科技金融、科技中介、商贸物流、法律服务等跟进落地，形成实体经济与生产性服务业相互支撑促进、配套式集聚、集群式发展的综合服务格局。

参考文献

［1］周立群等：《京津冀都市圈的崛起与中国经济发展》，经济科学出版社，2012。

［2］周立群、李家祥等：《滨海新区发展报告（2014）》，天津人民出版社，2014。
［3］周立群等：《中国区域经济新版图》，江苏人民出版社，2017。
［4］周彩云、周立群：《吸引北京高科技资源入津发展的现状与对策》，《天津政务参考》2018 年第 11 期。
［5］周彩云、周立群：《吸引与承接北京高科技创新资源入冀的建议》，《信息专报（中共河北省委办公厅）》2018 年第 9 期。
［6］王金杰、周立群：《非首都功能疏解与津冀承接平台的完善思路——京津冀协同发展战略实施五周年系列研究之一》，《天津社会科学》2019 年第 1 期。
［7］王金杰、周立群：《新常态下区域协同发展的取向和路径——以京津冀的探索和实践为例》，《江海学刊》2015 年第 4 期。
［8］薄文广、陈飞：《京津冀协同发展：挑战与困境》，《南开学报》（哲学社会科学版）2015 年第 1 期。
［9］张杰、郑若愚：《京津冀产业协同发展中的多重困局与改革取向》，《中共中央党校学报》2017 年第 4 期。
［10］天津市智能科技产业专家咨询委员会：《天津智能科技产业发展年度报告（2019）》，《天津》2019。
［11］天津市人民政府：《关于天津市 2018 年国民经济和社会发展计划执行情况与 2019 年国民经济和社会发展计划草案的报告》，（2019－02－15）［2019－06－26］. http：//www. tj. gov. cn/zw/zfgb/rdhwj/201903/t20190304_ 3650546. html。
［12］《GDP 增速全国垫底　天津深陷经济增长失速泥潭》，《华夏时报》2019 年 2 月 15 日。
［13］《天津经济增速降到多年来最低点，人民日报三问天津如何闯关》，澎湃新闻，2018－01－20［2019－06－26］. http：//news. 163. com/18/0120/07/D8IVDVM0000187VE. html。

B.6

广州建设科技教育文化中心目标内涵与路径策略

覃剑　尹涛*

摘　要： 培育提升科技教育文化中心功能是广州担当粤港澳大湾区发展核心引擎的重要支撑，是广州推动老城市焕发新活力的重要行动。作为国家中心城市，广州科技、教育、文化综合实力较强且较为均衡。面向未来，广州培育提升科技教育文化中心功能的基础在现代教育、重点在科技创新、气质在城市文化、关键在融通融合，目标是要建设成为中国特色社会主义科技教育文化融合发展的示范城市。为实现这一目标，广州应重点从建设世界科学家的理想城市、世界级大学科技园区、中国版“硅巷”、创新街区等方面着手突破。

关键词： 科技教育文化中心　城市功能　“硅巷”模式　广州

纵观纽约、伦敦、东京等全球顶级城市，在经历大规模基础设施建设和投资驱动发展阶段之后，城市综合竞争力越来越体现为科技创新、金融资本、文化软实力、现代教育、国际交往等功能及其这些功能形成辐射能级和影响力。在国内，科技、教育和文化资源也呈现向中心城市集聚的趋势。2019 年 2 月 18 日，《粤港澳大湾区发展规划纲要》（以下简称《纲要》）正式对外发布，提出广州进一步培育提升科技教育文化中心功能的新要求。事实上，在粤港澳大湾区主要城

---

* 覃剑，博士，广州市社会科学院区域经济研究所副所长副研究员，研究方向为城市与区域经济；尹涛，博士，广州市社会科学院副院长研究员，研究方向为产业经济。

市当中，广州在科技创新、教育科研和文化事业等方面都有较好的基础，且发展相对均衡，具备将“科技+教育+文化”融合起来打造科技教育文化中心的先发优势。因此，抓住粤港澳大湾区发展大机遇，发挥国家中心城市辐射带动作用，进一步集聚优质科技、教育、文化资源，对广州培育发展新动能、促进综合城市功能出新出彩、实现老城市新活力都具有十分重要意义。

一　广州建设科技教育文化中心的基础条件

（一）综合经济实力不断增强

改革开放以来，广州经济总体上呈现稳定较快的增长轨迹。2018 年，广州 GDP 同步增长 6.2%，GDP 从 1978 年的 43.09 亿元增长到 22859.35 亿元，三次产业结构从 1978 年的 11.67∶58.59∶29.74 演变为 0.98∶27.27∶71.75。常住人口城镇化率达到 86.4%，人均地区生产总值达到 155491 元，城市常住居民家庭人均消费支出 42180.96 元，其中教育文化娱乐支出所占比重达到 13.4%（见表 1）。从所处的经济发展水平和发展阶段来看，广州发展正逐步显现“创新+文化”双轮驱动发展的新特征，为建设科技教育文化中心提供了坚实基础。

表 1　2018 年我国部分城市的主要经济指标

城市	常住人口总量(万人)	地区生产总值(亿元)	地区人均GDP(万元)	GDP 增速(%)	一般公共预算收入(亿元)	常住人口城镇化率(%)
北京	2154.20	30320.00	14.00	6.6	5785.90	86.5
上海	2423.78	32679.87	13.50	6.6	7108.15	88.1
天津	1559.60	18809.64	12.10	3.6	2106.19	83.2
重庆	3101.79	20363.19	6.59	6.0	2265.50	65.5
广州	1490.44	22859.35	15.55	6.2	1632.30	86.4
武汉	1108.10	14847.29	13.51	8.0	1528.70	80.3
成都	1633.00	15342.77	9.50	8.0	1424.20	73.1
郑州	1013.60	10143.30	10.13	8.1	1152.10	73.4
西安	1000.37	8349.86	8.51	8.2	684.71	74.0

资料来源：各市 2018 年国民经济和社会发展统计公报。

（二）科技创新实力不断增强

根据国家和省的创新驱动发展战略部署要求，围绕建设国家创新中心城市的目标，广州加快推动广州科学城、南沙科学城、中新知识城、科技创新小镇、价值创新园区等一系列创新功能区和创新载体的建设，积极参与粤港澳大湾区综合新国家科学中心建设，不断加大创新投入力度，努力提升基础创新能力、完善国际创新合作网络、抢占创新产业发展前沿，着力打造国际科技创新枢纽，综合创新实力实现大幅度跃升。根据2017年12月上海市信息中心发布《2017全球科技创新中心评估报告》，广州位列全球城市排行榜第四十一位。根据国务院发展研究中心2018年11月发布的《2018年度全球主要城市硬科技创新指数》，广州跻身全球第九位。根据2018年11月英国《自然》增刊《2018自然指数——科研城市》，广州排在全球城市第二十五位（见表2）。

表2　广州在部分创新城市排行榜中的排名

发布时间	发布机构	指数报告	评价体系	广州排名
2018	英国《自然》增刊	《2018自然指数——科研城市》	根据国际高质量自然科学期刊所发表的科研论文，分析主要城市的研究机构、企业等高质量科研的产出绩效，进而得出科研实力排名	25
2018	国务院发展研究中心	《2018年度全球主要城市硬科技创新指数》	“硬科技”是指在信息技术、人工智能、生物技术、新材料、航空航天、智能制造、新能源、芯片等领域的高精尖原创技术。硬科技创新指数从创新投入、创新产出两大方面进行分析评价。创新投入指标细分为组织投入、人才投入和资金投入，创新产出指标细分为知识产出和商业转化	9
2017	上海市信息中心	《2017全球科技创新中心评估报告》	包括基础研究、创新环境、创新经济、产业技术4个一级指标和25个二级指标，主要对全球知名度较高、经济较发达、创新力较强的165个城市和都市圈进行评估	41
2018	首都科技发展战略研究院	《构建创新之城——中国创新城市TOP10的启示》	从创新资源、创新环境、创新服务和创新绩效4个维度选取26项具体指标构建“中国城市科技创新发展指标体系”	4

续表

发布时间	发布机构	指数报告	评价体系	广州排名
2018	福建师范大学等	《中国城市创新竞争力发展报告(2018)》	从创新基础竞争力、创新环境竞争力、创新投入竞争力、创新产出竞争力、创新可持续发展竞争力五大维度建立评价指标体系,对我国274个城市的创新竞争力开展综合评价	5

创新型企业枢纽地位基本形成。企业是市场创新的主体，近年来广州企业综合创新能力不断提升，研发型企业数量不断增加，企业内部设立的各类研发平台数量快速增加，创新型企业加速成长。2018 年，广州新增加的高新技术企业达 3104 家，高新技术企业总数已经达到 11794 家。在生物医药、人工智能、信息技术、云计算、新材料、新能源、大数据等战略性新兴产业领域，涌现出亿航智能、小马智行、小鹏汽车、云从科技、橙行智动、极飞科技、燃石医学等一批极具发展潜力的高成长、充满活力的创新性企业。根据 2018 年 11 月 20 日德勤对外发布的《2018 高科技高成长中国 50 强报告》，广州入选企业达 8 家，仅次于北京（12 家），其中广州慧正智联科技有限公司更是位居该榜单的第二位。

创新型活动枢纽地位初步形成。2018 年，广州专利申请量达到 173124 件，发明专利申请量达到 50169 件，分别增长 46.3% 和 35.8%（见表 3），增长速度在全国 19 个副省级及以上城市中位居第一。PCT 国际专利申请量仅次于北京和深圳，居全国主要城市第三位，企业发明专利申请量占总量的比重达到 63.4% 的新高水平。另外，广州拥有广东省绝大多数的高等院校和科研机构，2018 年拥有国家重点实验室 20 家、国家工程技术研究中心 18 家、国家级企业技术中心 27 家以及国家级、省级大学科技园 8 个，科技创新的知识储备和积淀基础雄厚。各类科技孵化平台和众创空间发展迅速，众创空间总数达 196 家，其中国家级众创空间 53 家，国家级孵化器 26 家，孵化面积 1050 万平方米。集聚了一批高层次创新型人才，拥有中国科学院院士和中国工程院院士 98 人，国家级高层次人才 490 人。

国际创新网络不断完善。近年来，广州开放式国际创新合作网络不断完善，吸引国际高端创新资源要素能力持续增强。面向欧美发达国家，成功引进斯坦福国际研究院、美国冷泉港实验室、广州万达匹兹堡大学国际医院、广州巴塞罗那国际医院，与英国伯明翰大学等建立政府间框架合作伙伴交流合作关系，与德国海德堡中德科教园签订协议；成立驻美国硅谷、波士顿和以色列特拉维夫办事处，积极推动项目合作与人才引进。面向“一带一路”沿线国家和地区，广州市各企事业单位与沿线国家和地区科研机构开展双边科研合作项目150余项。中国创新大会、《财富》国际科技头脑风暴大会创交会、海交会、小蛮腰科技大会、中国风险投资论坛等国际创新盛会成功推动广州与世界创新资源交流对接，促进广州融入全球创新网络。

表3　2017～2018年广州专利创造情况

指标	2017年	2018年	同比增长(%)
专利申请量(件)	118332	173124	46.3
发明专利申请量(件)	36941	50169	35.8
专利授权量(件)	60201	89826	49.2
发明专利授权量(件)	9345	10797	15.5
企业申请发明专利量占申请量的比重(%)	56.3	63.4	7.1

资料来源：《2017年广州市国民经济和社会发展统计公报》《2018年广州市国民经济和社会发展统计公报》。

（三）高等教育资源密集丰富

作为我国高等教育最发达的城市之一，2018年广州拥有80余所大专以上高等院校，中山大学、华南理工大学入选我国世界一流大学建设高校，暨南大学、华南师范大学入选我国世界一流学科建设高校。全市在校本专科学生的总人数达到108.64万人，数量位居全国第一。2003年1月，总面积达34.4平方公里的广州大学城正式启动规划建设，经过多年开发建设，其环境不断优化，已经集聚了中山大学、华南理工大学、暨南大学、华南师范大学等十余所国际国内知名高校，集中一批国家重点实验室、工程实验室等研发创新平台，研发的部分技术达到国际国内领先水平。集聚20多万高端创新人才、中青年创新人才、创新团队和高校师生，形成了促进科技创新的人才优势、技术优势和平台优势。依托中山大学及其周边地区科研优势，广州正在对标世界一流水平高起点规划建设中大国际创新谷，聚焦智能制造、信息技术、新能源、生物医药、创意设计等重点产业领域，建设集技术创新、技术转移、成果孵化、创业中心、人才创新基地于一体的新型科技创新园，可望为广州探索产学研融合发展新模式提供新路径、新模式。

在粤港澳大湾区建设推进实施的背景下，广州高等教育的国际和区域合作发展迎来了新的契机。香港中文大学与广州医科大学宣布合作建设高标准医学院、专科校区、专科医院和国际实验室。香港浸会大学与清华珠三角研究院、澳门大学与香雪制药深入开展产学研合作。2018 年 1 月，广州市政府与中国科学院大学签署框架协议，双方宣布将在广州共建中国科学院大学广州学院。2018 年 12 月，广州市政府、广州大学、香港科技大学共同宣布在南沙合作建设香港科技大学（广州）。同月，中国教育科学研究院与广州市人民政府签订共建教育综合改革实验区框架协议，双方将共建粤港澳大湾区教育研究中心，在南沙共建中国教育科学研究院。在加强引进国内外优质高等教育资源的同时，广州对本土高校的培育和发展也成效显著。广州大学围绕一流大学和一流学科建设目标发展迅速。华南理工大学广州国际校区加快建设，并将围绕高端装备制造、人工智能、量子通信、脑科学等新兴学科和交叉学科领域，开展顶尖创新人才培养、国际前沿科学研究、高水平科技成果转化等，携手剑桥大学、哈佛大学、南洋理工大学等著名高校合作打造国内顶尖、国际一流的国际化示范校区。2019 年 1 月，广州市政府正式批复建设广州交通大学，学校总用地规模达 66.7 公顷，将于 2020 年开始招生。2019 年 5 月，国家批准首批本科职业教育试点名单中的 15 所职业学院中，广州科技职业技术学院更名为广州科技职业技术大学，广州职业教育发展优势得到进一步认可。

（四）历史文化底蕴深厚

广州是我国首批公布的全国 24 个历史文化名城之一，已建成相对完备的公共文化设施体系，拥有最有特色、最具有竞争力的岭南文化中心地、古代海上丝路发源地、近现代民主革命策源地、改革开放前沿地“四地”资源优势。依托丰富的岭南文化资源和历史底蕴，广州在推动文商旅融合发展上动作频频。北京路文化旅游区跻身国家 4A 级旅游景区并获批国家级文化产业示范园区，被赋予在探索历史文化资源传承“活化”的新模式、探索品牌文化活动战略合作的新模式、探索“文化+”跨界融合发展新业态等十大方面开展探索创新的使命，为全国探索经验、提供示范。成立了广州市文化金融服务中心有限公司，并联合全国各地约20家文化金融中心、文化投资机构发起成立全国文化金融中心联盟，联动全国构建文化产业投融资体系，促进创新、金融和文化的跨界融合以及文化市场的繁荣发展。

近年来，广州文化产业发展迅速，文化影响力进一步提升，培育出网易、微信、酷狗、UC、YY语音、奥飞动漫、漫友文化、励丰文化等初具世界影响力的公司或品牌。《喜羊羊与灰太狼》《快乐酷宝》《猪猪侠》《巴啦啦小魔仙》入选中国动漫十大品牌。《南方日报》在我国省级党报品牌价值中排名第一位，《广州日报》在我国城市报业品牌价值中排名第一位。根据2018年6月20日世界品牌实验室发布的2018年《中国500最具价值品牌》报告，《南方日报》《南方都市报》《南方周末》的品牌总价值达到933.71亿元，南方报业传媒集团排在全国媒体机构第三位，仅次于中央广播电视总台和人民日报社，《南方日报》与《人民日报》《参考消息》占据全国平面媒体品牌价值三甲位置。中国（广州）国际纪录片节、中国国际儿童电影节、中国音乐金钟奖、中国国际演艺交易会、广州文化产业交易会、广州国际艺术博览会等品牌活动的国际影响力不断增强。为进一步提升文化产业发展水平，增强城市文化软实力，2018年，广州制定了《广州市关于加快文化产业创新发展的实施意见》，提出到2035年，推动文化产业成为全市重要的战略性支柱产业，稳步提升文化产业增加值在GDP中的比重，基本建成国际性文化产业枢纽城市。围绕实现这一目标，广州将培育20家数字内容领军企业，建设10个在国内外有较大影响力的市级以上数字内容产业园区，着力打造动漫游戏产业之都、全国艺术产业中心、全球文化创意设计之城、全球文化装备制造中心、全球文化会展中心、全国文化产业风投创投中心等。

二　广州建设科技教育文化中心的目标内涵

立足于广州的基础优势，借鉴国际先进城市发展经验，广州建设科技教育文化中心的目标是：以现代化的创新教育培养适应科技创新发展需要的高端人才、夯实科技创新的基础能力，以科技创新促进新技术新产业的发展，进而加速新旧产业更迭、新旧动能转换，以文化增强城市的感召力、创造力、影响力和认同度，加快构建良性循环的科技教育文化生态圈，促进科技、教育、文化融通贯通并形成整体性效应，率先探索建设我国科技教育文化融合发展示范城市。具体来看，广州建设科技教育文化中心的目标内涵主要包括四个方面。

（一）建设科技教育文化中心的基础在于现代教育

教育决定着人类的今天，也决定着人类的未来，是一个城市发展水平和发展潜力的重要标志。依托一流大学和一流学科，建设重大科研基础设施和大型科研仪器，实施国家重大科技项目乃至参与全球科研项目，可以有效增强城市的基础创新能力。发达的职业教育可以为企业源源不断地提供各类应用型人才和人力资源，进而促进产业的发展。德国正是依靠其发达的职业教育为“德国制造”和“德国品质”提供了一批优秀的产业工人和技术人才。事实上，国际化、品质化的基础教育不仅有利于提升城市市民的文化素养和持久竞争力，也是城市吸引国际人才安家落户的重要法宝。

（二）建设科技教育文化中心的重点在于科技创新

2019 年 4 月，习近平在出席第二届“一带一路”国际合作高峰论坛开幕式并发表主旨演讲时指出“创新就是生产力，企业赖之以强，国家赖之以盛”。对城市而言，科技创新与制度创新、管理创新、业态创新、文化创新和商业模式创新相互结合，可以推动城市从依靠劳动、资本投入为主导阶段迈向依靠知识和技术进步为主导阶段，促进城市经济向更加高级、高端、高质的阶段演进。面向未来，顺应数字化、网络化、智能化的发展大趋势，以智能、绿色、泛在为特征的群体性技术革命将引发国际产业分工重大调整，前沿性颠覆性技术不断涌现，导致全球创新版图加速重构。在此背景下，能否把握新一轮科技革命发展趋势强化科技创新驱动力，将直接决定城市竞争力的强弱及其在全球城市网络体系中的地位。因此，培育提升科技教育文化中心功能的重中之重在于强化科技创新功能，增强科技创新驱动力。

（三）建设科技教育文化中心的根本在于城市文化

城市文化是一个城市独树一帜的精神品格，是一座城市在长期发展中历史传统、文化底蕴、时代风貌和价值追求的综合体现。依托城市文化形成的文化软实力是城市迈向高级发展阶段的重要动力，最终将决定城市的历史地位。根据2019年3月11日上海交通大学与美国南加州大学联合发布的国际文化大都市评价报告，纽约、伦敦、巴黎、东京、旧金山、柏林、北京、洛杉矶、上海、罗马位居前十位。而对比2018年11月GaWC发布的2018年全球城市分级排名榜单的前十位城市伦敦、纽约、香港、北京、新加坡、上海、悉尼、巴黎、迪拜、东京可以发现，两个榜单具有较多的重合之处，这说明城市文化与城市综合竞争力息息相关。事实上，举世闻名的城市，往往都有扑面而来的精神气质。显然，要培育提升具有辨识度和鲜明气质的科技教育文化中心功能，必须依托丰厚的历史文化资源，提高市民精神文化素质，培育现代城市人文精神，以不断增强的文化软实力为城市的科技创新、经济发展和社会进步提供支撑和动力。

（四）建设科技教育文化中心的关键在于融通融合

科技、教育和文化之间具有千丝万缕的联系。教育既是科技转化为生产力的基础，其本身也是一种文化形态，教育发展可以推动科技创新能力提升以及社会文化的传承、保存、交流和创新。科技进步有助于教育现代化、文化推陈出新以及文化新业态发展，使教育和文化的影响力和传播力大大提升。深厚的历史文化底蕴和先进的文化理念是科技创新和现代化国际化教育发展的源头活水。因此，培育提升科技教育文化中心功能虽然包含了科技中心功能、教育中心功能和文化中心功能，但显然不是三者的简单加总和集合，更重要的是体现在科技、教育和文化功能的深度融合而形成的综合竞争力上，既要求城市要有深厚的历史底蕴，又要有充满活力的现代创新文化和创新精神。科技创新和文化软实力成为驱动城市发展的双轮动力。

三　粤港澳大湾区背景下广州建设科技教育文化中心的机遇

（一）粤港澳大湾区的中心城市效应

回顾我国城市发展经验，交通基础设施、公共服务基础设施、重大产业发展平台等往往首先围绕中心城市进行布局，进而使中心城市能够获取更多要素资源而率先发展，成为区域科技、教育、文化、经济、服务中心。在中心城市中，省会城市、经济特区、直辖市等特殊城市又会在行政资源、政策资源上更有优势，当前我国综合竞争力排名靠前的城市几乎都是这些类型的城市。

为进一步做大做强中心城市，新一轮的强省会城市战略正在开启，济南、成都、西安等城市通过行政区划调整和行政管理调整等方式努力增强省会城市辐射带动能力。城市群、都市圈、同城化发展也正掀起新一轮高潮，城市间专业化分工协作越来越紧密，中心城市正迎来集聚创新要素、提升经济密度、增强高端服务功能的新机遇。可以预见，在当前及未来一段时期，中心城市仍然在我国区域经济版图中充当领航者角色。

改革开放以来，广州先后被赋予广东省省会城市、全国首批沿海开放城市、国家计划单列市、华南地区中心城市、国家中心城市等定位，已经基本确立了中心城市的地位。《粤港澳大湾区发展规划纲要》又明确广州作为粤港澳大湾区四大中心城市之一，担当区域发展核心引擎的责任与使命。因此，培育提升科技教育文化中心功能，广州要善于运用中心城市和门户枢纽的优势地位，在向外拓展空间、辐射带动区域发展中增强集聚科技创新、教育科研、文化资源的能力，从交通枢纽型城市迈向科技教育文化枢纽型城市。

（二）粤港澳大湾区的协同发展效应

近年来，粤港澳三地协作对接发展虽然取得了显著成效，但市场互联互通水平有待进一步提升，生产要素高效便捷流动的良好局面尚未形成，部分地区和领域还存在同质化竞争和资源错配现象。随着《粤港澳大湾区发展规划纲要》及其配套政策、行动方案的出台，粤港澳将逐步实现制度规则联通、贯通、融通，推动市场一体化水平提升，使人流物流资金流信息流便捷高效流通，推动区域科技、教育和文化资源优化配置，为广州培育提升科技教育文化中心功能带来新机会。

围绕建设具有全球影响力的国际科技创新中心的目标定位，粤港澳大湾区将通过一系列的制度探索、创新与对接，促进粤港澳三地科技创新载体、平台、主体、成果共建共享与融通贯通，推动形成高度协同的区域创新市场。如香港与深圳在深港科技创新特别合作区共建深港协同创新中心、香港生产力促进局创新及技术中心，香港科技大学进驻建设重点实验室、工学院微电子分支机构、蓝海湾孵化器等。可以预见，随着粤港澳大湾区的建设，广州将有更多机会分享到香港乃至国际先进地区的创新模式和创新文化，进一步完善国际创新合作网络。

坚持以人民为中心的发展思想，围绕打造公共服务优质、宜居宜业宜游的优质生活圈，粤港澳大湾区将积极拓展教育、文化等领域的合作，推动高校合作办学、创建国际教育示范区、特色职业教育园区建设，共同塑造湾区人文精神、推动湾区文化繁荣发展，为广州发挥教育、文化优势提供了更大的可为空间。湾区的创新文化与广州的商业文化深度交融也将会促进广州文化创意产业发展、激活城市创新意识和精神。事实上，香港科技大学（南沙校区）、中央广播电视总台粤港澳大湾区总部在广州设立就是直接得益于粤港澳大湾区建设的推进。

（三）粤港澳大湾区的产业联动效应

围绕建设充满活力的世界城市群战略定位，粤港澳大湾区将促进产业优势互补、紧密协作、联动发展，携手构建具有国际竞争力的现代化产业体系。在此背景下，依托既有创新研发能力强、科研资源优势，在粤港澳大湾区产业对接中，广州将有更多机会承接区域产业链中两端研发设计与品牌营销等高附加值环节，将科研成果在更广阔的区域空间进行转化，尤其是与佛山、东莞以及珠江西岸城市可望形成“科研＋成果转化”的互动模式，进而强化自身的科技教育强市地位。

随着产业链分工的细化，广州、深圳、香港、澳门将有机会在人工智能、航空航天、生物技术、光电芯片、信息技术、新材料、新能源、智能制造等领域共建一批重大产业项目和工程，并形成各有特色、合作互补的新格局，深圳、香港和澳门的科技创新溢出效应也会推动广州科技创新能力的提升。广州各类高校和科研院所培养的人力资源将源源不断输入粤港澳大湾区当中，可为推动本区域形成实体经济、科技创新、现代金融和人力资源协同发展的现代化经济体系做出更大贡献。

在推动制造业结构调整和转型升级的过程中，粤港澳大湾区将努力推动制造业从加工制造环节向产业链两端的研发设计、品牌营销等环节延伸。可以预见，工业设计的市场需求将越来越大。而在工业设计领域当中，文化创意产业将大有可为。与此同时，在数字经济发展的背景下，粤港澳大湾区尤其是香港、深圳与广州各有优势，三地未来可望在数字文化装备、数字艺术展示等数字创意产业领域的合作迈上更高水平。

四 广州建设科技教育文化中心功能的路径与策略

（一）对标对表科学家的理想之城，打造粤港澳大湾区科技教育文化中心城市

建设国际科技创新中心，粤港澳大湾区必须有一批优秀的科学家作为支撑。2018 年 10 月，上海市科学学研究所与施普林格·自然集团（Springer Nature）共同发布《2018 全球科学家“理想之城”调查报告》，通过对全球主要国家和地区 654 名一线科学家的问卷调查显示，科学家在选择工作城市时，主要考虑的因素是该城市是否拥有领先的科研机构、领先的科研基础设施、广泛的国际交流合作机会、全球科技中心声誉、充分的科研工作机会和科研人员高收入等（见图 1）。

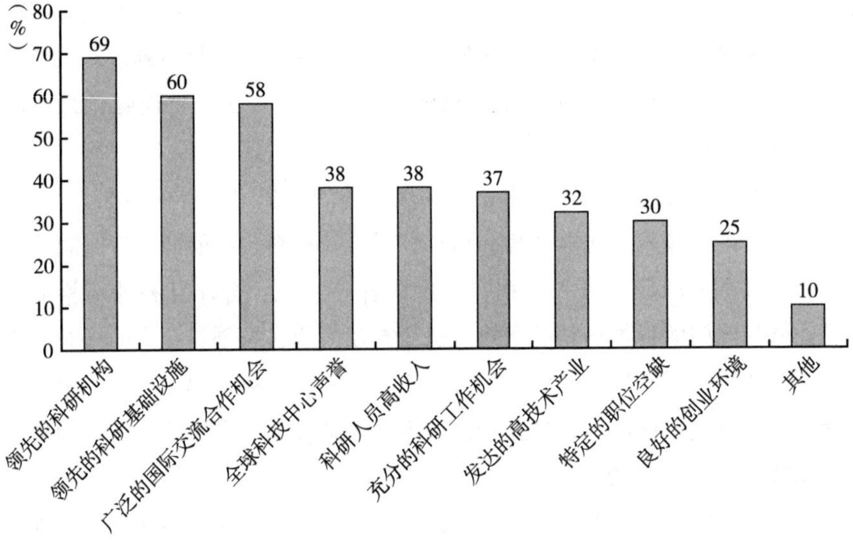

图 1 影响科学家选择理想工作城市的主要因素调查结果

资料来源：上海市科学学研究所：《2018 全球科学家“理想之城”调查报告》，2018 年 10 月 29 日发布。

科学家在选择生活城市时，主要考虑的因素是城市是否拥有开放包容的城市创新文化、生活的便利性、现代美丽时尚的都市风貌、清洁的空气和环境、交通的便利性、良好的子女教育环境和舒适的气候环境等（见图2）。

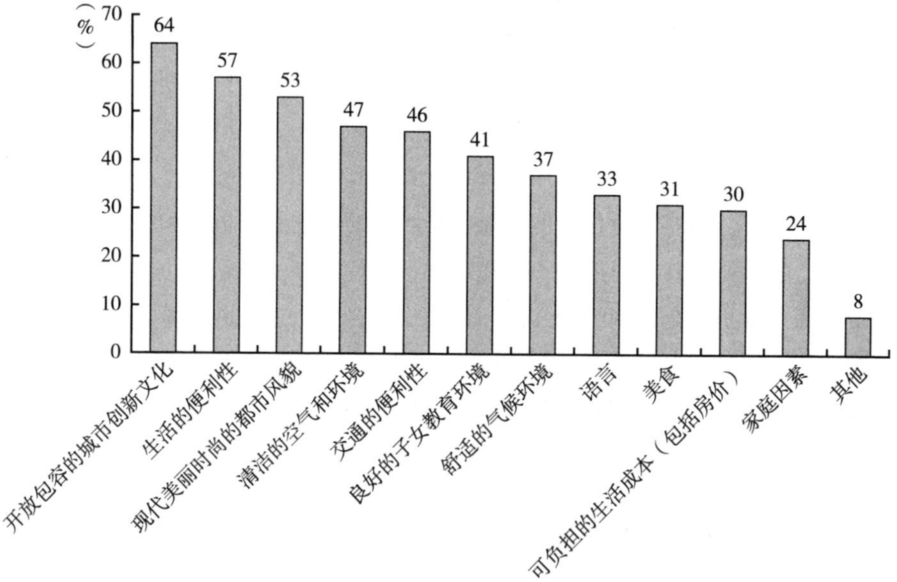

图2　影响科学家选择理想生活城市的主要因素调查结果

资料来源：上海市科学学研究所：《2018全球科学家“理想之城”调查报告》，2018年10月29日发布。

综合来看，广州集聚了广东省约70%的高校科研院所和国家、省部级重点实验室资源，是我国高等教育最发达的城市之一，同时又拥有开放包容的城市文化、便利的生活条件等，最有条件成为粤港澳大湾区科学家的理想之城。因此，广州培育提升科技教育文化中心功能，应将建设粤港澳大湾区科学家的理想之城作为重要目标，对照全球科学家选择工作城市和生活城市的主要影响因素，抓重点、补短板、强弱项：一是继续推动广州高等教育综合竞争力的提升。利用省会城市以及教育资源优势，启动实施“四个一批”工程，即推动一批优质中等专科学校升格为高等专科学校，推动一批优质高等专科学校升格为本科学院，推动一批优质本科学院升格为大学，推动一批优质大学和优质学科建设成为世界一流大学和一流学科。二是着力搭建世界一流的科研平台，努力营造优越的科研基础设施条件和兼容并蓄的创新体制环境、开放包容的城市文化环境，继续保持相对合理的房价水平，建立健全便利人才工作和生活的服务体系，面向全球吸引有创新创造活力的科学家，成为国际人才和创新高地。三是将小蛮腰科技大会打造成为全球科技界一年一度的盛会，成为全球科技、产业和资本的高层次对话平台，成为全球新科技、新技术、新产品以及各类创新指数、创新标准、创新报告的发布会，提升广州在全球科技创新中心城市体系中的美誉度和显示度。四是发挥中新广州知识城、广州科学城等区域全面创新改革和知识产权保护示范作用，率先探索有利科技创新的制度环境、政策环境和营商环境，培育专业化、国际化、品牌化的科技服务机构和组织，建立具有影响力的科技创新和科研知识转化市场，发挥其推动创新转化为现实价值的纽带作用。五是以全球视野加强国际科技创新合作，建立健全城市的国家科技创新合作网络。通过“走出去”和“引进来”共建新型科研机构、共同开展科技项目攻关、共同组织科技创新活动等形式，使世界级大脑和高水平专家的目光和时光更多聚焦在广州。

（二）对标对表世界级大学科技园区，打通科技创新与教育科研的经络

广州虽然拥有丰富的教育科研资源，但这种优势并没有转化成为科技创新优势。未来如果能打通两者之间联通的渠道，促进科技成果转移转化，广州在全球科技创新中心的地位势必会大大提升。为实现这一目标，未来可探索借鉴世界先进城市经验，抓住粤港澳大湾区构建开放型区域协同创新共同体的机遇，通过全球公开招标的形式，引入战略合作者共同建设1～2个专门面向高校科研院所的国际一流科技创新园，创新科研经费使用方式和科技成果转化支持扶持形式，面向全球吸引哈佛大学、牛津大学、斯坦福大学等共建创业学院、孵化器、众创空间等，面向粤港澳大湾区吸引香港和澳门顶尖大学、科研机构的科研创新创业团队到园区进行技术成果转化，打造成为粤港澳大湾区科技成果转移转化试验区和粤港澳大湾区构建开放型区域协同创新共同体的示范区。另外，积极探索吸引世界顶级理工院校来广州共建大学或科研院所，在培养优秀的应用科学人才、增强广州在应用科学领域优势的同时形成“鲇鱼效应”，为本土高校推动科研成果转化提供经验和示范。

（三）对标对表纽约硅巷发展模式，探索科技创新与商业文化的融合之路

广州历史文化底蕴深厚，但是文化产业尤其是文化创意产业发展却相对滞后，商业文化并未能很好激活整座城市的创新文化和创新基因。然而，面向未来随着新一轮科技革命引致新技术、新产业、新业态、新模式发展，为广州创新发展方式推动科技创新与商业文化融合、激活商业文化发展提供了新的机遇。事实上，回顾近年来中国孕育的独角兽企业榜单，广州上榜的独角兽企业大多来自电子商务、软件应用、文化娱乐等领域，代表了“科技 + 商业 + 文化”的独特发展模式。而同处在粤港澳大湾区的深圳上榜的独角兽企业则大多来自硬件、金融等领域，则代表了“科技 + 硬件 + 金融”的另一种新发展模式。事实上，广州和深圳的两种发展模式，分别与以美国硅巷为代表的“东岸模式”和以硅谷为代表的“西岸模式”有许多相似之处（见图 3）。

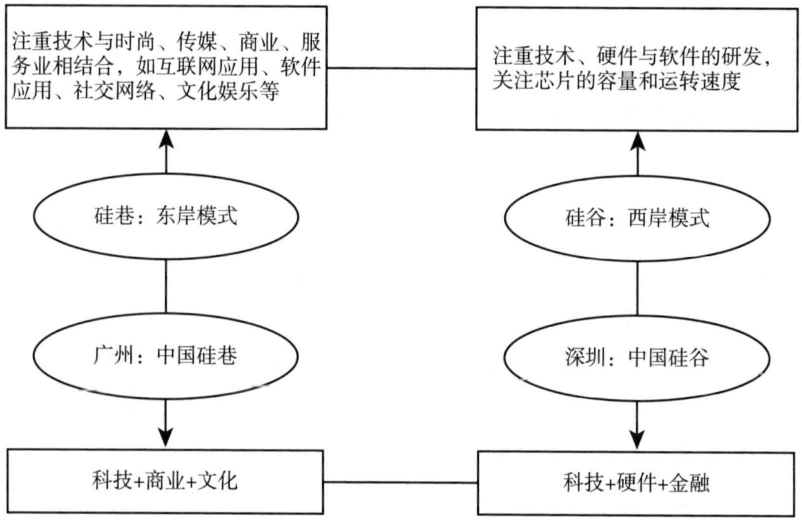

图 3　对标硅巷广州科技创新与商业文化融合发展模式

未来，在粤港澳大湾区中，立足各自优势所长，深圳将对标硅谷的发展模式，而广州则有极大机会对标硅巷发展模式，即更加注重新技术的应用，重点是将互联网新技术与时尚、传媒、商业、文化、服务业相结合，大力发展互联

网应用、软件应用、社交网络、文化娱乐、电子商务等行业，实现科技创新与商业文化的深度融合发展，开创出具有广州特色的新经济发展模式。为更好地实现这种新的发展模式，利用粤港澳大湾区建设契机与香港、深圳开展合作至关重要。广州具有浓厚的商业文化，香港具有独特的时尚创意文化，深圳具有极具活力的创新文化。因此，广州可通过吸引香港和深圳的文化产业龙头企业一起打造若干高水平的文化和科技深度融合示范园区，促进三地不同类型文化的叠加融合，在广州商业文化当中注入创新因子。

把握“互联网+”发展大趋势，探索在广州创建“中国互联网技术大学”，以互联网技术开发与应用为重点，为推动互联网、大数据、人工智能和实体经济深度融合提供支撑，为广州打造“中国硅巷”培养人才、培育产业、促进成果转化。在互联网应用、软件应用、社交网络、文化娱乐、电子商务等领域精心挖掘并培养出一批领袖企业和独角兽企业，通过积累形成优势。借鉴国际先进经验，积极探索“沙盒”监管模式，为科技创新与商业文化融合发展形成的新经济、新业态、新模式创造更加明确宽松自由的环境，打造粤港澳大湾区科技、商业和文化融合创新的试验场和示范区。

（四）对标对表世界知名创新街区，让科技教育文化回归中心城区发展

2014年，美国布鲁金斯学会发布一份名为《创新区的崛起》的研究报告，首次提出了“创新街区”（Innovation District）概念，并认为在中心城区高密度区域，依托便利的交通设施和互联网环境，整合创新企业、教育机构、金融机构、多元文化、消费性服务业等经济活动要素而建设的创新型街区可成为推动中心城区走向复兴的重要可行方案。创新街区的概念提出之后，在国外许多城市走向了实践，如伦敦的硅环、剑桥的肯德尔广场、波士顿的海港广场、西雅图的南湖等创新街区的建设都已经取得了成功。

广州推动老城市焕发新活力，重点任务之一是要加快推动老城区更新改造，为其注入发展新活力。借鉴国际先进经验，结合创建粤港澳大湾区科学家理想之城的目标，发挥中心城区工作生活便利优势，广州可通过高水平、高标准打造一批具有鲜明功能特征的创新街区、创意街区、创业街区、文化街区、历史街区等新型载体，布局有鲜明个性的实验室、中小企业孵化器、研究设

施、设计室、工作室等，将科技创新与历史文化有机融合起来，推动空间更新改造拓展新经济空间，让创新回归中心城区，推动老城区空间转换和功能提升。

借鉴国际创新街区的经验，广州探索建设创新街区可从微小处着手：一是推动中心城区尤其是老城区道路、管线、公园等基础设施更新，在公共空间实现5G信号全覆盖，免费提供高速的无线网络。二是设计建设一批开放式和开敞式的办公地和创新活动场，将室内进行的科技创新体现在城市的公共空间上，打造个性鲜明的科技界面，使科技对所有人显而易见，带动城市创新氛围的形成。三是挖掘并改造低效率或者正在衰退的城市空间，保留历史风情和文化底蕴，融入时尚气息，建设一批设计室、创意书店、咖啡馆、小酒吧等，使之成为创意工作者沟通交流、激发灵感的活力场所。四是针对广州立交桥众多的现实，借鉴布鲁克林桥下艺术新区等城市桥下空间对中心城区桥下空间进行微改造和功能开发，使之成为城市文化与科技潮流展示窗口和汇聚地。

参考文献

［1］原波、何显运：《德国双元制职业教育经验研究与借鉴》，《教育教学论坛》2019年第1期。

［2］范锐平：《加快建设独具人文魅力的世界文化名城》，《光明日报》2019年1月14日。

［3］邓智团：《创新街区研究：概念内涵、内生动力与建设路径》，《城市发展研究》2017年第8期。

［4］覃剑：《城市桥下空间功能开发与治理研究》，《建筑经济》2019年第5期。

B.7
重庆建设国家中心城市的新进展、主要特点与发展趋势

彭劲松　朱旭森　卢 飞 *

摘　要： 2018 年，重庆经济突破 2 万亿元大关，迈上新的发展台阶，但受内部因素和外部环境的交织作用，进入一个增速探底、发展方式转变、结构深度调整的关键期。重庆要在推进中央赋予国家战略中承担重要使命和责任，发挥综合集成优势，不断推进高质量发展。

关键词： 发展现状　四大周期　四大优势

重庆是中西部唯一的直辖市，是国家级中心城市，2018 年，面对错综复杂的国际形势，重庆坚持稳中求进的工作总基调，继续推进供给侧结构性改革，大力实施“八大行动计划”，以乡村振兴和城市提升两个工作面为工作切入点，积极推进国家中心城市高质量建设，取得了新的成效。

一　发展现状与基础

（一）经济发展

2018 年，重庆地区生产总值达突破 2 亿元大关，达到 20363. 19 亿元，增

* 彭劲松，硕士，重庆社会科学院城市发展研究所副所长、重庆城市提升战略研究中心主任，研究员，研究方向为城市经济与区域发展；朱旭森，硕士，重庆社会科学院副研究员，研究方向为经济地理和区域发展；卢飞，硕士，重庆社会科学院副研究员，研究方向为城市经济。

长6.0%（见图1），结束连续多年的两位数高速增长，回落到个位数，首次低于全国平均增速，进入一个增速探底、发展方式转变、结构深度调整的关键期。分产业看，第三产业增速最快，达到9.1%，第二产业为4.4%，第一产业为3.0%，三次产业的结构比为6.8∶40.9∶52.3。

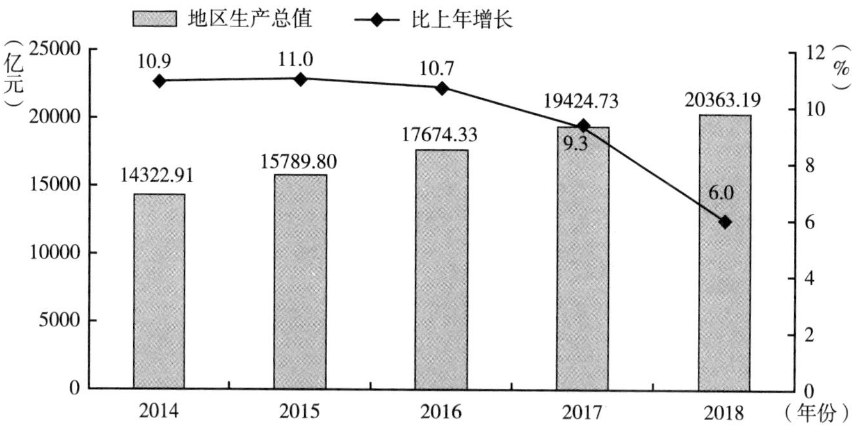

图1　2014～2018年重庆地区生产总值及增长率

资料来源：重庆市历年国民经济和社会发展统计公报。

2018年，重庆全市固定资产投资同比增长7.0%。第二产业、第三产业投资保持了稳中求进的良好态势，分别增长7.3%、7.4%，而第一产业投资则出现了负增长。分领域看，工业和基础设施依然是支撑全市固定资产投资的重要力量。随着全市投资和营商服务环境不断优化，重庆市的民间投资表现良好，全年民间投资增速达12.8%，高于全市投资增速5.8个百分点，占全市投资超过一半以上。

2018年，重庆市外贸在外部贸易环境不断恶化的情况下逆势上扬，全市外贸进出口达5222.62亿元，同比增长15.9%，达到近年来的一个较好的增长水平。积极吸引外商来渝投资，全年外商直接投资（FDI）完成32.5亿美元，增长43.8%，居中西部第一、全国第九。

2018年，重庆全市消费市场继续保持温和稳定。全市社会消费品零售总额同比增长8.7%。随着互联网基础设施和服务平台的不断构建完善，网络零售业发展迅猛，网上零售额增长增速是传统零售业增速3倍以上。全市电子商务交易额突破11000亿元，跨境电子商务进出口及结算超过200亿元。

（二）产业建设

2018 年，重庆市实现工业增加值 5997.70 亿元，同比增长 1.1%。全市重点支柱产业呈“七增两降”分化格局，其中，电子产业、装备产业、化工产业、医药产业、材料产业、消费品产业和能源工业七大产业分别增长 13.6%、3.2%、1.5%、9.3%、11.0%、1.9% 和 1.7%。作为工业发展的第一大支柱产业的汽摩产业呈现下降趋势，其中，汽车产业增加值下降 17.3%，摩托车产业增加值下降 0.3%。新动能培育发展势头良好，高技术产业增长和战略性新兴产业增长快于传统产业的增长速度，规模工业企业成为研究与开发投入的主要力量，相关企业的研发投入接近 320 亿元，增长 13.9%。

为保持产业发展的稳定性和连续性，重庆市加大了汽车产业结构调整和优化，加快以汽车产业转型升级建设步伐，先后出台了“1+2”政策体系，初步形成了产品结构比较合理的新能源汽车产业体系，包括长安汽车等 9 家乘用车企业、恒通等 3 家客车企业、庆铃等 5 家专用车企业，以及围绕汽车整车发展，大力扶持 30 余家具有较强市场竞争力的核心零部件配套生产企业。

重庆积极以制造业为核心，向研发和市场应用两个端头不断拓展延伸，积极打造全产业价值生态链。在研发领域，形成了中国汽车研究院、重庆车辆检测院等一批具有较强创新能力的新能源汽车测试、检测机构。在商业应用领域，依托长安汽车和力帆汽车的整车制造优势，培育了长安出行、盼达用车等网约车和分时租赁品牌商等。据统计，2019 年 1～4 月，重庆全市共生产新能源汽车 15146 辆，同比增长 32.6%；生产智能网联汽车 50600 辆，同比增长 10%。

智能制造产业也是重庆制造业发展的一个新兴增长点。2018 年，智能产业实现销售收入 4640 亿元，同比增长 19.2%，其中机器人、智能手机等产品产量增速较快。

（三）对外开放

重庆不断完善对外开放的基础设施条件，提升对外物流大通道，推进内陆开放高地建设迈向新的台阶。

一是开放大平台体系逐步形成。江津综保区、果园港保税物流中心（B型）获批，渝西地区的永川、荣昌两个园区升级为国家级高新技术产业开发区，全市形成了以两江新区为开发龙头的各类开放平台体系18个，建成4个国家级一类开放口岸，具有9类进口特殊商品指定口岸功能。这些重大开放平台的外贸进出口量占全市比重超过八成，外商直接投资（FDI）占全市比重超过七成，成为全市开放发展的主力军。

二是开放大通道进一步拓展。重庆立足处于“一带一路”和长江经济带联结点的独特优势，统筹铁、公、空、水等多种运输方式，大力发展多式联运，构建起全方位、立体化的开放大通道。其中，南向通道以中新互联互通“陆海新通道”为支撑，先后开通了铁、海、公等多式联运班列；西向通道以中欧班列（重庆）功能和网络体系建设为支撑，班列累计运行数量超过3000列，建设德国、俄罗斯等国外集散分拨点超过40个；东向通道主要依托长江黄金水道，北向通道正在构建联通中蒙俄经济走廊建设；空中走廊以国际航空枢纽建设为依托。

三是国际化营商环境建设取得新进展。深化国际贸易“单一窗口”建设，报检覆盖率和关区覆盖率达100%。深化7×24小时通关服务，加快推进智慧口岸建设，将进出口的整体通关时间压缩到原来的一半，在国内率先实现在线国际结算、提出进口药械全程追溯等9项创新功能。加快自贸试验区建设，在投资、贸易、金融、事中事后监管和陆上贸易规则等领域探索形成一系列的制度创新。获批汽车平行进口试点、深化服务贸易创新发展试点等试验。商事制度改革实现“三十一证合一”，企业开办审批时间压缩至5个工作日以内。自贸试验区建设取得新的进展，国内知名互联网企业百度、阿里巴巴、腾讯等区域总部机构先后入驻自贸试验区。在渝世界500强企业达287家，较2017年增加8家。

（四）城市建设

1. 城市空间格局不断优化。重庆全市面积8.24万平方公里，是由主城一个特大城市和若干个中小城镇构成的城市群。2018年，重庆市常住人口超过3100万人，城镇化率为65.50%。重庆主城区城镇化率达到90%，城市集聚能力显著提升，以主城区为核心的特大城市引领周边城市的都市圈发展格局正在形成。根据发展态势和发展形势需要，重庆将全域划分为主城区都市圈和渝东南、渝东北两个城镇群。其中，主城区都市圈包括主城区和西片区，面积约

2.87 万平方公里，重点是壮大城市规模，提升现代产业体系，建设文化形象鲜明、生态宜居、创新活力的现代化都市圈，成为成渝城市群高质量发展的重要引擎；渝东北城市群包括万州等 11 个区县，面积约 3.4 万平方公里，重点是以三峡库区水环境综合治理和生态修复为重点，促进三峡库区生态转型发展，提升库区生态文明建设水平；渝东南城市群包括黔江等 6 个区县，面积约 1.98 万平方公里，突出民俗特色和资源特色，发展绿色产业，打造建设武陵山区特色生态经济走廊。

2. 城市品质显著提升。积极推进城市提升行动计划，着力提升城市经济、人文、生态和生活品质。主城区发展主轴“两江四岸”治理提升、主城区“四山”综合整治有序推进，加快打造国际一流生态人文滨水空间。按照精细、智能和人性化的要求，大力提升城市综合管理水平。大力发展绿色建筑，推进建设施工现场综合管理，开展城市黑臭水体治理，建设城市慢行系统，推进悦来等海绵城市试点，不断提升城市的环境品质，城市居民的安全感、获得感和幸福感极大增强。

3. 城市综合交通建设提速。2018 年，重庆强化重点和骨干交通基础设施建设，持续弥补部分交通基础设施的短板，对外通达性和交通网络节点性功能进一步增强。航空方面，渝东北的巫山机场、渝东南的武隆机场在加快建设中；万州、黔江两个机场进行改扩建，提升客货运的吞吐能力，万州开通国际航线，架起了重庆地区江北国际机场、万州机场双口岸出入国门的空间走廊。铁路方面，陆续建成并投用了重庆西站、沙坪坝站等，开工建设渝湘高铁、重庆东站枢纽工程。公路方面，江习高速公路建成通车，新开工合璧津、巫镇、大内等 7 个项目，高速公路通道与网络进一步优化。轨道方面，积极推进城市轨道、市郊铁路和国铁干的融合，新开通轨道环线、4 号线，运营总里程达到 313.4 公里，轨道覆盖的平均距离达到 12.8 公里，单日最高客运量接近 300 万人次，轨道交通已成为主城区市民中长距离出行的主要选择。

4. 创新城市建设有力推进。重庆以全球视野谋划和推动创新，推进城市创新体系建设，深化国内外科技合作，化解创新投入强度和高水平的创新平台数量不足等瓶颈，着力强化科技创新对城市的引领带动能力。围绕全市特色优势产业，以两江新区、国家级农业科技园区、国家级经开区、国家级高新区等为载体，大力打造国家级技术创新中心、国家级重点实验室。大力引进世界高水平的高校和科研院所资源，先后吸引中国科学院、中国工程院等国家级科研院所，西北工业大学、华中科技大学等多所高校来渝设立教学和科研分支机构。与北京理工大学、中国兵器科学研究院等共建科技军民融合协同创新平台，推动军民在科技领域的深度融合。依托中德（重庆）国际技术转移中心、中匈（重庆）转移技术中心等，加强了与“一带一路”沿线国家科技创新合作。推进重庆大学、西南大学、重庆邮电大学的环大学创新创业生态圈建设。

二　面临的发展环境

（一）四大周期叠加导致增速下滑

2018 年，重庆工业、投资、消费和产出等主要经济指标增速低于预期，主观上既有产业技术结构调整迟滞、不到位的原因，客观上也受错综复杂的国际国内宏观形势变化影响，是产业、技术、金融和人口四大周期在时空交织叠加，由外部大环境和局部小气候综合作用所导致的结果。

1. 支柱产业发展处于全球性产业发展周期萎缩阶段的“末点”。在重庆，汽车制造和电子制造占据了工业的半壁江山，是重庆工业发展的两大驱动轮，特别是汽车工业，产业链很长，发展历史很悠久，在很长的一段时间都是重庆传统优势工业。2018 年，汽车工业的增速为 -17.3%，而电子信息产业也结束了几年前的几倍速的增长，增速回落到 13.6%，两大支柱产业增速回落是造成工业低速增长的主要因素。

据统计，2018 年，我国汽车整车销售 2808 万辆，同比下降 2.8%，这是我国汽车销售市场出现的首次下降，占汽车产销比重达 85% 的乘用车产销量也分别同比下降 5.2% 和 4.1%。事实上从 2016 年之后，汽车广泛进入中国家庭，也预示着全球传统汽车产业的衰退期已经到来。重庆汽车产业在全国市场竞争格局中仍只具备数量规模优势。据统计，重庆市的单车价值约为 8 万元，税收贡献约为 6000 元，远低于全国平均 14 万元和 1.8 万元水平，新能源汽车产量占比 1.9%，低于全国平均水平（2.7%）。重庆两大汽车生产商长安福特、长安股份在 2018 年产销双降，拉低全市工业产值增幅至少 3 个百分点，铃木、北汽银翔、力帆等车企均处于深度调整阶段，庆铃、上汽依维柯红岩等商用车企增速回落、支撑力削弱，重庆的支柱产业——汽车产业的确处于艰难时刻。

2. 遭遇全球技术发展周期边际递增阶段的青黄不接的“断点”。随着第四次科技革命的到来，大量新技术、新业态、新产业、新模式在经济社会中得到广泛应用，促进了产业的高端化、智能化、集约化、服务化和全球化。重庆推进产业新动能培育，首先得聚焦于我国拥有核心技术的“硬科技”产业发展，不独只是商业模式创新等“软科技”产业。

以 R&D 作为衡量创新的投入指标来看，2018 年，重庆 R&D 投入占 GDP 的比重为 1.95%，远低于北京、上海、深圳等一线城市，也低于武汉、西安、南京、杭州等省会城市。体现城市创新活力的独角兽企业，重庆仅只有一家企业上榜，远低于珠三角、长三角等发达城市群的一些城市。重庆整个城市技术发展结构处于青黄不接的“断点”，传统的比较庞大的产业技术作为一个变量，增长十分缓慢，而在新技术革命中孕育的战略新技术动力还在积蓄当中，尚未形成规模性集聚性优势。这场工业 4.0 新技术革命，完全颠覆了传统技术的发展路径依赖。在新的技术革命范式面前，弱者不恒弱，强者难恒强，优劣势转换不完全建立在原来的经济技术结构上，甚至有些劣势反而是一种优势，而传统的优势却成为新技术时代的包袱。重庆尚未很好融入这场正处于边际效应递增的技术革命进程中。

3. 企业资本渴求适逢我国金融发展周期结构性去杠杆“局点”。近两年，以推进结构性去杠杆，确保金融稳定为重点的防范和化解金融风险工作积极稳步推进，并取得了实质性成效。数据显示，我国广义货币供应量 M2 由多年的两位数高位增长向 2017 年、2018 年的 8% 水平回落，与 GDP 增速逼近，两者增速的“差口”大大缩小；与此同时，中国社会融资规模存量同比增速进入 10% 左右的增速区间，比 2017 年初高位时期回落 4.6 个百分点。

种种迹象表明，我国实体行业防范金融系统性风险、抑制金融泡沫扩大的攻坚战已经走到了决战的“局点”，金融结构去杠杆取得了阶段性成效。这一时期，银行收紧表内信贷，加强风险防控，但对正处于转轨转型、爬坡期，资金需求仍比较“饥渴”而抵押能力不够、信用水平不高的相当部分重庆企业，带来了流动性补充不足的“苦楚”。调研发现，重庆民营企业普遍存在短期流动资金需求较大，但正规渠道的融资渠道难以满足生产需求，融资难、融资贵的问题没有得到很好解决，影响了企业的生产经营。

4. 处于中国人口周期红利衰减的“拐点”。在经济社会活动中，人扮演着生产者和消费者的双重角色，发展经济学的奠基人刘易斯从城乡劳动力二元结构变化探析了人口变化对经济发展的“拐点性”影响，这一理论具有普遍性意义。有数据表明，包括我国在内的世界主要经济体，都是在人口红利进入拐点后，经济增长开始下台阶，由中高增速增长区间进入中低速增长区间。

2010 年，我国 15 ~ 64 岁劳动力占比由 74.5% 的峰值开始下行，也正是我国经济由两位数向个位数下降的“拐点”。美国在 2008 年劳动力“拐点”到来后，平均增速由 6.2% 下降到 2.6% 左右，日本在 1992 年劳动力拐点到来后，平均增速由 13.6% 下降到 0.6% 左右，其他发达经济体也有同样情形。2018 年，我国 65 周岁以上人口占比为 11.9%，重庆 65 周岁及以上人口占比 14.1%，高于全国平均水平 2.2 个百分点。重庆 15 ~ 59 周岁的劳动年龄人口占比仅为 61.3%，低于全国平均水平 3 个百分点。全国及重庆市人口红利，特别是劳动力“红利”的衰减，对经济中长期增长的影响是深远的。在外生因素没有出现显著性变化的前提下，这种下行态势殊难逆转。

（二）四大优势夯实持续发展基础

进入新时代，重庆既面临转型发展的挑战和压力，但同时也迎来国家对重庆的新一轮大力支持。重庆必须运用系统思维、创新思维，系统整合区位、生态、产业和体制四大独特优势，全力推进国家中心城市高质量发展。

1. 具有不可替代的区位优势。“一带一路”建设涉及 71 个国家，经济总量占全世界的 18% 左右，推进共建“一带一路”，形成共商共建共享的合作新机制，不仅是我国扩大对外开放的基本国策，也是将改革向纵深层面持续推进的重要内容。重庆处在“一带一路”和长江经济带所形成的“Y”字形布局的战略联结点上，在国家推进西部大开发战略，构建内陆和沿海均衡发展格局中具有独特而重要的作用。特别是随着国际陆海新通道建设上升为国家战略，重庆的区位优势更加凸显。重庆充分利用自身独特而不可替代的区位优势，加强大通道、大口岸、大平台建设，以重庆为国际物流枢纽集结地，构建面向欧洲、东南亚、中南半岛、俄罗斯远东地区、蒙古国等四通八达的大通道，打造人流、物流、商流、资金流、信息流等要素聚散的开放大口岸，有助于在西部内陆地区带头开放、带动开放，为西部内陆地区开发开放做出新贡献。

2. 具有鲜明独特的生态优势。重庆位于长江上游，其中三峡水利枢纽工程在重庆形成600多公里长的带状库区。保护好长江母亲河，重庆必须担负起上游生态环境保护的责任，这是全国生态安全发展的大局。在建设国家中心城市的进程中，重庆可充分利用得天独厚的自然山水资源优势，提升城市品质和城市环境，营造山环水绕、江峡相拥的城市美景，让山更青、水更绿、天更蓝、空气更清新，让生态宜居、绿色低碳、可持续发展等元素在建设国家中心城市中得到充分彰显。在筑牢长江上游重要生态屏障的同时，不断推进生态资源向生态经济方向发展，努力开发具有可持续循环的生态产品，这对优化发展环境、提升城市可持续发展竞争能力，也是一种极大的促进。

3. 具有雄厚发达的产业优势。重庆在近百余年发展历史中成为长江上游重要的工业城市，正朝着建设国家重要的现代制造业基地目标迈进。重庆产业门类比较健全、产业基础配套比较好、制造业基础扎实，在国家41个工业大类中重庆比较完整的门类有39个。特别是在长期产业变动调整中形成了电子信息产业和汽车制造业两大制造业集群，虽然近期出现了增速回调，但产量在全国和国际上仍占有比较重要的地位。重庆同时作为大山区、大库区，农业特色资源也十分丰富多样，重庆的现代山地特色高效农业、生态旅游业在乡村振兴的大背景下，也将迎来重要的增长空间。

4. 具有高位统筹的体制优势。重庆作为我国中西部地区唯一的直辖市，与西部其他省区相比，没有地市一级行政单位，行政层级少，行政服务和运行水平与其他省区相比更有效率。在建设国家中心城市的过程中，重庆立足直辖市的基本体制特征，结合城乡融合发展的客观需要，加大对乡村振兴和城市提升两个工作面的高位统筹。一方面通过提升城市经济、文化、生态和生活等城市功能品质；另一方面推进农业农村现代化，筑牢乡村的发展基础，建设城乡统筹的国家中心城市，让城市和农村各美其美，美美与共。

三　相关对策建议

（一）进一步优化区域空间布局

结合重庆正在推进的主城区都市圈建设，进一步优化城市区域空间布局的结构优化，构建“一核两副多中心”主城区都市圈的构架。一是做大做强主城区都市圈核心区的规模与体量，将位于渝西地区的璧山全域和江津的双福新区部分纳入重庆主城区，将重庆主城区向西拓展，在超过中梁山的同时，继续越过缙云山，进一步提升重庆建设国家中心城市的空间框架。由此将主城区空间由传统的“四山夹三槽”空间架构向“五山夹四槽”演进，即自东向西由明月山、铜锣山、中梁山和云雾山等五座南北大体平行走向的城市山脉夹住四大城市槽谷，都市圈主城区地理空间上的东、中、西部做新的概念重构。新的主城区东、中、西部地理空间概念应这样划分：东部为龙兴—鱼复—茶园—鹿角槽谷；中部为西永—大学城—金凤—白市驿槽谷、传统的中央槽谷；西部为璧山槽谷。二是建设主城区都市圈东西两翼两个城市副中心，其中，以永川为都市圈西部副中心，作为承接成渝城市群协作的桥头堡，以涪陵为都市圈东部副中心，作为传递主城核心区向渝东南、渝东北辐射的中继站。三是推进其他非核心区的中小城市结合城市自身特色、优势协同发展、融合发展。四是加快推进四川、贵州两省环主城区都市圈市区县及乡镇的协作关系，积极融入主城区都市圈，推进成渝城市群高质量一体化进程。五是加快都市圈基础设施建设，提升都市圈运行效率。加快地铁、城际列车和市郊列车的规划建设，尽快形成网络状的都市圈轨道交通体系，加快对城市智慧型设施的建设布局，推进智慧交通、智慧教育和智慧社区等公共服务的应用。

（二）构建完善现代产业体系

加大对汽车等优势产业改造和升级，以智能制造、互联网技术为切入点，加大研发投入力度，提升汽车产业的产品品质和品牌内涵，强化整车制造的质量和水平，加快中高端汽车整车产品的研发和市场投放，继续提升传统摩托车技术含量，在缩量的同时不断提质，重点在体育竞技型和游乐休闲型专用摩托车产品形成突破，提升高端市场占有率。提升重庆汽车零配件、汽车发动机系统、变速箱系统等关键汽车总成的自主生产制造能力。通过并购整合，提升全市汽车产业集中度，确立2～3家大型汽车为龙头的产业布局。围绕国民经济建设的重点领域和重点需求，加大发展基础装备制造业，在传统装备上，要以正在发展的轨道交通为重点做大轨道交通装备产业，围绕新能源的推广应用与生态环境保护日益加强的背景下，积极发展具有技术领先优势的节能环保和新能源装备产业，围绕航空航天产业的发展着力引进培育航空航天装备产业，围绕传统产业的数字化、智能改造大趋势，大力发展智能制造装备等，并着力提升关键基础件发展能力和水平。紧紧抓住全球新一轮科技革命和产业变革重大战略机遇，以重庆前期已经形成较大规模的电子信息产业为依托，积极向集成电路、新型显示、智能终端、智能传感器及仪器仪表等领域延伸，打造“芯屏器核网”智能产业集群。积极发展新能源汽车、生物医药、新材料和节能环保等新兴产业。以《军民融合发展战略行动计划》为引领，推进航天航空、通信制造、数字测绘和地理信息等产业，打造国家级军民融合产业技术转化示范基地。拓展数字经济和数字产业，建设数字经济研究院，提高数字资源的利用水平。

（三）加大开发开放力度

加快“水、陆、空、信息”等国际大通道建设，加密路线网络，提升通道等级，构建面向南亚、中亚、欧洲等地全面开放的交通体系，形成“一带一路”“陆海新通道”和长江经济带在重庆贯通融合的格局。建设国际信息门户枢纽，打造国际离岸数据中心和在岸数据中心，形成国际数据储备、集散和应用体系。加快内外开放平台建设，探索与“一带一路”和陆海新通道沿线国家和地区以产业园、飞地、开发区、自贸港等平台建设为基础加强合作。提升开放便利性，推动重庆电子口岸与“一带一路”和“陆海新通道”的互联互通，实现物流、通关通检等信息交换和业务协同，完善“单一窗口”集成性、追踪性、可溯性、时效性功能。深度融入全球产业链建设，发展内需导向和出口导向双轮驱动型经济：一方面加快现代服务业和战略性新兴产业发展，向产业链、价值链高端拓展，建成内陆服务贸易中心和先进制造业基地；另一方面，利用地理和交通区位优势，依托传统产业的技术积累、制造能力和配套体系，大力促进传统制造业提档升级，发展面向东盟和中亚等市场的出口导向型经济。加快吸引国际贸易，优化发展加工贸易和一般贸易，创新发展服务贸易，形成内陆国际贸易产业集群。加强国际人文交流合作，主动承接开展具有国际影响力的文化、旅游、会展、科技、交通等重大国际交流活动。

（四）着力提升城市生态品质

围绕全市正在构建的“一圈两群”区域发展新格局，不断优化全市生态、生产、生活空间，促进区域生态资源和生产要素合理配置。扎实推进主城区“两江四岸”治理提升和“四山”保护提升等工作，全力构建具有山水之城特征的生态网络体系，将城市的山清水秀和人文荟萃、宜居乐业等高度有机统一，创造国际化的城市生态品质、生活品质。建好具有山城文化特色的城市步道，利用城市各类边角地和闲置地建设社区体育文化公园，美化城市环境。推进城市公共交通建设，加大城市轨道向新城新区覆盖力度，提倡公共交通出行，降低城市碳排放，减少城市拥堵。推进海绵城市示范区建设，推进绿色节能建筑技术和材料，降低城市消耗，推进城市垃圾分类处置。加快长江绿色生态廊道建设，形成广阳岛等城市生态岛和长江风景眼等系列标识度高的生态地标。着力提升森林覆盖率与城市绿化覆盖率，建设更加集约、人性、活力的新型街区，彰显山水之城、美丽之地的独特魅力，最终形成兼具国际人文“气质”、山水特色“颜值”的“近悦远来的全球城市”。

（五）构建国际化的城市文化形象

注重城市内涵建设，培育城市精神，深入挖掘和继承重庆历史文脉，不断提升城市的精神气质，筑牢国际品质的城市文化根基。大力推进具有重庆特色的巴渝文化、抗战文化、三峡移民文化等具有较强影响力的文化建设，形成充满生命力和活力、积极向上、面貌精致美丽、文明而有涵养、人人向往的城市。加大对城市文化的整理与研究工作，保护并利用好城市优秀历史建筑，传承和丰富重庆的历史文化底蕴。保护重庆独特的山水自然条件和特色建筑，营造高低起伏、衔接流畅、多层次、立体的山水自然环境和建筑物完美融合的城市景象，对城市进行精细化管理，使城市形象更为精致、有品位。改善城市窗口形象，规范市容市貌，提升市民素质、员工素质和服务质量，提高执法和行政人员的素质和责任心、公正性。以国家级文明城市、卫生城市等创建为契机，不断提高市民的人文素养和知识水平，建设学习型城市和学习型社会。

参考文献

[1] 唐良智：《2019 年重庆市政府工作报告》，《重庆市人民政府公报》2019 年第 2 期。
[2] 彭劲松：《高水平打造重庆“两江四岸”推进城市高质量发展的思考》，《重庆经济》2019 年第 4 期。

B.8

成都市建设国家中心城市的进展、成效与展望

罗若愚　杨 静*

摘　要： 2018年是成都市经济社会发展的“全面落实年”，成都市紧扣“五中心一枢纽”中心城市建设的定位，稳步推进国家中心城市建设，在增强城市活力、促进新经济发展、改善营商环境和生态环境方面取得了新的突破性成就，凸显了成都发展的特色。然而成都中心城市建设依旧面临经济发展实力不强、“主干”引领辐射作用不明显、创新供给要素不充分、交通拥堵压力大、共享发展不理想的发展难题。未来成都的建设要注重提升经济实力，推动区域一体化发展，加大创新要素投入，合理规划城市交通体系，提升民众幸福感。

关键词： 成都市　中心城市建设　高质量发展　区域协调

一　成都建设国家中心城市的推进状况

国家中心城市是区域发展的“塔尖城市”，承担着国家发展的使命和功能。2018年成都市中心城市建设继续以建设“经济、科技、金融、文创、外交和国际交通枢纽”城市为定位，通过发展新经济、培育新科技、发展“交

---

* 罗若愚，博士，电子科技大学公共管理学院教授，研究方向为城市区域治理；杨静，电子科技大学公共管理学院硕士研究生，研究方向为区域治理。

子金融”、推进“三城三都”建设、加大对外开放等战略进行中心城市建设，取得了较好的发展成果。

（一）2018年成都市经济中心城市建设状况

2018年成都市以新发展理念为指导，推动经济平稳发展，各项经济指标都达到或者超过年初设立的目标。其中，地区生产总值突破1.5万亿元，达15342.77亿元，同比增长8%，高于全国1.4个百分点。固定资产投资8341.1亿元，同比增长10%，公共预算收入1424.2亿元，同比增长9.4%，社会消费品零售总额6801.8亿元，同比增长10%，物价水平上涨稳定，保持基本水平。

目前成都市大力发展经济，建立了“5+5+1”①的现代产业体系，全年五大先进制造业增加值增长10.8%，五大新型服务业增加值增长9%。同时新经济成为成都经济发展新的增长点，全年增加新经济企业4.1万户，为经济发展做出了突出的贡献。为了促进经济发展建立了66个产业功能区，覆盖成都五大区，实现产业的聚集和分工。建立了“总部经济”模式，实现“研发在成都，制造成德绵”，加快了地区的分工合作。促进民营经济健康发展，全年民营经济增加值7464.79亿元，同比增长8.1%，占GDP比重48.7%，民营经济已经成为成都市经济发展的重要组成部分（见图1）。

（二）2018年成都市科技中心城市建设状况

2018年成都市坚持西部“科技中心”城市建设，坚持“产学研”的发展方向，加大科技创新资源的投入力度，建设创新发展的基础，培育创新新动能，保护科技创新发展的知识产权，全市科技创新发展取得了新的发展成效。成都市加大对科技创新的投入力度，全年R&D投入增长12%，每万人发明专利拥有量22件，同比增长15.8%，新增国家企业技术中心7个，新型产业技术院8个，形成9项可全国推广的创新改革经验，建立各类产学研平台1200

① 5+5+1：第一个“5”指五大先进制造业，即电子信息、装备制造、医药健康、新型材料、绿色食品。第二个“5”指五大新兴服务业，即金融服务、现代物流、会展经济、文化旅游、生活服务。“1”指新经济产业，以“人工智能+、大数据+、5G+清洁能源+、供应链+”为代表。

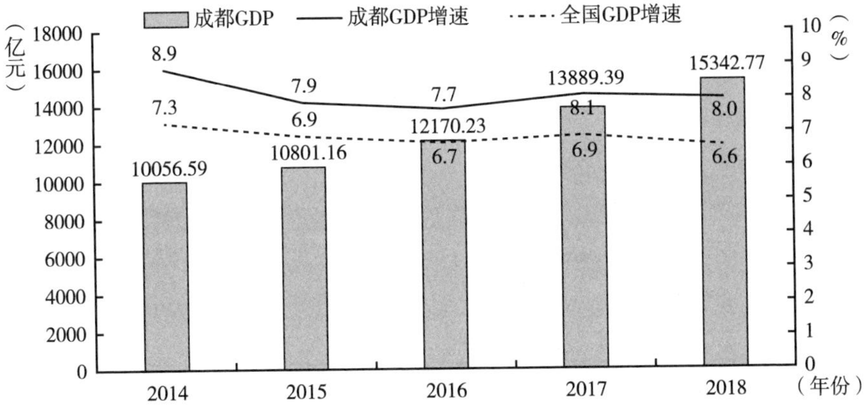

图1　成都市2014～2018年GDP和GDP增速及全国GDP增速

资料来源：2015～2019年成都市国民经济和社会发展统计公报。

个，完成火炬计划491项，完成技术攻关935项，获得年度国家科学技术奖29项。作为科技中心，成都市专利申请和专利授权数量连年攀升，2018年共受理申请107801件，授权57370件，申请总量有所回落，但授权专利数量大幅上升，同比增长39.63%（见图2）。同时成都还建立了知识产权交易中心，保护科技创新成果。科技创新企业发展迅速，截至2019年5月底，成都市入库科技型小中企业2703家、高新技术企业3112家、技术先进型服务业53家。全年共创造双创产品1980款，科技成果2234项，累计技术交易额3978亿元。为了扶持创新创业的发展，成都成立双创服务机构691家，各类双创载体289家，科技双创载体200家，培育双创企业团队28645家，汇集双创导师897位。同时成都不断促进校企联盟发展，实现百校千企共同创新发展。政府为了鼓励创新创业，通过“科创贷”“科创投”“科创券”为企业融资提供便利，累计信用贷款43.09亿元，投资总额6.44亿元，通过科创券为企业融资抵扣527.29万元。

（三）2018年成都市金融中心城市建设状况

2018年第10期“中国金融中心指数”“2018年天府金融指数”“全球金融中心指数”显示，成都金融业发展位居国内第六和全球第七十九，发展成效显著，同时成都金融中心建设也展现了新的发展状态。金融中心建设出现了由体量规模向核心功能转变，由传统金融向新金融业态转变，由自身吸附向对

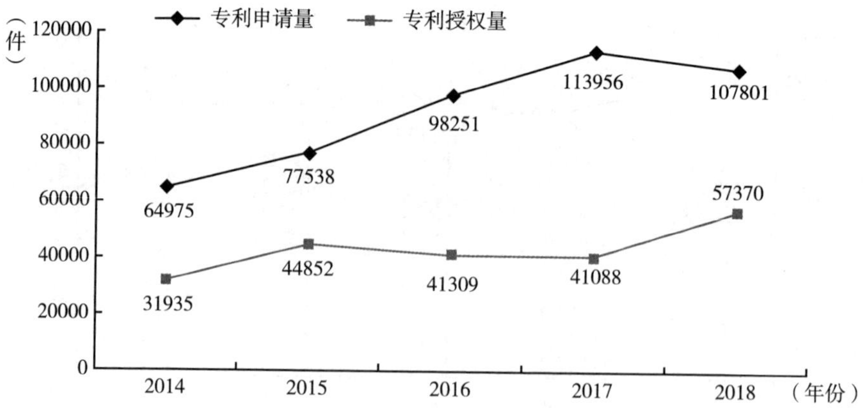

图2　2014～2018年成都市专利申请量和专利授权量情况

资料来源：2015～2019年成都市国民经济和社会发展公报。

外开放辐射转变的三大变化。成都市增强金融业“资本市场、财富管理、投创融资、金融结算和新型金融”五大核心功能，实现全年金融业增加值1750.02亿元，本外币存款余额37825.7亿元，贷款余额32637.2亿元。资本市场中新上市公司11家，组建纾困资金76亿元。投创融资活跃，全市直接融资3609.2亿元，开展跨境人民币结算811亿元。金融服务机构增加，截至2018年底，成都共有各类金融机构和服务机构2500多家，保险机构94家，银行金融机构84家，证券经营机构334家，地方金融机构900多家。同时成都着力构建“科技金融、消费金融、农村金融、供应链金融、绿色金融、文化金融”六大新金融产业生态圈，实现由传统金融向新金融业态的转变，以更好服务新经济、农村经济、文创产业。在对外开放辐射发展方面，成为首个承办泛美行理事会年会的中国城市，搭建了与资阳、眉山等市的合作协议，建立了一体化的金融服务市场，加强与国际的金融合作。

（四）2018年成都市文创中心城市建设状况

文化是一个城市独特的印记，承载着城市的历史和文明。文化与经济的发展可以相互促进，加强文化创新，可以为经济发展增添新的活力。2018年成都市凭借文化政策活力、人才活力、传播活力、产业活力的独特优势，在《中国新文创活力排行榜》位居首位。2018年全市文化创意产业发展再创新高，产业全年增加值1129.0亿元，同比增长43.79%，占GDP的7.4%。设立100亿元文创投资资金，认定文化创业园31个，引进文创龙头企业5个，引进知名音乐企业和重点项目142个，建立文创街区、文创小镇和文创空间800多个。推进“三城三都”① 建设，实现旅游收入3712.6亿元，其中入境旅游总收入14.5亿美元。建立世界赛事名城，分享体育经济蛋糕，打造体育经济消费产业，全年成功举办国际体育赛事21个，成功申办2021年第31届世界大学生夏季运动会和第12届世界运动会。建立国际音乐之都，举办音乐演艺活动1640余场次，引进咪咕音乐、成都演艺集团等企业103家，实现音乐产业总收入397.86亿元。建立国际消费之都，引进了300多个国际一线品牌，吸引200家首店落户，带动了消费业态和模式的创新。建立国际会展之都，举办重大活动689个，总收入突破千亿元，会展产业首次上升成为独立产业。文创对成都的影响越来越明显。

（五）2018年成都对外开放中心城市建设状况

2018年成都对外中心城市建设成效显著，根据《中国城市对外交往活力指数》显示，成都在对外交往活力指数综合排名中位居第五，在社会领域和政治领域得分排名第四，城市对外开放影响力逐步增强。成都发展外向型经济，进出口总额连年攀升，2018年进出口总额接近5000亿元大关，占全省外贸总额的83.87%，进出口总额的增长速度高达26.40%，增速在九大国家中心城市排名第二（见图3、图4）。促进自贸实验区的发展，改善自贸区营商环境，对自贸区实行税收减免政策，全年新增注册企业2.7万家，其中外资企业359家，新增注册资本7008.5亿元。吸引285家世界500强企业落户成都。加强与法国、意大利、韩国等国的合作园区建设，共计引进项目124个。成立“成都海外”工作站20个。在外交事务建设中，2018年成都新增奥地利驻蓉总领事馆，总领馆数量达17个，成为“领馆第三城”。随着“一路一带”建设的推进，成都市加强与沿海沿边城市的交流，国际朋友圈不断扩大，截至2018年底，已经与国外93个城市建立友好关系。中外交往不断加深，获批部分国家外国人144小时过境免签政

① 三城三都：三城，指世界文化名城、世界旅游名城、世界赛事名城；三都，指国际美食之都、国际音乐之都、国际会展之都。

策。成功举办第二届中国—中东欧国家艺术合作论坛、第四届阿拉伯艺术节、2018 年欧洲文化季、国际友城青年音乐周等国际交流活动，成都的国际影响力不断提升，成为西部对外交往中心城市。

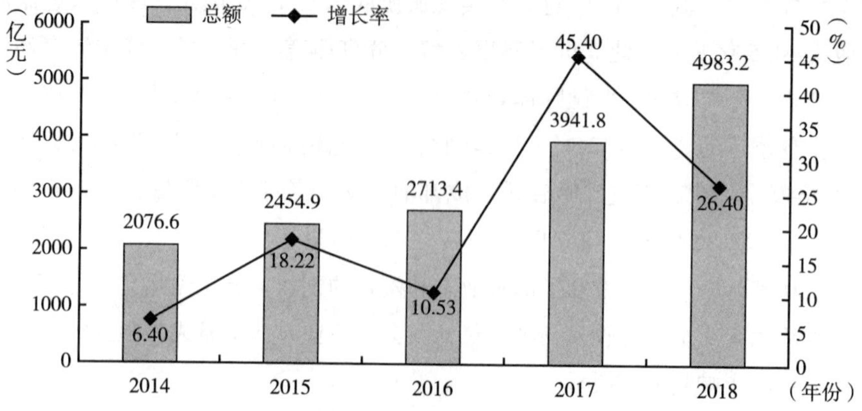

图 3　2014 ~ 2018 年成都市进出口总额和进出口总额增长率情况

资料来源：2015 ~ 2019 年成都市国民经济和社会发展统计公报。

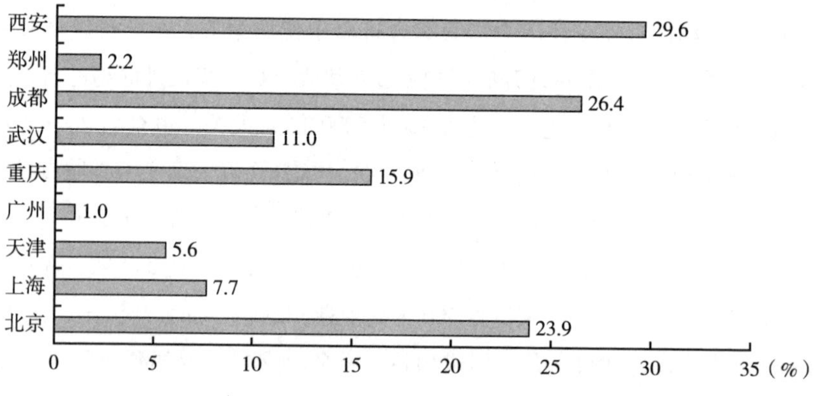

图 4　2018 年九大国家中心城市进出口总额增速情况

资料来源：根据九大国家中心城市 2019 年国民经济和社会发展统计公报整理。

（六）2018年成都综合交通通信枢纽中心城市建设状况

成都是西部开放门户，是连接“一路一带”沿边城市的重要枢纽，建立综合交通通信枢纽城市是成都遵守国家发展战略的需要，也是拉动内地经济发展的需要。成都综合交通通信枢纽城市的建设主要围绕着国际航空运输和铁路运输来提升其国际综合枢纽城市的地位，打造立体交通通信网络。在航空方面，2018年新增开飞往圣彼得堡、曼谷、吉普等12个城市的航线12条，国际航线总量达114条，国际航班网络进一步改善。从机场的吞吐量来看，双流国际机场全年旅客吞吐5295万人次，成为全球最繁忙机场第二十六名。在铁路运输方面，2018年成都打造了“7+5”① 国际铁路大通道，助力“国际陆海联运”走廊建设。全年国际班列开行2619列，同比增长159%，连接境内外城市共38个。其中中欧班列不断向北向南向西向东深入发展，总开行达1591列，同比增长85%。为了促进区域协调，新开通覆盖内江、自贡、泸州、德阳等14个沿边沿海城市的“蓉欧+”班列，形成了国际物流网络，实现城市间协同发展。从发展成果来看，全年实现社会客运周转量381.8亿吨公里、货运周转量1115.3亿人公里，同比增长7.3%、12.3%，综合交通通信枢纽城市地位得到提升。

二　2018年成都建设国家中心城市的主要成效

（一）城市发展活力旺盛，产业结构优化

西部大开发战略实施以来成都市一直保持较快的发展速度。经济增长的速度较多年份保持在8%以上，投资消费对经济的增长贡献能力持续增强，财政收入逐年增加，人民的收入水平提升明显，整个经济指标都呈现较快的增长速度，显示了成都的发展活力。在产业结构方面，三产全年增加值比值为3.4∶42.5∶54.1，第三产业对经济的贡献率逐步提升，增速9%，高于GDP增速1个百分点。三次产业结构调整优化，第三产业占比提升0.9个百分点。同时产业结构内部也实现了优化，先进制造业和服务业发展增度加快，对经济发展的贡献逐步提升。八大特色产业中的汽车产业、石化产业、建材产业和一些传统低级制造业和原料采掘业增加值占规模以上企业增加值比重进一步下降。五大先进制造业“电子信息、装备制造、医药健康、新型材料、绿色食品”总收入9705.4亿元，比上年增长10.9%。占全市工业增加值比重达

① “7+5”：7条国际铁路通道和5条国际铁海联运通道。

82%，高于其增长率2.4个百分点。高新技术产业增加值增长率15.3%，高于全市规模以上工业增加值增长率6.8个百分点。在服务业中，金融业、旅游业、邮电业都实现了较快的增长（参见表1、图5）。

表1　2014～2018年成都市经济发展指标情况

单位：%

年份	GDP增速速	固定资产投资增速	消费总额增速	财政收入增速
2018	8.00	9.40	10.00	10.00
2017	8.10	11.30	11.50	12.30
2016	7.70	7.00	10.40	14.30
2015	7.90	11.90	10.90	5.80
2014	8.90	14.10	12.10	1.80

资料来源：《2019年成都市国民经济和社会发展统计公报》。

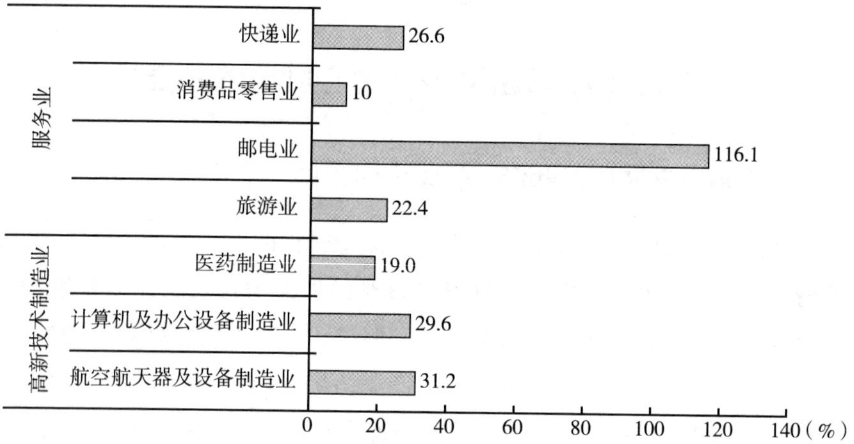

图5　2018年成都市高新技术制造业和服务业增长情况

资料来源：《2019年成都市国民经济和社会发展统计公报》。

（二）构建新经济政策体系，推动新经济发展

2018年成都市推进新经济发展成效显著，新经济发展活力旺盛。根据《2018中国新经济活力指数排行榜》显示，成都新经济活力位居全国第三。为了更好地引导新经济发展，成都市率先系统提出建立新经济城市，并挂牌成立

成都市新经济发展委员会，建立了以“六大经济形态”“七大应用场景”① 为基础的新经济政策体系，引导新经济的发展。2018 年成都市实施新经济企业“双百工程”，加强对重点企业和优秀人才进行扶持和培养，对新经济企业精准服务、建立新经济企业发展平台，创立天使基金对新经济发展进行扶持。全年成都市培育新经济企业 4.1 万户，245 家新经济企业共获得投资 170.21 亿元，百家规模以上企业累计收入 251.47 亿元，较上一年增长 40.24%。政府积极地在成都天府新区筹建“独角兽岛”，全年新培育独角兽企业 4 家。在新产品领域，城市轨道交通车辆、工业机器人、太阳能电池分别增产 31.6%、12.6%、110.1%。在新业态方面，全年成都网络零售业增长 29.4%，网上零售商品额达 669.5 亿元。同时政府为新经济发展提供良好的营商环境，实现服务功能的“三大转变”②，围绕新经济发展的“资本、技术、人才、数据”等要素出台扶持新经济发展的相关政策，谋划成都新经济 2.0 版。

（三）政府调节发力，营商环境改善明显

2018 年成都市致力于改善营商环境，根据《2019 中国城市营商环境指数评价报告》显示，成都在全国主要城市营商环境中排名第六，较上年提升 7 个位次（见表 2），在九大国家中心城市营商环境排名中由 2017 年的倒数第二名，上升至排名第五，营商环境状况向好发展。在政府服务方面，持续推动政府“放管服”改革，实现“证照分离”“四十三证合一”“一枚印章管审批”，便利企业的申报办理。加大力度推行“只跑一次”“一窗办理”改革，85% 的审批实现“跑一次”，95% 的公共服务实现网上办理。在增强市场活力方面，实施市场准入负面清单管理制度，放松对企业的管制。促进企业与“一带一路”沿线地区开展多种形式的合作交流。2018 年全年由于成都投资环境改善，带动企业在“一带一路”沿线国家投资建设项目 150 个，投资资金约 100 亿美元。在科研创新方面，成都市鼓励高校和企业创新创造，积极投建重点实验室并购置大型仪器

---

① 新经济“六大形态”是指重点发展数字经济、智能经济、绿色经济、创意经济、流量经济和共享经济，“七大应用场景”，即提升服务实体经济能力、推进智慧城市建设、科技创新创业、人力资本协同、消费提档升级、绿色低碳发展和现代供应链创新应用。

② 三大转变：一是从政策制定“配菜”变“点菜”，二是从“给优惠”向“给机会”转变，三是从“个别服务”向“生态营造”转变。

设备以便利开展科研工作，鼓励企业自主创新、自主研发，为创新型企业提供政策优惠和财税补贴，培育科技领军企业和标杆企业。在人才要素方面，推行人才“新政十二条”，建立“蓉城人才绿卡”服务体系，以筑巢引凤。目前成都市共用自主评选“蓉漂计划”专家659人、团队64个，拥有各类人才近500万人，为企业发展提供了优秀的人才基础。在法制环境方面，设立四川自贸区实验区人民法院和仲裁中心，成立成都知识产权法庭保障正常营商环境。

表2　中国城市营商环境指数和名次

城市	2017年名次	2018年名次	营商环境指数
深圳	3	1	0.611
上海	4	2	0.524
广州	1	3	0.512
北京	2	4	0.510
重庆	5	5	0.478
成都	13	6	0.405
南京	6	7	0.398
杭州	7	8	0.397
长沙	20	9	0.391
武汉	10	10	0.388
西安	12	11	0.377
青岛	9	12	0.375
昆明	22	13	0.359
贵阳	30	14	0.350
宁波	8	15	0.331
厦门	28	16	0.330
郑州	23	17	0.324
天津	11	18	0.322
大连	19	19	0.318
南昌	17	20	0.313

资料来源：《2019中国城市营商环境指数评价报告》。

（四）“蓝天保卫战”成效突出，生态环境改善明显

2018年成都坚持新的发展理念，加快公园城市建设，坚决落实绿色发展的理念，切实推进“三治一增”，以铁的决心改善成都生态环境。在国家中心城市建设中探索出一条实现绿色与发展“价值转换”的新路径。在污染治理

方面，“铁腕治霾、重拳治水、科学治堵”成效明显。开展“蓝天保卫战”行动，全年空气达标天数增加16天，空气优良天数达251天，有害物质PM10、PM2.5平均浓度下降8.0%、8.9%，SO_2、NO_2、CO平均浓度下降12.8%、9.4%、17.6%。荣获首批“全球绿色低碳领域先锋城市蓝天奖”。在水污染治理方面，着重解决黑臭水问题，地表水断面Ⅰ～Ⅲ类水质提升7.2%，锦江、沱江、金马河流域生态治理改善。建设了45个固体废物污染治理项目。在治堵方面，出台《2018年成都科学治堵工作实施方案》，科学治理交通拥堵。在生态环境建设方面，着力建设公园城市，落实“成都增绿十条”。2017年新增2万平方米以上公园6个，全年策划增绿项目839个，建成天府绿道2607公里，龙泉森林公园“增景增绿”近6.5万亩。全市取得森林覆盖率39.5%、建成区绿化面积覆盖率41.7%、人均公园面积12.7平方米的良好成绩。

三 成都建设国家中心城市的经验

（一）坚持新的发展理念，为建设高质量国家中心城市提供思想指导

成都的发展追求新的发展理念，努力走新时代高质量发展的成都路径。在国家中心城市建设中始终坚持创新驱动发展和产业转型的理念，加大对高新技术产业的培育，提高制造业的产业能级，加快发展新经济。以创新驱动发展战略引领新经济，创造新的发展模式，提高城市的创新力和创造力。始终坚持“一干多支”“五区协同”的协调发展理念，在成都市以“东进、南拓、西控、北改、中优”战略为指引，实现城市东南西北各区协同发展。在四川省推动“成都平原、川南、川东北、攀西、川西北”的产业分工合作、基础设施共同建设，实现五区协同发展。在国内外坚持对内对外开放战略，强化与重庆、西安、昆明、西宁、贵阳等周边城市的合作和交往，增强与“一带一路”沿边沿海城市的联系，建立共同的产业园和项目库。始终坚持绿色发展的理念，积极推进成都公园城市建设，实施保护生态环境的“三治一增”[①] 政策。始终坚持开放引领互利合作的理念，加强与周边国家的联系，构建西部内

① 三治一增：铁腕治霾、科学治堵、重拳治水、全域增绿。

陆开放高地。始终坚持共享发展的理念，改善民生，建立高品质的美丽宜居城市。

（二）坚持改革创新基本制度，为经济发展创造良好的空间

创新改革是未来城市发展的新动力和新优势，成都市国家中心城市建设也是在不断创新改革中寻求发展的新道路和新途径，破解在国家中心城市建设过程中的制度性阻碍，实现新的发展。2018 年成都市以“五项制度改革”为抓手，推动要素资源的高效率配置，改善经济社会发展环境。第一，推进财政预算改革，以绩效为导向建立财政预算管理体制和责任机制，实施严格的监管评价机制，避免财政资金的无效浪费投入，发挥财政政策调节经济平衡的最大杠杆作用。第二，推进国资经营评价制度改革，坚守效率优先的原则，关停低质低效企业。构建国资经营评价指标体系，推动国资国企实现专业化、国际化发展。第三，推动政务服务改革，提高公共服务能力，实现“证照分离”“四十三证合一”，便利企业的申报办理，实现“只跑一次”“不见面审批”，提高审批效率。第四，推动企业扶持激励制度和土地资源配置制度改革，给企业发展提供资金、技术、土地、人才等生产要素的帮扶和优惠，建立全生命周期企业帮扶制度，精准聚焦企业发展。第五，成都还进行了其他各领域的改革，旨在破解经济发展的障碍，实现经济高质量发展。

（三）强化政策引领作用，为国家中心城市建设指明方向

政府和市场是维护宏观经济运行平稳的两种手段。成都目前还处于建设中心城市的初级阶段，强化政策对中心城市的引领具有重大的意义。成都在建设国家中心城市发展过程中注重政策的引领作用，出台一系列规划文件和政策意见，实施各种制度，保障经济社会的平稳运行。通过制定一系列发展规划从宏观的角度对成都的建设给予指导。通过制定一系列具体的意见和方案，从微观角度对于经济转型、制造业升级、新经济发展、民营经济、对外开放、自贸区建设、文化建设、区域协同、环境保护等不同领域做了细致的规定，完善了国家中心城市建设的政策体系，强化了政策对国家中心城市建设的引领保障作用（见表 3）。

表 3　成都市出台引导经济社会发展的政策情况

政策类型	政策文件名称	发布时间	政策内容
发展规划类	《成渝城市群发展规划》	2016.4	成都要以建设国家中心城市为目标,增强成都"五中心一枢纽"功能,把成渝城市群建设成为国家级城市群
	《成都市国民经济与社会发展第十三个五年规划纲要》	2018.1	全面建设体现新理念的城市,全面加强改革,促进经济高质量发展,加快创新驱动发展,大力提升创新创业能力,建设开放门户,加强区域协调,促进民生发展
	《成都市城市总体规划(2016—2030年)》	2018.3	成都要建设国家中心城市、美丽宜居公园城市、国际门户枢纽城市、世界文化名城,迈向可持续发展的世界城市
经济类	《中共成都市委关于全面贯彻新发展理念加快推进高质量发展的决定》	2018.3	大力振兴实体经济,积极发展新经济,培育新动能,推动全市重点产业发展再上新台阶,谋划"5+5+1"的产业细分领域
	《成都市人民政府办公厅关于大力发展高新技术服务业支撑产业功能区及园区建设增强西部科技中心功能的实施意见》	2018.5	以产业功能区及园区为载体,建设"两核、多区、多点"的高新技术服务特色聚集区,构建"2+M+N的"高新技术服务业聚集区体系
	《中共成都市委成都市人民政府关于促进民营经济健康发展的意见》	2018.11	制定"民营经济健康发展25条",降低民营企业成本,解决融资难问题,支持民营经济创新创造,优化民营经济发展活力
区域协调类	《成都市人民政府关于加快总部经济发展做强国家中心城市核心功能支撑的意见》	2018.5	推进"总部成都"建设和总部经济发展,增强对现代产业体系的核心支撑作用。依托66个市级重点产业园(集聚区),打造总部经济骨干企业集群,辐射带动区域发展
	《关于加快推进成都平原经济区协同发展的实施意见》	2019.2	提升环成都经济圈各城市能级,推进成德、成眉、成资同城化突破,共同打造以成都为核心城市,以绵阳、德阳、乐山为区域中心城市,以眉山、遂宁、资阳、雅安为重要支撑,在西部地区最具综合竞争力、辐射带动力、国际影响力的现代化城市群
对外开放类	《中共成都市委成都市人民政府关于加快构建国际门户枢纽全面服务"一带一路"建设的意见》	2018.6	全面构建联通全球通江达海的战略大通道,积极推动国际贸易和投资优化升级、精准高效促进资源要素全球配置、全面深化高品质国际人文交流合作、加快形成法治化国际化便利化营商环境
	《建设西部对外交往中心行动计划(2017—2022年)》	2018.6	架设联通世界的"空中丝路",实施"极核型"企业招引计划,拓展国际交流合作新渠道

续表

政策类型	政策文件名称	发布时间	政策内容
生态类	《实施“成都治霾十条”推进铁腕治霾工作方案》	2017.6	提出推动源头治霾、分类治霾、协作治霾
	《实施“成都治水十条”推进重拳治水工作方案》	2017.6	提出治水十条,水污染防治“620”工程,强化生产、生活、生态用水治理

资料来源：成都市人民政府门户网站。

四　成都市建设国家中心城市面临的挑战

（一）经济要素的综合支撑能力较弱

地区生产总值、固定资产投资、公共预算收入、社会消费品零售总额、人均GDP这些经济指标反映了一个地区的综合经济实力。2018年成都市GDP达15342.8亿元，刚突破1.5万亿元，而北京、上海、广州、重庆早已经突破两万亿元大关。从固定资产投资的基本情况来看，成都2018年固定资产投资8341.1亿元，仅占天津固定资产投资的78.37%，占重庆的44.70%。从全年公共预算收入来看，成都市2018年公共预算收入1424.2亿元，在九大国家中心城市公共预算收入中仅仅高于郑州市和西安市，排名倒数第三，其收入总额仅约占北京总收入的25%，上海总收入的20%，重庆的63%。从人均GDP来看，成都仅高于重庆和西安。经济要素是国家中心城市建设的重要支撑，成都的综合经济指标还未能满足支撑成都建设成国家重要中心城市的要求（见表4）。

表4　2018年九大中心城市经济指标对比情况

城市	GDP(亿元)	固定资产投资(亿元)	社会消费品零售总额(亿元)	公共预算收入(亿元)	人均GDP(万元)
北京	30320.0	8062.1	11747.7	5785.9	13.5
上海	32679.9	7622.8	12668.7	7108.2	12.1
天津	18809.6	10642.7	5533.1	2106.2	15.5
广州	22859.4	6404.4	9256.2	1632.3	6.6
重庆	20363.2	18660.1	6960.1	2265.5	13.5
武汉	14847.3	8705.3	6843.9	1528.7	9.5

续表

城市	GDP(亿元)	固定资产投资(亿元)	社会消费品零售总额(亿元)	公共预算收入(亿元)	人均 GDP（万元）
成都	15342. 8	8341. 1	6801. 8	1424. 2	10. 1
郑州	10143. 3	8398. 5	4268. 1	1152. 1	8. 7
西安	8349. 9	8190. 7	4658. 7	684. 7	14. 0
成都排名	6	3	5	7	7

资料来源：根据九大国家中心城市国民经济和社会发展统计公报整理。

（二）主干辐射带动区域协调能力有待提升

2018 年成都市重视区域协同发展的建设，以“一干多支”“五区协同”区域发展理念指导区域实现共同发展。扎实推进“十大重点工程”助力乡村振兴。深度推进成德眉资同城化合作，打造区域副中心城市。推动各市（州）签署全面合作协议，实现共同发展。但是从整体效果来看，成都主干辐射带动区域协调发展的效果依然不明显。全省区经济发展差距依然比较大，省会成都市是四川省经济发展的支柱，全年地区生产总值 15342. 8 亿元，约为四川全省的 37. 72%，而次级城市绵阳、德阳、宜宾、南充等地地区生产总值仅占全省地区生产总值的 5. 66%、5. 44%、4. 89%、4. 83%。成都市 GDP 是这几个地区的六七倍。从反映人民生活水平的人均 GDP 角度考量，除了攀枝花地区由于储藏有钛、钒、石墨等矿产资源，人均 GDP 略低于成都之外，其他地区的人均 GDP 都与成都差距明显。从区域协同方面来讲，成都平原、川南、川东北、攀西、川西北全年的地区生产总值分别为 25665. 54 亿元、6539. 8 亿元、6394. 17 亿元、2706. 71 亿元、597. 87 亿元，仅成都平原 GDP 就占四川省 GDP 的 61%，比其他四区总和还要高 22 个百分点，排名第二和第五的川南和川西北地区生产总值仅占成都平原的 25. 48% 和 2. 33%，由此可见，成都对区域发展的辐射带动能力太弱，中心城市的辐射带动优势未发挥出来。同时区域协同机制不健全，存在产业同构和无序竞争的局面，交通设施、环境联治、公共服务均衡化和市场要素自由流动都存在一定的缺陷，区域的整体协调能力差，导致区域发展存在很大差距（见图 6、图 7）。

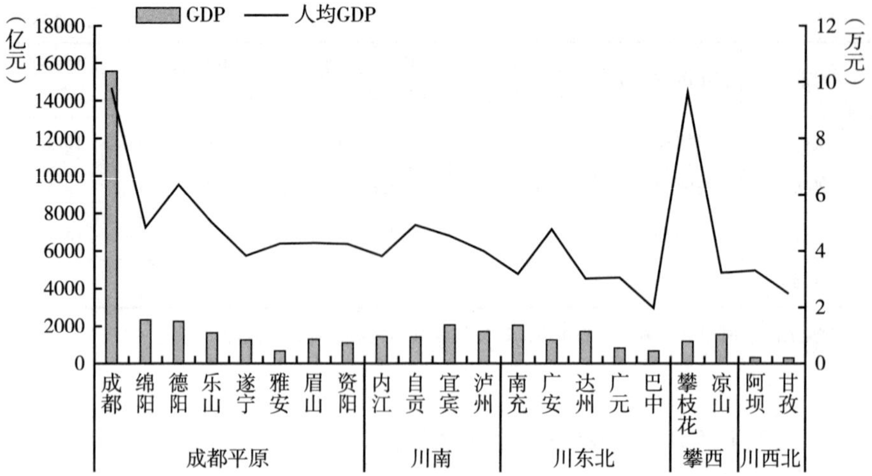

图 6　2018 年四川省各市 GDP 和人均 GDP 情况

资料来源：根据 2019 年四川省各市国民经济和社会发展统计公报整理。

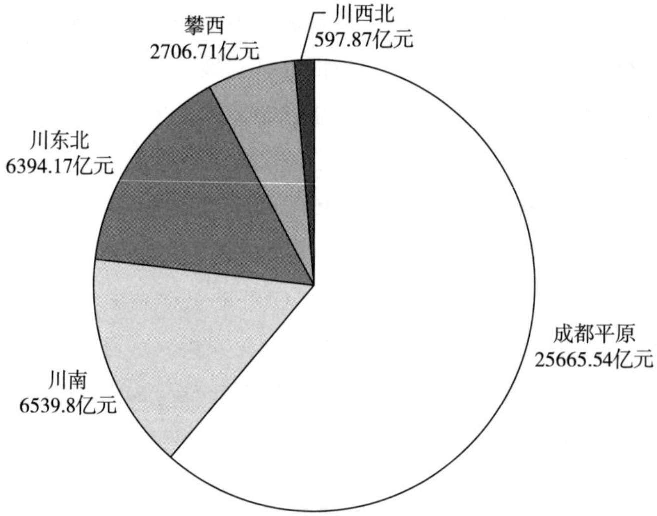

图 7　2018 年四川省五区 GDP 分布情况

（三）创新发展的供给要素能力不足

创新是未来城市发展的第一动力，各中心城市都在加大对创新的投入，给城市发展注入动力。成都在《2018 年城市创新力排名》中位居第十六位，在九大国家中心城市占位中仅超过郑州。研发投入 R&D 总额和研究生数量反映了一个地区对科技创新的重视程度和城市创新的上升空间。2017 年北京和上海以超过千亿元 R&D 研发投入稳居第一和第二名，成都市的 R&D 投入仅占这两个地区的 20% 和 27% 左右。成都市与同级别的武汉、重庆、西安比也有不小的差距。成都的 R&D 投入总额和投入强度都在九大中心城市中排名倒数第二，这与成都市建设科技新城的定位不匹配。成都在努力地打造新经济和高科技产业，科研投入经费的多少决定着新兴产业的生命力和活力。同时成都市科研创新环境较差，源头创新供给不足，国家级重大科技基础设施、创新基地资源不充分。人才要素集聚能力弱，领军人才不足，这些都限制了成都创新创造能力的提升（见图 8）。

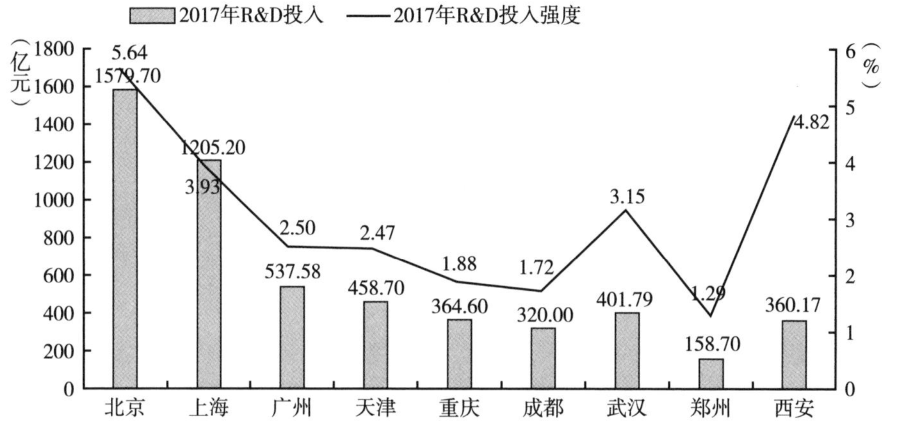

图 8　2017 年九大国家中心城市 R&D 投入总量和投入强度情况

资料来源：根据九大国家中心城市 2018 年统计年鉴整理。

（四）城市交通健康水平有待提升

近年来成都市经济发展迅速，人口吸虹能力增强，目前城市实际管理人口超过两千万，城市体量不断扩充。随着经济和人口的增长，不可避免会带来交通拥挤问题。交通拥挤不仅会给人们的生活带来不便，也会影响一个地区经济的发展。根据高德地图《2018 年主要城市交通分析报告》显示，成都高峰拥堵路程里程比在全国主要城市中排名第九，在交通健康指数方面排名第四十二位，交通健康指数 64.33%，时间—路网高延时运行时间占比 41.8%，空间—常发拥堵路程历程比 0.176%。成都市人均上班通勤的时间为 72.60 分钟，工作日平均上下班拥堵时长 32.78 分钟。按照交通健康状况的测算排名，成都目前还处于交通亚健康状态（见图 9）。

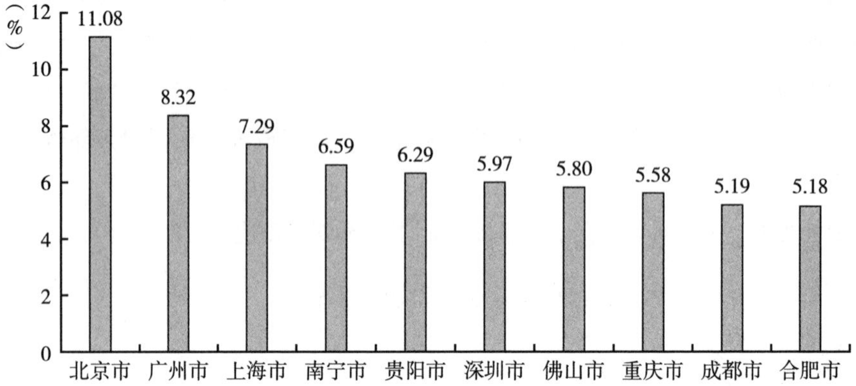

图 9　2018 年全国主要城市高峰拥堵路程里程比前 10 名

资料来源：高德地图《2018 年主要城市交通分析报告》。

（五）共享发展的力度需要加强

成都市经济发展有了较好的增长，但是发展成果还未达到人民共享的状态。成都市的城乡收入普遍较低，中小学教育资源不充分、医疗资源分布不均匀、养老基础设施不充分的问题依然存在。2018 年成都市居民的收入水平和消费水平虽然增长速度很快，但是由于本身基数较小，整体的收入水平与一线城市还有很大差距。幼儿园和中小学教学资源不充分，全年公办和公益性幼儿园覆盖 87.3%，很多地区幼儿上学难上学贵现象比较突出。中学和小学数量较少，导致“超大班额”的现象一直存在。在医疗卫生方面，成都市共有医疗卫生机构 10755 家，千人床位量 8.38 张，但是由于成都承载着大量外地就诊患者，医疗资源紧缺现象依然未得到改善。从地区分布来看，成都市部、省、市级三甲医院主要分布在二环以内，导致中心城区医院任务繁重，知名医学专家一号难求。在养老方面，成都市共有社区养老设施 2089 个，床位 3.0 万张，这些养老基础设施的供给难以满足人口老龄化对于养老基础设施的需求。

五　未来成都建设国家中心城市的展望和对策建议

（一）未来的展望

成都市经历多年的发展，逐步迈向高质量发展阶段。如今成都市已经成为西部发展的核心城市，发展潜力巨大。一方面成都发展受国家多重政策叠加影响较深，国家新一轮西部大开发、成渝城市群、长江经济带和西部地区“一带一路”、天府新区、自贸区建设的系统推进，为成都中心城市建设带来了机遇。另一方面，在政府层面，四川省主动融入国家发展大局，以新理念支撑建设中心城市，探索成都发展的道路，设计成都经济社会发展规划，出台各项促进经济社会发展的政策、意见、方案，给成都中心城市建设规划了蓝图。

成都市各项经济指标发展活力旺盛，但是整体发展实力不强。未来成都市中心城市建设步伐将会继续加快。目前成都市积极地发展先进制造业和服务业，以“六大经济形态”“七大应用场景”为抓手，发展新经济，未来这些先进的产业将会成为新时代经济发展的爆发点，支撑成都建设综合实力强的经济中心城市。科技水平将进一步得到提升，尽管目前成都市对创新投入的资金不足，企业的自主研发能力较弱，但是随着成都经济实力的增强，将可以为高校和企业的科技研发项目投入更多的资金。同时成都市建立了“校企联盟”，施行人才新政，这将会给成都的创新发展带来更多的人才，支撑科技中心城市的建设。在建设金融中心城市上，成都市确立了新时期金融业发展的“五大核心功能”，形成了“六大新金融产业生态圈”，同时规划了建设西部金融中心“十大工程”，这将会保障成都金融业在未来的繁荣发展。在建设文创中心上，成都市以独具特色的文化优势，将会形成文创核心聚集区，推动文创业走向专业化、国际化，展现成都人文魅力。在建设对外交往和国际枢纽中心城市上，成都将建成沟通五大洲主要城市的水陆空交通大网络，形成国际物流交往的大枢纽大通道，拓展对外开放空间，扩大交往的范围，促进成都国际影响力的提升。

（二）对策和建议

1. 高质量发展经济，提升城市整体实力

经济实力增强是一个地区发展建设的重要基础性指标。成都市的经济实力位居中西部地区的首位，但是从各类经济指标的对比结果来看，成都市经济实力与其他国家中心城市还有很大的差距，这是未来一段时期内成都面临的主要挑战。在未来发展中成都要在新理念的指导下，继续转变经济发展方式，引导成都三大产业迈向高质量发展的路径。第一，建立现代化经济体系，围绕“5+5+1”重点产业发展，建立完善的产业链，壮大产业实力。完善建设产业承载能力强的66个重点产业园区，优化产业功能区的布局，引进龙头企业，增强产业园的实力，努力打造综合实力强的四大产业新城。第二，加快产业转型升级，提升制造业的产业能级，推动五大产业实现产业的聚集，扩大产业规模，提高产业附加值，提高高新技术产业的研发制造能力，走高端的产业发展路径。同时也应该对重点产业进行高端化和数字化改造，增强产品的科技含量。第三，着重培育科技含量高、具有强势竞争力的“人工智能+、大数据+、5G+、清洁能源+、供应链+”新经济，发挥新经济在未来经济发展中的重要作用。第四，注重投资和消费对经济发展的拉动作用，以项目为引领进行投资建设，发挥投资对宏观经济发展的带动作用。壮大消费市场，支持建设国际化的成都品牌，助力成都“国际消费之都”的建设，增强成都市的整体经济实力。

2. 做强主干，引领区域协同一体化建设

成都市是四川省的“主干”城市，是成渝城市群的“核心城市”，是西部地区重要的中心城市和国际交往的内陆开放高地。成都的建设承担了多重的历史和现实使命，其中最重要的一项使命就是辐射带动地区的发展，实现地区的协调发展。未来成都的建设，要注重区域协调，努力实现区域发展一体化。第一，做强成都“主干”，发挥主干的引领作用。坚持多点多极战略，实现区域的均衡发展。重视区域协同发展的顶层设计，合理进行产业规划，走错位发展的战略，实现各区域产业的合理分工和协作，构建完善的产业生态链。第二，培育次级中心城市和卫星城市，重点推进同城化的深度建设，提升区域发展能级。第三，转变政府治理方式，优化区域的营商环境，实现要素市场的自由流动，为区域市场经济发展创造活力。第四，加大力度规划和建设服务全区的交通基础设施，实现城市铁路、高速公路的对接，大力发展城际公交，提供同城化服务。第五，共同制定区域协同规划，保障区域协同发展的有序推进。建立完善的各级各地政府之间的协调机制，搭建区域合作联盟，深化区域在产业链分工、科技创新、基础设施共建、环境联治等方面的合作，打造区域发展共同体。

3. 加大创新要素的投入，提升创新能力

科技是第一生产力，创新是唯一驱动力。成都市的高新技术产业和新经济的发展需要创新资源的强劲投入。针对成都目前发展的现状，成都市一方面要加大对于高校科研经费的投入力度，大力支持科研创新活动；另一方面要鼓励企业进行自主研发创新，加大对产品的科技投入，对科创型企业发展给予税收优惠，或者进行补贴，激发企业创新创造的活力。加大对教育资源的投入力度，为高校购买重大实验仪器，建立重点实验室，支持科研活动的开展。加大对研究生的招生力度，整合教育资源，建立一流大学和一流学科，为创新奠定基础。大力引进高端创新人才，完善人才引进方案。

4. 合理规划城市，提升空间承载力

成都市要合理地规划城市的空间结构，科学优化城市交通体系，学习借鉴城市交通疏堵之策。成都要解决城市交通拥挤的难题，一方面要合理地规划建设城市空间结构，合理地构建不同的产业区域，分流人群上班地点；另一方面要优化城市综合交通建设，推动城市交通加密成网，建设半小时轨道交通通勤圈。加大力度投资建设公交、地铁、有轨电车，提高其运营覆盖率，形成便捷的交通网络体系。大力推广智慧公交，连接地铁和有轨电车，优化公交的调度，缓解高峰时间段的拥堵状况，缩短通勤时间。同时也要学习其他城市的治堵之策，例如："交叉口渠化改善""早/晚高峰信号灯配时优化""区域关节点信号联控与分流"等措施科学治堵。

5. 提升人民幸福感，共享发展成果

成都市地区发展不均衡，造成城乡居民收入水平差别较大，教育、医疗和基础设施等资源分布不均衡，影响城乡居民生活幸福水平的提高。为了实现"有感发展"，成都市首先要稳步推进乡村振兴项目，发掘乡村发展潜力；支持部分企业到乡村建设生产加工基地，实现农村工业化，实现农民增产增收。其次要高质量发展教育事业，扩增扩建幼儿园和中小学，引进优秀教师资源，助力成都办好教育事业，提升人民的文化水平；同时要扩建重点医院，在不同区域合理配置优质医疗资源，打造"15 分钟医疗健康圈"满足民众需求。最后要积极发展老年人社会保障事业，加大财政投资力度支持老年基础设施建设，保障老年人的晚年生活。

参考文献

[1] 成都市人民政府:《2019 年成都市政府工作报告》, https: //www. is97. com/doc - 173925 - 1. html。

[2] 四川省人民政府:《2018 年成都 GDP 超 1. 5 万亿元同比增长 8. 0%》, http: //www. sc. gov. cn/10462/10464/10465/10595/2019/1/29/3b3fb4caca5b462fb292833ff6195d00. shtml。

[3] 侯初初:《牢记嘱托抢抓机遇　成都市高质量发展取得积极进展》, http: //sc. cri. cn/20190123/389e5237 - 7107 - ef37 - 998d - 9cb2cf81165c. html。

[4]《新经济企业不断涌现　成都“城市机会清单”扩容》, http: //www. p5w. net/news/gncj/201906/t20190613_ 2303777. htm。

[5]《“三城三都”建设按下“快进键”》, http: //sc. people. com. cn/n2/2019/0603/c379471 - 33003170. html。

[6] 温珙竹:《坚持把创造一流营商环境作为“头号工程”成都确立 2019 年为国际化营商环境建设年》, http: //www. sohu. com/a/294098142_ 120066169。

[7]《2018 年成都全方位对外开放成绩显著》, http: //www. yybnet. net/news/china/201903/8818265. html。

[8]《成都:担当“主干”责任为全省发展聚力赋能》, http: //sc. people. com. cn/n2/2018/1203/c379471 - 32357801. html。

[9] 《成都西部金融中心建设初现三“变”》, http: //scnews. newssc. org/system/20190222/000945142. html。

[10]《成都编制医疗卫生布局规划将建一批综合医院项目》, http: //sc. sina. com. cn/news/b/2018 - 05 - 01/detail - ifzvpatr7223565 - p2. shtml。

B.9

武汉国家中心城市建设的进展与前景

邓宏兵　李世冉*

摘　要：　无论从中部整体格局来看，还是从地理位置上看，武汉都处于特殊的空间枢纽位置。近年来，随着国家发展的重大战略逐渐从沿海向内陆延伸，武汉地处长江经济带、长江中游城市群以及武汉都市圈等重要核心位置，成为国家空间发展战略的重要增长极，在完善国家城镇空间格局体系过程中，承担着推动中部崛起、引领长江中游城市群发展，以及在长江经济带发展过程中起到核心门户的重要作用。武汉需要在明确自身优势与差距的前提下，通过叠加发展战略、发挥战略效应最大化等方式完成自身突破与转型升级，继而承担起国家空间支点的重大责任，完成建设国家中心城市的重大使命。

关键词：　国家中心城市　武汉都市圈　长江中游城市群

一　2018年武汉国家中心城市建设进展与成就

（一）2018年武汉国家中心城市建设进展

2018年，武汉市发展坚持以习近平新时代中国特色社会主义思想为指导，以党的十九大精神为指引，全面贯彻落实习近平总书记视察湖北重要讲话精神，

* 邓宏兵，博士，中国地质大学（武汉）区域经济与投资环境研究中心主任，教授、博士生导师，主要研究方向为区域经济与区域创新；李世冉，中国地质大学区域经济与投资环境研究中心博士，主要研究方向为区域经济。

全年保持经济稳定增长。促进改革创新、普惠民生、风险防范，聚焦三大战略性新兴产业发展。其中，智能制造业与规模以上服务业总产值分别增长 18.8% 和 23.6%，战略性新兴产业投资比上年增长 24.3%。集聚了由先进制造业、新经济、现代服务业构建的现代化产业体系，产业结构持续优化；招商引资力度持续加大，全年实现实际利用外资总额达 109.27 亿美元，同比增长 13.3%，新引进世界 500 强企业 10 家。积极落实脱贫攻坚行动，全年实现贫困村出列 87 个，脱贫人数达 2.16 万人，经济社会各项改革工作稳步推进，全市城乡居民收入保持平稳增长，加快推进“三化”大武汉建设，以高质量建设全面推动国家中心城市建设。

2018 年，武汉市 GDP 为 14847.29 亿元，人均 GDP 达到 12.39 万元，GDP 增速为 8.0%；全年全市居民人均可支配收入 42133 元，同比增长 9.0%，收入增速整体平稳，经济整体保持稳定增长。2014 ~ 2018 年，武汉地区生产总值在万亿元台阶上持续攀升，GDP 增速保持在 8.0% 左右，经济稳中求进的态势为武汉建设中心城市奠定了坚实的基础（见图 1）。

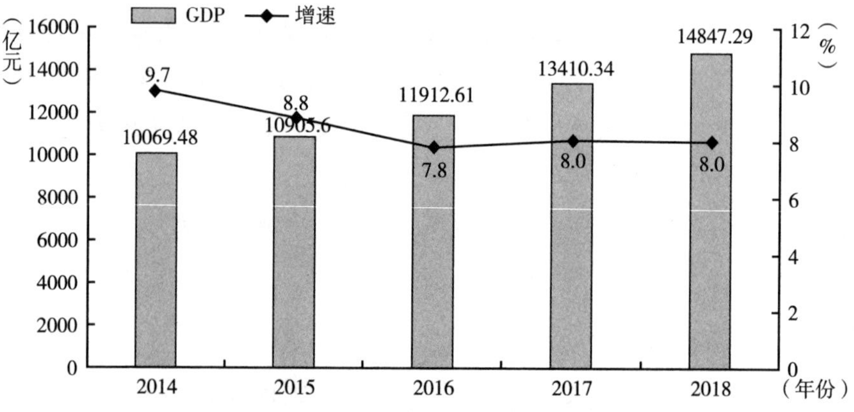

图 1　2014 ~ 2018 年武汉生产总值及其增速

资料来源：2015 ~ 2018 年武汉市统计年鉴、2015 ~ 2019 年武汉市国民经济和社会发展统计公报。

2018 年社会消费品零售总额 6843.9 亿元，同比增速为 10.5%，略高于收入增速，且 2014 ~ 2018 年武汉社会消费品零售总额攀升速度较快，2016 年开始增速基本控制在 10% 左右（见图 2）。据统计数据，武汉人均拥有零售商业面积大于 2 平方米，且商业网点达到 36.9 万个，全年武汉市城乡居民人均消费支出增速分别高于收入 0.3 个和 1.8 个百分点，说明居民消费需求仍较为旺

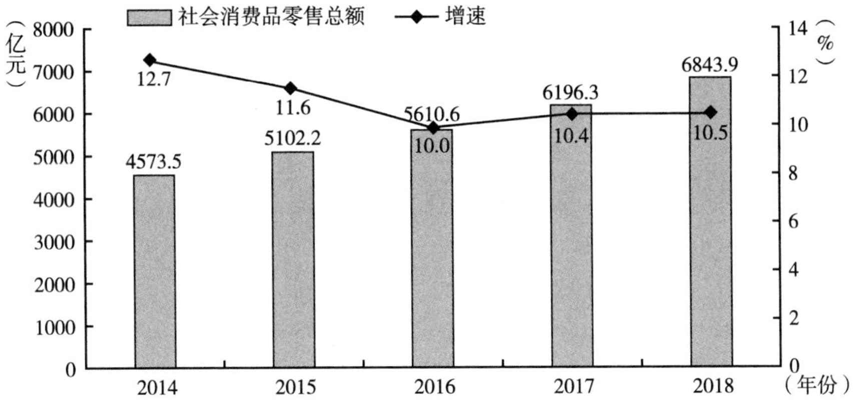

图 2　2014～2018 年武汉社会消费品零售总额及其增速

资料来源：2015～2018 年武汉市统计年鉴、2015～2019 年武汉市国民经济和社会发展统计公报。

盛，各项激发内需的政策措施仍在发挥作用。

改善型消费领跑全市居民的消费支出。2018 年武汉市居民居住支出占消费支出的比重为 27.4%，教育文化娱乐支出保持快速增长，占比为 10.5%，医疗保健上的支出增速较快，占消费支出的比重为 7.6%。2018 年武汉居民消费数据显示，12 个月份月度同比增长速度呈波动上升态势，其中 2 月、9 月、10 月同比增速最高，为 2.6%（图 3）。数据表明，武汉居民在满足基本需求后，全市城乡居民消费内容和水平向更高层次迈进。

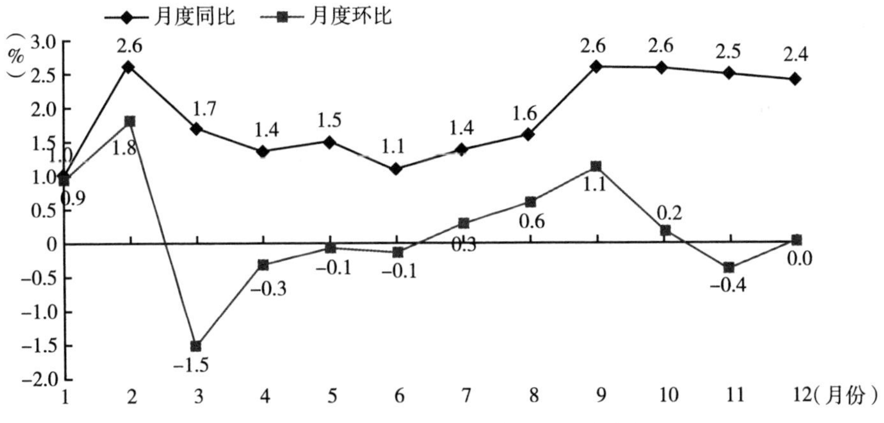

图 3　2018 年武汉居民消费价格月度数据

资料来源：2015～2018 年武汉市统计年鉴、2015～2019 年武汉市国民经济和社会发展统计公报。

统计结果显示，2018 年武汉全市城乡居民就业创业、收入均保持稳定增长，基本面向好，且全年新增加就业人数达 19.12 万人，城镇登记失业率为 2.14%，控制在目标范围以内；市场活力不断被激活，新增市场主体达 19.12 万户，同比增长了 5.2%，其中新登记的企业为 9.46 万户。全年居民收支还体现出武汉市向创新发展和高质量发展转型升级的特点。

产业优化布局与结构调整不断升级，且提供了更多高收入就业岗位。在生产总值构成中，2014 ~ 2018 年第三产业所占比重不断增大，2018 年比重达 54.6%（见图 4）。全年三大战略性新兴产业总产值均实现大幅增速，其中智能制造业营业收入增速最高，为 21.5%，在规模以上服务业中，旅游服务业营业收入同比增长了 23.6%，增幅最高，生产性服务业与科技性服务业增长速度紧随其后，分别为 21.2% 和 20.1%。同时，战略性新兴产业投资同比增长速度较快，增速为 24.3%。随着武汉加快构建先进制造业和新兴服务业为支撑的现代化产业体系，也为居民提供了优良的就业机会，其中从事信息传输、软件和信息技术服务业、金融业等人员所占比重较同期有明显提高。

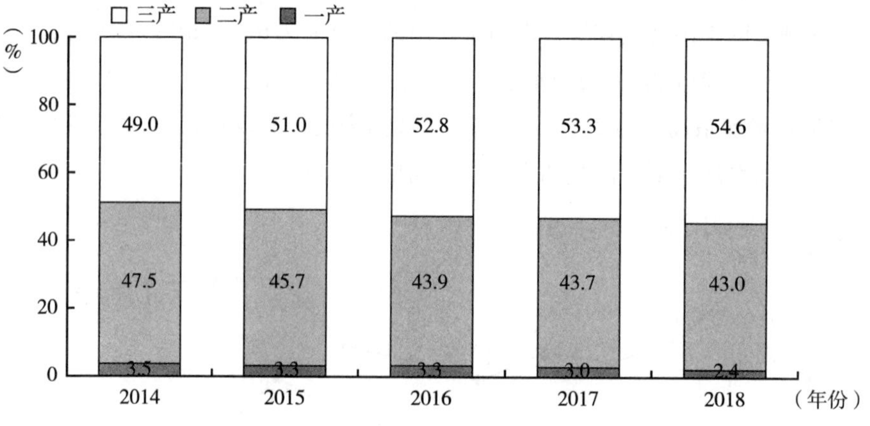

图 4　2014 ~ 2018 年武汉生产总值产业构成

资料来源：2015 ~ 2018 年武汉市统计年鉴、2015 ~ 2019 年武汉市国民经济和社会发展统计公报。

生态环境方面，2018 年全市环境空气质量与上年相比保持相对稳定，环境空气质量优良天数为 249 天，较 2017 年重度污染天数减少了 2 天，二氧化硫、二氧化氮、可吸入颗粒物等年均浓度均较上年有所下降；河流水质状况、湖泊水质状况均呈稳中向好态势。

科技创新方面，武汉市紧紧围绕科教兴国与创新驱动发展战略，以“五大工程、两大改革”为总抓手，积极推动国家知识产权强市建设，2018 年全市高新技术产业产值增长 13.5%，专利申请量和授权量增幅明显，2014～2018 年均呈现较为明显的上升态势（见图 5）。支持在武汉重点高校院所的科学研发，以专场对接活动为重点，大力实施高校院所科技成果转化对接，推进创新产业园区建设，新增加了省级及以上众创孵化机构 25 个；聚焦构建以信息技术、生命健康、智能制造三大重点产业为核心的现代化产业体系和未来产业布局优化，通过加快培育新的经济增长点，全力推动高新技术产业持续快速发展。

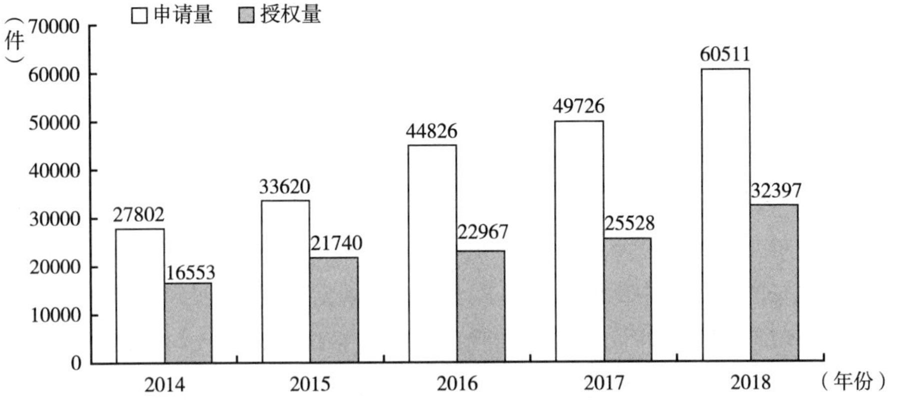

图 5　2014～2018 年武汉专利申请量和授权量

资料来源：2015～2018 年武汉市统计年鉴、2015～2019 年武汉市国民经济和社会发展统计公报。

（二）武汉建设国家中心城市的主要成就

近年来，武汉市发展坚持以习近平新时代中国特色社会主义思想为指导，以党的十九大精神为指引，在深刻认识建设国家中心城市的重大意义的基础之上，全面贯彻落实、有效对接国家发展战略，切实增强在国家城镇体系建设中的责任感。为早日建成国家中心城市，武汉市积极推进地区生产总值“万亿倍增”，在改革创新上着力聚焦、奋力赶超，以“行动政府”在复兴大武汉道路上迈出坚实步伐，在长江经济带和中部崛起中的核心带动作用更加凸显，在全国发展大局中的战略地位明显上升。

一是坚持与国家发展战略紧密对接、同频共振。国家发展战略中的“一带一路”倡议、长江经济带战略、中部崛起战略均与武汉息息相关，武汉面对重大战略机遇，充分发挥国家中心城市的核心作用。2018 年 11 月，中央全面深化改革委员会发布了《关于建立更加有效的区域协调发展新机制的意见》，把实施区域协调发展战略确立为新时代国家重大战略之一，有力指引了中部地区的发展，明确提出以武汉为中心，引领长江中游城市群发展，以驱动相关板块融合发展。通过自主创新示范区、自由贸易试验区、全面创新改革试验区、“两型”社会建设综合配套改革试验区等国家重大改革发展试点的平台，多角度叠加国家多重战略机遇，充分吸纳战略红利，从要素配置、政策配套、空间格局等多方面有效对接国家战略，建设全面开放的国家重大战略连接点，进而推动长江经济带、“一带一路”等的联动协同发展，成为重要节点综合战略枢纽。通过加大对外开放力度，实施对外开放平台功能，以提升武汉国家竞争力与影响力，打造面向国际、全球化的内陆开放高地。

二是超前布局武汉城市发展战略，增强城市未来发展竞争力。武汉始终坚持国家重大战略引领，为建设国家中心城市做超前规划，谋划武汉 2019、“万亿倍增”等重大发展战略，进而不断提高城市发展水平。继 2016 年 12 月国务院正式批复的《促进中部地区崛起“十三五”规划》，提出明确支持武汉建设国家中心城市之后，武汉正式迈向我国城镇体系塔尖，进入国家战略。2018 年 4 月，《武汉建设国家中心城市实施方案》正式提出，以城市总体规划的主动变革引领城市发展的战略转型，武汉建设国家中心城市将实施“三步走”战略：第一步到 2021 年，武汉地区生产总值要达到 2 万亿元左右，形成国家中心城市的基本框架；第二步到 2035 年，初步建成在全球范围内具有一定竞争力和影响力的国家中心城市，“三化”武汉基本建成，构建全国经济、高水平科技创新、商贸物流、综合交通枢纽等的中心地；第三步到 2049 年，在国家社会主义现代化进程中走在前列，成为具备国际影响力、全球竞争力和可持续发展能力的国家中心城市及世界亮点城市。

三是积极承担国家级改革试验，创新政策推进武汉国家中心城市高质量发展。武汉市自确立为国家中心城市以来，先后承担了 80 多项国家级改革试点。武汉坚持以问题为导向，将矛盾较为突出部位视为改革重点，在“三办”改革、取消 ETC 收费、放宽大学生落户、引导工商资本入乡、推进经济技术融合发展、税制改革、武汉“两型社会”建设综合配套改革、农村产权制度改革深入推进等多方面不断进行新的探索创新，投贷联动试点、外籍高层次人才引进服务政策完善、促进科教优势向经济优势转化的工研院模式在内的武汉改革举措均获得国家认可。其中以深化“放管服”为重点，深入实施“三办”改革，成了全国亮点。同时，武汉在全国率先建立税务部门协同注销机制，代开增值税电子普通发票；为了简化企业办事审批流程，率先实行“四十五证合一”；2017 年，率先创设网上群众工作部，利用“互联网 +”拓展网上群众路线，开创网络办理群众诉求新“闭环”；在强化司法体制改革方面，武汉承担了多个国家级试点，其中包括了武汉监察机关以公益诉讼办理了一批违建码头污染湖泊和长江水源地案件；在推进养老机构标准化建设方面，不仅将服务标准细化到 110 个流程，而且同时推广“互联网 + 居家养老”新模式；2018 年 4 月召开的市委常委会会议通过了《健康武汉 2035 规划》，在准确把握工作重点的同时，以抓好重大疫病防控为重心，发展健康产业，大力推动医疗与养老、旅游、互联网、体育的融合，倡导市民健康生活方式，更加注重医疗、医保、医药“三医”联动发展。一系列改革创新举措成为武汉城市发展的核心引擎，不仅强化了体制创新与有效供给，而且增强了内生动力，初步形成了较为先进的区域科技创新体系，为武汉城市创新驱动发展打下了坚实的地基。

四是着力构建优势产业集群，以巩固提升实体经济发展。武汉积极打造“大平台、大产业、大项目、大企业”工业重镇建设，以工业倍增与服务业升级计划提升产业综合竞争力，将现有支柱产业与战略性新兴产业深度融合，统筹发展产业体系的有机更迭，促使高新产业集群扎实推进。大批国家级制造业创新中心在武汉落地，2018 年 10 月 25 日，国家数字化设计与制造创新中心在武汉正式启动，该中心聚集 20 多位院士、专家和 70 多家龙头企业、科研院所的全国顶级资源，将致力于突破数字制造和智能制造关键领域核心工艺软件和核心工艺装备等方面的关键共性技术瓶颈，提升我国数字化智能化制造技术的核心竞争力。近年来，武汉市积极打造制造业创新中心矩阵，已形成两个国家制造业创新中心和 3 个省级制造业创新中心。2018 年 11 月，承载着推动我国信息光电子制造业“关键和共性技术协同研发”与“实现首次商业化”重任的国家光电信息中心总部落户武汉，助推信息光电子产业“缺芯”难题成功破解。截至此时，武汉成功获批武汉光电国家研究中心、国家信息光电子创新中心，成为继北京、上海以外，第三个拥有两家国家级制造业创新中心落户的城市。同时在北斗系统、智能网联汽车、氢能等领域已经布局创建省级创新中心。

二　武汉国家中心城市建设的特色、潜力与存在的主要问题

通过构建评价指标体系，在定量比较分析结果支撑下分析武汉国家中心城市建设的特色与潜力，进而分析存在的问题。

（一）武汉国家中心城市建设的特色与潜力分析

国家中心城市的发展基础是城市内涵和功能的具体体现，包含了经济发展水平、集聚水平、辐射带动水平以及交流水平；而在其快速成长阶段，充分体现了国家中心城市的潜力和竞争力，主要包括创新能力和信息共享能力两个方面；国家中心城市的建设目标体现着城市未来的发展方向，主要包括人文交流、生态宜居和绿色发展三个方面。基于此，本着科学性、系统性原则，建立国家中心城市综合评价指标体系（见表1），从基础、成长、目标三个层面分别反映国家中心城市发展过程中的城市现状、建设过程与最终状态。以武汉市为基准点，选取我国现有9个国家中心城市（北京、上海、天津、广州、重庆、成都、武汉、郑州、西安），运用层次分析法对9个国家中心城市综合体系中的各因子赋予相应权重，将城市综合能力作为决策层，基础职能、成长职能、目标职能作为目标层，经济发展中心、开放集聚中心、对外辐射中心、互动交往中心、科技创新中心、信息共享中心、宜居宜业中心、人文社会中心、绿色发展中心作为中间层，进行系统定量评价，以客观判断武汉国家中心城市建设的特色、潜力与存在的主要问题。

表1　国家中心城市综合评价指标体系

决策层	目标层	中间层	指标层	单位
城市综合能力	基础职能	经济发展中心	GDP	亿元
			人均GDP	万元
			第三产业产值占比	%
			地方财政收入	亿元
			GDP增长率	%

续表

决策层	目标层	中间层	指标层	单位
城市综合能力	基础职能	开放集聚中心	户籍人口	万人
			就业人口	万人
			常住外来人口	万人
			外资企业数量	个
			国企数量	个
		对外辐射中心	实际利用外资	亿美元
			社会消费品零售额	亿元
			城市外向功能	万人
			出口总额	亿美元
		互动交往中心	货运量	万吨
			客运量	万人次
	成长职能	科技创新中心	在读研究生数	万人
			科研机构数	个
			科研经费支出	亿元
			发明专利授权量	项
		信息共享中心	科技论文数	篇
			宽带用户数	万户
			人均移动电话数	个/人
	目标职能	宜居宜业中心	居民平均预期寿命	岁
			人均住房面积	平方米
			失业率	%
		人文社会中心	人均可支配收入	元
			公共交通里程	千米
			高等教育人数	万人
			文化产业 GDP	亿元
			医疗床位数	张
			公共图书馆藏书量	万册
			期刊出版量	亿册
			人均用水量	立方米
			人均用电量	千瓦时
		绿色发展中心	建成区绿化覆盖率	平方米
			人均公园绿地面积	平方米
			工业废水排放量	亿吨
			工业烟尘排放量	亿吨
			工业废物排放量	亿吨

资料来源：《2018 年武汉市统计公报》。

首先对逆向指标正向处理，包括失业率、人均用水量、人均用电量、人均公园绿地面积、工业废水排放量、工业烟尘排放量、工业废物排放量7个因子。由于各指标的性质不同及单位不同，通过对原始数据运用极值法，对各个指标数据进行无量纲化处理，以消除量纲不同所引起的误差。通过公式（1）对正向指标进行处理，通过公式（2）对负向指标进行处理。其中 $\max_{xij}$ 和 $\min_{xij}$ 分别为其中的最大值和最小值，X_{ij} 为处理后的标准值。处理后的数据取值为［0，1］，为了保证变量取值都大于零，本文采取用0.00001代替零值的方法，对零值进行处理。

$$X_{ij} = \frac{x_{ij} - \min_{xij}}{\max_{xij} - \min_{xij}} \tag{1}$$

$$X_{ij} = \frac{\max_{xij} - x_{ij}}{\max_{xij} - \min_{xij}} \tag{2}$$

为了克服主观确定权重的缺点，选用熵值法对指标权重进行确定。首先建立评价矩阵，建立 m 行 $\times n$ 列的原始数据矩阵 $X=(xij)\ m\times n$，m 为研究行政区的个数，n 为指标的个数；然后通过公式（3），运用标准化之后的标准值，进行信息熵的计算，其中，令 $k=(\ln m)^{-1}$，使 $0\leqslant Hj\leqslant 1$；最后通过公式（4）计算指标的权重。

$$\mathrm{Hj} = -k\sum_{i=1}^{m}\frac{Xij}{\sum_{i=1}^{m}Xij}\ln\frac{Xij}{\sum_{i=1}^{m}Xij} \tag{3}$$

$$\mathrm{Wj} = \frac{1-Hj}{\sum_{j=1}^{n}(1-Hj)} \tag{4}$$

根据各个因子的权重和9个国家中心城市的综合结果，最后计算得出各城市综合评价指数（见表2）。

表2　2018年国家中心城市综合评价指数

职能层	北京	上海	广州	成都	武汉	郑州	重庆	天津	西安
经济发展中心	0.8	0.8	0.7	0.5	0.5	0.6	0.4	0.2	0.4
开放集聚中心	0.55	0.65	0.38	0.45	0.09	0.25	0.45	0.33	0.12
对外辐射中心	0.55	1.00	0.45	0.18	0.01	0.13	0.29	0.15	0.05

续表

职能层	北京	上海	广州	成都	武汉	郑州	重庆	天津	西安
互动交往中心	0. 15	0. 52	0. 71	0. 59	0. 18	0. 26	0. 76	0. 55	0. 04
科技创新中心	0. 39	0. 21	0. 24	0. 24	0. 23	0. 15	0. 18	0. 04	0. 12
信息共享中心	0. 46	0. 32	0. 26	0. 26	0. 04	0. 03	0. 89	0. 03	0. 03
宜居宜业中心	0. 63	0. 71	0. 73	-0. 09	0. 33	0. 49	0. 13	0. 37	-0. 09
人文社会中心	0. 19	0. 49	0. 48	0. 48	0. 40	0. 38	0. 59	0. 19	0. 47
绿色发展中心	0. 50	0. 63	0. 68	0. 09	-0. 24	0. 12	0. 67	-0. 16	-0. 41
综合情况	0. 77	0. 76	0. 71	0. 47	0. 42	0. 33	0. 31	0. 28	0. 13
排名情况	1	2	3	4	5	6	7	8	9

通过对9个国家中心城市综合评价的比较分析（见图6），北京市城市综合水平最高，第二位是上海市，第三位是广州市，成都、武汉、郑州分别位列四至六位，重庆、天津、西安分别位列七至九位。国家中心城市综合指数的平均值为0.48，其中高于平均值的是北京、上海、广州，其余6个国家中心城市综合发展水平均低于国家平均水平，且前三位综合发展速度较快，结果说明其余6个城市综合发展不均衡问题依然突出。从分项职能来看，9个城市发展过程中更加注重基础职能的建设，而对成长职能的投入力度还不够。根据2018年9个国家中心城市的综合评价结果得出，多数城市发展依然将经济扩张作为发展的重心，对创新要素投入与绿色发展方面的关注还需进一步加强，应该更加关注创新、人文、绿色发展等方面的内容。

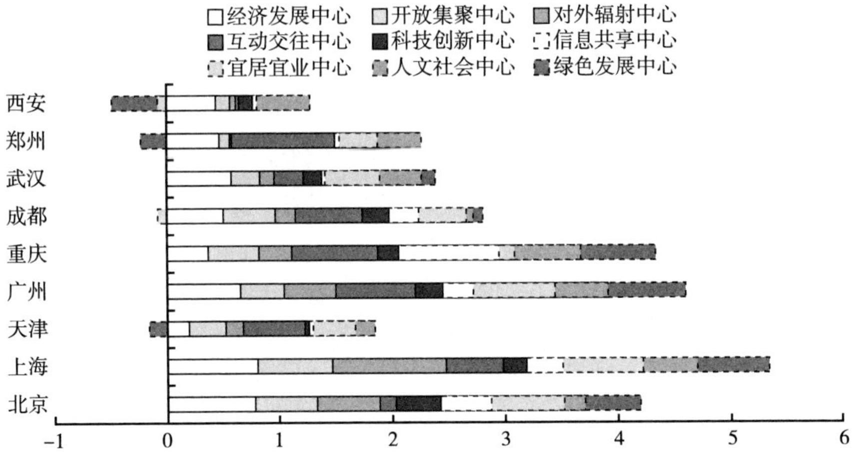

图6　2018年国家中心城市综合评价比较

从综合视角来看，武汉与国家中心城市综合平均水平相差较大。武汉在9个国家中心城市中列位第五，在第二批确立的4个国家中心城市中，武汉在区域中心城市中列第二（仅次于成都），而成都略高于武汉的综合评价指数，而且武汉相对于郑州、西安均表现出较大的领先优势。从平均职能水平来看，武汉有9项指标与国家中心城市平均水平有很大差距，同时，武汉也有7项指标在国家平均水平之上，说明武汉建设国家中心城市的过程中，优势与劣势并存，应充分发挥自身优势，认清发展短板，明确自身发展的核心职能定位。综合来看，武汉2018年建设国家中心城市的过程中，分解指标呈现两个层面：一个层面是有待提高性职能，包括开放集聚中心、互动交往中心、宜居宜业中心、信息共享中心和绿色发展中心；另一个层面是强化性职能，包括经济发展中心、对外辐射中心、科技创新中心、人文社会中心。

（二）武汉建设国家中心城市存在的问题

通过对9个国家中心城市的城市综合水平客观评价，以及武汉市综合对比分析，得出武汉在建设国家中心城市的过程中优势突出，但是短板依然明显，存在的主要问题如下。

第一，科教优势资源整合不足，成果转化落地有待提效。武汉市拥有丰富的科教、智库资源，但未能形成较为系统的科教智库系统。武汉作为中部地区中心城市之一、长江中游特大城市，应该充分发挥核心辐射带动作用，形成较为完善、具有决策研究比较优势的要地，并且充分利用科教资源优势，发展成为高质量智库的职能聚集地。根据以上研究结果发现，武汉未能通过富集的科教资源提升武汉城市的整体竞争力。同时，体现出的是武汉市在推进科技成果转化落地方面的质量和效率不足等问题，进而在整合科教资源、推进智库建设方面实施力度不够。

第二，开放水平需进一步强化。武汉虽然处于长江中游城市群，处于中国内陆地区，所处地理位置优越，但是与周边地区和国际交流较少，处于比较封闭的状况。在所有中心国家城市中，武汉的开放水平、互动交往等综合评比最低，由此可知武汉并没有将开放与交流放在主要位置，缺少地区及国家间的交流与合作。

第三，“三生”环境有待改善。虽然武汉大力发展基础建设，大力推进地铁建设，积极促进武汉交通等的便利，推动武汉快节奏发展。但是从综合评价得分结果可知，武汉的居住及就业环境与北、上、广、天和郑州差距较大。武汉对外交流与合作较少，对内的居住及就业环境一般，应引进外资或与外合作，改善地区的居住环境和就业环境，从而助推武汉城市影响力的提升。

三　武汉建设国家中心城市的辐射能力分析与评价

重点分析武汉市在武汉城市圈及长江经济带的辐射带动作用。

2016 年，国家发布长江经济带发展规划纲要，明确了武汉对长江经济带的核心引领作用。2018 年中央确定将区域协调发展战略确立为新时代国家重大战略之一，再次突出以武汉为中心，引领长江中游城市群发展。依据研究的科学性、系统性与可比较性原则，选取经济发展、城市规模、科技能力、对外开放、信息共享、交通通达六方面的 17 个指标反映武汉市综合实力发展情况（见表 3）。采用主成分分析法客观评析武汉建设国家中心城市对促进区域协调

表 3　武汉城市辐射力评价指标体系

目标层	准则层	领域层	指标层	单位
城市辐射力	内部经济实力（辐射源）	经济发展	人均 GDP	万元
			第三产业增加值占 GDP 比重	%
			人均固定资产投资额	元/人
			社会消费品零售总额	亿元
		城市规模	建成区面积	平方公里
			常住总人口	万人
		科技能力	高等学校数	个
			普通高校在校生人数	人
			专利授权量	件
			技术市场成交额	亿元
	外部联系程度（辐射流）	对外开放	进出口总额	亿美元
			实际利用外资额	亿美元
			国际旅游收入	亿美元
		信息共享	宽带用户数	万户
			邮电业务总量	亿元
		交通通达	地区客运总量	万人
			地区货运总量	万吨

资料来源：《2018 年武汉市统计公报》。

发展的辐射带动作用。选取长江经济带 11 直辖市和省会城市为研究对象，包括长沙、贵阳、成都、杭州、重庆、昆明、合肥、南昌、武汉、上海、南京，首先对原始数据进行标准化处理，然后运用主成分分析法对 11 个城市的综合辐射力进行客观评价。

根据计算得出，前四个主成分的累计贡献率为 97.07%，因此这四个主成分能较好地解释所选取的所有指标（限于篇幅，未列出），且所有指标对四个主成分均有贡献，所有指标对提取主成分的贡献程度，提取归纳对每个主成分贡献较大的变量，整理得出：F1 经济发展水平、F2 城市发展规模、F3 资本投入规模、F4 科技创新水平、E 综合辐射能力（见表 4）。

表 4　2018 年长江经济带省会以上城市辐射力四大主成分结果

	F1	排名	F2	排名	F3	排名	F4	排名	E	排名
上海市	6.876	1	-0.927	10	-0.501	10	-0.226	11	0.786	1
南京市	2.470	6	-0.199	8	0.879	4	0.309	5	0.577	4
杭州市	3.478	4	-1.339	11	1.097	3	1.663	1	0.663	2
合肥市	1.447	8	-0.040	7	0.750	5	0.349	4	0.353	8
南昌市	0.935	9	0.111	5	0.734	6	-0.218	10	0.141	11
武汉市	3.095	5	0.595	2	1.584	1	-0.075	9	0.378	6
长沙市	1.959	7	-0.274	9	0.536	7	0.187	7	0.640	3
重庆市	4.819	2	2.489	1	0.298	8	0.968	2	0.377	7
成都市	3.543	3	0.580	3	1.191	2	0.195	6	0.478	5
贵阳市	0.407	11	0.486	4	-1.004	11	0.852	3	0.169	10
昆明市	0.869	10	0.066	6	0.058	9	0.107	8	0.211	9

F1 综合反映了城市经济发展水平，主要贡献变量为人均 GDP、社会消费品零售总额、第三产业增加值占 GDP 比重以及邮电业务总量 4 个指标。由表 4 可知，上海、重庆、成都、杭州、武汉、南京、长沙、合肥的经济发展水平均大于 1，说明这 8 个城市经济发展水平均高于整体平均发展。武汉排名第五，且综合评价指数为 3.095，处于经济发展水平的第二阶梯，说明武汉在建设国家中心城市的过程中，经济发展水平稳中向好。

F2 综合反映了城市规模发展水平，主要贡献指标为建成区面积、普通高等学校在校生人数以及常住人口总数 3 个指标。其中综合排名中，武汉位列第二，武汉作为教育强省，科教资源丰裕，2018 年常住人口总数为 1108.1 万人，随着城市规模不断扩张，武汉实行总量与质量并行政策，对提升城市整体竞争力贡献度较大。

F3 主要贡献指标为人均固定资产投资额、地区客运总量以及地区货运总量，综合反映了资本投入规模水平。其中上海和贵阳为负值，说明在长江经济带 11 个省会中心城市中，只有这两个城市资本投入规模小于整体的平均水平。武汉市位列第一，由结果可知，武汉作为中部崛起、长江经济带、“一带一路”建设的多重重要节点城市，其资本投入规模体量较大。成都和杭州分别位列二、三位。

F4 主要贡献变量为专利授权量、技术市场成交额以及普通高等学校数，主要反映武汉科技创新能力。上海、南昌、武汉为负值，说明这三个城市科技创新能力低于整体水平，在科技创新能力为正的城市中，只有杭州结果大于 1。武汉作为中国重要的科教资源重地，拥有 88 所高校，但是科教创新能力却严重不足，这充分说明武汉科教、智库资源较为分散，科技成果转化落地效率有待提升。

城市综合辐射能力 E 是由 4 个主成分的权重所得，综合反映了长江经济带 11 个省会以上城市的经济发展、城市规模、资本投入、科技创新等整体水平。由表 4 可知，上海在政治、经济、文化、科技等方面综合发展能力较强，在长江经济带 11 个省会以上城市排名第一。其中武汉市处于综合辐射能力第二阶梯，综合排名第六，较第一阶梯的上海、杭州、长沙综合发展还有一定的差距，但是武汉辐射带动能力处于长江经济带整体的中等偏上水平。因此武汉作为中部地区的重要中心城市以及国家交通枢纽城市，需要精准定位发展短板，充分发挥人力资源、科教资源、智库资源等优势，提升辐射带动能力，在推动长江经济带发展的核心位置上发挥应有的作用。

四　武汉市国家中心城市建设发展态势与对策建议

（一）武汉市国家中心城市建设发展态势

2019 年是中华人民共和国成立 70 周年，武汉将举办第七届世界军人运动会，是建设好“三化”大武汉、国家中心城市至关重要的节点年份。武汉市正处于高质量发展的关键时期，紧密对接国家重大战略，落实全省“一芯两带三区”战略布局，深化供给侧结构性改革，全力推动高质量发展，与省政府工作保持高度一致，继续将国家重大战略叠加效应最大化、持续保持高质量发展的良好势头。深度领会习近平总书记先后两次视察武汉的重要精神，为武汉今后发展指明正确方向。

武汉建设国家中心城市的进程中，在不断强化责任的同时也注重超前布局，构建支撑武汉城市发展的产业体系与创新体系，重点围绕发挥改革创新这一核心引擎作用，大力发展战略性新兴产业，优化城市空间布局，统筹协调区域发展，以提升武汉整体国际化水平，增强城市未来发展的综合竞争能力。

未来武汉将继续拓宽领域，会在 20 个领域谋划建设制造业创新中心。计划在 2020 年形成两家以上国家级制造业创新中心，建设 5 个以上省级制造业创新中心，培育 5 个以上市级制造业创新中心，初步形成具有武汉特色的先进制造业创新体系，成为协同创新的技术策源地。武汉将继续坚持产业集约、集聚、集群发展，持续出台政策推进以城聚产、以产兴城、产城互动，有效推动城市功能和产业融合发展，进一步聚焦光电子信息、生物与健康、智能制造三大战略新兴产业。着力推进光电子信息、生物医药及医疗器械、汽车及零部件三大世界级产业集群快速建设，加快推进先进制造业与现代服务业深度融合发展，加快国家工业互联网顶级节点的建设和创新应用，推进规模以上工业企业技改项目全覆盖，以全面提升优势产业的综合竞争力。通过开展全面的质量提升行动，积极创建国家标准化改革创新先行区，打造具有国际竞争力的产业集群。

2018 年底，商务部发布了《关于开展步行街改造提升试点工作的通知》，江汉路将被改造提升为高品位步行街，入选全国首批 11 条试点步行街。2019 年武汉出台三年行动计划，拟打造国际消费中心城市，通过实施新消费促进、新商业地标建设、新零售之城建设、生活性服务业新供给 4 个专项行动，创造良好的消费环境，从供给端不断提升品质，从消费端创新发展模式，到 2021 年将武汉消费市场打造成为具有国际消费环境的现代商业化聚集地，以辐射国内消费市场、面向国家消费市场打响武汉品牌，这也将为武汉供应链创新与应用试点城市增添强有力的政策支持。

在招商引资方面，武汉将继续以创新全产业链发展为主要轴心，优化产业创新发展，力争实际到位资金年均增长约15%；在科技创新方面，武汉将打造“大学生最友好城市”，着力发展“菁英经济”，以百万大学生留汉创业就业工程与科技创新为核心，建设10家世界级产业研发中心与研发机构，大力发展高效高新产业，建设“中国制造2025”试点示范城市；航运是武汉未来发展的重点之一，武汉未来将继续全力优化营商环境，加大市场化改革力度，推进长江中游航运中心建设。

在交通环境方面，预计到2021年，武汉将全面建成运营400公里以上的轨道交通；在对外开放方面，通过加强对外贸易文化交流平台，支持企业“走出去”战略，如湖北自贸区武汉片区、中法武汉生态示范城等，以增加外贸出口总额，同时在有条件的国家建立专业性武汉产业园区，提升服务外包综合能力。同时中部地区涉外服务中心将建设在武汉，届时将引进更多领事机构和国际性组织落户，以提升对外交往层级，吸引更多海外学生来汉交流学习，打造“留学武汉”等更多品牌，同时实行高水平的贸易和投资自由化便利政策，大幅度放宽市场准入，加大武汉世界500强企业数量与质量，以扩大武汉的国际影响力。

同时武汉还将打造经济、科技创新、商贸物流、文化创意中心、建设世界一流的城市亮点区块；将水、陆、空统筹协调推进，建成国际性综合交通枢纽城市；打造美丽宜居之城、塑造国内外知名的滨水生态绿城等，这些超前布局将不断增强武汉城市综合竞争力，逐步成为面向未来的智慧城市。

（二）武汉市国家中心城市建设发展建议

1. 充分发挥国家战略的叠加效应，吸纳战略红利

武汉交通区位优势明显，人力资本富裕，历史人文资源丰富，辐射地域面积广阔，地区生产总值在亿万元台阶上稳步攀升，在建设国家中心城市过程中具有突出的比较优势，但是也存在城市建设管理相对滞后、创新产出不足、公共服务供给能力缺乏等发展短板，而武汉正面临着诸多国家战略叠加的重大机遇，因此，武汉需要从高度对接国家战略，从中部崛起、长江经济带发展、“一带一路”建设等重大国家战略规划中搭建平台，依托自身优势，从全局树立系统思维，精确把握发展短板，强化与战略平台的联通互动，努力在科技创新、信息枢纽等多方面开发潜力，以充分发挥武汉对长江经济带的核心促进作

用，与对武汉都市圈及长江中游城市群的辐射带动作用，使得与国家战略规划实现叠加效应的最大化。

2. 强化与周边城市的互联互通，加强武汉都市圈内部城市融合发展

从国家赋予武汉建设国家中心城市的功能定位来看，武汉是带动中部崛起的核心城市之一，且距离已经认可度较高的国家中心城市之间还存在较为明显的差距，因此，武汉需要加强与周边城市的联动发展。比如同为国家中心城市的郑州市，从建设国家中心的视角出发，郑州与武汉同处于国家区域协调发展格局的重要位置，且都属于带动中部崛起的重要核心城市；从城市空间发展来看，两市应该建立起较为密切的协调沟通机制，并充分发展自身优势，形成中部地区南北互相呼应的格局，从交通支撑上形成综合性运输枢纽；从统筹区域协调发展上，作为长江经济带、沿陇海经济带等的重要节点城市，两市联动发展有利于实现区域新的增长极，进而加快地区互联互通发展。同时，武汉作为关键要素支撑，要遵循城市群发展规划，推动武汉都市圈空间结构优化升级，以重点要素突破带动武汉都市圈整体快速向好发展。当前，武汉市的虹吸效应已然比较明显，综合实力较都市圈内其他城市差距较大，这不利于武汉与武汉都市圈内部的其他城市实现区域协调发展。因此，武汉在明确未来的城市发展功能与方向的基础上，强化基础设施支撑，提高与都市圈内部城市的有效衔接，从武汉都市圈一体化发展的整体利益和大格局出发，发挥武汉的核心城市作用，构建都市圈内部的利益共同体，形成可持续发展的创新模式。

3. 发挥科教强市优势，构建高质量智库支撑力量

武汉建设国家中心城市不仅是历史赋予武汉的重要使命，更是新时代国家给予武汉的战略使命，从建设国家中心城市这个迫切需要来看，作为长江经济带的核心城市需要高质量智库决策支撑，而从武汉智库发展的现状来看，缺少长期的、专注的、全方位的高质量研究智库。武汉作为教育强市，有丰富的科技教育资源，科技创新能力突出，科教综合实力在全国比较依然优势明显，面对建设国家中心城市的巨大社会需求，武汉应该切实加大高质量智库建设力度。首先，在深刻学习领会党的十九大关于加强中国特色新型智库建设的相关精神的基础上，更加系统地制定规划武汉市高质量智库发展规划；其次，由于武汉已有的智库资源较为分散低效，结合现有智库资源发展过程中出现的主要短板，重点整合湖北省智库资源与在汉高校智库资源，充分配置智库资源过程

中市场机制起到的决定性作用，使得武汉智库资源效率与质量并行；最后，积极构建并不断完善核心支撑智库资源，大力推进高质量智库的信息平台建设，实现并激励高质量智库成果的落地应用。

4. 创新绿色发展，提升武汉“三生”环境性能

从入选国家中心城市的客观指标来看，国家中心城市的人口规模更大，人口结构更加复杂，同时对宜居和宜业环境有更高层次的需求。但是，随着武汉城市规模的不断扩大，在享受人口红利的同时，原有的城市规模被不断地打破，导致城市公共产品供给出现不足现象，而且，由于城市管理部门等对城市规模扩张认识缺乏，造成管理模式转变相对滞后，城市环境没有得到相应的改善。从经济发展的角度来看，武汉生产性服务业领域的人力资本对于“三生”环境的要求较高，因此，需要在创新绿色产业对良好城市环境的要求基础之上，着力提升改善人们的“三生”环境。武汉要在增强经济、创新、开放等竞争能力的同时，重点提升生态宜居环境，以吸纳更多优秀人力资本来汉，使得武汉城市发展朝着更加文明、舒适、安全的方向发展。

参考文献

［1］李霞、戴胜利：《面向建设国家中心城市的智慧武汉发展评价及模式优化：理论与实证》，《中国软科学》2018 年第 1 期，第 77～89 页。

［2］田美玲、方世明：《武汉建设国家中心城市策略研究》，《北京规划建设》2017 年第 1 期，第 16～20 页。

［3］彭丽敏：《武汉建设国家中心城市的思考——以城市功能和国家战略的动态耦合为线索》，《城市发展研究》2013 年第 1 期，第 14～22 页。

［4］刘兰、罗凡：《武汉增强国家中心城市辐射力研究》，《江汉大学学报》（社会科学版）2015 年第 1 期，第 44～50＋124 页。

［5］李霞、戴胜利：《面向建设国家中心城市的智慧武汉发展评价及模式优化：理论与实证》，《中国软科学》2018 年第 1 期，第 77～89 页。

B.10
郑州建设国家中心城市的新成就、存在问题及对策建议

陈西川 *

摘　要：　随着郑州建设国家中心城市的稳步推进，支持郑州发展的国家战略已有中原城市群、郑州航空港综合经济实验区、郑洛新国家自主创新示范区、郑州自贸区等多项在相互叠加发挥作用，郑州在国家总体发展布局中的地位日益重要。本文分析郑州建设国家中心城市的历程，郑州建设国家中心城市的优势与基础、存在的问题与挑战，围绕国家对郑州建设国家中心城市的定位提出建议与重点努力方向。

关键词：　郑州　国家中心城市　中原城市群

一　郑州建设国家中心城市历程

（一）国家中心城市的提出及社会影响

中心城市是城市群功能分工和经济区生产布局的空间表现形式，是具有较强创新、服务和聚集扩散功能的区域经济中心。无论是区域中心城市还是国家中心城市，都具有中心城市的本质特征。国家中心城市是一国国际化和现代化水平的最高代表，不仅局限在国内，还要参与全球经济竞争，因而具有不同于

---

* 陈西川，管理学博士，郑州师范学院经济与管理学院院长、教授，研究方向为科技政策与科技管理、精益管理。

区域中心城市的功能与属性；国家中心城市是具有国家级战略功能的中心城市，在一定区域内居于社会经济的中心地位、能够辐射和带动周边区域经济发展的行政社会组织和经济组织的统一体。

2005 年，国家住房和城乡建设部在编制《全国城镇体系规划》时，首次提出建设国家中心城市这一概念。2008 年 12 月，“国家中心城市”正式出现在《珠江三角洲地区改革发展规划纲要》（以下简称《纲要》）中，《纲要》提出：“广州市要强化国家中心城市、综合性门户城市和区域文化教育中心的地位。”2010 年，住房和城乡建设部在《全国城镇体系规划（草案）》中明确提出建设北京、天津、上海、广州和重庆五大国家中心城市。

2016 年 2 月 5 日，国务院批复同意《广州市城市总体规划（2011—2020 年）》，将广州定位为国家历史文化名城、国家重要中心城市、国际商贸中心和综合交通枢纽。

2016 年 4 月 27 日，经国务院同意，国家发改委和住建部联合印发《成渝城市群发展规划》指导文件中，将成都定位为国家中心城市，要求成都“以建设国家中心城市为目标，增强成都西部地区重要的经济中心、科技中心、文创中心、对外交往中心和综合交通枢纽功能”。

2016 年 12 月 14 日，国家发改委出台了《关于支持武汉建设国家中心城市的指导意见》，明确提出“加快建成以全国经济中心、高水平科技创新中心、商贸物流中心和国际交往中心四大功能为支撑的国家中心城市”。

2016 年 12 月 20 日，国家发展和改革委员会正式印发了《促进中部地区崛起“十三五”规划》，明确提出“支持武汉、郑州建设国家中心城市”。

2017 年 1 月 22 日，国家发改委正式出台了《关于支持郑州建设国家中心城市的指导意见》，明确提出“郑州作为中原城市群核心城市，区位优势明显，腹地市场广阔，人力资源丰富，文化底蕴厚重”。

2018 年 2 月 2 日，经国务院同意，国家发展改革委、住房和城乡建设部印发《关中平原城市群发展规划》，明确指出“建设西安国家中心城市。加快西安中心城市建设步伐”“打造西部地区重要的经济中心、对外交往中心、丝路科创中心、丝路文化高地、内陆开放高地、国家综合交通枢纽”。

（二）郑州市的战略设想

1. 近期（启动开局阶段：2017～2020年）

开启郑州全面建设国家中心城市新征程，全面建成人民群众认可、经得起历史检验的高质量、高水平小康社会。综合竞争力持续增强，发展质量效益显著提升，生态环境有效改善，人民生活更有质量，各项事业全面发展。

2. 中期（加速推进阶段：2021～2035年）

郑州国家中心城市的地位更加突出，跻身国家创新型城市前列，建成国际综合枢纽、国际物流中心、国家重要的经济增长中心。争取提前五年，在2030年率先基本实现社会主义现代化。

3. 远期（全面建成阶段：2036～2050年）

到21世纪中叶，全面提升物质文明、政治文明、精神文明、社会文明、生态文明水平，实现治理体系和治理能力现代化，基本实现共同富裕，人民享有更加幸福安康的生活，建成社会主义现代化强市，成为具有全球影响力的世界城市。

二　郑州建设国家中心的定位、基础与优势

（一）中央对郑州国家中心城市建设的基本定位

国家发改委在《关于支持郑州建设国家中心城市的指导意见》中对郑州建设国家中心城市做出具体部署，要求郑州建设国际化现代都市，在综合经济实力上要全面提升，在经济发展新动能上要加快培育壮大，构建物流和交通枢纽，构筑内陆开放型经济高地，在引领中原城市群一体化发展、支撑中部崛起和服务全国发展大局中做出更大贡献。支持郑州“着力发展枢纽经济，着力提升科技创新能力，着力增强综合经济实力，努力建设具有创新活力、人文魅力、生态智慧、开放包容的国家中心城市”。

（二）郑州创建国家中心城市的基础与优势

1. 区位和交通枢纽优势显著

从全国区域分布看，郑州处于东南沿海和西部区域之间，属中部地区；从经济带分属上看，郑州同属沿陇海经济带和沿京广经济带，起着承东启西、连

南贯北的桥梁和纽带作用，位处推动中部崛起的核心区域。从中部区域看，郑州位于郑—汴—洛工业走廊和新—郑—漯产业发展带的交会点，是全国重要的铁路、航空、高速公路、电力、邮政电信枢纽城市，是国家首批跨境电子贸易试点城市和国家级互联网骨干直联点城市。郑州北站是亚洲最大的铁路编组站，郑州新郑国际机场是获批第五航权中国八大区域性枢纽机场之一，目前已开通航线236条，成为全国第二个实现航空、铁路、轨道交通、高速公路一体换乘机场，拥有铁路一类口岸和航空一类口岸各1个，铁路二类口岸和公路二类口岸各1个，具有良好的口岸经济发展基础，“四路协同”① 和境内外双枢纽、沿途多点集疏格局初步形成。中心城区“两横两纵+环线”快速路网体系基本形成，已开通至开封、焦作、许昌、新乡等多个地市的城际公交线，城市公交线路总长度超过5000公里，年运送乘客达10亿人次，成功创建“国家公交都市建设示范城市”。《郑州国际航空货运枢纽战略规划（2018—2035年）》《郑州铁路枢纽总图规划（2016—2030年）》成功获批，《畅通郑州白皮书（2019—2021年）》编制完成，“米”字形高铁网正在加快形成，交通枢纽优势日益提升。

2. 现代产业体系发展迅猛

至2018年底，郑州已初步形成电子信息、汽车及装备制造两个5000亿元级产值的产业集群，中牟汽车产业集聚区成为国家新型工业化产业示范基地。七大主导产业增加值增长7.6%，对全市工业增长的贡献率达到93.9%，郑州航空港经济综合实验区国家“双创”示范基地建设受到国务院表彰。郑东新区中央商务区成为“中国最具活力中央商务区”之一。国际物流园区晋升为国家级示范物流园区，同步成为陆港型、生产服务型、商贸服务型国家物流枢纽承载城市。新能源客车产销量突破2.5万辆，占全国的27%。全市三次产业结构比值从2015年末的2.1∶49.5∶48.4调整为1.81∶42.43∶55.76。

（三）郑州建设国家中心城市的进展

1. 经济社会发展主要指标实现历史性突破

至2018年底，伴随着郑州建设国家中心城市步伐的坚实推进，郑州站在

① “四路协同”：即“空中丝绸之路”（航空）、“陆上丝绸之路”（中欧班列）、“网上丝绸之路”和“海上丝绸之路”（郑州至连云港、青岛、天津等港口海铁联运班列累计已开行206班）。

了高质量发展的新起点。全市地区生产总值完成10143.3亿元，增长8.1%，在全国298个地级及以上城市排名中比上年前移1位，居第十六位；规模以上工业增加值增长6.8%，高耗能产业占比首次下降到40%以下；固定资产投资增长10.9%；工业投资增长11.8%，社会消费品零售总额增长9.7%；地方财政一般公共预算收入增长9%，达到1152.1亿元；税收占比74.6%，高出全省4个百分点。市场主体总量达到107.5万户，新增25.2万户，成为第8个超百万的省会城市；民营经济占GDP的比重达到58.9%，从业人员占城镇就业人员比重达87.3%。单位生产总值能耗降低率达到7%，万元工业增加值能耗下降14.8%。居民消费价格指数上涨2.4%，“衣食住行”等八大类商品价格均保持温和上涨。居民人均可支配收入完成33105元，增长8.3%，城乡居民收入比缩小到1.8。

2. 城市承载能力和服务功能日益完善

至2018年底，郑州市市域城市建成区面积1055.27平方公里，比上年扩大224.3平方公里，全市城镇化率达73.4%。教育、卫生、医疗、养老等公共服务设施加快布局，中央文化区（CCD）“四个中心”① 基本完工。

3. 空间布局和功能定位日益优化

2018年2月《郑州建设国家中心城市行动纲要（2017—2035年）》提出了“东扩、西拓、南延、北联、中优”的发展思路，持续优化市域空间布局，形成“双城引领②、三绿融合③、三轴交汇④、多极联动⑤”的空间形态，形成“主城区、航空城、多组团、多节点”的城镇体系；实施组团式发展，区分产业差异，明确发展定位，突出比较优势，彰显城市特色，以快速便捷的立体交

---

① “四个中心”规划范围为南水北调干渠以南，凯旋路以西，陇海路以北，用地面积约1.53平方公里。自西向东依次规划的项目是：奥体中心（体育场、体育馆、游泳馆）、文博艺术中心（美术馆、档案史志馆、博物馆、大剧院）、市民活动中心（科技馆、群艺馆、杂技馆、青少年活动中心、妇儿活动中心、健康中心）、现代传媒中心（报业大厦、广播电台、电视台）等16个单体项目。

② 双城引领：即优化主城，加快建设航空城（即面积达415平方公里的郑州航空港经济综合实验区），双城联动，引领城市与区域发展。

③ 三绿：黄河生态文化带、山区生态文化带和农区生态文化带。

④ 三轴：京广主轴、陇海主轴和机登洛次轴。

⑤ 多极：区域性功能中心、新的功能组团和外围特色小镇。

通为纽带，以大型绿地和生态为阻隔，推动新城组团与中心城区一体化发展；优先完成中牟、荥阳、新郑的撤县（市）改区，加快推进新密组团、登封组团、巩义组团建设，尽快实现全域城区化；加快中心城区功能疏解，以中心城区功能疏解为先导突破，有序推进产业转移，带动人口转移，优化城市布局，解决“大城市病”；优化省市公共服务机构布局，推动一般性批发市场和制造业外迁，加快火车站地区汽车中心站等长途客运站外迁，鼓励优质教育、医疗资源向新城组团转移。

三　郑州建设国家中心城市的目标

（一）积极推进创新创业中心建设，创新引领功能逐步提升

近年来，郑州市积极引导人才、技术、资金等创新要素向企业聚集，努力推动企业成为技术创新需求、研发投入、技术创新成果应用的主体；深入推进高校、科研院所与行业骨干企业联合搭建科技自主创新服务平台；积极构建财税、金融等政府各种政策投入，又有社会资本的多元化、多层次、多渠道的科技投入体系；实施人才强市战略，深入实施“智汇郑州·1125 聚才计划”“智汇郑州·1+7 人才引进计划”，加快引进培育创新创业大师人才及团队的步伐。创新创业引领功能逐步提升。至 2018 年底，全市组织实施科技项目比上年增长 8.8%，共 1336 项；其中省级以上项目增长 43.9%，共 436 项。有国家工程技术研究中心 6 个、国家级企业技术中心 19 个；省级工程技术研究中心 355 个、省级企业技术中心 280 个；省级重点实验室 117 个；获得国家科技进步奖 9 项，省级科技进步奖 38 项。全年专利申请量增长 38.8%，达到 70128 件；专利授权量增长 48.6%，达到 31585 件；全年签订技术合同增长 15.1%，达到 4349 份，技术合同成交金额增长 136.8%，达 82.4 亿元。2018 年，高新技术产业完成增加值 467.6 亿元，是 2010 年的 10.7 倍，有力支撑了郑州创业创新能力提升（见图 1）。

（二）积极推进经济增长中心建设，产业带动能力逐步提升

郑州市加快构建以先进制造业为支撑、以现代服务业为主导、以都市生态

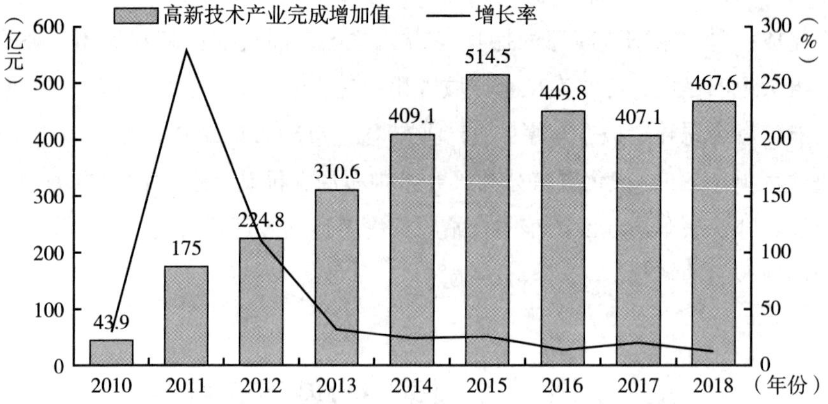

图1　2010～2018年郑州市高新技术产业完成增加值及增长率

资料来源：根据历年郑州市经济运行情况、郑州市国民经济和社会发展统计公报整理。

农业为基础，推动实体经济、科技创新、现代金融、人力资源协调发展；全市工信系统围绕工业稳增长、调结构、促转型，采取强化工业运行监测、推进招商引资和项目建设、加快产业转型升级、加快制造业创新发展、加强政策扶持引导等举措，推动产业集聚、提质转型，增强郑州产业在全省的要素集聚和辐射带动能力，推动产业发展水平加快向产业链中高端发展。通过增强微观主体活力，培育更加高效市场体系，将郑州打造成为中原经济区的经济增长极，带动中部地区崛起。至2018年底，全市年末总人口比上年增长2.6%，达到1013.6万人；全年完成生产总值比上年增长8.1%；人均生产总值比上年增长5.8%，城镇化率比上年提高1.2个百分点，达到73.4%；2018年，郑州市产业带动能力逐步提升（见图2）。

（三）积极推进华夏历史文明传承中心建设，城乡居民生活质量逐步提升

近年来，郑州以建设华夏历史文明传承创新中心为抓手，将保护和利用、传承与创新相结合，不断提升市民文明素质和城市文明程度，构建与国家中心城市定位相适应、体现社会主义核心价值观的开放包容文化，塑造现代化大都市人文精神，建设传统文化和现代文明交相辉映的国际文化大都市。通过打造

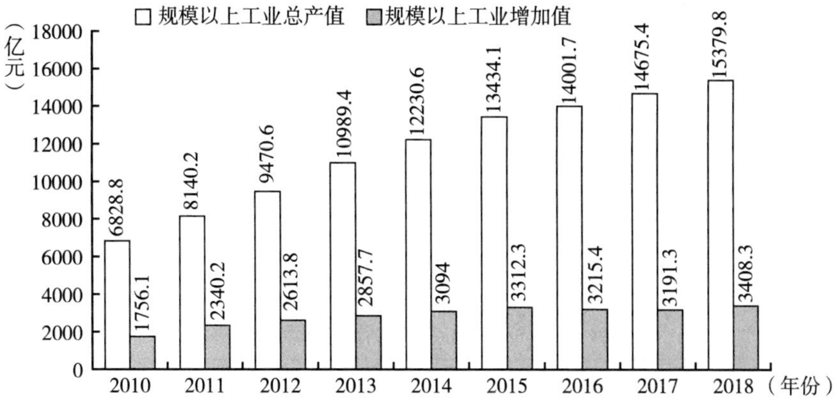

图2　2010～2018年郑州市郑州市规模以上工业总产值和增加值

资料来源：根据历年郑州市统计年鉴和郑州市国民经济和社会发展统计公报整理。

特色文化片区、推进文化精品工程、博物馆场馆建设、博物馆质量提升工程、积极申请世界文化遗产等措施，加强历史文化遗产的挖掘、保护和传承。以嵩山文化资源为依托，加大对外宣传力度，积极参与各类重大国际活动交流，开展多种多样的城市形象推介活动，中原文化的国际影响力进一步增强，中原文化与世界文化融合迈出坚实的步伐。至2018年底，全市共有艺术表演团体15个，公共图书馆17个，文化馆14个，博物馆38个，综合档案馆13个，已开放各类档案157.8万卷（件），有全国重点文物保护单位74处，国家级非物质文化遗产名录6个，全市广播、电视人口覆盖率达100%，有线电视用户155.8万户。居民生活质量逐步提升。

（四）积极推进国际综合交通和物流枢纽建设，辐射集聚功能逐步提升

以航空网为引领，以铁路网为骨架，以高等级公路网为支撑，通过打造联系全球、辐射全国的轮辐式航线网络，加快“米”字形高速铁路网和城际铁路网建设，持续完善市域内高速公路网格局、国道路网格局、市域内省道路网格局，构建以国际航空、高速铁路和高速公路为主体的现代化综合交通体系；优化“四港、多站”货运枢纽的综合布局，完善航空港、铁路港、公路港、海港“四港”功能，提升服务能力；推进“四枢、多站”建设，构建

四港联动、无缝衔接的综合枢纽体系；加强国际、国内和都市区运输大通道统筹布局，拓展国际航线，完善国内通道，构建结构合理、层次分明、功能完善、高度覆盖、深度通达的市域通道；着力形成“三网融合、四港联动、多式联运”的交通中枢，不断强化国家电力、信息、管道主枢纽建设，努力提升全球城市网络节点地位，建成国际综合枢纽城市。郑州市2013～2018交通运输情况见表1。

表1　2013～2018年郑州市交通运输情况

年份	货运周转量			客运周转量		
	铁路（亿吨公里）	航空（亿吨公里）	公路（亿吨公里）	铁路（亿人公里）	航空（亿人公里）	公路（亿人公里）
2013	217.2	0.5849	467.5	128	26.6	188
2014	199.9	4.7139	332.4	130.2	61.2	83.6
2015	172.7	5.4276	370	134.5	65.4	79.7
2016	176.8	14.7	494.8	138.2	65.9	107.7
2017	202.5	18.6	558.2	152.4	72.4	104.4
2018	213.8	29.1	621.4	157.1	87.3	97.1

资料来源：根据历年郑州市统计年鉴和郑州市国民经济和社会发展统计公报整理。

（五）积极推进内陆地区对外开放门户建设，商贸物流中心逐步提升

统筹推进郑州航空港经济综合实验区、郑州经济开发区、郑东新区等重要开放平台建设，打造开放平台支撑体系，进一步完善国际化口岸对外开放门户功能，建设完善郑州航空、铁路国际枢纽口岸，创新口岸通关物流机制，提升口岸跨境通关物流功能，强化口岸货运功能，完善口岸客运功能，打造国际邮件转运功能。加强与丝绸之路经济带沿线城市、长江经济带、京津冀地区、泛珠三角地区及东北地区的跨区域合作，推进交通基础设施、信息通信基础设施、口岸开放平台互联互通，强化重点领域互通合作，探索推进全球化口岸联盟。深度融入“一带一路”倡议，依托郑州优势旅游资源，搭建世界文明对话和文化交流的重要平台，密切人文交流，引进国外优质教育资源；营造国际营商环境，创新发展跨境E贸易产业，开展高水平国际经济交流合作，提升

城市国际化水平，建成国家内陆地区对外开放门户。郑州市2016～2018年货运变化见表2。

表2 郑州市2016～2018年商贸物流变化

年份	货运量			客运量		
	铁路（万吨）	航空（万吨）	公路（万吨）	铁路（万人）	航空（万人）	公路（万人）
2016	2750	19	19269	4875	479	11007
2017	3034.2	22.9	22073.2	5418.2	518.7	8815.4
2018	1920.3	31.5	25679	5780.5	813.1	8236

资料来源：根据历年郑州市统计年鉴和郑州市国民经济和社会发展统计公报整理。

四 郑州建设国家中心城市存在的问题及思考

（一）经济发展体量较小，城市综合承载力不足

郑州GDP尽管已突破万亿元，但与国内其他城市相比，GDP不到天津、重庆的50%，仅是武汉、成都的70%，GDP占全省的比重也远低于武汉、广州、成都和西安在各自省份中的占比。截至目前，在国家支持建设的国家中心城市中，郑州的区域面积较小，约为成都（14312平方公里）的一半。生态建设相对滞后，环境容量趋于饱和，生态环境承载能力薄弱。人均水资源占有量不足全国平均水平的1/10，空气质量在全国74个城市排名靠后。在全省和中原城市群中，郑州的人口和经济的首位度均不高；现代服务业中如金融、信息服务、科技研发等覆盖面小，综合服务功能水平存在短板，制约着城市对外辐射带动能力的提高。郑州市与其他国家中心城市的经济指标对比见表3。

表3 2018年郑州与其余八大国家中心城市经济指标比较

城市	GDP(亿元)	全部工业增加值(亿元)	固定资产投资(亿元)
北京	30320	4464.6	8062.2
上海	32679.87	8694.95	7623.4
天津	18809.64	6962.71	10643.3

续表

城市	GDP(亿元)	全部工业增加值(亿元)	固定资产投资(亿元)
广州	22859.35	5621.73	5938.4
重庆	20363.19	5997.7	18661.4
成都	15342.77	5663.75	8341.1
武汉	14847.29	5076.21	8706
郑州	10143.3	3746.2	8398.9
西安	8349.86	1874.36	8090.2

资料来源：根据各市2018年国民经济和社会发展统计公报整理。

（二）产业发展短板突出，发展潜力有待增强

郑州市工业大而不强，传统资源型产业占工业的比重仍在40%左右，大型龙头企业少，先进制造业和现代服务业的支撑主导作用还有待提高。第三产业占GDP比重达到50.7%，居全国35个大中城市第二十二位、省会城市第十七位。

1. 产业结构性问题依然存在

全市工业多布局在产业链的前端和价值链的中低端，产品附加值不高，高耗能产业占工业比重仍近40%，战略性新兴产业拉动作用不突出；服务业中传统商贸业、房地产业占比达到30%以上，科技服务、研发设计等新兴服务业占比偏低。

2. 现代服务业核心竞争力不足

服务业生产总值偏小，服务业固定资产投资中，金融、文化创意旅游、物流、科技服务业等产业投资占比偏低，产业发展后劲不足。从文化产业增加值占全市生产总值（GDP）的比重来看，郑州市落后于其他国家中心城市。文化企业经营规模偏小，竞争力和影响力弱，产业经营分散，产业规模化和集约化程度不高，大型骨干企业集团和具有国际国内知名文化品牌不多，缺乏“走出去”的雄厚实力。此外，文化产业与相关人才总量不足的矛盾比较突出，很大程度上制约了文化产业整体水平的提高。郑州市2010～2018年城镇及农村居民人均可支配收入见图3。

3. 农业发展质量仍有待提升

农业集约化、规模化水平亟待提高。郑州市农村土地流转率不到25%，

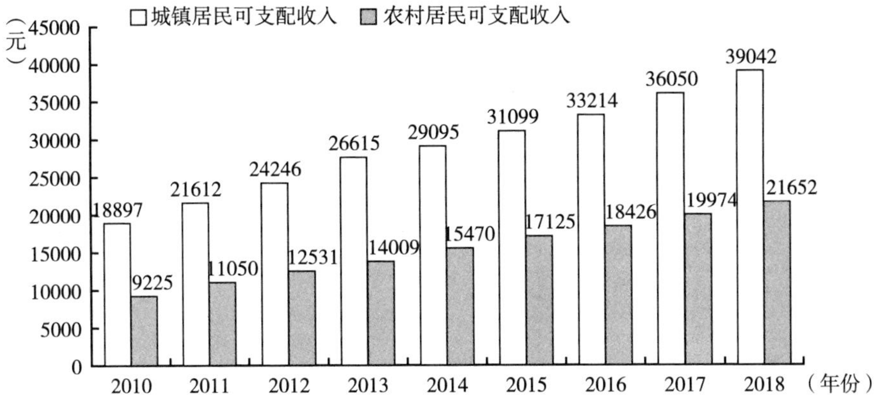

图3　2010～2018年郑州市城镇及农村居民人均可支配收入

资料来源：根据郑州市历年国民经济和社会发展统计公报整理。

远低于全省（38%）、全国（35%）的平均水平，农业土地亩均产出率低（3760元/亩），不到武汉（12980元/亩）的1/3，农业劳动生产率亟待提高。一产从业人员（91.7万人）是武汉市（45.6万人）两倍，但产业增加值不到武汉市1/2。从农业农村部公布的全国35个大中城市数据看，郑州农林牧渔业增加值的单位能耗最高、产出最低，其中单位产量耗能约是武汉市的4倍、成都市的3倍。

（三）科技创新基础仍较为薄弱，城市综合竞争力仍待提升

1. 全社会创新资源投入不足创新能力弱

郑州市研发活动主要集中在优势产业和大型企业，中小企业对研发普遍不够重视，企业自主创新意识亟待增强。创新主体整体能力有待提升。高新技术企业发展数量少、规模小、辐射力和带动力不强，创新型龙头企业、科技型企业发展速度慢、质量低。郑州市高端创新资源短缺，国家级大院大所只有12家，中科院系统的科研机构目前仅有1家，国家级重点实验室只有4家。在创新机制方面，郑州市激励创新、鼓励创业的发展环境亟待优化，与国内外加强交流与合作的体制、机制尚需完善，创新创业公共服务体系不够健全；驻郑高校、科研院所与产业发展结合不够紧密，科技成果转化率较低，支撑服务经济社会发展的能力有待加强。郑州市与其他国家中心城市产业结构和R&D经费支出及专利授权量对比见表4。

表 4 郑州市与其他国家中心城市产业结构（2018 年）和 R&D 经费支出（2017 年）及专利授权量（2018 年）对比

城市	第三产业增加值占GDP的比重（2018年）	R&D经费支出（亿元）（2017年）	R&D经费支出占GDP的比重（%）（2017年）	专利授权量（件）（2018年）
北京	80.98%	1579.7	5.64%	123000
上海	69.9%	1205.2	3.93%	92460
天津	58.6%	458.7	2.47%	54700
广州	71.75%	537.58	2.5%	89826
重庆	52.3%	364.6	1.88%	45688
成都	61.3%	331.3	2.39%	57370
武汉	54.6%	429.13	3.2%	32397
郑州	54.7%	158.7	1.29%（全省）	31583
西安	61.9%	360.17	4.82%	71250（申请量）

资料来源：根据各市 2016～2018 年国民经济和社会发展统计公报整理。

2. 郑洛新国家自主创新示范区核心区建设水平有待提高

目前，在自创区发展体制机制方面，核心区尚未真正建立充分适应自身建设发展需要、激发活力和动力、调动积极性和创造性的体制机制，一定程度上制约了自创区核心区的发展；在核心区的空间布局方面，99 平方公里的发展腹地（其中，建设用地规模 77 平方公里，基本农田 4.67 平方公里，其他不符合规划的有条件和限制用地约 17 平方公里）远远不能适应核心区建设与发展的实际需要；在各类创新型资源方面，高新技术产业发展人才总量不足，缺乏人力资源的支撑，高等院校数量、在校大学生人数、两院院士拥有量、千人计划专家数、高新技术企业数量、国家科技企业孵化器个数等，郑州市与其他国家中心城市相比都存在很大差距，不能满足科技创新需求和郑州片区的发展需求；在新兴产业总体规模方面，核心区战略性新兴产业整体规模偏小、数量少，缺少一批规模大、带动能力强的龙头企业，行业带动效应不强，产业体系有待完善。

（四）现代国际物流中心建设相对滞后，极具国际影响力的物流中心城市亟待加快构建

1. 郑州国际物流园区发展仍然存在短板与不足

郑州国际物流园区业务产业链条较短，投入产出比偏低；园区业务主要集

中在仓储、运输两大传统环节，物流项目整体呈现小而散的特征，总部型、平台型、供应链型项目少，龙头项目带动力不强，中小项目偏多，没有全面形成生产力，对营业收入、税收等贡献有限，亟须进行整合提升。园区智慧化程度整体偏低，骨干物流企业信息化程度高，中小物流企业信息化程度低；各类物流企业信息系统应用较广，政府物流公共信息服务平台建设滞后；园区物流信息综合服务商不足，为数众多的中小物流企业，产业层次低，物流信息化程度不高，信息集成整合能力较差，亟须进行资源整合和信息化改造。物流基础设施不完善，信息集成度不高。园区与主城区、航空港区、郑东新区及郑民高速、国道新107线等干线公路的连接还没有完全打通，公共停车场、公共货场、公共信息平台等物流专用设施也没有完全建设到位，雨雪雾等恶劣天气或运输高峰期，乱停乱放、交通拥堵等问题较为突出，园区整体支撑承载能力有待进一步提高。

2. 现代物流基础设施建设相对滞后

随着郑州交通枢纽地位的提升，物流基础设施总体规模小、结构不合理、配套不齐全、承载能力弱等问题，成为制约郑州现代物流业发展和现代国际物流中心建设的瓶颈。如目前郑州铁路集装箱中心站仅有两条装卸线在运营，随着中欧班列（郑州）的加密开行，铁路口岸装卸能力远不能满足实际需要。目前郑州物流业的运输、储存，大都处于较为低级阶段，物流基础设施与国家同类城市相比存在很大的差距，许多零担物流企业无稳定经营场所，严重制约零担物流企业发展。

3. 财政支持体系及多式联运间的衔接有待完善

目前郑州对航空、郑欧班列、口岸建设、跨境电子商务服务等方面的财政支持政策和支持体系比较分散，没有统领的物流政策支持体系对畅通国际物流通道、增强国际枢纽能级、提升口岸通关服务、提升物流现代化水平、创新物流组织模式等的各个环节进行系统的政策支持。在航空、铁路、公路等多种运输方式之间的衔接上主要存在标准不统一、衔接不顺畅、中转不高效、通关不便利等突出问题。尤其是铁路舱单与其他运输方式不能有效互认对接，成为制约郑州国际物流发展的主要障碍，机场、铁路及邮政口岸之间紧密连接、有效互动还不够充分。据郑州海关反映，海关监管与铁路部门安全检查存在冲突，为保证对货物的有效监管，海关会对集装箱施加关封或者关锁，而铁路为了防止偏重需对集装箱装载状态进行开箱检查。从公路运输等其他运输方式转关过来的集装箱已施加关封，铁路部门无法开箱检查货物的品名及进行装载加固，造成海关监管与运输安全的不协调。

（五）投资环境亟待优化，“互联网+政务服务”仍需不断推进

1. 政务服务效率亟待提升

近年来，郑州市着手开展电子政务的顶层设计和标准规范的编制工作，相继发布了一批电子政务领域的政策文件，由于各部门之间缺乏统一的标准体系的支撑，系统和数据标准不统一，严重影响了数据共享与业务协同工作的开展和推进，导致数据导引、数据获取、交互交换中发生迟滞、偏差，影响政务效率提升。

2. 政务服务窗口受理人员专业人才不足

电子政务建设是体系性工作，无论是基础性的云平台搭建、数据共享还是顶层规划设计都需要大量的具有先进电子政务理念的专业技术人才；由于前期信息化水平薄弱，窗口受理人员和专业技术人才严重不足，与先进城市的政务管理水平差距明显，与国家“互联网+政务服务”以及“放管服”改革的相关要求还存在很大差距，需加大包括资金、人才在内的各方支持力度，改善提升政务服务环境、投资环境。

（六）开放型经济发展缓慢，对外开放水平亟待提升

郑州市近年来对外开放工作已呈现良好发展态势，但与其他国家中心城市相比，有差距、存短板。

1. 中国（河南）自由贸易试验区郑州片区功能亟待提升

郑州片区对外开放水平整体偏低，对国际创新资源吸引力不足，对外资、外企、国际高端人才等创新资源或主体的吸引力较弱。跨部门沟通协调机制需进一步健全。改革创新试点任务牵头部门与配合部门的协调推进工作机制有待完善；郑州片区管委会与政府其他部门的沟通协调机制有待进一步加强；跨部门工作对接与信息共享方面需进一步完善，与开封片区、洛阳片区之间发展尚未形成合力；与境内外其他自贸试验区合作力度需持续加强；与中原经济区的协同联动发展还需进一步强化。

2. 郑州市城市国际化程度有待提高

郑州不临海，没有出海港口，海洋经济与口岸工业发展受限；虽然目前郑欧班列、跨境 E 贸易取得了不错成绩，郑州航空港经济综合实验区的功能也在不断提升，但与北京、上海、广州等航空港国际化程度高的城市相比，郑州的国际交往途径明显偏少，制约了郑州国际化程度的提升，限制了旅游、会展等一系列产业的提升发展。目前，郑州市服务业中有相当大一部分是房地产及其相关产业，服务经济和创意经济的层次不高、比重偏低、特色不明显、企业规模普遍较小，与郑州国际化程度有直接关系。

3. 对外贸易结构亟须优化

郑州市外贸进出口总额尽管高于周边城市，但贸易中对单一企业依赖程度过高问题仍然存在。单一企业富士康进出口占郑州市进出口总额的 80%，严重影响郑州市进出口平稳发展；对外招引高端制造业、现代服务业领域重大项目不多，产业转型升级后劲乏力，引进的国内外大型央企、行业领军企业偏少，对相关产业的辐射带动作用不强，制约了郑州市经济结构及对外贸易结构的调整，影响了郑州市经济对外开放的广度、深度。

（七）航空港实验区发展提升空间大，引领作用未能得到充分发挥

1. 航空枢纽建设、产业发展亟待加强

目前，在郑州航空港经济综合实验区入驻的基地公司只有南航河南航空有限公司一家合资基地航空公司，与支撑建设国际航空客货运枢纽的目标尚有差距，亟须扩大客货运基地公司的数量和规模；航空港实验区整体产业层次还处在产业链末端，创新型、龙头型、拉动型的重大项目缺乏，产业核心竞争力不强。

2. 国内外经济合作体制机制仍有待创新

航空枢纽地位的确立，某种程度上是业务范围的拓展，航空物流、装备制造、货运代理、高端技术维修、投融资等，一方面与专业人才有关，另一方面涉及各种制度与规定的衔接与创新，若没有完备的体制机制作为保障，经济合作的深度、广度和力度都会受到制约和影响，也影响枢纽功能的发挥。

3. 实验区国际航空物流中心集聚能力有待提升

市场主体小、散、弱，规模化、网络化的航空运输集团、大型航空物流综

合服务商不足；口岸基础设施建设缺乏有效衔接，多式联运发展较慢，通道不畅；国际化程度低，航空运输产业的集群效应不明显；口岸、企业、行业、信息平台之间的对接效率需要提升。国际航空物流中心的能力尚需进一步确认。

五　郑州建设国家中心城市的若干建议

（一）建设极具活力和区域竞争力的创新创业中心，打造郑州创新创业新引擎

1. 支持郑洛新国家自主创新示范区核心区扩区

郑州国家高新区作为郑洛新国家自主创新示范区的核心区域，总规划面积99平方公里，规模远小于火炬统计排名接近的武汉东湖高新区（518平方公里）、西安高新区（307平方公里）、济南高新区（191平方公里）、长沙高新区（140平方公里）。由于郑州高新区周边可供发展的空间遍布拟划定的永久基本农田，省市自身统筹能力受限，自创区国家战略的实施将受到重大影响。建议争取国家有关部门对国家自主创新示范区用地实施国家统筹。

2. 着力打造国家重要的创新创业中心

构筑开放式创新高地，全面融入全球创新体系，高标准建设中原科创谷，提升企业核心竞争力。强化协同创新，推进和鼓励企业、高校、科研院所联合构建产业技术创新战略联盟；提升国家技术转移郑州中心、国家专利审查协作河南中心等机构的辐射能级，建设全国重要的科技成果交易中心和转化高地。

3. 积极推进科技与金融结合

推动产、学、研、金深度结合，强化产业链、创新链、资金链“三链融合”。支持郑州市建设国家促进科技和金融结合试点城市，形成可复制的经验进行推广。设立郑洛新自主创新示范区科技成果转化引导基金，省市联动，引导社会资本支持科技创新，发展科技产业。发挥省科技金融引导专项资金作用，省市结合，开展“科技保”和“科技贷”业务，建立科技贷款风险补偿机制，引导银行加大对科技型企业的信贷支持力度，破解科技型中小企业贷款难题。鼓励银行业金融机构产品和服务方式创新，开展知识产权质押贷款、股

权质押贷款等贷款业务，为科技成果转化提供金融支持。培育和支持符合条件的科技型企业在境内外资本市场上市挂牌和融资。充分发挥河南省技术产权交易所的作用，为科技型中小企业融资提供服务。支持符合条件的科技型中小企业通过发行债券和实施资产证券化等方式拓宽融资渠道。鼓励发展股权投资基金和创业投资基金，规范发展股权众筹融资，完善科技型企业投融资机制，进一步完善科技信贷、科技保险等创新发展政策措施。积极争取在郑洛新国家自主创新示范区开展投贷联动试点。

（二）建设国家重要的经济增长中心，打造郑州产业转型升级新支撑

1. 发展先进制造业

全面对接“中国制造2025”国家战略和发展规划，强化谋划，做好顶层设计。结合郑州市新一轮城市总体规划编制，充分利用新技术、新产业、新业态、新模式等高质量发展要素，明确下一步重点发展的主导产业、新兴产业，谋定产业空间布局，提升国家中心城市产业辐射和带动作用；围绕重点工程等重要事项，以培育国家级、世界级产业集群为目标，加快产业优化升级，加快高质量发展。坚持质量第一、效益优先，以供给侧结构性改革为主线，加快传统产业的智能化、绿色化和技术改造，推进传统产业智能升级；可针对打造产业高质量发展的载体平台出台专门政策，整合人才、资金、土地、能源等资源要素，培育重点产业生态圈，形成产业可持续健康发展的总体格局。

2. 大力发展现代服务业

围绕国际枢纽物流中心、国家区域性现代金融中心，构建“融资多元、服务高效、一体联控”的金融服务体系；抓好国家现代物流创新发展试点城市建设，做强物流业，筑牢国际枢纽物流中心基础；继续做好安置房网签工作，促使房地产市场平稳健康发展；结合地方特色培育文化创意旅游业，针对河南实际，谋划健康养老产业发展，提升现代商贸会展业发展水平。

3. 补齐现代农业发展短板

精准支农惠农，用活用好财政支农资金，发展蔬菜、花卉、水果、食用菌等高效种植业、高效畜牧业；借鉴其他地区经验，在确保财政支农资金效能充分发挥功能的前提下，用以奖代补支持方式，有效推动农业项目建设；

制定符合郑州市发展实际的农业建设项目负面清单，激发社会力量推动都市生态农业发展活力，形成农业产业新增长点，推动郑州市农村发展、农民致富。

（三）建设华夏历史文明传承创新中心，打造宜居宜业宜游宜商的国际化大都市

1. 传承保护和创新发展古都文化、功夫文化、根亲文化和儒释道文化，提升凝聚荟萃、辐射带动和展示交流功能

郑州是华夏文明的重要发祥地、国家历史文化名城，是中国八大古都之一、国家重点支持的六个大遗址片区之一、世界历史都市联盟成员。在华夏民族传统宇宙观中，郑州地区是“天地之中心”，自古以来就是文明交流的十字要冲，域内留存了丰富的文化遗产。以此为依托提升嵩山论坛影响力，打造中华文明与世界文明对话交流的重要平台，培养高端文化人才，培养造就一批在国内外享有盛誉的文化名家、艺术大师和文化大使。

2. 大力发展数字传媒、创意设计、动漫游戏等文创产业

在技术革新的创客时代，那些既往“高新”的“智能技术”“互联网技术”“影像处理技术”的成本极大地降低。对于这些相对容易可得的技术，无论做什么，技术都能充分体现其应用性，能够解决实际应用场景中的问题，或是艺术表达中的某一技术环节。借助现代信息影像处理技术，推进文化旅游融合发展，创建国家全域旅游示范区，把郑州建成全球重要的宜居的文化旅游目的地城市。

（四）建设国际综合交通和物流枢纽，打造郑州综合交通枢纽升级版

1. 以“综合枢纽”战略引入基地货运航空公司，构建全球航空货运通道

随着“一带一路”建设深入，郑州将加快实施航空、铁路、公路国际国内“综合枢纽”战略，提升郑州主要节点城市辐射带动作用，推动跨区域基础设施协同共建和高效衔接，建设空中、陆上和网上丝绸之路，建成高效、便捷的铁路、航空、公路网络和功能完善的综合交通枢纽，构建多式联运体系，建设全方位的物流集疏网络。

2. 强化与国际物流集成商等货运服务企业合作，完善航空货运集疏体系

推进大型航空枢纽建设，强化陆空交通衔接，构建设施先进、网络完善、支撑有力、运行高效的航空货运集疏系统。打造交通物流信息平台，建设多式联运全国信息中心，打通物流信息链，推动大数据、物联网和新一代信息技术等前沿技术和交通物流深度融合。

（五）建设内陆地区对外开放门户，打造交换功能更加强大的国家商贸物流中心

1. 构建服务于国家战略的内陆地区全方位对外开放门户

大力发展口岸经济，构建服务于国家战略的内陆地区全方位对外开放门户。口岸是一个地区经济发展及对外开放程度的标志和门户。郑州依托空中国际物流走廊、铁路国际物流枢纽的构建，大力发展口岸经济，加速融入“一带一路”发展大格局。郑州机场口岸实施 7×24 小时通关服务，实行单证快速审结。郑州已成“国际物流通道枢纽”和“买全球、卖全球”全球网购商品集散分拨中心和丝绸之路经济带上最活跃的物流通道枢纽。

2. 完善复合型功能口岸平台建设

研究支持机场集团、陆港公司、保税集团和省内外大型龙头物流企业及国际战略投资者共同出资入股成立新机构，负责物流企业多式联运数据交易服务，提升现代综合交通枢纽和现代物流中心功能。

3. 打造交换功能更加强大的国家商贸物流中心

促进航空枢纽、铁路枢纽、公路枢纽一体化，统筹集疏网络建设，形成以航空枢纽为主体，陆空衔接、公铁集疏、内捷外畅的综合枢纽优势，构建网络通达、衔接高效、费用低廉、方式多样的多式联运国际物流中心；鼓励物流企业投资并购、资产重组、强强联合、战略协作，提升物流企业的规模化、集约化水平；围绕机场二期工程、富士康“五五”实施专案、三大片区开发、重大签约项目开工建设、重大招商项目引进落地、重大要素平台打造，巩固确立全球智能终端生产基地和国际航空物流中心的地位；依托“智汇郑州”人才工程“1+N”等政策体系，对商贸物流中心建设给予人才、土地、资金全方位支持。

参考文献

[1] 国家发展改革委:《国家发展改革委关于支持郑州建设国家中心城市的指导意见》(发改规划〔2017〕154 号)。

[2] 郑州市人民政府:《郑州建设国家中心城市行动纲要(2017—2035 年)的通知》。

B.11
西安国家中心城市建设的主要做法、机遇挑战及对策建议

王晓娟*

摘　要： 2018年，西安正式启动国家中心城市的建设，并在开局之年取得了初步的成效。经济指标取得新进展，经济结构调整加快，大西安发展要素加速聚集，开放水平明显提升，生态文明建设推进有力。与此同时，由于西安国家中心城市起步较晚，仍然存在着诸如经济基础实力较弱、科技成果产业化低，民营经济活力不足等问题。本报告针对当前西安国家中心城市建设中经济综合实力基础较弱，辐射带动能力发挥等亟待破解的重大问题，提出了建设大西安都市圈带动关中城市群加速崛起等具有针对性的对策建议。

关键词： 西安　国家中心城市　“一带一路”　国际化

一　西安国家中心城市建设开局良好

（一）主要经济指标再上新台阶

2018年是西安国家中心城市的开局之年，西安经济开始加速，西安地区生产总值迈上新台阶，实现了同比增长8.2%，比2017年提高了0.5个百分点，高于全国1.6个百分点，在全国副省级城市中增速位列第一。地区生产总

---

* 王晓娟，硕士，陕西省社会科学院助理研究员，研究方向为区域经济、金融投资。

值量达到8349.86亿元，进入全国城市20强。西安在关中城市群以及陕西的经济综合实力进一步凸显。2018年，西安的地区生产总值占陕西的34.2%，创历史新高。得益于“长安号”中欧货运班列的带动，西安的进出口总值取得了29.6%的超高速增长，增长速度位居副省级城市首位。进出口总额首次突破3000亿元大关。全社会固定资产投资、社会消费品零售总额和地方财政一般公共预算收入也取得了较高增长，增长率分别为8.4%、9.6%和10.8%。2018年，西安文化旅游迎来了大爆发，受益于西安网红城市效应、“西安年·最中国”“春满中国·醉西安”“唐都长安1400年”等旅游策划项目的宣传和影响力，西安迅速成为年度最火爆的旅游城市，荣获2018年度《中国国家旅游》“最佳文化旅游目的地”称号。2018年，西安接待游客数量和旅游收入迎来飞速增长，旅游人次突破2.47亿，增长率为36.7%，旅游总收入2554.81亿元，增长率为56.4%（见表1）。西安的国际化城市品牌和影响力进一步提升。

表1　2018年西安主要经济指标完成情况

主要指标	总额	增速(%)
地区生产总值(亿元)	8349.86	8.2
全社会固定资产投资(亿元)	8191.21	8.4
社会消费品零售总额(亿元)	4658.72	9.6
进出口总值(亿元)	3303.87	29.6
实际利用外商直接投资(亿美元)	63.54	14.9
旅游业总收入(亿元)	2554.81	56.4
地方财政一般公共预算收入(亿元)	684.71	10.8

资料来源：西安统计局网站。

（二）经济结构持续优化

2018年，在西安投资结构加速转变的有力带动下，西安的经济结构不断优化。西安经济的动力开始启动，投资动能快速转换，产业迈向高端化，科技创新涌动。主要表现在工业投资增速扭负为正加快，工业增长增加值稳步回升，成为西安经济的中流砥柱。2018年，西安一产增加值为258.82亿元；二产增加值为2925.61亿元，增长8.5%；三产增加值为5165.43亿元。三次产业比值为3.1∶35.0∶61.9。三次产业结构不断优化。第二产业恢复强势增长，工业投资加快，第三产业发展迅猛，比重同比提高0.4个百分点，拉动GDP的作用增强。特别是战略性新兴产业发展势头迅猛良好，为西安经济发展注入了强大的内生力量。产业加速迈向中高端，2018年，西安规模以上工业战略性新兴产业实现总产值2334.16亿元，占规上工业比重为40.7%，成为支撑西安工业经济发展的重要力量。在七大战略性新型产业中，新一代信息技术产业和新能源产业产值占比最高，分别是28.6%和22.8%，产值占到了总产值的半壁江山。从产业增长速度来看，高端装备制造业、新材料产业、新能源汽车产业和新能源产业增长速度相对较为迅速，分别是14.5%、15.1%、34.3%和14.1%，表现出较大的发展潜力。

表2　2018年西安规模以上工业战略性新兴产业指标统计

	工业总产值（亿元）	增速（%）	比重（%）	贡献率（%）	拉动点数（百分点）
规上工业	5734.50	12.2	—	—	—
规模以上工业战略性新兴产业	2334.16	11.1	40.7	37.3	4.5
新一代信息技术产业	668.22	1.0	28.6	2.8	0.3
高端装备制造业产业	222.37	14.5	9.5	12.1	1.3
新材料产业	237.27	15.1	10.2	13.4	1.5
生物产业	274.73	10.1	11.8	10.9	1.2
新能源汽车产业	247.67	34.3	10.6	27.2	3.0
新能源产业	531.23	14.1	22.8	28.3	3.1
节能环保产业	152.67	8.7	6.5	5.2	0.6

资料来源：西安统计局网站。

（三）大西安发展要素聚集

2018年以来，西安户籍新政成效进一步凸显，西安的人才“西引力”增强。2018年，西安新落户人口接近80万人。本科以上学历落户和人才引进占迁入人才的六成以上，较高质量的人才落户无疑会为西安国家中心城市的建设和发展贡献更多的力量。随着近年来西安营商环境的不断改善，各类创业人才也不断涌现。2018 年，西安新增市场主体实现了飞速增长，新登记市场主体达到 54.3 万户，同比增长 91.7%。科技创新成果层出不穷，支撑了西安科研新高地的建设，也助推和激发了“双创”的蓬勃发展，科研创新主体不断增多。科技部门数据显示，截至 2018 年底，西安累计建成了各类双创平台和载体 1156 个，建成总面积 3281 万平方米，入孵企业达 4.1 万家，就业人数达 40 余万人。2018 年，发明专利 26675 件，发明专利授权量 8096 件，技术合同成交额 1030 亿元，同比增长 21%。

（四）开放水平显著提升

2018 年，西安内陆型改革开放新高地建设深入推进。以“三个经济”为抓手，不断扩大对外开放，提升国际化水平，推进国家中心城市的开放步伐。强化自贸区开放平台建设，不断提升投资便利化，顺利吸收了三星二期、华为全球技术中心、阿里巴巴西部总部等一批重大项目落户西安，同时，继续吸引了更多的市场主体入驻自贸区。2018 年，自贸区新增企业主体 15000 余家，新增注册资本 2500 多亿元，其中新增外资企业 200 余家，注册资本在亿元以上的企业 347 家，市场主体的活力进一步显现。同时，围绕“一带一路”建设和国家中心城市，西安成功获批了省“一带一路”综合改革开放试验区、临空经济示范区、跨境电商综合试验区、跨境服务电子商务人民币结算平台、科技大市场等崭新的平台，这将进一步促进西安的开放发展。“长安号”中欧班列作为支撑西安对外贸易的重要抓手，2018 年取得了较大的发展，全年开行列车数量 1235 列，实现了开行数量、货运总量、重载率全国第一的重大突破。西安咸阳国际机场获批行使“第五航权”，极大地提高了西安的航空运行能力。2018 年，西安新增 7 条国际客运航线、总数达 64 条，航空旅客吞吐量跃居全国第七，货邮吞吐量突破 31 万吨，增速位居全国十大机场第一。随着第二国际商事法庭落户西安，西安新增国际友好城市和友好交流城市 8 个，吸引世界 500 强企业 215 家，实际利用外资 63.54 亿美元。西安在开放中赢得了口碑，积蓄了加速赶超的强大动能。

（五）生态文明建设推进有力

2018 年，西安国家生态文明建设示范区建设工作开始启动。以“两山”

理念为指导，西安深入推进生态文明建设“五大行动”，加快建设的步伐，努力将西安打造成生态宜居城市，荣获“2018 绿色发展示范城市”和“2018 首批生态型城市”称号。一年来，西安的城市面貌和精细化管理水平显著提升。西安通过加强园林化建设，为城市“增绿、添花、加彩”，建成绿地广场 62 个，免费开放公园 15 个，顺利通过国家园林城市复审。继续推进了“烟头革命”、城乡生活垃圾治理和两路两侧“三化”等重点工作，提升了西安作为国家中心城市的内在品质。“蓝天保卫”行动取得良好成效。按照铁腕治霾的工作思路，西安强力推动大气污染治理，超额完成了 2018 年度治理任务。根据 2018 年空气质量监测数据显示，西安空气质量优良天数 188 天，同比增加 8 天，收获了 21 个空气质量优级天。水环境治理稳步推进。西安坚持“五策治水”，积极推进实施了“八水绕长安”生态恢复工程、剿劣水“十大工程”和海绵城市建设。2018 年建成生态水面 2590 亩，在全市范围内推广应用雨水系统建设模式。浐灞区作为以生态命名的开发区，坚持“河流治理带动区域发展，新区开发支撑生态建设”的发展思路，逐步建立和形成了“城绿融合”的生态型宜居宜业的发展模式，荣获“2018 生态文明建设典范开发区”的称号。

二　西安国家中心城市建设的基本做法

（一）制定方案，确立目标

根据《关中平原城市群发展规划》确立的建设西安国家中心城市的建设目标，西安市委、市政府积极谋划，迅速启动了《西安国家中心城市建设实施方案》（以下简称《方案》）的制订，经过反复的研究和论证，方案于 2019 年初正式颁布实施。基于西安发展的历史和现实条件，《方案》提出了西安国家中心城市应按三步走的建设方案。《方案》明确指出，国家中心城市的建设是一个渐进的、长期的过程，因此，西安国家中心城市建设将分为三阶段组织实施。第一阶段：到 2020 年，国家中心城市建设迈出坚实步伐，形成大西安都市圈，基本建立“三中心两高地一枢纽”六维战略支撑体系，确立国家中心城市基本框架。第二阶段：到 2025 年，西安国家中心城市建设取得实质性进展，“核心带动、功能清晰、特色鲜明”的大西安空间格局基本形成，产业高端化发展取得明显成效，经济辐射带动能力明显增强，关中平原城市群分工更加有序、协作更加高效。第三阶段：到2035年，创新、协调、绿色、开放、共享发展走在全国前列，综合经济实力和发展活力明显增强，参与国际竞争的能力显著提升，在全国区域发展格局和国家治理体系中的地位更加凸显，创新型产业体系和基础设施支撑体系日趋健全，对内对外开放新格局有效构建，引领城市群发展的一体化体制机制不断完善，城市质量得到实质性提升，成为国家创新高地，基本实现现代化，建成“美丽中国”西安样板，全面建成代表国家形象、引领“一带一路”、具有重要国际影响力和竞争力的国家中心城市，为国际化大都市建设奠定坚实基础。《方案》目标的分步骤确立，为西安国家中心城市的建设勾画了清晰的发展线条，未来，西安将以三阶段目标实现为指引，有计划有步骤地推进西安国家中心城市建设目标的实现。

（二）深化改革创新，优化发展环境

2018年，西安围绕国家中心城市建设，进一步深化“放管服”改革，出台了优化提升营商环境组合方案，西安政务服务网建成投用，“最多跑一次”和“网上办”分别达90%和96%，企业开办平均时间从14.1天缩短到2.7天。西安营商环境综合排名一跃进入全国前十。随着西安营商环境的持续提升，吉利、亚马逊、阿里巴巴等重大项目纷纷落户西安，极大地促进了西安的产业投资，从而带动了西安投资创业主体的不断增加。据统计，2018年，西安新增市场主体达54.3万户，同比增长高达91.7%。同时，西安颁布实施了民营经济质量发展“30条措施”，开展了一系列促进非公民营经济发展的活动，其中，世界西商大会、对外开放暨民营经济发展大会，西安企业家节等活动的成功举办进一步增强了西安作为国家中心城市的影响力。依托雄厚的科技资源，西安继续深化科技体制改革，以打造丝路科创中心、全球硬科技之都为目标，为支撑西安国家中心城市和国际化大都市提供了内生动力。以推动国家全面创新改革试验区建设为抓手，西安坚持先行先试，为进一步促进科技创新资源的深度融合，首先出台了《西安市加快促进科技成果转移转化20条措施》、军民融合补短板促发展实施方案等一系列新政策，很好地促进了西安科技成果的转化，催生和培育了像中科院西安光机所“中科创星”等一大批创新创业团体，在科技成果转化方面走出了一条具有西安特色的发展道路。经过不断的创新改革和探索，2018 年，西安顺利通过国家全面创新改革试验系统评估，14 个优秀案例入选全国百佳，6 条创改经验在全国推广。

（三）抢抓机遇，全面追赶超越

抢抓国家战略叠加机遇。近年来，西安处于国家战略叠加期，国家“一带一路”倡议、国家向西开放战略、西安国家中心城市建设等战略，都为西安未来的发展提供了前所未有的机遇。西安紧密结合国家战略，提出要高标准建设“三中心二高地一枢纽”，引领、带动和辐射关中城市群。通过不断的建设和扩大内陆开放平台、优化物流枢纽的运营模式、打造自贸试验区的升级版等抓手，全力推进西安“三个经济”建设步伐，支撑西安作为“一带一路综合改革开放试验区”的建设，努力推动西安国家中心城市的高质量发展。抢抓开放大通道建设机遇。西安积极争取国家和陕西省级层面的支持，在基础设施投资方面，加快建设交通轨道、生态环保、市政建设等方面的重大项目，不断地畅通开放通道，补足了众多设施短板，畅通的开放大通道带来高水平开放平台的不断优化，覆盖领域越来越广。西安新筑铁路物流基地建成运营，同时，获批国家首批二手车出口业务试点，将内陆港的口岸功能再度放大。抢抓民营经济发展机遇。西安深刻学习和领会党和国家关于民营经济的一系列重要决策部署，积极推动调研和落实工作，努力为西安民营企业营造良好的发展环境。通过寻求西安民营经济发展的突破口，从营商环境、招商引资、人才引进、资金融通、科技创新等方面，激发民间市场主体的活力，全力引导和支持民营企业的健康发展，为西安国家中心城市建设和大西安的追赶超越贡献了重要的力量。

三　西安推进国家中心城市建设的制约和挑战

（一）经济综合实力基础较弱，辐射带动能力发挥有限

长期以来，西安与东部沿海地区的发展存在较大的差距，在市场经济作用下，这种发展的不平衡和不充分问题始终存在。国家提出建设西安国家中心城

市，旨在推进西部地区与东部沿海的协调和平衡，以此推动整个国家的区域经济均衡发展。西安在西北地区以及丝绸之路经济带，具有重要的区位和经济发展优势。国家需要西安去带动整个西北地区和丝绸之路经济带的区域发展。2018年是西安国家中心城市建设的开局之年，虽然西安区域经济开局良好，跑出经济加速度。但由于地处内陆，与其他国家中心城市相比，西安国家中心城市的建设和带动辐射作用的发挥，显得基础较弱，任务更重。从经济发展的基本要素来看，西安的地区生产总值、人口规模、区域面积等方面与其他国家中心城市都还有较大的差距，西安国家中心城市的建设阶段还处于做大自身，建设大西安的发展阶段，对周边关中平原城市群的资源、空间、人口还处于虹吸的阶段，作为关中平原城市群中心城市的辐射带动作用仍相当有限。而整个关中平原城市群以及更广阔的西北地区的国土面积大、经济密度低，因此，在未来较长的一段时间内，西安与关中城市群的关系仍然是“小马拉大车”。

（二）产业集群度较低，产业化能力明显不足

目前，西安形成了一批初具规模的产业集群，但产业规模和质量相对较弱。产业集群大多以央属企业为中心，核心技术和产品掌握在大企业手中，其他的中小企业大多提供较为低端的配套和服务，集群内中小企业存在着专业分工不明确、产品服务同质化严重等问题，上、中、下产业链之间的互补性不强，还有部分产业链关键环节缺失，关键技术和产品部件长期依赖外部，没有形成完整产业链，导致产业集群形成的整个产业链条的竞争力较弱，对西安经济发展的贡献较小。再有是龙头企业少，对产业的辐射带动力不足。据了解，战略性新兴产业产值过百亿元的企业仅有5家，分别为三星（中国）半导体有限公司、比亚迪汽车有限公司、隆基绿能科技股份有限公司、隆基乐叶光伏科技有限公司、西安中兴通讯终端科技有限公司。战略性新兴产业作为未来产业发展的方向，西安战略性新兴产业的要素还是略显不足，科技资源优势对战略性新兴产业的支撑作用仍然有限，不少战略性新兴产业的发展还是依靠政府的引导和支持，没有形成发展战略性新兴产业的自发性的生态循环机制。另外，西安相比国内发达城市，服务战略性新兴产业的专业型社会中介咨询服务机构发育迟缓，导致战略性新兴产业的发展受到一定程度的制约。

（三）科技实力与经济不匹配，科技成果转化不力

西安高校和科研院所密集，科技实力较为雄厚，具备发展经济的良好基础，特别是在军民融合发展方面还有非常大的发展空间。但长期以来，西安的科教和军工等优势资源都没有被充分地调动和发挥出来，表现出科技创新能力与经济实力的不平衡，西安的创造和制造水平较低。目前来看，西安的科研人员较为充沛，很多大公司的研发部门都落户在西安。但是，众多的研究成果与经济市场脱离，科研成果没有转化成有效的生产力，甚至存在一些科研成果在外地开花的尴尬现象。从企业的创新方面来看，西安的大企业和科技创新企业在数量和质量上都不够理想。由于科技体制机制的问题，西安部分企业的科技创新、成果转化的能力还很弱，需要在政策和体制机制层面，为企业提供科技资源、成果转化渠道等，打通科研机构与企业之间的沟通和联系，为科研成果和生产力之间架起一座桥梁。同时，企业自身在产学研创新、成果转化方面也需要继续努力，积极争取上市条件。

（四）民营经济发展相对滞后，企业实力和活力亟待提升

西安民营经济在扩大对外开放、加大技术创新、优化资源配置、推动企业转型升级等方面存在不少亟待解决的问题。目前，西安的民营非公经济仍以传统产业居多，所属行业主要集中于制造业、零售业、餐饮业等行业。西安民营经济横向纵向跟成都、武汉、郑州等城市的民营企业发展相比还有一定差距，民营企业活力还需提升。民营企业主要以小微型为主，比重较大，而大中型企业比重较小，仅为20%左右；从资产及营业收入总计看，也更为明显。民营企业在科技创新能力、技术人才等方面都存在着众多障碍和制约，特别是融资难融资贵的问题比较突出。而目前的各类民营经济相关的优惠政策落实还不太到位，制约了民营经济的发展壮大。此外，民营经济对新兴产业的涉足较少，产业结构层次低。民间投资结构比较集中。民间投资方向主要以房地产为主，而对技术和资金要求较高的战略性新兴行业，信息传输、软件和信息服务业等投入较少，投资分布过于集中且易受宏观政策影响，随着房地产业调控政策的不断出台，房地产投资增速放缓，必然会对民间投资带来较大的影响。

四　建设西安国家中心城市的对策建议

（一）建设大西安都市圈，带动关中城市群加速崛起

1. 加速推进西咸行政一体化

西安市委市政府的《西安国家中心城市建设实施方案》提出，到2020年，形成大西安都市圈。大西安都市圈的形成首先需要一个真正的大西安建设作为支撑，只有以大西安为中心的大西安都市圈，才能支撑和担当起国家中心城市的使命，才能使西安真正成为“一带一路”的核心、欧亚交流合作的国际化大都市。因此，以建设大西安为中心，在西安代管西咸新区的基础上，继续推进西咸一体化，有步骤开展行政区划的合理调整，实现大西安建设目标，支持大西安都市圈加快形成，进而带动和辐射周边城市群的发展壮大。

2. 推动设施交通互联互通

以全球视野高标准规划为起点，继续推动大西安基础设施和交通物流枢纽建设，实现城市品质国际接轨目标，全面建立品质卓越、内容全面、层级分明、辐射均衡的公共服务设施体系，提高国际化宜居生活水准，强化大西安都市圈城际的各类资源要素的双向流动。加快西安“米”字形高铁网、关中城际铁路网、高速公路网建设，进一步提高西安与关中平原城市群各城市间的快速通达能力，实现关中城市群区域交通一体化。在关中平原城市群交通互联互通的基础上，进一步推进多式联运信息平台互联互通，促进货源与“公”“铁”“空”“海”等运力资源有效匹配，打造“公空联运”卡车航班示范线路，推广“公空多式联运”服务模式。

3. 加快推动区域协同发展

西安作为关中城市群的核心城市，要担当国家中心城市的使命，必须以发展产业集群为抓手，集中优势资源推动产业高端化，发展高端制造业和现代服务业，可以开始将一些资源型产业或者劳动密集型产业有计划地向周边城市转移，从而带动关中城市群整个产业链条的配套服务能力。在政策和体制方面，建立起由西安牵头发起，关中城市群各市县共同参与的区域经济社会发展联盟，加强沟通和交通，建立起常态化的合作交流机制，便于在设施联通、产业

分工、科技交流、公共服务以及环境保护等方面形成建设合力，共同推动大项目的落地实施，形成关中城市群区域协同发展的长效机制。在空间建设方面，促进区域的联通和融合发展，加快推进西咸一体化、西铜同城化，形成区域发展共同体，从而带动和辐射整个关中地区，乃至西北地区的互动融合发展。

（二）以产业转型升级为契机，构建西安现代特色产业体系

1. 推动西安产业转型升级

以创建西安国家创新示范高地为目标和抓手，加快西安产业转型升级的步伐，坚持以转型促发展，调整产业结构，利用西安科技和军工的资源优势，推进科技创新向产业转化，同时，考虑产业空间布局，为转型的产业预留发展空间。紧密跟踪世界科技革命和新兴产业发展的趋势，构建和完善西安的现代产业体系。依托西安装备制造业的基础，通过实施企业技术改造提升工程，推进西安传统装备制造业向高端装备制造业转型升级，推动产业生产方式的高端化，建立起智能化、精细化和柔性化的生产方式，提升西安装备制造业的发展水平和行业影响力。引导和支持部分制造业向生产服务型产业转变，延长制造业生产和服务产业链条。培育和扩大战略性新兴产业，发展服务新兴产业的配套能力，激发科技、人才等要素对战略性新兴产业的支撑作用，不断拓展战略性新兴产业的发展空间。

2. 建立现代化特色产业体系

西安国家中心城市的高质量发展需要一个特色现代化产业体系的强力支撑。按照党的十九大提出的“四位协同”发展的产业体系的要求，加快以创新带动现代产业体系，更好地促进实体经济的壮大。立足西安在科技资源、产业基础以及未来产业革命的发展趋势，着重以 4 个万亿元级大产业为发展主体，推动高技术产业、先进制造业、现代服务业和文化旅游业的发展壮大，形成具有西安特色的有竞争力的现代产业体系。高新技术产业的发展坚持以新一代信息技术产业为核心，调动西安科技创新资源，聚力发展高端化信息技术产业，在无人机、新材料、集成电路、机器人等方面取得突破，培育西安高新技术产业发展的新动能。先进制造业的发展应围绕新能源汽车、人工智能、航空航天等产业为主，带动上下游产业的发展，逐步形成先进制造业产业集群。推动现代服务业高质量发展，重点培育商贸物流业、科技信息服务、金融服务等

与其他实体经济联系紧密的生产性服务业，为西安实体经济贡献力量。文化旅游业是西安独具优势的大产业，西安应不断创新，发挥西安历史文化资源优势，把西安打造成具有世界影响力的旅游时尚之都，通过旅游进一步带动关联产业的发展壮大。

3. 营造良好的产业发展环境

良好的产业发展环境需要政府的引导和支持。在产业政策方面，西安地方政府应制定合理的产业政策体系，建立市场准入和退出的动态管理制度，在财税、金融、人才、科技等方面全方位地为产业培育和发展提供政策支撑。建立产业项目的领导包抓制度，强化项目的绩效评估，对于重要项目，实行特事特办，调动各类资源，在土地、资金、管理等方面为项目争取绿色通道，提高项目的开工率和竣工投产率，推进重大产业项目的加快实施。不断克服长期以来的体制机制障碍，逐步完善信息咨询、担保、融资等服务体系，强化现有的知识产权保护，切实保护好产权所有者的合法权益，特别是要重点支持战略性新兴产业方面的科技成果优先实现产业化。进一步加大对外招商引资的力度，在招商引资的过程中，必须保证高质量的引资，开展精准化、专业化招商，着重围绕能够促进产业链条有效延伸的产业和企业进行招商，在做强西安产业链和产业集群上取得新突破。

（三）依托全面创新改革试验区建设，促进科技成果产业化

1. 加快科技创新改革

充分利用和发挥西安科教资源富集、创新实力雄厚、科创平台完备的优势，在搞活体制机制、营造环境氛围、精准制定政策、发挥主体作用等方面下功夫、求突破。围绕经济发展现实需要，进行科技攻关，推动旧动能向新动能不断转化，促进企业的转型升级。紧密跟踪科技前沿，进行前瞻性的理论创新研究，积极争取国家重点实验室、大科学装置、重大科技基础设施、前沿技术创新平台和产业创新平台落户西安，吸引国内外顶尖科学家、创新团队来西安开展科研工作，抢占创新发展的制高点，全力释放西安的科创优势，引领区域创新协同发展，使创新成为高质量发展的动力源泉。加快现有的研究中心和科学院的建设，着力建设好中科院西安科学园、中国西部科技创新港、西工大翱翔小镇等项目，打造丝路科创中心、国家创新高地等重要的科创平台和载体。

2. 推动军民融合创新发展

西安应继续发挥自身优势，着力破解体制机制难题，加速布局军民融合战略新兴产业，让军民融合发展作为追赶超越的“新引擎”。可借助军民融合契机，鼓励和引导非公企业进入军工产业，打通军用技术民用化通道，加强知识技术双向流动。把雄厚的科技资源转化为巨大的生产力，推动西安的经济发展跨上新台阶。充分利用现有的军民融合科技和平台资源，服务“民参军”企业，出台相关政策，鼓励有基础和有条件的民营企业进入军民融合产业领域。推动军工企业的混合所有制改革，发挥政府财政杠杆作用，引导社会资本投入军工企业，带动军民产业的融合发展。注重以试点和项目带动军民融合产业集群的形成，以“基地＋中心＋市场＋平台”的模式将军民融合的提升能力最大化发挥。加强人才引进和培养，吸引和留住更多的优秀管理人才和技术人才，逐步建立起人才信息库，形成服务军民融合创新发展的人才体系。

3. 打造硬科技之城

2017 年，西安明确提出要打造“硬科技之都”，并实施了“硬科技＋”“互联网＋”“军民融合＋”“高校＋”和“创业平台＋”等一系列发展战略。西安高校众多、科技创新力量丰富，还可以形成创新集群发挥更大的协同效果。西安立足国家中心城市定位，用“硬科技＋互联网”打造数字经济中国数谷。继续大力推动产学研融合，加快科技成果转化为现实的生产力，推动硬科技产业的长足发展。为科技与硬科技创业之间架起一座桥梁，营造融资、技术等方面创业生态服务环境，制定合理的支撑硬科技研发和产业发展的技术标准、知识产权保护等规章办法，把西安打造成硬科技制度供给高地。发挥和利用好硬科技智库、创新联盟、城市联盟等重要平台的作用，整合各类科技和人才高端资源，调动财政和金融的力量，推进各类科技平台和产业基地的成果、产品、业态和模式在西安就地转化，为西安硬科技发展汇聚能量。

（四）优化民间投资环境，发展壮大西安民营经济

1. 持续优化营商环境

认真学习和领悟习近平总书记在中央民营企业座谈会上的讲话精神，努力提高行政办事效率，认真研究当前西安民营经济发展在思想观念、体制机制、营商环境等方面的现实制约，做到有的放矢，制定符合西安实际的政策体系，

让民营经济能在西安国家中心城市建设中开辟一条新路径。深入推进“放管服”改革，不断创新服务方式，利用好互联网，建立起线上线下共同支撑的服务体系，改善针对民营企业的监管、税务、环保等方面的执法方式，为民营企业降低不必要的交易成本，努力做好民营企业的“金牌店小二”。将民营经济的发展纳入西安市委市政府的常态综合考核范畴，作为考核领导干部的重要指标之一，激发民营经济市场主体的活力，定期开展民营经济政策制度落实调查以及营商环境满意度调查大行动。强化政企互动和督促考核机制，实行严格问责追责，促进民营经济发展的鲜明导向和一流环境，真正使中央、省、市的惠企政策落地“最后一公里”的问题得以解决。

2. 打造新型民营经济示范城市

深入贯彻落实西安《关于推动民营经济高质量发展的若干意见》，全力消除民营企业发展“隐性障碍”。进一步把以前已经设定的有关支持民营经济发展、支持科技企业发展、支持文化企业发展的相关资金尽快有效整合，全方位支撑西安成为新型民营经济示范城市。实施民营企业发展成本降低计划。建立民营经济政府基金和行政收费的目录公示制度，杜绝公示目录之外的其他隐形收费。建立民营企业在用地上的减免优惠政策，保证中小微企业接电“零成本”。千方百计地降低中小微企业的融资成本，可以实施针对小微企业的融资奖补制度，缓解民营经济在融资过程中出现的“融资难、融资贵”问题。着力构建“亲清”政商关系，探索民营企业家参与民营经济政策制定的机制，保障民营企业合法权益的正当诉求途径。

3. 引导民营经济健康发展

深入挖掘和调动社会民间资本的潜力，引导民间蕴藏的资本进行有效投资，定期编制西安国家中心城市重大项目投资目录，明确扩大投资的重点方向，降低投资风险，减少投资限制，增强民营企业投资意愿、投资力度和投资积极性。探索发展混合所有制经济形式，为民营资本和民营企业参与西安的国企改革提供通道，允许民间资本以出资入股、认购可转债等多种方式进入竞争性行业，让各种不同类型的资本互为补充，融合发展。强化西安科技资源对民营经济的支撑作用，鼓励、支持和推动高校和科研单位的科技人才进入民营经济领域，为西安民营企业的发展做贡献。对服务民营经济的科技人才，可以赋予其更多的自主权，突破科研单位体制机制上的束缚，探索科技人才的成果处置权下放、收益归属权划分等方面的可行路径，进一步盘活科技资源，释放创新活力。逐步建立民营企业的市场退出机制，化解部分行业的产能过剩问题。引导和鼓励有条件的民营企业或者民营资本拓展产业发展空间，涉足养老健康产业、物联网、电子信息等新兴产业，加快民营经济的转型升级发展。

参考文献

[1] 张倪：《新晋国家中心城市：西安的使命与挑战》，《中国发展观察》2018 年第 5 期。

[2] 康乔娜：《书写自贸试验区建设的“西安方案”》，《大陆桥视野》2018 年第 1 期。

案 例 篇

Case Studies

B.12

广州：国家中心城市的更新与复兴

张大卫*

摘 要： 《粤港澳大湾区发展规划纲要》对广州有新定位。按照大湾区规划，中国的华南地区出现了广、深、港、澳四个中心城市，其“一国两制、三个关税区”的特殊性，在世界城市群中是仅有的。作为国家中心城市，广州基础雄厚，所具有的优势在一定时期内不可替代。广州是广深港澳四市中唯一拥有广阔经济腹地和多层级城市体系的中心城市，在竞争与合作中可以通过大都市圈规划来不断拓展自己发展的经济空间。广州应加快推进制度创新、科技创新和产业创新；加快城市更新步伐，使“老广”进一步焕发新活力；保持城市的年轻化；把广州建设成为有国际影响力的时尚中心和消费中心。

* 张大卫，经济学博士，博士生导师，中国国际经济交流中心副理事长兼秘书长、河南省原副省长，研究方向为区域经济、产业经济。本文是作者2019年6月21日在“2019广州：全球城市评价研究”学术会议上的演讲。

关键词： 广州 国家中心城市 粤港澳大湾区

一 广州市在粤港澳大湾区中的新定位

2019 年 2 月，中央正式向社会发布了《粤港澳大湾区发展规划纲要》（以下简称《纲要》），大湾区建设与“一带一路”建设、京津冀协同发展、长江经济带发展一起，成为国家区域发展的重大战略。

在《纲要》中，粤港澳大湾区的战略定位为：①充满活力的世界级城市群；②具有全球影响力的国际科技创新中心；③“一带一路”建设的重要支撑；④内地与港澳深度合作示范区；⑤宜居宜业宜游的优质生活圈。

这些定位，清晰地表达了国家制订大湾区规划的愿景。但建设大湾区的意义还不仅限于此，在《纲要》和中央最近出台的有关文件中，都明确揭示了这一区域战略所体现的国家意志。即丰富“一国两制”内涵，保持港澳长期稳定；落实新发展理念，发展新动能，实现创新驱动发展；深化改革，扩大开放，参与国际经济合作；助推“一带一路”建设，构筑海上丝绸之路对接融汇支撑区；带动珠江—西江经济带创新绿色发展。

重要意义也好，国家意志也好，广州都应从我国深化改革、扩大开放、经济持续健康发展、“一国两制”和促进祖国和平统一的大格局上，去把握这一区域战略的深刻内涵。

1. 促进创新、先进制造业、现代服务业等区域优势资源整合，激发市场活力，率先构筑现代化经济体系，培育带动国家经济持续增长的发动机。

2. 顺应经济全球化和国际贸易格局的变化，全面构建开放型经济新体制，打造国际性开放新高地，代表国家参与世界城市群竞争。

3. 加快“一国两制”框架下区域间制度磨合与融合，促进文明交流互鉴，为中华民族伟大复兴和构建人类命运共同体提供区域示范样板。

4. 推动经济社会协调发展，通过转变发展方式和产业变革，满足人民群众高品质生活对消费福利、人才、环境、生态及其他公共产品、公共服务的需要。

《纲要》在对粤港澳大湾区进行整体定位的同时，为强调发挥优势、合理分工、功能互补和错位发展，也概略地明确了广、深、港、澳的战略定位。广州是大湾区4个中心城市之一。《纲要》对广州市的定位主要有以下几个方面。

表1　粤港澳大湾区与其他世界级城市群竞争力对比

指标(2017年)	东京湾区	旧金山湾区	纽约湾区	粤港澳大湾区			
				大港区	内地九市	香港	澳门
人口(万人)	4347	473	2032	6951	6150	739	62
GDP(万亿美元)	1.82	0.48	1.74	1.51	1.12	0.34	0.05
人均GDP(万美元)	4.19	10.15	8.56	2.17	1.82	4.6	8.06
经济增速(%)	2.30	2.30	4.70	7.00	7.90	3.70	9.10
占地面积(万平方千米)	3.68	1.79	2.15	5.6	5.47	0.11	0.003
港口集装箱吞吐量(万标准箱)	798	242	671	7809	5719	2076	13
机场旅客吞吐量(亿人次)	1.24	0.79	1.32	2.02	1.22	0.73	0.07
全球金融中心指数排名	5	8	2	—	18(深圳) 28(广州)	3	—
全球创新指数排名	13	6	6	17(中国)	—	14	—
世界100强大学数量	2	2	3	4	0	4	0
世界500强企业总部数量	39	28	26	19	11	8	0

1. 国家中心城市和综合性门户城市；
2. 国际商贸中心、综合交通枢纽；
3. 科技文化教育中心；
4. 国际大都市。

对比21世纪以来历次修编后国务院批准的规划，可以看到有关广州市的定位在不断“升舱”。

与《纲要》中其他中心城市的定位相比，广州的优势在于被明确为国家中心城市；香港的优势在于被明确为“国际大都会”和国际金融、航运、贸易中心和国际航空枢纽，亚太区国际法律争议解决中心等；深圳的优势体现在“国家创新型城市”“现代化国际城市”“具有世界影响力的创新创意之都”等特定功能上（见图1、表2）。

2001~2011年规划（2005年）	2011~2020年规划（2016年）	2017~2035年规划（2018年）
广东省省会 华南地区中心城市之一 国家历史文化名城	广东省省会 国家历史文化名城 我国重要的中心城市 国际商贸中心和综合交通枢纽	广东省省会 国家重要中心城市 历史文化名城 国际综合交通枢纽，贸易中心、交往中心、科技产业创新中心、引领全球城市

图1　广州市历年规划纲要

表2　大湾区规划及四个中心城市战略定位

粤港澳大湾区	广州定位	深圳定位	香港定位	澳门定位
1. 充满活力的世界级城市群； 2. 具有全球影响力的国际科技创新中心； 3.“一带一路”建设的重要支撑； 4. 内地与港澳深度合作示范区； 5. 宜居宜业宜游的优质生活圈	1. 国家中心城市和综合性门户城市； 2. 国际商贸中心、综合交通枢纽； 3. 科技文化教育中心； 4. 国际大都市	1. 全国性经济中心城市； 2. 国际创新型城市； 3. 现代化国际城市； 4. 具有世界影响力的创新创意之都	1. 国际金融、航运、贸易中心和国际航空枢纽； 2. 全球离岸人民币业务枢纽，国际资产管理及风险管理中心； 3. 亚太区国际法律争议解决中心； 4. 国际大都会	1. 世界旅游休闲中心； 2. 中国与葡语国家合作服务平台； 3. 以中华文化为主流、多元文化共存的交流合作基地

从以上对比可以看出，仅凭广、深、港、澳四市的定位都不能单独担当起实现大湾区战略目标的历史使命。完成这一使命，必须靠四市协同、融合发力。

国际经验表明，过多的关税区、特区会造成城市间的经济隔离，形成中心城市孤立发展的状况。因而四市间要综合运用竞争与合作两种机制，使竞争成为合作的动力，用政府间、企业和公众广泛参与的合作来解决区域结构性矛盾。而广州则应紧扣国家中心城市的定位，抓住战略机遇，扬长补短，找准新时代发展路径。

二　广州成为国家中心城市的历史性思考

城市的存在不是孤立的。所谓中心城市，来自其在城市体系中的位置。中国的城市体系，有一个历史发育的过程。

1. 夏、商、周三代是中国城市的肇始期。由于政治上实行分封制，城市一般在空间上是割裂和封闭的。其往往是不同层级的政治中心，不具备自下而上的纵向联系和由此及彼的横向联系。

2. 自秦王朝实行郡县制直到明朝以前，国家虽废除了分封领地的制度，由于受小农经济社会形态的局限，大行政区内的城市间一般存有政治统辖的上下相属关系，但仍然缺乏自发、平等的经济联系。

3. 进入明代以后，随着中国商贸活动逐渐活跃和商业经济地位的提升，工商业城镇大量涌现。受政治和经济两种力量的交叉作用，城市空间体系开始复杂化，出现了如美国学者所说的行政隶属和经济联系两套体系。但一般而言，处于官衙所在地的城市以及由其所统辖的城市间，既存在行政隶属关系，也保持较密切的经济联系。管理较大区域的衙署所在地城市，往往具有行政和经济两套体系的“中心”功能。

4. 随着现代经济的发展，特别是在经济全球化条件下，资源在更大的地理空间配置，由行政中心统辖区内经济活动的城市体系发生了变化。城市特有的功能、与腹地间的联系、经济实力、交通的便利性、在全球供应链上的位置等，都会成为重要因素，使行政隶属的概念逐步弱化，而由市场分工形成的经济联系则日益紧密。一些成为经济中心的城市，地位可能会超过行政中心。如美国的纽约与华盛顿，中国的青岛与济南、大连与沈阳、厦门与福州等。

广州自秦始皇三十三年（公元前 214 年），秦将任嚣平定岭南后建城，即成为华南区域的中心城市。这里“介于岭海间，北负雄、韶，足以临吴、楚；东肩潮、惠，可以制瓯、闽；西固高、廉，扼交、邕之噤吭；南环琼岛，控黎夷之门户”。古人所言，讲的是广州所具有的区位优势和方舆上的军事控制能力。

而它“六脉皆通海，青山半入城”，“海、野、河、城层次渐进，底蕴丰厚；塔、楼、阁、台遥相呼应，各有含义，为岭南城市之表率”，讲的则是广州的深厚文化底蕴、鲜明城市特色和传统人居智慧在城建上的反映。

进入近现代社会，广州成为中国最先开放的城市和最先接触现代文明和开启国际贸易的城市，也是引领中国进入民主革命时代的城市之一。20 世纪 70 年代末以来，广州又因地近港澳和文化多元性的优势，开风气之先，引领了中国的改革与开放、繁荣与发展。其华南地区中心城市的地位，是唯一的、不容置疑的。

如今，在大湾区的规划中，中国的华南地区出现了广、深、港、澳四个中心城市，其“一国两制、三个关税区”的特殊性，在世界城市群中是仅有的。对广州来讲，特别有意味的是经过几十年的发展，当年的小渔村深圳迅速崛起，成为可与广州比肩的中心城市。对正在发生的变化，广州应客观分析，正确应对。

三　广州与深圳发展的关系

改革开放 40 年，深圳发生了沧海桑田之变。近年来，其又紧紧抓住了新科技革命和产业变革这一重大机遇，在经济结构调整中促进新旧动能转换。正是在这一背景下，深圳经济发展再次提质加速。2017 年，广州 GDP 被深圳超越；2018 年两市 GDP 和人均 GDP 的差距进一步扩大。（见表 3、图 2）

表 3　2017 年广州和深圳的经济结构

2017 年	GDP（亿元）	人均 GDP（元）	三次产业比重	常住人口（万人）	常住人口城镇化率	户籍人口（人）	户籍人口城镇化率	市辖区面积(平方公里)
广州	22859. 35	155491	0. 98∶27. 27∶71. 75	1490. 44	86. 38%	927. 69	79. 78%	7434. 4
深圳	24221. 98	189568	0. 4∶41. 1∶58. 8	1302. 66	100%	454. 7	34. 90%	1997. 47

资料来源：《2018 年广州统计年鉴》《2018 年深圳统计年鉴》。

深圳的奇迹具有不可复制性。广州地区生产总值被深圳超越，也有其深刻原因和内在的规律。认真分析起来，两市不同的经济结构和要素禀赋特征是关键。

（1）广州产业结构正处于调整期。作为老工业基地，工业经济中传统制造业比重较大。近年来，广州工业新旧动能转换加快，速度、效益、质量投资等指标也表现不俗。但 2018 年，35 个工业行业大类中，仍有 12 个行业出现负

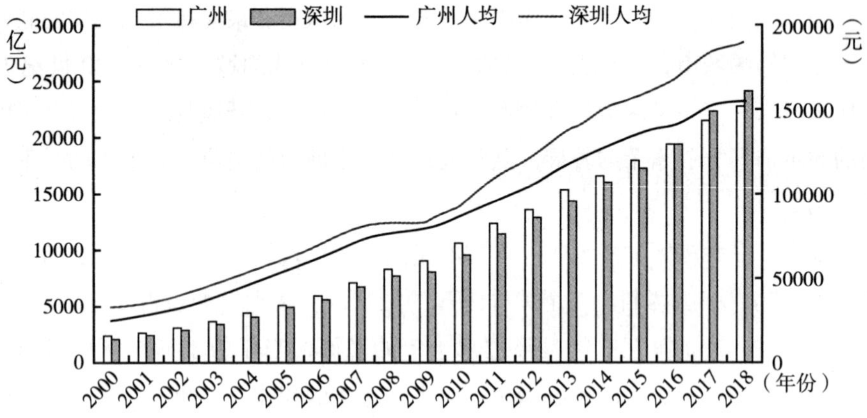

图 2 广州、深圳 2000～2018 年 GDP 和人均 GDP

资料来源：广州、深圳 2001～2018 年统计年鉴，2018 年国民经济和社会发展统计公报。

增长。广州全年工业增加值增长 5.5%，同期深圳工业增加值增长 9.5%，比广州高 4 个百分点。

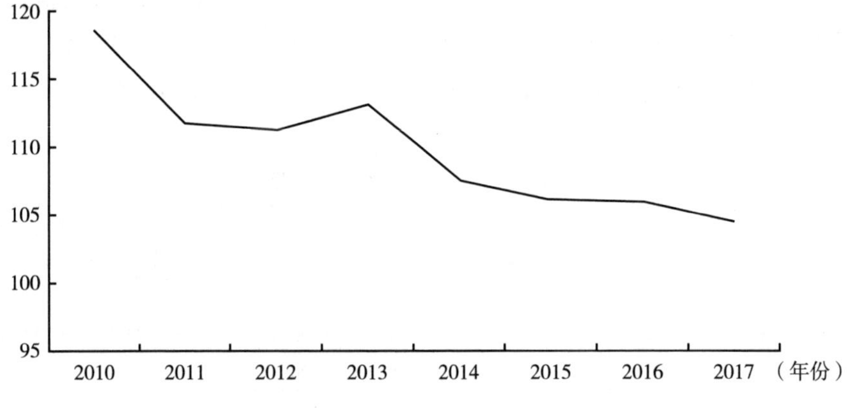

图 3 广州的工业总产值指数（2010～2017 年）

资料来源：根据《2018 年广州统计年鉴》计算。

（2）广州作为省会城市，服务业发展的基础好，规模大。2018 年广州第三产业增长6.6%，比重达到71.75%，比2017 年增加0.73 个百分点；深圳的增速为6.4%，比重达58.8%（参见图4）。

服务业增速加快和比重提高，是经济结构优化的结果，但在一般情况下，

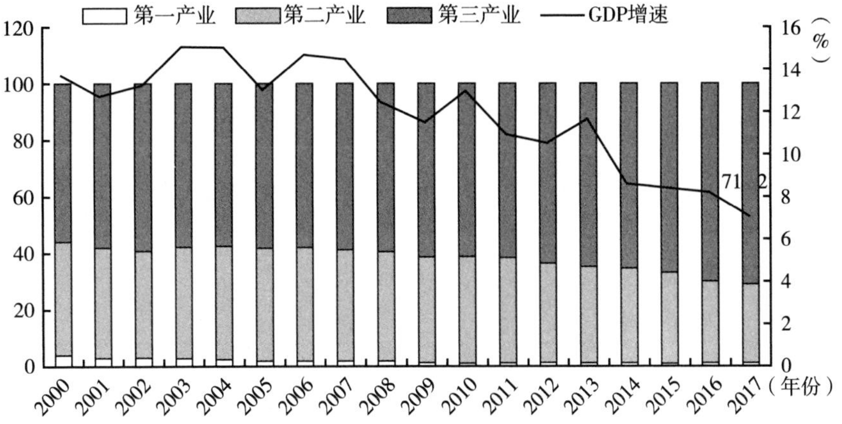

图4　2000～2017年广州三次产业结构和GDP增速

资料来源：根据《2018年广州统计年鉴》计算。

服务业效率往往低于工业部门的效率，这也会影响GDP的增速。

广深两市相比较，从创新动力、企业活力上看，深圳具有较强的产业发展后劲。

（1）形成了庞大的高端制造业产业集群。深圳规模以上工业增加值前十大行业依次为：计算机、通信和其他电子设备制造业，电气机械和器材制造业，专用设备制造业，电力、热力生产和供应业，石油和天然气开采业，橡胶和塑料制品业，通用设备制造业，金属制品业，汽车制造业，医药制造业。

其中，移动通信基站设备产量占全国产量的98.15%，移动通信手持机（手机）占全国产量的17.16%，工业机器人产量占全国的14.41%（参见表4）。

表4　深圳2018年主要工业产品产量与增速

名称	单位	产量	比上年增长(%)
移动通信基站设备	万信道	42427.60	63.5
新能源汽车	万辆	9.99	191.1
卫星导航定位接收机	万部	541.85	33.2
移动通信手持机(手机)	万台	30870.73	-15.3
民用无人机	万架	294.50	4.4
工业机器人	套	21283.00	34.0
电视接收机顶盒	万盒	9861.67	-0.9
半导体分立器件	亿只	98.88	-30.9

续表

名称	单位	产量	比上年增长(%)
集成电路	亿块	255.11	8.0
液晶显示器	亿片	11.08	-11.6
电子元件	亿只	1591.17	7.7
光纤	万千米	1240.71	12.8
服务器	万台	89.19	35.5
太阳能电池(光伏电池)	千瓦	239361.49	33.6
石墨及碳素制品	吨	12095.63	-31.4

资料来源:《深圳市2018年国民经济和社会发展统计公报》。

(2)上市公司数量大、市值高(见表5、图5)。

表5　截至2018年12月31日主要城市上市公司统计

	北京	上海	广州	深圳	天津	重庆
数量(家)	319	319	101	303	53	52
市值(亿元)	145807.7	44366.91	12284.24	54458.31	4511.002	5031.504

资料来源:《中国城市建设统计年鉴》。

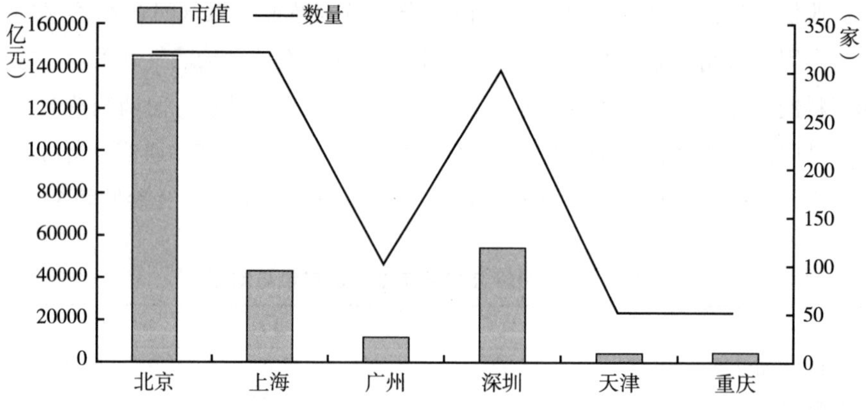

图5　2018年底主要城市上市公司总市值和上市公司数量

资料来源:《中国城市建设统计年鉴2018》。

深圳发展的态势令人鼓舞,但广州长期作为中心城市,其形成的优势和发展的后劲不能低估。

1. 有较大的发展空间

广州市总面积 7434. 4 平方公里，深圳仅有 1997. 47 平方公里，广州是深圳的 3. 72 倍；广州建成区面积 1294 平方公里，深圳建成区 973 平方公里。广州未建成区面积即潜在发展空间面积是深圳的 5. 99 倍。

2. 经济结构相对均衡

广州的产业体系健全，更具现代化经济体系的基本特征。工业部门的汽车制造业、电子产品制造业等战略性新兴产业发展势头良好，传统产业改造提升加快，基础性产业增长后劲充足。广州是千年商都，商业文化发达，商业场景众多，商业资本和产业结合更为紧密。2018 年，广州批发零售业商品销售总额是深圳的 2. 36 倍；快递业务量增长 28. 8%，突破 50 亿件，继续保持全国第一的位次。广州服务业比重虽高，但增长后劲强。而深圳产业体系的对外依存度高达 123. 79%（见表 6），为减少对国外市场的过度依赖，满足国内消费和产业升级的需要，下一步应围绕内需市场使产业结构有所调整。

表 6　广州、深圳 2018 年对外依存度

	GDP（亿元）	进口（亿元）	出口（亿元）	进出口差额(亿元)	进出口总额(亿元)	对美出口(亿元)	对香港出口(亿元)	对外贸依存度(%)
广州	22859. 35	4202. 57	5607. 58	1405. 01	9810. 15	821. 49	808. 72	42. 92
深圳	24221. 98	13709. 05	16274. 69	2565. 64	29983. 94	2383. 94	6758. 33	123. 79

资料来源：广州、深圳 2018 年经济社会统计公报。

3. 公共服务能力强

广州聚集了服务于华南乃至全国的优质医疗、教育、科技和文化资源，这种其他城市所不具备的公共服务能力，是广州最值得称道的软实力。

（1）医疗卫生

表 7　2018 年广州、深圳医疗卫生机构情况对比

	医院（家）	三甲医院（家）	全部床位（万张）	医院床位（万张）	每千人床位(张)	卫生技术人员(万人)	每千人卫生技术人员(人)
广州	255	57	9. 51	8. 6	5. 77	15. 65	10. 5
深圳	139	18	4. 76	4. 36	3. 35	9. 37	7. 19

资料来源：广州、深圳两市 2018 年统计公报。

在中国大陆地区《2018 顶级医院 100 强》中，广州有 11 家医院入围，次于北京 16 家、上海 13 家，排名第三。深圳仅有 1 家医院入围。

（2）教育

广州的高素质人才培养能力雄视华南，其 2018 年本专科招生、在校生、毕业生数量均是深圳的 10 倍以上。而其研究生招生、在校研究生和毕业研究生数量，也是深圳的 5 倍以上（见表 8）。

表 8　2018 年广州、深圳教育情况对比

单位：万人

	本专科招生	在校生	毕业生	研究生招生	在校研究生	毕业研究生
广州	32.36	108.64	29.04	3.74	10.11	2.54
深圳	2.71	8.82	2.31	0.65	1.76	0.49

资料来源：广州、深圳 2018 年经济社会统计公报。

（3）文化

广州从秦始皇时代筑番禺城至今已有两千多年的历史。中原文化与南越各民族文化融合，形成了独具特色的岭南—广府文化。广州面朝大海，背靠中华腹地，历史上在传承传播中华文化、文明的同时，也是接驳转化外来文化、文明的窗口。

广州是海上丝绸之路的重要起点。唐宋时代，就有阿拉伯商人在此开展贸易活动，在将中华文明推荐到欧洲的同时，也带来了印度、中亚、欧洲的宗教和文化。进入近现代社会，广州又是我国传统文化与西方工业文明最先产生碰撞的地方之一，在输入西方先进思想和科学技术的同时，无数中国的拓荒者也从这里走向东南亚和欧美国家。不同文明的交流互鉴，构筑了广州地域文化的特色和底蕴，使其具有很强的包容性和全球影响力，广州地区也已成为东西方文明、文化成功相互交融的典范。

4. 科技

广州有中山大学、华南理工大学、暨南大学等著名高校和中科院广州分院等众多国家一流科研机构，科技人才荟萃，科研设施完善，基础科学研究优势强，可以成为科学思想、科学发明的策源地。深圳是“东方硅谷”，其优势在于以企业为主体的创新活动，更有利于推动面向市场的技术创新。两城之间有良好的互补关系。

（1）专利

广州专利申请量、发明专利申请量、专利授权量、发明专利授权量虽仍与深圳有差距，但2018年普遍有了快于深圳的增长（见表9）。

表9　2018年广州、深圳专利申请情况比较

	专利申请量（万件）	增速（%）	专利授权量（万件）	增速（%）	发明专利申请量（万件）	增速（%）	发明专利授权量（万件）	增速（%）
广州	17.31	46.3	8.98	49.2	5.02	35.08	1.08	15.5
深圳	22.86	29.1	14.02	48.8	7	16.1	2.13	12.6

资料来源：广州、深圳2018年经济社会统计公报。

（2）科研机构

广州拥有的国家、省级高端科研平台数量远多于深圳（见表10）。

表10　广州、深圳科研机构数量

单位：个

城市	国家工程技术中心	国家级企业技术中心	国家重点实验室	省级工程技术研究中心	省级重点实验室	市级重点实验室
广州	18	27	20	956	233	165
深圳	7	26	14	218	24	238

注：广州是2018年的数据，深圳是2017年的数据。

资料来源：广州、深圳两市2018年经济社会统计公报及《深圳统计年鉴2018》。

5. 人口结构比较协调

2018年，广州1490.44万常住人口中，户籍人口达927.69万人，占62.2%；深圳1302.66万常住人口中，户籍人口达454.7万人，仅占34.9%。较为良好的人口稳定性，既是好的公共政策的结果，也是其进一步改善的前提。最重要的，是它有利于经济可持续发展和社会稳定和谐。

另外，从常住人口年龄结构看，在9个国家中心城市中，广州0~14岁人口占比为17.2%，仅低于郑州的19.3%，居第二位，甚至高于深圳；65岁以上人口占8.6%，为倒数第一位。这说明广州的人口老龄化程度较低，仍是一座“年轻”的城市，而且外来人口落户率高，劳动后备人口资源充足。这些体现“人口红利”的数据，都说明广州是一座成长性强和创新潜力巨大的城市（见表11）。

表11　国家中心城市常住人口年龄结构（2017年底）

地区	常住人口数（万人）	各年龄段人口数(万人)			比重(%)		
		0~14岁	15~64岁	65岁及以上	0~14岁	15~64岁	65岁及以上
北京市	2170.7	225.8	1706.2	238.8	10.4	78.6	11.0
上海市	2418	240.5	1832.7	344.8	9.9	75.8	14.3
天津市	1557	175.8	1205.5	175.7	11.3	77.4	11.3
重庆市	3075	504.1	2131.8	439.1	16.4	69.3	14.3
郑州市	988	190.7	694.6	102.7	19.3	70.3	10.4
武汉市	854	116.0	621.1	116.8	13.6	72.7	13.7
西安市	883	120.4	664.0	98.6	13.6	75.2	11.2
成都市	1604	253.9	1126.7	223.4	15.8	70.2	13.9
广州市	1450	249.5	1075.5	125.0	17.2	74.2	8.6

注：数据是根据2017年人口抽样调查汇总数据推算。

从以上分析可以看出，作为国家中心城市，广州的基础是雄厚的，所具有的优势在一定时期内是不可替代的。它在综合交通、文化、教育、医疗、科技等领域所具有的强大公共服务能力，华南地区别的城市还难以比肩。

特别是，广州是广、深、港、澳四市中唯一拥有广阔经济腹地和多层级城市体系的中心城市，在竞争与合作中，可以通过大都市圈规划来不断拓展自己发展的经济空间。经济社会发展是一个不断变化的运动过程，大可不必因GDP等个别指标一时被超越而生杞人之忧。

四　对广州的几点建议

粤港澳大湾区既是自然地理的概念，也是经济地理、文化地理和政治地理的概念。

从自然地理角度看，它有着背靠大陆腹地、面向西太平洋的良好区位，具有在蓝色港湾和珠江三角洲区域建设国际一流湾区和世界级城市群的良好自然禀赋。

从经济地理角度看，其位于我国开放前沿和“一带一路”的交会之地，是我国对外开放与交流合作的战略枢纽。经40年的改革开放，形成了特有的制度、体制、机制和市场的融合优势，已成为带动国家创新发展的引擎和辐射东亚、南亚、东南亚发展的经济支撑带。

从文化地理角度看，这一区域由于传统文化与工业文明、东方文化与西方文明的长期交融与碰撞，形成了积淀深厚、韵味悠长、包容互鉴、历久弥新的特定文化生态。它的发展、融合与传播寄托着民族的文化理想，有着很强的空间张力。

从政治地理角度看，它承担着经略南海，友邻东南亚区域，消解地缘政治冲突，维持长期繁荣稳定，以“一国两制”促进祖国和平统一的国家愿景和历史使命。是我国在全球化条件下将国家战略与参与全球治理实现互动的引领性平台。

大湾区的新使命，是通过竞合、融合，充分发挥要素优势、开放优势和文化优势，促进制度创新，深度与世界规则和标准对接，形成区域突破能力，推动中国实现现代化和伟大复兴。

广州是国家中心城市。国家赋予中心城市的任务主要有三：①国家战略要津；②代表国家参与全球竞争；③辐射带动大区域发展。为在建设粤港澳大湾区的进程中，更好地担负起国家中心城市的使命和责任，对广州提出以下建议。

1. 加快推进制度创新、科技创新和产业创新

一是加强与港澳的经济、文化联系，把握好与其开展制度层面合作的机会，充分利用港澳在体制、机制和营商环境方面的优势，主动对接国际规则、国际标准，以开阔的视野推动改革和制度创新，打造好外向型经济新体制和社会主义市场经济新体制的创新版、升级版，先行先试，为国家深化改革、扩大开放做示范。

二是抓住新科技革命和产业变革在重塑全球创新版图、全球经济结构、全球供应链时产生的历史机遇，提升创新资源管理能力，促进新动能发展和传统产业转型升级，实现新旧动能转换，牵手港澳深，整合区域创新、金融、商务

中介、自由贸易、综合交通等要素和产业优势，培育世界级先进制造业集群，形成全球产业引领能力和价值链管理能力。

三是打造以企业为主导和主体的创新平台，注重模式创新，发展以数字经济为主要特征的平台经济，促进经济组织和产业生态由线型结构、网状结构向矩阵型结构转变，把生产、交易、消费过程转化为跨区域和跨社群的价值创造、文化认同、资源共享、市场互动过程，使这些高度信息化和智能化的平台，成为广州特有的新生产关系网络节点和中心枢纽。

四是实现国家创新体系、产业创新体系和社会创新体系高效对接，搭建对接和相互转换的平台，减少国家创新战略、产业创新意愿及社会与市场创新能量之间的摩擦，提升创新效率，降低创新成本。

2. 加快城市更新步伐，使“老广”进一步焕发新活力

一是对城市进行智能化、低碳化、宜居化改造，加强对智慧城市、智慧交通、智慧市政、智慧管理的总体设计和统筹，避免城市智能化更新的过程被碎片化和概念化，为市民创造全龄化的便利、舒适、宜业宜居环境。

二是加强国际性综合交通枢纽和现代物流体系建设，形成强大的分拨、集疏、转运功能，发展枢纽经济。

三是促进城市产业升级，把先进制造业和现代服务业作为城市主要业态。根据广州的优势和特点，突出工业互联网、生命科学、人工智能、新能源、空间和海洋技术、新能源技术的产业化。将一般制造业向周边转移，在合理空间内形成科学的产业链、供应链布局，同时注重城市和产业对服务业生态的需要，形成合理的就业结构。

四是顺应技术进步对人工的替代和就业机会由制造业更多地转向服务业的趋势性变化，推动工作性质变革。加大政府、社会对人力资本、人力资源的投资，促进城市就业人口技能和职业素养提升，增加居民主动选择就业的机会。引导企业加强员工在职培训，使员工能适应技术进步和业态变化对岗位的新技能要求，支撑企业保持可持续的创新能力。

3. 保持城市的年轻化

一是大力发展新技术、新产业，特别是能吸引更多年轻人就业的新业态、新模式，为年轻人创造更多的创新创业创造空间和就业机会。

二是继续提升户籍人口占常住人口的比重，缩小常住人口与总人口的剪刀

差。将流动性就业人口更多地转化为新市民，使其子女成为能融入当地文化与生活环境、能接受本地化教育和平等享受城市公共服务的“广二代”“广三代”。发掘人力资源潜力，保持后备人力资源的充足与活力。

三是破除限制人才流入和人口流动的制度性障碍，在就业、住房、购房、购车、进城等政策上实行开明、开放、宽松的政策，实施包容审慎的管理，吸引国内外更多的人才和普通居民来广创业、就业、生活、消费。

4. 把广州建设成为有国际影响力的时尚中心和消费中心

一是煲好广州“岭南文化”“广府文化”这锅“老汤”，不断提鲜提纯，并在传承和传播、创新和弘扬上下功夫。保持文化的多元性特征，深化与港澳台文化、南洋文化的融合互动，加强与域外文化、文明的交流互鉴及接驳转换，打造世界多元文化、文明和谐共存共生的样板城市。用广州文化环境的包容性和生命力，打破“文明冲突”论的魔咒，促进形成交流与互鉴才是人类社会文明发展和文化进步主流的共识。

二是进一步提升广州的消费中心地位，促进与香港自由贸易港的合作，强化发展自由贸易理念，适时植入其在关税等方面的贸易制度，推动政府监管体系和制度创新，发展新贸易方式和新贸易业态。提升公共产品、公共服务供给能力，使其为大湾区及广义的华南地区提供优质便利可及的医疗、教育、养老、托幼、科技、文化、旅游等消费服务，提升广州作为国家中心城市的软实力和影响力。

三是发挥广州商业文化、消费文化底蕴深厚的优势，注重消费升级带来的消费情感、消费心理的需求变化，支持个性化设计、私人定制、消费体验、文化空间、消费社区发展，促进创意、时装、服饰、美妆、美食、戏剧、古典与流行音乐、茶楼文化、酒吧文化、健康养生、休闲旅游、社交沙龙、流行数码产品等业态的繁荣，为居民更多地提供创造、消费的选择机会与选择场景，使广州真正成为“低商务成本、高品质生活”，领导消费新潮流的时尚之都、魅力之都。

B.13 以文旅深度融合助推郑州高质量发展

孙先科　杜学霞*

摘　要：　文旅深度融合是未来旅游业的发展方向，是助推郑州高质量发展的重要动力。郑州文旅深度融合要注重发挥文化资源优势，以华夏历史文明传承创新为灵魂，以代表性文化事项为着力点；要与多种业态融合，走“文化旅游+”的道路；要着重聚焦“大融合”，谋划“大项目”，开发“大产品”，优化“大环境”；要框架高质量设计，产品高质量供给，产业高质量融合，品牌高质量塑造等；要坚持经济和文化可持续发展的原则。文旅深度融合将助推郑州高质量发展，弘扬和传播中华文化。

关键词：　文旅融合　高质量　文化旅游+　中华文化

随着大众旅游和全域旅游时代的到来，旅游业已经成为我国经济的支柱性产业。新常态下，文旅深度融合是助推旅游业发展的重要动力。郑州发展旅游业有明显的人口优势、区位优势和文化资源优势。郑州的旅游业也存在文化与旅游融合度不高、全域旅游意识不强、旅游品牌不突出等问题。如何充分发挥郑州的文化资源优势，解决当前旅游业面临的问题，如何以文旅深度融合助推高质量发展，推动国家中心城市建设，是非常值得我们深入探讨的问题。

---

* 孙先科，文学博士，郑州师范学院校长、教授、博士生导师，研究方向为现当代文学和文化；杜学霞，文学博士，郑州师范学院国家中心城市研究院教授，文艺学与中原文化。

一　我国旅游业发展总体态势

1. 我国已经进入大众旅游时代

大众旅游通常指大众在旅游业中参与率较高的一种旅游形式，这是由旅行成本的降低、生活水平的提高和交通技术的改进带来的。近些年，随着我国国民经济的高速增长，居民生活水平大幅度提高，以及我国航空和高铁等交通工具的大大进步，我国的旅游业一直呈现高速发展趋势。各种数据表明，我国的旅游业已经迈入了大众旅游时代，我国的旅游业也正在成为国民经济的重要产业。

2. 全域旅游已成为我国旅游业发展的重要战略之一

国家为了支持旅游业的发展，大力推进全域旅游。2018 年 3 月，国务院办公厅印发《关于促进全域旅游发展的指导意见》，就加快推动旅游业转型升级、提质增效，全面优化旅游发展环境，走全域旅游发展的新路子做出部署。全域旅游是我国新阶段旅游发展战略的再定位，是旅游业的一场具有深远意义的变革。

3. 旅游业是国民经济的重要增长极

2014 年，习近平主席提出国民经济发展进入了新常态，即从高速增长转为中高速增长，经济结构不断优化升级，第三产业消费需求逐步成为主体，从要素驱动、投资驱动转向创新驱动等。新常态下，我国旅游业仍有不俗的表现，其增长速度远高于 GDP 的增长速度。

从图 1 可以看出，全国旅游业的增速明显高于 GDP 的增速，总体呈现出高速增长的态势。资本具有明显的逐利性特点，各路资本疯狂涌入旅游业，旅游投资明显增长，这说明资本市场对我国旅游业的前景非常看好。以下是 2014 ~ 2020 年全国旅游业的投资规模及预测。

2014 年全国旅游业实际完成投资 7053 亿元，同比增长 32%；

2015 年全国旅游业完成投资 10072 亿元，同比增长 43%；

2016 年全国旅游业实际完成投资 12997 亿元，同比增长 29%；

2017 年，全国旅游投资总额超过 1.5 万亿元，同比增长 15%；

2018 年 1 ~ 7 月，总投资额已经达到 5800 亿元（部分数据）；

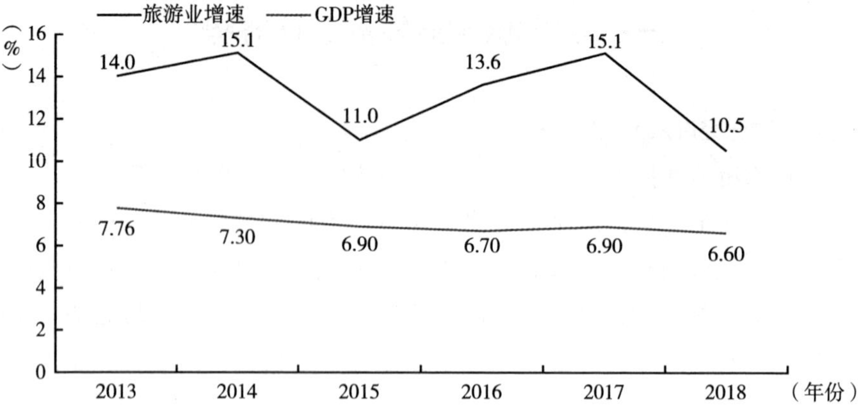

图1　2013～2018年来全国旅游业增速与GDP增速对比

资料来源：根据相关数据测算。

2020年有望达到2万亿元。

自2014年以来，国内旅游、入境旅游、出境旅游的增速也一直持续上涨，旅游业占GDP比重持续上升，说明在新常态下，旅游业在GDP中所占的比重不断增加，业已成为我国经济发展的重要增长极（见表1）。

表1　　2014～2018年全国旅游业收入情况

年份	全年旅游总收入（万亿元）	同比增长率（%）	全年GDP（万亿元）	全年全国旅游业对GDP的综合贡献量（万亿元）	占GDP的百分比(%)
2014	3.73	11	63.64	6.61	10.39
2015	4.13	10.7	67.67	7.34	10.85
2016	4.69	13.6	74.41	8.19	11.01
2017	5.4	15.1	82.71	9.13	11.04
2018	5.97	10.6	90.03	9.94	11.04

资料来源：根据相关数据测算。

4. 新常态下文旅融合的使命

2018 年 3 月，国家宣布文化部与国家旅游局正式合并为文化和旅游部。4 月，新成立的文化和旅游部正式挂牌。文化部与国家旅游局合并，是我国的重大举措，这标志着我国文化和旅游在体制上的融合。

文化部与国家旅游局两个部门合并，顺应了文化与旅游关联度越来越高的大格局、大趋势，其意义在于以下几个方面。其一，是文化产业与旅游产业两个产业关联度和重合度越来越高的实际需要，文化旅游将承担国家经济转型的使命，对助推中国经济高质量发展起重要作用。其二，基于我国旅游业发展的迫切需要。我国近年来旅游业虽然有不俗表现，但仍然存在产品质量不高、品牌效益不突出的现象，其中最集中和突出的问题是我国旅游业发展中文化和旅游的融合度不高，单纯的自然景观旅游不能满足普通民众对旅游的需要，亟待通过增加旅游中的文化内涵来提升旅游业。文旅融合后的旅游业，在“文化 +”和“旅游 +”的基础上，旅游业的文化内涵和经济内涵，是未来旅游业发展的出路和途径。其三，文化部和国家旅游局合并还显示了国家文化战略思维。文化旅游已不单单是文化经济，文化旅游还承担着传承、创新和弘扬中华优秀文化，提升国家文化软实力的重大使命。十八大以来，党中央、国务院大力提倡传承和弘扬中华优秀传统文化，文化旅游是传承、创新和弘扬中华优秀传统文化的重要途径和手段。就国内旅游而言，要赋予旅游业更多的文化内涵，向民众传播和普及中华优秀文化。同时，随着我国国际化程度越来越高，出境游和入境游的人数大大增长。出境游和入境游也成为传播和弘扬中华优秀文化的重要途径。因此，文化部和国家旅游局合并，是我国文旅融合迈出的第一步，此后还要不断加强文旅深度融合，不仅适应了新常态下国家战略发展的需要，有利于提升我国经济发展的质量，满足我国新常态下经济的转型需要，而且可以提升文化自觉，彰显文化自信，推动中华优秀文化走出去。

二　郑州旅游业发展现状和存在的问题

我们结合全国旅游业发展的情况，再来看看郑州 2014 ~ 2018 年来旅游业发展的情况（见表 2）。

表2　郑州2014～2018年旅游业增长情况

年份	旅游年收入(亿元)	同比增长(%)	旅游情况		国际旅游情况		国内旅游情况	
			人数(万人次)	同比增长(%)	人数(万人次)	同比增长(%)	人数(万人次)	同比增长(%)
2014	892.6	11.4	7766	10.6	45.1	2.7	7720.9	10.7
2015	1004.2	12.5	8674.4	11.7	47.3	4.9	8627.1	11.7
2016	1053.9	4.9	8933.6	3.0	48.1	1.7	8885.5	3.0
2017	1195	13.4	10092	13.0	50.3	4.6	10041.7	13.0
2018	1387.4	16.1	11410	13.1	52.7	4.8	11357.3	13.1

资料来源：根据郑州市文广旅游局提供的数据制作。

从表2可以看出，郑州2014～2018年来旅游业的增速保持着较高水平，说明郑州旅游业的发展有着良好的基础。

新常态下，虽然郑州这些年GDP增幅超过了全国GDP增幅，但是2018年GDP增幅仍低于郑州旅游业的增幅，这可以从表3看出来。

表3　“新常态”下郑州GDP的增速

年份	全市地区生产总值(亿元)	同比增长率(%)	全国GDP增幅
2014	6800	9.3%	7.3%
2015	7315.2	10.1%	6.9%
2016	7994.2	8.5%	6.7%
2017	9130.2	8.2%	6.8%
2018	10143.3	8.1%	6.6%

资料来源：根据郑州市相关部门发布的数据整理。

虽然，郑州旅游业目前增长高于GDP的增长，但也存在着很多困境和问题，这些困境与问题某种程度上与全国旅游业发展中存在的困境和问题有一致性，其困境和问题主要表现在如下几方面。

第一，文化与旅游融合度不够，没能充分发挥郑州文化资源优势。郑州作为国家历史文化名城，文化资源的丰厚自不待言。但是，在郑州旅游业实际发展中，文化资源优势并没有充分体现出来，特别是郑州在中原文化中的核心地位和在华夏历史文明中的核心地位并没有得到体现，这是导致郑州旅游业发展中文化与旅游融合度不高或者说文化和旅游离散的重要原因。这种状况，造成郑州本地人对自己的文化认同度也不够，说起自己所居住的郑州时，只知道嵩山、少林寺、黄河等的具体地点和景观，而不知道郑州是华夏历史文明的核心区域，不知道郑州是八大古都之一，不知道中华五千年的历史实际上源于黄帝文化；也造成了很多来郑州的外地人，不仅不熟悉郑州丰富的历史文化，反而觉得郑州是个没有文化的城市，来郑州旅游的人，也只想看看郑州的嵩山、少林寺、黄河等景点，而缺乏了解郑州文化的兴趣。

第二，没有及时把握和适应当前旅游分层化的发展趋势。随着我国大众旅游时代的到来，旅游民众对旅游出现了分层化的需求，这与不同的旅游者文化素养不同导致了旅游目的不同和对旅游的要求不同是一致的。但是，郑州目前的旅游品种明显存在“一刀切”“大锅烩”等思维，对旅游的分层化重视不够，没有组织力量去充分研究和积极应对，这一定程度上影响和制约了郑州文化旅游业的发展。

第三，没能做好全域旅游的“功课”。“全域旅游”是国家根据现阶段我国旅游业发展现状和未来旅游发展需求前景提出来的，是为了提升我国旅游发展的水平而开展的。但是目前郑州全域旅游方面并没有出现明显的成效，这与一些旅游企业和团体对全域旅游认识滞后、旅游服务意识不强有很大的关系。由于没能做好全域旅游的功课，导致郑州旅游业仍然过分依赖门票收入，而总体环境和服务未能跟上。

第四，知名品牌较少，也未能发挥知名品牌的带动作用。来郑州旅游的人们，一般想去的是中岳嵩山、少林寺、黄帝故里等地方。嵩山、少林寺、黄帝故里等确实也是郑州享誉全国乃至享誉世界的知名品牌。但整体看，郑州知名旅游品牌并不多，导致现有旅游品牌与郑州所拥有的文化资源明显不相匹配，郑州一些具有全国性影响的文化事项没有被重视，更谈不上深度发掘。知名品牌具有带动效果，能带动与之相关的一些文化产品。而郑州的知名文化品牌的带动力未能充分开发，带动力还不够。缺少知名品牌的带动，也是制约郑州旅游业发展的主要因素。

郑州旅游业发展中存在的上述问题，最根本的问题和症结其实还是文化和旅游的融合度不够，未能充分发挥郑州所拥有丰富的历史文化资源的优势。

三　文旅深度融合对郑州国家中心城市建设的推动力

新常态下，实现文旅深度融合，发挥郑州的人口优势、区位优势，尤其是文化资源优势，壮大郑州旅游业，弘扬中原文化和中华优秀文化，是建设国家中心城市的使命所在，也是建设郑州大都市区，实现中部崛起，积极融入国家“一带一路”倡议的使命所在。

下面几组数字可以看出郑州的人口优势和区位优势及在国家战略上的重要地位。

2017 年底，郑州获批建设国家中心城市，成为中国的国家 9 个中心城市之一。2018 年，郑州总人口达到了 1000 万，GDP 达到了一万亿元，这表明郑州城市建设和城市发展进入了新的阶段。2018 年底，省政府通过了《郑州大都市区空间规划（2018—2035 年）》，为郑州在国家中心城市建设的基础上，打造郑州大都市区（郑州大都市区以郑州为核心，包括郑州市域，开封、新乡、焦作、许昌四市中心城区和巩义市、武陟县、原阳县、新乡县、尉氏县、长葛市、平原城乡一体化示范区。郑州大都市区国土总面积约 1.59 万平方公里，占全省面积的 9.6%，集聚了全省近 20% 的人口和超过 30% 的经济总量，是中原城市群中经济实力最强、发展速度最快的区域，是新亚欧大陆桥经济走廊上最具发展活力的区域，插翅添翼。

郑州人口优势、区位优势都非常突出，郑州大力发展旅游业有雄厚基础和独特优势。

郑州的文化优势则更加突出。郑州是华夏历史文明的核心区域，有五次为都、八代为州的历史。这里是中华人文的始祖——黄帝的出生地和建都地，这里是夏朝大禹的建都地（登封告成镇是禹都阳城遗址），这里是商代早期都城亳都，这里是西周至春秋时代郑国国都，是战国时期韩国国都……可以说，华夏文明的每一个阶段都能看到郑州的身影。长期的历史发展留下了大量物质和非物质文化遗产。这里著名的物质文化遗产有黄帝故里，包含了仰韶、龙山和夏商四种不同时期考古学文化的大型古代聚落大河村遗址，有夏禹建都遗址、商代早期遗址、大运河通济渠郑州段、天地之中历史建筑群……这里的国家级非物质文化遗产有黄帝拜祖大典、超化吹歌、苌家拳、少林功夫、小相狮舞……

新常态下，郑州提升城市发展质量，提升城市文化品位，应充分发挥文化优势，尤其是应把文化旅游产业发展放在重要位置，通过旅游产业促进文化传承弘扬，通过文化资源挖掘和利用推进旅游产业的转型升级，从而真正实现文化旅游的融合发展。郑州文旅深度融合在推动郑州经济发展的同时，还将有助于实现中华优秀传统文化创造性转化、创新性发展，有助于弘扬历史上和当代的中原人文精神；由于郑州是“一带一路”重要的节点城市，文旅深度融合，也有助于郑州建设国际文化旅游名城，并推动中华优秀文化走出去。

四　文旅深度融合，打造高质量发展的郑州模式

郑州实现文旅深度融合有深厚基础。如前所述，郑州是华夏历史文明的核心区域，历史文化资源丰富。同时，郑州地处黄河中游，黄河滩涂、巍巍嵩山等是重要而丰富的自然景观旅游资源。文旅的深度融合，将裹挟着厚重的历史文化与自然资源融为一体，让自然与人文合二为一，让自然带给人美的享受，文化陶冶人的心灵。

那么，如何通过文旅深度融合，打造高质量发展的郑州模式呢？我们提出以下具体建议。

1. 以华夏历史文明传承和创新为灵魂。文旅融合，文化是灵魂，旅游是载体。以往的文化旅游，是举着文化的大旗发展旅游，现在是借助旅游的形式复兴文化。郑州作为华夏历史文明的核心区域，在实现文旅深度融合时，应注意以下几点：文化创意应该以华夏历史文明传承与创新为引领，有意识地突出郑州华夏历史文明核心区的地位；精品旅游线路要围绕展示和体验华夏历史文明中的主要文化事项做文章；文化理念应该把弘扬华夏历史文明、弘扬中原人文精神、弘扬中华文明精神作为重要目标；开展入境游要借“一带一路”的东风，重视和抢占沿线国家的文化旅游市场份额，加强与沿线国家的文化互动，实现中华文化与世界多元文化的交流和互鉴；等等。

2. 郑州文旅深度融合，应该选择代表性文化事项为着力点。就郑州而言，应发挥自己的文化资源优势，选取与华夏历史文明密切相关的、在国内和国际文化旅游中知名的旅游品牌和文旅事项来做大文章，实现文旅的深度融合。如

以黄帝文化、古都文化、少林文化等为资源，推动寻根问祖文化旅游、古都文化旅游、少林功夫文化旅游、大河文化旅游等具有国内国际知名的旅游品牌和旅游事项。同时，还应该通过大数据，分析不同旅游者的需求，进而分层化设计郑州文化旅游线路，以满足不同旅游者的旅游兴趣。

3. 文旅深度融合，应坚持“文化+”与“旅游+”的结合，推动文化和旅游与多业态的融合。以文化融入旅游，又让旅游与其他业态融合，将会产生文化旅游的“核裂变效应”。如坚持“文化+”和“旅游+”战略或者“文化+旅游+”战略，推动文化和旅游与农业、工业、服务业、体育健身等行业的深度融合；从投资主体方面看，应鼓励国有、集体、个体、外资等参与全域旅游开发；从整个业态看，要延伸产业链、提升价值链，培育新兴产业业态，从而支撑郑州市经济的高质量发展。

4. 郑州文旅深度融合，应该以建设国际文化大都市为重要目标。从目前看，郑州国际化程度还不算高，入境游人数也不算多。但是，随着郑州航空港的建设、每周八去八回的中欧班列（郑州）的运营、郑州买全球电商平台建设，作为“一带一路”的重要节点城市，郑州逐渐成为内陆开放高地，也将会越来越被世界各国人民认识和了解。“一带一路”涉及65个国家和地区，约44亿人口（约占全球人口的63%），旅游市场巨大，蕴含了巨大的文化旅游商机。郑州作为华夏历史文明的核心区域，应以前瞻性的眼光，抓住历史赋予的重大机遇，抢占文化旅游中的国际份额，并推进郑州国际文化大都市建设。郑州国际文化大都市建设，不仅是实现郑州文化旅游深度融合的重要途径，还是通过文旅深度融合推动郑州高质量发展的重要手段。

5. 郑州文旅深度融合的突破点应着重于：

——聚焦“大融合”。推动文旅融合、产城融合、产业融合，形成多领域、多产业和多区域融合式发展势头，成为撬动经济腾飞的重要支点。

——谋划“大项目”：发挥项目建设在优化结构中强大的引擎作用，推进文化旅游产业聚集发展，在更大时空更宽领域内更深层次地推动文化旅游产业提升。

——开发“大产品”：优化产品结构，塑造优质精品，满足消费者的高品质需要。

——优化“大环境”：通过服务质量提升，完善配套设施，形成优质发展环境。

6. 郑州文旅深度融合的路径在于：

——框架高质量设计，即制定旅游产业高质量发展的规划体系，整合区域旅游资源，推进体制机制改革，建立高质量发展示范区等，构建支撑经济高质量发展的总体框架。

——产品高质量供给，即实施差异化发展策略，推动旅游产品和服务的质量提升，培育优质旅游景区，提高旅游商品质量，推进重点旅游项目建设等，发挥经济高质量发展的引领功能。

——产业高质量融合，即以全域旅游发展为抓手，不断推进文化旅游与其他产业有机融合，创新融合方式方法，推进多要素集聚、多产业叠加，培育新业态，构建支撑经济高质量发展的新动力。

——品牌高质量塑造，即构建旅游整体品牌，打造组成多层次、全产业链的旅游品牌体系。创新文化旅游营销方式，强化宣传引导，讲好“郑州故事”，培育高质量发展的新亮点。

——公共服务体系高质量建设，即实现旅游集散咨询服务的“综合便捷”、旅游交通体系的“快进慢游”、旅游管理服务的“智慧智能”，构建高质量发展的新典范。

——乡村旅游高质量发展：通过构建乡村旅游片区、名村名镇建设、旅游扶贫等，以旅游推动乡村全面振兴，形成高质量发展的新内容。

——高质量保障措施：通过政策扶持、人才强旅、考核督导等方式，不断提升文化旅游产业品质，打造高质量发展新环境。

7. 郑州文旅深度融合的原则在于：坚持走经济和文化的可持续发展道路。党的十八大报告对推进中国特色社会主义事业、全面建成小康社会、实现社会主义现代化和中华民族伟大复兴做出的“五位一体”总体布局（“五位”是指经济建设、政治建设、文化建设、社会建设、生态文明建设），也充分体现了可持续发展的理念。习近平总书记也在不同场合反复提“可持续发展”的发展观。郑州的文旅深度融合也要走经济和文化的可持续发展道路。

五　文旅深度融合郑州模式的前景展望

郑州文旅深度融合，让文化旅游业成为提升郑州在国家中心城市建设的重要产业，进而通过国家中心城市建设带动郑州大都市区的经济发展，成为中部崛起的重要力量。

参考文献

[1] 胡晓芬、厉新建：《从八个视角看城市发展与文旅融合》，《中国文化报》2019年4月13日。

[2] 钟晟：《推进文旅融合　构筑中华民族精神家园》，《中国文化报》2019年7月26日。

[3] 钱春弦：《深化文旅融合，可以传承优秀传统文化》，《中国旅游报》2019年6月12日。

[4] 《亚洲文明对话大会2019北京共识》，新华网，http：//www.xinhuanet.com/world/2019-05/24/c_1124539189.htm，2019-5-24。

[5] 雒树刚：《以文旅融合促优质旅游》，《中国房地产》2019年第14期，第13页。

[6] 吴学安：《文化旅游联袂让诗和远方携手前行》，《中华读书报》2019年7月3日。

B.14
重庆大都市区一体化发展研究

涂建军　楚　杰　毛　凯　黄　艳　丁卫珍*

摘　要： 本报告运用城市中心性、场强和经济联系强度模型、威尔逊系数等数学模型，探究重庆大都市区的空间结构、一体化发展水平，提出大都市区一体化发展路径。结果表明：①重庆大都市区呈现“中心城 + 外围影响区”的城市空间结构。②“中心城”（主城建成区）的空间扩展方向以向西、向北为主，扩展重心路径为“渝北区、沙坪坝区、南岸区→江北区、沙坪坝区→江北区、渝北区、北碚区”；大都市区外围影响区的空间经济联系得到不断强化。③直辖以来重庆大都市区一体化综合水平显著提升，与建成区空间拓展、经济发展水平差异和国家战略、政府政策密切相关。④重庆大都市区一体化发展的关键路径是构建“一城—五片—多中心组团”的大都市区空间格局。

关键词： 大都市区　一体化发展　空间结构　重庆市

大都市区是城市演化过程中出现的一种特殊的地域空间组织形式，是城市经济社会发展到一定阶段的必然产物。多年来，世界各国相关专家、学者和城

* 涂建军，博士，西南大学经济管理学院教授、博士生导师，研究方向为城市与区域发展；楚杰，西南大学地理科学学院硕士研究生，研究方向为城市与区域发展；毛凯，西南大学地理科学学院硕士研究生，研究方向为城市与区域发展；黄艳，西南大学地理科学学院硕士研究生，研究方向为城市与区域发展；丁卫珍，西南大学地理科学学院硕士研究生，研究方向为城市与区域发展。

市管理、建设部门从理论和实践两方面探索了新的历史发展阶段中城市发展的总体趋势和突出特点，研究大都市区、都市圈、城市群、都市连绵区等不同空间组织形式的地域演进和组织规律，并取得了丰富的研究成果，对推动大都市区发展提供了理论依据与实践参考。

重庆市兼具一个特大城市和一个中等规模省域的双重特性，是国家中心城市和西部地区唯一直辖市。然而，重庆市主城区人口、经济、用地等总量规模较小，在一定程度上削弱了重庆经济、社会发展的规模效应。因此，重庆市推动一体化发展，需要以大都市区作为基本载体，促进区域内人口、用地、产业和交通等方面的合理布局，提升大都市区综合实力，这是推动重庆市各区域协调发展，实现重庆市全面、协调、可持续发展的必由路径。本报告从重庆大都市区的空间结构、一体化发展水平评价、影响因素和发展路径四个层面，探索重庆大都市区的空间特征、现状水平、发展轨迹以及驱动机制，为今后重庆市发展战略的制定提供实证基础。

一　研究方法与数据

（一）研究方法

1. 城市中心性

中心性是衡量中心地等级高低的指标，反映的是中心地为其以外地区服务的相对重要性。公式为：

$$U = \sum_{i=1}^{m} x_{ij} w_j \qquad (1)$$

公式（1）中，U 为城市中心性水平值，m 为年份，X_{ij}为第 i 个年份第 j 个指标的标准化值，W_j为第 j 项指标的权重（本报告涉及的权重计算均采用熵值法）。

2. 经济联系强度和经济联系隶属度模型

本报告采用城市人口规模、行政区划面积及 GDP 三个参量的经济联系强度模型公式和经济联系隶属度公式，并对权属进行修正。

经济距离是指中心城市与其他核心城镇之间的交流强度，核心城镇与中心城市距离越大，其与核心城镇间的交流强度变小，联系变少，其主要是对通勤时间的修正。本研究以空间距离为基础，通过两次修正得到经济距离，公式为：

$$E = \alpha \times \beta \times D \tag{2}$$

公式（2）中，E 为经济距离，D 是中心城市到城镇的空间距离，α、β 为修正权数。

经济联系强度模型用以表征区域的中心城市与周围核心城镇间绝对经济联系量，反映区域的中心城市对外经济联系范围，公式为：

$$T_{ij} = \frac{\sqrt[3]{P_i \times G_i \times R_i} \times \sqrt[3]{P_j \times G_j \times R_j}}{D_{ij}^{\ 2}} \tag{3}$$

经济联系隶属度模型，用以衡量一个区域周围核心城镇接受其中心城市经济辐射强度的大小，公式为：

$$L_{ij} = \frac{T_{ij}}{\sum_{i=1}^{n} T_{ij}} \tag{4}$$

其中，T 为经济联系强度，i 为大都市区周围核心城镇，j 为中心城市，P 为城市总人口，G 为城市 GDP，R 为行政区划面积，D 为经济距离，L_{ij} 为经济联系隶属度。

3. 城市经济场强模型

城市经济场强用来寻找区域中心城市对周围核心城镇作用力的“力场”中经济作用力迅速减少的位置，用来衡量大都市区中心城市对周围核心城镇经济作用的“力场图”，反映大都市区城镇间经济相互作用的空间结构，公式为：

$$S_j = \frac{\sqrt[3]{P_j \times G_j \times R_j}}{D_{ij}^{\ 2}} \tag{5}$$

其中，S 为城市场强，i 为大都市区周围核心城镇，j 为中心城市，P 为城市总人口，G 为城市 GDP，R 为行政区划面积，D 为经济距离。

4. 威尔逊系数

威尔逊系数是在变异系数的基础上所延伸的，是一种加权变异系数，它描述了具有相同性质的标志值数列的离散程度。公式为：

$$V_u = \frac{1}{x'} \times \sqrt{\sum_{i=1}^{n} \frac{(x_i - \bar{x})^2 p_i}{p}} \tag{6}$$

其中，x'为背景区域人均 GDP，x 为第 i 地区人均 GDP，p 为背景区域总人口，p_i为第 i 地区人口。当然，也可计入其他经济指标进行测算，如本报告综合运用 GDP 和人均 GDP 指标，如此便可更为全面地测算大都市区区域发展的差异程度。

5. 泰尔指数

泰尔指数是 1967 年由泰尔运用信息理论中的熵概念提出的可按加法原则分解的不平等系数，该指数因具有能将区域总体差异分解为组间与组内差异的优势，被逐步应用于区域差异测算的实证分析。公式为：

$$T = \frac{1}{N} \sum_{i \in N} \frac{y_i}{\mu} \ln \frac{y_i}{\mu} \tag{7}$$

公式（7）中，N代表所研究区域的个数，y为第i个区域的一体化水平，μ为重庆大都市区全区域一体化水平。对数离差值即泰尔指数 T。T 值越小表明区域差异越小，一体化水平越高，反之则区域差异越大，一体化水平越低。本报告通过测算重庆大都市区在经济发展、基础设施、公共服务 3 个方面的泰尔指数得到一体化综合指数来反映重庆大都市区的一体化水平。

（二）数据来源与处理

本文数据主要来源于 1997 ~ 2017 年中国城市统计年鉴、重庆市统计年鉴，部分数据来源于国家统计局网站（http：//data. stats. gov. cn/）。城市内交通数据来源于 http：//tools. 2345. com/jiaotong/lc. htm 和 https：//www. qichezhan. cn/，空间数据来自国家基础地理信息中心（http：//www. ngcc. cn/）。

本报告结合地理空间遥感技术（RS），运用 ENVI 软件对重庆主城区遥感数据进行处理，选取重庆直辖以来的遥感数据样本，经过辐射校正、几何校正、镶嵌裁剪和图像增强等预处理之后，建立 NDBI（归一化建筑指数）和

NDVI（归一化植被指数）模型，提取预处理后卫星遥感数据的城市面积和空间分布数据，得到重庆主城区城市建成区的空间结构演变。

二　重庆大都市区空间结构

大都市区不只是一个区域名称的概念，也是一个地区城镇化发展到成熟阶段的表现形式，更是推进城镇群建设的主体形态之一。大都市区是个复杂的系统，是以城市功能较强的中心城市为核心的。重庆大都市区现已形成以主城9区为“中心城”，以“中心城”外围12区（涪陵区、江津区、永川区、合川区、璧山区、綦江区、长寿区、大足区、潼南区、荣昌区、铜梁区、南川区）为影响区的城市区域，总面积2.87万平方公里。

（一）重庆大都市区“中心城”空间结构演变

大都市区的形成与发展是个动态演进的过程，任何一个大都市区都会经历从形成到成熟的变化过程。重庆主城建成区作为重庆大都市区的“中心城”，经历了改革开放以来，特别是直辖以来的快速发展，已经成为地区经济发展最为迅速、城镇化发展水平最高、城市空间拓展最为迅猛的地区，成为辐射、带动大都市区协调发展的坚强基石。

重庆主城区建成区空间拓展主要包括以下三个阶段。

第一阶段为1997～2005年：主城区城市空间拓展以向北、向西为主，至2005年，主城区核心区域向外延伸至缙云山与明月山之间，外围区域呈点状快速发展。城市建成区扩展主要位于渝北区、沙坪坝区和南岸区，沿交通干线延伸显著（见图1）。

第二阶段为2006～2010年：主城区建设发展转向西、北两方向。由于城市发展受交通因素的影响，城市建成区沿公路分布延伸明显，直接导致处于这两方向的沙坪坝区和江北区城市空间扩展速度最快，其中尤以江北区发展最为迅速，城市空间扩展强度最大（见图2）。

第三阶段为2011～2015年：经过2006～2010年的已建区内部空间消化，城区建设再次开始向外扩展，主要集中在两个方向：一是城市继续向西发展。随着中梁山多条隧道的打通，城区建设得以越过中梁山的地形限制，直达缙云山麓，实现了与中梁山—缙云山槽行谷地的联动发展。二是2010年后，随着两江新区（包括原来的北部新区）的成立与开发，主城区建设逐渐扩展到西北方向，涵盖江北区、渝北区和北碚区三个区域，现有江北金融城、悦来国际会展城和果园港地区得以迅速发展（见图3）。

图1　1997～2005年重庆主城建成区

图2　2006～2010年重庆主城建成区

图3　2011～2015年重庆主城建成区

（二）重庆大都市区外围影响区空间经济联系特征

重庆大都市区的一体化发展不仅体现在“中心城”（主城建成区）空间的进一步拓展，还表现在其外围影响区空间经济联系的强化。截至2016年末，重庆大都市区“中心城”人口规模达到851.80万，且城市化水平达到89.03%。除此之外，重庆大都市区“中心城”的城市中心性水平达到69.21（城市中心性水平指标体系构建及权重见表1）。

通过计算重庆大都市区“中心城”与周边核心区县的经济距离、重庆大都市区“中心城”与周边核心区县的经济联系强度和经济联系隶属度、重庆大都市区“中心城”对周边核心区县的场强，对比发现，重庆大都市区外围影响区12个区县的场强、经济联系强度和经济联系隶属度特征为：场强>1.50，经济联系强度>5.0，经济隶属度>0.3（见表2）。综合重庆大都市区“中心城”的人口规模、城市化水平和中心性，以及大都市区外围影响区的空间经济联系特征，进一步论证了重庆大都市区“中心城+外围影响区”的城市空间结构。

表1　城市中心性水平指标体系及各指标权重

目标层	准则层	指标层	权重
城市中心性水平	城市经济发展水平	地区生产总值(万元)	0.1355
		人均地区生产总值(元)	0.0958
		非农产业产值比重(%)	0.0935
		社会消费品零售总额(万元)	0.1105
	城市物质要素建设水平	常住人口城镇化率(%)	0.1002
		全社会固定资产投资额(万元)	0.0836
		建筑业总产值(万元)	0.0522
		交通便捷指数	0.0673
	城市公共服务与居民生活水平	各区县公共预算支出(万元)	0.0629
		中、小学在校人数(人)	0.0455
		城镇职工平均工资(元)	0.0793
		金融机构人均存款(元)	0.0737

注：交通便捷指数是将各区县高速公路里程数、等级公路里程数、高铁里程数、铁路里程数、交通出口（高速公路出口、高铁站、铁路站）总个数5个指标分别标准化后，参照《公路工程技术标准》（JTG B01—2014）的规定和国家铁路规定，并结合重庆路况，确定公路60km/h，铁路100km/h，高速公路120km/h，高速铁路200km/h，确定权重分别为0.19、0.13、0.32、0.16、0.2，最终加权求和得出。

表2　重庆大都市区“中心城”与周边核心区县的空间经济联系特征

区县	经济距离	场强	联系强度	隶属度(%)
璧山区	12.15	21.67	66.28	3.02
江津区	23.7	5.70	37.87	1.73
綦江区	47.7	1.51	7.04	0.32
合川区	22.4	6.38	35.44	1.61
永川区	29.4	3.70	17.81	0.81
铜梁区	46.68	1.57	5.71	0.31
长寿区	39.55	2.05	7.70	0.35
大足区	38.52	2.16	7.57	0.34
荣昌区	45.18	1.57	5.76	0.32
潼南区	41.7	1.84	5.94	0.37
南川区	131.4	1.90	5.80	0.33
涪陵区	32.36	3.06	20.52	0.93

三　重庆大都市区一体化水平评价

重庆大都市区一体化不仅体现在大都市区“中心城”（主城建成区）空间结构的拓展，“中心城”与外围影响区空间经济联系的加强，更体现在大都市区区域一体化水平的提高。重庆市雄厚的经济基础实力是推动重庆大都市区一体化发展的基础条件，新型城镇化建设稳步推进、区域发展战略的演变也成为助推重庆大都市区一体化发展的重要支撑。自2000年以来，重庆市经济发展实现了质的飞跃，全市GDP规模从2000年的1797亿元增加到2015年的15872.23亿元，增加了近8倍。此外，2015年重庆市社会固定资产投资达到15480.33亿元，相比于2000年的655.81亿元，增长了22.6倍。在重庆市经济发展水平日益提高的背景下，本报告从经济发展水平差异的单维视角和经济发展、基础设施、公共服务一体化水平测度的多维视角来评价重庆大都市区一体化水平。

（一）经济发展水平差异测度

地区经济发展水平是决定区域内部综合发展是否协调的关键因素。区域经济差异应包括各区域之间在经济增长总量、增长速度、经济结构乃至经济发展条件方面所存在的差异。以各区GDP和人均GDP为基础数据，利用威尔逊系数计算得出直辖以来重庆大都市区21个区之间的经济发展的差异值（威尔逊系数值）如图4所示。

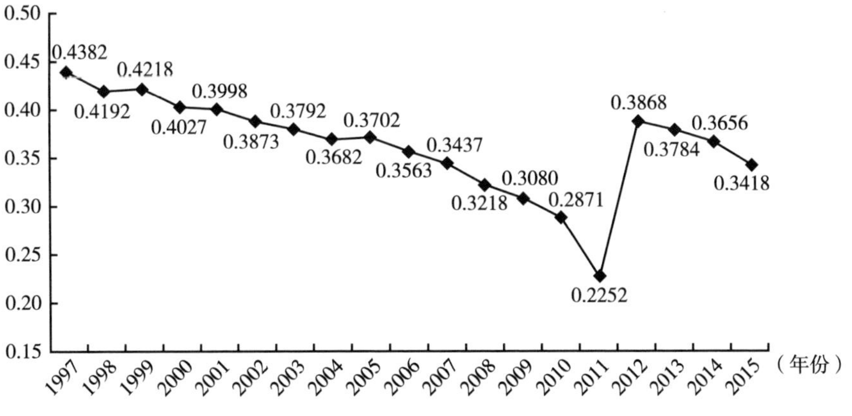

图4　重庆大都市区威尔逊指数（1997～2015年）

可以看出，直辖以来，重庆大都市区21个区之间的区域经济发展差异在这近20年间总体处于下降水平，从1997年的0.4382下降到2015年的0.3418，说明21个区之间的区域经济发展差异在不断缩小。需要指出的是，在2010年后，由于受到全球金融危机和“重庆市五大功能区”战略对大都市区的影响，大都市区威尔逊指数在2011～2012年出现了明显的回升，从2011年0.2252的历史最低位回升到2012年的0.3868，并在此后的2012～2015年继续下降。由此可以看出，国际环境、区域发展战略政策对区域一体化发展具有重要的影响。

（二）一体化发展水平测度

在对重庆大都市区21个区直辖以来的区域经济差异威尔逊指数演变历程研究的基础上，本报告运用区域协调发展指数（泰尔指数），从经济发展一体化、基础设施一体化、公共服务一体化三个方面（指标体系构建及权重见表3）分别计算出其泰尔指数在2000～2015年其变化趋势，从而得到一体化综合泰尔指数（见图5）。

表3　重庆大都市区一体化发展水平评价指标体系及权重

目标层	准则层	指标层	权重
区域一体化发展水平	经济发展一体化	非农产业GDP(万元)	0.1282
		人均GDP(元)	0.0392
		职工平均工资(元)	0.0131
		社会消费品零售总额(万元)	0.1571
	基础设施一体化	城镇化率(%)	0.0250
		全社会固定投资(万元)	0.1591
		等级公路里程(公里)	0.0365
		建筑业总产值(万元)	0.1793
	公共服务一体化	公共财政预算支出(万元)	0.0662
		中学以上在校学生数(人)	0.0914
		卫生机构个数(个)	0.0544
		公共图书馆藏书量(万册)	0.0504

可以看出，重庆大都市区一体化综合泰尔指数由2000年的0.028下降到2015年的0.008，区域一体化发展水平显著提升。从大都市区经济发展来看，

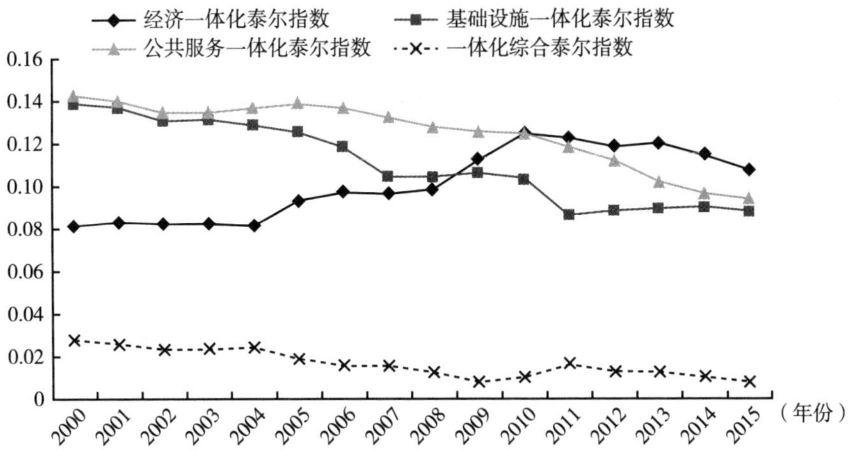

图 5　重庆大都市区一体化发展水平泰尔指数（2000～2015 年）

区域经济一体化泰尔指数经历了自 2004 年起先上升，后稳定，进而逐步下降的三个阶段，可以看出 2010 年后，大都市区经济发展差异开始缩小，经济一体化进程开始加速。大都市区基础设施和公共服务一体化发展历程大致相似，虽然在 2007～2011 年偶有起伏，但整体上相较于 2000 年，其一体化发展水平都有较大程度的提高。

四　重庆大都市区一体化发展路径分析

（一）构建一城—五片—多中心组团的大都市区空间布局

一是打造“一城”核心载体，即打造由大都市区“中心城”核心区构成的、承载国家中心城市功能的城市核心载体。

二是形成“五片”战略支撑。即在整个大都市区内部形成“1＋4”的城市空间格局。“1”是指在现有主城区空间范围的基础上，融合主城区外围地区 21 个镇街，实现主城区一体化发展。“4”是指在大都市区范围内形成的 4 个大的城市组团，分别是北部的铜梁—潼南组团、西部的永川—荣昌—大足组团、南部的綦江—南川组团、东部的长寿—涪陵组团。

三是构建“多中心组团式”网络结构。在“1＋4”大都市区总体空间格局的基础上，对每一个组团内部的空间结构进行深化。在主城区组团（即“1”）内部，形成以商圈、住宅区（大型聚居点）、产业园区等为中心的多级中心体系。铜梁—潼南组团以G93交通线为基础，形成以铜梁、潼南为中心的多级中心体系。永川—荣昌—大足组团以G85交通线为基础，形成以永川、荣昌、大足为中心的多级中心体系。綦江—南川组团以G210、G65交通线为基础，形成以綦江、南川、万盛为中心的多级中心体系。长寿—涪陵组团以G69、G50交通线为基础，形成以长寿、涪陵为中心的多级中心体系（多级中心体系指包括区域中心—县城—重点镇—重点村等在内的中心体系）。“4”个组团在大都市区范围内，由三环高速公路统一串联，形成继内环、外环后的又一环状空间结构，极大加强各组团之间的互联互通与交流协作。

（二）构建高效便捷的现代化综合交通运输体系

一是完善大都市区轨道交通网络体系，提高市民轨道出行比率。推动大都市区“中心城”形成以轨道＋步行、轨道＋公交为主的出行方式。

二是加快大都市区换乘场站和枢纽建设，实现交通出行零换乘。建设公众出行信息服务系统、车辆运营调度管理系统、安全监控系统和应急处置系统。加快建设公交换乘场站，重点解决重庆火车站、重庆北站、龙头寺、江北机场等交通节点与公交、轨道、出租车、市郊铁路等的换乘问题。

三是衔接市郊铁路与城市轨道，推动大都市区内部互联互通。优先利用国铁干线富余运输能力开行市郊列车，在干线铁路不能覆盖的区域新增布局市郊铁路线，并与干线铁路互联互通、与城市轨道交通便捷换乘，到2020年建成并开通市郊铁路璧山—铜梁、江津—九龙坡段，实现大都市区交通互联互通。

（三）优化产业分工，促进都市区产业集群与网络联动

一是大都市区“中心城”重点凸显出高端服务职能，着重布局金融服务、国际商务、高端商贸、文化创意、都市旅游等现代服务业，建设中央商务区与若干新兴现代服务业集聚区。

二是大都市区外围影响区要凸显先进制造与区域综合服务功能，布局电

子、汽摩、材料、航空设备、轨道交通设备等“国之重器”制造业，发展物流会展、仓储配送、软件研发、服务外包和服务贸易等区域综合性服务业。

三是大都市区一体化潜在拓展区则要凸显现代制造与本地服务功能，布局综合化工、钢铁、装备、消费品、电子配套及汽摩零部件等大型制造业，发展综合性物流、休闲旅游、商贸、现代农业等支撑产业，发挥工业经济主战场作用。

五 重庆大都市区一体化发展总体情况

重庆大都市区呈现出“中心城+外围影响区”的城市空间结构。重庆主城区建成区作为重庆大都市区“中心城”，其空间结构演变为重庆大都市区的形成与一体化发展奠定了基础，大都市区外围影响区的空间经济联系得到进一步强化，助推了重庆大都市区的一体化发展。

重庆主城建成区空间拓展主要包括三个阶段：第一阶段为1997~2005年，城市建成区扩展主要位于渝北区、沙坪坝区和南岸区，沿交通干线延伸显著，以外部蔓延为主；第二阶段为2006~2010年，主城区建设发展转向西、北两方向，沙坪坝区和江北区城市空间扩展速度最快，尤以江北区发展最为迅速，空间拓展模式由外围蔓延转向内部填充；第三阶段为2011~2015年，城市继续向西发展，2010年后，主城区建设逐渐扩展到西北方向，涵盖江北区、渝北区和北碚区三个区域。

直辖以来重庆大都市区21个区之间的经济发展差异整体处于下降水平，在2011~2012年出现了短暂的扩大，2012年后差距继续缩小。自2000年以来，重庆大都市区经济一体化水平在波动中前进，而基础设施和公共服务一体化水平同步提升，重庆大都市区一体化综合水平得到提升。影响重庆大都市区一体化水平的主要因素包括建成区空间拓展、社会经济发展水平差异和政府政策、发展战略等。

重庆大都市区一体化发展路径最重要的是构建“一城—五片—多中心组团”的大都市区空间布局，在整个大都市区内部形成“1+4”的城市空间格局，“1”是指在现有主城区空间范围的基础上，融合主城区外围地区21个镇街，实现主城区一体化发展；“4”是指在大都市区范围内形成的4个大的城市组团，分别是北部的铜梁—潼南组团、西部的永川—荣昌—大足组团、南部的綦江—南川组团、东部的长寿—涪陵组团，“4”个组团由三环高速公路统一串联，形成继内环、外环后的又一环状空间结构，进一步加强各组团之间的互联互通与交流协作。

由于数据的可获取性以及区域一体化的动态性特征，本研究还存在一些需要改进和完善的地方：①需要更深入探讨新形势下大都市区一体化发展的新格局。重庆市直辖以来，区域间经济联系在不断增强，要素向“中心城”集聚的趋势也越来越强，传统以行政界线为主的大都市区一体化格局不断发生变化，亟须研究大都市区一体化的新格局。②应对区域一体化水平进行动态的评价。本报告利用威尔逊系数和泰尔指数对重庆大都市区一体化水平进行评价，所用数据仅为 2016 年的截面数据，但是重庆大都市区一体化的空间范围是不断变化的，下一步应对不同时段的大都市区一体化水平进行评价。③可进一步借助网络大数据、人工智能平台进行研究。本报告利用遥感影像分析了重庆大都市区“中心城”的空间结构演变，用道路里程数据、经济数据等统计数据量化分析了城市空间经济联系，但区域间要素“流动”无时无刻不在进行，今后可借助实时大数据探究区域间人口、经济、交通的动态特征，并分析大都市区一体化的空间动态演变过程。

参考文献

［1］梁双波、曹有挥、吴威：《上海大都市区港口物流企业的空间格局演化》，《地理研究》2013 年第 8 期，第 1448 ~ 1456 页。

［2］宁越敏：《中国都市区和大城市群的界定——兼论大城市群在区域经济发展中的作用》，《地理科学》2011 年第 3 期，第 257 ~ 263 页。

［3］方创琳、Yehua Dennis Wei：《河西地区可持续发展能力评价及地域分异规律》，《地理学报》2001 年第 5 期，第 560 ~ 568 页。

［4］陈肖飞、张落成、姚士谋：《基于新经济地理学的长三角城市群空间格局及发展因素》，《地理科学进展》2015 年第 2 期，第 229 ~ 236 页。

［5］欧向军、薛丽萍、顾雯娟：《江苏省县市经济联系的空间特征》，《经济地理》2015 年第 8 期，第 24 ~ 31 页。

［6］闫广华：《沈阳都市圈的范围及城镇空间分布的分形研究》，《地理科学》2016

年第 11 期，第 1736 ~ 1742 页。

[7] 汪彬、陈耀：《京津冀城市群发展差距测算及协同发展研究》，《上海经济研究》2015 年第 8 期，第 109 ~ 116 页。

[8] 胡志远、欧向军：《基于泰尔指数的江苏省区域差异多指标测度》，《经济地理》2007 年第 5 期，第 719 ~ 724 页。

B.15 成都行政区划调整对公共服务供给的影响研究*

罗若愚　刘俊杰**

摘　要： 行政区划调整是政府改变城市发展的轨迹，重塑城市发展活力和区域发展格局的一种政策安排。现阶段促进城乡统筹，加快城乡一体化建设是行政区划调整的主要目标之一。行政区划调整可以降低行政成本，优化资源配置，改善公共服务供求矛盾。同时行政区划调整也会影响公共资源的供求结构以及公共服务设施的空间布局。本文以成都市为例，从纵向历史轨迹研究成都行政区划调整和公共服务供给体系变化的关系，探究公共服务的具体作用机理，并阐释行政区划调整对公共服务供给的双重影响。

关键词： 成都市　行政区划调整　城市空间结构　公共服务供给

作为政府治理社会的一项公共管理手段，行政区划调整主要通过系统性改变区域内的行政结构，进而带动城市空间结构的优化和升级。在城市化发展到一定阶段，城市区域空间扩大，城市人口增加，必然会对城市的公共服务产生较大影响。公共服务发展完善，又进一步影响城市居民生活的满意度和幸福度，是现代社会健康发展的重要指标，同时也是服务型政府建设的重要指标。

---

* 本文为教育部人文社会科学研究一般项目（19YJA630051）阶段性成果。

** 罗若愚，博士，电子科技大学公共管理学院教授，研究方向为城市与区域治理；刘俊杰，硕士，电子科技大学公共管理学院硕士，研究方向为城市与区域治理。

所以在行政区域调整的过程中应重视对公共服务的供给，缓解公共服务供给的空间结构不均衡的矛盾，以适应城市发展的需要。

一　成都市行政区划调整的过程及特征

（一）成都市行政区划调整的历史沿革

1. 第一次行政区划的调整。根据相关资料，从新中国成立到20世纪60年代是成都市行政区划的第一次调整时期，该时期主要是市辖区的调整。新中国成立初期，成都市有8个市辖区。1950～1960年不断对行政区划进行重划调整，成都市行政区划在1960年共分为东城区、西城区、郊区、青白江区和龙泉驿区5个组成区。在城市空间构造上，成都市沿用苏联模式，形成了核心放射的基本发展形态。同时为了适应国家五年计划，成都市重点对工业进行了布局，将工业区划分在西部城区，将居民区划分在东部城区，使得工业区与居民区的界线越来越明显（见表1）。

表1　成都市行政区划调整情况（新中国成立初期到20世纪60年代）

年份	行政区划调整后的变化
1950	划入华阳县的得胜乡部分和永丰乡入五、六区，同时将七、八两区并入
1952	撤销成都县，将原成都县属的天回泰华、金马、太平、红星等乡划入三区，划华阳县的保和、得胜、兴隆（龙潭寺）等乡入四区
1953	市辖区数量由原本的八区调整为东城、西城、望江、万年、龙潭五个区
1960	划温江县的簇桥公社入郊区。同年7月郊区更名为成都市金牛区。由1957年的三区发展为东城区、西城区、郊区、青白江区和龙泉驿区五区

资料来源：成都行政区划网。

2. 第二次行政区划的调整。成都市行政区划的第二次调整大致在20世纪70年代到90年代初。这一时期行政区划调整的主要表现是“划县入市”（见表2）。

在1976～1983年，金堂、双流两县以及简阳、温江的部分区域划归成都，并开始实行市领导县体制。这次的行政区划调整不仅扩大了成都市的区域范围，而且完善了城市的服务功能。

表 2　成都市行政区划调整情况（20 世纪 70 年代到 90 年代初）

年份	行政区划的具体调整
1976	金堂、双流两县划入成都；简阳洛带区划入龙泉驿区，仁寿县籍田区划入双流县
1983	温江地区（除广汉、什邡两县外）划入成都市，实行市领导县体制

资料来源：成都行政区划网。

3. 第三次行政区划调整。成都市大致在 20 世纪 90 年代到 21 世纪初，进行了第三次行政区划调整。这一时期行政区划调整主要表现在“行政区域界线调整”和“撤县设区”两个方面。在 1990 ~ 1994 年，成都市在行政区域界线调整方面，将原东城区、西城区、金牛区调整为锦江、青羊、金牛、武侯、成华区，并且采用城乡结合，以区带乡的管理体制对其行政区域进行管理。在“撤县建市”方面，选择了灌县等 4 个县进行了行政区划调整改革，使得行政区域的范围不断扩大。总体来讲，成都通过扩大行政区域边界和撤县设市，扩大了建成区的面积，使得城市由块状的空间结构向轴向结构发展延伸。

表 3　成都市行政区划调整情况（20 世纪 90 年代到 21 世纪初）

年份	行政调整方式	具体调整方案
1990	行政区域界线调整	将原东城区、西城区、金生区调整为锦江、青羊、金牛、武侯、成华区，采取了城乡结合，以区带乡体制
1994	撤县设市	灌县改为都江堰市，彭县、邛峡县、崇庆县相继“撤县建市”

资料来源：成都行政区划网。

4. 第四次行政区划的调整。第四次行政区划调整大致在 21 世纪初至今。在此期间，成都的行政区划调整最为频繁，调整的项目内容也最为丰富多样。主要表现形式是新城区建设、乡镇改革和区界重组。新城区建设主要表现为撤县设区和成立国家级新区。2002 年新都县及温江县相继开展撤县设区的工作；2013 年成立了国家级新区“天府新区”；2015 年双流县调整为双流区；2016 年郫县调整为郫都区。乡镇改革主要表现是乡镇建制改革。2004 年成都市通过撤销合并的形式改革了乡镇的行政管理机构，开始实行以街道办事处为基础的行政管理体制。区界重组大致开始于 21 世纪初，主要表现是城乡和不同区之间的面积变化调整。由于区界调整具有局部性和灵活性，所以区界重组将一直持续下去，以适应不断推进的城市化建设。

（二）成都市行政区划调整的特征

梳理历史文献，可以发现成都市行政区划的调整呈现阶段性特征。根据图1描绘的成都行政区划调整的时间轴，成都首先调整了行政区域的界线，调整的总体特征是城市的行政范围逐渐扩大到郊区。20世纪70年代初，伴随城市化的发展，成都开始在原成都区域边界建设卫星城。1983年成都进行行政建制改革，重组行政区界，实行市领导县的管理体制。行政区界的重组不仅影响了行政管理机构和人员设置安排，而且使得行政机关所在驻地发生迁移。进入21世纪，成都行政区划调整主要表现在两个方面，即“撤县设区”和“乡镇机构改革”，这两者之间开始时间较为接近，在项目整体建设中具有同步性特征。各项目在实施过程中基本不受其他项目影响，只是对行政区划变化方向做出适应性调整。调整的项目内容上具有协调性，没有单独的行政改革项目。

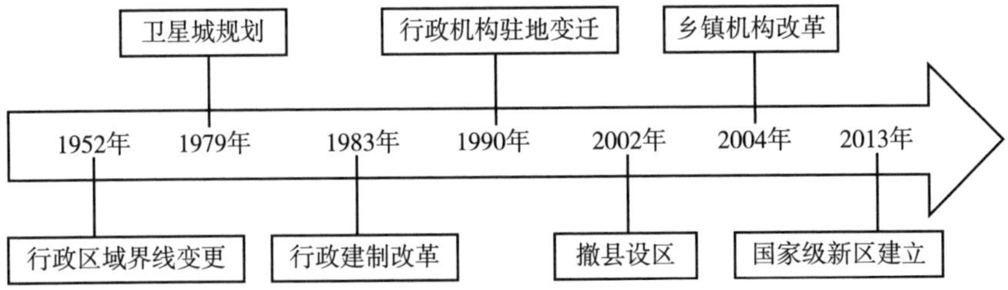

图1 成都市行政区划改革的时间轴

实质上成都行政区划调整的时空分布特征与中国城市发展战略和宏观经济政策演变密切相关。根据上述成都市行政区划调整的特征，大致可以将成都市行政区划调整划分为四个时期：城市地理空间扩展时期、城市行政机制变革时期、城市统筹城乡规划时期、城市区域转型发展时期。

1. 城市地理空间扩展时期

（1）行政区域边界的变更。行政区域边界是区与区之间的分界线，其主要作用是通过对其各辖区的划分，以方便对城市进行精细化的管理。成都市的行政区域边界变更始于1952年成都县改市调整，受宏观政策对行政区划的指导影响，其主要活跃期是从21世纪初到现在。其行政区域边界的变更主要是由行政撤并、区界重组和街道新增等所带来的行政区域边界的局部变化。行政撤并主要是撤销街道，归并乡镇。区界重组主要是通过街道合并组成新街道和扩大区镇的管辖区域。街道新增主要是增加新街道的数量。这三种形式都促进了行政区域边界的变更调整，优化了城市空间结构。

（2）卫星城的设立。卫星城要承担第二产业的职能，一方面疏解中心城区的工业，另一方面截流外来大型工业和人口进入中心城市。成都市对于卫星城的规划始于1979年前后。1996年，成都总体规划调整了卫星城设置和空间布局，建立了华阳、龙泉驿、新都、新繁、郫县、温江、双流、青白江8个卫星城镇。成都市在2003年总体规划中明确表示规划构建新都、温江、郫县等6个周边组团，重点向南、向北、向东三个方向发展。通过卫星城市的建设，成都形成了多核心的城市空间结构，有利于分解中心城市的发展压力，同时进一步拓展城市发展空间，优化城市的产业结构和人口结构，促进整个区域经济发展。

2. 城市行政机制变革时期

（1）行政建制变革。行政建制变革属于制度层面的变革，即通过顶层的设计规划，变更调整原有的行政管理体制，提高行政管理机构的工作效率和工作质量。成都市行政建制改革开始于1952年，活跃期主要集中在21世纪初期。这一时期在市级层面的行政建制改革主要体现在“县改市”“市领导县体制”“市代管县级市”，如在行政区划调整中，1952年撤销成都县并入成都市，部分县划入成都市郊区。1983年，撤销温江地区，其下辖的12个县全部划给成都市，并实行市领导县体制。2015年，开始实行市代管县级市制。目前成都共代管都江堰市、崇州市、彭州市、邛崃市、简阳市5个县级市。在区县级层面的行政建制改革主要是撤销乡镇建制，实行街道办事处管理体制。据成都市统计年鉴统计，从2000年到2010年成都市共减少乡镇政府42个，减少街道办事处4个。在2005年行政区划调整后，青羊区、锦江区、武侯区、金牛区、成华区基本没有乡镇，都以街道为行政单位；新都区、龙泉驿区、双流区、青白江区、温江区、郫都区虽然街道的数量有所增加，但行政体制改革方向整体呈现为乡镇合并、镇镇合并、以镇为主要行政区域单元的特征。2014年成都实施了5项改革，进行简政放权，全面改善了政府服务；精简、优化了行政审批制度，推行一站式服务，满足行政区划调整的需要。

（2）行政机关驻地变迁。成都市的行政机关变迁与行政区划调整具有趋同性。随着乡镇改革、撤县设区、重组街道等行政区划调整变革，必然会改变原行政单位的机构设置及人员构成。同时由于管辖区域的扩张，只有对行政机关驻地进行变迁，才能更便于对整个行政区域进行管理。成都市从 1990 年起就随着行政区划调整开始变迁行政机关驻地，21 世纪初为变迁调整活跃期。目前伴随行政区边界的变革，行政机构的撤并仍在进行中，行政机关也必将会随之变迁，以适应其管辖区域的变化。

3. 城市统筹城乡规划时期

（1）乡镇撤并、乡改镇、镇改街。2004 年成都开始进行乡镇改革，同年也进行了最大力度的行政调整，主要包括：乡镇数量调整、乡镇面积调整和乡镇人口数量的调整。在改革后，乡的数量由原来的 71 个减少为 27 个，镇的数量由原来的 247 个减少为 200 个，而乡镇的平均面积由原来的 37.5 平方千米增加为 49.7 平方千米，平均人口数量由 2.4 万增加到 3.2 万（见表 4）。在乡镇改革同时，成都市开始撤销乡镇建制，采用街道办事处管理体制，以适应城市管理的要求。街道的数量开始增加，同年成都市新增街道办事处 13 处。这些改革在实现财政集中和政务质量提升方面发挥了重要作用，同时也促进了城乡一体化发展。

表 4　2004 年成都市乡镇改革调整前后的比较

	乡镇改革前	乡镇改革后
乡的数量(个)	71	27
镇的数量(个)	247	200
乡镇平均面积(平方千米)	37.5	49.7
乡镇平均人口(万人)	2.4	3.2

资料来源：成都行政区划网。

（2）撤县设区。撤县设区是指市级行政单位将其下属的县级行政单位改设为区级行政单位。2002 年、2015 年以及 2016 年是成都市撤县设区改革的集中发生期。新都县、温江县在 2002 年撤县设区，双流县在 2015 年撤县设区，郫县在 2016 年撤县设区。通过撤县设区，周边的县可以深度融入中心城区。传统的县级公共服务会被强大的市级公共服务取代，这将会使得居民得到更大的实惠。

4. 城市区域转型发展时期

这一时期的行政区划调整主要表现为国家级新区的设立，时间上主要集中在 2013 年前后。如国家级新区天府新区成立于 2013 年，其设立主要受到经济社会发展的影响。城市化进程的加快，吸引了大量的外来人口聚集于市区，给城市的管理和公共服务的供给造成严重压力。成都国家新区的规划建设，可以分担中心城区的部分人口，同时还能截留部分外来人口，减轻中心城市的负担压力。同时新区设立承担国家重大发展和改革任务，在带动区域经济发展、引领全面改革开放、推动体制机制创新、促进产城融合和城乡一体发展等方面发挥着重要作用。

二　成都行政区划调整后公共服务供给的变化

（一）成都行政区划调整后公共服务供给的变化

根据图 2，成都行政区划调整对公共服务供给的影响可以分为短期影响和长期影响。短期影响主要体现在撤县设区和乡镇建制改革这两个方面。撤县设区在短期内就能够对变革后行政区域内的人均经济增长带来冲击效应，并带动社会性资本的流入。而乡镇建制改革更是能够直接改变城乡公共财政结构。从长期影响来看，主要表现在公共服务设施的空间布局及公共财政的支出偏好会受到行政区域扩张的影响。但是公共服务设施具有投入周期和建设周期长的特点，短期内行政区划调整对它的影响效果显示不出来。行政区边界的变革带来区域内公共服务供给主体的重新界定。由于一些县变为区后，它们原来作为县的一些行政权力仍然得以保留，导致城市和县级提供公共服务的责任重叠，反而对公共服务的供给产生不良影响。

1. 公共服务供给规模增加

行政区划调整激发了城市发展的活力，带动了区域经济社会的发展。根据相关统计年鉴资料显示，成都市在行政区划调整后，其公共服务支出水平不断提高。

这些公共服务支出，主要集中在教育、医疗、交通、养老保障等方面。成都市力图构建完善的公共服务体系，扩大公共服务的覆盖面（见表 5）。

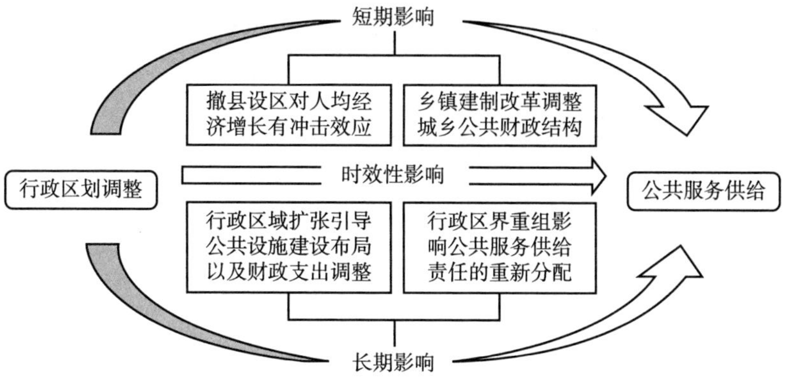

图 2　行政区划调整对公共服务的影响

表 5　成都市及各区一般公共服务支出（2013～2017 年）

单位：万元

	2013 年	2014 年	2015 年	2016 年	2017 年
成都市	1309986	1311174	1533158	1577380	1806007
锦江区	72683	70925	78118	73061	75409
青羊区	53233	54553	65651	68266	72293
金牛区	48426	53299	42861	45976	52883
武侯区	71676	71879	91841	112334	149060
成华区	51985	57053	58498	65773	79235
龙泉驿区	73272	67404	82088	87882	102863
青白江区	34226	34040	36423	39872	44384
新都区	59289	74804	64728	53759	74946
温江区	65486	58219	52890	57734	69222
双流区	96835	113709	179722	160054	213307
郫都区	59034	68488	97297	89472	73446

资料来源：2013～2017 年成都统计年鉴。

（1）医疗卫生服务能力得到提升。本报告主要采用成都市医疗卫生机构数量、卫生技术人员数和全年诊疗人次等相关指标来反映成都市医疗卫生服务能力。根据表 6，从卫生设施规模和数量上来看，2013～2018 年成都市卫生机构增加 2779 个，卫生技术人员增加了 4.9 万人；从每年在成都获取医疗卫生服务的诊疗人数来看，6 年内全年诊疗人次增加 4365 万，增长率 43%，这表明成都的医疗服务能力得到了极大的提升。

表 6 成都市医疗卫生服务指标统计（2013～2018 年）

年份	2013	2014	2015	2016	2017	2018
卫生机构(个)	7976	8190	8481	9853	10183	10755
医院、卫生院(个)	724	746	768	866	888	892
疾控预防控制中心(个)	22	22	22	23	23	23
妇幼保健院(个)	21	21	21	22	22	21
卫生机构床位数(万张)	10.1	10.8	11.5	12.8	13.5	14.3
卫生技术人员(万人)	12	12.8	13.5	14.8	15.8	16.9
全年诊疗(万人次)	10148	10928	11344	12762	13575	14513

资料来源：2013～2018 年成都统计年鉴。

（2）公共交通服务方面。撤县设区对公共交通带来的直接效益就是增加了中心城区公交线路的长度，随着新都、温江、双流、郫县等相继列入成都市辖区范围，成都市的整体区域面积扩大，必然要增加中心城区公交线路的长度，以改善各区县公交基础设施。成都在 2003 年基本建成了“一环＋八射”的都市区交通网络。2013～2017 年，中心城区公交线路增加了 8299 公里（参见表 7），实现了各市县交通网络的整合。高速公路网贯穿成都各县，城乡交通建设不断完善。同时，政府对农村交通建设也给予了偏向性财政资金支持，农村交通形成了新的路网，形成高达 98% 的农村客运同村率。通过改善城乡客运交通网，提升了城乡公共交通服务的效率和质量，方便了人民的工作生活。

表 7 成都市公共交通服务指标统计（2013～2017 年）

年份	2013	2014	2015	2016	2017
市辖区建成区面积(平方公里)	528.9	604.1	615.5	837.3	885.6
中心城区公交线路长度(公里)	4019	6421	6785	6777	12318
公共交通营运车辆(辆)	10176	11447	11294	10781	14402
铺装道路长度(公里)	2845	2633	2739	3700	4125

资料来源：2013～2018 年成都统计年鉴。

（3）社会保障与就业服务方面。成都市扎实推进就业与社保工作。全市参保职工人数和社保基金额度都不断得到提升，参加城镇基本养老和医疗保险的人数 2018 年比 2013 年分别增长了 303.4 万人和 295.6 万人，增长率分别为 49% 和 45%。从政府最低生活保障覆盖的居民人数来看，享受城镇和农村最低生活保障金的人数呈现逐年递减趋势，这说明成都的扶贫工作成效显著（见表 8）。此外，成都抓好重点群体就业创业，动态消除“零就业”家庭，新增城镇就业人数连年上升。最后成都市不断完善社会保障机制，建立了完善的工伤保险制度，社会保障基金监督等促进社保管理“精细化、规范化、专业化”建设。

表 8　成都市社会保障服务指标统计（2013～2018 年）

年份	2013	2014	2015	2016	2017	2018
参加城镇基本养老保险人数（万人）	514.5	547.5	570.8	657.1	719.6	817.9
参保职工（万人）	377.6	401.7	417.7	474.9	529.1	614.9
参加城镇基本医疗保险人数（万人）	555.2	5883.4	620.8	675.3	743.9	850.8
参保职工（万人）	416.7	442.2	468.7	506.5	562.0	655
政府最低生活保障覆盖城镇居民人数（万人）	4.1	3.6	3.4	3.4	2.8	2.5
政府最低生活保障覆盖农村居民人数（万人）	12.1	11.3	10.9	11.4	10.6	8.9

资料来源：2013～2018 年成都统计年鉴。

2. 公共服务供给结构失衡

（1）公共服务空间供给结构失衡。在城市空间格局中公共服务供给不平等现象更为明显。公共服务供给的空间不均衡性主要反映在各城区政府在公共服务财政支出不均等方面（见图 3）。

一般公共服务支出、社会保障与就业支出、教育支出、政府性基金支出这四项指标反映地区的公共服务供给水平。2017 年成都市在这四项指标上的财政支出情况，大致可以反映各城区公共服务的供给能力情况。

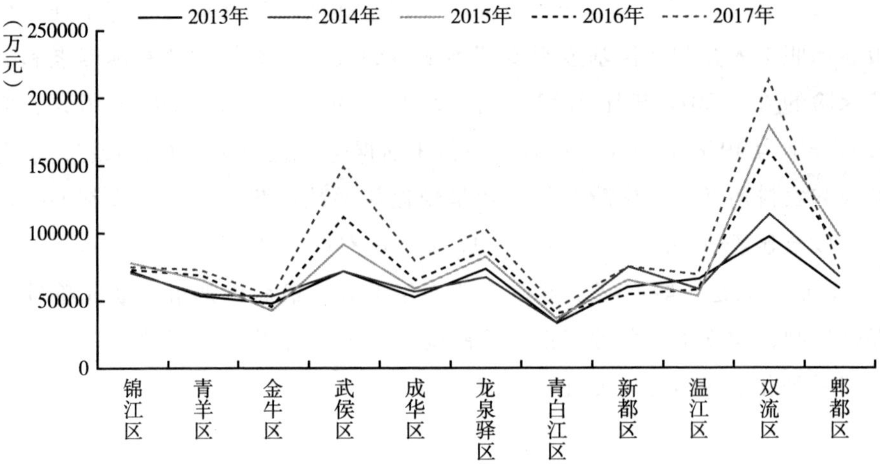

图 3　成都各区公共服务财政支出情况（2013 ~ 2017 年）

资料来源：2013 ~ 2017 年成都统计年鉴。

表 9　成都各区公共服务财政支出情况比较（2017 年）

单位：万元

	一般公共服务	教育	社会保障与就业	政府性基金
锦江区	75409	75260	72232	3798
青羊区	72293	88548	71414	24574
金牛区	52883	115650	54926	24281
武侯区	149060	134404	97265	31886
成华区	79235	102101	47236	254941
龙泉驿区	102863	178196	50568	759014
青白江区	44384	60713	34306	451752
新都区	74946	144248	55846	440341
温江区	69222	87425	29133	374261
双流区	213307	240321	87165	2690234
郫都区	73446	81372	54354	397226

资料来源：《成都统计年鉴 2017》。

根据表 9 的统计，可以反映出公共服务水平在整个市区的空间结构差异性。武侯区、双流区的整体公共服务支出水平较高，而青白江区和金牛区的整体公共服务水平较低。在公共服务项目上，各地区的投资比例也不相同。但从总体来讲各区都注重对公共教育服务的投资，而对社会保障与就业的重视程度相对较低。这种公共服务空间结构的不均衡性是由历史和现实等多种原因导致的，在具体实践中由于公共财政制度的差异性，各地区在公共服务支出中存在不同程度的财政倾斜，造成公共服务空间结构的不均衡。

（2）公共服务社会供给结构失衡。由于城乡二元结构和户籍制度约束，成都对于城乡居民、流动人口与户籍人口的公共服务供给不同，这种供给的差异就是公共服务社会供给结构的失衡。在成都行政区划调整过程中，城乡和户籍不同所带来的供给差异一直存在。

表 10　2013～2018 年成都行政区划调整后城乡居民收支结构变化

单位：元

年份	2013	2014	2015	2016	2017	2018
城镇居民人均可支配收入(元)	29968	32665	33476	35902	38918	42128
农村居民人均可支配收入(元)	12985	14478	17690	18605	20298	22135
城镇居民人均消费支出(元)	20362	21711	21825	23514	25314	27312
农村居民人均消费支出(元)	8866	9697	12711	13428	14616	15977

资料来源：2013～2018 年成都统计年鉴。

2013～2018 年内城乡居民人均可支配收入分别增长 41% 和 70%，人均消费支出分别增长 34% 和 80%，但是由于农村居民人均可支配收入和消费支出本身基数水平较低，所以城乡居民之间的收入差距依然很大（见表 10）。居民收入与支出之间存在差距导致公共服务支付水平的差距，而支付水平的差距影响其子女教育、就业服务与养老保障方面的公共服务的差距。

（二）成都市行政区划调整后公共服务供给的变化

目前成都市行政区划调整后公共服务供给主体向“多元化”方向发展，供给管理向“一站式”方向发展，供给方式向“分散”方向发展。

1. 公共服务供给主体向“多元化”方向发展

在推进城市化建设过程中，政府加大财政投资力度支持城市公共服务基础设施建设，优化了城市空间的发展环境。城市空间环境的优化又能吸引大量的人口、资本流入。如果仅靠政府这个单一主体提供公共服务，将很难满足居民对公共服务的需求。因此要解决公共服务供给的难题和困境，改善公共服务供求结构的空间失衡，必须寻求多元化的供给主体。成都市政府应该鼓励市场主体、非政府主体等共同参与公共服务供给，实现公共服务的成本由政府与社会“共同承担”。另外，通过“撤县设区”和新区建设，成都市不仅吸纳了高质量人才的流入，而且也吸纳了巨额的社会资本流入，这些资源的汇集能够促进本区域产业的优化升级，带动区域经济的发展。天府新区在建设过程中利用自身政策优势，吸引了社会资本和技术的聚集，在促进本地区经济转型升级的同时也促进了公共服务供给主体向“多元化”方向发展。

2. 公共服务供给管理向“一站式”方向发展

在行政区划调整过程中，行政机关通过撤销、调整和合并，实现了行政机构的精简改革、减少了相似功能部门的重复建设，这有利于政府各部门之间精细化和高效的管理。截至2018年底，成都市政府通过网站建设和市级政务云平台的搭建，实现了699项政务服务事项可在网上办理，91%的审批服务事项“最多跑一次”，改善了原来烦琐的政务服务模式，提高了公共服务的效率。

3. 公共服务供给方式向“分散”方向发展

城市化进程的加速，吸引大量人口聚集成都市，给中心城市造成了严重的公共服务供给压力。因此成都市在行政区划调整过程中，注重新区的规划和建设。合理地引导城市的要素资源的布局和流动，这促使政府对公共服务的投资由“集中式”向“分散化”转变。同时在城市规划设计中政府依据城市空间结构的变化，相应地在政策上给公共服务的发展提供更多的支持。这不仅能够改善城市公共服务的供给矛盾，还能够引导城市走上高质量可持续的发展路径。

三　成都市行政区划调整对公共服务供给的双重影响分析

（一）行政区划调整对公共服务供给的直接影响

1. 行政建制改革有助于节约公共服务成本

整合行政机构数量的行政建制改革主要意义在于提高公共服务的行政效率，建立一个人民满意的政府。成都的“以区带乡”和街道办事处管理制度就是为了缩小行政机关的管辖范围，实现“有限的政府”目标的同时，又能实现“有效的政府”目标。行政建制的变革提高了政府公共服务的供给效率，推动了多元供给主体间的有效合作，进一步降低了提供公共服务的行政成本。

表 11 成都市行政区划机构数量变化（2000～2005 年）

单位：个

研究区域	2000 年	2001 年	2002 年	2003 年	2004 年	2005 年
乡政府	37	25	22	22	3	3
镇政府	92	101	104	102	71	69
街道办事处	96	88	88	83	85	90

资料来源：2000～2005 年成都统计年鉴。

根据表 11 中行政区划机构数量变化的情况可以了解到，在 2000 年到 2005 年，成都市的行政区划数量明显在不断减少。其中变化最明显是的 2004 年，与上年相比乡政府减少了 19 个；镇政府减少了 31 个。原因在于同年成都在其辖区内实施了乡镇改革，撤乡并镇 78 个，乡镇建制改革为街道办事处管理体系。

2. “撤县设区”增加公共服务供给的投入

成都撤县设区以后，原县域内的公共服务基础设施将由“县管理”变为“城市统筹”。同时，原属于该县的管辖地区也将成为主城区，基础设施规划将逐步与主城区同步，主城区也能带动新城区的经济发展。此外，撤县设区能够积极引导社会性资本的流入。随着“撤县设区”区域基础设施的改善，将吸引大量的人口和社会资本的流入，从而使得地区财政收入增加，促进了社会对公共服务投资的增加。例如，2002 年新都县、温江县撤县设区后，该年其财政收入较上一年增长 1.18% 和 1.31%。2015 年双流县撤县设区改革，其财政收入较上一年增加 1.07%，同时其公共财政投入金额较上年增长 0.9%，达到 118.2 亿元。2016 年郫县撤县改区，其财政收入较上一年增加 0.96%，达 39.7 亿元。其公共财政支出金额也实现了增长，增长率为 1.057%，达 6.006 亿元。

3. 新城区规划有利于缓解公共服务供求矛盾

成都市新区的规划建设可以缓解城市公共服务供求矛盾。通过建立新区和卫星城，将部分人口和产业转移出去，可以缓解中心城市公共服务供给压力，扩大城市经济的发展空间。同时新城区也可以成为城乡协调发展的过渡带，帮助政府协调城市和郊区的公共服务，优化公共服务设施的空间布局结构。政府在新区建设过程中，增加对公共服务支出薄弱地区的资金支持，构建城市老城区与新城区的公共交通网络，帮助实现区域市场要素的自由流动。此外，随着新区的发展，必然会辐射带动郊区周边乡镇工业的发展，实现“以城带乡”“产城乡融合”。新区在带动乡镇工业发展的过程中，必然会缩小城乡收入差距，从而缓解城乡之间公共服务供给的差异。

（二）行政区划调整对公共服务供给的间接影响

1. 行政区划调整间接影响经济结构的优化

行政区划调整对城市经济结构的影响机理主要体现在行政边界的变化和行政管理体制的改革上。“撤县设区”以及建立新区和卫星城是对行政边界调整的两种重要措施，有利于扩大城市经济发展空间，使中心城区的经济辐射能够

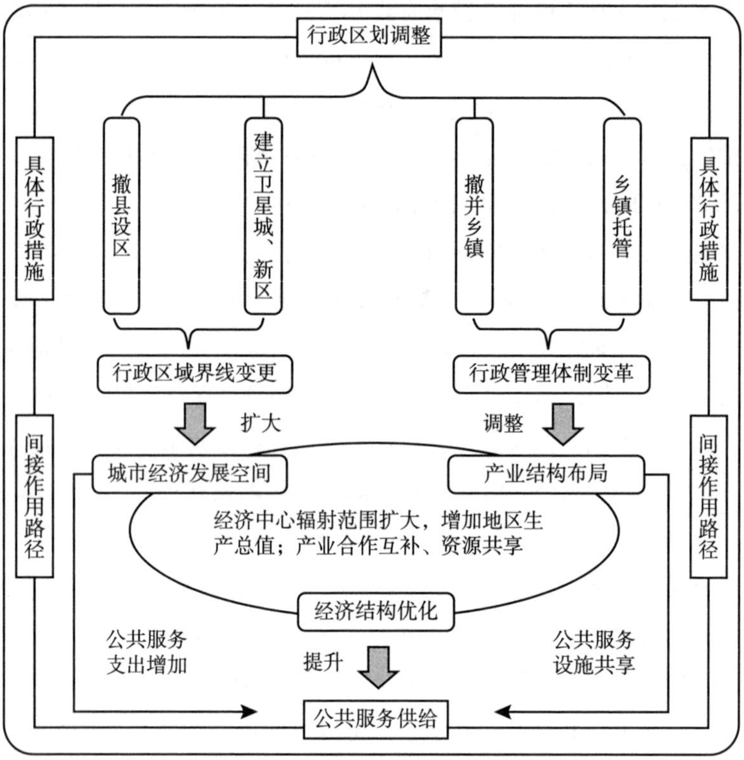

图 4　成都行政区划调整对城市经济结构的作用机理

带动新城区的经济增长，进而使当地政府公共服务供给能力得到提升。同时，通过“撤并乡镇”和“乡镇托管”，可以实现地区产业的合作发展，优化产业结构布局，改善区域经济结构，而经济结构的改善又能促进地区经济实力的提升。因此，行政区划调整对公共服务具有间接促进作用。

财政收入和地区 GDP 是主要的经济指标，同时它们也是影响公共服务供给能力的主要因素。根据图 5 和图 6，与 2011 年相比，2017 年成都及各区县的 GDP 和一般公共预算收入均有显著增长。研究表明，成都市的行政区划调整适应了经济发展的要求，对行政范围内的经济发展起到正向作用，进而提升了公共服务的供给能力。

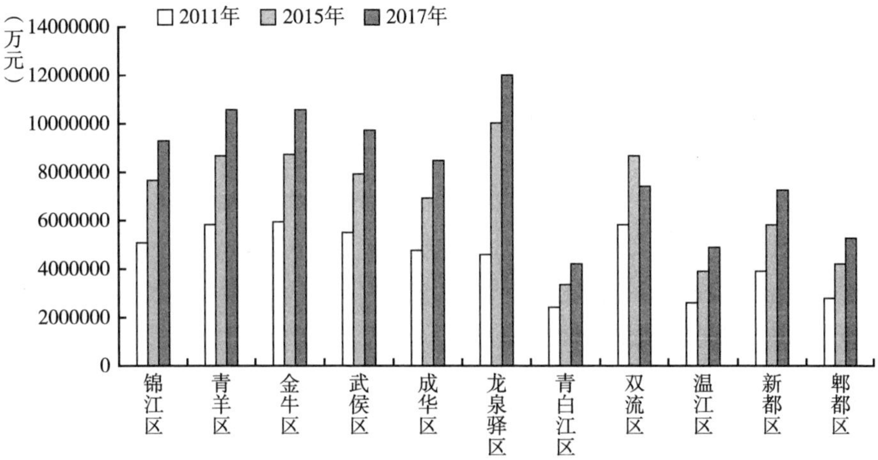

图 5　成都 2011 年、2015 年、2017 年各区生产总值情况

资料来源：2011 年、2015 年、2017 年成都统计年鉴。

2. 行政区划调整影响人口结构

行政区划影响人口流动主要是由其公共政策属性决定的，如建立国家新区和卫星城，这可能会带来大规模的人口流动。然而，公共服务系统的规划并不包括在新城新区的政策性规划中。由于一些公共服务项目，例如学校、医院和养老福利院，需要定点设施作为载体供应，而这类设施的建设周期较长。因此由于公共设施建设的滞后性可能会带来短期性的公共服务供求失衡，引发新的社会矛盾。此外，成都市实施乡镇建制变革、街道办事处管理体制改革，调整后城市土地利用规模扩大，吸引了农村剩余劳动力向城市转移。行政区划调整

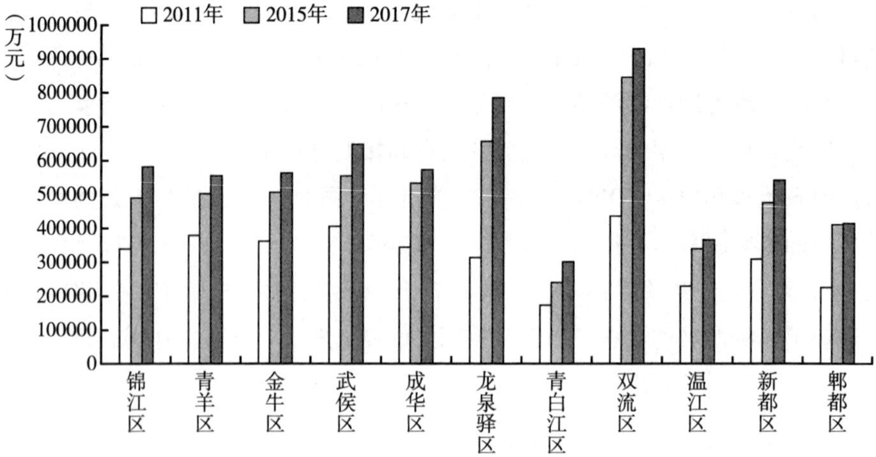

图6　成都2011年、2015年、2017年一般公共预算收入变化

资料来源：2011年、2015年、2017年成都统计年鉴。

促进人口聚集到城市，带来经济效益。但是由于公共服务的供给与居民的户籍状况有关，因此转移到城市的流动人口和农村人口不仅影响了城市居民享受公共服务的过程和效果，而且由于户籍制度的制约也使其难以平等地获取医疗、教育等公共服务（如图7）。

表12一方面反映了成都市行政区划调整促进了地区人口的增加，另一方面也反映了成都市各地区机械人口增长率存在较大的差距。2017年双流区增长率要比最低的青白江区高出90.12个百分点。面对快速增长的外来人口，一些区县的公共服务在短期内必然难以满足公众需求，而另外一些区县由于人口增加不明显，显然在公共服务方面会出现供过于求的现象，这表明公共服务的资源配置不能及时调整以适应人口空间结构的变化。

四　总结

本文通过对行政区划调整与公共服务关系的了解，发现行政区划调整对公共服务供给的直接影响主要表现在以下五个方面。第一，通过行政建制改革，提高了公共服务效率，降低了政府公共服务的行政成本。第二，通过行政区界的重组，可以实现城乡之间区域之间资源的合理配置，实现公共服务的一体

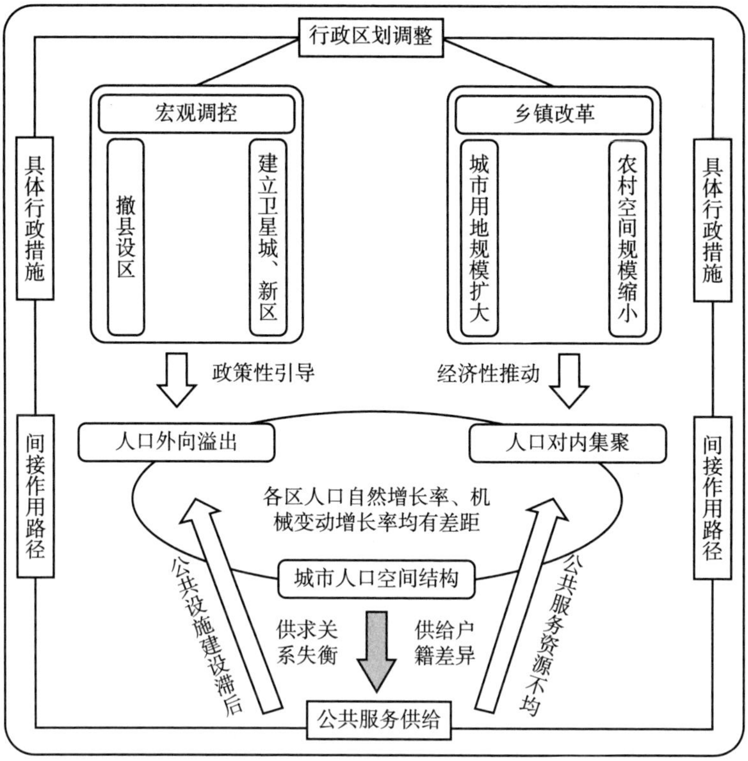

图7　成都行政区划调整对城市人口结构的作用机理

化。第三，通过撤县设区，能够引导社会资本和劳动力资源的流入，从而能够增加社会对公共服务的资本投入。第四，通过建立卫星城和新区，能够引导人口的合理流动，缓解中心城市公共服务压力，改善公共服务供求的结构关系。第五，通过行政机构的合并重组，能够提升公共服务的效率和质量。这些方面的改进，提升了成都市公共服务的整体供给水平。

表12　成都各区人口机械变动增长率（2013～2017年）

单位：%

年份	2013	2014	2015	2016	2017
成都市	9.69	14.3	8.77	11.01	25.02
锦江区	24.47	31.22	19.57	25.16	40.86
青羊区	28.49	31.66	18.96	17.39	30.59
金牛区	14.56	18.82	8.51	11	22.55

续表

年份	2013	2014	2015	2016	2017
武侯区	14.33	26.3	18.74	18.6	62.5
成华区	17.14	25.09	17.92	19.69	35.76
龙泉驿区	13.43	20.3	10.34	17.02	29.86
青白江区	2.63	2.5	0.03	2.33	2.01
双流区	15.97	25.02	19.48	25.93	92.13
温江区	14.82	27.67	20.15	26.76	49.92
新都区	9.87	8.43	15	15.71	26.28
郫都区	10.38	24.54	20.98	19.7	37.41

资料来源：2013～2017 年成都统计年鉴。

成都市政区划调整不仅直接给成都市公共服务的供给带来了积极的影响，而且也间接地给公共服务的供给带来了负面的影响。由于行政区划调整，导致原来的乡镇行政单位撤销或者合并，加剧了人口在不同区域之间的流动，整合了原有的公共服务供给机构和设施，这导致了公共服务供给的空间和社会结构失衡。

参考文献

[1] 佟岩、谢玉夫：《城市行政区划调整对空间布局优化效应的量化分析——以沈阳市为例》，《现代城市研究》2013 年第 7 期，第 37～42 页。

[2] 顾朝林、王颖、邵园、顾江：《基于功能区的行政区划调整研究——以绍兴城市群为例》，《地理学报》2015 年第 8 期，第 1187～1201 页。

[3] 胡德、刘君德：《政区等级、权力与区域经济关系——中国政府权力的空间过程及其影响》，《中国行政管理》2007 年第 6 期，第 11～13 页。

[4] 魏衡、魏清泉、曹天艳、赵静：《城市化进程中行政区划调整的类型、问题与发展》，《人文地理》2009 年第 6 期，第 55～58 页。

[5] 刘志慧：《撤县设区：现状·问题·对策》，《中共云南省委党校学报》2017 年第 2 期，第 164～168 页。

[6] 殷洁、罗小龙：《从撤县设区到区界重组——我国区县级行政区划调整的新趋势》，《城市规划》2013 年第 6 期，第 9～15 页。

[7] 赵培红、孙久文：《北京市行政区划调整对城市发展的影响及启示》，《城市观

察》2011 年第 5 期，第 107 ~ 117 页。

[8] 严雅娜：《基本公共服务均等化的财政对策研究》，山西财经大学博士学位论文，2017。

[9] 靳美娟、张志斌：《国内外城市空间结构研究综述》，《热带地理》2006 年第 2 期，第 134 ~ 138 + 172 页。

[10] 耿卫军：《“撤县设区”、行政区划体制转型与区域经济发展》，浙江财经大学硕士学位论文，2016。

[11] 尚正永、卢晓旭、张小林、吴启焰：《行政区划调整对城市地域结构演变的影响——以江苏省淮安市为例》，《经济地理》2015 年第 8 期，第 61 ~ 67 页。

[12] 李奕璇：《从宏观角度分析城市空间扩展对经济效应的影响》，《新西部（理论版）》2016 年第 16 期，第 61 + 50 页。

B.16 京津冀三地文化协同发展报告*

王华彪**

摘　要： 京津冀三地文化协同发展，要贯彻落实十九大提出的区域协调发展战略，深入推进“五个发展”理念和“五位一体”总体战略布局；牢牢扭住疏解北京非首都功能这个“牛鼻子”，确认三地协同发展的必要性，认真剖析当前三地文化发展中存在的主要问题；坚持高质量高标准，推动区域协同发展多出快出成果，打造三地文化命运共同体，为实现“中国梦”提供文化支持。

关键词： 京津冀　协同发展　文化生态　文化共兴

党的十九大提出“区域协同发展”“全面可持续发展”战略。强化京津冀三地文化协同发展，推动三地文化产业共兴，需要贯彻落实十九大提出的区域协调发展战略，深入推进“五个发展”理念和“五位一体”总体战略布局；需要以习近平新时代中国特色社会主义思想中文化发展方面的阐述为指导，牢牢扭住疏解北京非首都功能这个“牛鼻子”；需要确认三地协同发展的必要性，认真剖析当前三地文化发展中存在的主要问题；需要以协同发展理念推进三地文化共兴，推动区域协同发展多出快出成果，打造三地文化命运共同体，为实现“中国梦”提供文化支持。

---

* 基金项目：河北省文化艺术科学规划项目“京津冀协同发展视域下河北文化创意产业人才培养路径研究”（HB18－YB020）。

** 王华彪，硕士，河北建筑工程学院社科部（人文社科系）副教授，研究方向为哲学社会科学。

一　京津冀文化协同发展存在短板

改革开放以来，特别是在确立社会主义市场经济体制的目标以来，我国社会的物质财富得到迅猛发展，经济总量跃居世界第二。我国哲学社会科学工作者自觉坚持以科学的理论武装人、以正确的舆论引导人、以高尚的精神塑造人、以优秀的作品鼓舞人，科学研究取得了长足进步，推出了一批学术价值厚重、社会影响广泛的优秀成果，为全面建成小康社会提供了重要的理论支撑和智力支持。但与此同时，我们也应清醒地看到，随着改革的不断深化，京津冀三地的迅速转型和利益格局的巨大调整，形形色色的精神雾霾弥漫到哲学社会科学领域，信仰危机、学术研究中的“洋教条”、历史虚无主义、学术泡沫、学术不端等问题日趋严重，人民群众对祛除精神雾霾、营造精神生态和谐的呼声也越来越强烈。京津冀文化协同是全方位的协同，强调京津冀文化发展的系统性、关联性、平衡性和开放性，强调区域文化整体水平和质量的协同提升。

1. 三地文化发展差异明显。十九大提出区域协调发展战略，当前京津冀文化协同发展取得了显著成绩，但京津冀三地文化发展的水平和质量存在较大差异，距离京津冀协同发展的基本要求还有较大距离，尤其是北京作为我国的政治、科技、文化中心，相比天津和河北有着天然的优势；三地发展依然面临着行政体制障碍、经济基础差异大、文化协同标准模糊和发展时序安排混乱等问题。盲目建设、过度开发等问题已造成对传统文化生态环境的严重破坏。传统的文化正经受着考验。如我国传统文化中的仁义礼智，其核心是仁，而义、礼、智、信、忠等，都是仁在不同领域里所体现的重新命名。仁的精神要求推己及人，再扩展到推人及物，这是非常博大的。它的必要性就是非此不“和”，离开这条路走别的路一定是不能和谐的，因而就不能生生不息。在经济社会高速发展的今天，三地一大批真文物、老建筑被“假古董”“洋景观”取代，大量依靠口头和行为传承的文化遗产不断消失，许多传统技艺和表演传承困难，许多濒危的文化遗产亟待抢救保护，更多的文化遗产由于重视不够、经费不足、人员缺乏、保护不力、法治滞后等原因受到不同程度的损害。修复这些文化生态，需要迫不及待地推进三地文化协同发展。

2. 中西文化贸易的巨大逆差。西方所谓民主和普世价值及言论自由观对我们年青一代造成巨大困扰，庸俗、低俗、媚俗的文化侵蚀着三地，精神信仰的问题、道德的问题也从来没有像今天这样尖锐突出，文化生态环境面临污染危险，作为我国首都北京的周边区域城市，需要加强协同发展。另外，由于西方在文化生态的管理权、话语权上有着传统的优势，传播西方价值观念的文化产品大行其道，甚至中国的文化资源也被演变为占领中国文化市场的工具。典型代表就是美国根据中国元素生产的电影《花木兰》和《功夫熊猫》，它们借用我们熟悉和喜爱的形象潜移默化地推销了美国的价值观。对抗这些，需要我国盘活资源，强强联合，抱团取暖，争取国际话语权。在“众创时代”“互联网时代”“DT”时代，三地文化产业界人士贯彻落实十八大系列会议精神，尤其是贯彻五大发展理念，推进京津冀协同发展，是站在党和国家事业发展全局的高度，站在时代发展大局的高度，站在充分认识文化建设的战略高度，回应社会各界关切。

3. 社会信仰危机普遍存在。习近平总书记指出：“理想信念就是共产党人精神上的‘钙’，没有理想信念，理想信念不坚定，精神上就会‘缺钙’，就会得‘软骨病’。”改革开放后，市场经济在促进社会进步和思想解放的同时，它宣扬的个人主义、等价交换、利益最大化等原则，也严重冲击了社会主义理想信念建设，加剧了价值冲突。有人鼓吹这是一个“告别的时代”，告别理想、告别革命、告别英雄、告别主义……这是一个“渺茫的时代”，鼓吹“社会主义“失败论”“社会主义渺茫论”“共产主义渺茫论”……导致少部分学者缺少做学问应有的尊严感、使命感和批判精神。正如邓小平所说：“自由化的思想前几年有，现在也有，不仅社会上有，我们共产党内也有。自由化思潮一发展，我们的事业就会被冲乱。”因此，无论是一个党、一个国家，还是一个民族，都要有一种精神和信仰，这是实现共同理想和共同目标的精神支柱。

4. 历史虚无主义变种不断。清代学者龚自珍说：“欲要亡其国，必先灭其史。”历史虚无主义刮起一股以“反思历史”为名来重新“解读”历史，从而否定中国共产党执政合法性的社会思潮，社会危害甚大。在具体表现形式上表现为否定和歪曲中国革命历史、刻意虚构历史、为已被历史淘汰的旧势力评功摆好、“戏说”或“恶搞”历史、鼓吹“侵略有功论”等，他们颠倒黑白、混淆是非，严重消解了主流意识形态的历史根基，成为西方敌对势力分化中国的思想工具，在本质上是企图撬动中国共产党执政的合法性，使中国最终倒向西方资本主义怀抱。习近平在纪念毛泽东120周年诞辰大会上，提出了“两个三十年”重要问题。即一方面，不能用改革开放后的30年否定改革开放前的30年；另一方面，也不能用改革开放前的30年否定改革开放后的30年。

二　冀文化是协同发展战略的必然选择

2016年12月，国务院强调要“推进京津冀旅游一体化进程，打造世界一流旅游目的地”，为京津冀文化协同发展指明了方向。在资源整合上，北京是国家历史文化名城，文物古迹遗存丰富，天津的民俗文化、地域文化特色鲜明，推进“文化+旅游”，有利于三地连通文脉，打造区域文化旅游集群，实现“1+1+1>3”的综合效应。在市场分享上，随着京津冀“1小时交通圈”“四纵四横一环”城际铁路网络的建设完善，依托京津成熟的旅游消费市场和对“周边游”、生态游的庞大需求，将河北文化旅游打造成为京津冀旅游一体化的“第三极”。在借力发展上，京津两地的科技、人才、资金优势明显，通过文化协同发展，进一步承接两地在文化协同发展运作方面的“溢出效应”。故三地文化协同发展具有地缘相接的历史必然、共同利益的发展包容、唯物辩证的发展趋势、国家富强的精神支撑、传统文化的时代价值。

1. 地缘相接的历史必然。京津冀地缘相接、人缘相亲、地域一体、文化一脉，三地在历史上也渊源深厚。公元1272年，元朝统治者忽必烈下诏改京师中都为大都，当时元大都的设计者刘秉忠就是河北人；元朝时修建的今天北京环城水系通惠河的设计者郭守敬也是河北人；新中国成立后的1958～1966年，河北省省会就在天津。文化上，京津冀三地也是互通互融，河北现在传承的主要剧种例如京剧、河北梆子、评剧以及其他一些曲艺门类均发源于北京、天津两地。由此可见，京津冀三地在地域、历史、经济、政治等各个方面都是密切相连的。自古以来三地人员也来往密切，彼此联系，从未割裂。河北在三地文化共兴中一直扮演着服务于北京、天津的历史角色，主要呈现出单一性、功利性、非均衡性、被动性、滞后性的缺陷。

2. 共同利益的发展包容。京津冀三地的协同发展应遵循密切合作、优势互补、互联互通、互惠互利、和合大同的基本原则。一是基于共同的战略任务。习近平总书记在这方面为我们指明了方向，应该“在发展中传承文化生态，在开放中保护文化生态，在创新中培育文化生态，在包容中涵养文化生态，在传播中弘扬文化生态”，文化生态是我们人类生存和发展状态的一种体现。习近平总书记在中央政治局会议上在原有“新型工业化、信息化、城镇化、农业现代化道路”的基础上又提出了一个“绿色化”，这个“绿色化”不仅仅是简单的生态概念，也是对生态文化的最新要求，同时也是精神文明建设的一个载体。北京、天津饮用水的水源地绝大多数都在河北，如果河北生态环境遭到破害，北京、天津也要遭殃。二是基于避弱的木桶理论。美国著名经济学家彼得提出过一个“木桶理论”，这个原理的要求并不是简单地去提高自身的弱势，而是要设法发展自身的优势。河北应该在京津冀文化领域的协同发展中走在前，做表率。河北有着它自身的优势和劣势：优势是人口众多，文化底蕴深厚。近年来，河北的文化消费势头比较旺盛，同时，与北京、天津的文化交流和人员来往比较密切；劣势是河北是个农业大省，且经济欠发达，同时还不是文化强省，文化产品中以中低端的居多。河北是人口和文化资源大省，自身的文化传承如果出现问题，北京、天津也将受到影响。

3. 唯物辩证的发展趋势。当今的三地文化是一种新常态。“新”是一个动态概念，意思是“不同于以往”，强调的是“苟日新、日日新、又日新”，体现的是马克思主义哲学中“事物都是普遍运动发展联系的”唯物主义观点。“常”是一个静态概念，意思是“相对稳定”，强调的是“天行有常”“日月以为常”，体现的是辩证唯物主义中“绝对真理”的规定。“新”与“常”强调的都是外在，是客观。“态”就是心态、姿态，强调的是内在，是主观，是人的主观能动性在“新”和“常”的客观形势下的张扬。

4. 传统文化的时代价值。习近平总书记多次集中论述中华优秀传统文化，有的从哲学视角阐述了学习传统文化的重要性，有的阐述了中华传统文化及蕴含其中的理想信念在中华民族历史上的重要性，有的阐述了崇德向善是传承弘扬优秀传统文化的核心，有的阐述了中华文化在中华民族伟大复兴中的地位和作用及如何对待传统文化，有的从提高国家文化软实力角度阐述了传承弘扬传统文化的重要性及如何传承弘扬传统文化的问题，有的系统论述了传承保护历史文化遗产与城市建设的关系，有的阐述了弘扬优秀传统文化与增强文化自信的关系。弘扬民族传统文化，需要激发人民群众建设“两个百年”目标的热情；广泛开展文化志愿服务活动，目的是引导人们讲道德、尊道德、守道德，追求高尚的道德理想，为推动我国绿色发展提供道德支撑。

三 京津冀文化协同发展战略的对策建议

贯彻落实十九大及习总书记的讲话精神，促进京津冀区域文化产业的战略发展、一体发展，回应社会各界关切，恰逢其时，水到渠成。三地须站在党和国家事业发展全局的高度，站在时代发展大局的高度，站在充分认识文化建设的战略高度努力做到文化谋划共振、文化生态同筑、文化项目齐引和文化品牌共创。

1. 文化谋划共振。思路决定出路，思维的高度决定事业的广度。要有编制、深化规划的战略定力。千年大计，谋定后动，规划先行，编制规划，多方论证。中共中央总书记习近平同志强调，要从全局的高度和更长远的考虑来认识和做好京津冀协同发展工作，增强协同发展的自觉性、主动性、创造性。基于三地文化发展的统一共性和三地各自局部个性的兼容统一关系，推动三地文化协调发展需要在目标要求上坚持“一多结合”。

一是树立战略思维。战略思维，就是高瞻远瞩、统览全局，善于把握事物发展总体趋势和方向。习近平说：“我们要保持战略定力和坚定信念，坚定不移走自己的路，朝着自己的目标前进。”

二是树立系统思维。做到全局与局部相配套、当前与未来相协同、整体推进与重点突破相统一，我们一定可以聚合改革能量，激荡起书写历史的磅礴伟力。古人云，不谋全局者，不谋一隅；凡事预则立，不预则废。江河之所以能够冲开绝壁夺隘而出，是因为它们汇聚了奔涌向前、万壑归流的磅礴伟力。

三是树立辩证思维。树立对立统一的辩证思维，所谓对立，是指矛盾双方相互排斥、互相斗争。所谓统一是指如下两种情形：第一，矛盾双方在一定条件下相互依存，一方的存在以另一方的存在为前提，双方共处于一个统一体中；第二，矛盾着的双方，依据一定的条件，各向自己相反的方向转化。三地需要按照在区域协调发展和战略指导下，下好文化对立统一思维的一盘棋，做好 1 +1 +1 >3 的文化加法和乘法效应。

四是树立创新思维。《周易》里讲“日新之谓盛德”，意思就是要不断更新观念、创新思路。克服思维惯性，充分运用新方式新渠道新技术，抢占文化发展先机；要去除思维封闭，从高站位打开文化工作的思维空间。

五是树立协同思维。打破行政区划等人为界限和条块分割，建立高层协商机制和具体工作层面沟通协同机制，成立京津冀区域文化协同工作小组，推动建立三省市文化部门联席会议制度，实行国务院和三地双重管理，定期召开联席工作会议，就文化区域协同发展的重大事宜进行协商交流，在“区域一盘棋”的布局中统筹文化产业发展的诉求点。

2. 文化生态同筑。党的十八大以来，党中央、国务院高度重视林业和生态文明建设，把生态文明建设纳入中国特色社会主义“五位一体”总体布局，出台了《关于加快推进生态文明建设的意见》，对生态文明建设做出全面部署。按照全球经济发展的一般规律而言，后发展国家的追赶型经济发展大致经历三个阶段：模仿式发展的快速增长期、增长减速更加注重质量和效益的稳健增长期、接近或达到发达国家水平的基本稳定期，认真贯彻“两山理论”，既要金山银山，更要绿水青山。

一是优先发展生态。一个地区的文化底蕴、文化氛围，一座城市的文化品位、文化取向，越来越成为经济社会发展的重要条件。党的十八大提出“五位一体”建设战略，习近平总书记提出“五大发展战略”，对全面深化改革、进一步解放思想、进一步转变发展指导思想，明确提出坚持靠改革创新推动绿色崛起，京津冀三地开展文化生态同筑活动，与国家提出的“四个全面”发展战略是高度吻合的。深入研究解决全球化、市场化、信息化、城镇化条件下的文化生态问题，努力保持文化生态的持续、平衡和不断优化。

二是借力发展文化。三地应坚持把人作为文化生态链的核心，抓好专业和业余文化人才队伍建设，完善梯次结构，提升文化素养，强化文化使命，在继承、推广、弘扬、传播、创造中华优秀文化的行列中走在前、做表率。总结艺术创作规律和艺术人才成长规律。善于借智、借力和借势。借智就是但求所用不求所有；借力就是要借助社会各方面的力量包括民营的力量，来共同完成艺术创作和艺术生产；借势就是借助经济社会生态文明发展的趋势，要善于运用“无形的手”来做好“有形的事”。“智者借帆而行”，要借助各方面的力量从事艺术生产、创作和传播，发展先进文化、创新传统文化、扶持通俗文化、引导流行文化、改造落后文化、抵制有害文化、传播主流文化，共同推动文化的新发展新繁荣。

三是推动文化共兴。三地应遵循密切合作、优势互补、互联互通、互惠互利、和合大同的基本原则，遵循习近平总书记提出的“在发展中传承文化生态，在开放中保护文化生态，在创新中培育文化生态，在包容中涵养文化生态，在传播中弘扬文化生态”，文化生态是我们人类生存和发展状态的一种体现。对此，首先要做好文化生态涵养的总体设计，三地要认真分析有利条件和不利因素，制订详细方案，设计好传承保护和培育涵养文化生态的工作思路、具体路径和措施，明确目标、任务、要求和预期效果，提高工作的前瞻性。其次要在落细、落小、落实上下功夫。要把三地文化共兴融入具体的工作中。每一个剧目的创排，每一个展览的设计，每一个活动的开展，都要紧紧围绕促使观众、读者在每一次的文化体验中去感知、领悟中华优秀传统文化，使中华优秀传统文化价值的影响像空气一样无处不在、无时不有。

3. 文化项目齐引。河北应该在京津冀文化领域的协同发展中走在前、做表率。河北有着它自身的优势和劣势。优势是人口众多，文化底蕴深厚。近年来，河北的文化消费势头比较旺盛，同时，与北京、天津的文化交流和人员来往比较密切。劣势是河北是个农业大省，且经济欠发达，同时还不是文化强省，文化产品中的中低端产品居多。河北是人口和文化资源大省，自身的文化传承如果出现问题，北京、天津也将受到影响。

一是下好联合办奥“一盘棋”。在京张联合申办 2022 年冬季奥林匹克运动会布局中，中国将分三块比赛区域：北京市区承担 5 个冰上项目；北京延庆区小海坨山区，将举行雪橇、雪车和高山滑雪项目；位于张家口市距离北京市区约 220 公里的崇礼区太子城区域，承担跳台滑雪、单板滑雪、自由式滑雪、北欧两项、冬季两项和越野滑雪项目的比赛。目前这三块区域最缺的是一个宣传和提升文化体育品牌的平台，京冀两地应加强现代传媒，重新审视和宣传资源优势，广泛宣传，打造奥运体育品牌。

二是打造文化创意“一高地”。三地要加强高校、科研机构、企业之间的文化科研创新整合，建设集剧目创作、艺术交流、人才培养为一体的文化交流基地；着力创办高新技术创业服务中心、留学人员创业园、科研院所创业园等各种类型的科技企业“孵化器”和“创业园”。三地高校科研院所各级领导，尤其是党政一把手，要在提高文化创意科研素质上带好头，做好样子，从自身做起，以上率下，以实际行动影响和带动全体文化创意专业教师员工，成为勤学习、善思考、肯钻研、强科研的模范。

三是画好项目疏解“一张图”。三地要把握京张联合申奥与京津冀一体发展两大机遇，坚决执行京津冀规划一张图，京津冀三地发挥各自的比较优势。北京产业发展方向是“微笑曲线”的两个高端，而中间环节缺乏承载空间，已经成为制约北京综合实力提升的硬伤。津冀两地在各自创新驱动发展的同时，要自觉置身于国家战略全局之下，主动把服务首都疏解首都功能作为头等政治任务和发展的战略，不断满足承载北京教育、医疗、科研、养老、生态文明、文化等功能疏解的需求，尤其是河北在文化高新技术产业发展上，谋求建立高新技术产业园，打造京津冀重要的高新文化产业孵化和转化基地。

四是做好创新驱动“二重奏”。首先是政府引领推进创新驱动。三地教育行政机构要制定相关法规，完善相关可操作的制度，充分调动三方合作的积极性。三地企业应主动接纳高校文化创意专业师生到企业实习实训，定期鼓励师生参与企业的产学研协同发展中，并与高校保持深度合作，使企业真正成为学生实习实训的基地，为学生毕业后快速适应工作岗位提供平台。其次是考评激励刺激创新驱动。三地根据岗位职责和素质要求，制定文化创意专业岗位练兵考核评定标准，加大考核力度，重点掌握文化创意专业人员的能力素质、履行职责情况和工作实绩，并与晋职晋升衔接挂钩，有效激发文化创意专业人员立足本职岗位科研成长的内在动力；用考核科研比武奖惩机制激励专业人才成长成才，通过自身开展各种形式的科研考核比武竞赛和鼓励文化创意专业人才参加科技比武，激活文化创意专业人员开拓创新、锐意进取的内在动力；坚持唯才是举、鼓励创意、尊重创造，对勤奋好学、科研成绩突出的及时宣扬表彰，对有创新成果，为人才培养做出贡献的给予奖励；充分利用工作部署会、科研课题开题会、科研方案拟制研究会、科研成果现场推介会、阶段总结会、科研检查考核等有利时机，对全体文化专业技术人员进行传帮带，使他们从中看到科研水平差距，学到科研方法，丰富科研知识，增长科研才干，坚持经常抓、共同带、亲自帮、任务压，积极帮带科研人才成长。

4. 文化品牌共创。意识是价值选择的前提，是行动的先导。品牌是产业的先锋，是竞争的核心。古人讲：“虞舜不逢尧，耕耘处中田。太公未遭文，渔钓泾渭川。”机遇，是不可多得的战略资源。新常态下打造一流品牌就是一个新机遇，就是一个大舞台。正所谓“机不可失，失不再来”，要有“一万年太久，只争朝夕”的劲头，在打造品牌的机遇面前早抓一步、抢先一筹，推动文化发展快马一鞭、领先一步。

一是树立科技意识。科技意识一般是指对科学技术在生产活动中的地位和作用的认识。对这种认识除了理论上的阐述外，还可以从人们在生产活动中开展科研工作的积极性、宣传普及科学知识的自觉性和采用新技术的主动性表现出来。科技意识最重要的内容是“科学技术是第一生产力”的观点。邓小平提出这个观点时，看到了“最终可能是科学技术解决问题”的社会发展前景。“科学技术是第一生产力”的观点，对四个现代化建设具有重大意义。优势产业集聚能量，精品工程影响大众，品牌文化创造效益。

二是加大扶持力度。加大对文化创意的扶持力度，逐步推动文化创意形成新的高端产业形态。加强对吸纳原创人才、应用创意成果的文化创新企业、文化创新项目的奖励和支持，根据不同人群的多层次文化需求提供有针对性的文化服务，拓宽服务领域，提高服务质量，促进公益性文化事业繁荣发展。必须通过深化文化体制改革，繁荣发展文化创意事业，做大做强文化创意产业来创造文化环境，增强文化创新工作的综合实力和竞争力。

三是整合工作机制。组建“文产”论证、创意专家队伍，设立产业综合协调、项目论证规划、推介招商引资服务、统一行政执法等步调一致有人办事的工作机构，使“文产办”更好地承担起做大做强文化创意产业这一重任。采取全员聘用、岗位工资、业绩考核、项目负责等办法，增强活力，多出成果，多出精品，实现由群众文化向公共文化的转变。有计划地组织农民文化骨干进行系统学习和专业培训，充分发挥乡村文化能人传、帮、带作用。建立“文化志愿者”队伍，培育和发展农村业余演出队、放映队、特色文化示范户，形成专职文化队伍、志愿者队伍与农村文化骨干互补互动的良好局面，培养高素质的群众文化管理干部和群众文化专业骨干，造就一支支不走的文艺队伍，增强文化可持续发展能力。进一步放宽市场准入制度，建立多元化的投融资机制，鼓励吸引非文化民营企业、国内外知名品牌文化企业参与文化事业和文化创意产业的发展。要充分运用各类媒体、多种手段长期广泛宣传发动社会各界参与文化事业和文化创意产业的发展，做大做强文化创意产业的合力。

行之力则知愈进，知之深则行愈达。“滚石上山，爬坡过坎”是命题也是答案。以“功成不必在我”的历史耐心和“功成必定有我”的责任担当攻坚克难，形成协同发展“一盘棋”，迸发出高质量发展新活力。加快京津冀文化协同，应优先推进文化经济协同发展，持续优化京津冀三地文化协同发展的经济社会环境，培育壮大多元化京津冀文化协同发展主体，建立健全新时代文化协同治理体系和治理机制，促进三地文化共兴。加强三地协调发展，促进三地文化共兴，其核心是“强”。三地文化强是区域文化强的重要标志。当前，三地正处于由传统文化产业为主向新兴文化产业形态兴起的转型发展时期，面临着业态重塑、产业链再造的问题，推动文化协同发展，需要提炼各自发展经验，最大程度释放文化资源服务社会、推动发展的基本作用，在融合发展中达到互促共赢，产生叠加放大效应，助推三地文化产业升级，实现文化共兴。

参考文献

[1] 习近平：《在十八届中央政治局第一次集体学习时的讲话》，《人民日报》2012 年 11 月 19 日。

[2]《邓小平文选》第 3 卷，人民出版社，1993，第 39～44，124 页。

[3] 习近平：《稳扎稳打勇于担当敢于创新善作善成推动京津冀协同发展取得新的更大进展——在京津冀三省市考察并主持召开京津冀协同发展座谈会讲话》，《人民日报》2019 年 1 月 19 日。

[4] 习近平：《保持战略定力和坚定信念坚定不移走自己的路》，《党建》2014 年第 5 期，第 1～3 页。

[5] 人民日报评论部：《以系统思维聚合力——我们需要怎样的“改革思维”之四》，《人民日报》2014 年 3 月 13 日。

[6] 曾德贤等：《文化软实力：区域经济发展的强大动力》，《前沿》2012 年第 7 期，第 76 页。

[7] 刘建明等：《宣传舆论学大辞典》，经济日报出版社，1993，第 119 页。

B.17

河南跨境电子商务发展的思考和建议

尚国栋*

摘　要： 在当前国内外跨境电子商务业态快速发展的趋势下，本报告借鉴钻石模型理论，总结了河南省跨境电子商务发展具有的优势，梳理了当前存在的不足与短板，研究提出了下一步河南省跨境电子商务业态发展的一种可能性演化路径，并结合实际从理论创新、政策环境、产业培育、物流平台建设等方面给出了推动河南跨境电子商务产业发展的措施建议。

关键词： 钻石模型　国际贸易　跨境电子商务

近年来，随着经济全球化的不断深入和互联网信息技术的蓬勃发展，国际贸易的贸易方式、形式和特点都在发生革命性的变化。从宏观角度看，全球市场消费需求不断增长升级，贸易环境不断变化，对时效、标准、品质等方面的要求越来越高；从具体层面讲，贸易方式日益多元，贸易订单呈现碎片化、定制化、去中间化等趋势。这些都在深刻影响着当前国际贸易的规则和形态，也催生了跨境电子商务这一新兴业态。它通过降低国际贸易的门槛，减少贸易的中间环节，打破消费的时空限制，使“买全球、卖全球”成为现实。当前，跨境电子商务在国际贸易领域占有份额不断增加，影响越来越重要，将有望发展成为未来下一代贸易方式的主流形态。

本报告结合当前跨境电子商务业态发展的态势，借鉴钻石模型分析了河南省跨境电子商务发展的优势和短板，研究提出了下一步的发展目标和建议。

---

* 尚国栋，硕士，河南省人民政府办公厅副处长。

一　当前我国跨境电子商务发展的基本情况

目前，业界广泛接受并使用的跨境电子商务定义为：跨境电子商务，是指分属不同关境的交易主体，通过电子商务平台达成交易、进行支付结算，并通过跨境物流送达商品、完成交易的一种国际商业活动。跨境电子商务根据交易方和交易流程的不同，通常分为跨境 B2C、跨境 B2B、跨境 B2B2C 等。近年来，我国高度重视跨境电子商务的发展，将其作为构建开放型经济新体制、推动形成全面开放新格局的重要内容，始终秉承包容审慎的监管原则，以国际贸易自由化、便利化和业态创新为重点积极推进试点工作，实现了跨境电子商务的快速发展。

图 1、图 2、图 3 分别反映了 2011 ~2017 年我国跨境电子商务交易规模与货物贸易进出口总值的比较情况、跨境电子商务进出口交易额占比情况和业务模式占比情况。

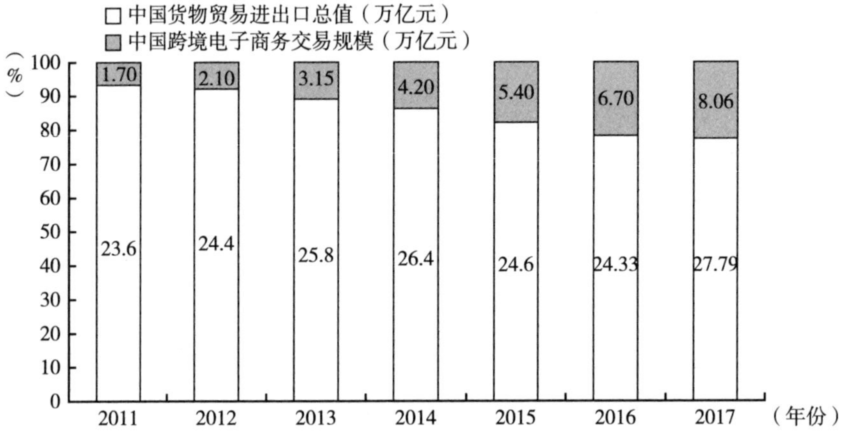

图 1　2011 ~2017 年我国跨境电子商务交易规模与货物贸易进出口总值比较

资料来源：中国电子商务研究中心《2017 年度中国电子商务市场数据监测报告》和中国海关统计数据。

可以看出，在贸易方式上，我国跨境电子商务占货物贸易进出口总值的比重逐年增加；进出口结构中，我国跨境电子商务以出口为主，但进口占比逐年

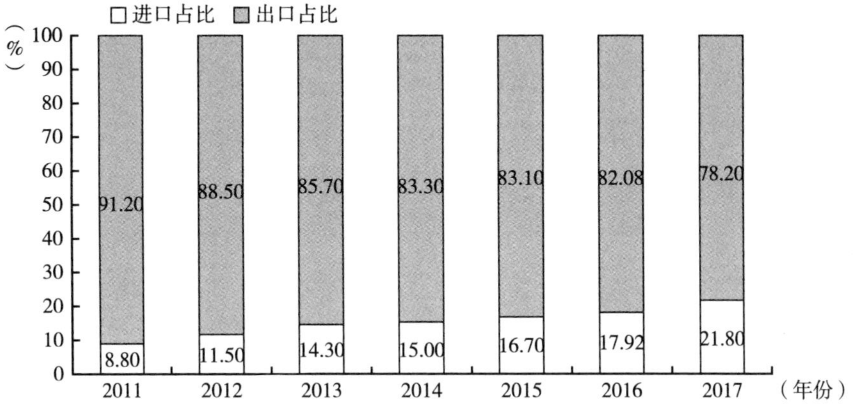

图2　2011～2017年我国跨境电子商务进出口交易额占比

资料来源：中国电子商务研究中心《2017年度中国电子商务市场数据监测报告》和中国海关统计数据。

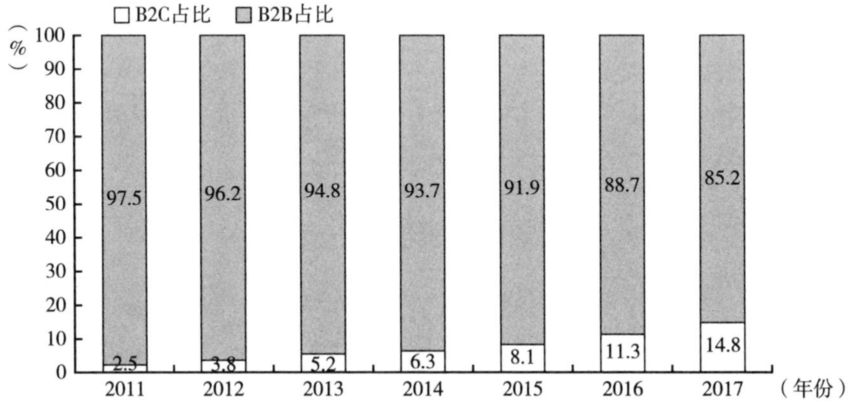

图3　2011～2017年我国跨境电子商务业务模式占比

资料来源：中国电子商务研究中心《2017年度中国电子商务市场数据监测报告》和中国海关统计数据。

增加；按业务模式分，我国跨境电子商务以B2B为主，但B2C（包含B2B2C）占比逐年提升。从河南省的情况看，近年来跨境电子商务发展也呈现出类似趋势，即以跨境电子商务B2B2C为主的跨境零售进口快速增长。这同时也说明，河南跨境电子商务的发展顺应了国际贸易发展的新趋势，抓住了国际贸易体系变革的机遇，发展重点与方向是正确的，未来发展前景乐观。

二 河南跨境电子商务发展的优势与短板

近年来，河南跨境电子商务业态发展迅速，年均保持30%以上的增速，2018年达到1285.9亿元（含B2B、B2C等），郑州市2018年跨境电商交易额570.2亿元，基本建成全球网购商品集疏分拨中心，业务覆盖196个国家和地区，网购保税进口累计业务总量、纳税总额居全国第一。河南跨境电子商务的发展得到了理论界、跨境电子商务行业和政府相关部门的高度肯定，也吸引了世界贸易组织、世界海关组织等国际组织的高度关注。跨境电子商务发展已经对河南的产业结构、对外开放度、城市发展乃至国际知名度和影响力产生了重大提升拉动作用，在河南新一轮高水平对外开放和构建开放型经济新体制中占有重要地位。同时，我们也要认识到，河南跨境电子商务发展并不是一帆风顺的，当前的成绩和地位也不是天然形成的。随着国家政策的推开和各地竞争的加剧，如果满足现状、停滞不前，就有可能面临“起个大早、赶个晚集”的尴尬局面。因此迫切需要开展持续性的、针对性的理论研究，梳理出河南跨境电子商务发展的优势和短板。下面就结合河南省情和跨境电子商务发展情况，借鉴波特钻石模型的理论框架，对其进行梳理分析。

（一）基于波特钻石模型的分析框架

波特钻石模型是由美国哈佛商学院著名的战略管理学家迈克尔·波特提出的。波特的钻石模型通常用于分析一个国家某种产业为什么会在国际上有较强的竞争力。该模型认为相关影响因素有：生产要素、需求条件、相关及联动产业和产业结构、同业竞争与合作，以及政府行为与机遇。借鉴这一理论，本报告分析提出了河南跨境电子商务发展优势与短板的分析框架，如图4所示。

以此框架为研究基础，接下来进一步分析河南跨境电子商务的优势与短板。

（二）优势

1. 不断创新的跨境电子商务业态。河南跨境电子商务的主要亮点是郑州试点首创的海关监管代码为“1210”的保税备货模式。该模式结合原有跨境

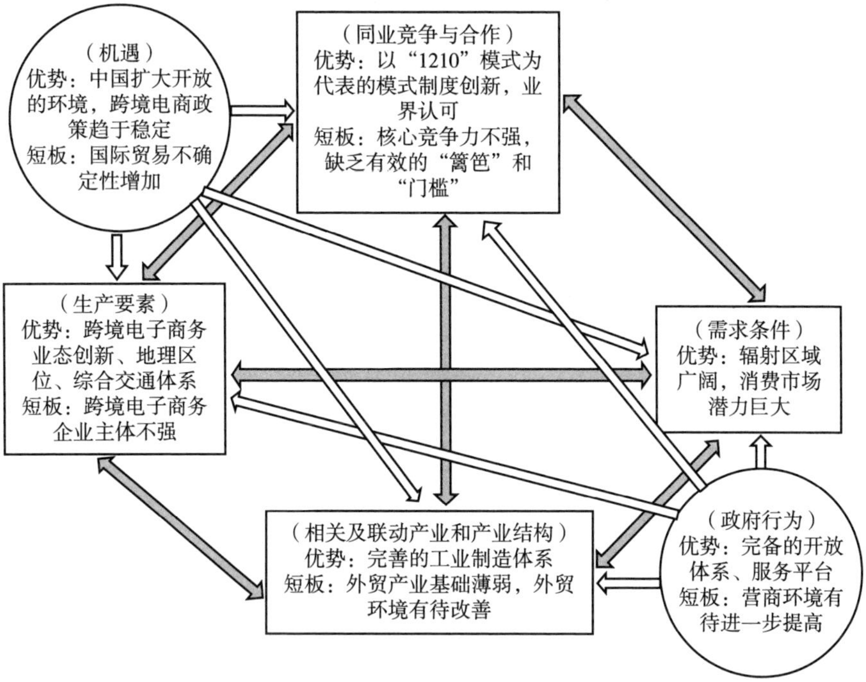

图4　河南跨境电子商务发展优势与短板分析框架

电子商务B2B、B2C的特点，在国外销售商（B）和国内消费者（C）中间创新地加入了一个中间服务商B（受监管的电商服务企业），由这个中间服务商提供商品采购、报关缴税等服务，承担销售主体接受监管、退货维权等职责。通过这个中间服务商，成功解决了企业关心的物流、成本问题，政府关心的税收、监管问题和消费者关心的质量安全、维权问题。以此为基础，郑州还试点提出了监管、征税、准入、风险、统计、结汇等方面的标准和规则，探索实施了“关检三个一”“查验双随机”“跨境秒通关”等创新举措，这些奠定了河南跨境电商在全国的创新引领地位。2017年，河南郑州在全国率先实现了“网购保税+线下提货”O2O新零售模式，提升了境外商品的快速购物体验。2018年，河南又积极贯彻落实国家“互联网+医疗健康”发展意见和国务院常务会议要求，通过讨论研究，向国家提出了开展跨境电商进口药品监管服务试点的申请，意在利用跨境电子商务渠道解决人民群众买药难、买药贵的问题。近期，郑州试点模式在广西南宁实现复制推广，中国－东盟（南宁）跨境电商产业园“南大门”成功投入运营。这一系列成果所体现的始终追赶业界前沿、通过实践不断突破自我的创新基因是河南跨境电子商务发展的宝贵精神力量，而其中涌现的敢于创新、善于创新的企业家团队则是河南跨境电子商务发展的基础优势和主体力量。

2. 优越的地理区位和发达的综合交通体系。因地处中部，河南与全国其他区域进行要素配置和资源交换的成本相对较低。特别是在“陆海内外联动、东西双向互济”的新一轮开放格局中，这种优势更加明显。近年来，河南持之以恒地加强综合交通体系建设，构建了路网密布、无缝衔接的公路、铁路、民航运输网络，为物流高效集疏提供了便利条件。河南发展跨境电子商务，无论是进口还是出口，都能以相对低的投入和成本对周边区域产生强大的带动辐射效应，推动我国中部乃至周边更大范围区域扩大国际经贸合作，全面融入经济全球化进程。

3. 潜力巨大的消费市场。河南本身有1亿人的消费市场，如果以郑州为中心，以500公里为半径可覆盖全国3.6亿人口，以1000公里为半径可覆盖7.9亿人口。优越的地理区位优势形成了得天独厚的市场覆盖能力，也使得河南发展跨境电子商务有着巨大的市场支撑和消费需求。

4. 完备的开放体系和服务平台。近年来，河南持续加快开放体系建设，已经形成“五区”（郑州航空港经济综合实验区、河南自贸试验区、郑洛新自创区、郑州跨境电子商务综合试验区、国家大数据综合试验区）联动、“四路”（空中、陆上、网上、海上丝绸之路）协同的对外开放新格局，郑州拥有九大功能性口岸，是内陆地区口岸数量最多、种类最全的城市。依托自贸区政策优势，已经建成了国际贸易“单一窗口”和跨境电子商务进出口业务全流程服务平台。

（三）短板

1. 尚未形成有效的“篱笆”和“门槛”。保税备货模式是一种商业模式的创新，这种创新虽然成功引发了商业业态的巨大变革，但它与技术创新、产品创新等不同，具有易于复制推广的特点，很难对同业者和后来者形成绝对领先优势。那些具有良好产业基础、开放条件和营商环境，并认识到发展跨境电子商务重要性的省份和地区，很有可能顺势而起、弯道超车，从而后发先至。

2018 年 7 月份，国务院又批准了在北京市等 22 个城市设立跨境电子商务综合试验区，至此全国跨境电子商务综合试验区达到 35 个。国家全面推开跨境电子商务的趋势已经非常明显，留给河南的时间窗口已经非常紧张了。

2. 外贸产业基础相对薄弱，外贸环境有待改善。河南包括郑州在内，过去对外开放度长期低于全国平均水平，外贸基础相对薄弱，产业结构外向度不高。如表 1 和图 5 所示，是根据地区生产总值和进出口总额测算出的第一批跨境电子商务试点城市以及河南、全国 2010 ~ 2017 年度外贸依存度数据（外贸依存度 = 对外贸易进出口总额/地区生产总值）。

表 1　第一批跨境电子商务试点城市及河南、全国 2010 ~ 2017 年度外贸依存度

单位：%

年份	2010	2011	2012	2013	2014	2015	2016	2017
上海	145.50	147.22	136.56	125.26	121.56	111.37	102.25	104.96
宁波	108.32	104.39	92.35	86.73	84.51	78.18	72.58	76.97
杭州	59.41	58.71	49.71	47.98	45.37	41.25	39.92	40.21
重庆	10.61	18.84	29.44	33.28	41.10	29.51	23.50	23.15
郑州	8.66	21.14	41.00	42.72	42.09	48.58	45.05	44.10
河南	5.26	7.74	10.95	11.56	11.43	12.43	11.69	11.76
全国	48.84	48.31	45.18	43.37	41.03	35.63	32.73	33.62

资料来源：国家统计年鉴、各地统计年鉴。

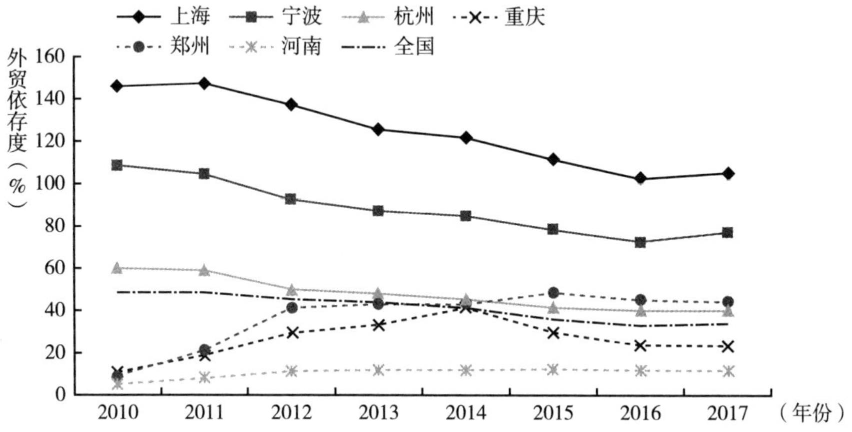

图 5　第一批跨境电子商务试点城市及河南、全国 2010 ~ 2017 年度外贸依存度

资料来源：国家统计年鉴、各地统计年鉴。

从图表中的数据看，得益于郑州航空港经济综合实验区建设和跨境电子商务产业发展，近年来郑州外贸依存度逐年提高，2014 年超过了全国平均水平。但河南全省外贸依存度依然低于全国平均水平，外贸基础和环境与沿海发达地区比还有很大差距，外向型产业和外贸服务环境还不足以为跨境电子商务的进一步发展，特别是在扩大出口方面，提供强大的产业基础和服务支撑。此外，跨境电子商务和外贸、物流专业高水平人才也相对匮乏，综合交通体系优势还没有完全转化为物流优势和供应链优势。

3. 跨境电子商务企业主体不强。河南近几年跨境电子商务发展成绩的取得，离不开聚美优品、小红书、网易考拉、唯品会、豌豆公主等知名电商企业和一大批物流服务商的支持。但是这些企业总部并不在河南，往往是根据业务发展的需要和各地支持政策的变化，动态调整战略重点和业务布局，不稳定性和变化性较大，这给河南跨境电子商务发展带来很大的不确定性。目前，河南本地从事跨境电子商务的企业相对规模小、业务不强，龙头型企业引领带动作用还未形成。

4. 营商环境有待进一步提高。随着开放的不断深入，河南的营商环境这几年已经有很大改善。但通过到沿海地区调研和与相关电商企业的沟通交流，客观上仍能感觉到与之存在差距。相关部门监管意识到位，但从心底里为企业服务的意识还不够主动；一些监管政策和执行标准有时过于苛刻和教条；部分承诺的配套支持政策因多种原因没有落实；企业缺乏稳定的政策预期，在业务扩展上容易存在保守观望情绪。这些细小但又很具体的问题汇集起来，就有可能成为制约河南跨境电子商务继续发展的重大阻碍。

三　河南发展跨境电子商务的目标

郑州和河南发展跨境电子商务，不应仅仅停留在高效便捷地购买全球高品质商品、满足人民群众高品质生活需求的阶段，而应将其作为推动经济结构调整、实现产业转型升级的重要抓手。通过发展跨境电子商务，进一步扩大对外开放，提高贸易自由化、便利化水平，使区域经济全面融入经济全球化，生产制造主动对接全球供应链，实现在全球市场内高效配置要素资源，提升河南全省的国际竞争力和国际化水平。图 6 反映的是郑州和河南跨境电子商务发展的目标定位演化。

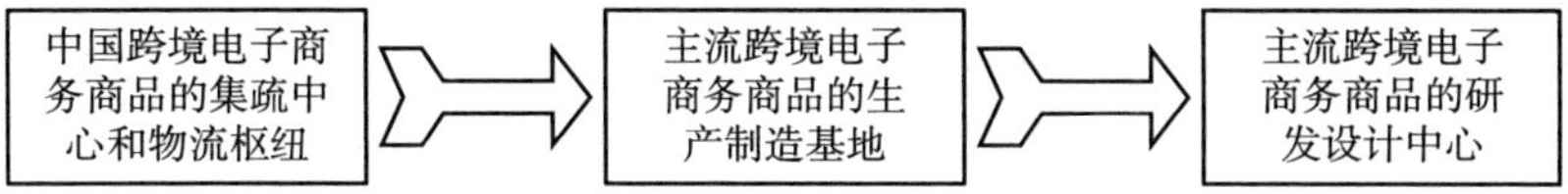

图6　郑州和河南发展跨境电子商务目标定位演化

首先，以郑州为中心，依托空港、口岸、高铁、公路等优势，努力建设中国跨境电子商务商品的集疏中心和物流枢纽，争取实现对华北、华中、西北大部分区域的辐射，成为这些区域跨境电子商务渠道进出口货物的配送中心和转运枢纽。其次，以物流枢纽为基础，抓住产业转移和消费升级的机遇，吸引跨境电子商务主流商品的生产企业在郑州周边落地布局，进行本地化制造，形成主流跨境电子商务商品的制造基地。最后，以制造基地为基础，吸引研发、设计、服务等高附加值产业、高精端行业落户河南，形成主流跨境电子商务商品的研发设计中心，推动河南产业层级的提升与进化。

四　下一步河南发展跨境电子商务的几点建议

当前，跨境电子商务发展面临难得的发展机遇和外部环境。2018 年 11 月 5 日，首届中国国际进口博览会在上海举行，会上提出了主动扩大进口、放宽市场准入等对外开放新举措。11 月 21 日，国务院出台了一系列有利于跨境电子商务发展的政策措施，包括延续实施进口现行监管政策、扩大适用范围、进一步扩大享受优惠政策的商品范围、提高单次和年度交易限值、支持出口、完善出口退税政策等。河南应该充分利用好机遇环境的窗口期，在关注业态发展动向，加强理论研究创新，制定针对性支持政策，培育龙头型领军企业，优化发展环境，夯实发展基础等方面下功夫。相关建议如下。

（一）加强理论创新研究，增强发展后劲。一是加强研究团队建设。跨境电子商务领域很多突破来源于国际贸易的实践和业界的创新，但其要发展壮大、走向国际贸易舞台就需要上升到理论层面，搭建科学的标准架构和厚实的体系支撑，这就需要建设一支既有深厚理论功底，又有丰富实际操作经验的研究队伍。二是加强对跨境电子商务全流程相关领域的研究。跨境电子商务要跨越不同关境、联通境内境外，就涉及全球贸易规则、关税政策、贸易通关便利化等；要通过电子商务平台达成交易、支付结算，就涉及电子订单、外汇管理与结算等；要通过跨境物流送达，就涉及物流、仓储、配送等。这些领域有很多具体问题，要深入细节流程中去，研究提出优化建议和实施方案。三是建立高效畅通的政策咨询与沟通机制。时刻关注一线的创新实践，及时跟踪服务，掌握行业内不同方面的动向，发挥好行业与监管部门之间的桥梁纽带作用，及时向有关部门提出政策咨询和建议，避免出现大的政策波动，为跨境电子商务发展营造良好政策环境。

（二）继续做强进口业务，努力做大出口业务。积极开展国际商贸交流与合作，“请进来”与“走出去”相结合，为跨境电子商务进出口业务创造平台、营造环境；利用各种展会搭建平台，鼓励电商企业将更多优质的国外商品选购进来，拓宽线上、线下销售渠道，扩大销售规模；争取跨境电子商务渠道进口药品试点尽快落地，着力丰富产业业态。充分发掘开发国内有特色、质量好的工业制品、消费品、手工制品、农产品等，注重树立品牌形象，将更多受国际市场欢迎的商品销售出去；在品牌宣传、检验标准、安全认证等方面为出口商品提供大力支持和便利化服务；支持海外仓等基础服务设施建设，复制国内模式做法，鼓励电商企业走出去。

（三）支持平台企业聚焦主业，完善服务功能。加快复制推广跨境电子商务“1210”保税备货和中大门模式，扩大试点服务区域和范围，不断提升业务规模；进一步完善跨境电子商务综合服务平台的报关、退税、外汇结算、金融服务等功能，深入推进贸易通关便利化；及时研究应对国际贸易体系中，特别是主要贸易对象出台的一些新政策（如中美贸易摩擦、欧盟 VAT 改革方案等），努力为跨境电商从业者提供系统解决方案；继续发挥现有与海关、检验检疫等监管部门的密切协调机制，将新模式、新业态发展的摩擦成本和内部阻力降到最低；加快建立完善的跨境电子商务统计体系，为政府部门决策提供科学数据支撑。

（四）多措并举，培育好龙头型企业和小微企业。充分发挥金融渠道作用，建立支持跨境电子商务产业发展的专项基金，力争通过入股、并购等金融手段引入规模大或有潜力的跨境电子商务领军企业；充分了解企业发展诉求，量身定制个性化的政策扶持方案，支持培育世界工厂网等一批本地跨境电子商务企业做大做强；借鉴杭州等地促进跨境电子商务加快发展的政策，在税收政策、配套资金、办公用房租金、仓储、物流补助、人才培训等方面制定出台相关政策，给予小微企业全方位的支持。

（五）做大做强郑州到周边主要城市的高铁物流。中国境内有目前全球总里程最长的高速铁路网络。据了解，一列 8 节车厢编组的高铁列车理论运输能力相当于一架波音 747 全货机，且成本方面远低于空运。我国高铁网络如果广泛开展货运业务，将会深刻改变国内现有物流格局，有可能形成像孟菲斯、法兰克福等航空物流枢纽一样的高铁物流枢纽。2018 年 5 月，中铁快运和顺丰合作开展“高铁极速达”物流服务，截至 11 月，运营线路已拓展至 413 条，58 个城市，完成超过 400 万票快递。郑州处于中国高铁网络的中心区域，据测算，高铁从郑州出发，5 小时左右可以通达周边 1200 公里区域内主要城市，10 小时左右可以覆盖全国大多数主要城市，非常适合开展高铁“当日达”（5 小时范围）、“次日达”（10 小时范围）等高时效物流服务。河南应主动加强与中国铁路总公司特别是中铁快运的合作，充分发挥区位优势和高铁网络优势，探索通过高铁行李专用柜、开通货运高铁专列等多种形式开拓物流市场，进一步提高郑州的物流集疏能力，力争形成以郑州为中心枢纽的高铁物流网络。

（六）推进“四路”协同，提高集疏效率，丰富商品品类。不同的运输方式在货物品类、运输效率和时效性等方面各有特点，通过科学安排、高效衔接可以形成紧密的互补协作关系，从而提升整体物流效率。从河南的情况看，“网上丝绸之路”将为其他三条丝绸之路提供日益增长的物流需求，并促进相互间的转换联运效率；其他三条丝绸之路则可以满足“网上丝绸之路”在商品种类、市场区域、运输时效等方面的不同要求，让“网上丝绸之路”更加快捷顺畅。推进空中、路上、海上、网上“四路”协同应是河南利用综合优势、发挥集成效应的战略选择（见图 7）。

推进“四路”协同，应在铁路港、航空港、保税园区间的高效协同上下功夫，推进相互间政策衔接、资源整合和系统集成，不断丰富完善“区港联动”“区区联动”的内容与功能；科学谋划、统筹推进河南连接全球主要市场的重大物流通道建设；以整体效率提升为目标，建设智能化物流网络平台，不断优化物流供应链；构建并加强空中、陆上、海上丝绸之路间的互补关系（图 7 中箭头④⑤⑥所示），促进其与跨境电子商务“网上丝绸之路”的共生关系（图 7 中箭头①②③所示）。

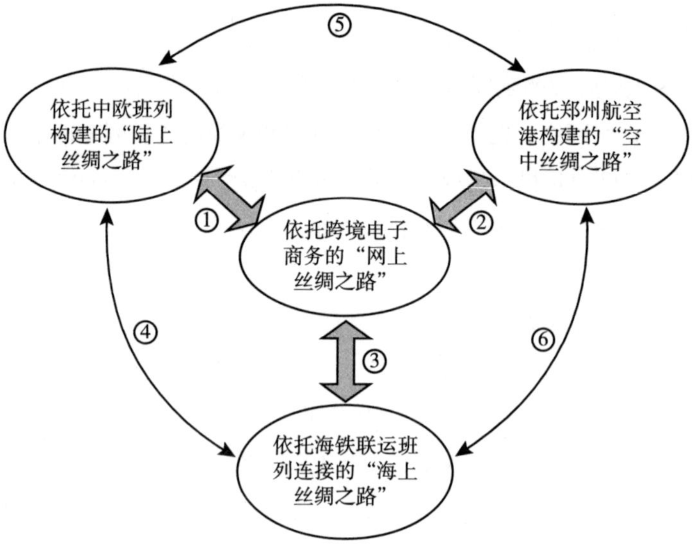

图 7 “四路”协同

参考文献

[1] 中国国际经济交流中心课题组：《E 国际贸易——下一代贸易方式的理论内涵与基础框架》，中国经济出版社，2018，第 43～44 页。

[2] 王外连、王明宇、刘淑贞：《中国跨境电子商务的现状分析及建议》，《电子商务》2013 年第 9 期，第 23～24 页。

[3] 孙志平、曹凯、刘怀丕：《中国为全球跨境电商发展难题提供解决方案》，中国国际电子商务网，http：//www.ec.com.cn/article/dssz/zhjg/201709/21676_1.html。

[4] 迈克尔·波特著，李明轩、邱如美译《国家竞争优势》，华夏出版社，2002，第 67～69 页。

B.18 打造郑州国家重要经济增长中心的思考与建议

喻新安　徐艳红*

摘　要： 郑州是国家支持建设的9个国家中心城市之一，是中原城市群核心城市，区位优势明显，承担着区域经济建设和发展的重大使命。目前郑州经济规模在河南省有一定优势，但与其他15个GDP超万亿元城市相比，总量不足，首位度不高。为支撑建设郑州国家中心城市，提升经济发展水平和辐射带动功能，在国家、河南省委省政府、郑州市委市政府高度重视和经济发展态势良好的状况下，需要破解产业发展质量不高、科技创新能力不强、国际化水平不高、综合承载力不足等问题，紧紧抓住新时期新机遇，通过进一步强化产业支撑、增强区位优势、坚持创新驱动、发挥龙头作用、提高国际化水平等，凸显郑州在全国经济版图和城市网络中的地位，逐步将郑州打造成为国家重要的经济增长中心，增强郑州的经济辐射力和影响力。

关键词： 经济增长中心　经济辐射力　区域经济　国家中心城市

一　打造郑州国家重要经济增长中心的背景

城市经济增长指在一个较长时间跨度上，城市地区生产总值（GDP）或人

---

* 喻新安，博士，二级研究员，中国区域经济学会副会长、河南省高校智库联盟理事长、郑州师范学院国家中心城市研究院首席专家，研究方向为区域经济、产业经济，经济体制改革；徐艳红，博士，讲师，研究方向为城市发展、城市生态。

均产出/收入的持续增加。1933 年德国经济地理学家克里斯泰勒首次提出城市中心性的概念。作为经济增长中心的城市，是某一区域活动的中心，并与周围区域具有紧密的联系，是该区域经济、政治、科技及商业服务等的重要集中地，对周边城市和地区具有直接的经济辐射带动作用。

郑州，不仅是河南省省会，更是新亚欧大陆桥重要节点城市、“一带一路”关键节点城市，国家“米”字形高铁网核心城市，并成为国家支持建设的 9 个国家中心城市之一。郑州区位与交通枢纽优势明显，经济发展潜力巨大。

2014 年 5 月，习近平总书记视察郑州时，提出郑州要“建成连通境内外、辐射东中西的物流通道枢纽，为丝绸之路经济带多作贡献”，向“买全球、卖全球”目标迈进，打造中部地区对外开放高地。

2016 年 12 月，国家明确提出支持郑州建设国家中心城市。国家发展改革委《关于支持郑州建设国家中心城市的复函》（发改规划〔2017〕154 号）文件中，批复同意支持郑州建设国家中心城市，同时提出郑州应“全面提升经济发展水平和辐射带动功能”的要求。

2018 年 11 月，中共中央、国务院《关于建立更加有效的区域协调发展新机制的意见》下发，郑州成为新时代国家建立更加有效的区域协调发展新机制的 12 个城市之一。

河南省委、省政府全力支持郑州国家中心城市建设，强调在引领中原城市群发展中，“让郑州这个龙头高高扬起来”。

郑州市委、市政府对建设国家中心城市高度重视，于 2018 年 2 月公布了《郑州建设国家中心城市行动纲要（2017—2035）》，明确提出郑州国家中心城市的功能定位为：国际综合枢纽、国际物流中心、国家重要的经济增长中心、国家极具活力的创新创业中心、国家内陆地区对外开放门户及华夏历史文明传承创新中心。郑州作为“国家重要的经济增长中心”这一定位成为全市干部群众的共识。

2018 年，郑州市 GDP 突破万亿元，人口超过千万，实现了量级和能级的跃升。社会各界对郑州发展的预期越来越高，也意味着郑州需要立足全国、放眼世界，以更高的站位、更宽的视野、更大的魄力，来谋划未来发展，勇挑“龙头”重担，叫响“郑中心”的名号。

适应新的形势，2019 年 6 月，中共河南省委、河南省人民政府下发《关于支持郑州建设国家中心城市的若干意见》（豫发〔2019〕18 号），明确“把郑州打造成为我省参与全球竞争、集聚高端资源的战略平台，形成我省的核心增长极”，“打造国家重要的经济增长中心”。

2019 年 7 月 24 日，河南省开放大会召开，省委书记王国生在大会讲话中要求郑州“对标一流、拉高标杆”，“在全国同类城市竞争中形成更多比较优势，在全省发挥更大辐射带动作用，展现国家中心城市的担当作为”。

无疑，在郑州“三中心一枢纽一门户”的城市总体定位中，列在第一位的，也是最为关键和要害的，是“国家重要的经济增长中心”。

二　郑州经济增长情况的比较分析

（一）郑州对河南省经济增长的贡献分析

郑州是全国重要的铁路、航空、高速公路、电力、邮政电信主要枢纽城市，是全国普通铁路和高速铁路网中唯一的“双十字”中心，随着郑济、郑万、郑合等高铁路网的建设，以郑州为中心的“米”字形高铁网正快速形成。同时，郑州作为河南省省会和政治、经济、文化及交通中心，对周边城市和地区具有较强的吸引力和辐射力。

GDP 是衡量一个国家或地区综合实力和发展水平的重要指标。城市对周边区域的科技、文化、投资、物流等多个领域的经济影响最终都会不同程度地体现在 GDP 上。城市经济规模越大，对区域经济增长的拉动越强。本报告针对“十二五”及“十二五”以来，河南省各省辖市 GDP 增长情况及经济贡献率进行对比，分析郑州对省内经济增长的贡献。

郑州作为河南省的政治、经济、文化中心，“十二五”期间，年均增速 11.1%，在省辖市里排名第三位，对全省经济发展做出了突出贡献（见表 1）。“十三五”以来，郑州经济持续保持了在省辖市的领先水平，GDP 在全省范围内优势明显。同时，郑州经济的快速发展，有效带动了周边南阳、洛阳、开封、许昌、新乡、平顶山等城市的发展，2016～2018 年河南各地市 GDP 均实现阶梯式增长，体现出国家中心城市较强的区域经济辐射力。从 GDP 增速上看，2016~2018年郑州的GDP增速分别为8.5%、8.2%、8.1%，增速分别处于全省第五位、第五位、第七位，增加态势虽略有下降，但各年度增速均高于全省GDP增速，各年度分别高于全省0.3个、0.4个、0.5个百分点，呈缓慢增长态势。

表1 河南各省辖市“十二五”时期经济增长情况及排序情况

省辖市	2015年GDP（亿元）	位次	2015年GDP增速(%)	位次	“十二五”时期年均增速(%)	位次
郑州市	7315.19	1	10.1	1	11.1	3
开封市	1604.84	13	9.4	3	10.8	5
洛阳市	3508.75	2	9.2	4	9.6	14
平顶山市	1705.78	12	6.7	15	7.7	18
安阳市	1884.48	8	7.4	14	8.8	17
鹤壁市	713.23	17	8.0	13	10.9	4
新乡市	1982.25	6	6.0	16	10.1	9
焦作市	1943.37	7	8.8	11	10.6	7
濮阳市	1333.64	14	9.5	2	11.2	1
许昌市	2170.60	4	9.0	6	11.2	1
漯河市	992.85	16	9.0	6	10.5	8
三门峡市	1260.55	15	3.5	18	9.3	16
南阳市	2875.02	3	9.1	5	9.5	15
商丘市	1803.93	11	8.7	12	10.0	10
信阳市	1877.75	9	8.9	9	9.7	12
周口市	2082.38	5	9.0	6	9.8	11
驻马店市	1807.09	10	8.9	9	9.7	12
济源市	494.41	18	6.0	16	10.8	5

根据表2所示，郑州、洛阳、南阳、许昌、周口、新乡的GDP位居河南省18个省辖市GDP排名前六位；2016~2018年，郑州GDP对河南省GDP贡献率分别为20.2%、20.6%、21.1%，呈不断增长态势，且远高于其他城市贡献率，是河南省第二大城市洛阳经济贡献率的两倍多。

表2　2016～2018年河南主要省辖市GDP及对河南省GDP贡献率

省辖市	2016年		2017年		2018年	
	GDP（亿元）	贡献率（%）	GDP（亿元）	贡献率（%）	GDP（亿元）	贡献率（%）
全　省	40249.23	—	44552.83	—	48055.86	—
郑　州	8113.97	20.2	9193.77	20.6	10143.32	21.1
洛　阳	3820.11	9.5	4290.19	9.6	4640.78	9.7
南　阳	3114.97	7.7	3345.30	7.5	3566.77	7.4
许　昌	2377.71	5.9	2632.92	5.9	2830.62	5.9
周　口	2263.86	5.6	2459.70	5.5	2687.22	5.6
新　乡	2166.97	5.4	2357.76	5.3	2526.55	5.3

资料来源：2016年和2017年数据分别来源于《2017年河南省统计年鉴》《2018年河南省统计年鉴》，2018年数据为初步统计数据。

（二）郑州在全国“万亿元俱乐部”中的位置分析

万亿元GDP是我国特大城市的“标牌”，也是多数城市追求的目标。“十二五”期间，全国有10个GDP超万亿元城市。“十三五”以来，我国经济依旧处于稳步发展中，GDP超万亿元的城市数量不断增加，除个别城市排名略有增加和下降一个名次外，其余城市排名基本稳定。

资料显示，南京、青岛于2016年迈入“GDP万亿元俱乐部”，2017年长沙、无锡GDP超过万亿元。郑州市2016年GDP为8114亿元，距离万亿GDP还有较大差距；但到2018年，郑州GDP达到10143亿元，并成为继宁波之后的第16个“GDP万亿元俱乐部”成员。同时，根据相关统计，2018年，GDP超万亿元的16个城市中，人口上千万的共有上海、北京、深圳、广州、天津、苏州、重庆、武汉、成都、郑州、杭州11个城市，郑州成为GDP过万亿、人口过千万的“双料”城市，成为中国当今的超级大城市之一。

从GDP增速分析，2016～2018年，万亿元俱乐部各个城市的GDP增速均呈现缓慢下降的态势，郑州的GDP增速虽略有下降，但增速一直保持在较高水平。在16个GDP超万亿元城市中，郑州的GDP增速位次不断上升，从2016年的第六位上升至2018年的第二位，比同年进入“GDP万亿元俱乐部”的宁波高1.1个百分点，与多数城市相比，郑州经济仍处于快速发展中（见表3）。

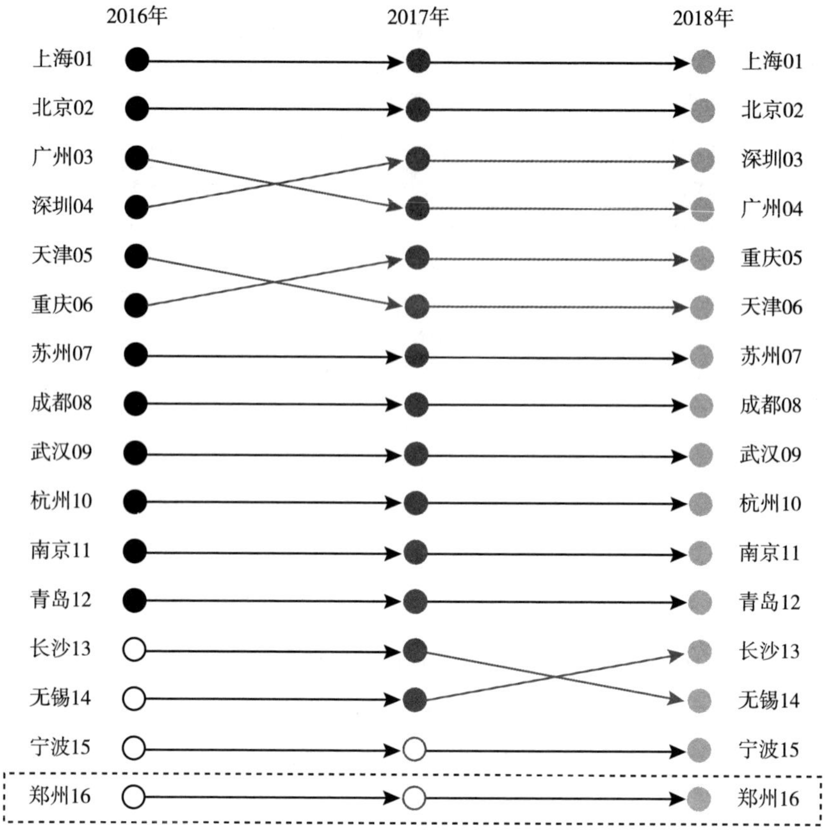

图1　2016～2018年“万亿元俱乐部城市”GDP排名

资料来源：2016年和2017年数据分别来源于各地市统计年鉴，2018年数据为初步统计数据。

表3　2016～2018年“万亿元俱乐部城市”GDP增速及位次

城市	2016年		2017年		2018年	
	GDP增速（%）	位次	GDP增速（%）	位次	GDP增速（%）	位次
上海	6.8	15	6.9	14	6.6	12
北京	6.7	16	6.7	15	6.6	13
深圳	9.0	4	8.8	3	7.6	6
广州	8.0	7	7.0	13	6.2	14
重庆	10.7	1	9.3	1	6.0	15

续表

城市	2016 年		2017 年		2018 年	
	GDP 增速（%）	位次	GDP 增速（%）	位次	GDP 增速（%）	位次
天津	9.0	5	3.6	16	3.6	16
苏州	7.5	12	7.1	12	7.0	9
成都	7.7	11	8.1	5	8.0	3
武汉	7.8	10	8.0	7	8.0	4
杭州	9.5	2	8.0	8	6.7	11
南京	8.0	8	8.1	6	8.0	5
青岛	7.9	9	7.5	10	7.4	7
长沙	9.4	3	9.0	2	8.5	1
无锡	7.5	13	7.4	11	7.4	8
宁波	7.1	14	7.8	9	7.0	10
郑州	8.5	6	8.2	4	8.1	2

资料来源：2016 年和 2017 年数据分别来源于各地市统计年鉴，2018 年数据为初步统计数据。

与同为中部省会城市的武汉和长沙相比，郑州 GDP 增速虽然保持在 8.0 以上，但 GDP 与武汉差距较大，约为其 68%，比长沙 GDP 略低，约为其 92%。从产业结构分析，2018 年郑州三大产业结构比例由 2016 年的 1.9∶46.8∶51.3，调整优化为 1.4∶43.9∶54.7，产业重心逐步转向第三产业，产业结构逐步高级化，形成了以电子信息工业、新材料产业、生物及医药产业、现代食品制造业、家居和品牌服装制造业、汽车及装备制造业、铝及铝精深加工业等为主导的七大产业体系，随着“三大改造”的深入推进，初步形成了电子信息、汽车及装备制造两个 5000 亿元级产业集群。同时，2018 年武汉的三大产业结构比例为 2.4∶43.0∶54.6、长沙为2.9∶42.4∶54.7，郑州三产比例与武汉和长沙相比相差不大。导致郑州 GDP 低于武汉、长沙的主要原因是：郑州的产业发展质量不高，传统产业仍占较大比重，新兴产业增速快但体量小，金融和实体经济的良性循环尚未形成。经济社会发展存在的这些不平衡不充分的矛盾和问题，造成与中部其他省会城市的差距。

在 16 个 GDP 超万亿元的城市中，郑州与长沙、南京、杭州、成都、武汉、广州均为省会城市。2016～2018 年，郑州在河南的经济首位度分别为 20.2%、20.6%、21.1%。与其他 6 个城市相比，2018 年郑州的经济首位度仅高于南京，高约 7.2 个百分点，但远低于其他 5 个城市（见图 2）。但郑州作为国家支持建设的9个国家中心城市之一、河南第一大城市，经济首位度与30%的目标仍有较大差距，仍需奋发图强，努力完成国家、河南省委省政府赋予的重任。

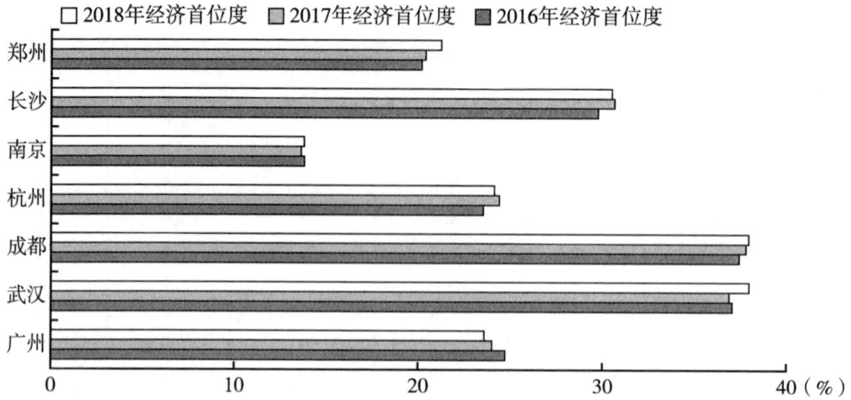

图2　2016~2018年“万亿元俱乐部”省会城市经济首位度对比

资料来源：2016年和2017年数据根据各地市及所在省统计年鉴相关数据计算，2018年数据为各地市及所在省初步统计数据。

（三）郑州经济增长现状总体判断

综合以上分析，“十三五”以来，郑州GDP有了较快发展，与省内其他城市相比，经济贡献率约为河南第二大城市洛阳的两倍，对河南省经济增长起到了较大的拉动作用，其作为河南省核心城市的地位不可动摇。

2018年郑州迈入“万亿元俱乐部”，成为GDP超万亿元、人口超千万的“双料”城市，郑州目前GDP增速虽保持在较为快速发展态势，但与其他15个“万亿元俱乐部”城市相比，郑州GDP仍有较大差距。尤其是与同为中部城市的武汉和长沙相比，差距仍较为明显。

三　打造郑州国家重要经济增长中心的综合考量

（一）打造郑州国家重要的经济增长中心的意义

（1）贯彻新经济理念，推动郑州国家中心城市建设迈上新台阶的现实需要

党的十九大指出，我国的经济发展已由高速增长阶段转向高质量发展阶段。

《国家发展改革委关于支持郑州建设国家中心城市的指导意见》指出，郑州建设国家中心城市仍需加快提升经济发展体量、科技创新水平、辐射带动能力。“十三五”以来，郑州经济快速发展，GDP 从 2016 年的 8114 亿元增长到 2018 年的 10143 亿元，全年居民人均可支配收入从 2016 年的 28039 元增长到 2018 年的 33105 元，均实现了较大幅度增长，迈上了新台阶。但同时也可以看到，郑州作为河南省省会城市，传统产业比重仍旧较大，在省内经济首位度不高，与其他 GDP 超万亿元的城市相比，差距还比较明显。为提高郑州经济发展的动能转化能力，提升郑州对周边区域的经济辐射影响力，必须牢固贯彻创新、协调、绿色、开放、共享的新发展理念，从质量改变、效率提升着手，开展动力变革，并将其落实到郑州经济高质量建设的过程中，推动郑州国家中心城市建设迈向新台阶，发挥引领中原发展、支撑中部崛起、服务全国大局的重任。

（2）全面提升经济发展水平和辐射带动功能，是促进区域协调发展的必然选择

《国家发展改革委关于支持郑州建设国家中心城市的指导意见》中，明确要求郑州建设国家中心城市必须坚持“开放引领、区域联动”的原则；《中共中央国务院关于建立更加有效的区域协调发展新机制的意见》在“推动国家重大区域战略融合发展”的任务中，提出了“以郑州为中心引领中原城市群发展，带动相关板块融合发展”的要求。目前我国经济呈现“南强北弱”特征，在 16 个“万亿元俱乐部”城市中，北方城市只有 4 个。郑州作为一座与胡焕庸线距离相对较短的北方城市，发展越快越好，越能增强集聚力，带动经济重心北移，为“协调东中西、平衡南北方”提供更大支撑。因此，为有效发挥郑州在区域协调发展中的作用，郑州应以打造国家重要的经济增长中心为目标，加快转换新旧动能，补齐科技创新发展和高端动能的短板，提升综合经济实力，逐步提升经济首位度，凝聚高端资源要素，从而更好发挥区域辐射带动作用。

（3）发挥强省会辐射带动作用，促进河南乃至中原城市群地区后发赶超的战略抉择

当前，“强省会战略”已成为中西部各省的集体路径选择。成都代管简阳、合肥拆吞巢湖、济南合并莱芜、西安代管西咸新区，中西部各省不约而同地做大中心城市，提升省会首位度，以增强其集聚辐射能力，形成了强省会崛起的时代趋势。与一些兄弟省会相比，郑州的城市首位度不高，2018 年郑州

经济首位度为21.1%，远低于多数省会城市30%左右的水平。河南作为全国经济大省，人均地区生产总值只有全国平均水平的80%，要实现后发赶超，迫切需要一个核心城市承接、吸引、集聚和消化各种资源，辐射、引领、带动全省经济发展。无论就河南自身发展需要，还是就支撑中部崛起、服务全国大局来看，都需要郑州这个龙头高高扬起来，实现由“弱核”到“强核”的转变。郑州要进一步扩充城市体量，加快郑州大都市区建设，同时增强郑州交通枢纽和载体平台作用，充分发挥地缘优势，让分享经济、总部经济、流量经济奔涌向前，引领中原地区更高质量一体化发展。

（二）打造郑州国家重要的经济增长中心的良好条件、突出短板和挑战与机遇

（1）良好条件

近年来，在河南省委省政府正确领导下，郑州市按照“五位一体”总体布局和“四个全面”战略布局，坚持开放创新双驱动，促进了经济社会持续健康发展，具备了打造成为国家重要经济增长中心的良好条件。

一是经济发展态势良好。“十三五”以来，郑州市经济运行呈现总体平稳、稳中有进的良好态势。2018年郑州GDP突破万亿元大关，在全国298个地级以上城市中排名第十六位。同时，现代产业体系构建进一步加快，航空港实验区电子信息先进制造业集群向高端拓展，高技术产业增加值快速增长，七大主导产业稳步发展，已形成电子信息、汽车及装备制造两个5000亿元级产业集群。

二是改革创新取得重大突破。供给侧结构性改革取得阶段性成果，“多证合一、一照一码”，“先照后证”稳步推进，国家“互联网+政务服务”示范工程成功申建，市场主体活力得到进一步释放，科技进步对经济增长贡献率达到63%。

三是对外开放水平不断提升。郑州国际陆港建设高水平推进，汽车、肉类等10个功能性口岸获批建设，郑州成为全国拥有商品口岸最多的内陆城市。跨境电子商务和中欧班列（郑州）的运行机制、经营规模位居全国前列。在2018年中国外贸百强城市评比中，郑州由第十九位升至第十六位，全市进出口额达615.1亿美元，继续位居中部六省省会城市第一位。

四是战略政策支撑更加完备。郑州航空港经济综合实验区、自贸区、自主创新示范区、跨境电商试验区、国家大数据试验区、通用航空产业综合试验区、国家综合交通枢纽示范城市、双创示范基地、新型智慧城市、中欧区域政策合作案例地区等先后获批，郑州成为全国政策叠加优势突出的内陆城市。

五是城市功能品质持续改善。大“井字 + 环线”快速骨干路网基本形成，一大批水电气暖设施建成投用，地下综合管廊、海绵城市建设取得新成效。城乡环境综合治理持续推进，生态水系、生态廊道建设和生态环境治理力度加大，城市精细化管理水平不断提升。

六是综合枢纽优势更加凸显。郑州被确定为全国12个最高等级国际性综合交通枢纽之一。着力构建多式联运枢纽体系，“米”字形高铁格局加快形成。2018年航空货邮吞吐量51.3万吨、客运量2733.5万人次，分别居全国大型机场第七位、第十二位。四通八达的公路网络日趋完善，国家级互联网骨干直联点投入使用，邮政电信业务量位居全国前列，管道运输中枢地位进一步确立。这些都为郑州打造成为国家重要经济增长中心奠定了坚实的基础，提供了政策保障。

（2）突出短板

对照国家中心城市定位，与国内先进城市相比，郑州发展还存在不少短板。

一是产业发展质量不高。产业结构不优，传统产业仍占较大比重，新兴产业增速快但体量小，战略性新兴产业增加值占规模以上工业比重尚未达到20%。六大高耗能产业占比超过30%，高新技术产业增加值占GDP的比重，分别低于武汉、长沙、合肥6.2个、19.6个、6.1个百分点。金融业发展较快，2018年郑州金融业增加值1145.8亿元，但金融和实体经济的良性循环尚未形成。投资特别是民间投资不足，民营和小微企业是实体经济的薄弱环节。

二是科技创新能力不强。科教创新基础薄弱，市内科技研究机构数量、高端创新人才、创新团队偏少，国家科技进步奖获奖数远低于武汉、长沙等中部省会城市，科技成果转化数量和高新技术产值尚与其他城市有较大差距。2017年郑州R&D投入102.8亿元，投入强度（R&D经费与区域生产总值的比值）为1.12%，与全国R&D经费投入强度2.13%相比，仍有较大差距。

三是国际化水平不高。如武汉有5家领事馆，成都有16家，郑州尚无一家。郑州国际友好城市数量（11个）低于武汉（22个）和成都（27个）。比如，郑州利用外资仅为武汉的1/3、西安的2/3，国际通航点不足成都的1/3、西安的1/2，入境旅游人数不到成都、武汉的1/5，常住外国人只有3300多人，远低于成都的1.75万人、武汉的1.5万人、西安的1.2万人，还没有一所外籍人员子女学校，举办影响力大的国际性活动不多。

四是综合承载力不足。在国家支持建设的国家中心城市中，郑州的区域面积最小，约为成都（14312平方公里）的一半。产业结构、能源结构、交通运输结构不优，大气、水体、土壤环境治理压力较大。环境容量趋于饱和，人均水资源占有量不足全国平均水平的1/10，空气质量在全国74个城市中排名靠后，生态建设相对滞后，生态环境承载能力薄弱。

五是民生保障还存在不少短板，就业、教育、医疗、住房、养老、家政等方面与群众期待还有差距，影响社会稳定的突出矛盾需要加快解决。

（3）挑战与机遇

当前，世界经济的复杂性、不稳定性、不确定性凸显，贸易保护主义加剧，“逆全球化”思维抬头。我国经济正由高速增长阶段向高质量发展阶段转变，呈现经济中高速增长、产业向中高端迈进的新特征。区域发展面临的人力资源、环境约束等方面的压力日益增强，城市竞争日趋激烈。国内外经济发展环境的深刻变化，对打造郑州国家重要的经济增长中心是严峻挑战。还要看到，以新一代信息技术、生物技术、新能源技术、新材料技术、智能制造技术等为代表的新一轮技术革命对区域发展产生深刻影响，并催生出新的结构性矛盾，对保持经济持续向好是新的挑战。对郑州这样传统产业占比大、科技创新资源相对匮乏的城市来说，由于对数据、知识等无形资本的供给能力较弱，更容易导致新形势下多种要素的供需结构失衡。

挑战同时也是机遇。新一轮技术革命和产业变革兴起及全球创新格局的调整，对打造郑州国家重要的经济增长中心也开启了新的“机会窗口”。郑州正处于加快转型攻坚、实现跨越发展的关键时期。“一带一路”建设的推进，有利于郑州在更大范围、更广领域利用两种资源、两个市场，为新技术利用、新动能转换、新产业发展创造条件。国家促进中部崛起、中原城市群建设等战略的深入实施，众多国家战略平台相继落地和加快推进，国家、省委省政府对郑州发展高度重视、大力支持，使郑州在全国经济版图和城市网络中的地位更加凸显，为打造郑州国家重要的经济增长中心提供了强大动力。

四　相关思考与建议

打造郑州国家重要的经济增长中心，有三个衡量维度：一是经济增速。在“十三五”的后两年和“十四五”期间，郑州市要保持高于河南全省1个以上百分点的增长速度，而不是“十三五”前三年的高于全省0.5个百分点及以下。根据河南经济增速预测，郑州今后几年要努力保持8.5%以上的增长速度。二是增速排序。在“十三五”的后两年和“十四五”期间，郑州市经济增速在省辖市之间比较，应该位居前三位，而不是“十三五”前三年的前五位。三是经济占比。要经过“十三五”的努力，力争郑州地区生产总值占河南全省地区生产总值的比重，由2018年的21.1%提高到30%左右。四是经济地位。就是在“万亿元级”城市俱乐部里，郑州的排序要前移，经济地位要进一步提高和加强。

要实现这几个目标，建议郑州市在经济发展方面采取一系列新的举措。

1. 强化产业支撑，增强经济增长拉动力

要把制造业发展放到更加突出的位置。推进先进制造业和现代服务业深度融合，加快传统优势产业转型升级，大力承接新兴产业布局和转移，建设数字经济发展核心区。充分借助现有高端设备制造业、新一代信息技术产业链，为创新产业集群的构建创造良好的实现环境，加快郑州七大主导产业结构的优化升级，努力在大数据、新一代人工智能、现代金融等方面实现突破。积极促进创新产业集群的形成与发展，支持郑州建设先进装备制造基地、新能源及网联汽车研发生产基地、生物医药研发和生产基地、人工智能发展高地、智能传感器创新中心等，促进经济结构进一步成熟和完善，提升郑州整体创新能力，达到整体产业结构升级，实现经济增长有效拉动。

2. 增强区位优势，打通经济增长通道

发挥区位优势，大力发展交通、通信等基础设施，增强与周边城市的经济联系强度和影响力。学习上海等城市经验，着力增强航空枢纽作用，增加连接全球主要枢纽机场的货运、客运航线，加强国际国内航线对接，强化郑州机场与高速铁路、城际铁路等便捷高效交通系统的无缝衔接。拓展铁路枢纽对外通道网络，巩固优化以郑州为中心的“米”字铁路枢纽通道。推进郑州与“一带一路”沿线重要口岸的互联互通，提升郑州在新亚欧大陆桥经济走廊建设中的重要节点作用。加快建设5G产业发展先行区和创新应用示范区、国家级智能传感器创新中心，构建顺畅的立体交通网络以及通信网络，打通郑州经济增长通道，增强经济发展后劲。

3. 坚持创新驱动，培育经济增长新动能

加快创新要素资源的聚集，全面提升经济发展核心竞争力，加快形成带动区域经济发展的动力源。支持开展一流大学、一流学科的“双一流”建设，支持国内外高水平大学和国家级科研院所在郑设立分支机构。加大科学技术研发投入，人才引进力度，借助郑州地区高校、科研院所、企业等单位的科技创新，建设数字经济区域总部和创新中心集群，促进产学研一体化结合发展，促进产业结构快速实现优化升级。用好自创区这个载体，争取国家级创新平台和企业研发中心落户，大力引进国内外优质高等教育资源，培育创新引领型主体、人才、平台、机构，让创新成为城市发展的不竭动力。

4. 发挥龙头作用，提升经济增长辐射力

郑州大都市区是随着区域经济一体化的快速发展而建立的，是在不断优化传统的城市体系基础上，可以充分利用郑州和开封、许昌、新乡、焦作地缘接近、经济社会联系紧密的优势，从竞争转向区域合作，逐步实施同城化。在郑州大都市区发展中，通过开展政府合作，发挥各地资源优势，优化区域劳动力资源配置，促进分工协作，降低交易成本和贸易成本；优化产业结构，促进区域产业集聚，实施产业错位发展，减少资源消耗，实现郑州大都市区深度融合，同时城市间良性竞争还可以进一步促进城市管理水平的上升，提升整个区域的竞争力，进一步扩大郑州的经济辐射范围。

5. 提高国际化水平，提高经济发展开放度

充分发挥“四路”“五区”战略叠加优势，更加主动参与全球资源配置和产业分工，提升全球城市网络节点地位。要全方位向国际化迈进，形成交通枢纽、开放平台、经济体系、营商环境、城市风貌的“五个国际化”。更加积极地开展国际交流交往，争取外事机构、国际组织分支机构、签证中心落地，积极申办国际会议、国际体育赛事、国际论坛等重大活动，打造国际会展名城，深化与友好城市交流合作，建设国际社区、国际医院、国际学校、国际商务楼宇和适合外国人的餐饮文化休闲场所，持续提升开放包容度、交往便利度、要素集聚度、城市美誉度，让外商在郑州投资顺心、生活舒心。

参考文献

［1］冯金钟：《关于推动我国经济高质量发展的若干思考》，《中国市场》2018 年第 18 期，第 14 ~ 15 页。

［2］刘海明、杨健、王灿雄、林强：《区域经济协同发展研究进展综述——兼论区域经济协同发展机制建立的必要性》，《中国集体经济》2010 年第 7 期，第 86 ~ 89 页。

［3］喻新安：《在动能转化的持续推动中实现区域协调发展》，《区域经济评论》2019 年第 1 期，第 15 ~ 18 页。

［4］赵大全：《实现经济高质量发展的思考与建议》，《经济研究参考》2018 年第 1 期，第 9 ~ 11，50 页。

［5］赵娴、林楠：《中国国家中心城市经济辐射力分析与评价》，《经济与管理研究》2013 年第 12 期，第 106 ~ 113 页。

［6］喻新安：《在高水平开放中跨越赶超》，《光明日报》2019 年 7 月 25 日。

B.19
郑州大都市区建设的主要任务

王建国*

摘　要： 建设郑州大都市区要牢固树立创新、协调、开放、绿色、共享的发展理念，按照以人为本、城镇引领、创新驱动、生态优先、共建共享的总体要求，着力构建与大都市区一体化融合发展相适应的交通运输体系、产业支撑体系、都市城镇体系、开放型经济体系和创新体系，为都市区建设和发展提供强力支撑。

关键词： 郑州都市区　建设任务　六大体系

随着国务院批复《中原城市群发展规划》正式提出郑州大都市区的概念，并确定了以郑州为核心，包括郑州市域，开封、新乡、焦作、许昌四市中心城区和巩义市、武陟县、原阳县、新乡县、尉氏县、长葛市、平原城乡一体化示范区的空间定位，标志着郑州大都市区建设进入实施阶段。郑州大都市的建设要牢固树立创新、协调、开放、绿色、共享的发展理念，按照以人为本、城镇引领、创新驱动、生态优先、共建共享的总体要求，进一步明确目标和任务，努力构建与大都市区一体化发展相适应的交通运输体系、产业支撑体系、都市城镇体系、开放型经济体系、创新体系和生态体系，将郑州大都市区逐步建设成为中部地区产业优化、生活优质、环境优美的发展高地。

一　构建国际化现代化立体综合交通枢纽体系

1. 推进大都市区交通一体化发展。郑州大都市区内拥有航空、铁路、高

---

* 王建国，硕士，河南省社会科学院城市与环境研究所所长、研究员研究方向为区域经济、城市经济。

速公路等多种交通运输方式，但是衔接还不够紧密，各种交通枢纽大多独立、分散建设，还没有形成真正意义上的一体化综合交通枢纽。未来，要立足于郑州大都市区的整体空间布局，适应交通运输产业转型升级需要，构建以轨道交通为骨干的多节点、网格状、全覆盖的交通网络，加强各种运输方式衔接，达到客运“零距离换乘”、货运“无缝衔接”，实现交通运输一体化发展。

推进大都市区交通一体化发展，一是在航空枢纽建设方面，抓住国家把郑州航空港经济综合试验区纳入国家战略的机遇，依托新郑国际机场，建设现代化的候机楼综合交通转换体系及集疏运网络体系，加强新郑机场与轨道、高速公路等多种交通方式的衔接，建设形成由京广高铁、郑开、郑焦、郑机城际、机场高速等组成的综合快速联络通道，显著提升大都市区航空枢纽的国际竞争力。加快郑州—卢森堡航空物流双枢纽建设，打造国际航空货运枢纽。二是在铁路枢纽建设方面，大力发展轨道交通，强化各类轨道交通的高效衔接，加强都市区中心城区与许昌、新乡、焦作等周边主要城镇之间快速交通联系。推动郑万高铁、郑合高铁、郑济高铁开工建设，加快建设郑州高铁南站、郑徐高铁开封北站、新焦济洛城际铁路等重点项目建设。三是在公路枢纽建设方面，完善公路交通网，继续加快高速公路建设，强化一般公路改造升级，增加农村公路供给，推动开港大道、官渡黄河大桥、许昌至机场快速通道、焦作至荥阳黄河公路大桥等重点项目建设，建设功能完善、内联外畅的公路交通网络。

2. 提升大都市区交通服务能力。郑州大都市区要着眼于郑州的“国家中心城市、国际航空大都市、世界文化旅游名城”等城市战略定位，围绕建设国内重要的田园都市、宜业宜居都市、畅通都市、创新都市、魅力都市等发展目标，以解决交通拥堵、环境污染等“大城市病”为首要任务，全面提升大都市区交通服务能力。

提升大都市区交通服务能力，一是要提高城市公共交通服务能力。加快城市轨道网建设，郑州市目前规划的城市轨道交通线路有 21 条，覆盖了郑州市区以及新密、荥阳、中牟、新郑等各个区域。除了加快建设这些规划中的轨道交通线路外，也要进一步加密城市轨道交通网，大力建设市域之间的轨道交通，加强郑州中心城区和周边城镇的轨道交通线建设，完善轨道站点交通接驳设施，实现轨道交通与其他交通方式便捷顺畅衔接。全面提升地面公交服务能力和水平，全面优化整合地面公交线路，科学配置地面公交运力，扩大公交线网和站点覆盖范围，加强城市轨道交通、地面公交等多种交通网络的融合衔接，提升公交换乘快捷性和便利性。二是要提高路网承载能力与运行水平。优化城市道路网络功能和级配结构，按照“窄马路、密路网”的布局理念，科学合理构建城市道路网系统。三是要完善新城区与县城综合交通体系建设。加快平原示范区、温县、武陟、禹州、长葛等城市的交通基础设施和公共交通服务配套建设，完善城市内部交通体系，构建以轨道交通及快速公交为主体的对外交通体系，增强新城区和县城的承接力和吸引力。

3. 推动现代物流设施建设。交通运输是物流发展的基础环节和重要载体，物流业的发展水平很大程度上受交通条件的限制，一些综合交通运输网络的货物运输枢纽往往也是物流集汇作业的节点，因此，在构建郑州大都市区现代化立体综合交通枢纽体系时就需要充分考虑现代物流设施的规划建设。

推动现代物流设施建设，一是要加快物流园区（货运枢纽）建设。完善物流园区规划，优化物流设施布局，将区域性物流园区向都市区中心城区外有序疏解。在郑州与焦作、开封、新乡、许昌等城市交汇的郑州北部、东部、南部等方向，规划布局若干大型综合性物流园区，在郑州市四环沿线规划建设一批服务于城市配送的物流园区。推动邮政集团加快对接万国邮联，构建辐射中西部的快件物流中心。二是要推进传统货运场站的转型升级。规范目前郑州市四环以内的物流和货运场站，推动传统货运场站向物流园区转型升级，积极打造与产业集聚区相配套的物流园区，重点建设具备多式联运功能的物流园区，提升货物运输衔接转换效率。三是推进城市配送发展。以快速消费品配送、冷藏货物配送等为重点，大力发展专业化城市配送，保障大都市区基本民生和城市运行需求。结合物联网加快发展末端配送网点建设，推广社区自提柜、冷链储藏柜、代收服务等新型社区化配送模式。

二　构建智慧化、国际化、高端化的产业支撑体系

1. 促进制造业高端化智能化发展。要以提高制造业创新能力和基础能力为重点，大力发展高端的先进制造业和战略性新兴产业。同时，要对传统制造业进行改造，推进制造业向集群化、智能化、绿色化、服务化升级，构建竞争优势明显的制造业体系。

为此，一要全面提升工业基础能力，实施关键基础材料、核心基础零部件（元器件）、先进基础工艺、产业技术基础等工业强基工程，突破制造业发展瓶颈。二要加快发展新型制造业，整合郑州、许昌、新乡、焦作等装备制造业优势资源，提高装备设计、制造和集成能力，推动制造业由生产型向生产服务型转变，引导制造企业延伸服务链条、促进服务增值。三要推动传统产业革新升级，重点推动铝工业、煤炭、轻工纺织等传统产业转型发展，推动开封碳素、新乡白鹭化纤、焦作奋安铝业高档铝型材等传统产业向绿色化、循环化、高端化发展。四要支持战略性新兴产业发展，重点推动先进材料、生物医药、先进机器人、物联网、智能微电网、基因检测等产业发展。

2. 推动服务业优质高效发展。推动服务业优质高效发展，要坚持市场需求引领、重点产业带动，以现代物流和现代金融引领生产性服务业提速发展，以精细化、品质提升为导向促进生活性服务业优质高效发展。

为此，一要促进生产性服务业专业化发展，重点发展现代物流、现代金融，加快壮大电子商务、信息服务、商贸服务、专业生产服务、服务外包等产业规模，加快推进开封国际农业会展中心、新乡国际商务中心等重点项目建设，打造中西部地区生产性服务业高地。二要提高生活性服务业品质，加快教育培训、健康养老、文化娱乐、体育健身、休闲旅游等领域服务业的发展，重点推动一批高端商业综合体建设。大力支持登封华夏历史文明传承创新示范工程建设、郑州国际文化创意产业园、宋都古城文化产业园、南太行生态旅游集聚带、省歌舞剧院、海昌极地海洋公园、禹州古镇体验景区、葛天源、双洎河国家湿地公园等文化旅游项目建设。推进商贸流通业转型升级，顺应消费升级趋势，大力发展居家养老业、医疗保健业，开拓个性化品质消费，提升安全消费水平。

3. 提高农业质量效益和竞争力。以集约、高效、绿色、可持续为方向，发展多种形式适度规模经营，推动农业与工业、服务业融合发展，提高农业质量效益和竞争力。

为此，一要推动都市生态农业发展。依托大都市区内的城乡一体化示范区，大力发展休闲观光、参与体验、民宿餐饮、生态景观等规模化、品牌化的都市生态农业园区。以“菜篮子”为主，突出产业和生态休闲功能，建设瑞之源、豫星、陉山福多多、佛耳湖观光游园等一批都市生态农业示范园区。二要推进农村一二三产业融合发展，加快发展农产品加工业和农业生产性服务业，拓展农业多种功效，推进农业与文化旅游、健康养生科普教育等深度融合，发展观光农业、体验农业、创意农业等新业态，提高农业综合效益。三要构建现代农业经营体系，以发展多种形式适度规模经营为引领，创新农业经营组织方式，构建以农户家庭经营为基础、互助与联合为纽带、社会化服务为支撑的现代农业经营体系。四是确保农产品质量安全，强化产地安全管理，建立全程可追溯、互联共享的农产品质量安全体系。

三　构建统筹城乡协调发展的都市城镇体系

1. 优化城市规模结构。在郑州大都市建设中，需要进一步完善和优化城市规模结构，以强化大都市区核心区的辐射带动作用为基础，以培育中心城市为重点，以建设中小城市和重点小城镇为支撑，优化城市规模结构，形成大中小城市和小城镇合理分布、协调发展的城镇化战略格局，强化城镇功能互补和内在联系，提高产业和人口集聚能力。

优化城市规模结构，一要优化提升核心区城市功能。优化郑州城市功能布局，统筹推进核心区有机更新、新城区有序拓展、航空城综合开发外围组团建设，适当疏解核心区非核心功能，强化与周边城镇高效通勤和一体发展，形成功能互补、生态隔离的现代都市区空间布局。二要做强做大中心城市。加快许昌、新乡、焦作等中心城市发展，结合这些城市自身特点和发展条件，适当扩大城市规模，加快产业转型升级，与邻近区县一体化发展，提升区域服务能力，分担核心区城市功能，形成带动区域发展的增长节点。三要培育发展一批中小城市。以武陟、长葛等县、市为重点，加大基础设施和公共服务设施建设力度，增加优质教育、医疗、文化等公共服务产品对中小城市的供给。推动基础条件好、经济实力强、具备行政区划调整条件的县有序改市，加快龙湖镇、回郭镇等特大镇改市试点工作。四是有重点地发展小城镇，因地制宜发展一批具有特色资源、区位优势的小城镇，通过规划引导、市场运作，培育成为交通枢纽、商贸物流、文化旅游、资源加工等专业特色镇。

2. 建设和谐宜居城市。郑州大都市区未来要进一步转变城市发展方式，加快新型城市建设，创新城市治理方式，加大“城市病”防治力度，不断提升城市环境质量、居民生活质量和城市竞争力，打造和谐宜居、富有活力、各具特色的城市。

为此，一要加快新型城市建设。根据资源环境承载力调节城市规模，实行绿色规划、绿色设计和绿色施工标准，加快建设生态廊道，实施生态系统修复工程，建设绿色城市。加强现代信息基础设施建设，推进大数据和物联网发展，建设智慧城市。发挥城市创新资源密集优势，建设创新城市。提高城市开放度和包容性，加强文化和自然遗产保护，延续历史文脉，建设人文城市。加强城市空间开发利用管制，建设密度较高、功效融合、公交导向的紧凑城市。二要加强城市基础设施建设。加强市政管网等地下基础设施革新与建设，因地制宜推进地下综合管廊建设。加强城市轨道交通、停车设施、城市步行、自行车交通等公共交通设施建设，严格执行新建小区停车位、充电桩等配建标准。加强城市防洪防涝与调蓄、公园绿地等生态设施建设，支持海绵城市发展，提高城市建筑和基础设施抗灾能力。三要加快城镇棚户区和危房革新。将棚户区改造与城市更新、产业转型升级相结合，加快推进集中成片棚户区和城中村革新，有序推进旧住宅小区综合整治、危旧住房和非成套住房革新。四要提升城市治理水平。创新城市治理方式，推进城市管理和执法体制改革。创新城市规划理念和方法，合理确定城市规模、开发边界、开发强度和保护性空间，加强对城市风貌整体性、文脉延续性的规划管控。全面推行城市科学设计，推进城市有机更新。推广发展适用经济的绿色建筑，推广装配式建筑和钢结构建筑，提高建筑技术水平和工程质量。

3. 推动城乡协调发展。城乡协调发展是社会经济发展的必然趋势，推动城乡协调发展，要把城市和农村发展作为一个有机整体，统筹进行规划，提升县域经济支撑辐射能力，促进公共资源在城乡间均衡配置，建设美丽乡村，拓展农村广阔发展空间，形成城乡共同发展新格局。

为此，一要发展特色县域经济。把县域作为如期实现全面建成小康社会目标的战略重点，不断完善其产业功能、服务功能和居住功能，提升其承接城市功效转移和辐射带动乡村发展能力。依托优势资源，促进农产品精深加工、农村服务业及劳动密集型产业发展，探索承接产业转移新模式，引导农村二、三产业向县城、重点乡镇及专业园区集中。扩大县域发展自主权，提高县级基本财力保障水平。二要加快建设美丽宜居乡村。推动农村集体经济改革创新，激发农村发展活力。科学规划村镇建设、农田保护和村落分布等空间布局，推进农村公路、饮水、环卫、宽带、危房等设施革新建设，改善农村医疗、教育条件，建立健全农村留守儿童和妇女、老人关爱服务体系。加强和改善农村社会治理，完善农村治安防控体系。加强农村文化建设，培育文明乡风、优良家风。开展农村人居环境综合整治行动，建设和谐幸福、美丽宜居乡村。三要促进城乡公共资源均衡配置。统筹城乡公共设施建设，推进交通、供电、信息、污水垃圾处理等基础设施向农村延伸对接，推动城市基本公共服务、生产生活社会服务网络和社会保障向农村延伸覆盖。

四　构建与国际接轨国内领先的开放型经济体系

1. 建设内陆开放高地。要利用郑州航空港经济综合实验区对外开放门户功能，创新开放型经济发展模式，探索内陆开放高地建设的新路径，为构建互利共赢、多元平衡、安全高效的开放型经济体系奠定坚实基础。

为此，一要强化郑州航空港开放优势。把郑州航空港经济综合实验区作为大都市区最大的开放品牌，以建设大枢纽、大物流、大产业、大都市为方向，提升郑州航空港多式联运物流功能，推进产业集聚和城市功能完善，增强航空港的国际影响力和区域带动力。打造以航空运输为主体的现代综合枢纽，构建以航空枢纽为主体，融合城市轨道交通、高速铁路、城际铁路等多种交通方式的综合枢纽。打通连接世界重要枢纽机场和主要经济体的航空物流通道，建设多式联运的国际物流中心。推动智能手机、航空维修、精密机械、生物医药等产业发展，建设以航空经济为引领的电子信息产业基地、航空维修基地和生物医药产业基地。二要完善提升对外开放支撑平台。加快建设郑州航空、铁路国际“双枢纽”口岸，推动郑州新郑综合保税区优化升级，提升郑欧班列品牌影响力，建设跨境电子商务综合试验区，积极申建内陆型自由贸易试验区，促进这些开放平台功能集合和联动发展，形成多层次、全覆盖、立体化的开放平台支撑体系。

2. 全面融入“一带一路”倡议。郑州大都市建设要积极融入“一带一路”倡议，服务国家重大战略，主动与亚投行、丝路基金等重大平台实施对接，深入推进与沿线国家和地区重要城市政府间的合作，增强中原腹地对

“一带一路”倡议的支撑。

为此，一要推进基础设施领域合作。深度参与国家战略性重大基础设施项目建设，积极参与中蒙俄、中巴、孟中印缅等经济走廊基础设施项目建设，畅通东联西进的出境出海通道。二要扩大对外经贸产业合作。支持农业、能源、物流、装备制造等优势产业积极“走出去”，到“一带一路”沿线国家从事经营活动，带动技术、标准、服务、品牌等输出。依托重大基础工程项目，推动装备制造领域优势企业到沿线国家投资建厂，积极参与国家级合作工业园开发。以“一带一路”沿线国家学生为重点实施留学计划，支持中医、武术、农业等特色院校赴沿线国家开展合作办学或设立分校。

3. 提升开放型经济发展水平。郑州大都市建设要根据经济全球化的新形势和经济转型升级的新需求，以更加开阔的视野和更加开放的姿态，充分利用国际国内两个市场、两种资源，积极参与全球产业分工格局重构，着力提高国际分工的地位，加快培育开放合作和竞争新优势。

一要持续推进开放招商。完善招商平台，改造提升和培育一批具有较强影响力的全国行业性展会、区域性招商平台，积极组织参加区域重大经贸活动。创新招商方式，推动“政策招商”向“产业招商”转变，拓展“贸易 + 投资”“技术 + 产业”等招商方式，实现企业集群式引进、产业链接式转移。提升招商层次，鼓励外资企业在大都市区设立研发中心、培训基地等功能性机构，支持国外优势企业和资本参与大都市区企业兼并重组。深化与央企的战略合作，促进央企扩大在大都市区的投资规模。二要优化开放营商环境。提升政府服务效能，引入国际通行的行业规范、管理标准和营商规则，打造法治化、国际化、便利化的营商环境。三要促进区域互动合作。顺应区域经济一体化发展趋势，主动对接长江经济带、京津冀经济区、淮河生态经济带、汉江生态经济带等重要经济区，在产业转移、要素集疏、人文交流、品牌培育等方面开展合作，提升对内开放合作水平。

五　构建科技创新链、人才支撑链、全民创业链“三链融合”的创新体系

1. 强化科技创新引领作用。郑州大都市区要适应我国经济社会发展要求，

充分发挥科技创新在全面创新中的引领作用，加强基础研究，强化原始创新、集成创新和引进消化吸收再创新，着力增强自主创新能力，为经济社会发展提供持久动力。

强化科技创新引领作用，一要大力提升原始创新能力。主动服务国家和省内的重大创新战略，开展一批科技前沿和战略必争领域的技术研究项目，力争在信息、基础材料、生物医学、农业生物遗传、能源等领域取得一批具有国际国内影响力的原始创新成果。二要强化企业创新主体地位和主导作用。鼓励企业开展基础性和前沿性创新研究，深入实施创新企业百强工程，形成一批有国际国内竞争力的创新型领军企业，支持科技型中小企业发展。三要积极推进产学研用协同创新。促进不同机构科技资源相互开放共享、向社会开放共享，推动形成以企业为主导、产学研用协同创新的新局面。

2. 推进大众创业万众创新。郑州大都市区实施创新驱动发展战略，就必须加快推进大众创业、万众创新，要把大众创业万众创新融入发展各领域各环节，鼓励支持各类主体开发新技术、新产品，促进形成新业态、新模式，打造经济发展的新引擎。

为此，一要建设创业创新公共服务平台。实施“双创”行动计划，大力发展面向大众、服务中小微企业的低成本、便利化、开放式服务平台。鼓励大型企业建立技术转移和服务平台，向创业者提供技术支撑服务。完善创业培育服务，打造创业服务与创业投资结合的开放式服务载体。二要全面推进众创众包众扶众筹。全面推进众创，培育一批基于互联网的新型孵化平台，推动技术、开发、营销等资源共享。积极推广众包，推广研发创意、生活服务众包，推动大众参与线上生产流通分工。建立立体式众扶，开放共享公共科技资源和信息资源，探索政府和公益机构、企业帮扶援助、个人互助互扶支持小微企业和创业者成长的方式。稳妥推进众筹，探索消费电子、智能家居、健康设备等实物众筹，开展股权众筹融资试点，推动设立网络借贷平台。三要倡导创新创业精神。树立创新创业的价值导向，加强各类媒体对创新创业的新闻宣传和舆论引导，保护企业家精神，宽容创业失败，包容创新对传统利益格局的挑战，依法保护企业家财产权和创新收益。

3. 强化人才对创新的支撑作用。实施人才优先发展战略，推进人才发展体制改革和政策创新，引进和集聚更多高端领军人才，形成具有国际国内影响力的人才制度优势。为此，一要让高校持续涌现创新活力。支持郑州大学、河南大学开展一流大学、一流学科建设，提高重点领域研究的国际国内影响力，强化与国际知名高校、科研院所合作交流，提升高等教育竞争力。二要强化创新型人才培养。进一步发挥好高校创新人才培养的枢纽作用，探索高校与科研机构、知名企业的高水平人才交叉培养的机制。加强对管理型、职业技能型人才的培养，积极构建创新人才终身学习和成长体系。三要吸引高端人才集聚。实施“智汇郑州·1125 聚才计划”，采用多种方式吸引国内外高级经营管理人才、高级专业技术人才和创业者到郑州大都市区创新创业。四要优化科技人才流动与配置机制。建立灵活多样的创新型人才聘用与流动方式，建立科研人员在事业单位和企业间流动通道，支持科技人员开展成果转化、创新创业。

参考文献

［1］姚阳：《新城市化发展模式与地方治理——美国大都市区发展的经验与启示》，《学术界》2013 年第 3 期。

［2］张强：《全球五大都市圈的特点、做法及经验》，《城市观察》2009 年第 1 期。

［3］王发曾、张改素等：《中原经济区城市体系空间组织》，《地理科学进展》2014 年第 2 期。

［4］杨姝琴：《广州增强国家中心城市辐射力研究》，《城市观察》2014 年第 6 期，第 166 ~ 177 页。

［5］李彤、韩宇：《构建环渤海世界级城市群综合交通体系研究探讨》，《城市》2011 年第 9 期。

［6］连维良、汪应洛：《城市规划郑州都市区建设的若干战略思考》，《城市规划》2012 年第 8 期。

［7］许学清：《科学建设郑州生态都市区的思考》，《城乡建设》2013 年第 11 期。

［8］黄涛、郭亚宣：《基于新型城镇化视野下的郑州都市区规划体系思考》，《现代城市研究》2016 年第 4 期。

［9］王建国：《推进中原城市群交通发展一体化》，《河南日报》2016 年 9 月 23 日。

B.20
基于对比的郑州国家中心城市建设研究

张 奕　苗金科*

摘　要： 国家中心城市是位于我国城镇体系塔尖的城市，是国家战略制高点的载体，是全国和全球城市网络体系的核心枢纽。目前，我国共有9个国家中心城市，即北京、上海、天津、重庆、广州、成都、武汉、郑州、西安。本报告从经济实力、综合交通、科教创新、对外开放、生态宜居、文化软实力6个方面，对郑州和其他8个国家中心城市进行对比研究，发现郑州整体发展水平较低。从而提出郑州建设国家中心城市的发展策略：发展枢纽经济，以综合交通枢纽带动经济增长；以创新驱动发展，建设“智力高地”和“创新高地”；深度融入“一带一路”建设，增强国际竞争力。

关键词： 国家中心城市　郑州　经济实力　综合交通　对外开放

2007年，《全国城镇体系规划（2006—2020）》明确提出“国家中心城市是全国城镇体系的核心，在我国金融、交通、文化和管理等方面都发挥着重要的中心和枢纽作用”。目前，全国已有9个国家中心城市，即北京、上海、天津、重庆、广州、成都、武汉、郑州、西安。2017年1月22日，国家发展和改革委员会正式批复同意了河南省政府《关于恳请支持郑州建设国家中心城市的函》，郑州步入了建设国家中心城市的新阶段。2018年，郑州在三个重要

---

* 张奕，硕士，郑州师范学院信息科学与技术学院讲师，研究方向为城市规划与设计；苗金科，硕士，郑州师范学院国家中心城市研究院讲师，研究方向为统计学。

的城市指标上有重大突破：第一个是常住人口突破1000万；第二个是建成区面积突破1000平方公里；第三个是GDP突破了1万亿元。三个指标一起突破具有历史性意义，标志着郑州的发展进入了一个新阶段。但是与其他国家中心城市相比还有一定差距，因此，郑州建设国家中心城市有必要借鉴其他国家中心城市的成功经验。

一　国家中心城市建设的相关理论

2007年，建设部在编制《全国城镇体系规划》过程中首次提出了国家中心城市这一概念，国外也有相关的世界城市的概念，这些世界城市在全球化进程中发挥着核心作用。国外学者也提出过相关观点，1986年弗里德曼（Friedman）提出把全球化进程与世界城市发展结合起来研究。1991年美国学者萨森（Sassen）从微观角度对全球城市进行研究，认为“在全球化加速发展过程中，全球城市发展的关键是完善的基础设施及服务，就像伦敦、东京、纽约等”。1996年，美国专家卡斯特尔（Castells）提出“基于动态角度把世界城市的发展理解为网络化过程，提高信息技术水平，加快生产服务流动，增强城市控制力”，形成以全球化、网络化和信息化为背景的社会形态的新理论。2010年克拉克提出“城市发展的全球化应该从人口、经济、文化、对外联系、城市政策等方面来研究”。

国内学者对国家中心城市这一概念的相关研究起步于20世纪90年代。2010年初，在城乡建设部编制的《全国城镇体系规划（2006—2020）》中，规划北京、天津、上海、重庆和广州为我国国家中心城市，自此我国学者从不同方面展开了对国家中心城市的研究。王国恩认为“国家中心城市带动区域融入全球化，在政治、经济、文化、国际交流等活动中发挥着核心作用”。姚华松、路洪卫等认为“国家中心城市在城市发展的各个领域代表着最高水平，是国家参与全球竞争与合作的重要载体”。田美玲认为“在全国和全球城镇网络中发挥着核心控制作用和重要的功能节点作用的特大中心城市可以被称为国家中心城市”。王新涛认为“国家中心城市是能够贯彻实施全国战略决策、带动区域发展、对外开放程度高、代表我国参与国内外合作交流竞争的中心城市”。

我国学者对于国家中心城市的评价也做了相关研究。周一星等学者的主要研究方向为中国主要城市的等级体系及中心性排序。肖耀球提出“基于对国际化职能效应和现代化城市质量两方面考虑的国际性城市评价指标体系”。刘玉芳提出“基于经济发展、社会进步、国际化水平与基础设施四个方面来构建国际性城市评价指标体系”。田美玲提出“基于国家中心城市的四大功能和八大中心来构建国家中心城市评价指标体系”。顾朝林等学者主要是通过网络数据挖掘方法，采集多源数据对国家地级市以上城市的中心性指数进行评价。和军等学者主要从政治级别、对外开放、经济发展、商贸辐射、社会服务 5 个方面选取指标来评价我国国家中心城市建设能力。

综上所述，国家中心城市应具有全球化、动态化、网络化的特征，在政治、经济、文化等方面居于核心地位，辐射和引领周边区域，能够代表国家参与国际竞争、合作和交流。参考国家中心城市的评价方法，本文分别从经济实力、综合交通、科教创新、对外开放、生态宜居、文化软实力 6 个方面对 9 个国家中心城市的发展建设进行对比分析。

二　国家中心城市建设的对比分析

（一）经济实力对比

经济实力是衡量城市发展的重要指标，国家中心城市更应该具有一定的经济实力来带动城市和区域经济的发展。从图 1 来看，国家中心城市中 GDP 居于前三位的是上、北、广，其中上海、北京超过了 3 万亿元，重庆在 2016 年之后超过天津，武汉和成都基本持平在 1.5 万亿元左右，2018 年郑州的 GDP 突破万亿元，位于第八，仅高于西安，与经济规模最好的上海市相差 2 倍，分别占成都和武汉的 66% 和 68%；从图 2 来看，十几年前各城市 GDP 平均增速超过 10%，创造了经济史上“中国奇迹”，2010 年开始整体趋于下降态势，增长速度换挡，我国经济由高速增长阶段向高质量转型发展，目前北京、上海稳定在 6% 左右。2018 年，广州、天津、重庆有所下降，分别是 5.75%、3.6%、6%，郑州、武汉、成都和西安均在 8% 左右，说明中部地区的经济增速较快，经济活力较强，发展势头迅猛。从图 3 来看，从人均 GDP 相比，广州市排名第一，2018 年人均 GDP 超过 15 万元，北京、上海、武汉、天津紧随其后，郑州位于第六，人均

GDP 超过 10 万元，高于成都、西安、重庆，说明郑州市民有一定的消费能力。在经济实力上对比分析，结合 GDP、GDP 增速和人均 GDP 的变化趋势分析，郑州与北京、上海、广州相差较大，与武汉、成都、重庆三个中西部城市相比 GDP 增速还有一定差距，人均 GDP 略高于成都、重庆，各项指标均高于西安。

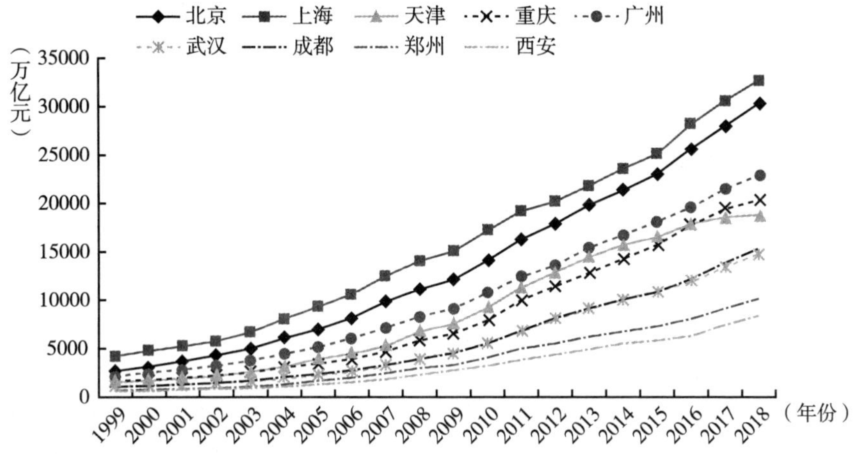

图 1　1999～2018 年国家中心城市 GDP 比较

资料来源：Wind，2018 年各城市国民经济和社会发展统计公报。

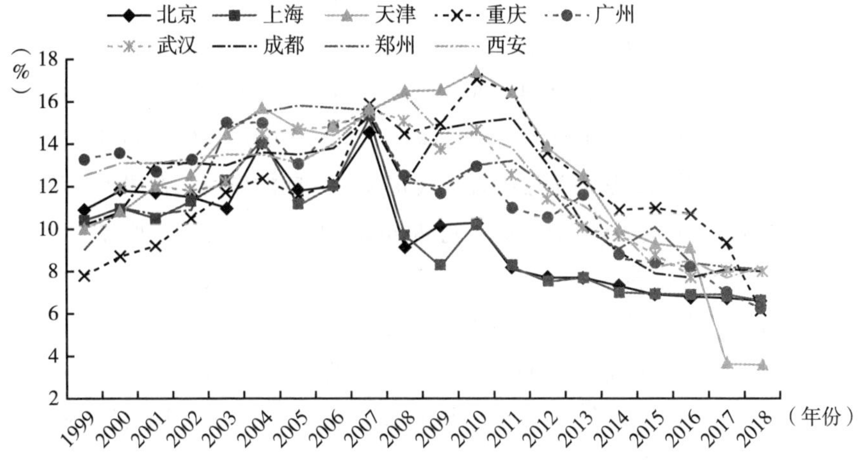

图 2　1999～2018 年国家中心城市 GDP 增速变化比较

资料来源：Wind，2018 年各城市国民经济和社会发展统计公报。

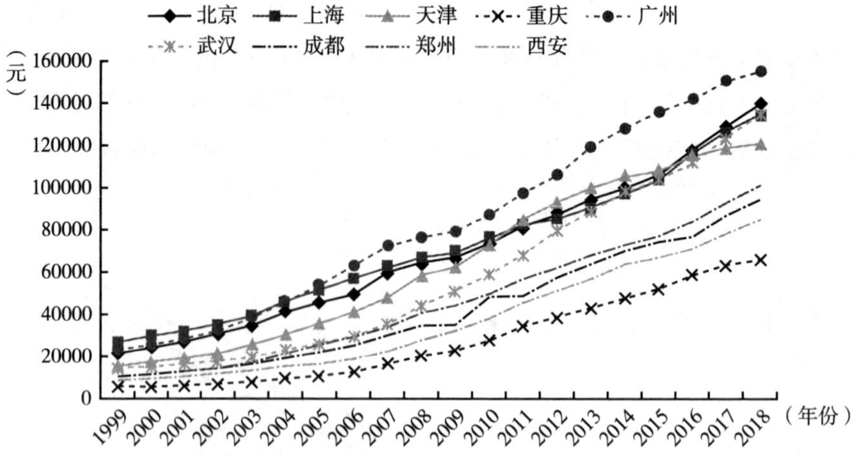

图3　1999～2018年国家中心城市人均GDP变化比较

资料来源：Wind，2018年各城市国民经济和社会发展统计公报。

根据图4所示，从产业结构来看，九大国家中心城市均以第三产业为主，形成了较为合理的产业结构。其中，郑州和武汉、成都产业结构比重相似，相比北、上、广第三产业比重偏低。结合表1来看，郑州的第三产业增加值较低，位居第八，仅高于西安，分别占武汉和成都的68%和67%。工业增长率西安第一，为9%；成都第二，为7.6%；郑州第三，为6.9%。说明西安、成都、郑州在工业企业盈利方面还有很强劲的增长势头，地区的发展水平和效益水平也处在提升的过程中。从建筑业增长率来看，郑州位于第一，为16.5%，远高于其他8个城市。说明郑州还在加快城镇化建设的进程中，同时创造更多的农村人口就业岗位，从而为维护社会稳定发挥一定的作用，在国民经济中处于经济繁荣的周期中。从交通运输、仓储和邮政业来看，无论从增加值还是增长率来看，郑州均排名靠后，对郑州GDP贡献仅占5%，说明对于郑州打造枢纽型网络城市发力不足。国家中心城市的建设离不开金融行业的发展和支撑。郑州的金融业增长值较低，为1145.8亿元，和北京、上海相差甚远，和天津、重庆也有一定差距，在第三产业中占比20.66%，对郑州GDP的贡献度占11%，北京和上海分别是17%和18%，郑州的金融业成长能力较弱，发展速度较慢，需要大力发展金融业，拉动地区经济增长。从图5来看，北京的上市公司317家，以超过14万亿元的市值领跑全国，归因于总部资源多数集中在

表 1　2018 年国家中心城市产业增加值及增速

2018 年增加值(亿元)		全国/增速(%)		北京/增速(%)		上海/增速(%)		天津/增速(%)		重庆/增速(%)	
GDP		900310.0	6.6	30320.0	6.6	32679.9	6.6	18809.6	3.6	20363.2	6.0
第一产业		64734.0	3.5	118.7	-2.3	104.4	6.9	172.7	0.1	1378.3	4.4
第二产业		366001.0	5.8	5647.7	4.2	9732.5	1.8	7609.8	1.0	8328.8	3.0
第三产业		469575.0	7.6	24553.6	7.3	22843.0	8.7	11027.1	5.9	10656.1	9.1
第二产业分解	工业	305160.0	6.1	4464.6	4.5	8695.0	1.9	6962.7	2.6	5997.7	1.1
	建筑业	61808.0	4.5	1274.9	3.3	1037.6	1.0	663.4	-16.7	2331.1	9.8
第三产业分解	交通运输、仓储和邮政业	40550.0	8.1	1346.2	7.0	1533.4	10.4	816.3	3.1	995.5	6.5
	批发和零售业	84201.0	6.2	2530.4	0.6	4581.5	3.3	2361.5	0.8	1710.0	5.9
	住宿和餐饮业	16023.0	6.5	440.8	1.6	—	—	327.9	4.5	457.2	5.3
	金融业	69100.0	4.4	5084.6	7.2	5781.6	5.7	1966.9	7.2	1942.3	6.9
	房地产业	59846.0	3.8	1748.3	-0.4	—	—	—	—	1134.7	0.6
	营利性服务业	—	—	—	—	—	—	—	—	—	—
	非营利性服务业	—	—	—	—	—	—	—	—	—	—
	其他服务业	19887.0	—	13311.5	—	10946.5	—	5538.2	—	44164.4	14.8
2018 年增加值(亿元)		广州/增速(%)		武汉/增速(%)		成都/增速(%)		郑州/增速(%)		西安/增速(%)	
GDP		22859.3	6.2	14847.3	8.0	15342.8	8.0	10143.3	8.1	8349.8	8.2
第一产业		223.4	2.5	362.0	2.9	522.6	3.6	147.1	2.1	258.8	3.3
第二产业		6234.1	5.4	6377.8	5.7	6516.2	7.0	4450.7	8.1	2925.6	8.5
第三产业		16401.8	6.6	8107.5	10.1	8304.0	9.0	5545.5	8.3	5165.4	8.3

续表

2018 年增加值(亿元)		广州/增速(%)		武汉/增速(%)		成都/增速(%)		郑州/增速(%)		西安/增速(%)	
第二产业分解	工业	5621.7	5.5	5076.2	5.9	5663.8	7.6	3746.2	6.9	1874.4	9.0
	建筑业	651.1	4.1	1301.5	4.9	926.8	3.7	708.6	16.5	1073.1	7.9
第三产业分解	交通运输、仓储和邮政业	1578.0	5.3	—	—	—	—	557.3	5.7	357.5	6.3
	批发和零售业	—	—	—	—	—	—	798.0	4.3	842.1	7.0
	住宿和餐饮业	—	—	—	—	—	—	380.4	5.8	204.9	5.8
	金融业	—	—	—	—	—	—	1145.8	5.8	874.9	5.3
	房地产业	—	—	—	—	—	—	693.9	8.5	643.2	5.8
	营利性服务业	—	—	—	—	—	—	924.3	21.3	964.6	22.9
	非营利性服务业	—	—	—	—	—	—	1036.4	5.2	1229.1	3.0
	其他服务业	14785.1	—	8107.5	—	8229.6	—	—	—	—	—

资料来源：Wind，2018 年各城市国民经济和社会发展统计公报。

北京，其中金融业市值占比过半。郑州的上市公司仅有23家，数量和市值均居于末位，不足京、沪的1/10，和中西部其他国家中心城市也存在一定的差距，说明郑州利用资本市场的融资能力有待提升。

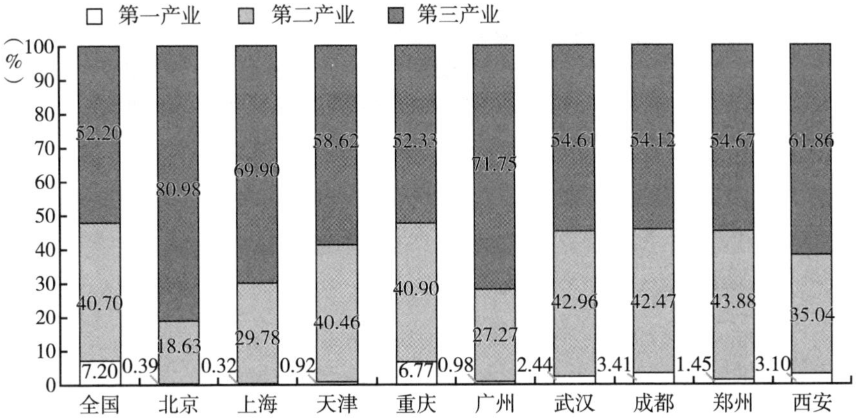

图4　2018年全国及9个国家中心城市GDP结构

资料来源：Wind，2018年各城市国民经济和社会发展统计公报。

（二）综合交通对比

国家中心城市拥有地理区位优势，建设集公路、铁路、空运、海运于一体的交通枢纽是发展的必备条件，依托于此，国家中心城市承担起区域间物流中转、交换、衔接的功能，发挥物流枢纽作用。同时，通过提升综合通信和信息共享，发展信息网络枢纽，形成集交通物流信息网络于一体的综合枢纽。从表2来看，郑州的旅客运输量与旅客周转量较低，说明郑州的旅游资源有待进一步整合提升。货物运输总量仅有2.76亿吨，但是货物周转量相对较高，这和郑州位于中部地区的地理优势和多式联运的交通息息相关，今后可以加大货物运输的优势，建设货物集装箱的货运枢纽。根据《畅通郑州白皮书（2019—2021）》显示，2018年，郑州机场共完成旅客吞吐量2733万人次，完成货邮吞吐量51.5万吨，客货运规模继续保持中部地区双料第一。并且郑州建有航空港经济综合试验区、中国（河南）自由贸易试验区、中国（郑州）跨境电子商务综合试验区。郑欧班列“新丝绸之路”的运营良好，每周“去九回八”，新开通中亚、东盟线

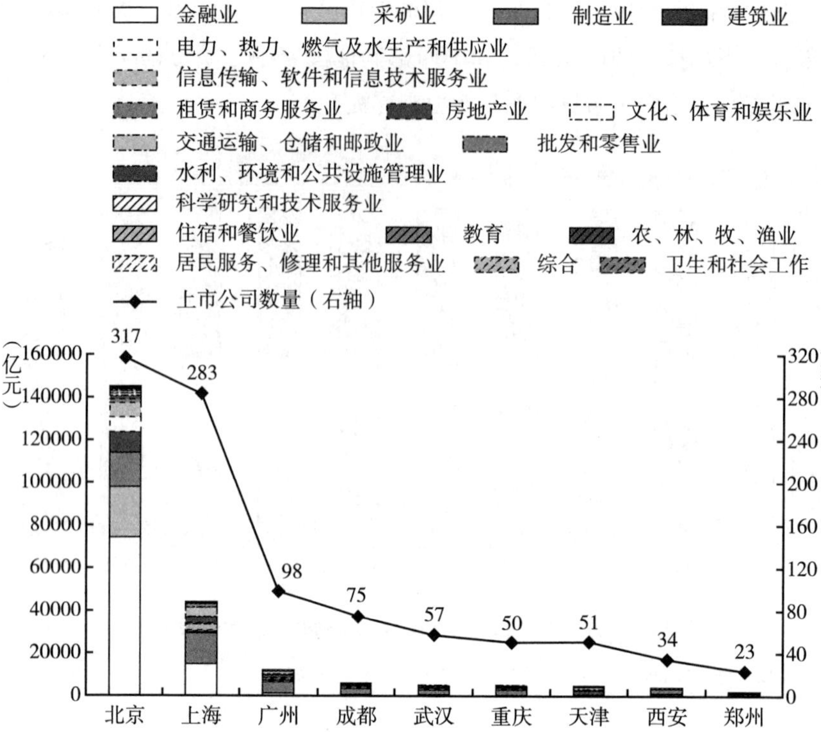

图5　2018年国家中心城市上市公司数量及各行业总市值情况

资料来源：Wind，截至2018年12月31日。

表2　2018年国家中心城市综合交通对比

2018年	北京	上海	天津	重庆	广州	武汉	成都	郑州	西安
货物运输总量(亿吨)	2.52	10.74	3.47	12.82	12.07*	6.25	—	2.76	2.62
货物周转量(亿吨公里)	780.70	—	1984.28	3593.64	—	3654.73	381.80	864.40	518.90
旅客运输量(亿人)	6.76	2.15	1.92	6.36	4.94*	2.86	—	1.48	2.61
旅客周转量(亿人公里)	2218.80	—	553.49	905.50	—	1232.52	1115.30	373.30	362.42
机动车保有量(万量)	608.40	393.42	298.69	630.21	—	312.30	548.40	404.10	325.63

注：*为2017年数据。

资料来源：2018年各城市国民经济和社会发展统计公报整理。

路，全年运行752班，从而加强了区域经济合作、提高了对外开放的程度。比起北上广这种终端型的枢纽，郑州更符合通过性枢纽的定位。

虽然与其他国家中心城市还有一定差距，但是郑州在交通枢纽功能上有一定的区位优势，拥有了“米”字形高铁网络，形成中原经济区“1小时经济圈”和覆盖中部地区“3小时经济圈”。郑州铁路枢纽在规划年度形成衔接西安、太原、武汉、重庆、石家庄、济南、徐州、阜阳（合肥）8个方向的铁路线，开设京广、郑太、郑万、郑阜、徐兰、郑济高铁，以及建设郑州—开封、机场、洛阳等城际铁路，未来将在郑州市内形成一条铁路环线，从而形成环形放射状铁路网。可在郑东新区、南部新城区和西部高新区等城市组团内设置客运站，扩大铁路网络覆盖服务范围。并且郑州的地铁1号线、2号线、5号线已开通，正在修建14条地铁线路。以上和郑州规划提出的“双城引领、多组团、多节点”的城市空间布局相呼应，推动郑州大都市区建设发展。郑州是国家“一带一路”倡议重要节点城市，郑州航空港经济综合实验区作为国务院批复的全国第一个以航空经济为主题的国家级功能区，郑州—卢森堡货物航运也获得国家支持，郑州机场已开通航线236条，国际及地区客运航线达30个城市以上，横跨欧美亚三大经济区，实现航空、铁路、轨道交通、高速公路一体化换乘，并且郑州机场已是国家一类航空口岸。同时，郑州至连云港、青岛、天津等港口海铁联运班列累计开行206班，基于关检互认、信息共享、海关一体化，郑州大力发展内陆港，建设一个能跟国际大交通接轨的枢纽。

（三）科教创新对比

建设国家中心城市，科技创新是内在动力，人才是关键。从表3来看，郑州拥有高等院校61所，其中211高校仅1所，专利授权31585件，与北京、上海、广州、武汉差距较大，尤其是高层次人才，郑州的研究生人数仅3万人，不足北京的1/10，郑州的高等教育院校数量太少，专利申请量和专利授权量也相对较少，说明科研成果转化率较低。郑州要借鉴其他国家中心城市的发展经验，例如武汉，作为全国第二大智力密集区和第三大科教中心，先后出台了“3551光谷人才计划”“创业十条”“青铜计划”“三权三归”“光谷基本法”“科技十条”等一系列政策制度，包括“光谷”未来科技城的建设，为科技创新提供了政策支持、智力支持和场地支持。广州建设了智慧城、科学城、中心广州知识城、高新区、琶洲互联网创新集聚区、国际创新城、大学城、生物岛等一系列科技创新的平台，并实施人才绿卡制度，使得近年来高新技术产业增长迅速。西安是西部科教中心，在国防科技工业尤其是航空航天科技方面成绩显著。借鉴武汉的经验，郑州建设了中原科创谷、北斗导航产业园、智慧城市产业园、大数据产业园、物联网产业园、轨道交通产业园、人工智能产业园等产业园区。郑州也出台了相关政策和计划，其中“四个一批”初显成效，使得高新技术企业数量增长 55%，共计 1329 家，科技型企业数量增长 32.7%，共计 4283 家。同时，实施“智汇郑州”30 条等相关策略，吸引来郑创业就业人才达 21 万。

表 3　2018 年国家中心城市科教创新水平对比

2018 年	北京	上海	天津	重庆	广州	武汉	成都	郑州	西安
专利申请量(件)	211000	150233	99000	72100	173124	60511	107801	70128	71250
专利授权量(件)	123000	92460	54700	45700	89826	32397	57370	31585	25042 *
普通高校数量(所)	92	64	56	65	83	84	64	61	63
211 大学数量(所)	26	10	4	2	4	7	5	1	7
普通高等学校在校学生数(万人)	58.1	51.8	52.3	76.3	108.6	96.9	91.3	99.3	127.1

注：＊为 2017 年数据。

资料来源：2018 年各城市国民经济和社会发展统计公报。

（四）对外开放对比

国家中心城市是代表国家参与到全球合作、竞争与交流中的，也是外向型经济和国际交往的重要门户。从图 6 看，北京和上海进出口总额和实际利用外资额领跑全国。在中部地区，郑州实际利用外资额居于末位，分别占武汉的 38.5% 和成都的 54.9%，说明郑州对外国企业的吸引力低。郑州进出口总额居于平均水平，略高于西安、武汉，说明郑州的对外贸易水平尚可。目前，对比中西部城市，武汉有 5 个外国领事馆，成都 16 个，郑州尚无外国领事馆入驻。2019 年 4 月，郑州河南联合签证中心将正式揭牌，可以办理法国、英国、日本、韩国、俄罗斯、新加坡、马来西亚、泰国、澳大利亚、柬埔寨、尼泊尔、以色列等国的签证业务，已是迈出对外开放的关键一步。在郑的世界 500

强企业数量仅有63家，是武汉的1/4。2018年，郑州接待外国游客人数50万人，友好城市数量仅有11个。综合以上，说明郑州的对外开放程度较低。

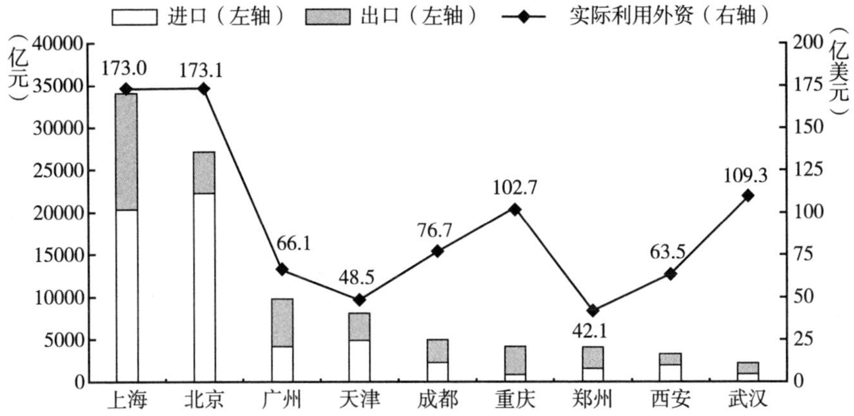

图6　2018年国家中心城市对外经济情况

资料来源：Wind，2018年各城市国民经济和社会发展统计公报。

（五）生态宜居对比

生态宜居城市是指坚持可持续发展理念，在尊重城市自然山水格局、顺应城市发展规律的基础上，建设生态良好、人文和谐、基础设施完善、安全有序、景观优美的人居环境，资源环境与经济社会的可持续发展。国家中心城市更需要打造生态宜居城市作为全国城市的示范。表4数据显示，在人口总数上，重庆、上海、北京的常住人口均超过2000万，位于前三；成都、天津、广州的常住人口在1500万左右；武汉、郑州、西安的常住人口突破1000万，跻身于超级大城市，在9个城市中，郑州人口总量处于偏小的行列。从城镇化率上看，上海、广州、北京均超过86%，天津和武汉超过80%，西安、郑州、成都均超过73%，仅高于重庆，九大国家中心城市均超过全国城镇化率。由此看出，郑州在人口结构和城镇化率方面和北、上、广相差较大，和西安、成都、武汉较为相近。2017年郑州的空气质量达到及好于二级的天数仅有166天，居于末位。城市城建区绿化覆盖率居于平均水平，能够基本满足生态园林城市创建的要求。2019年郑州市《政府工作报告》中指出“郑州市区新增绿

表 4　2017 年和 2018 年国家中心城市生态宜居程度对比

2018 年	北京	上海	天津	重庆	广州	武汉	成都	郑州	西安
常住人口(万人)	2154.20	2423.78	1559.60	3101.79	1490.44	1108.10	1633.00	1013.60	1000.37
城镇人口(万人)	1863.40	2120.88*	1296.81	2031.59	1287.44	889.69	1194.05	743.80	740.37
城镇化率(%)	86.50	87.7*	83.15	65.50	86.38	80.29	73.12	73.38	74.01
医院、卫生院数(个)	736	364	566	800	255	354*	892	349	343
执业医师数(万人)	10.9	7.49	4.3	7.63	5.41	3.82	6.2	4.2	3.38
2017 年	北京	上海	天津	重庆	广州	武汉	成都	郑州	西安
环境噪声等效声级 dB(A)	53.2	55.7	53.9	53.1	55.3	56.1	54.3	56	56.5
空气质量达到及好于二级(天)	226	275	209	277	294	255	235	166	294
城市建成区绿化覆盖率(%)	48.42	39.10	36.84	40.32	41.80*	43.70*	41.41*	40.33*	43.21*
城市实有道路面积(万平方米)	13959.79	10896.00	14742.12	19015.22	11525.00*	10154.00*	9590.00*	5820.85	7990.00*
每万人拥有公共汽车(台)	26.55	13.94	19.64	11.50	16.31**	13.40	16.18**	18.10**	12.52**

注：*为 2016 年数据，**为 2015 年数据。

资料来源：Wind，2017 年和 2018 年各城市国民经济和社会发展统计公报。

地1356万平方米，建成公园、微公园、游园411个，并且第十一届园博会闭幕后常态化开放”。从公共交通来看，郑州每万人拥有公交车数量相对较高，居民出行比较便利，成功创建“国家公交都市建设示范城市”。城市实有道路面积较小，结合以上建筑业较高的增长率，说明郑州还在加快推进城镇化的进程中。从医院、卫生院数来看，郑州高于西安和广州，接近于武汉和上海，虽然不具有明显优势，但是，陈润儿省长在《政府工作报告》提出“建设六大国家区域医疗中心，基于北京非首都功能疏解的背景下，依托郑州市现有的医疗资源，北京儿童医院郑州医院、阜外华中心血管病医院挂牌开诊，国家心血管病中心华中分中心正式运行”。郑州依托于承东启西连通南北的区位优势，成为全国层面的医疗中心指日可待。

（六）文化软实力对比

文化是一个城市的灵魂，对提升城市竞争力、吸引力和影响力有重要的作用，是一个城市软实力的体现。国家中心城市要发挥文化引领作用，需要大力保护历史文化遗产，打造特色文化地标，形成特定的城市文化，代表城市形象甚至中国形象。例如，北京作为全国文化中心，历史文化名城得到强有力的保护，公共文化服务体系建设相对完善，文化创意产业发展迅速，并且举办了很多有影响力的国际会议，如北京国际音乐节、北京文化创意产业博览会等。北京的图书馆、美术馆、文化馆、博物馆、艺术中心等各类公共文化设施基本实现全覆盖。上海以“红色文化”“海派文化”“江南文化”三大文化资源作为文化品牌建设的原动力，将上海建设成为全球文化交流中心。广州以新媒体为突破口，振兴“传媒之都”。重庆利用其丰富的自然人文资源打造世界级旅游文化。成都正形成以大熊猫文化、古蜀文化、三国文化等自然历史文化资源和宽窄巷子、锦里、东郊记忆等文化再生新兴资源相结合的一大批文创品牌，成为成都文创产业的重要支撑。成都是唯一被赋予“文创中心”功能定位的城市。武汉围绕“文化五城”建设，着重促进了十大文化及科技融合示范工程，武汉市被认为是第一批国家级文化及科技融合的示范基地。西安依托文化旅游资源，打造以西安为中心的“丝绸之路沿线旅游联合体”，促进旅游文化交流。郑州以建设华夏文明传承创新中心为抓手，努力塑造“天地之中、商城匠心”的城市性格，大力发展文化事业和文化产业，打造一批体现中原文化和郑州特色的文艺精品，发扬嵩山文化、黄帝文化、黄河文化、古都文化。开展黄帝故里拜祖大典、嵩山论坛、国际少林武术节等活动。从表5可以看出，郑州的博物馆、文化馆数量有限，公共图书馆数量尚可，档案馆数量较少，博物馆数量与北京、上海、西安差距较大，艺术表演团数量太少。需要深度挖掘郑州的历史文化资源，加大力度营造更好的人文氛围。

表5　2018年国家中心城市文化软实力对比

2018年文化业	上海	北京	广州	重庆	武汉	成都	天津	西安	郑州
公共图书馆(个)	23	24	14	43	2	22	29	13	17
档案馆(个)	49	18	27	45	—	—	—	—	13
博物馆(个)	131	179	31	100	10	35	65	134	38
群众艺术馆、文化馆(个)	25	20	13	41	1	22	17	14	14
艺术表演团(个)	329	—	7	13	—	—	103	—	15

资料来源：2018年各城市国民经济和社会发展统计公报。

三　郑州国家中心城市建设的不足与对策

（一）郑州国家中心城市建设的不足

根据以上数据及政策分析，郑州在建设国家中心城市的过程中还存在一些不足之处。一是综合经济实力较弱。与其他8个国家中心城市对比，郑州产业竞争力不强，行业聚集度低，没有形成在全国影响力大的核心市场。传统产业仍占较大比重，新兴产业虽然增速较快但是占比较小。第三产业中，金融、保险、信息技术等高端服务行业比较欠缺，上市公司数量过少，金融和实体经济未能形成良性循环。二是科教创新水平有待提升。郑州的国家重点院校和高层次研究机构欠缺，高层次人才培养能力较弱，智力支持不足，成果转化率低。高新技术产业体量较小，科创产业园也属于起步阶段。三是对外开放程度较低。郑州的行政级别较低，缺少外事外交活动，国际友好城市数量较少，尚无外国领事馆入驻。郑州进出口总额没有明显优势，实际利用外资金额较低，外向型经济薄弱，对外开放程度较低。

（二）郑州国家中心城市建设的对策

1. 以综合交通枢纽带动经济增长

郑州应该发挥综合交通枢纽优势，打造枢纽经济高地，发展航空经济、高铁经济、口岸经济等枢纽偏好型经济。例如，建设机场保税港、建设基地航空公司、飞机维修基地、机场大型购物中心；建设铁路集装箱的货运枢纽，形成仓储、物流、货运中心。进一步调整优化产业结构，以枢纽经济发展带动经济转型升级。郑州要发展先进制造业，“智能制造”提速增效，引进人工智能、智能终端、精密机械仪器制造、飞机及零部件制造等关联产业。发展“互联网+”金融、贸易、商务、会展、创意等，培育战略性新型产业集群，提高现代服务业的产业比重。带来物流业、会展业、金融业的发展，吸引更多的企业落户，提高就业率和经济收益，并且推动基础设施的完善，提升经济综合实力。

2. 以创新驱动发展，建设“智力高地”和“创新高地”

注重创新驱动发展、打造中部地区创新创业中心。由商品、资源、资本流量枢纽向信息、知识、人才流量控制节点转变。提升高校建设水平，把普通院校建设成高层次院校，加强与国内外高层次大学合作，与国内外科研机构合作建立河南分支，培养高层次人才，建立完善制度体系吸引人才；同时，基于郑州拥有一定数量的大中专院校，可以打造全国职业技术教育培训基地，培养高素质的技术技能人才；为推进“政产学研用”融合，促进科研成果转化；加大自创区发展力度，吸引高新技术企业，引进中国500强和世界500强公司，在郑州设立总部或分部；在新领域上进一步探索，例如新材料、人工智能、基因工程等。继续推进“四个一批”计划和“智汇郑州”工程，加快集聚高端创新资源，提升自主创新能力，把郑州打造成中部地区“智力高地”和“创新高地”。

3. 深度融入“一带一路”建设，增强国际竞争力

郑州市在政治领域影响力较低，需要积极引进国家重大组织机构入驻，积极承办重要外事活动、大型国际会议、国际赛事、国际性会展，加强对外交往联谊活动，加强对外经济合作。争取卢森堡领事馆入驻郑州，迈出对外开放的重要一步，逐步开放更多国家的签证业务。深度融入“一带一路”建设，扩大“四路协同”效应。“空中丝绸之路”强基扩面，增加国际航线和航班，建

设保税区和引进国内外知名航空物流服务企业相结合，加快组建本土客货运航空公司；“陆上丝绸之路”扩线提量，建设货物集装箱的货运枢纽，实施《郑州市推进中欧区域政策合作案例地区建设工作方案（2018—2020年）》，提升郑州的国际影响力；“网上丝绸之路”更加便捷便利，拓展跨境电商出口业务，引进跨境电商大型平台类、物流类、支付类总部企业入驻或设置河南分公司，完善跨境电商供应链体系，带动外贸转型升级，传统制造业与跨境电商相结合，产业优势与出口优势相互促进；“海上丝绸之路”无缝衔接，打造郑州内陆港，让港口功能平移至郑州内陆港，增加郑州海关报关放行的数量，加快建设内陆对外开放门户，进一步加大对外开放力度，增强国际竞争力。

本文通过对九大国家中心城市的研究分析，揭示了当前九大城市的发展水平。郑州整体发展水平较低，需要强化优势，补齐短板，提升城市建设水平，最终发展成为具有全国乃至全球影响力的国家中心城市。郑州建设国家中心城市要根据实际情况，立足中原地区，向武汉、成都、西安中西部城市汲取有益经验，兼顾高质量和高速度发展。把郑州打造为国际综合交通物流中枢、内陆地区对外开放的门户、全国重要的经济增长中心、全国极具活力的创新创业中心。国家中心城市是动态的发展，必然会受到国家和国际发展环境的影响，因此，有待尝试多视角、多空间范围、多层面的综合研究。

参考文献

[1] Fridmann, John. “The Word City Hypothesis,” *Development and Change*, 1986, 17 (1): 69 - 83.

[2] Sassen, Saskia. *The Global City: New York, London, Tokyo.* Princeton University Press, 1991.

[3] Castells, Manuel. *The Rise of the Network Society.* Wiley - Blackwell, 1996.

[4] Greg Clark. *Understanding OPEN Cities.* LERKO PRINT S. A. 2010. 10 - 11.

[5] 王国恩、王建军、周素红等：《基于国家中心城市定位的广州核心职能研究》，《城市规划》2009年第S2期，第13~19页。

[6] 田美玲：《国家中心城市及其竞争力的理论与实践研究》，华中师范大学博士学位论文，2014。

[7] 王新涛：《基于国家中心城市识别标准的郑州发展能力提升研究》，《区域经济

评论》2017 年第 4 期，第 75 ~ 81 页。
[8] 周一星、张莉、武悦：《城市中心性与我国城市中心性的等级体系》，《地域研究与开发》2001 年第 4 期，第 1 ~ 5 页。
[9] 肖耀球：《国际性城市评价体系研究》，《管理世界》2002 年第 4 期，第 140 ~ 141 页。
[10] 刘玉芳：《国际城市评价指标体系研究与探讨》，《城市规划》2007 年第 4 期，第 88 ~ 92 页。
[11] 田美玲、刘嗣明、朱媛媛：《国家中心城市评价指标体系与实证》，《统计与决策》2014 年第 9 期，第 37 ~ 39 页。
[12] 喻晓莹、喻新安：《郑州建设国家中心城市的独特优势与主要任务》，《区域经济评论》2018 年第 6 期，第 99 ~ 104 页。
[13] 易雪琴：《国家中心城市建设的国内经验及其对郑州的启示》，《中共郑州市委党校学报》2018 年第 153 期，第 90 ~ 94 页。

探 索 篇

Exploration Reports

B.21

大都市区一体化几个问题的思考

陈 耀*

摘 要： 大都市区在城市空间结构中处于中间层，是新型城镇化空间形态中的重要组成部分。根据国际国内经验，应先有都市区一体化，再有城市群的一体化，前者是后者的重要步骤和前提。大都市区一体化有利于中心城市的功能和能级提升，并能够带动周边地区发展，未来会成为国家新型城镇化推进的热点和重点。目前我国推进都市区一体化总体上有三个问题需要着力解决或破除，第一是核心城市集聚度过高；第二是区内各个城市之间功能定位不清，同质化严重；第三是中心城市综合实力弱，首位度低，对周边区域辐射带动作用有限。从根本上说一体化的难点和关键在体制机制，包括现有财税

* 陈耀，经济学博士，郑州师范学院国家中心城市研究院院长，中国社会科学院工业经济研究所研究员、教授、博士生导师，中国区域经济学会副会长兼秘书长，中国社会科学院西部发展研究中心副主任，研究方向为区域经济、产业空间组织和政府政策。

体制和行政区级别等体制。推动一体化的措施主要有：做好大都市区规划，重视培植外围次增长极，加强中心城区与周边城市及副中心的分工联动，形成功能产业差异化的互补。要减少行政干预，鼓励要素自由有序流动。要建立利益共享机制，包括产业转移与承接中的税收分成机制、生态受益区与受损区之间的生态补偿机制等。要建立城市首长或部门联席会，发挥社会机构的组织协调作用。郑州大都市区的一体化，应该围绕国家中心城市建设，强化中心城市引领和集聚辐射功能，并加快拓展周边城市的支撑空间，形成有影响力的现代化都市圈。

关键词： 大都市区（都市圈）　一体化　国家中心城市

大都市区或都市圈是工业化、城镇化发展到一定阶段的产物，中国的新型城镇化要以大都市区、城市群为主体形态，并着力推进都市区、城市群的一体化。本文重点探讨大都市区一体化的概念、理论和意义，推进大都市区一体化的难题和破解路径，以及关于郑州大都市区一体化的思路和建议。

一　大都市区一体化的概念、理论和意义

城市群、大都市区、国家中心城市等概念，学术界正在逐步理清，但迄今并没有一个统一的定义。笔者认为，“都市圈”跟“都市区”应该是一个概念，只是表述不一样而已，过去有人把都市圈讲得范围很大，实际上是把“都市圈”和“城市群”混在了一起，按照现在国家发改委的界定，都市区就是都市圈，这个“圈”的概念最早源于日本。日本最早关于都市圈的规划有非常细的标准界定，比如中心城市人口规模要达到多少，周边地区与中心城区的通勤人口和货物流向占多大比例，等等。

笔者认为，大都市区在城市空间结构里是处在一个中间层，是新型城镇化

空间形态中的重要组成部分，我们今天研讨的是大都市区一体化，再早一些时期我们讲的是城市群内部的一体化，现在看无论是主管部门还是地方实际操作层面，应该说过去都没有把时序搞清楚，一开始就推进城市群的一体化。现在按照国家的规划，全国划定了规模不等的 19 个城市群，其中像成渝城市群、中原城市群包含多达 30 多个城市，长三角城市群也有 26 个城市，地域范围非常之大，内部的差异性也非常大，所以虽然提出城市群一体化，但实际上推动起来没有抓手，很难形成联系紧密的城市化地区。

根据国际国内的经验，尤其是国外的经验，实际上应该先有都市区一体化，然后再有城市群的一体化，城市群的概念要大于都市区的概念，换言之，都市区的一体化是城市群一体化的一个重要步骤和前提。如美国东海岸城市群从东北部的波士顿，到西南部的纽约、费城、巴尔的摩，再到华盛顿，这一城市连绵带，建立在大纽约都会区、华盛顿都会区、波士顿都会区等基础上，并逐步形成各自特色和功能互补的一体化格局。

大都市区一体化有利于中心城市建设，它对于中心城市的功能和能级提升是有很大作用的，并能够带动周边地区发展，未来会成为国家新型城镇化推进的热点和重点。我国规划了 19 个城市群以后，各地的建设很难推动，一方面是由于空间尺度大，同时还要跨越省际行政区划，所以还是要从都市区、同城化这个角度着手，也就是说未来城镇化在现有的城市群内要先做都市圈一体化工作。

国家发改委发布的指导意见非常明确地讲我们要建设都市圈，但是这个都市圈前面有一个定语，要建设现代化都市圈，就是跟以往甚至跟国外讲的都市圈概念都有差异。指导意见有一个界定，明确是城市群内部以超大、特大城市或者辐射带动功能强的大城市为中心。就是对中心城市的体量提出了要求，超大城市是 1000 万人口以上的城市，特大城市是 500 万人以上的城市，大城市人口是 100 万到 500 万的城市，又分 100 万到 300 万、300 万到 500 万两个等级，应该说 300 万以上的城市都可以作为辐射带动功能强大的中心城市。我们讲的都市区要以 1 小时通勤圈为基本范围，这应该是一个基本的标准。“一小时”过去讲的是车程，现在讲的是“通勤”，就是我们上下班往返分别是一小时通勤范围的城镇化空间形态。

发改委的指导意见实际上把建设现代化都市圈作为新时代推进新型城镇化

的抓手，它的意义不仅在于可以优化城市空间结构，同时还在于可以激活有效投资和潜在的消费需求，增强内生动力。培育都市圈的基本思路是，通过促进中心城市与周边城镇同城化发展，以创新体制机制为抓手，推动现代化的都市圈发展。发展目标分为两个阶段，到 2022 年现代化都市圈要达到空间结构清晰、城市功能互补、产业分工协调、交通往来顺畅、公共服务均衡、环境和谐宜居等目标。到 2035 年，现代化都市圈基本形成，形成若干有全球影响力的都市圈。

现代化都市圈建设有七大任务，分别是基础设施一体化、产业分工协作、建设统一开放市场、公共服务共建共享、生态环境共保共治、城乡融合发展和一体化体制机制。国家已经提出培育现代化都市圈这个明确的指导意见，今后各个地区、各个省份会按照这个意见去着力推进。目前，在长三角城市群，除了上海都市圈的概念之外，南京都市圈、杭州都市圈、合肥都市圈也都在谋划。应该说都市圈一体化，实际上就是中心城市跟周边城市要尽快打破障碍，推进它们的协同发展、联动发展。

为什么现在又提出来大都市圈的概念呢？实际上跟我们的城镇化快速发展有密切关联，我们说大都市圈、大都市区的发展实际上就是城镇化、工业化发展到一定阶段后的产物。改革开放初期，我国城镇化率只有 17%，到了 2000 年是 29%，2017 年达到 58.52%，2018 年在 60% 左右了，也就是目前全国已有六成人口居住在城市。城镇化的快速发展大家应该都能实实在在地感受到，街道车辆拥堵、环境污染雾霾问题、房价高企问题、公共设施和服务不堪重负以及社会治理等问题显著。所以在城市化的推进过程中，城市化的空间形态也在发生变化，过去是城市单中心不断扩张蔓延，现在由单中心变成了多中心，以疏解中心城区功能、人口和产业过度集聚带来的问题，或者中心城区与周边城镇逐步实现同城化发展，形成了不同规模和能级的都市圈。

我国是一个拥有近 14 亿人口的大国，我们对城市规模的划分与国外明显不同，比如国外拥有 5 万人口就是不小的城市了，而在我国 5 万人只是镇级规模，我国最大的虎门镇常住人口达到 60 万。目前我们在原有大中小城市的基础上，还增加了特大城市和超大城市。过去 10 万人口属于小城市，现在 50 万以下属于小城市，特大城市是 500 万到 1000 万，超大城市是 1000 万以上。郑州市域常住人口已经突破 1000 万，按中心城区人口规模也应该属于特大城市了。目前国家规划的城市群有19个，其中最重要的有7个，也就是京津冀、长三角、珠三角，现在珠三角这一块叫粤港澳大湾区，然后是长江中游城市群、中原城市群、关中平原城市群、成渝城市群。这七大城市群都已明确其引领带动的中心城市，共有12个（京津冀和成渝城市群都有两个中心城市，大湾区有4个中心城市），除了香港、澳门和深圳，其中9个被确定为国家中心城市，比如郑州被明确确定为引领中原城市群发展的国家中心城市。总体看，目前7大城市群的布局相对均衡，三个在东部沿海地区，中西部地区各两个，有利于引领带动全国各地区协调发展（京津冀城市群要带动整个环渤海地区发展，应该说东北地区也能兼顾到）。

大都市圈的概念很早就有了，1957年法国地理经济学家戈特曼（Gottman）最早提出大都市圈（Megalopolis）概念，在他看来，大都市圈是“以一个或几个超级城市为核心，组成人口规模逾千万、政治经济影响力举足轻重的庞然大物”。我们现在基本上还是按照他这一思想来开展研究。关于都市区的理论有很多，比如美国经济学家约翰·弗里德曼（John Friedmann）借用熊彼特的创新思想创造了空间极化理论，提出中心—外围理论。还有法国经济学家佩鲁提出的“增长极”理论，美国诺贝尔经济学奖获得者缪尔达尔提出的“累积因果效应”以及克鲁格曼的新经济地理，等等。都市圈理论是以大都市为中心的城市空间形态为研究对象，该理论起源于德国经济学家冯·杜能的区位论，强调都市圈是一种圈层结构，由区域内不同等级、规模、职能及空间结构的城市体系构成，在一定地理或行政区域内，由一两个大城市或特大城市为核心，辐射并带动周边一定范围内的一批中小城市，使其成为有一定影响力、竞争力的区域城市群或城市带。

大都市区（都市圈）一体化主要是指大都市区内不同主体（政府、企业、居民、社团等）之间的协调联动和合作行为，旨在优化大都市区内的资源配置，提升整体竞争力。像国外的大伦敦、大纽约、大东京都市区，它的中心城市跟周边中小城市其实也是不同的行政区主体，所以它也有一个协同的问题，国际上的协同主要是通过建立联盟或者其他合作机制形成的。大都市区一体化的内容、任务主要是基础设施互联互通，产业分工协作，市场推进一体化，生态环境联防联控、共保共治，社会保障政策对接互认，等等。在我国，都市圈一体化现在有很多地方在积极探索和推进，仅2018年笔者就参与了几次调研，包括现在推进力度比较大、比较扎实的成都都市圈，作为中心城市的成都跟它邻近的周边城市眉山、资阳、德阳搞同城化，重点包括交通、产业、生态、社保、户籍、教育医疗等八大领域，每一个领域做得都非常扎实，通过推进同城化，使得中心城市发展品质和首位度不断提升，同时对周边这些城市发展也有很大的辐射带动作用。同城化、一体化的目标最终就是要实现中心城市和外围地区（包括城乡之间）人均收入水平和GDP差距的缩小，各地比较优势充分发挥，中心城市的引领和集聚辐射功能增强，既没有大城市病，也没有“乡村病”（贫瘠、荒芜、空心化）。

二　推进大都市区一体化的难题和破解路径

目前我国推进都市区的一体化，应该说还存在着很多难题，总体上看有三类问题需要着力解决或破除。一是核心城市集聚度过高，目前最突出的就是北京、上海，城市人口、产业、优质资源高度集中，核心功能与非核心功能无差异地不断集聚，导致大都市区内发展落差大，中心对周边和外围地区产生巨大的“虹吸效应”，这是我们推进一体化过程中解决难度比较大的问题。

二是大都市区内各个城市之间功能定位不清，同质化严重，这在那些缺乏突出中心城市的都市圈较为典型，比如成渝城市群中的“川南都市圈”（包含宜宾、自贡、内江、泸州等城市），由于城市规模、功能和产业相近，同质化现象严重，导致竞争远大于合作，不仅在产业发展、招商引资上恶性竞争，在基础设施规划布局和政策对接上也难以形成共识，因此需要我们研究这类都市圈一体化的办法。

三是中心城市综合实力弱，首位度低，“小马拉大车”，对周边城市区域辐射带动作用有限。我国首位度低的省会城市，东部突出的有济南、南京、石家庄，中部的郑州，西部的南宁、呼和浩特等。近些年省会城市都在努力提高首位度，有的比较成功，有的还未见效。值得提及的是，做大首位度要“取之有道”，不少城市希望通过撤县设区、合并城市来迅速做大，其中有的做法值得肯定，如合肥市合并巢湖市市区不仅有利于精兵简政，也有利于巢湖生态保护，并为省会城市发展提供了新空间，但总体上通过撤并做大的做法不值得鼓励，而且需要严格区划调整管制。做大首位度根本上要通过内生增长和创新驱动的力量，在这方面郑州市围绕建设国家中心城市，集聚资源创新发展，首位度不断提升，目前已经超过了20%，从2010年到2017年提高了约3个百分点，这是令人欣喜的发展。中心城市首位度提高了，才有实力带动周边发展，推进一体化进程。

从根本上说，都市圈一体化的难点和关键在于体制机制。改革开放初期，我国实行了“分灶吃饭”的财政体制，这种财政体制使得各个地区都要为了自己的财力去奋斗，企业只有在属地纳税，增加当地的就业，才能得到地方政府的鼓励，否则就会受到限制，这样就造成了重复建设、资源错配、低效投资等问题。另外一个一体化难题就是行政区的级别不对等，造成城市之间对接困难，很多周边地区跟中心城市很难对上话，缺乏合作的有效机制，这些都是推进一体化需要破解的难题。

在当前体制背景下，推进大都市区一体化，首先是要进一步细化现有城市群规划，要把率先推动都市圈的一体化作为城市群规划的重点。笔者对比过迄今已公布的几个城市群规划，其中中原城市群的规划应该说做得比较粗，规划范围大、涵盖城市多、可操作性低。如果能够围绕郑州大都市区一体化进一步做实规划，细化到城市区县，明确一体化的各个具体领域，无疑会更有利于中原城市群建设。所以推动城市群一体化应该首先做好大都市区规划。其次，还要重视培植外围次增长极，目前河南也在积极推进，如培育发展洛阳副中心，同时加强中心城区与周边城市及副中心的分工联动，形成功能产业差异化的互补。再次，要减少行政干预，鼓励要素自由有序流动。建立都市圈内的城市首长或部门联席会，发挥社会组织在推进一体化过程中的组织协调作用。

举几个国内和国外的例子。国内的如山东半岛城市群，这虽然是一个省内的城市群，但涵盖面积也非常大，中心城市除了省会济南，还有副省级城市青岛，以及烟台等，因此要实现整个半岛城市群的一体化，需要首先做好以这几个城市为核心的都市圈一体化，这样在规划中，明确划分了济南都市圈、青岛都市圈、烟台都市圈三个板块，这三个都市圈的一体化成为山东半岛城市群一体化的基础和前提。再看国外，国际上有影响力的五大城市群面积范围也非常大，也是由诸多都市圈构成的。美国规划了11个城市群，最重要的是东海岸以纽约为核心的东北部城市连绵带，还有中部以芝加哥为核心的五大湖区城市群，以及西部加州以洛杉矶为核心的西海岸城市群。但是美国的城市群从概念上讲是指都市连绵带，不是我们讲的都市区，与都市区概念类似的是大纽约区，即以纽约市为核心及其周边联系紧密的区域。美国东海岸城市群经过长时期的发展演变，已经形成明显的功能分工特征，如纽约为国际金融中心，波士顿为科技教育中心，费城和巴尔的摩为制造业和贸易中心，华盛顿是全美政治中心，大都市间功能互补，分工明确，值得我们借鉴。

三　关于郑州大都市区一体化的思路和建议

对于郑州大都市区的一体化，笔者认为还是应该围绕国家中心城市建设，要强化中心城市引领和集聚辐射功能，并加快拓展周边城市的支撑空间，形成有影响力的现代化都市圈。目前中央已明确未来国家城市群发展的重点是七大城市群，在七大城市群中特别明确了具有引领带动作用的中心城市，如郑州为引领中原城市群发展的中心城市。所以，推进郑州大都市区建设和中原城市群建设，都要首先把郑州中心城市建设好，要围绕郑州建设国家中心城市，推动郑州大都市区的一体化乃至中原城市群的一体化。

国家中心城市承担着国家使命，要有相当一部分服务全国的功能，我们现在对国家中心城市的功能做了具体分类，包括综合服务、科技创新、网络枢纽、开放交流、人文凝聚、生态宜居六大功能，每项功能里都有很多具体内涵。我们据此建立了完整的指标体系对全国 9 个国家中心城市进行评估，从评估结果看，总体上郑州在很多方面不如其他城市，但是也有一些相对强项，如 GDP、常住人口、外贸增速等超过西安，在网络枢纽方面也强一些。整体上，郑州正处在一个上升阶段。如郑州作为内陆城市要打造开放高地，其国际化程度明显较低，实际利用外资规模在九大中心城市中是最小的，国际友好交流城市数量也比较少；现在郑州的外国领事馆数量是零，可能很快会有所突破。郑州跟全国其他中心城市相比还存在明显短板，但是正进入快速上升通道，未来在综合服务功能、科技创新、开放交流等功能方面应是提升的重点。

按照国家有关都市圈发展的部署，郑州要培育发展现代化都市圈，首先要围绕建设国家中心城市，着眼承担的国家使命，增强城市服务全国的能力。郑州地理区位居中，是全国重要的综合交通枢纽，承东启西、连南贯北非常方便，交通便捷，所以郑州在服务全国上有很多领域都大有可为。

为了提升中心城市引领、集聚辐射功能和首位度，郑州未来的人口和经济集中度还可以继续提高。目前郑州以占全省 1/20 的土地面积，集聚了全省 1/10 的人口，产出了全省 1/5 的 GDP。但是，跟全国其他省会城市来比，郑州的集中度还不够，人口还可以继续集中，作为一个拥有 1 亿人口的大省，仅有 1/10 集中在省会城市，显然是低的，笔者认为可以提高到 20% 左右，经济首位度可以由 20% 提升到 30%。同时，城市建成区面积需要进一步扩容，现在郑州市建成区面积只有 1000 平方公里，发展空间与建设国家中心城市的要求显然不相匹配，跟很多省会城市比也小很多，未来至少要扩大到 1500～2000 平方公里。

此外，要研究明确郑州国家中心城市的核心功能，考虑逐步将一些非核心功能向周边城市疏解，以尽可能避免城市化快速推进导致的“城市病”，这也是推进郑州大都市区一体化的应有之义。郑州大都市区建设不能只是考虑到中心城市的集聚，还要带动开封、许昌、焦作、新乡等邻近周边城市的发展，所以有一些功能要考虑逐步向周边地区疏解，比如初级产品生产制造、大型公路物流仓储、都市型农业等。要认真研究国家关于都市圈的部署，争取把郑州大都市区打造成为全国现代化都市圈建设的示范区。

参考文献

[1] 陈耀、汪彬：《大城市群协同发展障碍及实现机制研究》，《区域经济评论》2016 年第 2 期。

[2] 陆大道：《大都市区的发展及其规划》，《经济地理》2009 年第 10 期。

[3] 覃成林：《中原城市群经济市场化与一体化研究》，《江西社会科学》2005 年第 12 期。

[4] 苗建军：《城市群利益冲突的理论与实证研究》，经济管理出版社，2014。

B.22 推动国家中心城市高质量发展要高度重视现代都市圈建设

赵 弘*

摘 要： 建设发展好国家中心城市，要充分认识、尊重和顺应城市发展规律。国家中心城市在许多方面都不同于中小城市，特别是在空间结构和交通结构两个方面，有其发展的内在要求。推动国家中心城市高质量发展，要深入研究和探索特大型城市发展的内在规律，在空间结构优化和交通结构优化这两个对城市发展具有根本性、持久性影响的关键问题上持续发力，建立健全适宜都市圈空间战略落地的体制机制，形成都市圈发展格局，推动城市高质量、可持续发展。

关键词： 国家中心城市 都市圈空间结构 市郊铁路建设

一 都市圈空间结构是提高城市承载能力和运行效率的一种重要空间战略

从特大城市发展规律看，许多国际大都市都经历了“单核心城市—多核心都市圈—城市群”的空间演变过程。城市在发展的初期，往往围绕中心城单核心向外拓展。随着城市规模不断扩大，一些城市面临功能集聚与运行效率的矛盾，出现“城市病”。为解决“城市病”，在中心城之外建设新城、卫星

* 赵弘，博士，北京市社会科学院副院长，研究员，主要研究方向为区域经济、产业经济、总部经济、城市治理等。

城来分担城市功能，甚至突破行政界限，在更大空间范围优化配置资源，协调人口资源环境关系，地域空间组织从量变到质变，形成跨区域的空间组织——“都市圈”。通过快速交通联系，都市圈中心城市的辐射半径可达到100公里。多个发达的中心城市都形成了各自的都市圈，其辐射范围相互交叠，构成了地域范围更广阔、承载能力更强劲的城市群（见表1）。如日本东京、大阪、名古屋三大城市都形成了各自的都市圈，每个都市圈均由中心城与周边卫星城、新城等通过快速交通连接构成，这三大都市圈共同支撑起日本太平洋沿岸城市群。

表1　国际大都市不同发展阶段的空间形态变化

发展阶段	单核心城市	多核心都市圈	城市群
动力机制	·集聚经济与规模效应催生城市，围绕中心城拓展 ·发展到一定阶段，可能产生集聚与效率的矛盾，出现城市病	·从“单核心”到“多核心”，突破行政界限，现代交通技术下，在100公里范围配置资源	·多个中心城市形成各自都市圈，辐射范围交叠，形成空间尺度更大的区
空间形态			

从纽约、伦敦、东京等国外特大城市发展历程和治理城市病的实践来看，特大城市在空间结构、交通结构等方面与中小城市存在根本上的差别。与中小城市相比，特大城市至少有两方面的独特性：一是对人口、资源的吸引力特别强劲。特大城市具有独特的品牌价值和城市魅力，形成吸引和集聚资源要素的强大“磁场”。二是城市功能多元化和复合性，教育、医疗、文化、科技、产业、居住等多元功能使城市人口规模巨大。所以特大型城市必须通过城市规划“对抗”人口在单一特定空间上的大规模集聚而带来的“规模不经济”问题。城市功能分散化布局和建立起与特大型城市交通需求相适应的交通供给结构，是避免和治理城市病的两大关键。

伦敦、纽约等国际大都市在城市化过程中都经历过空间结构和交通结构不合理而遭遇城市病困扰的城市发展历程。在探寻城市病治理办法的实践中，城市规划专家、城市经济专家等提出了不同的城市发展理论，也形成了不同的流派。比如“城市分散主义”认为不能任由城市自发膨胀，当城市规模达到一定程度以后，新增的部分应由城市周边的新城镇来承载。“城市集中主义”主张通过提高容积率、构建现代交通网、营造大面积绿地等途径，创造现代化生活环境。“分散”与“集中”这两种不同发展理念的交锋与融合，衍生了“分散化集中”理论，它强调通过生态空间将高密度的城市核心区与城市的其他功能中心区进行隔离，并通过城市间的公共交通系统，尤其是轨道交通系统将城市核心区与周边其他城市功能区连接起来，形成多中心、网络化的城市空间结构。

结合理论界的研究成果以及对国外特大城市实践的研究，我们认为，特大城市要实现高效可持续发展，必须做到两个方面。

一是要将多元化、复合性、极为丰富的城市功能在空间上进行分散化布局。采取分散组团式布局的思路，通过建设“新城”“卫星城”“业务核都市”等，引导城市功能与人口在空间上分散化布局，这是国际上许多城市解决“单核集聚”产生人口过多、交通拥堵等城市病的重要方式。比如，伦敦早在1946年就通过了《新城法》，掀起了“新城运动”，经历了四代卫星城的艰难探索。

（1）20世纪40年代，伦敦规划建设第一代卫星城。由于卫星城距离母城近，主要承担单一的居住功能，对母城有很强的依赖性，功能不完备，所以，第一代卫星城发展缓慢。

（2）20世纪50~60年代，伦敦规划建设第二代卫星城。在第一代卫星城单一居住功能的基础上，第二代卫星城增加了相当数量的产业和服务设施，独立性有所加强，但由于距离母城过近，规模扩大受限，第二代卫星城发展也不成功。

（3）20世纪60~70年代，伦敦规划建设新城，也可以看作第三代卫星城。这些新城、卫星城拉开了与母城的距离，除了居住功能外还配置了一些产业功能，居民可以就近工作。但当时认为这样的卫星城规模不宜过大，一般在3万~5万人。由于新城、卫星城规模过小，服务不完备，吸引力弱，第三代卫星城也没有发展起来。

（4）20世纪80年代以后，伦敦开始建设第四代卫星城。这一代卫星城的特征是，与母城拉开较远的距离，城市规模不断扩大，一般达到20万人左右；城市功能进一步增多，能够替代母城部分职能，成为伦敦大都市圈多中心区域网络的重要节点。第四代卫星城取得了成功。

经过几十年的实践探索，伦敦先后建设了33个新城、卫星城，这些新城、卫星城容纳了伦敦近1/4的城市居民，减轻了中心城的压力，也完备了伦敦都市圈的空间结构，有效缓解了伦敦的城市病。

二是要建立起与大都市空间结构、交通规模相适应的以轨道交通为主导的公共交通体系。一个城市的交通供给结构由这个城市的空间结构和城市交通需求规模所决定。清华大学交通研究所提供的数据显示：在等量空间资源条件下，小汽车一小时只能运输3000人，公共汽车一小时能运输3000～6000人，地面快轨一小时能运输1万～3万人，地铁（成网络）一小时则能运输3万～7万人。

从伦敦、纽约、东京等国际大都市治理城市病的历程看，建立起以轨道交通为主导的公共交通体系，是最终解决特大城市交通拥堵的根本出路，也是唯一出路。我们将其概括为“两个主导”：一是公共交通要在城市交通体系中占主导地位（70%～80%）；二是在公共交通结构中，各种轨道交通要占主导地位（70%～80%）。比如东京公共交通占城市交通的90%左右，其中轨道交通占公共交通的90%。所以，在“两个主导”中，第二个主导是关键、是根本，必须放在决定城市高效可持续发展的战略高度予以前瞻性规划，提前建设。

多年来，我国特大城市简单地强调地面公交的重要性，没有把城市交通供给的重心放在轨道交通建设上，导致城市轨道交通建设严重滞后，城市交通结构存在根本性缺陷。以北京为例，目前北京轨道交通体系存在两个短板：一是城市轨道交通密度偏低，大容量、高速化的轨道交通供给不足，城市交通承载力不强。目前全市城市轨道交通营运里程仅相当于东京的1/4（见图1）。二是市郊铁路建设滞后。伦敦、纽约、东京等国际大都市都有规模庞大、体系完善的市郊铁路系统，而北京市郊铁路建设相对落后，目前整体上处于起步阶段，线路少、里程短，疏解人口和引导城市功能空间布局的作用尚未发挥出来（见表2）。

从国外大都市轨道交通的运行范围来看，由于服务功能的差异，不同轨道

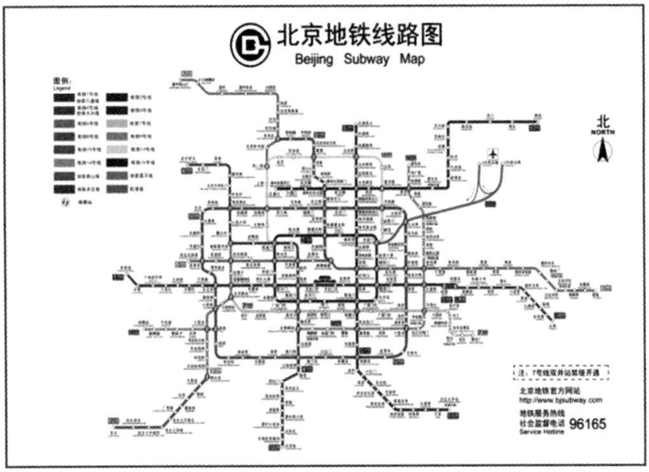

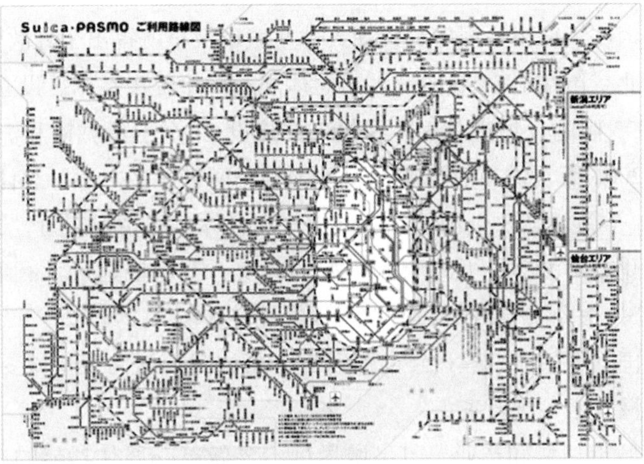

图 1　北京地铁线路图（上图）与东京湾地铁线路图（下图）

交通方式有其各自最佳效率的运营交通区间。其中，地铁是都市密集区内最主要的轨道交通方式，其特点是站距短、发车频次高、运行速度相对较慢，运营范围一般在半径 15 公里以内；快线铁路主要服务中心城区与近郊区之间的交通需求，其特点是站距长、速度快，运营范围一般在 15 ~ 30 公里；市郊铁路一般运营范围可达 30 ~ 70 公里，通常具有容量大、高速化、票价低的特点，主要服务中心城区与卫星城、新城之间的通勤需求。

上述城市功能分散化布局与轨道交通体系建设，是互为影响的一个事物的

表 2　部分国际大都市市郊铁路和地铁里程

城市	市郊铁路(km)	地铁(km)
伦敦	3650	402
纽约	3000	368
东京	2031	291
巴黎	1867	214
北京	238	609

资料来源：余柳、孙明正、王婷、鹿璐：《城市群交通一体化发展国际经验借鉴与中国路径探讨》，《道路交通与安全》2015 年第 4 期；潘昭宇、孙明正、白同舟、王永桑：《基于城市功能整合的“枢纽区域”研究》，《城市交通》2013 年第 1 期。

两个方面。

考察我国特大城市发展历程发现，这些城市很早就提出了分散化布局的思路。例如，北京市在 1983 版的《城市总体规划》中提出在郊区设立 13 个卫星城镇，在 1993 版的《城市总规》中提出要建设 14 个卫星城镇和 10 个边缘集团的目标，2004 版《城市总规》提出“两轴—两带—多中心”总体空间格局，规划建设 11 个新城和 8 个功能区。但从规划具体实施情况来看，我国特大城市空间分散化布局的理念并未得到很好的落实，卫星城建设没有取得预期成效，“单中心”发展格局始终没有取得根本性突破。

通过对国外卫星城镇建设经验的研究分析，我们认为卫星城要取得成功，需要认真把握 5 个关键要素。

第一是城市功能和产业。卫星城尽量不要做单一居住功能的布局，让一部分人能够在卫星城内实现职住平衡。例如，英国米尔顿·凯恩斯新城通常被称为伦敦第三代卫星城，距离伦敦市中心 80 公里，位于世界名校剑桥和牛津之间。凯恩斯新城利用优越的区位条件和先进的现代化基础设施，大力发展信息技术、商务咨询、金融保险、科技研发、教育培训等现代服务业，吸引了梅赛德斯 - 奔驰、大众集团、美孚石油、尼桑、雅马哈、达美乐比萨、BP 等数百家知名公司总部，入驻企业超过 5000 家，城市人口达 26 万，成为伦敦都市圈乃至英国知名的经济重镇。凯恩斯新城居民中有 2/3 实现了当地就业，但仍有 1/3 要到伦敦市就业；在凯恩斯新城的就业人口中，有 2/3 来自当地居民，但有 1/3 来自伦敦和周边其他区域。同时，卫星城还要有较好的公共服务基础，缩小与主城之间的公共服务落差，增强对主城疏解人口的吸引力。

第二是距离。卫星城与主城之间要保持一定的距离，以保证主城有足够的发展空间，同时要明确主城发展边界，通过严格划定生态红线，在主城周边建设大尺度的绿色生态空间，将主城与周边卫星城“隔离”起来，以避免主城“摊大饼”式蔓延。卫星城与主城的距离要适度，距离太近容易使卫星城与主城连在一起，太远则很难接受主城的辐射带动。从国际经验来看，卫星城与主城比较适宜的距离一般在 30 ~ 70 公里。

第三是通道。卫星城有没有吸引力，人们是否愿意去，关键是能否和主城保持紧密的联系。卫星城、新城只有能够和中心城区联动才会有吸引力，联动就要有通道。国外很多大都市的中心城区都建立了与周边新城、卫星城联系的大容量、高速化、一站式、低票价的市郊铁路。公路可以有，但不是主要的。因为公路在通勤高峰时段的交通容量有限，容易产生道路拥堵。

第四是规模。按照主城—卫星城、主城—新城的思路发展城市，中心城要控制，不能“摊大饼”。卫星城建设一般以中小城市为主，要承接一部分城市功能或发展一定的产业，所以规模不宜过小，否则难以有效发挥疏解主城人口和功能的作用；一般也不宜建设纯居住功能的卫星城，否则交通的需求量过大。同时，卫星城的总体规模也要加以控制，规模不能太大，过大的城市体量又会造成布局上的困难，居民从居住区到车站再到主城工作地点花费时间过多，会使卫星城失去了效率和吸引力。

第五是建设顺序。卫星城建设顺序对卫星城能否起到引导大都市城市空间结构优化作用，具有重要的影响。从国际经验来看，国外卫星城建设，一般是先修建轨道交通、车站等基础设施，然后建设公共服务设施，比如医院、学校等，最后才是建设住宅。这样的建设顺序使得住宅建设完成之前，卫星城就已经具备良好的交通条件和公共服务供给能力，有利于充分发挥轨道交通、公共服务对于城市分散化布局的引导作用，使得卫星城吸引主城人口前来居住生活的吸引力更强，最终达到吸引人口、资源分散化布局的目的。相反，如果建设顺序颠倒，先建设住宅，然后建设公共服务设施和交通设施，那么卫星城的居民到主城上班，就不得不选择汽车作为主要交通工具，这样很容易产生过度使用汽车带来的潮汐式交通拥堵现象，进而减弱卫星城的吸引力。以瑞典第三大城市马尔默为例，其卫星城建设的思路就是先建设市郊铁路车站，然后建设公共服务设施，最后建设住宅。

二 推动国家中心城市高质量发展、打造现代都市圈要抓住四个关键因素

一是创新城市发展理念，遵循特大城市发展的一般规律。城市有很强的集聚能力，各类功能和要素一定程度上的集聚可以产生规模经济，提高城市运行效率；但如果城市规模过大，功能和要素集聚过多、超过城市的承载能力，就会导致城市运行效率下降、运行成本提高，最终引发“城市病”。

因此，当城市功能和要素集聚到一定规模以后就要引导城市功能分散化布局。按照级差地租规律，一些非成本指向性的城市功能，或者有较强盈利能力的功能往往布局在城市中心区域，这些城市功能多是城市里面必不可少的功能，比如行政办公、金融商务等；其他城市功能，比如居住、教育、医疗、科技、经济等功能，可以通过在城市周边地区建设科教新城、医疗健康新城、产业新城等卫星城来安排，实现城市的功能分散布局。通过合理的城市空间布局，使城市内部各类功能和要素实现“大分散、小集中”，从而避免产生规模不经济的问题，确保有效提高城市运行效率和承载能力。

二是建设分散化、组团式、多中心的都市圈结构，提升区域整体承载力。都市圈是以具有很强辐射能力的中心城市为核心，与周边城市（新城、卫星城）分工合作，形成功能互补、相互依存的同城化区域。都市圈的形成和发展极大地优化了中心城市的功能布局，通过功能分散化，一方面有效避免了“城市病”的形成，另一方面有效辐射带动了周边区域的一体化发展，从而提升了都市圈的整体发展实力。都市圈和城市群是相互联系又有所区别的两个概念。都市圈是城市群发展的基础，只有以都市圈为基础建立起来的城市群，才更具有效率和生命力。

近年来，我国对城市群的研究逐渐增多，但对都市圈的重视和研究还不够，认知的“跳跃”不利于解决城市病问题。党的十九大提出要高质量发展，我们的子孙后代不能生活在无法逆转的城市病困境中。我国现阶段解决城市病，特别是未来防止（尤其是二三线、三四线城市）城市病问题发生，都必须把都市圈建设提升到应有的战略高度。

表3　都市圈与城市群的关系

	都市圈	城市群
功能	通过功能分散化、合理化布局，提升大城市的承载力与运行效率	不同大城市之间强化经济社会联系，提升区域竞争力
范围	一般半径70公里范围内	面积可达到5万～15万平方公里
规模	就业人口100万以上的大城市，多中心的效率开始超过单中心，可向都市圈发展	以若干都市圈为基础，形成城市群
核心支撑条件	以地铁、市郊铁路、轻轨为交通骨架，形成"1小时通勤圈"	城际铁路、干线铁路和高速公路构成骨架，交通一体化，但不要求"1小时通勤圈"
现实价值	对治理城市病具有直接、关键、决定性作用，是不可或缺、不可逾越的阶段	连接大城市，联动发展，同时不排斥中小城市直接参与都市圈分工

因此，推动国家中心城市高质量发展，应认真总结我国城市发展中的经验教训，重新认识都市圈建设的战略价值，重新研究都市圈与城市群之间的关系，借鉴国际化大都市在城市演进、拓展空间范围过程中的经验，亟待将都市圈建设放在首要地位，按照"分散紧凑型"理论，坚持大分散、小集中原则，通过规划建设新城、卫星城、微中心，构建"主城—新城""主城—卫星城""主城—微中心"的多中心、分散化、网络化的都市圈城市空间结构，提升区域整体承载能力（见表3）。

三是将市郊铁路建设放到突出位置，前瞻性规划建设市郊铁路。在都市圈范围内，主城与各功能组团之间要保持高效、紧密的联系，才能对城市功能和人口等形成吸引力，分散化、网络化的城市空间结构才能真正发展起来。公路的交通容量有限，且受天气等因素影响较大，依托公路保持主城与新城、卫星城的交通联系，可能会带来潮汐拥堵的问题。而轨道交通特别是市郊铁路由于其具有运量大、速度快、受天气因素影响小的特点，是支撑都市圈内主城与各功能组团高效联系的重要交通保障。因此，在都市圈空间格局下，保持主城与卫星城、新城的交通联系，要以轨道交通为主、公路交通为辅。

国家中心城市建设，需要借鉴东京都市圈、巴黎都市圈等国际大都市的发展经验，将市郊铁路建设放到更加突出和显著的位置，前瞻性地推进市郊铁路建设，加快构建适应特大城市交通规模、都市圈空间布局要求的交通结构，为现代化新型都市圈建设提供强有力的支撑。市郊铁路的规划实施应自成体系，确保独立建设、运营和管理。暂时没有条件的城市要在规划中预留路由，不能等到拥堵之后才“被动式”“补课式”寻找路由。市郊铁路建设与运营资金需求量大，仅靠政府单一投资渠道，难以满足建设发展需求。可以探索“轨道交通+土地”的综合开发模式，通过土地资源开发获得的收益，用以解决市郊铁路建设资金巨大的难题。

四是建立适宜都市圈空间战略落地的体制机制。都市圈的形成和演进需要经历一个漫长的过程，一般需要几十年甚至上百年的时间。推动国家中心城市高质量发展，需要保持充足的历史耐心和战略定力，要有“功成不必在我”的思想境界，坚持一张蓝图干到底，保障以国家中心城市为核心的都市圈空间规划能够顺利落地实施。

同时，都市圈的建设也是一项复杂的系统工程，既需要做好具有前瞻性的城市空间规划、轨道交通规划等，又要创新规划落实的机制保障，包括规划体检、城市体检、监督机制、追责机制等，避免任期制带来的短期化短视行为，否则只会成“饼”不会成“圈”。美国华盛顿特区没有出现城市病问题的一个重要原因，在于其能够持续严格落实城市规划。总体上看，在华盛顿城市发展的200多年里，城市的框架结构和空间大格局始终按照最初规划的目标一直延续下来，在历史发展的不同阶段会适当做一些调整完善，但总的格局没有变动。科学的规划和良好的执行力，避免了华盛顿市区“摊大饼”式扩张的冲动，而部分城市功能，比如居住、商业等，也得以在周边地区分散布局，沿6条放射轴线发展起一批卫星城，形成华盛顿都市圈。

借鉴国际经验，我们要建立常态化的规划体检评估机制，按照“一年一体检、五年一评估”的工作方式，对国家中心城市的城市总体规划、控制性详细规划等规划的实施情况进行体检和全面评估，形成体检、评估报告并提交相关部门审批。建立规划实施的监督机制和追责机制，通过论证会、听证会或其他方式，广泛征求各级人大、政府和社会公众意见，对于没有按照规划实施或落实规划不到位的，要坚决问责并及时纠偏，维护城市规划的刚性和权威，确保相关规划和都市圈空间战略真正落地实施。

参考文献

[1] 赵弘：《以现代都市圈建设推动京津冀协同发展》，《经济论坛》2018 年 7 期。

[2] 赵弘：《以可持续城市理念治理北京“城市病”问题》，《北京经济发展报告(2015～2016)》，社会科学文献出版社，2016。

[3] 李国平：《空间结构是影响城市发展的重要因素》，《北京日报》2017 年 8 月 28 日。

[4] 武剑红、沈砾子：《东京都市圈市郊铁路特点及对我国的启示》，《中国铁路》2019 年 9 期。

B.23
公路网建设、人口层级与高技术产业集聚

——基于京津冀人口流动的区位黏性分析*

杨　峥**

摘　要： 北京和天津两大直辖市相较于河北省，在政策、经济水平、社会环境等方面都具有一定的优势。市场机制下优质资源涌入发展较好的京津地区，加剧了河北省人才与资源流失，进一步导致发展的不均衡。一体化是区域行政边界不断消减、彼此融合的过程，空间集聚活动越来越依赖当地产业的组织方式。地区的持续增长必然依靠产业的创新优势来维持，高技术产业的知识关联效应则是经济集聚力的主要来源。本文测算了京津冀公路网络效率，然后从区位黏性这一全新视角分析了要素流动的内在机制。

关键词： 交通一体化　区位黏性　人口层级　产业集聚

京津冀协同发展，是习近平总书记亲自谋划、亲自部署、亲自推动的重大国家战略。党的十九大报告肯定了京津冀协同发展取得的成绩，也再次强调疏解北京非首都功能是实施京津冀协同发展战略的“牛鼻子”。设立雄安新区是

* 基金项目：天津市教委社科重大项目“天津市实现世界级制造业集群培育机制研究”；天津市哲学社会科学规划项目“经济新常态下天津市土地供给侧结构性改革与产业结构优化研究”（TJYY17－026）。

** 杨峥，博士，天津财经大学财税与公共管理学院，讲师，研究方向为财政理论与政策。

推动京津冀协同发展战略的重大举措，构建快捷高效的交通网络体系将为聚集人口和高端产业提供良好条件。按照《京津冀人才一体化发展规划（2017—2030年)》设定的目标，至2030年，三地区域人才结构更加合理，交通一体化势必成为适配京津冀人才空间布局的重中之重。《“十三五”时期京津冀国民经济和社会发展规划》作为全国第一个跨行政区域的发展规划，明确解决北京“大城市病”、有序疏解非首都功能必须打破行政边界的樊篱，共同打通“断头路”、拓宽“瓶颈路”。

阿肖尔（Aschauer)、博纳格利亚（Bonaglia)、德穆尔吉尔（Démurger）认为，交通基础设施建设力度不断增强极大改善了民生福祉，而且对于区域经济增长的贡献也功不可没。鲍德温（Baldwin）和霍尔（Holl）同样认为，交通改善对企业选址与产业布局的空间集聚平衡作用不可忽视。国内学界同样也注意到交通基础设施的网络外溢性与区域经济增长的紧密联系，特有的“中介效应”在扩大市场规模、提高经营效率以及增强市场活力等方面都扮演着重要角色。

理论上，随着交通体系的日趋完善，区际贸易成本逐渐消减。藤田昌久等研究发现，较高层级的城市不仅拥有较大的人口规模，也具有更为完整的产业体系。巴蒂（Batty）认为，规模各异的城镇能够共存于同一都市圈，这一有趣现象可能受组织机制支配。现实中，加大交通基础设施的公共支出究竟对人口空间分布、产业选址有何影响，答案却并非一目了然。美中不足的是，单中心的空间结构能否会就此瓦解而让位于协同发展模式，学界也未有过深入研究。有些计划和项目却偏离了整体的区域概念，各种实施路径常常莫衷一是。

基于此，本文在已有研究基础上尝试解决以下问题。第一，运用两阶段数据包络分析方法对京津冀公路网建设与空间需求匹配度进行系统考量；第二，采用分形理论对京津冀城镇层级体系的帕累托效率进行事实观察，为进一步优化空间布局提供定量判据；第三，基于新经济地理理论揭示要素集聚的内生机理与深层次动因，较好地衔接了理论模型与实证分析，从区域创新和产业升级的视角，探讨加快提升京津冀科技创新集聚优势的空间实施路径。

二　京津冀公路网建设效率评价

区域协同发展的主要动力在于科技创新，有效的交通基础设施网络是要素集聚创新与区域经济增长的“连接器”。交通基础设施投资持续增加以及不断攀升的公共债务，是近年来许多国家宏观经济政策的共同表征。我国地方政府一般公共预算中安排了交通运输支出，但土地资产由此产生的出让收入以及发挥金融属性获得的投融资平台抵押贷款，才是交通基础设施建设这一“城市硬件”的主要资金来源。尽管公共财政资金是有效提供交通基础设施的资金保障，但交通基础设施网络的效率评价并不是单纯比较公共支出投资强度，而是如何让辖区内的流动要素以此能更加有效地加以利用，并推动产业竞争优势不断增强。

（一）公路基础设施资金投入规模

《中国交通运输统计年鉴》统计了当年的公路建设投资完成额，只是时间上并不连续。《中国国土资源统计年鉴》无法清晰划分各地政府投向公路的财政性资金规模。《中国城市建设统计年鉴》中的全国城市维护建设资金（财政性资金），也只是笼统地按省列示出市政公用设施建设维护与管理支出。

为凸显出我国地方政府在公路建设过程中，多种资金融合以及建设周期长的特征，本文采用以地方财政交通运输支出滞后一期为因变量，公路里程为被解释变量的固定效应模型，用弹性系数的倒数估算出当年可能用于公路基础设施的财政资金投入。据此，再以公路里程（万公里）作为主要产出指标，用旅客周转量、货物周转量全面地显示财政资金对人流、物流的带动作用，从而客观反映流动要素对公路网的有效需求（见表1）。

（二）变量定义和研究模型

将地方政府用于公路建设的财政性资金使用过程分为产出和受益两个阶段（见图1），但与黄薇主观性赋权不同的是，以熵值法计算的综合得分体现出财政性资金在前后相继两个阶段中的重要程度。

表 1　2010～2017 年京津冀公路基础设施情况

	地方财政交通运输支出(亿元)			公路里程(万公里)			旅客周转量(亿人公里)			货物周转量(亿吨公里)		
年份	北京市	天津市	河北省	北京市	天津市	河北省	北京市	天津市	河北省	北京市	天津市	河北省
2010	154.99	46.95	155.72	876.93	10065.05	8071.11	390.19	269.03	1172.86	2.11	1.48	15.43
2011	199.12	97.37	261.36	999.6	10337.29	9630.43	412.33	285.1	1306.58	2.13	1.52	15.7
2012	243.76	87.21	287.04	1001.13	7844.06	10604.96	421.16	314.66	1369.2	2.15	1.54	16.3
2013	231.79	90.02	286.57	1051.14	3097.39	11674.06	254.04	267.09	1163.72	2.17	1.57	17.45
2014	214.55	94.95	310.23	1036.71	3602.38	12684.47	273.93	246.74	1276.66	2.18	1.61	17.92
2015	295.63	98.88	323.82	901.41	2519.22	12007.28	279.43	252.3	1213.21	2.19	1.66	18.46
2016	353.48	111.52	251.8	825.43	2302.32	12332.68	268.49	262.05	1238.12	2.2	1.68	18.84
2017	—	—	—	958.42	2169.54	13381.59	253.16	266.91	1282.78	2.22	1.65	19.17

资料来源：国家统计局。

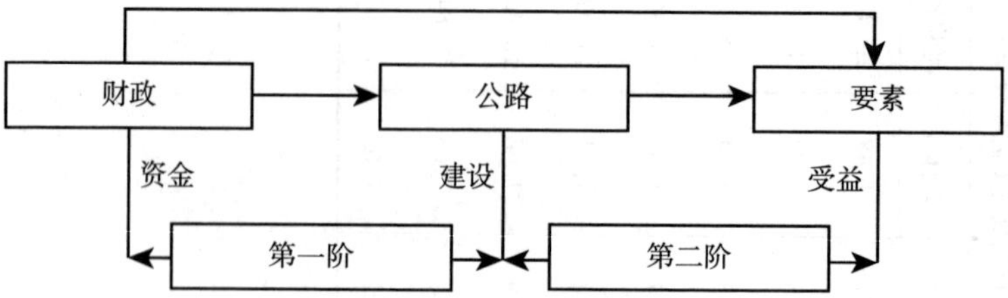

图1　公路网建设效率的两阶段分解

在一个经济系统中，有 n 个地区 m 项指标，第 j 项指标的熵值：

$$e_j = -\frac{\sum_{i=1}^{n}[p_{ij}\ln(p_{ij})]}{\ln(n)}$$

$p_{ij} = \frac{x'_{ij}}{\sum_{i=1}^{n} x'_{ij}}$，$x'_{ij}$ 是采用不同算法对正向、逆向指标进行标准化处理后的数据。

第 i 个地区公共服务产出或受益的综合得分：

$$s_i = \sum_{j=1}^{m}\left[\frac{p_{ij}(1-e_j)}{\sum_{j=1}^{m}(1-e_j)}\right]$$

据此即可分别计算出第一、第二阶段效率权重：

$$\lambda_1 = \frac{S_{产出}}{S_{产出}+S_{受益}}, \lambda_2 = \frac{S_{受益}}{S_{产出}+S_{受益}}$$

（三）京津冀公路网建设有效性实证结果

基于 CCR 产出导向模型分别计算出研究期内京津冀公路网建设、受益阶段的子效率和财政资金运用综合效率的全过程时空演变（见图 2）。

以往，河北省交通基础设施效率长期落后于北京和天津，《京津冀协同发展规划纲要》出台之后逐步得到提升。天津的交通基础设施效率甚至超过了北京，使得近年来天津产业快速发展，整个京津冀公路网建设的平均效率开始高于全国平均水平。

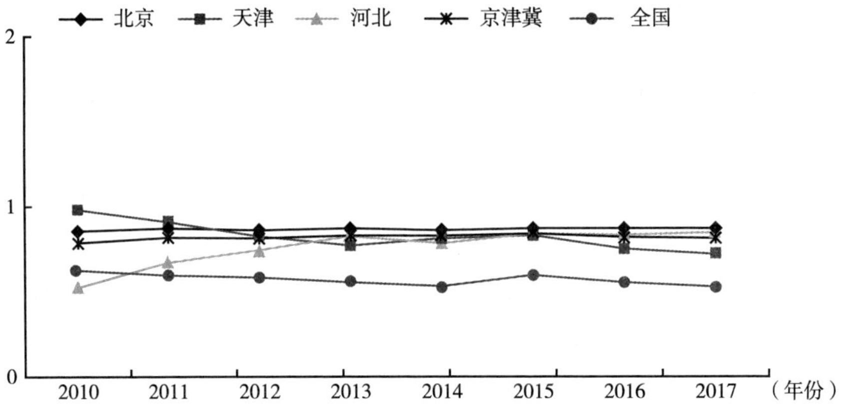

图 2　京津冀公路网建设两阶段综合效率比较

数据来源：作者基于 CCR 产出导向模型计算。

三　京津冀人口分布帕累托效率的事实观察

表面看来，多个不同层级、各司其职的城市和乡镇在较长时间内都处于基本稳定的状态。面对交通成本日益降低以及知识溢出叠加而来的技术创新冲击，原有的城镇体系空间结构是否还会因为公路网的不断完善而得以维持？巴蒂（Batty）认为，分形维数（fractal dimension）为解释空间结构分布的合理性、联系是否紧密提供了可靠的标准。在一个城镇体系的层次结构中，城市数量与规模之间的竞争关系遵循逆幂律法则：

$$N_r = P_r^{-D}$$

r 是某一城市在该城镇体系中的排位顺序（$r=1, 2, 3, \cdots$），N_r代表处于第 r 个层级上的城市数量，P_r是相互依存异质性城市 N_r的人口规模，D 为自相似层级的分析维数（fractal dimension）。用 *Hausdorff* 维数法确定一个空间分维，给定一个标度码尺（yardstick）r，大于 r 的地区个数 N（r）与 r 满足：$N(r) \propto r^{-D}$，$-D = \log N/\log r$。

人口流动受到集聚“拉力”与拥堵“推力”两种矛盾且本质上兼容的力量共同作用，因而考察人口分布的合理性时，必须在“混沌”不规则的空间形态中考虑其非平稳、不连续性特征，城镇体系可能并非是线性形态。基于巴蒂（Batty）和朗利（Longley）的做法，令 $f(D) = [c + d\sqrt{r}]/2$，估计方程变为非线性形式：$\ln N(r) = \ln\theta + (c/2)\ln r + ([c + d\sqrt{r}]/2)\ln r$。

待估参数：$d \to 0$，$c \to f(D)$。$(d\sqrt{r})/2$ 用于度量空间位序—规模的非线性特征，当 $c \to f(D) = 1$ 时达到最优分布的自然状态。

出于稳健性考虑，本文分别给出“十五”与“十二五”北京、天津与河北省地级市常住人口的检验结果，以及将北京、天津扩展至区县级口径的全域两种口径的分析结果。由于部分行政区划发生了变化，比如北京东城区和崇文区组成新东城区，北京西城区和宣武区合并成新西城区，为保持口径一致做了合并计算。

加巴克斯（Gabaix）和易卜拉欣莫夫（Ibragimov）、梁琦等等人采用 *Zipf* 维数法消除小样本情形下 OLS 线性估计的偏误。谈明洪、范存会证明，理论上 *Zipf* 维数与分形维数互为近似倒数关系，两者的乘积等于判定系数。基于此，本文将模型改进为 $ln(r-0.5)$ 做进一步估计（见表2）。

为了从多角度判断京津冀城镇层级体系的优劣，本文沿用人口规模的分形方法，对京津冀的 GDP 位序—规模进一步检验（见表3）。

首尔都市圈与京津冀“三足鼎立”的城市群形态类似，由首都首尔、港口城市仁川和土地面积较大的京畿道行政区构成，土地自然禀赋与京津冀地区比较接近。

实证结果表明（见表4），京津冀地区与首尔都市圈非线性模型的拟合优度，均比传统的线性模型有了改善，只是分形维数 $c \to f(D)$ 通过显著性检验的同时，人口规模的分维却没有给出比较有意义的结果，问题出于 $d \to 0$ 的假设条件并未成立。尽管采用了 $\ln(r-0.5)$ 的方法对模型修正以克服有偏问题，究其原因还是样本量过小导致的人口规模在城镇体系中的非线性分布特征没有完全显现。所有线性模型的分维都通过了显著性检验，不同统计口径得到的城镇体系人口位序—规模检验结论却截然不同。京津冀全域的人口分形维数 $f(D) > 1$，在省市一级 $f(D) < 1$。在行政级别上，北京、天津虽名曰为“市”，与河北省管辖的“市”并不属于同一层级，无论是从人口规模还是经

表 2　京津冀城镇体系人口规模位序 - 规模分形维数

		“十二五”全域		“十二五”省市		“十五”全域		“十五”省市	
传统模型 ln(*r*)									
线性	常数项	8.17	(49.84)***	7.842	(66.363)***	8.147	(50.177)***	7.531	(54.776)***
	$f(D)$	1.126	(−20.317)***	0.731	(−11.655)***	1.213	(−22.093)***	0.618	(−8.464)***
	R^2	0.91		0.92		0.92		0.86	
非线性	常数项	7.013	(65.927)***	7.587	(72.973)***	7.093	(50.721)***	7.23	(60.853)***
	$c \to f(D)$	0.376	(1.960)*	0.317	(−1.013)	0.029	(−0.118)	0.112	−0.314
	$d \to 0$	1.171	(−14.113)***	0.8313	(−3.793)***	1.067	(−9.788)***	0.978	(−3.909)***
	R^2	0.98		0.96		0.98		0.94	
修正有偏模型 ln(*r*−0.5)									
		“十二五”全域		“十二五”省市		“十五”全域		“十五”省市	
线性	常数项	7.752	(44.399)***	7.514	(66.11)***	7.701	(43.877)***	7.248	(57.911)***
	$f(D)$	0.998	(−16.764)***	0.59	(−9.478)***	1.077	(−17.987)***	0.496	(−7.234)***
	R^2	0.87		0.88		0.89		0.81	
非线性	常数项	7.103	(96.854)***	7.519	(112.884)***	7.076	(76.730)***	7.254	(92.481)***
	$c \to f(D)$	0.087	−0.669	0.467	(−2.773)**	0.143	(−0.872)	0.233	(−1.173)
	$d \to 0$	1.042	(−16.790)***	0.688	(−4.694)***	1.005	(−12.875)***	0.732	(−4.245)***
	R^2	0.98		0.96		0.98		0.93	

注：括号中的数字为系数的 t 统计量，*** $p<0.001$，** $p<0.01$，* $p<0.05$。

全域 = 北京 16 个区 + 天津 16 个区 + 河北省 11 个地级市共 44 个样本。

省市 = 北京 + 天津 + 河北省 11 个地级市共 13 个样本。

资料来源：作者根据历年北京统计年鉴、天津统计年鉴、河北经济年鉴数据计算。

表 3　京津冀城镇体系 GDP 位序 – 规模分形维数

传统模型 ln(r)									
		"十二五"全域		"十二五"省市		"十五"全域		"十五"省市	
线性	常数项	9.909	(57.326)***	10	(37.812)***	9.208	(39.158)***	8.962	(114.513)***
	$f(D)$	1.115	(−19.072)***	1.15	(−8.196)***	1.318	(39.158)***	1.164	(−28.033)***
	R^2	0.9		0.85		0.87		0.98	
非线性	常数项	8.213	(29.245)***	10.1	(28.047)***	7.408	(85.556)***	8.858	(93.475)***
	$c \to f(D)$	1.338	(2.859)***	2.749	(−2.534779)**	1.413	(9.126)***	1.862	(−6.523)***
	$d \to 0$	1.546	(−8.379)***	0.326	−0.429	1.789	(−26.930)***	0.339	(−1.697)
	R^2	0.96		0.83		0.99		0.99	
修正有偏模型 ln(r−0.5)									
		"十二五"全域		"十二五"省市		"十五"全域			
线性	常数项	9.909	(57.326)***	9.503	(43.678)***	8.706	(35.771)***	8.455	(92.713)***
	$f(D)$	1.115	(−19.072)***	0.941	(−16.696)***	1.165	(−14.134)***	0.95	(−19.022)***
	R^2	0.9		0.84		0.82		0.97	
非线性	常数项	8.321	(36.817)***	9.505	(42.149)***	7.743	(105.769)***	8.458	(147.128)***
	$c \to f(D)$	1.061	(2.707)***	1.629	(−2.857)**	0.706	(5.431)***	1.349	(−9.278)***
	$d \to 0$	1.432	(−8.919)***	0.244	(−0.491)	1.503	(−24.663)***	0.532	(−4.205)***
	R^2	0.96		0.82		0.99		0.99	

注：*** $p<0.001$，** $p<0.01$，* $p<0.05$；GDP 价格为当年价格；北京、天津区县的数据中扣除了划归市一级核算部分，区县 GDP 合计数略小于全市 GDP。

资料来源：作者根据历年北京统计年鉴、天津统计年鉴、河北经济年鉴数据计算。

表 4　首尔都市圈城镇体系人口位序－规模分形维数

传统模型 ln(r)					
模型类型	系数	“十二五”		“十五”	
线性	常数项	14.783	(77.058)***	14.749	(75.615)***
	$f(D)$	0.642	(−12.084)***	0.647	(−11.975)***
	R^2	0.63		0.63	
非线性	常数项	13.295	(49.6015)***	13.245	(48.445)***
	$c \to f(D)$	1.264	(3.288)***	1.282	(3.269)***
	$d \to 0$	0.909	(−6.799)***	0.919	(−6.739)***
	R^2	0.76		0.76	
修正有偏模型 ln(r − 0.5)					
模型类型	系数	“十二五”		“十五”	
线性	常数项	14.635	(77.426)***	14.6	(76.06)***
	$f(D)$	0.602	(−11.49)***	0.607	(−11.403)***
	R^2	0.61		0.6	
非线性	常数项	13.657	(66.149)***	13.616	(64.634)***
	$c \to f(D)$	0.748	(2.554)**	0.753	(2.519)**
	$d \to 0$	0.743	(−6.951)***	0.748	(−6.863)***
	R^2	0.75		0.74	

注：括号中的数字为系数的 t 统计量，*** $p<0.001$，** $p<0.01$，* $p<0.05$。

首尔都市圈共计 86 个样本，包括首尔 25 个区、仁川 8 个区和 2 个郡、京畿道包含 51 个市、邑。

资料来源：作者根据韩国统计局数据计算。

济总量排序，京津两地将无疑长期包揽“冠亚军”。首尔都市圈十多年来分形维数比较稳定，$f(D)<1$ 表明各地之间联系相对紧密。京津冀地区，无论是传统模型还是修正有偏模型，城镇体系分形维数都较“十五”时期有所降低。

《京津冀协同发展规划纲要》实施之前，从中央到地方政府都为推动京津冀协同发展实施了大规模的基础设施投资，为最终实现区域一体化付出了许多努力。然而，京津冀城镇体系趋于扁平化却是不争的事实，从二者系数的显著性可窥一斑，资源愈发向首位区靠近，中间城镇发展速度趋缓，与多中心城镇网络的全面协同发展相距甚远。如此中心－外围（core－periphery）式的单极发展必然导致区间差距不断扩大，这一结果是由于人口流动的区位黏性所致。克鲁格曼（Krugman）的区域竞争假设，人口和资本受区际交通条件的改善吸引，在空间上可以瞬时、无成本地流动。而现实中，“产业资本创新积累”与“人力资本蓄水池”增加了要素流动的“用脚投票”成本，也即区位黏性形成迁徙阻力，往往在短期内难以脱离当地产业价值链。

四　京津冀产业集聚创新

区域之间的有效合作得益于专业化分工，而当某一地区本身就具有“天然”竞争优势时（比如，北京的首都政治资源、天津的港口区位优势等），技能人才和研发资本将会不断涌入。为了更加接近较大的市场需求、降低交易成本，流动要素会选择那些已有较为完整产业链的区位。本地市场效应（Home Market Effect）带来更大份额的超常市场需求（Idiosyncratic Demand），众多新技术、新产业的不断涌现反过来进一步促进该地区产业集群的发展。为了更好地与理论分析有机结合起来，选择高技术产业单一部门逐个估计可以避免高估产业异质性问题对交通基础设施的贡献程度。

（一）高技术产业集聚经济的度量

借鉴谢子远和吴丽娟地方化经济的思路，某一地区高技术产业集聚经济公式：$loc_{ik}=s_{ik}/s_i$。s_{ik}代表地区 i 第 k 个行业（本文考察的是高技术行业）主营业务收入占该地区所有产业收入的比重（用规模以上工业企业主营业务收入代替)。s_i表示高技术产业占全国总收入的比重。数值越大说明高技术产业在该地区产业集中度高，优势越明显，也就是某一地区高技术产业的区位熵。

(二)模型设定与估计方法

除了传统的OLS方法，本文还列示了静态面板、动态GMM模型的估计结果。为测定京津冀公路建设对高技术产业集聚的影响程度，设定计量模型为：

$$loc_{itk} = \beta_0 + \beta_1 road_{it} + \beta_2 divs_{it} + \beta_3 X_{it} + \varepsilon_{it}$$

核心解释变量有三个。

1. 公路基础设施有效性(*road*)

大卫·李嘉图的比较优势理论提出，由于相对劳动生产率的差异，每个国家或地区都应集中生产具有比较优势而不是绝对优势的产品。针对京津冀而言，两市一省应该避免重复投资，并集中资源发挥自己的优势产业，利用本市的要素禀赋优势可以化解资源不足造成的发展难题。为此，选用测算的京津冀三地公路基础设施综合效率作为核心解释变量。

2. 消费多样性(*divs*)

消费者福利取决于商品多样性，与产地无关，也就是产业内贸易(Intra - Industry Trade)。一个辖区的价格指数随着产品多样性增加而降低，实际工资水平升高，可视为对消费者的补偿。为测算商品多样性偏好与支出份额的变化特征，采用城镇居民日常消费支出比重衡量。不仅反映偏好多样性程度，还代表该地区公路基础设施的实际使用效果，用以刻画贸易自由度。

3. 工具变量(*X*)

在GMM(I)模型中的工具变量包括：①中央政府的转移支付确实一定程度上缓解了京津冀之间的财政收入差距，但无论是财政收入总量还是人均财政收入规模的差距依然在扩大，经济发展较为落后的河北省对中央的转移支付有着很强的依赖。根据财政分权理论，由于信息不对称，中央政府不如地方政府更加了解当地的公共服务需求。近年来，中央的专项转移支付基本投向教育、医疗、社会保障等民生领域，较少涉及交通基础设施。为此，将地方财政收入总计加入工具变量当中。②交通基础设施的便利性与可达性是私人部门进行经济区位决策时的重要依据，对于地租的影响也毋庸置疑。土地出让成交价款既是我国财政管理体制下基础设施建设的重要资金来源，也可以侧面反映出流动要素在逐利原则下，对于当地公共服务“用脚投票”的选择结果。③GMM（II）添加了高产业集聚度的滞后项 $loc_{(-1)}$，以考察产业在地理上集聚、扩散、转移的动态因素。消费数据来自国家统计局，地方财政收入总计来源于《中国财政年鉴》，土地出让收入来源于《中国国土资源年鉴》。

（三）实证结果

普通面板的小样本量估计选择面板校正标准误（Panel Corrected Standard Errors）方法，权数选择按截面加权（cross - section weights）方式允许存在不同的截面异方差，以便有效处理面板数据的误差结构。

LM 检验结果表明随机效应优于混合效应模型。个体固定效应 F 检验和 χ^2 检验显示固定效应优于混合回归。Hausman 检验 p 值大于 0.01，不能拒绝存在随机效应的原假设。进一步通过最小二乘虚拟变量法（Leat Squares Dummy Variables，LSDV）认为个体效应较弱，表明拒绝京津冀差异较小的假设（见表 5）。

OLS 模型回归结果表明（见表 5），京津冀公路建设效率对当地高技术产业的集聚作用不明显，只有在随机效应模型中呈弱相关。添加了工具变量的 GMM 模型中（见表 6），J - statistic > 0.05 同样表明交通基础设施对于能否推动京津冀高技术产业的集聚并不明确。当然，掣肘于构建空间面板模型通常距离或 GDP 等空间权重矩阵，实际上经济或人口密度本身已经就是地理区位的决策结果。采用 1 或 0 的二进制邻接空间权值矩阵，显然容易忽略交通基础设施的全域网络属性，因而技术上无法使用空间面板模型来考虑京津冀交通基础设施网络的空间溢出效应。

五　政策建议

天津市在工业上的发展具有相当大的优势，占 GDP 比重超过四成。仓储和邮政业为河北省 GDP 贡献较大，得益于 2010 年成立的河北省物流标准化委员会，相继投资了石家庄、唐山、廊坊、邯郸、张家口五大物流枢纽城市，河北省的物流产业得以迅速发展。此外，以滨海国际机场为主导的空运以

表 5　京津冀高技术产业集聚估计结果

混合效应			LSDV 法混合效应						固定效应				随机效应			
	vote	*divs*		*vote*	*divs*	北京	天津	河北		常数项	*vote*	*divs*		常数项	*vote*	*divs*
系数	0.781	1.629	系数	0.523	−2.719	2.88	1.931	0.985	系数	2.66	0.293	−4.022	系数	−9.93	3.783	19.461
t	1.648	1.556	*t*	1.47	−0.575	1.363	1.028	0.5	*t*	3.353	2.026	−2.172	*t*	−3.54	2.547	3.547
Prob	0.119	0.139	*Prob*	0.165	0.575	0.196	0.323	0.626	*Prob*	0.005***	0.064	0.049*	*Prob*	0.003**	0.022*	0.003**
R^2	0.072		R^2	0.973					R^2	0.991			R^2	0.478		
Prob（*LM* 检验）	1.18		*Prob*（*LM* 检验）	16.873***					个体效应 *F* 检验	400.288***			*Hausman* 检验	0.000		

注：上标***、**、*分别表示1%、5%和10%的显著性水平。

资料来源：作者根据历年中国高技术产业统计年鉴数据计算。

表 6　京津冀高技术产业集聚度 GMM 模型估计结果

	混合效应				固定效应						随机效应					
	GMM(I)		GMM(II)		GMM(I)			GMM(II)			GMM(I)			GMM(II)		
	vote	*divs*	*vote*	*divs*	常数项	*vote*	*divs*	常数项	*vote*	*divs*	常数项	*vote*	*divs*	常数项	*vote*	*divs*
系数	2.309	−1.753	3.399	−3.937	3.771	9.232	−24.097	−6.415	2.61	13.214	−8.951	8.371	8.173	−23.5	17.401	25.374
t	1.213	−0.427	1.475	−0.802	0.057	0.406	−0.135	−0.813	1.331	0.851	−0.371	0.698	0.217	−1.783	1.637	1.056
Prob	0.243	0.675	0.164	0.437	0.956	0.692	0.895	0.435	0.213	0.415	0.716	0.496	0.831	0.1	0.128	0.312
J-statistic	0.064		7.683		0.000			0.033			0.000			0.221		

资料来源：作者计算。

及以天津港为主导的海运，适合成立跨境快递基地与河北省形成呼应，共同促进经济圈内交通物流行业蓬勃发展。

尽管目前来看，京津冀的发展水平与长三角之间仍然存在着一定差距，但是京津冀的发展优势也十分明显。第一，京津冀作为工业中心，具有比较完备的重工业现代化体系；第二，京津冀的文化氛围足够优越，以清华大学、北京大学为代表的众多国内一流高校，具有“高精尖”的设备且人才资源储备充足，具有发展高新技术的基础；第三，京津冀协调发展问题从来没有像今天这样受到广泛关注，众多利好政策的相继出台必然推动京津冀协同发展在万众期待中高速前行。

参考文献

［1］Aschauer. Infrastructure and Macroeconomic Performance: Direct and Indirect Effects, In The OECD Jobs Study: Investment, Productivity and Employment. OECD, Paris. 1993: 85 - 101.

［2］Bonaglia, Ferrara, Marcellino. “Public Capital and Economic Performance: Evidence from Italy,” *IGIER working paper*, 2000: 163.

［3］Démurger. “Infrastructure Development and Economic Growth: An Explanation for Regional Disparities in China?” *Journal of Comparative Economics*, 2001（1）: 95 - 117.

［4］Baldwin, R. E., Forslid, R., Martin, Ph., Ottaviano, G. I. P., Robert - Nicoud, F., *Economic Geography and Public Policy*. Princeton University Press, Princeton, NJ. 2003

［5］Holl Adelheid. “Transport Infrastructure, Agglomeration Economies, and Firm Birth: Empirical Evidence from Portugal,” *Journal of Regional Science*, 2004（l44）: 693 - 712.

［6］刘生龙、胡鞍钢：《基础设施的外部性在中国的检验：1988 ~ 2007》，《经济研究》2010 年第 3 期，第 4 ~ 15 页。

［7］张学良：《中国交通基础设施促进了区域经济增长吗》，《中国社会科学》2012 年第 3 期，第 60 ~ 77 页。

［8］张勋、王旭、万广华、孙芳城：《交通基础设施促进经济增长的一个综合框架》，《经济研究》2018 年第 1 期，第 50 ~ 64 页。

[9] Fujita, Krugman, Venables. *The Spatial Economy. Cities, Regions and International Trade*. Cambridge, MA: MIT Press. 1999.

[10] Batty. "Cities in Disequilibrium," *UCL Centre for Advanced Spatial Analysis, Working Papers Series*: Paper 202, 2015.

[11] 吴良镛:《京津冀地区城乡发展规划研究三期报告》，清华大学出版社，2013。

[12] 杨峥:《土地财政与最优城市规模》，《经济与管理研究》2012 年第 3 期，第 29 ~ 38 页。

B.24
国家中心城市建设视域下气候变化对航空安全发展的影响及政策建议*

孔 锋 李 航**

摘 要： 气候变化背景下极端天气事件增多，给航空安全带来了巨大挑战。本文从我国民航快速发展入手，基于增暖背景下的航空安全风险和经济损失风险趋于增大的趋势，从极端天气气候事件影响航空安全、飞机起飞限重天数、雾霾（低能见度）影响航空安全、航班飞行时间增加、高高原机场起飞条件变化、飞机腐蚀和晴空湍流颠簸7个方面分析了气候变化对航空安全的影响，并探析了航空业发展对气候变化的可能影响。最后基于气候变化和航空业的相互影响，提出了包括科学规划新建机场布局、航空气象数据共享平台建设、综合评估气候变化对航空影响、开发航空气象指数保险、制定航班延误的规范性操作、高度重视航空污染物排放影响和气候变化背景下的航空工作人员新风险应对培训在内的7点政策建议。本文对于全面了解气候变化和我国航空安全发展的相互影响具有参考价值。

关键词： 航空安全　气候变化　极端天气　国家安全　安全发展

* 本文由国家自然科学基金（41801064；71790611）、中国博士后科学基金资助项目（2019M650756）、中国气象局气候变化专项项目（CCSF201843；CCSF201844）和中亚大气科学研究基金（CAAS201804）资助。

** 孔锋，博士，清华大学公共管理学院助理研究员，研究方向为气候变化与自然灾害；李航，博士，中国民航大学中法联合空管应用数学研究中心助理研究员，研究方向为自然灾害学。

一　气候变化影响民航发展的背景

在城市发展竞争日趋激烈的当下，国家中心城市成为区域经济和社会发展的核心力量，不仅体现在人口数量和地域面积上，还更多承载着“引擎”性质的国家中心职能，已成为城市化体系的“塔尖”。国家中心城市是互联互通的关键节点，其在全球航空运行中起着重要的作用，同时航空业在引领、辐射、集散等主要功能定位上也推动着国家中心城市的快速发展。在我国，北京、天津、上海、广州、重庆、成都、武汉、郑州、西安 9 座城市已成为国家中心城市，且无一例外均有着规模庞大的航空运营吞吐量。航空业的持续发展一方面为全球带来了经济效益，尤其是临空经济、航空港经济等；另一方面提高了全球不同区域间的连通性，尤其是对内陆中心城市地区，同时还刺激了对新技术的投资，促进了区域经济发展的新旧动能转换。2014～2017 年，全球航班数量增长了 8%，预计 2017～2040 年可能增长 42%。近年来我国航班延误导致的旅客大范围滞留和冲突事件屡见不鲜，且国际上航空事故频率也趋于增多。其中由气候变化导致的极端对流和恶劣天气所引发的航班延误率占比不断攀升①。2011～2015 年，我国民航航班正常率逐年降低，平均正常率仅为 71.8%，其中天气原因是航班延误率增加的主要原因②。同时增暖背景下飞机起飞限重天数趋于增多，从长期来看，航空公司飞机起飞限重必将影响旅客行李减少，导致同等条件下的飞机票价和行李托运费趋于增长。目前，全球气候变化与航空业的相互影响还处于探索阶段。随着全球化进程的不断发展，我国对民航的依赖度不断增高。民航作为国家的战略性基础产业、窗口服务行业，其地位在国家经济社会发展和改革开放进程中越来越高，作用和责任越来越大，社会关注度越来越高。因此，必须高度重视气候变化对民航的影响。

---

① 周璞、张恬月、刘晓达：《成都双流机场跑道视程与低能见度的关系》，《陕西气象》2018 年第 3 期。

② 中国民用航空局：《2017 年民航行业发展统计公报》，《年度民航发展报告》，2017.

二 我国民航机场剧增，民航战略地位凸显

随着社会经济的发展和全球化进程的推进，我国民航业发展迅猛，越来越多的民众开始选择飞机出行，2017 年春节民航运送旅客 984 万人次，同比增长 15.1%，春节期间全国平均航班正常率 85.6%。截至 2015 年底，中国民航共有民航运输飞机 2650 架，颁证运输机场 210 个，通用机场 78 个，其中年旅客吞吐量 1000 万人次以上机场有 26 个。2015 年，中国民用航空运输总周转量达到 852 亿吨公里，比上年增长 13.8%，完成旅客运输量 4.4 亿人次，比上年增长 11.3%。

对于国家中心城市而言，民航的快速发展相比其他城市更为迅猛。以郑州为例，郑州新郑国际机场开通航线 143 条，联通欧美亚和全国 83 个主要城市，年吞吐量 1500 万人次以上，货物量 37 万吨以上，其增速连续 3 年居全国首位。2014 年郑州的航空港经济生产总值达 411 亿元以上，增长 18%，进出口总额达 379 亿美元，占全省进出口总额的约 55%。以智能手机为例，2014 年郑州航空港承担了约 1.43 亿部智能手机的运输，约占全球供货量的 1/8。北京 1985 年以来航空客运量的增长则更加迅猛（见图 1）。全国 2018 年航空新增旅客的客源地排名前 20 位包括了 9 大国家中心城市。

由此可见，国家中心城市的民航地位凸显。

从整体来看，目前我国的民航机场大致形成了五大机场群，即西北机场群、北方机场群、西南机场群、华东机场群和中南机场群。这五大机场群与我国五大战区在地理区位上具有较高的重合，且与国家中心城市紧密依托，为我国的国防安全建设发挥着重要作用，同时对于推进军民融合国家战略具有积极的作用。国务院办公厅发布的《关于促进通用航空业发展的指导意见》指出，截至 2020 年全国要建成 500 个以上通用机场，拥有各类运输飞机 4600 架，航班起降达到 1142 万架次，比 2015 年的 779 万架次增加 47%。中国沿边航空口岸在 2014 年占总口岸的 17%，货物吞度量占 12%，并持续增加。

国内航线则由 1990 年的 385 条增加到了 2016 年的 3055 条，增幅超过 6.9 倍。2010 年以来我国公民出境旅游基本保持 20% 左右的速度增长，自 2014 年开始，我国居民出境游总量超过 1 亿人次，123 个机场旅客吞吐量的增长速度

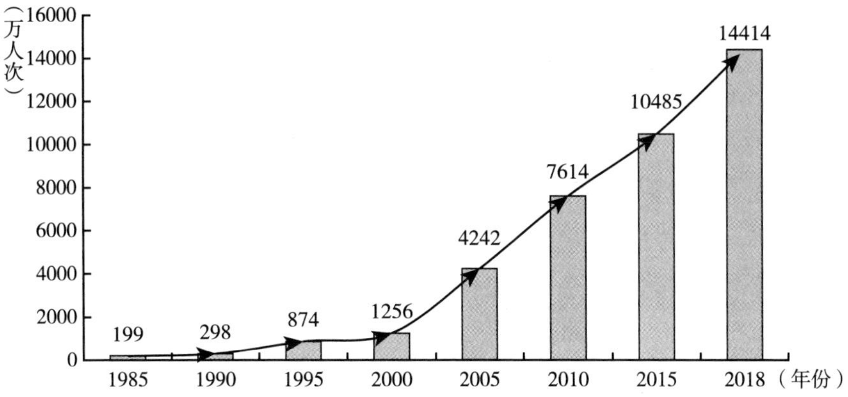

图1　1985～2018 年北京市航空客运量

资料来源：前瞻数据库。

超过了行业平均增长速度（11%）。我国国内的民航得到空前的发展，年均作业约 650 万小时。2020 年我国将初步建成民航强国，旅客运输量将达到 7.2 亿人次，2035 年达到 15 亿人次。这些数字均表明我国民航的蓬勃发展，战略地位日益凸显。在高速增长的经济形势下，可以预测我国未来 30 年内航空业会保持稳步增长的势头。

三　增暖背景下的天气原因导致的航班延误和事故风险升高

21 世纪以来受气候变化、城镇化步伐加快和人口激增等因素的影响，民用航空业风险造成的潜在经济损失呈快速增长态势。其中气候变化背景下的恶劣天气导致航班延误率和事故率居高不下，且缺乏有效的应对措施，加剧了机场公共安全风险。

（一）气候变化背景下的航空延误率趋于增多

国际航协统计了 2009～2013 年全球各地区百万架次航空事故率，其中欧洲、北美洲、南美洲、东亚、东南亚、地中海地区和非洲地区的百万架次航空事故率分别为 0.25、0.19、0.86、0.07、0.64、1.51、6.64。2013 年上述 7 个地区的百万架次航空事故率分别为 0.15、0.32、0.44、0.00、0.70、0.68、0.44。中国民航近 50 多年来，因不利气象条件导致的二等和重大以上飞行事故 40 起，占二等和重大以上飞行事故总数的 31.9%。2012～2016 年我国国内航空公司非正常航班次数明显增加，由 2012 年的 250.2 万班次，增加到 2016 年的 367.9 万班次，增加了 47%。航班延误原因中由天气原因导致的比例由 2012 年的 21.6% 增加到 2016 年的 56.5%。其中由气候变化导致的极端天气事件贡献明显增多，可以避免的比例占到 50% 以上。据中国民航公报显示 2018 年我国因天气原因导致航班不能正常完成的比例达 47.46%。在全世界范围来看，航班不正常起飞，比如航班晚点或延误，75% 以上是由恶劣天气造成的。

（二）极端天气因素导致的航空事故人员和经济损失巨大

航空史上迄今为止最惨重的空难就是由恶劣天气引发的。1977 年 3 月 27 日，加纳利群岛上的特内里费岛洛斯罗德奥斯机场被大雾笼罩，加之当时通信技术、雷达技术落后，两架波音 747 巨无霸客机在跑道上高速相撞，导致了 583 名乘客和机组人员丧生。1993 年 7 月 26 日，韩亚航空 733 号班机从首尔金浦国际机场飞往木浦市，降落前天气却瞬间转差，并伴有强风和暴雨，导致飞机爆炸，66 名乘客及 2 名机组人员死亡。2010 年 4 月 10 日，波兰总统乘坐的飞机由于降落地天气条件恶劣在俄罗斯坠毁，机载 96 人全部遇难。2019 年 5 月 5 日，俄罗斯一架客机从莫斯科谢列梅捷沃机场起飞后起火，飞机随后返航并在机场迫降。这起事故造成了 41 人死亡，事故主要原因是雷击。由此可见由极端天气因素导致的航空业人员伤亡和经济损失巨大。

（三）航班延误导致旅客滞留和公共安全风险增高

在世界各国，民航航班由于偶发机械故障、临时调度变动、天气恶劣等各方面原因延误或者变动航班的现象非常常见。随着我国民用航空的市场总量持续上升，班机延误给乘客带来不便甚至损失的事件也随之增加。气候变化背景下频发的极端天气导致航班延误，通常会造成长时间、大范围的旅客滞留，目前尚没有成熟的旅客滞留应对体制机制和赔偿方案，容易导致旅客和机场管理部门的冲突，如果不妥善处理这些矛盾，不仅影响民航营运，而且不利于社会和谐发展。2016 年 4 月 24 日，因天气原因，湖南长沙黄花机场飞往海南三亚的一个航班未能按时起飞，部分旅客因此情绪激动并与地勤发生冲突。2017年6月10日当天，我国多地出现了大暴雨天气，波及多个省份，华东地区多个机场航班起降被雷雨打乱，当日上海通行能力下降约50%，南京、杭州、广州、长沙等机场均受到影响，大量旅客长时间滞留，同年8月8日上海再度遭遇雷雨天气，通行能力再度下降50%。国际上通行的惯例是航空公司在一定的延误时间范围内，一般而言4小时以内，原则上只需表示歉意。但这并不代表航空公司就可以为所欲为，因为在一个竞争激烈的市场上，延误率比较高的航空公司没有生存的余地。对于国际通行惯例允许的时间范围以内，本来不必赔偿的延误，许多公司也在竞争压力下采取赠送饮料或者餐券的方式来安抚乘客。延误时间太长，航空公司就要承担赔偿责任。当前在我国，航空公司虽然在延误到过夜的情况下向被延误的乘客提供住宿和食品，但是他们并没有赔偿意识。民航总局对顾客24小时以前退票扣多少、24小时以内退票扣多少、两小时以内退票扣多少等都有明确规定。可是由于航班延误给乘客带来的风险，却基本上完全由乘客自己承担。需要注意的是，航空公司给被延误乘客提供的住宿和食品，只是人道的补偿，并不能弥补延误时间经济上的损失。民航服务双方风险补偿的这种不对称性，反映的正是“我单方面向你提供航空服务”的思维。因此，制定明确标准，规范民航服务，使得航空公司和乘客两方面都做到责、赔有据，减少依靠酌情权临时处理的不确定性，已成为刻不容缓的事情。

（四）恶劣天气影响航空工作人员操作事故风险增高

恶劣天气对航空从业人员会造成不良心理影响，容易增加事故风险。同时，航班延误导致的人员滞留问题尚未有成熟的解决机制，加剧了人员冲突和机场安全风险，对公共管理秩序产生恶劣影响。

回顾世界历史上的空难，事故调查和善后处理复杂而且漫长，一次航空事故就足以彻底抵消掉航空公司多年安全运营积攒的声誉，航空公司甚至整个航空业遭遇品牌危机。加之近年来，全球航空业整体走下坡路，航空公司面临安全和效益之间的平衡。因此，必须高度关注增暖背景下的气候变化对我国民航业的影响，将风险减到最小。

四　气候变化对航空业影响形势严峻

（一）增暖背景下的极端天气事件频发影响航空安全

由于全球气候变暖，雷暴、暴雨、冰雹、晴空湍流等极端天气事件频发以及由于大气环流、等压面高度等方面的改变，导致恶劣天气的变异特征增强，影响民航飞机在航路上飞行安全。雷暴、闪电、冰雹和大风四种灾害性对流天气对民航的影响显著，亟待开展增暖背景下的灾害风险评估，以保证运行安全，促进航班正常性和民航服务品质的提高。2017 年 6 月 21 日至 24 日华北、黄淮中东部和东北地区南部自西向东的一次强降雨过程，伴随着雷暴和大风，导致全国 16 家机场遭遇大面积延误，其中仅首都机场就取消航班 703 架次。

（二）全球变暖导致飞机起飞限重天数增加

随着气候变暖，空气会不断扩散，大气密度减小，在更稀薄的空气中，当飞机沿跑道前行时，机翼所产生的升力将会变小。因此，根据飞行器的型号、跑道长度、机场海拔等因素，如果温度过高，满载的飞机在某些时候可能无法安全起飞，必须清除超额重量，否则航班将不得不延误或取消。因此，对于特定机场跑道和特定机型而言，存在一个最高气温阈值，如果机场气温超过这个阈值，飞机的最大理论起飞重量就难以满足起飞条件。飞机起飞必须通过减少乘客或者货物来降低载荷，这无疑会对民航业造成一定的经济损失。

已有研究表明全球变暖导致的气温上升，将使得世界各地许多飞机在未来几十年里更加难以起飞。可见，高温导致的限重天数是量化气候增暖对飞机起飞影响的重要指标。我国学者周天军等基于集合模式预估数据，研究了未来不同温升目标下中国日最高温度变化，并选取北京、上海、昆明、拉萨、乌鲁木齐、香港和广州 7 个典型的民航机场，以波音 737 为例，讨论了温升阈值对这 7 个民航机场飞机最大起飞重量的影响。结果表明：在全球 1.5℃（2℃）温升阈值下，北京、上海、昆明、拉萨、乌鲁木齐等 5 个机场的夏季日最高气温将会增加 1.0℃～2.0℃（1.4℃～3.0℃），其中拉萨的增温幅度最大，这将导致北京、上海、拉萨三个机场的限重天数显著增加，乌鲁木齐机场在 2℃温升背景下将需要限重。其中拉萨机场对增暖最为敏感，在1.5℃和2℃全球温升情景下，拉萨机场的限重天数将由当前的7天分别增加到25天和46天。而香港和广州两地在两种温升背景下的日最高气温增幅差异不大。

气候变暖导致极端热浪的频率和强度增加，观测数据表明全球变暖使得全球80%地区的创纪录热浪发生概率有所提高。2017年7月上海最高气温达到40.9℃，创145年最高纪录。2017年9月，美国湾区多地出现创纪录历史高温，其中旧金山连续两日最高气温达到41℃，打破了自1874年有气温记录以来的历史最高纪录。2017年6月下旬，美国航空公司取消了40多架从亚利桑那州菲尼克斯出发的班机，原因是接近48.8℃的高温导致一些飞机无法起飞。2017年7月20日，由于机场气温异常偏高，导致美国菲尼克斯机场取消了40余架次航班，引起了公众和媒体的高度关注。

（三）增暖背景下雾霾天气增多影响航空安全

气候增暖背景下静稳天气增多，导致雾霾影响飞机飞行安全的风险增高。雾霾天气能见度通常低于10km，且变化缓慢，持续时间长，几乎不受日变化影响，且不容易消散。一方面雾霾天气导致飞机着陆时看不清跑道，使飞机偏离跑道或过早、过迟接地；另一方面雾霾天气导致飞行指挥员看不见飞机，容易造成指挥错误。此外，雾霾天气导致能见度达不到起飞或降落要求，增加了航班延误或取消频率。因此，增暖背景下的雾霾天气增多给航空飞行活动的安全带来了巨大挑战。数据显示，1951～1985年，发生过245次与气象有关的严重飞行事故，其中受能见度影响的47起，占19.2%，仅次于低云。

（四）增暖背景下航班飞行时间增加

全球气候变暖导致飞机飞行时间增加，并导致二氧化碳排放增多。由于全球变暖，飞机穿行的大气环境特征正在发生着变化。气候变化对航空的影响包括增强的湍流和增加的起飞重量限制，也导致了飞行时间的增加。风速是造成91%飞行时间差的原因。已有研究表明，当大气中的二氧化碳浓度加倍时，横渡大西洋的伦敦飞往纽约的航班发生了显著变化，即无论哪个季节，急流风的增强引起了东向航班航行时间显著缩短，而西向航班航行时间显著增加。东向航行缩短的时间和西向航行延长的时间并未相互抵消，而是使得往返航行时间增加。在冬季东西向往返时间增加了近 2 倍，东向航班航行时间约为 5.3 个小时，而西向航班航行时间则超过了 7 个小时。即使未来航班数量没有增加，所有横渡大西洋的航班飞机每年在空中的航行时间将额外增加 2000 小时，将额外燃烧 7200 万加仑的喷气燃料，额外花费近 2200 万美元，并额外排放 7000 千克二氧化碳。根据联合国政府间气候变化专门委员会（IPCC）数据显示，全球航空公司造成了约 3.5% 的温室气体排放，从而导致了气候变化。厄尔尼诺现象也对全球航空业产生了显著影响。太平洋赤道部分的水表层温度变化所产生的大气波会冲向东西半球更高纬度区域，从而改变高纬度环流性质，导致航空飞行时间的变化。已有研究数据显示，美国每天飞行约 3 万个商业航班。如果往返的总飞行时间存在一分钟的变化，商业航班每年在将多出 18.25 万小时飞行时间，导致消耗大约 10 亿加仑的附加喷射燃料，并且导致每年多排放 100 亿千克的二氧化碳。

（五）气候变化导致飞机腐蚀现象加剧

气候变化导致的大气环境变化加剧了飞机的电化学腐蚀、应力腐蚀和高温氧化腐蚀。电化学腐蚀的两个基本条件是电位差和电解质溶液。构成飞机的航空材料多为铝合金，客观上存在电化学腐蚀的可能。由于飞机飞行中时常穿越温度和湿度差异较大的气候带。在气候变化背景下，大气中的二氧化碳和二氧化硫等气体在空气湿度高的地区，会吸附在航空材料表面并发生电离。同时航空器结构连接的间隙，会导致电化学腐蚀蔓延的风险。海洋环境下大量存在的 Cl^- 离子，可以直接穿透目前大部分抗氧化防护涂层而破坏航空材料。同时，飞机穿越气候差异大的地区时容易造成飞机表面的积冰和积水问题，造成应力腐蚀。因此，气候变化导致的飞机电化学腐蚀和应力腐蚀风险将有可能增大。此外，气候变暖后极端高温频发会对飞机发动机产生高温氧化腐蚀，极大地消耗发动机的使用寿命，增加发动机安全风险。

（六）气候变化影响了高高原机场飞机起飞条件

高高原机场，是指海拔高度 2438 米及以上的机场。目前世界上运行中的高高原机场有 25 个，其中我国有 13 个；全球范围内海拔超过 3500 米的高高原机场 11 个，其中我国有 8 个；5 个海拔超过 4000 米的高高原机场，4 个都在我国。这些高高原机场集中在青藏高原和云贵高原，区域环境相比其他地区复杂，净空条件相对较差，天气特征复杂多变，地方性极端天气复杂特点突出，时常发生极端天气现象，极大地增加了航空安全保障的难度。同时高高原机场运行的飞机构型要求特殊。已有研究表明海拔较高地区对气候变化的响应较之低海拔地区敏感。未来随着气候增暖不断加剧，必将导致高高原机场基础设施、设备和起飞条件均产生不同程度变化。

（七）气候变化导致飞机飞行颠簸频率增多

气候变暖导致飞机遭遇晴空湍流现象频发，使得飞行更颠簸，甚至造成人员伤亡。二氧化碳增多会导致飞机遭遇晴空湍流现象频发。30000 英尺以上湍流源于高速气流带来的涡流与不稳定气流。高速气流是相对较窄、自西向东围绕地球的气流带，南北半球各有两条。高速气流跟随热带气团与极地气团的等温线传播，而气候变暖加快了高速气流的传播。不同强度的晴空湍流导致的飞行颠簸对旅客的影响不同。目前全球大气中二氧化碳的平均浓度是 400ppm，预计 21 世纪末期二氧化碳浓度将上升到 560ppm，是工业化之前水平的两倍。这将导致晴空湍流增多，飞机颠簸频率上升，其中轻度颠簸上升 59%，轻至中度颠簸上升 75%，重度颠簸将上升 149%。这意味着旅客将面临更多打翻饮料的困扰，听到更多系好安全带的警告。重度颠簸甚至会造成人员伤亡，必将给航空业带来严峻挑战。

五　航空业对气候变化的影响不容乐观

航空业也对气候变化产生显著影响。

首先，航空业产生的二氧化碳加剧了全球气候变暖和区域环境问题。其次，航空器的尾气排放导致酸雨和烟雾的大量形成。最后，航空业加剧了雾霾天气的发生。飞机由于自重大、耗油量大，其污染排放量也相当大。

此外，值得注意的是，航空业的社会认识是高端产业，以飞机为核心的临空经济区利益复杂，治理手段有限，而且目前技术手段有限，对高空污染物排放检测困难。而航空业近几十年来在航油和速度等技术上突破甚微，已步入中端产业和污染治理中的低端产业。

六　我国亟须开展气候变化对航空影响的科学评估

气象保障对于民航业尤为重要，越来越多的国家和组织正在采取行动，以适应和培养恢复力，抵御气候变化对航空业产生的影响。由于空中导航要求（例如安全、环境、经济、能力）相互冲突，运营计划并非总能发挥出全部潜力。在国际上，气候变化对民航业的影响逐渐受到重视。美国国家科学院于2012年颁布了《机场气候适应和恢复力》科学报告；欧洲航空安全组织（EUROCONTROL）也于2013年出台了题为“气候变化风险和恢复力”的评估报告。国际科学界围绕气候变化对航空业的影响问题的研究近年来亦不断有大量成果涌现，科学认知不断加深。而我国尚未有相应评估报告问世。在1880~2012年，全球陆地和海洋平均表面温度升高了0.85℃。1900~2015年，中国表面温度呈现（0.121℃±0.009℃）/10年的增温趋势。伴随平均温度的升高，极端天气和气候事件频发且强度不断增强。如何适应这种变化是包括航空业在内的社会各界必须面对的问题。伴随全球温度的升高，极端天气和气候事件等对民航业的影响越发显著，而关于气候变化对我国民航业的影响问题，国内目前的认知水平尚存在不足。受限于历史资料的获取和气候模式的水平，相关研究工作尚处于探索性阶段，因此，航空气象和气候变化的综合评估工作，亟待加强而且已经迫在眉睫，急需从其他行业吸收更广泛的专业知识和创新方法，创造潜在的新机会，以解决航空活动对环境的影响。

七　对策建议

2017年我国通用航空飞行小时数仅不到美国的3%，甚至明显落后于巴西和南非等发展中国家，发展严重滞后和不平衡。随着我国社会经济的发展，民航业发展潜力巨大。未来10~15年，中国民航仍将处于中高速发展阶段。因此，气象部门必须抓住民航发展机遇期，以“智慧气象”为理念，以“安全航空”为目标，以“气候变化”为抓手，全面参与到民航的发展建设中。主要建议如下。

（1）以军民融合战略为抓手，在充分考虑气候变化的基础上，三方协同科学规划未来新建机场布局。气候变化以其多样化的方式从功能和结构方面影响着航空业。在全面开展气候变化对航空业影响评估的基础上，需要高度关注气候变化对新建机场的多样性和复杂性影响，合理布局和规划民用和军用航空机场。中国气象局、中国民用航空局和军方需要协同合作，通过顶层设计、科学高效规划促进未来新建机场的安全运营。

（2）以中国气象局和中国民航部门为主，深化航空气象数据共享平台建设。虽然我国民航已建立了面向运输航空的基本气象服务体系，气象信息服务和天气预报能力不断提升，但仍存在民航气象信息共享不充分等问题，亟须利用互联网技术实现民航气象数据共享，提升气象服务能力，优化服务品质。因此，亟须以中国气象局和中国民航部门为主，通过协同设计、协同实施和协同推广来有序推动航空气象数据共享平台建设。

（3）系统开展气候变化对航空业影响的综合评估和区划工作，基于区块链技术搭建多方协同参与的航空气象服务平台。此外以中国气象局为核心的我国气象部门需要全面参与到我国新建机场规划中，新建机场需要充分考虑气候变化对飞机起飞的影响，并开展不同地区和季节民用航空的风险评估和区划工作，基于区块链技术尽快搭建多方协同参与的信息化程度高、资源集中、功能全面的航空气象服务平台。

（4）大力开发各类航空气象指数保险。采用非工程措施中的金融手段，大力发展各类航空气象指数保险，化解因气候变化导致的航空业长期风险。针对特殊航班运输任务，还应通过再保险手段进行风险转移。

（5）制定针对航班延误的详细可操作性的规范。航空公司通过顶层设计，逐步规范航班延误后的各项补偿性措施，建立具有行业条例功能的可操作保障规范。

（6）高度重视航空业污染物排放对雾霾产生的影响。目前北京正在建设的新机场位于北京城区出风口。一旦遭遇强劲北风，城区污染加剧。因此，需要全面深入研究飞机及临空经济区污染物排放在雾霾产生中的机理及其占比。

（7）定期对航空服务人员开展增暖背景下飞机飞行和地勤服务中新显现风险的应对培训。长期接触飞机噪声会产生各种健康风险，包括缺血性心脏病、睡眠障碍、烦躁和认知障碍等。以中国气象局、中国民航培训系统和医疗部门为核心，通过相互合作，优势互补，取长补短，开展变化环境背景下的新型风险应对培训。除应急技能培训外，尤其应增加空乘服务人员在恶劣环境下的心理调节培训。

综上所述，当前形势下，我国航空业一方面要加强自身能力建设，提高整个民航运输业和制造业绿色低碳发展能力及影响力；另一方面，也需要进一步统筹我国气候变化谈判，加大相应研究与参与谈判的力度，促进国际机制的公平性，有效维护国家整体利益和有关行业发展权益。

参考文献

[1] 周璞、张恬月、刘晓达：《成都双流机场跑道视程与低能见度的关系》，《陕西气象》2018 年第 3 期，第 20 ~ 24 页。

[2] 中国民用航空局：《2017 年民航行业发展统计公报》，2017。

B.25
国家中心城市建设与现代都市圈的协同发展
——以郑州为例

尚永珍*

摘　要： 在国家中心城市和都市圈建设双重战略叠加下，郑州面临前所未有的机遇和挑战，如何借力国家中心城市建设带动郑州都市圈快速协同发展极具探讨意义。本文通过对国家中心城市促进区域经济发展的机理分析，借鉴国外成熟都市圈发展的经验启示，探讨郑州在加快自身发展的同时带动周边地区发展的办法，为国家中心城市建设和现代都市圈的培育提供可借鉴的经验。

关键词： 国家中心城市　郑州都市圈　中心—外围　增长极

都市圈是城市发展到一定阶段的产物，是由中心城市和一定地理范围内的周边城市所组成的一种组团式新型城市发展模式。这种发展理念提倡使用城市间协同优化的区域共生模式取代单个城市相互独立、各自为政的发展方式，以便通过圈内合理的产业分工、公共服务资源最大限度地共享以及各种资源要素的无障碍自由流通实现更大区域范围的规模效应和集聚效应。2019 年 2 月，国家发改委印发《国家发展改革委关于培育发展现代化都市圈的指导意见》，指导意见中列出都市圈建设的具体时间表，提出 2020 年都市圈同城化取得明显进展，2035 年形成若干具有影响力的都市圈。从城镇化到城市群，从城市群到都市圈，我国的区域发展战略一步步细化。

---

* 尚永珍，中国社会科学院研究生院区域经济学博士生，主要从事区域经济研究。

建设国家中心城市是新时期国家促进区域协调发展和全面对外开放的又一重大战略，截至2018年2月，我国已对北京、天津、上海、广州、重庆、成都、武汉、郑州、西安9座城市明确提出建设国家中心城市的规划。这9座城市不仅肩负着国家中心城市建设的任务，同样也是都市圈发展的主力军，分别是我国已经成熟或初具规模的都市圈的中心城市。建设国家中心城市与培育发展现代化都市圈是我国区域协同发展方针指导下的两大具体战略，两者互为补充、相互促进。都市圈的发展状态很大程度上取决于中心城市势能的强弱，国家中心城市位于城镇体系的最高层，兼具对外开放和对内引领双重功能，国家中心城市的建设可以为都市圈培育具有强大经济势能和对外辐射能力的中心城市。同样国家中心城市的建设离不开强大腹地的有力支撑，培育发展现代化的都市圈，通过中心城市辐射效应的发挥带动周边城市融合发展，为国家中心城市功能的提升和完备奠定区域基础。

郑州都市圈又称郑州大都市区，位于中原城市群内部，依据国务院2016年批复的《中原城市群发展规划》，郑州都市圈范围包括河南省的郑州、开封、新乡、焦作、许昌5座地级市，面积31226平方公里。2016年12月26日，国家发改委印发《促进中部地区崛起“十三五”规划》，正式批复郑州建设国家中心城市。在国家中心城市和都市圈建设双重战略叠加下，郑州面临前所未有的机遇和挑战，如何借力国家中心城市建设带动郑州都市圈快速协同发展极具探讨意义。

国外关于中心对外围影响的讨论可以追溯到佩鲁（Perroux F.）的增长极理论，该理论认为经济增长通常是从一个或数个“增长中心”逐渐向其他部门或地区传导的，因此应选择特定的空间作为增长极以带动经济的发展。缪尔达尔（Myrdal）运用循环累积因果理论解释了区域经济发展不平衡问题，认为中心城市与周边城市之间既有回流效应也有扩散效应。弗里德曼（J. Friedman）提出“核心—边缘”理论，阐述了核心区与边缘区之间的相互作用和扩散的理论。克鲁格曼（Krugman）在梳理前人理论的基础上，建立了两部门的中心—外围模型，认为集聚的力量来自规模经济。还有国外学者通过对特别区域的分析，考察了中心与外围之间的关系。Richardson H W. 发现中心城市的扩散作用需在其成熟期才能发挥。Hughes 使用投入产出模型检验了华盛顿中心—外围的关系。Henry etc. 研究了美国和欧洲的城乡间作用，认为中心城市区的辐射作用强于回流作用。

中心与外围之间相互关系的研究，同样是我国区域经济学界研究的热点。一部分学者讨论了行政区域中心城市对周边区域经济发展的影响。柯善咨发现省会和地级中心城市对下级市县的经济增长有显著的回流效应。朱虹等对比北京和上海，发现北京以“空吸”效应为主，上海以“反哺”效应为主。伴随着城市群和都市圈等新型城市结构的发展，以城市群和都市圈为地域范围的实证研究逐渐展开。金祥荣和赵雪娇、王贤斌和吴子谦研究发现以城市群为尺度，中心城市发展对外围城市的经济增长呈现正向溢出效应。中心城市溢出效应的机理分析也是中心和外围关系研究中的一个重点，不同学者得出不同结论。程水红和曾菊新研究发现中心城市的技术扩散对区域经济增长均有显著的正向影响。何龙斌和李强认为中心城市的经济发展水平是影响边缘地区接受经济辐射的重要因素，产业结构和功能定位也会对其辐射能力产生影响。许治以北京和上海为例，认为国家中心城市对外有效的知识溢出是发挥其引领功能重要的路径。高玲玲基于新古典增长模型建模说明了中心城市影响区域经济的作用机制，认为中心城市通过资源配置效应和外部性效应影响整个地区的经济增长。阳国亮等发现在国家中心城市建设过程中产生的交易成本降低和市场开放度增强能显著促进区域协同增长。

一　国家中心城市促进区域经济发展的机理分析

国家中心城市的功能定位是世界城市体系的节点和国家战略布局在全国的空间支点，相对一般的区域中心城市具有更强大的辐射效应，能够通过多种机制在都市圈内起到引领、带动作用。

（一）知识溢出和技术扩散机制

马歇尔（Marshall）指出外部性是企业空间集聚的原因，索罗（Romer）的内生经济增长理论提出知识空间外溢导致规模报酬递增从而促进区域经济增长。与传统的物质资本投入相比，基于知识溢出和技术扩散的技术外部性是企业获得规模报酬的重要途径，也是中心带动外围，发挥中心引领功能的重要途径。国家中心城市是全国的科技创新中心，高端人才、一流高校、科研院所、企业总部集聚，创新科研成果丰富，相对一般的中心城市而言具有更强的知识溢出和技术扩散能力，能够为周边城市的发展提供智力支持，从而形成科技创新与经济增长的良性互动机制。

（二）降低交易成本机制

新经济地理学认为交易成本的高低是决定产业集聚和扩散的重要力量，都市圈的交易成本主要表现为货物的运输成本、人才的流动成本以及制度交易成本，国家中心城市强大的交通枢纽功能能够有效降低都市圈外部及内部的交易成本。首先，国家中心城市作为连接国内外的交通节点，缩短了地区间的空间距离，增强了都市圈与国内外的连通性，以高效便捷的运输方式降低货物的运输成本、人才的流动成本。其次，在都市圈内部，受制于行政区划限制形成的行政壁垒是阻碍都市圈协同发展的最大障碍，国家中心城市通过与周边城市的互联互通增强了城市间的经济联系，资源要素在圈内的自由流通具有降低行政壁垒产生的制度交易成本的功能。

（三）参与国际分工协作机制

我国制造业长期处于全球价值链的低端环节，通过人口红利和环境代价来换取经济的发展。国家中心城市是全球资源配置和产业分工体系的重要功能节点，代表国家参与国际分工与国际合作，是我国参与国际竞争与合作的重要平台。国家中心城市产业发展逐步转向高级化，国际影响力和竞争力日益提升，参与国际市场分工协作竞争日益频繁，正逐步转向全球价值链的中高端环节。其在国际分工的地位和深度融入国际的能力对都市圈内部其他城市的产业定位产生积极的影响，带动周边城市共同融入全球价值链。同时国家中心城市强大的科技创新能力能够提升周边产业的技术内涵，减少其对成本和资源环境的依赖性，在人口红利逐渐消失、资源环境承载能力接近上限的大背景下逐步摆脱其在国际分工中的劣势地位，实现在全球价值链分工地位的攀升。

二　国外都市圈发展的经验

纽约与东京为世界级的国家中心城市，也是两大都市圈的中心城市，对纽约都市圈与东京都市圈发展经验的总结，对于我国更好地发挥中心城市，尤其是国家中心城市对于都市圈发展的引领带动作用具有现实意义。

（一）强集聚与辐射能力的中心城市

东京是国际金融中心和日本政治、经济、文化中心，纽约是美国第一大城市、世界经济中心，也是世界三大金融中心之一，均具有强大的集聚力和辐射能力。强集聚能力是中心城市自身壮大发展、发挥辐射能力的前提，强辐射能力是中心城市作为圈内的经济增长极，发挥引领扩散功能、促进区域协调发展的基本要求。纽约都市圈和东京都市圈的发展经验均表明，中心城市与周边城市一般均遵循集聚—扩散—再集聚—再扩散的互动发展路径，初期是制造业的集聚，成熟期是生产性服务业的集聚，通过不断的循环往复促进整个都市圈的发展。例如，东京从最初的小渔村在 20 世纪 50 年代成为制造业的集聚地，80 年代开始东京由制造业中心转为经济中心，逐渐发展成为国际金融中心，是圈内经济实力最强、规模最大的国际型大都市。在这一过程中，东京不仅发展成为都市圈的经济核心，也不断带动周边城市产业的发展。

（二）完备的城市等级体系

都市圈的协同发展需要强大的中心城市，也需圈内处于不同等级的次中心城市、中小城市与之共同形成完备的城市等级体系，支撑都市圈的发展。规模大小不同、功能定位差异化的不同城市在都市圈内依据各自的绝对优势和相对优势形成了互补的经济发展方式。例如纽约都市圈以纽约为中心，以费城、波士顿、华盛顿为次中心，周边区域为中小城市，这些城市间经济联系紧密，分工不同。纽约形成以华尔街为代表的金融中心，费城为制造业中心，波士顿为科技与教育中心，华盛顿为全美的政治、文化中心。

（三）便捷的轨道交通

区域间便捷的交通网络体系是都市圈发展的基础，纽约都市圈与东京都市圈均形成了四通八达的网络化交通系统，但两者因人口密度不同，交通模式并不完全相同。纽约都市圈以公路和区域铁路为主，东京都市圈以轻轨、地铁、新干线组成的轨道交通为主，相比较而言，东京都市圈的交通网络布局对我国都市圈的发展更具借鉴意义。轨道交通是东京都市圈的枢纽，在东京市内及市郊之间主要由地铁、铁路干线和市郊铁路系统相互衔接，中心与周边之间主要通过铁路干线和城际高速公路连接。东京都市圈内轨道交通的长度和密度位居世界之首，采取放射线与环线相结合的方式，形成了密如蛛网但井然有序的交通运营网络，加快了都市圈内人口和要素的自由流动和资源要素在更大空间范围内的合理配置，从而为促进都市圈内合理的产业分工和城市功能定位奠定了基础。

三　郑州带动都市圈协同发展中存在的主要问题

（一）城市人口经济规模偏小、产业结构有待优化

中心城市经济和人口规模体现城市的集聚程度，是辐射效应发挥的基础，产业结构是否高端化决定中心与外围之间究竟是竞争关系还是合作关系。郑州市 2018 年地区生产总值 10143.3 亿元，全市年末总人口 1013.6 万人，首次全市地区生产总值突破万亿元，常住人口突破千万人，这对于郑州来说是里程碑式的进步，但 GDP 在全国排名第十七位，在 9 座国家中心城市中这两项指标排名仅高于西安，位列第八。从首位度来看，2018 年郑州 GDP 占河南省的 21%，人口占河南省的 9%，同期武汉都市圈的中心城市武汉，GDP 占湖北省的 38%，人口占湖北省的 19%。对比分析可以看出，郑州在河南省的首位度明显偏低。从产业结构来看，2018 年三次产业结构为 1.45∶43.88∶54.67，已经形成“三、二、一”的产业结构，但与其他中心城市相比，第三产业占比仍然相对偏低，制造业依然是郑州市的支柱产业。中心城市制造业占比较高易造成中心与外围之间竞争关系大于合作关系，不利于中心与外围之间形成分工协作、优势互补的产业模式。

（二）科技创新能力依然是最大的短板

无论是对照国家中心城市的功能要求还是与其他国家中心城市进行横向对比，科技创新能力都是郑州作为经济增长极的最大短板，创新能力的缺乏严重制约郑州对周边城市外溢效应的发挥。城市的科技创新能力主要涵盖创新资源、要素投入两方面。创新资源是城市科技创新能力存量的反映，一般使用

985 和 211 高校数量以及科研平台数量进行衡量，郑州市内虽然高校众多，但仅有郑州大学一所 211 高校。依据科技部最新公布的《2016 年国家重点实验室年度报告》，也仅有 1 个国家重点实验室，为国家中心城市中创新资源拥有数量最少的城市。要素投入是城市科技创新能力增量的反映，2017 年郑州市 R&D 投入强度为 1.74%，不仅没有达到全国 2.12% 的水平，与地理邻近的国家中心城市西安 4.82% 的投入强度也存在较大的差距。

（三）与周边城市协同发展机制有待完善

郑州对周边城市带动作用的发挥既取决于郑州自身经济势能的强弱，也与协同发展机制的完善与否密切相关。行政樊篱一直是我国区协同发展难以逾越的一大鸿沟，其根源还在于我国行政考核机制不健全所形成的不同行政区域之间的利益竞争机制。官员的晋升激励机制使得各地官员具有发展本地经济的强烈愿望，而忽视与周边地区的合作，加上市场机制尚不完善，难以通过市场力量形成跨行政区域的经济合作。即使在政府推动的跨区域经济合作中，合作双方因缺乏激励机制，往往经济发展状况好的一方主动性较低，合作框架与协议成为形式，并未落到实处。以郑汴一体化为例，自 2005 年被列入《河南省国民经济和社会发展第十一个五年规划纲要》以来，交通、通信、金融等多方面同城化快速形成，但深层次的产业对接仍有待发展。

（四）圈内城市间的连通性不强

交通是城市发展的翅膀，世界成熟的都市圈都很好地解决了交通的问题，建立了与其经济规模、人口数量相适应的立体交通体系。与其他国家中心城市相比，交通枢纽优势是郑州最具有竞争力的优势，但郑州连通四方的优势并未成为郑州都市圈的最大优势，主要原因在于圈内城市间基础设施的互联互通还没有达到应有的契合程度。从圈内的公路网建设来看，郑州都市圈内以平原为主，公路的建设条件得天独厚，已经形成高速公路、国省干线、县乡公路等都市圈多层次公路网，汽车是都市圈内许多居民的主要出行方式，但是各城市的连接点之间依然存在许多“瓶颈路”“断头路”，严重降低了都市圈的路网连通程度，对周边区域的发展形成一定制约。从轨道交通建设情况来看，郑州都市圈内轨道交通还处于发展建设中。郑州与开封、焦作之间已经形成“铁路、高速铁路、城际铁路”多种轨道交通并行的交通格局，但郑州与新乡、许昌之间的城际铁路尚未开通，且开封、焦作、新乡、许昌之间并无便捷的轨道交通连接。

四　以国家中心城市建设为契机，促进郑州都市圈协同发展的建议

国家中心城市建设是强化郑州带动功能，提升都市圈核心竞争力的重要突破口，因此应以国家中心城市建设为契机，强优势、补短板，促进郑州都市圈的协同发展。

（一）促进规模膨胀与产业结构高端化

纽约都市圈和东京都市圈的发展历程均证明强大的中心城市是都市圈发展的重要助推力，郑州今后面临的两个重要任务，一是做大首位度，二是加快产业高端化速度。也就是说未来郑州规模的提升不是简单的数量提升，而是要在增加数量的同时注重质量的优化，面临规模膨胀和转型升级的双重重任。

做大首位度首先要借力“区位优势”“政策扶持”“人口红利”及“郑州航空港建设”，加快郑州地区生产总值增长，并以地区生产总值的增长带动人口的增加。其次，要加快推进中牟、新郑、荥阳市三地撤县设区工作，破解郑州城区面积小的矛盾，撤县设区不仅可以为郑州提供更大的发展空间，而且可以增强都市圈内城市间的连通性，促进一体化发展。

加快产业高端化发展。应以先进制造业和现代服务业为主线，结合产业新领域，创新机制体制，以开放创新的理念促进郑州核心产业的快速发展，提升对周边产业的引领和服务能力。依托郑州航空港建设，大力发展航空物流、电子信息、跨境贸易、高端制造等高端临空产业，并吸引更多的企业总部、研发机构、物流中心、金融机构在郑州集聚，尤其是大力发展金融服务业，进一步加快郑州作为区域金融中心的建设步伐。

（二）增强创新引领发展能力

尽快补齐科技创新短板，既是郑州自身发展壮大的唯一途径，也是发挥辐射周边、带动区域发展的必由之路。针对目前郑州创新能力薄弱的现状，要通

过体制创新、方法创新吸引更多高端要素集聚，充分发挥后发优势，迎头赶上。一是要采取开放性的思维，尽其所能为高层次人才在社会保障、创新就业、住房补贴等多方面提供具有吸引力的优惠政策，在全国“人才大战”中赶超其他国家中心城市，抢占人才竞争制高点。二是充分发挥郑州交通枢纽优势，加强与国内科研院所的科技创新合作，吸引国内一流高校、科研机构在郑州建立分校、分支结构，借他山之石，琢郑州发展之玉，以多种形式弥补郑州人才短板。三是加大全社会 R&D 经费投入强度，尽快达到全国平均水平，在具体操作时应突出以企业为主体，以市场为导向的产学研深度结合，加速科研成果的产业化，深入推进创新驱动发展战略。

（三）探索区域经济合作新路径

郑州市是中原区域经济发展的中心，周边城市是郑州建设国家中心城市的重要经济腹地和支撑地，因此郑州应从大思维角度出发，突破制度障碍，积极探索、推动区域经济合作新路径，切实担当起“领头羊”的重任。首先，郑州应积极主动，与周边城市探索建立合理的利益分享机制。长久的区域经济合作是建立在双方共赢的基础上的，并不以牺牲任何一方的利益为代价，中心城市产业外迁至周边城市是区域经济合作最直接有效的方式，因此应遵循市场规律建立合理的利益分享机制，深化产业对接。其次，应由郑州牵头设立高效的协调机构，并在相关部门之间建立长效的对接机制。地方间政府的合作是一个从探索到逐渐规范的过程，在这期间畅通的协同运行机制是深化合作的有力保障，尤其是中心城市的协调工作中工作量大、任务重。因此，郑州应积极作为、勇于担当，形成强化工作落实的有效机制，通过平等协商调解政府间的各种分歧，有效而务实地推进都市圈的协同发展。

（四）推进交通一体化建设

推进郑州都市圈交通一体化，既有利于连通郑州发挥引领带动作用的交通渠道，也有利于都市圈内要素的自由流动和产业分工更加协调。依据都市圈目前基础设施建设状况，应从畅通公路网、推进城际铁路建设两方面加快推进郑州都市圈交通一体化。首先，从都市圈整体规划角度出发，对“断头路”和“瓶颈路”进行排查，加快对“瓶颈路”的扩容改造和“断头路”的连通，提升公路网络的联通程度。其次，推进城际铁路建设。借鉴东京都市圈轨道交通建设经验，科学编制城市轨道交通规划，既不能止步不前，也不能盲目推进，应确保轨道交通发展规划与郑州都市圈的实际需求相匹配，统筹布局城际铁路线路和站点。

参考文献

［1］Richardson, Harry W. "Growth pole spillovers: The Dynamics of Backwash and Spread," *Regional Studies*, 1976, 10 (1): 1 - 9.

［2］D. W. Hughes, D. W. holland, "Core - Periphery Economic Linkage: A Measure of Spread and Possible Backwash Effects for the Washington Economy," *Land Economics*, 1994 (3).

［3］Henry M S, Schmitt B, Kristensen K, et al. "Extending Carlino Mills Models to Examine Urban Size and Growth Impacts on Proximate Rural Areas," *Growth and Change*, 1999 (30): 26 - 48.

［4］柯善咨：《中国城市与区域经济增长的扩散回流与市场区效应》，《经济研究》2009 年第 8 期，第 85 ~ 98 页。

［5］朱虹、徐琰超、尹恒：《空吸抑或反哺：北京和上海的经济辐射模式比较》，《世界经济》2012 年第 3 期，第 111 ~ 124 页。

［6］金祥荣、赵雪娇：《中心城市的溢出效应与城市经济增长——基于中国城市群 2000 ~ 2012 年市级面板数据的经验研究》，《浙江大学学报》（人文社会科学版）2016 年第 5 期，第 170 ~ 181 页。

［7］王贤彬、吴子谦：《城市群中心城市驱动外围城市经济增长》，《产业经济评论》2018 年第 26（03）期，第 56 ~ 73 页。

［8］程水红、曾菊新：《中心城市技术空间扩散与经济增长实证分析——以海峡西岸经济区为例》，《经济地理》2017 年第 10 期。

［9］何龙斌、李强：《中心城市经济辐射机理与边缘地区接受辐射的实现条件》，《陕西理工大学学报》（社会科学版）2018 年第 5 期，第 7 ~ 13 + 32 页。

［10］许治：《国家中心城市技术扩散与区域经济增长——以北京、上海为例》，《科研管理》2013 年第 4 期，第 16 ~ 23 页。

［11］高玲玲：《中心城市与区域经济增长：理论与实证》，《经济问题探索》2015 年第 1 期。

［12］阳国亮、程皓、欧阳慧：《国家中心城市建设能促进区域协同增长吗》，《财经科学》2018 年第 5 期。

B.26
国家中心城市绿色发展评价指标体系研究

高 昕*

摘 要： 推动国家中心城市绿色发展具有重大的战略意义。本文围绕国家中心城市的战略定位，借鉴已有研究成果，构建绿色生产、绿色生活、绿色生态三个方面，涵盖32个具体测评指标的国家中心城市绿色发展评价指标体系。本研究采用综合指数法，依据现有9个国家中心城市统计年鉴、国民经济和社会发展统计公报数据，定量测度国家中心城市的绿色发展水平。结果显示，目前我国现有的9个国家中心城市的绿色发展水平差异性显著，其原因在于绿色发展理念、政策与技术供给的差异性。为此，推动国家中心城市绿色发展应在理念更新、政策供给、技术创新三个方面持续发力。

关键词： 国家中心城市 绿色发展 绿色生产 绿色生活

城市是人类文明的重要标志，城市的形成与发展既是人类占有改造自然环境的过程，也是人类认同适应自然环境的过程。国家中心城市作为国家发展战略的重要平台和战略支点，集中了空间、人口、资源、要素等优势，承载着率先践行新发展理念、引领区域协调发展、参与国际竞争合作、彰显国家综合实力等战略功能。截至2017年底，我国现有的9个国家中心城市的常住人口已经占到全国总人口的11.01%；在经济规模上，这9个城市的GDP总量占全国

---

* 高昕，经济学博士，黄河科技学院商学院副教授，研究方向为产业经济、农业农村发展。

GDP的比重达到19.4%；在人均GDP上，这9个城市的人均GDP是全国人均水平的1.76倍；在GDP增速上，这9个城市的GDP增长速度大多数超过全国平均水平；在财政收入上，这9个城市的一般公共预算收入占全国一般公共预算总收入的比重达到13.07%；在城镇化率上，这9个城市的常住人口城镇化率是全国平均水平的1.33倍。这些城市在经济社会发展的各项指标方面大多数走在全国前列，有些城市已跻身到全国乃至全球经济竞争力最强的城市行列，在我国区域和城镇发展中的“中心地位”已初步形成，并呈现加速发展的态势，其引领发展功能、国际竞争能力、辐射带动作用得到了充分彰显、提升与发挥。随着城市化进程的加速推进，加快推进国家中心城市绿色发展已经成为时代主题，这不仅是国家中心城市自身建设的应有之义，也是发挥其引领示范作用的重要途径。构建国家中心城市绿色发展评价指标体系，衡量国家中心城市绿色发展质量、监测国家中心城市绿色发展进程、引导国家中心城市绿色发展方向、识别国家中心城市绿色发展过程中的重大问题，具有重要的现实意义和理论价值。

近年来，随着绿色发展理念逐步深入人心，国内外一些机构和学者开始尝试构建城市绿色发展指标体系。2004年，欧盟围绕数量、质量、使用、规划发展管理四个方面构建了涵盖64个具体指标的城市绿色空间综合评价指标体系。2009年，美国绿色建筑委员会等构建了绿色社区认证体系，依据评价得分把社区分为认证级、银级、金级和铂金级四个层次。2011年，日本可持续建筑联合会提出了城市建成环境效率综合评价体系，采用5分制的形式评价城市建成环境效率。2011年，经济学人智库提出了包括8大类29项指标的绿色城市指数。上述这些国外城市绿色发展评价指标体系为构建中国城市绿色发展评价指标体系提供了有益的参考，但在构建中国国家中心城市绿色发展指标时，我们也需要立足中国基本国情，结合国家中心城市特殊的功能定位，甄别借鉴。

国内城市绿色发展起步较晚，其评价指标体系目前尚处在探索阶段。2011年，住房和城乡建设部等部委提出了绿色低碳重点小城镇建设评价指标（试行），构建了涵盖经济社会发展、土地资源利用、公共服务水平等7个类型62个具体指标的评价指标体系。2012年，北京师范大学联合有关单位，提出了中国绿色发展指数的概念，在城市层面设置了经济增长绿化度、资源环境承载力、政府政策支持度3个方面的43个指标。2016年，国家发展改革委员会、环境保护部等部门构建了涵盖资源利用、环境治理、生态保护、环境质量、绿色生活、增长质量、公众满意度7个方面56个绿色发展指标体系。同年，还出台了生态文明建设考核目标体系。2017年，国家标准化管理委员会从绿色生产、绿色生活和环境质量三个方面，选择12个二级指标、65个三级指标构建了绿色城市评价指标体系。在上述这些城市绿色发展指标体系中，住房和城乡建设部等发布的绿色低碳重点小城镇建设评价指标（试行）侧重于小城镇绿色发展评价，且定性指标多，定量指标少，可操作性欠佳。北京师范大学发布的中国绿色发展指数对城市产业发展关注多、对生态环境关注少，系统性表现不足。国家发展和改革委员会等部门发布的绿色发展指标体系和生态文明建设考核目标体系是中国生态文明建设评价考核的重要依据，可作为中国绿色城市指标体系构建的重要参考；国家标准化管理委员会发布的绿色城市评价指标具有系统性和完整性的特征，但缺乏不同类型、不同区域、不同阶段城市的差异性考量。此外，近年来，也有一些地方政府结合区域特征提出了相应的城市绿色发展评价指标体系，如上海市绿色发展指标体系、山东省绿色发展指标体系、陕西省绿色生态城区指标体系、安徽省绿色生态城市建设指标体系、成都市绿色发展指标体系等。还有一些学者以特定区域或城市为对象，构建了相应的城市绿色发展指标体系，主要包括邵全等的绿色北京指标体系（2015）、王婉晶等的绿色南京城市建设评价指标体系（2012）、耿直的长江上游四省市绿色发展评价指标（2019）、王国力和韩慧慧的京津冀地区城市绿色发展评价指标体系（2019）、马骍的云南省绿色经济发展评价指标体系（2018）、肖春梅和朱萍萍的新疆绿色发展评价指标体系（2018）、李雪的四川省绿色发展评价指标体系（2018）等。这些评价指标体系多是从特定区域或城市的实际情况出发构建的指标体系，具有一定的实用性和地域特色，但是各地区数据的统计口径和计算方法差异较大，不利于全国城市的评价和对比，具有一定的地域局限性。

国家中心城市作为我国城镇体系规划设置的最高层级，在引领绿色发展中发挥着极为重要的战略引领作用，目前我国9个国家中心城市虽然在总体战略定位上有共同之处，但在具体功能定位上却承载着不同的任务，且不同的国家中心城市因区位分布、文化背景、资源要素、禀赋条件、发展水平等的悬殊，其绿色发展任务、方向、路径等也各不相同。基于此，本文以9个国家中心城市为对象，构建其绿色发展评价指标体系，解析国家中心城市绿色发展水平及制约因素，掌握国家中心城市绿色发展现状，为深入贯彻落实“四个全面”战略布局，践行五大发展理念，推动国家中心城市高质量发展提供理论决策参考。

一　国家中心城市绿色发展评价指标的构建

（一）国家中心城市绿色发展的理论内涵

国家中心城市作为全国城镇体系的核心城市，是科技、金融、产业、生态、文化、交通、信息的中心和枢纽，具有全国范围的中心性和一定区域的国际性的基本特征以及引领、辐射和集散功能。与一般城市相比，国家中心城市在推动城乡融合发展、产业转型升级、人与自然和谐相处等方面发挥着更强大的引领示范、辐射带动作用。同时，由于国家中心城市都是人口、资源、交通等密集区，其生态环境问题高度敏感，是绿色发展最为前沿的阵地，其绿色发展状况既关乎自身的可持续发展，也直接影响和引领着整个国家绿色发展的方向与趋势。绿色发展作为一种发展方式的变革，涉及经济、社会、生态等诸多子系统，每个子系统之间相互联系又相互独立，其中经济系统、社会系统、生态系统的基础分别是生产、生活和环境。因此，城市绿色发展在某种意义上是城市绿色生产、绿色生活与绿色生态的集合，城市绿色生产、生活、生态的发展水平在一定程度上反映了城市绿色发展的绩效。

绿色生产是国家中心城市绿色发展的前提基础。生产是经济社会发展的前提与基础，没有生产就无从谈起发展。绿色生产以资源利用、动能培育、产出形态的绿色化为标志。衡量城市绿色生产水平需要从资源利用效率、产业结构形态、绿色动能培育等方面予以衡量。绿色生活是国家中心城市绿色发展的重要表现。城市生活的绿色化既是城市绿色发展目标之一，也是城市绿色发展的客观呈现。城市居民的收入水平、预期寿命、物资供给、文化产品、服务保障、消费理念等一方面构成了城市发展的重要目标，另一方面也反映了城市实现自我更新和可持续发展的能力，从而构成了城市绿色发展的重要表征。绿色生态是国家中心城市绿色发展的必要条件。生态资源既是人类赖以生存的基础条件，也是提高发展质量的重要保障。人类文明史事实上是人与自然的关系史，生态保护与经济发展相辅相成、辩证统一。空气、土壤、水等自然资源的利用状况、质量状况等深刻反映了绿色发展的层次与水平。

（二）国家中心城市绿色发展指标的选择原则

指标体系构建原则对于评价结果具有重要影响，结合城市绿色发展的内涵和国家中心城市的功能定位，我们借鉴国内外学者在绿色城市评价方面的研究成果，以指标可计算、数据可采集、方法可比对、结果可解释作为目标，遵循以下原则。

一是系统性与层次性相结合的原则。国家中心城市绿色发展涉及生产、生活、生态等诸多领域，且不同的领域相互制约、相互影响，每一领域的指标既相互独立、又相互关联，共同构成统一的整体系统。因此，在评价指标的选择中既要兼顾各指标的独立性，也要兼顾评价体系的整体性，从而全面系统反映国家中心城市绿色发展水平。

二是科学性与操作性相结合的原则。国家中心城市绿色发展具有内在的规律性，评价指标的选择要在充分挖掘国家中心城市绿色发展内在规律的基础上，在方法选择、指标确定等方面突出科学性和规范性。同时，指标的选择要充分考虑数据的可获得性，以便在实际运用中能够增强可操作性。

三是可比性与前瞻性相结合的原则。由于统计口径的差异，不同城市、不同指标的数值存在一定的差异性。为此，指标选择需要注重标准的统一性和可比性。为实现评价指导发展的目的，指标评价体系还需要具有一定的预见性和超前性，能够为未来国家中心城市绿色发展起到一定指导作用。

（三）国家中心城市绿色发展指标体系的构建

基于国家中心城市绿色发展的内涵和城市绿色发展评价指标体系构建原则，本文借鉴世界银行城市竞争力指数（2015 年），英国未来论坛可持续城市指数（2007 年），中国国家发展改革委员会绿色发展指标体系、生态文明建设考核目标体系，环保部生态文明试点示范市建设指标体系，国家标准化管理委员会绿色城市评价指标（2017 年）等 15 个方面的城市绿色发展指标体系，参考已有研究成果，从绿色生产、绿色生活和绿色生态三个方面选择国家中心城市人均 GDP、

GDP 增长率、第三产业比重、单位 GDP 能耗等 32 个指标，构建如表 1 所示的国家中心城市绿色发展评价指标体系，采用熵值法确定各指标权重。

表 1　国家中心城市绿色发展评价指标体系

一级指标	二级指标	三级指标	类型	权重
国家中心城市绿色发展指数	绿色生产指数 0.4624	人均 GDP(万元/人)	+	0.0257
		GDP 增长率(%)	+	0.0158
		第三产业比重(%)	+	0.0670
		单位 GDP 能耗(吨标准煤/万元)	-	0.0501
		万元工业产值氮氧化物排放量(千克)	-	0.0283
		万元工业产值工业烟(粉)尘排放量(千克)	-	0.0281
		万元工业产值工业废水排放量(吨)	+	0.0299
		一般工业固体物废弃物综合利用率(%)	+	0.0304
		R&D 经费投入强度(%)	+	0.0556
		万人发明专利拥有量(件)	+	0.0554
		每万人中大学生数(人)	+	0.0513
		城镇登记失业率(%)	-	0.0248
	绿色生活指数 0.2839	城镇居民人均可支配收入(元)	+	0.0390
		居民平均预期寿命(岁)	+	0.0317
		人口密度(人/平方公里)	-	0.0176
		人均日生活用水量(升)	-	0.0276
		供水普及率(%)	+	0.0169
		燃气普及率(%)	+	0.0283
		污水处理率(%)	+	0.0284
		生活垃圾无害化处理率(%)	+	0.0172
		城市天然气利用率(%)	+	0.0159
		人均生活污水排放量(吨)	-	0.0203
		人均生活氮氧化物排放量(千克)	-	0.0261
		人均生活烟尘排放量(千克)	-	0.0149
	绿色生态指数 0.2537	人均道路面积(平方米)	+	0.0258
		人均公园绿地面积(平方米)	+	0.0313
		建成区绿化覆盖率(%)	+	0.0295
		建成区绿地率(%)	+	0.0431
		空气质量综合指数	-	0.0236
		空气质量优良率(%)	+	0.0280
		城市噪声均值(分贝)	-	0.0391
		昼间道路交通噪声均值(分贝)	-	0.0333

以9个国家中心城市2018年统计年鉴和2018年国民经济和社会发展统计公报数据为基础，采用极值处理法对9个国家中心城市32项指标的2017年的原始数据进行处理，结合各指标的权重系数，计算得出各国家中心城市绿色发展综合指数，依据各指数值对9个国家中心城市绿色发展状况进行排名(见表2)。

表2　2017年9个国家中心城市绿色发展水平测度结果

	绿色生产指数	排名	绿色生活指数	排名	绿色生态指数	排名	绿色发展指数	排名
北京	0.3748	1	0.2404	1	0.1710	2	0.7862	1
广州	0.2363	3	0.1617	5	0.1513	3	0.5493	2
上海	0.2076	4	0.2291	2	0.0729	7	0.5096	3
武汉	0.1954	5	0.1799	3	0.0752	6	0.4506	4
西安	0.2618	2	0.1068	9	0.0612	8	0.4298	5
天津	0.1311	8	0.1749	4	0.1076	5	0.4135	6
成都	0.1760	6	0.1171	8	0.1179	4	0.4109	7
重庆	0.0445	9	0.1517	6	0.1735	1	0.3698	8
郑州	0.1453	7	0.1327	7	0.0541	9	0.3321	9

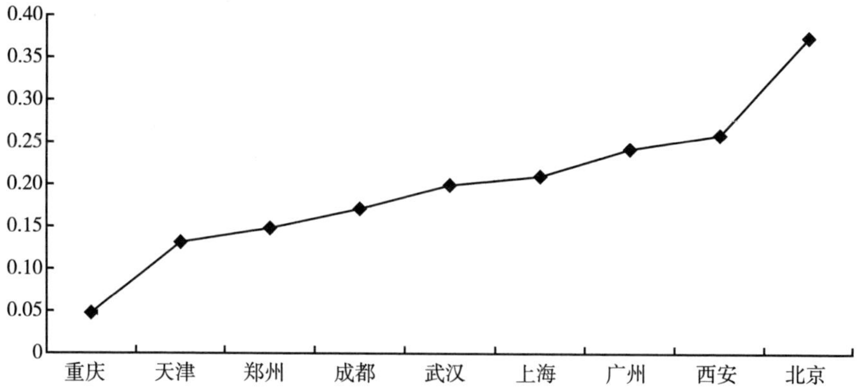

图1　国家中心城市2017年绿色生产指数

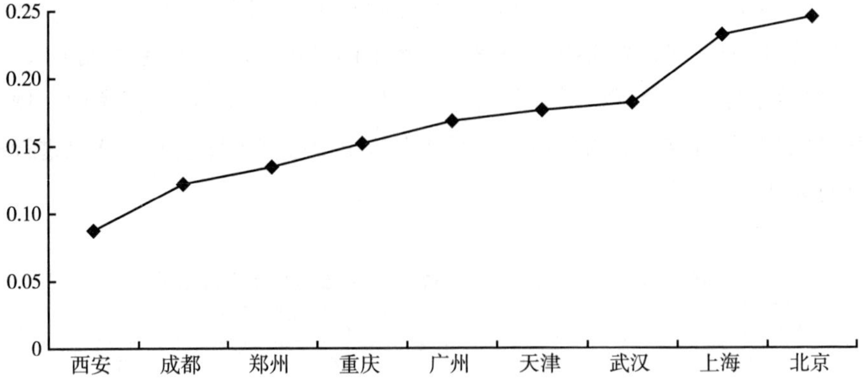

图 2　国家中心城市 2017 年绿色生活指数

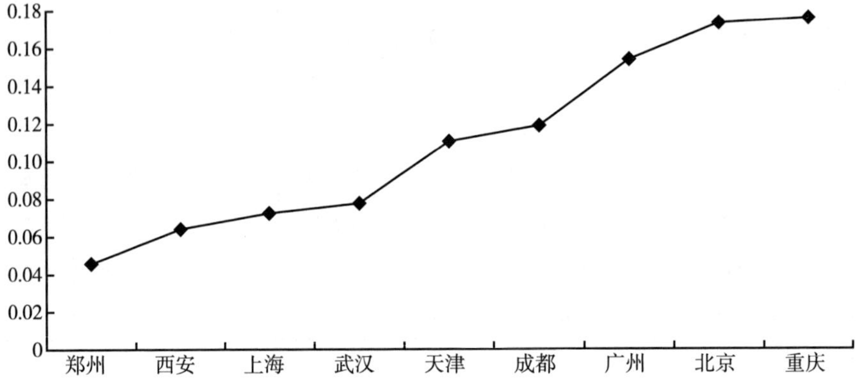

图 3　国家中心城市 2017 年绿色生态指数

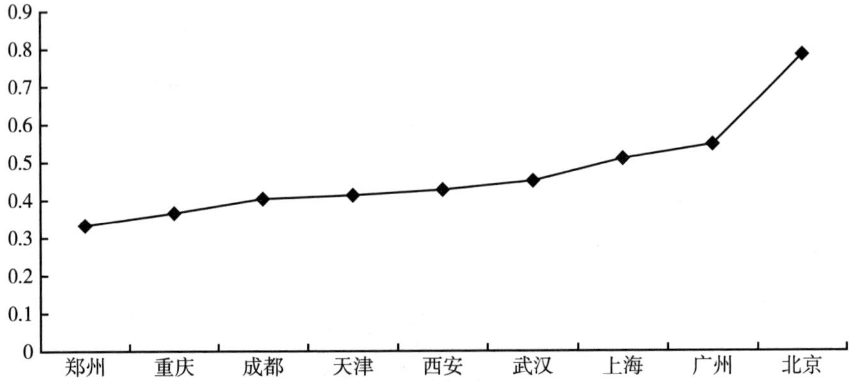

图 4　国家中心城市 2017 年绿色发展指数

二 国家中心城市绿色发展水平的多维分析

由于国家中心城市所处地理位置、自然环境、人口分布、能源储量、经济基础、新型技术开发运用和政策支持力度等因素存在不同程度的差异性，目前我国9个国家中心城市绿色发展水平参差不齐。

从绿色生产指数看（见图1），北京以0.3748排在9个国家中心城市的首位，重庆以0.0445排在最后一位。9个国家中心城市绿色生产指数的平均值为0.1970，其中北京、西安、广州和上海四个城市数值超过平均值，武汉、成都、郑州、天津和重庆得分低于平均值。9个国家中心城市绿色生产的差异性较为显著，从数值上看，北京市绿色生产水平接近平均水平的2倍，而重庆市则仅为平均水平的1/4稍多一点。进一步分析表明，绿色生产水平相对较低的重庆市、天津市和郑州市其主要制约因素在于绿色产业动能培育不足。2017年，重庆市和郑州市万人发明专利拥有量分别为9.1件和12.9件，而同年北京市这一数字已经达到111.2件；从R&D经费投入强度看，2017年郑州市科学研究与试验发展费用仅为158.7亿元，R&D经费投入强度仅为1.74%，而北京市同年的科学研究与试验发展费用为1595.3亿元，是郑州市的10倍，其R&D经费投入强度为5.64%，也是郑州市的3倍多。

从绿色生活指数看（见图2），9个国家中心城市的绿色生活指数排名依次是北京、上海、武汉、天津、广州、重庆、郑州、成都和西安，其绿色生产指数得分分别为0.2404、0.2291、0.1799、0.1749、0.1617、0.1517、0.1327、0.1171和0.1068。相对于绿色生产指数而言，9个国家中心城市绿色生活指数的差异性相对较小。各国家中心城市绿色生活水平存在差异的主要原因在于资源利用方式和污染物排放，西安市和郑州市2017年人均生活氮氧化物排放量分别为686千克和640千克，接近北京市的2倍。

从绿色生态指数看（见图3），重庆市以0.1735的数值位居9个国家中心城市首位，北京市以0.1710的数值排名第二位，郑州市和西安市分别以0.0541和0.0612的数值列倒数第一位和第二位。总体而言，9个国家中心城市绿色生态指数的差异性最大。9个国家中心城市绿色生态发展水平的区域差异一方面源于国家中心城市所处的地理位置和自然条件，另一方面源于不同中心城市的绿色生产生活状况。其中，重庆市位于我国西南部、长江上游地区，属亚热带季风性湿润气候，自然资源丰富，生态基础较好，因此，其绿色生态指数相对较高，而北京市绿色生态指数相对较高的原因得益于近年来实施的一系列绿色发展新政。

从绿色发展指数看（见图4），北京市以0.7862排名9个国家中心城市首位，比排名第二位的广州市多出0.2369，排名在第三位到第九位的城市分别是上海市、武汉市、西安市、天津市、成都市、重庆市和郑州市。对比9个国家中心城市的绿色发展水平，我们可以发现，作为首都的北京市，不论是绿色生产水平还是绿色生活水平，均排名9个国家中心城市首位，其绿色生态水平排在重庆市之后，位居第二位。由此也说明，在经济社会转型时期，加大绿色发展政策供给不失为推动城市绿色发展的重要路径。事实上，在推动绿色发展中，市场的“无形之手”绝非“上帝之手”，面对经济社会转型发展阶段物质主义的增长范式、利润挂帅的技术理性、区域发展的环境分异和物欲至上的消费观念，市场机制固然能对自然生态资源配置产生良好的效果，却无法完全限制宏观经济的规模以及对自然资源的过度耗损。绿水青山的隐性收益、环境污染的隐性成本以及资源环境的整体性、公共性和外部性决定了政府在推动绿色发展中不能缺位。

三　国家中心城市绿色发展的路径探索

我国国家中心城市绿色发展水平的多维测度结果表明，目前9个国家中心城市绿色发展呈现显著的差异性，产生这种差异性的主要原因在于绿色发展理念更新、绿色发展政策供给和绿色发展动能培育的差异性。因此，推动国家中心城市绿色发展需要从坚持理念先行、坚持政策引导、坚持科技支撑发展动能三个方面着力。

第一，坚持理念先行。诚如习近平总书记所言，进入工业文明时代以来，人类创造了前所未有的物质财富，也产生了难以弥补的生态创伤。随着我国社会主要矛盾转化为人民日益增长的美好生活需要和不平衡不充分的发展之间的矛盾，人民群众对优美生态环境的需要已经成为这一矛盾的重要方面，人们热切期盼加快提高生态环境质量，尤其期盼身边有清新空气、清澈水质、清洁环境。中国生态文明建设进入关键期、攻坚期、窗口期。世界各国中心城市的地方政府在执政理念上要牢固树立“保护生态环境就是保护生产力，改善生态环境就是发展生产力”的绿色发展理念。一是深化生态环境保护管理体制机制改革。建立健全政府各部门之间权责明晰、分工协作的责任体系和跨部门、跨行业、跨领域的一体化生态环境治理保护机制，以党和国家机构改革为契机，加快推进国家中心城市生态环境保护的组织体系优化，将资源管理、环境治理和生态保护等纳入一体，统一管理、统一部署。二是变革政府绩效考评机制。把环境治理、生态保护作为政府绩效考核的重要指标，将部门考核、公众评价、社会评价等统筹起来，针对不同区域采取差异化的考核机制，凸显“绿色政绩”在选人用人、干部任用、提拔晋升等方面的主导作用。三是推动绿色发展责任监督机制建设。结合生态环境建设滞后性、公众性、长期性的特征，建立领导干部绿色发展离任审计制度和责任终身追究制度，通过追责制度确保领导干部履职尽责，监督约束权力运行，进一步规范和强化国家中心城市政府的环境决策行为。同时要广泛引导社会公众树立绿色生活理念，在全社会倡导绿色消费理念，形成适度、科学、低碳、环保、循环的绿色消费方式。建立完善的生态伦理教育体系，加强环保科学教育，进一步传播生态科学知识，培育民众的节约意识、低碳意识、环保意识、生态意识，让绿色生活理念深入人心，让绿色生活方式推广普及。将环保科学教育纳入国民教育体系，树立个人生活要对环境负责任的观念，将绿色环保理念融入公民道德建设和精神文明建设，增强广大人民群众维护生态环境的自觉性、积极性、责任感与使命感，为公民养成绿色生活方式和行为习惯提供充满活力的、积极向上的文化氛围。

第二，坚持政策引导。推动国家中心城市绿色发展，需要坚定不移地推进供给侧结构性改革，充分发挥财税政策、金融政策、货币政策、产业政策的引导作用。把政策优化与市场引导有机结合起来，推动去产能、降成本、补短板。不同区域、不同阶段的国家中心城市应明确政策调控的重心与目标，围绕绿色发展的短板不足，以有效的政策供给，引导经济社会绿色发展。一是合理选择政策工具，支持城市绿色发展。充分利用价格、税收、补贴政策工具，引导和激励企业优化生产方式、公众优化生活方式，降低能源消耗、减少污染排放、提升利用效率。在国家中心城市探索实施水、电、气、热阶梯价格政策，合理分担能源消耗成本，促进节能意识转化为节能行为；对从事节能减排的企业实施相应的财政补贴政策，激励其进行技术创新、改造升级，大力提高可再生和清洁能源及节能环保产品的供应比例，降低或限制污染环境、安全度低的产品和非清洁能源在市场的流通和供应，激励引导企业走绿色发展之路，加速绿色转型，发展绿色生产。二是持续完善绿色采购。国家和地方政府要不断建立完善法律法规，鼓励各级政府机关、企事业单位、各人民团体采购具有环境认证的产品和服务，政府财政可以采取多种形式、多种手段引导和支持企业和居民使用节能环保的产品，对生产具有环境认证的产品和服务的企业进行奖励。政府要积极引导、合理利用社会资本参与公共性环境保护项目，同时管好、用好、放活社会资本。地方政府可以采取购买环保服务的方式，利用大企业内部设施处理城市废水和垃圾等；运用灵活的管理方式，鼓励民营企业为社会提供绿色服务，增加绿色投资项目的现金流和竞争力。运用税利债费等行政手段，提高企业绿色生产的收益或加大污染成本。通过制度形成公开透明的政府采购市场，形成公平公正公开的营商环境。三是建立绿色金融政策。通过贷款贴息或风险补偿等方式，发挥金融的带动作用，自发形成社会资本向环保项目投资，创新绿色金融工具，开发绿色债券、绿色贷款、绿色保险、绿色基金等新型金融工具，形成绿色金融体系。四是加强基础制度供给。完善碳排放权交易市场，分阶段、分步骤，循序渐进推动其制度体系、监管体系、报告制度、分配制度等方面的建设，以行业标准和交易机制统一性、政策法规和制度设计的有效性、配额分配和信息披露的透明性三个方面为核心，提升基础能力，充分发挥碳市场在减排温室气体中的作用，全力降低全社会减排成本。

第三，坚持科技支撑。推动国家中心城市绿色发展，要牢牢抓住科技创新这一关键，建立健全城市绿色发展科技支撑体系，依靠市场化技术实现城市发展绿色转型，运用核心关键技术推进城市绿色化变革，通过信息智能技术大幅提高城市绿色发展质量和效益，为国家中心城市绿色发展提供科学依据和技术支撑。一是建立以市场为导向的绿色技术创新体系。兼顾经济、社会、生态效益，依托有效的市场机制引导低碳技术与绿色技术的开发，持续加大节能环保、清洁生产、低碳高效产业技术的研发力度。把经济效益与生态效益结合起来，在国家中心城市大力推广高效节能技术的应用，将绿色理念、绿色技术、绿色工艺广泛运用到生产技术变革、产业转型升级中，贯通传统产业与绿色技术之间的联系，推动绿色产业发展的同时，提升传统产业的绿色发展水平。尤其是绿色发展水平相对较低的国家中心城市应结合区域发展特色，以产业结构转型升级为重点，加大科研投入力度，优化科研投入方式，推动传统产业升级换代，发展现代新兴产业形态，提升产业绿色发展质量。二是推进绿色技术支撑体系的系统集成。国家中心城市绿色发展作为一个系统工程，不仅需要转变生产方式、经营方式、生活方式，也需要知识创新、技术变革、产品升级。推动国家中心城市绿色技术的研发、应用、推广，需要构建系统集成的绿色技术支撑体系。要紧盯绿色技术基础领域和世界前沿，高起点、高标准打造绿色发展技术支撑体系，把人才、资源、信息、产品等要素集聚起来，把企业、高校、科研机构等研发主体联结起来，把研发、生产、销售、服务等环节贯通起来，形成系统化、集成化的绿色发展科技创新支撑体系。三是因地制宜打造引领产业发展的绿色核心技术体系。不同的国家中心城市的产业发展基础互有差异，各国家中心城市在推动绿色技术变革中，要相互借鉴、相互学习，同时更应立足本地实际，结合区域发展特点，围绕制约本地绿色发展的关键掣肘和突出矛盾，以问题为导向，持续打造引领产业发展转型的绿色核心技术体系。在绿色发展水平相对较低的国家中心城市，应明确阶段性的技术攻关重点，围绕新能源、新材料、高端装备制造等产业技术的研发应用，改造高耗能、高投入、高污染传统产业。同时加大人才技术储备力度，为绿色发展技术创新提供持续动力与源泉。在绿色发展水平相对较高的国家中心城市，要以世界前沿技术、关键技术、核心技术的开发应用为主线，引领世界科技前沿，服务国家重大战略。

参考文献

［1］陈春娣、荣冰凌、邓红兵：《欧盟国家城市绿色空间综合评价体系》，《中国园林》2009 年第 3 期，第 66 ~ 69 页。

［2］邵全、肖洋、刘娜：《绿色北京指标体系的构建与评价研究》，《生态经济》2015 年第 6 期，第 92 - 94 + 102 页。

［3］王婉晶、赵荣钦、揣小伟、高珊：《绿色南京城市建设评价指标体系研究》，《地域研究与开发》2012 年第 2 期，第 62 ~ 66 页。

［4］耿直：《长江上游四省市绿色发展水平及影响因素分析》，《武汉工程职业技术

学院学报》2019 年第 1 期，第 17 ~ 20 + 32 页。

[5] 王国力、韩慧慧：《京津冀地区城市绿色发展水平区域差异分析》，《辽宁师范大学学报》（自然科学版）2019 年第 1 期，第 106 ~ 111 页。

[6] 马骍：《云南省绿色经济发展评价指标体系研究》，《西南民族大学学报》（人文社科版）2018 年第 12 期，第 128 ~ 136 页。

[7] 肖春梅、朱萍萍：《新疆绿色发展水平综合评价与对策研究》，《石河子大学学报》（哲学社会科学版）2018 年第 3 期，第 41 ~ 49 页。

[8] 李雪：《四川省绿色发展水平评价与时空分异研究》，四川师范大学硕士学位论文，2018。

[9] 柴燕妮、魏冠军、侯伟、冯志贤、翟亮：《空间视角下的多尺度生态环境质量评价方法》，《生态学杂志》2018 年第 2 期，第 596 ~ 604 页。

B.27
国家中心城市建设背景下数据战略的国际借鉴

张 冰*

摘 要： 在信息时代背景下，城市数据是城市的重要资源、资本和资产，充分利用城市数据来用于政策决策、管理和创新，可以提高城市的竞争力，实现城市的可持续发展。本文分析了国际城市数据应用的典范——伦敦的城市数据战略，并借鉴伦敦的经验，对国家中心城市数据应用方面提出了6点建议：发挥中心城市政府主导地位，建立共享的城市数据平台，发展有活力的数据市场，构建有效的数据治理体系，保护公民的数据隐私，促进基于城市数据的协同创新。

关键词： 国家中心城市 伦敦城市数据 国际借鉴

2010年2月，建设部在《全国城镇体系规划（2010—2020年）》中首次提出建设国家中心城市，到2019年全国共明确定位9个国家中心城市，分别是北京、上海、重庆、广州、成都、武汉、郑州和西安。国家中心城市体现着全国城市发展的水平和品质，在当前和未来都将成为实施新发展理念的标杆。党的十九大报告提出建设“智慧社会”和数字中国，政府从互联网、信息化、大数据、人工智能等维度为城市持续赋能。在新时代背景下，城市数据是城市的重要资源、资本和资产，充分利用城市数据来用于政策决策，发展数据管

---

* 〔英〕张冰，英国赫瑞·瓦特大学博士，黄河科技学院中国（河南）创新发展研究院研究员，研究方向为金融学、城市经济。

理，推动数据创新，提升政府管理和公共服务的质量，创造新的商业机会和提高城市人民的生活质量。特别是在国家中心城市的建设过程中，创新发展理念，有效利用城市数据引领数据创新，实现城市数据价值的社会、经济和环境方面重要意义，对于全国其他城市具有引领、示范和辐射效应。

一 城市数据的经济和社会价值

1. 城市数据的定义和种类

城市数据是指利用新一代信息技术，由城市政府、事业单位、企业和个人收集整理的各种城市设施、组织和个人等主体和对象产生的大量动态和静态数据。城市数据有多种形式，包括政府公共服务部门的数据和私营部门组织，例如公用事业、基础设施供应商、零售商、土地开发商的数据。城市数据按照不同的来源和用途，可分为开放数据、私人数据、商业数据、传感器采集的数据和公民来源数据。开放数据即无隐私限制和非机密数据，来自公共和私营部门，可在不受任何限制的情况下提供，例如开放地图数据。私人数据是受限制和/或许可数据，以及目前私人持有的数据。商业数据指的是有许可证的数据，包括数据许可、收费数据等，例如城市居民的消费数据。传感器采集的数据是由公共、私营部门和公民拥有的传感器、执行器和设备收集的数据，例如城市夜光数据。公民来源数据包括公民应用数字技术产生的数据及社交媒体数据，例如手机数据。

2. 城市数据创造经济和社会价值的机制

充分利用城市数据可以提高城市治理水平，整合城市资源，提高资源配置效率，提升城市科技水平，促进城市产业转型升级，提升人民生活品质。城市数据的发布促进了一个创新生态系统来创造创新的产品和服务，这个系统包括政府、公司和一些非营利组织。数据驱动创新是基于发布的数据，以数据为驱动的创新，包括创新产品和服务，这种创新创造了社会和经济价值，产生了积极的经济和社会影响。图 1 描述了数据创新生态系统的三个阶段，从数据采集到数据处理，开发产品和服务，以及其经济和社会的价值流程。第一阶段关注数据的质量和可利用程度。如果数据有利用价值，在第二阶段将可以利用的城市数据开发产品和服务。第二阶段关注这些数据源如何转化为创新服务，以及产生数据驱动创新的产品与服务。第三阶段将第二阶段的产品、服务推广以及商业化，评估这些产品和服务的经济和社会影响。在这个数据生态系统中，城市作为数据的来源，公民作为最终创新产品和服务的最终用户。

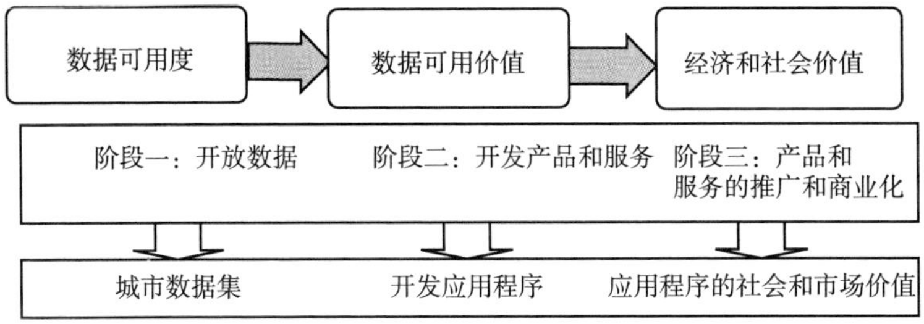

图1　城市数据创新生态系统

资料来源：A model of the analysis of data – driven innovation and value generation in smart cities' ecosytems（Alberto et al.，2017）作者根据翻译更新。

3. 城市数据应用过程中的关键因素

城市数据的应用过程中应注意以下 6 个关键因素。①是数据质量管理。利用城市数据的首要条件是高质量的城市数据。有些城市数据来自不同的数据采集设备，在收集数据的过程中会产生巨大差异。因此，为确保城市发展项目的成功，应考虑到现有数据的质量和找到提高数据质量的方法。②是整合不同来源的数据。不同类型的城市数据从各种城市的资源中收集而来，关键是将不同类型的数据集聚整合以提供高水平高质量的信息。不同的组织使用不同的数据结构，因此，不同领域内的数据集成和标准化是使用城市数据最紧迫的问题之一。③是了解公民、城市游客和员工的需求。以提升公共服务为目的数据应该是公民驱动的，而不是信息驱动的。确定对于公民、游客和员工最重要和有价值的信息，在基于数据的城市发展项目中是至关重要的，识别公民传递的信息直接关系到公共服务的价值及其吸引力。④是保护数据隐私。根据调查，公民有意愿接受以数据分析为基础创造的新产品和服务，同时也明确指出使用他们数据的先决条件应该是对他们隐私的保护。研究并解决数据隐私问题对于以城市数据为基础的城市发展项目至关重要。⑤是地理信息的可视化。使用城市数据的另外一个关键因素是利用地理信息系统（GIS）实现信息可视化和传递的有效性，比如城市建筑、不同公交线路的可视化信息等，信息可视化内容应清晰和充实。⑥是设计城市数据服务项目。充分利用城市数据创造价值，通过产品和服务的形式提供给公民和游客，提高城市运行的效率。这需要建立政府、研究机构和公民协同合作的有效机制。以上这六种关键因素密切相关，相辅相成。

二　城市数据战略的国际经验——以伦敦为例

伦敦是英国城市数据应用的典范，致力于通过开放数据等战略的实施，促进公众参与，助力解决城市难题，同时推动数据的创新应用，充分发掘城市数据的附加经济价值。2013 年的《智慧伦敦计划》注重开放数据的开放，以及利用数据推进伦敦的城市规划和运营，明确指出数据是城市规划和运营的支柱。使用伦敦的数据仪表板和其他数字工具，鼓励公众和开发人员参与伦敦的数据研发和应用。2018 智慧城市路线图《齐心协力建设更智慧的伦敦》阐述了伦敦对更好的数字服务、开放数据、互联互通、数字包容性、网络安全性、数据创新的规划。为了充分发挥跨域城市数据的潜力，提升城市数据的价值，伦敦市政府专门制定了 2016 年《城市数据战略》，其愿景是希望伦敦拥有世界上最具活力和生产力的城市数据市场。城市数据被视为伦敦基础设施的一部分，用来节约资金，培育创新，推动经济增长，以期伦敦因其数据影响力而享誉全球。

1. 伦敦的2016年《城市数据战略》

伦敦市政府利用 2016 年《城市数据战略》支持市政厅的施政举措和多方面的城市政策。在城市资产管理方面，利用数据开发和管理伦敦的基础设施，更有效地管理资产。能源方面，《伦敦能源计划》对一系列来源的复杂数据进行建模，以更好地了解伦敦的能源需求和供应方式，达到更有效地利用能源的目的。将城市数据和伦敦数据库置于智慧城市发展的中心，建立一个协调一致的城市平台开发方法和城市数据架构，能够整合数据流，优化城市服务。协作城市层面的战略决策，利用跨越商业以及学术界的数据和计算科学专业知识，更好地推进城市的战略发展，以及解决复杂城市系统中的问题。提升公共服务质量，从健康和社会关怀等服务的整合，到废物管理中的路线优化，利用城市数据共享和分析，有效地管理城市技术基础设施，提高服务效率和节约成本。该战略规划主要包括6个方面：发展伦敦数据市场、组织城市数据以扩大影响力、充分认识城市数据的价值、提升城市数据信任、建立积极有效的数据治理体系和数据技术路线图，具体内容如下。

（1）发展伦敦数据市场

建立和运营一个高效的城市数据市场，并创建支持工具，充分实现城市数据的价值。这就要求城市提供数据以创造更好的城市服务、建设更好的城市基础设施和服务经济发展，它还意味着提供改变组织文化和提高分析能力，推进各方都参与和发挥作用的开放式创新。更好的城市数据可以带来更好的城市服务、更好的城市政策，并可以促进创新。为了达到这一目标，伦敦市政府需要考虑构建以数据为基础的商业和金融模型、制定相关政策和数据许可协议，部署最先进的数据管理策略，以提供长期广泛使用数据的基础。伦敦市政府将建立一个强大的以价值为导向的合作伙伴网络，以降低数据基础设施开发的复杂性和成本，并确保伦敦数据的质量，创建新的数据驱动服务和智能基础设施。

（2）组织城市数据以扩大影响力

如果城市数据要在公共服务决策、基础设施投资决策和更广泛的创新中发挥强有力的支撑作用，就需要更好地组织城市数据，以便于更系统、更严格地用于管理城市服务和资产，还可以更有效地创建真正的“城市平台”和新的商业模式。伦敦市政府已经建立了以物联网和云计算为基础的伦敦数据库，使数据成为伦敦基础设施的核心部分。如图2所示，2010年开始筹建的伦敦数据库是世界上最早开放公共数据的平台之一，目前拥有827个数据集，涵盖经济、交通、环境、安保、医疗等8个领域，帮助解决城市挑战和提高公共服务水平。2013年开始筹建的第二代伦敦数据库与巴塞罗那等城市合作，作为耗资520万欧元的EU iCity项目的一部分，开发一个“城市平台”，测试从首都各地数以百万计的传感器设备中获取、捕获和存储不同类型的公共和私人数据。伦敦提供一个城市数据地图，并详细描述现有城市数据的架构特征，包括来源、数量、种类、时间因素和敏感性，以确定管理城市数据供应链所需的流程和资源。为了确保伦敦在数据驱动的世界中保持领先地位，伦敦加大了对数据基础设施的投资。在这一过程中，城市环境中的数据集成和呈现城市数据的统一标准尤为重要，因此伦敦提供“核心参考数据”，以支持整合不同来源的数据，发布城市数据基础设施中设计和服务交付的集成方法，以便确保数据标准的统一。

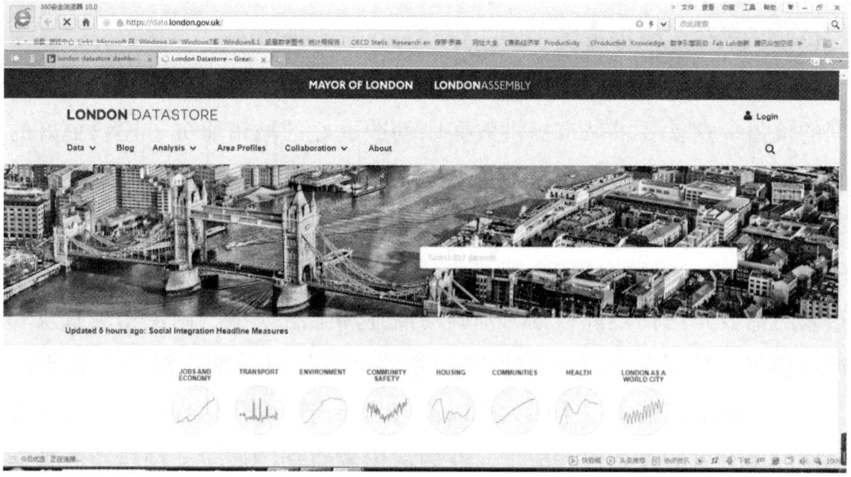

图 2　伦敦数据库截图

资料来源：英国大伦敦政府网站，于 2019 年 6 月 27 日登入，https：//data. london. gov. uk。

（3）充分认识城市数据的价值

衡量城市数据的价值必须考虑到社会、环境、经济以及金融领域。通过建立更好的以价值为基础的衡量方法和定价体系，促进所有合作伙伴正确理解数据价值以便在城市数据市场中进行交易。目前，人们对数据的用途知之甚少，包括私营部门和公共部门的情况都是如此，公共部门还没有把数据视为一种具有附加价值的资产，对于共享数据和开放数据以及随之而来的价值创造潜力的认识比较局限。因此就需要进行文化和组织机构变革，目前已经实施的变革方案包括伦敦基础设施地图应用程序，其数据来自一系列公用事业公司和公共部门以外的组织。通过深度挖掘数据来提升伦敦公共服务水平和推进智慧城市建设，以及通过展开学术研究和开发新产品来改善城市、企业及其居民生活品质来实现数据价值。为开放数据和商业数据制定必要的授权许可协议，以确保伦敦最大限度地利用和再利用各个城市数据集的潜力。

（4）提升城市数据信任

只有充分解决与个人数据有关的安全、隐私和信任问题，下一个数据利用时代及其创造服务的可能性才会成为现实。让公众充分理解如何利用他们的个人数据为经济、社会以及他们自己创造价值，将导致数据供应增加，并最终提升公众对服务的接受程度。公众是城市数据市场的重要组成部分，伦敦的城市数据有很大一部分是由公众提供的。基本上，这些数据主要来自服务、社交媒体、移动设备、车辆和智能卡的日常活动。未来，智能家居、其他智能城市服务、新型自主技术和人工智能也会增加个人数据的生成量。与数据创新启动中心（Digital Catapult）的个人数据和信任网络合作，以促进负责任的个人数据创新。建立一个消费者数据委员会，使伦敦市民能够参与讨论如何在城市数据市场上发布和使用他们的数据，并与一系列个人数据保护和消费者团体合作，以确保伦敦人更好地理解有关个人隐私权的法规。探索个人数据的隐私方面需求，为伦敦的数据基础设施制定数据管理策略，确保数据完整性并符合国家、欧洲和国际数据保护法规。建立一个数据伦理委员会，以解决与平衡隐私、数据安全和公共利益相关的法律和伦理挑战。

（5）建立积极有效的数据治理体系

积极治理伦敦城市数据市场，以便应对城市数据战略面临的挑战，预测并充分利用城市数据战略机遇。良好的治理将带来公众对监管和法律问题更好的理解，促进数据共享和公众利益的最大化，同时限制负面的效应。自开放数据的策略实施以来，伦敦城市数据市场的复杂性显著提升，治理体系不但要注重数据的质量和数据发布，也要注重数据操作的互通性和协调性等问题。伦敦建立城市数据委员会，显著加强围绕城市数据的治理，为伦敦数据创新中心制定战略方向。在伦敦数据库中设置城市数据交换部门，以鼓励城市数据市场中的所有合作伙伴制定其数据要求，明确对数据的预期需求及其用途，解决围绕数据共享和协调、衡量数据的价值和数据货币化带来的未决问题。要求伦敦金融城数据委员会制定一系列数据供应要求，涵盖公共部门供应合同和私营部门的商业模式，以防止有价值的数据被忽略。通过城市数据委员会，推动伦敦各政府部门（如税务部、就业和退休保障部）广泛获取数据，以克服目前阻碍部门内部和外部进一步数据共享、数据价值创造的障碍。组织城市数据委员会的一个小组，为与数据发布和数据共享相关的个人决策提供专业指导。

（6）数据技术路线图

通过技术路线图来有效协调城市的数据基础设施，这是伦敦整合数据，实现数字创新，提供真正的21世纪公共服务机会，提高城市经济竞争力的关键战略。该战略的核心是为组织和个人共享和利用数据提供先进的方式方法。伦敦需要通过下面一系列关联性的举措，改善城市的数据基础设施。包括共享数据：通过各种工具向城市数据合作伙伴（公民、城市管理者和其他第三方）共享信息和功能。构建伦敦超级云（全市范围内基于云的数字基础设施）：为公共服务和更广泛服务中的一系列数字创新应用打下基础。理解数据：有效地提高处理和分析能力，允许城市或公民对数据和信息进行优化和利用。存储数据：数据存储需要清晰分类以便进行搜索和可从单个点访问。高级分析：提供数据科学家需要的用于处理非结构化大数据的技术需要适当的软件、硬件和存储功能。2018年伦敦设立了数据分析和计划办公室，在市政厅和公共服务部门引入新的数据共享措施，旨在增加数据共享和协作。该计划重视与公共和技术部门建立合作伙伴关系，创建新的城市数据创新中心，以开发数据应用范例。

2. 伦敦数据政策的经济和社会价值

伦敦交通局的数据运用是伦敦城市数据战略的成功范例之一。伦敦交通局发布开放数据创造了一个提高交通质量的良性循环系统，为乘客提供可以嵌入应用程序的实时信息。到目前为止，伦敦交通局有超过80个数据源，涵盖运营和企业信息以及所有运输方式。大约75%的数据可通过应用程序接口获得，42%的伦敦人使用伦敦交通局数据驱动的应用程序，83%的人使用其网站。伦敦交通局与主要应用开发商和数字合作伙伴建立了重要的数据合作关系，有超过12000名注册开发人员。

伦敦交通局数据带来的经济效益可分为直接经济效益和广义的经济效益。直接经济效益包括就业率增长，创造更多的就业机会和增加新的业务部门。2016年伦敦数字部门的就业人数增长了13%，预计伦敦交通局开放数据将直接创造约500个新的工作岗位。在供应链和更广泛的经济领域，还创造了230个间接就业机会。许多公司在商业上使用和重复使用伦敦交通局数据，已经建立了一些新业务，将一系列新的应用程序和服务推向市场。其中许多公司总部设在伦敦，根据保守估计，这些公司更广泛的供应链和消费支出总增加值估计为1400万英镑/年。伦敦因伦敦交通局开放数据带来广义的经济效益包括新的发展机遇，以及鼓励和促进创新。伦敦交通局开放数据给乘客节省了时间，乘客可以通过应用程序更好地计划行程，这些应用程序帮助他们根据新信息调整路线，并在转乘不同的交通工具时提供更多的确定性，有助于避免交通阻塞和节省时间。在所有公共交通工具的应用上，节省的时间成本创造了7000万~9000万英镑的经济效益。并在转乘不同的交通工具时提供更多的确定性，有助于避免交通阻塞和节省乘客时间。

使用伦敦交通局开放数据乘客的直接和间接社会和环境效益包括乘客对旅程的满意度增加和过上更健康的生活。开放数据有助于整合第一英里和最后一英里，提倡使用公共交通设施，鼓励更健康绿色的出行方式，自2007年以来，将步行作为主要交通方式的人数增加了13%。

三　国家中心城市建设借鉴国际大都市数据战略的思考和建议

伦敦在城市建设的过程中，致力于通过城市数据等战略的实施，促进数据的创新应用，破解城市发展难题，充分发掘政府公共数据的经济价值和社会价值，推进城市可持续发展。在促进经济增长方面包括创建开放数据库应用程序的生态系统，为开放数据行业奠定基础，促进数据的创新应用，充分发掘城市数据的附加经济价值，企业可以利用与城市运营相关的开放数据资源提供开放数据服务和产品。在城市治理方面包括通过数据标准更好地跨地区分享信息，提高透明度，进行更好的信息共享。通过提供分析工具，利用城市网络扩大城市数据创新，改善运输和公共安全等主要部门的服务，更好地满足公民和企业的需求。我国国家中心城市在建设过程中，应借鉴伦敦的一些做法，充分利用城市数据，提高城市的竞争力，实现城市的可持续发展。

1. 发挥中心城市政府主导地位

从国家层面来看，英国政府2009年发布了《数字英国》，2017年又正式发布了《数字英国战略》。从城市层面来看，伦敦市政厅发布的2013年《智慧伦敦计划》，2016年《伦敦城市数据战略》和2018年《齐心协力建设更智慧的伦敦》，都致力于城市基础建设、推广全民数字应用，促进数据开放的共享和创新开发利用，形成了一系列以政府为主导的城市数据政策，促进城市数据的收集、整合、储存、共享和开发。我国在国家层面也高度重视数据的开发和利用，2016 年制定的《中华人民共和国国民经济和社会发展第十三个五年规划纲要》提出要将大数据作为基础性战略资源，全面实施促进大数据发展的行动。在国家中心城市的建设过程中，政府应该重视城市数据的价值，制定适合国家中心城市发展的数据政策，把城市数据作为城市的重要资源、资本和资产和城市创新发展的要素，制定城市数据战略，成立数据分析部门，充分挖掘城市数据的附加价值。

2. 建立共享的城市数据平台

伦敦数据库提供了 827 个数据集，涵盖八大经济社会领域，城市数据实时更新，有效促进了研究机构、公司和公民参与创新和新应用程序的开发。伦敦数据库吸引了伦敦的开发者，利用公共数据的获取创造了新的市场，并以数据为基础开发了许多应用程序，推动城市对现有资源的有效配置和合理化利用，帮助伦敦改善城市运行，改善生态环境，促进数字经济，促进能源节约等。同时伦敦作为一个大的数据开发基地，为其他英国城市数据开发提供一个范例。国家中心城市应该打破现有的城市部门间、行业间的数据壁垒，部门间的数据按照权限有序共享。整合数据资源，把多个渠道的数据标准化和规范化，建立数据管理流程和标准，确保数据质量。积极发布实时数据，开发通用、可互操作和易于使用的城市数据平台，并与其他城市和机构合作，释放更多数据来支持开发者开发新的商业模式，为城市居民创造更好、更便捷和更具成本效益的服务。

3. 发展有活力的数据市场

一个高效的数据市场可以推动政府、研究机构、公司和公民共同参与和发挥作用，促进开放式的数据创新。根据智研咨询（2018）发布的调查结果，中国大数据产业市场预计到 2020 年将达到 10100 亿元，2015 ~ 2020 年均复合增长率达到 29. 25% 。上海市积极开发城市数据市场，在 2016 年经上海市人民政府批准成立了上海数据交易中心（2016），利用“交易机构 + 创新基地 + 产业基金 + 发展联盟 + 研究中心”的机制，促进数据流通、跨区域的机构合作和数据互联和融合应用。目前中国其他中心城市还没有城市数据市场，国家中心城市应该起到创新示范作用，把城市数据作为城市重要的资产，发展有活力的数据市场和数据估值定价系统，委托专门机构进行经济分析，为城市数据市场建立货币化框架。同时构建城市数据以价值为基础的衡量方法和定价体系，以便所有的合作伙伴正确理解数据的价值并能够公开透明地在数据市场交易。

4. 构建有效的数据治理体系

在构建城市数据市场的同时，要考虑建立有效的数据治理体系，促进公众对数据监管和相关法律的理解，限制共享数据和数据应用的负面效应。国家中心城市可以建立与城市数据相关的监管机构，加强城市的数据治理，为城市数据创新中心指定战略方向。成立城市数据委员会或数据交换部门，理解对数据的预期需求及其用途，围绕数据共享和协调、衡量数据的价值和数据货币化带来的未决问题。通过城市数据委员会，统一多个公共机构在不同网站上发布数据标准，发布城市数据章程，设立城市数据的标准化格式，克服各部门数据共享的障碍，制定一套开放数据采用的标准和原则，提高数据的应用性。为开放城市数据制定必要的授权和许可证协议，以确保最大限度地利用和再利用城市数据的潜力。

5. 保护公民的数据隐私

城市数据的一个重要来源是公众的社交媒体、移动设备和智能服务等，因此保护公民数据的安全和隐私，是利用城市数据的重要前提。在以城市数据为基础的建设项目中，国家中心城市需要重视城市数据安全和隐私问题。制定全市范围的网络安全战略，协调应对公民的网络威胁。数据安全防御应从当前的事后防御，转变为主动、高效的事前防御，并对安全防御技术与管理进行持续性监管。加强数据权利，数据问责制和数据使用的公民信任度。比如建立一个消费者数据委员会，组织城市公众参与讨论在城市数据市场发布和使用他们数据的方法。与相关个人数据保护和消费者团体合作，确保公众理解有关个人隐私的法规。探索个人数据隐私方面的需求，为城市的数据基础设施制定数据管理策略。

6. 促进基于城市数据的协同创新

构建城市数字创新的生态体系，加强基于城市数据的政府、企业和学术界之间的协同创新和开放式创新，提升政府管理和公共服务的质量，给企业创造新的商业机会和提升城市人民的生活品质。国家中心城市可以利用开放式创新的模式，建立数据协同创新中心，政府通过城市数据，以协同创新中心为平台，鼓励学者、企业、开发人员和公众多方参与，群策群力激发城市创新应用。特别是在城市设计的过程中，城市的规划者不可能具备和理解当地市民的偏好和本地性知识，充分利用城市开源的数据分析内容，激发市民群体智慧，将本地信息、需求等传递给城市规划决策者，有助于他们做出最佳的城市规划决策。

参考文献

[1] 洪学海、范灵俊、洪筱楠、李国杰：《智慧城市建设中政府大数据开放与市场化利用》，《大数据》2016 年第 3 期，第 17 ~ 26 页。

[2] 德勤研究：《超级智能城市　更高质量的幸福社会》，2018。

[3] 本刊编辑部：《大数据服务城市可持续发展》，《中国建设信息化》2018 年第 19 期，第 3 页。

[4] 《上海数据交易中心成立》，新华网，http：//www. xinhuanet. com//politics/2016 – 04/01/c_ 128856527. htm。

[5] A. Abella, M. Ortiz – de – Urbina – Criado, C. De – Pablos – Heredero. "A model for the analysis of data – driven innovation and value generation in smart cities' ecosystems," *Cities*, 2017, (64)：47 – 53.

[6] Afzalan, N., Sanchez, T. W., & Evans – Cowley. "Creating smarter cities: Considerations for selecting online participatory tools," *Cities*, 2017, (67): 21 – 30.

[7] Aina, Y. A. "Achieving smart sustainable cities with GeoICT support: The Saudi evolving smart cities," *Cities*, 2017, (71): 49 – 58.

[8] Ben Sta, H. "Quality and the efficiency of data in "smart – cities"," *Future Generation Computer Systems*, 2017, (74): 409 – 416.

[9] Cicirelli, F., Guerrieri, A., Spezzano, G., & Vinci, A. "An edge – based platform for dynamic smart city applications," *Future Generation Computer Systems*, 2017, (76): 106 – 118.

[10] Deloitte LLP. "Assessing the value of TfL's open data and digital partnerships," July 2017.

B.28

中西部国家中心城市功能比较研究

——基于5个国家中心城市的面板数据

胡 星 王志博 李中明*

摘 要： 在构建基于综合经济能力、科技创新能力、国际竞争能力、辐射带动能力、交通通达能力、信息交流能力、可持续发展能力的国家中心城市功能考核指标评价体系基础上，运用熵权TOPSIS计算模型，以2013~2017年我国中西部地区5个国家中心城市（郑州、武汉、重庆、成都和西安）的相关指标数据为依据，对国家中心城市功能考核指标评价体系7个子系统和城市功能发展水平进行综合比较分析，并提出了进一步优化提升郑州国家中心城市功能的政策建议。

关键词： 国家中心城市 功能比较 优化提升

国家中心城市作为城市体系中综合实力最强的“塔尖”城市，是国家组织经济活动和配置资源的中枢，一般具有集聚辐射、服务带动、国际竞争、交通通达、科技创新、可持续发展等综合能力，发挥国家中心城市的多项综合性功能，对整体提升区域发展水平至关重要。自2010年2月起，住房与城乡建设部等多部门先后发文，将北京、天津、上海、广州和重庆五大城市建设为国家中心城市；2016年5月至2018年2月，国家发改委和住建部又先后发文支

---

* 胡星，经济学硕士，河南财经政法大学经济学院教授，研究方向为城市与区域经济发展；王志博，河南财经政法大学经济学院在校研究生；李中明，河南财经政法大学经济学院在校研究生。

持成都、武汉、郑州、西安建设国家中心城市。其中郑州市作为中部地区主要的核心城市，是我国通达南北、贯穿东西的基本枢纽之一，是“一带一路”的重要节点。郑州市建设国家中心城市对促进中部地区高质量可持续发展具有重要意义。

在九大国家中心城市中，北京、上海、天津和广州等首都和东南沿海城市，由于城市地理条件优势、发展时间长、政策优惠力度大等原因，其城市综合发展水平、科技文化和国际竞争力等方面远超中西部五大中心城市。因此，本文依据对国家中心城市建设的基本要求，建立了七大功能考察指标体系，每个功能层又包括 9 个具体指标，具体选取多个代表性指标数据对中西部 5 个国家中心城市七大功能发展水平进行实证测度和对比分析，以反映中心城市的综合经济能力、科技创新能力、国际竞争能力、辐射带动能力、交通通达能力、信息交流能力、可持续发展能力，并提出郑州等建设中的国家中心城市功能优化提升的对策建议，以进一步指导国家中心城市建设及区域协调发展。

一　中西部5个国家中心城市七大功能比较分析

1. 综合经济能力水平比较分析

2013 ~ 2018 年来，中西部 5 个国家中心城市 GDP 稳步上升（见图 1）。其中，2018 年郑州市 GDP 超过万亿元，达到 10143.32 亿元，是 2013 年的 1.64 倍，同比增长 10.3%；2018 年重庆市实现地区 GDP 20363.19 亿元，按可比价格计算，同比增长 6.0%，是 2013 年的 1.58 倍；2018 年武汉市 GDP 达到 14847.23 亿元，是 2013 年的 1.64 倍，同比增长 10.7%；2018 年成都市 GDP 达到 15342.77 亿元，是 2013 年的 1.68 倍，同比增长 10.5%；2018 年西安市 GDP 达到 8349.86 亿元，是 2013 年的 1.70 倍，同比增长 11.8%。2018 年重庆市 GDP 远远高于其他 4 个国家中心城市，但增长速度低于其他 4 个国家中心城市，成都和武汉市 GDP 基本持平。中西部 5 个国家中心城市 2013 ~ 2018 年历年 GDP 排名依次为重庆市、成都市、武汉市、郑州市和西安市。

在金融发展方面，2017 年重庆市金融机构存贷款在中西部 5 个中心城市排在第一位（63270.99 亿元），略高于成都市（62782.59 亿元），是西安市（37002.43 亿元）的 1.71 倍；2017 年成都市保险业务保费收入最高（952.25

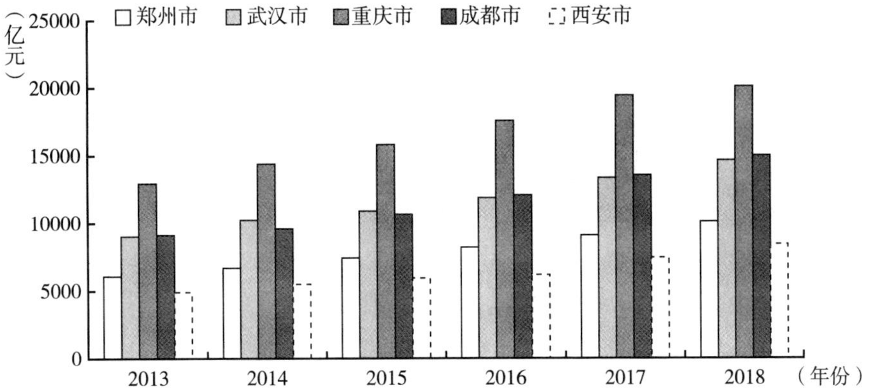

图1　2013～2018年中西部5个国家中心城市GDP

资料来源：历年中国统计年鉴及各市统计年鉴。

亿元），西安市最低（421.1亿元），前者是后者的2.26倍。2017年郑州市保险业务保费收入和金融机构存贷款分列第三名和第四名，说明郑州市金融业发展对其综合经济能力水平贡献度不高。综上可以明显看出，5个国家中心城市金融业发展差异显著，重庆、成都处于前列，西安市金融业发展较慢。在房地产开发投资方面，2017年郑州市房地产开发投资总额位列第二，达到了3358.84亿元，仅次于重庆市（3980.08亿元），是西安市房地产开发投资总额的1.44倍，可见房地产开发投资对重庆和郑州两市综合经济能力发展贡献度较大（见表1）。

表1　国家中心城市四大金融指标数据及排名（2017年）

	房地产开发投资总额（亿元）	排名	金融机构存贷款（亿元）	排名	保险业务保费收入（亿元）	排名	城镇居民可支配收入（元）	排名
郑州	3358.84	2	38342.36	4	655.74	3	36050	3
武汉	2686.36	3	48447.17	3	554.03	4	43404.96	1
重庆	3980.08	1	63270.99	1	744.75	2	32193	4
成都	2487.88	4	62782.59	2	952.25	1	38917.5	2
西安	2333.34	5	37002.43	5	421.1	5	30810	5

资料来源：2018年各市、直辖市统计年鉴。

2. 科技创新能力水平比较分析

在科研创新发展过程中，从2013～2015年的动态数据来看，5个国家中心城市规模以上工业企业科研人员数和研发投入额都在稳步提升，增长趋势明显。其中重庆市规模以上工业企业科研人员数明显高于其他4个中心城市，郑州、成都和西安科研人员数相差不大，但西安市科研人员数最少，2017年重庆市规模以上工业企业科研人员数（8.53万人）是西安市科研人员数（3.99万人）的2.14倍（见图2）。成都和重庆市规模以上工业企业研发投入额并驾齐驱，遥遥领先，武汉居中，郑州和西安市研发投入额较少，2017年成都市规模以上工业企业研发投入额（310.25亿元）是郑州市的3.00倍（见图3）。从各市发明专利/专利申请比值可以看出（见图4），2013～2017年武汉市和郑州市发明专利转化率不断提高，武汉市发明专利转化率从2013年的0.375上升到2017年的0.455，郑州市从2013年的0.290上升到2017年的0.344；2017年5个中心城市发明专利/专利申请比值依次排名为武汉（0.455）、西安（0.427）、成都（0.387）、郑州（0.344）和重庆（0.298）（见图4）。整体来看，各市科技创新能力水平差异显著，这与各中心城市科技发展基础和科技创新环境有关。

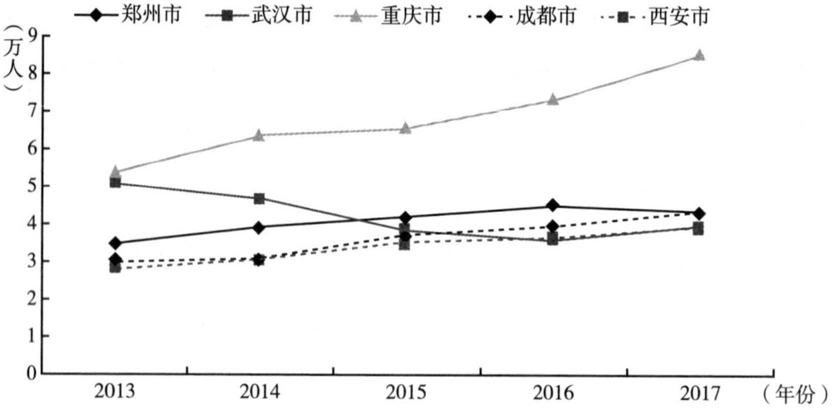

图2　2013～2017年中西部5个国家中心城市规模以上工业企业科研人员数

资料来源：历年中国统计年鉴及各市统计年鉴。

在教育方面，2013～2017年成都市教育经费占GDP比值最大，均值为0.0469，教育经费占GDP比值虽有所下降，但主要是因为成都市GDP增长较快，教育经费总额也在逐年增加；教育经费占GDP比值排名依次为成都、重

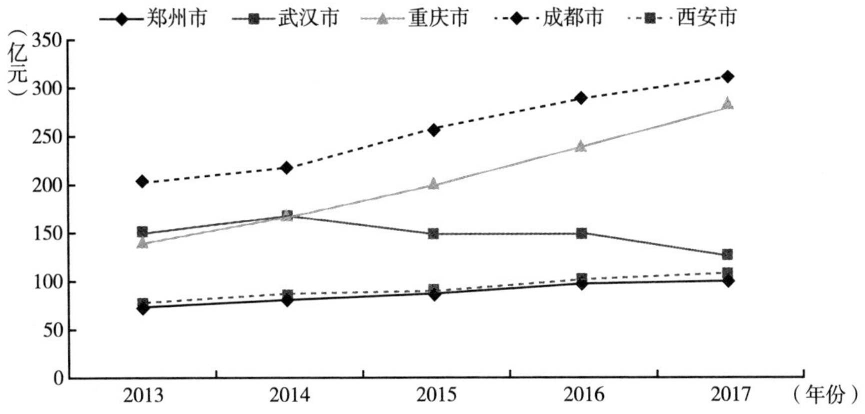

图 3　2013～2017 年中西部 5 个国家中心城市规模以上工业企业研发投入额

资料来源：历年中国统计年鉴及各市统计年鉴。

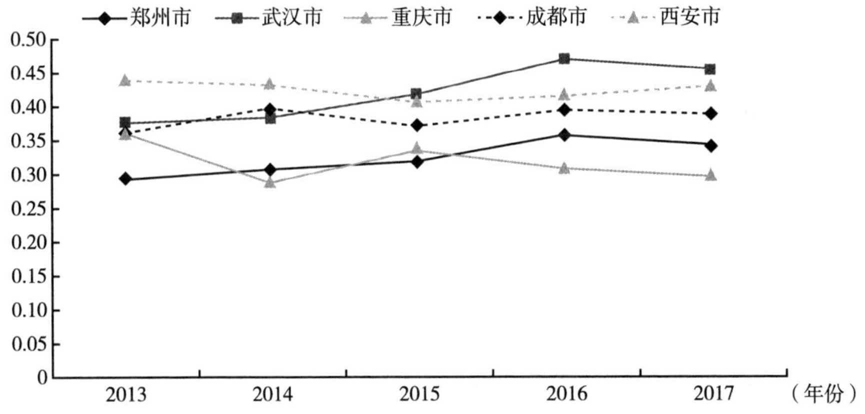

图 4　2013～2017 年中西部 5 个国家中心城市发明专利/专利申请比值

资料来源：历年中国统计年鉴及各市统计年鉴。

庆、郑州、武汉和西安（见图 5）。2013～2017 年武汉市高等学校专任教师数最多，重庆市最少，2017 年武汉市高等学校专任教师数达到 5.82 万人，重庆市为 4.17 万人，这与两市高校数量有直接关系；其中郑州市 2013～2017 年高等学校专任教师数增加明显，2017 年增加到 4.96 万人（见图 6）。

3. 国际竞争能力水平比较分析

从国际贸易发展来看，2013～2017 年 5 个国家中心城市国际货物进出口

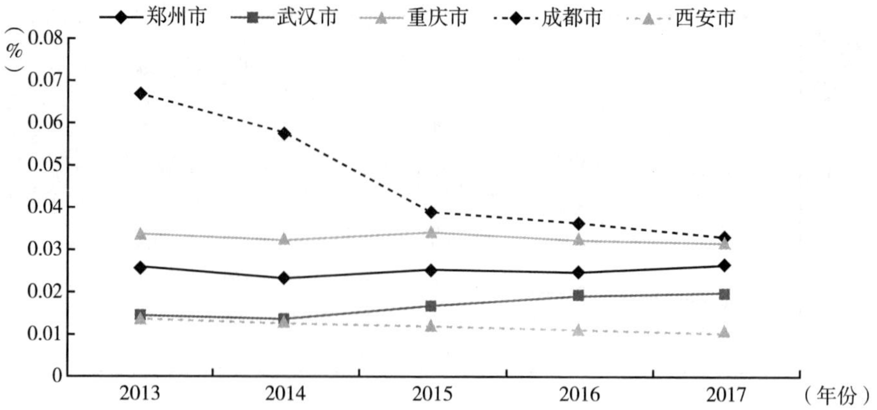

图5　2013～2017年中西部5个国家中心城市教育经费占GDP比值

资料来源：历年中国统计年鉴及各市统计年鉴。

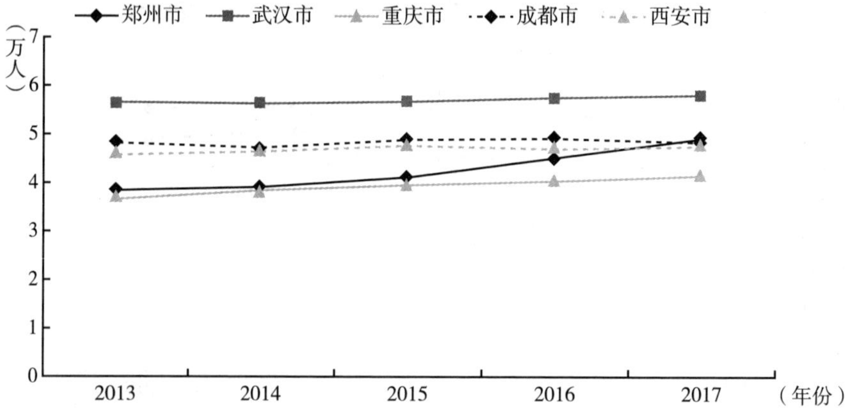

图6　2013～2017年中西部5个国家中心城市高等学校专任教师数

资料来源：历年中国统计年鉴及各市统计年鉴。

总额大致呈增长趋势，重庆市国际货物进出口总额虽然在2015年有所回落，但始终排在第一位；郑州市国际货物进出口总额在2015年超过成都，2017年达到596.3545亿美元，位列第二；成都市国际货物进出口总额稍有回落后回升，2017年达到583.0043亿美元，仅比郑州少13.3502亿美元，排在第三位；西安市在2014年超过武汉，2017年西安市国际货物进出口总额达到402.8038亿美元，武汉市为285.9100亿美元，分列第四、第五位（见图7）。在旅游业方面，2017 年有 3 个城市国际旅游创汇收入突破 2 亿美元，依次为武汉（2.50 亿美元）、西安（2.20 亿美元）和郑州（2.09 亿美元），重庆和成都分别为 1.95 亿美元和 1.31 亿美元；2017 年重庆市国际旅游总人次达到 358.35 亿人次，西安和成都国际旅游总人次分别超过 300 亿，武汉和郑州依次为 250.31 亿人次和 54.69 亿人次。数据表明国际旅游对重庆和西安市国际竞争能力贡献度较强，对郑州市国际竞争能力贡献度提高空间较大。

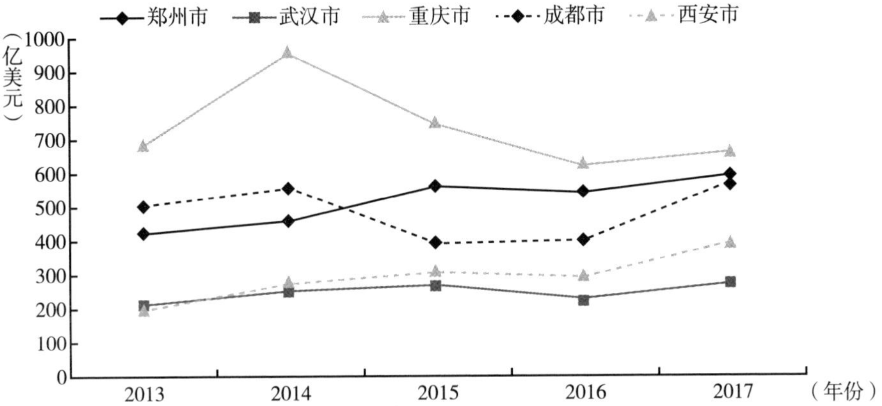

图 7　2013～2017 年中西部 5 个国家中心城市货物进出口总额

资料来源：历年中国统计年鉴及各市统计年鉴。

在外商投资方面，2017 年 5 个城市中 3 个城市实际利用外资额相差不多，依次为重庆（101.8255 亿美元）、成都（100.4100 亿美元）和武汉（96.4690 亿美元），西安市实际利用外资额（53.0680 亿美元）排在第四位，比第五位的郑州（40.4969 亿美元）多 12.5711 亿美元（见图 8）。2017 年郑州市规模以上工业企业外商投资企业数为 634 个（见图 9），远远高于其他 4 个国家中心城市，说明在外商投资方面 5 个城市总体差异较大，特别是郑州市实际利用外资额最少但规模以上工业企业外商投资企业数最多的现象值得深思。

在工业企业和社会生活方面，2013～2017 年 5 个城市规模以上工业企业主营业务收入都有不同程度提高，重庆市增长最为明显，从 2013 年的 15581.78 亿元增长到 2017 年的 20772.41 亿元，增长了 33.31%；郑州市规模以上工业企业主营业务收入位居第二，从 2013 年的 11016.27 亿元增长到 2017 年的 14738.92 亿元，增长了 33.79%；武汉市紧随其后，从 2013 年的

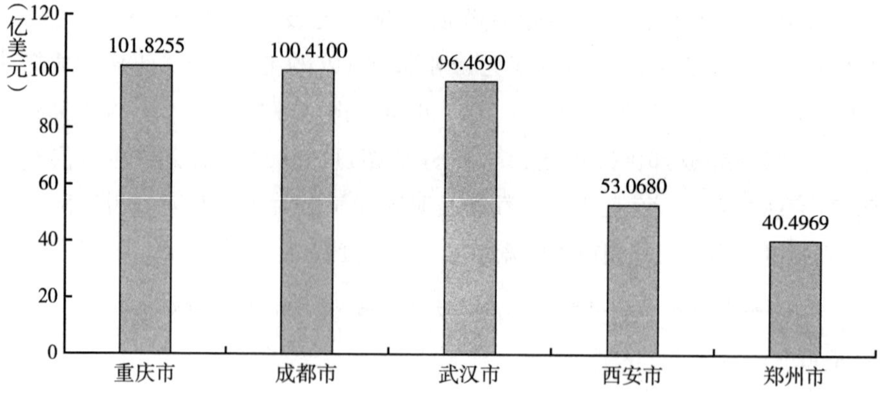

图8　2017年中西部5个国家中心城市实际利用外资额

资料来源：历年中国统计年鉴及各市统计年鉴。

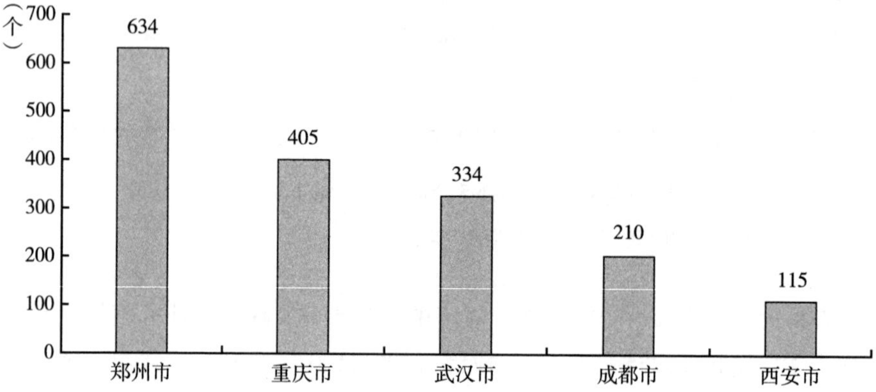

图9　2017年中西部5个国家中心城市规模以上工业企业外商投资企业数

资料来源：历年中国统计年鉴及各市统计年鉴。

10394.07亿元增长到2017年的14433.27亿元，增长了38.86%；成都市排在第四位，从2013年的8780.23亿元增长到2017年的12228.92亿元，增长了39.28%；排在第五位的是西安市，与其他4个城市相差较大，从2013年的4171.21亿元增长到2017年的5710.7亿元，增长了36.91%（见图10）。从2013~2017年社会消费品消费来看，郑州市社会消费品零售总额占市GDP比重最大，2017年占比56.88%；其他4个城市社会消费品零售总额占市GDP比重相差不大，2017年占比均超过40%，反映了我国城市人民物质文化生活水平有很大提高，社会商品购买力的实现程度高，以及零售市场消费规模状况很好（见图11）。

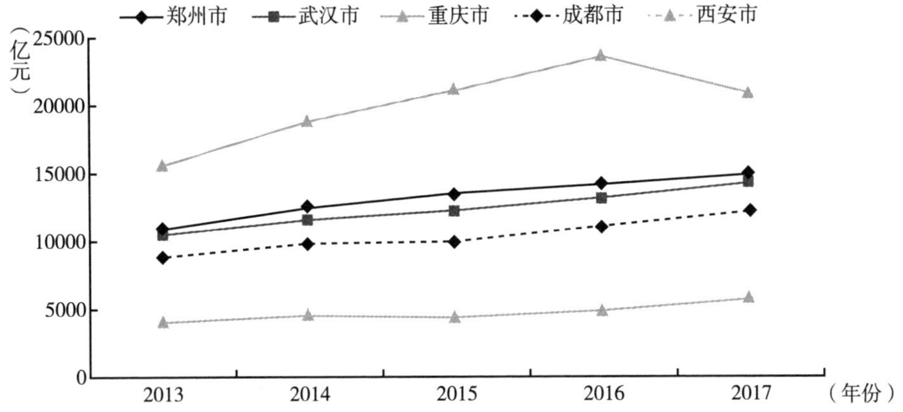

图10　2013～2017年中西部5个国家中心城市规模以上工业企业主营业务收入

资料来源：历年中国统计年鉴及各市统计年鉴。

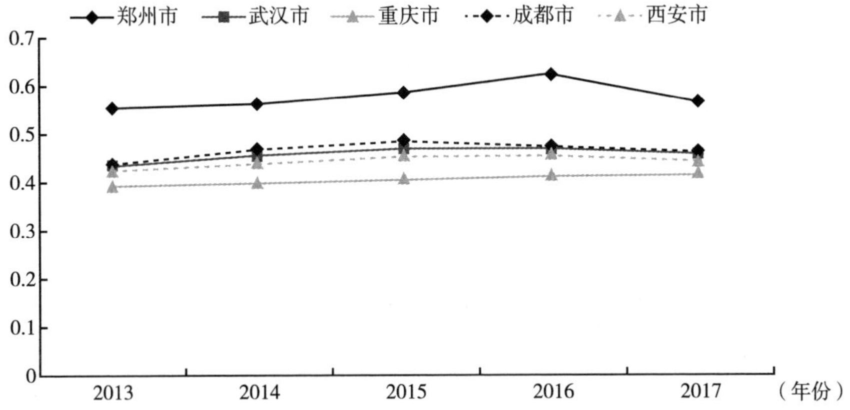

图11　2013～2017年中西部5个国家中心城市社会消费品零售总额占GDP比重

资料来源：历年中国统计年鉴及各市统计年鉴。

4. 辐射带动能力水平比较分析

5个国家中心城市提高辐射带动能力水平最基础要归结于人，图12可以明显看出，重庆市人口承载遥遥领先，2018年常住人口达到3101.7万人，主要是因为重庆是直辖市，第一批国家中心城市；其次是成都市，2018年常住人口达到1633万人，而武汉、郑州和西安2018年常住人口依次为1108.1万人、1013.6万人和1000.37万人，特别是郑州常住人口突破千万。从城市经济首位度来看，2013～2017年郑州城市首位度平均值为2.05，西安是1.97；而成都、重庆和武汉的城市首位度均值依次为6.39、5.15和3.22（见图13），5个中心城市都有所上升，但城市发展要素的集中程度和带动能力差距明显。

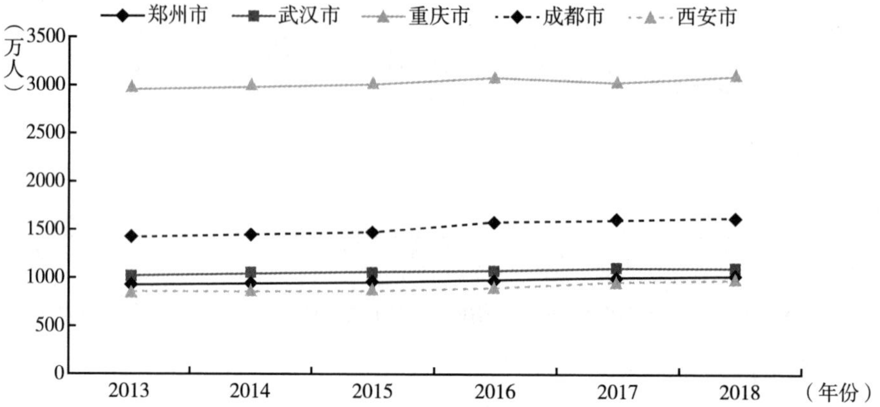

图12　2013～2018年中西部5个国家中心城市人口承载量——常住人口

资料来源：历年中国统计年鉴及各市统计年鉴。

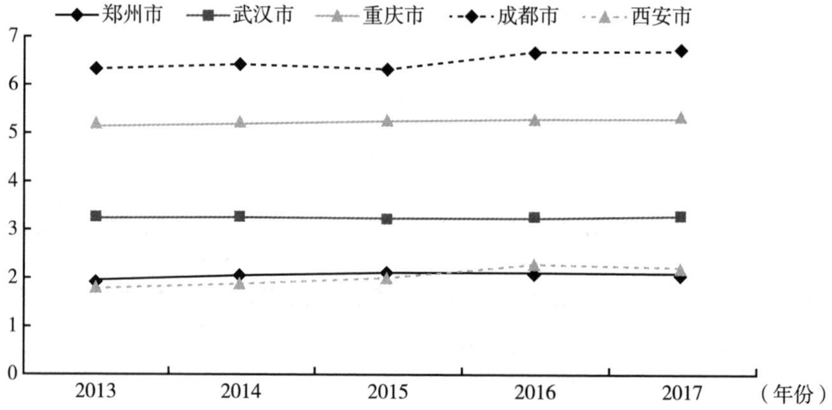

图13　2013～2017年中西部5个国家中心城市城市首位度

资料来源：历年中国统计年鉴及各市统计年鉴。

在城市发展和居民生活消费方面，2013～2017 年，5 个城市城镇居民人均消费支出水平和单位城区面积 GDP 都有大幅提升，除 2013 年人均消费支出外，武汉市一直处于首位；各市城镇居民人均消费支出水平均值排名依次为武汉（2.4236）、西安（2.3265）、成都（2.2545）、郑州（2.1733）和重庆（1.9787）（见图 14）；各市常住人口城镇化率水平均值排名依次为西安（72.90%）、成都（70.74%）、武汉（69.90%）、郑州（69.71%）和重庆（61.1%）；2017 年郑州市单位城区面积 GDP 上升到 18.36 万元，超过成都市（15.68 万元）位居第二位，而第一位武汉（21.35 万元）是第五位西安（10.94 万元）的 1.95 倍，第四位重庆为 12.69 万元（见图 15）。尽管近几年城市发展和居民生活消费水平有了整体性提高，特别是郑州各项指标数据都有大幅提升，但也表明 5 个城市之间发展水平不均衡，发展差异显著。

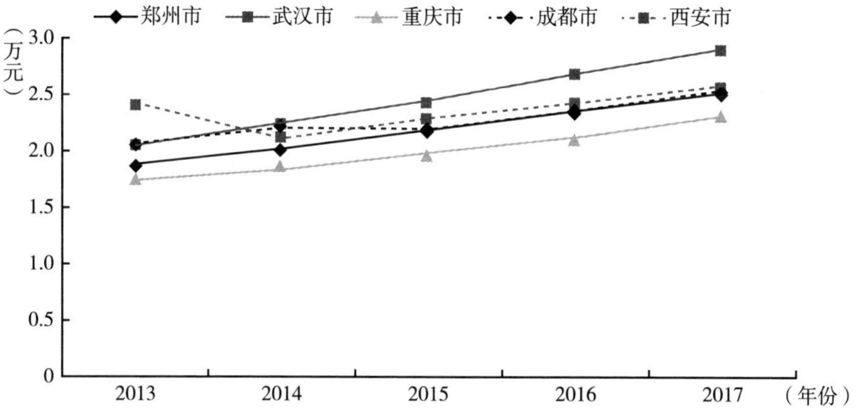

图 14　2013～2017 年中西部 5 个国家中心城市城镇居民人均消费支出水平

资料来源：历年中国统计年鉴及各市统计年鉴。

2013～2017 年 5 个城市第二三产业增加值占地区生产总值占比大致呈现先下降后回升的趋势，均值在 0.10 左右，说明 5 个城市第二三产业增加值占地区生产总值占比几乎没有差异；但是西安市从 2013 年的 0.1067 增加到 2017 年的 0.1526，第二三产业发展迅速，并且 2013～2017 年西安市现代服务业就业人员占比大幅提高，从 2013 年的 0.506 增加到 2017 年的 0.583（见图 16），在 2015 年超过武汉市位居首位，西安市第二三产业特别是现代服务业增速明显，主要因为西安是中国四大古都之一，“世界历史名城”和旅游胜地。郑州

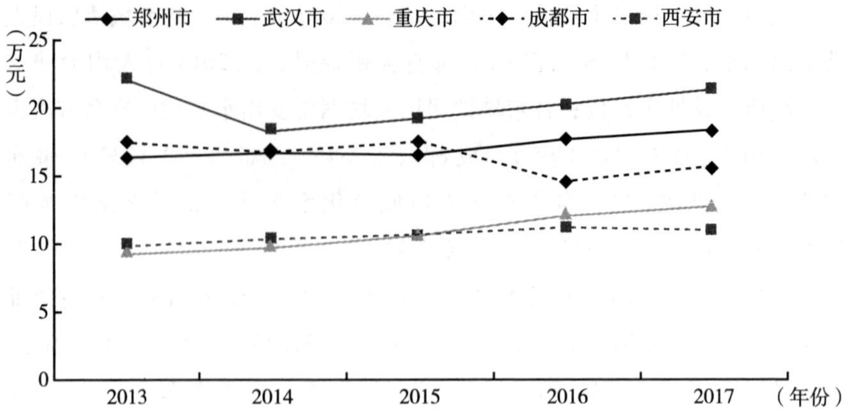

图 15　2013~2017 年中西部 5 个国家中心城市单位城区面积 GDP

资料来源：历年中国统计年鉴及各市统计年鉴。

市第二三产业也在稳步发展，2017 年第二三产业增加值占地区生产总值占比为 0.1111，超过均值（0.0960）1.51 个百分点，现代服务业就业人员占比为 0.5070，与武汉、成都相差较小，但第二三产业特别是现代服务业仍有待提高；而 2017 年重庆市第二三产业增加值占地区生产总值占比和现代服务业就业人员占比双低，依次为 0.0884 和 0.4538（见图 17），说明重庆第二三产业和现代服务业对地区辐射带动能力贡献度不高。

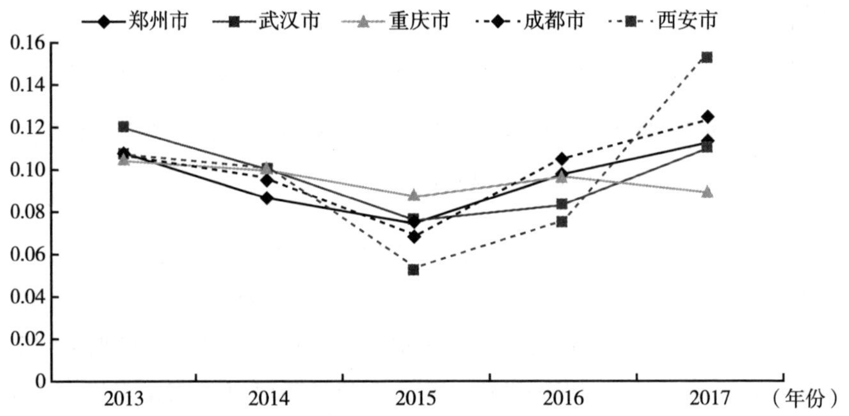

图 16　2013~2017 年中西部 5 个国家中心城市第二三产业增加值占地区生产总值比例

资料来源：历年中国统计年鉴及各市统计年鉴。

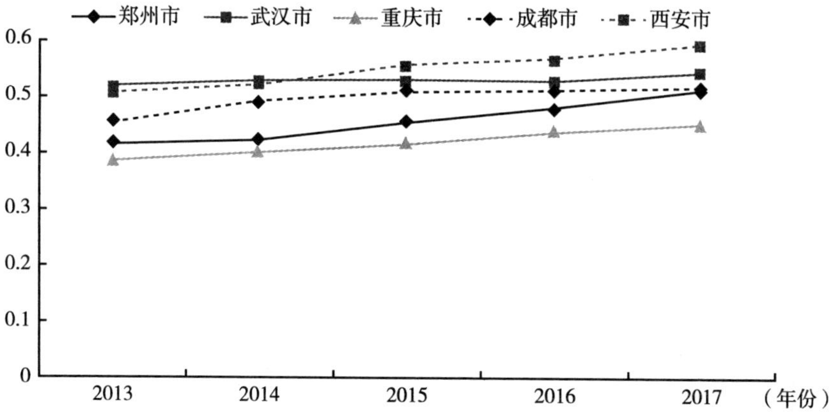

图 17　2013～2017 年中西部 5 个国家中心城市现代服务业就业人员占比

资料来源：历年中国统计年鉴及各市统计年鉴。

5. 交通通达能力水平比较分析

随着各市经济的发展和城镇居民可支配收入的增加，城市民用车辆在不断增加。重庆市民用车辆拥有量一直处在首位，在 2017 年达到 5674952 辆，第二位是成都市，2017 年达到 4941800 辆，郑州、武汉和西安 2017 年民用车辆拥有量依次为 3038852 辆、2750050 辆和 2716361 辆（见图 18）。各市高速公路、城市地铁的发展极大地提高了城市的交通通达能力，到 2018 年末，重庆

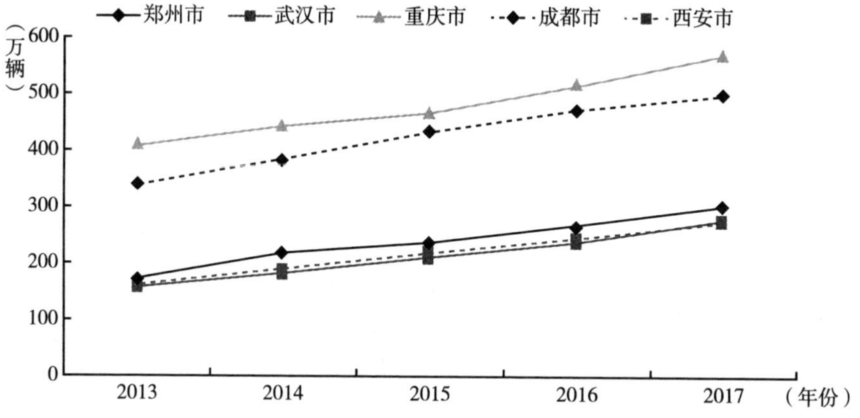

图 18　2013～2017 年中西部 5 个国家中心城市民用车辆拥有量

资料来源：历年中国统计年鉴及各市统计年鉴。

市高速公路通车里程达到3023公里，远远多于其他4个中心城市，郑州市位居第四位，仅比第五位西安（572公里）多10公里（见图19）。近几年各市城镇化率的提高，城市拥堵问题越来越受到社会各界关注，导致城市地铁发展迅速。2018年武汉市城市地铁通车运营里程最多，其次是成都和重庆，最后是郑州和西安，武汉市是西安市的2.15倍。

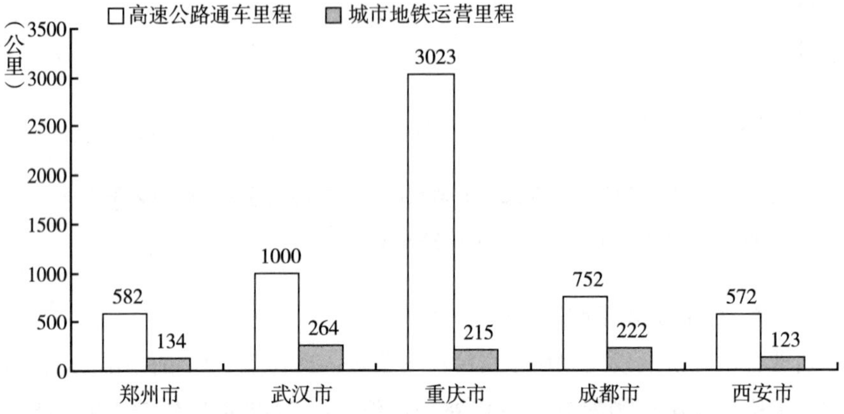

图19　2018年中西部5个国家中心城市高速公路、城市地铁通车运营里程

资料来源：历年中国统计年鉴及各市统计年鉴。

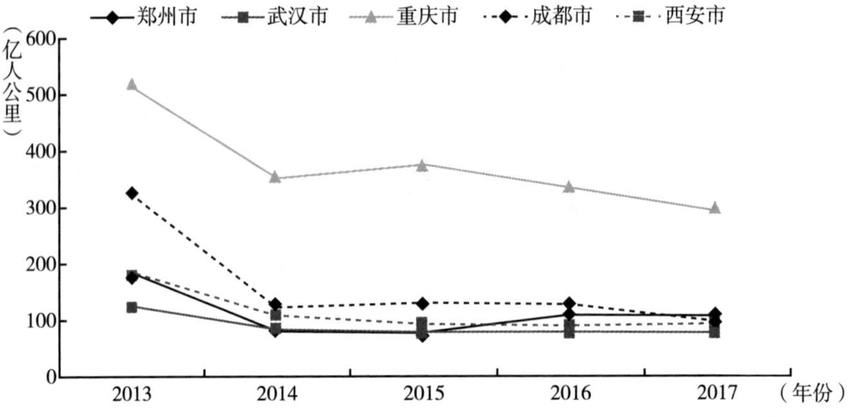

图20　2013～2017年中西部5个国家中心城市公路旅客周转量

资料来源：历年中国统计年鉴及各市统计年鉴。

随着人们物质生活水平的提高，2013～2017年公路旅客周转量明显下降，航空旅客周转量显著上升，而公路货物周转量逐渐上升。其中重庆市两项交通运输能力指标均居首位，郑州市公路货物周转量明显增加，2017年达到558亿吨公里（见图21），位列第三，相比武汉和成都相差较小。公路旅客周转量排名第二的成都市，其航空旅客吞吐量从2013年的1656.7万人增加到2017年的4976万人，位列第一，其他4个城市航空旅客吞吐量依次排名为西安（4186万人）、重庆（3966万人）、郑州（2596.58万人）和武汉（2312.94万人）（见图22）。在航空货运方面，2013～2017年郑州市航空货运周转量明显提升，从2013年的8.57亿吨公里增加到2017年的18.60亿吨公里，在2015年超过成都市居首位，2017年航空货运周转量超过第二位成都4.88亿吨公里，而武汉、重庆和西安航空货运周转量相差不大，依次为2.97亿吨公里、1.95亿吨公里和1.02亿吨公里（见图23）。2013～2017年各市铁路旅客发送量均值排名依次为武汉（1.42亿人）、成都（0.49亿人）、郑州（0.47亿人）、重庆（0.45亿人）和西安（0.38亿人）（见图24）。作为“中国铁路的心脏”的郑州，其全国重要的交通枢纽中心的作用不明显，对交通通达能力的贡献有待提高，而郑州航空港区依托新郑国际机场，航空货运周转量在中西部5个国家中心城市中居首，对郑州市交通通达能力的贡献很大。

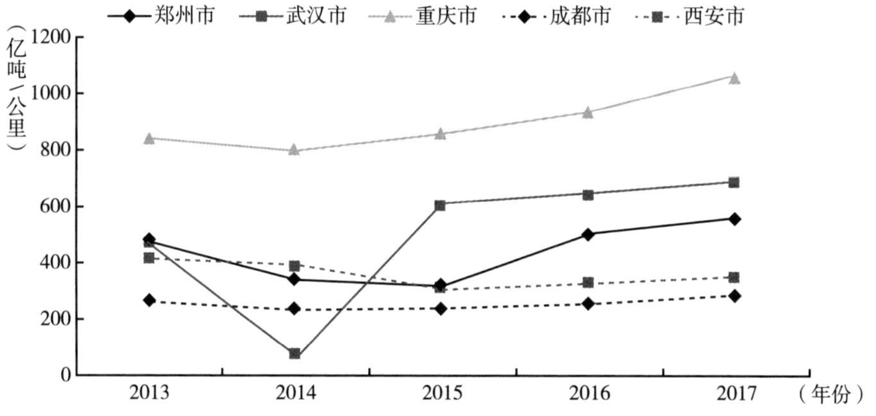

图21　2013～2017年中西部5个国家中心城市公路货物周转量

资料来源：历年中国统计年鉴及各市统计年鉴。

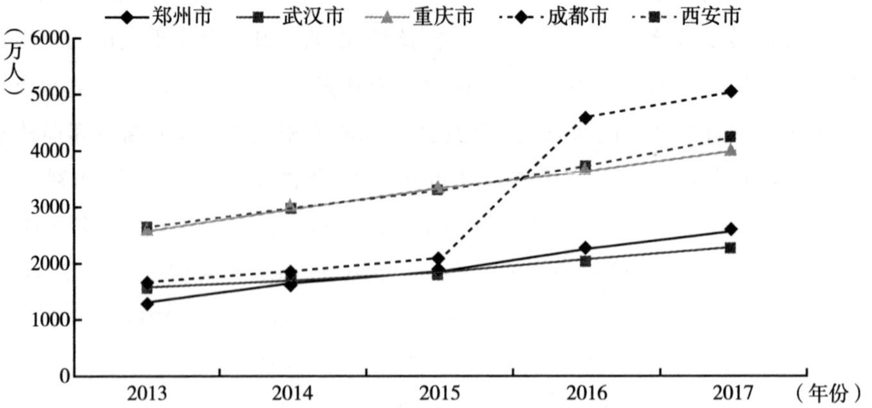

图 22　2013～2017 年中西部 5 个国家中心城市航空旅客吞吐量

资料来源：历年中国统计年鉴及各市统计年鉴。

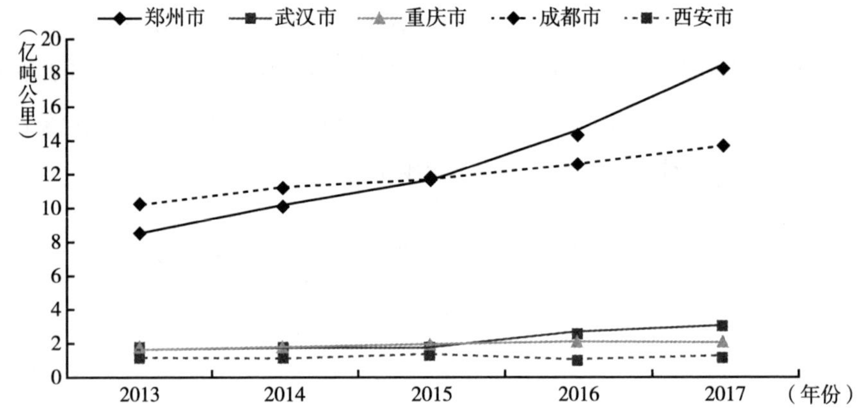

图 23　2013～2017 年中西部 5 个国家中心城市航空货运周转量

资料来源：历年中国统计年鉴及各市统计年鉴。

6. 信息交流能力水平比较分析

各市信息交流能力水平主要体现在互联网的应用、邮政电信业务等方面。随着互联网的发展与人们的信息文化交流逐渐频繁，2017 年郑州市国际互联网用户遥遥领先，达到 1735.26 万户，其次为成都市（1081.00 万户）和重庆市（1074.00 万户），最后是武汉（429.86 万户）和西安（343.42 万户）（见

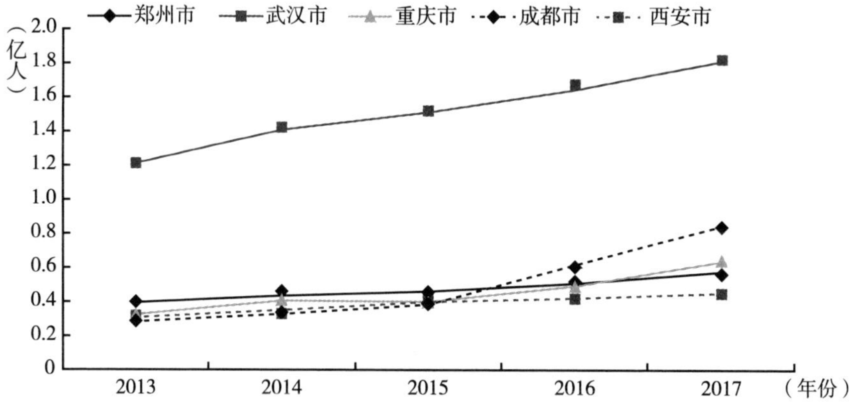

图 24　2013～2017 年中西部 5 个国家中心城市铁路旅客发送量

资料来源：历年中国统计年鉴及各市统计年鉴。

图 25）。从快递业来看，2017 年 5 个城市快递业务量、快递业务收入从高到低依次为：成都、武汉、郑州、重庆和西安（见图 26）。

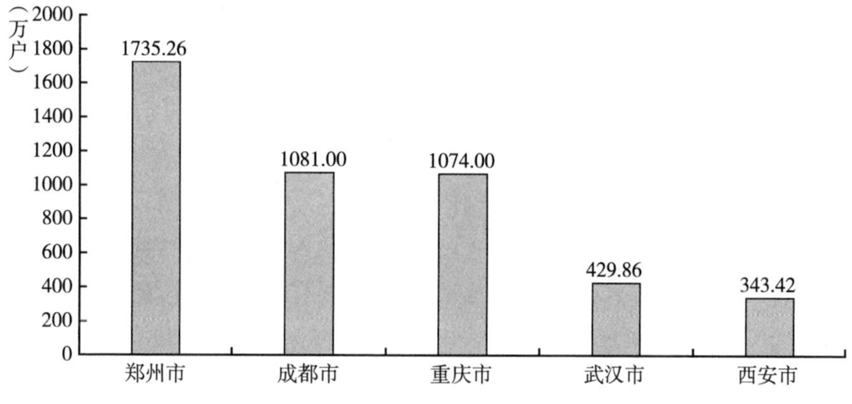

图 25　2017 年中西部 5 个国家中心城市国际互联网用户

资料来源：历年中国统计年鉴及各市统计年鉴。

从电信业来看，2013～2017 年 5 个城市人均电信业务消费量增长迅速，西安市始终居于首位，郑州市在 2016 年超过武汉市居第二位，2017 年郑州市人均电信业务消费量达到 0.3646 万元，仅比首位西安少 0.0056 万元，其他 3

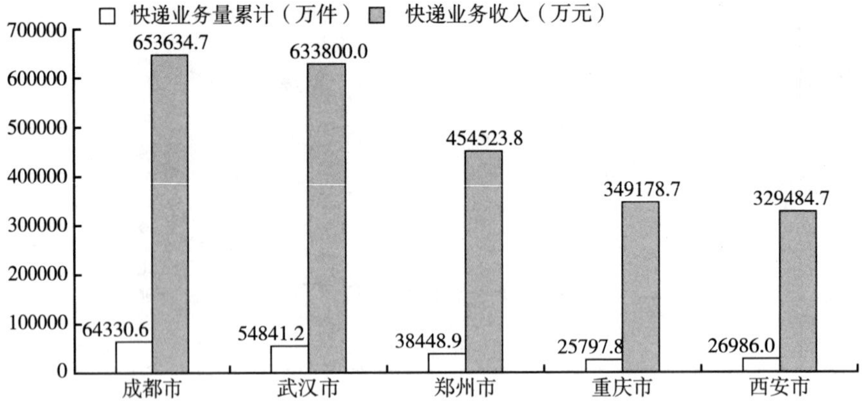

图 26　2017 年中西部 5 个国家中心城市快递业务量、快递业务收入

资料来源：历年中国统计年鉴及各市统计年鉴。

个城市排名依次为武汉（0.2949 万元）、重庆（0.1988 万元）和成都（0.1500 万元）（见图 27）。在移动通信方面，2013～2017 年西安市万人移动电话数明显高于其他四个城市，从 2013 年 1.93 万部增长到 2017 年的 2.52 万部，郑州市万人移动电话数明显从 2013 年 1.29 万部增长到 2017 年的 1.50 万部，排名最低的是重庆市，2017 年西安市万人移动电话数是重庆市（10649.46 部）的 2.36 倍（见图 28）。在信息服务业方面，成都市信息服务就业人员占比增长明显，从 2013 年的 0.0020 增长到 2017 年的 0.0345，位居首位，郑州市信息服务就业人员占比增长较快，从 2013 年的 0.0118 增长到 2017 年的 0.0202，在 2016 年超过重庆位居第二位，2017 年其他 3 个城市信息服务就业人员占比排名依次为重庆（0.0177）、西安（0.0154）和武汉（0.0151）（见图 29）。

7. 可持续发展能力水平比较分析

在能源利用效率方面，单位 GDP 能耗越低，说明能源利用效率越高。2013～2018 年 5 个中心城市单位 GDP 能耗显著降低，表明各城市能源利用效率普遍提高，具体来看，郑州市单位 GDP 能耗下降最明显，从 2013 年的 0.3853 万吨/亿元降低到 2018 年的 0.1884 万吨/亿元，能源利用效率最高；重庆市单位 GDP 能耗下降较明显，从 2013 年的 0.3079 万吨/亿元降低到 2018 年的 0.2017 万吨/亿元，能源利用效率次之；其他三个城市单位 GDP 能耗都有所降低，但成都

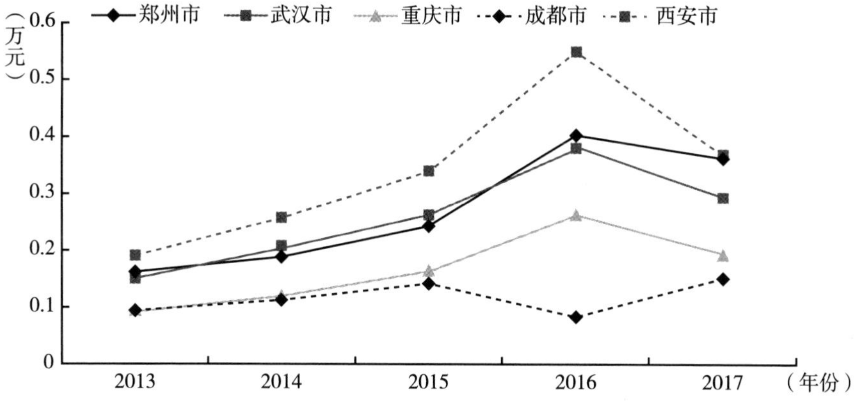

图 27　2013～2017 年中西部 5 个国家中心城市人均电信业务消费量

资料来源：历年中国统计年鉴及各市统计年鉴。

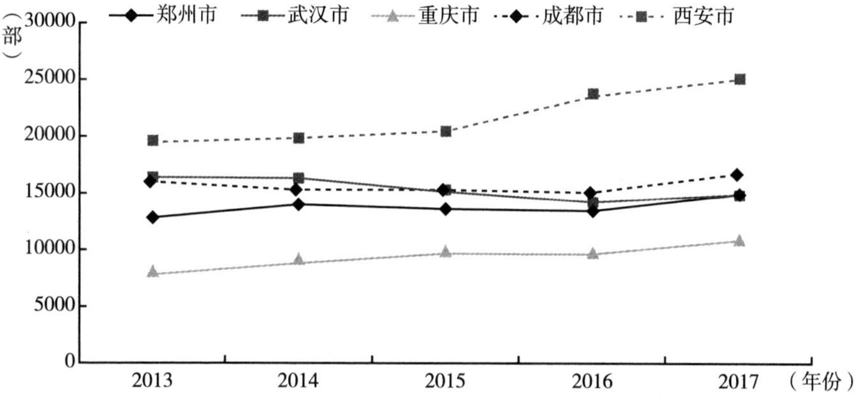

图 28　2013～2017 年中西部 5 个国家中心城市万人移动电话数

资料来源：历年中国统计年鉴及各市统计年鉴。

市能源利用效率提高较慢，2018 年能源利用效率排名依次为西安（0.3860 万吨/亿元）、武汉（0.3903 万吨/亿元）和成都（0.4500 万吨/亿元）（见图 30）。同样图 31 可以看出，2013～2017 年 5 个中心城市单位 GDP 天然气消耗量均值从小到大依次是郑州（14.14 立方米/万元）、武汉（14.66 立方米/万元）、成都（22.49 立方米/万元）、西安（32.55 立方米/万元）和重庆（54.83 立方米/万元），与 5 个城市天然气利用效率高低排名相同。2012～2017 年 5 个中心城市人

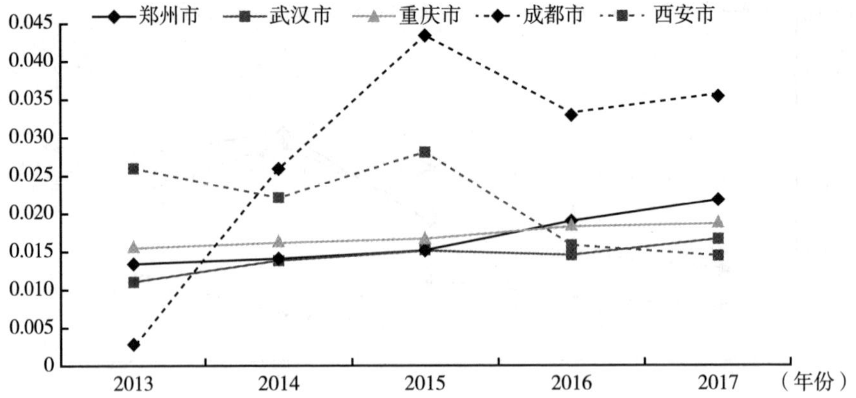

图 29　2013～2017 年中西部 5 个国家中心城市信息服务就业人员占比

资料来源：历年中国统计年鉴及各市统计年鉴。

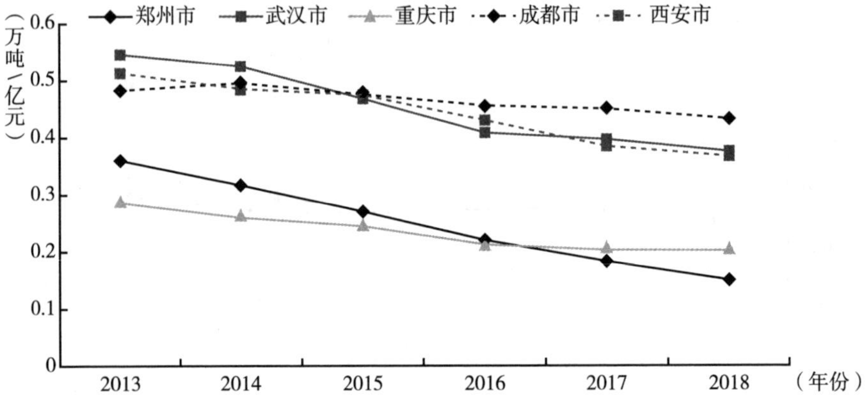

图 30　2013～2018 年中西部 5 个国家中心城市单位 GDP 能耗

资料来源：历年中国统计年鉴及各市统计年鉴。

均发电量（万千瓦时）均值排名依次为郑州（0.53 万千瓦时）、西安（0.48 万千瓦时）、武汉（0.44 万千瓦时）、重庆（0.29 万千瓦时）和成都（0.24 万千瓦时）（见图 32），首位郑州是第五位成都的 2.21 倍。

2017 年一般工业固体废物综合利用量最高的 3 个中西部国家中心城市依次为武汉（1403.2 万吨）、重庆（1402 万吨）和郑州（1332.33 万吨），郑州市虽位居第三，但与前两个城市差距较小；成都和西安一般工业固体废物综合

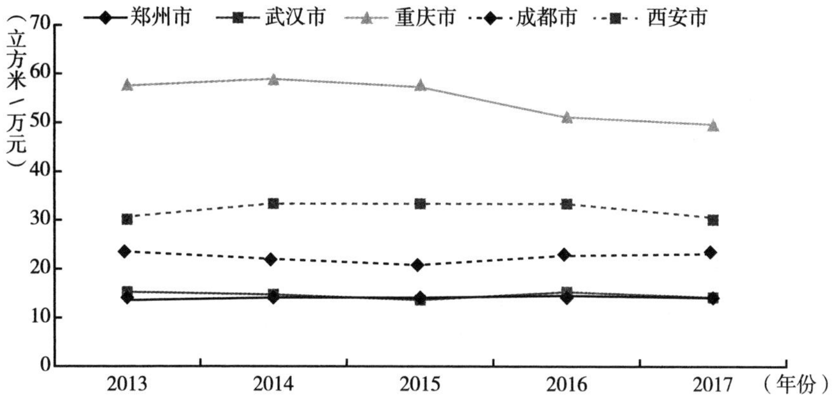

图31　2013～2017年中西部5个国家中心城市单位GDP天然气消耗量

资料来源：历年中国统计年鉴及各市统计年鉴。

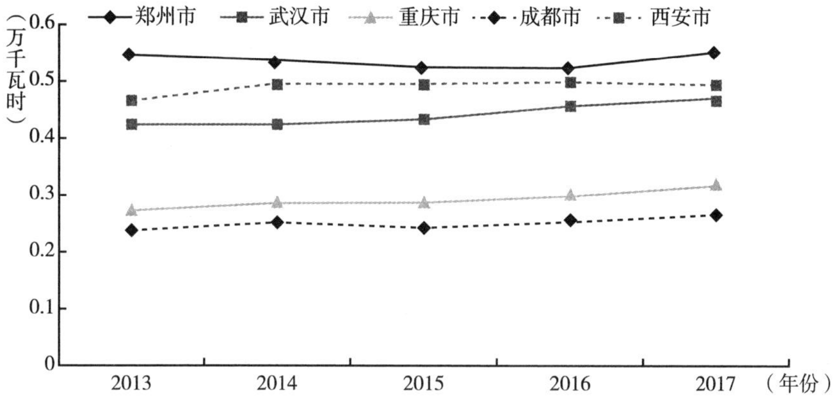

图32　2013～2017年中西部5个国家中心城市人均发电量

资料来源：历年中国统计年鉴及各市统计年鉴。

利用量较低，依次为200.76万吨和158.6万吨（见图33）。综上明显看出中西部国家中心城市可持续发展能力水平差异明显。在环境绿化保护方面，2013～2017年5个城市环境质量均有所改善，空气质量一、二级质量天数均值排名依次为重庆（262.2天）、武汉（203.8天）、成都（203天）、西安（190.2天）和郑州（146天）（见图34），最高天数是最低天数的1.80倍，郑州市空气质量达标率有待提高。

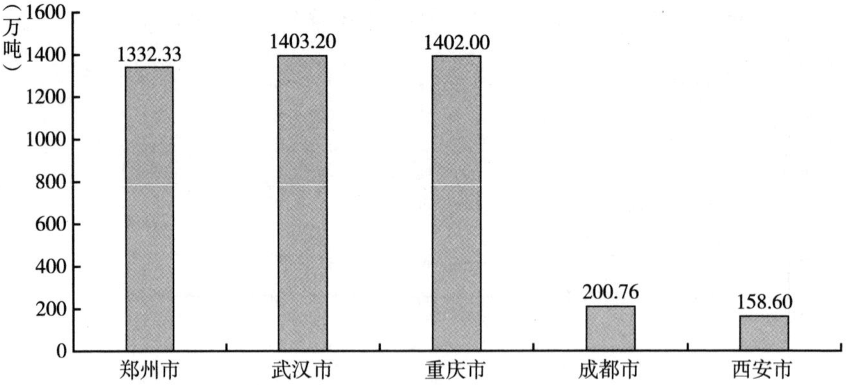

图 33　2017 年中西部 5 个国家中心城市一般工业固体废物综合利用量

资料来源：历年中国统计年鉴及各市统计年鉴。

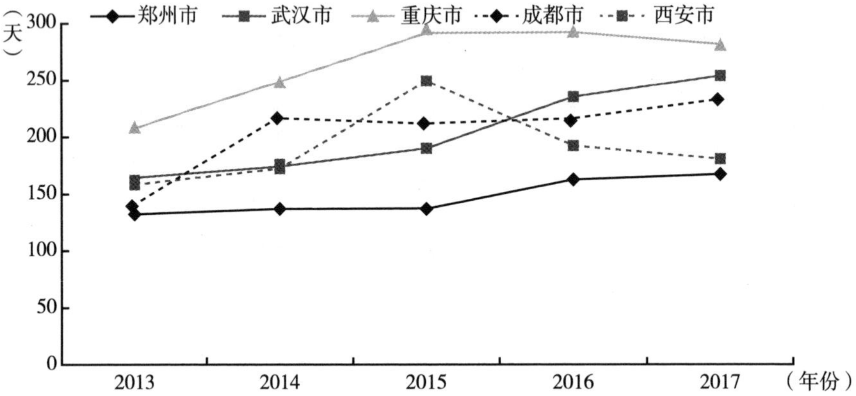

图 34　2013～2017 年中西部 5 个国家中心城市空气质量达标率（空气质量一、二级质量天数）

资料来源：历年中国统计年鉴及各市统计年鉴。

以 2018 年为例，选取部分原始数据对中西部 5 个国家中心城市主要功能进行简单比较（见表 2）。

基于构建国家中心城市功能考核评价指标体系测度体系，借助熵权 TOPSIS（具体过程略）对 2013～2017 年中国中西部 5 个国家中心城市功能考核评价各子系统指数及综合指数均值进行排名：重庆市（4.882）、武汉市（1.811）、成都市（1.342）、郑州市（1.174）和西安市（0.629）（见图 35）。

表 2　2018 年中西部 5 个国家中心城市主要功能指标对比

	郑州	武汉	重庆	成都	西安
人均 GDP(元)	100071.03	133988.71	65649.80	93954.50	83467.71
财政收入(亿元)	1152.1	2900.24	2265.5	1424.2	684.71
企业研发投入(亿元)	103.4	128.31	279.99	289.07	110.47
实际利用外资额(亿美元)	40.5	96.47	101.83	100.41	53.07
经济首位度	2.19	3.45	4.87	6.66	2.17
常住人口城镇化率(%)	73.38	80.29	65.77	73.12	74.01
现代服务业就业人员占比(%)	50.7	54.1	45.4	51.4	58.3
铁路旅客发送量(万人)	5751.86	18074.3	6349.24	8426.76	4500
信息服务人员占比(%)	2	1.5	1.8	3.5	1.5
单位 GDP 能耗(万吨/亿元)	0.155	0.376	0.196	0.433	0.367
城市空气质量达标率(空气质量一、二级质量天数)	168	249	316	251	188
第二三产业增加值与地区生产总值比值	0.0748	0.0733	0.0556	0.0476	0.0749

资料来源：根据历年中国统计年鉴及各省市统计年鉴整理而得。

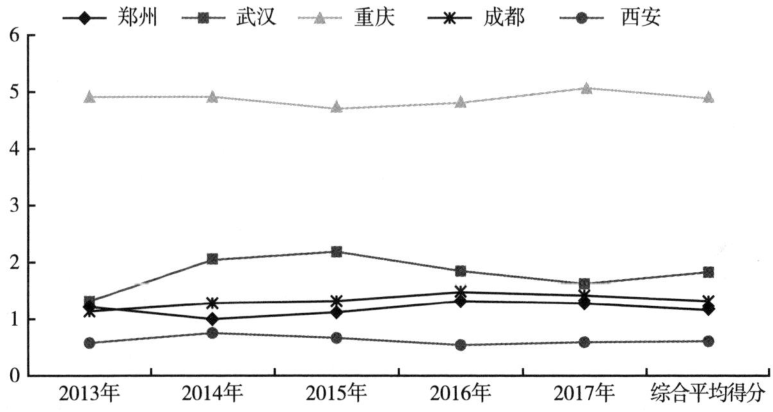

图 35　2013～2017 年中西部 5 个国家中心城市功能考核评价指标体系综合指数

资料来源：历年中国统计年鉴及各市统计年鉴。

从综合水平来看，2013～2017 年国家中心城市功能考核综合水平整体偏低，按照国家中心城市功能考核综合水平依次排名为重庆市、武汉市、成都市、郑州市、西安市，而且，中西部地区国家中心城市功能考核综合水平差异程度明显。

二　郑州建设国家中心城市功能优化提升建议

根据上述比较及研究结论，郑州应重点优化和提升其科技创新能力、国际竞争能力、辐射带动能力，进一步强化其交通通达能力，提高城市综合经济能力发展水平。为积极推进郑州等中西部国家中心城市功能水平的全面优化提升，提出以下政策建议。

1. 打造优势产业，促进郑州市综合经济高质量发展

中西部 5 个国家中心城市重庆市、武汉市、成都市和郑州市 GDP 均超过万亿元，但郑州市综合经济能力排名靠后，第二三产业对经济发展贡献度有待提高。在产业结构方面，郑州市应加大固定资产投资力度，特别是第二三产业，主要投资于先进智能制造业、新能源化工产业、电子信息产业等战略性新兴产业，努力实现“四化”生产；郑州市现代服务业就业人员占比和其他 4 个中心城市相比更加集中，要努力扩大信息、商务和科技服务业总量，克服服务业企业规模小的问题，实现生产性服务业发展规模与制造业相匹配。在金融业方面，郑州市需积极改善营商环境，完善金融市场体系和金融机构的政策举措，放宽金融市场准入机制，吸引国内外金融机构投资者进驻郑州，共同提高郑州市综合经济发展质量。

2. 注重科技创新，多方位提升科技创新能力

在科技创新能力方面，重庆市和武汉市科研创新能力较好，郑州市与之相比有一定差距。首先，郑州应进一步推动创新要素的集聚，加大创新人才引进和创新资金投入力度，大力吸引科研创新型人才，加大科技研发的投入力度，特别是为工业企业营造良好的科创环境，不断激发企业创新活力。其次，不断完善创新成果转化平台建设，提高授权专利占比，提高创新产出能力和科技竞争力。郑州还需尽快补齐短板，优化创新发展环境，深化创新体制机制改革，加大财政资金对创新的支持力度，政府、企业、大学、研发机构等多方位协同发展，提高政产学研用创新发展水平。从优势领域入手，依托郑洛新国家自主创新示范区，重点扶持培育创新龙头企业和创新产业集

群，以点带面提升郑州国家中心城市自主创新能力，引领支撑河南乃至中原经济区的创新发展。

3. 改善城市商业环境，提高国际竞争能力和信息化水平

郑州市国际竞争力的总体实力、区域实力以及信息技术等方面与重庆和成都有一定差距，但国际贸易方面表现出良好的攀升态势。一是改善商业环境，提高国际金融业发展水平，规范和提升金融监管质量和监管透明度，提高人民币在“一带一路”地区的结算地位，全面提高国际竞争能力。二是充分利用郑州自由贸易试验区的优势，重点发展先进制造业和国际服务业“走出去”，促进郑州市现代国际物流和国际商贸进一步发展，提升国际产能合作能力；充分发挥郑州商品交易所（中西部地区唯一的期货交易所）的期货交易功能，不断促进金融服务和实体经济的相互融合。三是打造国际信息化城市，加快信息基础设施建设，依据“互联网＋”思维范式发展云计算、大数据、人工智能等现代化信息技术，提升郑州市国际化开放程度和信息交流水平。

4. 进一步提升郑州的交通通达能力，发挥辐射带动作用

首先，优化空间结构，打造郑州大都市区，提高郑州城市首位度，进一步提升城镇化水平和质量，增强郑州市城市辐射力。郑州市是中部地区重要的经济中心城市，国家重要的综合交通、通信枢纽，要致力于完善郑州市城际交通网络，优化郑州与中原城市群互联互通网络运输模式，优化航空、高速公路、铁路和高铁运输效率，降低客货运输成本，提高郑州市对中原地区支撑和辐射作用。其次，在“一带一路”和中部崛起等国家战略指导下，郑州市要发挥国家综合交通枢纽示范工程城市的作用，陇海、京广铁路十字交汇，承载东西部产业转移与资源输出，同时也是南北经贸交流的纽带，郑州“米”字形高铁目前拥有8条城际铁路网，现在辐射全国经济、贸易以及创新型产业的“虹吸效应”。最后，郑州市建有中国首个国家级航空港经济综合实验区，要充分利用陆空对接、多式联运和内捷外畅的现代综合交通体系，以及郑州航空港、国际陆港、郑欧班列、跨境电子商务试验区等开放平台的优势，发挥航空运输货运中转和集疏能力，吸引高端要素聚集，形成以航空经济为引领的现代产业基地，建设内陆地区对外开放新高地。

参考文献

［1］张占仓：《建设国家中心城市的战略意义与推进对策》，《中州学刊》2017 年第 4 期，第 22 ~ 28 页。

［2］贺正楚：《长沙建设国家中心城市的对策研究》，《经济数学》2018 年第 1 期，第 44 ~ 57 页。

［3］于小琳、刘长、刘希玉：《中国四大经济强省科技创新能力比较及山东提升策略》，《中国科技论坛》2019 年第 2 期，第 100 ~ 108 页。

［4］王淑英、屈莹莹、WangShuying 等：《国家中心城市的金融集聚对经济效率的影响研究》，《工业技术经济》2017 年第 8 期，第 3 ~ 10 页。

［5］江昶：《国家治理现代化视域下的中国城市信息化建设研究》，《国家行政学院学报》2018 年第 6 期，第 181 ~ 193 页。

［6］徐爱民、刘冬明、黄元宰：《江苏省南通市优化城市建设增强中心功能研究》，《中国工程咨询》2017 年第 5 期，第 41 ~ 43 页。

［7］姚伟奇、李潭峰：《环鄱阳湖生态城市群交通体系规划研究》，《综合运输》2017 年第 12 期，第 13 ~ 18 页。

B.29

郑州国家中心城市与国家级中原城市群升级的战略与路径研究

刘战国*

摘　要： 随着我国经济重心战略西移，国家级中原城市群将成长为世界级城市群，郑州国家中心城市将成长为国际中心城市；制约中原城市群转型升级的主要矛盾是郑州中心城市经济实力较弱，“多中心大都市区、多核心大都市圈、一体化通勤圈”空间结构没有形成；未来应紧紧围绕构建世界级城市群和世界级中心城市战略目标加快转型升级，着力构建“多中心”大郑州都市区、“多核心同城化”大郑州都市圈、郑州洛阳双中心结构模式、外围副中心城市圈层、以轨道交通为主导的交通圈或通勤圈。

关键词： 郑州　国家中心城市　中原城市群

经济区是城市群的腹地和载体，城市群是经济区的主体。近年来我国工业化进入中后期阶段，城市群已经成为我国区域经济的主体形态。中心城市是城市群的核心增长极。

一　世界五大著名城市群的发展经验与启示

著名的世界五大城市群，分别为以纽约为中心的美国东北部大西洋沿岸城

* 刘战国，河南省人民政府发展研究中心研究员，研究方向为区域经济、城市发展。

市群（纽约大都市圈）、以芝加哥为中心的北美五大湖区城市群（北美五大湖大都市圈）、以东京为中心的日本太平洋沿岸城市群（东京大都市圈）、以巴黎为中心的欧洲西北部城市群（巴黎大都市圈）、以伦敦为中心的英国城市群（伦敦大都市圈）。

（一）经济高度集中、高度集聚、高度服务业化

①经济高度集中。巴黎都市区占法国国土面积的2%，人口却占到全国的19%，2005 年 GDP 占整个法国的28.6%。②中心城市的集中度高。纽约市以不到2%的国土面积，集聚了纽约都市圈38%的就业人口和34%的地区生产总值，其中曼哈顿地区集聚了纽约市 61% 就业人口和 71% 地区生产总值。③三次产业结构高度服务业化。处于后工业化社会，产业结构呈现高度服务业化，2004 年纽约都市圈三次产业就业结构为 0.2∶13.2∶86.6。

（二）首位城市为世界中心城市（或全球城市）

纽约、伦敦、东京、巴黎、芝加哥均为位居世界前列的世界城市，都具有全球影响力的经济中心、金融中心、贸易中心、交通枢纽、物流中心、总部经济中心、科创中心、政治文化中心。

（三）空间结构呈现“圈层结构”特点

世界各大城市群（大都市圈）均呈现圈层结构，如纽约大都市圈分为四层：第一层为核心 CBD；第二层为主城区；第三层为大都市区（通勤区），由近郊多中心和远郊卫星城组成，这些通勤区域构成纽约大都市圈的内圈，总面积为 10202 平方公里；第四层为纽约大都市圈，“跨越 10 个州、五大中心城市”的空间范围，形成纽约大都市圈的外环，总面积为 13.8 万平方公里。

（四）大都市区呈现“多中心”布局

世界各大城市群都经历过快速城镇化阶段，为了适应规模、功能和空间扩张的需要，实现经济与人文、生态环境的和谐发展，避免城市病，纷纷采取“大都市区近郊多中心、远郊卫星城、周边一体化”的空间布局战略。

（五）以轨道交通为主导的现代交通网络（或通勤圈）

都市圈区域一体化功能及各中心城市的高效分工协作，离不开发达的城际交通网，以轨道交通为主导的现代交通网是城市群的基础工程。例如，东京都市圈拥有约 2000 公里的轨道交通线路。

（六）注重以战略规划引领发展

大都市圈规划均具有前瞻性，东京是以政府为主导推动都市圈规划建设并取得成功的典型。以东京为核心的首都都市圈规划大约每 10 年修订一次，最终形成“多核多轴”网络化都市圈结构。

二　独特优势与终极目标：构建世界级中原城市群和郑州国际中心城市

（一）独特优势基础

当前我国区域经济发展呈现群雄并起的态势，加快中原崛起、建设世界级城市群和国际中心城市具有很多有利条件，河南省参与全国区域竞争的综合比较优势愈加凸显。

1. 交通区位独特，河南省地处中原，承东启西，连南贯北，高速公路、铁路、航空枢纽网络在全国举足轻重，全国第一个“米”字形高铁网络即将在河南形成，现代化国际化立体综合交通枢纽网络体系正在加速形成。

2. 人力资源丰富，河南是全国第一人口大省，劳动力资源丰富且成本低，随着基础教育、高等教育、职业教育不断加强，人力资源优势正在加速向人才资源优势转变。

3. 产业集群优势显著，河南省是全国经济第五大省、新兴的工业大省、产粮第二大省，现代产业体系完整，装备制造、电子信息、汽车、有色、食品、建材等产业集群优势明显，高新技术和战略新兴产业高速成长，现代物流、文化旅游、金融等现代服务业具有一定国际影响力，产业门类齐全，创新发展能力不断增强，转型升级不断加快，在全国全球产业链中的地位不断提升。

4. 市场优势显著，河南省庞大的人口规模和产业规模是一个巨大的市场，同时又可以很便利地辐射中西部地区乃至全国市场，已经成为国内外企业抢滩布局的热点区域。

5. 空间集聚优势显著，以郑州为中心的中原城市群涵盖省内外20多个省辖市，人口约1.9亿，是我国中西部地区规模最大的城市群，郑州中心城市和中原城市群双双进入国家战略重点。

6. 开放优势显著，随着国际航空和国际铁路的快速崛起，河南省从我国开放的大后方一跃成为开放的前沿阵地，郑州机场的枢纽地位持续上升，郑欧班列居全国前列，进出口和吸引外资在全国的位次持续攀升，成为我国经济由东向西梯次协调发展的战略支点和增长极，河南省已经成为内陆对外开放新高地。

7. 文化底蕴深厚。河南省是中华民族和华夏文明的重要发源地，河南省是华夏文明传承创新中心区，不断加快文化资源大省向文旅产业强省跨越。

8. 增长极优势。河南省坚持不懈地实施中心城市带动战略，建设郑州国家中心城市乃至世界城市，打造中西部地区增长极，提高郑州首位度。①打造以郑州为中心的国家级中原城市群，推进郑汴一体化，推进郑汴洛焦新许“1+5”一体化同城化，加快建设城际铁路网络；②拉大郑州市城市框架，建设郑东新区、郑西新区和航空港区；③建设国家金融中心、物流中心、商贸中心，提升城市辐射带动功能；④打造郑州国家国际综合交通枢纽，构建“米”字形高铁，建设空中丝绸之路，郑州国际机场客货运进入全国前列，郑欧班列居全国前列；⑤构建“三大一中”，建设国际航空大枢纽，带动航空大物流、航空大产业、航空大都市，成效显著。

以上独特比较优势，中原城市群和郑州国家中心城市适宜于承接国内国际高端产业转移，对国内外企业具有很强的吸引力，近年来国内外企业、资本、技术、人才等生产要素向河南省加速集聚，工业化城镇化进程加快，中原加速崛起的放大趋势已经形成，具备构建世界级中原城市群和郑州国际中心城市的潜力。中原城市群是中西部地区规模最大、区位优势最明显的城市群，近年来中原城市群在全国的战略地位逐步上升，有望成为沿海三大城市群之外的第四大城市群和经济增长极。

（二）大背景与大趋势

1. 从中原塌陷到中原崛起的大趋势。从 1992 年至 2018 年，河南省每年 GDP 增速都高于全国平均水平，年均比全国高出约 1.5 个百分点。

2. 国家战略重心向中西部地区转移。我国改革开放发展的确存在“东中西梯度转移”的规律。2005 年国家开始实施中部崛起战略。

3. 河南走向国家战略舞台的中心。最近十年，先后有近十项国家战略陆续落地河南：2009 年国家粮食生产核心区；2011 年中原经济区；2012 年郑州航空港经济综合试验区；2014 年郑州跨境电商试验区；2016 年郑洛新自主创新示范区、河南郑汴洛自贸区、大数据试验区，2015 年中国制造示范区；2017 年中原城市群、郑州国家中心城市。

4. 郑州市在全国中心城市中异军突起。近年来，郑州市 GDP 在全国位次持续攀升，2000～2010 年从 29 位上升到第二十二位，到 2018 年再上升到第十六位，几乎每年上升一位。2018 年郑州市 GDP 破万亿元，进入全国“GDP 万亿元俱乐部”，居全国第十六位；人口破千万，进入“人口千万俱乐部”，居全国第十二位，这是一次巨大的跨越，具有重大里程碑意义。郑州市在全国主要城市中异军突起，其实，这不是偶然现象，而是长期积累的结果，是量变到质变的结果，2001～2018 年郑州市 GDP 年均增速比全省高出约 1.5 个百分点，比全国高出约 3 个百分点（见图 1）。在全国的枢纽地位以及巨大的经济增长潜力是郑州市跻身 9 个国家中心城市之列的根基。2016 年升级为郑州国家级中心城市与国家级中原城市群，进入国家战略。

（三）郑州市未来升级目标：郑州国际中心城市

当前郑州已经从“三线城市”跻身“二线城市”行列，中心城市建设站在新起点，迈进新阶段，将攀上新高度，开始向 GDP 2 万亿元、人口 1500 万以上的“一线城市”进发，由国家中心城市向国际中心城市进发。力争 2035 年，GDP 达到 3 万亿元，进入全国前十位，人口达到 1500 万人，进入全国前八位。2050 年人口 2000 万人。

应明确郑州市终极目标为建设全球一流的国际中心城市。

1. 对标一流的国际中心城市。对标上海“五大中心”建设，即全球经济

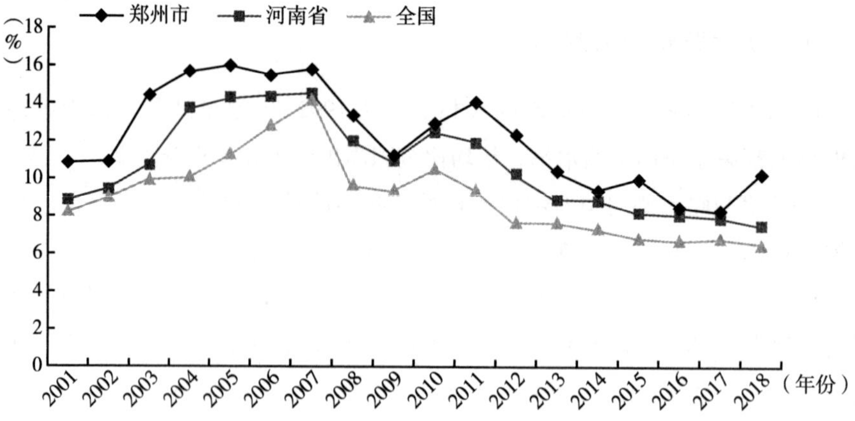

图1　2001～2018年郑州、河南、全国GDP增速趋势对比

中心、航运中心、贸易中心、金融中心、科创中心。尤其是对标深圳建设国际科技创新中心，对标杭州建设全球信息经济中心。对标京津冀、长三角、粤港澳大湾区，构建郑州黄河大湾区（郑汴洛焦新许1+5同城化）城市圈，打造国际科技创新中心、全球新经济中心。

2. 强化国际中心城市辐射带动功能。强化郑州国际综合枢纽功能，即国际航空枢纽、欧亚大陆桥铁路枢纽、陆海空多式联运枢纽、信息网络枢纽；强化开放门户功能，即中西部地区对外开放门户；提升世界产业基地功能，即战略新兴产业、先进制造业、现代服务业基地；强化国际贸易中心、国际金融中心、国际科创中心、国际文化中心等功能。

（四）中原城市群未来升级目标：世界级中原城市群

国家级城市群应具有位居国家前列的经济实力、跨省域的辐射带动能力和国家级中心城市，世界级城市群应该有世界级中心城市。

当前和今后几年，沿海地区三大城市群正在向世界级城市群转型升级，预计2020年发展成为真正的世界级城市群。

力争2020年基本发展成为国家级中原城市群。综合经济实力进入全国前五位、中西部地区第一位，郑州跻身于全国前十位城市行列。

力争2030年中原城市群建成世界级城市群，郑州建成世界城市或国际城市。

三　郑州中心城市和中原城市群升级的主要短板

按照国家级乃至世界级城市群的综合评价指标体系对中原城市群的发展现状进行评价分析，从中找出主要矛盾和问题。城市群及中心城市的人口、地区生产总值规模应居全国前列，这是成为国家级乃至世界级的物质基础和支撑条件。

（一）作为中心城市的郑州市规模小、实力弱、首位度低、发展滞后

中原城市群的缺陷也是非常明显的，最突出的矛盾就是中心城市总量规模较小、综合实力较弱，这是构建国家级中心城市和经济区的主要矛盾。

郑州作为中原城市群的中心城市，与北京、上海、广州、深圳、天津、重庆、成都、武汉等中心城市相比，人口规模和经济总量差距巨大，辐射带动能力弱，造成整个中原城市群内部经济协同不够，无法形成国家级乃至世界级的产业集群，综合竞争力弱、跨省域影响力小。

目前郑州与第一梯队的国际城市北、上、广、深的差距约 10 年；与第二梯队的武汉、成都、杭州等国家中心城市的差距约 5 年。

表 1　2018 年中国部分城市 GDP 排名

全国排名	城市	GDP(万亿元)
1	上海	3.3
2	北京	3
3	深圳	2.5
4	广州	2.3
8	武汉	1.53
9	成都	1.5
10	杭州	1.4
16	郑州	1.04

（二）“多中心”郑州大都市区空间结构框架体系没有形成

西方发达国家已经完成城镇化，其中心城市初期大都经历了摊大饼式城市

病，后期几乎无一例外地选择了“郊区多中心、卫星城多核心”的发展模式。为了适应中心城市集聚和扩张双向发展需要，我国主要中心城市几乎都把所辖县（市）行政区调整为市辖区，都市圈规划建设取向由“单中心”单极摊大饼模式转向“多中心、卫星城”多极协同模式。

反思郑州市的空间布局，始终没有突破传统行政区划的限制而建立“多中心、卫星城”的大都市圈空间布局。

（三）“多核心”郑州大都市圈没有形成

以中心城市为核心增长极，与周边城市协同联动发展，通过现代化综合交通网络，构成一体化或同城化的大都市圈，形成大城市群集聚增长核心，辐射带动外围圈层的城市协调发展，这是世界城市群发展壮大的一般规律。

反思郑州大都市圈建设，始终没有真正形成核心都市圈，中原城市群核心区 1 +5 城市圈中，郑汴洛焦新许等核心城市分工不明确，一体化或同城化协同程度较低，分工协作联系松散，以轨道交通为主导的 1 小时通勤圈尚未形成。

（四）大都市区或大都市圈的通勤圈没有形成

根据国内外经验，“多中心、多核心”大都市圈形成的必要条件是建立便捷的 1 小时交通圈和通勤圈。都市区或都市圈的空间范围大小均与通勤半径成正比，一般用时间来定义通勤圈，通常认为通勤上限时间为 1 个小时。

通勤圈的大小与通勤方式有关，现代大都市区或大都市圈一般都建立了以轨道交通为主导的通勤圈，所以国际上一般以轨道交通方式来确定通勤圈的空间范围，如伦敦通勤半径约为 70 公里，东京通勤半径约为 100 公里。随着轨道交通的现代化，运行速度进一步提高，我们可以将以轨道交通为主导的大都市区通勤圈的半径定义为 100 公里，大都市圈的通勤半径定义为 150 公里。

河南省高速公路四通八达，高速铁路网框架也基本形成，以地铁、轻轨、城际为主导的大众化市民化的轨道交通网络通勤系统尚未形成，郑州大都市区或大都市圈的空间扩展明显受限。

四　实施“一极一群”互动战略

城市群是区域经济的支柱和空间主体，中心城市是区域经济的心脏、引擎和增长极，中心城市和城市群是区域竞争和国际竞争的空间制高点。应借鉴京津冀、长三角、珠三角等世界级城市群一体化国际化发展经验，加快郑州进入国际中心城市之列，使之成为带动中原崛起的龙头，加快中原城市群进入世界级城市群之列，使之成为支撑中原崛起的主力军。

实现中原更加出彩、加快中原崛起必须培育国家级乃至世界级经济增长极，实施“一极一群”两大空间布局战略。

（一）实施中心城市带动战略，加快建设郑州国家中心城市乃至国际中心城市

郑州是中原城市群和中原经济区的增长极，其速度、规模、水平、层次决定中原崛起的进程。

1. 提升郑州国家中心城市乃至国际中心城市功能。对标北京、上海、广州、深圳四大国际城市，强化“一枢纽、一门户、三中心”（即国际综合交通枢纽、中西部地区对外开放门户、国际经济中心、国际金融中心、国际科创中心）综合功能。

2. 构建“多中心、卫星城、网络化”的大都市区空间格局。推进“县（市）改区”区划调整，开发郑东、郑西、郑南、滨黄新区、航空港五大新区。新的城市组团尽量布局在交通轴线与生态轴线的接合部，建设黄河生态文化产业带，沿黄河湾区布局科创产业带，建设嵩山国家公园，建设郑南新区—嵩山高新技术产业开发区。超前建设世界一流的地铁轻轨网络，构建覆盖周边卫星城的通勤圈，强化组团之间的分工协同一体化发展。

积极构建“2核+4次+6卫”大郑州都市区空间结构。①双核带动。构建中心城市和郑州航空港区两个核心增长极。②近郊四大次中心。分别在4个方向上规划建设郑东新区、郑西新区、郑南新区、滨黄新区四大次中心。③远郊6个卫星城。加快将中牟县、新郑市、荥阳市、新密市、登封市、巩义市变

更为“市辖区”，建设外围6大卫星城。

3. 强化枢纽比较优势，增强拉动作用。强化航空、铁路、公路、海运等多式联运国际综合交通枢纽优势。充分发挥郑州航空港经济综合实验区的龙头带动功能，加强国际航空大枢纽、航空大物流、航空大产业、航空大都市体系建设，推动航空货运进入全国前五位，客运进入全国前十位。郑欧班列保持全国领先。加快建成“米”字形高铁枢纽网络，加快建设中原城市群城际铁路和地铁轻轨网络。

4. 突破双一流高校和高端人才短板。营造优越的政策软环境，吸引国内外一流高校和研究机构集聚，吸引国内外各类高端人才集聚。

（二）实施城市群崛起战略，建设国家级乃至世界级的中原城市群

城市群的活力和竞争力来自一体化或同城化，一体化或同城化是城市群发展到高级阶段的必然趋势。实施城市群崛起战略，建设国家级乃至世界级的中原城市群，打造全国第四增长极、中西部地区最大增长极。

1. 加快推进1+5郑州大都市圈同城化。着力做大做强中原城市群核心区，构建“郑汴洛焦新许1+5同城化”大都市圈，加快建设同城化的城际铁路网络系统，构建半小时同城化通勤圈。

2. 推进“1+8中原城市群”核心区同城化。在1+5郑州大都市圈同城化基础上，适时推进“1+8大郑州都市圈”，将郑州定位为国家中心城市，将洛阳市定位为中原经济区的中心城市，形成郑州和洛阳“双中心”空间格局，将新乡、许昌、焦作、济源、平顶山、漯河等定位为中原经济区的6大核心城市。加快构建中原城市群轨道交通网络体系建设，加快推进“1+8大郑州都市圈”一体化乃至同城化发展，带动中原经济区周边区域快速发展。

3. 优先推进郑洛同城化。在郑汴一体化发展的基础上，推进郑洛同城化。郑州是枢纽城市，洛阳是工业科创城市，郑洛空间比邻，同城化有利于优势互补形成拳头，郑州和洛阳“双中心同城化结构模式”符合发展规律和趋势，加快推进郑洛同城化是构建世界级城市群产业科创中心的战略突破口，加快建设南线（航空港—新郑—新密—登封—偃师—洛阳）和北线沿黄河郑洛城际铁路，开发郑洛高新技术产业带，构建郑汴洛科创走廊。

4. 提升外围区域中心城市的功能定位。开放搞活中原城市群外围区域中心城市，在外围择优设立若干中原城市群副中心城市，使安阳、南阳、商丘、三门峡、信阳、濮阳、周口 7 大外围省辖市成为中原城市群的新增长极和新支柱，形成中心集聚、外围开花、群雄并起的新格局。

5. 积极谋划建设国家新区。借鉴全国 18 个国家新区建设经验，积极谋划创建“郑汴港国家新区”，或者郑许、郑新国家新区。建设郑汴洛国家黄河湿地公园。沿黄北岸建设国家农业高新技术产业示范区。

五　构建世界级中原城市群的四大支撑点

（一）构建中原城市群“郑州和洛阳双中心同城化结构模式”

根据中心城市空间布局形态，我国城市群划分为单中心、双中心、多中心、主副中心四种模式。

“双中心”结构模式，或双核结构模式、双子座的空间模式，是指在城市群内有两个规模实力最强大的核心首位城市，其经济实力、城市规模和辐射带动能力，都起着“双核”功能。“双中心”结构模式最典型的最常见的是“港城模式”，是指以区域中心城市和港口城市为主导的城市群空间结构。在世界范围内也有很多比较典型的双核结构模式案例：鹿特丹—伊斯堡、华盛顿—巴尔的摩、莱茵—鲁尔、伦敦—伯明翰、东京—横滨、首尔—仁川等。我国沿海地区的许多城市群都具有这种双核心港城模式特征，例如：珠三角城市群的广州和深圳；辽东半岛城市群的沈阳和大连；山东半岛城市群的济南和青岛；杭州湾城市群的杭州和宁波等；西部地区成渝城市群的重庆和成都也具有双核心港城模式特征。除了港城模式之外，还有其他双中心模式，例如东北的哈长城市群的哈尔滨和长春。总之，双核结构模式是对点轴系统理论的继承与发展，更能体现互补性、相互带动的区域经济发展新要求。

比较典型的是京津冀城市群“双中心”结构模式：京津冀城市群拥有北京和天津两个国家级中心城市，两个城市空间相邻，北京是政治中心和现代服务业中心，天津是港口城市和制造业中心，两者都具有全国影响力。

洛阳与郑州空间相邻，GDP 有一定差距但是差距没有超过 50%，洛阳与郑州的城市功能各具特色、错位发展、互补发展，郑州是省会城市、交通枢纽、商贸城市、先进制造业基地，洛阳是国家重要的装备制造业和重化工业基地，郑州洛阳与北京天津之间有许多相似性。中原城市群“双中心”结构是最优选择。

中原城市群可以采取郑州和洛阳“双中心”结构模式，其中，郑州市为国家中心城市，洛阳为中原经济区特色中心城市。实行郑洛“双中心”模式有利于弥补郑州经济实力弱的短板，构建郑洛工业走廊和都市连绵带。由于开封与郑州实现了同城化，就是一个城市区域，开封作为大郑州都市区的东部副中心可能更加确切，更符合客观现实。中原城市群采取“双中心”结构模式还有一个好处，可以把“副中心城市”设在中原城市群的外圈，激发外围城市发展活力和动力，这也符合副中心城市设置的一般规律，副中心城市一般设置在中心城市辐射带动作用衰竭的地带，即城市群的外围或外圈，或者设置在两大中心城市相互吸引均衡的“断裂带”上。

（二）构建中原城市群的外围“副中心城市圈层”

根据中心地理论，构建“圈层结构”的中原城市群，强化专业化分工协作，中心城市带动外围城市，外围城市支撑中心城市。第一层为中心区，建设大郑州都市区；第二层为（1 +5 +3）核心区，建设大郑州都市圈；第三层为外围区（1 +8 +7），外围拥有 7 大“副中心城市”。

把安阳、南阳、商丘、三门峡、信阳、濮阳、周口等外围省辖市设为中原城市群副中心城市，把驻马店、鹤壁设为中原城市群支柱城市。根据中心地理论“六边形模型”，周边 7 大省辖市均位于“米”字形高铁网络的重要节点，位于普铁、城际、高速公路、航空等综合交通网络的重要节点，在周边外围圈层设置 7 大副中心城市符合市场、交通、行政三个最优原则。根据两个中心城市之间相互吸引的“断裂点理论”，周边外围 7 大省辖市距离郑州较远，200 公里以上，受郑州中心城市的辐射带动较弱，受省外中心城市的辐射带动较强，处在郑州中心城市与省外中心城市相互吸引的断裂带上，设置 7 大副中心城市有利于辐射带动周边区域协同发展，有利于集聚外省要素资源。

应以开放的思维看待副中心，将安阳作为北京和石家庄的南部副中心，将三门峡作为西安的东部副中心，将信阳和南阳作为武汉的北部副中心。

（三）构建中原城市群轨道交通体系和通勤圈

积极构建“三级五网一体化”轨道交通体系，“三级”分别指中央、省、市三级政府分别管辖或负责构建“国家骨干网、城市群网、市域网”三级轨道交通网络。“五网”分别指普通客运铁路网络、国家高铁路客运网络、城市群城际铁路网络、城市都市圈轻轨网络、城市主城区地铁网络，简称“五网”（普铁、高铁、城铁、轻轨、地铁）。“一体化”是指“五网”无缝对接、互联互通、零换乘，构成一个高效运转的系统整体。

应突出三个政策关键点：①加快建设“米”字形高铁网络；②加快建设中心城市的地铁轻轨网络系统；③加快建设中原城市群城际铁路网络系统，建立半小时都市区、1 小时都市圈、1.5 小时城市群的大众化市民化现代化的轨道交通通勤网络系统。力争 2020 年建成放射加半圆的城际铁路系统，达到 1000 ~ 2000 公里；2030 年城际铁路或轻轨达到 3000 ~ 4000 公里，连通 80% 以上的县城。

（四）推进郑汴同城化，打造“郑汴港金三角”国家新区

郑州主城区为老中心，航空港区为新中心，开封市为副中心，呈三足鼎立之势，应充分发挥郑州航空港经济综合试验区的核心、龙头和增长极带动功能，加快规划建设“汴—港”产业带，建设“郑汴港金三角”新经济国家城市新区，打造郑汴同城化升级版。

参考文献

[1] 谢文蕙、邓卫：《城市经济学》，清华大学出版社，2013，第 79 ~ 98 页。

[2] 裘丽岚：《国内外城市群研究的理论与实践》，《城市观察》2011 年第 5 期，第 164 ~ 172 页。

[3] 杨卫东、郭虹：《中心城市经济理论与实践》，经济科学出版社，2011 年第 12 期，第 1 ~ 6 页。

[4] 王光荣:《论大城市多中心发展模式》,《天津师范大学学报》(社会科学版)2006 年第 4 期,第 24 页。
[5] 陆玉麒:《区域双核结构模式的形成机理》,《地理学报》2002 年第 1 期,第 85 ~ 95 页。
[6] 李小建:《经济地理学》,高等教育出版社,2013,第 58 ~ 114 页。

附　　录

Appendices

B.30
附录一　2018年国家中心城市主要统计数据汇总

指标	单位	北京	天津	上海	广州	重庆	成都	武汉	郑州	西安
年末常住人口数	万人	2154	1560	2424	1490	3102	1633	1108	1014	1000
城镇化率	%	86.5	83.15	88.1	86.38	65.5	73.12	80.29	73.38	74.01
地区生产总值	亿元	30320	18810	32680	22859	20363	15343	14847	10143	8350
GDP 同比增长	%	6.6	3.6	6.6	6.2	6.0	8.0	8.0	8.1	8.2
人均 GDP	元/人	140000	120606	135000	155491	65933	94782	135136	101349	85114
第二产业生产增加值	亿元	5648	7610	9733	6234	8329	6516	6378	4451	2926
第三产业生产增加值	亿元	24554	11027	22843	16402	10656	8304	8108	5546	5165
第三产业占比	%	81	58.6	69.9	71.75	52.3	54.1	54.6	54.7	61.9

续表

指标	单位	北京	天津	上海	广州	重庆	成都	武汉	郑州	西安
全社会固定资产投资增长率	%	-9.9	-5.6	5.2	8.2	7	10	10.6	10.9	8.4
社会消费品零售总额	亿元	11748	5533	12669	9256	8769	6802	6844	4268	4659
消费价格指数	%	102.5	102	101.6	102.4	102	101.4	101.9	102.4	101.9
地方财政一般公共预算收入	亿元	5786	2106	7108	1632	2266	1424	1529	1152	685
地方财政一般公共预算支出	亿元	7176	3105	8352	2506	4541	1837	1930	1763	1152
金融机构本外币存款余额	亿元	157092	30983	121112	54788	36887	37826	26332	21767	21267
金融机构本外币贷款余额	亿元	70484	34085	73272	40749	32248	32637	28271	21202	19892
进出口总值	亿元	27183	8077	85317	9810	5223	4983	2148	4105	3304
实际利用外资投资额	亿美元	173	49	173	66	102	120	109	42	64
入境国际旅游人数	万人	340	176	686	340	388	341	276	53	24738
客运总量	万人	67569	19200	21497	48048	63600	22558	28639	14830	26100
货运总量	万吨	25244	53548	107387	127752	128200	28934	62518	27631	26200
城市轨道交通运营里程	公里	636	220	705	456	313	225	355	95	127
人均公园绿地面积	平方米/人	16.3	11.48	8.2	17.06	16.36	12.7	9.61	12.5	11.92

续表

指标	单位	北京	天津	上海	广州	重庆	成都	武汉	郑州	西安
卫生机构数量	家	11100	5686	5298	3670	20524	10755	6340	4773	6638
国家级高新技术产业开发区、经济技术开发区总数	个	4	7	8	4	7	2	3	2	4
重点高等院校数（211、985高校）	所	26	4	10	4	2	5	7	1	6
普通高等院校数	所	58	56	64	22	65	64	67	61	63
普通高等学校在校生数	人	917000	591400	517800	1086400	762800	913000	1107000	993000	1271300
专利授权数	件	123000	54700	92460	89826	45700	57370	32397	31585	8096
城乡居民人均可支配收入	元	62361	39506	64183	55356	26386	36142	42133	33105	35432
城镇居民人均可支配收入	元	67990	42976	68034	59982	34889	42128	47359	39042	41657
农村居民人均可支配收入	元	—	23065	30375	26020	13781	22135	22652	21652	18008

注1：当前数据均来自已公布的统计公报、政府工作报告内容或根据相关资料按推算获取。

注2：本表内部分城市数据与其他城市发布口径略有出入，故各市数据一直沿用本市的发布口径。

注3：西安自2014年起不再将入境国际旅游人数与国内旅游人数分开统计，表中西安入境国际旅游人数一项24738万人为国内外游客总数。

B.31
附录二　中共中央国务院《关于建立更加有效的区域协调发展新机制的意见》

实施区域协调发展战略是新时代国家重大战略之一，是贯彻新发展理念、建设现代化经济体系的重要组成部分。党的十八大以来，各地区各部门围绕促进区域协调发展与正确处理政府和市场关系，在建立健全区域合作机制、区域互助机制、区际利益补偿机制等方面进行积极探索并取得一定成效。同时要看到，我国区域发展差距依然较大，区域分化现象逐渐显现，无序开发与恶性竞争仍然存在，区域发展不平衡不充分问题依然比较突出，区域发展机制还不完善，难以适应新时代实施区域协调发展战略需要。为全面落实区域协调发展战略各项任务，促进区域协调发展向更高水平和更高质量迈进，现就建立更加有效的区域协调发展新机制提出如下意见。

一　总体要求

（一）指导思想。以习近平新时代中国特色社会主义思想为指导，全面贯彻党的十九大和十九届二中、三中全会精神，认真落实党中央、国务院决策部署，坚持新发展理念，紧扣我国社会主要矛盾变化，按照高质量发展要求，紧紧围绕统筹推进“五位一体”总体布局和协调推进“四个全面”战略布局，立足发挥各地区比较优势和缩小区域发展差距，围绕努力实现基本公共服务均等化、基础设施通达程度比较均衡、人民基本生活保障水平大体相当的目标，深化改革开放，坚决破除地区之间利益樊篱和政策壁垒，加快形成统筹有力、竞争有序、绿色协调、共享共赢的区域协调发展新机制，促进区域协调发展。

（二）基本原则

——坚持市场主导与政府引导相结合。充分发挥市场在区域协调发展新机制建设中的主导作用，更好发挥政府在区域协调发展方面的引导作用，促进区域协调发展新机制有效有序运行。

——坚持中央统筹与地方负责相结合。加强中央对区域协调发展新机制的顶层设计，明确地方政府的实施主体责任，充分调动地方按照区域协调发展新机制推动本地区协调发展的主动性和积极性。

——坚持区别对待与公平竞争相结合。进一步细化区域政策尺度，针对不同地区实际制定差别化政策，同时更加注重区域一体化发展，维护全国统一市场的公平竞争，防止出现制造政策洼地、地方保护主义等问题。

——坚持继承完善与改革创新相结合。坚持和完善促进区域协调发展行之有效的机制，同时根据新情况新要求不断改革创新，建立更加科学、更加有效的区域协调发展新机制。

——坚持目标导向与问题导向相结合。瞄准实施区域协调发展战略的目标要求，破解区域协调发展机制中存在的突出问题，增强区域发展的协同性、联动性、整体性。

（三）总体目标

——到 2020 年，建立与全面建成小康社会相适应的区域协调发展新机制，在建立区域战略统筹机制、基本公共服务均等化机制、区域政策调控机制、区域发展保障机制等方面取得突破，在完善市场一体化发展机制、深化区域合作机制、优化区域互助机制、健全区际利益补偿机制等方面取得新进展，区域协调发展新机制在有效遏制区域分化、规范区域开发秩序、推动区域一体化发展中发挥积极作用。

——到 2035 年，建立与基本实现现代化相适应的区域协调发展新机制，实现区域政策与财政、货币等政策有效协调配合，区域协调发展新机制在显著缩小区域发展差距和实现基本公共服务均等化、基础设施通达程度比较均衡、人民基本生活保障水平大体相当中发挥重要作用，为建设现代化经济体系和满足人民日益增长的美好生活需要提供重要支撑。

——到本世纪中叶，建立与全面建成社会主义现代化强国相适应的区域协调发展新机制，区域协调发展新机制在完善区域治理体系、提升区域治理能力、实现全体人民共同富裕等方面更加有效，为把我国建成社会主义现代化强国提供有力保障。

二　建立区域战略统筹机制

（四）推动国家重大区域战略融合发展。以“一带一路”建设、京津冀协同发展、长江经济带发展、粤港澳大湾区建设等重大战略为引领，以西部、东北、中部、东部四大板块为基础，促进区域间相互融通补充。以“一带一路”建设助推沿海、内陆、沿边地区协同开放，以国际经济合作走廊为主骨架加强重大基础设施互联互通，构建统筹国内国际、协调国内东中西和南北方的区域发展新格局。以疏解北京非首都功能为“牛鼻子”推动京津冀协同发展，调整区域经济结构和空间结构，推动河北雄安新区和北京城市副中心建设，探索超大城市、特大城市等人口经济密集地区有序疏解功能、有效治理“大城市病”的优化开发模式。充分发挥长江经济带横跨东中西三大板块的区位优势，以共抓大保护、不搞大开发为导向，以生态优先、绿色发展为引领，依托长江黄金水道，推动长江上中下游地区协调发展和沿江地区高质量发展。建立以中心城市引领城市群发展、城市群带动区域发展新模式，推动区域板块之间融合互动发展。以北京、天津为中心引领京津冀城市群发展，带动环渤海地区协同发展。以上海为中心引领长三角城市群发展，带动长江经济带发展。以香港、澳门、广州、深圳为中心引领粤港澳大湾区建设，带动珠江—西江经济带创新绿色发展。以重庆、成都、武汉、郑州、西安等为中心，引领成渝、长江中游、中原、关中平原等城市群发展，带动相关板块融合发展。加强“一带一路”建设、京津冀协同发展、长江经济带发展、粤港澳大湾区建设等重大战略的协调对接，推动各区域合作联动。推进海南全面深化改革开放，着力推动自由贸易试验区建设，探索建设中国特色自由贸易港。

（五）统筹发达地区和欠发达地区发展。推动东部沿海等发达地区改革创新、新旧动能转换和区域一体化发展，支持中西部条件较好地区加快发展，鼓励国家级新区、自由贸易试验区、国家级开发区等各类平台大胆创新，在推动区域高质量发展方面发挥引领作用。坚持“输血”和“造血”相结合，推动欠发达地区加快发展。建立健全长效普惠性的扶持机制和精准有效的差别化支持机制，加快补齐基础设施、公共服务、生态环境、产业发展等短板，打赢精准脱贫攻坚战，确保革命老区、民族地区、边疆地区、贫困地区与全国同步实现全面建成小康社会。健全国土空间用途管制制度，引导资源枯竭地区、产业衰退地区、生态严重退化地区积极探索特色转型发展之路，推动形成绿色发展方式和生活方式。以承接产业转移示范区、跨省合作园区等为平台，支持发达地区与欠发达地区共建产业合作基地和资源深加工基地。建立发达地区与欠发达地区区域联动机制，先富带后富，促进发达地区和欠发达地区共同发展。

（六）推动陆海统筹发展。加强海洋经济发展顶层设计，完善规划体系和管理机制，研究制定陆海统筹政策措施，推动建设一批海洋经济示范区。以规划为引领，促进陆海在空间布局、产业发展、基础设施建设、资源开发、环境保护等方面全方位协同发展。编制实施海岸带保护与利用综合规划，严格围填海管控，促进海岸地区陆海一体化生态保护和整治修复。创新海域海岛资源市场化配置方式，完善资源评估、流转和收储制度。推动海岸带管理立法，完善海洋经济标准体系和指标体系，健全海洋经济统计、核算制度，提升海洋经济监测评估能力，强化部门间数据共享，建立海洋经济调查体系。推进海上务实合作，维护国家海洋权益，积极参与维护和完善国际和地区海洋秩序。

三　健全市场一体化发展机制

（七）促进城乡区域间要素自由流动。实施全国统一的市场准入负面清单制度，消除歧视性、隐蔽性的区域市场准入限制。深入实施公平竞争审查制度，消除区域市场壁垒，打破行政性垄断，清理和废除妨碍统一市场和公平竞争的各种规定和做法，进一步优化营商环境，激发市场活力。全面放宽城市落户条件，完善配套政策，打破阻碍劳动力在城乡、区域间流动的不合理壁垒，促进人力资源优化配置。加快深化农村土地制度改革，推动建立城乡统一的建设用地市场，进一步完善承包地所有权、承包权、经营权三权分置制度，探索宅基地所有权、资格权、使用权三权分置改革。引导科技资源按照市场需求优化空间配置，促进创新要素充分流动。

（八）推动区域市场一体化建设。按照建设统一、开放、竞争、有序的市场体系要求，推动京津冀、长江经济带、粤港澳等区域市场建设，加快探索建立规划制度统一、发展模式共推、治理方式一致、区域市场联动的区域市场一体化发展新机制，促进形成全国统一大市场。进一步完善长三角区域合作工作机制，深化三省一市在规划衔接、跨省重大基础设施建设、环保联防联控、产业结构布局调整、改革创新等方面合作。

（九）完善区域交易平台和制度。建立健全用水权、排污权、碳排放权、用能权初始分配与交易制度，培育发展各类产权交易平台。进一步完善自然资源资产有偿使用制度，构建统一的自然资源资产交易平台。选择条件较好地区建设区域性排污权、碳排放权等交易市场，推进水权、电力市场化交易，进一步完善交易机制。建立健全用能预算管理制度。促进资本跨区域有序自由流动，完善区域性股权市场。

四　深化区域合作机制

（十）推动区域合作互动。深化京津冀地区、长江经济带、粤港澳大湾区等合作，提升合作层次和水平。积极发展各类社会中介组织，有序发展区域性行业协会商会，鼓励企业组建跨地区跨行业产业、技术、创新、人才等合作平台。加强城市群内部城市间的紧密合作，推动城市间产业分工、基础设施、公共服务、环境治理、对外开放、改革创新等协调联动，加快构建大中小城市和小城镇协调发展的城镇化格局。积极探索建立城市群协调治理模式，鼓励成立多种形式的城市联盟。

（十一）促进流域上下游合作发展。加快推进长江经济带、珠江—西江经济带、淮河生态经济带、汉江生态经济带等重点流域经济带上下游间合作发展。建立健全上下游毗邻省市规划对接机制，协调解决地区间合作发展重大问题。完善流域内相关省市政府协商合作机制，构建流域基础设施体系，严格流域环境准入标准，加强流域生态环境共建共治，推进流域产业有序转移和优化升级，推动上下游地区协调发展。

（十二）加强省际交界地区合作。支持晋陕豫黄河金三角、粤桂、湘赣、川渝等省际交界地区合作发展，探索建立统一规划、统一管理、合作共建、利益共享的合作新机制。加强省际交界地区城市间交流合作，建立健全跨省城市政府间联席会议制度，完善省际会商机制。

（十三）积极开展国际区域合作。以“一带一路”建设为重点，实行更加积极主动的开放战略，推动构建互利共赢的国际区域合作新机制。充分发挥“一带一路”国际合作高峰论坛、上海合作组织、中非合作论坛、中俄东北—远东合作、长江—伏尔加河合作、中国—东盟合作、东盟与中日韩合作、中日韩合作、澜沧江—湄公河合作、图们江地区开发合作等国际区域合作机制作用，加强区域、次区域合作。支持沿边地区利用国际合作平台，积极主动开展国际区域合作。推进重点开发开放试验区建设，支持边境经济合作区发展，稳步建设跨境经济合作区，更好发挥境外产能合作园区、经贸合作区的带动作用。

五　优化区域互助机制

（十四）深入实施东西部扶贫协作。加大东西部扶贫协作力度，推动形成专项扶贫、行业扶贫、社会扶贫等多方力量多种举措有机结合互为支撑的“三位一体”大扶贫格局。强化以企业合作为载体的扶贫协作，组织企业到贫困地区投资兴业、发展产业、带动就业。完善劳务输出精准对接机制，实现贫困人口跨省稳定就业。进一步加强扶贫协作双方党政干部和专业技术人员交流，推动人才、资金、技术向贫困地区和边境地区流动，深化实施携手奔小康行动。积极引导社会力量广泛参与深度贫困地区脱贫攻坚，帮助深度贫困群众解决生产生活困难。

（十五）深入开展对口支援。深化全方位、精准对口支援，推动新疆、西藏和青海、四川、云南、甘肃四省藏区经济社会持续健康发展，促进民族交往交流交融，筑牢社会稳定和长治久安基础。强化规划引领，切实维护规划的严肃性，进一步完善和规范对口支援规划的编制实施和评估调整机制。加强资金和项目管理，科学开展绩效综合考核评价，推动对口支援向更深层次、更高质量、更可持续方向发展。

（十六）创新开展对口协作（合作）。面向经济转型升级困难地区，组织开展对口协作（合作），构建政府、企业和相关研究机构等社会力量广泛参与的对口协作（合作）体系。深入开展南水北调中线工程水源区对口协作，推动水源区绿色发展。继续开展对口支援三峡库区，支持库区提升基本公共服务供给能力，加快库区移民安稳致富，促进库区社会和谐稳定。进一步深化东部发达省市与东北地区对口合作，开展干部挂职交流和系统培训，建设对口合作重点园区，实现互利共赢。

六 健全区际利益补偿机制

（十七）完善多元化横向生态补偿机制。贯彻绿水青山就是金山银山的重要理念和山水林田湖草是生命共同体的系统思想，按照区际公平、权责对等、试点先行、分步推进的原则，不断完善横向生态补偿机制。鼓励生态受益地区与生态保护地区、流域下游与流域上游通过资金补偿、对口协作、产业转移、人才培训、共建园区等方式建立横向补偿关系。支持在具备重要饮用水功能及生态服务价值、受益主体明确、上下游补偿意愿强烈的跨省流域开展省际横向生态补偿。在京津冀水源涵养区、安徽浙江新安江、广西广东九洲江、福建广东汀江—韩江、江西广东东江、广西广东西江流域等深入开展跨地区生态保护补偿试点，推广可复制的经验。

（十八）建立粮食主产区与主销区之间利益补偿机制。研究制定粮食主产区与主销区开展产销合作的具体办法，鼓励粮食主销区通过在主产区建设加工园区、建立优质商品粮基地和建立产销区储备合作机制以及提供资金、人才、技术服务支持等方式开展产销协作。加大对粮食主产区的支持力度，促进主产区提高粮食综合生产能力，充分调动主产区地方政府抓粮食生产和农民种粮的积极性，共同维护国家粮食安全。

（十九）健全资源输出地与输入地之间利益补偿机制。围绕煤炭、石油、天然气、水能、风能、太阳能以及其他矿产等重要资源，坚持市场导向和政府调控相结合，加快完善有利于资源集约节约利用和可持续发展的资源价格形成机制，确保资源价格能够涵盖开采成本以及生态修复和环境治理等成本。鼓励资源输入地通过共建园区、产业合作、飞地经济等形式支持输出地发展接续产业和替代产业，加快建立支持资源型地区经济转型长效机制。

七 完善基本公共服务均等化机制

（二十）提升基本公共服务保障能力。在基本公共服务领域，深入推进财政事权和支出责任划分改革，逐步建立起权责清晰、财力协调、标准合理、保障有力的基本公共服务制度体系和保障机制。规范中央与地方共同财政事权事项的支出责任分担方式，调整完善转移支付体系，基本公共服务投入向贫困地区、薄弱环节、重点人群倾斜，增强市县财政特别是县级财政基本公共服务保障能力。强化省级政府统筹职能，加大对省域范围内基本公共服务薄弱地区扶持力度，通过完善省以下财政事权和支出责任划分、规范转移支付等措施，逐步缩小县域间、市地间基本公共服务差距。

（二十一）提高基本公共服务统筹层次。完善企业职工基本养老保险基金中央调剂制度，尽快实现养老保险全国统筹。完善基本医疗保险制度，不断提高基本医疗保险统筹层级。巩固完善义务教育管理体制，增加中央财政对义务教育转移支付规模，强化省、市统筹作用，加大对“三区三州”等深度贫困地区和集中连片特困地区支持力度。

（二十二）推动城乡区域间基本公共服务衔接。加快建立医疗卫生、劳动就业等基本公共服务跨城乡跨区域流转衔接制度，研究制定跨省转移接续具体办法和配套措施，强化跨区域基本公共服务统筹合作。鼓励京津冀、长三角、珠三角地区积极探索基本公共服务跨区域流转衔接具体做法，加快形成可复制可推广的经验。

八　创新区域政策调控机制

（二十三）实行差别化的区域政策。充分考虑区域特点，发挥区域比较优势，提高财政、产业、土地、环保、人才等政策的精准性和有效性，因地制宜培育和激发区域发展动能。坚持用最严格制度最严密法治保护生态环境的前提下，进一步突出重点区域、行业和污染物，有效防范生态环境风险。加强产业转移承接过程中的环境监管，防止跨区域污染转移。对于生态功能重要、生态环境敏感脆弱区域，坚决贯彻保护生态环境就是保护生产力、改善生态环境就是发展生产力的政策导向，严禁不符合主体功能定位的各类开发活动。相关中央预算内投资和中央财政专项转移支付继续向中西部等欠发达地区和东北地区等老工业基地倾斜，研究制定深入推进西部大开发和促进中部地区崛起的政策措施。动态调整西部地区有关产业指导目录，对西部地区优势产业和适宜产业发展给予必要的政策倾斜。在用地政策方面，保障跨区域重大基础设施和民生工程用地需求，对边境和特殊困难地区实行建设用地计划指标倾斜。研究制定鼓励人才到中西部地区、东北地区特别是“三区三州”等深度贫困地区工作的优惠政策，支持地方政府根据发展需要制定吸引国内外人才的区域性政策。

（二十四）建立区域均衡的财政转移支付制度。根据地区间财力差异状况，调整完善中央对地方一般性转移支付办法，加大均衡性转移支付力度，在充分考虑地区间支出成本因素、切实增强中西部地区自我发展能力的基础上，将常住人口人均财政支出差异控制在合理区间。严守生态保护红线，完善主体功能区配套政策，中央财政加大对重点生态功能区转移支付力度，提供更多优质生态产品。省级政府通过调整收入划分、加大转移支付力度，增强省以下政府区域协调发展经费保障能力。

（二十五）建立健全区域政策与其他宏观调控政策联动机制。加强区域政策与财政、货币、投资等政策的协调配合，优化政策工具组合，推动宏观调控政策精准落地。财政、货币、投资政策要服务于国家重大区域战略，围绕区域规划及区域政策导向，采取完善财政政策、金融依法合规支持、协同制定引导性和约束性产业政策等措施，加大对跨区域交通、水利、生态环境保护、民生等重大工程项目的支持力度。对因客观原因造成的经济增速放缓地区给予更有针对性的关心、指导和支持，在风险可控的前提下加大政策支持力度，保持区域经济运行在合理区间。加强对杠杆率较高地区的动态监测预警，强化地方金融监管合作和风险联防联控，更加有效防范和化解系统性区域性金融风险。

九　健全区域发展保障机制

（二十六）规范区域规划编制管理。加强区域规划编制前期研究，完善区域规划编制、审批和实施工作程序，实行区域规划编制审批计划管理制度，进一步健全区域规划实施机制，加强中期评估和后期评估，形成科学合理、管理严格、指导有力的区域规划体系。对实施到期的区域规划，在后评估基础上，确需延期实施的可通过修订规划延期实施，不需延期实施的要及时废止。根据国家重大战略和重大布局需要，适时编制实施新的区域规划。

（二十七）建立区域发展监测评估预警体系。围绕缩小区域发展差距、区域一体化、资源环境协调等重点领域，建立区域协调发展评价指标体系，科学客观评价区域发展的协调性，为区域政策制定和调整提供参考。引导社会智库研究发布区域协调发展指数。加快建立区域发展风险识别和预警预案制度，密切监控突出问题，预先防范和妥善应对区域发展风险。

（二十八）建立健全区域协调发展法律法规体系。研究论证促进区域协调发展的法规制度，明确区域协调发展的内涵、战略重点和方向，健全区域政策制定、实施、监督、评价机制，明确有关部门在区域协调发展中的职责，明确地方政府在推进区域协调发展中的责任和义务，发挥社会组织、研究机构、企业在促进区域协调发展中的作用。

十　切实加强组织实施

（二十九）加强组织领导。坚持和加强党对区域协调发展工作的领导，充分发挥中央与地方区域性协调机制作用，强化地方主体责任，广泛动员全社会力量，共同推动建立更加有效的区域协调发展新机制，为实施区域协调发展战略提供强有力的保障。中央和国家机关有关部门要按照职能分工，研究具体政策措施，协同推动区域协调发展。各省、自治区、直辖市要制定相应落实方案，完善相关配套政策，确保区域协调发展新机制顺畅运行。

（三十）强化协调指导。国家发展改革委要会同有关部门加强对区域协调发展新机制实施情况跟踪分析和协调指导，研究新情况、总结新经验、解决新问题，重大问题要及时向党中央、国务院报告。

（2018 年 11 月 18 日）

B.32

附录三　国家发展改革委《关于培育发展现代都市圈的指导意见》（发改规划［2019］328号）

各省、自治区、直辖市人民政府，国务院有关部门，铁路总公司：

城市群是新型城镇化主体形态，是支撑全国经济增长、促进区域协调发展、参与国际竞争合作的重要平台。都市圈是城市群内部以超大特大城市或辐射带动功能强的大城市为中心、以1小时通勤圈为基本范围的城镇化空间形态。近年来，都市圈建设呈现较快发展态势，但城市间交通一体化水平不高、分工协作不够、低水平同质化竞争严重、协同发展体制机制不健全等问题依然突出。为加快培育发展现代化都市圈，经国务院同意，现提出以下意见。

一　总体要求

（一）指导思想。

以习近平新时代中国特色社会主义思想为指导，全面贯彻党的十九大和十九届二中、三中全会精神，坚持和加强党的全面领导，坚持以人民为中心的发展思想，坚持稳中求进工作总基调，坚持新发展理念，坚持推动高质量发展，坚持以供给侧结构性改革为主线，坚持市场化改革、扩大高水平开放，以促进中心城市与周边城市（镇）同城化发展为方向，以创新体制机制为抓手，以推动统一市场建设、基础设施一体高效、公共服务共建共享、产业专业化分工协作、生态环境共保共治、城乡融合发展为重点，培育发展一批现代化都市圈，形成区域竞争新优势，为城市群高质量发展、经济转型升级提供重要支撑。

（二）基本原则。

——坚持尊重规律、顺势而为。遵循城镇化发展规律，顺应产业升级、人口流动和空间演进趋势，充分考虑不同都市圈现有基础和发展潜力的差异性，科学确定都市圈功能定位、发展目标和实现路径，因地制宜推动都市圈建设。

——坚持深化改革、创新发展。以强化制度、政策和模式创新为引领，坚决破除制约各类资源要素自由流动和高效配置的体制机制障碍，科学构建都市圈协同发展机制，加快推进都市圈发展。

——坚持功能互补、共建共享。统筹都市圈整体利益和各城市比较优势，强化城市间专业化分工协作，促进城市功能互补、产业错位布局、基础设施和公共服务共建共享，在深化合作中实现互利共赢。

——坚持市场主导、政府引导。充分发挥市场配置资源的决定性作用，更好发挥政府在规划政策引领、空间开发管制、公共资源配置、体制机制改革等方面的作用，使都市圈建设成为市场主导、自然发展的过程，成为政府引导、高质量发展的过程。

——坚持统筹谋划、地方负责。统筹全国都市圈建设的总体方向、战略布局和制度安排，强化分类指导；因地制宜推进都市圈建设，避免一哄而上；尊重基层首创精神，鼓励先行先试，及时推广成功经验。

（三）主要目标。

到2022年，都市圈同城化取得明显进展，基础设施一体化程度大幅提高，阻碍生产要素自由流动的行政壁垒和体制机制障碍基本消除，成本分担和利益共享机制更加完善，梯次形成若干空间结构清晰、城市功能互补、要素流动有序、产业分工协调、交通往来顺畅、公共服务均衡、环境和谐宜居的现代化都市圈。到2035年，现代化都市圈格局更加成熟，形成若干具有全球影响力的都市圈。

二　推进基础设施一体化

以增强都市圈基础设施连接性贯通性为重点，以推动一体化规划建设管护为抓手，织密网络、优化方式、畅通机制，加快构建都市圈公路和轨道交通网。

（四）畅通都市圈公路网。增加城市间公路通道，密切城际公路联系，加快构建高速公路、国省干线、县乡公路等都市圈多层次公路网。鼓励地方对高频次通行车辆实施高速公路收费优惠政策，加快推广 ETC 应用，推动取消高速公路省界收费站，提升都市圈内高速公路通勤效率。实施“断头路”畅通工程和“瓶颈路”拓宽工程，全面摸排都市圈内各类“断头路”和“瓶颈路”，加快打通“断头路”，提升都市圈路网联通程度，推进“瓶颈路”改造扩容，畅通交界地区公路联系，全面取缔跨行政区道路非法设置限高、限宽等路障设施。打造一体化公路客运网络，完善充电桩、加气站、公交站场等布局，支持毗邻城市（镇）开行城际公交，加快推动近郊班线公交化。优化交界地区公交线网，促进与市域公交网络快速接驳。加快推进都市圈内城市间公交一卡互通、票制资费标准一致，健全运营补偿和结算机制，推动信息共享和监管协同。

（五）打造轨道上的都市圈。统筹考虑都市圈轨道交通网络布局，构建以轨道交通为骨干的通勤圈。在有条件地区编制都市圈轨道交通规划，推动干线铁路、城际铁路、市域（郊）铁路、城市轨道交通“四网融合”。探索都市圈中心城市轨道交通适当向周边城市（镇）延伸。统筹布局都市圈城际铁路线路和站点，完善城际铁路网络规划，有序推进城际铁路建设，充分利用普速铁路和高速铁路等提供城际列车服务。创新运输服务方式，提升城际铁路运输效率。大力发展都市圈市域（郊）铁路，通过既有铁路补强、局部线路改扩建、站房站台改造等方式，优先利用既有资源开行市域（郊）列车；有序新建市域（郊）铁路，将市域（郊）铁路运营纳入城市公共交通系统。探索都市圈轨道交通运营管理“一张网”，推动中心城市、周边城市（镇）、新城新区等轨道交通有效衔接，加快实现便捷换乘，更好适应通勤需求。

（六）提升都市圈物流运行效率。打造“通道 + 枢纽 + 网络”的物流运行体系，推动物流资源优化配置。统筹布局货运场站、物流中心等，鼓励不同类型枢纽协同或合并建设，支持城市间合作共建物流枢纽。结合发展需要适当整合迁移或新建枢纽设施，完善既有物流设施枢纽功能，提高货物换装的便捷性、兼容性和安全性。畅通货运场站周边道路，补齐集疏运“最后一公里”短板。提高物流活动系统化组织水平。加强干支衔接和组织协同，大力发展多式联运，推动港口型枢纽统筹对接船期、港口装卸作业、堆存仓储安排和干线铁路运输计划；鼓励空港型枢纽开展陆空联运、铁空联运、空空中转。加强现代信息技术和智能化装备应用，实行多式联运“一单制”。

（七）统筹市政和信息网络建设。强化都市圈内市政基础设施协调布局，统筹垃圾处理厂、污水及污泥处理处置设施、变电站、危险品仓库等市政基础设施规划建设。推动供水、供电、供气、供热、排水等各类市政管网合理衔接，鼓励兼并重组、规模化市场化运营。完善都市圈信息网络一体化布局，推进第五代移动通信和新一代信息基础设施布局。探索取消都市圈内固定电话长途费，推动都市圈内通信业务异地办理和资费统一，持续推进网络提速降费。

三　强化城市间产业分工协作

以推动都市圈内各城市间专业化分工协作为导向，推动中心城市产业高端化发展，夯实中小城市制造业基础，促进城市功能互补、产业错位布局和特色化发展。

（八）促进城市功能互补。增强中心城市核心竞争力和辐射带动能力，推动超大特大城市非核心功能向周边城市（镇）疏解，推动中小城市依托多层次基础设施网络增强吸纳中心城市产业转移承接能力，构建大中小城市和小城镇特色鲜明、优势互补的发展格局。统筹整合都市圈内新区、园区等各类平台，支持建设一体化发展和承接产业转移示范区，推动创新链和产业链融合发展。鼓励建立联合招商、共同开发、利税共享的产业合作发展机制。

（九）推动中心城市产业高端化发展。加快推动中心城市集聚创新要素、提升经济密度、增强高端服务功能。通过关键共性技术攻关、公共创新平台建设等方式，加快制造业转型升级，重塑产业竞争新优势。以科技研发、工业设计、金融服务、文化创意、商务会展等为重点发展生产性服务业，推动服务业与制造业深度融合，形成以现代服务经济为主的产业结构。

（十）夯实中小城市制造业基础。充分利用中小城市土地、人力等综合成本低的优势，优化营商环境，积极承接中心城市产业转移，推动制造业规模化、特色化、集群化发展，形成以先进制造为主的产业结构。适度提高制造类企业集中的开发区配套用地比例，采取整体出让、集中开发等方式，推动生产制造和生活服务等功能适度混合。强化与中心城市公共服务连通共享，提高中小城市对工程师、技术工人、高校毕业生等人才的吸引力。

四　加快建设统一开放市场

以打破地域分割和行业垄断、清除市场壁垒为重点，加快清理废除妨碍统一市场和公平竞争的各种规定和做法，营造规则统一开放、标准互认、要素自由流动的市场环境。

（十一）加快人力资源市场一体化。放开放宽除个别超大城市外的城市落户限制，在具备条件的都市圈率先实现户籍准入年限同城化累积互认，加快消除城乡区域间户籍壁垒，统筹推进本地人口和外来人口市民化，促进人口有序流动、合理分布和社会融合。推动人力资源信息共享、公共就业服务平台共建。

（十二）推动技术市场一体化。支持联合建设科技资源共享服务平台，鼓励共建科技研发和转化基地。探索建立企业需求联合发布机制和财政支持科技成果共享机制。清理城市间因技术标准不统一形成的各种障碍。建立都市圈技术交易市场联盟，构建多层次知识产权交易市场体系。鼓励发展跨地区知识产权交易中介服务，支持金融机构开展知识产权质押融资、科技型中小企业履约保证保险等业务。推动科技创新券在城市间政策衔接、通兑通用。

（十三）推动金融服务一体化。加强金融基础设施、信息网络、服务平台一体化建设，鼓励金融机构在都市圈协同布局，探索银行分支机构在都市圈内跨行政区开展业务，加快实现存取款等金融服务同城化。强化金融监管合作和风险联防联控，建立金融风险联合处置机制，合力打击非法集资等金融违法活动。

（十四）统一市场准入标准。消除商事主体异地迁址变更登记隐形阻碍，探索“一照多址、一证多址”企业开办经营模式，加快取消具有相应资质的设计、施工企业异地备案手续，推动各类审批流程标准化和审批信息互联共享。建立都市圈市场监管协调机制，统一监管标准，推动执法协作及信息共享。加快完善都市圈信用体系，实施守信联合激励和失信联合惩戒。联合打击侵权假冒行为，探索建立食品药品联动实时监控平台，推进食品安全检验检测结果互认。

五　推进公共服务共建共享

以都市圈公共服务均衡普惠、整体提升为导向，统筹推动基本公共服务、社会保障、社会治理一体化发展，持续提高共建共享水平。

（十五）促进优质公共服务资源共享。鼓励都市圈内开展多层次多模式合作办学办医，支持有条件的中小学和三级医院推进集团化办学办医，开展远程教学医疗和教师、医护人员异地交流，支持中心城市三级医院异地设置分支机构。在都市圈内率先实现与产业链相配套的中高职学校紧缺专业贯通招生。推动病历跨地区、跨机构互通共享，推动医学检验检查结果跨地区、跨机构互认。推动公共服务从按行政等级配置向按常住人口规模配置转变。允许镇区人口10万以上的特大镇按同等城市标准配置教育医疗资源，鼓励有条件的小城镇布局三级医院，降低与大中城市公共服务落差。增加健康、养老、家政等服务多元化供给，鼓励都市圈城市联建共建养老机构，加快城市设施适老化和无障碍改造。推动博物馆、剧院、体育场馆等共建共享。

（十六）加快社会保障接轨衔接。建设涵盖各类社会保障信息的统一平台，加强都市圈异地居住退休人员养老保险信息交换，推广通过公安信息比对进行社会保险待遇资格认证模式，加快实现养老补贴跟着老人走。扩大异地就医直接结算联网定点医疗机构数量。鼓励有条件的中心城市与毗邻城市开展基本医疗保险异地门诊即时结算合作。加快推动都市圈医保目录和报销政策统筹衔接。推动工伤认定政策统一、结果互认。推动公共租赁住房保障范围常住人口全覆盖，提高住房公积金统筹层次，建立住房公积金异地信息交换和核查机制，推行住房公积金转移接续和异地贷款。

（十七）推动政务服务联通互认。全面取消没有法律法规规定的证明事项。除法律法规另有规定或涉密等外，政务服务事项全部纳入平台办理，全面实现同城化“一网通办”。进一步便利跨省市户口迁移网上审批，居民身份证、普通护照、机动车驾驶证异地申领，异地驾考和机动车异地年检、违章联网办理。建立健全民生档案异地查询联动机制。

（十八）健全跨行政区社会治理体系。完善突发公共事件联防联控、灾害事件预防处理和紧急救援等联动机制。加强交界地区城市管理联动，强化社区自治和服务功能，建立健全治安维稳、行政执法等协作机制，建立健全安全隐患排查和社区人居环境综合整治机制。建立重大工程项目选址协商机制，充分征求毗邻城市意见。积极利用信息技术手段，推动都市圈治理精细化。

六 强化生态环境共保共治

以推动都市圈生态环境协同共治、源头防治为重点，强化生态网络共建和环境联防联治，在一体化发展中实现生态环境质量同步提升，共建美丽都市圈。

（十九）构建绿色生态网络。严格保护跨行政区重要生态空间，加强中心城市生态用地维护与建设，编制实施都市圈生态环境管控方案，联合实施生态系统保护和修复工程。加强区域生态廊道、绿道衔接，促进林地绿地湿地建设、河湖水系疏浚和都市圈生态环境修复。

（二十）推动环境联防联治。以都市圈为单元制定城市空气质量达标时间表，强化工业源、移动源和生活源排放污染治理，实现核发机动车注册登记环保标准互认与车用燃料标准统一。加快消除都市圈内劣Ⅴ类水质断面。全面开展生活垃圾分类，基本完成存量生活垃圾场治理任务。鼓励既有建筑节能化改造，城镇新建建筑100%落实强制性节能标准。将建设用地土壤环境管理要求纳入城市规划和供地管理。

（二十一）建立生态环境协同共治机制。加快生态环境监测网络一体化建设，协商建立都市圈大气污染、流域水污染、土壤污染、噪声污染综合防治和利益协调机制。探索生态保护性开发模式，建立生态产品价值实现机制、市场化生态补偿机制。

七 率先实现城乡融合发展

以促进城乡要素自由流动、平等交换和公共资源合理配置为重点，建立健全城乡融合发展体制机制，构筑功能一体、空间融合的城乡体系，在都市圈率先实现城乡融合发展。

（二十二）建立健全城乡融合发展体制机制。建立健全有利于城乡要素合理配置的体制机制，促进人才、资金、科技、信息等要素更多向乡村流动。建立健全有利于城乡基本公共服务普惠共享的体制机制，推动公共服务向农村延伸、社会事业向农村覆盖。建立健全有利于城乡基础设施一体化发展的体制机制，加快基础设施和市政公用设施向乡村延伸，推动乡村基础设施提档升级。建立健全有利于乡村经济多元化发展的体制机制，促进农业全产业链发展。建立健全有利于农民收入持续增长的体制机制，持续缩小城乡居民生活水平差距。

（二十三）搭建城乡融合发展平台。在都市圈内培育建设联结城乡的功能平台，推动城乡要素跨界配置和产业有机融合发展。有序发展特色小城镇，实施特色小镇高质量发展工程，打造一批功能多样、产业集聚、设施完善的创新创业平台。优化提升现代农业产业园等园区，有序建设农村产业融合发展示范园，推动农业现代化。

八　构建都市圈一体化发展机制

加快构建都市圈协商合作、规划协调、政策协同、社会参与等机制，凝神聚力推进都市圈建设重点任务落地。

（二十四）创新协商合作机制。都市圈建设由相关地方负责统筹推进，建立城市间多层次合作协商机制。有条件的地方可以探索设立都市圈发展及重点领域协调推进机制，负责推动落实都市圈一体化发展重大事项。

（二十五）健全规划协调机制。围绕提升都市圈发展质量和现代化水平，探索编制都市圈发展规划或重点领域专项规划。强化都市圈规划与城市群规划、城市规划的有机衔接，确保协调配合、同向发力。国家发展改革委会同有关部门要加强对都市圈规划编制的统筹指导，研究制定支持都市圈建设的政策措施。

（二十六）强化政策协同机制。积极构建都市圈互利共赢的税收分享机制和征管协调机制，加强城市间税收优惠政策协调。鼓励社会资本参与都市圈建设与运营。允许都市圈内城乡建设用地增减挂钩节余指标跨地区调剂。健全都市圈商品房供应体系，强化城市间房地产市场调控政策协同。

（二十七）完善社会参与机制。都市圈规划编制实施和相关配套政策的出台，要广泛听取社会各界特别是利益相关方意见建议，主动接受社会监督，及时回应社会关切。鼓励智库参与都市圈建设决策咨询，建立健全第三方评估机制。加强舆论引导，创新宣传方式，营造有利于都市圈建设的氛围，增强都市圈内社会各方的认同感和积极性，汇聚形成共同参与和支持都市圈建设的强大合力。

城镇化是现代化的必由之路，是我国发展最大的潜力所在。建设现代化都市圈是推进新型城镇化的重要手段，既有利于优化人口和经济的空间结构，又有利于激活有效投资和潜在消费需求，增强内生发展动力。各地区各部门要统一思想认识、加强组织领导、强化责任意识，用改革的办法和创新的精神，积极培育发展现代化都市圈。

B.33

附录四　国家中心城市建设大事记

1. 2018 年 2 月 11 日，习近平总书记在成都天府新区视察，对成都工作提出了一系列重大要求，明确表示支持成都建设全面体现新发展理念的城市，为成都国家中心城市建设指明了政治方向、提供了根本遵循。

2. 2018 年 3 月 26 日，上海出台《上海加快实施人才高峰工程行动方案》，提出上海要在“人才高地”基础上筑起“人才高峰”，聚天下英才而用之。

3. 2018 年 4 月 26 日，习近平总书记在武汉主持召开深入推动长江经济带发展座谈会，为长江经济带发展进一步指引方向，做出部署；为新时代武汉高质量发展定向导航、把脉施治，武汉发展站上新起点，迈入新境界。

4. 2018 年 6 月 1 日，长三角主要领导座谈会审议通过《长三角地区一体化发展三年行动计划（2018—2020 年）》，进一步明确了长三角一体化发展的任务书、时间表和路线图。

5. 2018 年 7 月 6 日至 7 日，成都市第十三届委员会第三次全体会议审议通过《中共成都市委关于全面贯彻新发展理念加快推动高质量发展的决定》《中共成都市委关于深入贯彻落实习近平总书记来川视察重要指示精神加快建设美丽宜居公园城市的决定》，对加快建设全面体现新发展理念的国家中心城市做出了全面部署。

6. 2018 年 7 月 11 日，上海市人民政府印发《上海市清洁空气行动计划（2018—2022 年）》，提出到 2020 年，PM2.5 年均浓度力争达到 37 微克/立方米以下；空气质量优良率（AQI）力争达到 80% 左右，基本消除重污染天气。到 2022 年，PM2.5 年均浓度力争达到 35 微克/立方米以下，AQI 进一步提升。

7. 2018 年 7 月 29 日，成都市政府印发《2018 年成都科学治堵工作实施方案》，提出要全方位提升道路通行效率，探索“快速连续、便捷转换”三环路交通组织模式、“高峰限货、分道通行”绕城高速交通组织模式和“窄马路、密路网”小街区通行模式，提升路网资源使用效率。

8. 2018 年 7 月 30 日至 31 日，中国共产党西安市第十三届委员会第五次全体会议审议通过《中共西安市委关于加快国家中心城市建设推动高质量发展的决定》，讨论了《西安国家中心城市建设实施方案》，进一步明确了西安建设国家中心城市的路线图和时间表。

9. 2018 年 8 月 20 日，天津市人民政府印发《天津市打好污染防治攻坚战八个作战计划》，系统梳理了天津市生态环境领域的突出问题，统筹谋划未来三年生态环境保护工作，延续深化大气、水、土壤污染防治“三个十条”，形成蓝天、碧水、净土等三大保卫战和柴油货车污染治理、水源地保护、黑臭水体治理、渤海综合治理和农业农村污染治理等五个攻坚战三年作战计划。

10. 2018 年 8 月 27 日，郑州市人民政府印发《郑州市人口发展规划（2016—2030 年）》，明确到 2020 年，郑州市全面两孩政策效应充分发挥，生育水平向合理区间回归，流动人口逐步趋于稳定，常住人口总量保持适度增长，人口素质不断提高、结构逐步优化、分布更加合理。到 2030 年，人口自身均衡发展的态势基本形成，人口与经济社会、资源环境的协调程度进一步提高。

11. 2018 年 10 月 8 日，郑州市人民政府印发《郑州市信息安全产业发展规划（2018—2025 年）》，提出力争通过 3 + 5（2018—2020、2021—2025）两个发展阶段，郑州市信息安全产业基本呈现技术先进、应用广泛，产业链完整，产业生态完善，产业竞争力领跑全国第一方阵，把郑州打造成信息安全产业之都。

12. 2018 年 10 月 18 日，中国（四川）—东盟自由贸易合作中心在成都天府新城会议中心正式揭牌，该中心将打造成与东盟国家地区贸易、投资、文化、技术合作等方面的综合性重要战略合作平台，将成为全面提升成都对外开放水平的重要载体。

13. 2018 年 10 月 24 日，习近平总书记在广州视察，强调广州要实现老城市新活力，着力在综合城市功能、城市文化综合实力、现代服务业、现代化国际化营商环境方面出新出彩，为广州发展指明了前进方向，提供了根本遵循。

14. 2018 年 10 月 30 日，成都首个全球跨境电商服务资源中心正式启用，明确将引入具有全国资源的行业组织或中介机构代为运营，招引一批国际国内知名平台、供应链、金融、贸易等跨境电商企业集聚发展。

15. 2018 年 10 月 30 日，武汉市人民政府印发《武汉市国际化水平提升计划（2018—2020 年）》，提出要把武汉建设成为中部国际交通枢纽、国际经贸合作高地、国际交往中心、具有全球影响力的产业创新中心和国际人才汇聚高地。

16. 2018 年 11 月 18 日，中共中央、国务院发布《关于建立更加有效的区域协调发展新机制的意见》，提出以北京、天津为中心引领京津冀城市群发展，带动环渤海地区协同发展；以上海为中心引领长三角城市群发展，带动长江经济带发展；以香港、澳门、广州、深圳为中心引领粤港澳大湾区建设，带动珠江—西江经济带创新绿色发展；以重庆、成都、武汉、郑州、西安等为中心，引领成渝、长江中游、中原、关中平原等城市群发展，带动相关板块融合发展。

17. 2018 年 11 月 8 日至 11 日，全球硬科技创新暨“一带一路”创新合作大会在西安召开，会上展示了以西安硬科技“八路军”产业发展代表性企业及成就为重点的国内外硬科技领域前沿新技术、新产品。

18. 2018 年 12 月 7 日，河南省委常委会审议通过《郑州大都市区空间规划（2018—2035 年）》，进一步明晰了郑州未来的发展目标、战略路径和主要任务。

19. 2018 年 12 月 14 日，西安市人民政府出台《西安市加快促进科技成果转移转化 20 条措施》，要求进一步激发科技成果转移转化主体活力，深化产学研协同创新，营造转移转化良好环境，加快科技成果向现实生产力转移转化，支撑丝路科技创新中心建设，实现追赶超越发展。

20. 2018 年 12 月 20 日，北京市人民政府印发《中国（北京）跨境电子商务综合试验区实施方案》，要求全面推进中国（北京）跨境电子商务综合试验区建设，进一步提升首都开放型经济发展水平。

21. 2018 年 12 月 21 日，重庆市人民政府印发《重庆市加快新能源和智能网联汽车产业发展若干政策措施（2018—2022 年）》，提出加快新能源和智能网联汽车产业发展，培育新的增长动能。

22. 2018 年 12 月 29 日，重庆市人民政府印发《重庆市深化科技奖励制度改革实施方案》，明确重庆市科学技术奖设立科技突出贡献奖、自然科学奖、技术发明奖、科技进步奖、国际科技合作奖和企业技术创新奖 6 类奖项，其中自然科学奖、技术发明奖、科技进步奖“三大奖”总数每年不超过150项。

23. 2018年12月29日，西安市人民政府印发《西安市“铁腕治霾·保卫蓝天”三年行动方案（2018—2020年）（修订版）》，要求坚持全民共治、源头防治、标本兼治，持续实施大气污染防治行动，改善全市空气质量。

24. 2019年1月2日，天津市人民政府印发《关于支持金融机构和金融人才在津发展的政策措施》，要求完善支持金融业发展的政策体系，大力推进金融创新运营示范区建设。

25. 2019年1月5日，西安市人民政府印发《西安国家中心城市建设实施方案》，详细阐述了西安建设国家中心城市的“1610”战略。

26. 2019年1月10日，广州市人民政府印发《广州综合交通枢纽总体规划（2018—2035年）》，明确广州作为全国三大综合交通枢纽之一，到2020年将基本建成国际性综合交通枢纽，到2035年建成全球交通枢纽。

27. 2019年1月14日，广州市人民政府印发《关于支持广州区域金融中心建设的若干规定》，要求加快广州区域金融中心建设，完善现代金融服务体系，集聚金融资源，推动经济高质量发展，服务粤港澳大湾区建设。

28. 2019年2月18日，国务院印发《粤港澳大湾区发展规划纲要》，明确广州作为区域发展的核心引擎之一，继续发挥比较优势做优做强，增强对周边区域发展的辐射带动作用。

29. 2019年2月21日，郑州市第十五届人民代表大会第二次会议表决通过《2019年郑州市政府工作报告》，指出截止到2018年底，郑州实现了地区生产总值破万亿元、常住人口破千万、人均生产总值破10万元“三大突破”，出彩郑州站在了高质量发展的新起点。

30. 2019年2月21日，国家发展改革委印发《关于培育发展现代化都市圈的指导意见》，提出以促进中心城市与周边城市（镇）同城化发展为方向，以创新体制机制为抓手，以推动统一市场建设、基础设施一体高效、公共服务共建共享、产业专业化分工协作、生态环境共保共治、城乡融合发展为重点，培育发展一批现代化都市圈，形成区域竞争新优势，为城市群高质量发展、经济转型升级提供重要支撑。

31. 2019年4月1日，成都市政府发布《关于进一步加快建设国家西部金融中心的若干意见》，并集中出台《关于推广交子金融“5+2”平台构建中小微企业全生命周期投融资服务体系的实施意见》《关于扩大金融服务业对外开放助力实体经济高质量发展的若干政策措施》《关于支持金融科技产业创新发展的若干政策措施》《成都市引进培育交子金融人才实施办法》四项配套文件。

32. 2019 年 4 月 3 日，北京市人民政府印发《2019 年北京市交通综合治理行动计划》，要求全面提升北京市交通综合治理能力，营造良好出行环境。

33. 2019 年 4 月 12 日，武汉市人民政府印发《武汉市大健康产业发展规划（2019—2035 年）》，确定了构建生物医药、医疗器械、医药流通、生物农业和健康服务五大领域协同发展的“一城一园三区”新格局，加快建成世界级万亿大健康产业集群。

34. 2019 年 5 月 7 日，郑州市人民政府印发《郑州市高新技术企业倍增计划实施方案（2019—2021 年）》，要求进一步加大高新技术企业培育力度，促进高新技术企业健康快速发展，力争用三年时间实现全市高新技术企业数量倍增。

35. 2019 年 5 月 13 日，中共中央总书记习近平主持召开中共中央政治局会议，会议审议通过了《长江三角洲区域一体化发展规划纲要》，会议指出，长三角一体化发展具有极大的区域带动和示范作用，要紧扣“一体化”和“高质量”两个关键，带动整个长江经济带和华东地区发展，形成高质量发展的区域集群。

36. 2019 年 5 月 23 日，天津市委常委会讨论了《关于天津港建设世界一流港口的实施方案（2019—2023 年）》，强调要深入贯彻落实习近平总书记关于天津港“要志在万里，努力打造世界一流的智慧港口、绿色港口”的重要指示精神，坚持国家战略、天津实施的思路理念，将天津港作为国家的核心战略资源和京津冀、“三北”地区的海上门户，进一步畅通铁路和公路通道，努力打造完备的港口集疏运体系。

37. 2019 年 5 月 27 日，上海市人民政府印发《上海市推进运输结构调整实施方案（2018—2020 年）》，提出到 2020 年，运输结构调整取得突破性进展，上海港口铁路集疏运量有明显增加。

38. 2019 年 6 月 20 日，广州市政府 75 次常务会议审议并原则通过《广州市协同构建粤港澳大湾区具有国际竞争力的现代产业体系行动计划》，提出以先进制造业、战略性新兴产业、现代服务业、海洋经济、都市现代农业为主导，形成“一核、一廊、三翼、多极驱动”产业空间布局。开展先进制造业高质量发展行动、战略性新兴产业引领壮大行动、现代服务业出新出彩行动等9个重点行动，细化为40项具体任务。

39. 2019年6月25日，上海市人民政府发布《关于支持浦东新区改革开放再出发实现新时代高质量发展的若干意见》。提出上海要担起新使命、实现新作为，必须继续高举浦东开发开放旗帜，推动浦东新区更好发挥排头兵和试验田的作用，为全市高质量发展做出更大贡献，勇当新时代全国改革开放和创新发展的标杆。

40. 2019年7月4日，河南省委、省政府印发《关于支持郑州建设国家中心城市的若干意见》，提出把郑州打造成为河南省参与全球竞争、集聚高端资源的战略平台，形成河南省的核心增长极，引领带动中原城市群和中部地区高质量发展。

41. 2019年7月4日，郑州市人民政府印发《中国（河南）自由贸易试验区郑州片区三年行动计划（2019—2021年）》，明确了三年行动目标，提出申建自由贸易港，并明确郑州片区将聚焦先进制造业、现代服务业等重点产业，推进贸易、物流、金融、文化、信息、专业服务、制造业7大新经济产业集群建设，以跨境电商、平行进口汽车试点为突破口，创新产业监管和支持政策，打造内陆开放型经济新高地。

42. 2019年7月5日，天津市政府印发《关于推进现代都市型农业绿色发展的实施意见》，提出全面建立以绿色生态为导向的制度体系，加快形成与资源环境承载力相匹配、与生产生活生态相协调的现代都市型农业绿色发展新格局。

43. 2019年7月29日，广州市人民政府印发《关于进一步加快促进科技创新的政策措施》，出台12条重磅内容，包括面向港澳开放市科技计划（专项、基金）、协同推进市财政科研资金跨境使用、对境外高端人才给予个税补贴、3年内新增3万套人才公寓和公共租赁住房等。

44. 2019年8月2日，重庆市人民政府印发《重庆市营商环境优化提升工作方案》，要求力争通过3年左右的努力，全市营商环境短板弱项显著改善，进入全国先进行列。

皮书起源

“皮书”起源于十七、十八世纪的英国，主要指官方或社会组织正式发表的重要文件或报告，多以“白皮书”命名。在中国，“皮书”这一概念被社会广泛接受，并被成功运作、发展成为一种全新的出版形态，则源于中国社会科学院社会科学文献出版社。

皮书定义

皮书是对中国与世界发展状况和热点问题进行年度监测，以专业的角度、专家的视野和实证研究方法，针对某一领域或区域现状与发展态势展开分析和预测，具备原创性、实证性、专业性、连续性、前沿性、时效性等特点的公开出版物，由一系列权威研究报告组成。

皮书作者

皮书系列的作者以中国社会科学院、著名高校、地方社会科学院的研究人员为主，多为国内一流研究机构的权威专家学者，他们的看法和观点代表了学界对中国与世界的现实和未来最高水平的解读与分析。

皮书荣誉

皮书系列已成为社会科学文献出版社的著名图书品牌和中国社会科学院的知名学术品牌。2016 年，皮书系列正式列入“十三五”国家重点出版规划项目；2013~2019 年，重点皮书列入中国社会科学院承担的国家哲学社会科学创新工程项目；2019 年，64 种院外皮书使用“中国社会科学院创新工程学术出版项目”标识。

中国皮书网

（网址：www.pishu.cn）

发布皮书研创资讯，传播皮书精彩内容
引领皮书出版潮流，打造皮书服务平台

栏目设置

关于皮书：何谓皮书、皮书分类、皮书大事记、皮书荣誉、
皮书出版第一人、皮书编辑部

最新资讯：通知公告、新闻动态、媒体聚焦、网站专题、视频直播、下载专区

皮书研创：皮书规范、皮书选题、皮书出版、皮书研究、研创团队

皮书评奖评价：指标体系、皮书评价、皮书评奖

互动专区：皮书说、社科数托邦、皮书微博、留言板

所获荣誉

2008 年、2011 年，中国皮书网均在全国新闻出版业网站荣誉评选中获得“最具商业价值网站”称号；

2012 年，获得“出版业网站百强”称号。

网库合一

2014 年，中国皮书网与皮书数据库端口合一，实现资源共享。

S 基本子库
SUB DATABASE

中国社会发展数据库（下设12个子库）

全面整合国内外中国社会发展研究成果，汇聚独家统计数据、深度分析报告，涉及社会、人口、政治、教育、法律等12个领域，为了解中国社会发展动态、跟踪社会核心热点、分析社会发展趋势提供一站式资源搜索和数据分析与挖掘服务。

中国经济发展数据库（下设12个子库）

基于"皮书系列"中涉及中国经济发展的研究资料构建，内容涵盖宏观经济、农业经济、工业经济、产业经济等12个重点经济领域，为实时掌控经济运行态势、把握经济发展规律、洞察经济形势、进行经济决策提供参考和依据。

中国行业发展数据库（下设17个子库）

以中国国民经济行业分类为依据，覆盖金融业、旅游、医疗卫生、交通运输、能源矿产等100多个行业，跟踪分析国民经济相关行业市场运行状况和政策导向，汇集行业发展前沿资讯，为投资、从业及各种经济决策提供理论基础和实践指导。

中国区域发展数据库（下设6个子库）

对中国特定区域内的经济、社会、文化等领域现状与发展情况进行深度分析和预测，研究层级至县及县以下行政区，涉及地区、区域经济体、城市、农村等不同维度。为地方经济社会宏观态势研究、发展经验研究、案例分析提供数据服务。

中国文化传媒数据库（下设18个子库）

汇聚文化传媒领域专家观点、热点资讯，梳理国内外中国文化发展相关学术研究成果、一手统计数据，涵盖文化产业、新闻传播、电影娱乐、文学艺术、群众文化等18个重点研究领域。为文化传媒研究提供相关数据、研究报告和综合分析服务。

世界经济与国际关系数据库（下设6个子库）

立足"皮书系列"世界经济、国际关系相关学术资源，整合世界经济、国际政治、世界文化与科技、全球性问题、国际组织与国际法、区域研究6大领域研究成果，为世界经济与国际关系研究提供全方位数据分析，为决策和形势研判提供参考。

法律声明